THE NORTON ANTHOLOGY OF

AMERICAN LITERATURE

NINTH EDITION

VOLUME D: 1914–1945

VOLUME A

American Literature, Beginnings to 1820 • GUSTAFSON

VOLUME B

American Literature 1820–1865 • LEVINE

VOLUME C

American Literature 1865–1914 • ELLIOTT

VOLUME D

American Literature 1914–1945

LOEFFELHOLZ

VOLUME E

American Literature since 1945

HUNGERFORD

Michael A. Elliott
PROFESSOR OF ENGLISH AND AMERICAN STUDIES
EMORY UNIVERSITY

Sandra M. Gustafson
PROFESSOR OF ENGLISH AND AMERICAN STUDIES
UNIVERSITY OF NOTRE DAME

Amy Hungerford
PROFESSOR OF ENGLISH AND AMERICAN STUDIES
AND DIRECTOR OF THE DIVISION OF THE HUMANITIES
YALE UNIVERSITY

Mary Loeffelholz
PROFESSOR OF ENGLISH
NORTHEASTERN UNIVERSITY

THE NORTON ANTHOLOGY OF AMERICAN LITERATURE

NINTH EDITION

Robert S. Levine, *General Editor*
PROFESSOR OF ENGLISH AND
DISTINGUISHED UNIVERSITY PROFESSOR AND
DISTINGUISHED SCHOLAR-TEACHER
University of Maryland, College Park

VOLUME D: 1914–1945

W • W • NORTON & COMPANY
NEW YORK • LONDON

W. W. Norton & Company has been independent since its founding in 1923, when William Warder Norton and Mary D. Herter Norton first published lectures delivered at the People's Institute, the adult education division of New York City's Cooper Union. The firm soon expanded its program beyond the Institute, publishing books by celebrated academics from America and abroad. By midcentury, the two major pillars of Norton's publishing program—trade books and college texts—were firmly established. In the 1950s, the Norton family transferred control of the company to its employees, and today—with a staff of four hundred and a comparable number of trade, college, and professional titles published each year—W. W. Norton & Company stands as the largest and oldest publishing house owned wholly by its employees.

Printed in the United States of America

Editor: Julia Reidhead
Managing Editor, College: Marian Johnson
Manuscript Editors: Kurt Wildermuth, Harry Haskell, Michael Fleming, Candace Levy
Assistant Editor: Rachel Taylor
Managing Editor, College Digital Media: Kim Yi
Media Editor: Carly Fraser Doria
Assistant Media Editor: Ava Bramson
Media Project Editor: Kristin Sheerin
Marketing Manager, Literature: Kimberly Bowers
Production Manager: Sean Mintus
Art Director: Debra Morton Hoyt
Text Design: Jo Anne Metsch
Cover Design: Tiani Kennedy
Photo Editor: Cat Abelman
Photo Research: Julie Tesser
Permissions Manager: Megan Jackson Schindel
Permissions Clearing: Margaret Gorenstein
Composition: Westchester Book Group

ISBN: 978-0-393-26449-4

W. W. Norton & Company, Inc., 500 Fifth Avenue, New York, NY 10110
wwnorton.com

W. W. Norton & Company Ltd., 15 Carlisle Street, London W1D 3BS

1 2 3 4 5 6 7 8 9 0

Contents

Preface to the Ninth Edition

The Ninth Edition of *The Norton Anthology of American Literature* is the first for me as General Editor; for the Eighth Edition, I served as Associate General Editor under longstanding General Editor Nina Baym. On the occasion of a new general editorship, we have undertaken one of the most extensive revisions in our long publishing history. Three new section editors have joined the team: Sandra M. Gustafson, Professor of English and Concurrent Professor of American Studies at the University of Notre Dame, who succeeds Wayne Franklin and Philip Gura as editor of "American Literature, Beginnings to 1820"; Michael A. Elliott, Professor of English at Emory University, who succeeds Nina Baym, Robert S. Levine, and Jeanne Campbell Reesman as editor of "American Literature, 1865–1914"; and Amy Hungerford, Professor of English and American Studies at Yale University, who succeeds Jerome Klinkowitz and Patricia B. Wallace as editor of "American Literature since 1945." These editors join Robert S. Levine, editor of "American Literature, 1820–1865," and Mary Loeffelholz, editor of "American Literature, 1914–1945." Each editor, new or continuing, is a well-known expert in the relevant field or period and has ultimate responsibility for his or her section of the anthology, but we have worked closely from first to last to rethink all aspects of this new edition. Volume introductions, author headnotes, thematic clusters, annotations, illustrations, and bibliographies have all been updated and revised. We have also added a number of new authors, selections, and thematic clusters. We are excited about the outcome of our collaboration and anticipate that, like the previous eight editions, this edition of *The Norton Anthology of American Literature* will continue to lead the field.

From the anthology's inception in 1979, the editors have had three main aims: first, to present a rich and substantial enough variety of works to enable teachers to build courses according to their own vision of American literary history (thus, teachers are offered more authors and more selections than they will probably use in any one course); second, to make the anthology self-sufficient by featuring many works in their entirety along with extensive selections for individual authors; third, to balance traditional interests with developing critical concerns in a way that allows for the complex, rigorous, and capacious study of American literary traditions. As early as 1979, we anthologized work by Anne Bradstreet, Mary Rowlandson, Sarah Kemble Knight, Phillis Wheatley, Margaret Fuller, Harriet Beecher Stowe, Frederick Douglass, Sarah Orne Jewett, Kate Chopin, Mary E. Wilkins Freeman, Booker T. Washington, Charles W. Chesnutt, Edith Wharton,

W. E. B. Du Bois, and other writers who were not yet part of a standard canon. Yet we never shortchanged writers—such as Franklin, Emerson, Whitman, Hawthorne, Melville, Dickinson, Hemingway, Fitzgerald, and Faulkner—whose work many students expected to read in their American literature courses, and whom most teachers then and now would not think of doing without.

The so-called canon wars of the 1980s and 1990s usefully initiated a review of our understanding of American literature, a review that has enlarged the number and diversity of authors now recognized as contributors to the totality of American literature. The traditional writers look different in this expanded context, and they also appear different according to which of their works are selected. Teachers and students remain committed to the idea of the literary—that writers strive to produce artifacts that are both intellectually serious and formally skillful—but believe more than ever that writers should be understood in relation to their cultural and historical situations. We address the complex interrelationships between literature and history in the volume introductions, author headnotes, chronologies, and some of the footnotes. As in previous editions, we have worked with detailed suggestions from many teachers on how best to present the authors and selections. We have gained insights as well from the students who use the anthology. Thanks to questionnaires, face-to-face and phone discussions, letters, and email, we have been able to listen to those for whom this book is intended. For the Ninth Edition, we have drawn on the careful commentary of over 240 reviewers and reworked aspects of the anthology accordingly.

Our new materials continue the work of broadening the canon by representing thirteen new writers in depth, without sacrificing widely assigned writers, many of whose selections have been reconsidered, reselected, and expanded. Our aim is always to provide extensive enough selections to do the writers justice, including complete works wherever possible. Our Ninth Edition offers complete longer works, including Hawthorne's *The Scarlet Letter* and Kate Chopin's *The Awakening*, and such new and recently added works as Margaret Fuller's *The Great Lawsuit*, Abraham Cahan's *Yekl: A Tale of the New York Ghetto*, Nella Larsen's *Passing*, Katherine Anne Porter's *Pale Horse, Pale Rider*, Nathanael West's *The Day of the Locust*, and August Wilson's *Fences*. Two complete works—Eugene O'Neill's *Long Day's Journey into Night* and Tennessee Williams's *A Streetcar Named Desire*—are exclusive to *The Norton Anthology of American Literature*. Charles Brockden Brown, Louisa May Alcott, Upton Sinclair, and Junot Díaz are among the writers added to the prior edition, and to this edition we have introduced John Rollin Ridge, Constance Fenimore Woolson, George Saunders, and Natasha Tretheway, among others. We have also expanded and in some cases reconfigured such central figures as Franklin, Hawthorne, Dickinson, Twain, and Hemingway, offering new approaches in the headnotes, along with some new selections. In fact, the headnotes and, in many cases, selections for such frequently assigned authors as William Bradford, Washington Irving, James Fenimore Cooper, William Cullen Bryant, Lydia Maria Child, Henry Wadsworth Longfellow, Ralph Waldo Emerson, Harriet Beecher Stowe, Mark Twain, William Dean Howells, Henry James, Kate Chopin, W. E. B. Du Bois, Edith Wharton, Willa Cather, and William

Faulkner have been revised, updated, and in some cases entirely rewritten in light of recent scholarship. The Ninth Edition further expands its selections of women writers and writers from diverse ethnic, racial, and regional backgrounds—always with attention to the critical acclaim that recognizes their contributions to the American literary record. New and recently added writers such as Samson Occom, Jane Johnston Schoolcraft, John Rollin Ridge, and Sarah Winnemucca, along with the figures represented in "Voices from Native America," enable teachers to bring early Native American writing and oratory into their syllabi, or should they prefer, to focus on these selections as a freestanding unit leading toward the moment after 1945 when Native writers fully entered the mainstream of literary activity.

We are pleased to continue our popular innovation of topical gatherings of short texts that illuminate the cultural, historical, intellectual, and literary concerns of their respective periods. Designed to be taught in a class period or two, or used as background, each of the sixteen clusters consists of brief, carefully excerpted primary and (in one case) secondary texts, about six to ten per cluster, and an introduction. Diverse voices—many new to the anthology—highlight a range of views current when writers of a particular time period were active, and thus allow students better to understand some of the large issues that were being debated at particular historical moments. For example, in "Slavery, Race, and the Making of American Literature," texts by David Walker, William Lloyd Garrison, Angelina Grimké, Sojourner Truth, James M. Whitfield, and Martin R. Delany speak to the great paradox of pre–Civil War America: the contradictory rupture between the realities of slavery and the nation's ideals of freedom.

The Ninth Edition strengthens this feature with eight new and revised clusters attuned to the requests of teachers. To help students address the controversy over race and aesthetics in *Adventures of Huckleberry Finn*, we have revised a cluster in Volume C that shows what some of the leading critics of the past few decades thought was at stake in reading and interpreting slavery and race in Twain's canonical novel. New to Volume A is "American Literature and the Varieties of Religious Expression," which includes selections by Elizabeth Ashbridge, John Woolman, and John Marrant, while Volume B offers "Science and Technology in the Pre–Civil War Nation." Volume C newly features "Becoming American in the Gilded Age," and we continue to include the useful "Modernist Manifestos" in Volume D. We have added to the popular "Creative Nonfiction" in Volume E new selections by David Foster Wallace and Hunter S. Thompson, who join such writers as Jamaica Kincaid and Joan Didion.

The Ninth Edition features an expanded illustration program, both of the black-and-white images, 145 of which are placed throughout the volumes, and of the color plates so popular in the last two editions. In selecting color plates—from Elizabeth Graham's embroidered map of Washington, D.C., at the start of the nineteenth century to Jeff Wall's "After 'Invisible Man'" at the beginning of the twenty-first—the editors aim to provide images relevant to literary works in the anthology while depicting arts and artifacts representative of each era. In addition, graphic works—segments from the colonial children's classic *The New-England Primer* and from Art Spiegelman's canonical graphic novel, *Maus*, and a facsimile page of Emily

Dickinson manuscript, along with the many new illustrations—open possibilities for teaching visual texts.

Period-by-Period Revisions

Volume A, Beginnings to 1820. Sandra M. Gustafson, the new editor of Volume A, has substantially revised the volume. Prior editions of Volume A were broken into two historical sections, with two introductions and a dividing line at the year 1700; Gustafson has dropped that artificial divide to tell a more coherent and fluid story (in her new introduction) about the variety of American literatures during this long period. The volume continues to feature narratives by early European explorers of the North American continent as they encountered and attempted to make sense of the diverse cultures they met, and as they sought to justify their aim of claiming the territory for Europeans. These are precisely the issues foregrounded by the revised cluster "First Encounters: Early European Accounts of Native America," which gathers writings by Hernán Cortés, Samuel de Champlain, Robert Juet, and others, including the newly added Thomas Harriot. In addition to the standing material from *The Bay Psalm Book*, we include new material by Roger Williams; additional poems by Annis Boudinot Stockton; Abigail Adams's famous letter urging her husband to "Remember the Ladies"; an additional selection from Olaudah Equiano on his post-emancipation travels; and Charles Brockden Brown's "Memoirs of Carwin the Biloquist" (the complete "prequel" to his first novel, *Wieland*). We continue to offer the complete texts of Rowlandson's enormously influential *A Narrative of the Captivity and Restoration of Mrs. Mary Rowlandson*, Benjamin Franklin's *Autobiography* (which remains one of the most compelling works on the emergence of an "American" self), Royall Tyler's popular play *The Contrast*, and Hannah Foster's novel *The Coquette*, which uses a real-life tragedy to meditate on the proper role of well-bred women in the new republic and testifies to the existence of a female audience for the popular novels of the period. New to this volume is Washington Irving, a writer who looks back to colonial history and forward to Jacksonian America. The inclusion of Irving in both Volumes A and B, with one key overlapping selection, points to continuities and changes between the two volumes.

Five new and revised thematic clusters of texts highlight themes central to Volume A. In addition to "First Encounters," we have included "Native American Oral Literature," "American Literature and the Varieties of Religious Expression," "Ethnographic and Naturalist Writings," and "Native American Eloquence: Negotiation and Resistance." "Native American Oral Literature" features creation stories, trickster tales, oratory, and poetry from a spectrum of traditions, while "Native American Eloquence" collects speeches and accounts by Canassatego and Native American women (both new to the volume), Pontiac, Chief Logan (as cited by Thomas Jefferson), and Tecumseh, which, as a group, illustrate the centuries-long pattern of initial peaceful contact between Native Americans and whites mutating into bitter and violent conflict. This cluster, which focuses on Native Americans' points of view, complements "First Encounters," which focuses on European colonizers' points of view. The Native American presence in the volume is further expanded with increased representation of Samson Occom, which includes an excerpt from his sermon at the execution of Moses Paul, and the inclusion of Sagoyewatha in "American Literature and the Varieties of Religious Expression." Strategically located between the Congregationalist Protestant (or late-Puritan) Jonathan Edwards and the Enlightenment figure Franklin, this cluster brings together works from the perspectives of the major religious groups of the early Americas, including Quakerism (poems by Francis Daniel Pastorius, selections from autographical narratives of Elizabeth Ashbridge and John Woolman), Roman Catholicism (poems by Sor Juana, two Jesuit Relations, with biographical accounts of Father Isaac Jogues and Kateri Tekakwitha), dissenting Protestantism (Marrant), Judaism (Rebecca Samuel), and indigenous beliefs (Sagoyewatha). The new cluster "Ethnographic and Naturalist Writings" includes writings by Sarah Kemble Knight and William Byrd, along with new selections by Alexander Hamilton, William Bartram, and Hendrick Aupaumut. With this cluster, the new cluster on science and technology in Volume B, and a number of new selections and revisions in Volumes C, D, and E, the Ninth Edition pays greater attention to the impact of science on American literary traditions.

Volume B, American Literature, 1820–1865. Under the editorship of Robert S. Levine, this volume over the past several editions has become more diverse. Included here are the complete texts of Emerson's *Nature*, Hawthorne's *Scarlet Letter*, Thoreau's *Walden*, Douglass's *Narrative*, Whitman's *Song of Myself*, Melville's *Benito Cereno* and *Billy Budd*, Rebecca Harding Davis's *Life in the Iron Mills*, and Margaret Fuller's *The Great Lawsuit*. At the same time, aware of the important role of African American writers in the period, and the omnipresence of race and slavery as literary and political themes, we have recently added two major African American writers, William Wells Brown and Frances E. W. Harper, along with Douglass's novella *The Heroic Slave*. Thoreau's "Plea for Captain John Brown," a generous selection from Stowe's *Uncle Tom's Cabin*, and the cluster "Slavery, Race, and the Making of American Literature" also help remind students of how central slavery was to the literary and political life of the nation during this period. "Native Americans: Resistance and Removal" gathers oratory and writings—by Native Americans such as Black Hawk and whites such as Ralph Waldo Emerson—protesting Andrew Jackson's ruthless national policy of Indian removal. Newly added is a selection from *The Life and Adventures of Joaquín Murieta*, by the Native American writer John Rollin Ridge. This potboiler of a novel, set in the new state of California, emerged from the debates that began during the Indian removal period. Through the figure of the legendary Mexican bandit Murieta, who fights back against white expansionists, Ridge responds to the violence encouraged by Jackson and subsequent white leaders as they laid claim to the continent. Political themes, far from diluting the literary imagination of American authors, served to inspire some of the most memorable writing of the pre–Civil War Period.

Women writers recently added to Volume B include Lydia Huntley Sigourney, the Native American writer Jane Johnston Schoolcraft, and Louisa May Alcott. Recently added prose fiction includes chapters from Cooper's *The Last of the Mohicans*, Sedgwick's *Hope Leslie*, and Melville's *Moby-Dick*, along with Poe's "The Black Cat" and Hawthorne's "Wakefield." For the first time, we print Melville's "Hawthorne and His Mosses" as it appeared in the 1850 *Literary World*. Poetry by Emily Dickinson is now presented in the texts established by R. W. Franklin and includes a facsimile page from Fascicle 10. For this edition we have added several poems by Dickinson that were inspired by the Civil War. Other selections added to this edition include Fanny Fern's amusing sketch "Writing 'Compositions,'" the chapter in Frederick Douglass's *My Bondage and My Freedom* on his resistance to the slave-breaker Covey, three poems by Melville ("Dupont's Round Fight," "A Utilitarian View of the Monitor's Fight," and "Art"), and Whitman's "The Sleepers."

Perhaps the most significant addition to Volume B is the cluster "Science and Technology in the Pre–Civil War Nation," with selections by the canonical writers Charles Dickens, Edgar Allan Poe, and Frederick Douglass, by the scientists Jacob Bigelow and Alexander Humboldt, and by the editor-writer Harriet Farley. The cluster calls attention to the strong interest in science and technology throughout this period and should provide a rich context for reconsidering works such as Thoreau's *Walden* and Melville's "The Paradise of Bachelors and the Tartarus of Maids." In an effort to underscore the importance of science and technology to Poe and Hawthorne in particular, we have added two stories that directly address these topics: Poe's "The Facts in the Case of M. Valdemar" and Hawthorne's "The Artist of the Beautiful" (which reads nicely in relation to his "The Birth-Mark" and "Rappaccini's Daughter"). Emerson, Whitman, and Dickinson are among the many other authors in Volume B who had considerable interest in science.

Volume C, American Literature, 1865–1914. Newly edited by Michael A. Elliott, the volume includes expanded selections of key works, as well as new ones that illustrate how many of the struggles of this period prefigure our own. In addition to complete longer works such as Twain's *Adventures of Huckleberry Finn*, Chopin's *The Awakening*, James's *Daisy Miller*, and Stephen Crane's *Maggie: A Girl of the Streets*, the Ninth Edition now includes the complete text of *Yekl: A Tale of the New York Ghetto*, a highly influential novella of immigrant life that depicts the pressures facing newly arrived Jews in the nation's largest metropolis. Also new is a substantial selection from Sarah Orne Jewett's *The Country of the Pointed Firs*, a masterpiece of literary regionalism that portrays a remote seaside community facing change.

Americans are still reflecting on the legacy of the Civil War, and we have added two works approaching that subject from different angles. Constance Fenimore Woolson's "Rodman the Keeper" tells the story of a Union veteran who maintains a cemetery in the South. In "The Private History of a Campaign That Failed," Mark Twain reflects with wit and insight on his own brief experience in the war. In the Eighth Edition, we introduced a section on the critical controversy surrounding race and the conclusion of *Adventures of Huckleberry Finn*. That section remains as important as ever, and new additions incorporate a recent debate about the value of an expurgated edition of the novel.

We have substantially revised clusters designed to give students a sense of the cultural context of the period. New selections in "Realism and Naturalism" demonstrate what was at stake in the debate over realism, among them a feminist response from Charlotte Perkins Gilman. "Becoming American in the Gilded Age," a new cluster, introduces students to writing about wealth and citizenship at a time when the nation was undergoing transformation. Selections from one of Horatio Alger's popular novels of economic uplift, Andrew Carnegie's "Gospel of Wealth," and Charles W. Chesnutt's "The Future American" together reveal how questions about the composition of the nation both influenced the literature of this period and prefigured contemporary debates on immigration, cultural diversity, and the concentration of wealth.

The turn of the twentieth century was a time of immense literary diversity. "Voices from Native America" brings together a variety of expressive forms—oratory, memoir, ethnography—through which Native Americans sought to represent themselves. It includes new selections by Francis LaFlesche, Zitkala Ša, and Chief Joseph. For the first time, we include the complete text of José Martí's "Our America," in a new translation by Martí biographer Alfred J. López. By instructor request, we have added fiction and nonfiction by African American authors: Charles W. Chesnutt's "Po' Sandy," Pauline Hopkins's "Talma Gordon," and expanded selections from W. E. B. Du Bois's *Souls of Black Folk* and James Weldon Johnson's *Autobiography of an Ex-Colored Man*.

Volume D, American Literature 1914–1945. Edited by Mary Loeffelholz, Volume D offers a number of complete longer works—Eugene O'Neill's *Long Day's Journey into Night* (exclusive to the Norton Anthology), William Faulkner's *As I Lay Dying*, and Willa Cather's *My Ántonia*. To these we have added Nella Larsen's *Passing*, which replaces *Quicksand*, and Nathanael West's *The Day of the Locust*. We added *Passing* in response to numerous requests from instructors and students who regard it as one of the most compelling treatments of racial passing in American literature. The novel also offers rich descriptions of the social and racial geographies of Chicago and New York City. West's darkly comic *The Day of the Locust* similarly offers rich descriptions of the social and racial geography of Los Angeles. West's novel can at times seem bleak and not "politically correct," but in many ways it is the first great American novel about the film industry, and it also has much to say about the growth of California in the early decades of the twentieth century. New selections by Zora Neale Hurston ("Sweat") and John Steinbeck ("The Chrysanthemums") further contribute to the volume's exploration of issues connected with racial and social geographies.

Selections by Ezra Pound, T. S. Eliot, Marianne Moore, Hart Crane, and Langston Hughes encourage students and teachers to contemplate the interrelation of modernist aesthetics with ethnic, regional, and popular writing. In "Modernist Manifestos," F. T. Marinetti, Mina Loy, Ezra Pound, Willa Cather, William Carlos Williams, and Langston Hughes show how the manifesto as a form exerted a powerful influence on international modernism in all the arts. Another illuminating cluster addresses central events of the modern period. In "World War I and Its Aftermath," writings by Ernest Hemingway, Gertrude Stein, Jessie Redmon Fauset, and others explore sharply divided views on the U.S. role in World War I, as well as the radicalizing effect of modern warfare—with 365,000 American casualties—on contemporary writing. We have added to this edition a chapter from Hemingway's first novel, *The Sun Also Rises*, which speaks to the impact of the war on sexuality and gender. Other recent and new additions to Volume D include Faulkner's popular "A Rose for Emily," Katherine Anne Porter's novella *Pale Horse, Pale Rider*, Gertrude Stein's "Objects," Marianne Moore's ambitious longer poem "Marriage," poems by Edgar Lee Masters and Edwin Arlington Robinson, and Jean Toomer's "Blood Burning Moon."

Volume E, American Literature, 1945 to the Present. Amy Hungerford, the new editor of Volume E, has revised the volume to present a wider range of writing in poetry, prose, drama, and nonfiction. As before, the volume offers the complete texts of Tennessee Williams's *A Streetcar Named Desire* (exclusive to this anthology), Arthur Miller's *Death of a Salesman*, Allen Ginsberg's *Howl*, Sam Shepard's *True West*, August Wilson's *Fences*, David Mamet's *Glengarry Glen Ross*, and Louise Glück's long poem *October*. A selection from Art Spiegelman's prize-winning *Maus* opens possibilities for teaching the graphic novel. We also include teachable stand-alone segments from influential novels by Saul Bellow (*The Adventures of Augie March*) and Kurt Vonnegut (*Slaughterhouse-Five*), and, new to this edition, Jack Kerouac (*On the Road*) and Don DeLillo (*White Noise*). The selection from one of DeLillo's most celebrated novels tells what feels like a contemporary story about a nontraditional family navigating an environmental disaster in a climate saturated by mass media. Three newly added stories—Patricia Highsmith's "The Quest for *Blank Claveringi*," Philip K. Dick's "Precious Artifact," and George Saunders's "CivilWarLand in Bad Decline"—reveal the impact of science fiction, fantasy, horror, and (especially in the case of Saunders) mass media on literary fiction. Also appearing for the first time are Edward P. Jones and Lydia Davis, contemporary masters of the short story, who join such short fiction writers as Ann Beattie and Junot Díaz. Recognized literary figures in all genres, ranging from Robert Penn Warren and Elizabeth Bishop to Leslie Marmon Silko and Toni Morrison, continue to be richly represented. In response to instructors' requests, we now include Flannery O'Connor's "A Good Man Is Hard to Find" and James Baldwin's "Sonny's Blues."

One of the most distinctive features of twentieth- and twenty-first-century American literature is a rich vein of African American poetry. This edition adds two contemporary poets from this living tradition: Natasha Trethewey and Tracy K. Smith. Trethewey's selections include personal and historical elegies; Smith draws on cultural materials as diverse as David Bowie's music and the history of the Hubble Space Telescope. These writers join African American poets whose work has long helped define the anthology—Rita Dove, Gwendolyn Brooks, Robert Hayden, Audre Lorde, and others.

This edition gives even greater exposure to literary and social experimentation during the 1960s, 1970s, and beyond. The work of two avant-garde playwrights joins "Postmodern Manifestos" (which pairs nicely with "Modernist Manifestos" in Volume D). Introduced to the anthology through their short, challenging pieces, Charles Ludlam and Richard Foreman cast the mechanics of performance in a new light. Reading their thought pieces in relation to the volume's complete plays helps raise new questions about how the seemingly more traditional dramatic works engage structures of time, plot, feeling, and spectatorship. To our popular cluster "Creative Nonfiction" we have added a new selection by Joan Didion, from "Slouching Towards

Bethlehem," which showcases her revolutionary style of journalism as she comments on experiments with public performance and communal living during the 1960s. A new selection from David Foster Wallace in the same cluster pushes reportage on the Maine Lobster Festival into philosophical inquiry: how can we fairly assess the pain of other creatures? This edition also introduces poet Frank Bidart through his most famous work—*Ellen West*—in which the poet uses experimental forms of verse he pioneered during the 1970s to speak in the voice of a woman battling anorexia. Standing authors in the anthology, notably John Ashbery and Amiri Baraka, fill out the volume's survey of radical change in the forms, and social uses, of literary art.

We are delighted to offer this revised Ninth Edition to teachers and students, and we welcome your comments.

Additional Resources from the Publisher

The Ninth Edition retains the paperback splits format, popular for its flexibility and portability. This format accommodates the many instructors who use the anthology in a two-semester survey, but allows for mixing and matching the five volumes in a variety of courses organized by period or topic, at levels from introductory to advanced. We are also pleased to offer the Ninth Edition in an ebook format. The Digital Anthologies include all the content of the print volumes, with print-corresponding page and line numbers for seamless integration into the print-digital mixed classroom. Annotations are accessible with a click or a tap, encouraging students to use them with minimal interruption to their reading of the text. The e-reading platform facilitates active reading with a powerful annotation tool and allows students to do a full-text search of the anthology and read online or off. The Digital Editions can be accessed from any computer or device with an Internet browser and are available to students at a fraction of the print price at digital.wwnorton.com/americanlit9pre1865 and digital.wwnorton.com/americanlit9post1865. For exam copy access to the Digital Editions and for information on making the Digital Editions available through the campus bookstore or packaging the Digital Editions with the print anthology, instructors should contact their Norton representative.

To give instructors even more flexibility, Norton is making available the full list of 254 Norton Critical Editions. A Norton Critical Edition can be included for free with either package (Volumes A and B; Volumes C, D, E) or any individual split volume. Each Norton Critical Edition gives students an authoritative, carefully annotated text accompanied by rich contextual and critical materials prepared by an expert in the subject. The publisher also offers the much-praised guide *Writing about American Literature*, by Karen Gocsik (University of California–San Diego) and Coleman Hutchison (University of Texas–Austin), free with either package or any individual split volume.

In addition to the Digital Editions, for students using *The Norton Anthology of American Literature*, the publisher provides a wealth of free resources at digital.wwnorton.com/americanlit9pre1865 and digital.wwnorton.com/americanlit9post1865. There students will find more than seventy reading-comprehension quizzes on the period introductions and widely taught works with extensive feedback that points them back to the text. Ideal for self-study or homework assignments, Norton's sophisticated quizzing engine allows instructors to track student results and improvement. For over thirty works in the anthology, the sites also offer Close Reading Workshops that walk students step-by-step through analysis of a literary work. Each workshop prompts students to read, reread, consider contexts, and answer questions along the way, making these perfect assignments to build close-reading skills.

The publisher also provides extensive instructor-support materials. New to the Ninth Edition is an online Interactive Instructor's Guide at iig.wwnorton.com/americanlit9/full. Invaluable for course preparation, this resource provides hundreds of teaching notes, discussion questions, and suggested resources from the much-praised *Teaching with* The Norton Anthology of American Literature: *A Guide for Instructors* by Edward Whitley (Lehigh University). Also at this searchable and sortable site are quizzes, images, and lecture PowerPoints for each introduction, topic cluster, and twenty-five widely taught works. A PDF of *Teaching with NAAL* is available for download at wwnorton.com/instructors.

Finally, Norton Coursepacks bring high-quality digital media into a new or existing online course. The coursepack includes all the reading comprehension quizzes (customizable within the coursepack), the Writing about Literature video series, a bank of essay and exam questions, bulleted summaries of the period introductions, and "Making Connections" discussion or essay prompts to encourage students to draw connections across the anthology's authors and works. Coursepacks are available in a variety of formats, including Blackboard, Canvas, Desire2Learn, and Moodle, at no cost to instructors or students.

Editorial Procedures

As in past editions, editorial features—period introductions, headnotes, annotations, and bibliographies—are designed to be concise yet full and to give students necessary information without imposing a single interpretation. The editors have updated all apparatus in response to new scholarship: period introductions have been entirely or substantially rewritten, as have many headnotes. All selected bibliographies and each period's general-resources bibliographies, categorized by Reference Works, Histories, and Literary Criticism, have been thoroughly updated. The Ninth Edition retains three editorial features that help students place their reading in historical and cultural context—a Texts/Contexts timeline following each period introduction, a map on the front endpaper of each volume, and a chronological chart, on the back endpaper, showing the lifespans of many of the writers anthologized.

Whenever possible, our policy has been to reprint texts as they appeared in their historical moment. There is one exception: we have modernized most spellings and (very sparingly) the punctuation in Volume A on the principle that archaic spellings and typography pose unnecessary problems for beginning students. We have used square brackets to indicate titles supplied by the editors for the convenience of students. Whenever a portion of a text has been omitted, we have indicated that omission with three asterisks.

If the omitted portion is important for following the plot or argument, we give a brief summary within the text or in a footnote. After each work, we cite the date of first publication on the right; in some instances, the latter is followed by the date of a revised edition for which the author was responsible. When the date of composition is known and differs from the date of publication, we cite it on the left.

The editors have benefited from commentary offered by hundreds of teachers throughout the country. Those teachers who prepared detailed critiques, or who offered special help in preparing texts, are listed under Acknowledgments, on a separate page. We also thank the many people at Norton who contributed to the Ninth Edition: Julia Reidhead, who supervised the Ninth Edition; Marian Johnson, managing editor, college; Carly Fraser Doria, media editor; Kurt Wildermuth, Michael Fleming, Harry Haskell, Candace Levy, manuscript editors; Rachel Taylor and Ava Bramson, assistant editors; Sean Mintus, production manager; Cat Abelman, photo editor; Julie Tesser, photo researcher; Debra Morton Hoyt, art director; Tiani Kennedy, cover designer; Megan Jackson Schindel, permissions manager; and Margaret Gorenstein, who cleared permissions. We also wish to acknowledge our debt to the late George P. Brockway, former president and chairman at Norton, who invented this anthology, and to the late M. H. Abrams, Norton's advisor on English texts. All have helped us create an anthology that, more than ever, testifies to the continuing richness of American literary traditions.

ROBERT S. LEVINE, General Editor

Acknowledgments

Among our many critics, advisors, and friends, the following were of especial help toward the preparation of the Ninth Edition, either with advice or by providing critiques of particular periods of the anthology: Melissa Adams-Campbell (Northern Illinois University); Rolena Adorno (Yale University); Heidi Ajrami (Victoria College); Simone A. James Alexander (Seton Hall University); Brian Anderson (Central Piedmont Community College); Lena Andersson (Fulton-Montgomery Community College); Marilyn Judith Atlas (Ohio University); Sylvia Baer (Gloucester County College); George H. Bailey (Northern Essex Community College); Margarita T. Barceló (MSU Denver); Peter Bellis (University of Alabama–Birmingham); Randall Blankenship (Valencia College); Susanne Bloomfield (University of Nebraska–Kearney); David Bordelon (Ocean County College); Patricia Bostian (Central Piedmont Community College); Maria Brandt (Monroe Community College); Tamara Ponzo Brattoli (Joliet Junior College); Joanna Brooks (San Diego State University); David Brottman (Iowa State University); Arthur Brown (University of Evansville); Martin Brückner (University of Delaware); Judith Budz (Fitchburg State University); Dan Butcher (University of Alabama–Birmingham); Maria J. Cahill (Edison State College); Ann Cameron (Indiana University–Kokomo); Brad Campbell (Cal Poly); Mark Canada (University of North Carolina–Pembroke); Gerry Canavan (Marquette University); Ann Capel (Gadsden State Community College, Ayers Campus); Elisabeth Ceppi (Portland State University); Tom Cerasulo (Elms College); Mark Cirino (University of Evansville); Josh Cohen (Emory University); Matt Cohen (University of Texas–Austin); William Corley (Cal Poly Pomona and U.S. Naval Academy); David Cowart (University of South Carolina); Paul Crumbley (Utah State University); Ryan Cull (New Mexico State University); Sue Currell (University of Sussex); Kathleen Danker (South Dakota State University); Clark Davis (University of Denver); Eve Davis (Virginia Union University); Matthew R. Davis (University of Wisconsin–Stevens Point); Laura Dawkins (Murray State University); Bruce J. Degi (Metropolitan State University of Denver); Jerry DeNuccio (Graceland University); Lisa DeVries (Victoria College); Lorraine C. DiCicco (King's University College); Joshua A. Dickson (SUNY Jefferson); Rick Diguette (Georgia Perimeter College); Raymond F. Dolle (Indiana State University); James Donelan (UC Santa Barbara); Clark Draney (College of Southern Idaho); John Dudley (University of South Dakota); Sara Eaton (North Central College); Julia Eichelberger (College of Charleston); Marilyn Elkins (California State University–Los Angeles); Sharyn Emery (Indiana

University Southeast); Hilary Emmett (University of East Anglia); Terry Engebresten (Idaho State University); Patrick Erben (University of West Georgia); Timothy J. Evans (College of William & Mary); Duncan Faherty (CUNY); Laura Fine (Meredith College); Daniel Fineman (Occidental College); Pat Gantt (Utah State University); Xiongya Gao (Southern University at New Orleans); Becky Jo Gesteland (Weber State University); Paul Gilmore (Rutgers University); Len Gougeon (University of Scranton); Carey Goyette (Clinton Community College); Sarah Graham (University of Leicester); Alan Gravano (Marshall University); James N. Green (Library Company of Philadelphia); Laura Morgan Green (Northeastern University); John Gruesser (Kean University); Bernabe G. Gutierrez (Laredo Community College); Julia Hans (Fitchburg State University); Stephanie Hawkins (University of North Texas); Catherine F. Heath (Victoria College); Roger Hechy (SUNY Oneonta); Terry Heller (Coe College); Carl Herzig (St. Ambrose University); Eric Heyne (University of Alaska–Fairbanks); Thomas Alan Holmes (East Tennessee State University); Greg Horn (Southwest Virginia Community College); Ruth Y. Hsu (University of Hawaii–Manoa); Kate Huber (Temple University); Zach Hutchins (Colorado State University); Thomas Irwin (University of Missouri–St. Louis); Elizabeth Janoski (Lackawanna College); Andrew Jenkins (College of Central Florida); Luke Johnson (Mesabi Range College); Mark Johnson (San Jacinto College); Paul Jones (Ohio University); Roger Walton Jones (Ranger College); Jennifer Jordan-Henley (Roane State Community College); Mark Kamrath (University of Central Florida); Rachel Key (El Centro College); Julie H. Kim (Northeastern Illinois University); Vincent King (Black Hills State University); Denis Kohn (Baldwin Wallace University); Gary Konas (University of Wisconsin–La Crosse); Michael Kowalewski (Carleton College); Michael Lackey (University of Minnesota–Morris); Jennifer Ladino (University of Idaho); Thomas W. LaFleur (Laredo Community College); Andrew Lanham (Yale University); Christopher Leise (Whitman College); Beth Leishman (Northwest MS Community College); Jennifer Levi (Cecil College); Alfred J. López (Purdue University); Paul Madachy (Prince George's Community College); Etta Madden (Missouri State University); Marc Malandra (Biola University); David Malone (Union University); Matt Martin (Wesleyan College); Stephen Mathewson (Central New Mexico Community College); Liz Thompson Mayo (Jackson State Community College); David McCracken (Coker College); Kathleen McDonald (Norwich University); John McGreevy (University of Notre Dame); Dana McMichael (Abilene Christian University); Sandra Measels (Holmes Community College); Eric Mein (Normandale Community College); Christine Mihelich (Marywood University); Deborah M. Mix (Ball State University); Aaron Moe (Washington State University); Joelle Moen (Brigham Young University–Idaho); Lisa Muir (Wilkes Community College); Lori Muntz (Iowa Wesleyan College); Justine Murison (University of Illinois); Jillmarie Murphy (Union College); Harold Nelson (Minot State University); Howard Nelson (Cayuga Community College); Lance Newman (Westminster College); Taryn Okuma (The Catholic University of America); Stanley Orr (University of Hawai'i–West O'ahu); Samuel Otter (University of California–Berkeley); Susan Scott Parrish (University of Michigan); Martha H. Patterson (McKendree University); Michelle Paulsen (Victoria College); Daniel G. Payne (SUNY Oneonta); Ian Peddie (Georgia

Gwinnett College); Aaron Matthew Percich (West Virginia University); Tom Perrin (Huntingdon College); Sandra Petrulionis (Penn State–Altoona); Christopher Phillips (Lafayette College); Maria Pollack (Hudson Valley Community College); Kenneth M. Price (University of Nebraska); Marty G. Price (Mississippi State University); Kieran Quinlan (University of Alabama–Birmingham); Wesley Raabe (Kent State University); Maria Ramos (J. Sargeant Reynolds Community College); Palmer Rampell (Yale University); Rick Randolph (Kauai Community College); Kimberly Reed (Lipscomb University); Joan Reeves (Northeast Alabama Community College); Elizabeth Renker (The Ohio State University); Joseph Rezek (Boston University); Anne Boyd Rioux (University of New Orleans); Marc Robinson (Yale University); Jane Rosecrans (J. Sargeant Reynolds Community College); Phillip Round (University of Iowa); Jeffrey Rubinstein (Hillborough Community College); Maureen Ryan (University of Southern Mississippi); Jamie Sadler (Richmond Community College); Gordon Sayre (University of Oregon); Jennifer Schell (University of Alaska–Fairbanks); Jim Schrantz (Tarrant County College); Joshua Schuster (University of Western Ontario); Marc Seals (University of Wisconsin–Baraboo/Sauk County); Carl Sederholm (Brigham Young University); Larry Severeid (Utah State University–Eastern); Anna Shectman (Yale University); Deborah Sims (USC and UCR); Claudia Slate (Florida Southern College); Brenda R. Smith (Kent State University–Stark); Martha Nell Smith (University of Maryland); Eric Sterling (Auburn University Montgomery); Julia Stern (Northwestern University); Billy J. Stratton (University of Denver); Steve Surryhne (California State University–San Francisco); Timothy Sweet (West Virginia University); David Taylor (University of North Texas); Jan Thompson (University of Nebraska–Kearney); Robin Thompson (Governors State University); Marjory Thrash (Pearl River Community College); Nicole Tonkovich (UC San Diego); Steve Tracy (University of Massachusetts–Amherst); Alan Trusky (Forence-Darlington Tech College); April Van Camp (Indian River State College); Joanne van der Woude (University of Groningen); Abram van Engen (Washington University); Laura Veltman (California Baptist University); Eliza Waggoner (Miami University–Middletown); Catherine Waitinas (Cal Poly State University); Laura Dassow Walls (University of Notre Dame); Raquel Wanzo (Laney College); Bryan Waterman (New York University); Stephanie Wells (Orange Coast College); Jeff Westover (Boise State University); Belinda Wheeler (Paine College); Chris Wheeler (Horry-Georgetown Technical College); Steven J. Whitton (Jacksonville State University); Elizabeth Wiet (Yale University); Jason Williams (Brigham Young University–Idaho); Barbara Williamson (Spokane Falls Community College); Gaye Winter (Mississippi Gulf Coast Community College); Kelly Wisecup (University of North Texas); Aiping Zhang (California State University–Chico).

THE NORTON ANTHOLOGY OF

AMERICAN LITERATURE

NINTH EDITION

VOLUME D: 1914–1945

PHILLIES

American Literature 1914–1945

THE TWO WARS AS HISTORICAL MARKERS

The conflict eventually known as World War I broke out in Europe in 1914, with Great Britain, France, and Russia fighting against Germany. The United States, which belatedly entered the war in 1917, on the side of Britain and France, had ended its last full-scale conflict, the Civil War, some fifty years previously. In the interval, the country's industrial power had grown immensely. So had its major cities, swelled on the Eastern seaboard by immigrants increasingly from southern and eastern Europe, and on the West Coast, from Asia. In 1914 the country's network of transcontinental railroads linked its productive farms, small towns, and industry to urban centers. Henry Ford had begun the transformation of the automobile from an exotic luxury technology into a consumer good with the 1908 introduction of the Model T, and by 1912 an American entrepreneur had dreamed up the first transcontinental highway. Aviation pioneers were rapidly building on the Wright brothers' first successful powered airplane flights of 1903. Like the Civil War, World War I would mobilize the country's industries and technologies, spur their development, and uproot both soldiers and civilians. On an even larger scale, World War II would do the same.

These events were momentous both in themselves and as harbingers of transformations to come. At the end of World War I, however, the United States was still in the main a nation of small farms and small towns, with about two-thirds of its population living in rural districts or towns of fewer than twenty-five thousand inhabitants. Although several waves of immigration had altered the makeup of the population, the

Night Hawks (detail), Edward Hopper, 1942. For more information about this painting, see the color insert in this volume.

NAACP—Silent March, 1917. On July 28, 1917, under the leadership of the National Association for the Advancement of Colored People, some ten thousand African Americans marched down New York City's Fifth Avenue to protest the race riots of that summer in East Saint Louis, during which an estimated one hundred black citizens were lynched and thousands of others were left homeless.

majority of Americans were still of English or German ancestry and about one American in ten was of African descent. The majority was deeply distrustful of international politics, and after the war ended, many attempted to steer the nation back to prewar modes of life. In 1924 Congress enacted a sweeping exclusionary immigration act, extending the reach of previous restrictions. The act prohibited all Asian immigration and set quotas for other countries on the basis of their existing U.S. immigrant populations, intending thereby to control the ethnic makeup of the United States (and indeed the proportion of Americans born outside the United States did decline markedly from 1910 to 1940). The immediate postwar years also saw the so-called Red Scare, when labor union headquarters were raided and immigrant radicals were deported by a government fearful of the influence of the newly Communist Soviet Union (formerly tsarist Russia).

For other Americans, however, the war helped accelerate long-sought changes in the forms of political and social life. The long struggle to win American women the vote—given a final push by women's work as nurses and ambulance drivers during the war—ended in 1920 with the passage of the Nineteenth Amendment to the Constitution. The National Association for the Advancement of Colored People (NAACP), founded in 1909, successfully argued during World War I for the commissioning of black officers in the U.S. armed forces; as they would again after World War II, African Americans who fought abroad returned to fight for their rights at

Suffragettes Picket the White House, 1917. Members of the National Woman's Party regularly demonstrated in front of the White House during Woodrow Wilson's administration. After the U.S. entry into World War I heightened concerns for domestic order, pro-suffrage picketers were arrested and jailed.

home. Despite the government's restrictions on leftist political activity, many Americans—among them writers and intellectuals as well as labor activists and urban immigrants—looked to the Soviet Union and the international Communist movement for a model in combating inequality and fostering workers' rights in the United States. Other Americans went abroad, for shorter or longer stretches of time, in order to taste the expatriate life (made cheaper in war-ravaged economies by the solid American dollar) in Europe's battered but still vibrant cities and countryside. Some Americans traveled physical and social distances almost as great within the boundaries of the United States, as African Americans began to migrate in large numbers out of the segregated South and young people everywhere increasingly attended college away from home and moved to the cities. African Americans, emancipated urban women, and the restless young faced off against rural and urban traditionalists over the question of who, exactly, was truly "American."

These conflicts over the shape of the future acquired new urgency when the stock market crashed in 1929 and led to an economic depression with a 25 percent unemployment rate—a percentage even larger in its impact, by present-day standards, because women in general were not in the workforce. Known as the Great Depression, this period of economic hardship did not fully end until the United States entered World War II, following the Japanese attack on the American fleet at Pearl Harbor on December 7, 1941. Japan's ally Germany also declared war on the United States, thus involving the country in another European conflict. The war unified the country politically; revitalized industry, which devoted itself to goods needed for the war effort; and put people to work, including women who went into the labor force in unprecedented numbers. Germany surrendered in the spring of 1945. The war ended in August 1945 following the detonation of two atomic bombs over the Japanese cities of Hiroshima and Nagasaki. Europe was in ruins and the United States had become the world's major industrial and political power. The two wars, then, bracket a period during which the United States became a fully modern nation.

In the arena of literature and culture, the period demarcated by the two world wars is known as the era of modernism. Far too broad and widespread to be understood as a single movement, *modernism* nevertheless names a recognizable international phenomenon, a wave of challenges mounted against traditional authority in almost every realm—the arts, religion, science, politics, and social conventions. American literature in these decades registers all sides of the era's struggles and debates, while sharing a commitment to explore the many meanings of modernity. Some writers rejoiced while others lamented; some anticipated future utopias and others believed that civilization had collapsed; but the period's most influential voices, believing that old forms would not work for new times, were inspired by the possibility of creating something entirely new.

Within this period, three issues stand out as dividing various writers and schools of writers, all of them related to the accelerating transformations and conflicts of modernity. One issue centered on the uses of literary tradition. To some, a work registering its allegiance to literary history—through allusion to canonical works of the past, or by using traditional poetic forms and poetic language, or by relying on traditional forms of narrative authority—seemed imitative and old-fashioned. To others, a work failing to honor literary tradition was simply bad or incompetent writing. For still others, literary history was best appreciated oppositionally: modernist works often allude to previous literature ironically, or deliberately fracture traditional literary formulas. A related issue involved the place of popular culture in serious literature. Throughout the era, popular culture gained momentum and influence. Some writers regarded it as crucial for the future of literature that popular art forms, such as film and jazz, be embraced; to others, serious literature by definition had to reject what they saw as the cynical commercialism of popular culture.

Another issue was the question of how far literature should engage itself in political and social struggle. Should art be a domain unto itself, exploring aesthetic questions and enunciating transcendent truths, or should art participate in the politics of the times? For some, a work that was political in aim counted as propaganda, not art; others thought that apolitical literature was evasive and irresponsible; some viewed the call to keep art out of politics as covertly political, a conservative mandate to preserve the status quo, even if it did not acknowledge itself as such.

CHANGING TIMES

The transformations of the first half of the twentieth century were driven both by ideas and by changes in the economic and technological underpinnings of daily life. Much social energy in the 1920s went into enlarging the boundaries for acceptable self-expression. Adherents of small-town values such as the work ethic, social conformity, duty, and respectability clashed ideologically not only with internationally minded radicals but also with newly affluent young people who argued for more diverse, permissive, and tolerant styles of life. To some extent this debate recapitulated the long-standing American conflict between the claims of the individual and those of society, a conflict going back to the seventeenth-century religious conflicts over autonomy of conscience that were later epitomized in Ralph Waldo Emerson's call, in the 1840s: "Whosoever would be a man, must be a non-conformist."

The 1920s saw significant changes in sexual mores, with increasing numbers of young people no longer under the watchful eyes of their small-town elders. These social changes found their most influential theorist in the Austrian psychiatrist Sigmund Freud (1858–1939), inventor of the practice of psychoanalysis. According to Freud, many modern neuroses could be traced to repression and inhibition. Freud developed the idea of the self as grounded in an "unconscious," where forbidden desires, traumas, and unacceptable emotions—mostly sexual in nature and derived from childhood experiences—were stored. Freudian analysis aimed at helping people become aware of their repressed feelings and so less likely to reenact in the present the traumas of the past. Americanized Freudian ideas provided the psychological underpinning for much literature of the interwar era, whether the focus was the individual trapped in a repressive culture or the repressive culture itself.

The middle-class double sexual standard had, in fact, always granted considerable sexual freedom to men; now, however, women—enfranchised and liberated by automobiles and job possibilities away from home—began to demand similar freedom for themselves. Women's demands went well beyond the erotic, however, encompassing education, professional work, mobility, and whatever else seemed like social goods hitherto reserved for men. Female dress changed: long, heavy, restricting garments gave way to short, lightweight, easily worn store-bought clothing. The combination of expanding urban life with new psychologies oriented to self-expression also brought into being new social possibilities for women and men whose sexual desires did not conform to traditional patterns. Freud was only one of a number of thinkers in the period who urged a measure of toleration for sexual minorities, especially homosexuals—a term that entered specialized English usage in the 1890s and came into wider circulation in the years following World War I. Although the legal risks and social stigma borne by homosexuals remained very much in force, gay enclaves became more visible in American life and gay lives became more imaginable as a theme in American literature.

African Americans, like women, became mobile in these years as never before. Around 1915, as a direct result of the industrial needs of World War I, opportunities opened for African Americans in the factories of the North, and what became known as the Great Migration out of the South began. Not only did migration give the lie to southern white claims that African Americans were content with southern segregationist practices, but it also damaged the South's economy by draining off an important segment of its

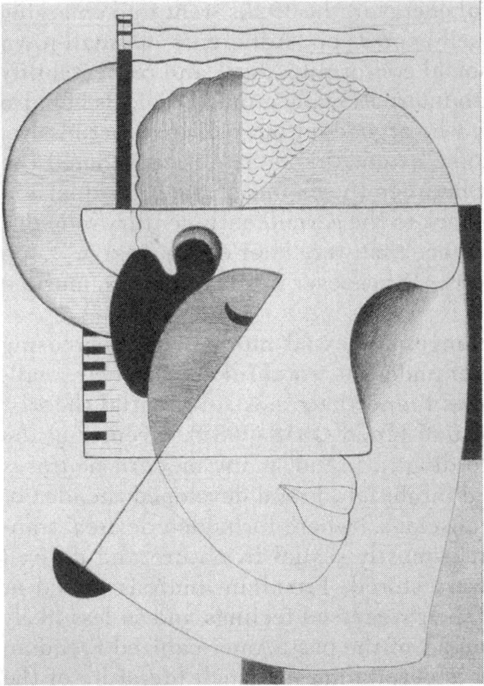

Lenox Avenue, Sargent Claude Johnson, 1938. Johnson's lithograph pays tribute to the clubs, ballrooms, and bars of New York City's Lenox Avenue, hub of the Harlem Renaissance. During the Great Depression, the Federal Art Project enlisted many notable artists to create graphic works celebrating American cultural and natural landmarks.

working population. Even though African Americans faced racism, segregation, and racial violence in the North, a black American presence soon became powerfully visible in American cultural life. Harlem, a section of New York City, attained an almost wholly black population of over 150,000 by the mid-1920s; from this "city within a city," African Americans wrote, performed, composed, and painted. Here as well they founded two major journals of opinion and culture, *The Crisis* (in 1910) and *Opportunity* (in 1923). This cultural outpouring influenced writers, painters, and musicians of other ethnicities and became known collectively as the Harlem Renaissance.

The famous black intellectual W. E. B. Du Bois had argued in *The Souls of Black Folk* (1903) that African Americans had a kind of double consciousness—of themselves as Americans and as blacks. This doubleness contributed to debates within the African American cultural community. The Harlem Renaissance sparked arguments between those who wanted to claim membership in the culture at large and those who wanted to stake out a separate artistic domain; between those who wanted to celebrate rural African American folkways and those committed to urban intellectuality; between those who wanted to join the American mainstream and those who, disgusted by American race prejudice, aligned themselves with worldwide revolutionary movements; between those who celebrated a "primitive" African heritage and those who rejected the idea as a degrading stereotype. African American women, as Nella Larsen's novel *Passing* (1929) testifies, could experience these divisions with special intensity. Women were very much called on in efforts to "uplift," advance, and educate the black community, but these communal obligations could be felt as constraints on individual freedom and exploration; meanwhile the white social world, given to exoticizing or sexualizing black women, offered few alternatives.

Class inequality, as well as American racial divisions, continued to generate intellectual and artistic debate in the interwar years. The nineteenth-century United States had been host to many radical movements—labor activism, utopianism, socialism, anarchism—inspired by diverse sources. In the twentieth century, especially following the rise of the Soviet Union, the American left increasingly drew its intellectual and political program from the Marxist tradition. The German philosopher Karl Marx (1818–1883) located the roots of human behavior in economics. He claimed that industrializing societies were structurally divided into two antagonistic classes based on different relations to the means of production—capital versus labor. The Industrial Revolution arose from the accumulation of surplus capital by industrialists paying the least possible amount to workers; the next stage in world history would be when workers took control of the means of production for themselves. Because, to Marx, the ideas and ideals of any particular society could represent the interests of only its dominant class, he derided individualism as a middle-class or "bourgeois" value that could only discourage worker solidarity.

Marx's ideas formed the basis for Communist political parties across Europe. In 1917, a Communist revolution in Russia led by Vladimir Ilyich Lenin (1870–1914) overthrew the tsarist regime, instituted the "dictatorship of the proletariat" that Marx had called for, and engineered the development of communism as a unified international movement. Americans who thought of themselves as Marxists in the 1920s and 1930s were usually connected with the Communist Party and subjected to government surveillance and occasional violence, as were socialists, anarchists, union organizers, and others who opposed unfettered American capitalism and marketplace competition. Although politics directed from outside the national boundaries was, almost by definition, "un-American," many adherents of these movements hoped to make the United States conform to its stated ideals, guaranteeing liberty and justice for all.

A defining conflict between American ideals and American realities for writers of the 1920s was the Sacco-Vanzetti case. Nicola Sacco and Bartolomeo Vanzetti were Italian immigrants, not Communists but avowed anarchists; on April 15, 1920, they were arrested near Boston after a murder during a robbery. They were accused of that crime, then tried and condemned to death in 1921; but it was widely believed that they had not received a fair trial and that their political beliefs had been held against them. After a number of appeals, they were executed in 1927, maintaining their innocence to the end. John Dos Passos and Katherine Anne Porter were among the many writers and intellectuals who demonstrated in their defense; several were arrested and jailed. It is estimated that well over a hundred poems (including works by William Carlos Williams, Edna St. Vincent Millay, and Carl Sandburg) along with six plays and eight novels of the time treated the incident from a sympathetic perspective.

Like the Sacco-Vanzetti case in the 1920s, the Scottsboro case in the 1930s brought many American writers and intellectuals, black and white, together in a cause—here, the struggle against racial bias in the justice system. In 1931 nine black youths were indicted in Scottsboro, Alabama, for the alleged rape of two white women in a railroad freight car. They were all found guilty, and some were sentenced to death. The U.S. Supreme Court reversed convictions twice; in a second trial one of the alleged victims retracted her testimony; in 1937 charges against five of the defendants were dropped. But four went to jail, in many people's view unfairly. American

Communists were especially active in the Scottsboro defense; but people across the political spectrum saw the case as crucial to the question of whether black people could receive fair trials in the American South. The unfair trial of an African American man became a literary motif in much writing of the period and beyond, including Richard Wright's *Native Son* (1940), William Faulkner's *Intruder in the Dust* (1948), and Harper Lee's *To Kill a Mockingbird* (1960).

SCIENCE AND TECHNOLOGY

Technology played a vital, although often invisible, role in all these events, because it linked places and spaces, contributing to the shaping of culture as a national phenomenon rather than a series of local manifestations. Without new modes of production, transportation, and communication, modern America in all its complexity could not have existed. Electricity for lights and appliances, along with the telephone—nineteenth-century inventions—expanded into American homes during these years, improving life for many but widening the gap between those plugged into the new networks and those outside them. The phonograph record and the record player (early devices for recording and playing music), the motion picture (which acquired sound in 1929), and the radio brought mass popular culture into being. Although the nineteenth-century dream of forging a scattered population into a single nation could now be realized more instantaneously and directly than was ever possible with print media, many intellectuals suspected that mass culture would create a robotic, passive population vulnerable to demagoguery.

The most powerful technological innovation, however, the automobile, encouraged activity, not passivity. Automobiles put Americans on the road, dramatically reshaped the structure of American industry and occupations, and altered the national topography as well. Along with work in automobile factories themselves, millions of other jobs—in steel mills, parts factories, highway construction and maintenance, gas stations, machine shops, roadside restaurants, motels—depended on the automobile. The road itself became—and has remained—a potent symbol of the United States and of modernity as well. Cities grew, suburbs came into being, small towns died, and new towns arose, all according to the placement of highways, which rapidly supplanted the railroad in shaping the patterns of twentieth-century American urban expansion. The United States had become a nation of migrants as much as or more than it was a nation of immigrants.

In tandem with the impact of technological change on daily life, one of the most important developments in the interwar period was the growth of modern "big" science. At the end of the nineteenth century and beginning of the twentieth, scientists discovered that the atom was not the smallest possible unit of matter, that matter was not indestructible, that both time and space were relative to an observer's position, that some phenomena were so small that attempts at measurement would alter them, that some outcomes could be predicted only in terms of statistical probability, that the universe might be infinite in size and yet infinitely expanding; hence, much of the commonsense basis of nineteenth-century science had to be put aside in favor of far more powerful but also far less commonsensical theories. Among many results, scientists and literary intellectuals became less able to communicate with each other, and their worldviews began to diverge. Writers responded with ambivalence to the new science, sometimes drawing on scientific images and ideas—"the imagination uses the phraseology of science," wrote the poet (and physician) William Carlos Williams—sometimes deploring the lost authority of traditional, humanistic explanations of the concrete, experienced world and felt human life. Gertrude Stein's radical literary experiments were partly inspired by her laboratory experiences in neuroanatomy at Harvard University and the Johns Hopkins Medical School. Poets like Ezra Pound, T. S. Eliot, and Wallace Stevens, however, along with many of their readers, questioned the capacity of science to provide accounts of subjective experience and moral issues, and they elevated the metaphorical language of poetry over the supposed literal accuracy of scientific description. The increased specialization of intellectual activity divided educated people into what the British novelist and physicist C. P. Snow was later to call the "two cultures"—science versus letters.

THE 1930s

The Great Depression was a worldwide phenomenon and fostered social unrest that led to the rise of fascist dictatorships in Europe, including those of Francisco Franco in Spain, Benito Mussolini in Italy, and Adolf Hitler in Germany. Hitler's program, which was to make Germany rich and strong by conquering the rest of Europe, led inexorably to World War II.

In the United States, the Depression made politics and economics the salient issues of public life and overrode questions of individual freedom with fear of mass collapse. Free-enterprise capitalism had always justified itself by arguing that the system not only made a small number of individuals immensely wealthy, but also guaranteed better lives for all. This assurance now rang hollow. The suicides of millionaire bankers

The Bread Line, New York, Clare Leighton, 1932. Leighton, who was born in England and became a U.S. citizen in 1939, made her reputation as an illustrator of rural life and work. This wood engraving's line of idled men dwarfed by their urban surroundings represents Depression-era New York City as the dark antithesis of Leighton's traditional subjects.

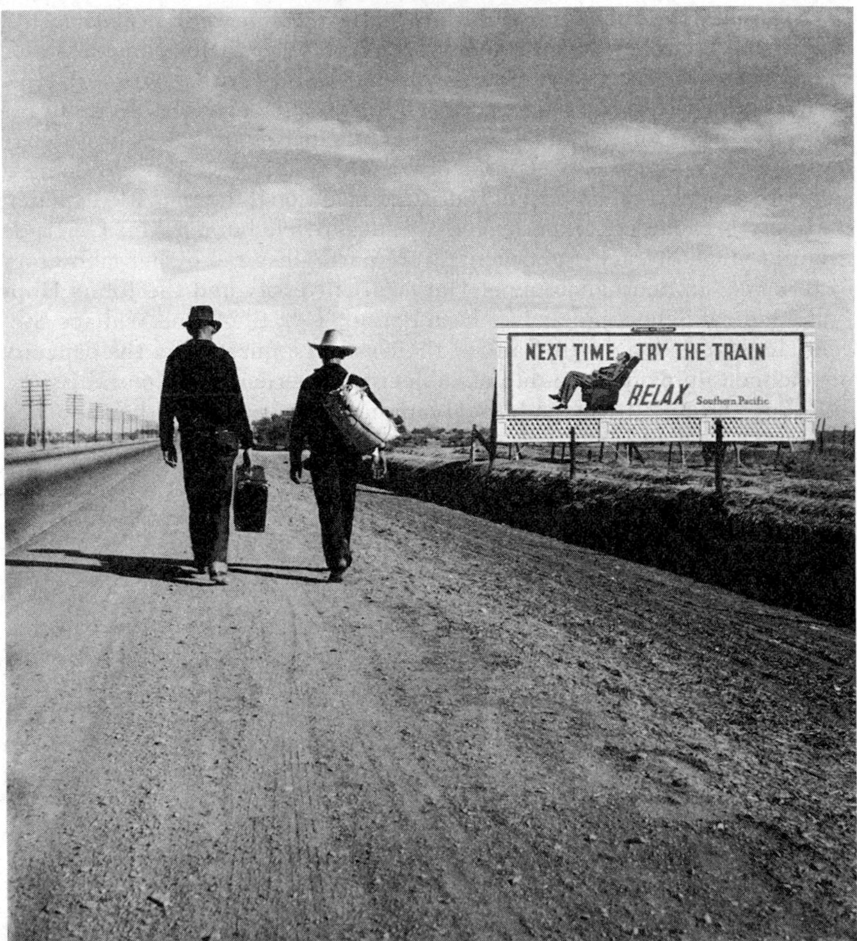

Towards Los Angeles, Dorothea Lange 1937. During the Great Depression, the Farm Security Administration (FSA)—one of many new government agencies created in response to the economic emergency—employed a number of well-known documentary photographers. Lange produced memorable portraits of migrants displaced by the Dust Bowl under the FSA's sponsorship.

and stockbrokers made the headlines, but more compelling was the enormous toll among ordinary people who lost their homes, jobs, farms, and life savings in the stock market crash. Conservatives advised waiting until things got better; radicals espoused immediate social revolution. In this polarized atmosphere, the election of Franklin Delano Roosevelt to the presidency in 1932 was a victory for American pragmatism; his series of liberal reforms—Social Security, programs creating jobs in the public sector, welfare, and unemployment insurance—cushioned the worst effects of the Depression and avoided the civil strife that many had thought inevitable.

The terrible economic situation in the United States produced a significant increase in Communist Party membership and prestige in the 1930s. Numerous intellectuals allied themselves with its causes, even if they did not actually become party members. An old radical journal, *The Masses*, later *The New Masses*, became the official literary voice of the party, and various other radical groups founded journals to represent their viewpoints. Visitors to the Soviet Union returned with glowing reports about a true workers' democracy and prosperity for all. The appeal of communism was significantly enhanced by its claim to be an opponent of fascism. Communists fought against Franco in the Spanish Civil War of 1936 and 1937. Hitler's nightmare policies of genocide and racial superiority, and his plans for a general European war to secure more room for the superior German "folk," became increasingly evident as European refugees began to flee to the United States in the 1930s, and many believed that the USSR would be the only country able to withstand the German war machine. But Soviet communism showed another side to Americans when American Communists were ordered to break up the meetings of other radical groups; when Josef Stalin, the Soviet dictator, instituted a series of brutal purges in the Soviet Union, beginning in 1936; and when in 1939 he signed a pact promising not to go to war against Germany. The disillusionment and betrayal felt by many radicals over these acts led many 1930s left-wing activists to become staunch anti-Communists after World War II.

AMERICAN VERSIONS OF MODERNISM

In English-language literary contexts, *modernism* is sometimes used as a catchall term for any kind of literary production in the interwar period that deals with the modern world. More narrowly, it refers to work that represents the transformation of traditional society under the pressures of modernity, and that breaks down traditional literary forms in doing so. Much modernist literature of this kind, which critics increasingly now set apart as "high modernism," is in a sense antimodern: it interprets modernity as an experience of loss. As its title underlines, T. S. Eliot's *The Waste Land*—the great poem of high modernism—represents the modern world as a scene of ruin.

Scholars of international modernism frequently trace its rise back to the later nineteenth century, citing the works of French symbolists in literature, Friedrich Nietzsche in philosophy, and Charles Darwin in science as examples of radically antitraditional modes of thought and artistic practice. As an artistic movement, however, modernism reached a defining level of international coherence and momentum in response to World War I, which was far more devastating to the Continent than it was to the United States. Modernism involved other art forms—sculpture, painting, dance—as well as literature. The poetry of William Butler Yeats; James Joyce's *Ulysses* (1922); Marcel Proust's *Remembrance of Things Past* (1913–27); Thomas Mann's novels and short stories, including *The Magic Mountain* (1927)—these were only a few of the literary products of this movement in England and on the Continent. In painting, artists like Pablo Picasso, Juan Gris, and Georges Braque invented cubism; in the 1920s the surrealistic movement known as Dadaism emerged. The American public was introduced to modern art at the famous New York Armory Show of 1913, which featured cubist paintings and caused an uproar. Marcel Duchamp's *Nude Descending a Staircase*, which, to the untrained eye, looked like a mass of crudely drawn rectangles, was especially provocative. Composers like Igor Stravinsky similarly produced music in a "modern" mode, featuring dissonance and discontinuity rather than neat formal structure and appealing tonal harmonies. His composition *The Rite of Spring* (1913) provoked a riot in the Paris concert hall where it was premiered.

At the heart of the high modernist aesthetic lay the conviction that the previously sustaining structures of human life, whether social, political, religious, or artistic, had been destroyed or shown up as falsehoods or, at best, arbitrary and fragile human constructions. Order, sequence, and unity in works of art might well express human desires for coherence rather than reliable intuitions of reality. Generalization, abstraction, and high-flown writing might conceal rather than convey the real. The traditional form of a story, with its beginnings, complications, and resolutions, might be an artifice imposed on the flux and fragmentation of experience. To the extent that art falsely presented such an order as given or natural, it had to be renovated.

Thus a key formal characteristic typical of high modernist works, whether in painting, sculpture, or musical composition, is its construction out of fragments—fragments of myth or history, fragments of experience or perception, fragments of previous artistic works. Modernist literature is often notable for what it omits: the explanations, interpretations, connections, summaries, and distancing that provide continuity, perspective, and security in earlier literatures. A modernist work may seem to begin arbitrarily, to advance without explanation, and to end without resolution, consisting of vivid segments juxtaposed without cushioning or integrating transitions. There may be abrupt shifts in perspective, voice, and tone. Its rhetoric may be understated, ironic. It may suggest rather than assert, making use of symbols and images instead of statements. Its elements may be drawn from disparate areas of experience. The effect may be shocking and unsettling; the experience of reading will be challenging and difficult. Faced with intuiting connections left unstated, the reader of a modernist work is often said to participate in the creative work of making the poem or story.

Some high modernist works, however, order their discontinuous elements into conspicuous larger patterns, patterns often drawn from world literature, mythologies, and religions. As its title advertises, Joyce's *Ulysses* maps the lives of its modern characters onto Homer's *Odyssey*; Eliot's *The Waste Land* layers the Christian narrative of death and resurrection over a broad range of quest myths. The question for readers lies in the meaning of these borrowed structures and mythic parallels: do they reveal profound similarities or ironic contrasts between the modern world and earlier times? For some writers and readers, the adaptability of ancient stories to modern circumstances testified to their deep truth, underlying the surface buzz and confusion of modernity; for others, such parallels indicated Christianity to be only a myth, one of many human constructions aimed at creating order out of, and finding purpose in, history's flux.

If meaning is a human construction, then meaning cannot be separated from the difficult process of its making; if meaning lies obscured deep underneath the ruins of modern life, then it must be effortfully sought out. Modernist literature therefore tended to foreground the search for meaning over didactic statement, and the subject matter of modernist writing often became, by extension, the literary work itself. While there have long been paintings about painting and poems about poetry, high modernist writing was especially self-reflexive, concerned with its own nature as art and with its questioning of previous traditions of literature. Ironically—because this subject matter was motivated by deep concern about the interrelation of literature and life—this subject often had the effect of limiting the audience for a modernist work; high modernism demanded of its ideal readers an encyclopedic knowledge of the traditions it fragmented or ironized. Nevertheless, over time, the principles of modernism became increasingly influential.

Modernist techniques transformed fiction as well as poetry in this period. Prose writers strove for directness, compression, and vividness. They were often sparing of words. The average novel became quite a bit shorter than it had been in the nineteenth century, when a novel was expected to fill two or even three volumes. The modernist aesthetic gave a new significance to the short story, which had previously been thought of as a relatively slight artistic form. (Poems too became shorter, as narrative poems lost ground to lyrics and the repetitive patterns of rhyme and meter that had helped sustain long poems in previous centuries lost ground to free verse.) Victorian or realistic fiction achieved its effects by accumulation and saturation; modern fiction preferred suggestion. Victorian fiction often featured an authoritative narrator; modern fiction tended to be written in the first person or to limit the reader to one character's point of view on the action. This limitation accorded with the modernist sense that truth does not exist objectively but is the product of the mind's interaction with reality. The selected point of view is often that of a naive or marginal person—a child or an outsider—to convey better the reality of confusion and dissent rather than the myth of certainty and consensus. In both poetry and fiction, modernists tended to emphasize the concrete sensory image or detail over general statement. Allusions to literary, historical, philosophical, or religious details of the past often keep company, in modernist works, with vignettes of contemporary life, chunks of popular culture, dream imagery, and symbolism drawn from the author's private repertory of life experiences. A work built from these various materials may move across time and space, shift from the public to the personal, and open up literature as a field for every sort of concern. The inclusion of material previously deemed "unliterary" in works of high seriousness extended to language that might previously have been thought improper, including representations of the speech of the uneducated and the inarticulate, the colloquial, slangy, and the popular. Traditional realistic fiction had incorporated colloquial and dialect speech, often to comic effect, in its representation of the broad tapestry of social life; but such speakers were usually framed by a narrator's educated literary voice, conveying truth and authority over subordinate voices. In modernist writing like William Faulkner's *As I Lay Dying*, these voices assume the full burden of the narrative's authority; this is what Ernest Hemingway had in mind when he asserted that the American literary tradition began with *Huckleberry Finn*.

"Serious" literature between the two world wars thus found itself in a difficult relationship with the culture at large. If it attacked the old-style ideals of polite literature, it felt itself attacked in turn by the ever-growing industry of popular literature. The reading audience in America was vast, but it preferred kinds of books different from those turned out by literary high modernists; tales of romance or adventure, historical novels, crime fiction, and Westerns became popular modes, enjoying a success that most serious writers could only dream of. The problem was that often they did dream of it; unrealistically, perhaps, the Ezra Pounds and Nathanael Wests of the era imagined themselves having an audience of millions. When, on occasion, this dream came true—as it did for F. Scott Fitzgerald and Ernest Hemingway—writers often accused themselves, and were accused by others, of having sold out.

Serious writers in these years were, in fact, being published and read as writers had not been in earlier times. Modernist works were widely reviewed and referred to in magazines and newspapers of general circulation, where experimental writers like Gertrude Stein enjoyed a notoriety much in excess of their sales. Outside the mass periodical market, the number of so-called little magazines—that is, magazines of very small circulations devoted to the publication of works for a small audience (sometimes the works of a specific group of authors)—was in the hundreds. *Poetry: A Magazine of Verse* began in 1912. *The Little Review* followed in 1914. Then came the *Seven Arts* in 1916, the *Dial* in 1917, the *Frontier* in 1920, *Reviewer* and *Broom* in 1921, *Fugitive* in 1922, *This Quarter* in 1925, *Transition* and *Hound and Horn* in 1927, and many more. The culture that did not listen attentively to serious writers or make them rich still gave them plenty of opportunity to be read, and it allowed them (in such neighborhoods as Greenwich Village in New York City) a freedom in lifestyle that was new in American history. In addition, such major publishers as New Directions, Random House, Scribner, and Harper, and such stylish periodicals as *Vanity Fair*, were actively looking for serious fiction and poetry to feature alongside best sellers like *Gone with the Wind* (1936) and *Anthony Adverse* (1933). Some writers in the period were able to use these opportunities to cross over the hierarchies separating high modernism from middlebrow and popular culture.

***Broom* Magazine Cover,** Enrico Prampolini, 1922. *Broom* was among the most internationally ambitious of modernism's little magazines, publishing authors such as Gertrude Stein, Wallace Stevens, and Jean Toomer alongside work by artists like Man Ray and Picasso. This cover complemented an essay by Harold Loeb, *Broom*'s editor, that celebrated the modernist beauty of engines, motors, and airplanes.

Vanity Fair published Gertrude Stein, E. E. Cummings, Sherwood Anderson, and Edna St. Vincent Millay. By the 1930s, American literary modernism had its recognized celebrities in authors like Stein, Fitzgerald, and Hemingway, and a substantial supporting community of publishers, critics, and readers.

MODERNISM ABROAD AND ON NATIVE GROUNDS

The profession of authorship in the United States has always defined itself in part as a patriotic enterprise aimed at developing a cultural life for the nation and embodying national values. High modernism, however, was a self-consciously international movement, and the leading American exponents of high modernism tended to be permanent expatriates, such as Gertrude Stein, Ezra Pound, H.D., and T. S. Eliot. These writers left the United States because they found the country lacking in a tradition of high culture and indifferent, if not actively hostile, to artistic achievement. They also believed that a national culture could never be more than parochial. In London in the first two decades of the twentieth century and in Paris during the 1920s, they found a vibrant community of dedicated artists and a society that respected them and allowed them a great deal of personal freedom. Yet they seldom thought of themselves as deserting their nation, and only Eliot gave up American citizenship (sometimes, too, the traffic went in the other direction, as when the British-born poet Mina Loy became an American citizen). They thought of themselves as bringing the United States into the larger context of European culture. The ranks of these permanent expatriates were swelled by American writers who lived abroad for some part of the period, among them Ernest Hemingway, Sherwood Anderson, F. Scott Fitzgerald, Claude McKay, Katherine Anne Porter, Nella Larsen, Robert Frost, and Eugene O'Neill.

Those writers who came back, however, and those who never left took seriously the task of integrating modernist ideas and methods with American subject matter. Not every experimental modernist writer disconnected literary ambitions from national belonging: Hart Crane, Marianne Moore, and William Carlos Williams, for example, all wanted to write overtly "American" works. Some writers—as the title of John Dos Passos's *U.S.A.* clearly shows—attempted to speak for the nation as a whole. Crane's long poem *The Bridge* and Williams's *Paterson* both take an American city as symbol and expand it to the nation, following the model established by Walt Whitman. F. Scott Fitzgerald's *The Great Gatsby* is similarly ambitious, and many writers addressed the whole nation in individual works—for example, E. E. Cummings's "next to of course god america i" and Claude McKay's "America." And a profoundly modern writer like William Faulkner cannot be extricated from his commitment to writing about his native South.

Like Faulkner, many writers of the period chose to identify themselves with the American scene and to root their work in a specific region, continuing a tradition of regionalist American writing that burgeoned in the years following the American Civil War. Their perspectives on their various regions were sometimes celebratory and sometimes critical. Carl Sandburg, Edgar Lee Masters, Sherwood Anderson, and Willa Cather worked with the Midwest; Cather grounded her later work in the Southwest; John Steinbeck wrote about California; Edwin Arlington Robinson and Robert Frost identified their work with New England. An especially strong center of regional literary activity emerged in the South, which had a weak literary tradition up to the Civil War. Thomas Wolfe's was an Appalachian South of hardy mountain people. Katherine Anne Porter wrote about her native Texas as a heterogeneous combination of frontier, plantation, and Hispanic cultures. Zora Neale Hurston drew on her childhood memories of the all-black town of Eatonville, Florida, for much of her best-known fiction, including her novel *Their Eyes Were Watching God*. William Faulkner depicted a South at once grounded in his native state of Mississippi and also expanded into a mythic region anguished by racial and historical conflict.

As the pairing of Hurston and Faulkner suggests, the history of race in the United States was central to the specifically national subject matter to which many American modernists remained committed. Although race as a subject potentially implicated all American writers, it was African Americans whose contributions most signally differentiated American modernism from that of Europe. The numerous writers associated with the Harlem Renaissance made it impossible ever to think of a national literature without the work of black Americans. Countee Cullen, Langston Hughes, and Zora Neale Hurston attained particular prominence at the time; but others, including Claude McKay and Nella Larsen, were also well known. All were influenced by the values of modernism: both Hughes, for example, with his incorporation of blues rhythms into poetry, and Hurston, with her poetic depictions of folk culture, applied modernist techniques to represent twentieth-century African American lives. Writers associated with the Renaissance expressed protest and anger—Hughes, in particular, wrote a number of powerful antilynching and anticapitalist poems; but the movement's writers also articulated the hopes of racial uplift and, like Hurston, focused on the vitality of black culture more than on the burdens of racism. At least part of this approach was strategic—the bulk of the readership for Harlem authors was white. The note of pure anger was not expressed until Richard Wright, who had come to literary maturity in Chicago, published *Native Son* in 1940. Contributions to the Harlem Renaissance came from artists in many media; an influence equal to or greater than that of the writers came from musicians. Jazz and blues, African American in origin, are felt by many to be the most authentically American art forms the nation has ever produced. African American singers and musicians in this period achieved worldwide reputations and were often much more highly regarded abroad than in the United States.

American literary women had been active on the national scene from Anne Bradstreet forward. Their increasing prominence in the nineteenth century generated a backlash from some male modernists, who asserted their own artistic seriousness by identifying women writers with the didactic, popular writing against which they rebelled. But women refused to stay on the sidelines and associated themselves with all the important literary trends of the era: H.D. and Amy Lowell with imagism, Marianne Moore and Gertrude Stein with high modernism, Willa Cather with mythic regionalism, Zora Neale Hurston and Nella Larsen with the Harlem Renaissance, Katherine Anne Porter with psychological fiction, Edna St. Vincent

Millay with social and sexual liberation. Many of these writers concentrated on depictions of women characters or women's thoughts and experiences. Yet few labeled themselves feminists. The passage of the suffrage amendment in 1920 had taken some of the energy out of feminism that would not return until the 1960s. Some women writers found social causes like labor and racism more important than women's rights; others focused their energies on struggles less amenable to public, legal remedies, as when Mina Loy's "Feminist Manifesto" sought to represent motherhood as compatible with an energetic vision of female sexuality. Nevertheless, these literary women were clearly pushing back the boundaries of the permissible, demanding new cultural freedom for women and taking positions on public causes.

MODERN LITERATURE ON STAGE AND SCREEN

Drama in America was slow to develop as a self-conscious literary form. It was not until 1920 (the year of Eugene O'Neill's *Beyond the Horizon*) that the United States produced a world-class playwright. This is not to say that *theater*—productions and performances—was new to American life. After the American Revolution, theaters—at first with itinerant English actors and companies, then with American—opened throughout the East; among early centers were Boston and Philadelphia as well as New York City. As the country expanded westward, so did its theater, together with other kinds of performance: burlesques, showboats on the Mississippi, minstrel shows, pantomimes. As the nineteenth century went on, the activity became centered more and more in New York—especially within the few blocks known as Broadway. Managers originated plays there and then sent them out to tour through the rest of the country, as Eugene O'Neill's father did with his *Count of Monte Cristo*.

Innovations in American theater are often launched in reaction against Broadway, a pattern observable as early as 1915 with the formation of the Washington Square Players and the Provincetown Players (organized by Susan Glaspell and others), both located in New York's Greenwich Village and both dedicated to the production of plays that more conservative managers refused. The Provincetown Players produced the first works of Glaspell and Eugene O'Neill. These fledgling companies, and others like them, often knew better what they opposed than what they wanted. European influence was important to them. By 1915, Henrik Ibsen in Europe and George Bernard Shaw in England had shown that the theater could be an arena for serious ideas; meanwhile the psychological dramas of August Strindberg, the symbolic work of Maurice Maeterlinck, and the sophisticated criticism of Arthur Schnitzler provided other models. The American tours of European companies, in particular the Moscow Art Theatre in 1923, further exposed Americans to the theatrical avant-garde.

Just as his contemporaries in poetry and fiction were changing and questioning their forms, so Eugene O'Neill sought to refine his. He experimented less in language than in dramatic structure and in new production methods available through technology (e.g., lighting) or borrowed from the stylized realism of German expressionism. Playwrights such as Sidney Howard

Eugene O'Neill and the Provincetown Players, 1916. O'Neill (on ladder) and members of the company preparing the stage for *Bound East for Cardiff,* O'Neill's first play produced by the players, at the company's first New York City theater, on Macdougal Street in Greenwich Village.

(1891–1939), Lillian Hellman (1905–1984), and Robert Sherwood (1896–1955) wrote serious realistic plays. George Kaufman and his many collaborators, especially Moss Hart, invented a distinctively American form, the wisecracking domestic and social comedy, while S. N. Behrman and Philip Barry wrote higher comedies of ideas. The musical comedy was another distinctively American invention: beginning as a revue of jokes, songs, and dances, it progressed steadily toward an integration of its various elements, reaching new heights with the work of George and Ira Gershwin in the 1920s and 1930s and of Oscar Hammerstein, in collaboration with Jerome Kern or Richard Rodgers, from the 1920s on into the 1950s.

Social commentary and satire had been conspicuous in American drama since the early 1920s, beginning, perhaps, with Elmer Rice's fiercely expressionistic play about a rebellious nonentity, *The Adding Machine* (1923). During the Depression social criticism became a much more important dramatic theme, with political plays performed by many radical groups. Among the most significant was Clifford Odets's *Waiting for Lefty* (1935), which dramatized a taxi drivers' strike meeting and turned the stage into a platform for argument. The Federal Theatre Project of 1935–39, established by President Franklin Roosevelt's administration to provide employment to theater artists of all kinds during the Great Depression, produced plays by Odets, O'Neill, and other contemporary authors, alongside new productions of Shakespeare and Aristophanes. The Negro Theatre Unit, a major creative arm of the project, produced works by African American writers, like W. E. B. Du Bois's *Haiti* (1938), as well as innovative productions with black casts, most famously the all-black version of Shakespeare's *Macbeth* adapted by Orson Welles in 1936.

With the rise of the film industry, many popular playwrights and authors of fiction found new outlets for their work in Hollywood. Robert Sherwood became a screenwriter and had a number of his plays adapted into films; Sidney Howard won the Academy Award in 1940 for his adaptation of *Gone with the Wind*. Where writers like William Faulkner and F. Scott Fitzgerald experienced Hollywood as a graveyard of serious literary ambition, Katherine Anne Porter found in the film industry not only financial rewards but also a springboard to wider critical and popular appreciation for her work as a whole. The motion picture industry in turn provided American writers with important new subject matter: Hollywood-based novels of the period include Fitzgerald's *The Last Tycoon* (completed after his death and published in 1941), Nathanael West's *The Day of the Locust* (newly added to this volume), and Budd Schulberg's *What Makes Sammy Run?* (1941)—all of which were later turned into films. The adaptation of literary works from one medium to another accelerated in the first half of the twentieth century. Writers explored the commercial and artistic possibilities emerging in the new relationships among literature's printed page, the stage, and the screen in ways that look forward to the hyperreal, media-saturated generic experimentation that would characterize much American literature in the second half of the twentieth century.

1914–1945

TEXTS	CONTEXTS
1910 Edwin Arlington Robinson, **"Miniver Cheevy"**	
1914 Robert Frost, **"Home Burial"** • Carl Sandburg, **"Chicago"**	**1914–18** World War I
1915 Edgar Lee Masters, ***Spoon River Anthology*** • Ezra Pound begins ***Cantos***	**1915** Great Migration of African Americans from the rural South to northern industrial cities
1916 Susan Glaspell, ***Trifles*** • Robert Frost, **"Birches"**	
	1917 United States declares war on Germany • revolution in Russia brings Communist Party to power
1918 Willa Cather, ***My Ántonia*** • Carl Sandburg, **"Grass"**	**1918** Daylight Savings Time instituted to allow more daylight for war production
1919 Sherwood Anderson, ***Winesburg, Ohio*** • Amy Lowell, **"Madonna of the Evening Flowers"**	**1919** Senate limits U.S. participation in League of Nations; does not ratify Versailles Treaty to end World War I
1920 Pound, **"Hugh Selwyn Mauberley"**	**1920** 18th Amendment prohibits the manufacture, sale, and transportation of alcoholic beverages • 19th Amendment gives women the vote
	1920–27 Sacco-Vanzetti trial
1921 T. S. Eliot, ***The Waste Land*** • Claude McKay, **"Africa, America"** • Marianne Moore, **"Poetry"** • Langston Hughes, **"The Negro Speaks of Rivers"**	
	1922 Fascism rises in Europe; Mussolini becomes dictator of Italy
1923 Wallace Stevens, **"Sunday Morning"** • Jean Toomer, ***Cane***	
1924 H.D. (Hilda Doolittle), **"Helen"**	**1924** Exclusionary immigration act bars Asians from the United States
1925 Countee Cullen, **"Heritage"** • Gertrude Stein, ***The Making of Americans*** • Alain Locke publishes *The New Negro*, leading anthology of the Harlem Renaissance	
1926 Ernest Hemingway, ***The Sun Also Rises*** • Hart Crane, ***The Bridge***	
1927 Zora Neale Hurston, **"The Eatonville Anthology"**	**1927** *The Jazz Singer*, first full-length "talkie," is released
1929 Nella Larsen, ***Passing***	**1929** Stock market crashes; Great Depression begins

Boldface titles indicate works in the anthology.

TEXTS	CONTEXTS
1930 Katherine Anne Porter, **"Flowering Judas"**	1930 Sinclair Lewis is first American to win Nobel Prize for literature
1931 E. E. Cummings, **"i sing of Olaf glad and big"** • F. Scott Fitzgerald, **"Babylon Revisited"**	1931 Scottsboro trial
1932 Sterling Brown, **"He Was a Man"**	1932 Franklin Delano Roosevelt's New Deal introduces Social Security, welfare, and unemployment insurance
1933 Gertrude Stein, *The Autobiography of Alice B. Toklas*	1933 Adolf Hitler's Nationalist Socialist (Nazi) Party comes to power in Germany • 18th Amendment repealed
1934 William Carlos Williams, **"This Is Just to Say"**	1934 Wheeler-Howard (Indian Reorganization) Act passed, ending Dawes era
1936 Ernest Hemingway, "The Snows of Kilimanjaro"	1936 Hitler begins armed occupation of Europe 1936–39 Spanish Civil War: U.S. volunteers among those fighting against General Franco, who becomes dictator of Spain
1937 Thomas Wolfe, **"The Lost Boy"**	1937 Stalin's purges
1938 John Dos Passos, ***U.S.A.*** • William Faulkner, **"Barn Burning"**	
1939 Richard Wright, **"The Man Who Was Almost a Man"** • Nathanael West, ***The Day of the Locust***	1939–45 World War II • the Holocaust
1940 Eugene O'Neill, ***Long Day's Journey into Night***	
	1941 Japan bombs Pearl Harbor, Hawaii • United States enters war against Japan and its allies, Germany and Italy
1942 Wallace Stevens, **"Of Modern Poetry"**	1942 President Roosevelt orders internment of Japanese Americans in camps
1943 Langston Hughes, **"Madam and Her Madam"**	
1944 H.D. (Hilda Doolittle), ***The Walls Do Not Fall*** • Marianne Moore, **"In Distrust of Merits"**	1944 D Day; Allied invasion of Normandy
	1945 German forces surrender in spring; Japan surrenders in August following explosion of two nuclear bombs over Japanese cities

EDGAR LEE MASTERS
1868–1950

Few books of poetry published in the United States have had an immediate impact like that of *Spoon River Anthology.* Its lack of rhyme and verse, its rough, flat, unpoetic diction, its forthright presentation of private yet ordinary lives, its representation of sex as a basic human motive, and its deeply critical view of small-town values—these traits of the volume ran counter to public expectations of what poetry should be like. But controversy was good for sales; the book went through nineteen printings in its first edition, a record for poetry up until then.

Edgar Lee Masters was practicing law in Chicago at the time of its publication in 1915. He was born in Kansas and grew up in two small Illinois towns, Petersburg and Lewiston. His father was a lawyer and politician, his mother a lover of music and literature homesick for her native New England. Masters attended Knox College in Galesburg, Illinois, for a year and then studied law in his father's office. He passed his bar exams and entered the legal profession to please his father, but broke decisively with both parents when he moved to Chicago in 1891.

In Chicago, Masters met many of the writers and intellectuals involved in the Chicago Renaissance, a movement aiming to make the city a cultural center. He worked with Harriet Monroe, editor of *Poetry: A Magazine of Verse,* an important little magazine of the era, and began to publish poetry of his own. A friend, William Marion Reedy, publisher of the influential St. Louis weekly *Reedy's Mirror,* gave him a copy of J. W. Mackail's *Selected Epigrams from the Greek Anthology.* In this collection of some four thousand short poems written between 700 B.C.E. and 1000 C.E., Masters found interconnected autobiographical poems, where the speaker in one poem talked bluntly about speakers in other poems. This structure showed Masters how to give poetic shape to a naturalistic vision more commonly associated with fiction.

All the speakers in *Spoon River Anthology* are dead, buried in the cemetery on "the hill," which is the title of the first poem in the book: "All, all, are sleeping on the hill." These lifelong friends and neighbors continue their loves and quarrels beyond the grave. Their dissonant voices converge in a lament for suppressed and wasted lives, only rarely varied by joy or gusto. Sex has driven them, but given little pleasure. They long for the sympathy that they withhold from each other. Yet the poems as a group are compassionate, not judgmental.

Masters's dramatic sense, his ability to condense and convey a whole life through the narration of one incident, contributed to the craft of the short story as well as to a new sense of what poetry might consist of. His work was immediate inspiration for hostile depictions of small-town and small-minded America in the work of such 1920s writers as Sherwood Anderson and Sinclair Lewis. None of Masters's many other books of verse, except the sequel *The New Spoon River* in 1924, attained the reputation of *Spoon River Anthology.* He was, however, a prolific writer in other modes. He composed several novels; biographies of Abraham Lincoln, Vachel Lindsay (the Chicago poet), Walt Whitman, and Mark Twain; and his own autobiography, *Across Spoon River,* in 1936.

In all, he wrote more than fifty books, committing himself after the success of *Spoon River Anthology* to a full-time literary career. He married twice and had four children. He gave up the law, left Chicago, and settled in New York City in 1920, living in later life at the Chelsea Hotel, a favorite residence for writers.

The text of the poems included here is that of *Spoon River Anthology* (1915).

Trainor, the Druggist

Only the chemist can tell, and not always the chemist,
What will result from compounding
Fluids or solids.
And who can tell
How men and women will interact
On each other, or what children will result?
There were Benjamin Pantier and his wife,
Good in themselves, but evil toward each other:
He oxygen, she hydrogen,
Their son, a devastating fire.
I Trainor, the druggist, a mixer of chemicals,
Killed while making an experiment,
Lived unwedded.

1915

"Butch" Weldy

After I got religion and steadied down
They gave me a job in the canning works,
And every morning I had to fill
The tank in the yard with gasoline,
That fed the blow-fires in the sheds
To heat the soldering irons.
And I mounted a rickety ladder to do it,
Carrying buckets full of the stuff.
One morning, as I stood there pouring,
The air grew still and seemed to heave,
And I shot up as the tank exploded,
And down I came with both legs broken,
And my eyes burned crisp as a couple of eggs.
For someone left a blow-fire going,
And something sucked the flame in the tank.
The Circuit Judge said whoever did it
Was a fellow-servant of mine, and so
Old Rhodes' son didn't have to pay me.
And I sat on the witness stand as blind
As Jack the Fiddler, saying over and over,
"I didn't know him at all."

1915

Margaret Fuller[1] Slack

I would have been as great as George Eliot[2]
But for an untoward fate.
For look at the photograph of me made by Penniwit,
Chin resting on hand, and deep-set eyes—
Gray, too, and far-searching.
But there was the old, old problem:
Should it be celibacy, matrimony or unchastity?
Then John Slack, the rich druggist, wooed me,
Luring me with the promise of leisure for my novel,
And I married him, giving birth to eight children,
And had no time to write.
It was all over with me, anyway,
When I ran the needle in my hand
While washing the baby's things,
And died from lock-jaw, an ironical death.
Hear me, ambitious souls,
Sex is the curse of life!

1915

Nellie Clark

I was only eight years old;
And before I grew up and knew what it meant
I had no words for it, except
That I was frightened and told my Mother;
And that my Father got a pistol
And would have killed Charlie, who was a big boy,
Fifteen years old, except for his Mother.
Nevertheless the story clung to me.
But the man who married me, a widower of thirty-five,
Was a newcomer and never heard it
Till two years after we were married.
Then he considered himself cheated,
And the village agreed that I was not really a virgin.
Well, he deserted me, and I died
The following winter.

1915

1. New England feminist, writer, and journalist (1810–1850); symbol of an emancipated and intellectual woman.
2. English novelist (1819–1880), whose real name was Mary Ann Evans; author of such classics as *The Mill on the Floss* (1860) and *Middlemarch* (1871–72).

Abel Melveny

I bought every kind of machine that's known—
Grinders, shellers, planters, mowers,
Mills and rakes and ploughs and threshers—
And all of them stood in the rain and sun,
Getting rusted, warped and battered,
For I had no sheds to store them in,
And no use for most of them.
And toward the last, when I thought it over,
There by my window, growing clearer
About myself, as my pulse slowed down,
And looked at one of the mills I bought—
Which I didn't have the slightest need of,
As things turned out, and I never ran—
A fine machine, once brightly varnished,
And eager to do its work,
Now with its paint washed off—
I saw myself as a good machine
That Life had never used.

1915

EDWIN ARLINGTON ROBINSON

1869–1935

regional/NE

Surveying Edwin Arlington Robinson's poetry after his death, Robert Frost observed that Robinson "could make lyric talk like drama." Like Frost, Robinson made his name as a New England regional poet. Along with Edgar Lee Masters and Sherwood Anderson, Robinson focused his most compelling work on wasted or impoverished lives played out in a small-town setting. His brief narrative and portrait poems, composed in traditionally rhymed and metered forms, often represent these blighted lives from the communal viewpoint of a tragic chorus, as in "Richard Cory" and "Eros Turannos"—a collective *we* bearing ironic witness to forms of suffering it cannot fully comprehend.

Robinson was raised in Gardiner, Maine, which became "Tilbury Town" in his poems. His father's lumber business and land speculations failed during the Great Panic of 1893. One of his brothers, a physician, became a drug addict; the other, a businessman, became an alcoholic. Robinson, by nature a scholar and book lover, was able to afford just two years at Harvard, where he continued an ambitious program of largely self-directed reading that included classical works in many languages as well as such American writers as Hawthorne, Whitman, Emerson, and Henry James. He was also drawn to the bleak vision of the British novelist Thomas

Hardy. These influences were distilled in the gloomy, austere, yet sonorous verse of his second book, *The Children of the Night* (1897)—*The Torrent and the Night Before* had been published the previous year, at his own expense.

Robinson moved from Gardiner to New York City shortly after *The Children of the Night* appeared. The volume came to the attention of no less a patron than President Theodore Roosevelt, whose son Kermit urged him to find a way of relieving Robinson's financial anxieties. Like Nathaniel Hawthorne and Herman Melville before him, Robinson in 1905 reluctantly accepted a political appointment in the U.S. Customs Service, which he resigned with Roosevelt's departure from office in 1909. *The Town Down River* (1910) and *The Man against the Sky* (1916) brought Robinson increasing numbers of readers and critical notice. His *Collected Poems* (1921) won the first of his three Pulitzer Prizes.

By this time Robinson was over fifty and feeling increasingly distanced from the free verse of his modernist contemporaries. His own efforts turned in the direction of narrative poems, including a trilogy of long poems in imitation of medieval narratives that began with *Merlin* (1917) and ended with *Tristram* (1927), another Pulitzer Prize winner. These works found popular audiences, but many critics and fellow poets were less enthusiastic to see Robinson embrace without irony the romantic nostalgia he had satirized in "Miniver Cheevy." The prizes and honors of Robinson's final decades represented, to a large extent, belated recognition of his earlier poetry. Reviewing his *Collected Poems* in 1922, the poet and critic Yvor Winters praised Robinson for inheriting and extending the twisted, hard, epigrammatic New England tradition of Emerson and Emily Dickinson: to that tradition, Winters wrote, Robinson contributed his own "polished stoniness of mind."

The text of the poems included here is that of *Collected Poems of Edwin Arlington Robinson* (1921, 1937).

Luke Havergal

Go to the western gate, Luke Havergal,—
There where the vines cling crimson on the wall,—
And in the twilight wait for what will come.
The wind will moan, the leaves will whisper some,—
Whisper of her, and strike you as they fall;
But go, and if you trust her she will call.
Go to the western gate, Luke Havergal—
Luke Havergal.

No, there is not a dawn in eastern skies
To rift the fiery night that's in your eyes;
But there, where western glooms are gathering,
The dark will end the dark, if anything:
God slays Himself with every leaf that flies,
And hell is more than half of paradise.
No, there is not a dawn in eastern skies—
In eastern skies.

Out of a grave I come to tell you this,—
Out of a grave I come to quench the kiss

That flames upon your forehead with a glow
That blinds you to the way that you must go.
Yes, there is yet one way to where she is,—
Bitter, but one that faith may never miss.
Out of a grave I come to tell you this—
To tell you this.

There is the western gate, Luke Havergal,
There are the crimson leaves upon the wall.
Go,—for the winds are tearing them away,—
Nor think to riddle the dead words they say,
Nor any more to feel them as they fall;
But go! and if you trust her she will call.
There is the western gate, Luke Havergal—
Luke Havergal.

1896

Richard Cory

"communal viewpoint of a tragic chorus"

Whenever Richard Cory went down town,
We people on the pavement looked at him:
He was a gentleman from sole to crown,
Clean favored, and imperially slim.

And he was always quietly arrayed,
And he was always human when he talked;
But still he fluttered pulses when he said,
"Good-morning," and he glittered when he walked.

And he was rich—yes, richer than a king,—
And admirably schooled in every grace:
In fine, we thought that he was everything
To make us wish that we were in his place.

So on we worked, and waited for the light,
And went without the meat, and cursed the bread;
And Richard Cory, one calm summer night,
Went home and put a bullet through his head.

1896

Miniver Cheevy

Satire

Miniver Cheevy, child of scorn,
   Grew lean while he assailed the seasons;
He wept that he was ever born,
   And he had reasons.

Miniver loved the days of old
  When swords were bright and steeds were prancing;
The vision of a warrior bold
  Would set him dancing.

Miniver sighed for what was not,
  And dreamed, and rested from his labors;
He dreamed of Thebes and Camelot,[1]
  And Priam's neighbors.[2]

Miniver mourned the ripe renown
  That made so many a name so fragrant;
He mourned Romance, now on the town,
  And Art, a vagrant.

Miniver loved the Medici,[3]
  Albeit he had never seen one;
He would have sinned incessantly
  Could he have been one.

Miniver cursed the commonplace
  And eyed a khaki suit with loathing;
He missed the mediæval grace
  Of iron clothing.

Miniver scorned the gold he sought,
  But sore annoyed was he without it;
Miniver thought, and thought, and thought,
  And thought about it.

Miniver Cheevy, born too late,
  Scratched his head and kept on thinking;
Miniver coughed, and called it fate,
  And kept on drinking.

1910

Eros Turannos[1]

She fears him, and will always ask
  What fated her to choose him;
She meets in his engaging mask
  All reasons to refuse him;
But what she meets and what she fears

1. Thebes was an ancient city in Boeotia, rival of Athens and Sparta for supremacy in Greece and the setting of Sophocles's tragedies about Oedipus. Camelot is the legendary court of King Arthur and the knights of the Round Table.
2. The neighbors of King Priam in Homer's *Iliad* are his heroic compatriots in the doomed city of Troy.
3. Family of wealthy merchants, politicians, churchmen, and art patrons in 16th-century Florence.
1. Love, the tyrant (Latin).

Are less than are the downward years,
Drawn slowly to the foamless weirs
  Of age, were she to lose him.

Between a blurred sagacity
  That once had power to sound him,
And Love, that will not let him be
  The Judas[2] that she found him,
Her pride assuages her almost,
As if it were alone the cost.—
He sees that he will not be lost,
  And waits and looks around him.

A sense of ocean and old trees
  Envelops and allures him;
Tradition, touching all he sees,
  Beguiles and reassures him;
And all her doubts of what he says
Are dimmed with what she knows of days—
Till even prejudice delays
  And fades, and she secures him.

The falling leaf inaugurates
  The reign of her confusion;
The pounding wave reverberates
  The dirge of her illusion;
And home, where passion lived and died,
Becomes a place where she can hide,
While all the town and harbor side
  Vibrate with her seclusion.

We tell you, tapping on our brows,
  The story as it should be,—
As if the story of a house
  Were told, or ever could be;
We'll have no kindly veil between
Her visions and those we have seen,—
As if we guessed what hers have been,
  Or what they are or would be.

Meanwhile we do no harm; for they
  That with a god have striven,
Not hearing much of what we say,
  Take what the god has given;
Though like waves breaking it may be
Or like a changed familiar tree,
Or like a stairway to the sea
  Where down the blind are driven.

1914, 1921

2. One of the twelve apostles in the New Testament; he betrayed Jesus Christ.

WILLA CATHER
1873–1947

Willa Cather was born in Virginia, the oldest child of Charles and Mary Virginia Cather, who moved with their family to the Nebraska Divide when she was nine years old. After a year of farming, they relocated to the town of Red Cloud, and her father went into the real estate business. At sixteen, Cather moved on her own to Lincoln, the state capital and seat of the University of Nebraska; she attended preparatory school for one year and graduated from the university in 1895. In college she studied the classics and participated in the lively contemporary cultural life of the city by reviewing books, plays, and musical performances. Following graduation, she eked out a year as a journalist in Red Cloud and Lincoln before moving to Pittsburgh, Pennsylvania, to work as an editor of a women's magazine, the *Home Monthly,* a position she left five years later to teach high-school English and Latin. During this time she also wrote poems and stories, gathering poems into *April Twilights,* in 1903, and stories (including the early version of "The Sculptor's Funeral") into *The Troll Garden,* in 1905. Also in Pittsburgh, in 1899, she met Isabelle McClung, from a prominent, wealthy family. She lived in the McClung home from 1901 to 1906, when she moved to New York City to write for the journal *McClure's.* Throughout her life, Cather remained devoted to McClung, experiencing her marriage in 1916 as a severe personal loss and being devastated by her death in 1938.

Having long wished to write novels, Cather took a leave of absence from *McClure's* in 1911, and wrote *Alexander's Bridge* (1912). This novel was successful, but it was the next three that made her reputation. Each focused on a western heroine: Alexandra Bergson in *O Pioneers!* (1913), Thea Kronborg in *The Song of the Lark* (1915), and Ántonia Shimerda in *My Ántonia* (1918). While Alexandra is extraordinary as the most successful farmer—the only woman farmer—on the Nebraska Divide, and Thea is extraordinary as a gifted opera singer, Ántonia has no unusual gifts; for Cather and the novel's many readers she stands for the entire experience of European settlement of the Great Plains. These three novels also manifest Cather's lyrical yet understated prose writing; they contain a wealth of detail about the lives of Nebraska settlers—Bohemian Czech, German, Danish, Swedish, Norwegian, French, Russian, and "Americans" from the East—as they learned to farm on the prairie and built communities in which their various ethnicities met and mingled. Cather's is no melting pot ethos, however; rather she sees the frontier as a shifting kaleidoscope of overlapping social groups and individuals. Recognizing that even by the second decade of the twentieth century this period in U.S. history had disappeared, Cather approached her characters with deep respect for what they had endured and accomplished.

Whether these novels (or any of Cather's other work) reflect a lesbian sensibility has been a matter of much critical debate. Her *Selected Letters* (2013), long withheld from publication, confirm that Cather's central emotional involvements in her life were with women; in 1908 she began to share an apartment with Edith Lewis, a Nebraskan whom she had met in 1903, and they lived together until Cather's death. (They lived mostly in New York City, but Cather also traveled a great deal: to Europe, to New England, to the Southwest, and back to Red Cloud to visit her family.) Estrangement from conventional sexuality and sex roles is typical of many of her main characters, male and female; but heterosexual romance and sexual behavior is

Illustration for *My Ántonia*, W. T. Benda. For the first edition of *My Ántonia*, Cather commissioned a set of drawings by Wladyslaw T. Benda, a Polish immigrant who was part of the New York City art scene. Known to Cather through his work for *McClure's*, Benda simplified his often dramatic visual style to match Cather's spare narration.

equally present in her novels. It seems fair to say that close friendship, much more than romantic or sexual love, is the great ideal in her fiction.

Around 1922, according to Cather, the world broke in two; she suffered from the combined effects of poor health, dissatisfaction with the progress of her career, and alarm at the increasing mechanization and mass-produced quality of American life. She joined the Episcopal Church, and her novels took a new direction. Although her books had always celebrated alternative values to the material and conventional, this theme became much more urgent, while the motif of heroic womanhood—which had led many to call her a feminist, though Cather herself kept aloof from all movements—receded. Important books from her "middle period" include *A Lost Lady* (1923) and *The Professor's House* (1925), which deal with spiritual and cultural crises in the lives of the main characters.

Published in 1927, the novel *Death Comes for the Archbishop* initiated another stage. Like many other writers and artists in the 1920s, Cather had become entranced with the American Southwest—especially New Mexico; her first trip to the region in 1912 figured in her depiction (in *The Song of the Lark*) of Thea Kronborg finding spiritual renewal in this landscape. *Death Comes for the Archbishop,* partly written at Mary Austin's home in Santa Fe, is based on the career of Jean Baptiste Lamy (1814–1888), archbishop of New Mexico, and the priest Joseph Marchebeuf, his close friend and collaborator. Another historical novel, *Shadows on the Rock* (1931) is set even further back in time, in seventeenth-century Quebec. In both books, a composite image of high French culture, ceremonial spirituality, and the American landscape contrasts with the material trivia and empty banality of contemporary life.

Inspired by the classical Latin works that she loved so much, Cather believed in the ideas of art and the artist and strove to attain an artistic height from which she might survey the entire human scene. She tried to imbue the particularities of her stories with what she thought of as universal significance. In *My Ántonia,* which continues to be the favorite novel for most Cather readers, Jim Burden reflects on the aspirations of the poet Virgil to bring the muse to his own country for the first time; by country, Virgil means "not a nation or even a province, but the little rural neighborhood" where he was born. This is clearly what is intended in *My Ántonia;* the idea of combining artistic transcendence with local, especially rural, specificity, speaks to Cather's own goals. It is a measure of her ambition that she thinks of her work in Virgilian terms, since Virgil was the greatest of the Latin poets.

Politically, culturally, and aesthetically, Cather was in many respects deeply conservative as well as conflicted—a sophisticated populist, an agrarian urbanite. She believed in high art and superior people, but also thought great human gifts were more often found among the obscure and ordinary than among those with great advantages. Her vision of the United States seldom focused on Native Americans and African Americans; yet she preferred immigrants from Europe to migrants from the East Coast. She appreciated popular legends and folktales, which appear along with classical myth and allusion in her work. Her subtle experiments with formal structure include the retrospective narrative of *My Ántonia,* the imbedded Southwestern story of Tom Outland in *The Professor's House,* and the seemingly unplotted, episodic chronicle form of *Death Comes for the Archbishop.* She once described her work as deliberately "unfurnished," meaning that it was cut down to only those details absolutely necessary; "suggestion rather than enumeration" was another way she described her goal (see "The Novel Démeublé," p. 324). The resulting spareness and clarity of her fiction puts it in the modernist tradition.

The text of *My Ántonia* is that of the first edition (1918). The text of "The Sculptor's Funeral" is that published in *Youth and the Bright Medusa* (1920).

My Ántonia

Optima dies . . . prima fugit
—VIRGIL[1]

Introduction

Last summer I happened to be crossing the plains of Iowa in a season of intense heat, and it was my good fortune to have for a traveling companion James Quayle Burden—Jim Burden, as we still call him in the West. He and I are old friends—we grew up together in the same Nebraska town—and we had much to say to each other. While the train flashed through never-ending miles of ripe wheat, by country towns and bright-flowered pastures and oak groves wilting in the sun, we sat in the observation car, where the woodwork was hot to the touch and red dust lay deep over everything. The dust and heat, the burning wind, reminded us of many things. We were talking about what it is like to spend one's childhood in little towns like these, buried in wheat and corn, under stimulating extremes of climate: burning summers when the world lies green and billowy beneath a brilliant sky, when one is fairly stifled in vegetation, in the color and smell of strong weeds and heavy harvests; blustery winters with little snow, when the whole country is stripped bare and gray as sheet-iron. We agreed that no one who had not grown up in a little prairie town could know anything about it. It was a kind of freemasonry,[2] we said.

Although Jim Burden and I both live in New York, and are old friends, I do not see much of him there. He is legal counsel for one of the great Western railways, and is sometimes away from his New York office for weeks together. That is one reason why we do not often meet. Another is that I do not like his wife.

When Jim was still an obscure young lawyer, struggling to make his way in New York, his career was suddenly advanced by a brilliant marriage.[3] Genevieve Whitney was the only daughter of a distinguished man. Her marriage

1. Roman poet (70–19 B.C.E.) "The best days . . . are the first to flee" (Latin); from the *Georgics* (29 B.C.), a long didactic poem idealizing farm life.
2. A secret fraternal organization; here a reference to secret, shared knowledge.
3. In the 1926 edition, Cather revised and shortened the *Introduction,* omitting most of the characterization of Burden's wife and details of his career as an advocate of "mines and timber and oil."

with young Burden was the subject of sharp comment at the time. It was said she had been brutally jilted by her cousin, Rutland Whitney, and that she married this unknown man from the West out of bravado. She was a restless, headstrong girl, even then, who liked to astonish her friends. Later, when I knew her, she was always doing something unexpected. She gave one of her town houses for a Suffrage headquarters, produced one of her own plays at the Princess Theater, was arrested for picketing during a garment-makers' strike, etc. I am never able to believe that she has much feeling for the causes to which she lends her name and her fleeting interest. She is handsome, energetic, executive, but to me she seems unimpressionable and temperamentally incapable of enthusiasm. Her husband's quiet tastes irritate her, I think, and she finds it worth while to play the patroness to a group of young poets and painters of advanced ideas and mediocre ability. She has her own fortune and lives her own life. For some reason, she wishes to remain Mrs. James Burden.

As for Jim, no disappointments have been severe enough to chill his naturally romantic and ardent disposition. This disposition, though it often made him seem very funny when he was a boy, has been one of the strongest elements in his success. He loves with a personal passion the great country through which his railway runs and branches. His faith in it and his knowledge of it have played an important part in its development. He is always able to raise capital for new enterprises in Wyoming or Montana, and has helped young men out there to do remarkable things in mines and timber and oil. If a young man with an idea can once get Jim Burden's attention, can manage to accompany him when he goes off into the wilds hunting for lost parks or exploring new canyons, then the money which means action is usually forthcoming. Jim is still able to lose himself in those big Western dreams. Though he is over forty now, he meets new people and new enterprises with the impulsiveness by which his boyhood friends remember him. He never seems to me to grow older. His fresh color and sandy hair and quick-changing blue eyes are those of a young man, and his sympathetic, solicitous interest in women is as youthful as it is Western and American.

During that burning day when we were crossing Iowa, our talk kept returning to a central figure, a Bohemian[4] girl whom we had known long ago and whom both of us admired. More than any other person we remembered, this girl seemed to mean to us the country, the conditions, the whole adventure of our childhood. To speak her name was to call up pictures of people and places, to set a quiet drama going in one's brain. I had lost sight of her altogether, but Jim had found her again after long years, had renewed a friendship that meant a great deal to him, and out of his busy life had set apart time enough to enjoy that friendship. His mind was full of her that day. He made me see her again, feel her presence, revived all my old affection for her.

"I can't see," he said impetuously, "why you have never written anything about Ántonia."

I told him I had always felt that other people—he himself, for one—knew her much better than I. I was ready, however, to make an agreement with

4. From Bohemia, a region in the Czech Republic. Immigrants to the United States from this part of eastern Europe began to arrive in great numbers during the 1880s, which is when the novel begins.

him; I would set down on paper all that I remembered of Ántonia if he would do the same. We might, in this way, get a picture of her.

He rumpled his hair with a quick, excited gesture, which with him often announces a new determination, and I could see that my suggestion took hold of him. "Maybe I will, maybe I will!" he declared. He stared out of the window for a few moments, and when he turned to me again his eyes had the sudden clearness that comes from something the mind itself sees. "Of course," he said, "I should have to do it in a direct way, and say a great deal about myself. It's through myself that I knew and felt her, and I've had no practice in any other form of presentation."

I told him that how he knew her and felt her was exactly what I most wanted to know about Ántonia. He had had opportunities that I, as a little girl who watched her come and go, had not.

Months afterward Jim Burden arrived at my apartment one stormy winter afternoon, with a bulging legal portfolio sheltered under his fur overcoat. He brought it into the sitting-room with him and tapped it with some pride as he stood warming his hands.

"I finished it last night—the thing about Ántonia," he said. "Now, what about yours?"

I had to confess that mine had not gone beyond a few straggling notes.

"Notes? I didn't make any." He drank his tea all at once and put down the cup. "I didn't arrange or rearrange. I simply wrote down what of herself and myself and other people Ántonia's name recalls to me. I suppose it hasn't any form. It hasn't any title, either." He went into the next room, sat down at my desk and wrote on the pinkish face of the portfolio the word, "Ántonia." He frowned at this a moment, then prefixed another word, making it "My Ántonia." That seemed to satisfy him.

"Read it as soon as you can," he said, rising, "but don't let it influence your own story."

My own story was never written, but the following narrative is Jim's manuscript, substantially as he brought it to me.

Book I. The Shimerdas

I

I first heard of Ántonia[5] on what seemed to me an interminable journey across the great midland plain of North America. I was ten years old then; I had lost both my father and mother within a year, and my Virginia relatives were sending me out to my grandparents, who lived in Nebraska. I traveled in the care of a mountain boy, Jake Marpole, one of the "hands" on my father's old farm under the Blue Ridge, who was now going West to work for my grandfather. Jake's experience of the world was not much wider than mine. He had never been in a railway train until the morning when we set out together to try our fortunes in a new world.

5. "The Bohemian name *Ántonia* is strongly accented on the first syllable, like the English name *Anthony,* and the *i* is, of course, given the sound of long *e.* The name is pronounced An'-ton-ee-ah" [Cather's note].

We went all the way in day-coaches,[6] becoming more sticky and grimy with each stage of the journey. Jake bought everything the newsboys offered him: candy, oranges, brass collar buttons, a watch-charm, and for me a "Life of Jesse James,"[7] which I remember as one of the most satisfactory books I have ever read. Beyond Chicago we were under the protection of a friendly passenger conductor, who knew all about the country to which we were going and gave us a great deal of advice in exchange for our confidence. He seemed to us an experienced and worldly man who had been almost everywhere; in his conversation he threw out lightly the names of distant States and cities. He wore the rings and pins and badges of different fraternal orders to which he belonged. Even his cuff-buttons were engraved with hieroglyphics, and he was more inscribed than an Egyptian obelisk. Once when he sat down to chat, he told us that in the immigrant car ahead there was a family from "across the water" whose destination was the same as ours.

"They can't any of them speak English, except one little girl, and all she can say is 'We go Black Hawk, Nebraska.' She's not much older than you, twelve or thirteen, maybe, and she's as bright as a new dollar. Don't you want to go ahead and see her, Jimmy? She's got the pretty brown eyes, too!"

This last remark made me bashful, and I shook my head and settled down to "Jesse James." Jake nodded at me approvingly and said you were likely to get diseases from foreigners.

I do not remember crossing the Missouri River, or anything about the long day's journey through Nebraska. Probably by that time I had crossed so many rivers that I was dull to them. The only thing very noticeable about Nebraska was that it was still, all day long, Nebraska.

I had been sleeping, curled up in a red plush seat, for a long while when we reached Black Hawk. Jake roused me and took me by the hand. We stumbled down from the train to a wooden siding, where men were running about with lanterns. I couldn't see any town, or even distant lights; we were surrounded by utter darkness. The engine was panting heavily after its long run. In the red glow from the fire-box, a group of people stood huddled together on the platform, encumbered by bundles and boxes. I knew this must be the immigrant family the conductor had told us about. The woman wore a fringed shawl tied over her head, and she carried a little tin trunk in her arms, hugging it as if it were a baby. There was an old man, tall and stooped. Two half-grown boys and a girl stood holding oil-cloth bundles, and a little girl clung to her mother's skirts. Presently a man with a lantern approached them and began to talk, shouting and exclaiming. I pricked up my ears, for it was positively the first time I had ever heard a foreign tongue.

Another lantern came along. A bantering voice called out: "Hello, are you Mr. Burden's folks? If you are, it's me you're looking for. I'm Otto Fuchs. I'm Mr. Burden's hired man, and I'm to drive you out. Hello, Jimmy, ain't you scared to come so far west?"

I looked up with interest at the new face in the lantern light. He might have stepped out of the pages of "Jesse James." He wore a sombrero hat, with a wide leather band and a bright buckle, and the ends of his mustache were twisted up stiffly, like little horns. He looked lively and ferocious, I

6. Railroad passenger cars with no sleeping compartments.

7. Notorious American bandit (1847–1882) whose gang robbed banks and trains.

thought, and as if he had a history. A long scar ran across one cheek and drew the corner of his mouth up in a sinister curl. The top of his left ear was gone, and his skin was brown as an Indian's. Surely this was the face of a desperado. As he walked about the platform in his high-heeled boots, looking for our trunks, I saw that he was a rather slight man, quick and wiry, and light on his feet. He told us we had a long night drive ahead of us, and had better be on the hike. He led us to a hitching-bar where two farm wagons were tied, and I saw the foreign family crowding into one of them. The other was for us. Jake got on the front seat with Otto Fuchs, and I rode on the straw in the bottom of the wagon-box, covered up with a buffalo hide. The immigrants rumbled off into the empty darkness, and we followed them.

I tried to go to sleep, but the jolting made me bite my tongue, and I soon began to ache all over. When the straw settled down I had a hard bed. Cautiously I slipped from under the buffalo hide, got up on my knees and peered over the side of the wagon. There seemed to be nothing to see; no fences, no creeks or trees, no hills or fields. If there was a road, I could not make it out in the faint starlight. There was nothing but land: not a country at all, but the material out of which countries are made. No, there was nothing but land—slightly undulating, I knew, because often our wheels ground against the brake as we went down into a hollow and lurched up again on the other side. I had the feeling that the world was left behind, that we had got over the edge of it, and were outside man's jurisdiction. I had never before looked up at the sky when there was not a familiar mountain ridge against it. But this was the complete dome of heaven, all there was of it. I did not believe that my dead father and mother were watching me from up there; they would still be looking for me at the sheep-fold down by the creek, or along the white road that led to the mountain pastures. I had left even their spirits behind me. The wagon jolted on, carrying me I knew not whither. I don't think I was homesick. If we never arrived anywhere, it did not matter. Between that earth and that sky I felt erased, blotted out. I did not say my prayers that night: here, I felt, what would be would be.

II

I do not remember our arrival at my grandfather's farm sometime before daybreak, after a drive of nearly twenty miles with heavy work-horses. When I awoke, it was afternoon. I was lying in a little room, scarcely larger than the bed that held me, and the window-shade at my head was flapping softly in a warm wind. A tall woman, with wrinkled brown skin and black hair, stood looking down at me; I knew that she must be my grandmother. She had been crying, I could see, but when I opened my eyes she smiled, peered at me anxiously, and sat down on the foot of my bed.

"Had a good sleep, Jimmy?" she asked briskly. Then in a very different tone she said, as if to herself, "My, how you do look like your father!" I remembered that my father had been her little boy; she must often have come to wake him like this when he overslept. "Here are your clean clothes," she went on, stroking my coverlid with her brown hand as she talked. "But first you come down to the kitchen with me, and have a nice warm bath behind the stove. Bring your things; there's nobody about."

"Down to the kitchen" struck me as curious; it was always "out in the kitchen" at home.[8] I picked up my shoes and stockings and followed her through the living-room and down a flight of stairs into a basement. This basement was divided into a dining-room at the right of the stairs and a kitchen at the left. Both rooms were plastered and whitewashed—the plaster laid directly upon the earth walls, as it used to be in dugouts. The floor was of hard cement. Up under the wooden ceiling there were little half-windows with white curtains, and pots of geraniums and wandering Jew[9] in the deep sills. As I entered the kitchen I sniffed a pleasant smell of gingerbread baking. The stove was very large, with bright nickel trimmings, and behind it there was a long wooden bench against the wall, and a tin washtub, into which grandmother poured hot and cold water. When she brought the soap and towels, I told her that I was used to taking my bath without help.

"Can you do your ears, Jimmy? Are you sure? Well, now, I call you a right smart little boy."

It was pleasant there in the kitchen. The sun shone into my bath-water through the west half-window, and a big Maltese cat came up and rubbed himself against the tub, watching me curiously. While I scrubbed, my grandmother busied herself in the dining-room until I called anxiously, "Grandmother, I'm afraid the cakes are burning!" Then she came laughing, waving her apron before her as if she were shooing chickens.

She was a spare, tall woman, a little stooped, and she was apt to carry her head thrust forward in an attitude of attention, as if she were looking at something, or listening to something, far away. As I grew older, I came to believe that it was only because she was so often thinking of things that were far away. She was quick-footed and energetic in all her movements. Her voice was high and rather shrill, and she often spoke with an anxious inflection, for she was exceedingly desirous that everything should go with due order and decorum. Her laugh, too, was high, and perhaps a little strident, but there was a lively intelligence in it. She was then fifty-five years old, a strong woman, of unusual endurance.

After I was dressed I explored the long cellar next to the kitchen. It was dug out under the wing of the house, was plastered and cemented, with a stairway and an outside door by which the men came and went. Under one of the windows there was a place for them to wash when they came in from work.

While my grandmother was busy about supper I settled myself on the wooden bench behind the stove and got acquainted with the cat—he caught not only rats and mice, but gophers, I was told. The patch of yellow sunlight on the floor traveled back toward the stairway, and grandmother and I talked about my journey, and about the arrival of the new Bohemian family; she said they were to be our nearest neighbors. We did not talk about the farm in Virginia, which had been her home for so many years. But after the men came in from the fields, and we were all seated at the supper-table, then she asked Jake about the old place and about our friends and neighbors there.

My grandfather said little. When he first came in he kissed me and spoke kindly to me, but he was not demonstrative. I felt at once his deliberateness

8. Farm kitchens in the South typically were detached from the main house.

9. A type of showy, trailing plant.

and personal dignity, and was a little in awe of him. The thing one immediately noticed about him was his beautiful, crinkly, snow-white beard. I once heard a missionary say it was like the beard of an Arabian sheik. His bald crown only made it more impressive.

Grandfather's eyes were not at all like those of an old man; they were bright blue, and had a fresh, frosty sparkle. His teeth were white and regular—so sound that he had never been to a dentist in his life. He had a delicate skin, easily roughened by sun and wind. When he was a young man his hair and beard were red; his eyebrows were still coppery.

As we sat at the table Otto Fuchs and I kept stealing covert glances at each other. Grandmother had told me while she was getting supper that he was an Austrian who came to this country a young boy and had led an adventurous life in the Far West among mining-camps and cow outfits. His iron constitution was somewhat broken by mountain pneumonia, and he had drifted back to live in a milder country for a while. He had relatives in Bismarck, a German settlement to the north of us, but for a year now he had been working for grandfather.

The minute supper was over, Otto took me into the kitchen to whisper to me about a pony down in the barn that had been bought for me at a sale; he had been riding him to find out whether he had any bad tricks, but he was a "perfect gentleman," and his name was Dude. Fuchs told me everything I wanted to know: how he had lost his ear in a Wyoming blizzard when he was a stage-driver, and how to throw a lasso. He promised to rope a steer for me before sundown next day. He got out his "chaps" and silver spurs to show them to Jake and me, and his best cowboy boots, with tops stitched in bold design—roses, and true-lover's knots, and undraped female figures. These, he solemnly explained, were angels.

Before we went to bed Jake and Otto were called up to the living-room for prayers. Grandfather put on silver-rimmed spectacles and read several Psalms. His voice was so sympathetic and he read so interestingly that I wished he had chosen one of my favorite chapters in the Book of Kings. I was awed by his intonation of the word "Selah." *"He shall choose our inheritance for us, the excellency of Jacob whom He loved. Selah."*[1] I had no idea what the word meant; perhaps he had not. But, as he uttered it, it became oracular, the most sacred of words.

Early the next morning I ran out of doors to look about me. I had been told that ours was the only wooden house west of Black Hawk—until you came to the Norwegian settlement, where there were several. Our neighbors lived in sod houses and dugouts—comfortable, but not very roomy. Our white frame house, with a story and half-story above the basement, stood at the east end of what I might call the farmyard, with the windmill close by the kitchen door. From the windmill the ground sloped westward, down to the barns and granaries and pig-yards. This slope was trampled hard and bare, and washed out in winding gullies by the rain. Beyond the corncribs, at the bottom of the shallow draw,[2] was a muddy little pond, with rusty willow bushes growing about it. The road from the post-office came directly by our door, crossed the

1. Psalms 47.4. The meaning of *Selah* is still unknown.

2. A gully that draws runoff water from rain and thaws.

farmyard, and curved round this little pond, beyond which it began to climb the gentle swell of unbroken prairie to the west. There, along the western skyline, it skirted a great cornfield, much larger than any field I had ever seen. This cornfield, and the sorghum patch behind the barn, were the only broken[3] land in sight. Everywhere, as far as the eye could reach, there was nothing but rough, shaggy, red grass, most of it as tall as I.

North of the house, inside the ploughed fire-breaks, grew a thick-set strip of box-elder trees, low and bushy, their leaves already turning yellow. This hedge was nearly a quarter of a mile long, but I had to look very hard to see it at all. The little trees were insignificant against the grass. It seemed as if the grass were about to run over them, and over the plum-patch behind the sod chicken-house.

As I looked about me I felt that the grass was the country, as the water is the sea. The red of the grass made all the great prairie the color of winestains, or of certain seaweeds when they are first washed up. And there was so much motion in it; the whole country seemed, somehow, to be running.

I had almost forgotten that I had a grandmother, when she came out, her sunbonnet on her head, a grain-sack in her hand, and asked me if I did not want to go to the garden with her to dig potatoes for dinner. The garden, curiously enough, was a quarter of a mile from the house, and the way to it led up a shallow draw past the cattle corral. Grandmother called my attention to a stout hickory cane, tipped with copper, which hung by a leather thong from her belt. This, she said, was her rattlesnake cane. I must never go to the garden without a heavy stick or a corn-knife; she had killed a good many rattlers on her way back and forth. A little girl who lived on the Black Hawk road was bitten on the ankle and had been sick all summer.

I can remember exactly how the country looked to me as I walked beside my grandmother along the faint wagon-tracks on that early September morning. Perhaps the glide of long railway travel was still with me, for more than anything else I felt motion in the landscape; in the fresh, easy-blowing morning wind, and in the earth itself, as if the shaggy grass were a sort of loose hide, and underneath it herds of wild buffalo were galloping, galloping . . .

Alone, I should never have found the garden—except, perhaps, for the big yellow pumpkins that lay about unprotected by their withering vines—and I felt very little interest in it when I got there. I wanted to walk straight on through the red grass and over the edge of the world, which could not be very far away. The light air about me told me that the world ended here: only the ground and sun and sky were left, and if one went a little farther there would be only sun and sky, and one would float off into them, like the tawny hawks which sailed over our heads making slow shadows on the grass. While grandmother took the pitchfork we found standing in one of the rows and dug potatoes, while I picked them up out of the soft brown earth and put them into the bag, I kept looking up at the hawks that were doing what I might so easily do.

When grandmother was ready to go, I said I would like to stay up there in the garden awhile.

She peered down at me from under her sunbonnet. "Aren't you afraid of snakes?"

"A little," I admitted, "but I'd like to stay anyhow."

3. I.e., plowed. Plowing land for the first time is extremely difficult work.

"Well, if you see one, don't have anything to do with him. The big yellow and brown ones won't hurt you; they're bull-snakes and help to keep the gophers down. Don't be scared if you see anything look out of that hole in the bank over there. That's a badger hole. He's about as big as a big 'possum, and his face is striped, black and white. He takes a chicken once in a while, but I won't let the men harm him. In a new country a body feels friendly to the animals. I like to have him come out and watch me when I'm at work."

Grandmother swung the bag of potatoes over her shoulder and went down the path, leaning forward a little. The road followed the windings of the draw; when she came to the first bend she waved at me and disappeared. I was left alone with this new feeling of lightness and content.

I sat down in the middle of the garden, where snakes could scarcely approach unseen, and leaned my back against a warm yellow pumpkin. There were some ground-cherry bushes growing along the furrows, full of fruit. I turned back the papery triangular sheaths that protected the berries and ate a few. All about me giant grasshoppers, twice as big as any I had ever seen, were doing acrobatic feats among the dried vines. The gophers scurried up and down the ploughed ground. There in the sheltered draw-bottom the wind did not blow very hard, but I could hear it singing its humming tune up on the level, and I could see the tall grasses wave. The earth was warm under me, and warm as I crumbled it through my fingers. Queer little red bugs came out and moved in slow squadrons around me. Their backs were polished vermilion, with black spots. I kept as still as I could. Nothing happened. I did not expect anything to happen. I was something that lay under the sun and felt it, like the pumpkins, and I did not want to be anything more. I was entirely happy. Perhaps we feel like that when we die and become a part of something entire, whether it is sun and air, or goodness and knowledge. At any rate, that is happiness; to be dissolved into something complete and great. When it comes to one, it comes as naturally as sleep.

III

On Sunday morning Otto Fuchs was to drive us over to make the acquaintance of our new Bohemian neighbors. We were taking them some provisions, as they had come to live on a wild place where there was no garden or chicken-house, and very little broken land. Fuchs brought up a sack of potatoes and a piece of cured pork from the cellar, and grandmother packed some loaves of Saturday's bread, a jar of butter, and several pumpkin pies in the straw of the wagon-box. We clambered up to the front seat and jolted off past the little pond and along the road that climbed to the big cornfield.

I could hardly wait to see what lay beyond that cornfield; but there was only red grass like ours, and nothing else, though from the high wagon-seat one could look off a long way. The road ran about like a wild thing, avoiding the deep draws, crossing them where they were wide and shallow. And all along it, wherever it looped or ran, the sunflowers grew; some of them were as big as little trees, with great rough leaves and many branches which bore dozens of blossoms. They made a gold ribbon across the prairie. Occasionally one of the horses would tear off with his teeth a plant full of blossoms, and walk along munching it, the flowers nodding in time to his bites as he ate down toward them.

The Bohemian family, grandmother told me as we drove along, had bought the homestead of a fellow-countryman, Peter Krajiek, and had paid him more than it was worth. Their agreement with him was made before they left the old country, through a cousin of his, who was also a relative of Mrs. Shimerda. The Shimerdas were the first Bohemian family to come to this part of the county. Krajiek was their only interpreter, and could tell them anything he chose. They could not speak enough English to ask for advice, or even to make their most pressing wants known. One son, Fuchs said, was well-grown, and strong enough to work the land; but the father was old and frail and knew nothing about farming. He was a weaver by trade; had been a skilled workman on tapestries and upholstery materials. He had brought his fiddle with him, which wouldn't be of much use here, though he used to pick up money by it at home.

"If they're nice people, I hate to think of them spending the winter in that cave of Krajiek's," said grandmother. "It's no better than a badger hole; no proper dugout at all. And I hear he's made them pay twenty dollars for his old cookstove that ain't worth ten."

"Yes'm," said Otto; "and he's sold 'em his oxen and his two bony old horses for the price of good work-teams. I'd have interfered about the horses—the old man can understand some German—if I'd 'a' thought it would do any good. But Bohemians has a natural distrust of Austrians."[4]

Grandmother looked interested. "Now, why is that, Otto?"

Fuchs wrinkled his brow and nose. "Well, ma'm, it's politics. It would take me a long while to explain."

The land was growing rougher; I was told that we were approaching Squaw Creek, which cut up the west half of the Shimerdas' place and made the land of little value for farming. Soon we could see the broken, grassy clay cliffs which indicated the windings of the stream, and the glittering tops of the cottonwoods and ash trees that grew down in the ravine. Some of the cottonwoods had already turned, and the yellow leaves and shining white bark made them look like the gold and silver trees in fairy tales.

As we approached the Shimerdas' dwelling, I could still see nothing but rough red hillocks, and draws with shelving banks and long roots hanging out where the earth had crumbled away. Presently, against one of those banks, I saw a sort of shed, thatched with the same wine-colored grass that grew everywhere. Near it tilted a shattered windmill-frame, that had no wheel. We drove up to this skeleton to tie our horses, and then I saw a door and window sunk deep in the draw-bank. The door stood open, and a woman and a girl of fourteen ran out and looked up at us hopefully. A little girl trailed along behind them. The woman had on her head the same embroidered shawl with silk fringes that she wore when she had alighted from the train at Black Hawk. She was not old, but she was certainly not young. Her face was alert and lively, with a sharp chin and shrewd little eyes. She shook grandmother's hand energetically.

"Very glad, very glad!" she ejaculated. Immediately she pointed to the bank out of which she had emerged and said, "House no good, house no good!"

4. Bohemia shared a border with Austria and for centuries had been involved in warfare with that nation. At the time in which *My Ántonia* is set, Bohemia was a dominion of the Austro-Hungarian Empire ruled by the Hapsburg monarchy.

Grandmother nodded consolingly. "You'll get fixed up comfortable after while, Mrs. Shimerda; make good house."

My grandmother always spoke in a very loud tone to foreigners, as if they were deaf. She made Mrs. Shimerda understand the friendly intention of our visit, and the Bohemian woman handled the loaves of bread and even smelled them, and examined the pies with lively curiosity, exclaiming, "Much good, much thank!"—and again she wrung grandmother's hand.

The oldest son, Ambrož,—they called it Ambrosch,—came out of the cave and stood beside his mother. He was nineteen years old, short and broad-backed, with a close-cropped, flat head, and a wide, flat face. His hazel eyes were little and shrewd, like his mother's, but more sly and suspicious; they fairly snapped at the food. The family had been living on corncakes and sorghum molasses for three days.

The little girl was pretty, but Án-tonia—they accented the name thus, strongly, when they spoke to her—was still prettier. I remembered what the conductor had said about her eyes. They were big and warm and full of light, like the sun shining on brown pools in the wood. Her skin was brown, too, and in her cheeks she had a glow of rich, dark color. Her brown hair was curly and wild-looking. The little sister, whom they called Yulka (Julka), was fair, and seemed mild and obedient. While I stood awkwardly confronting the two girls, Krajiek came up from the barn to see what was going on. With him was another Shimerda son. Even from a distance one could see that there was something strange about this boy. As he approached us, he began to make uncouth noises, and held up his hands to show us his fingers, which were webbed to the first knuckle, like a duck's foot. When he saw me draw back, he began to crow delightedly, "Hoo, hoo-hoo, hoo-hoo!" like a rooster. His mother scowled and said sternly, "Marek!" then spoke rapidly to Krajiek in Bohemian.

"She wants me to tell you he won't hurt nobody, Mrs. Burden. He was born like that. The others are smart. Ambrosch, he make good farmer." He struck Ambrosch on the back, and the boy smiled knowingly.

At that moment the father came out of the hole in the bank. He wore no hat, and his thick, iron-gray hair was brushed straight back from his forehead. It was so long that it bushed out behind his ears, and made him look like the old portraits I remembered in Virginia. He was tall and slender, and his thin shoulders stooped. He looked at us understandingly, then took grandmother's hand and bent over it. I noticed how white and well-shaped his own hands were. They looked calm, somehow, and skilled. His eyes were melancholy, and were set back deep under his brow. His face was ruggedly formed, but it looked like ashes—like something from which all the warmth and light had died out. Everything about this old man was in keeping with his dignified manner. He was neatly dressed. Under his coat he wore a knitted gray vest, and, instead of a collar, a silk scarf of a dark bronze-green, carefully crossed and held together by a red coral pin. While Krajiek was translating for Mr. Shimerda, Ántonia came up to me and held out her hand coaxingly. In a moment we were running up the steep drawside together, Yulka trotting after us.

When we reached the level and could see the gold tree-tops, I pointed toward them, and Ántonia laughed and squeezed my hand as if to tell me how glad she was I had come. We raced off toward Squaw Creek and did not stop until the ground itself stopped—fell away before us so abruptly that the next step would have been out into the tree-tops. We stood panting on the edge of the ravine, looking down at the trees and bushes that grew below us. The wind was so strong that I had to hold my hat on, and the girls' skirts were blown out before them. Ántonia seemed to like it; she held her little sister by the hand and chattered away in that language which seemed to me spoken so much more rapidly than mine. She looked at me, her eyes fairly blazing with things she could not say.

"Name? What name?" she asked, touching me on the shoulder. I told her my name, and she repeated it after me and made Yulka say it. She pointed into the gold cottonwood tree behind whose top we stood and said again, "What name?"

We sat down and made a nest in the long red grass. Yulka curled up like a baby rabbit and played with a grasshopper. Ántonia pointed up to the sky and questioned me with her glance. I gave her the word, but she was not satisfied and pointed to my eyes. I told her, and she repeated the word, making it sound like "ice." She pointed up to the sky, then to my eyes, then back to the sky, with movements so quick and impulsive that she distracted me, and I had no idea what she wanted. She got up on her knees and wrung her hands. She pointed to her own eyes and shook her head, then to mine and to the sky, nodding violently.

"Oh," I exclaimed, "blue; blue sky."

She clapped her hands and murmured, "Blue sky, blue eyes," as if it amused her. While we snuggled down there out of the wind she learned a score of words. She was quick, and very eager. We were so deep in the grass that we could see nothing but the blue sky over us and the gold tree in front of us. It was wonderfully pleasant. After Ántonia had said the new words over and over, she wanted to give me a little chased[5] silver ring she wore on her middle finger. When she coaxed and insisted, I repulsed her quite sternly. I didn't want her ring, and I felt there was something reckless and extravagant about her wishing to give it away to a boy she had never seen before. No wonder Krajiek got the better of these people, if this was how they behaved.

While we were disputing about the ring, I heard a mournful voice calling, "Án-tonia, Án-tonia!" She sprang up like a hare. "*Tatinek,*[6] Tatinek!" she shouted, and we ran to meet the old man who was coming toward us. Ántonia reached him first, took his hand and kissed it. When I came up, he touched my shoulder and looked searchingly down into my face for several seconds. I became somewhat embarrassed, for I was used to being taken for granted by my elders.

We went with Mr. Shimerda back to the dugout, where grandmother was waiting for me. Before I got into the wagon, he took a book out of his pocket, opened it, and showed me a page with two alphabets, one English and the other Bohemian. He placed this book in my grandmother's hands, looked at her entreatingly, and said with an earnestness which I shall never forget, "Te-e-ach, te-e-ach my Án-tonia!"

5. Embossed.
6. Father (Czech); affectionate term equivalent to *daddy*.

IV

On the afternoon of that same Sunday I took my first long ride on my pony, under Otto's direction. After that Dude and I went twice a week to the post-office, six miles east of us, and I saved the men a good deal of time by riding on errands to our neighbors. When we had to borrow anything, or to send about word that there would be preaching at the sod schoolhouse, I was always the messenger. Formerly Fuchs attended to such things after working hours.

All the years that have passed have not dimmed my memory of that first glorious autumn. The new country lay open before me: there were no fences in those days, and I could choose my own way over the grass uplands, trusting the pony to get me home again. Sometimes I followed the sunflower-bordered roads. Fuchs told me that the sunflowers were introduced into that country by the Mormons; that at the time of the persecution, when they left Missouri and struck out into the wilderness to find a place where they could worship God in their own way, the members of the first exploring party, crossing the plains to Utah, scattered sunflower seed as they went. The next summer, when the long trains of wagons came through with all the women and children, they had the sunflower trail to follow. I believe that botanists do not confirm Jake's story, but insist that the sunflower was native to those plains. Nevertheless, that legend has stuck in my mind, and sunflower-bordered roads always seem to me the roads to freedom.

I used to love to drift along the pale yellow cornfields, looking for the damp spots one sometimes found at their edges, where the smartweed soon turned a rich copper color and the narrow brown leaves hung curled like cocoons about the swollen joints of the stem. Sometimes I went south to visit our German neighbors and to admire their catalpa grove, or to see the big elm tree that grew up out of a deep crack in the earth and had a hawk's nest in its branches. Trees were so rare in that country, and they had to make such a hard fight to grow, that we used to feel anxious about them, and visit them as if they were persons. It must have been the scarcity of detail in that tawny landscape that made detail so precious.

Sometimes I rode north to the big prairie-dog town to watch the brown, earth-owls fly home in the late afternoon and go down to their nests underground with the dogs. Ántonia Shimerda liked to go with me, and we used to wonder a great deal about these birds of subterranean habit. We had to be on our guard there, for rattlesnakes were always lurking about. They came to pick up an easy living among the dogs and owls, which were quite defenseless against them; took possession of their comfortable houses and ate the eggs and puppies. We felt sorry for the owls. It was always mournful to see them come flying home at sunset and disappear under the earth. But, after all, we felt, winged things who would live like that must be rather degraded creatures. The dog-town was a long way from any pond or creek. Otto Fuchs said he had seen populous dog-towns in the desert where there was no surface water for fifty miles; he insisted that some of the holes must go down to water—nearly two hundred feet, hereabouts. Ántonia said she didn't believe it; that the dogs probably lapped up the dew in the early morning, like the rabbits.

Ántonia had opinions about everything, and she was soon able to make them known. Almost every day she came running across the prairie to have her reading lesson with me. Mrs. Shimerda grumbled, but realized it was important that one member of the family should learn English. When the lesson was over, we used to go up to the watermelon patch behind the garden. I split the melons with an old corn-knife, and we lifted out the hearts and ate them with the juice trickling through our fingers. The white Christmas melons we did not touch, but we watched them with curiosity. They were to be picked late, when the hard frosts had set in, and put away for winter use. After weeks on the ocean, the Shimerdas were famished for fruit. The two girls would wander for miles along the edge of the cornfields, hunting for ground-cherries.

Ántonia loved to help grandmother in the kitchen and to learn about cooking and house-keeping. She would stand beside her, watching her every movement. We were willing to believe that Mrs. Shimerda was a good housewife in her own country, but she managed poorly under new conditions: the conditions were bad enough, certainly!

I remember how horrified we were at the sour, ashy-gray bread she gave her family to eat. She mixed her dough, we discovered, in an old tin peck-measure[7] that Krajiek had used about the barn. When she took the paste out to bake it, she left smears of dough sticking to the sides of the measure, put the measure on the shelf behind the stove, and let this residue ferment. The next time she made bread, she scraped this sour stuff down into the fresh dough to serve as yeast.

During those first months the Shimerdas never went to town. Krajiek encouraged them in the belief that in Black Hawk they would somehow be mysteriously separated from their money. They hated Krajiek, but they clung to him because he was the only human being with whom they could talk or from whom they could get information. He slept with the old man and the two boys in the dugout barn, along with the oxen. They kept him in their hole and fed him for the same reason that the prairie dogs and the brown owls housed the rattlesnakes—because they did not know how to get rid of him.

V

We knew that things were hard for our Bohemian neighbors, but the two girls were light-hearted and never complained. They were always ready to forget their troubles at home, and to run away with me over the prairie, scaring rabbits or starting up flocks of quail.

I remember Ántonia's excitement when she came into our kitchen one afternoon and announced: "My papa find friends up north, with Russian mans. Last night he take me for see, and I can understand very much talk. Nice mans, Mrs. Burden. One is fat and all the time laugh. Everybody laugh. The first time I see my papa laugh in this kawn-tree. Oh, very nice!"

I asked her if she meant the two Russians who lived up by the big dog-town. I had often been tempted to go to see them when I was riding in that direction, but one of them was a wild-looking fellow and I was a little afraid

7. Equal to two gallons. The implication is that the container is an unsuitable size for bread making. The sourdough bread of the Shimerda family is also seen as an inferior product.

of him. Russia seemed to me more remote than any other country—farther away than China, almost as far as the North Pole. Of all the strange, uprooted people among the first settlers, those two men were the strangest and the most aloof. Their last names were unpronounceable, so they were called Pavel and Peter. They went about making signs to people, and until the Shimerdas came they had no friends. Krajiek could understand them a little, but he had cheated them in a trade, so they avoided him. Pavel, the tall one, was said to be an anarchist; since he had no means of imparting his opinions, probably his wild gesticulations and his generally excited and rebellious manner gave rise to this supposition. He must once have been a very strong man, but now his great frame, with big, knotty joints, had a wasted look, and the skin was drawn tight over his high cheek-bones. His breathing was hoarse, and he always had a cough.

Peter, his companion, was a very different sort of fellow; short, bow-legged, and as fat as butter. He always seemed pleased when he met people on the road, smiled and took off his cap to every one, men as well as women. At a distance, on his wagon, he looked like an old man; his hair and beard were of such a pale flaxen color that they seemed white in the sun. They were as thick and curly as carded wool. His rosy face, with its snub nose, set in this fleece, was like a melon among its leaves. He was usually called "Curly Peter," or "Rooshian Peter."

The two Russians made good farmhands, and in summer they worked out together. I had heard our neighbors laughing when they told how Peter always had to go home at night to milk his cow. Other bachelor homesteaders used canned milk, to save trouble. Sometimes Peter came to church at the sod schoolhouse. It was there I first saw him, sitting on a low bench by the door, his plush cap in his hands, his bare feet tucked apologetically under the seat.

After Mr. Shimerda discovered the Russians, he went to see them almost every evening, and sometimes took Ántonia with him. She said they came from a part of Russia where the language was not very different from Bohemian, and if I wanted to go to their place, she could talk to them for me. One afternoon, before the heavy frosts began, we rode up there together on my pony.

The Russians had a neat log house built on a grassy slope, with a windlass well beside the door. As we rode up the draw we skirted a big melon patch, and a garden where squashes and yellow cucumbers lay about on the sod. We found Peter out behind his kitchen, bending over a washtub. He was working so hard that he did not hear us coming. His whole body moved up and down as he rubbed, and he was a funny sight from the rear, with his shaggy head and bandy legs. When he straightened himself up to greet us, drops of perspiration were rolling from his thick nose down on to his curly beard. Peter dried his hands and seemed glad to leave his washing. He took us down to see his chickens, and his cow that was grazing on the hillside. He told Ántonia that in his country only rich people had cows, but here any man could have one who would take care of her. The milk was good for Pavel, who was often sick, and he could make butter by beating sour cream with a wooden spoon. Peter was very fond of his cow. He patted her flanks and talked to her in Russian while he pulled up her lariat pin and set it in a new place.

After he had shown us his garden, Peter trundled a load of watermelons up the hill in his wheelbarrow. Pavel was not at home. He was off somewhere helping to dig a well. The house I thought very comfortable for two men who were "batching." Besides the kitchen, there was a living-room, with a wide double bed built against the wall, properly made up with blue gingham sheets and pillows. There was a little storeroom, too, with a window, where they kept guns and saddles and tools, and old coats and boots. That day the floor was covered with garden things, drying for winter; corn and beans and fat yellow cucumbers. There were no screens or window-blinds in the house, and all the doors and windows stood wide open, letting in flies and sunshine alike.

Peter put the melons in a row on the oil-cloth-covered table and stood over them, brandishing a butcher knife. Before the blade got fairly into them, they split of their own ripeness, with a delicious sound. He gave us knives, but no plates, and the top of the table was soon swimming with juice and seeds. I had never seen any one eat so many melons as Peter ate. He assured us that they were good for one—better than medicine; in his country people lived on them at this time of year. He was very hospitable and jolly. Once, while he was looking at Ántonia, he sighed and told us that if he had stayed at home in Russia perhaps by this time he would have had a pretty daughter of his own to cook and keep house for him. He said he had left his country because of a "great trouble."

When we got up to go, Peter looked about in perplexity for something that would entertain us. He ran into the storeroom and brought out a gaudily painted harmonica, sat down on a bench, and spreading his fat legs apart began to play like a whole band. The tunes were either very lively or very doleful, and he sang words to some of them.

Before we left, Peter put ripe cucumbers into a sack for Mrs. Shimerda and gave us a lard-pail full of milk to cook them in. I had never heard of cooking cucumbers, but Ántonia assured me they were very good. We had to walk the pony all the way home to keep from spilling the milk.

VI

One afternoon we were having our reading lesson on the warm, grassy bank where the badger lived. It was a day of amber sunlight, but there was a shiver of coming winter in the air. I had seen ice on the little horse-pond that morning, and as we went through the garden we found the tall asparagus, with its red berries, lying on the ground, a mass of slimy green.

Tony was barefooted, and she shivered in her cotton dress and was comfortable only when we were tucked down on the baked earth, in the full blaze of the sun. She could talk to me about almost anything by this time. That afternoon she was telling me how highly esteemed our friend the badger was in her part of the world, and how men kept a special kind of dog, with very short legs, to hunt him. Those dogs, she said, went down into the hole after the badger and killed him there in a terrific struggle underground; you could hear the barks and yelps outside. Then the dog dragged himself back, covered with bites and scratches, to be rewarded and petted by his master. She knew a dog who had a star on his collar for every badger he had killed.

The rabbits were unusually spry that afternoon. They kept starting up all about us, and dashing off down the draw as if they were playing a game of some kind. But the little buzzing things that lived in the grass were all dead—all but one. While we were lying there against the warm bank, a little insect of the palest, frailest green hopped painfully out of the buffalo grass and tried to leap into a bunch of bluestem. He missed it, fell back, and sat with his head sunk between his long legs, his antennæ quivering, as if he were waiting for something to come and finish him. Tony made a warm nest for him in her hands; talked to him gayly and indulgently in Bohemian. Presently he began to sing for us—a thin, rusty little chirp. She held him close to her ear and laughed, but a moment afterward I saw there were tears in her eyes. She told me that in her village at home there was an old beggar woman who went about selling herbs and roots she had dug up in the forest. If you took her in and gave her a warm place by the fire, she sang old songs to the children in a cracked voice, like this. Old Hata, she was called, and the children loved to see her coming and saved their cakes and sweets for her.

When the bank on the other side of the draw began to throw a narrow shelf of shadow, we knew we ought to be starting homeward; the chill came on quickly when the sun got low, and Ántonia's dress was thin. What were we to do with the frail little creature we had lured back to life by false pretenses? I offered my pockets, but Tony shook her head and carefully put the green insect in her hair, tying her big handkerchief down loosely over her curls. I said I would go with her until we could see Squaw Creek, and then turn and run home. We drifted along lazily, very happy, through the magical light of the late afternoon.

All those fall afternoons were the same, but I never got used to them. As far as we could see, the miles of copper-red grass were drenched in sunlight that was stronger and fiercer than at any other time of the day. The blond cornfields were red gold, the haystacks turned rosy and threw long shadows. The whole prairie was like the bush that burned with fire and was not consumed.[8] That hour always had the exultation of victory, of triumphant ending, like a hero's death—heroes who died young and gloriously. It was a sudden transfiguration, a lifting-up of day.

How many an afternoon Ántonia and I have trailed along the prairie under that magnificence! And always two long black shadows flitted before us or followed after, dark spots on the ruddy grass.

We had been silent a long time, and the edge of the sun sank nearer and nearer the prairie floor, when we saw a figure moving on the edge of the upland, a gun over his shoulder. He was walking slowly, dragging his feet along as if he had no purpose. We broke into a run to overtake him.

"My papa sick all the time," Tony panted as we flew. "He not look good, Jim."

As we neared Mr. Shimerda she shouted, and he lifted his head and peered about. Tony ran up to him, caught his hand and pressed it against her cheek. She was the only one of his family who could rouse the old man from the torpor in which he seemed to live. He took the bag from his belt and showed us three rabbits he had shot, looked at Ántonia with a wintry flicker of a smile and began to tell her something. She turned to me.

"My *tatinek* make me little hat with the skins, little hat for win-ter!" she exclaimed joyfully. "Meat for eat, skin for hat,"—she told off these benefits on her fingers.

Her father put his hand on her hair, but she caught his wrist and lifted it carefully away, talking to him rapidly. I heard the name of old Hata. He

8. In Exodus 3.2, God's angel appeared to Moses in the middle of a bush that burned, but "was not consumed."

untied the handkerchief, separated her hair with his fingers, and stood looking down at the green insect. When it began to chirp faintly, he listened as if it were a beautiful sound.

I picked up the gun he had dropped; a queer piece from the old country, short and heavy, with a stag's head on the cock. When he saw me examining it, he turned to me with his faraway look that always made me feel as if I were down at the bottom of a well. He spoke kindly and gravely, and Ántonia translated:—

"My *tatinek* say when you are big boy, he give you his gun. Very fine, from Bohemie. It was belong to a great man, very rich, like what you not got here; many fields, many forests, many big house. My papa play for his wedding, and he give my papa fine gun, and my papa give you."

I was glad that this project was one of futurity. There never were such people as the Shimerdas for wanting to give away everything they had. Even the mother was always offering me things, though I knew she expected substantial presents in return. We stood there in friendly silence, while the feeble minstrel sheltered in Ántonia's hair went on with its scratchy chirp. The old man's smile, as he listened, was so full of sadness, of pity for things, that I never afterward forgot it. As the sun sank there came a sudden coolness and the strong smell of earth and drying grass. Ántonia and her father went off hand in hand, and I buttoned up my jacket and raced my shadow home.

VII

Much as I liked Ántonia, I hated a superior tone that she sometimes took with me. She was four years older than I, to be sure, and had seen more of the world; but I was a boy and she was a girl, and I resented her protecting manner. Before the autumn was over she began to treat me more like an equal and to defer to me in other things than reading lessons. This change came about from an adventure we had together.

One day when I rode over to the Shimerdas' I found Ántonia starting off on foot for Russian Peter's house, to borrow a spade Ambrosch needed. I offered to take her on the pony, and she got up behind me. There had been another black frost the night before, and the air was clear and heady as wine. Within a week all the blooming roads had been despoiled—hundreds of miles of yellow sunflowers had been transformed into brown, rattling, burry stalks.

We found Russian Peter digging his potatoes. We were glad to go in and get warm by his kitchen stove and to see his squashes and Christmas melons, heaped in the store-room for winter. As we rode away with the spade, Ántonia suggested that we stop at the prairie-dog town and dig into one of the holes. We could find out whether they ran straight down, or were horizontal, like mole-holes; whether they had underground connections; whether the owls had nests down there, lined with feathers. We might get some puppies, or owl eggs, or snake-skins.

The dog-town was spread out over perhaps ten acres. The grass had been nibbled short and even, so this stretch was not shaggy and red like the surrounding country, but gray and velvety. The holes were several yards apart, and were disposed with a good deal of regularity, almost as if the town had been laid out in streets and avenues. One always felt that an orderly and very sociable kind of life was going on there. I picketed Dude down in a draw, and we went wandering about, looking for a hole that would be easy to dig. The dogs were out, as usual, dozens of them, sitting up on their hind legs over the doors of their houses. As we approached, they barked, shook their tails at us, and scurried underground. Before the mouths of the holes were little patches of sand and gravel, scratched up, we supposed, from a long way below the surface. Here and there, in the town, we came on larger gravel patches, several yards away from any hole. If the dogs had scratched the sand up in excavating, how had they carried it so far? It was on one of these gravel beds that I met my adventure.

We were examining a big hole with two entrances. The burrow sloped into the ground at a gentle angle, so that we could see where the two corridors united, and the floor was dusty from use, like a little highway over which much travel went. I was walking backward, in a crouching position, when I heard Ántonia scream. She was standing opposite me, pointing behind me and shouting something in Bohemian. I whirled round, and there, on one of those dry gravel beds, was the biggest snake I had ever seen. He was sunning himself, after the cold night, and he must have been asleep when Ántonia screamed. When I turned he was lying in long loose waves, like a letter "W." He twitched and began to coil slowly. He was not merely a big snake, I thought—he was a circus monstrosity. His abominable muscularity, his loathsome, fluid motion, somehow made me sick. He was as thick as my leg, and looked as if millstones couldn't crush the disgusting vitality out of him. He lifted his hideous little head, and rattled. I didn't run because I didn't think of it—if my back had been against a stone wall I couldn't have felt more cornered. I saw his coils tighten—now he would spring, spring his length, I remembered. I ran up and drove at his head with my spade, struck him fairly across the neck, and in a minute he was all about my feet in wavy loops. I struck now from hate. Ántonia, barefooted as she was, ran up behind me. Even after I had pounded his ugly head flat, his body kept on coiling and winding, doubling and falling back on itself. I walked away and turned my back. I felt seasick. Ántonia came after me, crying, "O Jimmy, he not bite you? You sure? Why you not run when I say?"

"What did you jabber Bohunk[9] for? You might have told me there was a snake behind me!" I said petulantly.

"I know I am just awful, Jim, I was so scared." She took my handkerchief from my pocket and tried to wipe my face with it, but I snatched it away from her. I suppose I looked as sick as I felt.

"I never know you was so brave, Jim," she went on comfortingly. "You is just like big mans; you wait for him lift his head and then you go for him. Ain't you feel scared a bit? Now we take that snake home and show everybody. Nobody ain't seen in this kawn-tree so big snake like you kill."

She went on in this strain until I began to think that I had longed for this opportunity, and had hailed it with joy. Cautiously we went back to the snake; he was still groping with his tail, turning up his ugly belly in the light. A faint, fetid smell came from him, and a thread of green liquid oozed from his crushed head.

"Look, Tony, that's his poison," I said.

9. Bohemian (slang).

I took a long piece of string from my pocket, and she lifted his head with the spade while I tied a noose around it. We pulled him out straight and measured him by my riding-quirt;[1] he was about five and a half feet long. He had twelve rattles, but they were broken off before they began to taper, so I insisted that he must once have had twenty-four. I explained to Ántonia how this meant that he was twenty-four years old, that he must have been there when white men first came, left on from buffalo and Indian times. As I turned him over I began to feel proud of him, to have a kind of respect for his age and size. He seemed like the ancient, eldest Evil. Certainly his kind have left horrible unconscious memories in all warm-blooded life. When we dragged him down into the draw, Dude sprang off to the end of his tether and shivered all over—wouldn't let us come near him.

We decided that Ántonia should ride Dude home, and I would walk. As she rode along slowly, her bare legs swinging against the pony's sides, she kept shouting back to me about how astonished everybody would be. I followed with the spade over my shoulder, dragging my snake. Her exultation was contagious. The great land had never looked to me so big and free. If the red grass were full of rattlers, I was equal to them all. Nevertheless, I stole furtive glances behind me now and then to see that no avenging mate, older and bigger than my quarry, was racing up from the rear.

The sun had set when we reached our garden and went down the draw toward the house. Otto Fuchs was the first one we met. He was sitting on the edge of the cattle-pond, having a quiet pipe before supper. Ántonia called him to come quick and look. He did not say anything for a minute, but scratched his head and turned the snake over with his boot.

"Where did you run onto that beauty, Jim?"

"Up at the dog-town," I answered laconically.

"Kill him yourself? How come you to have a weepon?"

"We'd been up to Russian Peter's, to borrow a spade for Ambrosch."

Otto shook the ashes out of his pipe and squatted down to count the rattles. "It was just luck you had a tool," he said cautiously. "Gosh! I wouldn't want to do any business with that fellow myself, unless I had a fence-post along. Your grandmother's snake-cane wouldn't more than tickle him. He could stand right up and talk to you, he could. Did he fight hard?"

Ántonia broke in: "He fight something awful! He is all over Jimmy's boots. I scream for him to run, but he just hit and hit that snake like he was crazy."

Otto winked at me. After Ántonia rode on he said: "Got him in the head first crack, didn't you? That was just as well."

We hung him up to the windmill, and when I went down to the kitchen I found Ántonia standing in the middle of the floor, telling the story with a great deal of color.

Subsequent experiences with rattlesnakes taught me that my first encounter was fortunate in circumstance. My big rattler was old, and had led too easy a life; there was not much fight in him. He had probably lived there for years, with a fat prairie dog for breakfast whenever he felt like it, a sheltered home, even an owl-feather bed, perhaps, and he had forgot that the world doesn't owe rattlers a living. A snake of his size, in fighting trim, would be more than any boy could handle. So in reality it was a mock adventure;

1. A whip with a short handle and rawhide lash.

the game was fixed for me by chance, as it probably was for many a dragon-slayer. I had been adequately armed by Russian Peter; the snake was old and lazy; and I had Ántonia beside me, to appreciate and admire.

That snake hung on our corral fence for several days; some of the neighbors came to see it and agreed that it was the biggest rattler ever killed in those parts. This was enough for Ántonia. She liked me better from that time on, and she never took a supercilious air with me again. I had killed a big snake—I was now a big fellow.

VIII

While the autumn color was growing pale on the grass and cornfields, things went badly with our friends the Russians. Peter told his troubles to Mr. Shimerda: he was unable to meet a note which fell due on the first of November; had to pay an exorbitant bonus on renewing it, and to give a mortgage on his pigs and horses and even his milk cow. His creditor was Wick Cutter, the merciless Black Hawk money-lender, a man of evil name throughout the county, of whom I shall have more to say later. Peter could give no very clear account of his transactions with Cutter. He only knew that he had first borrowed two hundred dollars, then another hundred, then fifty—that each time a bonus was added to the principal, and the debt grew faster than any crop he planted. Now everything was plastered with mortgages.

Soon after Peter renewed his note, Pavel strained himself lifting timbers for a new barn, and fell over among the shavings with such a gush of blood from the lungs that his fellow-workmen thought he would die on the spot. They hauled him home and put him into his bed, and there he lay, very ill indeed. Misfortune seemed to settle like an evil bird on the roof of the log house, and to flap its wings there, warning human beings away. The Russians had such bad luck that people were afraid of them and liked to put them out of mind.

One afternoon Ántonia and her father came over to our house to get buttermilk, and lingered, as they usually did, until the sun was low. Just as they were leaving, Russian Peter drove up. Pavel was very bad, he said, and wanted to talk to Mr. Shimerda and his daughter; he had come to fetch them. When Ántonia and her father got into the wagon, I entreated grandmother to let me go with them: I would gladly go without my supper, I would sleep in the Shimerdas' barn and run home in the morning. My plan must have seemed very foolish to her, but she was often large-minded about humoring the desires of other people. She asked Peter to wait a moment, and when she came back from the kitchen she brought a bag of sandwiches and doughnuts for us.

Mr. Shimerda and Peter were on the front seat; Ántonia and I sat in the straw behind and ate our lunch as we bumped along. After the sun sank, a cold wind sprang up and moaned over the prairie. If this turn in the weather had come sooner, I should not have got away. We burrowed down in the straw and curled up close together, watching the angry red die out of the west and the stars begin to shine in the clear, windy sky. Peter kept sighing and groaning. Tony whispered to me that he was afraid Pavel would never get well. We lay still and did not talk. Up there the stars grew magnificently bright. Though we had come from such different parts of the world, in both of us there was some dusky superstition that those shining groups have their influence upon what is and what is not to be. Perhaps Russian Peter, come from farther away than any of us, had brought from his land, too, some such belief.

The little house on the hillside was so much the color of the night that we could not see it as we came up the draw. The ruddy windows guided us—the light from the kitchen stove, for there was no lamp burning.

We entered softly. The man in the wide bed seemed to be asleep. Tony and I sat down on the bench by the wall and leaned our arms on the table in front of us. The firelight flickered on the hewn logs that supported the thatch overhead. Pavel made a rasping sound when he breathed, and he kept moaning. We waited. The wind shook the doors and windows impatiently, then swept on again, singing through the big spaces. Each gust, as it bore down, rattled the panes, and swelled off like the others. They made me think of defeated armies, retreating; or of ghosts who were trying desperately to get in for shelter, and then went moaning on. Presently, in one of those sobbing intervals between the blasts, the coyotes tuned up with their whining howl; one, two, three, then all together—to tell us that winter was coming. This sound brought an answer from the bed,—a long complaining cry,—as if Pavel were having bad dreams or were waking to some old misery. Peter listened, but did not stir. He was sitting on the floor by the kitchen stove. The coyotes broke out again; yap, yap, yap—then the high whine. Pavel called for something and struggled up on his elbow.

"He is scared of the wolves," Ántonia whispered to me. "In his country there are very many, and they eat men and women." We slid closer together along the bench.

I could not take my eyes off the man in the bed. His shirt was hanging open, and his emaciated chest, covered with yellow bristle, rose and fell horribly. He began to cough. Peter shuffled to his feet, caught up the tea-kettle and mixed him some hot water and whiskey. The sharp smell of spirits[2] went through the room.

Pavel snatched the cup and drank, then made Peter give him the bottle and slipped it under his pillow, grinning disagreeably, as if he had outwitted some one. His eyes followed Peter about the room with a contemptuous, unfriendly expression. It seemed to me that he despised him for being so simple and docile.

Presently Pavel began to talk to Mr. Shimerda, scarcely above a whisper. He was telling a long story, and as he went on, Ántonia took my hand under the table and held it tight. She leaned forward and strained her ears to hear him. He grew more and more excited, and kept pointing all around his bed, as if there were things there and he wanted Mr. Shimerda to see them.

"It's wolves, Jimmy," Ántonia whispered. "It's awful, what he says!"

The sick man raged and shook his fist. He seemed to be cursing people who had wronged him. Mr. Shimerda caught him by the shoulders, but could hardly hold him in bed. At last he was shut off by a coughing fit which fairly choked him. He pulled a cloth from under his pillow and held it to his mouth. Quickly it was covered with bright red spots—I thought I had never seen any blood so bright. When he lay down and turned his face to the wall,

2. Alcohol.

all the rage had gone out of him. He lay patiently fighting for breath, like a child with croup. Ántonia's father uncovered one of his long bony legs and rubbed it rhythmically. From our bench we could see what a hollow case his body was. His spine and shoulder-blades stood out like the bones under the hide of a dead steer left in the fields. The sharp backbone must have hurt him when he lay on it.

Gradually, relief came to all of us. Whatever it was, the worst was over. Mr. Shimerda signed to us that Pavel was asleep. Without a word Peter got up and lit his lantern. He was going out to get his team to drive us home. Mr. Shimerda went with him. We sat and watched the long bowed back under the blue sheet, scarcely daring to breathe.

On the way home, when we were lying in the straw, under the jolting and rattling Ántonia told me as much of the story as she could. What she did not tell me then, she told later; we talked of nothing else for days afterward.

When Pavel and Peter were young men, living at home in Russia, they were asked to be groomsmen for a friend who was to marry the belle of another village. It was in the dead of winter and the groom's party went over to the wedding in sledges. Peter and Pavel drove in the groom's sledge, and six sledges followed with all his relatives and friends.

After the ceremony at the church, the party went to a dinner given by the parents of the bride. The dinner lasted all afternoon; then it became a supper and continued far into the night. There was much dancing and drinking. At midnight the parents of the bride said good-bye to her and blessed her. The groom took her up in his arms and carried her out to his sledge and tucked her under the blankets. He sprang in beside her, and Pavel and Peter (our Pavel and Peter!) took the front seat. Pavel drove. The party set out with singing and the jingle of sleigh-bells, the groom's sledge going first. All the drivers were more or less the worse for merry-making, and the groom was absorbed in his bride.

The wolves were bad that winter, and every one knew it, yet when they heard the first wolf-cry, the drivers were not much alarmed. They had too much good food and drink inside them. The first howls were taken up and echoed and with quickening repetitions. The wolves were coming together. There was no moon, but the starlight was clear on the snow. A black drove came up over the hill behind the wedding party. The wolves ran like streaks of shadow; they looked no bigger than dogs, but there were hundreds of them.

Something happened to the hindmost sledge: the driver lost control,—he was probably very drunk,—the horses left the road, the sledge was caught in a clump of trees, and overturned. The occupants rolled out over the snow, and the fleetest of the wolves sprang upon them. The shrieks that followed made everybody sober. The drivers stood up and lashed their horses. The groom had the best team and his sledge was lightest—all the others carried from six to a dozen people.

Another driver lost control. The screams of the horses were more terrible to hear than the cries of the men and women. Nothing seemed to check the wolves. It was hard to tell what was happening in the rear; the people who were falling behind shrieked as piteously as those who were already lost. The little bride hid her face on the groom's shoulder and sobbed. Pavel sat still and watched his horses. The road was clear and white, and the groom's three blacks went like the wind. It was only necessary to be calm and to guide them carefully.

At length, as they breasted a long hill, Peter rose cautiously and looked back. "There are only three sledges left," he whispered.

"And the wolves?" Pavel asked.

"Enough! Enough for all of us."

Pavel reached the brow of the hill, but only two sledges followed him down the other side. In that moment on the hilltop, they saw behind them a whirling black group on the snow. Presently the groom screamed. He saw his father's sledge overturned, with his mother and sisters. He sprang up as if he meant to jump, but the girl shrieked and held him back. It was even then too late. The black ground-shadows were already crowding over the heap in the road, and one horse ran out across the fields, his harness hanging to him, wolves at his heels. But the groom's movement had given Pavel an idea.

They were within a few miles of their village now. The only sledge left out of six was not very far behind them, and Pavel's middle horse was failing. Beside a frozen pond something happened to the other sledge; Peter saw it plainly. Three big wolves got abreast of the horses, and the horses went crazy. They tried to jump over each other, got tangled up in the harness, and overturned the sledge.

When the shrieking behind them died away, Pavel realized that he was alone upon the familiar road. "They still come?" he asked Peter.

"Yes."

"How many?"

"Twenty, thirty—enough."

Now his middle horse was being almost dragged by the other two. Pavel gave Peter the reins and stepped carefully into the back of the sledge. He called to the groom that they must lighten—and pointed to the bride. The young man cursed him and held her tighter. Pavel tried to drag her away. In the struggle, the groom rose. Pavel knocked him over the side of the sledge and threw the girl after him. He said he never remembered exactly how he did it, or what happened afterward. Peter, crouching in the front seat, saw nothing. The first thing either of them noticed was a new sound that broke into the clear air, louder than they had ever heard before—the bell of the monastery of their own village, ringing for early prayers.

Pavel and Peter drove into the village alone, and they had been alone ever since. They were run out of their village. Pavel's own mother would not look at him. They went away to strange towns, but when people learned where they came from, they were always asked if they knew the two men who had fed the bride to the wolves. Wherever they went, the story followed them. It took them five years to save money enough to come to America. They worked in Chicago, Des Moines, Fort Wayne, but they were always unfortunate. When Pavel's health grew so bad, they decided to try farming.

Pavel died a few days after he unburdened his mind to Mr. Shimerda, and was buried in the Norwegian graveyard. Peter sold off everything, and left the country—went to be cook in a railway construction camp where gangs of Russians were employed.

At his sale we bought Peter's wheelbarrow and some of his harness. During the auction he went about with his head down, and never lifted his eyes. He seemed not to care about anything. The Black Hawk money-lender who held mortgages on Peter's live-stock was there, and he bought in the sale notes at about fifty cents on the dollar. Every one said Peter kissed the cow before she was led away by her new owner. I did not see him do it, but this I know: after all his furniture and his cook-stove and pots and pans had been hauled off by the purchasers, when his house was stripped and bare, he sat down on the floor with his clasp-knife and ate all the melons that he had put away for winter. When Mr. Shimerda and Krajiek drove up in their wagon to take Peter to the train, they found him with a dripping beard, surrounded by heaps of melon rinds.

The loss of his two friends had a depressing effect upon old Mr. Shimerda. When he was out hunting, he used to go into the empty log house and sit there, brooding. This cabin was his hermitage until the winter snows penned him in his cave. For Ántonia and me, the story of the wedding party was never at an end. We did not tell Pavel's secret to any one, but guarded it jealously—as if the wolves of the Ukraine had gathered that night long ago, and the wedding party been sacrificed, to give us a painful and peculiar pleasure. At night, before I went to sleep, I often found myself in a sledge drawn by three horses, dashing through a country that looked something like Nebraska and something like Virginia.

IX

The first snowfall came early in December. I remember how the world looked from our sitting-room window as I dressed behind the stove that morning: the low sky was like a sheet of metal; the blond cornfields had faded out into ghostliness at last; the little pond was frozen under its stiff willow bushes. Big white flakes were whirling over everything and disappearing in the red grass.

Beyond the pond, on the slope that climbed to the cornfield, there was, faintly marked in the grass, a great circle where the Indians used to ride. Jake and Otto were sure that when they galloped round that ring the Indians tortured prisoners, bound to a stake in the center; but grandfather thought they merely ran races or trained horses there. Whenever one looked at this slope against the setting sun, the circle showed like a pattern in the grass; and this morning, when the first light spray of snow lay over it, it came out with wonderful distinctness, like strokes of Chinese white on canvas. The old figure stirred me as it had never done before and seemed a good omen for the winter.

As soon as the snow had packed hard I began to drive about the country in a clumsy sleigh that Otto Fuchs made for me by fastening a wooden goods-box on bobs.[3] Fuchs had been apprenticed to a cabinet-maker in the old country and was very handy with tools. He would have done a better job if I hadn't hurried him. My first trip was to the post-office, and the next day I went over to take Yulka and Ántonia for a sleigh-ride.

It was a bright, cold day. I piled straw and buffalo robes into the box, and took two hot bricks wrapped in old blankets. When I got to the Shimerdas' I did not go up to the house, but sat in my sleigh at the bottom of the draw and called. Ántonia and Yulka came running out, wearing little rabbit-skin hats their father had made for them. They had heard about my sledge from

3. Short runners. The sleigh probably had two pairs, one front and one back.

Ambrosch and knew why I had come. They tumbled in beside me and we set off toward the north, along a road that happened to be broken.

The sky was brilliantly blue, and the sunlight on the glittering white stretches of prairie was almost blinding. As Ántonia said, the whole world was changed by the snow; we kept looking in vain for familiar landmarks. The deep arroyo[4] through which Squaw Creek wound was now only a cleft between snowdrifts—very blue when one looked down into it. The tree-tops that had been gold all the autumn were dwarfed and twisted, as if they would never have any life in them again. The few little cedars, which were so dull and dingy before, now stood out a strong, dusky green. The wind had the burning taste of fresh snow; my throat and nostrils smarted as if some one had opened a hartshorn[5] bottle. The cold stung, and at the same time delighted one. My horse's breath rose like steam, and whenever we stopped he smoked all over. The cornfields got back a little of their color under the dazzling light, and stood the palest possible gold in the sun and snow. All about us the snow was crusted in shallow terraces, with tracings like ripple-marks at the edges, curly waves that were the actual impression of the stinging lash in the wind.

The girls had on cotton dresses under their shawls; they kept shivering beneath the buffalo robes and hugging each other for warmth. But they were so glad to get away from their ugly cave and their mother's scolding that they begged me to go on and on, as far as Russian Peter's house. The great fresh open, after the stupefying warmth indoors, made them behave like wild things. They laughed and shouted, and said they never wanted to go home again. Couldn't we settle down and live in Russian Peter's house, Yulka asked, and couldn't I go to town and buy things for us to keep house with?

All the way to Russian Peter's we were extravagantly happy, but when we turned back,—it must have been about four o'clock,—the east wind grew stronger and began to howl; the sun lost its heartening power and the sky became gray and somber. I took off my long woolen comforter and wound it around Yulka's throat. She got so cold that we made her hide her head under the buffalo robe. Ántonia and I sat erect, but I held the reins clumsily, and my eyes were blinded by the wind a good deal of the time. It was growing dark when we got to their house, but I refused to go in with them and get warm. I knew my hands would ache terribly if I went near a fire. Yulka forgot to give me back my comforter, and I had to drive home directly against the wind. The next day I came down with an attack of quinsy,[6] which kept me in the house for nearly two weeks.

The basement kitchen seemed heavenly safe and warm in those days—like a tight little boat in a winter sea. The men were out in the fields all day, husking corn, and when they came in at noon, with long caps pulled down over their ears and their feet in red-lined over-shoes, I used to think they were like Arctic explorers.

In the afternoons, when grandmother sat upstairs darning, or making husking-gloves, I read "The Swiss Family Robinson"[7] aloud to her, and I felt that the Swiss family had no advantages over us in the way of an adventurous

4. A water-carved gully (Spanish).
5. Ammonia preparation used as a stimulant via nasal inhalation.
6. Severe sore throat.
7. Popular children's novel (1813), by Swiss writer Johann Rudolph Wyss, about how a family wrecked on a desert island manages to survive.

life. I was convinced that man's strongest antagonist is the cold. I admired the cheerful zest with which grandmother went about keeping us warm and comfortable and well-fed. She often reminded me, when she was preparing for the return of the hungry men, that this country was not like Virginia; and that here a cook had, as she said, "very little to do with."[8] On Sundays she gave us as much chicken as we could eat, and on other days we had ham or bacon or sausage meat. She baked either pies or cake for us every day, unless, for a change, she made my favorite pudding, striped with currants and boiled in a bag.

Next to getting warm and keeping warm, dinner and supper were the most interesting things we had to think about. Our lives centered around warmth and food and the return of the men at nightfall. I used to wonder, when they came in tired from the fields, their feet numb and their hands cracked and sore, how they could do all the chores so conscientiously: feed and water and bed the horses, milk the cows, and look after the pigs. When supper was over, it took them a long while to get the cold out of their bones. While grandmother and I washed the dishes and grandfather read his paper upstairs, Jake and Otto sat on the long bench behind the stove, "easing"[9] their inside boots, or rubbing mutton tallow into their cracked hands.

Every Saturday night we popped corn or made taffy, and Otto Fuchs used to sing, "For I Am a Cowboy and Know I've Done Wrong," or, "Bury Me Not on the Lone Prairee." He had a good baritone voice and always led the singing when we went to church services at the sod schoolhouse.

I can still see those two men sitting on the bench; Otto's close-clipped head and Jake's shaggy hair slicked flat in front by a wet comb. I can see the sag of their tired shoulders against the whitewashed wall. What good fellows they were, how much they knew, and how many things they had kept faith with!

Fuchs had been a cowboy, a stage-driver, a bar-tender, a miner; had wandered all over that great Western country and done hard work everywhere, though, as grandmother said, he had nothing to show for it. Jake was duller than Otto. He could scarcely read, wrote even his name with difficulty, and he had a violent temper which sometimes made him behave like a crazy man—tore him all to pieces and actually made him ill. But he was so soft-hearted that any one could impose upon him. If he, as he said, "forgot himself" and swore before grandmother, he went about depressed and shamefaced all day. They were both of them jovial about the cold in winter and the heat in summer, always ready to work overtime and to meet emergencies. It was a matter of pride with them not to spare themselves. Yet they were the sort of men who never get on, somehow, or do anything but work hard for a dollar or two a day.

On those bitter, starlit nights, as we sat around the old stove that fed us and warmed us and kept us cheerful, we could hear the coyotes howling down by the corrals, and their hungry, wintry cry used to remind the boys of wonderful animal stories; about gray wolves and bears in the Rockies, wildcats and panthers in the Virginia mountains. Sometimes Fuchs could be persuaded to talk about the outlaws and desperate characters he had known. I remember one funny story about himself that made grandmother,

8. I.e., the range of foodstuffs available on the prairie is extremely limited.

9. Manipulating the inside of the boot to soften it.

who was working her bread on the bread-board, laugh until she wiped her eyes with her bare arm, her hands being floury. It was like this:—

When Otto left Austria to come to America, he was asked by one of his relatives to look after a woman who was crossing on the same boat, to join her husband in Chicago. The woman started off with two children, but it was clear that her family might grow larger on the journey. Fuchs said he "got on fine with the kids," and liked the mother, though she played a sorry trick on him. In mid-ocean she proceeded to have not one baby, but three! This event made Fuchs the object of undeserved notoriety, since he was traveling with her. The steerage stewardess was indignant with him, the doctor regarded him with suspicion. The first-cabin passengers, who made up a purse for the woman, took an embarrassing interest in Otto, and often inquired of him about his charge. When the triplets were taken ashore at New York, he had, as he said, "to carry some of them." The trip to Chicago was even worse than the ocean voyage. On the train it was very difficult to get milk for the babies and to keep their bottles clean. The mother did her best, but no woman, out of her natural resources, could feed three babies. The husband, in Chicago, was working in a furniture factory for modest wages, and when he met his family at the station he was rather crushed by the size of it. He, too, seemed to consider Fuchs in some fashion to blame. "I was sure glad," Otto concluded, "that he didn't take his hard feeling out on that poor woman; but he had a sullen eye for me, all right! Now, did you ever hear of a young feller's having such hard luck, Mrs. Burden?"

Grandmother told him she was sure the Lord had remembered these things to his credit, and had helped him out of many a scrape when he didn't realize that he was being protected by Providence.

X

For several weeks after my sleigh-ride, we heard nothing from the Shimerdas. My sore throat kept me indoors, and grandmother had a cold which made the housework heavy for her. When Sunday came she was glad to have a day of rest. One night at supper Fuchs told us he had seen Mr. Shimerda out hunting.

"He's made himself a rabbit-skin cap, Jim, and a rabbit-skin collar that he buttons on outside his coat. They ain't got but one overcoat among 'em over there, and they take turns wearing it. They seem awful scared of cold, and stick in that hole in the bank like badgers."

"All but the crazy boy," Jake put in. "He never wears the coat. Krajiek says he's turrible strong and can stand anything. I guess rabbits must be getting scarce in this locality. Ambrosch come along by the cornfield yesterday where I was at work and showed me three prairie dogs he'd shot. He asked me if they was good to eat. I spit and made a face and took on, to scare him, but he just looked like he was smarter'n me and put 'em back in his sack and walked off."

Grandmother looked up in alarm and spoke to grandfather. "Josiah, you don't suppose Krajiek would let them poor creatures eat prairie dogs, do you?"

"You had better go over and see our neighbors to-morrow, Emmaline," he replied gravely.

Fuchs put in a cheerful word and said prairie dogs were clean beasts and ought to be good for food, but their family connections were against them.

I asked what he meant, and he grinned and said they belonged to the rat family.

When I went downstairs in the morning, I found grandmother and Jake packing a hamper basket in the kitchen.

"Now, Jake," grandmother was saying, "if you can find that old rooster that got his comb froze, just give his neck a twist, and we'll take him along. There's no good reason why Mrs. Shimerda couldn't have got hens from her neighbors last fall and had a henhouse going by now. I reckon she was confused and didn't know where to begin. I've come strange to a new country myself, but I never forgot hens are a good thing to have, no matter what you don't have."

"Just as you say, mam," said Jake, "but I hate to think of Krajiek getting a leg of that old rooster." He tramped out through the long cellar and dropped the heavy door behind him.

After breakfast grandmother and Jake and I bundled ourselves up and climbed into the cold front wagon-seat. As we approached the Shimerdas' we heard the frosty whine of the pump and saw Ántonia, her head tied up and her cotton dress blown about her, throwing all her weight on the pump-handle as it went up and down. She heard our wagon, looked back over her shoulder, and catching up her pail of water, started at a run for the hole in the bank.

Jake helped grandmother to the ground, saying he would bring the provisions after he had blanketed his horses. We went slowly up the icy path toward the door sunk in the drawside. Blue puffs of smoke came from the stovepipe that stuck out through the grass and snow, but the wind whisked them roughly away.

Mrs. Shimerda opened the door before we knocked and seized grandmother's hand. She did not say "How do!" as usual, but at once began to cry, talking very fast in her own language, pointing to her feet which were tied up in rags, and looking about accusingly at every one.

The old man was sitting on a stump behind the stove, crouching over as if he were trying to hide from us. Yulka was on the floor at his feet, her kitten in her lap. She peeped out at me and smiled, but, glancing up at her mother, hid again. Ántonia was washing pans and dishes in a dark corner. The crazy boy lay under the only window, stretched on a gunnysack[1] stuffed with straw. As soon as we entered he threw a grainsack over the crack at the bottom of the door. The air in the cave was stifling, and it was very dark, too. A lighted lantern, hung over the stove, threw out a feeble yellow glimmer.

Mrs. Shimerda snatched off the covers of two barrels behind the door, and made us look into them. In one there were some potatoes that had been frozen and were rotting, in the other was a little pile of flour. Grandmother murmured something in embarrassment, but the Bohemian woman laughed scornfully, a kind of whinny-laugh, and catching up an empty coffee-pot from the shelf, shook it at us with a look positively vindictive.

Grandmother went on talking in her polite Virginia way, not admitting their stark need or her own remissness, until Jake arrived with the hamper, as if in direct answer to Mrs. Shimerda's reproaches. Then the poor woman broke down. She dropped on the floor beside her crazy son, hid her face on

1. Large sack made from gunny, a coarse heavy fabric.

her knees, and sat crying bitterly. Grandmother paid no heed to her, but called Ántonia to come and help empty the basket. Tony left her corner reluctantly. I had never seen her crushed like this before.

"You not mind my poor *mamenka,* Mrs. Burden. She is so sad," she whispered, as she wiped her wet hands on her skirt and took the things grandmother handed her.

The crazy boy, seeing the food, began to make soft, gurgling noises and stroked his stomach. Jake came in again, this time with a sack of potatoes. Grandmother looked about in perplexity.

"Haven't you got any sort of cave or cellar outside, Ántonia? This is no place to keep vegetables. How did your potatoes get frozen?"

"We get from Mr. Bushy, at the post-office,—what he throw out. We got no potatoes, Mrs. Burden," Tony admitted mournfully.

When Jake went out, Marek crawled along the floor and stuffed up the door-crack again. Then, quietly as a shadow, Mr. Shimerda came out from behind the stove. He stood brushing his hand over his smooth gray hair, as if he were trying to clear away a fog about his head. He was clean and neat as usual, with his green neckcloth and his coral pin. He took grandmother's arm and led her behind the stove, to the back of the room. In the rear wall was another little cave; a round hole, not much bigger than an oil barrel, scooped out in the black earth. When I got up on one of the stools and peered into it, I saw some quilts and a pile of straw. The old man held the lantern. "Yulka," he said in a low, despairing voice, "Yulka; my Ántonia!"

Grandmother drew back. "You mean they sleep in there,—your girls?" He bowed his head.

Tony slipped under his arm. "It is very cold on the floor, and this is warm like the badger hole. I like for sleep there," she insisted eagerly. "My *mamenka* have nice bed, with pillows from our own geese in Bohemie. See, Jim?" She pointed to the narrow bunk which Krajiek had built against the wall for himself before the Shimerdas came.

Grandmother sighed. "Sure enough, where *would* you sleep, dear! I don't doubt you're warm there. You'll have a better house after while, Ántonia, and then you'll forget these hard times."

Mr. Shimerda made grandmother sit down on the only chair and pointed his wife to a stool beside her. Standing before them with his hand on Ántonia's shoulder, he talked in a low tone, and his daughter translated. He wanted us to know that they were not beggars in the old country; he made good wages, and his family were respected there. He left Bohemia with more than a thousand dollars in savings, after their passage money was paid. He had in some way lost on exchange in New York, and the railway fare to Nebraska was more than they had expected. By the time they paid Krajiek for the land, and bought his horses and oxen and some old farm machinery, they had very little money left. He wished grandmother to know, however, that he still had some money. If they could get through until spring came, they would buy a cow and chickens and plant a garden, and would then do very well. Ambrosch and Ántonia were both old enough to work in the fields, and they were willing to work. But the snow and the bitter weather had disheartened them all.

Ántonia explained that her father meant to build a new house for them in the spring; he and Ambrosch had already split the logs for it, but the logs were all buried in the snow, along the creek where they had been felled.

While grandmother encouraged and gave them advice, I sat down on the floor with Yulka and let her show me her kitten. Marek slid cautiously toward us and began to exhibit his webbed fingers. I knew he wanted to make his queer noises for me—to bark like a dog or whinny like a horse,—but he did not dare in the presence of his elders. Marek was always trying to be agreeable, poor fellow, as if he had it on his mind that he must make up for his deficiencies.

Mrs. Shimerda grew more calm and reasonable before our visit was over, and, while Ántonia translated, put in a word now and then on her own account. The woman had a quick ear, and caught up phrases whenever she heard English spoken. As we rose to go, she opened her wooden chest and brought out a bag made of bed-ticking, about as long as a flour sack and half as wide, stuffed full of something. At sight of it, the crazy boy began to smack his lips. When Mrs. Shimerda opened the bag and stirred the contents with her hand, it gave out a salty, earthy smell, very pungent, even among the other odors of that cave. She measured a teacup full, tied it up in a bit of sacking, and presented it ceremoniously to grandmother.

"For cook," she announced. "Little now; be very much when cook," spreading out her hands as if to indicate that the pint would swell to a gallon. "Very good. You no have in this country. All things for eat better in my country."

"Maybe so, Mrs. Shimerda," grandmother said drily. "I can't say but I prefer our bread to yours, myself."

Ántonia undertook to explain. "This very good, Mrs. Burden,"—she clasped her hands as if she could not express how good,—"it make very much when you cook, like what my mama say. Cook with rabbit, cook with chicken, in the gravy,—oh, so good!"

All the way home grandmother and Jake talked about how easily good Christian people could forget they were their brothers' keepers.

"I will say, Jake, some of our brothers and sisters are hard to keep: Where's a body to begin, with these people? They're wanting in everything, and most of all in horse-sense. Nobody can give 'em that, I guess. Jimmy, here, is about as able to take over a homestead as they are. Do you reckon that boy Ambrosch has any real push in him?"

"He's a worker, all right, mam, and he's got some ketch-on[2] about him; but he's a mean one. Folks can be mean enough to get on in this world; and then, ag'in, they can be too mean."

That night, while grandmother was getting supper, we opened the package Mrs. Shimerda had given her. It was full of little brown chips that looked like the shavings of some root. They were as light as feathers, and the most noticeable thing about them was their penetrating, earthy odor. We could not determine whether they were animal or vegetable.

"They might be dried meat from some queer beast, Jim. They ain't dried fish, and they never grew on stalk or vine. I'm afraid of 'em. Anyhow, I shouldn't want to eat anything that had been shut up for months with old clothes and goose pillows."

She threw the package into the stove, but I bit off a corner of one of the chips I held in my hand, and chewed it tentatively. I never forgot the strange taste; though it was many years before I knew that those little brown shav-

2. Alertness (slang); literally, the ability to catch on.

ings, which the Shimerdas had brought so far and treasured so jealously, were dried mushrooms. They had been gathered, probably, in some deep Bohemian forest. . . . . .

XI

During the week before Christmas, Jake was the most important person of our household, for he was to go to town and do all our Christmas shopping. But on the 21st of December, the snow began to fall. The flakes came down so thickly that from the sitting-room windows I could not see beyond the windmill—its frame looked dim and gray, unsubstantial like a shadow. The snow did not stop falling all day, or during the night that followed. The cold was not severe, but the storm was quiet and resistless. The men could not go farther than the barns and corral. They sat about the house most of the day as if it were Sunday; greasing their boots, mending their suspenders, plaiting whiplashes.

On the morning of the 22d, grandfather announced at breakfast that it would be impossible to go to Black Hawk for Christmas purchases. Jake was sure he could get through on horseback, and bring home our things in saddle-bags; but grandfather told him the roads would be obliterated, and a newcomer in the country would be lost ten times over. Anyway, he would never allow one of his horses to be put to such a strain.

We decided to have a country Christmas, without any help from town. I had wanted to get some picture-books for Yulka and Ántonia; even Yulka was able to read a little now. Grandmother took me into the ice-cold storeroom, where she had some bolts of gingham and sheeting. She cut squares of cotton cloth and we sewed them together into a book. We bound it between pasteboards, which I covered with brilliant calico, representing scenes from a circus. For two days I sat at the dining-room table, pasting this book full of pictures for Yulka. We had files of those good old family magazines which used to publish colored lithographs of popular paintings, and I was allowed to use some of these. I took "Napoleon Announcing the Divorce to Josephine"[3] for my frontispiece. On the white pages I grouped Sunday-School cards and advertising cards which I had brought from my "old country." Fuchs got out the old candle-moulds and made tallow candles. Grandmother hunted up her fancy cake-cutters and baked gingerbread men and roosters, which we decorated with burnt sugar and red cinnamon drops.

On the day before Christmas, Jake packed the things we were sending to the Shimerdas in his saddle-bags and set off on grandfather's gray gelding. When he mounted his horse at the door, I saw that he had a hatchet slung to his belt, and he gave grandmother a meaning look which told me he was planning a surprise for me. That afternoon I watched long and eagerly from the sitting-room window. At last I saw a dark spot moving on the west hill, beside the half-buried cornfield, where the sky was taking on a coppery flush from the sun that did not quite break through. I put on my cap and ran out to meet Jake. When I got to the pond I could see that he was bringing in a little cedar tree across his pommel. He used to help my father cut Christmas trees for me in Virginia, and he had not forgotten how much I liked them.

3. Josephine (1763–1814), empress of France and wife of Napoleon Bonaparte, who married her in 1796 and divorced her in 1809 to marry Marie Louise, daughter of the Austrian emperor. In American popular culture, she became a symbol of the deserted wife.

By the time we had placed the cold, fresh-smelling little tree in a corner of the sitting-room, it was already Christmas Eve. After supper we all gathered there, and even grandfather, reading his paper by the table, looked up with friendly interest now and then. The cedar was about five feet high and very shapely. We hung it with the gingerbread animals, strings of popcorn, and bits of candle which Fuchs had fitted into pasteboard sockets. Its real splendors, however, came from the most unlikely place in the world—from Otto's cowboy trunk. I had never seen anything in that trunk but old boots and spurs and pistols, and a fascinating mixture of yellow leather thongs, cartridges, and shoemaker's wax. From under the lining he now produced a collection of brilliantly colored paper figures, several inches high and stiff enough to stand alone. They had been sent to him year after year, by his old mother in Austria. There was a bleeding heart, in tufts of paper lace; there were the three kings, gorgeously appareled, and the ox and the ass and the shepherds; there was the Baby in the manger, and a group of angels, singing; there were camels and leopards, held by the black slaves of the three kings. Our tree became the talking tree of the fairy tale; legends and stories nestled like birds in its branches. Grandmother said it reminded her of the Tree of Knowledge. We put sheets of cotton wool under it for a snow-field, and Jake's pocket-mirror for a frozen lake.

I can see them now, exactly as they looked, working about the table in the lamplight: Jake with his heavy features, so rudely moulded that his face seemed, somehow, unfinished; Otto with his half-ear and the savage scar that made his upper lip curl so ferociously under his twisted mustache. As I remember them, what unprotected faces they were; their very roughness and violence made them defenseless. These boys had no practiced manner behind which they could retreat and hold people at a distance. They had only their hard fists to batter at the world with. Otto was already one of those drifting, case-hardened laborers who never marry or have children of their own. Yet he was so fond of children!

XII

On Christmas morning, when I got down to the kitchen, the men were just coming in from their morning chores—the horses and pigs always had their breakfast before we did. Jake and Otto shouted "Merry Christmas"! to me, and winked at each other when they saw the waffle-irons on the stove. Grandfather came down, wearing a white shirt and his Sunday coat. Morning prayers were longer than usual. He read the chapters from St. Matthew about the birth of Christ, and as we listened it all seemed like something that had happened lately, and near at hand. In his prayer he thanked the Lord for the first Christmas, and for all that it had meant to the world ever since. He gave thanks for our food and comfort, and prayed for the poor and destitute in great cities, where the struggle for life was harder than it was here with us. Grandfather's prayers were often very interesting. He had the gift of simple and moving expression. Because he talked so little, his words had a peculiar force; they were not worn dull from constant use. His prayers reflected what he was thinking about at the time, and it was chiefly through them that we got to know his feelings and his views about things.

After we sat down to our waffles and sausage, Jake told us how pleased the Shimerdas had been with their presents; even Ambrosch was friendly and went to the creek with him to cut the Christmas tree. It was a soft gray day outside, with heavy clouds working across the sky, and occasional squalls of snow. There were always odd jobs to be done about the barn on holidays, and the men were busy until afternoon. Then Jake and I played dominoes, while Otto wrote a long letter home to his mother. He always wrote to her on Christmas Day, he said, no matter where he was, and no matter how long it had been since his last letter. All afternoon he sat in the dining-room. He would write for a while, then sit idle, his clenched fist lying on the table, his eyes following the pattern of the oilcloth. He spoke and wrote his own language so seldom that it came to him awkwardly. His effort to remember entirely absorbed him.

At about four o'clock a visitor appeared: Mr. Shimerda, wearing his rabbit-skin cap and collar, and new mittens his wife had knitted. He had come to thank us for the presents, and for all grandmother's kindness to his family. Jake and Otto joined us from the basement and we sat about the stove, enjoying the deepening gray of the winter afternoon and the atmosphere of comfort and security in my grandfather's house. This feeling seemed completely to take possession of Mr. Shimerda. I suppose, in the crowded clutter of their cave, the old man had come to believe that peace and order had vanished from the earth, or existed only in the old world he had left so far behind. He sat still and passive, his head resting against the back of the wooden rocking-chair, his hands relaxed upon the arms. His face had a look of weariness and pleasure, like that of sick people when they feel relief from pain. Grandmother insisted on his drinking a glass of Virginia apple-brandy after his long walk in the cold, and when a faint flush came up in his cheeks, his features might have been cut out of a shell, they were so transparent. He said almost nothing, and smiled rarely; but as he rested there we all had a sense of his utter content.

As it grew dark, I asked whether I might light the Christmas tree before the lamp was brought. When the candle ends sent up their conical yellow flames, all the colored figures from Austria stood out clear and full of meaning against the green boughs. Mr. Shimerda rose, crossed himself, and quietly knelt down before the tree, his head sunk forward. His long body formed a letter "S." I saw grandmother look apprehensively at grandfather. He was rather narrow in religious matters, and sometimes spoke out and hurt people's feelings. There had been nothing strange about the tree before, but now, with some one kneeling before it,—images, candles, . . . Grandfather merely put his fingertips to his brow and bowed his venerable head, thus Protestantizing the atmosphere.[4]

We persuaded our guest to stay for supper with us. He needed little urging. As we sat down to the table, it occurred to me that he liked to look at us, and that our faces were open books to him. When his deep-seeing eyes rested on me, I felt as if he were looking far ahead into the future for me, down the road I would have to travel.

4. Traditional forms of Protestantism (the Burdens are Baptists) strongly opposed modes of worship involving images, statues, and rituals, which were interpreted as superstitions. It is therefore notable when, at the end of the chapter, Grandfather justifies Mr. Shimerda's making the sign of the cross.

At nine o'clock Mr. Shimerda lighted one of our lanterns and put on his overcoat and fur collar. He stood in the little entry hall, the lantern and his fur cap under his arm, shaking hands with us. When he took grandmother's hand, he bent over it as he always did, and said slowly, "Good wo-man!" He made the sign of the cross over me, put on his cap and went off in the dark. As we turned back to the sitting-room, grandfather looked at me searchingly. "The prayers of all good people are good," he said quietly.

XIII

The week following Christmas brought in a thaw, and by New Year's Day all the world about us was a broth of gray slush, and the guttered slope between the windmill and the barn was running black water. The soft black earth stood out in patches along the roadsides. I resumed all my chores, carried in the cobs and wood and water, and spent the afternoons at the barn, watching Jake shell corn with a hand-sheller.

One morning, during this interval of fine weather, Ántonia and her mother rode over on one of their shaggy old horses to pay us a visit. It was the first time Mrs. Shimerda had been to our house, and she ran about examining our carpets and curtains and furniture, all the while commenting upon them to her daughter in an envious, complaining tone. In the kitchen she caught up an iron pot that stood on the back of the stove and said: "You got many, Shimerdas no got." I thought it weak-minded of grandmother to give the pot to her.

After dinner, when she was helping to wash the dishes, she said, tossing her head: "You got many things for cook. If I got all things like you, I make much better."

She was a conceited, boastful old thing, and even misfortune could not humble her. I was so annoyed that I felt coldly even toward Ántonia and listened unsympathetically when she told me her father was not well.

"My papa sad for the old country. He not look good. He never make music any more. At home he play violin all the time; for weddings and for dance. Here never. When I beg him for play, he shake his head no. Some days he take his violin out of his box and make with his fingers on the strings, like this, but never he make the music. He don't like this kawn-tree."

"People who don't like this country ought to stay at home," I said severely. "We don't make them come here."

"He not want to come, nev-er!" she burst out. "My *mamenka* make him come. All the time she say: 'America big country; much money, much land for my boys, much husband for my girls.' My papa, he cry for leave his old friends what make music with him. He love very much the man what play the long horn like this"—she indicated a slide trombone. "They go to school together and are friends from boys. But my mama, she want Ambrosch for be rich, with many cattle."

"Your mama," I said angrily, "wants other people's things."

"Your grandfather is rich," she retorted fiercely. "Why he not help my papa? Ambrosch be rich, too, after while, and he pay back. He is very smart boy. For Ambrosch my mama come here."

Ambrosch was considered the important person in the family. Mrs. Shimerda and Ántonia always deferred to him, though he was often surly with them and contemptuous toward his father. Ambrosch and his mother had everything their own way. Though Ántonia loved her father more than she did any one else, she stood in awe of her elder brother.

After I watched Ántonia and her mother go over the hill on their miserable horse, carrying our iron pot with them, I turned to grandmother, who had taken up her darning, and said I hoped that snooping old woman wouldn't come to see us any more.

Grandmother chuckled and drove her bright needle across a hole in Otto's sock. "She's not old, Jim, though I expect she seems old to you. No, I wouldn't mourn, if she never came again. But, you see, a body never knows what traits poverty might bring out in 'em. It makes a woman grasping to see her children want for things. Now read me a chapter in 'The Prince of the House of David.'[5] Let's forget the Bohemians."

We had three weeks of this mild, open weather. The cattle in the corral ate corn almost as fast as the men could shell it for them, and we hoped they would be ready for an early market. One morning the two big bulls, Gladstone and Brigham Young,[6] thought spring had come, and they began to tease and butt at each other across the barbed wire that separated them. Soon they got angry. They bellowed and pawed up the soft earth with their hoofs, rolling their eyes and tossing their heads. Each withdrew to a far corner of his own corral, and then they made for each other at a gallop. Thud, thud, we could hear the impact of their great heads, and their bellowing shook the pans on the kitchen shelves. Had they not been dehorned, they would have torn each other to pieces. Pretty soon the fat steers took it up and began butting and horning each other. Clearly, the affair had to be stopped. We all stood by and watched admiringly while Fuchs rode into the corral with a pitchfork and prodded the bulls again and again, finally driving them apart.

The big storm of the winter began on my eleventh birthday, the 20th of January. When I went down to breakfast that morning, Jake and Otto came in white as snow-men, beating their hands and stamping their feet. They began to laugh boisterously when they saw me, calling:—

"You've got a birthday present this time, Jim, and no mistake. They was a full-grown blizzard ordered for you."

All day the storm went on. The snow did not fall this time, it simply spilled out of heaven, like thousands of feather-beds being emptied. That afternoon the kitchen was a carpenter-shop; the men brought in their tools and made two great wooden shovels with long handles. Neither grandmother nor I could go out in the storm, so Jake fed the chickens and brought in a pitiful contribution of eggs.

Next day our men had to shovel until noon to reach the barn—and the snow was still falling! There had not been such a storm in the ten years my grandfather had lived in Nebraska. He said at dinner that we would not try to reach the cattle—they were fat enough to go without their corn for a day or two; but to-morrow we must feed them and thaw out their water-tap so that they could drink. We could not so much as see the corrals, but we knew the steers were over there, huddled together under the north bank.

5. Best-selling American novel of 1855, by Joseph Holt Ingraham (1809–1860); based on the life of Jesus Christ. A pious household like the Burdens' would oppose novel reading in general; biblical novels would be exceptions.

6. Mormon leader (1801–1877) who led the Mormons to Salt Lake City in 1846–47 and directed the settlement there. William Gladstone (1809–1898), English statesman who was prime minister four times. The two bulls are humorously named.

Our ferocious bulls, subdued enough by this time, were probably warming each other's backs. "This'll take the bile out of 'em!" Fuchs remarked gleefully.

At noon that day the hens had not been heard from. After dinner Jake and Otto, their damp clothes now dried on them, stretched their stiff arms and plunged again into the drifts. They made a tunnel under the snow to the henhouse, with walls so solid that grandmother and I could walk back and forth in it. We found the chickens asleep; perhaps they thought night had come to stay. One old rooster was stirring about, pecking at the solid lump of ice in their water-tin. When we flashed the lantern in their eyes, the hens set up a great cackling and flew about clumsily, scattering down-feathers. The mottled, pinheaded, guinea-hens, always resentful of captivity, ran screeching out into the tunnel and tried to poke their ugly, painted faces through the snow walls. By five o'clock the chores were done—just when it was time to begin them all over again! That was a strange, unnatural sort of day.

XIV

On the morning of the 22d I wakened with a start. Before I opened my eyes, I seemed to know that something had happened. I heard excited voices in the kitchen—grandmother's was so shrill that I knew she must be almost beside herself. I looked forward to any new crisis with delight. What could it be, I wondered, as I hurried into my clothes. Perhaps the barn had burned; perhaps the cattle had frozen to death; perhaps a neighbor was lost in the storm.

Down in the kitchen grandfather was standing before the stove with his hands behind him. Jake and Otto had taken off their boots and were rubbing their woolen socks. Their clothes and boots were steaming, and they both looked exhausted. On the bench behind the stove lay a man, covered up with a blanket. Grandmother motioned me to the dining-room. I obeyed reluctantly. I watched her as she came and went, carrying dishes. Her lips were tightly compressed and she kept whispering to herself: "Oh, dear Saviour!" "Lord, Thou knowest!"

Presently grandfather came in and spoke to me: "Jimmy, we will not have prayers this morning, because we have a great deal to do. Old Mr. Shimerda is dead, and his family are in great distress. Ambrosch came over here in the middle of the night, and Jake and Otto went back with him. The boys have had a hard night, and you must not bother them with questions. That is Ambrosch, asleep on the bench. Come in to breakfast, boys."

After Jake and Otto had swallowed their first cup of coffee, they began to talk excitedly, disregarding grandmother's warning glances. I held my tongue, but I listened with all my ears.

"No, sir," Fuchs said in answer to a question from grandfather, "nobody heard the gun go off. Ambrosch was out with the ox team, trying to break a road, and the women folks was shut up tight in their cave. When Ambrosch come in it was dark and he didn't see nothing, but the oxen acted kind of queer. One of 'em ripped around and got away from him—bolted clean out of the stable. His hands is blistered where the rope run through. He got a lantern and went back and found the old man, just as we seen him."

"Poor soul, poor soul!" grandmother groaned. "I'd like to think he never done it. He was always considerate and un-wishful to give trouble. How could he forget himself and bring this on us!"

"I don't think he was out of his head for a minute, Mrs. Burden," Fuchs declared. "He done everything natural. You know he was always sort of fixy,[7] and fixy he was to the last. He shaved after dinner, and washed hisself all over after the girls was done the dishes. Ántonia heated the water for him. Then he put on a clean shirt and clean socks, and after he was dressed he kissed her and the little one and took his gun and said he was going out to hunt rabbits. He must have gone right down to the barn and done it then. He layed down on that bunk-bed, close to the ox stalls, where he always slept. When we found him, everything was decent except,"—Fuchs wrinkled his brow and hesitated,—"except what he couldn't nowise foresee. His coat was hung on a peg, and his boots was under the bed. He'd took off that silk neckcloth he always wore, and folded it smooth and stuck his pin through it. He turned back his shirt at the neck and rolled up his sleeves."

"I don't see how he could do it!" grandmother kept saying.

Otto misunderstood her. "Why, mam, it was simple enough; he pulled the trigger with his big toe. He layed over on his side and put the end of the barrel in his mouth, then he drew up one foot and felt for the trigger. He found it all right!"

"Maybe he did," said Jake grimly. "There's something mighty queer about it."

"Now what do you mean, Jake?" grandmother asked sharply.

"Well, mam, I found Krajiek's axe under the manger, and I picks it up and carries it over to the corpse, and I take my oath it just fit the gash in the front of the old man's face. That there Krajiek had been sneakin' round, pale and quiet, and when he seen me examinin' the axe, he begun whimperin', 'My God, man, don't do that!' 'I reckon I'm a-goin' to look into this,' says I. Then he begun to squeal like a rat and run about wringin' his hands. 'They'll hang me!' says he. 'My God, they'll hang me sure!'"

Fuchs spoke up impatiently. "Krajiek's gone silly, Jake, and so have you. The old man wouldn't have made all them preparations for Krajiek to murder him, would he? It don't hang together. The gun was right beside him when Ambrosch found him."

"Krajiek could 'a' put it there, couldn't he?" Jake demanded.

Grandmother broke in excitedly: "See here, Jake Marpole, don't you go trying to add murder to suicide. We're deep enough in trouble. Otto reads you too many of them detective stories."

"It will be easy to decide all that, Emmaline," said grandfather quietly. "If he shot himself in the way they think, the gash will be torn from the inside outward."

"Just so it is, Mr. Burden," Otto affirmed. "I seen bunches of hair and stuff sticking to the poles and straw along the roof. They was blown up there by gunshot, no question."

Grandmother told grandfather she meant to go over to the Shimerdas with him.

"There is nothing you can do," he said doubtfully. "The body can't be touched until we get the coroner here from Black Hawk, and that will be a matter of several days, this weather."

7. Finicky, fastidious.

"Well, I can take them some victuals, anyway, and say a word of comfort to them poor little girls. The oldest one was his darling, and was like a right hand to him. He might have thought of her. He's left her alone in a hard world." She glanced distrustfully at Ambrosch, who was now eating his breakfast at the kitchen table.

Fuchs, although he had been up in the cold nearly all night, was going to make the long ride to Black Hawk to fetch the priest and the coroner. On the gray gelding, our best horse, he would try to pick his way across the country with no roads to guide him.

"Don't you worry about me, Mrs. Burden," he said cheerfully, as he put on a second pair of socks. "I've got a good nose for directions, and I never did need much sleep. It's the gray I'm worried about. I'll save him what I can, but it'll strain him, as sure as I'm telling you!"

"This is no time to be over-considerate of animals, Otto; do the best you can for yourself. Stop at the Widow Steavens's for dinner. She's a good woman, and she'll do well by you."

After Fuchs rode away, I was left with Ambrosch. I saw a side of him I had not seen before. He was deeply, even slavishly, devout. He did not say a word all morning, but sat with his rosary in his hands, praying, now silently, now aloud. He never looked away from his beads, nor lifted his hands except to cross himself. Several times the poor boy fell asleep where he sat, wakened with a start, and began to pray again.

No wagon could be got to the Shimerdas' until a road was broken, and that would be a day's job. Grandfather came from the barn on one of our big black horses, and Jake lifted grandmother up behind him. She wore her black hood and was bundled up in shawls. Grandfather tucked his bushy white beard inside his overcoat. They looked very Biblical as they set off, I thought. Jake and Ambrosch followed them, riding the other black and my pony, carrying bundles of clothes that we had got together for Mrs. Shimerda. I watched them go past the pond and over the hill by the drifted cornfield. Then, for the first time, I realized that I was alone in the house.

I felt a considerable extension of power and authority, and was anxious to acquit myself creditably. I carried in cobs[8] and wood from the long cellar, and filled both the stoves. I remembered that in the hurry and excitement of the morning nobody had thought of the chickens, and the eggs had not been gathered. Going out through the tunnel, I gave the hens their corn, emptied the ice from their drinking-pan, and filled it with water. After the cat had had his milk, I could think of nothing else to do, and I sat down to get warm. The quiet was delightful, and the ticking clock was the most pleasant of companions. I got "Robinson Crusoe"[9] and tried to read, but his life on the island seemed dull compared with ours. Presently, as I looked with satisfaction about our comfortable sitting-room, it flashed upon me that if Mr. Shimerda's soul were lingering about in this world at all, it would be here, in our house, which had been more to his liking than any other in the neighborhood. I remembered his contented face when he was with us on Christmas Day. If he could have lived with us, this terrible thing would never have happened.

8. After the corn kernels have been scraped from them, the cobs can be used for fuel.

9. A 1719 novel by English writer Daniel Defoe (1660?–1731), based on the true adventures of Alexander Selkirk in 1704. The story tells how Robinson Crusoe, shipwrecked on an uninhabited island, learns to survive.

I knew it was homesickness that had killed Mr. Shimerda, and I wondered whether his released spirit would not eventually find its way back to his own country. I thought of how far it was to Chicago, and then to Virginia, to Baltimore,—and then the great wintry ocean. No, he would not at once set out upon that long journey. Surely, his exhausted spirit, so tired of cold and crowding and the struggle with the ever-falling snow, was resting now in this quiet house.

I was not frightened, but I made no noise. I did not wish to disturb him. I went softly down to the kitchen which, tucked away so snugly underground, always seemed to me the heart and center of the house. There, on the bench behind the stove, I thought and thought about Mr. Shimerda. Outside I could hear the wind singing over hundreds of miles of snow. It was as if I had let the old man in out of the tormenting winter, and were sitting there with him. I went over all that Ántonia had ever told me about his life before he came to this country; how he used to play the fiddle at weddings and dances. I thought about the friends he had mourned to leave, the trombone-player, the great forest full of game,—belonging, as Ántonia said, to the "nobles,"—from which she and her mother used to steal wood on moonlight nights. There was a white hart that lived in that forest, and if any one killed it, he would be hanged, she said. Such vivid pictures came to me that they might have been Mr. Shimerda's memories, not yet faded out from the air in which they had haunted him.

It had begun to grow dark when my household returned, and grandmother was so tired that she went at once to bed. Jake and I got supper, and while we were washing the dishes he told me in loud whispers about the state of things over at the Shimerdas'. Nobody could touch the body until the coroner came. If any one did, something terrible would happen, apparently. The dead man was frozen through, "just as stiff as a dressed turkey you hang out to freeze," Jake said. The horses and oxen would not go into the barn until he was frozen so hard that there was no longer any smell of blood. They were stabled there now, with the dead man, because there was no other place to keep them. A lighted lantern was kept hanging over Mr. Shimerda's head. Ántonia and Ambrosch and the mother took turns going down to pray beside him. The crazy boy went with them, because he did not feel the cold. I believed he felt cold as much as any one else, but he liked to be thought insensible to it. He was always coveting distinction, poor Marek!

Ambrosch, Jake said, showed more human feeling than he would have supposed him capable of; but he was chiefly concerned about getting a priest, and about his father's soul, which he believed was in a place of torment and would remain there until his family and the priest had prayed a great deal for him.[1] "As I understand it," Jake concluded, "it will be a matter of years to pray his soul out of Purgatory, and right now he's in torment."

"I don't believe it," I said stoutly. "I almost know it isn't true." I did not, of course, say that I believed he had been in that very kitchen all afternoon, on his way back to his own country. Nevertheless, after I went to bed, this idea of punishment and Purgatory came back on me crushingly. I remembered the account of Dives[2] in torment, and shuddered. But Mr. Shimerda had not

1. The Catholic Shimerdas believe that suicide is a mortal sin.

2. In Luke 16.19–31, Jesus recounts the story of Dives, a rich, selfish man who suffers the torments of hell, and Lazarus, a beggar who goes to heaven.

been rich and selfish; he had only been so unhappy that he could not live any longer.

XV

Otto Fuchs got back from Black Hawk at noon the next day. He reported that the coroner would reach the Shimerdas' sometime that afternoon, but the missionary priest was at the other end of his parish, a hundred miles away, and the trains were not running. Fuchs had got a few hours' sleep at the livery barn in town, but he was afraid the gray gelding had strained himself. Indeed, he was never the same horse afterward. That long trip through the deep snow had taken all the endurance out of him.

Fuchs brought home with him a stranger, a young Bohemian who had taken a homestead near Black Hawk, and who came on his only horse to help his fellow-countrymen in their trouble. That was the first time I ever saw Anton Jelinek. He was a strapping young fellow in the early twenties then, handsome, warm-hearted, and full of life, and he came to us like a miracle in the midst of that grim business. I remember exactly how he strode into our kitchen in his felt boots and long wolf-skin coat, his eyes and cheeks bright with the cold. At sight of grandmother, he snatched off his fur cap, greeting her in a deep, rolling voice which seemed older than he.

"I want to thank you very much, Mrs. Burden, for that you are so kind to poor strangers from my kawn-tree."

He did not hesitate like a farmer boy, but looked one eagerly in the eye when he spoke. Everything about him was warm and spontaneous. He said he would have come to see the Shimerdas before, but he had hired out to husk corn all the fall, and since winter began he had been going to the school by the mill, to learn English, along with the little children. He told me he had a nice "lady-teacher" and that he liked to go to school.

At dinner grandfather talked to Jelinek more than he usually did to strangers.

"Will they be much disappointed because we cannot get a priest?" he asked.

Jelinek looked serious. "Yes, sir, that is very bad for them. Their father has done a great sin," he looked straight at grandfather. "Our Lord has said that."

Grandfather seemed to like his frankness. "We believe that, too, Jelinek. But we believe that Mr. Shimerda's soul will come to its Creator as well off without a priest. We believe that Christ is our only intercessor."

The young man shook his head. "I know how you think. My teacher at the school has explain. But I have seen too much. I believe in prayer for the dead. I have seen too much."

We asked him what he meant.

He glanced around the table. "You want I shall tell you? When I was a little boy like this one, I begin to help the priest at the altar. I make my first communion very young; what the Church teach seem plain to me. By 'n' by war-times come, when the Austrians fight us. We have very many soldiers in camp near my village, and the cholera[3] break out in that camp, and the men die like flies. All day long our priest go about there to give the Sacrament

3. A highly contagious gastrointestinal disease that causes severe and often fatal dehydration.

to dying men, and I go with him to carry the vessels with the Holy Sacrament. Everybody that go near that camp catch the sickness but me and the priest. But we have no sickness, we have no fear, because we carry that blood and that body of Christ, and it preserve us." He paused, looking at grandfather. "That I know, Mr. Burden, for it happened to myself. All the soldiers know, too. When we walk along the road, the old priest and me, we meet all the time soldiers marching and officers on horse. All those officers, when they see what I carry under the cloth, pull up their horses and kneel down on the ground in the road until we pass. So I feel very bad for my kawntreeman to die without the Sacrament, and to die in a bad way for his soul, and I feel sad for his family."

We had listened attentively. It was impossible not to admire his frank, manly faith.

"I am always glad to meet a young man who thinks seriously about these things," said grandfather, "and I would never be the one to say you were not in God's care when you were among the soldiers."

After dinner it was decided that young Jelinek should hook our two strong black farmhorses to the scraper and break a road through to the Shimerdas', so that a wagon could go when it was necessary. Fuchs, who was the only cabinet-maker in the neighborhood, was set to work on a coffin.

Jelinek put on his long wolfskin coat, and when we admired it, he told us that he had shot and skinned the coyotes, and the young man who "batched" with him, Jan Bouska, who had been a fur-worker in Vienna, made the coat. From the windmill I watched Jelinek come out of the barn with the blacks, and work his way up the hillside toward the cornfield. Sometimes he was completely hidden by the clouds of snow that rose about him; then he and the horses would emerge black and shining.

Our heavy carpenter's bench had to bc brought from the barn and carried down into the kitchen. Fuchs selected boards from a pile of planks grandfather had hauled out from town in the fall to make a new floor for the oats bin. When at last the lumber and tools were assembled, and the doors were closed again and the cold drafts shut out, grandfather rode away to meet the coroner at the Shimerdas', and Fuchs took off his coat and settled down to work. I sat on his work-table and watched him. He did not touch his tools at first, but figured for a long while on a piece of paper, and measured the planks and made marks on them. While he was thus engaged, he whistled softly to himself, or teasingly pulled at his half-ear. Grandmother moved about quietly, so as not to disturb him. At last he folded his ruler and turned a cheerful face to us.

"The hardest part of my job's done," he announced. "It's the head end of it that comes hard with me, especially when I'm out of practice. The last time I made one of these, Mrs. Burden," he continued, as he sorted and tried his chisels, "was for a fellow in the Black Tiger mine, up above Silverton, Colorado. The mouth of that mine goes right into the face of the cliff, and they used to put us in a bucket and run us over on a trolley and shoot us into the shaft. The bucket traveled across a box cañon three hundred feet deep, and about a third full of water. Two Swedes had fell out of that bucket once, and hit the water, feet down. If you'll believe it, they went to work the next day. You can't kill a Swede. But in my time a little Eyetalian tried the high dive, and it turned out different with him. We was snowed in then, like we are now, and I happened to be the only man in camp that could make a coffin for him. It's a handy thing to know, when you knock about like I've done."

"We'd be hard put to it now, if you didn't know, Otto," grandmother said.

"Yes,'m," Fuchs admitted with modest pride. "So few folks does know how to make a good tight box that'll turn water. I sometimes wonder if there'll be anybody about to do it for me. However, I'm not at all particular that way."

All afternoon, wherever one went in the house, one could hear the panting wheeze of the saw or the pleasant purring of the plane. They were such cheerful noises, seeming to promise new things for living people: it was a pity that those freshly planed pine boards were to be put underground so soon. The lumber was hard to work because it was full of frost, and the boards gave off a sweet smell of pine woods, as the heap of yellow shavings grew higher and higher. I wondered why Fuchs had not stuck to cabinet-work, he settled down to it with such ease and content. He handled the tools as if he liked the feel of them; and when he planed, his hands went back and forth over the boards in an eager, beneficent way as if he were blessing them. He broke out now and then into German hymns, as if this occupation brought back old times to him.

At four o'clock Mr. Bushy, the postmaster, with another neighbor who lived east of us, stopped in to get warm. They were on their way to the Shimerdas'. The news of what had happened over there had somehow got abroad through the snow-blocked country. Grandmother gave the visitors sugar-cakes and hot coffee. Before these callers were gone, the brother of the Widow Steavens, who lived on the Black Hawk road, drew up at our door, and after him came the father of the German family, our nearest neighbors on the south. They dismounted and joined us in the dining-room. They were all eager for any details about the suicide, and they were greatly concerned as to where Mr. Shimerda would be buried. The nearest Catholic cemetery was at Black Hawk, and it might be weeks before a wagon could get so far. Besides, Mr. Bushy and grandmother were sure that a man who had killed himself could not be buried in a Catholic graveyard. There was a burying-ground over by the Norwegian church, west of Squaw Creek; perhaps the Norwegians would take Mr. Shimerda in.

After our visitors rode away in single file over the hill, we returned to the kitchen. Grandmother began to make the icing for a chocolate cake, and Otto again filled the house with the exciting, expectant song of the plane. One pleasant thing about this time was that everybody talked more than usual. I had never heard the postmaster say anything but "Only papers, to-day," or, "I've got a sackful of mail for ye," until this afternoon. Grandmother always talked, dear woman; to herself or to the Lord, if there was no one else to listen; but grandfather was naturally taciturn, and Jake and Otto were often so tired after supper that I used to feel as if I were surrounded by a wall of silence. Now every one seemed eager to talk. That afternoon Fuchs told me story after story; about the Black Tiger mine, and about violent deaths and casual buryings, and the queer fancies of dying men. You never really knew a man, he said, until you saw him die. Most men were game, and went without a grudge.

The postmaster, going home, stopped to say that grandfather would bring the coroner back with him to spend the night. The officers of the Norwegian church, he told us, had held a meeting and decided that the Norwegian graveyard could not extend its hospitality to Mr. Shimerda.

Grandmother was indignant. "If these foreigners are so clannish, Mr. Bushy, we'll have to have an American graveyard that will be more liberal-minded. I'll get right after Josiah to start one in the spring. If anything was to happen to me, I don't want the Norwegians holding inquisitions over me to see whether I'm good enough to be laid amongst 'em."

Soon grandfather returned, bringing with him Anton Jelinek, and that important person, the coroner. He was a mild, flurried old man, a Civil War veteran, with one sleeve hanging empty. He seemed to find this case very perplexing, and said if it had not been for grandfather he would have sworn out a warrant against Krajiek. "The way he acted, and the way his axe fit the wound, was enough to convict any man."

Although it was perfectly clear that Mr. Shimerda had killed himself, Jake and the coroner thought something ought to be done to Krajiek because he behaved like a guilty man. He was badly frightened, certainly, and perhaps he even felt some stirrings of remorse for his indifference to the old man's misery and loneliness.

At supper the men ate like vikings, and the chocolate cake, which I had hoped would linger on until to-morrow in a mutilated condition, disappeared on the second round. They talked excitedly about where they should bury Mr. Shimerda; I gathered that the neighbors were all disturbed and shocked about something. It developed that Mrs. Shimerda and Ambrosch wanted the old man buried on the southwest corner of their own land; indeed, under the very stake that marked the corner. Grandfather had explained to Ambrosch that some day, when the country was put under fence and the roads were confined to section lines, two roads would cross exactly on that corner. But Ambrosch only said, "It makes no matter."

Grandfather asked Jelinek whether in the old country there was some superstition to the effect that a suicide must be buried at the cross-roads.

Jelinek said he didn't know; he seemed to remember hearing there had once been such a custom in Bohemia. "Mrs. Shimerda is made up her mind," he added. "I try to persuade her, and say it looks bad for her to all the neighbors; but she say so it must be. 'There I will bury him, if I dig the grave myself,' she say. I have to promise her I help Ambrosch make the grave to-morrow."

Grandfather smoothed his beard and looked judicial. "I don't know whose wish should decide the matter, if not hers. But if she thinks she will live to see the people of this country ride over that old man's head, she is mistaken."

XVI

Mr. Shimerda lay dead in the barn four days, and on the fifth they buried him. All day Friday Jelinek was off with Ambrosch digging the grave, chopping out the frozen earth with old axes. On Saturday we breakfasted before daylight and got into the wagon with the coffin. Jake and Jelinek went ahead on horseback to cut the body loose from the pool of blood in which it was frozen fast to the ground.

When grandmother and I went into the Shimerdas' house, we found the women-folk alone; Ambrosch and Marek were at the barn. Mrs. Shimerda sat crouching by the stove, Ántonia was washing dishes. When she saw me she ran out of her dark corner and threw her arms around me. "Oh, Jimmy," she sobbed, "what you tink for my lovely papa!" It seemed to me that I could feel her heart breaking as she clung to me.

Mrs. Shimerda, sitting on the stump by the stove, kept looking over her shoulder toward the door while the neighbors were arriving. They came on horseback, all except the post-master, who brought his family in a wagon over the only broken wagon-trail. The Widow Steavens rode up from her farm eight miles down the Black Hawk road. The cold drove the women into the cave-house, and it was soon crowded. A fine, sleety snow was beginning to fall, and every one was afraid of another storm and anxious to have the burial over with.

Grandfather and Jelinek came to tell Mrs. Shimerda that it was time to start. After bundling her mother up in clothes the neighbors had brought, Ántonia put on an old cape from our house and the rabbit-skin hat her father had made for her. Four men carried Mr. Shimerda's box up the hill; Krajiek slunk along behind them. The coffin was too wide for the door, so it was put down on the slope outside. I slipped out from the cave and looked at Mr. Shimerda. He was lying on his side, with his knees drawn up. His body was draped in a black shawl, and his head was bandaged in white muslin, like a mummy's; one of his long, shapely hands lay out on the black cloth; that was all one could see of him.

Mrs. Shimerda came out and placed an open prayer-book against the body, making the sign of the cross on the bandaged head with her fingers. Ambrosch knelt down and made the same gesture, and after him Ántonia and Marek. Yulka hung back. Her mother pushed her forward, and kept saying something to her over and over. Yulka knelt down, shut her eyes, and put out her hand a little way, but she drew it back and began to cry wildly. She was afraid to touch the bandage. Mrs. Shimerda caught her by the shoulders and pushed her toward the coffin, but grandmother interfered.

"No, Mrs. Shimerda," she said firmly, "I won't stand by and see that child frightened into spasms. She is too little to understand what you want of her. Let her alone."

At a look from grandfather, Fuchs and Jelinek placed the lid on the box, and began to nail it down over Mr. Shimerda. I was afraid to look at Ántonia. She put her arms round Yulka and held the little girl close to her.

The coffin was put into the wagon. We drove slowly away, against the fine, icy snow which cut our faces like a sand-blast. When we reached the grave, it looked a very little spot in that snow-covered waste. The men took the coffin to the edge of the hole and lowered it with ropes. We stood about watching them, and the powdery snow lay without melting on the caps and shoulders of the men and the shawls of the women. Jelinek spoke in a persuasive tone to Mrs. Shimerda, and then turned to grandfather.

"She says, Mr. Burden, she is very glad if you can make some prayer for him here in English, for the neighbors to understand."

Grandmother looked anxiously at grandfather. He took off his hat, and the other men did likewise. I thought his prayer remarkable. I still remember it. He began, "Oh, great and just God, no man among us knows what the sleeper knows, nor is it for us to judge what lies between him and Thee." He prayed that if any man there had been remiss toward the stranger come to a far country, God would forgive him and soften his heart. He recalled the promises to the widow and the fatherless, and asked God to smooth the way before this widow and her children, and to "incline the hearts of men to deal justly with her." In closing, he said we were leaving Mr. Shimerda at "Thy judgment seat, which is also Thy mercy seat."

All the time he was praying, grandmother watched him through the black fingers of her glove, and when he said "Amen," I thought she looked satisfied with him. She turned to Otto and whispered, "Can't you start a hymn, Fuchs? It would seem less heathenish."

Fuchs glanced about to see if there was general approval of her suggestion, then began, "Jesus, Lover of my Soul," and all the men and women took it up after him. Whenever I have heard the hymn since, it has made me remember that white waste and the little group of people; and the bluish air, full of fine, eddying snow, like long veils flying:—

"While the nearer waters roll,
While the tempest still is high."

• • • • •

Years afterward, when the open-grazing days were over, and the red grass had been ploughed under and under until it had almost disappeared from the prairie; when all the fields were under fence, and the roads no longer ran about like wild things, but followed the surveyed section-lines, Mr. Shimerda's grave was still there, with a sagging wire fence around it, and an unpainted wooden cross. As grandfather had predicted, Mrs. Shimerda never saw the roads going over his head. The road from the north curved a little to the east just there, and the road from the west swung out a little to the south; so that the grave, with its tall red grass that was never mowed, was like a little island; and at twilight, under a new moon or the clear evening star, the dusty roads used to look like soft gray rivers flowing past it. I never came upon the place without emotion, and in all that country it was the spot most dear to me. I loved the dim superstition, the propitiatory intent, that had put the grave there; and still more I loved the spirit that could not carry out the sentence—the error from the surveyed lines, the clemency of the soft earth roads along which the home-coming wagons rattled after sunset. Never a tired driver passed the wooden cross, I am sure, without wishing well to the sleeper.

XVII

When spring came, after that hard winter, one could not get enough of the nimble air. Every morning I wakened with a fresh consciousness that winter was over. There were none of the signs of spring for which I used to watch in Virginia, no budding woods or blooming gardens. There was only—spring itself; the throb of it, the light restlessness, the vital essence of it everywhere; in the sky, in the swift clouds, in the pale sunshine, and in the warm, high wind—rising suddenly, sinking suddenly, impulsive and playful like a big puppy that pawed you and then lay down to be petted. If I had been tossed down blindfold on that red prairie, I should have known that it was spring.

Everywhere now there was the smell of burning grass. Our neighbors burned off their pasture before the new grass made a start, so that the fresh growth would not be mixed with the dead stand of last year. Those light, swift fires, running about the country, seemed a part of the same kindling that was in the air.

The Shimerdas were in their new log house by then. The neighbors had helped them to build it in March. It stood directly in front of their old cave, which they used as a cellar. The family were now fairly equipped to begin their struggle with the soil. They had four comfortable rooms to live in, a new windmill,—bought on credit,—a chicken-house and poultry. Mrs. Shimerda had paid grandfather ten dollars for a milk cow, and was to give him fifteen more as soon as they harvested their first crop.

When I rode up to the Shimerdas' one bright windy afternoon in April, Yulka ran out to meet me. It was to her, now, that I gave reading lessons; Ántonia was busy with other things. I tied my pony and went into the kitchen where Mrs. Shimerda was baking bread, chewing poppy seeds as she worked. By this time she could speak enough English to ask me a great many questions about what our men were doing in the fields. She seemed to think that my elders withheld helpful information, and that from me she might get valuable secrets. On this occasion she asked me very craftily when grandfather expected to begin planting corn. I told her, adding that he thought we should have a dry spring and that the corn would not be held back by too much rain, as it had been last year.

She gave me a shrewd glance. "He not Jesus," she blustered; "he not know about the wet and the dry."

I did not answer her; what was the use? As I sat waiting for the hour when Ambrosch and Ántonia would return from the fields, I watched Mrs. Shimerda at her work. She took from the oven a coffee-cake which she wanted to keep warm for supper, and wrapped it in a quilt stuffed with feathers. I have seen her put even a roast goose in this quilt to keep it hot. When the neighbors were there building the new house they saw her do this, and the story got abroad that the Shimerdas kept their food in their feather beds.

When the sun was dropping low, Ántonia came up the big south draw with her team. How much older she had grown in eight months! She had come to us a child, and now she was a tall, strong young girl, although her fifteenth birthday had just slipped by. I ran out and met her as she brought her horses up to the windmill to water them. She wore the boots her father had so thoughtfully taken off before he shot himself, and his old fur cap. Her outgrown cotton dress switched about her calves, over the boot-tops. She kept her sleeves rolled up all day, and her arms and throat were burned as brown as a sailor's. Her neck came up strongly out of her shoulders, like the bole of a tree out of the turf. One sees that draft-horse neck among the peasant women in all old countries.

She greeted me gayly, and began at once to tell me how much ploughing she had done that day. Ambrosch, she said, was on the north quarter, breaking sod with the oxen.

"Jim, you ask Jake how much he ploughed to-day. I don't want that Jake get more done in one day than me. I want we have very much corn this fall."

While the horses drew in the water, and nosed each other, and then drank again, Ántonia sat down on the windmill step and rested her head on her hand. "You see the big prairie fire from your place last night? I hope your grandpa ain't lose no stacks?"

"No, we didn't. I came to ask you something, Tony. Grandmother wants to know if you can't go to the term of school that begins next week over at the sod schoolhouse. She says there's a good teacher, and you'd learn a lot."

Ántonia stood up, lifting and dropping her shoulders as if they were stiff. "I ain't got time to learn. I can work like mans now. My mother can't say no more how Ambrosch do all and nobody to help him. I can work as much as him. School is all right for little boys. I help make this land one good farm."

She clucked to her team and started for the barn. I walked beside her, feeling vexed. Was she going to grow up boastful like her mother, I wondered? Before we reached the stable, I felt something tense in her silence, and glancing up I saw that she was crying. She turned her face from me and looked off at the red streak of dying light, over the dark prairie.

I climbed up into the loft and threw down the hay for her, while she unharnessed her team. We walked slowly back toward the house. Ambrosch had come in from the north quarter, and was watering his oxen at the tank.

Ántonia took my hand. "Sometime you will tell me all those nice things you learn at the school, won't you, Jimmy?" she asked with a sudden rush of feeling in her voice. "My father, he went much to school. He know a great deal; how to make the fine cloth like what you not got here. He play horn and violin, and he read so many books that the priests in Bohemie come to talk to him. You won't forget my father, Jim?"

"No," I said, "I will never forget him."

Mrs. Shimerda asked me to stay for supper. After Ambrosch and Ántonia had washed the field dust from their hands and faces at the wash-basin by the kitchen door, we sat down at the oilcloth-covered table. Mrs. Shimerda ladled meal mush out of an iron pot and poured milk on it. After the mush we had fresh bread and sorghum molasses, and coffee with the cake that had been kept warm in the feathers. Ántonia and Ambrosch were talking in Bohemian; disputing about which of them had done more ploughing that day. Mrs. Shimerda egged them on, chuckling while she gobbled her food.

Presently Ambrosch said sullenly in English: "You take them ox to-morrow and try the sod plough. Then you not be so smart."

His sister laughed. "Don't be mad. I know it's awful hard work for break sod. I milk the cow for you to-morrow, if you want."

Mrs. Shimerda turned quickly to me. "That cow not give so much milk like what your grandpa say. If he make talk about fifteen dollars, I send him back the cow."

"He doesn't talk about the fifteen dollars," I exclaimed indignantly. "He doesn't find fault with people."

"He say I break his saw when we build, and I never," grumbled Ambrosch.

I knew he had broken the saw, and then hid it and lied about it. I began to wish I had not stayed for supper. Everything was disagreeable to me. Ántonia ate so noisily now, like a man, and she yawned often at the table and kept stretching her arms over her head, as if they ached. Grandmother had said, "Heavy field work'll spoil that girl. She'll lose all her nice ways and get rough ones." She had lost them already.

After supper I rode home through the sad, soft spring twilight. Since winter I had seen very little of Ántonia. She was out in the fields from sun-up until sun-down. If I rode over to see her where she was ploughing, she stopped at the end of a row to chat for a moment, then gripped her plough-handles, clucked to her team, and waded on down the furrow, making me feel that she was now grown up and had no time for me. On Sundays she helped her mother make garden or sewed all day. Grandfather was pleased with Ántonia. When we complained of her, he only smiled and said, "She will help some fellow get ahead in the world."

Nowadays Tony could talk of nothing but the prices of things, or how much she could lift and endure. She was too proud of her strength. I knew, too, that Ambrosch put upon her some chores a girl ought not to do, and that the farmhands around the country joked in a nasty way about it. Whenever I saw her come up the furrow, shouting to her beasts, sun-burned, sweaty, her dress open at the neck, and her throat and chest dust-plastered, I used to think of the tone in which poor Mr. Shimerda, who could say so little, yet managed to say so much when he exclaimed, "My Án-tonia!"

XVIII

After I began to go to the country school, I saw less of the Bohemians. We were sixteen pupils at the sod schoolhouse, and we all came on horseback and brought our dinner. My schoolmates were none of them very interesting, but I somehow felt that by making comrades of them I was getting even with Ántonia for her indifference. Since the father's death, Ambrosch was more than ever the head of the house and he seemed to direct the feelings as well as the fortunes of his women-folk. Ántonia often quoted his opinions to me, and she let me see that she admired him, while she thought of me only as a little boy. Before the spring was over, there was a distinct coldness between us and the Shimerdas. It came about in this way.

One Sunday I rode over there with Jake to get a horse-collar which Ambrosch had borrowed from him and had not returned. It was a beautiful blue morning. The buffalo-peas were blooming in pink and purple masses along the roadside, and the larks, perched on last year's dried sunflower stalks, were singing straight at the sun, their heads thrown back and their yellow breasts a-quiver. The wind blew about us in warm, sweet gusts. We rode slowly, with a pleasant sense of Sunday indolence.

We found the Shimerdas working just as if it were a week-day. Marek was cleaning out the stable, and Ántonia and her mother were making garden, off across the pond in the draw-head. Ambrosch was up on the wind-mill tower, oiling the wheel. He came down, not very cordially. When Jake asked for the collar, he grunted and scratched his head. The collar belonged to grandfather, of course, and Jake, feeling responsible for it, flared up.

"Now, don't you say you haven't got it, Ambrosch, because I know you have, and if you ain't a-going to look for it, I will."

Ambrosch shrugged his shoulders and sauntered down the hill toward the stable. I could see that it was one of his mean days. Presently he returned, carrying a collar that had been badly used—trampled in the dirt and gnawed by rats until the hair was sticking out of it.

"This what you want?" he asked surlily.

Jake jumped off his horse. I saw a wave of red come up under the rough stubble on his face. "That ain't the piece of harness I loaned you, Ambrosch;

or if it is, you've used it shameful. I ain't a-going to carry such a looking thing back to Mr. Burden."

Ambrosch dropped the collar on the ground. "All right," he said coolly, took up his oil-can, and began to climb the mill. Jake caught him by the belt of his trousers and yanked him back. Ambrosch's feet had scarcely touched the ground when he lunged out with a vicious kick at Jake's stomach. Fortunately Jake was in such a position that he could dodge it. This was not the sort of thing country boys did when they played at fisticuffs, and Jake was furious. He landed Ambrosch a blow on the head—it sounded like the crack of an axe on a cow-pumpkin. Ambrosch dropped over, stunned.

We heard squeals, and looking up saw Ántonia and her mother coming on the run. They did not take the path around the pond, but plunged through the muddy water, without even lifting their skirts. They came on, screaming and clawing the air. By this time Ambrosch had come to his senses and was sputtering with nose-bleed. Jake sprang into his saddle. "Let's get out of this, Jim," he called.

Mrs. Shimerda threw her hands over her head and clutched as if she were going to pull down lightning. "Law, law!" she shrieked after us. "Law for knock my Ambrosch down!"

"I never like you no more, Jake and Jim Burden," Ántonia panted. "No friends any more!"

Jake stopped and turned his horse for a second. "Well, you're a damned ungrateful lot, the whole pack of you," he shouted back. "I guess the Burdens can get along without you. You've been a sight of trouble to them, anyhow!"

We rode away, feeling so outraged that the fine morning was spoiled for us. I hadn't a word to say, and poor Jake was white as paper and trembling all over. It made him sick to get so angry. "They ain't the same, Jimmy," he kept saying in a hurt tone. "These foreigners ain't the same. You can't trust 'em to be fair. It's dirty to kick a feller. You heard how the women turned on you—and after all we went through on account of 'em last winter! They ain't to be trusted. I don't want to see you get too thick with any of 'em."

"I'll never be friends with them again, Jake," I declared hotly. "I believe they are all like Krajiek and Ambrosch underneath."

Grandfather heard our story with a twinkle in his eye. He advised Jake to ride to town to-morrow, go to a justice of the peace, tell him he had knocked young Shimerda down, and pay his fine. Then if Mrs. Shimerda was inclined to make trouble—her son was still under age—she would be forestalled. Jake said he might as well take the wagon and haul to market the pig he had been fattening. On Monday, about an hour after Jake had started, we saw Mrs. Shimerda and her Ambrosch proudly driving by, looking neither to the right nor left. As they rattled out of sight down the Black Hawk road, grandfather chuckled, saying he had rather expected she would follow the matter up.

Jake paid his fine with a ten-dollar bill grandfather had given him for that purpose. But when the Shimerdas found that Jake sold his pig in town that day, Ambrosch worked it out in his shrewd head that Jake had to sell his pig to pay his fine. This theory afforded the Shimerdas great satisfaction, apparently. For weeks afterward, whenever Jake and I met Ántonia on her way to the post-office, or going along the road with her work-team, she would clap her hands and call to us in a spiteful, crowing voice:—

"Jake-y, Jake-y, sell the pig and pay the slap!"

Otto pretended not to be surprised at Ántonia's behavior. He only lifted his brows and said, "You can't tell me anything new about a Czech; I'm an Austrian."

Grandfather was never a party to what Jake called our feud with the Shimerdas. Ambrosch and Ántonia always greeted him respectfully, and he asked them about their affairs and gave them advice as usual. He thought the future looked hopeful for them. Ambrosch was a far-seeing fellow; he soon realized that his oxen were too heavy for any work except breaking sod, and he succeeded in selling them to a newly arrived German. With the money he bought another team of horses, which grandfather selected for him. Marek was strong, and Ambrosch worked him hard; but he could never teach him to cultivate corn, I remember. The one idea that had ever got through poor Marek's thick head was that all exertion was meritorious. He always bore down on the handles of the cultivator and drove the blades so deep into the earth that the horses were soon exhausted.

In June Ambrosch went to work at Mr. Bushy's for a week, and took Marek with him at full wages. Mrs. Shimerda then drove the second cultivator; she and Ántonia worked in the fields all day and did the chores at night. While the two women were running the place alone, one of the new horses got colic and gave them a terrible fright.

Ántonia had gone down to the barn one night to see that all was well before she went to bed, and she noticed that one of the roans was swollen about the middle and stood with its head hanging. She mounted another horse, without waiting to saddle him, and hammered on our door just as we were going to bed. Grandfather answered her knock. He did not send one of his men, but rode back with her himself, taking a syringe and an old piece of carpet he kept for hot applications when our horses were sick. He found Mrs. Shimerda sitting by the horse with her lantern, groaning and wringing her hands. It took but a few moments to release the gases pent up in the poor beast, and the two women heard the rush of wind and saw the roan visibly diminish in girth.

"If I lose that horse, Mr. Burden," Ántonia exclaimed, "I never stay here till Ambrosch come home! I go drown myself in the pond before morning."

When Ambrosch came back from Mr. Bushy's, we learned that he had given Marek's wages to the priest at Black Hawk, for masses for their father's soul. Grandmother thought Ántonia needed shoes more than Mr. Shimerda needed prayers, but grandfather said tolerantly, "If he can spare six dollars, pinched as he is, it shows he believes what he professes."

It was grandfather who brought about a reconciliation with the Shimerdas. One morning he told us that the small grain was coming on so well, he thought he would begin to cut his wheat on the first of July. He would need more men, and if it were agreeable to every one he would engage Ambrosch for the reaping and thrashing, as the Shimerdas had no small grain of their own.

"I think, Emmaline," he concluded, "I will ask Ántonia to come over and help you in the kitchen. She will be glad to earn something, and it will be a good time to end misunderstandings. I may as well ride over this morning and make arrangements. Do you want to go with me, Jim?" His tone told me that he had already decided for me.

After breakfast we set off together. When Mrs. Shimerda saw us coming, she ran from her door down into the draw behind the stable, as if she did not want to meet us. Grandfather smiled to himself while he tied his horse, and we followed her.

Behind the barn we came upon a funny sight. The cow had evidently been grazing somewhere in the draw. Mrs. Shimerda had run to the animal, pulled up the lariat pin, and, when we came upon her, she was trying to hide the cow in an old cave in the bank. As the hole was narrow and dark, the cow held back, and the old woman was slapping and pushing at her hind quarters, trying to spank her into the draw-side.

Grandfather ignored her singular occupation and greeted her politely. "Good-morning, Mrs. Shimerda. Can you tell me where I will find Ambrosch? Which field?"

"He with the sod corn." She pointed toward the north, still standing in front of the cow as if she hoped to conceal it.

"His sod corn will be good for fodder this winter," said grandfather encouragingly. "And where is Ántonia?"

"She go with." Mrs. Shimerda kept wiggling her bare feet about nervously in the dust.

"Very well. I will ride up there. I want them to come over and help me cut my oats and wheat next month. I will pay them wages. Good-morning. By the way, Mrs. Shimerda," he said as he turned up the path, "I think we may as well call it square about the cow."

She started and clutched the rope tighter. Seeing that she did not understand, grandfather turned back. "You need not pay me anything more; no more money. The cow is yours."

"Pay no more, keep cow?" she asked in a bewildered tone, her narrow eyes snapping at us in the sunlight.

"Exactly. Pay no more, keep cow." He nodded.

Mrs. Shimerda dropped the rope, ran after us, and crouching down beside grandfather, she took his hand and kissed it. I doubt if he had ever been so much embarrassed before. I was a little startled, too. Somehow, that seemed to bring the Old World very close.

We rode away laughing, and grandfather said: "I expect she thought we had come to take the cow away for certain, Jim. I wonder if she wouldn't have scratched a little if we'd laid hold of that lariat rope!"

Our neighbors seemed glad to make peace with us. The next Sunday Mrs. Shimerda came over and brought Jake a pair of socks she had knitted. She presented them with an air of great magnanimity, saying, "Now you not come any more for knock my Ambrosch down?"

Jake laughed sheepishly. "I don't want to have no trouble with Ambrosch. If he'll let me alone, I'll let him alone."

"If he slap you, we ain't got no pig for pay the fine," she said insinuatingly.

Jake was not at all disconcerted. "Have the last word, mam," he said cheerfully. "It's a lady's privilege."

XIX

July came on with that breathless, brilliant heat which makes the plains of Kansas and Nebraska the best corn country in the world. It seemed as if we could hear the corn growing in the night; under the stars one caught a faint crackling in the dewy, heavy-odored cornfields where the feathered stalks stood so juicy and green. If all the great plain from the Missouri to the Rocky Mountains had been under glass, and the heat regulated by a thermometer, it could not have been better for the yellow tassels that were ripening and fertilizing the silk day by day. The cornfields were far apart in those times, with miles of wild grazing land between. It took a clear, meditative eye like my grandfather's to foresee that they would enlarge and multiply until they would be, not the Shimerdas' cornfields, or Mr. Bushy's, but the world's cornfields; that their yield would be one of the great economic facts, like the wheat crop of Russia, which underlie all the activities of men, in peace or war.

The burning sun of those few weeks, with occasional rains at night, secured the corn. After the milky ears were once formed, we had little to fear from dry weather. The men were working so hard in the wheatfields that they did not notice the heat,—though I was kept busy carrying water for them,—and grandmother and Ántonia had so much to do in the kitchen that they could not have told whether one day was hotter than another. Each morning, while the dew was still on the grass, Ántonia went with me up to the garden to get early vegetables for dinner. Grandmother made her wear a sunbonnet, but as soon as we reached the garden she threw it on the grass and let her hair fly in the breeze. I remember how, as we bent over the pea-vines, beads of perspiration used to gather on her upper lip like a little mustache.

"Oh, better I like to work out of doors than in a house!" she used to sing joyfully. "I not care that your grandmother say it makes me like a man. I like to be like a man." She would toss her head and ask me to feel the muscles swell in her brown arm.

We were glad to have her in the house. She was so gay and responsive that one did not mind her heavy, running step, or her clattery way with pans. Grandmother was in high spirits during the weeks that Ántonia worked for us.

All the nights were close[4] and hot during that harvest season. The harvesters slept in the hayloft because it was cooler there than in the house. I used to lie in my bed by the open window, watching the heat lightning play softly along the horizon, or looking up at the gaunt frame of the windmill against the blue night sky. One night there was a beautiful electric storm, though not enough rain fell to damage the cut grain. The men went down to the barn immediately after supper, and when the dishes were washed Ántonia and I climbed up on the slanting roof of the chicken-house to watch the clouds. The thunder was loud and metallic, like the rattle of sheet iron, and the lightning broke in great zigzags across the heavens, making everything stand out and come close to us for a moment. Half the sky was checkered with black thunderheads, but all the west was luminous and clear: in the lightning-flashes it looked like deep blue water, with the sheen of moonlight on it; and the mottled part of the sky was like marble pavement, like the quay of some splendid sea-coast city, doomed to destruction. Great warm splashes of rain fell on our upturned faces. One black cloud, no bigger than a little boat, drifted out into the clear space unattended, and kept moving westward. All about us we could hear the felty beat of the raindrops on the soft dust of the farmyard. Grandmother came to the door and said it was late, and we would get wet out there.

4. Humid.

"In a minute we come," Ántonia called back to her. "I like your grandmother, and all things here," she sighed. "I wish my papa live to see this summer. I wish no winter ever come again."

"It will be summer a long while yet," I reassured her. "Why aren't you always nice like this, Tony?"

"How nice?"

"Why, just like this; like yourself. Why do you all the time try to be like Ambrosch?"

She put her arms under her head and lay back, looking up at the sky. "If I live here, like you, that is different. Things will be easy for you. But they will be hard for us."

Book II. The Hired Girls

I

I had been living with my grandfather for nearly three years when he decided to move to Black Hawk. He and grandmother were getting old for the heavy work of a farm, and as I was now thirteen they thought I ought to be going to school. Accordingly our homestead was rented to "that good woman, the Widow Steavens," and her bachelor brother, and we bought Preacher White's house, at the north end of Black Hawk. This was the first town house one passed driving in from the farm, a landmark which told country people their long ride was over.

We were to move to Black Hawk in March, and as soon as grandfather had fixed the date he let Jake and Otto know of his intention. Otto said he would not be likely to find another place that suited him so well; that he was tired of farming and thought he would go back to what he called the "wild West." Jake Marpole, lured by Otto's stories of adventure, decided to go with him. We did our best to dissuade Jake. He was so handicapped by illiteracy and by his trusting disposition that he would be an easy prey to sharpers.[5] Grandmother begged him to stay among kindly, Christian people, where he was known; but there was no reasoning with him. He wanted to be a prospector. He thought a silver mine was waiting for him in Colorado.

Jake and Otto served us to the last. They moved us into town, put down the carpets in our new house, made shelves and cupboards for grandmother's kitchen, and seemed loath to leave us. But at last they went, without warning. Those two fellows had been faithful to us through sun and storm, had given us things that cannot be bought in any market in the world. With me they had been like older brothers; had restrained their speech and manners out of care for me, and given me so much good comradeship. Now they got on the west-bound train one morning, in their Sunday clothes, with their oilcloth valises—and I never saw them again. Months afterward we got a card from Otto, saying that Jake had been down with mountain fever but now they were both working in the Yankee Girl mine, and were doing well. I wrote to them at that address, but my letter was returned to me, "unclaimed." After that we never heard from them.

5. Swindlers.

Black Hawk, the new world in which we had come to live, was a clean, well-planted little prairie town, with white fences and good green yards about the dwellings, wide, dusty streets, and shapely little trees growing along the wooden sidewalks. In the center of the town there were two rows of new brick "store" buildings, a brick schoolhouse, the court-house, and four white churches. Our own house looked down over the town, and from our upstairs windows we could see the winding line of the river bluffs, two miles south of us. That river was to be my compensation for the lost freedom of the farming country.

We came to Black Hawk in March, and by the end of April we felt like town people. Grandfather was a deacon in the new Baptist Church, grandmother was busy with church suppers and missionary societies, and I was quite another boy, or thought I was. Suddenly put down among boys of my own age, I found I had a great deal to learn. Before the spring term of school was over I could fight, play "keeps," tease the little girls, and use forbidden words as well as any boy in my class. I was restrained from utter savagery only by the fact that Mrs. Harling, our nearest neighbor, kept an eye on me, and if my behavior went beyond certain bounds I was not permitted to come into her yard or to play with her jolly children.

We saw more of our country neighbors now than when we lived on the farm. Our house was a convenient stopping-place for them. We had a big barn where the farmers could put up their teams, and their women-folk more often accompanied them, now that they could stay with us for dinner, and rest and set their bonnets right before they went shopping. The more our house was like a country hotel, the better I liked it. I was glad, when I came home from school at noon, to see a farm wagon standing in the back yard, and I was always ready to run downtown to get beefsteak or baker's bread for unexpected company. All through that first spring and summer I kept hoping that Ambrosch would bring Ántonia and Yulka to see our new house. I wanted to show them our red plush furniture, and the trumpet-blowing cherubs the German paper-hanger[6] had put on our parlor ceiling.

When Ambrosch came to town, however, he came alone, and though he put his horses in our barn, he would never stay for dinner, or tell us anything about his mother and sisters. If we ran out and questioned him as he was slipping through the yard, he would merely work his shoulders about in his coat and say, "They all right, I guess."

Mrs. Steavens, who now lived on our farm, grew as fond of Ántonia as we had been, and always brought us news of her. All through the wheat season, she told us, Ambrosch hired his sister out like a man, and she went from farm to farm, binding sheaves or working with the thrashers. The farmers liked her and were kind to her; said they would rather have her for a hand than Ambrosch. When fall came she was to husk corn for the neighbors until Christmas, as she had done the year before; but grandmother saved her from this by getting her a place to work with our neighbors, the Harlings.

II

Grandmother often said that if she had to live in town, she thanked God she lived next the Harlings. They had been farming people, like ourselves,

6. Specialist in decorating with wallpaper.

and their place was like a little farm, with a big barn and a garden, and an orchard and grazing lots,—even a windmill. The Harlings were Norwegians, and Mrs. Harling had lived in Christiania[7] until she was ten years old. Her husband was born in Minnesota. He was a grain merchant and cattle buyer, and was generally considered the most enterprising business man in our county.[8] He controlled a line of grain elevators in the little towns along the railroad to the west of us, and was away from home a great deal. In his absence his wife was the head of the household.

Mrs. Harling was short and square and sturdy-looking, like her house. Every inch of her was charged with an energy that made itself felt the moment she entered a room. Her face was rosy and solid, with bright, twinkling eyes and a stubborn little chin. She was quick to anger, quick to laughter, and jolly from the depths of her soul. How well I remember her laugh; it had in it the same sudden recognition that flashed into her eyes, was a burst of humor, short and intelligent. Her rapid footsteps shook her own floors, and she routed lassitude and indifference wherever she came. She could not be negative or perfunctory about anything. Her enthusiasm, and her violent likes and dislikes, asserted themselves in all the every-day occupations of life. Wash-day was interesting, never dreary, at the Harlings'. Preserving-time was a prolonged festival, and house-cleaning was like a revolution. When Mrs. Harling made garden that spring, we could feel the stir of her undertaking through the willow hedge that separated our place from hers.

Three of the Harling children were near me in age. Charley, the only son,—they had lost an older boy,—was sixteen; Julia, who was known as the musical one, was fourteen when I was; and Sally, the tomboy with short hair, was a year younger. She was nearly as strong as I, and uncannily clever at all boys' sports. Sally was a wild thing, with sun-burned yellow hair, bobbed about her ears, and a brown skin, for she never wore a hat. She raced all over town on one roller skate, often cheated at "keeps," but was such a quick shot one couldn't catch her at it.

The grown-up daughter, Frances, was a very important person in our world. She was her father's chief clerk, and virtually managed his Black Hawk office during his frequent absences. Because of her unusual business ability, he was stern and exacting with her. He paid her a good salary, but she had few holidays and never got away from her responsibilities. Even on Sundays she went to the office to open the mail and read the markets. With Charley, who was not interested in business, but was already preparing for Annapolis,[9] Mr. Harling was very indulgent; bought him guns and tools and electric batteries, and never asked what he did with them.

Frances was dark, like her father, and quite as tall. In winter she wore a sealskin coat and cap, and she and Mr. Harling used to walk home together in the evening, talking about grain-cars and cattle, like two men. Sometimes she came over to see grandfather after supper, and her visits flattered him. More than once they put their wits together to rescue some unfortunate farmer from the clutches of Wick Cutter, the Black Hawk money-lender.

7. Now Oslo, capital of Norway.
8. Successful plains agriculture required middlemen to store and market the grain and livestock that large farms were producing.
9. I.e., U.S. Naval Academy, in Annapolis, Maryland.

Grandfather said Frances Harling was as good a judge of credits as any banker in the country. The two or three men who had tried to take advantage of her in a deal acquired celebrity by their defeat. She knew every farmer for miles about; how much land he had under cultivation, how many cattle he was feeding, what his liabilities were. Her interest in these people was more than a business interest. She carried them all in her mind as if they were characters in a book or a play.

When Frances drove out into the country on business, she would go miles out of her way to call on some of the old people, or to see the women who seldom got to town. She was quick at understanding the grandmothers who spoke no English, and the most reticent and distrustful of them would tell her their story without realizing they were doing so. She went to country funerals and weddings in all weathers. A farmer's daughter who was to be married could count on a wedding present from Frances Harling.

In August the Harlings' Danish cook had to leave them. Grandmother entreated them to try Ántonia. She cornered Ambrosch the next time he came to town, and pointed out to him that any connection with Christian Harling would strengthen his credit and be of advantage to him. One Sunday Mrs. Harling took the long ride out to the Shimerdas' with Frances. She said she wanted to see "what the girl came from" and to have a clear understanding with her mother. I was in our yard when they came driving home, just before sunset. They laughed and waved to me as they passed, and I could see they were in great good humor. After supper, when grandfather set off to church, grandmother and I took my short cut through the willow hedge and went over to hear about the visit to the Shimerdas.

We found Mrs. Harling with Charley and Sally on the front porch, resting after her hard drive. Julia was in the hammock—she was fond of repose—and Frances was at the piano, playing without a light and talking to her mother through the open window.

Mrs. Harling laughed when she saw us coming. "I expect you left your dishes on the table to-night, Mrs. Burden," she called. Frances shut the piano and came out to join us.

They had liked Ántonia from their first glimpse of her; felt they knew exactly what kind of girl she was. As for Mrs. Shimerda, they found her very amusing. Mrs. Harling chuckled whenever she spoke of her. "I expect I am more at home with that sort of bird than you are, Mrs. Burden. They're a pair, Ambrosch and that old woman!"

They had had a long argument with Ambrosch about Ántonia's allowance for clothes and pocket-money. It was his plan that every cent of his sister's wages should be paid over to him each month, and he would provide her with such clothing as he thought necessary. When Mrs. Harling told him firmly that she would keep fifty dollars a year for Ántonia's own use, he declared they wanted to take his sister to town and dress her up and make a fool of her. Mrs. Harling gave us a lively account of Ambrosch's behavior throughout the interview; how he kept jumping up and putting on his cap as if he were through with the whole business, and how his mother tweaked his coat-tail and prompted him in Bohemian. Mrs. Harling finally agreed to pay three dollars a week for Ántonia's services—good wages in those days—and to keep her in shoes. There had been hot dispute about the shoes, Mrs. Shimerda finally saying persuasively that she would send Mrs. Harling three fat geese every year to "make even." Ambrosch was to bring his sister to town next Saturday.

"She'll be awkward and rough at first, like enough," grandmother said anxiously, "but unless she's been spoiled by the hard life she's led, she has it in her to be a real helpful girl."

Mrs. Harling laughed her quick, decided laugh. "Oh, I'm not worrying, Mrs. Burden! I can bring something out of that girl. She's barely seventeen, not too old to learn new ways. She's good-looking, too!" she added warmly.

Frances turned to grandmother. "Oh, yes, Mrs. Burden, you didn't tell us that! She was working in the garden when we got there, barefoot and ragged. But she has such fine brown legs and arms, and splendid color in her cheeks—like those big dark red plums."

We were pleased at this praise. Grandmother spoke feelingly. "When she first came to this country, Frances, and had that genteel old man to watch over her, she was as pretty a girl as ever I saw. But, dear me, what a life she's led, out in the fields with those rough thrashers! Things would have been very different with poor Ántonia if her father had lived."

The Harlings begged us to tell them about Mr. Shimerda's death and the big snowstorm. By the time we saw grandfather coming home from church we had told them pretty much all we knew of the Shimerdas.

"The girl will be happy here, and she'll forget those things," said Mrs. Harling confidently, as we rose to take our leave.

III

On Saturday Ambrosch drove up to the back gate, and Ántonia jumped down from the wagon and ran into our kitchen just as she used to do. She was wearing shoes and stockings, and was breathless and excited. She gave me a playful shake by the shoulders. "You ain't forget about me, Jim?"

Grandmother kissed her. "God bless you, child! Now you've come, you must try to do right and be a credit to us."

Ántonia looked eagerly about the house and admired everything. "Maybe I be the kind of girl you like better, now I come to town," she suggested hopefully.

How good it was to have Ántonia near us again; to see her every day and almost every night! Her greatest fault, Mrs. Harling found, was that she so often stopped her work and fell to playing with the children. She would race about the orchard with us, or take sides in our hay-fights in the barn, or be the old bear that came down from the mountain and carried off Nina. Tony learned English so quickly that by the time school began she could speak as well as any of us.

I was jealous of Tony's admiration for Charley Harling. Because he was always first in his classes at school, and could mend the water-pipes or the door-bell and take the clock to pieces, she seemed to think him a sort of prince. Nothing that Charley wanted was too much trouble for her. She loved to put up lunches for him when he went hunting, to mend his ball-gloves and sew buttons on his shooting-coat, baked the kind of nut-cake he liked, and fed his setter dog when he was away on trips with his father. Ántonia had made herself cloth working-slippers out of Mr. Harling's old coats, and in these she went padding about after Charley, fairly panting with eagerness to please him.

Next to Charley, I think she loved Nina best. Nina was only six, and she was rather more complex than the other children. She was fanciful, had all sorts of unspoken preferences, and was easily offended. At the slightest disappointment or displeasure her velvety brown eyes filled with tears, and she would lift her chin and walk silently away. If we ran after her and tried to appease her, it did no good. She walked on unmollified. I used to think that no eyes in the world could grow so large or hold so many tears as Nina's. Mrs. Harling and Ántonia invariably took her part. We were never given a chance to explain. The charge was simply: "You have made Nina cry. Now, Jimmy can go home, and Sally must get her arithmetic." I liked Nina, too; she was so quaint and unexpected, and her eyes were lovely; but I often wanted to shake her.

We had jolly evenings at the Harlings when the father was away. If he was at home, the children had to go to bed early, or they came over to my house to play. Mr. Harling not only demanded a quiet house, he demanded all his wife's attention. He used to take her away to their room in the west ell, and talk over his business with her all evening. Though we did not realize it then, Mrs. Harling was our audience when we played, and we always looked to her for suggestions. Nothing flattered one like her quick laugh.

Mr. Harling had a desk in his bedroom, and his own easy-chair by the window, in which no one else ever sat. On the nights when he was at home, I could see his shadow on the blind, and it seemed to me an arrogant shadow. Mrs. Harling paid no heed to any one else if he was there. Before he went to bed she always got him a lunch of smoked salmon or anchovies and beer. He kept an alcohol lamp in his room, and a French coffee-pot, and his wife made coffee for him at any hour of the night he happened to want it.

Most Black Hawk fathers had no personal habits outside their domestic ones; they paid the bills, pushed the baby carriage after office hours, moved the sprinkler about over the lawn, and took the family driving on Sunday. Mr. Harling, therefore, seemed to me autocratic and imperial in his ways. He walked, talked, put on his gloves, shook hands, like a man who felt that he had power. He was not tall, but he carried his head so haughtily that he looked a commanding figure, and there was something daring and challenging in his eyes. I used to imagine that the "nobles" of whom Antonia was always talking probably looked very much like Christian Harling, wore caped overcoats like his, and just such a glittering diamond upon the little finger.

Except when the father was at home, the Harling house was never quiet. Mrs. Harling and Nina and Ántonia made as much noise as a houseful of children, and there was usually somebody at the piano. Julia was the only one who was held down to regular hours of practicing, but they all played. When Frances came home at noon, she played until dinner was ready. When Sally got back from school, she sat down in her hat and coat and drummed the plantation melodies that negro minstrel troupes brought to town. Even Nina played the Swedish Wedding March.

Mrs. Harling had studied the piano under a good teacher, and somehow she managed to practice every day. I soon learned that if I were sent over on an errand and found Mrs. Harling at the piano, I must sit down and wait quietly until she turned to me. I can see her at this moment; her short, square person planted firmly on the stool, her little fat hands moving quickly and neatly over the keys, her eyes fixed on the music with intelligent concentration.

IV

> "I won't have none of your weevily wheat, and I won't have none of your barley,
> But I'll take a measure of fine white flour, to make a cake for Charley."

We were singing rhymes to tease Ántonia while she was beating up one of Charley's favorite cakes in her big mixing-bowl. It was a crisp autumn evening, just cold enough to make one glad to quit playing tag in the yard, and retreat into the kitchen. We had begun to roll popcorn balls with syrup when we heard a knock at the back door, and Tony dropped her spoon and went to open it. A plump, fair-skinned girl was standing in the doorway. She looked demure and pretty, and made a graceful picture in her blue cashmere dress and little blue hat, with a plaid shawl drawn neatly about her shoulders and a clumsy pocketbook in her hand.

"Hello, Tony. Don't you know me?" she asked in a smooth, low voice, looking in at us archly.

Ántonia gasped and stepped back. "Why, it's Lena! Of course I didn't know you, so dressed up!"

Lena Lingard laughed, as if this pleased her. I had not recognized her for a moment, either. I had never seen her before with a hat on her head—or with shoes and stockings on her feet, for that matter. And here she was, brushed and smoothed and dressed like a town girl, smiling at us with perfect composure.

"Hello, Jim," she said carelessly as she walked into the kitchen and looked about her. "I've come to town to work, too, Tony."

"Have you, now? Well, ain't that funny!" Ántonia stood ill at ease, and didn't seem to know just what to do with her visitor.

The door was open into the dining-room, where Mrs. Harling sat crocheting and Frances was reading. Frances asked Lena to come in and join them.

"You are Lena Lingard, aren't you? I've been to see your mother, but you were off herding cattle that day. Mama, this is Chris Lingard's oldest girl."

Mrs. Harling dropped her worsted and examined the visitor with quick, keen eyes. Lena was not at all disconcerted. She sat down in the chair Frances pointed out, carefully arranging her pocketbook and gray cotton gloves on her lap. We followed with our popcorn, but Ántonia hung back—said she had to get her cake into the oven.

"So you have come to town," said Mrs. Harling, her eyes still fixed on Lena. "Where are you working?"

"For Mrs. Thomas, the dressmaker. She is going to teach me to sew. She says I have quite a knack. I'm through with the farm. There ain't any end to the work on a farm, and always so much trouble happens. I'm going to be a dressmaker."

"Well, there have to be dressmakers. It's a good trade. But I wouldn't run down the farm, if I were you," said Mrs. Harling rather severely. "How is your mother?"

"Oh, mother's never very well; she has too much to do. She'd get away from the farm, too, if she could. She was willing for me to come. After I learn to do sewing, I can make money and help her."

"See that you don't forget to," said Mrs. Harling skeptically, as she took up her crocheting again and sent the hook in and out with nimble fingers.

"No, 'm, I won't," said Lena blandly. She took a few grains of the popcorn we pressed upon her, eating them discreetly and taking care not to get her fingers sticky.

Frances drew her chair up nearer to the visitor. "I thought you were going to be married, Lena," she said teasingly. "Didn't I hear that Nick Svendsen was rushing you pretty hard?"

Lena looked up with her curiously innocent smile. "He did go with me quite a while. But his father made a fuss about it and said he wouldn't give Nick any land if he married me, so he's going to marry Annie Iverson. I wouldn't like to be her; Nick's awful sullen, and he'll take it out on her. He ain't spoke to his father since he promised."

Frances laughed. "And how do you feel about it?"

"I don't want to marry Nick, or any other man," Lena murmured. "I've seen a good deal of married life, and I don't care for it. I want to be so I can help my mother and the children at home, and not have to ask lief[1] of anybody."

"That's right," said Frances. "And Mrs. Thomas thinks you can learn dressmaking?"

"Yes, 'm. I've always liked to sew, but I never had much to do with. Mrs. Thomas makes lovely things for all the town ladies. Did you know Mrs. Gardener is having a purple velvet made? The velvet came from Omaha. My, but it's lovely!" Lena sighed softly and stroked her cashmere folds. "Tony knows I never did like out-of-door work," she added.

Mrs. Harling glanced at her. "I expect you'll learn to sew all right, Lena, if you'll only keep your head and not go gadding about to dances all the time and neglect your work, the way some country girls do."

"Yes, 'm. Tiny Soderball is coming to town, too. She's going to work at the Boys' Home Hotel. She'll see lots of strangers," Lena added wistfully.

"Too many, like enough," said Mrs. Harling. "I don't think a hotel is a good place for a girl; though I guess Mrs. Gardener keeps an eye on her waitresses."

Lena's candid eyes, that always looked a little sleepy under their long lashes, kept straying about the cheerful rooms with naïve admiration. Presently she drew on her cotton gloves. "I guess I must be leaving," she said irresolutely.

Frances told her to come again, whenever she was lonesome or wanted advice about anything. Lena replied that she didn't believe she would ever get lonesome in Black Hawk.

She lingered at the kitchen door and begged Ántonia to come and see her often. "I've got a room of my own at Mrs. Thomas's, with a carpet."

Tony shuffled uneasily in her cloth slippers. "I'll come sometime, but Mrs. Harling don't like to have me run much," she said evasively.

"You can do what you please when you go out, can't you?" Lena asked in a guarded whisper. "Ain't you crazy about town, Tony? I don't care what

1. Leave, permission.

anybody says, I'm done with the farm!" She glanced back over her shoulder toward the dining-room, where Mrs. Harling sat.

When Lena was gone, Frances asked Ántonia why she hadn't been a little more cordial to her.

"I didn't know if your mother would like her coming here," said Ántonia, looking troubled. "She was kind of talked about, out there."

"Yes, I know. But mother won't hold it against her if she behaves well here. You needn't say anything about that to the children. I guess Jim has heard all that gossip?"

When I nodded, she pulled my hair and told me I knew too much, anyhow. We were good friends, Frances and I.

I ran home to tell grandmother that Lena Lingard had come to town. We were glad of it, for she had a hard life on the farm.

Lena lived in the Norwegian settlement west of Squaw Creek, and she used to herd her father's cattle in the open country between his place and the Shimerdas'. Whenever we rode over in that direction we saw her out among her cattle, bareheaded and barefooted, scantily dressed in tattered clothing, always knitting as she watched her herd. Before I knew Lena, I thought of her as something wild, that always lived on the prairie, because I had never seen her under a roof. Her yellow hair was burned to a ruddy thatch on her head; but her legs and arms, curiously enough, in spite of constant exposure to the sun, kept a miraculous whiteness which somehow made her seem more undressed than other girls who went scantily clad. The first time I stopped to talk to her, I was astonished at her soft voice and easy, gentle ways. The girls out there usually got rough and mannish after they went to herding. But Lena asked Jake and me to get off our horses and stay awhile, and behaved exactly as if she were in a house and were accustomed to having visitors. She was not embarrassed by her ragged clothes, and treated us as if we were old acquaintances. Even then I noticed the unusual color of her eyes—a shade of deep violet—and their soft, confiding expression.

Chris Lingard was not a very successful farmer, and he had a large family. Lena was always knitting stockings for little brothers and sisters, and even the Norwegian women, who disapproved of her, admitted that she was a good daughter to her mother. As Tony said, she had been talked about. She was accused of making Ole Benson lose the little sense he had—and that at an age when she should still have been in pinafores.

Ole lived in a leaky dugout somewhere at the edge of the settlement. He was fat and lazy and discouraged, and bad luck had become a habit with him. After he had had every other kind of misfortune, his wife, "Crazy Mary," tried to set a neighbor's barn on fire, and was sent to the asylum at Lincoln. She was kept there for a few months, then escaped and walked all the way home, nearly two hundred miles, traveling by night and hiding in barns and haystacks by day. When she got back to the Norwegian settlement, her poor feet were as hard as hoofs. She promised to be good, and was allowed to stay at home—though every one realized she was as crazy as ever, and she still ran about barefooted through the snow, telling her domestic troubles to her neighbors.

Not long after Mary came back from the asylum, I heard a young Dane, who was helping us to thrash, tell Jake and Otto that Chris Lingard's oldest girl had put Ole Benson out of his head, until he had no more sense than his crazy wife. When Ole was cultivating his corn that summer, he used to get discouraged in the field, tie up his team, and wander off to wherever Lena Lingard was herding. There he would sit down on the draw-side and help her watch her cattle. All the settlement was talking about it. The Norwegian preacher's wife went to Lena and told her she ought not to allow this; she begged Lena to come to church on Sundays. Lena said she hadn't a dress in the world any less ragged than the one on her back. Then the minister's wife went through her old trunks and found some things she had worn before her marriage.

The next Sunday Lena appeared at church, a little late, with her hair done up neatly on her head, like a young woman, wearing shoes and stockings, and the new dress, which she had made over for herself very becomingly. The congregation stared at her. Until that morning no one—unless it were Ole—had realized how pretty she was, or that she was growing up. The swelling lines of her figure had been hidden under the shapeless rags she wore in the fields. After the last hymn had been sung, and the congregation was dismissed, Ole slipped out to the hitch-bar and lifted Lena on her horse. That, in itself, was shocking; a married man was not expected to do such things. But it was nothing to the scene that followed. Crazy Mary darted out from the group of women at the church door, and ran down the road after Lena, shouting horrible threats.

"Look out, you Lena Lingard, look out! I'll come over with a corn-knife one day and trim some of that shape off you. Then you won't sail round so fine, making eyes at the men! . . ."

The Norwegian women didn't know where to look. They were formal housewives, most of them, with a severe sense of decorum. But Lena Lingard only laughed her lazy, good-natured laugh and rode on, gazing back over her shoulder at Ole's infuriated wife.

The time came, however, when Lena didn't laugh. More than once Crazy Mary chased her across the prairie and round and round the Shimerdas' cornfield. Lena never told her father; perhaps she was ashamed; perhaps she was more afraid of his anger than of the cornknife. I was at the Shimerdas' one afternoon when Lena came bounding through the red grass as fast as her white legs could carry her. She ran straight into the house and hid in Ántonia's feather-bed. Mary was not far behind; she came right up to the door and made us feel how sharp her blade was, showing us very graphically just what she meant to do to Lena. Mrs. Shimerda, leaning out of the window, enjoyed the situation keenly, and was sorry when Ántonia sent Mary away, mollified by an apronful of bottle-tomatoes. Lena came out from Tony's room behind the kitchen, very pink from the heat of the feathers, but otherwise calm. She begged Ántonia and me to go with her, and help get her cattle together; they were scattered and might be gorging themselves in somebody's cornfield.

"Maybe you lose a steer and learn not to make somethings with your eyes at married men," Mrs. Shimerda told her hectoringly.

Lena only smiled her sleepy smile. "I never made anything to him with my eyes. I can't help it if he hangs around, and I can't order him off. It ain't my prairie."

V

After Lena came to Black Hawk I often met her downtown, where she would be matching sewing silk or buying "findings" for Mrs. Thomas. If I happened to walk home with her, she told me all about the dresses she was helping to make, or about what she saw and heard when she was with Tiny Soderball at the hotel on Saturday nights.

The Boys' Home was the best hotel on our branch of the Burlington, and all the commercial travelers[2] in that territory tried to get into Black Hawk for Sunday. They used to assemble in the parlor after supper on Saturday nights. Marshall Field's[3] man, Anson Kirkpatrick, played the piano and sang all the latest sentimental songs. After Tiny had helped the cook wash the dishes, she and Lena sat on the other side of the double doors between the parlor and the dining-room, listening to the music and giggling at the jokes and stories. Lena often said she hoped I would be a traveling man when I grew up. They had a gay life of it; nothing to do but ride about on trains all day and go to theaters when they were in big cities. Behind the hotel there was an old store building, where the salesmen opened their big trunks and spread out their samples on the counters. The Black Hawk merchants went to look at these things and order goods, and Mrs. Thomas, though she was "retail trade," was permitted to see them and to "get ideas." They were all generous, these traveling men; they gave Tiny Soderball handkerchiefs and gloves and ribbons and striped stockings, and so many bottles of perfume and cakes of scented soap that she bestowed some of them on Lena.

One afternoon in the week before Christmas I came upon Lena and her funny, square-headed little brother Chris, standing before the drug-store, gazing in at the wax dolls and blocks and Noah's arks arranged in the frosty show window. The boy had come to town with a neighbor to do his Christmas shopping, for he had money of his own this year. He was only twelve, but that winter he had got the job of sweeping out the Norwegian church and making the fire in it every Sunday morning. A cold job it must have been, too!

We went into Duckford's dry-goods store, and Chris unwrapped all his presents and showed them to me—something for each of the six younger than himself, even a rubber pig for the baby. Lena had given him one of Tiny Soderball's bottles of perfume for his mother, and he thought he would get some handkerchiefs to go with it. They were cheap, and he hadn't much money left. We found a tableful of handkerchiefs spread out for view at Duckford's. Chris wanted those with initial letters in the corner, because he had never seen any before. He studied them seriously, while Lena looked over his shoulder, telling him she thought the red letters would hold their color best. He seemed so perplexed that I thought perhaps he hadn't enough money, after all. Presently he said gravely,—

"Sister, you know mother's name is Berthe. I don't know if I ought to get B for Berthe, or M for Mother."

Lena patted his bristly head. "I'd get the B, Chrissy. It will please her for you to think about her name. Nobody ever calls her by it now."

2. Traveling salesmen.
3. Prominent Chicago-based merchant (1834–1906) who pioneered many modern retailing practices; best known now for the department-store chain bearing his name.

That satisfied him. His face cleared at once, and he took three reds and three blues. When the neighbor came in to say that it was time to start, Lena wound Chris's comforter about his neck and turned up his jacket collar—he had no overcoat—and we watched him climb into the wagon and start on his long, cold drive. As we walked together up the windy street, Lena wiped her eyes with the back of her woolen glove. "I get awful homesick for them, all the same," she murmured, as if she were answering some remembered reproach.

VI

Winter comes down savagely over a little town on the prairie. The wind that sweeps in from the open country strips away all the leafy screens that hide one yard from another in summer, and the houses seem to draw closer together. The roofs, that looked so far away across the green tree-tops, now stare you in the face, and they are so much uglier than when their angles were softened by vines and shrubs.

In the morning, when I was fighting my way to school against the wind, I couldn't see anything but the road in front of me; but in the late afternoon, when I was coming home, the town looked bleak and desolate to me. The pale, cold light of the winter sunset did not beautify—it was like the light of truth itself. When the smoky clouds hung low in the west and the red sun went down behind them, leaving a pink flush on the snowy roofs and the blue drifts, then the wind sprang up afresh, with a kind of bitter song, as if it said: "This is reality, whether you like it or not. All those frivolities of summer, the light and shadow, the living mask of green that trembled over everything, they were lies, and this is what was underneath. This is the truth." It was as if we were being punished for loving the loveliness of summer.

If I loitered on the playground after school, or went to the post-office for the mail and lingered to hear the gossip about the cigar-stand, it would be growing dark by the time I came home. The sun was gone; the frozen streets stretched long and blue before me; the lights were shining pale in kitchen windows, and I could smell the suppers cooking as I passed. Few people were abroad, and each one of them was hurrying toward a fire. The glowing stoves in the houses were like magnets. When one passed an old man, one could see nothing of his face but a red nose sticking out between a frosted beard and a long plush cap. The young men capered along with their hands in their pockets, and sometimes tried a slide on the icy sidewalk. The children, in their bright hoods and comforters, never walked, but always ran from the moment they left their door, beating their mittens against their sides. When I got as far as the Methodist Church, I was about halfway home. I can remember how glad I was when there happened to be a light in the church, and the painted glass window shone out at us as we came along the frozen street. In the winter bleakness a hunger for color came over people, like the Laplander's craving for fats and sugar. Without knowing why, we used to linger on the sidewalk outside the church when the lamps were lighted early for choir practice or prayer-meeting, shivering and talking until our feet were like lumps of ice. The crude reds and greens and blues of that colored glass held us there.

On winter nights, the lights in the Harlings' windows drew me like the painted glass. Inside that warm, roomy house there was color, too. After supper I used to catch up my cap, stick my hands in my pockets, and dive through the willow hedge as if witches were after me. Of course, if Mr. Harling was at home, if his shadow stood out on the blind of the west room, I did not go in, but turned and walked home by the long way, through the street, wondering what book I should read as I sat down with the two old people.

Such disappointments only gave greater zest to the nights when we acted charades, or had a costume ball in the back parlor, with Sally always dressed like a boy. Frances taught us to dance that winter, and she said, from the first lesson, that Ántonia would make the best dancer among us. On Saturday nights, Mrs. Harling used to play the old operas for us,—"Martha," "Norma," "Rigoletto,"[4]—telling us the story while she played. Every Saturday night was like a party. The parlor, the back parlor, and the dining-room were warm and brightly lighted, with comfortable chairs and sofas, and gay pictures on the walls. One always felt at ease there. Ántonia brought her sewing and sat with us—she was already beginning to make pretty clothes for herself. After the long winter evenings on the prairie, with Ambrosch's sullen silences and her mother's complaints, the Harlings' house seemed, as she said, "like Heaven" to her. She was never too tired to make taffy or chocolate cookies for us. If Sally whispered in her ear, or Charley gave her three winks, Tony would rush into the kitchen and build a fire in the range on which she had already cooked three meals that day.

While we sat in the kitchen waiting for the cookies to bake or the taffy to cool, Nina used to coax Ántonia to tell her stories—about the calf that broke its leg, or how Yulka saved her little turkeys from drowning in the freshet, or about old Christmases and weddings in Bohemia. Nina interpreted the stories about the crêche fancifully, and in spite of our derision she cherished a belief that Christ was born in Bohemia a short time before the Shimerdas left that country. We all liked Tony's stories. Her voice had a peculiarly engaging quality; it was deep, a little husky, and one always heard the breath vibrating behind it. Everything she said seemed to come right out of her heart.

One evening when we were picking out kernels for walnut taffy, Tony told us a new story.

"Mrs. Harling, did you ever hear about what happened up in the Norwegian settlement last summer, when I was thrashing there? We were at Iversons', and I was driving one of the grain wagons."

Mrs. Harling came out and sat down among us. "Could you throw the wheat into the bin yourself, Tony?" She knew what heavy work it was.

"Yes, mam, I did. I could shovel just as fast as that fat Andern boy that drove the other wagon. One day it was just awful hot. When we got back to the field from dinner, we took things kind of easy. The men put in the horses and got the machine going, and Ole Iverson was up on the deck, cutting bands. I was sitting against a straw stack, trying to get some shade. My wagon wasn't going out first, and somehow I felt the heat awful that day. The sun was so hot like it was going to burn the world up. After a while I see a man coming across the stubble, and when he got close I see it was a tramp.[5] His

4. Prominent 19th-century operas, which are still performed. *Martha,* by Friedrich von Flotow (1812–1883), first performed in 1847. *Norma,* by Vincenzo Bellini (1801–1835), first performed in 1831. *Rigoletto,* by Giuseppe Verdi (1813–1901), first performed in 1851.

5. Vagabond.

toes stuck out of his shoes, and he hadn't shaved for a long while, and his eyes was awful red and wild, like he had some sickness. He comes right up and begins to talk like he knows me already. He says: 'The ponds in this country is done got so low a man couldn't drownd himself in one of 'em.'

"I told him nobody wanted to drownd themselves, but if we didn't have rain soon we'd have to pump water for the cattle.

"'Oh, cattle,' he says, 'you'll all take care of your cattle! Ain't you got no beer here?' I told him he'd have to go to the Bohemians for beer; the Norwegians didn't have none when they thrashed. 'My God!' he says, 'so it's Norwegians now, is it? I thought this was Americy.'

"Then he goes up to the machine and yells out to Ole Iverson, 'Hello, partner, let me up there. I can cut bands, and I'm tired of trampin'. I won't go no farther.'

"I tried to make signs to Ole, 'cause I thought that man was crazy and might get the machine stopped up. But Ole, he was glad to get down out of the sun and chaff—it gets down your neck and sticks to you something awful when it's hot like that. So Ole jumped down and crawled under one of the wagons for shade, and the tramp got on the machine. He cut bands all right for a few minutes, and then, Mrs. Harling, he waved his hand to me and jumped head-first right into the thrashing machine after the wheat.

"I begun to scream, and the men run to stop the horses, but the belt had sucked him down, and by the time they got her stopped he was all beat and cut to pieces. He was wedged in so tight it was a hard job to get him out, and the machine ain't never worked right since."

"Was he clear dead, Tony?" we cried.

"Was he dead? Well, I guess so! There, now, Nina's all upset. We won't talk about it. Don't you cry, Nina. No old tramp won't get you while Tony's here."

Mrs. Harling spoke up sternly. "Stop crying, Nina, or I'll always send you upstairs when Ántonia tells us about the country. Did they never find out where he came from, Ántonia?"

"Never, mam. He hadn't been seen nowhere except in a little town they call Conway. He tried to get beer there, but there wasn't any saloon. Maybe he came in on a freight, but the brakeman hadn't seen him. They couldn't find no letters nor nothing on him; nothing but an old penknife in his pocket and the wishbone of a chicken wrapped up in a piece of paper, and some poetry."

"Some poetry?" we exclaimed.

"I remember," said Frances. "It was 'The Old Oaken Bucket,'[6] cut out of a newspaper and nearly worn out. Ole Iverson brought it into the office and showed it to me."

"Now, wasn't that strange, Miss Frances?" Tony asked thoughtfully. "What would anybody want to kill themselves in summer for? In thrashing time, too! It's nice everywhere then."

"So it is, Ántonia," said Mrs. Harling heartily. "Maybe I'll go home and help you thrash next summer. Isn't that taffy nearly ready to eat? I've been smelling it a long while."

6. Popular poem by the American writer Samuel Woodworth (1785–1842), first published in 1826.

There was a basic harmony between Ántonia and her mistress. They had strong, independent natures, both of them. They knew what they liked, and were not always trying to imitate other people. They loved children and animals and music, and rough play and digging in the earth. They liked to prepare rich, hearty food and to see people eat it; to make up soft white beds and to see youngsters asleep in them. They ridiculed conceited people and were quick to help unfortunate ones. Deep down in each of them there was a kind of hearty joviality, a relish of life, not over-delicate, but very invigorating. I never tried to define it, but I was distinctly conscious of it. I could not imagine Ántonia's living for a week in any other house in Black Hawk than the Harlings'.

VII

Winter lies too long in country towns; hangs on until it is stale and shabby, old and sullen. On the farm the weather was the great fact, and men's affairs went on underneath it, as the streams creep under the ice. But in Black Hawk the scene of human life was spread out shrunken and pinched, frozen down to the bare stalk.

Through January and February I went to the river with the Harlings on clear nights, and we skated up to the big island and made bonfires on the frozen sand. But by March the ice was rough and choppy, and the snow on the river bluffs was gray and mournful-looking. I was tired of school, tired of winter clothes, of the rutted streets, of the dirty drifts and the piles of cinders that had lain in the yards so long. There was only one break in the dreary monotony of that month; when Blind d'Arnault, the negro pianist, came to town. He gave a concert at the Opera House on Monday night, and he and his manager spent Saturday and Sunday at our comfortable hotel. Mrs. Harling had known d'Arnault for years. She told Ántonia she had better go to see Tiny that Saturday evening, as there would certainly be music at the Boys' Home.

Saturday night after supper I ran downtown to the hotel and slipped quietly into the parlor. The chairs and sofas were already occupied, and the air smelled pleasantly of cigar smoke. The parlor had once been two rooms, and the floor was sway-backed where the partition had been cut away. The wind from without made waves in the long carpet. A coal stove glowed at either end of the room, and the grand piano in the middle stood open.

There was an atmosphere of unusual freedom about the house that night, for Mrs. Gardener had gone to Omaha for a week. Johnnie had been having drinks with the guests until he was rather absent-minded. It was Mrs. Gardener who ran the business and looked after everything. Her husband stood at the desk and welcomed incoming travelers. He was a popular fellow, but no manager.

Mrs. Gardener was admittedly the best-dressed woman in Black Hawk, drove the best horse, and had a smart trap and a little white-and-gold sleigh. She seemed indifferent to her possessions, was not half so solicitous about them as her friends were. She was tall, dark, severe, with something Indian-like in the rigid immobility of her face. Her manner was cold, and she talked little. Guests felt that they were receiving, not conferring, a favor when they stayed at her house. Even the smartest traveling men were flattered when Mrs. Gardener stopped to chat with them for a moment. The patrons of the hotel were divided into two classes; those who had seen Mrs. Gardener's diamonds, and those who had not.

When I stole into the parlor Anson Kirkpatrick, Marshall Field's man, was at the piano, playing airs from a musical comedy then running in Chicago. He was a dapper little Irishman, very vain, homely as a monkey, with friends everywhere, and a sweetheart in every port, like a sailor. I did not know all the men who were sitting about, but I recognized a furniture salesman from Kansas City, a drug man, and Willy O'Reilly, who traveled for a jewelry house and sold musical instruments. The talk was all about good and bad hotels, actors and actresses and musical prodigies. I learned that Mrs. Gardener had gone to Omaha to hear Booth and Barrett, who were to play there next week, and that Mary Anderson was having a great success in "A Winter's Tale,"[7] in London.

The door from the office opened, and Johnnie Gardener came in, directing Blind d'Arnault,—he would never consent to be led. He was a heavy, bulky mulatto, on short legs, and he came tapping the floor in front of him with his gold-headed cane. His yellow face was lifted in the light, with a show of white teeth, all grinning, and his shrunken, papery eyelids lay motionless over his blind eyes.

"Good evening, gentlemen. No ladies here? Good-evening, gentlemen. We going to have a little music? Some of you gentlemen going to play for me this evening?" It was the soft, amiable negro voice, like those I remembered from early childhood, with the note of docile subservience in it. He had the negro head, too; almost no head at all; nothing behind the ears but folds of neck under close-clipped wool. He would have been repulsive if his face had not been so kindly and happy. It was the happiest face I had seen since I left Virginia.

He felt his way directly to the piano. The moment he sat down, I noticed the nervous infirmity of which Mrs. Harling had told me. When he was sitting, or standing still, he swayed back and forth incessantly, like a rocking toy. At the piano, he swayed in time to the music, and when he was not playing, his body kept up this motion, like an empty mill grinding on. He found the pedals and tried them, ran his yellow hands up and down the keys a few times, tinkling off scales, then turned to the company.

"She seems all right, gentlemen. Nothing happened to her since the last time I was here. Mrs. Gardener, she always has this piano tuned up before I come. Now, gentlemen, I expect you've all got grand voices. Seems like we might have some good old plantation songs to-night."

The men gathered round him, as he began to play "My Old Kentucky Home."[8] They sang one negro melody after another, while the mulatto sat rocking himself, his head thrown back, his yellow face lifted, its shriveled eyelids never fluttering.

He was born in the Far South, on the d'Arnault plantation, where the spirit if not the fact of slavery persisted. When he was three weeks old he

7. A play by William Shakespeare (1564–1616). Edwin Booth (1833–1893) and Lawrence Barrett (1838–1891), American actors who had a long partnership performing Shakespearean plays. The dates of these actors' lives allow for rather precise dating of the novel. Anderson was an English actress.

8. Nostalgic popular song about the South by Stephen Foster (1826–1864), who composed for minstrel shows in which white performers acted in blackface. Foster's songs were often mistaken for folk songs and, as Cather shows here, were performed by black musicians as well as white.

had an illness which left him totally blind. As soon as he was old enough to sit up alone and toddle about, another affliction, the nervous motion of his body, became apparent. His mother, a buxom young negro wench who was laundress for the d'Arnaults, concluded that her blind baby was "not right" in his head, and she was ashamed of him. She loved him devotedly, but he was so ugly, with his sunken eyes and his "fidgets," that she hid him away from people. All the dainties she brought down from the "Big House" were for the blind child, and she beat and cuffed her other children whenever she found them teasing him or trying to get his chicken-bone away from him. He began to talk early, remembered everything he heard, and his mammy said he "wasn't all wrong." She named him Samson, because he was blind, but on the plantation he was known as "yellow Martha's simple child." He was docile and obedient, but when he was six years old he began to run away from home, always taking the same direction. He felt his way through the lilacs, along the boxwood hedge, up to the south wing of the "Big House," where Miss Nellie d'Arnault practiced the piano every morning. This angered his mother more than anything else he could have done; she was so ashamed of his ugliness that she couldn't bear to have white folks see him. Whenever she caught him slipping away from the cabin, she whipped him unmercifully, and told him what dreadful things old Mr. d'Arnault would do to him if he ever found him near the "Big House." But the next time Samson had a chance, he ran away again. If Miss d'Arnault stopped practicing for a moment and went toward the window, she saw this hideous little pickaninny, dressed in an old piece of sacking, standing in the open space between the hollyhock rows, his body rocking automatically, his blind face lifted to the sun and wearing an expression of idiotic rapture. Often she was tempted to tell Martha that the child must be kept at home, but somehow the memory of his foolish, happy face deterred her. She remembered that his sense of hearing was nearly all he had,—though it did not occur to her that he might have more of it than other children.

One day Samson was standing thus while Miss Nellie was playing her lesson to her music-master. The windows were open. He heard them get up from the piano, talk a little while, and then leave the room. He heard the door close after them. He crept up to the front windows and stuck his head in: there was no one there. He could always detect the presence of any one in a room. He put one foot over the window sill and straddled it. His mother had told him over and over how his master would give him to the big mastiff if he ever found him "meddling." Samson had got too near the mastiff's kennel once, and had felt his terrible breath in his face. He thought about that, but he pulled in his other foot.

Through the dark he found his way to the Thing, to its mouth. He touched it softly, and it answered softly, kindly. He shivered and stood still. Then he began to feel it all over, ran his finger tips along the slippery sides, embraced the carved legs, tried to get some conception of its shape and size, of the space it occupied in primeval night. It was cold and hard, and like nothing else in his black universe. He went back to its mouth, began at one end of the keyboard and felt his way down into the mellow thunder, as far as he could go. He seemed to know that it must be done with the fingers, not with the fists or the feet. He approached this highly artificial instrument through a mere instinct, and coupled himself to it, as if he knew it was to piece him out and make a whole creature of him. After he had tried over all the sounds, he began to finger out passages from things Miss Nellie had been practicing, passages that were already his, that lay under the bones of his pinched, conical little skull, definite as animal desires. The door opened; Miss Nellie and her music-master stood behind it, but blind Samson, who was so sensitive to presences, did not know they were there. He was feeling out the pattern that lay all ready-made on the big and little keys. When he paused for a moment, because the sound was wrong and he wanted another, Miss Nellie spoke softly. He whirled about in a spasm of terror, leaped forward in the dark, struck his head on the open window, and fell screaming and bleeding to the floor. He had what his mother called a fit. The doctor came and gave him opium.

When Samson was well again, his young mistress led him back to the piano. Several teachers experimented with him. They found he had absolute pitch, and a remarkable memory. As a very young child he could repeat, after a fashion, any composition that was played for him. No matter how many wrong notes he struck, he never lost the intention of a passage, he brought the substance of it across by irregular and astonishing means. He wore his teachers out. He could never learn like other people, never acquired any finish. He was always a negro prodigy who played barbarously and wonderfully. As piano playing, it was perhaps abominable, but as music it was something real, vitalized by a sense of rhythm that was stronger than his other physical senses,—that not only filled his dark mind, but worried his body incessantly. To hear him, to watch him, was to see a negro enjoying himself as only a negro can. It was as if all the agreeable sensations possible to creatures of flesh and blood were heaped up on those black and white keys, and he were gloating over them and trickling them through his yellow fingers.

In the middle of a crashing waltz d'Arnault suddenly began to play softly, and, turning to one of the men who stood behind him, whispered, "Somebody dancing in there." He jerked his bullet head toward the dining-room. "I hear little feet,—girls, I 'spect."

Anson Kirkpatrick mounted a chair and peeped over the transom. Springing down, he wrenched open the doors and ran out into the dining-room. Tiny and Lena, Ántonia and Mary Dusak, were waltzing in the middle of the floor. They separated and fled toward the kitchen, giggling.

Kirkpatrick caught Tiny by the elbows. "What's the matter with you girls? Dancing out here by yourselves, when there's a roomful of lonesome men on the other side of the partition! Introduce me to your friends, Tiny."

The girls, still laughing, were trying to escape. Tiny looked alarmed. "Mrs. Gardener wouldn't like it," she protested. "She'd be awful mad if you was to come out here and dance with us."

"Mrs. Gardener's in Omaha, girl. Now, you're Lena, are you?—and you're Tony and you're Mary. Have I got you all straight?"

O'Reilly and the others began to pile the chairs on the tables. Johnnie Gardener ran in from the office.

"Easy, boys, easy!" he entreated them. "You'll wake the cook, and there'll be the devil to pay for me. She won't hear the music, but she'll be down the minute anything's moved in the dining-room."

"Oh, what do you care, Johnnie? Fire the cook and wire Molly to bring another. Come along, nobody'll tell tales."

Johnnie shook his head. "'S a fact, boys," he said confidentially. "If I take a drink in Black Hawk, Molly knows it in Omaha!"

His guests laughed and slapped him on the shoulder. "Oh, we'll make it all right with Molly. Get your back up, Johnnie."

Molly was Mrs. Gardener's name, of course. "Molly Bawn" was painted in large blue letters on the glossy white side of the hotel bus, and "Molly" was engraved inside Johnnie's ring and on his watch-case—doubtless on his heart, too. He was an affectionate little man, and he thought his wife a wonderful woman; he knew that without her he would hardly be more than a clerk in some other man's hotel.

At a word from Kirkpatrick, d'Arnault spread himself out over the piano, and began to draw the dance music out of it, while the perspiration shone on his short wool and on his uplifted face. He looked like some glistening African god of pleasure, full of strong, savage blood. Whenever the dancers paused to change partners or to catch breath, he would boom out softly, "Who's that goin' back on me? One of these city gentlemen, I bet! Now, you girls, you ain't goin' to let that floor get cold?"

Ántonia seemed frightened at first, and kept looking questioningly at Lena and Tiny over Willy O'Reilly's shoulder. Tiny Soderball was trim and slender, with lively little feet and pretty ankles—she wore her dresses very short. She was quicker in speech, lighter in movement and manner than the other girls. Mary Dusak was broad and brown of countenance, slightly marked by smallpox, but handsome for all that. She had beautiful chestnut hair, coils of it; her forehead was low and smooth, and her commanding dark eyes regarded the world indifferently and fearlessly. She looked bold and resourceful and unscrupulous, and she was all of these. They were handsome girls, had the fresh color of their country up-bringing, and in their eyes that brilliancy which is called,—by no metaphor, alas!—"the light of youth."

D'Arnault played until his manager came and shut the piano. Before he left us, he showed us his gold watch which struck the hours, and a topaz ring, given him by some Russian nobleman who delighted in negro melodies, and had heard d'Arnault play in New Orleans. At last he tapped his way upstairs, after bowing to everybody, docile and happy. I walked home with Ántonia. We were so excited that we dreaded to go to bed. We lingered a long while at the Harlings' gate, whispering in the cold until the restlessness was slowly chilled out of us.

VIII

The Harling children and I were never happier, never felt more contented and secure, than in the weeks of spring which broke that long winter. We were out all day in the thin sunshine, helping Mrs. Harling and Tony break the ground and plant the garden, dig around the orchard trees, tie up vines and clip the hedges. Every morning, before I was up, I could hear Tony singing in the garden rows. After the apple and cherry trees broke into bloom, we ran about under them, hunting for the new nests the birds were building, throwing clods at each other, and playing hide-and-seek with Nina. Yet the summer which was to change everything was coming nearer every day. When boys and girls are growing up, life can't stand still, not even in the quietest of country towns; and they have to grow up, whether they will or no. That is what their elders are always forgetting.

It must have been in June, for Mrs. Harling and Ántonia were preserving cherries, when I stopped one morning to tell them that a dancing pavilion had come to town. I had seen two drays hauling the canvas and painted poles up from the depot.

That afternoon three cheerful-looking Italians strolled about Black Hawk, looking at everything, and with them was a dark, stout woman who wore a long gold watch chain about her neck and carried a black lace parasol. They seemed especially interested in children and vacant lots. When I overtook them and stopped to say a word, I found them affable and confiding. They told me they worked in Kansas City in the winter, and in summer they went out among the farming towns with their tent and taught dancing. When business fell off in one place, they moved on to another.

The dancing pavilion was put up near the Danish laundry, on a vacant lot surrounded by tall, arched cottonwood trees. It was very much like a merry-go-round tent, with open sides and gay flags flying from the poles. Before the week was over, all the ambitious mothers were sending their children to the afternoon dancing class. At three o'clock one met little girls in white dresses and little boys in the round-collared shirts of the time, hurrying along the sidewalk on their way to the tent. Mrs. Vanni received them at the entrance, always dressed in lavender with a great deal of black lace, her important watch chain lying on her bosom. She wore her hair on the top of her head, built up in a black tower, with red coral combs. When she smiled, she showed two rows of strong, crooked yellow teeth. She taught the little children herself, and her husband, the harpist, taught the older ones.

Often the mothers brought their fancy-work[9] and sat on the shady side of the tent during the lesson. The popcorn man wheeled his glass wagon under the big cottonwood by the door, and lounged in the sun, sure of a good trade when the dancing was over. Mr. Jensen, the Danish laundryman, used to bring a chair from his porch and sit out in the grass plot. Some ragged little boys from the depot sold pop and iced lemonade under a white umbrella at the corner, and made faces at the spruce youngsters who came to dance. That vacant lot soon became the most cheerful place in town. Even on the hottest afternoons the cottonwoods made a rustling shade, and the air smelled of popcorn and melted butter, and Bouncing Bets wilting in the sun. Those hardy flowers had run away from the laundry-man's garden, and the grass in the middle of the lot was pink with them.

The Vannis kept exemplary order, and closed every evening at the hour suggested by the City Council. When Mrs. Vanni gave the signal, and the harp struck up "Home, Sweet Home,"[1] all Black Hawk knew it was ten o'clock. You could set your watch by that tune as confidently as by the Round House[2] whistle.

At last there was something to do in those long, empty summer evenings, when the married people sat like images on their front porches, and the boys

9. Embroidery.

1. Extremely popular song featured in the play *Clari; or, The Maid of Milan* (first produced in 1823) by the American John Howard Payne (1791–1852).

2. Circular building for housing and repairing locomotives.

and girls tramped and tramped the board sidewalks—northward to the edge of the open prairie, south to the depot, then back again to the post-office, the ice-cream parlor, the butcher shop. Now there was a place where the girls could wear their new dresses, and where one could laugh aloud without being reproved by the ensuing silence. That silence seemed to ooze out of the ground, to hang under the foliage of the black maple trees with the bats and shadows. Now it was broken by light-hearted sounds. First the deep purring of Mr. Vanni's harp came in silvery ripples through the blackness of the dusty-smelling night; then the violins fell in—one of them was almost like a flute. They called so archly, so seductively, that our feet hurried toward the tent of themselves. Why hadn't we had a tent before?

Dancing became popular now, just as roller skating had been the summer before. The Progressive Euchre[3] Club arranged with the Vannis for the exclusive use of the floor on Tuesday and Friday nights. At other times any one could dance who paid his money and was orderly; the railroad men, the Round House mechanics, the delivery boys, the ice-man, the farmhands who lived near enough to ride into town after their day's work was over.

I never missed a Saturday night dance. The tent was open until midnight then. The country boys came in from farms eight and ten miles away, and all the country girls were on the floor,—Ántonia and Lena and Tiny, and the Danish laundry girls and their friends. I was not the only boy who found these dances gayer than the others. The young men who belonged to the Progressive Euchre Club used to drop in late and risk a tiff with their sweethearts and general condemnation for a waltz with "the hired girls."

IX

There was a curious social situation in Black Hawk. All the young men felt the attraction of the fine, well-set-up country girls who had come to town to earn a living, and, in nearly every case, to help the father struggle out of debt, or to make it possible for the younger children of the family to go to school.

Those girls had grown up in the first bitter-hard times, and had got little schooling themselves. But the younger brothers and sisters, for whom they made such sacrifices and who have had "advantages," never seem to me, when I meet them now, half as interesting or as well educated. The older girls, who helped to break up the wild sod, learned so much from life, from poverty, from their mothers and grandmothers; they had all, like Ántonia, been early awakened and made observant by coming at a tender age from an old country to a new. I can remember a score of these country girls who were in service in Black Hawk during the few years I lived there, and I can remember something unusual and engaging about each of them. Physically they were almost a race apart, and out-of-door work had given them a vigor which, when they got over their first shyness on coming to town, developed into a positive carriage and freedom of movement, and made them conspicuous among Black Hawk women.

That was before the day of High-School athletics. Girls who had to walk more than half a mile to school were pitied. There was not a tennis court in the town; physical exercise was thought rather inelegant for the daughters of

3. Card game for four players.

well-to-do families. Some of the High-School girls were jolly and pretty, but they stayed indoors in winter because of the cold, and in summer because of the heat. When one danced with them their bodies never moved inside their clothes; their muscles seemed to ask but one thing—not to be disturbed. I remember those girls merely as faces in the schoolroom, gay and rosy, or listless and dull, cut off below the shoulders, like cherubs, by the ink-smeared tops of the high desks that were surely put there to make us round-shouldered and hollow-chested.

The daughters of Black Hawk merchants had a confident, uninquiring belief that they were "refined," and that the country girls, who "worked out," were not. The American[4] farmers in our country were quite as hard-pressed as their neighbors from other countries. All alike had come to Nebraska with little capital and no knowledge of the soil they must subdue. All had borrowed money on their land. But no matter in what straits the Pennsylvanian or Virginian found himself, he would not let his daughters go out into service. Unless his girls could teach a country school, they sat at home in poverty. The Bohemian and Scandinavian girls could not get positions as teachers, because they had had no opportunity to learn the language. Determined to help in the struggle to clear the homestead from debt, they had no alternative but to go into service. Some of them, after they came to town, remained as serious and as discreet in behavior as they had been when they ploughed and herded on their father's farm. Others, like the three Bohemian Marys, tried to make up for the years of youth they had lost. But every one of them did what she had set out to do, and sent home those hard-earned dollars. The girls I knew were always helping to pay for ploughs and reapers, brood-sows, or steers to fatten.

One result of this family solidarity was that the foreign farmers in our county were the first to become prosperous. After the fathers were out of debt, the daughters married the sons of neighbors,—usually of like nationality,—and the girls who once worked in Black Hawk kitchens are to-day managing big farms and fine families of their own; their children are better off than the children of the town women they used to serve.

I thought the attitude of the town people toward these girls very stupid. If I told my schoolmates that Lena Lingard's grandfather was a clergyman, and much respected in Norway, they looked at me blankly. What did it matter? All foreigners were ignorant people who couldn't speak English. There was not a man in Black Hawk who had the intelligence or cultivation, much less the personal distinction, of Ántonia's father. Yet people saw no difference between her and the three Marys; they were all Bohemians, all "hired girls."

I always knew I should live long enough to see my country girls come into their own, and I have. To-day the best that a harassed Black Hawk merchant can hope for is to sell provisions and farm machinery and automobiles to the rich farms where that first crop of stalwart Bohemian and Scandinavian girls are now the mistresses.

The Black Hawk boys looked forward to marrying Black Hawk girls, and living in a brand-new little house with best chairs that must not be sat upon, and hand-painted china that must not be used. But sometimes a young fellow would look up from his ledger, or out through the grating of his father's bank, and let his eyes follow Lena Lingard, as she passed the window with

4. I.e., born in America, nonimmigrant.

her slow, undulating walk, or Tiny Soderball, tripping by in her short skirt and striped stockings.

The country girls were considered a menace to the social order. Their beauty shone out too boldly against a conventional background. But anxious mothers need have felt no alarm. They mistook the mettle of their sons. The respect for respectability was stronger than any desire in Black Hawk youth.

Our young man of position was like the son of a royal house; the boy who swept out his office or drove his delivery wagon might frolic with the jolly country girls, but he himself must sit all evening in a plush parlor where conversation dragged so perceptibly that the father often came in and made blundering efforts to warm up the atmosphere. On his way home from his dull call, he would perhaps meet Tony and Lena, coming along the sidewalk whispering to each other, or the three Bohemian Marys in their long plush coats and caps, comporting themselves with a dignity that only made their eventful histories the more piquant. If he went to the hotel to see a traveling man on business, there was Tiny, arching her shoulders at him like a kitten. If he went into the laundry to get his collars, there were the four Danish girls, smiling up from their ironing-boards, with their white throats and their pink cheeks.

The three Marys were the heroines of a cycle of scandalous stories, which the old men were fond of relating as they sat about the cigar-stand in the drug-store. Mary Dusak had been housekeeper for a bachelor rancher from Boston, and after several years in his service she was forced to retire from the world for a short time. Later she came back to town to take the place of her friend, Mary Svoboda, who was similarly embarrassed.[5] The three Marys were considered as dangerous as high explosives to have about the kitchen, yet they were such good cooks and such admirable house-keepers that they never had to look for a place.

The Vannis' tent brought the town boys and the country girls together on neutral ground. Sylvester Lovett, who was cashier in his father's bank, always found his way to the tent on Saturday night. He took all the dances Lena Lingard would give him, and even grew bold enough to walk home with her. If his sisters or their friends happened to be among the onlookers on "popular nights," Sylvester stood back in the shadow under the cottonwood trees, smoking and watching Lena with a harassed expression. Several times I stumbled upon him there in the dark, and I felt rather sorry for him. He reminded me of Ole Benson, who used to sit on the draw-side and watch Lena herd her cattle. Later in the summer, when Lena went home for a week to visit her mother, I heard from Ántonia that young Lovett drove all the way out there to see her, and took her buggy-riding. In my ingenuousness I hoped that Sylvester would marry Lena, and thus give all the country girls a better position in the town.

Sylvester dallied about Lena until he began to make mistakes in his work; had to stay at the bank until after dark to make his books balance. He was daft about her, and every one knew it. To escape from his predicament he ran away with a widow six years older than himself, who owned a half-section.[6] This remedy worked, apparently. He never looked at Lena again,

5. Both women had out-of-wedlock babies.
6. One-half of a square mile, or 320 acres.

nor lifted his eyes as he ceremoniously tipped his hat when he happened to meet her on the sidewalk.

So that was what they were like, I thought, these white-handed, high-collared clerks and bookkeepers! I used to glare at young Lovett from a distance and only wished I had some way of showing my contempt for him.

X

It was at the Vannis' tent that Ántonia was discovered. Hitherto she had been looked upon more as a ward of the Harlings than as one of the "hired girls." She had lived in their house and yard and garden; her thoughts never seemed to stray outside that little kingdom. But after the tent came to town she began to go about with Tiny and Lena and their friends. The Vannis often said that Ántonia was the best dancer of them all. I sometimes heard murmurs in the crowd outside the pavilion that Mrs. Harling would soon have her hands full with that girl. The young men began to joke with each other about "the Harlings' Tony" as they did about "the Marshalls' Anna" or "the Gardeners' Tiny."

Ántonia talked and thought of nothing but the tent. She hummed the dance tunes all day. When supper was late, she hurried with her dishes, dropped and smashed them in her excitement. At the first call of the music, she became irresponsible. If she hadn't time to dress, she merely flung off her apron and shot out of the kitchen door. Sometimes I went with her; the moment the lighted tent came into view she would break into a run, like a boy. There were always partners waiting for her; she began to dance before she got her breath.

Ántonia's success at the tent had its consequences. The iceman lingered too long now, when he came into the covered porch to fill the refrigerator. The delivery boys hung about the kitchen when they brought the groceries. Young farmers who were in town for Saturday came tramping through the yard to the back door to engage dances, or to invite Tony to parties and picnics. Lena and Norwegian Anna dropped in to help her with her work, so that she could get away early. The boys who brought her home after the dances sometimes laughed at the back gate and wakened Mr. Harling from his first sleep. A crisis was inevitable.

One Saturday night Mr. Harling had gone down to the cellar for beer. As he came up the stairs in the dark, he heard scuffling on the back porch, and then the sound of a vigorous slap. He looked out through the side door in time to see a pair of long legs vaulting over the picket fence. Ántonia was standing there, angry and excited. Young Harry Paine, who was to marry his employer's daughter on Monday, had come to the tent with a crowd of friends and danced all evening. Afterward, he begged Ántonia to let him walk home with her. She said she supposed he was a nice young man, as he was one of Miss Frances's friends, and she didn't mind. On the back porch he tried to kiss her, and when she protested,—because he was going to be married on Monday,—he caught her and kissed her until she got one hand free and slapped him.

Mr. Harling put his beer bottles down on the table. "This is what I've been expecting, Ántonia. You've been going with girls who have a reputation for being free and easy, and now you've got the same reputation. I won't have this and that fellow tramping about my back yard all the time. This is the end of it, to-night. It stops, short. You can quit going to these dances, or you can hunt another place. Think it over."

The next morning when Mrs. Harling and Frances tried to reason with Ántonia, they found her agitated but determined. "Stop going to the tent?" she panted. "I wouldn't think of it for a minute! My own father couldn't make me stop! Mr. Harling ain't my boss outside my work. I won't give up my friends, either. The boys I go with are nice fellows. I thought Mr. Paine was all right, too, because he used to come here. I guess I gave him a red face for his wedding, all right!" she blazed out indignantly.

"You'll have to do one thing or the other, Ántonia," Mrs. Harling told her decidedly. "I can't go back on what Mr. Harling has said. This is his house."

"Then I'll just leave, Mrs. Harling. Lena's been wanting me to get a place closer to her for a long while. Mary Svoboda's going away from the Cutters' to work at the hotel, and I can have her place."

Mrs. Harling rose from her chair. "Ántonia, if you go to the Cutters to work, you cannot come back to this house again. You know what that man is. It will be the ruin of you."

Tony snatched up the tea-kettle and began to pour boiling water over the glasses, laughing excitedly. "Oh, I can take care of myself! I'm a lot stronger than Cutter is. They pay four dollars there, and there's no children. The work's nothing; I can have every evening, and be out a lot in the afternoons."

"I thought you liked children. Tony, what's come over you?"

"I don't know, something has." Ántonia tossed her head and set her jaw. "A girl like me has got to take her good times when she can. Maybe there won't be any tent next year. I guess I want to have my fling, like the other girls."

Mrs. Harling gave a short, harsh laugh. "If you go to work for the Cutters, you're likely to have a fling that you won't get up from in a hurry."

Frances said, when she told grandmother and me about this scene, that every pan and plate and cup on the shelves trembled when her mother walked out of the kitchen. Mrs. Harling declared bitterly that she wished she had never let herself get fond of Ántonia.

XI

Wick Cutter was the money-lender who had fleeced poor Russian Peter. When a farmer once got into the habit of going to Cutter, it was like gambling or the lottery; in an hour of discouragement he went back.

Cutter's first name was Wycliffe,[7] and he liked to talk about his pious bringing-up. He contributed regularly to the Protestant churches, "for sentiment's sake," as he said with a flourish of the hand. He came from a town in Iowa where there were a great many Swedes, and could speak a little Swedish, which gave him a great advantage with the early Scandinavian settlers.

In every frontier settlement there are men who have come there to escape restraint. Cutter was one of the "fast set" of Black Hawk business men. He was an inveterate gambler, though a poor loser. When we saw a light burning in his office late at night, we knew that a game of poker was going on. Cutter boasted that he never drank anything stronger than sherry, and he said he got his start in life by saving the money that other young men spent for cigars. He

7. After John Wycliffe (1328–1384), English religious reformer.

was full of moral maxims for boys. When he came to our house on business, he quoted "Poor Richard's Almanack"[8] to me, and told me he was delighted to find a town boy who could milk a cow. He was particularly affable to grandmother, and whenever they met he would begin at once to talk about "the good old times" and simple living. I detested his pink, bald head, and his yellow whiskers, always soft and glistening. It was said he brushed them every night, as a woman does her hair. His white teeth looked factory-made. His skin was red and rough, as if from perpetual sunburn; he often went away to hot springs to take mud baths. He was notoriously dissolute with women. Two Swedish girls who had lived in his house were the worse for the experience. One of them he had taken to Omaha and established in the business for which he had fitted her.[9] He still visited her.

Cutter lived in a state of perpetual warfare with his wife, and yet, apparently, they never thought of separating. They dwelt in a fussy, scroll-work house, painted white and buried in thick evergreens, with a fussy white fence and barn. Cutter thought he knew a great deal about horses, and usually had a colt which he was training for the track. On Sunday mornings one could see him out at the fair grounds, speeding around the race-course in his trotting-buggy, wearing yellow gloves and a black-and-white-check traveling cap, his whiskers blowing back in the breeze. If there were any boys about, Cutter would offer one of them a quarter to hold the stop-watch, and then drive off, saying he had no change and would "fix it up next time." No one could cut his lawn or wash his buggy to suit him. He was so fastidious and prim about his place that a boy would go to a good deal of trouble to throw a dead cat into his back yard, or to dump a sackful of tin cans in his alley. It was a peculiar combination of old-maidishness and licentiousness that made Cutter seem so despicable.

He had certainly met his match when he married Mrs. Cutter. She was a terrifying-looking person; almost a giantess in height, raw-boned, with iron-gray hair, a face always flushed, and prominent, hysterical eyes. When she meant to be entertaining and agreeable, she nodded her head incessantly and snapped her eyes at one. Her teeth were long and curved, like a horse's; people said babies always cried if she smiled at them. Her face had a kind of fascination for me; it was the very color and shape of anger. There was a gleam of something akin to insanity in her full, intense eyes. She was formal in manner, and made calls in rustling, steel-gray brocades and a tall bonnet with bristling aigrettes.[1]

Mrs. Cutter painted china so assiduously that even her washbowls and pitchers, and her husband's shaving-mug, were covered with violets and lilies. Once when Cutter was exhibiting some of his wife's china to a caller, he dropped a piece. Mrs. Cutter put her handkerchief to her lips as if she were going to faint and said grandly: "Mr. Cutter, you have broken all the Commandments—spare the finger-bowls!"

They quarreled from the moment Cutter came into the house until they went to bed at night, and their hired girls reported these scenes to the town at large. Mrs. Cutter had several times cut paragraphs about unfaithful

8. A farmer's almanac written and published in Philadelphia by Benjamin Franklin from 1733 to 1758; it was famous for maxims and proverbs through which Franklin taught an ethic of hard work and prudence.
9. I.e., prostitution.
1. Sprays of feathers.

husbands out of the newspapers and mailed them to Cutter in a disguised handwriting. Cutter would come home at noon, find the mutilated journal in the paper-rack, and triumphantly fit the clipping into the space from which it had been cut. Those two could quarrel all morning about whether he ought to put on his heavy or his light underwear, and all evening about whether he had taken cold or not.

The Cutters had major as well as minor subjects for dispute. The chief of these was the question of inheritance: Mrs. Cutter told her husband it was plainly his fault they had no children. He insisted that Mrs. Cutter had purposely remained childless, with the determination to outlive him and to share his property with her "people," whom he detested. To this she would reply that unless he changed his mode of life, she would certainly outlive him. After listening to her insinuations about his physical soundness, Cutter would resume his dumb-bell practice for a month, or rise daily at the hour when his wife most liked to sleep, dress noisily, and drive out to the track with his trotting-horse.

Once when they had quarreled about house-hold expenses, Mrs. Cutter put on her brocade and went among their friends soliciting orders for painted china, saying that Mr. Cutter had compelled her "to live by her brush." Cutter wasn't shamed as she had expected; he was delighted!

Cutter often threatened to chop down the cedar trees which half-buried the house. His wife declared she would leave him if she were stripped of the "privacy" which she felt these trees afforded her. That was his opportunity, surely; but he never cut down the trees. The Cutters seemed to find their relations to each other interesting and stimulating, and certainly the rest of us found them so. Wick Cutter was different from any other rascal I have ever known, but I have found Mrs. Cutters all over the world; sometimes founding new religions, sometimes being forcibly fed—easily recognizable, even when superficially tamed.

XII

After Ántonia went to live with the Cutters, she seemed to care about nothing but picnics and parties and having a good time. When she was not going to a dance, she sewed until midnight. Her new clothes were the subject of caustic comment. Under Lena's direction she copied Mrs. Gardener's new party dress and Mrs. Smith's street costume so ingeniously in cheap materials that those ladies were greatly annoyed, and Mrs. Cutter, who was jealous of them, was secretly pleased.

Tony wore gloves now, and high-heeled shoes and feathered bonnets, and she went downtown nearly every afternoon with Tiny and Lena and the Marshalls' Norwegian Anna. We High-School boys used to linger on the playground at the afternoon recess to watch them as they came tripping down the hill along the board sidewalk, two and two. They were growing prettier every day, but as they passed us, I used to think with pride that Ántonia, like Snow-White in the fairy tale, was still "fairest of them all."

Being a Senior now, I got away from school early. Sometimes I overtook the girls down-town and coaxed them into the ice-cream parlor, where they would sit chattering and laughing, telling me all the news from the country. I remember how angry Tiny Soderball made me one afternoon. She declared she had heard grandmother was going to make a Baptist preacher of me. "I guess you'll have to stop dancing and wear a white necktie then. Won't he look funny, girls?"

Lena laughed. "You'll have to hurry up, Jim. If you're going to be a preacher, I want you to marry me. You must promise to marry us all, and then baptize the babies."

Norwegian Anna, always dignified, looked at her reprovingly.

"Baptists don't believe in christening babies, do they, Jim?"

I told her I didn't know what they believed, and didn't care, and that I certainly wasn't going to be a preacher.

"That's too bad," Tiny simpered. She was in a teasing mood. "You'd make such a good one. You're so studious. Maybe you'd like to be a professor. You used to teach Tony, didn't you?"

Ántonia broke in. "I've set my heart on Jim being a doctor. You'd be good with sick people, Jim. Your grandmother's trained you up so nice. My papa always said you were an awful smart boy."

I said I was going to be whatever I pleased. "Won't you be surprised, Miss Tiny, if I turn out to be a regular devil of a fellow?"

They laughed until a glance from Norwegian Anna checked them; the High-School Principal had just come into the front part of the shop to buy bread for supper. Anna knew the whisper was going about that I was a sly one. People said there must be something queer about a boy who showed no interest in girls of his own age, but who could be lively enough when he was with Tony and Lena or the three Marys.

The enthusiasm for the dance, which the Vannis had kindled, did not at once die out. After the tent left town, the Euchre Club became the Owl Club, and gave dances in the Masonic Hall once a week. I was invited to join, but declined. I was moody and restless that winter, and tired of the people I saw every day. Charley Harling was already at Annapolis, while I was still sitting in Black Hawk, answering to my name at roll-call every morning, rising from my desk at the sound of a bell and marching out like the grammar-school children. Mrs. Harling was a little cool toward me, because I continued to champion Ántonia. What was there for me to do after supper? Usually I had learned next day's lessons by the time I left the school building, and I couldn't sit still and read forever.

In the evening I used to prowl about, hunting for diversion. There lay the familiar streets, frozen with snow or liquid with mud. They led to the houses of good people who were putting the babies to bed, or simply sitting still before the parlor stove, digesting their supper. Black Hawk had two saloons. One of them was admitted, even by the church people, to be as respectable as a saloon could be. Handsome Anton Jelinek, who had rented his homestead and come to town, was the proprietor. In his saloon there were long tables where the Bohemian and German farmers could eat the lunches they brought from home while they drank their beer. Jelinek kept rye bread on hand, and smoked fish and strong imported cheeses to please the foreign palate. I liked to drop into his bar-room and listen to the talk. But one day he overtook me on the street and clapped me on the shoulder.

"Jim," he said, "I am good friends with you and I always like to see you. But you know how the church people think about saloons. Your grandpa has always treated me fine, and I don't like to have you come into my place, because I know he don't like it, and it puts me in bad with him."

So I was shut out of that.

One could hang about the drug-store, and listen to the old men who sat there every evening, talking politics and telling raw stories. One could go to the cigar factory and chat with the old German who raised canaries for sale, and look at his stuffed birds. But whatever you began with him, the talk went back to taxidermy. There was the depot, of course; I often went down to see the night train come in, and afterward sat awhile with the disconsolate telegrapher who was always hoping to be transferred to Omaha or Denver, "where there was some life." He was sure to bring out his pictures of actresses and dancers. He got them with cigarette coupons and nearly smoked himself to death to possess these desired forms and faces. For a change, one could talk to the station agent; but he was another malcontent; spent all his spare time writing letters to officials requesting a transfer. He wanted to get back to Wyoming where he could go trout-fishing on Sundays. He used to say "there was nothing in life for him but trout streams, ever since he'd lost his twins."

These were the distractions I had to choose from. There were no other lights burning downtown after nine o'clock. On starlight nights I used to pace up and down those long, cold streets, scowling at the little, sleeping houses on either side, with their storm-windows and covered back porches. They were flimsy shelters, most of them poorly built of light wood, with spindle porch-posts horribly mutilated by the turning-lathe. Yet for all their frailness, how much jealousy and envy and unhappiness some of them managed to contain! The life that went on in them seemed to me made up of evasions and negations; shifts to save cooking, to save washing and cleaning, devices to propitiate the tongue of gossip. This guarded mode of existence was like living under a tyranny. People's speech, their voices, their very glances, became furtive and repressed. Every individual taste, every natural appetite, was bridled by caution. The people asleep in those houses, I thought, tried to live like the mice in their own kitchens; to make no noise, to leave no trace, to slip over the surface of things in the dark. The growing piles of ashes and cinders in the back yards were the only evidence that the wasteful, consuming process of life went on at all. On Tuesday nights the Owl Club danced; then there was a little stir in the streets, and here and there one could see a lighted window until midnight. But the next night all was dark again.

After I refused to join "the Owls," as they were called, I made a bold resolve to go to the Saturday night dances at Firemen's Hall. I knew it would be useless to acquaint my elders with any such plan. Grandfather didn't approve of dancing anyway; he would only say that if I wanted to dance I could go to the Masonic Hall, among "the people we knew." It was just my point that I saw altogether too much of the people we knew.

My bedroom was on the ground floor, and as I studied there, I had a stove in it. I used to retire to my room early on Saturday night, change my shirt and collar and put on my Sunday coat. I waited until all was quiet and the old people were asleep, then raised my window, climbed out, and went softly through the yard. The first time I deceived my grandparents I felt rather shabby, perhaps even the second time, but I soon ceased to think about it.

The dance at the Firemen's Hall was the one thing I looked forward to all the week. There I met the same people I used to see at the Vannis' tent.

Sometimes there were Bohemians from Wilber, or German boys who came down on the afternoon freight from Bismarck. Tony and Lena and Tiny were always there, and the three Bohemian Marys, and the Danish laundry girls.

The four Danish girls lived with the laundryman and his wife in their house behind the laundry, with a big garden where the clothes were hung out to dry. The laundryman was a kind, wise old fellow, who paid his girls well, looked out for them, and gave them a good home. He told me once that his own daughter died just as she was getting old enough to help her mother, and that he had been "trying to make up for it ever since." On summer afternoons he used to sit for hours on the sidewalk in front of his laundry, his newspaper lying on his knee, watching his girls through the big open window while they ironed and talked in Danish. The clouds of white dust that blew up the street, the gusts of hot wind that withered his vegetable garden, never disturbed his calm. His droll expression seemed to say that he had found the secret of contentment. Morning and evening he drove about in his spring wagon, distributing freshly ironed clothes, and collecting bags of linen that cried out for his suds and sunny drying-lines. His girls never looked so pretty at the dances as they did standing by the ironing-board, or over the tubs, washing the fine pieces, their white arms and throats bare, their cheeks bright as the brightest wild roses, their gold hair moist with the steam or the heat and curling in little damp spirals about their ears. They had not learned much English, and were not so ambitious as Tony or Lena; but they were kind, simple girls and they were always happy. When one danced with them, one smelled their clean, freshly ironed clothes that had been put away with rosemary leaves from Mr. Jensen's garden.

There were never girls enough to go round at those dances, but every one wanted a turn with Tony and Lena. Lena moved without exertion, rather indolently, and her hand often accented the rhythm softly on her partner's shoulder. She smiled if one spoke to her, but seldom answered. The music seemed to put her into a soft, waking dream, and her violet-colored eyes looked sleepily and confidingly at one from under her long lashes. When she sighed she exhaled a heavy perfume of sachet powder. To dance "Home, Sweet Home," with Lena was like coming in with the tide. She danced every dance like a waltz, and it was always the same waltz—the waltz of coming home to something, of inevitable, fated return. After a while one got restless under it, as one does under the heat of a soft, sultry summer day.

When you spun out into the floor with Tony, you didn't return to anything. You set out every time upon a new adventure. I liked to schottische[2] with her; she had so much spring and variety, and was always putting in new steps and slides. She taught me to dance against and around the hard-and-fast beat of the music. If, instead of going to the end of the railroad, old Mr. Shimerda had stayed in New York and picked up a living with his fiddle, how different Ántonia's life might have been!

Ántonia often went to the dances with Larry Donovan, a passenger conductor who was a kind of professional ladies' man, as we said. I remember how admiringly all the boys looked at her the night she first wore her velveteen dress, made like Mrs. Gardener's black velvet. She was lovely to see,

2. A group dance in the round, like a polka only somewhat slower.

with her eyes shining, and her lips always a little parted when she danced. That constant, dark color in her cheeks never changed.

One evening when Donovan was out on his run, Ántonia came to the hall with Norwegian Anna and her young man, and that night I took her home. When we were in the Cutters' yard, sheltered by the evergreens, I told her she must kiss me good-night.

"Why, sure Jim." A moment later she drew her face away and whispered indignantly, "Why, Jim! You know you ain't right to kiss me like that. I'll tell your grandmother on you!"

"Lena Lingard lets me kiss her," I retorted, "and I'm not half as fond of her as I am of you."

"Lena does?" Tony gasped. "If she's up to any of her nonsense with you, I'll scratch her eyes out!" She took my arm again and we walked out of the gate and up and down the sidewalk. "Now, don't you go and be a fool like some of these town boys. You're not going to sit around here and whittle store-boxes and tell stories all your life. You are going away to school and make something of yourself. I'm just awful proud of you. You won't go and get mixed up with the Swedes, will you?"

"I don't care anything about any of them but you," I said. "And you'll always treat me like a kid, I suppose."

She laughed and threw her arms around me. "I expect I will, but you're a kid I'm awful fond of, anyhow! You can like me all you want to, but if I see you hanging round with Lena much, I'll go to your grandmother, as sure as your name's Jim Burden! Lena's all right, only—well, you know yourself she's soft that way. She can't help it. It's natural to her."

If she was proud of me, I was so proud of her that I carried my head high as I emerged from the dark cedars and shut the Cutters' gate softly behind me. Her warm, sweet face, her kind arms, and the true heart in her; she was, oh, she was still my Ántonia! I looked with contempt at the dark, silent little houses about me as I walked home, and thought of the stupid young men who were asleep in some of them. I knew where the real women were, though I was only a boy; and I would not be afraid of them, either!

I hated to enter the still house when I went home from the dances, and it was long before I could get to sleep. Toward morning I used to have pleasant dreams: sometimes Tony and I were out in the country, sliding down straw-stacks as we used to do; climbing up the yellow mountains over and over, and slipping down the smooth sides into soft piles of chaff.

One dream I dreamed a great many times, and it was always the same. I was in a harvest-field full of shocks, and I was lying against one of them. Lena Lingard came across the stubble barefoot, in a short skirt, with a curved reaping-hook in her hand, and she was flushed like the dawn, with a kind of luminous rosiness all about her. She sat down beside me, turned to me with a soft sigh and said, "Now they are all gone, and I can kiss you as much as I like."

I used to wish I could have this flattering dream about Ántonia, but I never did.

XIII

I noticed one afternoon that grandmother had been crying. Her feet seemed to drag as she moved about the house, and I got up from the table where

I was studying and went to her, asking if she didn't feel well, and if I couldn't help her with her work.

"No, thank you, Jim. I'm troubled, but I guess I'm well enough. Getting a little rusty in the bones, maybe," she added bitterly.

I stood hesitating. "What are you fretting about, grandmother? Has grandfather lost any money?"

"No, it ain't money. I wish it was. But I've heard things. You must 'a' known it would come back to me sometime." She dropped into a chair, and covering her face with her apron, began to cry. "Jim," she said, "I was never one that claimed old folks could bring up their grandchildren. But it came about so; there wasn't any other way for you, it seemed like."

I put my arms around her. I couldn't bear to see her cry.

"What is it, grandmother? Is it the Firemen's dances?"

She nodded.

"I'm sorry I sneaked off like that. But there's nothing wrong about the dances, and I haven't done anything wrong. I like all those country girls, and I like to dance with them. That's all there is to it."

"But it ain't right to deceive us, son, and it brings blame on us. People say you are growing up to be a bad boy, and that ain't just to us."

"I don't care what they say about me, but if it hurts you, that settles it. I won't go to the Firemen's Hall again."

I kept my promise, of course, but I found the spring months dull enough. I sat at home with the old people in the evenings now, reading Latin that was not in our High-School course. I had made up my mind to do a lot of college requirement work in the summer, and to enter the freshman class at the University without conditions in the fall. I wanted to get away as soon as possible.

Disapprobation hurt me, I found,—even that of people whom I did not admire. As the spring came on, I grew more and more lonely, and fell back on the telegrapher and the cigar-maker and his canaries for companionship. I remember I took a melancholy pleasure in hanging a May-basket for Nina Harling that spring. I bought the flowers from an old German woman who always had more window plants than any one else, and spent an afternoon trimming a little work-basket. When dusk came on, and the new moon hung in the sky, I went quietly to the Harlings' front door with my offering, rang the bell, and then ran away as was the custom. Through the willow hedge I could hear Nina's cries of delight, and I felt comforted.

On those warm, soft spring evenings I often lingered downtown to walk home with Frances, and talked to her about my plans and about the reading I was doing. One evening she said she thought Mrs. Harling was not seriously offended with me.

"Mama is as broad-minded as mothers ever are, I guess. But you know she was hurt about Ántonia, and she can't understand why you like to be with Tiny and Lena better than with the girls of your own set."

"Can you?" I asked bluntly.

Frances laughed. "Yes, I think I can. You knew them in the country, and you like to take sides. In some ways you're older than boys of your age. It will be all right with mama after you pass your college examinations and she sees you're in earnest."

"If you were a boy," I persisted, "you wouldn't belong to the Owl Club, either. You'd be just like me."

She shook her head. "I would and I wouldn't. I expect I know the country girls better than you do. You always put a kind of glamour over them. The trouble with you, Jim, is that you're romantic. Mama's going to your Commencement. She asked me the other day if I knew what your oration is to be about. She wants you to do well."

I thought my oration very good. It stated with fervor a great many things I had lately discovered. Mrs. Harling came to the Opera House to hear the Commencement exercises, and I looked at her most of the time while I made my speech. Her keen, intelligent eyes never left my face. Afterward she came back to the dressing-room where we stood, with our diplomas in our hands, walked up to me, and said heartily: "You surprised me, Jim. I didn't believe you could do as well as that. You didn't get that speech out of books." Among my graduation presents there was a silk umbrella from Mrs. Harling, with my name on the handle.

I walked home from the Opera House alone. As I passed the Methodist Church, I saw three white figures ahead of me, pacing up and down under the arching maple trees, where the moonlight filtered through the lush June foliage. They hurried toward me; they were waiting for me—Lena and Tony and Anna Hansen.

"Oh, Jim, it was splendid!" Tony was breathing hard, as she always did when her feelings outran her language. "There ain't a lawyer in Black Hawk could make a speech like that. I just stopped your grandpa and said so to him. He won't tell you, but he told us he was awful surprised himself, didn't he, girls?"

Lena sidled up to me and said teasingly: "What made you so solemn? I thought you were scared. I was sure you'd forget."

Anna spoke wistfully. "It must make you happy, Jim, to have fine thoughts like that in your mind all the time, and to have words to put them in. I always wanted to go to school, you know."

"Oh, I just sat there and wished my papa could hear you! Jim,"—Ántonia took hold of my coat lapels,—"there was something in your speech that made me think so about my papa!"

"I thought about your papa when I wrote my speech, Tony," I said. "I dedicated it to him."

She threw her arms around me, and her dear face was all wet with tears.

I stood watching their white dresses glimmer smaller and smaller down the sidewalk as they went away. I have had no other success that pulled at my heartstrings like that one.

XIV

The day after Commencement I moved my books and desk upstairs, to an empty room where I should be undisturbed, and I fell to studying in earnest. I worked off a year's trigonometry that summer, and began Virgil[3] alone. Morning after morning I used to pace up and down my sunny little room, looking off at the distant river bluffs and the roll of the blond pastures between, scanning the Æneid aloud and committing long passages to memory. Sometimes in the evening Mrs. Harling called to me as I passed her

3. Roman poet (70–19 B.C.E.), most famous for his epic, the *Aeneid*, about the founding of Rome by the Trojan hero Aeneas. The poem was part of a basic classical education in the United States, and Jim Burden would be studying it in its original Latin. See also p. 34, epigraph and n. 1.

gate, and asked me to come in and let her play for me. She was lonely for Charley, she said, and liked to have a boy about. Whenever my grandparents had misgivings, and began to wonder whether I was not too young to go off to college alone, Mrs. Harling took up my cause vigorously. Grandfather had such respect for her judgment that I knew he would not go against her.

I had only one holiday that summer. It was in July. I met Ántonia downtown on Saturday afternoon, and learned that she and Tiny and Lena were going to the river next day with Anna Hansen—the elder[4] was all in bloom now, and Anna wanted to make elder-blow wine.

"Anna's to drive us down in the Marshalls' delivery wagon, and we'll take a nice lunch and have a picnic. Just us; nobody else. Couldn't you happen along, Jim? It would be like old times."

I considered a moment. "Maybe I can, if I won't be in the way."

On Sunday morning I rose early and got out of Black Hawk while the dew was still heavy on the long meadow grasses. It was the high season for summer flowers. The pink bee-bush stood tall along the sandy roadsides, and the cone-flowers and rose mallow grew everywhere. Across the wire fence, in the long grass, I saw a clump of flaming orange-colored milkweed, rare in that part of the State. I left the road and went around through a stretch of pasture that was always cropped short in summer, where the gaillardia came up year after year and matted over the ground with the deep, velvety red that is in Bokhara carpets. The country was empty and solitary except for the larks that Sunday morning, and it seemed to lift itself up to me and to come very close.

The river was running strong for midsummer; heavy rains to the west of us had kept it full. I crossed the bridge and went upstream along the wooded shore to a pleasant dressing-room I knew among the dogwood bushes, all overgrown with wild grapevines. I began to undress for a swim. The girls would not be along yet. For the first time it occurred to me that I would be homesick for that river after I left it. The sandbars, with their clean white beaches and their little groves of willows and cottonwood seedlings, were a sort of No Man's Land, little newly-created worlds that belonged to the Black Hawk boys. Charley Harling and I had hunted through these woods, fished from the fallen logs, until I knew every inch of the river shores and had a friendly feeling for every bar and shallow.

After my swim, while I was playing about indolently in the water, I heard the sound of hoofs and wheels on the bridge. I struck downstream and shouted, as the open spring wagon came into view on the middle span. They stopped the horse, and the two girls in the bottom of the cart stood up, steadying themselves by the shoulders of the two in front, so that they could see me better. They were charming up there, huddled together in the cart and peering down at me like curious deer when they come out of the thicket to drink. I found bottom near the bridge and stood up, waving to them.

"How pretty you look!" I called.

"So do you!" they shouted altogether, and broke into peals of laughter. Anna Hansen shook the reins and they drove on, while I zigzagged back to my inlet and clambered up behind an overhanging elm. I dried myself in the sun, and dressed slowly, reluctant to leave that green enclosure where the sunlight flickered so bright through the grapevine leaves and the woodpecker

4. A shrub that bears flowers used for a mild, sweet wine as well as edible berries.

hammered away in the crooked elm that trailed out over the water. As I went along the road back to the bridge I kept picking off little pieces of scaly chalk from the dried water gullies, and breaking them up in my hands.

When I came upon the Marshalls' delivery horse, tied in the shade, the girls had already taken their baskets and gone down the east road which wound through the sand and scrub. I could hear them calling to each other. The elder bushes did not grow back in the shady ravines between the bluffs, but in the hot, sandy bottoms along the stream, where their roots were always in moisture and their tops in the sun. The blossoms were unusually luxuriant and beautiful that summer.

I followed a cattle path through the thick underbrush until I came to a slope that fell away abruptly to the water's edge. A great chunk of the shore had been bitten out by some spring freshet, and the scar was masked by elder bushes, growing down to the water in flowery terraces. I did not touch them. I was overcome by content and drowsiness and by the warm silence about me. There was no sound but the high, sing-song buzz of wild bees and the sunny gurgle of the water underneath. I peeped over the edge of the bank to see the little stream that made the noise; it flowed along perfectly clear over the sand and gravel, cut off from the muddy main current by a long sandbar. Down there, on the lower shelf of the bank, I saw Ántonia, seated alone under the pagoda-like elders. She looked up when she heard me, and smiled, but I saw that she had been crying. I slid down into the soft sand beside her and asked her what was the matter.

"It makes me homesick, Jimmy, this flower, this smell," she said softly. "We have this flower very much at home, in the old country. It always grew in our yard and my papa had a green bench and a table under the bushes. In summer, when they were in bloom, he used to sit there with his friend that played the trombone. When I was little I used to go down there to hear them talk—beautiful talk, like what I never hear in this country."

"What did they talk about?" I asked her.

She sighed and shook her head. "Oh, I don't know! About music, and the woods, and about God, and when they were young." She turned to me suddenly and looked into my eyes. "You think, Jimmy, that maybe my father's spirit can go back to those old places?"

I told her about the feeling of her father's presence I had on that winter day when my grandparents had gone over to see his dead body and I was left alone in the house. I said I felt sure then that he was on his way back to his own country, and that even now, when I passed his grave, I always thought of him as being among the woods and fields that were so dear to him.

Ántonia had the most trusting, responsive eyes in the world; love and credulousness seemed to look out of them with open faces. "Why didn't you ever tell me that before? It makes me feel more sure for him." After a while she said: "You know, Jim, my father was different from my mother. He did not have to marry my mother, and all his brothers quarreled with him because he did. I used to hear the old people at home whisper about it. They said he could have paid my mother money, and not married her.[5] But he was older than she was, and he was too kind to treat her like that. He lived in his mother's house, and she was a poor girl come in to do the work. After my

5. Implying that he had gotten her pregnant.

father married her, my grandmother never let my mother come into her house again. When I went to my grandmother's funeral was the only time I was ever in my grandmother's house. Don't that seem strange?"

While she talked, I lay back in the hot sand and looked up at the blue sky between the flat bouquets of elder. I could hear the bees humming and singing, but they stayed up in the sun above the flowers and did not come down into the shadow of the leaves. Ántonia seemed to me that day exactly like the little girl who used to come to our house with Mr. Shimerda.

"Some day, Tony, I am going over to your country, and I am going to the little town where you lived. Do you remember all about it?"

"Jim," she said earnestly, "if I was put down there in the middle of the night, I could find my way all over that little town; and along the river to the next town, where my grandmother lived. My feet remember all the little paths through the woods, and where the big roots stick out to trip you. I ain't never forgot my own country."

There was a crackling in the branches above us, and Lena Lingard peered down over the edge of the bank.

"You lazy things!" she cried. "All this elder, and you two lying there! Didn't you hear us calling you?" Almost as flushed as she had been in my dream, she leaned over the edge of the bank and began to demolish our flowery pagoda. I had never seen her so energetic; she was panting with zeal, and the perspiration stood in drops on her short, yielding upper lip. I sprang to my feet and ran up the bank.

It was noon now, and so hot that the dogwoods and scrub-oaks began to turn up the silvery under-side of their leaves, and all the foliage looked soft and wilted. I carried the lunch-basket to the top of one of the chalk bluffs, where even on the calmest days there was always a breeze. The flat-topped, twisted little oaks threw light shadows on the grass. Below us we could see the windings of the river, and Black Hawk, grouped among its trees, and, beyond, the rolling country, swelling gently until it met the sky. We could recognize familiar farmhouses and windmills. Each of the girls pointed out to me the direction in which her father's farm lay, and told me how many acres were in wheat that year and how many in corn.

"My old folks," said Tiny Soderball, "have put in twenty acres of rye. They get it ground at the mill, and it makes nice bread. It seems like my mother ain't been so homesick, ever since father's raised rye flour for her."

"It must have been a trial for our mothers," said Lena, "coming out here and having to do everything different. My mother had always lived in town. She says she started behind in farm-work, and never has caught up."

"Yes, a new country's hard on the old ones, sometimes," said Anna thoughtfully. "My grandmother's getting feeble now, and her mind wanders. She's forgot about this country, and thinks she's at home in Norway. She keeps asking mother to take her down to the waterside and the fish market. She craves fish all the time. Whenever I go home I take her canned salmon and mackerel."

"Mercy, it's hot!" Lena yawned. She was supine under a little oak, resting after the fury of her elder-hunting, and had taken off the high-heeled slippers she had been silly enough to wear. "Come here, Jim. You never got the sand out of your hair." She began to draw her fingers slowly through my hair.

Ántonia pushed her away. "You'll never get it out like that," she said sharply. She gave my head a rough touzling and finished me off with something like a box on the ear. "Lena, you oughtn't to try to wear those slippers any more. They're too small for your feet. You'd better give them to me for Yulka."

"All right," said Lena good-naturedly, tucking her white stockings under her skirt. "You get all Yulka's things, don't you? I wish father didn't have such bad luck with his farm machinery; then I could buy more things for my sisters. I'm going to get Mary a new coat this fall, if the sulky plough's never paid for!"

Tiny asked her why she didn't wait until after Christmas, when coats would be cheaper. "What do you think of poor me?" she added; "with six at home, younger than I am? And they all think I'm rich, because when I go back to the country I'm dressed so fine!" She shrugged her shoulders. "But, you know, my weakness is playthings. I like to buy them playthings better than what they need."

"I know how that is," said Anna. "When we first came here, and I was little, we were too poor to buy toys. I never got over the loss of a doll somebody gave me before we left Norway. A boy on the boat broke her, and I still hate him for it."

"I guess after you got here you had plenty of live dolls to nurse, like me!" Lena remarked cynically.

"Yes, the babies came along pretty fast, to be sure. But I never minded. I was fond of them all. The youngest one, that we didn't any of us want, is the one we love best now."

Lena sighed. "Oh, the babies are all right; if only they don't come in winter. Ours nearly always did. I don't see how mother stood it. I tell you what girls," she sat up with sudden energy, "I'm going to get my mother out of that old sod house where she's lived so many years. The men will never do it. Johnnie, that's my oldest brother, he's wanting to get married now, and build a house for his girl instead of his mother. Mrs. Thomas says she thinks I can move to some other town pretty soon, and go into business for myself. If I don't get into business, I'll maybe marry a rich gambler."

"That would be a poor way to get on," said Anna sarcastically. "I wish I could teach school, like Selma Kronn. Just think! She'll be the first Scandinavian girl to get a position in the High School. We ought to be proud of her."

Selma was a studious girl, who had not much tolerance for giddy things like Tiny and Lena; but they always spoke of her with admiration.

Tiny moved about restlessly, fanning herself with her straw hat. "If I was smart like her, I'd be at my books day and night. But she was born smart—and look how her father's trained her! He was something high up in the old country."

"So was my mother's father," murmured Lena, "but that's all the good it does us! My father's father was smart, too, but he was wild. He married a Lapp.[6] I guess that's what's the matter with me; they say Lapp blood will out."

"A real Lapp, Lena?" I exclaimed. "The kind that wear skins?"

"I don't know if she wore skins, but she was a Lapp all right, and his folks felt dreadful about it. He was sent up north on some Government job he had, and fell in with her. He would marry her."

6. Nomadic people of northern Scandinavia.

"But I thought Lapland women were fat and ugly, and had squint eyes, like Chinese?" I objected.

"I don't know, maybe. There must be something mighty taking about the Lapp girls, though; mother says the Norwegians up north are always afraid their boys will run after them."

In the afternoon, when the heat was less oppressive, we had a lively game of "Pussy Wants a Corner," on the flat bluff-top, with the little trees for bases. Lena was Pussy so often that she finally said she wouldn't play any more. We threw ourselves down on the grass, out of breath.

"Jim," Ántonia said dreamily, "I want you to tell the girls about how the Spanish first came here, like you and Charley Harling used to talk about. I've tried to tell them, but I leave out so much."

They sat under a little oak, Tony resting against the trunk and the other girls leaning against her and each other, and listened to the little I was able to tell them about Coronado[7] and his search for the Seven Golden Cities. At school we were taught that he had not got so far north as Nebraska, but had given up his quest and turned back somewhere in Kansas. But Charley Harling and I had a strong belief that he had been along this very river. A farmer in the county north of ours, when he was breaking sod, had turned up a metal stirrup of fine workmanship, and a sword with a Spanish inscription on the blade. He lent these relics to Mr. Harling, who brought them home with him. Charley and I scoured them, and they were on exhibition in the Harling office all summer. Father Kelly, the priest, had found the name of the Spanish maker on the sword, and an abbreviation that stood for the city of Cordova.[8]

"And that I saw with my own eyes," Ántonia put in triumphantly. "So Jim and Charley were right, and the teachers were wrong!"

The girls began to wonder among themselves. Why had the Spaniards come so far? What must this country have been like, then? Why had Coronado never gone back to Spain, to his riches and his castles and his king? I couldn't tell them. I only knew the school books said he "died in the wilderness, of a broken heart."

"More than him has done that," said Ántonia sadly, and the girls murmured assent.

We sat looking off across the country, watching the sun go down. The curly grass about us was on fire now. The bark of the oaks turned red as copper. There was a shimmer of gold on the brown river. Out in the stream the sandbars glittered like glass, and the light trembled in the willow thickets as if little flames were leaping among them. The breeze sank to stillness. In the ravine a ringdove mourned plaintively, and somewhere off in the bushes an owl hooted. The girls sat listless, leaning against each other. The long fingers of the sun touched their foreheads.

Presently we saw a curious thing: There were no clouds, the sun was going down in a limpid, gold-washed sky. Just as the lower edge of the red disc rested on the high fields against the horizon, a great black figure suddenly appeared on the face of the sun. We sprang to our feet, straining our eyes toward it. In a moment we realized what it was. On some upland farm, a

7. Francisco Vázquez de Coronado (c. 1510–1554), Spanish governor of a Mexican province, who set out in 1840 in quest of the fabled Seven Cities and their immense wealth.

8. In Spain.

plough had been left standing in the field. The sun was sinking just behind it. Magnified across the distance by the horizontal light, it stood out against the sun, was exactly contained within the circle of the disc; the handles, the tongue, the share—black against the molten red. There it was, heroic in size, a picture writing on the sun.[9]

Even while we whispered about it, our vision disappeared; the ball dropped and dropped until the red tip went beneath the earth. The fields below us were dark, the sky was growing pale, and that forgotten plough had sunk back to its own littleness somewhere on the prairie.

XV

Late in August the Cutters went to Omaha for a few days, leaving Ántonia in charge of the house. Since the scandal about the Swedish girl, Wick Cutter could never get his wife to stir out of Black Hawk without him.

The day after the Cutters left, Ántonia came over to see us. Grandmother noticed that she seemed troubled and distracted. "You've got something on your mind, Ántonia," she said anxiously.

"Yes, Mrs. Burden. I couldn't sleep much last night." She hesitated, and then told us how strangely Mr. Cutter had behaved before he went away. He put all the silver in a basket and placed it under her bed, and with it a box of papers which he told her were valuable. He made her promise that she would not sleep away from the house, or be out late in the evening, while he was gone. He strictly forbade her to ask any of the girls she knew to stay with her at night. She would be perfectly safe, he said, as he had just put a new Yale lock on the front door.

Cutter had been so insistent in regard to these details that now she felt uncomfortable about staying there alone. She hadn't liked the way he kept coming into the kitchen to instruct her, or the way he looked at her. "I feel as if he is up to some of his tricks again, and is going to try to scare me, somehow."

Grandmother was apprehensive at once. "I don't think it's right for you to stay there, feeling that way. I suppose it wouldn't be right for you to leave the place alone, either, after giving your word. Maybe Jim would be willing to go over there and sleep, and you could come here nights. I'd feel safer, knowing you were under my own roof. I guess Jim could take care of their silver and old usury notes as well as you could."

Ántonia turned to me eagerly. "Oh, would you, Jim? I'd make up my bed nice and fresh for you. It's a real cool room, and the bed's right next the window. I was afraid to leave the window open last night."

I liked my own room, and I didn't like the Cutters' house under any circumstances; but Tony looked so troubled that I consented to try this arrangement. I found that I slept there as well as anywhere, and when I got home in the morning, Tony had a good breakfast waiting for me. After prayers she sat down at the table with us, and it was like old times in the country.

The third night I spent at the Cutters', I awoke suddenly with the impression that I had heard a door open and shut. Everything was still, however, and I must have gone to sleep again immediately.

9. In Cather's agrarian mythology, the land is conquered or tamed by the plow, not the sword.

The next thing I knew, I felt some one sit down on the edge of the bed. I was only half awake, but I decided that he might take the Cutters' silver, whoever he was. Perhaps if I did not move, he would find it and get out without troubling me. I held my breath and lay absolutely still. A hand closed softly on my shoulder, and at the same moment I felt something hairy and cologne-scented brushing my face. If the room had suddenly been flooded with electric light, I couldn't have seen more clearly the detestable bearded countenance that I knew was bending over me. I caught a handful of whiskers and pulled, shouting something. The hand that held my shoulder was instantly at my throat. The man became insane; he stood over me, choking me with one fist and beating me in the face with the other, hissing and chuckling and letting out a flood of abuse.

"So this is what she's up to when I'm away, is it? Where is she, you nasty whelp, where is she? Under the bed, are you, hussy? I know your tricks! Wait till I get at you! I'll fix this rat you've got in here. He's caught, all right!"

So long as Cutter had me by the throat, there was no chance for me at all. I got hold of his thumb and bent it back, until he let go with a yell. In a bound, I was on my feet, and easily sent him sprawling to the floor. Then I made a dive for the open window, struck the wire screen, knocked it out, and tumbled after it into the yard.

Suddenly I found myself running across the north end of Black Hawk in my nightshirt, just as one sometimes finds one's self behaving in bad dreams. When I got home I climbed in at the kitchen window. I was covered with blood from my nose and lip, but I was too sick to do anything about it. I found a shawl and an overcoat on the hatrack, lay down on the parlor sofa, and in spite of my hurts, went to sleep.

Grandmother found me there in the morning. Her cry of fright awakened me. Truly, I was a battered object. As she helped me to my room, I caught a glimpse of myself in the mirror. My lip was cut and stood out like a snout. My nose looked like a big blue plum, and one eye was swollen shut and hideously discolored. Grandmother said we must have the doctor at once, but I implored her, as I had never begged for anything before, not to send for him. I could stand anything, I told her, so long as nobody saw me or knew what had happened to me. I entreated her not to let grandfather, even, come into my room. She seemed to understand, though I was too faint and miserable to go into explanations. When she took off my nightshirt, she found such bruises on my chest and shoulders that she began to cry. She spent the whole morning bathing and poulticing me, and rubbing me with arnica.[1] I heard Ántonia sobbing outside my door, but I asked grandmother to send her away. I felt that I never wanted to see her again. I hated her almost as much as I hated Cutter. She had let me in for all this disgustingness. Grandmother kept saying how thankful we ought to be that I had been there instead of Ántonia. But I lay with my disfigured face to the wall and felt no particular gratitude. My one concern was that grandmother should keep every one away from me. If the story once got abroad, I would never hear the last of it. I could well imagine what the old men down at the drug-store would do with such a theme.

1. A medicinal herb; here in the form of a soothing lotion.

While grandmother was trying to make me comfortable, grandfather went to the depot and learned that Wick Cutter had come home on the night express from the east, and had left again on the six o'clock train for Denver that morning. The agent said his face was striped with court-plaster, and he carried his left hand in a sling. He looked so used up, that the agent asked him what had happened to him since ten o'clock the night before; whereat Cutter began to swear at him and said he would have him discharged for incivility.

That afternoon, while I was asleep, Ántonia took grandmother with her, and went over to the Cutters' to pack her trunk. They found the place locked up, and they had to break the window to get into Ántonia's bedroom. There everything was in shocking disorder. Her clothes had been taken out of her closet, thrown into the middle of the room, and trampled and torn. My own garments had been treated so badly that I never saw them again; grandmother burned them in the Cutters' kitchen range.

While Ántonia was packing her trunk and putting her room in order, to leave it, the front-door bell rang violently. There stood Mrs. Cutter,—locked out, for she had no key to the new lock—her head trembling with rage. "I advised her to control herself, or she would have a stroke," grandmother said afterwards.

Grandmother would not let her see Ántonia at all, but made her sit down in the parlor while she related to her just what had occurred the night before. Ántonia was frightened, and was going home to stay for a while, she told Mrs. Cutter; it would be useless to interrogate the girl, for she knew nothing of what had happened.

Then Mrs. Cutter told her story. She and her husband had started home from Omaha together the morning before. They had to stop over several hours at Waymore Junction to catch the Black Hawk train. During the wait, Cutter left her at the depot and went to the Waymore bank to attend to some business. When he returned, he told her that he would have to stay overnight there, but she could go on home. He bought her ticket and put her on the train. She saw him slip a twenty-dollar bill into her handbag with her ticket. That bill, she said, should have aroused her suspicions at once—but did not.

The trains are never called at little junction towns; everybody knows when they come in. Mr. Cutter showed his wife's ticket to the conductor, and settled her in her seat before the train moved off. It was not until nearly nightfall that she discovered she was on the express bound for Kansas City, that her ticket was made out to that point, and that Cutter must have planned it so. The conductor told her the Black Hawk train was due at Waymore twelve minutes after the Kansas City train left. She saw at once that her husband had played this trick in order to get back to Black Hawk without her. She had no choice but to go on to Kansas City and take the first fast train for home.

Cutter could have got home a day earlier than his wife by any one of a dozen simpler devices; he could have left her in the Omaha hotel, and said he was going on to Chicago for a few days. But apparently it was part of his fun to outrage her feelings as much as possible.

"Mr. Cutter will pay for this, Mrs. Burden. He will pay!" Mrs. Cutter avouched, nodding her horselike head and rolling her eyes.

Grandmother said she hadn't a doubt of it.

Certainly Cutter liked to have his wife think him a devil. In some way he depended upon the excitement he could arouse in her hysterical nature. Perhaps he got the feeling of being a rake more from his wife's rage and amazement than from any experiences of his own. His zest in debauchery might wane, but never Mrs. Cutter's belief in it. The reckoning with his wife at the end of an escapade was something he counted on—like the last powerful liqueur after a long dinner. The one excitement he really couldn't do without was quarreling with Mrs. Cutter!

Book III. Lena Lingard

I

At the University I had the good fortune to come immediately under the influence of a brilliant and inspiring young scholar. Gaston Cleric had arrived in Lincoln only a few weeks earlier than I, to begin his work as head of the Latin Department. He came West at the suggestion of his physicians, his health having been enfeebled by a long illness in Italy. When I took my entrance examinations he was my examiner, and my course was arranged under his supervision.

I did not go home for my first summer vacation, but stayed in Lincoln, working off a year's Greek, which had been my only condition on entering the Freshman class. Cleric's doctor advised against his going back to New England, and except for a few weeks in Colorado, he, too, was in Lincoln all that summer. We played tennis, read, and took long walks together. I shall always look back on that time of mental awakening as one of the happiest in my life. Gaston Cleric introduced me to the world of ideas; when one first enters that world everything else fades for a time, and all that went before is as if it had not been. Yet I found curious survivals; some of the figures of my old life seemed to be waiting for me in the new.

In those days there were many serious young men among the students who had come up to the University from the farms and the little towns scattered over the thinly settled State. Some of those boys came straight from the cornfields with only a summer's wages in their pockets, hung on through the four years, shabby and underfed, and completed the course by really heroic self-sacrifice. Our instructors were oddly assorted; wandering pioneer schoolteachers, stranded ministers of the Gospel, a few enthusiastic young men just out of graduate schools. There was an atmosphere of endeavor, of expectancy and bright hopefulness about the young college that had lifted its head from the prairie only a few years before.

Our personal life was as free as that of our instructors. There were no college dormitories; we lived where we could and as we could. I took rooms with an old couple, early settlers in Lincoln, who had married off their children and now lived quietly in their house at the edge of town, near the open country. The house was inconveniently situated for students, and on that account I got two rooms for the price of one. My bedroom, originally a linen closet, was unheated and was barely large enough to contain my cot bed, but it enabled me to call the other room my study. The dresser, and the great walnut wardrobe which held all my clothes, even my hats and shoes, I had pushed out of the way, and I considered them non-existent, as children eliminate incongruous objects when they are playing house. I worked at a commodious green-topped table placed directly in front of the west window which looked out over the prairie. In the corner at my right were all my books, in shelves I had made and painted myself. On the blank wall at my left the dark, old-fashioned wall-paper was covered by a large map of ancient Rome, the work of some German scholar. Cleric had ordered it for me when he was sending for books from abroad. Over the bookcase hung a photograph of the Tragic Theater at Pompeii,[2] which he had given me from his collection.

When I sat at work I half faced a deep, upholstered chair which stood at the end of my table, its high back against the wall. I had bought it with great care. My instructor sometimes looked in upon me when he was out for an evening tramp, and I noticed that he was more likely to linger and become talkative if I had a comfortable chair for him to sit in, and if he found a bottle of Bénédictine[3] and plenty of the kind of cigarettes he liked, at his elbow. He was, I had discovered, parsimonious about small expenditures—a trait absolutely inconsistent with his general character. Sometimes when he came he was silent and moody, and after a few sarcastic remarks went away again, to tramp the streets of Lincoln, which were almost as quiet and oppressively domestic as those of Black Hawk. Again, he would sit until nearly midnight, talking about Latin and English poetry, or telling me about his long stay in Italy.

I can give no idea of the peculiar charm and vividness of his talk. In a crowd he was nearly always silent. Even for his classroom he had no platitudes, no stock of professorial anecdotes. When he was tired his lectures were clouded, obscure, elliptical; but when he was interested they were wonderful. I believe that Gaston Cleric narrowly missed being a great poet, and I have sometimes thought that his bursts of imaginative talk were fatal to his poetic gift. He squandered too much in the heat of personal communication. How often I have seen him draw his dark brows together, fix his eyes upon some object on the wall or a figure in the carpet, and then flash into the lamplight the very image that was in his brain. He could bring the drama of antique life before one out of the shadows—white figures against blue backgrounds. I shall never forget his face as it looked one night when he told me about the solitary day he spent among the sea temples at Paestum:[4] the soft wind blowing through the roofless columns, the birds flying low over the flowering marsh grasses, the changing lights on the silver, cloud-hung mountains. He had willfully stayed the short summer night there, wrapped in his coat and rug, watching the constellations on their path down the sky until "the bride of old Tithonus"[5] rose out of the sea, and the mountains stood sharp in the dawn. It was there he caught the fever which held him back on the eve of his departure for Greece and of which he lay ill so long in Naples. He was still, indeed, doing penance for it.

2. Ancient city in southwest Italy, which was buried by an eruption of Mount Vesuvius in 79 C.E.; its buildings were preserved in superb condition.

3. After-dinner liqueur made in France by Benedictine monks.

4. Coastal town in southern Italy containing Roman temples from the 5th and 6th centuries B.C.E.

5. I.e., Eos, the goddess of the dawn. In Greek myth Tithonus was the son of the king of Troy.

I remember vividly another evening, when something led us to talk of Dante's veneration for Virgil.[6] Cleric went through canto after canto of the "Commedia," repeating the discourse between Dante and his "sweet teacher," while his cigarette burned itself out unheeded between his long fingers. I can hear him now, speaking the lines of the poet Statius,[7] who spoke for Dante: *"I was famous on earth with the name which endures longest and honors most. The seeds of my ardor were the sparks from that divine flame whereby more than a thousand have kindled; I speak of the Æneid, mother to me and nurse to me in poetry."*

Although I admired scholarship so much in Cleric, I was not deceived about myself; I knew that I should never be a scholar. I could never lose myself for long among impersonal things. Mental excitement was apt to send me with a rush back to my own naked land and the figures scattered upon it. While I was in the very act of yearning toward the new forms that Cleric brought up before me, my mind plunged away from me, and I suddenly found myself thinking of the places and people of my own infinitesimal past. They stood out strengthened and simplified now, like the image of the plough against the sun. They were all I had for an answer to the new appeal. I begrudged the room that Jake and Otto and Russian Peter took up in my memory, which I wanted to crowd with other things. But whenever my consciousness was quickened, all those early friends were quickened within it, and in some strange way they accompanied me through all my new experiences. They were so much alive in me that I scarcely stopped to wonder whether they were alive anywhere else, or how.

II

One March evening in my Sophomore year I was sitting alone in my room after supper. There had been a warm thaw all day, with mushy yards and little streams of dark water gurgling cheerfully into the streets out of old snow-banks. My window was open, and the earthy wind blowing through made me indolent. On the edge of the prairie, where the sun had gone down, the sky was turquoise blue, like a lake, with gold light throbbing in it. Higher up, in the utter clarity of the western slope, the evening star hung like a lamp suspended by silver chains—like the lamp engraved upon the title-page of old Latin texts, which is always appearing in new heavens, and waking new desires in men. It reminded me, at any rate, to shut my window and light my wick in answer. I did so regretfully, and the dim objects in the room emerged from the shadows and took their place about me with the helpfulness which custom breeds.

I propped my book open and stared listlessly at the page of the Georgics where tomorrow's lesson began. It opened with the melancholy reflection that, in the lives of mortals, the best days are the first to flee. *"Optima dies . . . prima fugit."* I turned back to the beginning of the third book, which we had read in class that morning. *"Primus ego in patriam mecum . . . deducam Musas"*; "for I shall be the first, if I live, to bring the Muse into my

6. Dante Alighieri (1265–1321), Italian poet, famous for the *Divine Comedy,* a long poem recounting the poet's journey through Hell (*Inferno*), Purgatory (*Purgatorio*), and Heaven (*Paradiso*). Virgil is his guide in Hell and Purgatory.

7. Roman poet (c. 45–96 C.E.) who, in Cantos 21 and 22 of the *Purgatorio,* meets Virgil and speaks the quoted lines.

country." Cleric had explained to us that "patria" here meant, not a nation or even a province, but the little rural neighborhood on the Mincio where the poet was born. This was not a boast, but a hope, at once bold and devoutly humble, that he might bring the Muse (but lately come to Italy from her cloudy Grecian mountains), not to the capital, the *palatia Romana,* but to his own little "country"; to his father's fields, "sloping down to the river and to the old beech trees with broken tops."

Cleric said he thought Virgil, when he was dying at Brindisi, must have remembered that passage. After he had faced the bitter fact that he was to leave the Æneid unfinished, and had decreed that the great canvas, crowded with figures of gods and men, should be burned rather than survive him unperfected, then his mind must have gone back to the perfect utterance of the Georgics, where the pen was fitted to the matter as the plough is to the furrow; and he must have said to himself with the thankfulness of a good man, "I was the first to bring the Muse into my country."

We left the classroom quietly, conscious that we had been brushed by the wing of a great feeling, though perhaps I alone knew Cleric intimately enough to guess what that feeling was. In the evening, as I sat staring at my book, the fervor of his voice stirred through the quantities on the page before me. I was wondering whether that particular rocky strip of New England coast about which he had so often told me was Cleric's *patria*. Before I had got far with my reading I was disturbed by a knock. I hurried to the door and when I opened it saw a woman standing in the dark hall.

"I expect you hardly know me, Jim."

The voice seemed familiar, but I did not recognize her until she stepped into the light of my doorway and I beheld—Lena Lingard! She was so quietly conventionalized by city clothes that I might have passed her on the street without seeing her. Her black suit fitted her figure smoothly, and a black lace hat, with pale-blue forget-me-nots, sat demurely on her yellow hair.

I led her toward Cleric's chair, the only comfortable one I had, questioning her confusedly.

She was not disconcerted by my embarrassment. She looked about her with the naïve curiosity I remembered so well. "You are quite comfortable here, aren't you? I live in Lincoln now, too, Jim. I'm in business for myself. I have a dressmaking shop in the Raleigh Block, out on O Street. I've made a real good start."

"But, Lena, when did you come?"

"Oh, I've been here all winter. Didn't your grandmother ever write you? I've thought about looking you up lots of times. But we've all heard what a studious young man you've got to be, and I felt bashful. I didn't know whether you'd be glad to see me." She laughed her mellow, easy laugh, that was either very artless or very comprehending, one never quite knew which. "You seem the same, though,—except you're a young man, now, of course. Do you think I've changed?"

"Maybe you're prettier—though you were always pretty enough. Perhaps it's your clothes that make a difference."

"You like my new suit? I have to dress pretty well in my business." She took off her jacket and sat more at ease in her blouse, of some soft, flimsy silk. She was already at home in my place, had slipped quietly into it, as she did into everything. She told me her business was going well, and she had saved a little money.

"This summer I'm going to build the house for mother I've talked about so long. I won't be able to pay up on it at first, but I want her to have it before she is too old to enjoy it. Next summer I'll take her down new furniture and carpets, so she'll have something to look forward to all winter."

I watched Lena sitting there so smooth and sunny and well cared-for, and thought of how she used to run barefoot over the prairie until after the snow began to fly, and how Crazy Mary chased her round and round the cornfields. It seemed to me wonderful that she should have got on so well in the world. Certainly she had no one but herself to thank for it.

"You must feel proud of yourself, Lena," I said heartily. "Look at me; I've never earned a dollar, and I don't know that I'll ever be able to."

"Tony says you're going to be richer than Mr. Harling some day. She's always bragging about you, you know."

"Tell me, how *is* Tony?"

"She's fine. She works for Mrs. Gardener at the hotel now. She's housekeeper. Mrs. Gardener's health isn't what it was, and she can't see after everything like she used to. She has great confidence in Tony. Tony's made it up with the Harlings, too. Little Nina is so fond of her that Mrs. Harling kind of overlooked things."

"Is she still going with Larry Donovan?"

"Oh, that's on, worse than ever! I guess they're engaged. Tony talks about him like he was president of the railroad. Everybody laughs about it, because she was never a girl to be soft. She won't hear a word against him. She's so sort of innocent."

I said I didn't like Larry, and never would.

Lena's face dimpled. "Some of us could tell her things, but it wouldn't do any good. She'd always believe him. That's Ántonia's failing, you know; if she once likes people, she won't hear anything against them."

"I think I'd better go home and look after Ántonia," I said.

"I think you had." Lena looked up at me in frank amusement. "It's a good thing the Harlings are friendly with her again. Larry's afraid of them. They ship so much grain, they have influence with the railroad people. What are you studying?" She leaned her elbows on the table and drew my book toward her. I caught a faint odor of violet sachet. "So that's Latin, is it? It looks hard. You do go to the theater sometimes, though, for I've seen you there. Don't you just love a good play, Jim? I can't stay at home in the evening if there's one in town. I'd be willing to work like a slave, it seems to me, to live in a place where there are theaters."

"Let's go to a show together sometime. You are going to let me come to see you, aren't you?"

"Would you like to? I'd be ever so pleased. I'm never busy after six o'clock, and I let my sewing girls go at half-past five. I board, to save time, but sometimes I cook a chop for myself, and I'd be glad to cook one for you. Well,"—she began to put on her white gloves,—"it's been awful good to see you, Jim."

"You needn't hurry, need you? You've hardly told me anything yet."

"We can talk when you come to see me. I expect you don't often have lady visitors. The old woman downstairs didn't want to let me come up very much.

I told her I was from your home town, and had promised your grandmother to come and see you. How surprised Mrs. Burden would be!" Lena laughed softly as she rose.

When I caught up my hat she shook her head. "No, I don't want you to go with me. I'm to meet some Swedes at the drug-store. You wouldn't care for them. I wanted to see your room so I could write Tony all about it, but I must tell her how I left you right here with your books. She's always so afraid some one will run off with you!" Lena slipped her silk sleeves into the jacket I held for her, smoothed it over her person, and buttoned it slowly. I walked with her to the door. "Come and see me sometimes when you're lonesome. But maybe you have all the friends you want. Have you?" She turned her soft cheek to me. "Have you?" she whispered teasingly in my ear. In a moment I watched her fade down the dusky stairway.

When I turned back to my room the place seemed much pleasanter than before. Lena had left something warm and friendly in the lamplight. How I loved to hear her laugh again! It was so soft and unexcited and appreciative—gave a favorable interpretation to everything. When I closed my eyes I could hear them all laughing—the Danish laundry girls and the three Bohemian Marys. Lena had brought them all back to me. It came over me, as it had never done before, the relation between girls like those and the poetry of Virgil. If there were no girls like them in the world, there would be no poetry. I understood that clearly, for the first time. This revelation seemed to me inestimably precious. I clung to it as if it might suddenly vanish.

As I sat down to my book at last, my old dream about Lena coming across the harvest field in her short skirt seemed to me like the memory of an actual experience. It floated before me on the page like a picture, and underneath it stood the mournful line: *Optima dies . . . prima fugit.*

III

In Lincoln the best part of the theatrical season came late, when the good companies stopped off there for one-night stands, after their long runs in New York and Chicago. That spring Lena went with me to see Joseph Jefferson in "Rip Van Winkle," and to a war play called "Shenandoah."[8] She was inflexible about paying for her own seat; said she was in business now, and she wouldn't have a schoolboy spending his money on her. I liked to watch a play with Lena; everything was wonderful to her, and everything was true. It was like going to revival meetings with some one who was always being converted. She handed her feelings over to the actors with a kind of fatalistic resignation. Accessories of costume and scene meant much more to her than to me. She sat entranced through "Robin Hood"[9] and hung upon the lips of the contralto who sang, "Oh, Promise Me!"

Toward the end of April, the billboards, which I watched anxiously in those days, bloomed out one morning with gleaming white posters on which two

8. A four-act play (1889), by American playwright Bronson Howard (1842–1908), about lovers separated by the Civil War. Jefferson (1829–1905), a well-known American comedian who from 1865 on mainly played the role of Rip Van Winkle in a stage version of Washington Irving's 1819 story.

9. A three-act comic opera (1890), by American Reginald De Koven (1859–1920). "Oh, Promise Me!" was its most popular song.

names were impressively printed in blue Gothic letters: the name of an actress of whom I had often heard, and the name "Camille."[1]

I called at the Raleigh Block for Lena on Saturday evening, and we walked down to the theater. The weather was warm and sultry and put us both in a holiday humor. We arrived early, because Lena liked to watch the people come in. There was a note on the programme, saying that the "incidental music" would be from the opera "Traviata,"[2] which was made from the same story as the play. We had neither of us read the play, and we did not know what it was about—though I seemed to remember having heard it was a piece in which great actresses shone. "The Count of Monte Cristo," which I had seen James O'Neill play that winter, was by the only Alexandre Dumas[3] I knew. This play, I saw, was by his son, and I expected a family resemblance. A couple of jack-rabbits, run in off the prairie, could not have been more innocent of what awaited them than were Lena and I.

Our excitement began with the rise of the curtain, when the moody Varville, seated before the fire, interrogated Nanine. Decidedly, there was a new tang about this dialogue. I had never heard in the theater lines that were alive, that presupposed and took for granted, like those which passed between Varville and Marguerite in the brief encounter before her friends entered.[4] This introduced the most brilliant, worldly, the most enchantingly gay scene I had ever looked upon. I had never seen champagne bottles opened on the stage before—indeed, I had never seen them opened anywhere. The memory of that supper makes me hungry now; the sight of it then, when I had only a students' boarding-house dinner behind me, was delicate torment. I seem to remember gilded chairs and tables (arranged hurriedly by footmen in white gloves and stockings), linen of dazzling whiteness, glittering glass, silver dishes, a great bowl of fruit, and the reddest of roses. The room was invaded by beautiful women and dashing young men, laughing and talking together. The men were dressed more or less after the period in which the play was written; the women were not. I saw no inconsistency. Their talk seemed to open to one the brilliant world in which they lived; every sentence made one older and wiser, every pleasantry enlarged one's horizon. One could experience excess and satiety without the inconvenience of learning what to do with one's hands in a drawing-room! When the characters all spoke at once and I missed some of the phrases they flashed at each other, I was in misery. I strained my ears and eyes to catch every exclamation.

The actress who played Marguerite was even then old-fashioned, though historic. She had been a member of Daly's[5] famous New York company, and afterward a "star" under his direction. She was a woman who could not be taught, it is said, though she had a crude natural force which carried with

1. *La Dame aux Camélias* (The lady of the camellias) was a play based on the novel (1848) by the French writer Alexandre Dumas, *fils* (1824–1895). It was brought to the United States in an English version in 1853. The actress is probably Clara Morris (1848–1925).

2. Verdi's 1853 opera was also based on the Dumas novel.

3. French writer (*père,* 1802–1870) who published *The Count of Monte Cristo* in 1844–45. O'Neill (1847–1920), father of Eugene O'Neill, performed the leading role for more than a quarter century, starting in 1883.

4. The story is about the romance between Marguerite Gautier, a woman of the world, and the young Armand Duval. Armand's father persuades her to give Armand up. Other characters are Varville, her patron; Nanine, her maid; and Gaston, a friend.

5. John Augustin Daly (1838–1899), playwright, producer, and director in the American theater.

people whose feelings were accessible and whose taste was not squeamish. She was already old, with a ravaged countenance and a physique curiously hard and stiff. She moved with difficulty—I think she was lame—I seem to remember some story about a malady of the spine. Her Armand was disproportionately young and slight, a handsome youth, perplexed in the extreme. But what did it matter? I believed devoutly in her power to fascinate him, in her dazzling loveliness. I believed her young, ardent, reckless, disillusioned, under sentence, feverish, avid of pleasure. I wanted to cross the footlights and help the slim-waisted Armand in the frilled shirt to convince her that there was still loyalty and devotion in the world. Her sudden illness, when the gayety was at its height, her pallor, the handkerchief she crushed against her lips, the cough she smothered under the laughter while Gaston kept playing the piano lightly—it all wrung my heart. But not so much as her cynicism in the long dialogue with her lover which followed. How far was I from questioning her unbelief! While the charmingly sincere young man pleaded with her—accompanied by the orchestra in the old "Traviata" duet, *"misterioso, misterioso!"*—she maintained her bitter skepticism, and the curtain fell on her dancing recklessly with the others, after Armand had been sent away with his flower.

Between the acts we had no time to forget. The orchestra kept sawing away at the "Traviata" music, so joyous and sad, so thin and far-away, so clap-trap and yet so heart-breaking. After the second act I left Lena in tearful contemplation of the ceiling, and went out into the lobby to smoke. As I walked about there I congratulated myself that I had not brought some Lincoln girl who would talk during the waits about the Junior dances, or whether the cadets would camp at Plattsmouth. Lena was at least a woman, and I was a man.

Through the scene between Marguerite and the elder Duval, Lena wept unceasingly, and I sat helpless to prevent the closing of that chapter of idyllic love, dreading the return of the young man whose ineffable happiness was only to be the measure of his fall.

I suppose no woman could have been further in person, voice, and temperament from Dumas' appealing heroine than the veteran actress who first acquainted me with her. Her conception of the character was as heavy and uncompromising as her diction; she bore hard on the idea and on the consonants. At all times she was highly tragic, devoured by remorse. Lightness of stress or behavior was far from her. Her voice was heavy and deep: "Ar-r-r-mond!" she would begin, as if she were summoning him to the bar of Judgment. But the lines were enough. She had only to utter them. They created the character in spite of her.

The heartless world which Marguerite reentered with Varville had never been so glittering and reckless as on the night when it gathered in Olympe's salon for the fourth act. There were chandeliers hung from the ceiling, I remember, many servants in livery, gaming-tables where the men played with piles of gold, and a staircase down which the guests made their entrance. After all the others had gathered round the card tables, and young Duval had been warned by Prudence, Marguerite descended the staircase with Varville; such a cloak, such a fan, such jewels—and her face! One knew at a glance how it was with her. When Armand, with the terrible words, "Look, all of you, I owe this woman nothing!" flung the gold and bank-notes at the half-swooning Marguerite, Lena cowered beside me and covered her face with her hands.

The curtain rose on the bedroom scene. By this time there wasn't a nerve in me that hadn't been twisted. Nanine alone could have made me cry. I loved Nanine tenderly; and Gaston, how one clung to that good fellow! The New Year's presents were not too much; nothing could be too much now. I wept unrestrainedly. Even the handkerchief in my breast-pocket, worn for elegance and not at all for use, was wet through by the time that moribund woman sank for the last time into the arms of her lover.

When we reached the door of the theater, the streets were shining with rain. I had prudently brought along Mrs. Harling's useful Commencement present, and I took Lena home under its shelter. After leaving her, I walked slowly out into the country part of the town where I lived. The lilacs were all blooming in the yards, and the smell of them after the rain, of the new leaves and the blossoms together, blew into my face with a sort of bitter sweetness. I tramped through the puddles and under the showery trees, mourning for Marguerite Gauthier as if she had died only yesterday, sighing with the spirit of 1840, which had sighed so much, and which had reached me only that night, across long years and several languages, through the person of an infirm old actress. The idea is one that no circumstances can frustrate. Wherever and whenever that piece is put on, it is April.

IV

How well I remember the stiff little parlor where I used to wait for Lena: the hard horse-hair furniture, bought at some auction sale, the long mirror, the fashion-plates on the wall. If I sat down even for a moment I was sure to find threads and bits of colored silk clinging to my clothes after I went away. Lena's success puzzled me. She was so easy-going; had none of the push and self-assertiveness that get people ahead in business. She had come to Lincoln, a country girl, with no introductions except to some cousins of Mrs. Thomas who lived there, and she was already making clothes for the women of "the young married set." She evidently had great natural aptitude for her work. She knew, as she said, "what people looked well in." She never tired of poring over fashion books. Sometimes in the evening I would find her alone in her work-room, draping folds of satin on a wire figure, with a quite blissful expression of countenance. I couldn't help thinking that the years when Lena literally hadn't enough clothes to cover herself might have something to do with her untiring interest in dressing the human figure. Her clients said that Lena "had style," and overlooked her habitual inaccuracies. She never, I discovered, finished anything by the time she had promised, and she frequently spent more money on materials than her customer had authorized. Once, when I arrived at six o'clock, Lena was ushering out a fidgety mother and her awkward, overgrown daughter. The woman detained Lena at the door to say apologetically:—

"You'll try to keep it under fifty for me, won't you, Miss Lingard? You see, she's really too young to come to an expensive dressmaker, but I knew you could do more with her than anybody else."

"Oh, that will be all right, Mrs. Herron. I think we'll manage to get a good effect," Lena replied blandly.

I thought her manner with her customers very good, and wondered where she had learned such self-possession.

Sometimes after my morning classes were over, I used to encounter Lena downtown, in her velvet suit and a little black hat, with a veil tied smoothly over her face, looking as fresh as the spring morning. Maybe she would be carrying home a bunch of jonquils or a hyacinth plant. When we passed a candy store her footsteps would hesitate and linger. "Don't let me go in," she would murmur. "Get me by if you can." She was very fond of sweets, and was afraid of growing too plump.

We had delightful Sunday breakfasts together at Lena's. At the back of her long work-room was a bay-window, large enough to hold a box-couch and a reading-table. We breakfasted in this recess, after drawing the curtains that shut out the long room, with cutting-tables and wire women and sheet-draped garments on the walls. The sunlight poured in, making everything on the table shine and glitter and the flame of the alcohol lamp disappear altogether. Lena's curly black water-spaniel, Prince, breakfasted with us. He sat beside her on the couch and behaved very well until the Polish violin-teacher across the hall began to practice, when Prince would growl and sniff the air with disgust. Lena's landlord, old Colonel Raleigh, had given her the dog, and at first she was not at all pleased. She had spent too much of her life taking care of animals to have much sentiment about them. But Prince was a knowing little beast, and she grew fond of him. After breakfast I made him do his lessons; play dead dog, shake hands, stand up like a soldier. We used to put my cadet cap on his head—I had to take military drill at the University—and give him a yard-measure to hold with his front leg. His gravity made us laugh immoderately.

Lena's talk always amused me. Ántonia had never talked like the people about her. Even after she learned to speak English readily there was always something impulsive and foreign in her speech. But Lena had picked up all the conventional expressions she heard at Mrs. Thomas's dressmaking shop. Those formal phrases, the very flower of small-town proprieties, and the flat commonplaces, nearly all hypocritical in their origin, became very funny, very engaging, when they were uttered in Lena's soft voice, with her caressing intonation and arch naïveté. Nothing could be more diverting than to hear Lena, who was almost as candid as Nature, call a leg a "limb" or a house a "home."

We used to linger a long while over our coffee in that sunny corner. Lena was never so pretty as in the morning; she wakened fresh with the world every day, and her eyes had a deeper color then, like the blue flowers that are never so blue as when they first open. I could sit idle all through a Sunday morning and look at her. Ole Benson's behavior was now no mystery to me.

"There was never any harm in Ole," she said once. "People needn't have troubled themselves. He just liked to come over and sit on the draw-side and forget about his bad luck. I liked to have him. Any company's welcome when you're off with cattle all the time."

"But wasn't he always glum?" I asked. "People said he never talked at all."

"Sure he talked, in Norwegian. He'd been a sailor on an English boat and had seen lots of queer places. He had wonderful tattoos. We used to sit and look at them for hours; there wasn't much to look at out there. He was like a picture book. He had a ship and a strawberry girl on one arm, and on the other a girl standing before a little house, with a fence and gate and all, waiting for her sweetheart. Farther up his arm, her sailor had come back and was kissing her. 'The Sailor's Return,' he called it."

I admitted it was no wonder Ole liked to look at a pretty girl once in a while, with such a fright at home.

"You know," Lena said confidentially, "he married Mary because he thought she was strong-minded and would keep him straight. He never could keep straight on shore. The last time he landed in Liverpool he'd been out on a two years' voyage. He was paid off one morning, and by the next he hadn't a cent left, and his watch and compass were gone. He'd got with some women, and they'd taken everything. He worked his way to this country on a little passenger boat. Mary was a stewardess, and she tried to convert him on the way over. He thought she was just the one to keep him steady. Poor Ole! He used to bring me candy from town, hidden in his feed-bag. He couldn't refuse anything to a girl. He'd have given away his tattoos long ago, if he could. He's one of the people I'm sorriest for."

If I happened to spend an evening with Lena and stayed late, the Polish violin-teacher across the hall used to come out and watch me descend the stairs, muttering so threateningly that it would have been easy to fall into a quarrel with him. Lena had told him once that she liked to hear him practice, so he always left his door open, and watched who came and went.

There was a coolness between the Pole and Lena's landlord on her account. Old Colonel Raleigh had come to Lincoln from Kentucky and invested an inherited fortune in real estate, at the time of inflated prices. Now he sat day after day in his office in the Raleigh Block, trying to discover where his money had gone and how he could get some of it back. He was a widower, and found very little congenial companionship in this casual Western city. Lena's good looks and gentle manners appealed to him. He said her voice reminded him of Southern voices, and he found as many opportunities of hearing it as possible. He painted and papered her rooms for her that spring, and put in a porcelain bathtub in place of the tin one that had satisfied the former tenant. While these repairs were being made, the old gentleman often dropped in to consult Lena's preferences. She told me with amusement how Ordinsky, the Pole, had presented himself at her door one evening, and said that if the landlord was annoying her by his attentions, he would promptly put a stop to it.

"I don't exactly know what to do about him," she said, shaking her head, "he's so sort of wild all the time. I wouldn't like to have him say anything rough to that nice old man. The Colonel is long-winded, but then I expect he's lonesome. I don't think he cares much for Ordinsky, either. He said once that if I had any complaints to make of my neighbors, I mustn't hesitate."

One Saturday evening when I was having supper with Lena we heard a knock at her parlor door, and there stood the Pole, coatless, in a dress shirt and collar. Prince dropped on his paws and began to growl like a mastiff, while the visitor apologized, saying that he could not possibly come in thus attired, but he begged Lena to lend him some safety pins.

"Oh, you'll have to come in, Mr. Ordinsky, and let me see what's the matter." She closed the door behind him. "Jim, won't you make Prince behave?"

I rapped Prince on the nose, while Ordinsky explained that he had not had his dress clothes on for a long time, and to-night, when he was going to play for a concert, his waistcoat had split down the back. He thought he could pin it together until he got it to a tailor.

Lena took him by the elbow and turned him round. She laughed when she saw the long gap in the satin. "You could never pin that, Mr. Ordinsky. You've kept it folded too long, and the goods is all gone along the crease. Take it off. I can put a new piece of lining-silk in there for you in ten minutes." She disappeared into her work-room with the vest, leaving me to confront the Pole, who stood against the door like a wooden figure. He folded his arms and glared at me with his excitable, slanting brown eyes. His head was the shape of a chocolate drop, and was covered with dry, straw-colored hair that fuzzed up about his pointed crown. He had never done more than mutter at me as I passed him, and I was surprised when he now addressed me.

"Miss Lingard," he said haughtily, "is a young woman for whom I have the utmost, the utmost respect."

"So have I," I said coldly.

He paid no heed to my remark, but began to do rapid finger-exercises on his shirt-sleeves, as he stood with tightly folded arms.

"Kindness of heart," he went on, staring at the ceiling, "sentiment, are not understood in a place like this. The noblest qualities are ridiculed. Grinning college boys, ignorant and conceited, what do they know of delicacy!"

I controlled my features and tried to speak seriously.

"If you mean me, Mr. Ordinsky, I have known Miss Lingard a long time, and I think I appreciate her kindness. We come from the same town, and we grew up together."

His gaze traveled slowly down from the ceiling and rested on me. "Am I to understand that you have this young woman's interests at heart? That you do not wish to compromise her?"

"That's a word we don't use much here, Mr. Ordinsky. A girl who makes her own living can ask a college boy to supper without being talked about. We take some things for granted."

"Then I have misjudged you, and I ask your pardon,"—he bowed gravely. "Miss Lingard," he went on, "is an absolutely trustful heart. She has not learned the hard lessons of life. As for you and me, *noblesse oblige,*"[6]—he watched me narrowly.

Lena returned with the vest. "Come in and let us look at you as you go out, Mr. Ordinsky. I've never seen you in your dress suit," she said as she opened the door for him.

A few moments later he reappeared with his violin case—a heavy muffler about his neck and thick woolen gloves on his bony hands. Lena spoke encouragingly to him, and he went off with such an important, professional air, that we fell to laughing as soon as we had shut the door. "Poor fellow," Lena said indulgently, "he takes everything so hard."

After that Ordinsky was friendly to me, and behaved as if there were some deep understanding between us. He wrote a furious article, attacking the musical taste of the town, and asked me to do him a great service by taking it to the editor of the morning paper. If the editor refused to print it, I was to tell him that he would be answerable to Ordinsky "in person." He declared that he would never retract one word, and that he was quite prepared to

6. Rank carries its obligations (French).

lose all his pupils. In spite of the fact that nobody ever mentioned his article to him after it appeared—full of typographical errors which he thought intentional—he got a certain satisfaction from believing that the citizens of Lincoln had meekly accepted the epithet "coarse barbarians." "You see how it is," he said to me, "where there is no chivalry, there is no *amour propre*."[7] When I met him on his rounds now, I thought he carried his head more disdainfully than ever, and strode up the steps of front porches and rang doorbells with more assurance. He told Lena he would never forget how I had stood by him when he was "under fire."

All this time, of course, I was drifting. Lena had broken up my serious mood. I wasn't interested in my classes. I played with Lena and Prince, I played with the Pole, I went buggy-riding with the old Colonel, who had taken a fancy to me and used to talk to me about Lena and the "great beauties" he had known in his youth. We were all three in love with Lena.

Before the first of June, Gaston Cleric was offered an instructorship at Harvard College, and accepted it. He suggested that I should follow him in the fall, and complete my course at Harvard. He had found out about Lena—not from me—and he talked to me seriously.

"You won't do anything here now. You should either quit school and go to work, or change your college and begin again in earnest. You won't recover yourself while you are playing about with this handsome Norwegian. Yes, I've seen her with you at the theater. She's very pretty, and perfectly irresponsible, I should judge."

Cleric wrote my grandfather that he would like to take me East with him. To my astonishment, grandfather replied that I might go if I wished. I was both glad and sorry on the day when the letter came. I stayed in my room all evening and thought things over; I even tried to persuade myself that I was standing in Lena's way—it is so necessary to be a little noble!—and that if she had not me to play with, she would probably marry and secure her future.

The next evening I went to call on Lena. I found her propped up on the couch in her bay window, with her foot in a big slipper. An awkward little Russian girl whom she had taken into her work-room had dropped a flat-iron on Lena's toe. On the table beside her there was a basket of early summer flowers which the Pole had left after he heard of the accident. He always managed to know what went on in Lena's apartment.

Lena was telling me some amusing piece of gossip about one of her clients, when I interrupted her and picked up the flower basket.

"This old chap will be proposing to you some day, Lena."

"Oh, he has—often!" she murmured.

"What! After you've refused him?"

"He doesn't mind that. It seems to cheer him to mention the subject. Old men are like that, you know. It makes them feel important to think they're in love with somebody."

"The Colonel would marry you in a minute. I hope you won't marry some old fellow; not even a rich one."

Lena shifted her pillows and looked up at me in surprise. "Why, I'm not going to marry anybody. Didn't you know that?"

7. Self-respect (French).

"Nonsense, Lena. That's what girls say, but you know better. Every handsome girl like you marries, of course."

She shook her head. "Not me."

"But why not? What makes you say that?" I persisted.

Lena laughed. "Well, it's mainly because I don't want a husband. Men are all right for friends, but as soon as you marry them they turn into cranky old fathers, even the wild ones. They begin to tell you what's sensible and what's foolish, and want you to stick at home all the time. I prefer to be foolish when I feel like it, and be accountable to nobody."

"But you'll be lonesome. You'll get tired of this sort of life, and you'll want a family."

"Not me. I like to be lonesome. When I went to work for Mrs. Thomas I was nineteen years old, and I had never slept a night in my life when there weren't three in the bed. I never had a minute to myself except when I was off with the cattle."

Usually, when Lena referred to her life in the country at all, she dismissed it with a single remark, humorous or mildly cynical. But to-night her mind seemed to dwell on those early years. She told me she couldn't remember a time when she was so little that she wasn't lugging a heavy baby about, helping to wash for babies, trying to keep their little chapped hands and faces clean. She remembered home as a place where there were always too many children, a cross man, and work piling up around a sick woman.

"It wasn't mother's fault. She would have made us comfortable if she could. But that was no life for a girl! After I began to herd and milk I could never get the smell of the cattle off me. The few underclothes I had I kept in a cracker box. On Saturday nights, after everybody was in bed, then I could take a bath if I wasn't too tired. I could make two trips to the windmill to carry water, and heat it in the wash-boiler on the stove. While the water was heating, I could bring in a washtub out of the cave, and take my bath in the kitchen. Then I could put on a clean nightgown and get into bed with two others, who likely hadn't had a bath unless I'd given it to them. You can't tell me anything about family life. I've had plenty to last me."

"But it's not all like that," I objected.

"Near enough. It's all being under somebody's thumb. What's on your mind, Jim? Are you afraid I'll want you to marry me some day?"

Then I told her I was going away.

"What makes you want to go away, Jim? Haven't I been nice to you?"

"You've been just awfully good to me, Lena," I blurted. "I don't think about much else. I never shall think about much else while I'm with you. I'll never settle down and grind if I stay here. You know that." I dropped down beside her and sat looking at the floor. I seemed to have forgotten all my reasonable explanations.

Lena drew close to me, and the little hesitation in her voice that had hurt me was not there when she spoke again.

"I oughtn't to begun it, ought I?" she murmured. "I oughn't to have gone to see you that first time. But I did want to. I guess I've always been a little foolish about you. I don't know what first put it into my head, unless it was Ántonia, always telling me I mustn't be up to any of my nonsense with you. I let you alone for a long while, though, didn't I?"

She was a sweet creature to those she loved, that Lena Lingard!

At last she sent me away with her soft, slow, renunciatory kiss. "You aren't sorry I came to see you that time?" she whispered. "It seemed so natural. I used to think I'd like to be your first sweetheart. You were such a funny kid!" She always kissed one as if she were sadly and wisely sending one away forever.

We said many good-byes before I left Lincoln, but she never tried to hinder me or hold me back. "You are going, but you haven't gone yet, have you?" she used to say.

My Lincoln chapter closed abruptly. I went home to my grandparents for a few weeks, and afterward visited my relatives in Virginia until I joined Cleric in Boston. I was then nineteen years old.

Book IV. The Pioneer Woman's Story

I

Two years after I left Lincoln I completed my academic course at Harvard. Before I entered the Law School I went home for the summer vacation. On the night of my arrival Mrs. Harling and Frances and Sally came over to greet me. Everything seemed just as it used to be. My grandparents looked very little older. Frances Harling was married now, and she and her husband managed the Harling interests in Black Hawk. When we gathered in grandmother's parlor, I could hardly believe that I had been away at all. One subject, however, we avoided all evening.

When I was walking home with Frances, after we had left Mrs. Harling at her gate, she said simply, "You know, of course, about poor Ántonia."

Poor Ántonia! Every one would be saying that now, I thought bitterly. I replied that grandmother had written me how Ántonia went away to marry Larry Donovan at some place where he was working; that he had deserted her, and that there was now a baby. This was all I knew.

"He never married her," Frances said. "I haven't seen her since she came back. She lives at home, on the farm, and almost never comes to town. She brought the baby in to show it to mama once. I'm afraid she's settled down to be Ambrosch's drudge for good."

I tried to shut Ántonia out of my mind. I was bitterly disappointed in her. I could not forgive her for becoming an object of pity, while Lena Lingard, for whom people had always foretold trouble, was now the leading dressmaker of Lincoln, much respected in Black Hawk. Lena gave her heart away when she felt like it, but she kept her head for her business and had got on in the world.

Just then it was the fashion to speak indulgently of Lena and severely of Tiny Soderball, who had quietly gone West to try her fortune the year before. A Black Hawk boy, just back from Seattle, brought the news that Tiny had not gone to the coast on a venture, as she had allowed people to think, but with very definite plans. One of the roving promoters that used to stop at Mrs. Gardener's hotel owned idle property along the waterfront in Seattle, and he had offered to set Tiny up in business in one of his empty buildings. She was now conducting a sailors' lodging-house. This, every one said, would be the end of Tiny. Even if she had begun by running a decent place, she couldn't keep it up; all sailors' boarding-houses were alike.

When I thought about it, I discovered that I had never known Tiny as well as I knew the other girls. I remembered her tripping briskly about the dining-room on her high heels, carrying a big tray full of dishes, glancing rather pertly at the spruce traveling men, and contemptuously at the scrubby ones—who were so afraid of her that they didn't dare to ask for two kinds of pie. Now it occurred to me that perhaps the sailors, too, might be afraid of Tiny. How astonished we would have been, as we sat talking about her on Frances Harling's front porch, if we could have known what her future was really to be! Of all the girls and boys who grew up together in Black Hawk, Tiny Soderball was to lead the most adventurous life and to achieve the most solid worldly success.

This is what actually happened to Tiny: While she was running her lodging-house in Seattle, gold was discovered in Alaska.[8] Miners and sailors came back from the North with wonderful stories and pouches of gold. Tiny saw it and weighed it in her hands. That daring which nobody had ever suspected in her, awoke. She sold her business and set out for Circle City, in company with a carpenter and his wife whom she had persuaded to go along with her. They reached Skaguay in a snowstorm, went in dog sledges over the Chilkoot Pass, and shot the Yukon in flatboats. They reached Circle City on the very day when some Siwash Indians came into the settlement with the report that there had been a rich gold strike farther up the river, on a certain Klondike Creek. Two days later Tiny and her friends, and nearly every one else in Circle City, started for the Klondike fields on the last steamer that went up the Yukon before it froze for the winter. That boatload of people founded Dawson City. Within a few weeks there were fifteen hundred homeless men in camp. Tiny and the carpenter's wife began to cook for them, in a tent. The miners gave her a lot, and the carpenter put up a log hotel for her. There she sometimes fed a hundred and fifty men a day. Miners came in on snowshoes from their placer claims twenty miles away to buy fresh bread from her, and paid for it in gold.

That winter Tiny kept in her hotel a Swede whose legs had been frozen one night in a storm when he was trying to find his way back to his cabin. The poor fellow thought it great good fortune to be cared for by a woman, and a woman who spoke his own tongue. When he was told that his feet must be amputated, he said he hoped he would not get well; what could a working-man do in this hard world without feet? He did, in fact, die from the operation, but not before he had deeded Tiny Soderball his claim on Hunker Creek. Tiny sold her hotel, invested half her money in Dawson building lots, and with the rest she developed her claim. She went off into the wilds and lived on it. She bought other claims from discouraged miners, traded or sold them on percentages.

After nearly ten years in the Klondike, Tiny returned, with a considerable fortune, to live in San Francisco. I met her in Salt Lake City in 1908. She was a thin, hard-faced woman, very well-dressed, very reserved in manner. Curiously enough, she reminded me of Mrs. Gardener, for whom she had worked in Black Hawk so long ago. She told me about some of the desperate chances she had taken in the gold country, but the thrill of them was quite gone. She said frankly that nothing interested her much now but making money. The

8. In the winter of 1897–98.

only two human beings of whom she spoke with any feeling were the Swede, Johnson, who had given her his claim, and Lena Lingard. She had persuaded Lena to come to San Francisco and go into business there.

"Lincoln was never any place for her," Tiny remarked. "In a town of that size Lena would always be gossiped about. Frisco's the right field for her. She has a fine class of trade. Oh, she's just the same as she always was! She's careless, but she's level-headed. She's the only person I know who never gets any older. It's fine for me to have her there; somebody who enjoys things like that. She keeps an eye on me and won't let me be shabby. When she thinks I need a new dress, she makes it and sends it home—with a bill that's long enough, I can tell you!"

Tiny limped slightly when she walked. The claim on Hunker Creek took toll from its possessors. Tiny had been caught in a sudden turn of weather, like poor Johnson. She lost three toes from one of those pretty little feet that used to trip about Black Hawk in pointed slippers and striped stockings. Tiny mentioned this mutilation quite casually—didn't seem sensitive about it. She was satisfied with her success, but not elated. She was like some one in whom the faculty of becoming interested is worn out.

II

Soon after I got home that summer I persuaded my grandparents to have their photographs taken, and one morning I went into the photographer's shop to arrange for sittings. While I was waiting for him to come out of his developing-room, I walked about trying to recognize the likenesses on his walls: girls in Commencement dresses, country brides and grooms holding hands, family groups of three generations. I noticed, in a heavy frame, one of those depressing "crayon enlargements" often seen in farmhouse parlors, the subject being a round-eyed baby in short dresses. The photographer came out and gave a constrained, apologetic laugh.

"That's Tony Shimerda's baby. You remember her; she used to be the Harling's Tony. Too bad! She seems proud of the baby, though; wouldn't hear to a cheap frame for the picture. I expect her brother will be in for it Saturday."

I went away feeling that I must see Ántonia again. Another girl would have kept her baby out of sight, but Tony, of course, must have its picture on exhibition at the town photographer's, in a great gilt frame. How like her! I could forgive her, I told myself, if she hadn't thrown herself away on such a cheap sort of fellow.

Larry Donovan was a passenger conductor, one of those train-crew aristocrats who are always afraid that some one may ask them to put up a car-window, and who, if requested to perform such a menial service, silently point to the button that calls the porter. Larry wore this air of official aloofness even on the street, where there were no car-windows to compromise his dignity. At the end of his run he stepped indifferently from the train along with the passengers, his street hat on his head and his conductor's cap in an alligator-skin bag, went directly into the station and changed his clothes. It was a matter of the utmost importance to him never to be seen in his blue trousers away from his train. He was usually cold and distant with men, but with all women he had a silent, grave familiarity, a special handshake, accompanied by a significant, deliberate look. He took women, married or single, into his confidence; walked them up and down in the moonlight, telling them what a mistake he had made by not entering the office branch of the service, and how much better fitted he was to fill the post of General Passenger Agent in Denver than the roughshod man who then bore that title. His unappreciated worth was the tender secret Larry shared with his sweethearts, and he was always able to make some foolish heart ache over it.

As I drew near home that morning, I saw Mrs. Harling out in her yard, digging round her mountain-ash tree. It was a dry summer, and she had now no boy to help her. Charley was off in his battleship, cruising somewhere on the Caribbean sea. I turned in at the gate—it was with a feeling of pleasure that I opened and shut that gate in those days; I liked the feel of it under my hand. I took the spade away from Mrs. Harling, and while I loosened the earth around the tree, she sat down on the steps and talked about the oriole family that had a nest in its branches.

"Mrs. Harling," I said presently, "I wish I could find out exactly how Ántonia's marriage fell through."

"Why don't you go out and see your grandfather's tenant, the Widow Steavens? She knows more about it than anybody else. She helped Ántonia get ready to be married, and she was there when Ántonia came back. She took care of her when the baby was born. She could tell you everything. Besides, the Widow Steavens is a good talker, and she has a remarkable memory."

III

On the first or second day of August I got a horse and cart and set out for the high country, to visit the Widow Steavens. The wheat harvest was over, and here and there along the horizon I could see black puffs of smoke from the steam thrashing-machines. The old pasture land was now being broken up into wheatfields and cornfields, the red grass was disappearing, and the whole face of the country was changing. There were wooden houses where the old sod dwellings used to be, and little orchards, and big red barns; all this meant happy children, contented women, and men who saw their lives coming to a fortunate issue. The windy springs and the blazing summers, one after another, had enriched and mellowed that flat tableland; all the human effort that had gone into it was coming back in long, sweeping lines of fertility. The changes seemed beautiful and harmonious to me; it was like watching the growth of a great man or of a great idea. I recognized every tree and sandbank and rugged draw. I found that I remembered the conformation of the land as one remembers the modeling of human faces.

When I drew up to our old windmill, the Widow Steavens came out to meet me. She was brown as an Indian woman, tall, and very strong. When I was little, her massive head had always seemed to me like a Roman senator's. I told her at once why I had come.

"You'll stay the night with us, Jimmy? I'll talk to you after supper. I can take more interest when my work is off my mind. You've no prejudice against hot biscuit for supper? Some have, these days."

While I was putting my horse away I heard a rooster squawking. I looked at my watch and sighed; it was three o'clock, and I knew that I must eat him at six.

After supper Mrs. Steavens and I went upstairs to the old sitting-room, while her grave, silent brother remained in the basement to read his farm papers. All the windows were open. The white summer moon was shining outside, the windmill was pumping lazily in the light breeze. My hostess put the lamp on a stand in the corner, and turned it low because of the heat. She sat down in her favorite rocking-chair and settled a little stool comfortably under her tired feet. "I'm troubled with callouses, Jim; getting old," she sighed cheerfully. She crossed her hands in her lap and sat as if she were at a meeting of some kind.

"Now, it's about that dear Ántonia you want to know? Well, you've come to the right person. I've watched her like she'd been my own daughter.

"When she came home to do her sewing that summer before she was to be married, she was over here about every day. They've never had a sewing machine at the Shimerdas', and she made all her things here. I taught her hemstitching, and I helped her to cut and fit. She used to sit there at that machine by the window, pedaling the life out of it—she was so strong—and always singing them queer Bohemian songs, like she was the happiest thing in the world.

" 'Ántonia,' I used to say, 'don't run that machine so fast. You won't hasten the day none that way.'

"Then she'd laugh and slow down for a little, but she'd soon forget and begin to pedal and sing again. I never saw a girl work harder to go to housekeeping right and well-prepared. Lovely table linen the Harlings had given her, and Lena Lingard had sent her nice things from Lincoln. We hemstitched all the tablecloths and pillow-cases, and some of the sheets. Old Mrs. Shimerda knit yards and yards of lace for her underclothes. Tony told me just how she meant to have everything in her house. She'd even bought silver spoons and forks, and kept them in her trunk. She was always coaxing brother to go to the post-office. Her young man did write her real often, from the different towns along his run.

"The first thing that troubled her was when he wrote that his run had been changed, and they would likely have to live in Denver. 'I'm a country girl,' she said, 'and I doubt if I'll be able to manage so well for him in a city. I was counting on keeping chickens, and maybe a cow.' She soon cheered up, though.

"At last she got the letter telling her when to come. She was shaken by it; she broke the seal and read it in this room. I suspected then that she'd begun to get faint-hearted, waiting; though she'd never let me see it.

"Then there was a great time of packing. It was in March, if I remember rightly, and a terrible muddy, raw spell, with the roads bad for hauling her things to town. And here let me say, Ambrosch did the right thing. He went to Black Hawk and bought her a set of plated silver in a purple velvet box, good enough for her station. He gave her three hundred dollars in money; I saw the check. He'd collected her wages all those first years she worked out, and it was but right. I shook him by the hand in this room. 'You're behaving like a man, Ambrosch,' I said, 'and I'm glad to see it, son.'

" 'Twas a cold, raw day he drove her and her three trunks into Black Hawk to take the night train for Denver—the boxes had been shipped before. He stopped the wagon here, and she ran in to tell me good-bye. She threw her arms around me and kissed me, and thanked me for all I'd done for her. She was so happy she was crying and laughing at the same time, and her red cheeks was all wet with rain.

"'You're surely handsome enough for any man,' I said, looking her over.

"She laughed kind of flighty like, and whispered, 'Good-bye, dear house!' and then ran out to the wagon. I expect she meant that for you and your grandmother, as much as for me, so I'm particular to tell you. This house had always been a refuge to her.

"Well, in a few days we had a letter saying she got to Denver safe, and he was there to meet her. They were to be married in a few days. He was trying to get his promotion before he married, she said. I didn't like that, but I said nothing. The next week Yulka got a postal card, saying she was 'well and happy.' After that we heard nothing. A month went by, and old Mrs. Shimerda began to get fretful. Ambrosch was as sulky with me as if I'd picked out the man and arranged the match.

"One night brother William came in and said that on his way back from the fields he had passed a livery team from town, driving fast out the west road. There was a trunk on the front seat with the driver, and another behind. In the back seat there was a woman all bundled up; but for all her veils, he thought 't was Ántonia Shimerda, or Ántonia Donovan, as her name ought now to be.

"The next morning I got brother to drive me over. I can walk still, but my feet ain't what they used to be, and I try to save myself. The lines outside the Shimerdas' house was full of washing, though it was the middle of the week. As we got nearer I saw a sight that made my heart sink—all those underclothes we'd put so much work on, out there swinging in the wind. Yulka came bringing a dishpanful of wrung clothes, but she darted back into the house like she was loath to see us. When I went in, Ántonia was standing over the tubs, just finishing up a big washing. Mrs. Shimerda was going about her work, talking and scolding to herself. She didn't so much as raise her eyes. Tony wiped her hand on her apron and held it out to me, looking at me steady but mournful. When I took her in my arms she drew away. 'Don't, Mrs. Steavens,' she says, 'you'll make me cry, and I don't want to.'

"I whispered and asked her to come out of doors with me. I knew she couldn't talk free before her mother. She went out with me, bareheaded, and we walked up toward the garden.

"'I'm not married, Mrs. Steavens,' she says to me very quiet and natural-like, 'and I ought to be.'

"'Oh, my child,' says I, 'what's happened to you? Don't be afraid to tell me!'

"She sat down on the draw-side, out of sight of the house. 'He's run away from me,' she said. 'I don't know if he ever meant to marry me.'

"'You mean he's thrown up his job and quit the country?' says I.

"'He didn't have any job. He'd been fired; blacklisted for knocking down fares.[9] I didn't know. I thought he hadn't been treated right. He was sick when I got there. He'd just come out of the hospital. He lived with me till my money gave out, and afterwards I found he hadn't really been hunting work at all. Then he just didn't come back. One nice fellow at the station told me, when I kept going to look for him, to give it up. He said he was afraid Larry'd gone bad and wouldn't come back any more. I guess he's gone to Old Mexico.

9. Selling tickets at reduced prices and keeping the money for himself.

The conductors get rich down there, collecting half-fares off the natives and robbing the company. He was always talking about fellows who had got ahead that way.'

"I asked her, of course, why she didn't insist on a civil marriage at once—that would have given her some hold on him. She leaned her head on her hands, poor child, and said, 'I just don't know, Mrs. Steavens. I guess my patience was wore out, waiting so long. I thought if he saw how well I could do for him, he'd want to stay with me.'

"Jimmy, I sat right down on that bank beside her and made lament. I cried like a young thing. I couldn't help it. I was just about heart-broke. It was one of them lovely warm May days, and the wind was blowing and the colts jumping around in the pastures; but I felt bowed with despair. My Ántonia, that had so much good in her, had come home disgraced. And that Lena Lingard, that was always a bad one, say what you will, had turned out so well, and was coming home here every summer in her silks and her satins, and doing so much for her mother. I give credit where credit is due, but you know well enough, Jim Burden, there is a great difference in the principles of those two girls. And here it was the good one that had come to grief! I was poor comfort to her. I marveled at her calm. As we went back to the house, she stopped to feel of her clothes to see if they was drying well, and seemed to take pride in their whiteness—she said she'd been living in a brick block, where she didn't have proper conveniences to wash them.

"The next time I saw Ántonia, she was out in the fields ploughing corn. All that spring and summer she did the work of a man on the farm; it seemed to be an understood thing. Ambrosch didn't get any other hand to help him. Poor Marek had got violent and been sent away to an institution a good while back. We never even saw any of Tony's pretty dresses. She didn't take them out of her trunks. She was quiet and steady. Folks respected her industry and tried to treat her as if nothing had happened. They talked, to be sure; but not like they would if she'd put on airs. She was so crushed and quiet that nobody seemed to want to humble her. She never went anywhere. All that summer she never once came to see me. At first I was hurt, but I got to feel that it was because this house reminded her of too much. I went over there when I could, but the times when she was in from the fields were the times when I was busiest here. She talked about the grain and the weather as if she'd never had another interest, and if I went over at night she always looked dead weary. She was afflicted with toothache; one tooth after another ulcerated, and she went about with her face swollen half the time. She wouldn't go to Black Hawk to a dentist for fear of meeting people she knew. Ambrosch had got over his good spell long ago, and was always surly. Once I told him he ought not to let Ántonia work so hard and pull herself down. He said, 'If you put that in her head, you better stay home.' And after that I did.

"Ántonia worked on through harvest and thrashing, though she was too modest to go out thrashing for the neighbors, like when she was young and free. I didn't see much of her until late that fall when she begun to herd Ambrosch's cattle in the open ground north of here, up toward the big dog town. Sometimes she used to bring them over the west hill, there, and I would run to meet her and walk north a piece with her. She had thirty cattle in her bunch; it had been dry, and the pasture was short, or she wouldn't have brought them so far.

"It was a fine open fall, and she liked to be alone. While the steers grazed, she used to sit on them grassy banks along the draws and sun herself for hours. Sometimes I slipped up to visit with her, when she hadn't gone too far.

"'It does seem like I ought to make lace, or knit like Lena used to,' she said one day, 'but if I start to work, I look around and forget to go on. It seems such a little while ago when Jim Burden and I was playing all over this country. Up here I can pick out the very places where my father used to stand. Sometimes I feel like I'm not going to live very long, so I'm just enjoying every day of this fall.'

"After the winter begun she wore a man's long overcoat and boots, and a man's felt hat with a wide brim. I used to watch her coming and going, and I could see that her steps were getting heavier. One day in December, the snow began to fall. Late in the afternoon I saw Ántonia driving her cattle homeward across the hill. The snow was flying round her and she bent to face it, looking more lonesome-like to me than usual. 'Deary me,' I says to myself, 'the girl's stayed out too late. It'll be dark before she gets them cattle put into the corral.' I seemed to sense she'd been feeling too miserable to get up and drive them.

"That very night, it happened. She got her cattle home, turned them into the corral, and went into the house, into her room behind the kitchen, and shut the door. There, without calling to anybody, without a groan, she lay down on the bed and bore her child.

"I was lifting supper when old Mrs. Shimerda came running down the basement stairs, out of breath and screeching:—

"'Baby come, baby come!' she says. 'Ambrosch much like devil!'

"Brother William is surely a patient man. He was just ready to sit down to a hot supper after a long day in the fields. Without a word he rose and went down to the barn and hooked up his team. He got us over there as quick as it was humanly possible. I went right in, and began to do for Ántonia; but she laid there with her eyes shut and took no account of me. The old woman got a tubful of warm water to wash the baby. I overlooked what she was doing and I said out loud:—

"'Mrs. Shimerda, don't you put that strong yellow soap near that baby. You'll blister its little skin.' I was indignant.

"'Mrs. Steavens,' Ántonia said from the bed, 'if you'll look in the top tray of my trunk, you'll see some fine soap.' That was the first word she spoke.

"After I'd dressed the baby, I took it out to show it to Ambrosch. He was muttering behind the stove and wouldn't look at it.

"'You'd better put it out in the rain barrel,' he says.

"'Now, see here, Ambrosch,' says I, 'there's a law in this land, don't forget that. I stand here a witness that this baby has come into the world sound and strong, and I intend to keep an eye on what befalls it.' I pride myself I cowed him.

"Well, I expect you're not much interested in babies, but Ántonia's got on fine. She loved it from the first as dearly as if she'd had a ring on her finger, and was never ashamed of it. It's a year and eight months old now, and no baby was ever better cared-for. Ántonia is a natural-born mother. I wish she could marry and raise a family, but I don't know as there's much chance now."

I slept that night in the room I used to have when I was a little boy, with the summer wind blowing in at the windows, bringing the smell of the ripe fields. I lay awake and watched the moonlight shining over the barn and the stacks and the pond, and the windmill making its old dark shadow against the blue sky.

IV

The next afternoon I walked over to the Shimerdas'. Yulka showed me the baby and told me that Ántonia was shocking wheat on the southwest quarter. I went down across the fields, and Tony saw me from a long way off. She stood still by her shocks, leaning on her pitchfork, watching me as I came. We met like the people in the old song, in silence, if not in tears. Her warm hand clasped mine.

"I thought you'd come, Jim. I heard you were at Mrs. Steavens's last night. I've been looking for you all day."

She was thinner than I had ever seen her, and looked, as Mrs. Steavens said, "worked down," but there was a new kind of strength in the gravity of her face, and her color still gave her that look of deep-seated health and ardor. Still? Why, it flashed across me that though so much had happened in her life and in mine, she was barely twenty-four years old.

Ántonia stuck her fork in the ground, and instinctively we walked toward that unploughed patch at the crossing of the roads as the fittest place to talk to each other. We sat down outside the sagging wire fence that shut Mr. Shimerda's plot off from the rest of the world. The tall red grass had never been cut there. It had died down in winter and come up again in the spring until it was as thick and shrubby as some tropical gardengrass. I found myself telling her everything: why I had decided to study law and to go into the law office of one of my mother's relatives in New York City; about Gaston Cleric's death from pneumonia last winter, and the difference it had made in my life. She wanted to know about my friends and my way of living, and my dearest hopes.

"Of course it means you are going away from us for good," she said with a sigh. "But that don't mean I'll lose you. Look at my papa here; he's been dead all these years, and yet he is more real to me than almost anybody else. He never goes out of my life. I talk to him and consult him all the time. The older I grow, the better I know him and the more I understand him."

She asked me whether I had learned to like big cities. "I'd always be miserable in a city. I'd die of lonesomeness. I like to be where I know every stack and tree, and where all the ground is friendly. I want to live and die here. Father Kelly says everybody's put into this world for something, and I know what I've got to do. I'm going to see that my little girl has a better chance than ever I had. I'm going to take care of that girl, Jim."

I told her I knew she would. "Do you know, Ántonia, since I've been away, I think of you more often than of any one else in this part of the world. I'd have liked to have you for a sweetheart, or a wife, or my mother or my sister—anything that a woman can be to a man. The idea of you is a part of my mind; you influence my likes and dislikes, all my tastes, hundreds of times when I don't realize it. You really are a part of me."

She turned her bright, believing eyes to me, and the tears came up in them slowly. "How can it be like that, when you know so many people, and when I've disappointed you so? Ain't it wonderful, Jim, how much people can mean to each other? I'm so glad we had each other when we were little. I can't wait till my little girl's old enough to tell her about all the things we used to do. You'll always remember me when you think about old times, won't you? And I guess everybody thinks about old times, even the happiest people."

As we walked homeward across the fields, the sun dropped and lay like a great golden globe in the low west. While it hung there, the moon rose in the east, as big as a cartwheel, pale silver and streaked with rose color, thin as a bubble or a ghost-moon. For five, perhaps ten minutes, the two luminaries confronted each other across the level land, resting on opposite edges of the world. In that singular light every little tree and shock of wheat, every sunflower stalk and clump of snow-on-the-mountain, drew itself up high and pointed; the very clods and furrows in the fields seemed to stand up sharply. I felt the old pull of the earth, the solemn magic that comes out of those fields at night-fall. I wished I could be a little boy again, and that my way could end there.

We reached the edge of the field, where our ways parted. I took her hands and held them against my breast, feeling once more how strong and warm and good they were, those brown hands, and remembering how many kind things they had done for me. I held them now a long while, over my heart. About us it was growing darker and darker, and I had to look hard to see her face, which I meant always to carry with me; the closest, realest face, under all the shadows of women's faces, at the very bottom of my memory.

"I'll come back," I said earnestly, through the soft, intrusive darkness.

"Perhaps you will"—I felt rather than saw her smile. "But even if you don't, you're here, like my father. So I won't be lonesome."

As I went back alone over that familiar road, I could almost believe that a boy and girl ran along beside me, as our shadows used to do, laughing and whispering to each other in the grass.

Book V. Cuzak's Boys

I

I told Ántonia I would come back, but life intervened, and it was twenty years before I kept my promise. I heard of her from time to time; that she married, very soon after I last saw her, a young Bohemian, a cousin of Anton Jelinek; that they were poor, and had a large family. Once when I was abroad I went into Bohemia, and from Prague I sent Ántonia some photographs of her native village. Months afterward came a letter from her, telling me the names and ages of her many children, but little else; signed, "Your old friend, Ántonia Cuzak." When I met Tiny Soderball in Salt Lake, she told me that Ántonia had not "done very well"; that her husband was not a man of much force, and she had had a hard life. Perhaps it was cowardice that kept me away so long. My business took me West several times every year, and it was always in the back of my mind that I would stop in Nebraska some day and go to see Ántonia. But I kept putting it off until the next trip. I did not want to find her aged and broken; I really dreaded it. In the course of twenty crowded years one parts with many illusions. I did not wish to lose the early ones. Some memories are realities, and are better than anything that can ever happen to one again.

I owe it to Lena Lingard that I went to see Ántonia at last. I was in San Francisco two summers ago when both Lena and Tiny Soderball were in town. Tiny lives in a house of her own, and Lena's shop is in an apartment house just around the corner. It interested me, after so many years, to see the two women together. Tiny audits Lena's accounts occasionally, and invests her money for her; and Lena, apparently, takes care that Tiny doesn't grow too miserly. "If there's anything I can't stand," she said to me in Tiny's presence, "it's a shabby rich woman." Tiny smiled grimly and assured me that Lena would never be either shabby or rich. "And I don't want to be," the other agreed complacently.

Lena gave me a cheerful account of Ántonia and urged me to make her a visit.

"You really ought to go, Jim. It would be such a satisfaction to her. Never mind what Tiny says. There's nothing the matter with Cuzak. You'd like him. He isn't a hustler, but a rough man would never have suited Tony. Tony has nice children—ten or eleven of them by this time, I guess. I shouldn't care for a family of that size myself, but somehow it's just right for Tony. She'd love to show them to you."

On my way East I broke my journey at Hastings, in Nebraska, and set off with an open buggy and a fairly good livery team to find the Cuzak farm. At a little past midday, I knew I must be nearing my destination. Set back on a swell of land at my right, I saw a wide farmhouse, with a red barn and an ash grove, and cattle yards in front that sloped down to the high road. I drew up my horses and was wondering whether I should drive in here, when I heard low voices. Ahead of me, in a plum thicket beside the road, I saw two boys bending over a dead dog. The little one, not more than four or five, was on his knees, his hands folded, and his close-clipped, bare head drooping forward in deep dejection. The other stood beside him, a hand on his shoulder, and was comforting him in a language I had not heard for a long while. When I stopped my horses opposite them, the older boy took his brother by the hand and came toward me. He, too, looked grave. This was evidently a sad afternoon for them.

"Are you Mrs. Cuzak's boys?" I asked.

The younger one did not look up; he was submerged in his own feelings, but his brother met me with intelligent gray eyes. "Yes, sir."

"Does she live up there on the hill? I am going to see her. Get in and ride up with me."

He glanced at his reluctant little brother. "I guess we'd better walk. But we'll open the gate for you."

I drove along the side-road and they followed slowly behind. When I pulled up at the windmill, another boy, barefooted and curly-headed, ran out of the barn to tie my team for me. He was a handsome one, this chap, fair-skinned and freckled, with red cheeks and a ruddy pelt as thick as a lamb's wool, growing down on his neck in little tufts. He tied my team with two flourishes of his hands, and nodded when I asked him if his mother was at home. As he glanced at me, his face dimpled with a seizure of irrelevant merriment, and he shot up the windmill tower with a lightness that struck me as disdainful. I knew he was peering down at me as I walked toward the house.

Ducks and geese ran quacking across my path. White cats were sunning themselves among yellow pumpkins on the porch steps. I looked through the wire screen into a big, light kitchen with a white floor. I saw a long table, rows of wooden chairs against the wall; and a shining range in one corner. Two girls were washing dishes at the sink, laughing and chattering, and a little one, in a short pinafore, sat on a stool playing with a rag baby. When I asked for their mother, one of the girls dropped her towel, ran across the floor with noiseless bare feet, and disappeared. The older one, who wore shoes and stockings, came to the door to admit me. She was a buxom girl with dark hair and eyes, calm and self-possessed.

"Won't you come in? Mother will be here in a minute."

Before I could sit down in the chair she offered me, the miracle happened; one of those quiet moments that clutch the heart, and take more courage than the noisy, excited passages in life. Ántonia came in and stood before me; a stalwart, brown woman, flat-chested, her curly brown hair a little grizzled. It was a shock, of course. It always is, to meet people after long years, especially if they have lived as much and as hard as this woman had. We stood looking at each other. The eyes that peered anxiously at me were—simply Ántonia's eyes. I had seen no others like them since I looked into them last, though I had looked at so many thousands of human faces. As I confronted her, the changes grew less apparent to me, her identity stronger. She was there, in the full vigor of her personality, battered but not diminished, looking at me, speaking to me in the husky, breathy voice I remembered so well.

"My husband's not at home, sir. Can I do anything?"

"Don't you remember me, Ántonia? Have I changed so much?"

She frowned into the slanting sunlight that made her brown hair look redder than it was. Suddenly her eyes widened, her whole face seemed to grow broader. She caught her breath and put out two hard-worked hands.

"Why, it's Jim! Anna, Yulka, it's Jim Burden!" She had no sooner caught my hands than she looked alarmed. "What's happened? Is anybody dead?"

I patted her arm. "No. I didn't come to a funeral this time. I got off the train at Hastings and drove down to see you and your family."

She dropped my hand and began rushing about. "Anton, Yulka, Nina, where are you all? Run, Anna, and hunt for the boys. They're off looking for that dog, somewhere. And call Leo. Where is that Leo!" She pulled them out of corners and came bringing them like a mother cat bringing in her kittens. "You don't have to go right off, Jim? My oldest boy's not here. He's gone with papa to the street fair at Wilber. I won't let you go! You've got to stay and see Rudolph and our papa." She looked at me imploringly, panting with excitement.

While I reassured her and told her there would be plenty of time, the barefooted boys from outside were slipping into the kitchen and gathering about her.

"Now, tell me their names, and how old they are."

As she told them off in turn, she made several mistakes about ages, and they roared with laughter. When she came to my light-footed friend of the windmill, she said, "This is Leo, and he's old enough to be better than he is."

He ran up to her and butted her playfully with his curly head, like a little ram, but his voice was quite desperate. "You've forgot! You always forget mine. It's mean! Please tell him, mother!" He clenched his fists in vexation and looked up at her impetuously.

She wound her forefinger in his yellow fleece and pulled it, watching him. "Well, how old are you?"

"I'm twelve," he panted, looking not at me but at her; "I'm twelve years old, and I was born on Easter day!"

She nodded to me. "It's true. He was an Easter baby."

The children all looked at me, as if they expected me to exhibit astonishment or delight at this information. Clearly, they were proud of each other, and of being so many. When they had all been introduced, Anna, the eldest daughter, who had met me at the door, scattered them gently, and came bringing a white apron which she tied round her mother's waist.

"Now, mother, sit down and talk to Mr. Burden. We'll finish the dishes quietly and not disturb you."

Ántonia looked about, quite distracted. "Yes, child, but why don't we take him into the parlor, now that we've got a nice parlor for company?"

The daughter laughed indulgently, and took my hat from me. "Well, you're here, now, mother, and if you talk here, Yulka and I can listen, too. You can show him the parlor after while." She smiled at me, and went back to the dishes, with her sister. The little girl with the rag doll found a place on the bottom step of an enclosed back stairway, and sat with her toes curled up, looking out at us expectantly.

"She's Nina, after Nina Harling," Ántonia explained. "Ain't her eyes like Nina's? I declare, Jim, I loved you children almost as much as I love my own. These children know all about you and Charley and Sally, like as if they'd grown up with you. I can't think of what I want to say, you've got me so stirred up. And then, I've forgot my English so. I don't often talk it any more. I tell the children I used to speak real well." She said they always spoke Bohemian at home. The little ones could not speak English at all—didn't learn it until they went to school.

"I can't believe it's you, sitting here, in my own kitchen. You wouldn't have known me, would you, Jim? You've kept so young, yourself. But it's easier for a man. I can't see how my Anton looks any older than the day I married him. His teeth have kept so nice. I haven't got many left. But I feel just as young as I used to, and I can do as much work. Oh, we don't have to work so hard now! We've got plenty to help us, papa and me. And how many have you got, Jim?"

When I told her I had no children she seemed embarrassed. "Oh, ain't that too bad! Maybe you could take one of my bad ones, now? That Leo; he's the worst of all." She leaned toward me with a smile. "And I love him the best," she whispered.

"Mother!" the two girls murmured reproachfully from the dishes.

Ántonia threw up her head and laughed. "I can't help it. You know I do. Maybe it's because he came on Easter day, I don't know. And he's never out of mischief one minute!"

I was thinking, as I watched her, how little it mattered—about her teeth, for instance. I know so many women who have kept all the things that she had lost, but whose inner glow has faded. Whatever else was gone, Ántonia had not lost the fire of life. Her skin, so brown and hardened, had not that look of flabbiness, as if the sap beneath it had been secretly drawn away.

While we were talking, the little boy whom they called Jan came in and sat down on the step beside Nina, under the hood of the stairway. He wore a funny long gingham apron, like a smock, over his trousers, and his hair was clipped so short that his head looked white and naked. He watched us out of his big, sorrowful gray eyes.

"He wants to tell you about the dog, mother. They found it dead," Anna said, as she passed us on her way to the cupboard.

Ántonia beckoned the boy to her. He stood by her chair, leaning his elbows on her knees and twisting her apron strings in his slender fingers, while he told her his story softly in Bohemian, and the tears brimmed over and hung on his long lashes. His mother listened, spoke soothingly to him, and in a whisper promised him something that made him give her a quick, teary smile. He slipped away and whispered his secret to Nina, sitting close to her and talking behind his hand.

When Anna finished her work and had washed her hands, she came and stood behind her mother's chair. "Why don't we show Mr. Burden our new fruit cave?" she asked.

We started off across the yard with the children at our heels. The boys were standing by the windmill, talking about the dog; some of them ran ahead to open the cellar door. When we descended, they all came down after us, and seemed quite as proud of the cave as the girls were. Ambrosch, the thoughtful-looking one who had directed me down by the plum bushes, called my attention to the stout brick walls and the cement floor. "Yes, it is a good way from the house," he admitted. "But, you see, in winter there are nearly always some of us around to come out and get things."

Anna and Yulka showed me three small barrels; one full of dill pickles, one full of chopped pickles, and one full of pickled watermelon rinds.

"You wouldn't believe, Jim, what it takes to feed them all!" their mother exclaimed. "You ought to see the bread we bake on Wednesdays and Saturdays! It's no wonder their poor papa can't get rich, he has to buy so much sugar for us to preserve with. We have our own wheat ground for flour,—but then there's that much less to sell."

Nina and Jan, and a little girl named Lucie, kept shyly pointing out to me the shelves of glass jars. They said nothing, but glancing at me, traced on the glass with their finger-tips the outline of the cherries and strawberries and crab-apples within, trying by a blissful expression of countenance to give me some idea of their deliciousness.

"Show him the spiced plums, mother. Americans don't have those," said one of the older boys. "Mother uses them to make *kolaches*,"[1] he added.

Leo, in a low voice, tossed off some scornful remark in Bohemian.

I turned to him. "You think I don't know what *kolaches* are, eh? You're mistaken, young man. I've eaten your mother's *kolaches* long before that Easter day when you were born."

"Always too fresh, Leo," Ambrosch remarked with a shrug.

Leo dived behind his mother and grinned out at me.

We turned to leave the cave; Ántonia and I went up the stairs first, and the children waited. We were standing outside talking, when they all came running up the steps together, big and little, tow heads and gold heads and brown, and flashing little naked legs; a veritable explosion of life out of the dark cave into the sunlight. It made me dizzy for a moment.

1. Fruit-filled sweet rolls.

The boys escorted us to the front of the house, which I hadn't yet seen; in farmhouses, somehow, life comes and goes by the back door. The roof was so steep that the eaves were not much above the forest of tall hollyhocks, now brown and in seed. Through July, Ántonia said, the house was buried in them; the Bohemians, I remembered, always planted hollyhocks. The front yard was enclosed by a thorny locust hedge, and at the gate grew two silvery, moth-like trees of the mimosa family. From here one looked down over the cattle yards, with their two long ponds, and over a wide stretch of stubble which they told me was a rye-field in summer.

At some distance behind the house were an ash grove and two orchards; a cherry orchard, with gooseberry and currant bushes between the rows, and an apple orchard, sheltered by a high hedge from the hot winds. The older children turned back when we reached the hedge, but Jan and Nina and Lucie crept through it by a hole known only to themselves and hid under the low-branching mulberry bushes.

As we walked through the apple orchard, grown up in tall bluegrass, Ántonia kept stopping to tell me about one tree and another. "I love them as if they were people," she said, rubbing her hand over the bark. "There wasn't a tree here when we first came. We planted every one, and used to carry water for them, too—after we'd been working in the fields all day. Anton, he was a city man, and he used to get discouraged. But I couldn't feel so tired that I wouldn't fret about these trees when there was a dry time. They were on my mind like children. Many a night after he was asleep I've got up and come out and carried water to the poor things. And now, you see, we have the good of them. My man worked in the orange groves in Florida, and he knows all about grafting. There ain't one of our neighbors has an orchard that bears like ours."

In the middle of the orchard we came upon a grape-arbor, with seats built along the sides and a warped plank table. The three children were waiting for us there. They looked up at me bashfully and made some request of their mother.

"They want me to tell you how the teacher has the school picnic here every year. These don't go to school yet, so they think it's all like the picnic."

After I had admired the arbor sufficiently, the youngsters ran away to an open place where there was a rough jungle of French pinks, and squatted down among them, crawling about and measuring with a string. "Jan wants to bury his dog there," Ántonia explained. "I had to tell him he could. He's kind of like Nina Harling; you remember how hard she used to take little things? He has funny notions, like her."

We sat down and watched them. Ántonia leaned her elbows on the table. There was the deepest peace in that orchard. It was surrounded by a triple enclosure; the wire fence, then the hedge of thorny locusts, then the mulberry hedge which kept out the hot winds of summer and held fast to the protecting snows of winter. The hedges were so tall that we could see nothing but the blue sky above them, neither the barn roof nor the windmill. The afternoon sun poured down on us through the drying grape leaves. The orchard seemed full of sun, like a cup, and we could smell the ripe apples on the trees. The crabs hung on the branches as thick as beads on a string, purple-red, with a thin silvery glaze over them. Some hens and ducks had crept through the hedge and were pecking at the fallen apples.

The drakes were handsome fellows, with pinkish gray bodies, their heads and necks covered with iridescent green feathers which grew close and full, changing to blue like a peacock's neck. Ántonia said they always reminded her of soldiers—some uniform she had seen in the old country, when she was a child.

"Are there any quail left now?" I asked. I reminded her how she used to go hunting with me the last summer before we moved to town. "You weren't a bad shot, Tony. Do you remember how you used to want to run away and go for ducks with Charley Harling and me?"

"I know, but I'm afraid to look at a gun now." She picked up one of the drakes and ruffled his green capote with her fingers. "Ever since I've had children, I don't like to kill anything. It makes me kind of faint to wring an old goose's neck. Ain't that strange, Jim?"

"I don't know. The young Queen of Italy said the same thing once, to a friend of mine. She used to be a great huntswoman, but now she feels as you do, and only shoots clay pigeons."

"Then I'm sure she's a good mother," Ántonia said warmly.

She told me how she and her husband had come out to this new country when the farm land was cheap and could be had on easy payments. The first ten years were a hard struggle. Her husband knew very little about farming and often grew discouraged. "We'd never have got through if I hadn't been so strong. I've always had good health, thank God, and I was able to help him in the fields until right up to the time before my babies came. Our children were good about taking care of each other. Martha, the one you saw when she was a baby, was such a help to me, and she trained Anna to be just like her. My Martha's married now, and has a baby of her own. Think of that, Jim!

"No, I never got down-hearted. Anton's a good man, and I loved my children and always believed they would turn out well. I belong on a farm. I'm never lonesome here like I used to be in town. You remember what sad spells I used to have, when I didn't know what was the matter with me? I've never had them out here. And I don't mind work a bit, if I don't have to put up with sadness." She leaned her chin on her hand and looked down through the orchard, where the sunlight was growing more and more golden.

"You ought never to have gone to town, Tony," I said, wondering at her.

She turned to me eagerly. "Oh, I'm glad I went! I'd never have known anything about cooking or housekeeping if I hadn't. I learned nice ways at the Harlings', and I've been able to bring my children up so much better. Don't you think they are pretty well-behaved for country children? If it hadn't been for what Mrs. Harling taught me, I expect I'd have brought them up like wild rabbits. No, I'm glad I had a chance to learn; but I'm thankful none of my daughters will ever have to work out. The trouble with me was, Jim, I never could believe harm of anybody I loved."

While we were talking, Ántonia assured me that she could keep me for the night. "We've plenty of room. Two of the boys sleep in the haymow till cold weather comes, but there's no need for it. Leo always begs to sleep there, and Ambrosch goes along to look after him."

I told her I would like to sleep in the haymow, with the boys.

"You can do just as you want to. The chest is full of clean blankets, put away for winter. Now I must go, or my girls will be doing all the work, and I want to cook your supper myself."

As we went toward the house, we met Ambrosch and Anton, starting off with their milking-pails to hunt the cows. I joined them, and Leo accompanied us at some distance, running ahead and starting up at us out of clumps of ironweed, calling, "I'm a jack rabbit," or, "I'm a big bull-snake."

I walked between the two older boys—straight, well-made fellows, with good heads and clear eyes. They talked about their school and the new teacher, told me about the crops and the harvest, and how many steers they would feed that winter. They were easy and confidential with me, as if I were an old friend of the family—and not too old. I felt like a boy in their company, and all manner of forgotten interests revived in me. It seemed, after all, so natural to be walking along a barbed-wire fence beside the sunset, toward a red pond, and to see my shadow moving along at my right, over the close-cropped grass.

"Has mother shown you the pictures you sent her from the old country?" Ambrosch asked. "We've had them framed and they're hung up in the parlor. She was so glad to get them. I don't believe I ever saw her so pleased about anything." There was a note of simple gratitude in his voice that made me wish I had given more occasion for it.

I put my hand on his shoulder. "Your mother, you know, was very much loved by all of us. She was a beautiful girl."

"Oh, we know!" They both spoke together; seemed a little surprised that I should think it necessary to mention this. "Everybody liked her, didn't they? The Harlings and your grandmother, and all the town people."

"Sometimes," I ventured, "it doesn't occur to boys that their mother was ever young and pretty."

"Oh, we know!" they said again, warmly. "She's not very old now," Ambrosch added. "Not much older than you."

"Well," I said, "if you weren't nice to her, I think I'd take a club and go for the whole lot of you. I couldn't stand it if you boys were inconsiderate, or thought of her as if she were just somebody who looked after you. You see I was very much in love with your mother once, and I know there's nobody like her."

The boys laughed and seemed pleased and embarrassed. "She never told us that," said Anton. "But she's always talked lots about you, and about what good times you used to have. She has a picture of you that she cut out of the Chicago paper once, and Leo says he recognized you when you drove up to the windmill. You can't tell about Leo, though; sometimes he likes to be smart."

We brought the cows home to the corner nearest the barn, and the boys milked them while night came on. Everything was as it should be: the strong smell of sunflowers and ironweed in the dew, the clear blue and gold of the sky, the evening star, the purr of the milk into the pails, the grunts and squeals of the pigs fighting over their supper. I began to feel the loneliness of the farm-boy at evening, when the chores seem everlastingly the same, and the world so far away.

What a tableful we were at supper; two long rows of restless heads in the lamplight, and so many eyes fastened excitedly upon Ántonia as she sat at the head of the table, filling the plates and starting the dishes on their way. The children were seated according to a system; a little one next an older one, who was to watch over his behavior and to see that he got his food. Anna and

Yulka left their chairs from time to time to bring fresh plates of *kolaches* and pitchers of milk.

After supper we went into the parlor, so that Yulka and Leo could play for me. Ántonia went first, carrying the lamp. There were not nearly chairs enough to go round, so the younger children sat down on the bare floor. Little Lucie whispered to me that they were going to have a parlor carpet if they got ninety cents for their wheat. Leo, with a good deal of fussing, got out his violin. It was old Mr. Shimerda's instrument, which Ántonia had always kept, and it was too big for him. But he played very well for a self-taught boy. Poor Yulka's efforts were not so successful. While they were playing, little Nina got up from her corner, came out into the middle of the floor, and began to do a pretty little dance on the boards with her bare feet. No one paid the least attention to her, and when she was through she stole back and sat down by her brother.

Ántonia spoke to Leo in Bohemian. He frowned and wrinkled up his face. He seemed to be trying to pout, but his attempt only brought out dimples in unusual places. After twisting and screwing the keys, he played some Bohemian airs, without the organ to hold him back, and that went better. The boy was so restless that I had not had a chance to look at his face before. My first impression was right; he really was faun-like. He hadn't much head behind his ears, and his tawny fleece grew down thick to the back of his neck. His eyes were not frank and wide apart like those of the other boys, but were deep-set, gold-green in color, and seemed sensitive to the light. His mother said he got hurt oftener than all the others put together. He was always trying to ride the colts before they were broken, teasing the turkey gobbler, seeing just how much red the bull would stand for, or how sharp the new axe was.

After the concert was over Ántonia brought out a big boxful of photographs; she and Anton in their wedding clothes, holding hands; her brother Ambrosch and his very fat wife, who had a farm of her own, and who bossed her husband, I was delighted to hear; the three Bohemian Marys and their large families.

"You wouldn't believe how steady those girls have turned out," Ántonia remarked. "Mary Svoboda's the best butter-maker in all this country, and a fine manager. Her children will have a grand chance."

As Ántonia turned over the pictures the young Cuzaks stood behind her chair, looking over her shoulder with interested faces. Nina and Jan, after trying to see round the taller ones, quietly brought a chair, climbed up on it, and stood close together, looking. The little boy forgot his shyness and grinned delightedly when familiar faces came into view. In the group about Ántonia I was conscious of a kind of physical harmony. They leaned this way and that, and were not afraid to touch each other. They contemplated the photographs with pleased recognition; looked at some admiringly, as if these characters in their mother's girlhood had been remarkable people. The little children, who could not speak English, murmured comments to each other in their rich old language.

Ántonia held out a photograph of Lena that had come from San Francisco last Christmas. "Does she still look like that? She hasn't been home for six years now." Yes, it was exactly like Lena, I told her; a comely woman, a trifle too plump, in a hat a trifle too large, but with the old lazy eyes, and the old dimpled ingenuousness still lurking at the corners of her mouth.

There was a picture of Frances Harling in a be-frogged[2] riding costume that I remembered well. "Isn't she fine!" the girls murmured. They all assented. One could see that Frances had come down as a heroine in the family legend. Only Leo was unmoved.

"And there's Mr. Harling, in his grand fur coat. He was awfully rich, wasn't he, mother?"

"He wasn't any Rockefeller," put in Master Leo, in a very low tone, which reminded me of the way in which Mrs. Shimerda had once said that my grandfather "wasn't Jesus." His habitual skepticism was like a direct inheritance from that old woman.

"None of your smart speeches," said Ambrosch severely.

Leo poked out a supple red tongue at him, but a moment later broke into a giggle at a tintype of two men, uncomfortably seated, with an awkward-looking boy in baggy clothes standing between them; Jake and Otto and I! We had it taken, I remembered, when we went to Black Hawk on the first Fourth of July I spent in Nebraska. I was glad to see Jake's grin again, and Otto's ferocious mustaches. The young Cuzaks knew all about them.

"He made grandfather's coffin, didn't he?" Anton asked.

"Wasn't they good fellows, Jim?" Ántonia eyes filled. "To this day I'm ashamed because I quarreled with Jake that way. I was saucy and impertinent to him, Leo, like you are with people sometimes, and I wish somebody had made me behave."

"We aren't through with you, yet," they warned me. They produced a photograph taken just before I went away to college; a tall youth in striped trousers and a straw hat, trying to look easy and jaunty.

"Tell us, Mr. Burden," said Charley, "about the rattler you killed at the dog town. How long was he? Sometimes mother says six feet and sometimes she says five."

These children seemed to be upon very much the same terms with Ántonia as the Harling children had been so many years before. They seemed to feel the same pride in her, and to look to her for stories and entertainment as we used to do.

It was eleven o'clock when I at last took my bag and some blankets and started for the barn with the boys. Their mother came to the door with us, and we tarried for a moment to look out at the white slope of the corral and the two ponds asleep in the moonlight, and the long sweep of the pasture under the star-sprinkled sky.

The boys told me to choose my own place in the haymow, and I lay down before a big window, left open in warm weather, that looked out into the stars. Ambrosch and Leo cuddled up in a hay-cave, back under the eaves, and lay giggling and whispering. They tickled each other and tossed and tumbled in the hay; and then, all at once, as if they had been shot, they were still. There was hardly a minute between giggles and bland slumber.

I lay awake for a long while, until the slow-moving moon passed my window on its way up the heavens. I was thinking about Ántonia and her children; about Anna's solicitude for her, Ambrosch's grave affection, Leo's jealous, animal little love. That moment, when they all came tumbling out of the cave into the light, was a sight any man might have come far to see.

2. Decorated with ornamental braiding.

Ántonia had always been one to leave images in the mind that did not fade—that grew stronger with time. In my memory there was a succession of such pictures, fixed there like the old woodcuts of one's first primer: Ántonia kicking her bare legs against the sides of my pony when we came home in triumph with our snake; Ántonia in her black shawl and fur cap, as she stood by her father's grave in the snowstorm; Ántonia coming in with her work-team along the evening sky-line. She lent herself to immemorial human attitudes which we recognize by instinct as universal and true. I had not been mistaken. She was a battered woman now, not a lovely girl; but she still had that something which fires the imagination, could still stop one's breath for a moment by a look or gesture that somehow revealed the meaning in common things. She had only to stand in the orchard, to put her hand on a little crab tree and look up at the apples, to make you feel the goodness of planting and tending and harvesting at last. All the strong things of her heart came out in her body, that had been so tireless in serving generous emotions.

It was no wonder that her sons stood tall and straight. She was a rich mine of life, like the founders of early races.

II

When I awoke in the morning long bands of sunshine were coming in at the window and reaching back under the eaves where the two boys lay. Leo was wide awake and was tickling his brother's leg with a dried cone-flower he had pulled out of the hay. Ambrosch kicked at him and turned over. I closed my eyes and pretended to be asleep. Leo lay on his back, elevated one foot, and began exercising his toes. He picked up dried flowers with his toes and brandished them in the belt of sunlight. After he had amused himself thus for some time, he rose on one elbow and began to look at me, cautiously, then critically, blinking his eyes in the light. His expression was droll; it dismissed me lightly. "This old fellow is no different from other people. He doesn't know my secret." He seemed conscious of possessing a keener power of enjoyment than other people; his quick recognitions made him frantically impatient of deliberate judgments. He always knew what he wanted without thinking.

After dressing in the hay, I washed my face in cold water at the windmill. Breakfast was ready when I entered the kitchen, and Yulka was baking griddle-cakes. The three older boys set off for the fields early. Leo and Yulka were to drive to town to meet their father, who would return from Wilber on the noon train.

"We'll only have a lunch at noon," Ántonia said, "and cook the geese for supper, when our papa will be here. I wish my Martha could come down to see you. They have a Ford car now, and she don't seem so far away from me as she used to. But her husband's crazy about his farm and about having everything just right, and they almost never get away except on Sundays. He's a handsome boy, and he'll be rich some day. Everything he takes hold of turns out well. When they bring that baby in here, and unwrap him, he looks like a little prince; Martha takes care of him so beautiful. I'm reconciled to her being away from me now, but at first I cried like I was putting her into her coffin."

We were alone in the kitchen, except for Anna, who was pouring cream into the churn. She looked up at me. "Yes, she did. We were just ashamed of mother. She went round crying, when Martha was so happy, and the rest of us were all glad. Joe certainly was patient with you, mother."

Ántonia nodded and smiled at herself. "I know it was silly, but I couldn't help it. I wanted her right here. She'd never been away from me a night since she was born. If Anton had made trouble about her when she was a baby, or wanted me to leave her with my mother, I wouldn't have married him. I couldn't. But he always loved her like she was his own."

"I didn't even know Martha wasn't my full sister until after she was engaged to Joe," Anna told me.

Toward the middle of the afternoon the wagon drove in, with the father and the eldest son. I was smoking in the orchard, and as I went out to meet them, Ántonia came running down from the house and hugged the two men as if they had been away for months.

"Papa" interested me, from my first glimpse of him. He was shorter than his older sons; a crumpled little man, with run-over boot heels, and he carried one shoulder higher than the other. But he moved very quickly, and there was an air of jaunty liveliness about him. He had a strong, ruddy color, thick black hair, a little grizzled, a curly mustache, and red lips. His smile showed the strong teeth of which his wife was so proud, and as he saw me his lively, quizzical eyes told me that he knew all about me. He looked like a humorous philosopher who had hitched up one shoulder under the burdens of life, and gone on his way having a good time when he could. He advanced to meet me and gave me a hard hand, burned red on the back and heavily coated with hair. He wore his Sunday clothes, very thick and hot for the weather, an unstarched white shirt, and a blue necktie with big white dots, like a little boy's, tied in a flowing bow. Cuzak began at once to talk about his holiday—from politeness he spoke in English.

"Mama, I wish you had see the lady dance on the slack-wire in the street at night. They throw a bright light on her and she float through the air something beautiful, like a bird! They have a dancing bear, like in the old country, and two three merry-go-around, and people in balloons, and what you call the big wheel, Rudolph?"

"A Ferris wheel," Rudolph entered the conversation in a deep baritone voice. He was six foot two, and had a chest like a young black-smith. "We went to the big dance in the hall behind the saloon last night, mother, and I danced with all the girls, and so did father. I never saw so many pretty girls. It was a Bohunk crowd, for sure. We didn't hear a word of English on the street, except from the show people, did we, papa?"

Cuzak nodded. "And very many send word to you, Ántonia. You will excuse"—turning to me—"if I tell her." While we walked toward the house he related incidents and delivered messages in the tongue he spoke fluently, and I dropped a little behind, curious to know what their relations had become—or remained. The two seemed to be on terms of easy friendliness, touched with humor. Clearly, she was the impulse, and he the corrective. As they went up the hill he kept glancing at her sidewise, to see whether she got his point, or how she received it. I noticed later that he always looked at people sidewise, as a work-horse does at its yoke-mate. Even when he sat opposite me in the kitchen, talking, he would turn his head a little toward the clock or the stove and look at me from the side, but with frankness and good-nature. This trick did not suggest duplicity or secretiveness, but merely long habit, as with the horse.

He had brought a tintype of himself and Rudolph for Ántonia's collection, and several paper bags of candy for the children. He looked a little disappointed when his wife showed him a big box of candy I had got in Denver—she hadn't let the children touch it the night before. He put his candy away in the cupboard, "for when she rains," and glanced at the box, chuckling. "I guess you must have hear about how my family ain't so small," he said.

Cuzak sat down behind the stove and watched his women-folk and the little children with equal amusement. He thought they were nice, and he thought they were funny, evidently. He had been off dancing with the girls and forgetting that he was an old fellow, and now his family rather surprised him; he seemed to think it a joke that all these children should belong to him. As the younger ones slipped up to him in his retreat, he kept taking things out of his pockets; penny dolls, a wooden clown, a balloon pig that was inflated by a whistle. He beckoned to the little boy they called Jan, whispered to him, and presented him with a paper snake, gently, so as not to startle him. Looking over the boy's head he said to me, "This one is bashful. He gets left."

Cuzak had brought home with him a roll of illustrated Bohemian papers. He opened them and began to tell his wife the news, much of which seemed to relate to one person. I heard the name Vasakova, Vasakova, repeated several times with lively interest, and presently I asked him whether he were talking about the singer, Maria Vasak.

"You know? You have heard, maybe?" he asked incredulously. When I assured him that I had heard her, he pointed out her picture and told me that Vasak had broken her leg, climbing in the Austrian Alps, and would not be able to fill her engagements. He seemed delighted to find that I had heard her sing in London and in Vienna; got out his pipe and lit it to enjoy our talk the better. She came from his part of Prague. His father used to mend her shoes for her when she was a student. Cuzak questioned me about her looks, her popularity, her voice; but he particularly wanted to know whether I had noticed her tiny feet, and whether I thought she had saved much money. She was extravagant, of course but he hoped she wouldn't squander everything, and have nothing left when she was old. As a young man, working in Wienn, he had seen a good many artists who were old and poor, making one glass of beer last all evening, and "it was not very nice, that."

When the boys came in from milking and feeding, the long table was laid, and two brown geese, stuffed with apples, were put down sizzling before Ántonia. She began to carve, and Rudolph, who sat next his mother, started the plates on their way. When everybody was served, he looked across the table at me.

"Have you been to Black Hawk lately, Mr. Burden? Then I wonder if you've heard about the Cutters?"

No, I had heard nothing at all about them.

"Then you must tell him, son, though it's a terrible thing to talk about at supper. Now, all you children be quiet, Rudolph is going to tell about the murder."

"Hurrah! The murder!" the children murmured, looking pleased and interested.

Rudolph told his story in great detail, with occasional promptings from his mother or father.

Wick Cutter and his wife had gone on living in the house that Ántonia and I knew so well, and in the way we knew so well. They grew to be very old people. He shriveled up, Ántonia said, until he looked like a little old yellow monkey, for his beard and his fringe of hair never changed color. Mrs. Cutter remained flushed and wild-eyed as we had known her, but as the years passed she became afflicted with a shaking palsy which made her nervous nod continuous instead of occasional. Her hands were so uncertain that she could no longer disfigure china, poor woman! As the couple grew older, they quarreled more and more about the ultimate disposition of their "property." A new law was passed in the State, securing the surviving wife a third of her husband's estate under all conditions. Cutter was tormented by the fear that Mrs. Cutter would live longer than he, and that eventually her "people," whom he had always hated so violently, would inherit. Their quarrels on this subject passed the boundary of the close-growing cedars, and were heard in the street by whoever wished to loiter and listen.

One morning, two years ago, Cutter went into the hardware store and bought a pistol, saying he was going to shoot a dog, and adding that he "thought he would take a shot at an old cat while he was about it." (Here the children interrupted Rudolph's narrative by smothered giggles.)

Cutter went out behind the hardware store, put up a target, practiced for an hour or so, and then went home. At six o'clock that evening, when several men were passing the Cutter house on their way home to supper, they heard a pistol shot. They paused and were looking doubtfully at one another, when another shot came crashing through an upstairs window. They ran into the house and found Wick Cutter lying on a sofa in his upstairs bedroom, with his throat torn open, bleeding on a roll of sheets he had placed beside his head.

"Walk in, gentlemen," he said weakly. "I am alive, you see, and competent. You are witnesses that I have survived my wife. You will find her in her own room. Please make your examination at once, so that there will be no mistake."

One of the neighbors telephoned for a doctor, while the others went into Mrs. Cutter's room. She was lying on her bed, in her nightgown and wrapper, shot through the heart. Her husband must have come in while she was taking her afternoon nap and shot her, holding the revolver near her breast. Her nightgown was burned from the powder.

The horrified neighbors rushed back to Cutter. He opened his eyes and said distinctly, "Mrs. Cutter is quite dead, gentlemen, and I am conscious. My affairs are in order." Then, Rudolph said, "he let go and died."

On his desk the coroner found a letter, dated at five o'clock that afternoon. It stated that he had just shot his wife; that any will she might secretly have made would be invalid, as he survived her. He meant to shoot himself at six o'clock and would, if he had strength, fire a shot through the window in the hope that passers-by might come in and see him "before life was extinct," as he wrote.

"Now, would you have thought that man had such a cruel heart?" Ántonia turned to me after the story was told. "To go and do that poor woman out of any comfort she might have from his money after he was gone!"

"Did you ever hear of anybody else that killed himself for spite, Mr. Burden?" asked Rudolph.

I admitted that I hadn't. Every lawyer learns over and over how strong a motive hate can be, but in my collection of legal anecdotes I had nothing to match this one. When I asked how much the estate amounted to, Rudolph said it was a little over a hundred thousand dollars.

Cuzak gave me a twinkling, sidelong glance. "The lawyers, they got a good deal of it, sure," he said merrily.

A hundred thousand dollars; so that was the fortune that had been scraped together by such hard dealing, and that Cutter himself had died for in the end!

After supper Cuzak and I took a stroll in the orchard and sat down by the windmill to smoke. He told me his story as if it were my business to know it.

His father was a shoemaker, his uncle a furrier, and he, being a younger son, was apprenticed to the latter's trade. You never got anywhere working for your relatives, he said, so when he was a journeyman he went to Vienna and worked in a big fur shop, earning good money. But a young fellow who liked a good time didn't save anything in Vienna; there were too many pleasant ways of spending every night what he'd made in the day. After three years there, he came to New York. He was badly advised and went to work on furs during a strike, when the factories were offering big wages. The strikers won, and Cuzak was blacklisted. As he had a few hundred dollars ahead, he decided to go to Florida and raise oranges. He had always thought he would like to raise oranges! The second year a hard frost killed his young grove, and he fell ill with malaria. He came to Nebraska to visit his cousin, Anton Jelinek, and to look about. When he began to look about, he saw Ántonia, and she was exactly the kind of girl he had always been hunting for. They were married at once, though he had to borrow money from his cousin to buy the wedding-ring.

"It was a pretty hard job, breaking up this place and making the first crops grow," he said, pushing back his hat and scratching his grizzled hair. "Sometimes I git awful sore on this place and want to quit, but my wife she always say we better stick it out. The babies come along pretty fast, so it look like it be hard to move, anyhow. I guess she was right, all right. We got this place clear now. We pay only twenty dollars an acre then, and I been offered a hundred. We bought another quarter[3] ten years ago, and we got it most paid for. We got plenty boys; we can work a lot of land. Yes, she is a good wife for a poor man. She ain't always so strict with me, neither. Sometimes maybe I drink a little too much beer in town, and when I come home she don't say nothing. She don't ask me no questions. We always get along fine, her and me, like at first. The children don't make trouble between us, like sometimes happens." He lit another pipe and pulled on it contentedly.

I found Cuzak a most companionable fellow. He asked me a great many questions about my trip through Bohemia, about Vienna and the Ringstrasse and the theaters.

"Gee! I like to go back there once, when the boys is big enough to farm the place. Sometimes when I read the papers from the old country, I pretty near

3. I.e., a quarter section, equal to one-quarter of a square mile, or 160 acres.

run away," he confessed with a little laugh. "I never did think how I would be a settled man like this."

He was still, as Ántonia said, a city man. He liked theaters and lighted streets and music and a game of dominoes after the day's work was over. His sociability was stronger than his acquisitive instinct. He liked to live day by day and night by night, sharing in the excitement of the crowd.—Yet his wife had managed to hold him here on a farm, in one of the loneliest countries in the world.

I could see the little chap, sitting here every evening by the windmill, nursing his pipe and listening to the silence; the wheeze of the pump, the grunting of the pigs, an occasional squawking when the hens were disturbed by a rat. It did rather seem to me that Cuzak had been made the instrument of Ántonia's special mission. This was a fine life, certainly, but it wasn't the kind of life he had wanted to live. I wondered whether the life that was right for one was ever right for two!

I asked Cuzak if he didn't find it hard to do without the gay company he had always been used to. He knocked out his pipe against an upright, sighed, and dropped it into his pocket.

"At first I near go crazy with lonesomeness," he said frankly, "but my woman is got such a warm heart. She always make it as good for me as she could. Now it ain't so bad; I can begin to have some fun with my boys, already!"

As we walked toward the house, Cuzak cocked his hat jauntily over one ear and looked up at the moon. "Gee!" he said in a hushed voice, as if he had just wakened up, "it don't seem like I am away from there twenty-six year!"

III

After dinner the next day I said good-bye and drove back to Hastings to take the train for Black Hawk. Ántonia and her children gathered round my buggy before I started, and even the little ones looked up at me with friendly faces. Leo and Ambrosch ran ahead to open the lane gate. When I reached the bottom of the hill, I glanced back. The group was still there by the windmill. Ántonia was waving her apron.

At the gate Ambrosch lingered beside my buggy, resting his arm on the wheel-rim. Leo slipped through the fence and ran off into the pasture.

"That's like him," his brother said with a shrug. "He's a crazy kid. Maybe he's sorry to have you go, and maybe he's jealous. He's jealous of anybody mother makes a fuss over, even the priest."

I found I hated to leave this boy, with his pleasant voice and his fine head and eyes. He looked very manly as he stood there without a hat, the wind rippling his shirt about his brown neck and shoulders.

"Don't forget that you and Rudolph are going hunting with me up on the Niobrara[4] next summer," I said. "Your father's agreed to let you off after harvest."

He smiled. "I won't likely forget. I've never had such a nice thing offered to me before. I don't know what makes you so nice to us boys," he added, blushing.

"Oh, yes you do!" I said, gathering up my reins.

4. River flowing east from Wyoming across Nebraska.

He made no answer to this, except to smile at me with unabashed pleasure and affection as I drove away.

My day in Black Hawk was disappointing. Most of my old friends were dead or had moved away. Strange children, who meant nothing to me, were playing in the Harlings' big yard when I passed; the mountain ash had been cut down, and only a sprouting stump was left of the tall Lombardy poplar that used to guard the gate. I hurried on. The rest of the morning I spent with Anton Jelinek, under a shady cottonwood tree in the yard behind his saloon. While I was having my mid-day dinner at the hotel, I met one of the old lawyers who was still in practice, and he took me up to his office and talked over the Cutter case with me. After that, I scarcely knew how to put in the time until the night express was due.

I took a long walk north of the town, out into the pastures where the land was so rough that it had never been ploughed up, and the long red grass of early times still grew shaggy over the draws and hillocks. Out there I felt at home again. Overhead the sky was that indescribable blue of autumn; bright and shadowless, hard as enamel. To the south I could see the dun-shaded river bluffs that used to look so big to me, and all about stretched drying cornfields, of the pale-gold color I remembered so well. Russian thistles were blowing across the uplands and piling against the wire fences like barricades. Along the cattle paths the plumes of golden-rod were already fading into sun-warmed velvet, gray with gold threads in it. I had escaped from the curious depression that hangs over little towns, and my mind was full of pleasant things; trips I meant to take with the Cuzak boys, in the Bad Lands and up on the Stinking Water. There were enough Cuzaks to play with for a long while yet. Even after the boys grew up, there would always be Cuzak himself! I meant to tramp along a few miles of lighted streets with Cuzak.

As I wandered over those rough pastures, I had the good luck to stumble upon a bit of the first road that went from Black Hawk out to the north country; to my grandfather's farm, then on to the Shimerdas' and to the Norwegian settlement. Everywhere else it had been ploughed under when the highways were surveyed; this half-mile or so within the pasture fence was all that was left of that old road which used to run like a wild thing across the open prairie, clinging to the high places and circling and doubling like a rabbit before the hounds. On the level land the tracks had almost disappeared—were mere shadings in the grass, and a stranger would not have noticed them. But wherever the road had crossed a draw, it was easy to find. The rains had made channels of the wheel-ruts and washed them so deep that the sod had never healed over them. They looked like gashes torn by a grizzly's claws, on the slopes where the farm wagons used to lurch up out of the hollows with a pull that brought curling muscles on the smooth hips of the horses. I sat down and watched the haystacks turn rosy in the slanting sunlight.

This was the road over which Ántonia and I came on that night when we got off the train at Black Hawk and were bedded down in the straw, wondering children, being taken we knew not whither. I had only to close my eyes to hear the rumbling of the wagons in the dark, and to be again overcome by that obliterating strangeness. The feelings of that night were so near that I could reach out and touch them with my hand. I had the sense of coming home to myself, and of having found out what a little circle man's experience is. For Ántonia and for me, this had been the road of Destiny; had taken us to those early accidents of fortune which predetermined for us all that we can ever be. Now I understood that the same road was to bring us together again. Whatever we had missed, we possessed together the precious, the incommunicable past.

1918

The Sculptor's Funeral

A group of the townspeople stood on the station siding of a little Kansas town, awaiting the coming of the night train, which was already twenty minutes overdue. The snow had fallen thick over everything; in the pale starlight the line of bluffs across the wide, white meadows south of the town made soft, smoke-colored curves against the clear sky. The men on the siding stood first on one foot and then on the other, their hands thrust deep into their trousers pockets, their overcoats open, their shoulders screwed up with the cold; and they glanced from time to time toward the southeast, where the railroad track wound along the river shore. They conversed in low tones and moved about restlessly, seeming uncertain as to what was expected of them. There was but one of the company who looked as if he knew exactly why he was there, and he kept conspicuously apart; walking to the far end of the platform, returning to the station door, then pacing up the track again, his chin sunk in the high collar of his overcoat, his burly shoulders drooping forward, his gait heavy and dogged. Presently he was approached by a tall, spare, grizzled man clad in a faded Grand Army suit,[1] who shuffled out from the group and advanced with a certain deference, craning his neck forward until his back made the angle of a jackknife three-quarters open.

"I reckon she's a goin' to be pretty late again tonight, Jim," he remarked in a squeaky falsetto. "S'pose it's the snow?"

"I don't know," responded the other man with a shade of annoyance, speaking from out an astonishing cataract of red beard that grew fiercely and thickly in all directions.

The spare man shifted the quill toothpick he was chewing to the other side of his mouth. "It ain't likely that anybody from the East will come with the corpse, I s'pose," he went on reflectively.

"I don't know," responded the other, more curtly than before.

"It's too bad he didn't belong to some lodge or other. I like an order funeral[2] myself. They seem more appropriate for people of some repytation," the spare man continued, with an ingratiating concession in his shrill voice, as he carefully placed his toothpick in his vest pocket. He always carried the flag at the G.A.R. funerals in the town.

1. Quasi-military, uniform-inspired suit worn by members of the Grand Army of the Republic (G.A.R.), a fraternal organization for northern veterans of the Civil War founded in 1866.
2. Lodge, order: fraternal organizations.

The heavy man turned on his heel, without replying, and walked up the siding. The spare man rejoined the uneasy group. "Jim's ez full ez a tick, ez ushel," he commented commiseratingly.

Just then a distant whistle sounded, and there was a shuffling of feet on the platform. A number of lanky boys, of all ages, appeared as suddenly and slimily as eels wakened by the crack of thunder; some came from the waiting-room, where they had been warming themselves by the red stove, or half asleep on the slat benches; others uncoiled themselves from baggage trucks or slid out of express wagons. Two clambered down from the driver's seat of a hearse that stood backed up against the siding. They straightened their stooping shoulders and lifted their heads, and a flash of momentary animation kindled their dull eyes at that cold, vibrant scream, the world-wide call for men. It stirred them like the note of a trumpet; just as it had often stirred the man who was coming home tonight, in his boyhood.

The night express shot, red as a rocket, from out the eastward marsh lands and wound along the river shore under the long lines of shivering poplars that sentinelled the meadows, the escaping steam hanging in gray masses against the pale sky and blotting out the Milky Way. In a moment the red glare from the headlight streamed up the snow-covered track before the siding and glittered on the wet, black rails. The burly man with the disheveled red beard walked swiftly up the platform toward the approaching train, uncovering his head as he went. The group of men behind him hesitated, glanced questioningly at one another, and awkwardly followed his example. The train stopped, and the crowd shuffled up to the express car just as the door was thrown open, the man in the G.A.R. suit thrusting his head forward with curiosity. The express messenger appeared in the doorway, accompanied by a young man in a long ulster and travelling cap.

"Are Mr. Merrick's friends here?" inquired the young man.

The group on the platform swayed uneasily. Philip Phelps, the banker, responded with dignity: "We have come to take charge of the body. Mr. Merrick's father is very feeble and can't be about."

"Send the agent out here," growled the express messenger, "and tell the operator to lend a hand."

The coffin was got out of its rough-box and down on the snowy platform. The townspeople drew back enough to make room for it and then formed a close semicircle about it, looking curiously at the palm leaf which lay across the black cover. No one said anything. The baggage man stood by his truck, waiting to get at the trunks. The engine panted heavily, and the fireman dodged in and out among the wheels with his yellow torch and long oil-can, snapping the spindle boxes. The young Bostonian, one of the dead sculptor's pupils who had come with the body, looked about him helplessly. He turned to the banker, the only one of that black, uneasy, stoop-shouldered group who seemed enough of an individual to be addressed.

"None of Mr. Merrick's brothers are here?" he asked uncertainly.

The man with the red beard for the first time stepped up and joined the others. "No, they have not come yet; the family is scattered. The body will be taken directly to the house." He stooped and took hold of one of the handles of the coffin.

"Take the long hill road up, Thompson, it will be easier on the horses," called the liveryman as the undertaker snapped the door of the hearse and prepared to mount to the driver's seat.

Laird, the red-bearded lawyer, turned again to the stranger: "We didn't know whether there would be any one with him or not," he explained. "It's a long walk, so you'd better go up in the hack." He pointed to a single battered conveyance, but the young man replied stiffly: "Thank you, but I think I will go up with the hearse. If you don't object," turning to the undertaker, "I'll ride with you."

They clambered up over the wheels and drove off in the starlight up the long, white hill toward the town. The lamps in the still village were shining from under the low, snow-burdened roofs; and beyond, on every side, the plains reached out into emptiness, peaceful and wide as the soft sky itself, and wrapped in a tangible, white silence.

When the hearse backed up to a wooden sidewalk before a naked, weather-beaten frame house, the same composite, ill-defined group that had stood upon the station siding was huddled about the gate. The front yard was an icy swamp, and a couple of warped planks, extending from the sidewalk to the door, made a sort of rickety footbridge. The gate hung on one hinge, and was opened wide with difficulty. Steavens, the young stranger, noticed that something black was tied to the knob of the front door.

The grating sound made by the casket, as it was drawn from the hearse, was answered by a scream from the house; the front door was wrenched open, and a tall, corpulent woman rushed out bare-headed into the snow and flung herself upon the coffin, shrieking: "My boy, my boy! And this is how you've come home to me!"

As Steavens turned away and closed his eyes with a shudder of unutterable repulsion, another woman, also tall, but flat and angular, dressed entirely in black, darted out of the house and caught Mrs. Merrick by the shoulders, crying sharply: "Come, come, mother; you mustn't go on like this!" Her tone changed to one of obsequious solemnity as she turned to the banker: "The parlour is ready, Mr. Phelps."

The bearers carried the coffin along the narrow boards, while the undertaker ran ahead with the coffin-rests. They bore it into a large, unheated room that smelled of dampness and disuse and furniture polish, and set it down under a hanging lamp ornamented with jingling glass prisms and before a "Rogers group" of John Alden and Priscilla, wreathed with smilax.[3] Henry Steavens stared about him with the sickening conviction that there had been a mistake, and that he had somehow arrived at the wrong destination. He looked at the clover-green Brussels,[4] the fat plush upholstery, among the hand-painted china placques and panels and vases, for some mark of identification,—for something that might once conceivably have belonged to Harvey Merrick. It was not until he recognized his friend in the crayon portrait of a little boy in kilts and curls, hanging above the piano, that he felt willing to let any of these people approach the coffin.

3. A flowering vine; also the name of a nymph turned into the flower in Greek mythology. "Rogers group": plaster figurines of literary and historical subjects, mass-produced by John Rogers from 1859 to 1892. John Alden and Priscilla were Pilgrims on the *Mayflower* whose love was treated in Henry Wadsworth Longfellow's best-selling 1858 narrative poem *The Courtship of Miles Standish*.

4. Carpeting developed in Europe and mass-produced in the United States beginning in the mid-19th century.

"Take the lid off, Mr. Thompson; let me see my boy's face," wailed the elder woman between her sobs. This time Steavens looked fearfully, almost beseechingly into her face, red and swollen under its masses of strong, black, shiny hair. He flushed, dropped his eyes, and then, almost incredulously, looked again. There was a kind of power about her face—a kind of brutal handsomeness, even; but it was scarred and furrowed by violence, and so colored and coarsened by fiercer passions that grief seemed never to have laid a gentle finger there. The long nose was distended and knobbed at the end, and there were deep lines on either side of it; her heavy, black brows almost met across her forehead, her teeth were large and square, and set far apart—teeth that could tear. She filled the room; the men were obliterated, seemed tossed about like twigs in an angry water, and even Steavens felt himself being drawn into the whirlpool.

The daughter—the tall, raw-boned woman in crêpe, with a mourning comb in her hair which curiously lengthened her long face—sat stiffly upon the sofa, her hands, conspicuous for their large knuckles, folded in her lap, her mouth and eyes drawn down, solemnly awaiting the opening of the coffin. Near the door stood a mulatto woman, evidently a servant in the house, with a timid bearing and an emaciated face pitifully sad and gentle. She was weeping silently, the corner of her calico apron lifted to her eyes, occasionally suppressing a long, quivering sob. Steavens walked over and stood beside her.

Feeble steps were heard on the stairs, and an old man, tall and frail, odorous of pipe smoke, with shaggy, unkept gray hair and a dingy beard, tobacco stained about the mouth, entered uncertainly. He went slowly up to the coffin and stood rolling a blue cotton handkerchief between his hands, seeming so pained and embarrassed by his wife's orgy of grief that he had no consciousness of anything else.

"There, there, Annie, dear, don't take on so," he quavered timidly, putting out a shaking hand and awkwardly patting her elbow. She turned and sank upon his shoulder with such violence that he tottered a little. He did not even glance toward the coffin, but continued to look at her with a dull, frightened, appealing expression, as a spaniel looks at the whip. His sunken cheeks slowly reddened and burned with miserable shame. When his wife rushed from the room, her daughter strode after her with set lips. The servant stole up to the coffin, bent over it for a moment, and then slipped away to the kitchen, leaving Steavens, the lawyer, and the father to themselves. The old man stood looking down at his dead son's face. The sculptor's splendid head seemed even more noble in its rigid stillness than in life. The dark hair had crept down upon the wide forehead; the face seemed strangely long, but in it there was not that repose we expect to find in the faces of the dead. The brows were so drawn that there were two deep lines above the beaked nose, and the chin was thrust forward defiantly. It was as though the strain of life had been so sharp and bitter that death could not at once relax the tension and smooth the countenance into perfect peace—as though he were still guarding something precious, which might even yet be wrested from him.

The old man's lips were working under his stained beard. He turned to the lawyer with timid deference: "Phelps and the rest are comin' back to set up with Harve, ain't they?" he asked. "Thank 'ee, Jim, thank 'ee." He brushed the hair back gently from his son's forehead. "He was a good boy, Jim; always a good boy. He was ez gentle ez a child and the kindest of 'em all—only we didn't none of us ever onderstand him." The tears trickled slowly down his beard and dropped upon the sculptor's coat.

"Martin, Martin! Oh, Martin! come here," his wife wailed from the top of the stairs. The old man started timorously: "Yes, Annie, I'm coming." He turned away, hesitated, stood for a moment in miserable indecision; then reached back and patted the dead man's hair softly, and stumbled from the room.

"Poor old man, I didn't think he had any tears left. Seems as if his eyes would have gone dry long ago. At his age nothing cuts very deep," remarked the lawyer.

Something in his tone made Steavens glance up. While the mother had been in the room, the young man had scarcely seen any one else; but now, from the moment he first glanced into Jim Laird's florid face and bloodshot eyes, he knew that he had found what he had been heartsick at not finding before—the feeling, the understanding, that must exist in some one, even here.

The man was red as his beard, with features swollen and blurred by dissipation, and a hot, blazing blue eye. His face was strained—that of a man who is controlling himself with difficulty—and he kept plucking at his beard with a sort of fierce resentment. Steavens, sitting by the window, watched him turn down the glaring lamp, still its jangling pendants with an angry gesture, and then stand with his hands locked behind him, staring down into the master's face. He could not help wondering what link there had been between the porcelain vessel and so sooty a lump of potter's clay.

From the kitchen an uproar was sounding; when the dining-room door opened, the import of it was clear. The mother was abusing the maid for having forgotten to make the dressing for the chicken salad which had been prepared for the watchers. Steavens had never heard anything in the least like it; it was injured, emotional, dramatic abuse, unique and masterly in its excruciating cruelty, as violent and unrestrained as had been her grief of twenty minutes before. With a shudder of disgust the lawyer went into the dining-room and closed the door into the kitchen.

"Poor Roxy's getting it now," he remarked when he came back. "The Mericks took her out of the poor-house years ago; and if her loyalty would let her, I guess the poor old thing could tell tales that would curdle your blood. She's the mulatto woman who was standing in here a while ago, with her apron to her eyes. The old woman is a fury; there never was anybody like her. She made Harvey's life a hell for him when he lived at home; he was so sick ashamed of it. I never could see how he kept himself sweet."

"He was wonderful," said Steavens slowly, "wonderful; but until tonight I have never known how wonderful."

"That is the eternal wonder of it, anyway; that it can come even from such a dung heap as this," the lawyer cried, with a sweeping gesture which seemed to indicate much more than the four walls within which they stood.

"I think I'll see whether I can get a little air. The room is so close I am beginning to feel rather faint," murmured Steavens, struggling with one of the windows. The sash was stuck, however, and would not yield, so he sat down dejectedly and began pulling at his collar. The lawyer came over, loosened the sash with one blow of his red fist and sent the window up a few inches. Steavens thanked him, but the nausea which had been gradually climbing into his throat for the last half hour left him with but one desire—a desperate feeling that he must get away from this place with what was left of Harvey Merrick. Oh, he comprehended well enough now the quiet bitterness of the smile that he had seen so often on his master's lips!

Once when Merrick returned from a visit home, he brought with him a singularly feeling and suggestive bas-relief[5] of a thin, faded old woman, sitting and sewing something pinnned to her knee; while a full-lipped, full-blooded little urchin, his trousers held up by a single gallows,[6] stood beside her, impatiently twitching her gown to call her attention to a butterfly he had caught. Steavens, impressed by the tender and delicate modelling of the thin, tired face, had asked him if it were his mother. He remembered the dull flush that had burned up in the sculptor's face.

The lawyer was sitting in a rocking-chair beside the coffin, his head thrown back and his eyes closed. Steavens looked at him earnestly, puzzled at the line of the chin, and wondering why a man should conceal a feature of such distinction under that disfiguring shock of beard. Suddenly, as though he felt the young sculptor's keen glance, Jim Laird opened his eyes.

"Was he always a good deal of an oyster?" he asked abruptly. "He was terribly shy as a boy."

"Yes, he was an oyster, since you put it so," rejoined Steavens. "Although he could be very fond of people, he always gave one the impression of being detached. He disliked violent emotion; he was reflective, and rather distrustful of himself—except, of course, as regarded his work. He was sure enough there. He distrusted men pretty thoroughly and women even more, yet somehow without believing ill of them. He was determined, indeed, to believe the best; but he seemed afraid to investigate."

"A burnt dog dreads the fire," said the lawyer grimly, and closed his eyes.

Steavens went on and on, reconstructing that whole miserable boyhood. All this raw, biting ugliness had been the portion of the man whose mind was to become an exhaustless gallery of beautiful impressions—so sensitive that the mere shadow of a poplar leaf flickering against a sunny wall would be etched and held there for ever. Surely, if ever a man had the magic word in his finger tips, it was Merrick. Whatever he touched, he revealed its holiest secret; liberated it from enchantment and restored it to its pristine loveliness. Upon whatever he had come in contact with, he had left a beautiful record of the experience—a sort of ethereal signature; a scent, a sound, a color that was his own.

Steavens understood now the real tragedy of his master's life; neither love nor wine, as many had conjectured; but a blow which had fallen earlier and cut deeper than anything else could have done—a shame not his, and yet so unescapably his, to hide in his heart from his very boyhood. And without—the frontier warfare; the yearning of a boy, cast ashore upon a desert of newness and ugliness and sordidness, for all that is chastened and old, and noble with traditions.

5. Low relief (French); a sculpture in which an image is slightly raised against a background.

6. I.e., a single suspender.

At eleven o'clock the tall, flat woman in black announced that the watchers were arriving, and asked them to "step into the dining-room." As Steavens rose, the lawyer said dryly: "You go on—it'll be a good experience for you. I'm not equal to that crowd tonight; I've had twenty years of them."

As Steavens closed the door after him he glanced back at the lawyer, sitting by the coffin in the dim light, with his chin resting on his hand.

The same misty group that had stood before the door of the express car shuffled into the dining-room. In the light of the kerosene lamp they separated and became individuals. The minister, a pale, feeble-looking man with white hair and blond chin-whiskers, took his seat beside a small side table and placed his Bible upon it. The Grand Army man sat down behind the stove and tilted his chair back comfortably against the wall, fishing his quill toothpick from his waistcoat pocket. The two bankers, Phelps and Elder, sat off in a corner behind the dinner-table, where they could finish their discussion of the new usury law and its effect on chattel security loans.[7] The real estate agent, an old man with a smiling, hypocritical face, soon joined them. The coal and lumber dealer and the cattle shipper sat on opposite sides of the hard coal-burner, their feet on the nickel-work.[8] Steavens took a book from his pocket and began to read. The talk around him ranged through various topics of local interest while the house was quieting down. When it was clear that the members of the family were in bed, the Grand Army man hitched his shoulders and, untangling his long legs, caught his heels on the rounds of his chair.

"S'pose there'll be a will, Phelps?" he queried in his weak falsetto.

The banker laughed disagreeably, and began trimming his nails with a pearl-handled pocket-knife.

"There'll scarcely be any need for one, will there?" he queried in his turn.

The restless Grand Army man shifted his position again, getting his knees still nearer his chin. "Why, the ole man says Harve's done right well lately," he chirped.

The other banker spoke up. "I reckon he means by that Harve ain't asked him to mortgage any more farms lately, so as he could go on with his education."

"Seems like my mind don't reach back to a time when Harve wasn't bein' edycated," tittered the Grand Army man.

There was a general chuckle. The minister took out his handkerchief and blew his nose sonorously. Banker Phelps closed his knife with a snap. "It's too bad the old man's sons didn't turn out better," he remarked with reflective authority. "They never hung together. He spent money enough on Harve to stock a dozen cattle-farms, and he might as well have poured it into Sand Creek. If Harve had stayed at home and helped nurse what little they had, and gone into stock on the old man's bottom farm, they might all have been well fixed. But the old man had to trust everything to tenants and was cheated right and left."

"Harve never could have handled stock none," interposed the cattleman. "He hadn't it in him to be sharp. Do you remember when he bought Sander's

7. Loans backed by the debtor's personal property. Kansas revised its laws regulating interest on loans and prohibiting usury (excessive interest) in 1889.

8. Cast-iron stoves were often finished with nickel trim work, sometimes including footrests.

mules for eight-year olds, when everybody in town knew that Sander's father-in-law give 'em to his wife for a wedding present eighteen years before, an' they was full-grown mules then?"

The company laughed discreetly, and the Grand Army man rubbed his knees with a spasm of childish delight.

"Harve never was much account for anything practical, and he shore was never fond of work," began the coal and lumber dealer. "I mind the last time he was home; the day he left, when the old man was out to the barn helpin' his hand hitch up to take Harve to the train, and Cal Moots was patchin' up the fence; Harve, he come out on the step and sings out, in his ladylike voice: 'Cal Moots, Cal Moots! please come cord my trunk.'"

"That's Harve for you," approved the Grand Army man. "I kin hear him howlin' yet, when he was a big feller in long pants and his mother used to whale him with a rawhide in the barn for lettin' the cows git foundered in the cornfield when he was drivin' 'em home from pasture. He killed a cow of mine that-a-way onct—a pure Jersey and the best milker I had, an' the ole man had to put up for her. Harve, he was watchin' the sun set acrost the marshes when the anamile got away."

"Where the old man made his mistake was in sending the boy East to school," said Phelps, stroking his goatee and speaking in a deliberate, judicial tone. "There was where he got his head full of nonsense. What Harve needed, of all people, was a course in some first-class Kansas City business college."

The letters were swimming before Steavens's eyes. Was it possible that these men did not understand, that the palm on the coffin meant nothing to them? The very name of their town would have remained for ever buried in the postal guide had it not been now and again mentioned in the world in connection with Harvey Merrick's. He remembered what his master had said to him on the day of his death, after the congestion of both lungs had shut off any probability of recovery, and the sculptor had asked his pupil to send his body home. "It's not a pleasant place to be lying while the world is moving and doing and bettering," he had said with a feeble smile, "but it rather seems as though we ought to go back to the place we came from, in the end. The townspeople will come in for a look at me; and after they have had their say, I shan't have much to fear from the judgment of God!"

The cattleman took up the comment. "Forty's young for a Merrick to cash in; they usually hang on pretty well. Probably he helped it along with whisky."

"His mother's people were not long lived, and Harvey never had a robust constitution," said the minister mildly. He would have liked to say more. He had been the boy's Sunday-school teacher, and had been fond of him; but he felt that he was not in a position to speak. His own sons had turned out badly, and it was not a year since one of them had made his last trip home in the express car, shot in a gambling-house in the Black Hills.

"Nevertheless, there is no disputin' that Harve frequently looked upon the wine when it was red, also variegated, and it shore made an oncommon fool of him," moralized the cattleman.

Just then the door leading into the parlour rattled loudly and every one started involuntarily, looking relieved when only Jim Laird came out. The

Grand Army man ducked his head when he saw the spark in his blue, blood-shot eye. They were all afraid of Jim; he was a drunkard, but he could twist the law to suit his client's needs as no other man in all western Kansas could do, and there were many who tried. The lawyer closed the door behind him, leaned back against it and folded his arms, cocking his head a little to one side. When he assumed this attitude in the court-room, ears were always pricked up, as it usually foretold a flood of withering sarcasm.

"I've been with you gentlemen before," he began in a dry, even tone, "when you've sat by the coffins of boys born and raised in this town; and, if I remember rightly, you were never any too well satisfied when you checked them up. What's the matter, anyhow? Why is it that reputable young men are as scarce as millionaires in Sand City? It might almost seem to a stranger that there was some way something the matter with your progressive town. Why did Ruben Sayer, the brightest young lawyer you ever turned out, after he had come home from the university as straight as a die, take to drinking and forge a check and shoot himself? Why did Bill Merrit's son die of the shakes in a saloon in Omaha? Why was Mr. Thomas's son, here, shot in a gambling-house? Why did young Adams burn his mill to beat the insurance companies and go to the pen?"

The lawyer paused and unfolded his arms, laying one clenched fist quietly on the table. "I'll tell you why. Because you drummed nothing but money and knavery into their ears from the time they wore knickerbockers; because you carped away at them as you've been carping here tonight, holding our friends Phelps and Elder up to them for their models, as our grandfathers held up George Washington and John Adams. But the boys were young, and raw at the business you put them to, and how could they match coppers with such artists as Phelps and Elder? You wanted them to be successful rascals; they were only unsuccessful ones—that's all the difference. There was only one boy ever raised in this borderland between ruffianism and civilization who didn't come to grief, and you hated Harvey Merrick more for winning out than you hated all the other boys who got under the wheels. Lord, Lord, how you did hate him! Phelps, here, is fond of saying that he could buy and sell us all out any time he's a mind to; but he knew Harve wouldn't have given a tinker's damn for his bank and all his cattlefarms put together; and a lack of appreciation, that way, goes hard with Phelps.

"Old Nimrod thinks Harve drank too much; and this from such as Nimrod and me!

"Brother Elder says Harve was too free with the old man's money—fell short in filial consideration, maybe. Well, we can all remember the very tone in which brother Elder swore his own father was a liar, in the county court; and we all know that the old man came out of that partnership with his son as bare as a sheared lamb. But maybe I'm getting personal, and I'd better be driving ahead at what I want to say."

The lawyer paused a moment, squared his heavy shoulders, and went on: "Harvey Merrick and I went to school together, back East. We were dead in earnest, and we wanted you all to be proud of us some day. We meant to be great men. Even I, and I haven't lost my sense of humor, gentlemen, I meant to be a great man. I came back here to practice, and I found you didn't in the least want me to be a great man. You wanted me to be a shrewd lawyer—oh, yes! Our veteran here wanted me to get him an increase of pension, because he had dyspepsia; Phelps wanted a new county survey that would put the widow Wilson's little bottom farm inside his south line; Elder wanted to lend money at 5 per cent a month, and get it collected; and Stark here wanted to wheedle old women up in Vermont into investing their annuities in real-estate mortgages that are not worth the paper they are written on. Oh, you needed me hard enough, and you'll go on needing me!

"Well, I came back here and became the damned shyster you wanted me to be. You pretend to have some sort of respect for me; and yet you'll stand up and throw mud at Harvey Merrick, whose soul you couldn't dirty and whose hands you couldn't tie. Oh, you're a discriminating lot of Christians! There have been times when the sight of Harvey's name in some Eastern paper has made me hang my head like a whipped dog; and, again, times when I liked to think of him off there in the world, away from all this hog-wallow, climbing the big, clean up-grade he'd set for himself.

"And we? Now that we've fought and lied and sweated and stolen, and hated as only the disappointed strugglers in a bitter, dead little Western town know how to do, what have we got to show for it? Harvey Merrick wouldn't have given one sunset over your marshes for all you've got put together, and you know it. It's not for me to say why, in the inscrutable wisdom of God, a genius should ever have been called from this place of hatred and bitter waters; but I want this Boston man to know that the drivel he's been hearing here tonight is the only tribute any truly great man could have from such a lot of sick, side-tracked, burnt-dog, land-poor sharks as the here-present financiers of Sand City—upon which town may God have mercy!"

The lawyer thrust out his hand to Steavens as he passed him, caught up his overcoat in the hall, and had left the house before the Grand Army man had had time to lift his ducked head and crane his long neck about at his fellows.

Next day Jim Laird was drunk and unable to attend the funeral services. Steavens called twice at his office, but was compelled to start East without seeing him. He had a presentiment that he would hear from him again, and left his address on the lawyer's table; but if Laird found it, he never acknowledged it. The thing in him that Harvey Merrick had loved must have gone under ground with Harvey Merrick's coffin; for it never spoke again, and Jim got the cold he died of driving across the Colorado mountains to defend one of Phelps's sons who had got into trouble out there by cutting government timber.

1905, 1920

AMY LOWELL
1874–1925

Born in Brookline, Massachusetts, the fifth and last child, twelve years younger than her nearest sibling, Amy Lowell hailed from one of Boston's wealthiest and most prestigious and powerful families. The first Lowell arrived at Massachusetts Bay Colony in 1639; from the revolutionary years on, when a Lowell was made a judge by George Washington, no era was without one or more Lowells prominent in the intellectual, religious, political, philanthropic, and commercial life of New England. In the early nineteenth century her paternal grandfather and his brothers established the Lowell textile mills in Lowell, Massachusetts—the town itself had been founded by the Lowells in 1653. The success of these mills changed the economy of New England. Profits were invested in utilities, highways, railroads, and banks. In the same generation her maternal grandfather, Abbot Lawrence, established a second New England textile dynasty. All the Lowell men went to Harvard. Traditionally, those who were not in business became Unitarian ministers or scholars—the poet James Russell Lowell was her great-uncle; her father, Augustus, was important to the founding of the Massachusetts Institute of Technology; her brother Percival was a pioneering scholar of Japanese and Korean civilization and an astronomer (he founded the Lowell Observatory); her brother Abbot Lawrence was president of Harvard from 1909 to 1933.

But none of the millionaires, manufacturers, philanthropists, statesmen, ambassadors, judges, and scholars in Amy Lowell's background could give this energetic and unusually intelligent young woman a model to follow. They were all men, and the rules for Lowell women were different. Women in the family were expected to marry well, imbue their children with a strong sense of family pride, oversee the running of several homes, and participate in upper-class Boston's busy social world. None of this interested Lowell in the least. Yet she believed in the importance of her heritage and shared the self-confidence and drive to contribute notably to public life characteristic of Lowell men.

Resisting the kind of formal education available to women of her class at the time, she attended school only between the ages of ten and seventeen. She educated herself through the use of her family's extensive private library as well as the resources of the Boston Athenaeum, a dues-paying library club founded by one of her ancestors early in the nineteenth century. She had enjoyed writing from childhood on, but did not venture into professional authorship until 1912, at the age of thirty-eight. In that year, her first book of poems—*A Dome of Many-Coloured Glass*—achieved both popular and critical success.

The year 1912 was the year that Harriet Monroe launched her influential little magazine, *Poetry*, and when in January 1913 Lowell read H.D.'s imagistic poetry she was converted to this new style. She decided to devote her popularity and social prominence to popularizing imagism and with characteristic energy and self-confidence journeyed to England to meet H.D., Ezra Pound, D. H. Lawrence, Richard Aldington, and other participants in the informal movement. When Pound abandoned imagism for vorticism, Lowell became the chief spokesperson for the movement, editing several imagist anthologies. Two volumes of original criticism by Lowell—*Six French Poets* (1915) and *Tendencies in Modern American Poetry* (1917)—also forwarded the cause. Pound, upstaged as a publicist, enviously renamed the movement "Amygism." Lowell retorted that "it was not until I entered the arena and Ezra dropped out that Imagism had to be considered seriously."

Lowell's own poetry—published in *Sword Blades and Poppy Seed* (1914), *Men, Women, and Ghosts* (1916), *Can Grande's Castle* (1918), *Pictures of the Floating World* (1919), and *Legends* (1921)—was never exclusively imagistic but included long historical narrative poems and journalistic prose poems and used standard verse patterns, blank verse, and a Whitmanesque free verse resembling the open line developed by Carl Sandburg. Her best poems tend to enclose sharp imagistic representation within this relatively fluid line, thereby achieving an effect of simultaneous compactness and flexibility. Like many women poets, she worked with a symbolic vocabulary of flowers and color.

Lowell enjoyed her success and cheerfully went on the lecture circuit as a celebrity, making innumerable close friendships as a result of her warmth and generosity. Despite health problems that plagued her for most of her life, she remained full of energy and zest. She depended for support on the companionship of Ada Dwyer Russell, a former actress, for whom she wrote many of her most moving appreciations of female beauty. Although she traveled widely in Europe, she was ultimately committed to New England and the Lowell heritage, both of which fused in an attachment to her home, Sevenels, in Brookline. A devotee of Romantic poetry and especially of Keats, she had begun to collect Keats manuscripts in 1905; these now form the basis of the great collection at Harvard University. In addition to all her other activities in the 1920s, she worked on a two-volume biography of Keats that greatly extended the published information about the poet when it appeared in 1925, although its psychological approach offended many traditional critics.

Lowell was just fifty-one when she died. Despite continued sniping from the high modernist poets who thought her work was too accessible, her poetry continued to be both popular and critically esteemed until the 1950s, when scholars focused the canon on a very small number of writers. The efforts of feminists to rediscover and republicize the work of neglected women authors as well as the researches of literary historians into the whole picture of American literary achievement have together brought her work back into the spotlight that it occupied during her lifetime.

The texts printed here are from Lowell's *Complete Poems* (1955).

The Captured Goddess

Over the housetops,
Above the rotating chimney-pots,
I have seen a shiver of amethyst,
And blue and cinnamon have flickered
A moment,
At the far end of a dusty street.

Through sheeted rain
Has come a lustre of crimson,
And I have watched moonbeams
Hushed by a film of palest green.

It was her wings,
Goddess!
Who stepped over the clouds,
And laid her rainbow feathers
Aslant on the currents of the air.
I followed her for long,

With gazing eyes and stumbling feet.
I cared not where she led me,
My eyes were full of colors:
Saffrons, rubies, the yellows of beryls,
And the indigo-blue of quartz;
Flights of rose, layers of chrysoprase,
Points of orange, spirals of vermilion,
The spotted gold of tiger-lily petals,
The loud pink of bursting hydrangeas.
I followed,
And watched for the flashing of her wings.

In the city I found her,
The narrow-streeted city.
In the market-place I came upon her,
Bound and trembling.
Her fluted wings were fastened to her sides with cords,
She was naked and cold,
For that day the wind blew
Without sunshine.

Men chaffered for her,
They bargained in silver and gold,
In copper, in wheat,
And called their bids across the market-place.

The Goddess wept.

Hiding my face I fled,
And the grey wind hissed behind me,
Along the narrow streets.

1914

Venus Transiens

Tell me,
Was Venus more beautiful
Than you are,
When she topped
The crinkled waves,
Drifting shoreward
On her plaited shell?
Was Botticelli's[1] vision
Fairer than mine;
And were the painted rosebuds
He tossed his lady,
Of better worth

1. Sandro Botticelli (c. 1440–1510), Italian Renaissance painter among whose works is the *Birth of Venus*, depicting the Greek goddess of love and beauty rising from the ocean on a seashell.

Than the words I blow about you
To cover your too great loveliness
As with a gauze
Of misted silver?

For me,
You stand poised
In the blue and buoyant air,
Cinctured by bright winds,
Treading the sunlight.
And the waves which precede you
Ripple and stir
The sands at my feet.

1919

Madonna of the Evening Flowers

All day long I have been working,
Now I am tired.
I call: "Where are you?"
But there is only the oak tree rustling in the wind.
The house is very quiet,
The sun shines in on your books,
On your scissors and thimble just put down,
But you are not there.
Suddenly I am lonely:
Where are you?
I go about searching.

Then I see you,
Standing under a spire of pale blue larkspur,
With a basket of roses on your arm.
You are cool, like silver,
And you smile.
I think the Canterbury bells[1] are playing little tunes.

You tell me that the peonies need spraying,
That the columbines have overrun all bounds,
That the pyrus japonica should be cut back and rounded.
You tell me these things.
But I look at you, heart of silver,
White heart-flame of polished silver,
Burning beneath the blue steeples of the larkspur,
And I long to kneel instantly at your feet,
While all about us peal the loud, sweet *Te Deums* of the
Canterbury bells.

1919

1. Little bell-shaped blue flowers. Lowell puns on the bells of Canterbury Cathedral in England pealing out religious music.

September, 1918

This afternoon was the colour of water falling through sunlight;
The trees glittered with the tumbling of leaves;
The sidewalks shone like alleys of dropped maple leaves;
And the houses ran along them laughing out of square, open windows.
Under a tree in the park,
Two little boys, lying flat on their faces,
Were carefully gathering red berries
To put in a pasteboard box.

Some day there will be no war.
Then I shall take out this afternoon
And turn it in my fingers,
And remark the sweet taste of it upon my palate,
And note the crisp variety of its flights of leaves.
To-day I can only gather it
And put it into my lunch-box,
For I have time for nothing
But the endeavour to balance myself
Upon a broken world.

1919

St. Louis

June

Flat,
Flat,
Long as sight
Either way,
An immense country,
With a great river
Steaming it full of moist, unbearable heat.
The orchards are little quincunxes of Noah's Ark trees,
The plows and horses are children's toys tracing amusingly shallow lines upon an illimitable surface.
Great chunks of life to match the country,
Great lungs to breathe this hot, wet air.

But it is not mine.
Mine is a land of hills
Lying couchant in the angles of heraldic beasts
About white villages.
A land of singing elms and pine-trees.
A restless up and down land

Always mounting, dipping, slipping into a different contour,
Where the roads turn every hundred yards or so,
Where brooks rattle forgotten Indian names to tired farm-houses,
And faint spires of old meeting-houses
Flaunt their golden weather-cocks in a brave show of challenge at a sunset sky.

Here the heat stuffs down with the thickness of boiled feathers,
The river runs in steam.
There, lilacs are in bloom,
Cool blue-purples, wine-reds, whites,
Flying colour to quiet dooryards.
Grown year on year to a suddenness of old perfection,
Saying "Before! Before!" to each new Spring.
Here is "Now,"
But "Before" is mine with the lilacs,
With the white sea of everywhither,
With the heraldic, story-telling hills.

1927

New Heavens for Old

I am useless,
What I do is nothing.
What I think has no savour.
There is an almanac between the windows:
It is of the year when I was born.
My fellows call to me to join them,
They shout for me,
Passing the house in a great wind of vermillion banners.
They are fresh and fulminant,
They are indecent and strut with the thought of it.
They laugh, and curse, and brawl,
And cheer a holocaust of "Who comes Firsts!" at the iron fronts of the houses at the two edges of the street.
Young men with naked hearts jeering between iron house-fronts,
Young men with naked bodies beneath their clothes
Passionately conscious of them,
Ready to strip off their clothes,
Ready to strip off their customs, their usual routine,
Clamouring for the rawness of life,
In love with appetite,
Proclaiming it as a creed,
Worshipping youth,
Worshipping themselves.
They call for the women and the women come,
They bare the whiteness of their lusts to the dead gaze of the old house-fronts,

They roar down the street like flame,
They explode upon the dead houses like new, sharp fire.

But I—
I arrange three roses in a Chinese vase:
A pink one,
A red one,
A yellow one.
I fuss over their arrangement.
Then I sit in a South window
And sip pale wine with a touch of hemlock in it,
And think of Winter nights,
And field-mice crossing and re-crossing
The spot which will be my grave.

1927

GERTRUDE STEIN
1874–1946

Among modernists active between the wars, Gertrude Stein was more radically experimental than most. She pushed language to its limits—and kept on pushing. Her work was sometimes literal nonsense, often funny, and always exciting to those who thought of writing as a craft and language as a medium. As Sherwood Anderson wrote, "she is laying word against word, relating sound to sound, feeling for the taste, the smell, the rhythm of the individual word. She is attempting to do something for the writers of our English speech that may be better understood after a time, and she is not in a hurry."

Stein's grandparents were well-off German Jewish immigrants who, at the time of her birth, were established in business in Baltimore. Born in Allegheny, Pennsylvania, she was the youngest of seven children; the family lived abroad from 1875 to 1879 and then settled in northern California. Her parents died when she was an adolescent, leaving their five surviving children well provided for. Stein made a family with her favorite brother, Leo, for many years. When he went to Harvard in 1892 she followed and was admitted to Harvard's "annex for women"—later Radcliffe College. She studied there with the great psychologist William James; some of her early writings—for example, *Three Lives* (1909) and *The Making of Americans,* which she completed in 1908 but did not publish until 1925—are probably trying to apply his theories of consciousness: consciousness as unique to each individual, as an ongoing stream, a perpetual present. In *Three Lives,* also, Stein set herself the difficult task of representing the consciousnesses of three ordinary, working-class women whose lives and minds were not the conventional material of serious literature.

When Leo moved on to Johns Hopkins to study biology, Stein followed, enrolling in the medical school. At the end of her fourth year, she failed intentionally, for several reasons: Leo had become interested in art and decided to go to Europe, she

Gertrude Stein and Picasso's Portrait, Man Ray, 1922. Man Ray, one of the most important of modernist photographers, posed Stein at home in front of her 1906 portrait by Pablo Picasso. Stein in her turn composed many "portraits" in writing of her artist friends, including Picasso and Henri Matisse.

had begun to write, and she had become erotically involved with two women (the story of this triangle formed the basis of her novel *Q.E.D.*, published posthumously in 1950). In early 1903 Leo settled in Paris; Stein joined him that fall. They began to collect modern art and became good friends with many of the brilliant aspiring painters of the day, including Pablo Picasso, Georges Braque, and Henri Matisse. Stein's friendship with the painters was extremely important for her development, for she reproduced some of their experiments in the very different medium of words. Because of them, she came to think of words as tangible entities in themselves as well as vehicles conveying meaning or representing reality. The cubist movement in painting also affected her. Painters like Picasso and Braque believed that so-called representational paintings conveyed not what people actually saw but rather what they had learned to *think* they saw. The cubists wanted to reproduce a pure visual experience unmediated by cultural ideas. To see a "person" is to see a cultural construct. So they painted a human form reduced to various geometrical shapes as they might be seen from different angles when the form moved or the observer changed position. The degree to which their paintings shocked an audience measured, to Picasso and Braque, the degree to which that audience had lost its original perceiving power.

In 1909 the long companionship of Stein and her brother was complicated when Alice B. Toklas joined the household as Gertrude Stein's lover; she became her secretary, housekeeper, typist, editor, and lifelong companion. Leo moved out in 1913, and the art collection was divided, but the apartment at 27 rue de Fleurus continued to serve as a gathering place for French artists and intellectuals, American expatriates, and American visitors. Without much expectation that her work would achieve any wide audience, Stein continued to write and to advise younger writers like Ernest Hemingway and F. Scott Fitzgerald. "A great deal of description," she said about a draft of Hemingway's first novel, "and not particularly good description.

Begin over again and concentrate." The need to concentrate and distill—the idea that description was too often an indulgence—was a lesson the younger writer took to heart.

In the 1920s Stein and Toklas began spending summers in the south of France, where they bought a small house in 1929. They lived there during the war, when they could not return to Paris. Devoted to their adopted country, Stein and Toklas did what they could for France during both world wars. They visited and entertained American soldiers, many of whom continued to write to the couple for years after they had returned to the United States and some of whom visited when they had occasion to return to France. Even though Stein returned to the United States only once, in 1934, on what turned into a very successful lecture tour, she and Toklas always thought of themselves as Americans.

Being American is one topic of investigation that threads itself throughout Stein's body of experimental writing; the other is love. *The Making of Americans*, the most ambitious work of Stein's early career, linked these two concerns by wrenching a familiar novelistic form, that of the multigenerational family saga, into a strange and monumental new shape. Stein called the story of Martha Hersland and her family "a decent family progress," but it is a progress built on repetition—not only the repetition of human character from one generation to the next but also repetition in the words and sentences of Stein's prose. *The Making of Americans* identifies repeating with loving, with the process of writing, with human history, and with the rhythms of life itself: "Repeating is a wonderful thing in living being."

Stein's 1914 *Tender Buttons*, a cubist prose-poem presenting verbal collages of domestic objects, also celebrated her loving relationship with Alice B. Toklas. From its title forward, the work incorporates semiprivate erotic wordplay into its playful catalog of Stein and Toklas's shared life. *Tender Buttons* looked forward to Stein's innovative work of the 1920s, in which she treated words as things, ignoring or defying the connection between words and meanings, continually undercutting expectations about order, coherence, and associations.

In the 1930s Stein turned her writing toward more accessible forms and more public purposes—including self-promotion. Her gossipy, intimate, irreverent autobiography, written as *The Autobiography of Alice B. Toklas* (1933), was serialized in *The Atlantic Monthly* and became a best seller in the United States. In 1934 the opera *Four Saints in Three Acts*, for which she had written a libretto set to music by the American composer Virgil Thomson (1896–1989), opened on Broadway, with an all-black cast daringly chosen to portray Stein's roster of white European saints. *Everybody's Autobiography* (1937) recounted Stein's triumphant American lecture tour of 1934–35. Stein returned to American history for one of her last major works, the libretto to *The Mother of Us All* (set to music once again by Virgil Thomson and premiered in 1947), which centered on the life and work of the suffragist Susan B. Anthony (1820–1906).

By the time of her death Stein had become a public personality. In the later twentieth century, the women's and gay liberation movements contributed to a new appreciation of her radical individualism. Avant-garde American writing and art, such as the L=A=N=G=U=A=G=E school of contemporary poetry and the hypnotically repetitive operas of Philip Glass, continue to register the influence of Stein's experimental work.

The text of *The Making of Americans* is from the first edition (1925). The text of *Tender Buttons* is from the first edition (1914).

From The Making of Americans[1]

[INTRODUCTION]

Once an angry man dragged his father along the ground through his own orchard. "Stop!" cried the groaning old man at last, "Stop! I did not drag my father beyond this tree."

It is hard living down the tempers we are born with. We all begin well, for in our youth there is nothing we are more intolerant of than our own sins writ large in others and we fight them fiercely in ourselves; but we grow old and we see that these our sins are of all sins the really harmless ones to own, nay that they give a charm to any character, and so our struggle with them dies away.

I am writing for myself and strangers. This is the only way that I can do it. Everybody is a real one to me, everybody is like some one else too to me. No one of them that I know can want to know it and so I write for myself and strangers.

Every one is always busy with it, no one of them then ever want to know it that every one looks like some one else and they see it. Mostly every one dislikes to hear it. It is very important to me to always know it, to always see it which one looks like others and to tell it. I write for myself and strangers. I do this for my own sake and for the sake of those who know I know it that they look like other ones, that they are separate and yet always repeated.[2] There are some who like it that I know they are like many others and repeat it, there are many who never can really like it.

There are many that I know and they know it. They are all of them repeating and I hear it. I love it and I tell it, I love it and now I will write it. This is now the history of the way some of them are it.

I write for myself and strangers. No one who knows me can like it. At least they mostly do not like it that every one is of a kind of men and women and I see it. I love it and I write it.

I want readers so strangers must do it. Mostly no one knowing me can like it that I love it that every one is a kind of men and women, that always I am looking and comparing and classifying of them, always I am seeing their repeating. Always more and more I love repeating, it may be irritating to hear from them but always more and more I love it of them. More and more I love it of them, the being in them, the mixing in them, the repeating in them, the deciding the kinds of them every one is who has human being.

This is now a little of what I love and how I write it. Later there will be much more of it.

There are many ways of making kinds of men and women. Now there will be descriptions of every kind of way every one can be a kind of men and women.

This is now a history of Martha Hersland. This is now a history of Martha and of every one who came to be of her living.

1. This long book—over nine hundred pages—tells the story of Martha Hersland, who represents Stein herself, and her family. *Making* refers both to family history and to making the book.

2. Differences within basic similarities among people correspond to the differences within similar sentences employed as the chief experimental technique of *The Making of Americans.*

There will then be soon much description of every way one can think of men and women, in their beginning, in their middle living, and their ending.[3]

Every one then is an individual being. Every one then is like many others always living, there are many ways of thinking of every one, this is now a description of all of them. There must then be a whole history of each one of them. There must then now be a description of all repeating. Now I will tell all the meaning to me in repeating, the loving there is in me for repeating.

Every one is one inside them, every one reminds some one of some other one who is or was or will be living. Every one has it to say of each one he is like such a one I see it in him, every one has it to say of each one she is like some one else I can tell by remembering. So it goes on always in living, every one is always remembering some one who is resembling to the one at whom they are then looking. So they go on repeating, every one is themselves inside them and every one is resembling to others, and that is always interesting. There are many ways of making kinds of men and women. In each way of making kinds of them there is a different system of finding them resembling. Sometime there will be here every way there can be of seeing kinds of men and women. Sometime there will be then a complete history of each one. Every one always is repeating the whole of them and so sometime some one who sees them will have a complete history of every one. Sometime some one will know all the ways there are for people to be resembling, some one sometime then will have a completed history of every one.

Soon now there will be a history of the way repeating comes out of them comes out of men and women when they are young, when they are children, they have then their own system of being resembling; this will soon be a description of the men and women in beginning, the being young in them, the being children.

There is then now and here the loving repetition, this is then, now and here, a description of the loving of repetition and then there will be a description of all the kinds of ways there can be seen to be kinds of men and women. Then there will be realised the complete history of every one, the fundamental character of every one, the bottom nature in them, the mixtures in them, the strength and weakness of everything they have inside them, the flavor of them, the meaning in them, the being in them, and then you have a whole history then of each one. Everything then they do in living is clear to the completed understanding, their living, loving, eating, pleasing, smoking, thinking, scolding, drinking, working, dancing, walking, talking, laughing, sleeping, everything in them. There are whole beings then, they are themselves inside them, repeating coming out of them makes a history of each one of them.

Always from the beginning there was to me all living as repeating. This is now a description of my feeling. As I was saying listening to repeating is often irritating,[4] always repeating is all of living, everything in a being is always repeating, more and more listening to repeating gives to me completed understanding. Each one slowly comes to be a whole one to me. Each one slowly

3. Here Stein expands her intention to encompass every variation of human life. The repetition of present participles (*-ing*) emphasizes current action, present time.

4. Stein is aware that her techniques may irritate readers, just as human sameness may cause people to be irritated with each other.

comes to be a whole one in me. Soon then it commences to sound through my ears and eyes and feelings the repeating that is always coming out from each one, that is them, that makes then slowly of each one of them a whole one. Repeating then comes slowly then to be to one who has it to have loving repeating as natural being comes to be a full sound telling all the being in each one such a one is ever knowing. Sometimes it takes many years of knowing some one before the repeating that is that one gets to be a steady sounding to the hearing of one who has it as a natural being to love repeating that slowly comes out from every one. Sometimes it takes many years of knowing some one before the repeating in that one comes to be a clear history of such a one. Natures sometimes are so mixed up in some one that steady repeating in them is mixed up with changing. Soon then there will be a completed history of each one. Sometimes it is difficult to know it in some, for what these are saying is repeating in them is not the real repeating of them, is not the complete repeating for them. Sometimes many years of knowing some one pass before repeating of all being in them comes out clearly from them. As I was saying it is often irritating to listen to the repeating they are doing, always then that one that has it as being to love repeating that is the whole history of each one, such a one has it then that this irritation passes over into patient completed understanding. Loving repeating is one way of being. This is now a description of such feeling.

There are many that I know and they know it. They are all of them repeating and I hear it. I love it and I tell it. I love it and now I will write it. This is now a history of my love of it. I hear it and I love it and I write it. They repeat it. They live it and I see it and I hear it. They live it and I hear it and I see it and I love it and now and always I will write it. There are many kinds of men and women and I know it. They repeat it and I hear it and I love it. This is now a history of the way they do it. This is now a history of the way I love it.[5]

Now I will tell of the meaning to me in repeating, of the loving there is in me for repeating.

Sometimes every one becomes a whole one to me. Sometimes every one has a completed history for me. Slowly each one is a whole one to me, with some, all their living is passing before they are a whole one to me. There is a completed history of them to me then when there is of them a completed understanding of the bottom nature in them of the nature or natures mixed up in them with the bottom nature of them or separated in them. There is then a history of the things they say and do and feel, and happen to them. There is then a history of the living in them. Repeating is always in all of them. Repeating in them comes out of them, slowly making clear to any one that looks closely at them the nature and the natures mixed up in them. This sometime comes to be clear in every one.

Often as I was saying repeating is very irritating to listen to from them and then slowly it settles into a completed history of them. Repeating is a wonderful thing in living being. Sometime then the nature of every one comes to be clear to some one listening to the repeating coming out of each one.

This is then now to be a little description of the loving feeling for understanding of the completed history of each one that comes to one who listens

5. In telling about others with such care, Stein shows her love for them; hence the tale is about her love as well as their lives.

always steadily to all repeating. This is the history then of the loving feeling in me of repeating, the loving feeling in me for completed understanding of the completed history of every one as it slowly comes out in every one as patiently and steadily I hear it and see it as repeating in them. This is now a little a description of this loving feeling. This is now a little a history of it from the beginning.

* * *

1906–08 1925

From Tender Buttons

Objects

A CARAFE, THAT IS A BLIND GLASS

A kind in glass and a cousin, a spectacle and nothing strange a single hurt color and an arrangement in a system to pointing. All this and not ordinary, not unordered in not resembling. The difference is spreading.

GLAZED GLITTER

Nickel, what is nickel, it is originally rid of a cover.

The change in that is that red weakens an hour. The change has come. There is no search. But there is, there is that hope and that interpretation and sometime, surely any is unwelcome, sometime there is breath and there will be a sinecure and charming very charming is that clean and cleansing. Certainly glittering is handsome and convincing.

There is no gratitude in mercy and in medicine. There can be breakages in Japanese. That is no programme. That is no color chosen. It was chosen yesterday, that showed spitting and perhaps washing and polishing. It certainly showed no obligation and perhaps if borrowing is not natural there is some use in giving.

A SUBSTANCE IN A CUSHION

The change of color is likely and a difference a very little difference is prepared. Sugar is not a vegetable.

Callous is something that hardening leaves behind what will be soft if there is a genuine interest in there being present as many girls as men. Does this change. It shows that dirt is clean when there is a volume.

A cushion has that cover. Supposing you do not like to change, supposing it is very clean that there is no change in appearance, supposing that there is regularity and a costume is that any the worse than an oyster and an exchange. Come to season that is there any extreme use in feather and cotton. Is there not much more joy in a table and more chairs and very likely roundness and a place to put them.

A circle of fine card board and a chance to see a tassel.

What is the use of a violent kind of delightfulness if there is no pleasure in not getting tired of it. The question does not come before there is a quotation.

In any kind of place there is a top to covering and it is a pleasure at any rate there is some venturing in refusing to believe nonsense. It shows what use there is in a whole piece if one uses it and it is extreme and very likely the little things could be dearer but in any case there is a bargain and if there is the best thing to do is to take it away and wear it and then be reckless be reckless and resolved on returning gratitude.

Light blue and the same red with purple makes a change. It shows that there is no mistake. Any pink shows that and very likely it is reasonable. Very likely there should not be a finer fancy present. Some increase means a calamity and this is the best preparation for three and more being together. A little calm is so ordinary and in any case there is sweetness and some of that.

A seal and matches and a swan and ivy and a suit.

A closet, a closet does not connect under the bed. The band if it is white and black, the band has a green string. A sight a whole sight and a little groan grinding makes a trimming such a sweet singing trimming and a red thing not a round thing but a white thing, a red thing and a white thing.

The disgrace is not in carelessness nor even in sewing it comes out out of the way.

What is the sash like. The sash is not like anything mustard it is not like a same thing that has stripes, it is not even more hurt than that, it has a little top.

A BOX

Out of kindness comes redness and out of rudeness comes rapid same question, out of an eye comes research, out of selection comes painful cattle. So then the order is that a white way of being round is something suggesting a pin and is it disappointing, it is not, it is so rudimentary to be analysed and see a fine substance strangely, it is so earnest to have a green point not to red but to point again.

A PIECE OF COFFEE

More of double.

A place in no new table.

A single image is not splendor. Dirty is yellow. A sign of more in not mentioned. A piece of coffee is not a detainer. The resemblance to yellow is dirtier and distincter. The clean mixture is whiter and not coal color, never more coal color than altogether.

The sight of a reason, the same sight slighter, the sight of a simpler negative answer, the same sore sounder, the intention to wishing, the same splendor, the same furniture.

The time to show a message is when too late and later there is no hanging in a blight.

A not torn rose-wood color. If it is not dangerous then a pleasure and more than any other if it is cheap is not cheaper. The amusing side is that the sooner there are no fewer the more certain is the necessity dwindled. Supposing that the case contained rose-wood and a color. Supposing that there was no reason for a distress and more likely for a number, supposing that there was no astonishment, is it not necessary to mingle astonishment.

The settling of stationing cleaning is one way not to shatter scatter and scattering. The one way to use custom is to use soap and silk for cleaning. The one way to see cotton is to have a design concentrating the illusion and the illustration. The perfect way is to accustom the thing to have a lining and the shape of a ribbon and to be solid, quite solid in standing and to use heaviness in morning. It is light enough in that. It has that shape nicely. Very nicely may not be exaggerating. Very strongly may be sincerely fainting. May be strangely flattering. May not be strange in everything. May not be strange to.

DIRT AND NOT COPPER

Dirt and not copper makes a color darker. It makes the shape so heavy and makes no melody harder.

It makes mercy and relaxation and even a strength to spread a table fuller. There are more places not empty. They see cover.

NOTHING ELEGANT

A charm a single charm is doubtful. If the red is rose and there is a gate surrounding it, if inside is let in and there places change then certainly something is upright. It is earnest.

MILDRED'S UMBRELLA

A cause and no curve, a cause and loud enough, a cause and extra a loud clash and an extra wagon, a sign of extra, a sac a small sac and an established color and cunning, a slender grey and no ribbon, this means a loss a great loss a restitution.

A METHOD OF A CLOAK

A single climb to a line, a straight exchange to a cane, a desperate adventure and courage and a clock, all this which is a system, which has feeling, which has resignation and success, all makes an attractive black silver.

A RED STAMP

If lilies are lily white if they exhaust noise and distance and even dust, if they dusty will dirt a surface that has no extreme grace, if they do this and it is not necessary it is not at all necessary if they do this they need a catalogue.

A BOX

A large box is handily made of what is necessary to replace any substance. Suppose an example is necessary, the plainer it is made the more reason there is for some outward recognition that there is a result.

A box is made sometimes and them to see to see to it neatly and to have the holes stopped up makes it necessary to use paper.

A custom which is necessary when a box is used and taken is that a large part of the time there are three which have different connections. The one is on the table. The two are on the table. The three are on the table.

The one, one is the same length as is shown by the cover being longer. The other is different there is more cover that shows it. The other is different and that makes the corners have the same shade the eight are in singular arrangement to make four necessary.

Lax, to have corners, to be lighter than some weight, to indicate a wedding journey, to last brown and not curious, to be wealthy, cigarettes are established by length and by doubling.

Left open, to be left pounded, to be left closed, to be circulating in summer and winter, and sick color that is grey that is not dusty and red shows, to be sure cigarettes do measure an empty length sooner than a choice in color.

Winged, to be winged means that white is yellow and pieces pieces that are brown are dust color if dust is washed off, then it is choice that is to say it is fitting cigarettes sooner than paper.

An increase why is an increase idle, why is silver cloister, why is the spark brighter, if it is brighter is there any result, hardly more than ever.

A PLATE

An occasion for a plate, an occasional resource is in buying and how soon does washing enable a selection of the same thing neater. If the party is small a clever song is in order.

Plates and a dinner set of colored china. Pack together a string and enough with it to protect the centre, cause a considerable haste and gather more as it is cooling, collect more trembling and not any even trembling, cause a whole thing to be a church.

A sad size a size that is not sad is blue as every bit of blue is precocious. A kind of green a game in green and nothing flat nothing quite flat and more round, nothing a particular color strangely, nothing breaking the losing of no little piece.

A splendid address a really splendid address is not shown by giving a flower freely, it is not shown by a mark or by wetting.

Cut cut in white, cut in white so lately. Cut more than any other and show it. Show it in the stem and in starting and in evening coming complication.

A lamp is not the only sign of glass. The lamp and the cake are not the only sign of stone. The lamp and the cake and the cover are not the only necessity altogether.

A plan a hearty plan, a compressed disease and no coffee, not even a card or a change to incline each way, a plan that has that excess and that break is the one that shows filling.

A SELTZER BOTTLE

Any neglect of many particles to a cracking, any neglect of this makes around it what is lead in color and certainly discolor in silver. The use of this is manifold. Supposing a certain time selected is assured, suppose it is even necessary, suppose no other extract is permitted and no more handling is needed, suppose the rest of the message is mixed with a very long slender needle and even if it could be any black border, supposing all this altogether made a dress and suppose it was actual, suppose the mean way to state it was occasional, if you suppose this in August and even more melodiously, if you suppose this even in the necessary incident of there certainly being no middle in summer and winter, suppose this and an elegant settlement a very elegant settlement is more than of consequence, it is not final and sufficient and substituted. This which was so kindly a present was constant.

A LONG DRESS

What is the current that makes machinery, that makes it crackle, what is the current that presents a long line and a necessary waist. What is this current.

What is the wind, what is it.

Where is the serene length, it is there and a dark place is not a dark place, only a white and red are black, only a yellow and green are blue, a pink is scarlet, a bow is every color. A line distinguishes it. A line just distinguishes it.

A RED HAT

A dark grey, a very dark grey, a quite dark grey is monstrous ordinarily, it is so monstrous because there is no red in it. If red is in everything it is not necessary. Is that not an argument for any use of it and even so is there any place that is better, is there any place that has so much stretched out.

A BLUE COAT

A blue coat is guided guided away, guided and guided away, that is the particular color that is used for that length and not any width not even more than a shadow.

A PIANO

If the speed is open, if the color is careless, if the selection of a strong scent is not awkward, if the button holder is held by all the waving color and there is no color, not any color. If there is no dirt in a pin and there can be none scarcely, if there is not then the place is the same as up standing.

This is no dark custom and it even is not acted in any such a way that a restraint is not spread. That is spread, it shuts and it lifts and awkwardly not awkwardly the centre is in standing.

A CHAIR

A widow in a wise veil and more garments shows that shadows are even. It addresses no more, it shadows the stage and learning. A regular arrangement, the severest and the most preserved is that which has the arrangement not more than always authorized.

A suitable establishment, well housed, practical, patient and staring, a suitable bedding, very suitable and not more particularly than complaining, anything suitable is so necessary.

A fact is that when the direction is just like that, no more, longer, sudden and at the same time not any sofa, the main action is that without a blaming there is no custody.

Practice measurement, practice the sign that means that really means a necessary betrayal, in showing that there is wearing.

Hope, what is a spectacle, a spectacle is the resemblance between the circular side place and nothing else, nothing else.

To choose it is ended, it is actual and more and more than that it has it certainly has the same treat, and a seat all that is practiced and more easily much more easily ordinarily.

Pick a barn, a whole barn, and bend more slender accents than have ever been necessary, shine in the darkness necessarily.

Actually not aching, actually not aching, a stubborn bloom is so artificial and even more than that, it is a spectacle, it is a binding accident, it is animosity and accentuation.

If the chance to dirty diminishing is necessary, if it is why is there no complexion, why is there no rubbing, why is there no special protection.

A FRIGHTFUL RELEASE

A bag which was left and not only taken but turned away was not found. The place was shown to be very like the last time. A piece was not exchanged, not a bit of it, a piece was left over. The rest was mismanaged.

A PURSE

A purse was not green, it was not straw color, it was hardly seen and it had a use a long use and the chain, the chain was never missing, it was not misplaced, it showed that it was open, that is all that it showed.

A MOUNTED UMBRELLA

What was the use of not leaving it there where it would hang what was the use if there was no chance of ever seeing it come there and show that it was handsome and right in the way it showed it. The lesson is to learn that it does show it, that it shows it and that nothing, that there is nothing, that there is no more to do about it and just so much more is there plenty of reason for making an exchange.

A CLOTH

Enough cloth is plenty and more, more is almost enough for that and besides if there is no more spreading is there plenty of room for it. Any occasion shows the best way.

MORE

An elegant use of foliage and grace and a little piece of white cloth and oil.

Wondering so winningly in several kinds of oceans is the reason that makes red so regular and enthusiastic. The reason that there is more snips are the same shining very colored rid of no round color.

A NEW CUP AND SAUCER

Enthusiastically hurting a clouded yellow bud and saucer, enthusiastically so is the bite in the ribbon.

OBJECTS

Within, within the cut and slender joint alone, with sudden equals and no more than three, two in the centre make two one side.

If the elbow is long and it is filled so then the best example is all together.

The kind of show is made by squeezing.

EYE GLASSES

A color in shaving, a saloon is well placed in the centre of an alley.

A CUTLET

A blind agitation is manly and uttermost.

CARELESS WATER

No cup is broken in more places and mended, that is to say a plate is broken and mending does do that it shows that culture is Japanese. It shows the whole element of angels and orders. It does more to choosing and it does more to that ministering counting. It does, it does change in more water.

Supposing a single piece is a hair supposing more of them are orderly, does that show that strength, does that show that joint, does that show that balloon famously. Does it.

A PAPER

A courteous occasion makes a paper show no such occasion and this makes readiness and eyesight and likeness and a stool.

A DRAWING

The meaning of this is entirely and best to say the mark, best to say it best to shown sudden places, best to make bitter, best to make the length tall and nothing broader, anything between the half.

WATER RAINING

Water astonishing and difficult altogether makes a meadow and a stroke.

COLD CLIMATE

A season in yellow sold extra strings makes lying places.

MALACHITE

The sudden spoon is the same in no size. The sudden spoon is the wound in the decision.

AN UMBRELLA

Coloring high means that the strange reason is in front not more in front behind. Not more in front in peace of the dot.

A PETTICOAT

A light white, a disgrace, an ink spot, a rosy charm.

A WAIST

A star glide, a single frantic sullenness, a single financial grass greediness.

Object that is in wood. Hold the pine, hold the dark, hold in the rush, make the bottom.

A piece of crystal. A change, in a change that is remarkable there is no reason to say that there was a time.

A woolen object gilded. A country climb is the best disgrace, a couple of practices any of them in order is so left.

A TIME TO EAT

A pleasant simple habitual and tyrannical and authorised and educated and resumed and articulate separation. This is not tardy.

A LITTLE BIT OF A TUMBLER

A shining indication of yellow consists in there having been more of the same color than could have been expected when all four were bought. This was the hope which made the six and seven have no use for any more places and this necessarily spread into nothing. Spread into nothing.

A FIRE

What was the use of a whole time to send and not send if there was to be the kind of thing that made that come in. A letter was nicely sent.

A HANDKERCHIEF

A winning of all the blessings, a sample not a sample because there is no worry.

RED ROSES

A cool red rose and a pink cut pink, a collapse and a sold hole, a little less hot.

IN BETWEEN

In between a place and candy is a narrow foot-path that shows more mounting than anything, so much really that a calling meaning a bolster measured a whole thing with that. A virgin a whole virgin is judged made and so between curves and outlines and real seasons and more out glasses and a perfectly unprecedented arrangement between old ladies and mild colds there is no satin wood shining.

COLORED HATS

Colored hats are necessary to show that curls are worn by an addition of blank spaces, this makes the difference between single lines and broad stomachs, the least thing is lightening, the least thing means a little flower and a big delay a big delay that makes more nurses than little women really little women. So clean is a light that nearly all of it shows pearls and little ways. A large hat is tall and me and all custard whole.

A FEATHER

A feather is trimmed, it is trimmed by the light and the bug and the post, it is trimmed by little leaning and by all sorts of mounted reserves and loud volumes. It is surely cohesive.

A BROWN

A brown which is not liquid not more so is relaxed and yet there is a change, a news is pressing.

A LITTLE CALLED PAULINE

A little called anything shows shudders.

Come and say what prints all day. A whole few watermelon. There is no pope.

No cut in pennies and little dressing and choose wide soles and little spats really little spices.

A little lace makes boils. This is not true.

Gracious of gracious and a stamp a blue green white bow a blue green lean, lean on the top.

If it is absurd then it is leadish and nearly set in where there is a tight head.

A peaceful life to arise her, noon and moon and moon. A letter a cold sleeve a blanket a shaving house and nearly the best and regular window.

Nearer in fairy sea, nearer and farther, show white has lime in sight, show a stitch of ten. Count, count more so that thicker and thicker is leaning.

I hope she has her cow. Bidding a wedding, widening received treading, little leading mention nothing.

Cough out cough out in the leather and really feather it is not for.

Please could, please could, jam it not plus more sit in when.

A SOUND

Elephant beaten with candy and little pops and chews all bolts and reckless reckless rats, this is this.

A TABLE

A table means does it not my dear it means a whole steadiness. Is it likely that a change.

A table means more than a glass even a looking glass is tall. A table means necessary places and a revision a revision of a little thing it means it does mean that there has been a stand, a stand where it did shake.

SHOES

To be a wall with a damper a stream of pounding way and nearly enough choice makes a steady midnight. It is pus.

A shallow hole rose on red, a shallow hole in and in this makes ale less. It shows shine.

A DOG

A little monkey goes like a donkey that means to say that means to say that more sighs last goes. Leave with it. A little monkey goes like a donkey.

A WHITE HUNTER

A white hunter is nearly crazy.

A LEAVE

In the middle of a tiny spot and nearly bare there is a nice thing to say that wrist is leading. Wrist is leading.

SUPPOSE AN EYES

Suppose it is within a gate which open is open at the hour of closing summer that is to say it is so.

All the seats are needing blackening. A white dress is in sign. A soldier a real soldier has a worn lace a worn lace of different sizes that is to say if he can read, if he can read he is a size to show shutting up twenty-four.

Go red go red, laugh white.

Suppose a collapse in rubbed purr, in rubbed purr get.

Little sales ladies little sales ladies little saddles of mutton.

Little sales of leather and such beautiful beautiful, beautiful beautiful.

A SHAWL

A shawl is a hat and hurt and a red balloon and an under coat and a sizer a sizer of talks.

A shawl is a wedding, a piece of wax a little build. A shawl.

Pick a ticket, pick it in strange steps and with hollows. There is hollow hollow belt, a belt is a shawl.

A plate that has a little bobble, all of them, any so.

Please a round it is ticket.

It was a mistake to state that a laugh and a lip and a laid climb and a depot and a cultivator and little choosing is a point it.

BOOK

Book was there, it was there. Book was there. Stop it, stop it, it was a cleaner, a wet cleaner and it was not where it was wet, it was not high, it was directly placed back, not back again, back it was returned, it was needless, it put a bank, a bank when, a bank care.

Suppose a man a realistic expression of resolute reliability suggests pleasing itself white all white and no head does that mean soap. It does not so. It means kind wavers and little chance to beside beside rest. A plain.

Suppose ear rings that is one way to breed, breed that. Oh chance to say, oh nice old pole. Next best and nearest a pillar. Chest not valuable, be papered.

Cover up cover up the two with a little piece of string and hope rose and green, green.

Please a plate, put a match to the seam and really then really then, really then it is a remark that joins many many lead games. It is a sister and sister and a flower and a flower and a dog and a colored sky a sky colored grey and nearly that nearly that let.

PEELED PENCIL, CHOKE

Rub her coke.

IT WAS BLACK, BLACK TOOK

Black ink best wheel bale brown.

Excellent not a hull house, not a pea soup, no bill no care, no precise no past pearl pearl goat.

THIS IS THIS DRESS, AIDER

Aider, why aider why whow, whow stop touch, aider whow, aider stop the muncher, muncher munchers.

A jack in kill her, a jack in, makes a meadowed king, makes a to let.

1914

World War I and Its Aftermath

By some measures, World War I was a relatively contained event for citizens of the United States. The official American combat presence in the war lasted only seventeen months, from the declaration of war by the U.S. Congress on April 6, 1917, to the armistice declared in western Europe on November 11, 1918. The arrival of the first waves of United States forces in the summer and fall of 1917 helped break what had become an immensely bloody and costly stalemate between the Central Powers (Germany, Austria-Hungary, and Turkey) and the Allies (Great Britain, France, Russia, Italy, and Japan) along the line of trenches extending across western Europe. With the full weight of American industrial, financial, and agricultural power now fortifying the Allies, and with American president Woodrow Wilson having proposed a relatively merciful set of conditions for their surrender, the Central Powers began negotiating in earnest for peace. By the war's end, some 365,000 American soldiers had been killed or wounded in carrying out President Wilson's famous call to "make the world safe for democracy." American casualty rates were high, but the war had not devastated either the landscape or the economy of the United States. The American Civil War, by contrast, had raged over American soil for four years, from 1861 to 1865, costing the armies on both sides a total of more than 1.1 million killed and wounded (and many civilian casualties as well), and wrecked the Southern economy for decades.

The impact of World War I on the United States and its literature, however, was deep and broad. From the moment war broke out, Americans plunged into debate over the responsibilities of the United States in relation to the rest of the world. Some Americans, including writers and artists who had lived abroad or who felt specially connected to Great Britain and France, vociferously argued for an early U.S. entry into the war on the Allied side: during her American tour of 1916, for example, the pioneering modern dancer Isadora Duncan concluded her recitals with an impassioned solo on the French national anthem, the *Marseillaise,* coupled with a speech urging Americans to join the fight for the Allies. Some, like the poet Alan Seeger, acted on their loyalties by joining the French Foreign Legion or the ambulance corps of the Red Cross as volunteers early in the war. Still other Americans, however, felt that the United States ought to keep its distance from the war: why should Americans go to the rescue of a European continent entangled in ancient alliances and dynastic rivalries, decaying empires and stifling class hierarchies? In the conflict's early stages, antiwar Americans included committed left-wing activists and writers who saw revolutionary possibilities in the prospect of Europe's advanced capitalist societies destroying one another; Americans who had emigrated from Germany and other of the Central Powers; and religious pacifists and humanitarian liberals who believed that human progress could and should make war obsolete.

As the conflict went on, though, the German strategy of attacking merchant ships at sea—including ships carrying U.S. citizens as passengers—hardened American public opinion against the Central Powers and enabled President Wilson to obtain an overwhelming congressional majority in favor of American entry into the war. With war declared, the U.S. government acted quickly, on a wide front, to mobilize American society. For the first time since the Civil War, the U.S. Congress enacted a law to conscript men into the armed forces. A host of new government agencies sprang up to coordinate the American economy in the war effort: the Council of National Defense, the War Industries Board, the War Trade Board, the

Food Administration. Other government agencies, like the Committee on Public Information, set out to sell the war to the American public with the aid of new twentieth-century media like films and newsreels. When some newspapers and magazines refused the government's invitation to self-censor their views on the war, Congress responded with the Espionage Act of June 1917, which outlawed statements intended "to interfere with the operation or success of the military or naval forces."

Writers and artists on the left protested these restrictions on freedom of speech, but they were not the only Americans to experience the contradiction between the war's declared aim of making the world safe for democracy abroad and their daily lives. Anti-immigrant feeling rose, especially against German-Americans; Woodrow Wilson declared to Congress in 1918 that "Any man who carries a hyphen about him carries a dagger that he is ready to plunge into the vitals of this Republic." Militant suffragists denounced the hypocrisy of crusading for democracy abroad while denying the vote to women at home. While some leaders of organized labor allied themselves with management and government in the war effort, others dissented. The draft and the growth of war-related industries opened up jobs that drew black Americans from the rural South to the cities of the North, where their growing urban communities came under white attack in a series of race riots both before and after the war. African Americans who volunteered for or were drafted into the segregated armed forces also registered the contradiction between American ideals of democracy and their treatment as second-class citizens. Many men and women caught up in it found that the fundamental conditions of modern warfare undermined clean-cut, idealistic notions of the war's aims. In E. E. Cummings's

"Destroy This Mad Brute." U.S. Army recruitment poster, H. R. Hopps, 1917. Propaganda on both sides of the conflict demonized opponents as rapists and brutalizers of helpless civilians. This famous poster would later be cited in Nazi propaganda as evidence of Anglo-American hatred of the German people.

The Enormous Room, the French military bureaucracy oppresses the common soldiers of its own army no less than those of the enemy; in Ernest Hemingway's experience of the Italian front as recorded in his letters, the sheer firepower of modern artillery far exceeds his commanders' ability to make sense of either their immediate tactical situation or the war's ultimate purpose. Katherine Anne Porter's *Pale Horse, Pale Rider* depicts the coercive patriotism of the war's domestic front.

The waste and futility that marked so much of the military effort expended in World War I not only eroded popular deference to the wisdom of generals and politicians but also licensed rebellion against literary traditions. Cummings's multilingual, colloquial literary style in *The Enormous Room* defies the routines of bureaucratic language even as his autobiographical narrator refuses to defer to his jailors. Gertrude Stein's matter-of-fact, concrete, at times gossipy tone in *The Autobiography of Alice B. Toklas* declines to moralize the end of the war as a high drama of ideals achieved. Whether they witnessed World War I at firsthand or from a distance, Americans saw the home of nineteenth-century European high culture at once exploded into bits and, in another way, bound together by a shared nightmare. Both Europe's fragmentation and the grip of the war's shared experiences found their way into high modernist works of postwar American writing like T. S. Eliot's *The Waste Land* and Ezra Pound's "Hugh Selwyn Mauberley."

ALAN SEEGER

Born in New York City, Alan Seeger (1888–1916) was educated at private schools before entering Harvard in 1906, where he became one of the editors of the *Harvard Monthly* and a contributor of poetry to its pages; among his Harvard classmates was T. S. Eliot. Looking for literary circles, Seeger returned to New York after graduating from Harvard, and in 1912 moved on to Paris. Although Paris by that time was a hub of artistic experimentation and the home of radical American modernists like Gertrude Stein, Seeger's own artistic tastes were less adventurous, and he seems to have made little contact with Paris's innovators before the outbreak of World War I inspired him to join the French Foreign Legion. Seeger's wartime letters to newspapers in the United States acknowledged some of the miseries of trench combat for the soldier "[e]xposed to all the dangers of war, but with none of its enthusiasm or splendid *élan*"; his poetry, however, romanticized the sacrifices of military service. Published after Seeger's death in combat, "I Have a Rendezvous with Death . . ." became one of the most widely anthologized American poems of the war. Reviewing Seeger's poems after his death, his former classmate T. S. Eliot declared them "high-flown, heavily decorated and solemn"—and "so out of date as to be almost a positive quality."

I Have a Rendezvous with Death . . .

I have a rendezvous with Death
At some disputed barricade,
When Spring comes back with rustling shade
And apple-blossoms fill the air—
I have a rendezvous with Death
When Spring brings back blue days and fair.

It may be he shall take my hand
And lead me into his dark land
And close my eyes and quench my breath—
It may be I shall pass him still.
I have a rendezvous with Death
On some scarred slope of battered hill,
When Spring comes round again this year
And the first meadow-flowers appear.

God knows 'twere better to be deep
Pillowed in silk and scented down,
Where Love throbs out in blissful sleep,
Pulse nigh to pulse, and breath to breath,
Where hushed awakenings are dear . . .
But I've a rendezvous with Death
At midnight in some flaming town,
When Spring trips north again this year,
And I to my pledged word am true,
I shall not fail that rendezvous.

1917

ERNEST HEMINGWAY

Denied entry into the U.S. armed forces because of poor eyesight, Ernest Hemingway (1899–1961) volunteered for the ambulance corps of the Red Cross and was sent to Italy in June 1918. On July 8, 1918, he was seriously wounded: hit by shrapnel from a mortar shell, he was awarded the Italian Silver Medal for Valor and spent several months recovering before returning home to Oak Park, Illinois, in January 1919. Hemingway's parents published some of his letters from the hospital in local newspapers; whether or not he knew this as he was writing, the letters seem to aim at a public tone of ironic, disillusioned courage and objective description. Hemingway drew on his experiences on the Italian front and in the military hospital for the character Frederic Henry, a wounded American officer, in his novel *A Farewell to Arms* (1929).

Letter of August 18, 1918, to His Parents

* * *

You know they say there isn't anything funny about this war. And there isn't. I wouldn't say it was hell, because that's been a bit overworked since Gen. Sherman's time,[1] but there have been about 8 times when I would have welcomed Hell. Just on a chance that it couldn't come up to the phase of war I was experiencing. F'r example. In the trenches during an attack when a shell makes a direct hit in a group where you're standing. Shells aren't bad except direct hits. You must take chances on the fragments of the bursts. But when there is a direct hit your pals get spattered all over you. Spattered is literal. During the six days I was up in the Front line trenches, only 50 yds from the Austrians, I got the rep. of having a charmed life. The rep of having one doesn't mean much but having one does! I hope I have one. That knocking sound is my knuckles striking the wooden bed tray.

It's too hard to write on two sides of the paper so I'll skip.

Well I can now hold up my hand and say I've been shelled by high explosive, shrapnel and gas. Shot at by trench mortars, snipers and machine guns, and as an added attraction an aeroplane machine gunning the lines. I've never had a hand grenade thrown at me, but a rifle grenade struck rather close. Maybe I'll get a hand grenade later. Now out of all that mess to only be struck by a trench mortar and a machine gun bullet while advancing toward the rear, as the Irish say, was fairly lucky. What, Family?

The 227 wounds I got from the trench mortar didn't hurt a bit at the time, only my feet felt like I had rubber boots full of water on. Hot water. And my knee cap was acting queer. The machine gun bullet just felt like a sharp smack on my leg with an icy snow ball. However it spilled me. But I got up again and got my wounded into the dug out. I kind of collapsed at the dug out. The Italian I had with me had bled all over my coat and my pants looked like somebody had made current jelly in them and then punched holes to let the pulp out. Well the Captain who was a great pal of mine, It was his dug out said "Poor Hem he'll be R.I.P. soon." Rest In Peace, that is. You see they thought I was shot through the chest on account of my bloody coat. But I made them take my coat and shirt off. I wasn't wearing any undershirt, and the old torso was intact. Then they said I'd probably live. That cheered me up any amount. I told him in Italian that I wanted to see my legs, though I was afraid to look at them. So we took off my trousers and the old limbs were still there but gee they were a mess. They couldn't figure out how I had walked 150 yards with a load with both knees shot through and my right shoe punctured two big places. Also over 200 flesh wounds. "Oh," says I, "My Captain, it is of nothing. In America they all do it! It is thought well not to allow the enemy to perceive that they have captured our goats!"[2]

1. William Tecumseh Sherman (1820–1891), a general in the Union Army during the Civil War noted for the destructiveness of his campaign in Georgia, said that "war is . . . hell" in an 1880 speech.

2. Hemingway plays with his Italian commander's ignorance of the American idiom "to get someone's goat"—i.e., to make someone betray anger or irritation.

The goat speech required some masterful lingual ability but I got it across and then went to sleep for a couple of minutes. After I came to they carried me on a stretcher three kilometers to a dressing station. The stretcher bearers had to go over lots because the road was having the "entrails" shelled out of it. Whenever a big one would come, Whee - whoosh - Boom - they'd lay me down and get flat. My wounds were now hurting like 227 little devils were driving nails into the raw. The dressing station had been evacuated during the attack so I lay for two hours in a stable, with the roof shot off, waiting for an ambulance. When it came I ordered it down the road to get the soldiers that had been wounded first. It came back with a load and then they lifted me in. The shelling was still pretty thick and our batteries were going off all the time way back of us and the big 250's and 350's[3] going over head for Austria with a noise like a railway train. Then we'd hear the bursts back of the lines. Then there would come a big Austrian shell and then the crash of the burst. But we were giving them more and bigger stuff than they sent. Then a battery of field guns would go off, just back of the shed—boom, boom, boom, boom, and the Seventy-Fives or 149's[4] would go whipping over to the Austrian lines, and the star shells going up all the time and the machines going like rivetters, tat-a-tat, tat-a-tat.

* * *

I sent you that cable so you wouldn't worry. I've been in the Hospital a month and 12 days and hope to be out in another month. The Italian Surgeon did a peach of a job on my right knee joint and right foot. Took 28 stitches and assures me that I will be able to walk as well as ever. The wounds all healed up clean and there was no infection. He has my right leg in a plaster splint now so that the joint will be all right. I have some snappy souvenirs that he took out at the last operation.

I wouldn't really be comfortable now unless I had some pain. The Surgeon is going to cut the plaster off in a week now and will allow me on crutches in 10 days.

I'll have to learn to walk again.

* * *

3. Large artillery shells of 250 and 350 millimeters in diameter (about 10 and 14 inches, respectively).
4. Medium-caliber artillery guns designed to move with military units in the field and firing ammunition of 75 and 149 millimeters (about 3 and 6 inches, respectively).

E. E. CUMMINGS

Following the U.S. entry into World War I, E. E. Cummings (1894–1962) volunteered for the Ambulance Corps of the American Red Cross in France. In Paris he befriended another American volunteer, William Slater Brown, who like Cummings was fluent in French. Brown and Cummings socialized with French soldiers, imbibing some of their cynicism about the war and about France's military bureaucracy;

French wartime censors, reading Brown's letters, imprisoned both men. *The Enormous Room* records Cummings's ensuing three months in French jails and prison camps. The novelist John Dos Passos, reviewing *The Enormous Room* for *The Dial*, praised its "reckless," colloquial, and vividly personal style in rendering Cummings's encounter with "a bit of the underside of History." In this excerpt from an early chapter, Cummings is held in a detainment cell previously inhabited by both German and French prisoners.

From The Enormous Room

Chapter Two

EN ROUTE

I put the bed-roll down. I stood up.

I was myself.

An uncontrollable joy gutted me after three months of humiliation, of being bossed and herded and bullied and insulted. I was myself and my own master.

In this delirium of relief (hardly noticing what I did) I inspected the pile of straw, decided against it, set up my bed, disposed the roll on it, and began to examine my cell.

I have mentioned the length and breadth. The cell was ridiculously high; perhaps ten feet. The end with the door in it was peculiar. The door was not placed in the middle of this end, but at one side, allowing for a huge iron can waist-high which stood in the other corner. Over the door and across the end, a grating extended. A slit of sky was always visible.

Whistling joyously to myself, I took three steps which brought me to the door end. The door was massively made, all of iron or steel I should think. It delighted me. The can excited my curiosity. I looked over the edge of it. At the bottom reposefully lay a new human turd.

* * *

It was then that I noticed the walls. Arm-high they were covered with designs, mottos, pictures. The drawing had all been done in pencil. I resolved to ask for a pencil at the first opportunity.

There had been Germans and Frenchmen imprisoned in this cell. On the right wall, near the door-end, was a long selection from Goethe, laboriously copied. Near the other end of this wall a satiric landscape took place. The technique of this landscape frightened me. There were houses, men, children. And there were trees. I began to wonder what a tree looks like, and laughed copiously.

The back wall had a large and exquisite portrait of a German officer.

The left wall was adorned with a yacht, flying a number—13. "My beloved boat" was inscribed in German underneath. Then came a bust of a German soldier, very idealized, full of unfear. After this, a masterful crudity—a doughnut-bodied rider, sliding with fearful rapidity down the acute backbone of a totally transparent sausage-shaped horse who was moving simultaneously in five directions. The rider had a bored expression as he supported the stiff reins in one fist. His further leg assisted in his flight. He wore a German soldier's cap and was smoking. I made up my mind to copy the horse and rider at once, so soon that is as I should have obtained a pencil.

Last, I found a drawing surrounded by a scrolled motto. The drawing was a potted plant with four blossoms. The four blossoms were elaborately dead. Their death was drawn with a fearful care. An obscure deliberation was exposed in the depiction of their drooping petals. The pot tottered very crookedly on a sort of table, as near as I could see. All around ran a funereal scroll. I read: "Mes derniers adieux à ma femme aimée, Gaby."[1] A fierce hand, totally distinct from the former, wrote in proud letters above: "Tombé pour désert. Six ans de prison—dégradation militaire."[2]

It must have been five o'clock. Steps. A vast cluttering of the exterior of the door—by whom? Whang opens the door. Turnkey-creature extending a piece of chocolat with extreme and surly caution. I say "Merci"[3] and seize chocolat, Klang shuts the door.

I am lying on my back, the twilight does mistily bluish miracles thru the slit over the whang-klang. I can just see leaves, meaning trees.

Then from the left and way off, faintly, broke a smooth whistle, cool like a peeled willow-branch, and I found myself listening to an air from Pétrouchka, Pétrouchka, which we saw in Paris at the Châtelet, mon ami et moi[4]. . .

The voice stopped in the middle—and I finished the air. This code continued for a half-hour.

It was dark.

I had laid a piece of my piece of chocolat on the window-sill. As I lay on my back, a little silhouette came along the sill and ate that piece of a piece, taking something like four minutes to do so. He then looked at me, I then smiled at him, and we parted, each happier than before.

My cellule[5] was cool, and I fell asleep easily.

* * *

I contemplate the bowl which contemplates me. A glaze of greenish grease seals the mystery of its content. I induce two fingers to penetrate the seal. They bring me up a flat sliver of choux[6] and a large, hard, thoughtful, solemn, uncooked bean. To pour the water off (it is warmish and sticky) without committing a nuisance is to lift the cover off Ça Pue.[7] I did.

Thus leaving beans and cabbage-slivers. Which I ate hurryingly, fearing a ventral misgiving.

I pass a lot of time cursing myself about the pencil, looking at my walls, my unique interior.

Suddenly I realize the indisputable grip of nature's humorous hand. One evidently stands on Ça Pue in such cases. Having finished, panting with stink, I tumble on the bed and consider my next move.

The straw will do. Ouch, but it's Dirty.—Several hours elapse . . .

Stepsandfumble. Klang. Repetition of promise to Monsieur Savy, etc.

1. My last farewell to my beloved wife, Gaby (French).
2. Condemned for desertion. Six years in prison—military degradation (French); i.e., loss of rank.
3. Thanks (French).
4. My friend and I (French). *Pétrouchka*: is a modernist ballet set to music by Igor Stravinsky and choreographed by Mikhail Fokine (1911). "Châtelet": i.e., the *Théâtre du Châtelet*, the musical theater of Paris.
5. Cell (French).
6. Cabbage (French). Cummings is looking at a bowl of soup brought to him by his jailors.
7. It Stinks (French); Cummings's nickname for the iron can that serves as his lavatory.

Turnkeyish and turnkeyish. Identical expression. One body collapses sufficiently to deposit a hunk of bread and a piece of water.

Give your bowl.

I gave it, smiled and said: "Well, how about that pencil?"

"Pencil?" T-c[8] looked at t-c.

They recited then the following word: "Tomorrow." Klangandfootsteps.

So I took matches, burnt, and with just 60 of them wrote the first stanza of a ballade. Tomorrow I will write the second. Day after tomorrow the third. Next day the refrain. After—oh, well.

My whistling of Pétrouchka brought no response this evening.

So I climbed on Ça Pue, whom I now regarded with complete friendliness; the new moon was unclosing sticky wings in dusk, a far noise from near things.

I sang a song the "dirty Frenchmen" taught us, mon ami et moi. The song says Bon soir, Madame la Lune.[9] . . . I did not sing out loud, simply because the moon was like a mademoiselle, and I did not want to offend the moon. My friends: the silhouette and la lune, not counting Ça Pue, whom I regarded almost as a part of me.

Then I lay down, and heard (but could not see) the silhouette eat something or somebody . . . and saw, but could not hear, the incense of Ça Pue mount gingerly upon the taking air of twilight.

The next day.—Promise to M. Savy. Whang. "My pencil?"—"You don't need any pencil, you're going away."—"When?"—"Directly."—"How directly?"—"In an hour or two: your friend has already gone before. Get ready."

Klangandsteps.

Everyone very sore about me. Je m'en fous pas mal,[1] however.

One hour I guess.

Steps. Sudden throwing of door open. Pause.

"Come out, American."

* * *

1922

8. Cummings's abbreviation of "Turnkey-creature," his contemptuous term for his jailors.
9. Good evening, Madame Moon (French); title of a popular prewar French cabaret tune.
1. I don't give a damn (French).

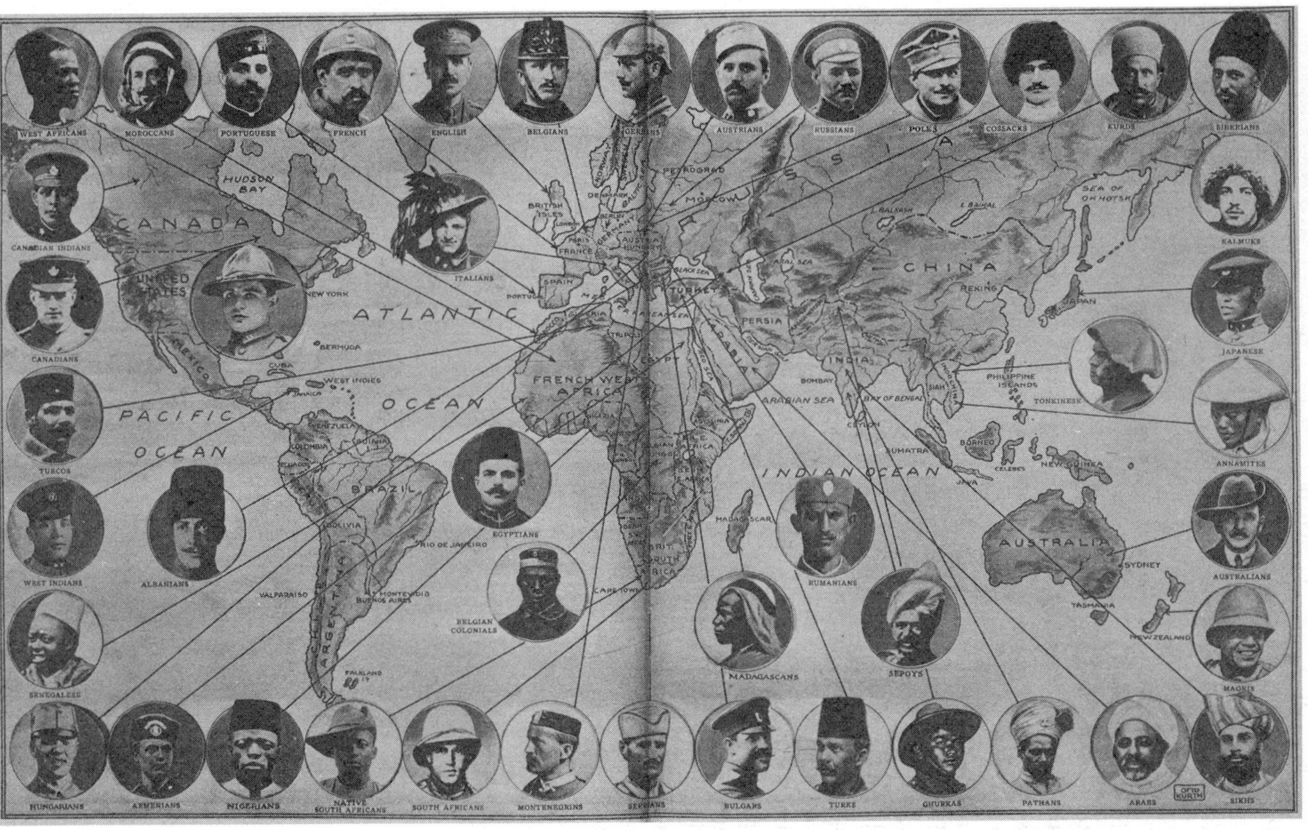

"War of the Races," *New York Times*, December 31, 1919. The *Times*'s composite "Ethnological Map of the World" frames an idealized white American soldier among representatives of the many nations involved in the war.

JESSIE REDMON FAUSET

One of the central writers of the Harlem Renaissance, Jessie Redmon Fauset (1882?–1961) was the first black woman to attend Cornell University. She taught Latin and French in high schools in Washington D.C. and New York City before becoming literary editor at *The Crisis* magazine, the journal of the National Association for the Advancement of Colored People (NAACP). Her career as a novelist began with *There Is Confusion* (1924), a group portrait of young African Americans in the black communities of New York and Washington D.C. Like her other novels—including *Plum Bun* (1928), *The Chinaberry Tree* (1931), and *Comedy: American Style* (1933)—*There Is Confusion* concerns itself primarily with the dilemmas of a literate, ambitious black middle class. Although some critics, both in her own time and afterward, lamented Fauset's focus on genteel characters, she represents her urban middle-class communities as buzzing with debate over the standing of African Americans nationwide. In *There Is Confusion*, her characters monitor reports of lynching from the South, argue over whether blacks should enlist in World War I to fight on behalf of a segregated country, and trade reports of postwar repression aimed at African Americans. In this excerpt, Peter Bye, the well-educated but drifting son of a proud Philadelphia family, has enlisted in a black regiment sent to France, where he finds the Allied armies painfully divided by race. For African American soldiers in Fauset's novel, the willingness of French women to associate openly with black men comes as a revelation; white American soldiers retaliate violently to enforce the racial segregation they are accustomed to at home.

From There Is Confusion

* * *

This town, the end of Brittany and the furthest western outpost of France, always remained in Peter's memory as a horrible prelude to a most horrible war. Brest[1] up to the time that Europe had gone so completely and so suddenly insane, had been the typical, stupid, monotonous French town with picturesquely irregular pavements, narrow tortuous streets, dark, nestling little shops and the inevitable public square. Around and about the city to all sides stretched well ordered farms.

Then came the march of two million American soldiers across the town and the surrounding country. Under their careless feet the farms became mud, so that the name Brest recalls to the minds of thousands nothing if not a picture of the deepest, slimiest, stickiest mud that the world has known. All about were people, people, too many people, French and Americans. And finally the relations between the two nations, allies though they were, developed from misunderstandings into hot irritations, from irritations into clashes. First white Americans and Frenchmen

1. Major port city in northwestern France.

Negro Soldier, 1934, Malvin Gray Johnson. Johnson was a notable painter of the Harlem Renaissance and worked with the Federal Art Project during the Great Depression.

clashed; separate restaurants and accommodations had to be arranged. Then came the inevitable clash between white and colored Americans; petty jealousies and meannesses arose over the courtesies of Frenchwomen and the lack of discrimination in the French cafés. The Americans found a new and inexplicable irritation in the French colored colonials.[2] Food was bad, prices were exorbitant; officers became tyrants. Everyone was at once in Brest and constantly about to leave it; real understanding and acquaintanceship were impossible.

Peter thought Dante might well have included this place in the description of his Inferno.[3] Here were Disease and Death, Mutilation and Murder. Stevedores and even soldiers became cattle and beasts of burden. Many black men were slaves. The thing from which France was to be defended could hardly be worse than this welter of human misunderstandings, the clashing of unknown tongues, the cynical investigations of the government, the immanence of war and the awful, persistent wretchedness of the weather.

The long wait turned into sudden activity and Peter's outfit was ordered to Lathus, thence to La Courtine,[4] one of the large training centers.

* * *

At Lathus, Harley Alexander met him in the little *place*.[5] "Seems to me you're got up regardless," Peter had commented. Alexander, one of the trimmest men in the regiment, was looking unusually shipshape, almost dapper.

The other struck him familiarly across the shoulder. "And that ain't all. Say, fellow, there's a band concert to-night right here in this little old square. I'm goin' and I'm goin' to take a lady."

"Lady! Where'd you get her?"

2. Africans and other people of color from France's overseas colonies; some white American troops resented their relative social freedom in wartime France.

3. Dante Alighieri (1265–1321), Italian poet. The *Inferno*, the first part of Dante's epic *Divine Comedy* (1310–14), tells of Dante's journey through hell.

4. Towns in central France.

5. Town square (French).

"Right here. These girls are all right. Not afraid of a dark skin. 'How should we have fear, m'soo,' one of them says to me, 'when you fight for our *patrie*[6] and when you are so *beau*? '*Beau*' that's handsome, ain't it? Say this is some country to fight for; got some sense of appreciation. Better come along, old scout. There's a pile of loots[7] getting ready to come, each with a French dame in tow."

"I'll be there," Peter told him, laughing. "But count me out with the ladies. I can't get along with the domestic brand and I know I'll be out of luck with the foreign ones."

Some passing thought wiped the joy of anticipation from Harley's face. "My experience is that these foreign ones are a damn sight less foolish than some domestic ones I've met. Well, me for the concert."

But that band concert never came off. At sunset a company of white American Southerners marched into Lathus down the main street, past the little *place*. There was a sudden uproar.

"Look! Darkies and white women! Come on, fellows, kill the damned niggers!"

There was a hasty onslaught in which the colored soldiers even taken by surprise gave as good as they took. Between these two groups from the same soil there was grimmer, more determined fighting than was seen at Verdun.[8] The French civil population stood on the church-steps opposite the square and watched with amazement.

"*Nom de dieu!*[9] Are they crazy, then, these Americans, that they kill each other!"

The next day saw Peter's company on its way to La Courtine, a training center, where there were no women. Thence they moved presently to the front in the Metz[1] sector.

* * *

1924

6. The fatherland (French).
7. Shortened, Americanized version of *poilus*, nickname for French infantrymen.
8. The battle of Verdun, one of the longest and bloodiest of World War I.
9. Name of God! (French).
1. City in northeastern France, near the German border.

JOHN ALLAN WYETH JR.

Like Alan Seeger, John Allan Wyeth Jr. (1894–1981) was born in New York City and attended an Ivy League college where he wrote poetry and had a more famous literary classmate: for Wyeth, the school was Princeton and his classmate the great modernist critic and journalist Edmund Wilson (1895–1972), who remembered Wyeth as the "aesthete" of his year. Unlike Seeger, Wyeth turned his combat experience in World War I—he enlisted in 1917, was sent to France in

1918, and saw the bloody battles on the Somme and at Verdun—into innovative rather than dated poetry. His only published book of poems, *This Man's Army: A War in Fifty-Odd Sonnets* (1928), transformed a literary form traditionally associated with love into a vehicle for colloquial dialogue and biting observation of men at war.

Fromereville[1]

War in Heaven[2]

A reek of steam—the bath-house rang with cries.
"Come across with the soap."
"Like hell, what makes you think it's yours?"
"Don't turn *off the water*, that ain't fair
I'm all *covered* with soap."
"Hurry up, get out of the way."
"Thank God you're takin' a bath."
"He wants to surprise us."
"Oh is that so, well anyway I don't stink like you."

"Air raid!"

We ran out into the square,
naked and cold like souls on Judgment Day.
Over us, white clouds blazoned on blue skies,
and a green balloon on fire[3]—we watched it shrink
into flame and a fall of smoke. Around us, brute
guns belching puffs of shrapnel in the air,
where one plane swooping like a bird of prey
spat fire into a dangling parachute.

1928

1. Village in the Alsatian region of France, near the German border; site of a large American station in World War I.
2. In John Milton's epic poem *Paradise Lost* (1667), the angel Raphael tells Adam and Eve the story of the war in heaven between the armies of God and those of Satan and the fallen angels.
3. Manned observation balloons were widely used in World War I to spy on the enemy's trench deployments. Under attack, their crews could attempt to escape by parachute.

GERTRUDE STEIN

One of the most accessible of Gertrude Stein's major works, *The Autobiography of Alice B. Toklas* is written in the voice of Stein's lover of several decades. Some of its most memorable recollections are of Toklas and Stein's time in France during World War I. Stein (1874–1946) and Toklas were traveling in England when the war broke out; as soon as the initial German advance on Paris was halted they returned to France, where they helped transport supplies for war relief efforts and provided warm hospitality to American soldiers after the U.S. entry into the war. When the Armistice was declared, they visited the frontline villages and the blasted landscapes left behind by trench warfare and bombardment. Back in Paris, they witnessed the parades celebrating victory and the influx of diplomats struggling to forge a lasting peace. *The Autobiography of Alice B. Toklas* appeared in 1933, as Hitler and the Nazi Party were coming to power in Germany.

From The Autobiography of Alice B. Toklas

Time went on, we were very busy and then came the armistice.[1] We were the first to bring the news to many small villages. The french soldiers in the hospitals were relieved rather than glad. They seemed not to feel that it was going to be such a lasting peace. I remember one of them saying to Gertrude Stein when she said to him, well here is peace, at least for twenty years, he said.

The next morning we had a telegram from Mrs. Lathrop.[2] Come at once want you to go with the french armies to Alsace.[3] We did not stop on the way. We made it in a day. Very shortly after we left for Alsace.

* * *

Soon we came to the battle-fields and the lines of trenches of both sides. To any one who did not see it as it was then it is impossible to imagine it. It was not terrifying it was strange. We were used to ruined houses and even ruined towns but this was different. It was a landscape. And it belonged to no country.

I remember hearing a french nurse once say and the only thing she did say of the front was, c'est un paysage passionant, an absorbing landscape. And that was what it was as we saw it. It was strange. Camouflage, huts, everything was there. It was wet and dark and there were a few people, one did not know whether they were chinamen or europeans. Our fan-belt had stopped working. A staff car stopped and fixed it with a hairpin, we still wore hairpins.

Another thing that interested us enormously was how different the camouflage of the french looked from the camouflage of the germans, and then once we came across some very very neat camouflage and it was american.[4] The idea was the same but as after all it was different nationalities who did it the difference was inevitable. The colour schemes were different, the designs were different, the way of placing them was different, it made plain the whole theory of art and its inevitability.

* * *

1. The November 11, 1918, armistice ending combat in World War I.
2. Isabel Stevens Lathrop (1868–1964), chair of the Paris depot of the American Fund for French Wounded, was one of many socially well-connected American women involved in war relief.
3. Region of eastern France, on the German border.
4. Camouflage was invented in response to another innovation of World War I, airplane attacks on ground positions.

Our business in Alsace was not hospitals but refugees. The inhabitants were returning to their ruined homes all over the devastated country and it was the aim of the A.F.F.W.[5] to give a pair of blankets, underclothing and children's and babies' woollen stockings and babies' booties to every family. There was a legend that the quantity of babies' booties sent to us came from the gifts sent to Mrs. Wilson[6] who was supposed at that time to be about to produce a little Wilson. There were a great many babies' booties but not too many for Alsace.

* * *

We once more returned to a changed Paris. We were restless. Gertrude Stein began to work very hard, it was at this time that she wrote her Accents in Alsace and other political plays, the last plays in Geography and Plays.[7] We were still in the shadow of war work and we went on doing some of it, visiting hospitals and seeing the soldiers left in them, now pretty well neglected by everybody. We had spent a great deal of our money during the war and we were economising, servants were difficult to get if not impossible, prices were high. We settled down for the moment with a femme de ménage[8] for only a few hours a day. I used to say Gertrude Stein was the chauffeur and I was the cook. We used to go over early in the morning to the public markets and get in our provisions. It was a confused world.

Jessie Whitehead[9] had come over with the peace commission as secretary to one of the delegations and of course we were very interested in knowing all about the peace. It was then that Gertrude Stein described one of the young men of the peace commission who was holding forth, as one who knew all about the war, he had been here ever since the peace. Gertrude Stein's cousins came over, everybody came over, everybody was dissatisfied and every one was restless. It was a restless and disturbed world.

* * *

As I say we were restless and we were economical and all day and all evening we were seeing people and at last there was the defile, the procession under the Arc de Triomphe,[1] of the allies.

The members of the American Fund for French Wounded were to have seats on the benches that were put up the length of the Champs Elysées[2] but quite rightly the people of Paris objected as these seats would make it impossible for them to see the parade and so Clemenceau promptly had them taken down. Luckily for us Jessie Whitehead's room in her hotel looked right over the Arc de Triomphe and she asked us to come to it to see the parade. We accepted gladly. It was a wonderful day.

5. American Fund for French Wounded.
6. Edith Bolling Galt Wilson (1872–1961), second wife of U.S. president Woodrow Wilson.
7. Published in 1922.
8. Cleaning woman (French).
9. Jessie Marie Whitehead, daughter of the mathematician and philosopher Alfred North Whitehead and Evelyn Whitehead, friends of Stein and Toklas in England.
1. Triumphal Arch (French), monument in central Paris originally dedicated to Napoleon's military victories.
2. Elysian Fields (French), major avenue in central Paris.

We got up at sunrise, as later it would have been impossible to cross Paris in a car. This was one of the last trips Auntie[3] made. By this time the red cross was painted off it but it was still a truck. Very shortly after it went its honourable way and was succeeded by Godiva, a two-seated runabout,[4] also a little ford. She was called Godiva because she had come naked into the world and each of our friends gave us something with which to bedeck her.

Auntie then was making practically her last trip. We left her near the river and walked up to the hotel. Everybody was on the streets, men, women, children, soldiers, priests, nuns, we saw two nuns being helped into a tree from which they would be able to see. And we ourselves were admirably placed and we saw perfectly.

We saw it all, we saw first the few wounded from the Invalides[5] in their wheeling chairs wheeling themselves. It is an old french custom that a military procession should always be preceded by the veterans from the Invalides. They all marched past through the Arc de Triomphe. Gertrude Stein remembered that when as a child she used to swing on the chains that were around the Arc de Triomphe her governess had told her that no one must walk underneath since the german armies had marched under it after 1870.[6] And now everybody except the germans were passing through.

All the nations marched differently, some slowly, some quickly, the french carry their flags the best of all, Pershing[7] and his officer carrying the flag behind him were perhaps the most perfectly spaced. It was this scene that Gertrude Stein described in the movie she wrote about this time that I have published in Operas and Plays in the Plain Edition.[8]

However it all finally came to an end. We wandered up and we wandered down the Champs Elysées and the war was over and the piles of captured cannon that had made two pyramids were being taken away and peace was upon us.

1933

3. Stein and Toklas's Ford truck, which they had used for Red Cross relief transport in the war.
4. Small, lightweight automobile. "Godiva": after Lady Godiva, who according to medieval legend rode naked through the streets of Coventry, England, to persuade her husband to forgive his tenants' debts.
5. Hôtel des Invalides, home for disabled war veterans built by Louis XIV in 1670.
6. Paris surrendered to German forces during the Franco-Prussian War of 1870–71.
7. General John J. Pershing, leader of the American Expeditionary Forces from 1917 to 1918.
8. Published in 1932.

ROBERT FROST
1874–1963

Although he identified himself with New England, Robert Frost was born in California and lived there until his father died, when Frost was eleven. The family then moved to New England, where his mother supported them by teaching school. Frost graduated from high school in 1891 in Lawrence, Massachusetts, sharing the post of valedictorian with Elinor White, whom he married three years later. Occasional attendance at Dartmouth College and Harvard, and a variety of different jobs including an attempt to run a farm in Derry, New Hampshire, marked the next twenty years. Frost made a new start in 1912, taking his family, which included four children, to England. There he worked on his poetry and found a publisher for his first book, *A Boy's Will* (1913). Ezra Pound reviewed it favorably, excited (as he put it in a letter) by this "VURRY Amur'k'n talent." Pound recommended Frost's poems to American editors and helped get his second book, *North of Boston*, published in 1914. *North of Boston* was widely praised by critics in America and England when it appeared; the favorable reception persuaded Frost to return home. He bought another farm in New Hampshire and prospered financially through sales of his books and papers, along with teaching and lecturing at various colleges. The success he enjoyed for the rest of his life, however, came too late to cancel the bitterness left by his earlier struggles. Moreover, he endured personal tragedy: a son committed suicide, and a daughter had a complete mental collapse.

The clarity of Frost's diction, the colloquial rhythms, the simplicity of his images, and above all the folksy speaker—these are intended to make the poems look natural, unplanned. In the context of the modernist movement, however, they can be seen as a thoughtful reply to high modernism's fondness for obscurity and difficulty. In addition, by investing in the New England terrain, Frost rejected modernist internationalism and revitalized the tradition of New England regionalism. Readers who accepted Frost's persona and his setting as typically American accepted the powerful myth that rural New England was the heart of America.

Frost played the rhythms of ordinary speech against formal patterns of line and verse and contained them within traditional poetic forms. The interaction of colloquial diction with blank verse is especially central to his dramatic monologues. To Frost traditional forms were the essence of poetry, material with which poets responded to flux and disorder (what, adopting scientific terminology, he called "decay") by forging something permanent. Poetry, he wrote, was "one step backward taken," resisting time—a "momentary stay against confusion."

Throughout the 1920s Frost's poetic practice changed very little; later books—including *Mountain Interval* (1916), *New Hampshire* (1923), and *West-Running Brook* (1928)—confirmed the impression he had created in *North of Boston*. Most of his poems fall into a few types. Nature lyrics describing or commenting on a scene or event—like "Stopping by Woods on a Snowy Evening," "Birches," and "After Apple-Picking"—are probably the best known. There are also dramatic narratives in blank verse about country people, like "The Death of the Hired Man," and poems of commentary or generalization, like "The Gift Outright," which he read at John F. Kennedy's presidential inauguration in 1961. He could also be humorous or sardonic, as in "Fire and Ice." In the nature lyrics, a comparison often emerges between the outer scene and the psyche, a comparison of what Frost in one poem called "outer and inner weather."

Because he presented himself as a New Englander reading a New England landscape, Frost is often interpreted as an ideological descendent of the nineteenth-century American Transcendentalists. But he is far less affirmative about the universe than they; for where they, looking at nature, discerned a benign creator, he saw "no expression, nothing to express." Frost did share with Emerson and Thoreau, however, the belief that collective enterprises could do nothing but weaken the individual self. He avoided political movements precisely because they were movements, group undertakings. In the 1930s he parted company with many American writers by opposing both the social programs of Franklin Roosevelt's New Deal and artistic programs similarly aimed, he thought, at the lessening of social grievances rather than the exploration of enduring human grief. In *A Further Range* (1936), for which he won the third of his four Pulitzer Prizes, Frost invited readers "to a one-man revolution"—the "only revolution that is coming," he declared. Left-leaning critics replied by denouncing the volume's "reactionary" constriction of Frost's poetic voice to that of a head-shaking Yankee skeptic. Frost deeply resented this criticism and responded to it with a newly didactic kind of poetry. In the last twenty years of his life, Frost increased his activities as a teacher and lecturer—at Amherst, at Dartmouth, at Harvard, at the Bread Loaf School of English at Middlebury College in Vermont, and in poetry readings and talks around the country.

The text of the poems included here is that of *The Poetry of Robert Frost* (1969).

The Pasture

I'm going out to clean the pasture spring;
I'll only stop to rake the leaves away
(And wait to watch the water clear, I may):
I shan't be gone long.—You come too.
I'm going out to fetch the little calf
That's standing by the mother. It's so young
It totters when she licks it with her tongue.
I shan't be gone long.—You come too.

1913

Mowing

There was never a sound beside the wood but one,
And that was my long scythe whispering to the ground.
What was it it whispered? I knew not well myself;
Perhaps it was something about the heat of the sun,
Something, perhaps, about the lack of sound—
And that was why it whispered and did not speak.
It was no dream of the gift of idle hours,
Or easy gold at the hand of fay or elf:
Anything more than the truth would have seemed too weak
To the earnest love that laid the swale[1] in rows,

1. Grasses in a marshy meadow.

Not without feeble-pointed spikes of flowers
(Pale orchises), and scared a bright green snake.
The fact is the sweetest dream that labor knows.
My long scythe whispered and left the hay to make.

1913

Mending Wall

Something there is that doesn't love a wall,
That sends the frozen-ground-swell under it,
And spills the upper boulders in the sun,
And makes gaps even two can pass abreast.
The work of hunters is another thing:
I have come after them and made repair
Where they have left not one stone on a stone,
But they would have the rabbit out of hiding,
To please the yelping dogs. The gaps I mean,
No one has seen them made or heard them made,
But at spring mending-time we find them there.
I let my neighbor know beyond the hill;
And on a day we meet to walk the line
And set the wall between us once again.
We keep the wall between us as we go.
To each the boulders that have fallen to each.
And some are loaves and some so nearly balls
We have to use a spell to make them balance:
"Stay where you are until our backs are turned!"
We wear our fingers rough with handling them.
Oh, just another kind of outdoor game,
One on a side. It comes to little more:
There where it is we do not need the wall:
He is all pine and I am apple orchard.
My apple trees will never get across
And eat the cones under his pines, I tell him.
He only says, "Good fences make good neighbors."
Spring is the mischief in me, and I wonder
If I could put a notion in his head:
"*Why* do they make good neighbors? Isn't it
Where there are cows? But here there are no cows.
Before I built a wall I'd ask to know
What I was walling in or walling out,
And to whom I was like to give offense.
Something there is that doesn't love a wall,
That wants it down." I could say "Elves" to him,
But it's not elves exactly, and I'd rather
He said it for himself. I see him there
Bringing a stone grasped firmly by the top
In each hand, like an old-stone savage armed.
He moves in darkness as it seems to me,

Not of woods only and the shade of trees.
He will not go behind his father's saying,
And he likes having thought of it so well
He says again, "Good fences make good neighbors."

1914

The Death of the Hired Man

Mary sat musing on the lamp-flame at the table
Waiting for Warren. When she heard his step,
She ran on tip-toe down the darkened passage
To meet him in the doorway with the news
And put him on his guard. "Silas is back."
She pushed him outward with her through the door
And shut it after her. "Be kind," she said.
She took the market things from Warren's arms
And set them on the porch, then drew him down
To sit beside her on the wooden steps.

"When was I ever anything but kind to him?
But I'll not have the fellow back," he said.
"I told him so last haying, didn't I?
If he left then, I said, that ended it.
What good is he? Who else will harbor him
At his age for the little he can do?
What help he is there's no depending on.
Off he goes always when I need him most.
He thinks he ought to earn a little pay,
Enough at least to buy tobacco with,
So he won't have to beg and be beholden.
'All right,' I say, 'I can't afford to pay
Any fixed wages, though I wish I could.'
'Someone else can.' 'Then someone else will have to.'
I shouldn't mind his bettering himself
If that was what it was. You can be certain,
When he begins like that, there's someone at him
Trying to coax him off with pocket-money,—
In haying time, when any help is scarce.
In winter he comes back to us. I'm done."

"Sh! not so loud: he'll hear you," Mary said.

"I want him to: he'll have to soon or late."

"He's worn out. He's asleep beside the stove.
When I came up from Rowe's I found him here,
Huddled against the barn-door fast asleep,
A miserable sight, and frightening, too—
You needn't smile—I didn't recognize him—

I wasn't looking for him—and he's changed.
Wait till you see."

"Where did you say he'd been?"

"He didn't say. I dragged him to the house,
And gave him tea and tried to make him smoke.
I tried to make him talk about his travels.
Nothing would do: he just kept nodding off."

"What did he say? Did he say anything?"

"But little."

"Anything? Mary, confess
He said he'd come to ditch the meadow for me."

"Warren!"

"But did he? I just want to know."

"Of course he did. What would you have him say?
Surely you wouldn't grudge the poor old man
Some humble way to save his self-respect.
He added, if you really care to know,
He meant to clear the upper pasture, too.
That sounds like something you have heard before?
Warren, I wish you could have heard the way
He jumbled everything. I stopped to look
Two or three times—he made me feel so queer—
To see if he was talking in his sleep.
He ran on Harold Wilson—you remember—
The boy you had in haying four years since.
He's finished school, and teaching in his college.
Silas declares you'll have to get him back.
He says they two will make a team for work:
Between them they will lay this farm as smooth!
The way he mixed that in with other things.
He thinks young Wilson a likely lad, though daft
On education—you know how they fought
All through July under the blazing sun,
Silas up on the cart to build the load,
Harold along beside to pitch it on."

"Yes, I took care to keep well out of earshot."

"Well, those days trouble Silas like a dream.
You wouldn't think they would. How some things linger!
Harold's young college-boy's assurance piqued him.
After so many years he still keeps finding
Good arguments he sees he might have used.

I sympathize. I know just how it feels
To think of the right thing to say too late.
Harold's associated in his mind with Latin.
He asked me what I thought of Harold's saying
He studied Latin, like the violin,
Because he liked it—that an argument!
He said he couldn't make the boy believe
He could find water with a hazel prong—
Which showed how much good school had ever done him.
He wanted to go over that. But most of all
He thinks if he could have another chance
To teach him how to build a load of hay—"

"I know, that's Silas' one accomplishment.
He bundles every forkful in its place,
And tags and numbers it for future reference,
So he can find and easily dislodge it
In the unloading. Silas does that well.
He takes it out in bunches like big birds' nests.
You never see him standing on the hay
He's trying to lift, straining to lift himself."

"He thinks if he could teach him that, he'd be
Some good perhaps to someone in the world.
He hates to see a boy the fool of books.
Poor Silas, so concerned for other folk,
And nothing to look backward to with pride,
And nothing to look forward to with hope,
So now and never any different."

Part of a moon was falling down the west,
Dragging the whole sky with it to the hills.
Its light poured softly in her lap. She saw it
And spread her apron to it. She put out her hand
Among the harplike morning-glory strings,
Taut with the dew from garden bed to eaves,
As if she played unheard some tenderness
That wrought on him beside her in the night.
"Warren," she said, "he has come home to die:
You needn't be afraid he'll leave you this time."

"Home," he mocked gently.

"Yes, what else but home?
It all depends on what you mean by home.
Of course he's nothing to us, any more
Than was the hound that came a stranger to us
Out of the woods, worn out upon the trail."

"Home is the place where, when you have to go there,
They have to take you in."

"I should have called it
Something you somehow haven't to deserve."

Warren leaned out and took a step or two,
Picked up a little stick, and brought it back
And broke it in his hand and tossed it by.
"Silas has better claim on us you think
Than on his brother? Thirteen little miles
As the road winds would bring him to his door.
Silas has walked that far no doubt today.
Why doesn't he go there? His brother's rich,
A somebody—director in the bank."

"He never told us that."

"We know it though."

"I think his brother ought to help, of course.
I'll see to that if there is need. He ought of right
To take him in, and might be willing to—
He may be better than appearances.
But have some pity on Silas. Do you think
If he had any pride in claiming kin
Or anything he looked for from his brother,
He'd keep so still about him all this time?"

"I wonder what's between them."

"I can tell you.
Silas is what he is—we wouldn't mind him—
But just the kind that kinsfolk can't abide.
He never did a thing so very bad.
He don't know why he isn't quite as good
As anybody. Worthless though he is,
He won't be made ashamed to please his brother."

"*I* can't think Si ever hurt anyone."

"No, but he hurt my heart the way he lay
And rolled his old head on that sharp-edged chair-back.
He wouldn't let me put him on the lounge.
You must go in and see what you can do.
I made the bed up for him there tonight.
You'll be surprised at him—how much he's broken.
His working days are done; I'm sure of it."

"I'd not be in a hurry to say that."

"I haven't been. Go, look, see for yourself.
But, Warren, please remember how it is:
He's come to help you ditch the meadow.
He has a plan. You mustn't laugh at him.

He may not speak of it, and then he may.
I'll sit and see if that small sailing cloud
Will hit or miss the moon."

It hit the moon.
Then there were three there, making a dim row,
The moon, the little silver cloud, and she.
Warren returned—too soon, it seemed to her,
Slipped to her side, caught up her hand and waited.

"Warren?" she questioned.

"Dead," was all he answered.

1914

Home Burial[1]

He saw her from the bottom of the stairs
Before she saw him. She was starting down,
Looking back over her shoulder at some fear.
She took a doubtful step and then undid it
To raise herself and look again. He spoke
Advancing toward her: "What is it you see
From up there always—for I want to know."
She turned and sank upon her skirts at that,
And her face changed from terrified to dull.
He said to gain time: "What is it you see,"
Mounting until she cowered under him.
"I will find out now—you must tell me, dear."
She, in her place, refused him any help
With the least stiffening of her neck and silence.
She let him look, sure that he wouldn't see,
Blind creature; and awhile he didn't see.
But at last he murmured, "Oh," and again, "Oh."

"What is it—what?" she said.

"Just that I see."

"You don't," she challenged. "Tell me what it is."

"The wonder is I didn't see at once.
I never noticed it from here before.
I must be wonted to it—that's the reason.
The little graveyard where my people are!
So small the window frames the whole of it.
Not so much larger than a bedroom, is it?

1. The title refers to the rural custom of burying family members on the home property.

There are three stones of slate and one of marble,
Broad-shouldered little slabs there in the sunlight
On the sidehill. We haven't to mind *those*.
But I understand: it is not the stones,
But the child's mound——"

"Don't, don't, don't, don't," she cried.

She withdrew shrinking from beneath his arm
That rested on the banister, and slid downstairs;
And turned on him with such a daunting look,
He said twice over before he knew himself:
"Can't a man speak of his own child he's lost?"

"Not you!—Oh, where's my hat? Oh, I don't need it!
I must get out of here. I must get air.—
I don't know rightly whether any man can."

"Amy! Don't go to someone else this time.
Listen to me. I won't come down the stairs."
He sat and fixed his chin between his fists.
"There's something I should like to ask you, dear."

"You don't know how to ask it."

"Help me, then."

Her fingers moved the latch for all reply.

"My words are nearly always an offense.
I don't know how to speak of anything
So as to please you. But I might be taught
I should suppose. I can't say I see how.
A man must partly give up being a man
With womenfolk. We could have some arrangement
By which I'd bind myself to keep hands off
Anything special you're a-mind to name.
Though I don't like such things 'twixt those that love.
Two that don't love can't live together without them.
But two that do can't live together with them."
She moved the latch a little. "Don't—don't go.
Don't carry it to someone else this time.
Tell me about it if it's something human.
Let me into your grief. I'm not so much
Unlike other folks as your standing there
Apart would make me out. Give me my chance.
I do think, though, you overdo it a little.
What was it brought you up to think it the thing
To take your mother-loss of a first child
So inconsolably—in the face of love.
You'd think his memory might be satisfied——"

"There you go sneering now!"
"I'm not, I'm not!
You make me angry. I'll come down to you.
God, what a woman! And it's come to this,
A man can't speak of his own child that's dead."

"You can't because you don't know how to speak.
If you had any feelings, you that dug
With your own hand—how could you?—his little grave;
I saw you from that very window there,
Making the gravel leap and leap in air,
Leap up, like that, like that, and land so lightly
And roll back down the mound beside the hole.
I thought, Who is that man? I didn't know you.
And I crept down the stairs and up the stairs
To look again, and still your spade kept lifting.
Then you came in. I heard your rumbling voice
Out in the kitchen, and I don't know why,
But I went near to see with my own eyes.
You could sit there with the stains on your shoes
Of the fresh earth from your own baby's grave
And talk about your everyday concerns.
You had stood the spade up against the wall
Outside there in the entry, for I saw it."

"I shall laugh the worst laugh I ever laughed.
I'm cursed. God, if I don't believe I'm cursed."

"I can repeat the very words you were saying:
'Three foggy mornings and one rainy day
Will rot the best birch fence a man can build.'
Think of it, talk like that at such a time!
What had how long it takes a birch to rot
To do with what was in the darkened parlor?
You *couldn't* care! The nearest friends can go
With anyone to death, comes so far short
They might as well not try to go at all.
No, from the time when one is sick to death,
One is alone, and he dies more alone.
Friends make pretense of following to the grave,
But before one is in it, their minds are turned
And making the best of their way back to life
And living people, and things they understand.
But the world's evil. I won't have grief so
If I can change it. Oh, I won't, I won't!"

"There, you have said it all and you feel better.
You won't go now. You're crying. Close the door.
The heart's gone out of it: why keep it up?
Amy! There's someone coming down the road!"

"*You*—oh, you think the talk is all. I must go—
Somewhere out of this house. How can I make you——"

"If—you—do!" She was opening the door wider.
"Where do you mean to go? First tell me that.
I'll follow and bring you back by force. I *will*!——"

1914

After Apple-Picking

My long two-pointed ladder's sticking through a tree
Toward heaven still,
And there's a barrel that I didn't fill
Beside it, and there may be two or three
Apples I didn't pick upon some bough.
But I am done with apple-picking now.
Essence of winter sleep is on the night,
The scent of apples: I am drowsing off.
I cannot rub the strangeness from my sight
I got from looking through a pane of glass
I skimmed this morning from the drinking trough
And held against the world of hoary grass.
It melted, and I let it fall and break.
But I was well
Upon my way to sleep before it fell,
And I could tell
What form my dreaming was about to take.
Magnified apples appear and disappear,
Stem end and blossom end,
And every fleck of russet showing clear.
My instep arch not only keeps the ache,
It keeps the pressure of a ladder-round.
I feel the ladder sway as the boughs bend.
And I keep hearing from the cellar bin
The rumbling sound
Of load on load of apples coming in.
For I have had too much
Of apple-picking: I am overtired
Of the great harvest I myself desired.
There were ten thousand thousand fruit to touch,
Cherish in hand, lift down, and not let fall.
For all
That struck the earth,
No matter if not bruised or spiked with stubble,
Went surely to the cider-apple heap
As of no worth.
One can see what will trouble
This sleep of mine, whatever sleep it is.
Were he not gone,
The woodchuck could say whether it's like his
Long sleep, as I describe its coming on,
Or just some human sleep.

1914

The Wood-Pile

Out walking in the frozen swamp one gray day,
I paused and said, "I will turn back from here.
No, I will go on farther—and we shall see."
The hard snow held me, save where now and then
One foot went through. The view was all in lines
Straight up and down of tall slim trees
Too much alike to mark or name a place by
So as to say for certain I was here
Or somewhere else: I was just far from home.
A small bird flew before me. He was careful
To put a tree between us when he lighted,
And say no word to tell me who he was
Who was so foolish as to think what *he* thought.
He thought that I was after him for a feather—
The white one in his tail; like one who takes
Everything said as personal to himself.
One flight out sideways would have undeceived him.
And then there was a pile of wood for which
I forgot him and let his little fear
Carry him off the way I might have gone,
Without so much as wishing him good-night.
He went behind it to make his last stand.
It was a cord of maple, cut and split
And piled—and measured, four by four by eight.
And not another like it could I see.
No runner tracks in this year's snow looped near it.
And it was older sure than this year's cutting,
Or even last year's or the year's before.
The wood was gray and the bark warping off it
And the pile somewhat sunken. Clematis
Had wound strings round and round it like a bundle.
What held it, though, on one side was a tree
Still growing, and on one a stake and prop,
These latter about to fall. I thought that only
Someone who lived in turning to fresh tasks
Could so forget his handiwork on which
He spent himself, the labor of his ax,
And leave it there far from a useful fireplace
To warm the frozen swamp as best it could
With the slow smokeless burning of decay.

1914

The Road Not Taken

Two roads diverged in a yellow wood,
And sorry I could not travel both
And be one traveler, long I stood
And looked down one as far as I could
To where it bent in the undergrowth;

Then took the other, as just as fair,
And having perhaps the better claim,
Because it was grassy and wanted wear;
Though as for that, the passing there
Had worn them really about the same,

And both that morning equally lay
In leaves no step had trodden black.
Oh, I kept the first for another day!
Yet knowing how way leads on to way,
I doubted if I should ever come back.

I shall be telling this with a sigh
Somewhere ages and ages hence:
Two roads diverged in a wood, and I—
I took the one less traveled by,
And that has made all the difference.

1916

The Oven Bird

There is a singer everyone has heard,
Loud, a mid-summer and a mid-wood bird,
Who makes the solid tree trunks sound again.
He says that leaves are old and that for flowers
Mid-summer is to spring as one to ten.
He says the early petal-fall is past,
When pear and cherry bloom went down in showers
On sunny days a moment overcast;
And comes that other fall we name the fall.
He says the highway dust is over all.
The bird would cease and be as other birds
But that he knows in singing not to sing.
The question that he frames in all but words
Is what to make of a diminished thing.

1916

Birches

When I see birches bend to left and right
Across the lines of straighter darker trees,
I like to think some boy's been swinging them.
But swinging doesn't bend them down to stay
As ice storms do. Often you must have seen them
Loaded with ice a sunny winter morning
After a rain. They click upon themselves
As the breeze rises, and turn many-colored
As the stir cracks and crazes their enamel.
Soon the sun's warmth makes them shed crystal shells
Shattering and avalanching on the snow crust—
Such heaps of broken glass to sweep away
You'd think the inner dome of heaven had fallen.
They are dragged to the withered bracken by the load,
And they seem not to break; though once they are bowed
So low for long, they never right themselves:
You may see their trunks arching in the woods
Years afterwards, trailing their leaves on the ground
Like girls on hands and knees that throw their hair
Before them over their heads to dry in the sun.
But I was going to say when Truth broke in
With all her matter of fact about the ice storm,
I should prefer to have some boy bend them
As he went out and in to fetch the cows—
Some boy too far from town to learn baseball,
Whose only play was what he found himself,
Summer or winter, and could play alone.
One by one he subdued his father's trees
By riding them down over and over again
Until he took the stiffness out of them,
And not one but hung limp, not one was left
For him to conquer. He learned all there was
To learn about not launching out too soon
And so not carrying the tree away
Clear to the ground. He always kept his poise
To the top branches, climbing carefully
With the same pains you use to fill a cup
Up to the brim, and even above the brim.
Then he flung outward, feet first, with a swish,
Kicking his way down through the air to the ground.
So was I once myself a swinger of birches.
And so I dream of going back to be.
It's when I'm weary of considerations,
And life is too much like a pathless wood
Where your face burns and tickles with the cobwebs
Broken across it, and one eye is weeping
From a twig's having lashed across it open.
I'd like to get away from earth awhile
And then come back to it and begin over.
May no fate willfully misunderstand me

And half grant what I wish and snatch me away
Not to return. Earth's the right place for love:
I don't know where it's likely to go better.
I'd like to go by climbing a birch tree,
And climb black branches up a snow-white trunk
Toward heaven, till the tree could bear no more,
But dipped its top and set me down again.
That would be good both going and coming back.
One could do worse than be a swinger of birches.

1916

"Out, Out—"[1]

The buzz saw snarled and rattled in the yard
And made dust and dropped stove-length sticks of wood,
Sweet-scented stuff when the breeze drew across it.
And from there those that lifted eyes could count
Five mountain ranges one behind the other
Under the sunset far into Vermont.
And the saw snarled and rattled, snarled and rattled,
As it ran light, or had to bear a load.
And nothing happened: day was all but done.
Call it a day, I wish they might have said
To please the boy by giving him the half hour
That a boy counts so much when saved from work.
His sister stood beside them in her apron
To tell them "Supper." At the word, the saw,
As if to prove saws knew what supper meant,
Leaped out at the boy's hand, or seemed to leap—
He must have given the hand. However it was,
Neither refused the meeting. But the hand!
The boy's first outcry was a rueful laugh,
As he swung toward them holding up the hand,
Half in appeal, but half as if to keep
The life from spilling. Then the boy saw all—
Since he was old enough to know, big boy
Doing a man's work, though a child at heart—
He saw all spoiled. "Don't let him cut my hand off—
The doctor, when he comes. Don't let him, sister!"
So. But the hand was gone already.
The doctor put him in the dark of ether.
He lay and puffed his lips out with his breath.
And then—the watcher at his pulse took fright.
No one believed. They listened at his heart.
Little—less—nothing!—and that ended it.
No more to build on there. And they, since they
Were not the one dead, turned to their affairs.

1916

1. From Shakespeare's *Macbeth* 5.5.23–24: "Out, out, brief candle! / Life's but a walking shadow."

Fire and Ice

Some say the world will end in fire,
Some say in ice.
From what I've tasted of desire
I hold with those who favor fire.
But if it had to perish twice,
I think I know enough of hate
To say that for destruction ice
Is also great
And would suffice.

1923

Nothing Gold Can Stay

Nature's first green is gold,
Her hardest hue to hold.
Her early leaf's a flower;
But only so an hour.
Then leaf subsides to leaf.
So Eden sank to grief,
So dawn goes down to day.
Nothing gold can stay.

1923

Stopping by Woods on a Snowy Evening

Whose woods these are I think I know.
His house is in the village, though;
He will not see me stopping here
To watch his woods fill up with snow.

My little horse must think it queer
To stop without a farmhouse near
Between the woods and frozen lake
The darkest evening of the year.

He gives his harness bells a shake
To ask if there is some mistake.
The only other sound's the sweep
Of easy wind and downy flake.

The woods are lovely, dark, and deep,
But I have promises to keep,
And miles to go before I sleep.
And miles to go before I sleep.

1923

Desert Places

Snow falling and night falling fast, oh, fast
In a field I looked into going past,
And the ground almost covered smooth in snow,
But a few weeds and stubble showing last.

The woods around it have it—it is theirs.
All animals are smothered in their lairs.
I am too absent-spirited to count;
The loneliness includes me unawares.

And lonely as it is, that loneliness
Will be more lonely ere it will be less—
A blanker whiteness of benighted snow
With no expression, nothing to express.

They cannot scare me with their empty spaces
Between stars—on stars where no human race is.
I have it in me so much nearer home
To scare myself with my own desert places.

1936

Design

I found a dimpled spider, fat and white,
On a white heal-all,[1] holding up a moth
Like a white piece of rigid satin cloth—
Assorted characters of death and blight
Mixed ready to begin the morning right,
Like the ingredients of a witches' broth—
A snow-drop spider, a flower like a froth,
And dead wings carried like a paper kite.

What had that flower to do with being white,
The wayside blue and innocent heal-all?
What brought the kindred spider to that height,
Then steered the white moth thither in the night?
What but design of darkness to appall?—
If design govern in a thing so small.

1922, 1936

1. Common wildflower whose blossom is normally violet or blue.

Neither Out Far Nor In Deep

The people along the sand
All turn and look one way.
They turn their back on the land.
They look at the sea all day.

As long as it takes to pass
A ship keeps raising its hull;
The wetter ground like glass
Reflects a standing gull.

The land may vary more;
But wherever the truth may be—
The water comes ashore,
And the people look at the sea.

They cannot look out far.
They cannot look in deep.
But when was that ever a bar
To any watch they keep?

1936

Provide, Provide

The witch that came (the withered hag)
To wash the steps with pail and rag
Was once the beauty Abishag,[1]

The picture pride of Hollywood.
Too many fall from great and good
For you to doubt the likelihood.

Die early and avoid the fate.
Or if predestined to die late,
Make up your mind to die in state.

Make the whole stock exchange your own!
If need be occupy a throne,
Where nobody can call *you* crone.

Some have relied on what they knew,
Others on being simply true.
What worked for them might work for you.

1. A beautiful maiden brought to comfort King David in his old age (1 Kings 1.2–4).

No memory of having starred
Atones for later disregard
Or keeps the end from being hard.

Better to go down dignified
With boughten friendship at your side
Than none at all. Provide, provide!

1934, 1936

The Gift Outright

The land was ours before we were the land's.
She was our land more than a hundred years
Before we were her people. She was ours
In Massachusetts, in Virginia,
But we were England's, still colonials,
Possessing what we still were unpossessed by,
Possessed by what we now no more possessed.
Something we were withholding made us weak
Until we found out that it was ourselves
We were withholding from our land of living,
And forthwith found salvation in surrender.
Such as we were we gave ourselves outright
(The deed of gift was many deeds of war)
To the land vaguely realizing westward,
But still unstoried, artless, unenhanced,
Such as she was, such as she would become.

1942

Directive

Back out of all this now too much for us,
Back in a time made simple by the loss
Of detail, burned, dissolved, and broken off
Like graveyard marble sculpture in the weather,
There is a house that is no more a house
Upon a farm that is no more a farm
And in a town that is no more a town.
The road there, if you'll let a guide direct you
Who only has at heart your getting lost,
May seem as if it should have been a quarry—
Great monolithic knees the former town
Long since gave up pretense of keeping covered.
And there's a story in a book about it:
Besides the wear of iron wagon wheels

The ledges show lines ruled southeast-northwest,
The chisel work of an enormous Glacier
That braced his feet against the Arctic Pole.
You must not mind a certain coolness from him
Still said to haunt this side of Panther Mountain.
Nor need you mind the serial ordeal
Of being watched from forty cellar holes
As if by eye pairs out of forty firkins.[1]
As for the woods' excitement over you
That sends light rustle rushes to their leaves,
Charge that to upstart inexperience.
Where were they all not twenty years ago?
They think too much of having shaded out
A few old pecker-fretted[2] apple trees.
Make yourself up a cheering song of how
Someone's road home from work this once was,
Who may be just ahead of you on foot
Or creaking with a buggy load of grain.
The height of the adventure is the height
Of country where two village cultures faded
Into each other. Both of them are lost.
And if you're lost enough to find yourself
By now, pull in your ladder road behind you
And put a sign up closed to all but me.
Then make yourself at home. The only field
Now left's no bigger than a harness gall.[3]
First there's the children's house of make-believe,
Some shattered dishes underneath a pine,
The playthings in the playhouse of the children.
Weep for what little things could make them glad.
Then for the house that is no more a house,
But only a belilaced cellar hole,
Now slowly closing like a dent in dough.
This was no playhouse but a house in earnest.
Your destination and your destiny's
A brook that was the water of the house,
Cold as a spring as yet so near its source,
Too lofty and original to rage.
(We know the valley streams that when aroused
Will leave their tatters hung on barb and thorn.)
I have kept hidden in the instep arch
Of an old cedar at the waterside
A broken drinking goblet like the Grail[4]
Under a spell so the wrong ones can't find it,

1. Small wooden tubs for butter or lard.
2. Marked up with small holes by woodpeckers.
3. Sore on a horse's skin caused by the rubbing of the harness.
4. The cup used by Jesus at the Last Supper. According to legend, the Grail later disappeared from its keepers because of their moral impurity, and various knights, including those of King Arthur's Round Table, went in quest of it. From this, the quest for the Grail has come to symbolize any spiritual search.

So can't get saved, as Saint Mark[5] says they mustn't.
(I stole the goblet from the children's playhouse.)
Here are your waters and your watering place.
Drink and be whole again beyond confusion.

1947

The Figure a Poem Makes[1]

Abstraction is an old story with the philosophers, but it has been like a new toy in the hands of the artists of our day. Why can't we have any one quality of poetry we choose by itself? We can have in thought. Then it will go hard if we can't in practice. Our lives for it.

Granted no one but a humanist much cares how sound a poem is if it is only *a* sound. The sound is the gold in the ore. Then we will have the sound out alone and dispense with the inessential. We do till we make the discovery that the object in writing poetry is to make all poems sound as different as possible from each other, and the resources for that of vowels, consonants, punctuation, syntax, words, sentences, meter are not enough. We need the help of context—meaning—subject matter. That is the greatest help towards variety. All that can be done with words is soon told. So also with meters—particularly in our language where there are virtually but two, strict iambic and loose iambic. The ancients with many were still poor if they depended on meters for all tune. It is painful to watch our sprung-rhythmists[2] straining at the point of omitting one short from a foot for relief from monotony. The possibilities for tune from the dramatic tones of meaning struck across the rigidity of a limited meter are endless. And we are back in poetry as merely one more art of having something to say, sound or unsound. Probably better if sound, because deeper and from wider experience.

Then there is this wildness whereof it is spoken. Granted again that it has an equal claim with sound to being a poem's better half. If it is a wild tune, it is a poem. Our problem then is, as modern abstractionists, to have the wildness pure; to be wild with nothing to be wild about. We bring up as aberrationists, giving way to undirected associations and kicking ourselves from one chance suggestion to another in all directions as of a hot afternoon in the life of a grasshopper. Theme alone can steady us down. Just as the first mystery was how a poem could have a tune in such a straightness as meter, so the second mystery is how a poem can have wildness and at the same time a subject that shall be fulfilled.

It should be of the pleasure of a poem itself to tell how it can. The figure a poem makes. It begins in delight and ends in wisdom. The figure is the same as for love. No one can really hold that the ecstasy should be static and stand still in one place. It begins in delight, it inclines to the impulse, it assumes direction with the first line laid down, it runs a course of lucky

5. A reference to Mark 4.11–12; see also Mark 16.16.
1. This essay was published as an introduction to *The Collected Poems of Robert Frost* (1939).
2. *Sprung rhythm* was a term invented by the English poet Gerard Manley Hopkins (1844–1889) for meters depending not on repeated units of syllables and accents, as in traditional verse, but on irregularities.

events, and ends in a clarification of life—not necessarily a great clarification, such as sects and cults are founded on, but in a momentary stay against confusion. It has denouement. It has an outcome that though unforeseen was predestined from the first image of the original mood—and indeed from the very mood. It is but a trick poem and no poem at all if the best of it was thought of first and saved for the last. It finds its own name as it goes and discovers the best waiting for it in some final phrase at once wise and sad—the happy-sad blend of the drinking song.

No tears in the writer, no tears in the reader. No surprise for the writer, no surprise for the reader. For me the initial delight is in the surprise of remembering something I didn't know I knew. I am in a place, in a situation, as if I had materialized from cloud or risen out of the ground. There is a glad recognition of the long lost and the rest follows. Step by step the wonder of unexpected supply keeps growing. The impressions most useful to my purpose seem always those I was unaware of and so made no note of at the time when taken, and the conclusion is come to that like giants we are always hurling experience ahead of us to pave the future with against the day when we may want to strike a line of purpose across it for somewhere. The line will have the more charm for not being mechanically straight. We enjoy the straight crookedness of a good walking stick. Modern instruments of precision are being used to make things crooked as if by eye and hand in the old days.

I tell how there may be a better wildness of logic than of inconsequence. But the logic is backward, in retrospect, after the act. It must be more felt than seen ahead like prophecy. It must be a revelation, or a series of revelations, as much for the poet as for the reader. For it to be that there must have been the greatest freedom of the material to move about in it and to establish relations in it regardless of time and space, previous relation, and everything but affinity. We prate of freedom. We call our schools free because we are not free to stay away from them till we are sixteen years of age. I have given up my democratic prejudices and now willingly set the lower classes free to be completely taken care of by the upper classes. Political freedom is nothing to me. I bestow it right and left. All I would keep for myself is the freedom of my material—the condition of body and mind now and then to summon aptly from the vast chaos of all I have lived through.

Scholars and artists thrown together are often annoyed at the puzzle of where they differ. Both work from knowledge; but I suspect they differ most importantly in the way their knowledge is come by. Scholars get theirs with conscientious thoroughness along projected lines of logic; poets theirs cavalierly and as it happens in and out of books. They stick to nothing deliberately, but let what will stick to them like burrs where they walk in the fields. No acquirement is on assignment, or even self-assignment. Knowledge of the second kind is much more available in the wild free ways of wit and art. A school boy may be defined as one who can tell you what he knows in the order in which he learned it. The artist must value himself as he snatches a thing from some previous order in time and space into a new order with not so much as a ligature clinging to it of the old place where it was organic.

More than once I should have lost my soul to radicalism if it had been the originality it was mistaken for by its young converts. Originality and initiative are what I ask for my country. For myself the originality need be no more than the freshness of a poem run in the way I have described: from delight to wisdom. The figure is the same as for love. Like a piece of ice on a hot stove the poem must ride on its own melting. A poem may be worked over once it is in being, but may not be worried into being. Its most precious quality will remain its having run itself and carried away the poet with it. Read it a hundred times: it will forever keep its freshness as a petal keeps its fragrance. It can never lose its sense of a meaning that once unfolded by surprise as it went.

1939

SUSAN GLASPELL

1876–1948

Susan Glaspell—journalist, novelist, short-story writer, playwright, theatrical producer and director, actor—was a multitalented professional who eventually published more than fifty short stories, nine novels, and fourteen plays. Feminist rediscovery of *Trifles*, her first play—written and produced in 1916 and turned into a prize-winning short story, "A Jury of Her Peers," in 1917—has made this her best-known work today.

Born and raised in Davenport, Iowa, Glaspell worked for a year on the Davenport *Morning Republican* after high school graduation, then attended Drake University in Des Moines from 1895 to 1899. In college she wrote for the campus newspaper as well as various Des Moines papers; after graduation she worked for two years on the Des Moines *Daily News*. In 1901 she abandoned journalism, returning to Davenport with a plan to earn her living as a fiction writer. Her early stories, combining regional midwestern settings with romantic plots, found favor with the editors of such popular magazines as *Harper's*, the *Ladies' Home Journal*, the *American Magazine*, and the *Woman's Home Companion*. In 1909 she published her first novel, *The Glory of the Conquered*.

In 1913 she married the recently divorced George Cram Cook, a Harvard-educated native of Davenport, who was a writer and theatrical director much interested in modernist experimentation. The two moved to the East Coast, traveled widely, and collaborated on many projects. They helped found both the Washington Square Players in 1914 and the group that came to be known as the Provincetown Players in 1916.

The Provincetown Players, named for the New England seaport town where many of the members spent their summers, aimed to foster an American theater by producing plays by American playwrights only. Eugene O'Neill became the best-known dramatist of the group; Glaspell was a close second. She not only wrote plays but also acted in them, directed them, and helped produce them. From 1916 to 1922 she wrote nine plays, including *Trifles,* for the Provincetown Players; in 1922 Cook and Glaspell withdrew from the group, finding that it had become too commercially successful to suit their experimental aims.

Cook died in 1924; a later close relationship, with the novelist and playwright Norman Matson, ended in 1932. Throughout the 1930s and 1940s, Glaspell, now a year-round resident of Provincetown, continued to write and publish. Her novel *Judd*

Rankin's Wife (1928) was made into a movie. She won the 1930 Pulitzer Prize for drama for *Alison's Room,* a play loosely based on the life of Emily Dickinson. Her last novel, *Judd Rankin's Daughter,* appeared in 1945, three years before she died at the age of seventy-two.

For Glaspell, the influence of such European playwrights as Henrik Ibsen and August Strindberg opened the door to much grimmer writing in a play like *Trifles* than in her popular short stories, with their formulaic happy endings. Her realism—her unsparing depiction of women's narrow, thwarted, isolated, and subjugated lives in rural, regional settings—produces effects unlike the nostalgic celebrations of woman-centered societies often associated with women regionalists. The efficiently plotted *Trifles* also features a formal device found in other Glaspell works, including *Alison's Room:* the main character at its center never appears.

The text is from *Plays by Susan Glaspell* (1987).

Trifles

Characters

GEORGE HENDERSON, *County Attorney*
HENRY PETERS, *Sheriff*
LEWIS HALE, *a Neighboring Farmer*
MRS PETERS
MRS HALE

SCENE: *The kitchen in the now abandoned farmhouse of* John Wright, *a gloomy kitchen, and left without having been put in order—unwashed pans under the sink, a loaf of bread outside the bread-box, a dish-towel on the table—other signs of incompleted work. At the rear the outer door opens and the* SHERIFF *comes in followed by the* COUNTY ATTORNEY *and* HALE. *The* SHERIFF *and* HALE *are men in middle life, the* COUNTY ATTORNEY *is a young man; all are much bundled up and go at once to the stove. They are followed by the two women—the* SHERIFF's *wife first; she is a slight wiry woman, a thin nervous face.* MRS HALE *is larger and would ordinarily be called more comfortable looking, but she is disturbed now and looks fearfully about as she enters. The women have come in slowly, and stand close together near the door.*

COUNTY ATTORNEY [*rubbing his hands*] This feels good. Come up to the fire, ladies.

MRS PETERS [*after taking a step forward*] I'm not—cold.

SHERIFF [*unbuttoning his overcoat and stepping away from the stove as if to mark the beginning of official business*] Now, Mr Hale, before we move things about, you explain to Mr Henderson just what you saw when you came here yesterday morning.

COUNTY ATTORNEY By the way, has anything been moved? Are things just as you left them yesterday?

SHERIFF [*looking about*] It's just the same. When it dropped below zero last night I thought I'd better send Frank out this morning to make a fire for us—no use getting pneumonia with a big case on, but I told him not to touch anything except the stove—and you know Frank.

COUNTY ATTORNEY Somebody should have been left here yesterday.

SHERIFF Oh—yesterday. When I had to send Frank to Morris Center for that man who went crazy—I want you to know I had my hands full yesterday. I knew you could get back from Omaha by today and as long as I went over everything here myself—

COUNTY ATTORNEY Well, Mr Hale, tell just what happened when you came here yesterday morning.

HALE Harry and I had started to town with a load of potatoes. We came along the road from my place and as I got here I said, 'I'm going to see if I can't get John Wright to go in with me on a party telephone.'[1] I spoke to Wright about it once before and he put me off, saying folks talked too much anyway, and all he asked was peace and quiet—I guess you know about how much he talked himself; but I thought maybe if I went to the house and talked about it before his wife, though I said to Harry that I didn't know as what his wife wanted made much difference to John—

COUNTY ATTORNEY Let's talk about that later, Mr Hale. I do want to talk about that, but tell now just what happened when you got to the house.

HALE I didn't hear or see anything; I knocked at the door, and still it was all quiet inside. I knew they must be up, it was past eight o'clock. So I knocked again, and I thought I heard somebody say, 'Come in.' I wasn't sure. I'm not sure yet, but I opened the door—this door [*indicating the door by which the two women are still standing*] and there in that rocker—[*pointing to it*] sat Mrs Wright.

[*They all look at the rocker.*]

COUNTY ATTORNEY What—was she doing?

HALE She was rockin' back and forth. She had her apron in her hand and was kind of—pleating it.

COUNTY ATTORNEY And how did she—look?

HALE Well, she looked queer.

COUNTY ATTORNEY How do you mean—queer?

HALE Well, as if she didn't know what she was going to do next. And kind of done up.

COUNTY ATTORNEY How did she seem to feel about your coming?

HALE Why, I don't think she minded—one way or other. She didn't pay much attention. I said. 'How do. Mrs Wright it's cold, ain't it?' And she said, 'Is it?'—and went on kind of pleating at her apron. Well, I was surprised: she didn't ask me to come up to the stove, or to set down, but just sat there, not even looking at me, so I said, 'I want to see John.' And then she—laughed. I guess you would call it a laugh. I thought of Harry and the team outside, so I said a little sharp: 'Can't I see John?' 'No,' she says, kind o' dull like. 'Ain't he home?' says I. 'Yes,' says she, 'he's home.' 'Then why can't I see him?' I asked her, out of patience. ''Cause he's dead,' says she. *'Dead?'* says I. She just nodded her head, not getting a bit excited, but rockin' back and forth. 'Why—where is he?' says I, not knowing what to say. She just pointed upstairs—like that [*himself pointing to the room above*] I got up, with the idea of going up there. I walked from there to here—then I says, 'Why, what did he die of?' 'He died of a rope round his neck,' says she, and just went on pleatin' at her apron. Well, I went out

1. A single telephone line shared by several households.

and called Harry. I thought I might—need help. We went upstairs and there he was lyin'—

COUNTY ATTORNEY I think I'd rather have you go into that upstairs, where you can point it all out. Just go on now with the rest of the story.

HALE Well, my first thought was to get that rope off. It looked . . . [*stops, his face twitches*] . . . but Harry, he went up to him, and he said, 'No, he's dead all right, and we'd better not touch anything.' So we went back down stairs. She was still sitting that same way. 'Has anybody been notified?' I asked. 'No,' says she unconcerned. 'Who did this, Mrs Wright?' said Harry. He said it business-like—and she stopped pleatin' of her apron. 'I don't know,' she says. 'You don't *know*?' says Harry. 'No,' says she. 'Weren't you sleepin' in the bed with him?' says Harry. 'Yes,' says she, 'but I was on the inside.' 'Somebody slipped a rope round his neck and strangled him and you didn't wake up?' says Harry. 'I didn't wake up,' she said after him. We must 'a looked as if we didn't see how that could be, for after a minute she said, 'I sleep sound.' Harry was going to ask her more questions but I said maybe we ought to let her tell her story first to the coroner, or the sheriff, so Harry went fast as he could to Rivers' place, where there's a telephone.

COUNTY ATTORNEY And what did Mrs Wright do when she knew that you had gone for the coroner?

HALE She moved from that chair to this one over here [*pointing to a small chair in the corner*] and just sat there with her hands held together and looking down. I got a feeling that I ought to make some conversation, so I said I had come in to see if John wanted to put in a telephone, and at that she started to laugh, and then she stopped and looked at me—scared. [*the* COUNTY ATTORNEY, *who has had his notebook out, makes a note*] I dunno, maybe it wasn't scared. I wouldn't like to say it was. Soon Harry got back, and then Dr Lloyd came, and you, Mr Peters, and so I guess that's all I know that you don't.

COUNTY ATTORNEY [*looking around*] I guess we'll go upstairs first—and then out to the barn and around there. [*to the* SHERIFF] You're convinced that there was nothing important here—nothing that would point to any motive.

SHERIFF Nothing here but kitchen things.

[*The* COUNTY ATTORNEY, *after again looking around the kitchen, opens the door of a cupboard closet. He gets up on a chair and looks on a shelf. Pulls his hand away, sticky.*]

COUNTY ATTORNEY Here's a nice mess.

[*The women draw nearer.*]

MRS PETERS [*to the other woman*] Oh, her fruit: it did freeze. [*to the* LAWYER] She worried about that when it turned so cold. She said the fire'd go out and her jars would break.

SHERIFF Well, can you beat the women! Held for murder and worryin' about her preserves.

COUNTY ATTORNEY I guess before we're through she may have something more serious than preserves to worry about.

HALE Well, women are used to worrying over trifles.

[*The two women move a little closer together.*]

COUNTY ATTORNEY [*with the gallantry of a young politician*] And yet, for all their worries, what would we do without the ladies? [*the women do not unbend. He goes to the sink, takes a dipperful of water from the pail and pouring it into a basin, washes his hands. Starts to wipe them on the roller-towel, turns it for a cleaner place*] Dirty towels! [*kicks his foot against the pans under the sink*] Not much of a housekeeper, would you say, ladies?

MRS HALE [*stiffly*] There's a great deal of work to be done on a farm.

COUNTY ATTORNEY To be sure. And yet [*with a little bow to her*] I know there are some Dickson county farmhouses which do not have such roller towels.

[*He gives it a pull to expose its length again.*]

MRS HALE Those towels get dirty awful quick. Men's hands aren't always as clean as they might be.

COUNTY ATTORNEY Ah, loyal to your sex. I see. But you and Mrs Wright were neighbors. I suppose you were friends, too.

MRS HALE [*shaking her head*] I've not seen much of her of late years. I've not been in this house—it's more than a year.

COUNTY ATTORNEY And why was that? You didn't like her?

MRS HALE I liked her all well enough. Farmers' wives have their hands full, Mr Henderson. And then—

COUNTY ATTORNEY Yes—?

MRS HALE [*looking about*] It never seemed a very cheerful place.

COUNTY ATTORNEY No—it's not cheerful. I shouldn't say she had the homemaking instinct.

MRS HALE Well, I don't know as Wright had, either.

COUNTY ATTORNEY You mean that they didn't get on very well?

MRS HALE No. I don't mean anything. But I don't think a place'd be any cheerfuller for John Wright's being in it.

COUNTY ATTORNEY I'd like to talk more of that a little later. I want to get the lay of things upstairs now.

[*He goes to the left, where three steps lead to a stair door.*]

SHERIFF I suppose anything Mrs Peters does'll be all right. She was to take in some clothes for her, you know, and a few little things. We left in such a hurry yesterday.

COUNTY ATTORNEY Yes, but I would like to see what you take, Mrs Peters, and keep an eye out for anything that might be of use to us.

MRS PETERS Yes, Mr Henderson.

[*The women listen to the men's steps on the stairs, then look about the kitchen.*]

MRS HALE I'd hate to have men coming into my kitchen, snooping around and criticising.

[*She arranges the pans under sink which the* lawyer *had shoved out of place.*]

MRS PETERS Of course it's no more than their duty.

MRS HALE Duty's all right, but I guess that deputy sheriff that came out to make the fire might have got a little of this on. [*gives the roller towel a pull*] Wish I'd thought of that sooner. Seems mean to talk about her for not having things slicked up when she had to come away in such a hurry.

MRS PETERS [*who has gone to a small table in the left rear corner of the room, and lifted one end of a towel that covers a pan*] She had bread set.

[*Stands still.*]

MRS HALE [*eyes fixed on a loaf of bread beside the bread-box, which is on a low shelf at the other side of the room. Moves slowly toward it*] She was going to put this in there. [*picks up loaf, then abruptly drops it. In a manner of returning to familiar things*] It's a shame about her fruit. I wonder if it's all gone. [*gets up on the chair and looks*] I think there's some here that's all right, Mrs Peters. Yes—here; [*holding it toward the window*] this is cherries, too. [*looking again*] I declare I believe that's the only one. [*gets down, bottle in her hand. Goes to the sink and wipes it off on the outside*] She'll feel awful bad after all her hard work in the hot weather. I remember the afternoon I put up my cherries last summer.

[*She puts the bottle on the big kitchen table, center of the room. With a sigh, is about to sit down in the rocking-chair. Before she is seated realizes what chair it is; with a slow look at it, steps back. The chair which she has touched rocks back and forth.*]

MRS PETERS Well, I must get those things from the front room closet. [*she goes to the door at the right, but after looking into the other room, steps back*] You coming with me, Mrs Hale? You could help me carry them.

[*They go in the other room; reappear,* MRS PETERS *carrying a dress and skirt,* MRS HALE *following with a pair of shoes.*]

MRS PETERS My, it's cold in there.

[*She puts the clothes on the big table and hurries to the stove.*]

MRS HALE [*examining the skirt*] Wright was close.[2] I think maybe that's why she kept so much to herself. She didn't even belong to the Ladies Aid. I suppose she felt she couldn't do her part, and then you don't enjoy things when you feel shabby. She used to wear pretty clothes and be lively, when she was Minnie Foster, one of the town girls singing in the choir. But that—oh, that was thirty years ago. This all you was to take in?

MRS PETERS She said she wanted an apron. Funny thing to want, for there isn't much to get you dirty in jail, goodness knows. But I suppose just to make her feel more natural. She said they was in the top drawer in this cupboard. Yes, here. And then her little shawl that always hung behind the door. [*opens stair door and looks*] Yes, here it is.

[*Quickly shuts door leading upstairs.*]

MRS HALE [*abruptly moving toward her*] Mrs Peters?

MRS PETERS Yes, Mrs Hale?

MRS HALE Do you think she did it?

MRS PETERS [*in a frightened voice*] Oh, I don't know.

MRS HALE Well, I don't think she did. Asking for an apron and her little shawl. Worrying about her fruit.

MRS PETERS [*starts to speak, glances up, where footsteps are heard in the room above. In a low voice*] Mr Peters says it looks bad for her. Mr Henderson is awful sarcastic in a speech and he'll make fun of her sayin' she didn't wake up.

MRS HALE Well, I guess John Wright didn't wake when they was slipping that rope under his neck.

MRS PETERS No, it's strange. It must have been done awful crafty and still. They say it was such a—funny way to kill a man, rigging it all up like that.

2. Miserly.

MRS HALE That's just what Mr Hale said. There was a gun in the house. He says that's what he can't understand.

MRS PETERS Mr Henderson said coming out that what was needed for the case was a motive; something to show anger, or—sudden feeling.

MRS HALE [*who is standing by the table*] Well, I don't see any signs of anger around here. [*she puts her hand on the dish-towel which lies on the table, stands looking down at table, one half of which is clean, the other half messy*] It's wiped to here. [*makes a move as if to finish work, then turns and looks at loaf of bread outside the bread-box. Drops towel. In that voice of coming back to familiar things.*] Wonder how they are finding things upstairs. I hope she had it a little more red-up[3] up there. You know, it seems kind of *sneaking*. Locking her up in town and then coming out here and trying to get her own house to turn against her!

MRS PETERS But Mrs Hale, the law is the law.

MRS HALE I s'pose 'tis. [*unbuttoning her coat*] Better loosen up your things, Mrs Peters. You won't feel them when you go out.

[MRS PETERS *takes off her fur tippet,*[4] *goes to hang it on hook at back of room, stands looking at the under part of the small corner table.*]

MRS PETERS She was piecing a quilt.

[*She brings the large sewing basket and they look at the bright pieces.*]

MRS HALE It's log cabin pattern. Pretty, isn't it? I wonder if she was goin' to quilt it or just knot it?

[*Footsteps have been heard coming down the stairs. The* SHERIFF *enters followed by* HALE *and the* COUNTY ATTORNEY.]

SHERIFF They wonder if she was going to quilt it or just knot it!

[*The men laugh, the women look abashed.*]

COUNTY ATTORNEY [*rubbing his hands over the stove*] Frank's fire didn't do much up there, did it? Well, let's go out to the barn and get that cleared up.

[*The men go outside.*]

MRS HALE [*resentfully*] I don't know as there's anything so strange, our takin' up our time with little things while we're waiting for them to get the evidence. [*she sits down at the big table smoothing out a block with decision*] I don't see as it's anything to laugh about.

MRS PETERS [*apologetically*] Of course they've got awful important things on their minds.

[*Pulls up a chair and joins* MRS HALE *at the table.*]

MRS HALE [*examining another block*] Mrs Peters, look at this one. Here, this is the one she was working on, and look at the sewing! All the rest of it has been so nice and even. And look at this! It's all over the place! Why, it looks as if she didn't know what she was about!

[*After she has said this they look at each other, then start to glance back at the door. After an instant* MRS HALE *has pulled at a knot and ripped the sewing.*]

MRS PETERS Oh, what are you doing, Mrs Hale?

MRS HALE [*mildly*] Just pulling out a stitch or two that's not sewed very good. [*threading a needle*] Bad sewing always made me fidgety.

MRS PETERS [*nervously*] I don't think we ought to touch things.

3. Tidy.

4. Short cape, falling just below the shoulders.

MRS HALE I'll just finish up this end. [*suddenly stopping and leaning forward*] Mrs Peters?

MRS PETERS Yes, Mrs Hale?

MRS HALE What do you suppose she was so nervous about?

MRS PETERS Oh—I don't know. I don't know as she was nervous. I sometimes sew awful queer when I'm just tired. [MRS HALE *starts to say something, looks at* MRS PETERS, *then goes on sewing*] Well I must get these things wrapped up. They may be through sooner than we think. [*putting apron and other things together*] I wonder where I can find a piece of paper, and string.

MRS HALE In that cupboard, maybe.

MRS PETERS [*looking in cupboard*] Why, here's a bird-cage. [*holds it up*] Did she have a bird, Mrs Hale?

MRS HALE Why, I don't know whether she did or not—I've not been here for so long. There was a man around last year selling canaries cheap, but I don't know as she took one; maybe she did. She used to sing real pretty herself.

MRS PETERS [*glancing around*] Seems funny to think of a bird here. But she must have had one, or why would she have a cage? I wonder what happened to it.

MRS HALE I s'pose maybe the cat got it.

MRS PETERS No, she didn't have a cat. She's got that feeling some people have about cats—being afraid of them. My cat got in her room and she was real upset and asked me to take it out.

MRS HALE My sister Bessie was like that. Queer, ain't it?

MRS PETERS [*examining the cage*] Why, look at this door. It's broke. One hinge is pulled apart.

MRS HALE [*looking too*] Looks as if someone must have been rough with it.

MRS PETERS Why, yes.

[*She brings the cage forward and puts it on the table.*]

MRS HALE I wish if they're going to find any evidence they'd be about it. I don't like this place.

MRS PETERS But I'm awful glad you came with me, Mrs Hale. It would be lonesome for me sitting here alone.

MRS HALE It would, wouldn't it? [*dropping her sewing*] But I tell you what I do wish, Mrs Peters. I wish I had come over sometimes when *she* was here. I—[*looking around the room*]—wish I had.

MRS PETERS But of course you were awful busy. Mrs Hale—your house and your children.

MRS HALE I could've come. I stayed away because it weren't cheerful—and that's why I ought to have come. I—I've never liked this place. Maybe because it's down in a hollow and you don't see the road. I dunno what it is, but it's a lonesome place and always was. I wish I had come over to see Minnie Foster sometimes. I can see now—[*shakes her head*]

MRS PETERS Well, you mustn't reproach yourself, Mrs Hale. Somehow we just don't see how it is with other folks until—something comes up.

MRS HALE Not having children makes less work—but it makes a quiet house, and Wright out to work all day, and no company when he did come in. Did you know John Wright, Mrs Peters?

MRS PETERS Not to know him; I've seen him in town. They say he was a good man.

MRS HALE Yes—good; he didn't drink, and kept his word as well as most, I guess, and paid his debts. But he was a hard man, Mrs Peters. Just to pass the time of day with him—[*shivers*] Like a raw wind that gets to the bone. [*pauses, her eye falling on the cage*] I should think she would a wanted a bird. But what do you suppose went with it?

MRS PETERS I don't know, unless it got sick and died.

[*She reaches over and swings the broken door, swings it again, both women watch it.*]

MRS HALE You weren't raised round here, were you? [MRS PETERS *shakes her head*] You didn't know—her?

MRS PETERS Not till they brought her yesterday.

MRS HALE She—come to think of it, she was kind of like a bird herself—real sweet and pretty, but kind of timid and—fluttery. How—she—did—change. [*silence: then as if struck by a happy thought and relieved to get back to everyday things*] Tell you what, Mrs Peters, why don't you take the quilt in with you? It might take up her mind.

MRS PETERS Why, I think that's a real nice idea, Mrs Hale. There couldn't possibly be any objection to it, could there? Now, just what would I take? I wonder if her patches are in here—and her things.

[*They look in the sewing basket.*]

MRS HALE Here's some red. I expect this has got sewing things in it. [*brings out a fancy box*] What a pretty box. Looks like something somebody would give you. Maybe her scissors are in here. [*Opens box. Suddenly puts her hand to her nose*] Why—[MRS PETERS *bends nearer, then turns her face away*] There's something wrapped up in this piece of silk.

MRS PETERS Why, this isn't her scissors.

MRS HALE [*lifting the silk*] Oh, Mrs Peters—it's—

[MRS PETERS *bends closer.*]

MRS PETERS It's the bird.

MRS HALE [*jumping up*] But, Mrs Peters—look at it! It's neck! Look at its neck! It's all—other side *to*.

MRS PETERS Somebody—wrung—its—neck.

[*Their eyes meet. A look of growing comprehension, of horror. Steps are heard outside.* MRS HALE *slips box under quilt pieces, and sinks into her chair. Enter* SHERIFF *and* COUNTY ATTORNEY. MRS PETERS *rises.*]

COUNTY ATTORNEY [*as one turning from serious things to little pleasantries*] Well ladies, have you decided whether she was going to quilt it or knot it?

MRS PETERS We think she was going to—knot it.

COUNTY ATTORNEY Well, that's interesting, I'm sure. [*seeing the bird-cage*] Has the bird flown?

MRS HALE [*putting more quilt pieces over the box*] We think the—cat got it.

COUNTY ATTORNEY [*preoccupied*] Is there a cat?

[MRS HALE *glances in a quick covert way at* MRS PETERS.]

MRS PETERS Well, not *now*. They're superstitious, you know. They leave.

COUNTY ATTORNEY [*to* SHERIFF PETERS, *continuing an interrupted conversation*] No sign at all of anyone having come from the outside. Their own rope. Now let's go up again and go over it piece by piece. [*they start upstairs*] It would have to have been someone who knew just the—

[MRS PETERS *sits down. The two women sit there not looking at one another, but as if peering into something and at the same time holding back. When they talk now it is in the manner of feeling their way over strange ground, as if afraid of what they are saying, but as if they can not help saying it.*]

MRS HALE She liked the bird. She was going to bury it in that pretty box.

MRS PETERS [*in a whisper*] When I was a girl—my kitten—there was a boy took a hatchet, and before my eyes—and before I could get there—[*covers her face an instant*] If they hadn't held me back I would have—[*catches herself, looks upstairs where steps are heard, falters weakly*]—hurt him.

MRS HALE [*with a slow look around her*] I wonder how it would seem never to have had any children around. [*pause*] No, Wright wouldn't like the bird—a thing that sang. She used to sing. He killed that, too.

MRS PETERS [*moving uneasily*] We don't know who killed the bird.

MRS HALE I knew John Wright.

MRS PETERS It was an awful thing was done in this house that night, Mrs Hale. Killing a man while he slept, slipping a rope around his neck that choked the life out of him.

MRS HALE His neck. Choked the life out of him.

[*Her hand goes out and rests on the bird-cage.*]

MRS PETERS [*with rising voice*] We don't know who killed him. We don't *know*.

MRS HALE [*her own feeling not interrupted*] If there'd been years and years of nothing, then a bird to sing to you, it would be awful—still, after the bird was still.

MRS PETERS [*something within her speaking*] I know what stillness is. When we homesteaded in Dakota, and my first baby died—after he was two years old, and me with no other then—

MRS HALE [*moving*] How soon do you suppose they'll be through, looking for the evidence?

MRS PETERS I know what stillness is. [*pulling herself back*] The law has got to punish crime, Mrs Hale.

MRS HALE [*not as if answering that*] I wish you'd seen Minnie Foster when she wore a white dress with blue ribbons and stood up there in the choir and sang. [*a look around the room*] Oh, I *wish* I'd come over here once in a while! That was a crime! That was a crime! Who's going to punish that?

MRS PETERS [*looking upstairs*] We mustn't—take on.

MRS HALE I might have known she needed help! I know how things can be—for women. I tell you, it's queer. Mrs Peters. We live close together and we live far apart. We all go through the same things—it's all just a different kind of the same thing. [*brushes her eyes, noticing the bottle of fruit, reaches out for it*] If I was you, I wouldn't tell her her fruit was gone. Tell her it *ain't*. Tell her it's all right. Take this in to prove it to her. She—she may never know whether it was broke or not.

MRS PETERS [*takes the bottle, looks about for something to wrap it in; takes petticoat from the clothes brought from the other room, very nervously begins winding this around the bottle. In a false voice*] My, it's a good thing the men couldn't hear us. Wouldn't they just laugh! Getting all stirred up over a little thing like a—dead canary. As if that could have anything to do with—with—wouldn't they *laugh!*

[*The men are heard coming down stairs.*]

MRS HALE [*under her breath*] Maybe they would—maybe they wouldn't.

COUNTY ATTORNEY No, Peters, it's all perfectly clear except a reason for doing it. But you know juries when it comes to women. If there was some definite thing. Something to show—something to make a story about—a thing that would connect up with this strange way of doing it—

[*The women's eyes meet for an instant. Enter* HALE *from outer door.*]

HALE Well. I've got the team around. Pretty cold out there.

COUNTY ATTORNEY I'm going to stay here a while by myself. [*to the* SHERIFF] You can send Frank out for me, can't you? I want to go over everything. I'm not satisfied that we can't do better.

SHERIFF Do you want to see what Mrs Peters is going to take in?

[*The* LAWYER *goes to the table, picks up the apron, laughs.*]

COUNTY ATTORNEY Oh, I guess they're not very dangerous things the ladies have picked out. [*Moves a few things about, disturbing the quilt pieces which cover the box. Steps back*] No, Mrs Peters doesn't need supervising. For that matter, a sheriff's wife is married to the law. Ever think of it that way, Mrs Peters?

MRS PETERS Not—just that way.

SHERIFF [*chuckling*] Married to the law. [*moves toward the other room*] I just want you to come in here a minute, George. We ought to take a look at these windows.

COUNTY ATTORNEY [*scoffingly*] Oh, windows!

SHERIFF We'll be right out, Mr Hale.

[HALE *goes outside. The* SHERIFF *follows the* COUNTY ATTORNEY *into the other room. Then* MRS HALE *rises, hands tight together, looking intensely at* MRS PETERS, *whose eyes make a slow turn, finally meeting* MRS HALE'S. *A moment* MRS HALE *holds her, then her own eyes point the way to where the box is concealed. Suddenly* MRS PETERS *throws back quilt pieces and tries to put the box in the bag she is wearing. It is too big. She opens box, starts to take bird out, cannot touch it, goes to pieces, stands there helpless. Sound of a knob turning in the other room.* MRS HALE *snatches the box and puts it in the pocket of her big coat. Enter* COUNTY ATTORNEY *and* SHERIFF.]

COUNTY ATTORNEY [*facetiously*] Well, Henry, at least we found out that she was not going to quilt it. She was going to—what is it you call it, ladies?

MRS HALE [*her hand against her pocket*] We call it—knot it, Mr Henderson.

CURTAIN

1916

SHERWOOD ANDERSON
1876–1941

Sherwood Anderson was approaching middle age when he abandoned a successful business career to become a writer. Living in Chicago, New Orleans, and Paris, meeting literary people, he worked furiously to make up for his late start, producing novels, short stories, essays, and an autobiography. His short fiction provided a model for younger writers, whose careers he encouraged by literary advice and by practical help in getting published as well. *Winesburg, Ohio,* which appeared in 1919 when he was forty-three years old, remains a major work of experimental fiction and was in its time a bold treatment of small-town life in the American Midwest in the tradition of Edgar Lee Masters's *Spoon River Anthology.*

Anderson was born in southern Ohio, the third of seven children in a family headed by a father whose training and skill as a harness maker were becoming useless in the new world of the automobile. Anderson's father kept his family on the move in search of work; the stamina and tenderness of his mother supplied coherence and security in this nomadic life. Not until 1892, when Anderson was sixteen, did they settle down in the town of Clyde, Ohio, which became the model for Winesburg. Anderson never finished high school. He held a variety of jobs, living in Chicago with an older brother in 1896 and again in 1900 when he worked as an advertising copywriter.

His first wife came from a successful Ohio business family; the couple settled in Ohio where Anderson managed a mail-order house as well as two paint firms. But he found increasingly that the need to write conflicted with his career. In 1912 he left his business and his marriage, returning to Chicago, where he met the writers and artists whose activities were creating the Chicago Renaissance. These included the novelists Floyd Dell and Theodore Dreiser; the poets Edgar Lee Masters, Vachel Lindsay, and Carl Sandburg; and the editors Harriet Monroe of *Poetry* and Margaret C. Anderson of the *Little Review.* His first major publication was *Windy McPherson's Son* (1916), the story of a man who runs away from a small Iowa town in futile search for life's meaning; his second was *Marching Men* (1917), about a charismatic lawyer who tries—unsuccessfully—to reorganize the factory system in a small town. These books reveal three of Anderson's preoccupations: the individual quest for self and social betterment, the small-town environment, and the distrust of modern industrial society. Missing, however, is the interest in human psychology and the sense of conflict between inner and outer worlds that appear in *Winesburg* and later works.

In 1916 Anderson began writing and publishing the tales that were brought together in *Winesburg, Ohio.* The formal achievement of the book lay in its articulation of individual tales to a loose but coherent structure. The lives of a number of people living in the town of Winesburg are observed by the naive adolescent George Willard, a reporter for the local newspaper. Their stories contribute to his understanding of life and to his preparation for a career as a writer. The book ends when his mother dies and he leaves Winesburg. With the help of the narrator, whose vision is larger than George's, the reader can see how the lives of the characters have been profoundly distorted by the frustration and suppression of so many of their desires. Anderson calls these characters "grotesques," but the intention of *Winesburg, Ohio* is to show that life in all American small towns is grotesque in the same way. Anderson's attitude toward the characters mixes compassion for the individual with dismay at a social order that can do so much damage. His criticism is

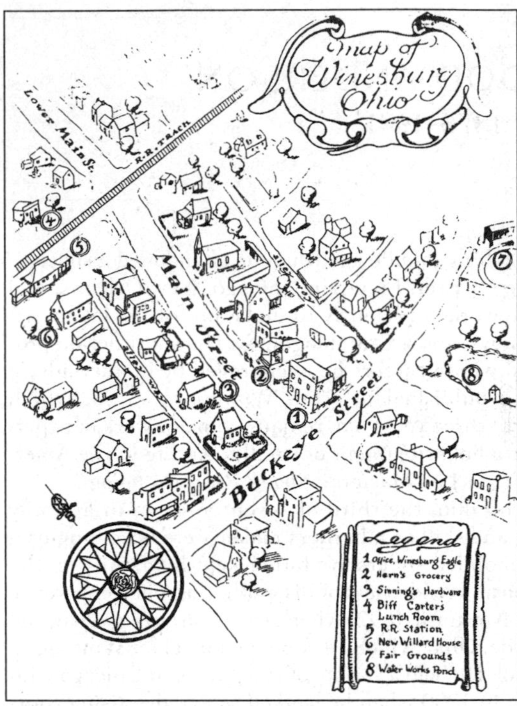

Winesburg, Ohio, Harald Toksvig, 1919. Toksvig's map was printed in the first edition of *Winesburg, Ohio.*

not specifically political, however; he is measuring society by a utopian standard of free emotional and sensual expression.

Stylistically Anderson strove for the simplest possible prose, using brief or at least uncomplex sentences and an unsophisticated vocabulary appropriate to the muffled awareness and limited resources of his typical characters. Structurally, his stories build toward a moment when the character breaks out in some frenzied gesture of release that is revelatory of a hidden inner life. In both style and structure Anderson's works were important influences on other writers: he encouraged simplicity and directness of style, made attractive the use of the point of view of outsider characters as a way of criticizing conventional society, and gave the craft of the short story a decided push toward stories presenting a slice of life or a significant moment as opposed to panorama and summary.

Winesburg, Ohio appeared near the beginning of Anderson's literary career, and although he continued writing for two decades, he never repeated its success. His best later work was in short stories, published in three volumes: *The Triumph of the Egg* (1921), *Horses and Men* (1923), and *Death in the Woods and Other Stories* (1933). He also wrote a number of novels, including *Poor White* (1920), *Many Marriages* (1923), *Beyond Desire* (1932), and *Kit Brandon* (1936), as well as free verse, prose poems, plays, and essays. A series of autobiographical volumes advertised his career, attempted to define the writer's vocation in America, and discussed his impact on other writers. The more he claimed, however, the less other writers were willing to allow him; both Hemingway and Faulkner, for example, whom he had met in Chicago and New Orleans, respectively, satirized his cult of the simple and thereby disavowed his influence. (In fact, he *had* stimulated and helped both of them—stimulated Hemingway in his quest for stylistic simplicity, Faulkner in his search for the proper subject matter.) During the 1930s Anderson, along with many other writers, was active in liberal causes, and he died at sea on the way to South America while on a goodwill mission for the State Department.

The text is that of *Winesburg, Ohio* (1919).

From Winesburg, Ohio

Hands

Upon the half decayed veranda of a small frame house that stood near the edge of a ravine near the town of Winesburg, Ohio, a fat little old man walked nervously up and down. Across a long field that had been seeded for clover but that had produced only a dense crop of yellow mustard weeds, he could see the public highway along which went a wagon filled with berry pickers returning from the fields. The berry pickers, youths and maidens, laughed and shouted boisterously. A boy clad in a blue shirt leaped from the wagon and attempted to drag after him one of the maidens who screamed and protested shrilly. The feet of the boy in the road kicked up a cloud of dust that floated across the face of the departing sun. Over the long field came a thin girlish voice. "Oh, you Wing Biddlebaum, comb your hair, it's falling into your eyes," commanded the voice to the man, who was bald and whose nervous little hands fiddled about the bare white forehead as though arranging a mass of tangled locks.

Wing Biddlebaum, forever frightened and beset by a ghostly band of doubts, did not think of himself as in any way a part of the life of the town where he had lived for twenty years. Among all the people of Winesburg but one had come close to him. With George Willard, son of Tom Willard, the proprietor of the new Willard House, he had formed something like a friendship. George Willard was the reporter on the *Winesburg Eagle* and sometimes in the evenings he walked out along the highway to Wing Biddlebaum's house. Now as the old man walked up and down on the veranda, his hands moving nervously about, he was hoping that George Willard would come and spend the evening with him. After the wagon containing the berry pickers had passed, he went across the field through the tall mustard weeds and climbing a rail fence peered anxiously along the road to the town. For a moment he stood thus, rubbing his hands together and looking up and down the road, and then, fear overcoming him, ran back to walk again upon the porch on his own house.

In the presence of George Willard, Wing Biddlebaum, who for twenty years had been the town mystery, lost something of his timidity, and his shadowy personality, submerged in a sea of doubts, came forth to look at the world. With the young reporter at his side, he ventured in the light of day into Main Street or strode up and down on the rickety front porch of his own house, talking excitedly. The voice that had been low and trembling became shrill and loud. The bent figure straightened. With a kind of wriggle, like a fish returned to the brook by the fisherman, Biddlebaum the silent began to talk, striving to put into words the ideas that had been accumulated by his mind during long years of silence.

Wing Biddlebaum talked much with his hands. The slender expressive fingers, forever active, forever striving to conceal themselves in his pockets or behind his back, came forth and became the piston rods of his machinery of expression.

The story of Wing Biddlebaum is a story of hands. Their restless activity, like unto the beating of the wings of an imprisoned bird, had given him his name. Some obscure poet of the town had thought of it. The hands alarmed their owner. He wanted to keep them hidden away and looked with amazement at the quiet inexpressive hands of other men who worked beside him in the fields, or passed, driving sleepy teams on country roads.

When he talked to George Willard, Wing Biddlebaum closed his fists and beat with them upon a table or on the walls of his house. The action made him more comfortable. If the desire to talk came to him when the two were walking in the fields, he sought out a stump or the top board of a fence and with his hands pounding busily talked with renewed ease.

The story of Wing Biddlebaum's hands is worth a book in itself. Sympathetically set forth it would tap many strange, beautiful qualities in obscure men. It is a job for a poet. In Winesburg the hands had attracted attention merely because of their activity. With them Wing Biddlebaum had picked as high as a hundred and forty quarts of strawberries in a day. They became his distinguishing feature, the source of his fame. Also they made more grotesque an already grotesque and elusive individuality. Winesburg was proud of the hands of Wing Biddlebaum in the same spirit in which it was proud of Banker White's new stone house and Wesley Moyer's bay stallion, Tony Tip, that had won the two-fifteen trot at the fall races in Cleveland.

As for George Willard, he had many times wanted to ask about the hands. At times an almost overwhelming curiosity had taken hold of him. He felt that there must be a reason for their strange activity and their inclination to keep hidden away and only a growing respect for Wing Biddlebaum kept him from blurting out the questions that were often in his mind.

Once he had been on the point of asking. The two were walking in the fields on a summer afternoon and had stopped to sit upon a grassy bank. All afternoon Wing Biddlebaum had talked as one inspired. By a fence he had stopped and beating like a giant woodpecker upon the top board had shouted at George Willard, condemning his tendency to be too much influenced by the people about him. "You are destroying yourself," he cried. "You have the inclination to be alone and to dream and you are afraid of dreams. You want to be like others in town here. You hear them talk and you try to imitate them."

On the grassy bank Wing Biddlebaum had tried again to drive his point home. His voice became soft and reminiscent, and with a sigh of contentment he launched into a long rambling talk, speaking as one lost in a dream.

Out of the dream Wing Biddlebaum made a picture for George Willard. In the picture men lived again in a kind of pastoral golden age. Across a green open country came clean-limbed young men, some afoot, some mounted upon horses. In crowds the young men came to gather about the feet of an old man who sat beneath a tree in a tiny garden and who talked to them.[1]

Wing Biddlebaum became wholly inspired. For once he forgot the hands. Slowly they stole forth and lay upon George Willard's shoulders. Something new and bold came into the voice that talked. "You must try to forget all you have learned," said the old man. "You must begin to dream. From this time on you must shut your ears to the roaring of the voices."

1. Biddlebaum's picture invokes ideals of the Greek Golden Age generally, and more particularly the image of the Athenian philosopher Socrates (469–399 B.C.E) teaching young Greek aristocrats.

Pausing in his speech, Wing Biddlebaum looked long and earnestly at George Willard. His eyes glowed. Again he raised the hands to caress the boy and then a look of horror swept over his face.

With a convulsive movement of his body, Wing Biddlebaum sprang to his feet and thrust his hands deep into his trousers pockets. Tears came to his eyes. "I must be getting along home. I can talk no more with you," he said nervously.

Without looking back, the old man had hurried down the hillside and across a meadow, leaving George Willard perplexed and frightened upon the grassy slope. With a shiver of dread the boy arose and went along the road toward town. "I'll not ask him about his hands," he thought, touched by the memory of the terror he had seen in the man's eyes. "There's something wrong, but I don't want to know what it is. His hands have something to do with his fear of me and of everyone."

And George Willard was right. Let us look briefly into the story of the hands. Perhaps our talking of them will arouse the poet who will tell the hidden wonder story of the influence for which the hands were but fluttering pennants of promise.

In his youth Wing Biddlebaum had been a school teacher in a town in Pennsylvania. He was not then known as Wing Biddlebaum, but went by the less euphonic name of Adolph Myers.[2] As Adolph Myers he was much loved by the boys of his school.

Adolph Myers was meant by nature to be a teacher of youth. He was one of those rare, little-understood men who rule by a power so gentle that it passes as a lovable weakness. In their feeling for the boys under their charge such men are not unlike the finer sort of women in their love of men.

And yet that is but crudely stated. It needs the poet there. With the boys of his school, Adolph Myers had walked in the evening or had sat talking until dusk upon the schoolhouse steps lost in a kind of dream. Here and there went his hands, caressing the shoulders of the boys, playing about the tousled heads. As he talked his voice became soft and musical. There was a caress in that also. In a way the voice and the hands, the stroking of the shoulders and the touching of the hair was a part of the schoolmaster's effort to carry a dream into the young minds. By the caress that was in his fingers he expressed himself. He was one of those men in whom the force that creates life is diffused, not centralized. Under the caress of his hands doubt and disbelief went out of the minds of the boy and they began also to dream.

And then the tragedy. A half-witted boy of the school became enamored of the young master. In his bed at night he imagined unspeakable things and in the morning went forth to tell his dreams as facts. Strange, hideous accusations fell from his loose-hung lips. Through the Pennsylvania town went a shiver. Hidden, shadowy doubts that had been in men's minds concerning Adolph Myers were galvanized into beliefs.

The tragedy did not linger. Trembling lads were jerked out of bed and questioned. "He put his arms about me," said one. "His fingers were always playing in my hair," said another.

2. Both his adopted surname and his original one underline Biddlebaum's foreignness by labeling him as German and, probably, Jewish.

One afternoon a man of the town, Henry Bradford, who kept a saloon, came to the schoolhouse door. Calling Adolph Myers into the school yard he began to beat him with his fists. As his hard knuckles beat down into the frightened face of the schoolmaster, his wrath became more and more terrible. Screaming with dismay, the children ran here and there like disturbed insects "I'll teach you to put your hands on my boy, you beast," roared the saloon keeper, who, tired of beating the master, had begun to kick him about the yard.

Adolph Myers was driven from the Pennsylvania town in the night. With lanterns in their hands a dozen men came to the door of the house where he lived alone and commanded that he dress and come forth. It was raining and one of the men had a rope in his hands. They had intended to hang the schoolmaster, but something in his figure, so small, white, and pitiful, touched their hearts and they let him escape. As he ran away into the darkness they repented of their weakness and ran after him, swearing and throwing sticks and great balls of soft mud at the figure that screamed and ran faster and faster into the darkness.

For twenty years Adolph Myers had lived alone in Winesburg. He was but forty but looked sixty-five. The name of Biddlebaum he got from a box of goods seen at a freight station as he hurried through an eastern Ohio town. He had an aunt in Winesburg, a black-toothed old woman who raised chickens, and with her he lived until she died. He had been ill for a year after the experience in Pennsylvania, and after his recovery worked as a day laborer in the fields, going timidly about and striving to conceal his hands. Although he did not understand what had happened he felt that the hands must be to blame. Again and again the fathers of the boys had talked of the hands. "Keep your hands to yourself," the saloon keeper had roared, dancing with fury in the schoolhouse yard.

Upon the veranda of his house by the ravine, Wing Biddlebaum continued to walk up and down until the sun had disappeared and the road beyond the field was lost in the grey shadows. Going into his house he cut slices of bread and spread honey upon them. When the rumble of the evening train that took away the express cars loaded with the day's harvest of berries had passed and restored the silence of the summer night, he went again to walk upon the veranda. In the darkness he could not see the hands and they became quiet. Although he still hungered for the presence of the boy, who was the medium through which he expressed his love of man, the hunger became again a part of his loneliness and his waiting. Lighting a lamp, Wing Biddlebaum washed the few dishes soiled by his simple meal and, setting up a folding cot by the screen door that led to the porch, prepared to undress for the night. A few stray white bread crumbs lay on the cleanly washed floor by the table; putting the lamp upon a low stool he began to pick up the crumbs, carrying them to his mouth one by one with unbelievable rapidity. In the dense blotch of light beneath the table, the kneeling figure looked like a priest engaged in some service of his church. The nervous expressive fingers, flashing in and out of the light, might well have been mistaken for the fingers of the devotee going swiftly through decade after decade of his rosary.[3]

3. String of beads used by Roman Catholics to keep track of prayers, divided into sections ("decades") of ten beads.

Mother

Elizabeth Willard, the mother of George Willard, was tall and gaunt and her face was marked with smallpox scars. Although she was but forty-five, some obscure disease had taken the fire out of her figure. Listlessly she went about the disorderly old hotel looking at the faded wall-paper and the ragged carpets and, when she was able to be about, doing the work of a chambermaid among beds soiled by the slumbers of fat traveling men. Her husband, Tom Willard, a slender, graceful man with square shoulders, a quick military step, and a black mustache, trained to turn sharply up at the ends, tried to put the wife out of his mind. The presence of the tall ghostly figure, moving slowly through the halls, he took as a reproach to himself. When he thought of her he grew angry and swore. The hotel was unprofitable and forever on the edge of failure and he wished himself out of it. He thought of the old house and the woman who lived there with him as things defeated and done for. The hotel in which he had begun life so hopefully was now a mere ghost of what a hotel should be. As he went spruce and businesslike through the streets of Winesburg, he sometimes stopped and turned quickly about as though fearing that the spirit of the hotel and of the woman would follow him even into the streets. "Damn such a life, damn it!" he sputtered aimlessly.

Tom Willard had a passion for village politics and for years had been the leading Democrat in a strongly Republican community. Some day, he told himself, the tide of things political will turn in my favor and the years of ineffectual service count big in the bestowal of rewards. He dreamed of going to Congress and even of becoming governor. Once when a younger member of the party arose at a political conference and began to boast of his faithful service, Tom Willard grew white with fury. "Shut up, you," he roared, glaring about. "What do you know of service? What are you but a boy? Look at what I've done here! I was a Democrat here in Winesburg when it was a crime to be a Democrat. In the old days they fairly hunted us with guns."

Between Elizabeth and her one son George there was a deep unexpressed bond of sympathy, based on a girlhood dream that had long ago died. In the son's presence she was timid and reserved, but sometimes while he hurried about town intent upon his duties as a reporter, she went into his room and closing the door knelt by a little desk, made of a kitchen table, that sat near a window. In the room by the desk she went through a ceremony that was half a prayer, half a demand, addressed to the skies. In the boyish figure she yearned to see something half forgotten that had once been a part of herself recreated. The prayer concerned that. "Even though I die, I will in some way keep defeat from you," she cried, and so deep was her determination that her whole body shook. Her eyes glowed and she clenched her fists. "If I am dead and see him becoming a meaningless drab figure like myself, I will come back," she declared. "I ask God now to give me that privilege. I demand it. I will pay for it. God may beat me with his fists. I will take any blow that may befall if but this my boy be allowed to express something for us both." Pausing uncertainly, the woman stared about the boy's room. "And do not let him become smart and successful either," she added vaguely.

The communion between George Willard and his mother was outwardly a formal thing without meaning. When she was ill and sat by the window in her room he sometimes went in the evening to make her a visit. They sat by a window that looked over the roof of a small frame building into Main Street. By turning their heads they could see, through another window, along an alleyway that ran behind the Main Street stores and into the back door of Abner Groff's bakery. Sometimes as they sat thus a picture of village life presented itself to them. At the back door of his shop appeared Abner Groff with a stick or an empty milk bottle in his hand. For a long time there was a feud between the baker and a grey cat that belonged to Sylvester West, the druggist. The boy and his mother saw the cat creep into the door of the bakery and presently emerge followed by the baker who swore and waved his arms about. The baker's eyes were small and red and his black hair and beard were filled with flour dust. Sometimes he was so angry that, although the cat had disappeared, he hurled sticks, bits of broken glass, and even some of the tools of his trade about. Once he broke a window at the back of Sinning's Hardware Store. In the alley the grey cat crouched behind barrels filled with torn paper and broken bottles above which flew a black swarm of flies. Once when she was alone, and after watching a prolonged and ineffectual outburst on the part of the baker, Elizabeth Willard put her head down on her long white hands and wept. After that she did not look along the alleyway any more, but tried to forget the contest between the bearded man and the cat. It seemed like a rehearsal of her own life, terrible in its vividness.

In the evening when the son sat in the room with his mother, the silence made them both feel awkward. Darkness came on and the evening train came in at the station. In the street below feet tramped up and down upon a board sidewalk. In the station yard, after the evening train had gone, there was a heavy silence. Perhaps Skinner Leason, the express agent, moved a truck the length of the station platform. Over on Main Street sounded a man's voice, laughing. The door of the express office banged. George Willard arose and crossing the room fumbled for the doorknob. Sometimes he knocked against a chair, making it scrape along the floor. By the window sat the sick woman, perfectly still, listless. Her long hands, white and bloodless, could be seen drooping over the ends of the arms of the chair. "I think you had better be out among the boys. You are too much indoors," she said, striving to relieve the embarrassment of the departure. "I thought I would take a walk," replied George Willard, who felt awkward and confused.

One evening in July, when the transient guests who made the New Willard House their temporary homes had become scarce, and the hallways, lighted only by kerosene lamps turned low, were plunged in gloom, Elizabeth Willard had an adventure. She had been ill in bed for several days and her son had not come to visit her. She was alarmed. The feeble blaze of life that remained in her body was blown into a flame by her anxiety and she crept out of bed, dressed and hurried along the hallway toward her son's room, shaking with exaggerated fears. As she went along she steadied herself with her hand, slipped along the papered walls of the hall and breathed with difficulty. The air whistled through her teeth. As she hurried forward she thought how foolish she was. "He is concerned with boyish affairs," she told herself. "Perhaps he has now begun to walk about in the evening with girls."

Elizabeth Willard had a dread of being seen by guests in the hotel that had once belonged to her father and the ownership of which still stood recorded in her name in the county courthouse. The hotel was continually losing patronage because of its shabbiness and she thought of herself as also shabby. Her own room was in an obscure corner and when she felt able to work she voluntarily worked among the beds, preferring the labor that could be done when the guests were abroad seeking trade among the merchants of Winesburg.

By the door of her son's room the mother knelt upon the floor and listened for some sound from within. When she heard the boy moving about and talking in low tones a smile came to her lips. George Willard had a habit of talking aloud to himself and to hear him doing so had always given his mother a peculiar pleasure. The habit in him, she felt, strengthened the secret bond that existed between them. A thousand times she had whispered to herself of the matter. "He is groping about, trying to find himself," she thought. "He is not a dull clod, all words and smartness. Within him there is a secret something that is striving to grow. It is the thing I let be killed in myself."

In the darkness in the hallway by the door the sick woman arose and started again toward her own room. She was afraid that the door would open and the boy come upon her. When she had reached a safe distance and was about to turn a corner into a second hallway she stopped and bracing herself with her hands waited, thinking to shake off a trembling fit of weakness that had come upon her. The presence of the boy in the room had made her happy. In her bed, during the long hours alone, the little fears that had visited her had become giants. Now they were all gone. "When I get back to my room I shall sleep," she murmured gratefully.

But Elizabeth Willard was not to return to her bed and to sleep. As she stood trembling in the darkness the door of her son's room opened and the boy's father, Tom Willard, stepped out. In the light that streamed out at the door he stood with the knob in his hand and talked. What he said infuriated the woman.

Tom Willard was ambitious for his son. He had always thought of himself as a successful man, although nothing he had ever done had turned out successfully. However, when he was out of sight of the New Willard House and had no fear of coming upon his wife, he swaggered and began to dramatize himself as one of the chief men of the town. He wanted his son to succeed. He it was who had secured for the boy the position on the *Winesburg Eagle*. Now, with a ring of earnestness in his voice, he was advising concerning some course of conduct. "I tell you what, George, you've got to wake up," he said sharply. "Will Henderson has spoken to me three times concerning the matter. He says you go along for hours not hearing when you are spoken to and acting like a gawky girl. What ails you?" Tom Willard laughed good-naturedly. "Well, I guess you'll get over it," he said. "I told Will that. You're not a fool and you're not a woman. You're Tom Willard's son and you'll wake up. I'm not afraid. What you say clears things up. If being a newspaper man had put the notion of becoming a writer into your mind that's all right. Only I guess you'll have to wake up to do that too, eh?"

Tom Willard went briskly along the hallway and down a flight of stairs to the office. The woman in the darkness could hear him laughing and talking with a guest who was striving to wear away a dull evening by dozing in a chair by the office door. She returned to the door of her son's room. The weakness had passed from her body as by a miracle and she stepped boldly along. A thousand ideas raced through her head. When she heard the scraping of a chair and the sound of a pen scratching upon paper, she again turned and went back along the hallway to her own room.

A definite determination had come into the mind of the defeated wife of the Winesburg Hotel keeper. The determination was the result of long years of quiet and rather ineffectual thinking. "Now," she told herself, "I will act. There is something threatening my boy and I will ward it off." The fact that the conversation between Tom Willard and his son had been rather quiet and natural, as though an understanding existed between them, maddened her. Although for years she had hated her husband, her hatred had always before been a quite impersonal thing. He had been merely a part of something else that she hated. Now, and by the few words at the door, he had become the thing personified. In the darkness of her own room she clenched her fists and glared about. Going to a cloth bag that hung on a nail by the wall she took out a long pair of sewing scissors and held them in her hand like a dagger. "I will stab him," she said aloud. "He has chosen to be the voice of evil and I will kill him. When I have killed him something will snap within myself and I will die also. It will be a release for all of us."

In her girlhood and before her marriage with Tom Willard, Elizabeth had borne a somewhat shaky reputation in Winesburg. For years she had been what is called "stage-struck" and had paraded through the streets with traveling men guests at her father's hotel, wearing loud clothes and urging them to tell her of life in the cities out of which they had come. Once she startled the town by putting on men's clothes and riding a bicycle down Main Street.

In her own mind the tall girl had been in those days much confused. A great restlessness was in her and it expressed itself in two ways. First there was an uneasy desire for change, for some big definite movement to her life. It was this feeling that had turned her mind to the stage. She dreamed of joining some company and wandering over the world, seeing always new faces and giving something out of herself to all people. Sometimes at night she was quite beside herself with the thought, but when she tried to talk of the matter to the members of the theatrical companies that came to Winesburg and stopped at her father's hotel, she got nowhere. They did not seem to know what she meant, or if she did get something of her passion expressed, they only laughed. "It's not like that," they said. "It's as dull and uninteresting as this here. Nothing comes of it."

With the traveling men when she walked about with them, and later with Tom Willard, it was quite different. Always they seemed to understand and sympathize with her. On the side streets of the village, in the darkness under the trees, they took hold of her hand and she thought that something unexpressed in herself came forth and became a part of an unexpressed something in them.

And then there was the second expression of her restlessness. When that came she felt for a time released and happy. She did not blame the men who walked with her and later she did not blame Tom Willard. It was always the same, beginning with kisses and ending, after strange wild emotions, with peace and then sobbing repentance. When she sobbed she put her hand upon the face of the man and had always the same thought. Even though he were large and bearded she thought he had become suddenly a little boy. She wondered why he did not sob also.

In her room, tucked away in a corner of the old Willard House, Elizabeth Willard lighted a lamp and put it on a dressing table that stood by the door. A thought had come into her mind and she went to a closet and brought out a small square box and set it on the table. The box contained material for make-up and had been left with other things by a theatrical company that had once been stranded in Winesburg. Elizabeth Willard had decided that she would be beautiful. Her hair was still black and there was a great mass of it braided and coiled about her head. The scene that was to take place in the office below began to grow in her mind. No ghostly worn-out figure should confront Tom Willard, but something quite unexpected and startling. Tall and with dusky cheeks and hair that fell in a mass from her shoulders, a figure should come striding down the stairway before the startled loungers in the hotel office. The figure would be silent—it would be swift and terrible. As a tigress whose cub had been threatened would she appear, coming out of the shadows, stealing noiselessly along and holding the long wicked scissors in her hand.

With a little broken sob in her throat Elizabeth Willard blew out the light that stood upon the table and stood weak and trembling in the darkness. The strength that had been a miracle in her body left and she half reeled across the floor, clutching at the back of the chair in which she had spent so many long days staring out over the tin roofs into the main street of Winesburg. In the hallway there was the sound of footsteps and George Willard came in at the door. Sitting in a chair beside his mother he began to talk. "I'm going to get out of here," he said. "I don't know where I shall go or what I shall do but I am going away."

The woman in the chair waited and trembled. An impulse came to her. "I suppose you had better wake up," she said. "You think that? You will go to the city and make money, eh? It will be better for you, you think, to be a business man, to be brisk and smart and alive?" She waited and trembled.

The son shook his head. "I suppose I can't make you understand, but oh, I wish I could," he said earnestly. "I can't even talk to father about it. I don't try. There isn't any use. I don't know what I shall do. I just want to go away and look at people and think."

Silence fell upon the room where the boy and woman sat together. Again, as on the other evenings, they were embarrassed. After a time the boy tried again to talk. "I suppose it won't be for a year or two but I've been thinking about it," he said, rising and going toward the door. "Something father said makes it sure that I shall have to go away." He fumbled with the door knob. In the room the silence became unbearable to the woman. She wanted to cry out with joy because of the words that had come from the lips of her son, but the expression of joy had become impossible to her. "I think you had better go out among the boys. You are too much indoors," she said. "I thought I would go for a little walk," replied the son stepping awkwardly out of the room and closing the door.

Adventure

Alice Hindman, a woman of twenty-seven when George Willard was a mere boy, had lived in Winesburg all her life. She clerked in Winney's Dry Goods Store and lived with her mother, who had married a second husband.

Alice's step-father was a carriage painter, and given to drink. His story is an odd one. It will be worth telling some day.

At twenty-seven Alice was tall and somewhat slight. Her head was large and overshadowed her body. Her shoulders were a little stooped and her hair and eyes brown. She was very quiet but beneath a placid exterior a continual ferment went on.

When she was a girl of sixteen and before she began to work in the store, Alice had an affair with a young man. The young man, named Ned Currie, was older than Alice. He, like George Willard, was employed on the *Winesburg Eagle* and for a long time he went to see Alice almost every evening. Together the two walked under the trees through the streets of the town and talked of what they would do with their lives. Alice was then a very pretty girl and Ned Currie took her into his arms and kissed her. He became excited and said things he did not intend to say and Alice, betrayed by her desire to have something beautiful come into her rather narrow life, also grew excited. She also talked. The outer crust of her life, all of her natural diffidence and reserve, was torn away and she gave herself over to the emotions of love. When, late in the fall of her sixteenth year, Ned Currie went away to Cleveland where he hoped to get a place on a city newspaper and rise in the world, she wanted to go with him. With a trembling voice she told him what was in her mind. "I will work and you can work," she said. "I do not want to harness you to a needless expense that will prevent your making progress. Don't marry me now. We will get along without that and we can be together. Even though we live in the same house no one will say anything. In the city we will be unknown and people will pay no attention to us."

Ned Currie was puzzled by the determination and abandon of his sweetheart and was also deeply touched. He had wanted the girl to become his mistress but changed his mind. He wanted to protect and care for her. "You don't know what you're talking about," he said sharply; "you may be sure I'll let you do no such thing. As soon as I get a good job I'll come back. For the present you'll have to stay here. It's the only thing we can do."

On the evening before he left Winesburg to take up his new life in the city, Ned Currie went to call on Alice. They walked about through the streets for an hour and then got a rig from Wesley Moyer's livery and went for a drive in the country. The moon came up and they found themselves unable to talk. In his sadness the young man forgot the resolutions he had made regarding his conduct with the girl.

They got out of the buggy at a place where a long meadow ran down to the bank of Wine Creek and there in the dim light became lovers. When at midnight they returned to town they were both glad. It did not seem to them that anything that could happen in the future could blot out the wonder and beauty of the thing that had happened. "Now we will have to stick to each other, whatever happens we will have to do that," Ned Currie said as he left the girl at her father's door.

The young newspaper man did not succeed in getting a place on a Cleveland paper and went west to Chicago. For a time he was lonely and wrote to Alice almost every day. Then he was caught up by the life of the city; he began to make friends and found new interests in life. In Chicago he boarded at a house where there were several women. One of them attracted his attention and he forgot Alice in Winesburg. At the end of a year he had stopped writing letters, and only once in a long time, when he was lonely or when he went into one of the city parks and saw the moon shining on the grass as it had shone that night on the meadow by Wine Creek, did he think of her at all.

In Winesburg the girl who had been loved grew to be a woman. When she was twenty-two years old her father, who owned a harness repair shop, died suddenly. The harness maker was an old soldier, and after a few months his wife received a widow's pension. She used the first money she got to buy a loom and became a weaver of carpets, and Alice got a place in Winney's store. For a number of years nothing could have induced her to believe that Ned Currie would not in the end return to her.

She was glad to be employed because the daily round of toil in the store made the time of waiting seem less long and uninteresting. She began to save money, thinking that when she had saved two or three hundred dollars she would follow her lover to the city and try if her presence would not win back his affections.

Alice did not blame Ned Currie for what had happened in the moonlight in the field, but felt that she could never marry another man. To her the thought of giving to another what she still felt could belong only to Ned seemed monstrous. When other young men tried to attract her attention she would have nothing to do with them. "I am his wife and shall remain his wife whether he comes back or not," she whispered to herself, and for all of her willingness to support herself could not have understood the growing modern idea of a woman's owning herself and giving and taking for her own ends in life.

Alice worked in the dry goods store from eight in the morning until six at night and on three evenings a week went back to the store to stay from seven until nine. As time passed and she became more and more lonely she began to practice the devices common to lonely people. When at night she went upstairs into her own room she knelt on the floor to pray and in her prayers whispered things she wanted to say to her lover. She became attached to inanimate objects, and because it was her own, could not bear to have anyone touch the furniture of her room. The trick of saving money, begun for a purpose, was carried on after the scheme of going to the city to find Ned Currie had been given up. It became a fixed habit, and when she needed new clothes she did not get them. Sometimes on rainy afternoons in the store she got out her bank book and, letting it lie open before her, spent hours dreaming impossible dreams of saving money enough so that the interest would support both herself and her future husband.

"Ned always liked to travel about," she thought. "I'll give him the chance. Some day when we are married and I can save both his money and my own, we will be rich. Then we can travel together all over the world."

In the dry goods store weeks ran into months and months into years as Alice waited and dreamed of her lover's return. Her employer, a grey old man with false teeth and a thin grey mustache that drooped down over his mouth, was not given to conversation, and sometimes, on rainy days and in the winter when a storm raged in Main Street, long hours passed when no customers came in. Alice arranged and rearranged the stock. She stood near the front window where she could look down the deserted street and thought of the evenings when she had walked with Ned Currie and of what he had said. "We will have to stick to each other now." The words echoed and re-echoed through the mind of the maturing woman. Tears came into her eyes. Sometimes when her employer had gone out and she was alone in the store she put her head on the counter and wept. "Oh, Ned, I am waiting," she whispered over and over, and all the time the creeping fear that he would never come back grew stronger within her.

In the spring when the rains have passed and before the long hot days of summer have come, the country about Winesburg is delightful. The town lies in the midst of open fields, but beyond the fields are pleasant patches of woodlands. In the wooded places are many little cloistered nooks, quiet places where lovers go to sit on Sunday afternoons. Through the trees they look out across the fields and see farmers at work about the barns or people driving up and down on the roads. In the town bells ring and occasionally a train passes, looking like a toy thing in the distance.

For several years after Ned Currie went away Alice did not go into the wood with other young people on Sunday, but one day after he had been gone for two or three years and when her loneliness seemed unbearable, she put on her best dress and set out. Finding a little sheltered place from which she could see the town and a long stretch of the fields, she sat down. Fear of age and ineffectuality took possession of her. She could not sit still, and arose. As she stood looking out over the land something, perhaps the thought of never ceasing life as it expresses itself in the flow of the season, fixed her mind on the passing years. With a shiver of dread, she realized that for her the beauty and freshness of youth had passed. For the first time she felt that she had been cheated. She did not blame Ned Currie and did not know what to blame. Sadness swept over her. Dropping to her knees, she tried to pray, but instead of prayers words of protest came to her lips. "It is not going to come to me. I will never find happiness. Why do I tell myself lies?" she cried, and an odd sense of relief came with this, her first bold attempt to face the fear that had become a part of her everyday life.

In the year when Alice Hindman became twenty-five two things happened to disturb the dull uneventfulness of her days. Her mother married Bush Milton, the carriage painter of Winesburg, and she herself became a member of the Winesburg Methodist Church. Alice joined the church because she had become frightened by the loneliness of her position in life. Her mother's second marriage had emphasized her isolation. "I am becoming old and queer. If Ned comes he will not want me. In the city where he is living men are perpetually young. There is so much going on that they do not have time to grow old," she told herself with a grim little smile, and went resolutely about the business of becoming acquainted with people. Every Thursday evening when the store had closed she went to a prayer meeting in the basement of the church and on Sunday evening attended a meeting of an organization called The Epworth League.

When Will Hurley, a middle-aged man who clerked in a drug store and who also belonged to the church, offered to walk home with her she did not protest. "Of course I will not let him make a practice of being with me, but if he comes to see me once in a long time there can be no harm in that," she told herself, still determined in her loyalty to Ned Currie.

Without realizing what was happening, Alice was trying feebly at first, but with growing determination, to get a new hold upon life. Beside the drug clerk she walked in silence, but sometimes in the darkness as they went stolidly along she put out her hand and touched softly the folds of his coat. When he left her at the gate before her mother's house she did not go indoors, but stood for a moment by the door. She wanted to call to the drug clerk, to ask him to sit with her in the darkness on the porch before the house, but was afraid he would not understand. "It is not him that I want," she told herself; "I want to avoid being so much alone. If I am not careful I will grow unaccustomed to being with people."

During the early fall of her twenty-seventh year a passionate restlessness took possession of Alice. She could not bear to be in the company of the drug clerk, and when, in the evening, he came to walk with her she sent him away. Her mind became intensely active and when, weary from the long hours of standing behind the counter in the store, she went home and crawled into bed, she could not sleep. With staring eyes she looked into the darkness. Her imagination, like a child awakened from long sleep, played about the room. Deep within her there was something that would not be cheated by phantasies and that demanded some definite answer from life.

Alice took a pillow into her arms and held it tightly against her breasts. Getting out of bed, she arranged a blanket so that in the darkness it looked like a form lying between the sheets and, kneeling beside the bed, she caressed it, whispering words over and over, like a refrain. "Why doesn't something happen? Why am I left here alone?" she muttered. Although she sometimes thought of Ned Currie, she no longer depended on him. Her desire had grown vague. She did not want Ned Currie or any other man. She wanted to be loved, to have something answer the call that was growing louder and louder within her.

And then one night when it rained Alice had an adventure. It frightened and confused her. She had come home from the store at nine and found the house empty. Bush Milton had gone off to town and her mother to the house of a neighbor. Alice went upstairs to her room and undressed in the darkness. For a moment she stood by the window hearing the rain beat against the glass and then a strange desire took possession of her. Without stopping to think of what she intended to do, she ran downstairs through the dark house and out into the rain. As she stood on the little grass plot before the house and felt the cold rain on her body a mad desire to run naked through the streets took possession of her.

She thought that the rain would have some creative and wonderful effect on her body. Not for years had she felt so full of youth and courage. She wanted to leap and run, to cry out, to find some other lonely human and embrace him. On the brick sidewalk before the house a man stumbled homeward. Alice started to run. A wild, desperate mood took possession of her. "What do I care who it is. He is alone, and I will go to him," she thought; and then without stopping to consider the possible result of her madness, called softly. "Wait!" she cried. "Don't go away. Whoever you are, you must wait."

The man on the sidewalk stopped and stood listening. He was an old man and somewhat deaf. Putting his hand to his mouth, he shouted, "What? What say?" he called.

Alice dropped to the ground and lay trembling. She was so frightened at the thought of what she had done that when the man had gone on his way she did not dare get to her feet, but crawled on hands and knees through the grass to the house. When she got to her own room she bolted the door and drew her dressing table across the doorway. Her body shook as with a chill and her hands trembled so that she had difficulty getting into her night-dress. When she got into bed she buried her face in the pillow and wept broken-heartedly. "What is the matter with me? I will do something dreadful if I am not careful," she thought, and turning her face to the wall, began trying to force herself to face bravely the fact that many people must live and die alone, even in Winesburg.

1919

CARL SANDBURG
1878–1967

Son of an immigrant Swedish blacksmith who had settled in Galesburg, Illinois, Carl Sandburg was an active populist and socialist, a journalist, and an important figure in the Chicago Renaissance of arts and letters. During the 1920s and 1930s he was one of the most widely read poets in the nation. His poetic aim was to celebrate the working people of America in poems that they could understand. He wrote sympathetically and affirmatively of the masses, using a long verse line unfettered by rhyme or regular meter, a line deriving from Whitman but with cadences closer to the rhythms of ordinary speech. "Simple poems for simple people," he said.

Sandburg's irregular schooling included brief attendance at Lombard College, but he was too restless to work through to a degree. He held a variety of jobs before moving to Chicago in 1913; he was in the army during the Spanish-American War, served as a war correspondent for the Galesburg *Evening Mail,* worked for the Social Democratic Party in Wisconsin, was secretary to the Socialist mayor of Milwaukee, and wrote editorials for the Milwaukee *Leader.* He had long been writing poetry but achieved success with the 1914 publication of his poem "Chicago" in *Poetry* magazine.

Poetry was one element in a surge of artistic activity in Chicago following the 1893 World's Fair. Such midwesterners as the architect Frank Lloyd Wright; the novelists Theodore Dreiser, Henry Blake Fuller, and Floyd Dell; and the poets Edgar Lee Masters and Vachel Lindsay believed not only that Chicago was a great city but that, since the Midwest was America's heartland, it was in this region that the cultural life of the nation ought to center. Two literary magazines—*Poetry,* founded in 1912 by Harriet Monroe, and the *Little Review,* founded by Margaret C. Anderson in 1914—helped bring this informal movement to international attention. Nothing could be more apt to local interests than a celebratory poem called "Chicago."

Four volumes of poetry by Sandburg appeared in the next ten years: *Chicago Poems* (1914), *Cornhuskers* (1918), *Smoke and Steel* (1920), and *Slabs of the Sunburnt West* (1922). These present a panorama of America, concentrating on the prairies and cities of the Midwest. Like Whitman, Sandburg was aware that American life was increasingly urban, and he had little interest in the small town and its conventional middle class. The cities of the Midwest seemed to display both the vitality of the masses and their exploitation in an inequitable class system. Unlike many radicals whose politics were formed after the turn of the twentieth century, Sandburg believed that the people themselves, rather than a cadre of intellectuals acting on behalf of the people, would ultimately shape their own destiny. His political poems express appreciation for the people's energy and outrage at the injustices they suffer. They also balance strong declarative statements with passages of precise description. Other poems show Sandburg working in more lyrical or purely imagistic modes.

If the early "Chicago" is his best-known poem, his most ambitious is the book-length *The People, Yes* (1936), a collage of prose vignettes, anecdotes, and poetry, making use of his researches into American folk song. Sandburg had published these researches in *The American Songbag* in 1927, and he also composed a multivolume biography of Abraham Lincoln between 1926 and 1939. The purpose of this painstaking work was to present Lincoln as an authentic folk hero, a great man who had risen from among the people of the American heartland and represented its best values. He wrote features, editorials, and columns for the *Chicago Daily News* between 1922 and 1930, and pursued other literary projects as well. After World War II, when it became common for poets to read their works at campuses around the country, he enjoyed bringing his old-style populist radicalism to college students.

The text of the poems here is that of *The Complete Poems of Carl Sandburg* (1970).

Chicago

Hog Butcher for the World,
Tool Maker, Stacker of Wheat,
Player with Railroads and the Nation's Freight Handler;
Stormy, husky, brawling,
City of the Big Shoulders:

They tell me you are wicked and I believe them, for I have seen
your painted women under the gas lamps luring the farm
boys.
And they tell me you are crooked and I answer: Yes, it is true I
have seen the gunman kill and go free to kill again.
And they tell me you are brutal and my reply is: On the faces of
women and children I have seen the marks of wanton hunger.
And having answered so I turn once more to those who sneer at
this my city, and I give them back the sneer and say to them:
Come and show me another city with lifted head singing so
proud to be alive and coarse and strong and cunning.
Flinging magnetic curses amid the toil of piling job on job, here
is a tall bold slugger set vivid against the little soft cities;

Fierce as a dog with tongue lapping for action, cunning as a
    savage pitted against the wilderness,
        Bareheaded,
        Shoveling,
        Wrecking,
        Planning,
        Building, breaking, rebuilding,
Under the smoke, dust all over his mouth, laughing with white
    teeth,
Under the terrible burden of destiny laughing as a young man
    laughs,
Laughing even as an ignorant fighter laughs who has never lost
    a battle,
Bragging and laughing that under his wrist is the pulse, and
    under his ribs the heart of the people,
        Laughing!
Laughing the stormy, husky, brawling laughter of Youth, half-
    naked, sweating, proud to be Hog Butcher, Tool Maker,
    Stacker of Wheat, Player with Railroads and Freight
    Handler to the Nation.

1914, 1916

Fog

The fog comes
on little cat feet.

It sits looking
over harbor and city
on silent haunches
and then moves on.

1916

Cool Tombs

When Abraham Lincoln was shoveled into the tombs, he forgot the copperheads and the assassin[1] . . . in the dust, in the cool tombs.

And Ulysses Grant lost all thought of con men and Wall Street, cash and collateral turned ashes[2] . . . in the dust, in the cool tombs.

1. President Lincoln (1809–1865) was opposed by southern sympathizers in the North, called Copperheads, and assassinated by John Wilkes Booth. The copperhead is a poisonous snake.

2. The second administration of President Grant (1822–1885) was riddled with bribery and political corruption. After leaving office, Grant was exploited in business and declared bankruptcy.

Pocahontas' body, lovely as a poplar, sweet as a red haw in November or a pawpaw[3] in May, did she wonder? does she remember? . . . in the dust, in the cool tombs?

Take any streetful of people buying clothes and groceries, cheering a hero or throwing confetti and blowing tin horns . . . tell me if the lovers are losers . . . tell me if any get more than the lovers . . . in the dust . . . in the cool tombs.

1918

Grass[1]

Pile the bodies high at Austerlitz and Waterloo.
Shovel them under and let me work—
I am the grass; I cover all.

And pile them high at Gettysburg
And pile them high at Ypres and Verdun.
Shovel them under and let me work.
Two years, ten years, and passengers ask the conductor:
What place is this?
Where are we now?

I am the grass.
Let me work.

1918

3. A fruit native to the eastern United States. Pocahontas (1595?–1617), daughter of the Native American chief Powhatan, intervened to save the life of Captain John Smith. "Red haw": a type of American hawthorn tree.

1. The proper names in this poem are all famous battlefields in the Napoleonic Wars, the American Civil War, and World War I.

WALLACE STEVENS
1879–1955

Wallace Stevens was raised in Reading, Pennsylvania, and attended Harvard for three years as a special student before leaving in 1900 to find a career. His father, a self-made lawyer and businessman, advised Stevens to approach his Harvard studies both broadly and practically. Cautioning Stevens that "you are not out on a pic-nic—but really preparing for the campaign of life—where self sustenance is essential and where everything depends upon yourself," he also encouraged his son's pursuit of a wide-ranging liberal education. Anticipating that Stevens's "power of painting pictures in words" might one day make him famous, his father suggested that he "Paint truth but not always in drab clothes"—"A little romance is essential to ecstasy." As a young man, Stevens wrestled with both sides of his father's values. Drawn equally to a life of aesthetic dreaming and practical work, Stevens admonished himself "not to be a dilettante—half dream, half deed. I must be all dream or all deed." Ultimately, however, he straddled these worlds more successfully than perhaps any other American poet of the twentieth century.

After moving to New York City for a brief attempt at journalism, Stevens went to law school. He started publishing in little magazines in 1914 and frequented literary gatherings in New York, becoming friends with William Carlos Williams and Marianne Moore, among others. In 1916 he began to work for the Hartford Accident and Indemnity Company and moved with his wife to Hartford, Connecticut. They made that city their lifelong home, Stevens writing his poetry at night and during summers. Visiting Florida frequently on business from 1922 onward, he experienced the contrast between the South's lush tropical climate and the chilly austerity of New England that he would turn into a metaphor for opposing ways of imagining the world in poems like "The Snow Man" and "Sunday Morning." A good businessman, Stevens by the mid-1930s was prosperous. He continued to work for the same company until his death, eventually becoming a vice president.

Stevens's first volume of poetry, *Harmonium*, appeared in 1923. The poems in that book are dazzling in their wit, imagery, and color; they found Stevens an audience, although some critics saw in them so much display as to make their "seriousness" questionable. But Stevens's purpose in part was to show that display was a valid poetic exercise—that poetry existed to illuminate the world's surfaces as well as its depths. Anything but drab, the poems of *Harmonium* abound in allusions to music and painting; are packed with sense images, especially of sound and color; and are elegant and unexpectedly funny. Consider the surprise and humor in the titles of the selections printed here as well as these: "Floral Decorations for Bananas," "Palace of the Babies," "The Bird with the Coppery, Keen Claws," "Frogs Eat Butterflies, Snakes Eat Frogs, Hogs Eat Snakes, Men Eat Hogs." Stevens's line is simple—either blank verse or brief stanzas, sparsely rhymed—so that the reader's attention is directed to vocabulary and imagery more often than prosody. Invented words are frequent, some employed simply for the pleasure of their sound effects.

Harmonium interspersed brief lyrics with more extended meditative poems, some of which became in the following decades not only landmarks of Stevens's career but also touchstones for critics attempting to define the ambitions of twentieth-century poetry more broadly. "Peter Quince at the Clavier" along with "Sunday Morning" articulated Stevens's paradoxical belief that the only immortal beauty is that found in earthly nature and mortal human life. In "Sunday Morning," the speaker replies to human yearnings for "imperishable bliss" by asserting that the annual return of "April's green" will outlast every human myth or image of permanence, including Christianity's faith in the resurrection of Christ.

Stevens thought of the twentieth century as "an age of disbelief," and he did not much regret the loss. "To see the gods dispelled in mid-air and dissolve like clouds is one of the great human experiences," he wrote near the end of his life. Stevens's hope that with the fading of traditional religion poetry might become the forger of new faiths coincided with the convictions of such other modernist poets as T. S. Eliot (before his conversion to Anglo-Catholicism) and Ezra Pound. From the beginning of his career to the end, Stevens played variations on the proposition that poetry gestures toward a "supreme fiction," embraced without the need of final belief. All gods, Stevens thought, borrowed their power from the human world. The modern poet's role was to return that borrowed glory to its origins and, in doing so, to provide men and women with "a style of bearing themselves in reality."

Reality was an important word for Stevens throughout his career, often paired with *imagination*. Stevens inherited the central conviction of the nineteenth-century British romantic poets and American transcendentalists, that reality comes to human beings through acts of perception and imaginative ordering that at least half create—as the poet William Wordsworth (1770–1850) famously phrased it—what we experience. Placing a jar on a hill in Tennessee ("Anecdote of the Jar") reorders the world perceived around it; the singer's voice (as in "The Idea of Order at Key West") creates the world for her and her audience.

In the six years following the appearance of *Harmonium* Stevens published little new work. During the years leading up to World War II, however, Stevens's concern for the pressures of reality deepened, and his style altered. New volumes and major works began appearing with *Ideas of Order* in 1935, *Owl's Clover* in 1936, *The Man with a Blue Guitar* in 1937, and *Parts of a World* in 1942. The poems became increasingly discursive and philosophical; the conspicuous effects diminished, the diction became plainer. Although he would always remain distanced from political movements, World War II drew Stevens to articulate his own distinctive concern for the active role that poetry might play in the world: "It has to think about war / And it has to find what will suffice" ("Of Modern Poetry").

After World War II, long poems in this discursive, philosophical style became increasingly central to Stevens's work. "Notes Toward a Supreme Fiction" anchored *Transport to Summer* (1947), and *An Ordinary Evening in New Haven* (1950) included "The Auroras of Autumn" and "An Ordinary Evening in New Haven." A book collecting his occasional lectures appeared as *The Necessary Angel* in 1951. A final collection, *The Rock* (1954) appeared in the same year as his *Collected Poems*. Circling around the image of a rock covered with fallen leaves (a pun, among other things, on the leaves of a book), these last poems explored both "an end of the imagination" and the unending work of reclothing the world in images.

Stevens had always been something of a late bloomer as a poet—*Harmonium* appeared when he was forty-four—and his reputation rose steeply in the last decade of his life. He received the Bollingen Prize for lifetime achievement in poetry in 1950 and the National Book Award for *Auroras of Autumn* in 1951. His *Collected Poems* (1954) was recognized with the Pulitzer Prize as well as a second National Book Award in 1955, and has been celebrated as one of the most important books of American poetry in the twentieth century.

The text of the poems included here is that of *The Collected Poems of Wallace Stevens* (1954).

The Snow Man

One must have a mind of winter
To regard the frost and the boughs
Of the pine-trees crusted with snow;

And have been cold a long time
To behold the junipers shagged with ice,
The spruces rough in the distant glitter

Of the January sun; and not to think
Of any misery in the sound of the wind,
In the sound of a few leaves,

Which is the sound of the land
Full of the same wind
That is blowing in the same bare place

For the listener, who listens in the snow,
And, nothing himself, beholds
Nothing that is not there and the nothing that is.

1931

A High-Toned Old Christian Woman

Poetry is the supreme fiction, madame.
Take the moral law and make a nave[1] of it
And from the nave build haunted heaven. Thus,
The conscience is converted into palms,
Like windy citherns[2] hankering for hymns.
We agree in principle. That's clear. But take
The opposing law and make a peristyle,[3]
And from the peristyle project a masque[4]
Beyond the planets. Thus, our bawdiness,
Unpurged by epitaph, indulged at last,
Is equally converted into palms,
Squiggling like saxophones. And palm for palm,
Madame, we are where we began. Allow,
Therefore, that in the planetary scene
Your disaffected flagellants, well-stuffed,
Smacking their muzzy[5] bellies in parade,
Proud of such novelties of the sublime,
Such tink and tank and tunk-a-tunk-tunk,
May, merely may, madame, whip from themselves
A jovial hullabaloo among the spheres.
This will make widows wince. But fictive things
Wink as they will. Wink most when widows wince.

1923

The Emperor of Ice-Cream

Call the roller of big cigars,
The muscular one, and bid him whip
In kitchen cups concupiscent curds.
Let the wenches dawdle in such dress
As they are used to wear, and let the boys
Bring flowers in last month's newspapers.
Let be be finale of seem.
The only emperor is the emperor of ice-cream.

1. Main body of a church building, especially the vaulted central portion of a Christian Gothic church.
2. I.e., citterns; pear-shaped guitars.
3. Colonnade surrounding a building, especially the cells or main chamber of an ancient Greek temple—an "opposing law" to a Christian church.
4. Spectacle or entertainment consisting of music, dancing, mime, and often poetry.
5. Sodden with drunkenness.

Take from the dresser of deal,[1]
Lacking the three glass knobs, that sheet
On which she embroidered fantails[2] once
And spread it so as to cover her face.
If her horny feet protrude, they come
To show how cold she is, and dumb.
Let the lamp affix its beam.
The only emperor is the emperor of ice-cream.

1923

Disillusionment of Ten O'Clock

The houses are haunted
By white night-gowns.
None are green,
Or purple with green rings,
Or green with yellow rings,
Or yellow with blue rings.
None of them are strange,
With socks of lace
And beaded ceintures.
People are not going
To dream of baboons and periwinkles.
Only, here and there, an old sailor,
Drunk and asleep in his boots,
Catches tigers
In red weather.

1931

Sunday Morning[1]

I

Complacencies of the peignoir, and late
Coffee and oranges in a sunny chair,
And the green freedom of a cockatoo
Upon a rug mingle to dissipate
The holy hush of ancient sacrifice.
She dreams a little, and she feels the dark
Encroachment of that old catastrophe,
As a calm darkens among water-lights.
The pungent oranges and bright, green wings

1. Plain, unfinished wood.
2. Stevens explained that "the word fantails does not mean fan, but fantail pigeons."
1. This poem was first published in *Poetry* magazine in 1915; the editor, Harriet Monroe, printed only five of its eight stanzas but arranged them in the order Stevens suggested when consenting to the deletions (I, VIII, IV, V, and VII); he restored the deleted stanzas and the original sequence in subsequent printings.

Seem things in some procession of the dead,
Winding across wide water, without sound.
The day is like wide water, without sound,
Stilled for the passing of her dreaming feet
Over the seas, to silent Palestine,
Dominion of the blood and sepulchre.

II

Why should she give her bounty to the dead?
What is divinity if it can come
Only in silent shadows and in dreams?
Shall she not find in comforts of the sun,
In pungent fruit and bright, green wings, or else
In any balm or beauty of the earth,
Things to be cherished like the thought of heaven?
Divinity must live within herself:
Passions of rain, or moods in falling snow;
Grievings in loneliness, or unsubdued
Elations when the forest blooms; gusty
Emotions on wet roads on autumn nights;
All pleasures and all pains, remembering
The bough of summer and the winter branch.
These are the measures destined for her soul.

III

Jove[2] in the clouds had his inhuman birth.
No mother suckled him, no sweet land gave
Large-mannered motions to his mythy mind.
He moved among us, as a muttering king,
Magnificent, would move among his hinds,
Until our blood, commingling, virginal,
With heaven, brought such requital to desire
The very hinds[3] discerned it, in a star.
Shall our blood fail? Or shall it come to be
The blood of paradise? And shall the earth
Seem all of paradise that we shall know?
The sky will be much friendlier then than now,
A part of labor and a part of pain,
And next in glory to enduring love,
Not this dividing and indifferent blue.

IV

She says, "I am content when wakened birds,
Before they fly, test the reality
Of misty fields, by their sweet questionings;
But when the birds are gone, and their warm fields
Return no more, where, then, is paradise?"
There is not any haunt of prophecy,

2. Supreme god in Roman mythology.
3. Farmhands; an allusion to the shepherds who saw the star of Bethlehem that signaled the birth of Jesus.

Nor any old chimera[4] of the grave,
Neither the golden underground, nor isle
Melodious, where spirits gat them home,
Nor visionary south, nor cloudy palm
Remote on heaven's hill,[5] that has endured
As April's green endures; or will endure
Like her remembrance of awakened birds,
Or her desire for June and evening, tipped
By the consummation of the swallow's wings.

V

She says, "But in contentment I still feel
The need of some imperishable bliss."
Death is the mother of beauty; hence from her,
Alone, shall come fulfillment to our dreams
And our desires. Although she strews the leaves
Of sure obliteration on our paths,
The path sick sorrow took, the many paths
Where triumph rang its brassy phrase, or love
Whispered a little out of tenderness,
She makes the willow shiver in the sun
For maidens who were wont to sit and gaze
Upon the grass, relinquished to their feet.
She causes boys to pile new plums and pears
On disregarded plate. The maidens taste
And stray impassioned in the littering leaves.

VI

Is there no change of death in paradise?
Does ripe fruit never fall? Or do the boughs
Hang always heavy in that perfect sky,
Unchanging, yet so like our perishing earth,
With rivers like our own that seek for seas
They never find, the same receding shores
That never touch with inarticulate pang?
Why set the pear upon those river-banks
Or spice the shores with odors of the plum?
Alas, that they should wear our colors there,
The silken weavings of our afternoons,
And pick the strings of our insipid lutes!
Death is the mother of beauty, mystical,
Within whose burning bosom we devise
Our earthly mothers waiting, sleeplessly.

VII

Supple and turbulent, a ring of men
Shall chant in orgy on a summer morn
Their boisterous devotion to the sun,

4. In Greek mythology, a monster with a lion's head, goat's body, and serpent's tail.

5. Versions of Paradise in diverse world religions.

Not as a god, but as a god might be,
Naked among them, like a savage source.
Their chant shall be a chant of paradise,
Out of their blood, returning to the sky;
And in their chant shall enter, voice by voice,
The windy lake wherein their lord delights,
The trees, like serafin,[6] and echoing hills,
That choir among themselves long afterward.
They shall know well the heavenly fellowship
Of men that perish and of summer morn.
And whence they came and whither they shall go
The dew upon their feet shall manifest.

VIII

She hears, upon that water without sound,
A voice that cries, "The tomb in Palestine
Is not the porch of spirits lingering.
It is the grave of Jesus, where he lay."
We live in an old chaos of the sun,
Or old dependency of day and night,
Or island solitude, unsponsored, free,
Of that wide water, inescapable.
Deer walk upon our mountains, and the quail
Whistle about us their spontaneous cries;
Sweet berries ripen in the wilderness;
And, in the isolation of the sky,
At evening, casual flocks of pigeons make
Ambiguous undulations as they sink,
Downward to darkness, on extended wings.

1915, 1923

Anecdote of the Jar

I placed a jar in Tennessee,
And round it was, upon a hill.
It made the slovenly wilderness
Surround that hill.

The wilderness rose up to it,
And sprawled around, no longer wild.
The jar was round upon the ground
And tall and of a port in air.

It took dominion everywhere.
The jar was gray and bare.
It did not give of bird or bush,
Like nothing else in Tennessee.

1923

6. I.e., seraphim; angels.

Thirteen Ways of Looking at a Blackbird

I

Among twenty snowy mountains,
The only moving thing
Was the eye of the blackbird.

II

I was of three minds,
Like a tree
In which there are three blackbirds.

III

The blackbird whirled in the autumn winds.
It was a small part of the pantomime.

IV

A man and a woman
Are one.
A man and a woman and a blackbird
Are one.

V

I do not know which to prefer,
The beauty of inflections
Or the beauty of innuendoes,
The blackbird whistling
Or just after.

VI

Icicles filled the long window
With barbaric glass.
The shadow of the blackbird
Crossed it, to and fro.
The mood
Traced in the shadow
An indecipherable cause.

VII

O thin men of Haddam,[1]
Why do you imagine golden birds?
Do you not see how the blackbird
Walks around the feet
Of the women about you?

1. A city in Connecticut.

VIII

I know noble accents
And lucid, inescapable rhythms;
But I know, too,
That the blackbird is involved
In what I know.

IX

When the blackbird flew out of sight,
It marked the edge
Of one of many circles.

X

At the sight of blackbirds
Flying in a green light,
Even the bawds of euphony
Would cry out sharply.

XI

He rode over Connecticut
In a glass coach.
Once, a fear pierced him,
In that he mistook
The shadow of his equipage
For blackbirds.

XII

The river is moving.
The blackbird must be flying.

XIII

It was evening all afternoon.
It was snowing
And it was going to snow.
The blackbird sat
In the cedar-limbs.

1931

The Idea of Order at Key West[1]

She sang beyond the genius of the sea.
The water never formed to mind or voice,
Like a body wholly body, fluttering
Its empty sleeves; and yet its mimic motion
Made constant cry, caused constantly a cry,
That was not ours although we understood,
Inhuman, of the veritable ocean.

The sea was not a mask. No more was she.
The song and water were not medleyed sound
Even if what she sang was what she heard,
Since what she sang was uttered word by word.
It may be that in all her phrases stirred
The grinding water and the gasping wind;
But it was she and not the sea we heard.

For she was the maker of the song she sang.
The ever-hooded, tragic-gestured sea
Was merely a place by which she walked to sing.
Whose spirit is this? we said, because we knew
It was the spirit that we sought and knew
That we should ask this often as she sang.

If it was only the dark voice of the sea
That rose, or even colored by many waves;
If it was only the outer voice of sky
And cloud, of the sunken coral water-walled,
However clear, it would have been deep air,
The heaving speech of air, a summer sound
Repeated in a summer without end
And sound alone. But it was more than that,
More even than her voice, and ours, among
The meaningless plungings of water and the wind,
Theatrical distances, bronze shadows heaped
On high horizons, mountainous atmospheres
Of sky and sea.
It was her voice that made
The sky acutest at its vanishing.
She measured to the hour its solitude.
She was the single artificer of the world
In which she sang. And when she sang, the sea,
Whatever self it had, became the self
That was her song, for she was the maker. Then we,
As we beheld her striding there alone,
Knew that there never was a world for her
Except the one she sang and, singing, made.

1. One of the islands off the southern coast of Florida, where Stevens vacationed. The poem begins with the scene of a woman walking by the sea and singing.

Ramon Fernandez,[2] tell me, if you know,
Why, when the singing ended and we turned
Toward the town, tell why the glassy lights,
The lights in the fishing boats at anchor there,
As the night descended, tilting in the air,
Mastered the night and portioned out the sea,
Fixing emblazoned zones and fiery poles,
Arranging, deepening, enchanting night.

Oh! Blessed rage for order, pale Ramon,
The maker's rage to order words of the sea,
Words of the fragrant portals, dimly-starred,
And of ourselves and of our origins,
In ghostlier demarcations, keener sounds.

1936

Of Modern Poetry

The poem of the mind in the act of finding
What will suffice. It has not always had
To find: the scene was set; it repeated what
Was in the script.
Then the theatre was changed
To something else. Its past was a souvenir.
It has to be living, to learn the speech of the place.
It has to face the men of the time and to meet
The women of the time. It has to think about war
And it has to find what will suffice. It has
To construct a new stage. It has to be on that stage
And, like an insatiable actor, slowly and
With meditation, speak words that in the ear,
In the delicatest ear of the mind, repeat,
Exactly, that which it wants to hear, at the sound
Of which, an invisible audience listens,
Not to the play, but to itself, expressed
In an emotion as of two people, as of two
Emotions becoming one. The actor is
A metaphysician in the dark, twanging
An instrument, twanging a wiry string that gives
Sounds passing through sudden rightnesses, wholly
Containing the mind, below which it cannot descend,
Beyond which it has no will to rise.
It must
Be the finding of a satisfaction, and may
Be of a man skating, a woman dancing, a woman
Combing. The poem of the act of the mind.

1942

2. A French literary critic and essayist (1894–1944). Stevens said that he had invented the name and that its coincidence with a real person was accidental.

The Plain Sense of Things

After the leaves have fallen, we return
To a plain sense of things. It is as if
We had come to an end of the imagination,
Inanimate in an inert savoir.[1]

It is difficult even to choose the adjective
For this blank cold, this sadness without cause.
The great structure has become a minor house.
No turban walks across the lessened floors.

The greenhouse never so badly needed paint.
The chimney is fifty years old and slants to one side.
A fantastic effort has failed, a repetition
In a repetitiousness of men and flies.

Yet the absence of the imagination had
Itself to be imagined. The great pond,
The plain sense of it, without reflections, leaves,
Mud, water like dirty glass, expressing silence

Of a sort, silence of a rat come out to see,
The great pond and its waste of the lilies, all this
Had to be imagined as an inevitable knowledge,
Required, as a necessity requires.

1954

1. Knowledge (French).

WILLIAM CARLOS WILLIAMS
1883–1963

A modernist known for his disagreements with all the other modernists, William Carlos Williams thought of himself as the most underrated poet of his generation. His reputation has risen dramatically since World War II as a younger generation of poets testified to the influence of his work on their idea of what poetry should be. The simplicity of his verse forms, the matter-of-factness of both his subject matter and his means of describing it, seemed to bring poetry into natural relation with everyday life. He is now judged to be among the most important poets writing between the wars. His career continued into the 1960s, taking new directions as he produced, along with shorter lyrics, his epic five-part poem *Paterson*.

He was born in 1883 in Rutherford, New Jersey, a town near the city of Paterson. His maternal grandmother, an Englishwoman deserted by her husband, had come to

America with her son, married again, and moved to Puerto Rico. Her son—Williams's father—married a woman descended on one side from French Basque people, on the other from Dutch Jews. This mix of origins always fascinated Williams and made him feel that he was different from what he thought of as mainstream Americans—that is, northeasterners or midwesterners of English descent. After the family moved to New Jersey, Williams's father worked as a salesman for a perfume company; in childhood his father was often away from home, and the two women—mother and grandmother—were the most important adults to him.

Except for a year in Europe, Williams attended local schools. He entered the School of Dentistry at the University of Pennsylvania directly after graduating from high school but soon switched to medicine. In college he met and became friends with Ezra Pound; Hilda Doolittle, later to become known as the poet H.D.; and the painter Charles Demuth. These friendships did much to steer him toward poetry, and even as he completed his medical work, interned in New York City, and did postgraduate study in Leipzig, Germany, he was reconceiving his commitment to medicine as a means of self-support in the more important enterprise of becoming a poet. Although he never lost his sense that he was a doctor in order to be a poet, his patients knew him as a dedicated old-fashioned physician, who made house calls, listened to people's problems, and helped them through life's crises. Pediatrics was his specialty; and in the course of his career, he delivered more than two thousand babies.

In 1912, after internship and study abroad, Williams married his fiancée of several years, Florence Herman. Despite strains in their relationship caused by Williams's continuing interest in other women, the marriage lasted and became, toward the end of Williams's life, the subject of some beautiful love poetry, including "Asphodel, that Greeny Flower." In the meantime women and the mixed belittlement–adoration accorded them by men (including the poet) were persistent themes in his work. The couple settled in Rutherford, where Williams opened his practice. Except for a trip to Europe in 1924, when he saw Pound and met James Joyce, among others, and trips for lectures and poetry readings later in his career, Williams remained in Rutherford all his life, continuing his medical practice until poor health forced him to retire. He wrote at night, and spent weekends in New York City with friends who were writers and artists—the avant-garde painters Marcel Duchamp and Francis Picabia, the poets Marianne Moore and Wallace Stevens, and others. At their gatherings he acquired a reputation for outspoken hostility to most of the "-isms" of the day.

The characteristic Williams style emerged clearly in the landmark volume of mixed prose and poetry *Spring and All* (1923; see pp. 286 and 326). This book demonstrates that the gesture of staying at home was more for him than a practical assessment of his chances of self-support. Interested, like his friend Ezra Pound, in making a new kind of poetry, Williams also wanted always to speak as an American within an American context. He staked this claim in the title of one of his books of essays, *In the American Grain* (1925), and in his choice of his own region as the setting and subject of *Paterson* (1946–58), a long poem about his native city incorporating a great variety of textual fragments—letters, newspaper accounts, poetry—in a modernist collage.

Williams detested Eliot's *The Waste Land*, describing its popularity as a "catastrophe and" deploring not only its internationalism but also its pessimism and deliberate obscurity. To him these characteristics were un-American. Yet Williams was not a sentimental celebrant of American life. He objected to Robert Frost's homespun poetry—which might be thought of as similar to his own work—for nostalgically evoking a bygone rural America rather than engaging with what he saw as the real American present. His America was made up of small cities like Paterson, with immigrants, factories, and poor working-class people struggling to get by. The sickness and suffering he saw as a physician entered into his poetry, as did his personal life; but the overall impact of his poetry is social rather than autobiographical.

The social aspect of Williams's poetry rises from its accumulation of detail; he opposed the use of poetry for general statements and abstract critique. "No ideas but in things," he wrote—a line that became one of the most influential mottos of twentieth-century American poetry. "Not ideas about the thing but the thing itself," echoed Wallace Stevens; yet there is a world of difference between Williams's plainspoken and often opinionated writing and Stevens's cool elegance. Williams drew his vocabulary from up-to-date local speech and searched for a poetic line derived from the cadences of street talk. But he rejected "free verse" as an absurdity; rhythm within the line, and linking one line to another, was the heart of poetic craft to him. While working on *Paterson,* he invented the "triadic" or "stepped line," a long line broken into three segments, which he used in many poems, including several of the selections printed here.

Williams published fiction and essays as well as poetry, especially during the 1930s. Books of short stories (*The Edge of the Knife,* 1932, and *Life along the Passaic River,* 1938) and novels (*White Mule,* 1937, and *In the Money,* 1940) appeared in these years. He was also involved with others in the establishment of several little magazines, each designed to promulgate counterstatements to the powerful influences of Pound, Eliot, and the New Critics. All the time he remained active in his community and in political events; in the 1930s and 1940s he aligned himself with liberal Democratic and, on occasion, leftist issues but always from the vantage point of an unreconstructed individualism. Some of his affiliations were held against him in the McCarthy era and to his great distress he was deprived in 1948 of the post of consultant in poetry at the Library of Congress.

It was also in 1948 that he had a heart attack, and in 1951 the first of a series of strokes required him to turn over his medical practice to one of his two sons and made writing increasingly difficult. Nevertheless, he persevered in his work on *Paterson,* whose five books were published in 1946, 1948, 1949, 1951, and 1958. *The Desert Music* (1954) and *Pictures from Brueghel* (1962), containing new poetry, also appeared; but by 1961 Williams had to stop writing. By the time of his death a host of younger poets, including Allen Ginsberg, Denise Levertov, Charles Olson, and Robert Creeley, had been inspired by his example. He won the National Book Award in 1950, the Bollingen Prize in 1953, and the Pulitzer Prize in 1962.

The texts of the poems included here are those of *The Collected Poems of William Carlos Williams,* Volume 1: *1909–1939* (1986), edited by A. Walton Litz and Christopher MacGowan, and *The Collected Poems of William Carlos Williams,* Volume 2: *1939–1962* (1988), edited by Christopher MacGowan.

The Young Housewife

At ten A.M. the young housewife
moves about in negligee behind
the wooden walls of her husband's house.
I pass solitary in my car.

Then again she comes to the curb
to call the ice-man, fish-man, and stands
shy, uncorseted, tucking in
stray ends of hair, and I compare her
to a fallen leaf.

The noiseless wheels of my car
rush with a crackling sound over
dried leaves as I bow and pass smiling.

1916, 1917

Portrait of a Lady

Your thighs are appletrees
whose blossoms touch the sky.
Which sky? The sky
where Watteau[1] hung a lady's
slipper. Your knees
are a southern breeze—or
a gust of snow. Agh! what
sort of man was Fragonard?[2]
—as if that answered
anything. Ah, yes—below
the knees, since the tune
drops that way, it is
one of those white summer days,
the tall grass of your ankles
flickers upon the shore—
Which shore?—
the sand clings to my lips—
Which shore?
Agh, petals maybe. How
should I know?
Which shore? Which shore?
I said petals from an appletree.

1920, 1934

Queen-Anne's-Lace[1]

Her body is not so white as
anemone petals nor so smooth—nor
so remote a thing. It is a field
of the wild carrot taking
the field by force; the grass
does not raise above it.
Here is no question of whiteness,

1. Jean Antoine Watteau (1684–1721), French artist who painted elegantly dressed lovers in idealized rustic settings.

2. Jean Honoré Fragonard (1732–1806), French painter who depicted fashionable lovers in paintings more wittily and openly erotic than Watteau's. Fragonard's *The Swing* depicts a girl who has kicked her slipper into the air.

1. A common wildflower whose white bloom is composed of numerous tiny blossoms, each with a dark spot at the center, joined to the stalk by fibrous stems.

white as can be, with a purple mole
at the center of each flower.
Each flower is a hand's span
of her whiteness. Wherever
his hand has lain there is
a tiny purple blemish. Each part
is a blossom under his touch
to which the fibres of her being
stem one by one, each to its end,
until the whole field is a
white desire, empty, a single stem,
a cluster, flower by flower,
a pious wish to whiteness gone over—
or nothing.

1921

The Widow's Lament in Springtime

Sorrow is my own yard
where the new grass
flames as it has flamed
often before but not
with the cold fire
that closes round me this year.
Thirtyfive years
I lived with my husband.
The plumtree is white today
with masses of flowers.
Masses of flowers
load the cherry branches
and color some bushes
yellow and some red
but the grief in my heart
is stronger than they
for though they were my joy
formerly, today I notice them
and turn away forgetting.
Today my son told me
that in the meadows,
at the edge of the heavy woods
in the distance, he saw
trees of white flowers.
I feel that I would like
to go there
and fall into those flowers
and sink into the marsh near them.

1921

Spring and All[1]

By the road to the contagious hospital[2]
under the surge of the blue
mottled clouds driven from the
northeast—a cold wind. Beyond, the
waste of broad, muddy fields
brown with dried weeds, standing and fallen

patches of standing water
the scattering of tall trees

All along the road the reddish
purplish, forked, upstanding, twiggy
stuff of bushes and small trees
with dead, brown leaves under them
leafless vines—

Lifeless in appearance, sluggish
dazed spring approaches—

They enter the new world naked,
cold, uncertain of all
save that they enter. All about them
the cold, familiar wind—

Now the grass, tomorrow
the stiff curl of wildcarrot leaf

One by one objects are defined—
It quickens: clarity, outline of leaf

But now the stark dignity of
entrance—Still, the profound change
has come upon them: rooted, they
grip down and begin to awaken

1923

To Elsie[1]

The pure products of America
go crazy—
mountain folk from Kentucky

1. In the volume *Spring and All* (as originally published, 1923), prose statements were interspersed through the poems, which were identified by roman numerals. Williams added titles later and used the volume's title for the opening poem. For examples of the prose sections of *Spring and All*, see "Modernist Manifestos," p. 326.
2. I.e., a hospital for treating contagious diseases.
1. In *Spring and All,* this poem was originally numbered XVIII. Elsie, from the State Orphanage, worked for the Williams family as a nursemaid.

or the ribbed north end of
Jersey
with its isolate lakes and

valleys, its deaf-mutes, thieves
old names
and promiscuity between

devil-may-care men who have taken
to railroading
out of sheer lust of adventure—

and young slatterns, bathed
in filth
from Monday to Saturday

to be tricked out that night
with gauds
from imaginations which have no

peasant traditions to give them
character
but flutter and flaunt

sheer rags—succumbing without
emotion
save numbed terror

under some hedge of choke-cherry
or viburnum—
which they cannot express—

Unless it be that marriage
perhaps
with a dash of Indian blood

will throw up a girl so desolate
so hemmed round
with disease or murder

that she'll be rescued by an
agent—
reared by the state and

sent out at fifteen to work in
some hard-pressed
house in the suburbs—

some doctor's family, some Elsie—
voluptuous water
expressing with broken

brain the truth about us—
her great
ungainly hips and flopping breasts

addressed to cheap
jewelry
and rich young men with fine eyes

as if the earth under our feet
were
an excrement of some sky

and we degraded prisoners
destined
to hunger until we eat filth

while the imagination strains
after deer
going by fields of goldenrod in

the stifling heat of September
Somehow
it seems to destroy us

It is only in isolate flecks that
something
is given off

No one
to witness
and adjust, no one to drive the car

1923

The Red Wheelbarrow[1]

so much depends
upon

a red wheel
barrow

glazed with rain
water

beside the white
chickens

1923

1. Numbered XXII in *Spring and All*.

The Dead Baby

Sweep the house
under the feet of the curious
holiday seekers—
sweep under the table and the bed
the baby is dead—

The mother's eyes where she sits
by the window, unconsoled—
have purple bags under them
the father—
tall, wellspoken, pitiful
is the abler of these two—

Sweep the house clean
here is one who has gone up
(though problematically)
to heaven, blindly
by force of the facts—
a clean sweep
is one way of expressing it—

Hurry up! any minute
they will be bringing it
from the hospital—
a white model of our lives
a curiosity—
surrounded by fresh flowers

1927, 1935

This Is Just to Say

I have eaten
the plums
that were in
the icebox

and which
you were probably
saving
for breakfast

Forgive me
they were delicious
so sweet
and so cold

1934

A Sort of a Song

Let the snake wait under
his weed
and the writing
be of words, slow and quick, sharp
to strike, quiet to wait,
sleepless.

—through metaphor to reconcile
the people and the stones.
Compose. (No ideas
but in things) Invent!
Saxifrage is my flower that splits
the rocks.

1944

The Dance

In Brueghel's great picture, The Kermess,[1]
the dancers go round, they go round and
around, the squeal and the blare and the
tweedle of bagpipes, a bugle and fiddles
tipping their bellies (round as the thick-
sided glasses whose wash they impound)
their hips and their bellies off balance
to turn them. Kicking and rolling about
the Fair Grounds, swinging their butts, those
shanks must be sound to bear up under such
rollicking measures, prance as they dance
in Brueghel's great picture, The Kermess.

1944

Burning the Christmas Greens

Their time past, pulled down
cracked and flung to the fire
—go up in a roar
All recognition lost, burnt clean
clean in the flame, the green
dispersed, a living red,
flame red, red as blood wakes
on the ash—

1. *The Wedding Dance* by the Flemish painter Pieter Brueghel (or Breughel) the Elder (c. 1525–1569).

and ebbs to a steady burning
the rekindled bed become
a landscape of flame

At the winter's midnight
we went to the trees, the coarse
holly, the balsam and
the hemlock for their green

At the thick of the dark
the moment of the cold's
deepest plunge we brought branches
cut from the green trees

to fill our need, and over
doorways, about paper Christmas
bells covered with tinfoil
and fastened by red ribbons

we stuck the green prongs
in the windows hung
woven wreaths and above pictures
the living green. On the

mantle we built a green forest
and among those hemlock
sprays put a herd of small
white deer as if they

were walking there. All this!
and it seemed gentle and good
to us. Their time past,
relief! The room bare. We

stuffed the dead grate
with them upon the half burnt out
log's smoldering eye, opening
red and closing under them

and we stood there looking down.
Green is a solace
a promise of peace, a fort
against the cold (though we

did not say so) a challenge
above the snow's
hard shell. Green (we might
have said) that, where

small birds hide and dodge
and lift their plaintive

rallying cries, blocks for them
and knocks down

the unseeing bullets of
the storm. Green spruce boughs
pulled down by a weight of
snow—Transformed!

Violence leaped and appeared.
Recreant! roared to life
as the flame rose through and
our eyes recoiled from it.

In the jagged flames green
to red, instant and alive. Green!
those sure abutments . . . Gone!
lost to mind

and quick in the contracting
tunnel of the grate
appeared a world! Black
mountains, black and red—as

yet uncolored—and ash white,
an infant landscape of shimmering
ash and flame and we, in
that instant, lost,

breathless to be witnesses,
as if we stood
ourselves refreshed among
the shining fauna of that fire.

1944

Landscape with the Fall of Icarus[1]

According to Brueghel[2]
when Icarus fell
it was spring

a farmer was ploughing
his field
the whole pageantry

1. In Greek mythology, a young man whose father made wings for him with feathers held together by wax. Icarus flew too close to the sun, the wax melted, and he fell into the sea and drowned.

2. A landscape by Flemish painter Pieter Brueghel the Elder (c. 1525–1569) in which Icarus is depicted by a tiny leg sticking out of the sea in one corner of the picture.

of the year was
awake tingling
near

the edge of the sea
concerned
with itself

sweating in the sun
that melted
the wings' wax

unsignificantly
off the coast
there was

a splash quite unnoticed
this was
Icarus drowning

1962

EZRA POUND
1885–1972

Ezra Loomis Pound was born in Hailey, Idaho. When he was still an infant his parents settled in a comfortable suburb near Philadelphia where his father was an assayer at the regional branch of the U.S. Mint. "I knew at fifteen pretty much what I wanted to do," he wrote in 1913; what he wanted was to become a poet. He had this goal in mind as an undergraduate at the University of Pennsylvania (where he met and became lifelong friends with William Carlos Williams and had a romance with Hilda Doolittle, who was later to become the poet H.D.) and at Hamilton College; it also motivated his graduate studies in languages—French, Italian, Old English, and Latin—at the University of Pennsylvania, where he received an M.A. in 1906. He planned to support himself as a college teacher while writing.

The poetry that he had in mind in these early years was in vogue at the turn of the twentieth century—melodious in versification and diction, romantic in themes, world-weary in tone—poetry for which the term *decadent* was used. A particular image of the poet went with such poetry: the poet committed to art for its own sake, careless of convention, and continually shocking the respectable middle class. A rebellious and colorful personality, Pound delighted in this role but quickly found that it was not compatible with the sober behavior expected from professors of language. He lost his first teaching job, at Wabash College in Indiana, in fewer than six months.

Convinced that his country had no place for him—and that a country with no place for him had no place for art—he went to Europe in 1908. He settled in London and quickly became involved in its literary life, and especially prominent in movements to revolutionize poetry and identify good new poets. He supported himself by teaching and reviewing for several journals. For a while he acted as secretary to the great Irish poet William Butler Yeats. He married Dorothy Shakespear, daughter of a close friend of Yeats, in 1914. Ten years later he became involved with the American expatriate Olga Rudge and maintained relationships with both women thereafter.

As an advocate of the new, he found himself propagandizing against the very poetry that had made him want to be a poet at the start, and this contradiction remained throughout his life: on the one hand, a desire to "make it new"; on the other, a deep attachment to the old. Many of his critical essays were later collected and published in books such as *Make It New* (1934), *The ABC of Reading* (1934), *Polite Essays* (1937), and *Literary Essays* (1954). He was generous in his efforts to assist other writers in their work and in their attempts to get published; he was helpful to H.D., T. S. Eliot, James Joyce, William Carlos Williams, Robert Frost, Ernest Hemingway, and Marianne Moore, to name just a few.

Pound first campaigned for "imagism," his name for a new kind of poetry. Rather than describing something—an object or situation—and then generalizing about it, imagist poets attempted to present the object directly, avoiding the ornate diction and complex but predictable verse forms of traditional poetry. Any significance to be derived from the image had to appear inherent in its spare, clean presentation. "Go in fear of abstractions," Pound wrote (see "A Retrospect," p. 321). Elaborate grammatical constructions seemed artificial; hence this new poetry tended to work by juxtaposition of fragments. Although imagism lasted only briefly as a formal movement, most subsequent twentieth-century poetry showed its influence. Pound soon moved on to "vorticism," which, although still espousing direct and bare presentation, sought for some principle of dynamism and energy in the image. In his imagist phase Pound was connected with H.D. and Richard Aldington, a British poet who became H.D.'s husband; as a vorticist he was allied with the iconoclastic writer and artist Wyndham Lewis.

Pound thought of the United States as a culturally backward nation and longed to produce a sophisticated, worldly poetry on behalf of his country. Walt Whitman was his symbol of American poetic narrowness. His major works during his London years consisted of free translations from languages unknown to most Westerners: Provençal, Chinese, Japanese. He also experimented with the dramatic monologue form developed by the English Victorian poet Robert Browning. Poems from these years appeared in his volumes *A Lume Spento* (By the spent light; Italian), which appeared in 1908, *A Quinzaine for This Yule* (1908), and *Personae* (1910). *Persona* means "mask," and the poems in this last volume developed the dramatic monologue as a means for the poet to assume various identities and to engage in acts of historical reconstruction and empathy.

Although the imagist view of poetry would seem to exclude the long poem as a workable form, Pound could not overcome the traditional belief that a really great poem had to be long. He hoped to write such a poem himself, a poem for his time, which would unite biography and history by representing the total content of his mind and memory. To this end he began working on his *Cantos* in 1915. The cantos were separate poems of varying lengths, combining reminiscence, meditation, description, and transcriptions from books Pound was reading, all of which were to be forged into unity by the heat of the poet's imagination. Ultimately, he produced 116 cantos, whose intricate obscurities continue to fascinate and challenge critics. The London period came to a close with two poems of disillusionment, "Hugh Selwyn Mauberley (Life and Contacts)" and "Mauberley," which described the decay of Western civilization in the aftermath of the Great War.

Looking for an explanation of what had gone wrong, Pound came upon the "social credit" theories of Major Clifford Hugh Douglas, a social economist who attributed all the ills of civilization to the interposition of money between human exchanges of goods. At this point, poetry and politics fused in Pound's work, and he began to search for a society in which art was protected from money and to record this search in poems and essays. This became a dominant theme in the *Cantos*. Leaving England for good in 1920, he lived on the Mediterranean Sea, in Paris for a time, and then settled in the small Italian town of Rapallo in 1925. His survey of history having persuaded him that the ideal society was a hierarchy with a strong leader and an agricultural economy, he greeted the Italian Fascist dictator Benito Mussolini as a deliverer. He looked for other strong leaders in world history and idealized them in the *Cantos*. During World War II he voluntarily served the Italian government by making numerous English-language radio broadcasts beamed at England and the United States in which he vilified Jews, President Franklin D. Roosevelt, and American society in general. When the U.S. Army occupied Italy, Pound was arrested, held for weeks in an open-air cage at the prison camp near Pisa, and finally brought to the United States to be tried for treason. The trial did not take place, however, because the court accepted a psychiatric report to the effect that Pound was "insane and mentally unfit to be tried." From 1946 to 1958 he was a patient and a prisoner in St. Elizabeth's Hospital for the criminally insane in Washington, D.C. During those years he received visits, wrote letters, composed cantos, and continued his polemic against American society.

In 1948 the *Pisan Cantos* (LXXIV–LXXXIV) won the Library of Congress's newly established Bollingen Prize for poetry, an event that provoked tremendous debate about Pound's stature as a poet as well as a citizen. Ten years later the efforts of a committee of writers succeeded in winning Pound's release; he returned to Italy, where he died at the age of eighty-seven. He remains one of the most controversial poets of the era.

The texts of the poems included here are those of *Personae: The Collected Poems* (rev., 1949) and *The Cantos* (1976).

To Whistler, American[1]

On the loan exhibit of his paintings at the Tate Gallery.

You also, our first great
Had tried all ways;
Tested and pried and worked in many fashions,
And this much gives me heart to play the game.

Here is a part that's slight, and part gone wrong,
And much of little moment, and some few
Perfect as Dürer![2]
"In the Studio" and these two portraits,[3] if I had my choice!
And then these sketches in the mood of Greece?

You had your searches, your uncertainties,
And this is good to know—for us, I mean,
Who bear the brunt of our America
And try to wrench her impulse into art.

1. James Abbott McNeill Whistler (1834–1903), expatriate American painter.
2. Albrecht Dürer (1471–1528), German painter and engraver.
3. "'Brown and Gold—de Race,' 'Grenat et Or—Le Petit Cardinal' ('Garnet and Gold—The Little Cardinal')" [Pound's note]. Titles and subjects of the portraits.

You were not always sure, not always set
To hiding night or tuning "symphonies";[4]
Had not one style from birth, but tried and pried
And stretched and tampered with the media.

You and Abe Lincoln from that mass of dolts
Show us there's chance at least of winning through.

1912, 1949

Portrait d'une Femme[1]

Your mind and you are our Sargasso Sea,[2]
London has swept about you this score years
And bright ships left you this or that in fee:
Ideas, old gossip, oddments of all things,
Strange spars of knowledge and dimmed wares of price.
Great minds have sought you—lacking someone else.
You have been second always. Tragical?
No. You preferred it to the usual thing:
One dull man, dulling and uxorious,
One average mind—with one thought less, each year.
Oh, you are patient, I have seen you sit
Hours, where something might have floated up.
And now you pay one. Yes, you richly pay.
You are a person of some interest, one comes to you
And takes strange gain away:
Trophies fished up; some curious suggestion;
Fact that leads nowhere; and a tale or two,
Pregnant with mandrakes,[3] or with something else
That might prove useful and yet never proves,
That never fits a corner or shows use,
Or finds its hour upon the loom of days:
The tarnished, gaudy, wonderful old work;
Idols and ambergris and rare inlays,
These are your riches, your great store; and yet
For all this sea-hoard of deciduous things,
Strange woods half sodden, and new brighter stuff:
In the slow float of differing light and deep,
No! there is nothing! In the whole and all,
Nothing that's quite your own.
Yet this is you.

1912

4. Whistler painted many night scenes and titled many paintings "symphonies."
1. Portrait of a lady (French).
2. Sea in the North Atlantic where boats were becalmed; named for its large masses of floating seaweed.
3. Herb used as a cathartic; believed in legend to have human properties, to shriek when pulled from the ground, and to promote pregnancy.

A Virginal[1]

No, no! Go from me. I have left her lately.
I will not spoil my sheath with lesser brightness,
For my surrounding air hath a new lightness;
Slight are her arms, yet they have bound me straitly
And left me cloaked as with a gauze of æther;
As with sweet leaves; as with subtle clearness.
Oh, I have picked up magic in her nearness
To sheathe me half in half the things that sheathe her.
No, no! Go from me. I have still the flavour,
Soft as spring wind that's come from birchen bowers.
Green come the shoots, aye April in the branches,
As winter's wound with her sleight hand she staunches,
Hath of the trees a likeness of the savour:
As white their bark, so white this lady's hours.

1912

A Pact

I make a pact with you, Walt Whitman—
I have detested you long enough.
I come to you as a grown child
Who has had a pig-headed father;
I am old enough now to make friends.
It was you that broke the new wood,
Now is a time for carving.
We have one sap and one root—
Let there be commerce between us.

1913, 1916

In a Station of the Metro[1]

The apparition of these faces in the crowd;
Petals on a wet, black bough.

1913, 1916

The River-Merchant's Wife: A Letter[1]

While my hair was still cut straight across my forehead
I played about the front gate, pulling flowers.

1. A small pianolike instrument popular in the 16th and 17th centuries.
1. Paris subway.
1. Adaptation from the Chinese of Li Po (701–762), named Rihaku in Japanese, from the papers of Ernest Fenollosa, an American scholar whose widow gave his papers on Japan and China to Pound.

You came by on bamboo stilts, playing horse,
You walked about my seat, playing with blue plums.
And we went on living in the village of Chŭkan:
Two small people, without dislike or suspicion.

At fourteen I married My Lord you.
I never laughed, being bashful.
Lowering my head, I looked at the wall.
Called to, a thousand times, I never looked back.

At fifteen I stopped scowling,
I desired my dust to be mingled with yours
Forever and forever and forever.
Why should I climb the look out?

At sixteen you departed,
You went into far Ku-tŭ-en, by the river of swirling eddies,
And you have been gone five months.
The monkeys make sorrowful noise overhead.

You dragged your feet when you went out.
By the gate now, the moss is grown, the different mosses,
Too deep to clear them away!
The leaves fall early this autumn, in wind.
The paired butterflies are already yellow with August
Over the grass in the West garden;
They hurt me. I grow older.
If you are coming down through the narrows of the river Kiang,
Please let me know beforehand,
And I will come out to meet you
    As far as Chŭ-fū-Sa.

By Rihaku

1915

Villanelle: The Psychological Hour[1]

I

I had over-prepared the event,
    that much was ominous.
With middle-ageing care
    I had laid out just the right books.
I had almost turned down the pages.

Beauty is so rare a thing.
So few drink of my fountain.

1. The poem is not in the traditional villanelle stanza pattern.

So much barren regret,
So many hours wasted!
And now I watch, from the window,
 the rain, the wandering busses.
"Their little cosmos is shaken"—
 the air is alive with that fact.
In their parts of the city
 they are played on by diverse forces.
How do I know?
 Oh, I know well enough.
For them there is something afoot.
 As for me;
I had over-prepared the event—

Beauty is so rare a thing.
So few drink of my fountain.

Two friends: a breath of the forest . . .
Friends? Are people less friends
 because one has just, at last, found them?
Twice they promised to come.

"Between the night and morning?"[2]

Beauty would drink of my mind.
Youth would awhile forget
 my youth is gone from me.

II

("Speak up! You have danced so stiffly?
 Someone admired your works,
 And said so frankly.
"Did you talk like a fool,
 The first night?
 The second evening?"

"*But* they promised again:
 'To-morrow at tea-time.' ")

III

Now the third day is here—
 no word from either;
No word from her nor him,
Only another man's note:
 "Dear Pound, I am leaving England."

1916

2. In "The People," an uncollected poem published in 1916, William Butler Yeats complained of an "unmannerly town" that can ruin one's reputation "Between the night and the morning."

Hugh Selwyn Mauberley[1] (Life and Contacts)[2]

"Vocat æestus in umbram"
—Nemesianus,[3] *Ec. IV*

E. P. Ode pour l'election de Son Sepulchre[4]

For three years, out of key with his time,
He strove to resuscitate the dead art
Of poetry; to maintain "the sublime"
In the old sense. Wrong from the start—

No, hardly, but seeing he had been born
In a half savage country, out of date;
Bent resolutely on wringing lilies from the acorn;
Capaneus,[5] trout for factitious bait;

Ἴδμεν γάρ τοι πάνθ',ὅσ ἐνὶ Τροίῃ[6]
Caught in the unstopped ear;
Giving the rocks small lee-way
The chopped seas held him, therefore, that year.

His true Penelope was Flaubert,[7]
He fished by obstinate isles;
Observed the elegance of Circe's[8] hair
Rather than the mottoes on sun-dials.

Unaffected by "the march of events,"
He passed from men's memory in *l'an trentuniesme*
De son eage,[9] the case presents
No adjunct to the Muses' diadem.

1. This poem was published in 1920 when Pound was on the verge of leaving London. He declared that the poem was modeled partly on the technique of Henry James's prose fiction: it presents its subject through the medium of a character's mind or voice, a "center of consciousness" whose mind and standards are also part of the subject being treated and are exposed themselves to scrutiny and assessment. In "Hugh Selwyn Mauberley" the first thirteen lyrics are presented through "E. P." In the next section, titled "Mauberley" (I through "Medallion"), the persona of "E. P." is absorbed in the fictitious poet Mauberley, a second persona.
2. Echo of a conventional subtitle of literary biographies, "Life and Letters." In the 1957 edition, Pound reversed the sequence, claiming that "Contacts and Life" followed the "order of the subject matter." To the American edition of *Personae* in 1926 Pound added the following note: "The sequence is so distinctly a farewell to London that the reader who chooses to regard this as an exclusively American edition may as well omit it."
3. Carthaginian poet (3rd century). The Latin, from his *Eclogues* (4.38), reads "The heat calls us into the shade."
4. Adaptation of the title of an ode by Pierre de Ronsard (1524–1585), "On the Selection of His Tomb" (*Odes* 4.5).
5. One of the seven champions who attack Thebes in Aeschylus's tragedy *The Seven Against Thebes* (476 B.C.E.) and who is struck down by Zeus.
6. For we know all the toils [endured] in wide Troy (Greek). In Homer's *Odyssey* (12.189) part of the sirens' song to detain Odysseus. Odysseus stopped his comrades' ears with wax to prevent their succumbing to the lure.
7. Gustave Flaubert (1821–1880), French novelist who cultivated form and stylistic precision. Penelope was Odysseus's wife; she remained faithful during his long absence, despite appeals from many suitors.
8. Sorceress with whom Odysseus lived for a year before returning home.
9. The thirty-first year of his age (Old French); adapted from *The Testament* by the 15th-century French poet François Villon.

II

The age demanded an image
Of its accelerated grimace,
Something for the modern stage,
Not, at any rate, an Attic grace;

Not, not certainly, the obscure reveries
Of the inward gaze;
Better mendacities
Than the classics in paraphrase!

The "age demanded" chiefly a mould in plaster,
Made with no loss of time,
A prose kinema,[1] not, not assuredly, alabaster
Or the "sculpture" of rhyme.

III

The tea-rose tea-gown, etc.
Supplants the mousseline of Cos,[2]
The pianola "replaces"
Sappho's barbitos.[3]

Christ follows Dionysus,[4]
Phallic and ambrosial
Made way for macerations[5]
Caliban casts out Ariel.[6]

All things are a flowing,
Sage Heracleitus[7] says;
But a tawdry cheapness
Shall outlast our days.

Even the Christian beauty
Defects—after Samothrace;[8]
We see τὸ καλὸν[9]
Decreed in the market place.

Faun's flesh is not to us,
Nor the saint's vision.
We have the press for wafer;
Franchise for circumcision.

1. Movement (Greek) and early spelling of *cinema,* "motion pictures."
2. Gauzelike fabric for which the Aegean island Cos was famous.
3. Lyrelike instrument used by the Greek poet Sappho (fl. 600 B.C.E.).
4. Greek god of fertility, regenerative suffering, wine, and poetic inspiration; his rites were characterized by frenzies and ecstasies.
5. Wasting, fasting. Pound contrasts Christian asceticism to Dionysian rites.
6. Characters in Shakespeare's *Tempest;* Caliban is earthbound and Ariel is a spirit of air.
7. Greek philosopher (fl. 500 B.C.E.) who taught that all reality is flux or "a flowing."
8. North Aegean island, center of religious mystery cults.
9. The beautiful (Greek).

All men, in law, are equals.
Free of Pisistratus,[1]
We choose a knave or an eunuch
To rule over us.

O bright Apollo,
τίν' ἄνδρα, τίν' ἥρωα, τινα θεόν,[2]
What god, man, or hero
Shall I place a tin wreath upon!

IV

These fought in any case,
and some believing,
pro domo,[3] in any case . . .

Some quick to arm,
some for adventure,
some from fear of weakness,
some from fear of censure,
some for love of slaughter, in imagination,
learning later . . .
some in fear, learning love of slaughter;

Died some, pro patria,
non "dulce" non "et decor"[4] . . .
walked eye-deep in hell
believing in old men's lies, then unbelieving
came home, home to a lie,
home to many deceits,
home to old lies and new infamy;
usury age-old and age-thick
and liars in public places.

Daring as never before, wastage as never before.
Young blood and high blood,
fair cheeks, and fine bodies;

fortitude as never before

frankness as never before,
disillusions as never told in the old days,
hysterias, trench confessions,
laughter out of dead bellies.

1. Athenian tyrant and art patron (fl. 6th century B.C.E.).
2. What man, what hero, what god (Greek). Pound's version of Pindar's "What god, what hero, what man shall we loudly praise" (*Olympian Odes* 2.2).
3. For the home (Latin).
4. For one's native land, not sweetly, not gloriously (Latin). Adapted from Horace, "it is sweet and glorious to die for one's fatherland" (*Odes* 3.2.13).

V

There died a myriad,
And of the best, among them,
For an old bitch gone in the teeth,
For a botched civilization,

Charm, smiling at the good mouth,
Quick eyes gone under earth's lid,

For two gross of broken statues,
For a few thousand battered books.

Yeux Glauques[5]

Gladstone[6] was still respected,
When John Ruskin produced
"King's Treasuries"; Swinburne
And Rossetti still abused.

Fœtid Buchanan lifted up his voice
When that faun's head of hers
Became a pastime for
Painters and adulterers.

The Burne-Jones cartoons[7]
Have preserved her eyes;
Still, at the Tate, they teach
Cophetua to rhapsodize;

Thin like brook-water,
With a vacant gaze.
The English Rubaiyat was still-born[8]
In those days.

The thin, clear gaze, the same
Still darts out faun-like from the half-ruin'd face,
Questing and passive . . .
"Ah, poor Jenny's[9] case" . . .

5. The brilliant yellow-green eyes of Elizabeth Siddal, the favorite model of the Pre-Raphaelite painters and later the wife of the painter and poet Dante Gabriel Rossetti (1828–1882). She was the model for the beggar maid in *Cophetua and the Beggar Maid* (now hanging in the Tate Gallery, London), by Sir Edward Burne-Jones (1833–1898).
6. William E. Gladstone (1809–1898) was four times prime minister of Britain.
7. Drawings. The Pre-Raphaelites, including the poet Algernon Swinburne (1837–1909), were attacked as "The Fleshly School of Poetry" by Robert W. Buchanan (1841–1901) in 1871 and were defended by the critic John Ruskin (1819–1900), whose *Sesame and Lilies* (1865) contains a chapter titled "Kings' Treasuries," calling for the diffusion of literature and the improvement of English tastes in the arts.
8. Edward FitzGerald (1809–1883) translated *The Rubáiyát of Omar Khayyám* in 1859, but it was not read ("still-born") until discovered later by the Pre-Raphaelites.
9. Prostitute, heroine of a poem by Rossetti.

Bewildered that a world
Shows no surprise
At her last maquero's[1]
Adulteries.

"Siena mi fe'; Disfecemi Maremma"[2]

Among the pickled fœtuses and bottled bones,
Engaged in perfecting the catalogue,
I found the last scion of the
Senatorial families of Strasbourg, Monsieur Verog.[3]

For two hours he talked of Gallifet;[4]
Of Dowson; of the Rhymers' Club;
Told me how Johnson (Lionel)[5] died
By falling from a high stool in a pub . . .

But showed no trace of alcohol
At the autopsy, privately performed—
Tissue preserved—the pure mind
Arose toward Newman[6] as the whiskey warmed.

Dowson found harlots cheaper than hotels;
Headlam for uplift; Image[7] impartially imbued
With raptures for Bacchus, Terpsichore[8] and the Church
So spoke the author of "The Dorian Mood,"

M. Verog, out of step with the decade,
Detached from his contemporaries,
Neglected by the young,
Because of these reveries.

Brennbaum

The sky-like limpid eyes,
The circular infant's face,
The stiffness from spats to collar
Never relaxing into grace;

1. Pimp's.
2. Siena made me, Maremma unmade me (Medieval Italian); spoken by a Sienese woman, condemned by her husband to die in Maremma marshes for her infidelity, in Dante's *Purgatory* (5.134).
3. Victor Plarr (1863–1929), French poet ("In the Dorian Mood," 1896) and raconteur from Strasbourg, later librarian of the Royal College of Surgeons and member of the Rhymers' Club.
4. Marquis de Galliffet (1830–1909), French general at the battle of Sedan, which the French lost, in the Franco-Prussian War.
5. Two members of the Rhymers' Club were Roman Catholic poets and heavy drinkers. Ernest Dowson (1867–1900), of whom Plarr published a memoir. Lionel Johnson (1867–1902), whose *Poetical Works* Pound edited in 1915.
6. John Henry Newman (1801–1890), editor and Roman Catholic convert and intellectual, later cardinal.
7. Two more members of the Rhymers' Club. The Reverend Stewart D. Headlam (1847–1924), forced to resign his curacy for lecturing on the dance to workers' clubs. Selwyn Image (1849–1930), founder with Headlam of the Church and Stage Guild.
8. Greek Muse of the dance.

The heavy memories of Horeb, Sinai and the forty years,[9]
Showed only when the daylight fell
Level across the face
Of Brennbaum "The Impeccable."

Mr. Nixon

In the cream gilded cabin of his steam yacht
Mr. Nixon advised me kindly, to advance with fewer
Dangers of delay. "Consider
"Carefully the reviewer.

"I was as poor as you are;
"When I began I got, of course,
"Advance on royalties, fifty at first," said Mr. Nixon,
"Follow me, and take a column,
"Even if you have to work free.

"Butter reviewers. From fifty to three hundred
"I rose in eighteen months;
"The hardest nut I had to crack
"Was Dr. Dundas.

"I never mentioned a man but with the view
"Of selling my own works.
"The tip's a good one, as for literature
"It gives no man a sinecure.

"And no one knows, at sight, a masterpiece.
"And give up verse, my boy,
"There's nothing in it."

. . . .

Likewise a friend of Blougram's once advised me:[1]
Don't kick against the pricks,
Accept opinion. The "Nineties"[2] tried your game
And died, there's nothing in it.

X

Beneath the sagging roof
The stylist has taken shelter,
Unpaid, uncelebrated,
At last from the world's welter

9. The Israelites wandered in the wilderness for forty years. Moses saw the burning bush at Horeb (Exodus 3.2); he received the Ten Commandments at Sinai (Exodus 19.20ff.).

1. In Robert Browning's "Bishop Blougram's Apology," the bishop rationalized doctrinal laxity.
2. The 1890s.

Nature receives him;
With a placid and uneducated mistress
He exercises his talents
And the soil meets his distress.

The haven from sophistications and contentions
Leaks through its thatch;
He offers succulent cooking;
The door has a creaking latch.

XI

"Conservatrix of Milésien"[3]
Habits of mind and feeling,
Possibly. But in Ealing[4]
With the most bank-clerky of Englishmen?

No, "Milésian" is an exaggeration.
No instinct has survived in her
Older than those her grandmother
Told her would fit her station.

XII

"Daphne with her thighs in bark
Stretches toward me her leafy hands,"[5]
Subjectively. In the stuffed-satin drawing-room
I await The Lady Valentine's commands,

Knowing my coat has never been
Of precisely the fashion
To stimulate, in her,
A durable passion;

Doubtful, somewhat, of the value
Of well-gowned approbation
Of literary effort,
But never of The Lady Valentine's vocation:

Poetry, her border of ideas,
The edge, uncertain, but a means of blending
With other strata
Where the lower and higher have ending;

A hook to catch the Lady Jane's attention,
A modulation toward the theatre,

3. I.e., conservator of the erotic, for which the Ionian city of Miletus and Aristides's *Milesian Tales* (2nd century B.C.E.) were known.
4. London suburb.
5. In Greek mythology, the nymph Daphne changed into a laurel tree to escape Apollo. Pound's lines are a translation of Théophile Gautier's version of Ovid's story in *Le Château de Souvenir*.

Also, in the case of revolution,
A possible friend and comforter.

. . . .

Conduct, on the other hand, the soul
"Which the highest cultures have nourished"[6]
To Fleet St. where
Dr. Johnson[7] flourished;

Beside this thoroughfare
The sale of half-hose has
Long since superseded the cultivation
Of Pierian roses.[8]

Envoi (1919)[9]

Go, dumb-born book,
Tell her that sang me once that song of Lawes:
Hadst thou but song
As thou hast subjects known,
Then were there cause in thee that should condone
Even my faults that heavy upon me lie,
And build her glories their longevity.

Tell her that sheds
Such treasure in the air,
Recking naught else but that her graces give
Life to the moment,
I would bid them live
As roses might, in magic amber laid,
Red overwrought with orange and all made
One substance and one colour
Braving time.

Tell her that goes
With song upon her lips
But sings not out the song, nor knows
The maker of it, some other mouth,
May be as fair as hers,
Might, in new ages, gain her worshippers,
When our two dusts with Waller's shall be laid,
Siftings on siftings in oblivion,
Till change hath broken down
All things save Beauty alone.

1920

6. A translation of two lines from "Complainte de Pianos" by French poet Jules Laforgue (1860–1887).
7. Samuel Johnson (1709–1784), man of letters in mid-18th-century London. "Fleet St.": newspaper publishing center in London.
8. Roses of Pieria, place near Mount Olympus in Greece, where the Muses were worshiped.
9. This section of the poem is modeled on "Go, Lovely Rose" by Edmund Waller (1606–1687), whose poems were set to music by Henry Lawes (1596–1662).

From The Cantos

I[1]

And then went down to the ship,
Set keel to breakers, forth on the godly sea, and
We set up mast and sail on that swart ship,
Bore sheep aboard her, and our bodies also
Heavy with weeping, and winds from sternward
Bore us out onward with bellying canvas,
Circe's[2] this craft, the trim-coifed goddess.
Then sat we amidships, wind jamming the tiller,
Thus with stretched sail, we went over sea till day's end.
Sun to his slumber, shadows o'er all the ocean,
Came we then to the bounds of deepest water,
To the Kimmerian[3] lands, and peopled cities
Covered with close-webbed mist, unpierced ever
With glitter of sun-rays
Nor with stars stretched, nor looking back from heaven
Swartest night stretched over wretched men there
The ocean flowing backward, came we then to the place
Aforesaid by Circe.
Here did they rites, Perimedes and Eurylochus,[4]
And drawing sword from my hip
I dug the ell-square pitkin;[5]
Poured we libations unto each the dead,
First mead then sweet wine, water mixed with white flour.
Then prayed I many a prayer to the sickly death's-heads;
As set in Ithaca, sterile bulls of the best
For sacrifice, heaping the pyre with goods,
A sheep to Tiresias only, black and a bell-sheep.[6]
Dark blood flowed in the fosse,[7]
Souls out of Erebus,[8] cadaverous dead, of brides
Of youths and of the old who had borne much;
Souls stained with recent tears, girls tender,
Men many, mauled with bronze lance heads,
Battle spoil, bearing yet dreory[9] arms,
These many crowded about me; with shouting,
Pallor upon me, cried to my men for more beasts;
Slaughtered the herds, sheep slain of bronze;
Poured ointment, cried to the gods,

1. Lines 1–68 are an adaptation of book 11 of Homer's *Odyssey,* which recounts Odysseus's voyage to Hades, the underworld of the dead. Odysseus was a native of Ithaca, in Greece.
2. Odysseus lived for a year with Circe before he determined to return to Ithaca. She instructed him to get directions for his trip home by visiting the Theban prophet Tiresias in the underworld.
3. Mythical people living in a foggy region at the edge of the earth.
4. Two of Odysseus's companions.
5. Small pit, one ell (forty-five inches) on each side.
6. The prophet Tiresias is likened to a sheep that leads the herd.
7. Ditch, trench.
8. Land of the dead, Hades.
9. Bloody.

To Pluto the strong, and praised Proserpine;[1]
Unsheathed the narrow sword,
I sat to keep off the impetuous impotent dead,
Till I should hear Tiresias.
But first Elpenor[2] came, our friend Elpenor,
Unburied, cast on the wide earth,
Limbs that we left in the house of Circe,
Unwept, unwrapped in sepulchre, since toils urged other.
Pitiful spirit. And I cried in hurried speech:
"Elpenor, how art thou come to this dark coast?
"Cam'st thou afoot, outstripping seamen?"
          And he in heavy speech:
"Ill fate and abundant wine. I slept in Circe's ingle.[3]
"Going down the long ladder unguarded,
"I fell against the buttress,
"Shattered the nape-nerve, the soul sought Avernus.[4]
"But thou, O King, I bid remember me, unwept, unburied,
"Heap up mine arms, be tomb by sea-bord, and inscribed:
"*A man of no fortune, and with a name to come.*
"And set my oar up, that I swung mid fellows."

And Anticlea[5] came, whom I beat off, and then Tiresias Theban,
Holding his golden wand, knew me, and spoke first:
"A second time?[6] why? man of ill star,
"Facing the sunless dead and this joyless region?
"Stand from the fosse, leave me my bloody bever[7]
"For soothsay."
          And I stepped back,
And he strong with the blood, said then: "Odysseus
"Shalt return through spiteful Neptune,[8] over dark seas,
"Lose all companions." And then Anticlea came.
Lie quiet Divus. I mean, that is Andreas Divus,
In officina Wecheli, 1538, out of Homer.[9]
And he sailed, by Sirens and thence outward and away
And unto Circe.
          Venerandam,[1]
In the Cretan's phrase, with the golden crown, Aphrodite,
Cypri munimenta sortita est,[2] mirthful, orichalchi,[3] with golden

1. Goddess of regeneration and wife of Pluto, god of the underworld.
2. Odysseus's companion who fell to his death from the roof of Circe's house and was left unburied by his friends.
3. Corner, house.
4. Lake near Naples, the entrance to Hades.
5. Odysseus's mother. In the *Odyssey,* Odysseus weeps at the sight of her but obeys Circe's instructions to speak to no one until Tiresias has first drunk the libation of blood that will enable him to speak.
6. They met once before on earth.
7. Libation.
8. God of the sea, who was to delay Odysseus's return by a storm at sea.
9. Pound acknowledges using the Renaissance Latin translation of Homer, produced in the workshop ("officina") of Wechel in Paris in 1538, by Andreas Divus.
1. Commanding reverence; a phrase describing Aphrodite, the goddess of love, in the Latin translation of the second Homeric Hymn by Georgius Dartona Cretensis (the "Cretan" in line 73).
2. The fortresses of Cyprus were her appointed realm (Latin).
3. Of copper (Latin); a reference to gifts presented to Aphrodite in the second Homeric Hymn.

Girdles and breast bands, thou with dark eyelids
Bearing the golden bough of Argicida.[4] So that:

1925

XVII[1]

So that the vines burst from my fingers
And the bees weighted with pollen
More heavily in the vine-shoots:
    chirr—chirr—chir-rikk—a purring sound,
And the birds sleepily in the branches.
    ZAGREUS! IO ZAGREUS.[2]
With the first pale-clear of the heaven
And the cities set in their hills,
And the goddess of the fair knees[3]
Moving there, with the oak-woods behind her,
The green slope, with white hounds
            leaping about her;
And thence down to the creek's mouth, until evening,
Flat water before me,
        and the trees growing in water,
Marble trunks out of stillness,[4]
On past the palazzi,
                in the stillness,
The light now, not of the sun.
                    Chrysophrase,[5]
And the water green clear, and blue clear;
On, to the great cliffs of amber.
                        Between them,
Cave of Nerea,[6]
    she like a great shell curved,
And the boat drawn without sound,

4. Aeneas offered the Golden Bough to Proserpine before descending to the underworld. Pound associates Persephone with Aphrodite, goddess of love and slayer of the Greeks (Argi) during the Trojan War, and associates the Golden Bough, sacred to the goddess Diana, with the magic wand of the god Hermes, slayer of the many-eyed Argus ("Argicida") and liberator of Io.

1. This canto represents Pound's treatment of ancient myth and Renaissance history. Three sequences figure in this canto: Ulysses's (Odysseus's) voyage through the Mediterranean in search of home in Ithaca, Jason's voyage to the islands of Colchis in search of the Golden Fleece, and a ship's entrance into Venice. Among the personae that Pound assumes, besides Ulysses and Jason, are Dionysus (Zagreus), the Greek god of wine, rebirth, and ecstasy; Actaeon, who saw the goddess Diana bathing and was punished by being turned into a stag that was torn apart by his hounds; and Hades (Pluto), god of the underworld, who loved Koré (Persephone, goddess of regeneration) and who kidnaped her from a meadow but was later forced to allow her to return to earth for several months each year.

2. Zagreus! I am Zagreus. (Greek). A sacrificial god often identified in a Greek myth with Dionysus, Zagreus was the offspring of Persephone (Koré) and Zeus; Zeus raped her before she was kidnaped by Hades.

3. Diana, goddess of the hunt.

4. The first glimpse of Venice. The marble façades and columns of its *palazzi* (palaces) are presented in accordance with the theories of the landscape painter and art critic Adrian Stokes (1854–1935), a friend of Pound's. Stokes (*The Stones of Rimini,* 1934) stressed the affinity of Venetian arts with the salt sea and the origin of marble from sunken forests and watery limestone: "Amid the sea Venice is built from the essence of the sea."

5. Green semiprecious stone.

6. Possibly the nymph Calypso, the temptress and death goddess who detained Ulysses for seven years in her island cave.

Without odour of ship-work,
Nor bird-cry, nor any noise of wave moving,
Nor splash of porpoise, nor any noise of wave moving,
Within her cave, Nerea,
                    she like a great shell curved
In the suavity of the rock,
                         cliff green-gray in the far,
In the near, the gate-cliffs of amber,
And the wave
                    green clear, and blue clear,
And the cave salt-white, and glare-purple,
            cool, porphyry smooth,
            the rock sea-worn.
No gull-cry, no sound of porpoise,
Sand as of malachite,[7] and no cold there,
        the light not of the sun.

Zagreus, feeding his panthers,
        the turf clear as on hills under light.
And under the almond-trees, gods,
        with them, *choros nympharum.*[8] Gods,
Hermes and Athene,[9]
                As shaft of compass,
Between them, trembled—
To the left is the place of fauns,
                sylva nympharum;[1]
The low wood, moor-scrub,
      the doe, the young spotted deer,
      leap up through the broom-plants,
                as dry leaf amid yellow.
And by one cut of the hills,
      the great alley of Memnons.[2]
Beyond, sea, crests seen over dune
Night sea churning shingle,
To the left, the alley of cypress.
                         A boat came,
One man holding her sail,
Guiding her with oar caught over gunwale, saying:
"   There, in the forest of marble,
"   the stone trees—out of water—
"   the arbours of stone—
"   marble leaf, over leaf,
"   silver, steel over steel,
"   silver beaks rising and crossing,
"   prow set against prow,

7. Green mineral.
8. Chorus of nymphs (Greek).
9. Ulysses's protectors. Hermes (messenger of the gods, patron of merchants and thieves) freed Ulysses from the bonds of Calypso. Athene (goddess of wisdom) calmed the waves for his final voyage home to Ithaca (*Odyssey* 5).
1. Forest of the nymphs (Greek).
2. Commander of Ethiopian troops in the defense of Troy, he was called "son of dawn." His statue near Thebes, here likened to a row of cypress trees, reputedly issued a musical sound at daybreak.

"   stone, ply over ply,
"   the gilt beams flare of an evening"
Borso, Carmagnola, the men of craft, *i vitrei*,[3]
Thither, at one time, time after time,
And the waters richer than glass,
Bronze gold, the blaze over the silver,
Dye-pots in the torch-light,
The flash of wave under prows,
And the silver beaks rising and crossing.
          Stone trees, white and rose-white in the darkness,
Cypress there by the towers,
          Drift under hulls in the night.

          "In the gloom the gold
Gathers the light about it."[4] . . .

Now supine in burrow, half over-arched bramble,
One eye for the sea, through that peek-hole,
Gray light, with Athene.
Zothar and her elephants, the gold loin-cloth,
The sistrum,[5] shaken, shaken,
          the cohorts of her dancers.
And Aletha,[6] by bend of the shore,
          with her eyes seaward,
     and in her hands sea-wrack
Salt-bright with the foam.
Koré through the break meadow,
          with green-gray dust in the grass:
"For this hour, brother of Circe."[7]
Arm laid over my shoulder,
Saw the sun for three days, the sun fulvid,
As a lion lift over sand-plain;
                    and that day,
And for three days, and none after,
Splendour, as the splendour of Hermes,
And shipped thence
                    to the stone place,
Pale white, over water,
                    known water,
And the white forest of marble, bent bough over bough,
The pleached arbour of stone,
Thither Borso, when they shot the barbed arrow at him,
And Carmagnola, between the two columns,

3. Glassmakers, for whom Venice is famous. Borse d'Este (1431–1471) of Ferrara, patron of learning whose assassination was attempted in Venice. Francesco Bussone da Carmagnola (1390?–1432), mercenary soldier, tried and executed for treason in Venice.
4. Quoted from an earlier canto (XI) where "about" reads "against."
5. An Egyptian metal rattle.
6. Zothar (line 88) and Aletha are probably invented names.
7. I.e., Aetes, king of Colchis, who maintained a cult of the sun (his father) on his island, and held possession of the Golden Fleece sought by Jason. Circe was the enchantress who detained Ulysses for a year, then instructed him to consult Tiresias in the underworld to learn his route home and told him how to enter the world of the dead through the Grove of Persephone.

Sigismundo,[8] after that wreck in Dalmatia.
Sunset like the grasshopper flying.

1933

XLV

With *Usura*[1]

With usura hath no man a house of good stone
each block cut smooth and well fitting
that design might cover their face,
with usura
hath no man a painted paradise on his church wall
harpes et luz[2]
or where virgin receiveth message
and halo projects from incision,[3]
with usura
seeth no man Gonzaga[4] his heirs and his concubines
no picture is made to endure nor to live with
but it is made to sell and sell quickly
with usura, sin against nature,
is thy bread ever more of stale rags
is thy bread dry as paper,
with no mountain wheat, no strong flour
with usura the line grows thick
with usura is no clear demarcation
and no man can find site for his dwelling.
Stonecutter is kept from his stone
weaver is kept from his loom
WITH USURA
wool comes not to market
sheep bringeth no gain with usura
Usura is a murrain,[5] usura
blunteth the needle in the maid's hand
and stoppeth the spinner's cunning. Pietro Lombardo[6]
came not by usura
Duccio came not by usura
nor Pier della Francesca; Zuan Bellin'[7] not by usura

8. Sigismondo Malatesta (1417–1468), Renaissance ruler of Rimini whom Pound admired. An art patron, antipapist, and builder of the Tempio Malatestiana in Rimini, he fought for Venice and other cities and in 1464 reached the Dalmatian coast in an unsuccessful crusade.
1. Usury, or lending money at interest (Latin). Pound interpreted this practice as the root of all corruption in the modern world, the cause of the separation of the worker—whether farmer, laborer, or artist—from the work.
2. Harps and lutes (Latin). In medieval and Renaissance depictions of Paradise, the angels are shown playing on such instruments.
3. Description of scenes in religious paintings, especially the Annunciation, in which the Virgin Mary is informed that she is to be the mother of Christ.
4. Luigi Gonzaga (1267–1360), prince of Mantua and founder of a dynasty that ruled that Italian city until the 18th century.
5. A plague (archaic).
6. Italian sculptor (1435–1515).
7. Duccio di Buoninsegna (1260?–1318?), Piero della Francesca (1420?–1492), and Giovanni Bellini (1430?–1516) were Italian painters from Florence and nearby towns.

nor was 'La Calumnia'[8] painted.
Came not by usura Angelico; came not Ambrogio Praedis,[9]
Came no church of cut stone signed: *Adamo me fecit.*[1]
Not by usura St Trophime
Not by usura Saint Hilaire,[2]
Usura rusteth the chisel
It rusteth the craft and the craftsman
It gnaweth the thread in the loom
None learneth to weave gold in her pattern;
Azure hath a canker by usura; cramoisi[3] is unbroidered
Emerald findeth no Memling[4]
Usura slayeth the child in the womb
It stayeth the young man's courting
It hath brought palsey to bed, lyeth
between the young bride and her bridegroom
CONTRA NATURAM[5]
They have brought whores for Eleusis[6]
Corpses are set to banquet
at behest of usura.

N.B. Usury: A charge for the use of purchasing power, levied without regard to production; often without regard to the possibilities of production. (Hence the failure of the Medici bank.[7])

1937

8. Rumor (Italian); allegorical painting by Sandro Botticelli (1445–1510), one of the greatest of the Italian Renaissance painters.
9. Fra Angelico (1387?–1455) and Praedis (1455?–1506) were Italian painters.
1. Adam made me (Latin); words carved into the church of San Zeno Maggiore in Verona, Italy. To Pound, a symbol of the architect's pride in and feeling of connection with his work.
2. Medieval churches in the French cities of Arles and Poitiers, respectively.
3. Heavy crimson cloth (French).
4. Hans Memling (1430?–1495), Flemish painter.
5. Against nature (Latin).
6. City in ancient Greece, northwest of Athens, where secret religious rites in honor of Demeter and Persephone, the goddess of fertility and her daughter, were celebrated by priestesses every spring. The substitution of whores for priestesses represents the degradation of ancient rituals.
7. A bank operated from 1397 to 1494 by the Medici family of Florence; it anticipated modern banking techniques.

Modernist Manifestos

As an artistic movement, or set of movements, given to asserting its breaks with past traditions, modernism in the early twentieth century often proclaimed itself in the writing of manifestos. The modernist manifesto is a public declaration of artistic convictions, relatively brief, often highly stylized or epigrammatic in the mode of other forms of modernist writing, and almost always an aggressively self-conscious declaration of artistic independence.

The word *manifesto,* derived from Latin and meaning "to make public," first entered English usage in the seventeenth century to describe printed declarations of belief and advocacy. Early manifestos tended to be weapons forged by dissenting groups in religious and political struggles, a tradition that continued into the nineteenth century with perhaps the most famous political manifesto of the era, Karl Marx's *Communist Manifesto* (1848). In the nineteenth century, artistic groups also began to issue manifestos. The preface to the second edition of *Lyrical Ballads* (1800) by the poets William Wordsworth and Samuel Taylor Coleridge, for example, defended their "experiment" with a new kind of poetry; in the United States, Ralph Waldo Emerson's *Nature* (1836), the founding document of American transcendentalism, called for spiritual and artistic renewal; inspired partly by Emerson's example, Margaret Fuller's "The Great Lawsuit: MAN *versus* MEN. WOMAN *versus* WOMEN" (1843) linked women's pursuit of political rights to their pursuit of artistic expression and intellectual independence. In late-nineteenth-century Paris, the "Symbolist Manifesto" (1886), by the poet Jean Moréas, turned the genre of the manifesto in some of its characteristically high modernist directions. Attacking not so much oppressive social conditions as oppressive conceptions of literature, the symbolists declared their hostility to realism's "plain meanings, declamations, false sentimentality and matter-of-fact description" in order to claim for poetry a freer, less moralizing play of verbal imagination.

The writers of manifestos did not have one particular audience in mind; it was enough for them to get their positions into the public realm. But manifestos also worked to bring like-minded people together; a poet might publish a manifesto in a journal of poetry, a political radical in a radical journal, and so on. In the modernist period, manifestos increasingly reached an international community of self-consciously avant-garde, cosmopolitan artists. The Italian writer F. T. Marinetti published his "Manifesto of Futurism" in French; Ezra Pound's "A Retrospect" ranged freely over his contemporaries in British and American modernist poetry as well as over Pound's admired writers of the past in several languages—Dante, Goethe, Shakespeare; Willa Cather similarly juxtaposed American fiction with French, Russian, and British works in "The Novel Démeublé."

Hostility is often a rhetorical tool of the manifesto, and it was especially so in the modernist period. Modernist manifestos often tried to grab their audiences by the lapels, to separate not only the new from the old but also a creative *us* from a "vulgar" or hidebound *them.* The us–them divide was intended to offend traditionalists as well as to unite the believers in new artistic movements, and it often succeeded in both aims. Marinetti's "Manifesto of Futurism" set the tone in 1909 by declaring that "No work without an aggressive character can be a masterpiece" and exalting "scorn for women" along with modern technology. By 1918, Ezra Pound in "A Retrospect" could manage to insult in one sentence both traditional poetic forms and would-be imitators of his own free verse: "The actual language and phrasing" of the new poetry, Pound complained, "is often as bad as that of our elders without even the excuse that the words are shoveled in to fill a metric pattern or to complete the noise of a rhyme-sound." The modernist boundary between *us* and *them,* Pound's "Retrospect" implies, will always be in motion, always pushing forward and leaving someone behind.

At the same time, however, the very aggression of some high modernist manifestos encouraged some members of their audience to talk back with equal vigor. Marinetti denounced advocates of women's suffrage but recognized a counterpart to his own aggressive tactics in London's most radical suffragettes, to the point of joining them on a march that was broken up by mounted police. The Anglo-American poet Mina Loy wrote and privately circulated her "Feminist Manifesto" as an enthusiastic member of Marinetti's circle; his take-no-prisoners example licensed her rhetoric of destruction and demolition, which she aimed not only at the institutions of sexism but also at less confrontational versions of feminism.

Other influential modernist manifestos were more measured in their language or more subtle in their explorations of the relationship between modernist destruction and cultural production. William Carlos Williams's exuberant prose interludes in *Spring and All* asserted, with the aid of language borrowed from evolutionary biology, that modernism's sudden "SPRING" into the new was the explosive culmination of many small, repeated movements in the past. The title metaphor of Willa Cather's "The Novel Démeublé"—the novel "unfurnished"—suggested that modernism might prune the decorative excesses of nineteenth-century realism without abandoning its basic structure. And Langston Hughes, although he railed against "the mountain standing in the way of any true Negro art in America," ultimately envisioned the mountain—the internal and external struggles of black Americans to cast off white denigrations of African American culture—as the foundation of a higher and broader modernist art: "We build our temples for tomorrow, strong as we know how, and we stand on top of the mountain, free within ourselves."

F. T. MARINETTI

Marinetti (1876–1944) published two obscure volumes of poetry in his native Italian before "The Founding and Manifesto of Futurism" appeared in *Le Figaro,* an influential Parisian journal, in February 1909. The futurist manifesto attracted an international circle of artists and writers into Marinetti's orbit, including painters, architects, poets, sculptors, playwrights, and film directors. Across all the arts, futurism scorned traditional standards of artistic beauty, celebrated modern technologies of speed, and aimed to shock audiences: futurist painters adopted the mixed perspectives of cubism to celebrate speeding trains, and futurist theater drew on cabaret, variety shows, and circuses in staging free-form events that violated traditional theater's boundary between actors and audience. Futurism's aesthetic of aggression had unsettling political implications as well: true to his manifesto's declaration that war is "the only hygiene" of the world, Marinetti welcomed the technologically enhanced slaughter of World War I and supported the rise of Mussolini's Italian fascism.

From Manifesto of Futurism

1. We intend to sing the love of danger, the habit of energy and fearlessness.

2. Courage, audacity, and revolt will be essential elements of our poetry.

3. Up to now literature has exalted a pensive immobility, ecstasy, and sleep. We intend to exalt aggressive action, a feverish insomnia, the racer's stride, the mortal leap, the punch and the slap.

4. We say that the world's magnificence has been enriched by a new beauty; the beauty of speed. A racing car whose hood is adorned with great pipes, like serpents of explosive breath—a roaring car that seems to ride on grapeshot—is more beautiful than the *Victory of Samothrace.*[1]

5. We want to hymn the man at the wheel, who hurls the lance of his spirit across the Earth, along the circle of its orbit.

6. The poet must spend himself with ardor, splendor, and generosity, to swell the enthusiastic fervor of the primordial elements.

7. Except in struggle, there is no more beauty. No work without an aggressive character can be a masterpiece. Poetry must be conceived as a violent attack on unknown forces, to reduce and prostrate them before man.

8. We stand on the last promontory of the centuries! . . . Why should we look back, when what we want is to break down the mysterious doors of the Impossible? Time and Space died yesterday. We already live in the absolute, because we have created eternal, omnipresent speed.

9. We will glorify war—the world's only hygiene—militarism, patriotism, the destructive gesture of freedom-bringers, beautiful ideas worth dying for, and scorn for woman.

10. We will destroy the museums, libraries, academies of every kind, will fight moralism, feminism, every opportunistic or utilitarian cowardice.

11. We will sing of great crowds excited by work, by pleasure, and by riot; we will sing of the multicolored, polyphonic tides of revolution in the modern capitals; we will sing of the vibrant nightly fervor of arsenals and shipyards blazing with violent electric moons; greedy railway stations that devour smoke-plumed serpents; factories hung on clouds by the crooked lines of their smoke; bridges that stride the rivers like giant gymnasts, flashing in the sun with a glitter of knives; adventurous steamers that sniff the horizon; deep-chested locomotives whose wheels paw the tracks like the hooves of enormous steel horses bridled by tubing; and the sleek flight of planes whose propellers chatter in the wind like banners and seem to cheer like an enthusiastic crowd.

* * *

1909

1. Famous Greek statue of Nike, the winged goddess of victory, from the 2nd or 3rd century B.C.E.; discovered on the island of Samothrace in 1863, it became an icon of 19th-century high artistic taste.

MINA LOY

"Feminist Manifesto" was written during Loy's association with F. T. Marinetti but never published during her lifetime (1882–1966); it survives in a copy sent to a friend, the writer Mabel Dodge Luhan, in 1914. Loy's central demand is sexual freedom, the end of the divide between "the mistress" and "the mother," and the destruction of women's attachment to ideals of their own purity. Loy's modernist call for women's free sexual expression appeals to elite women's sense of race and class privilege: echoing nineteenth-century alarms that granting women life choices beyond marriage and childbearing would lead to white "race suicide," Loy urges "superior" women to embrace maternity as both a responsibility and an aspect of their own sexual development.

Feminist Manifesto

The feminist movement as at present instituted is
Inadequate

Women if you want to realise yourselves—you are on the eve of a devastating psychological upheaval—all your pet illusions must be unmasked—the lies of centuries have got to go—are you prepared for the **Wrench**—? There is no half-measure—NO scratching on the surface of the rubbish heap of tradition, will bring about **Reform**, the only method is **Absolute Demolition**

Cease to place your confidence in economic legislation, vice-crusades & uniform education[1]—you are glossing over **Reality**.
Professional & commercial careers are opening up for you—
Is that all you want ?

1. Securing women's legal right to own property, gaining access to education for women (especially higher education) on the same terms as men, and suppressing prostitution were all important goals of 19th- and early 20th-century feminist movements.

And if you honestly desire to find your level without prejudice—be <u>**Brave**</u> & deny at the outset—that pathetic clap-trap war cry <u>**Woman**</u> <u>**is**</u> <u>**the**</u> <u>**equal**</u> <u>**of**</u> <u>**man**</u>—

for

She is <u>**NOT!**</u>

The man who lives a life in which his activities conform to a social code which is a protectorate of the feminine element— ——is no longer <u>**masculine**</u>
The women who adapt themselves to a theoretical valuation of their sex as a <u>**relative**</u> <u>**impersonality**</u>, are not yet <u>**Feminine**</u>
Leave off looking to men to find out what you are <u>**not**</u> —seek within yourselves to find out what you <u>**are**</u>
As conditions are at present constituted—you have the choice between <u>**Parasitism**</u>, & <u>**Prostitution**</u> —or Negation

Men & women are enemies, with the enmity of the exploited for the parasite, the parasite for the exploited—at present they are at the mercy of the advantage that each can take of the others sexual dependence—. The only point at which the interests of the sexes merge—is the sexual embrace.

The first illusion it is to your interest to demolish is the division of women into two classes <u>**the**</u> <u>**mistress,**</u> <u>**&**</u> <u>**the**</u> <u>**mother**</u> every well-balanced & developed woman knows that is not true, Nature has endowed the complete woman with a faculty for expressing herself through <u>all</u> her functions—there are <u>**no**</u> <u>**restrictions**</u> the woman who is so incompletely evolved as to be un-self-conscious in sex, will prove a restrictive influence on the temperamental expansion of the next generation; the woman who is a poor mistress will be an incompetent mother—an inferior mentality—& will enjoy an inadequate apprehension of <u>**Life**</u> .

To obtain results you must make sacrifices & the first & greatest sacrifice you have to make is of your "virtue"
The fictitious value of woman as identified with her physical purity—is too easy a stand-by——rendering her lethargic in the acquisition of intrinsic merits of character by which she could obtain a concrete value— therefore, the first self-enforced law for the female sex, as a protection against the man made bogey of virtue—which is the principle instrument of her subjection, would be the unconditional surgical destruction of virginity through-out the female population at puberty—.

The value of man is assessed entirely according to his use or interest to the community, the value of woman, depends entirely on chance, her success or insuccess in manoeuvering a man into taking the life-long responsibility of her—
The advantages of marriage of too ridiculously ample—compared to all other trades—for under modern conditions a woman can accept preposterously luxurious support from a man (with-out return of any sort—even offspring)—as a thank offering for her virginity
The woman who has not succeeded in striking that advantageous bargain—is prohibited from any but surreptitious re-action to Life-stimuli—**& entirely debarred maternity.**
Every woman has a right to maternity—
Every woman of superior intelligence should realize her race-responsibility, in producing children in adequate proportion to the unfit or degenerate members of her sex—

Each child of a superior woman should be the result of a definite period of psychic development in her life—& not necessarily of a possibly irksome & outworn continuance of an alliance—spontaneously adapted for vital creation in the beginning but not necessarily harmoniously balanced as the parties to it—follow their individual lines of personal evolution—

For the harmony of the race, each individual should be the expression of an easy & ample interpenetration of the male & female temperaments—free of stress
Woman must become more responsible for the child than man—
Women must destroy in themselves, the desire to be loved—

The feeling that it is a personal insult when a man transfers his attentions from her to another woman
The desire for comfortable protection instead of an intelligent curiosity & courage in meeting & resisting the pressure of life sex or so called love must be reduced to its initial element, honour, grief, sentimentality, pride & consequently jealousy must be detached from it.
Woman for her happiness must retain her deceptive fragility of appearance, combined with indomitable will, irreducible courage, & abundant health the outcome of sound nerves—
Another great illusion that woman must use all her introspective clear-sightedness & unbiassed bravery to destroy—for the sake of her self respect is the impurity of sex the realisation in defiance of superstition that there is nothing impure in sex—except in the mental attitude to it—will constitute an incalculable & wider social regeneration than it is possible for our generation to imagine.

1914 1982

EZRA POUND

"A Retrospect" summarizes Pound's (1885–1972) early declarations of the principles of Imagism. His famous list of "Don'ts," originally published in 1913, cautioned poets against superfluous words, rigid metrical rhythms, and the use of abstract rhetoric rather than "direct treatment" of poetic subjects. Pound's own poetry by 1918 was taking a turn away from Imagism's characteristic emphasis on representing "an intellectual and emotional complex in an instant of time" and toward longer poems, more engaged with history and the inherited materials of art.

From A Retrospect

There has been so much scribbling about a new fashion in poetry, that I may perhaps be pardoned this brief recapitulation and retrospect.

In the spring or early summer of 1912, "H. D.," Richard Aldington and myself decided[1] that we were agreed upon the three principles following:

1. Direct treatment of the 'thing' whether subjective or objective.
2. To use absolutely no word that does not contribute to the presentation.
3. As regarding rhythm: to compose in the sequence of the musical phrase, not in sequence of a metronome.

Upon many points of taste and of predilection we differed, but agreeing upon these three positions we thought we had as much right to a group name, at least as much right, as a number of French "schools" proclaimed by Mr Flint in the August number of Harold Monro's[2] magazine for 1911.

This school has since been "joined" or "followed" by numerous people who, whatever their merits, do not show any signs of agreeing with the second specification. Indeed *vers libre*[3] has become as prolix and as verbose as any of the flaccid varieties that preceded it. It has brought faults of its own. The actual language and phrasing is often as bad as that of our elders without even the excuse that the words are shovelled in to fill a metric pattern or to complete the noise of a rhyme-sound. Whether or no the phrases followed by the followers are musical must be left to the reader's decision. At times I can find a marked metre in "vers libres," as stale and hackneyed as any pseudo-Swinburnian,[4] at times the writers seem to follow no musical structure whatever. But it is, on the whole, good that the field should be ploughed. Perhaps a few good poems have come from the new method, and if so it is justified.

Criticism is not a circumscription or a set of prohibitions. It provides fixed points of departure. It may startle a dull reader into alertness. That little of it which is good is mostly in stray phrases; or if it be an older artist helping a younger it is in great measure but rules of thumb, cautions gained by experience.

I set together a few phrases on practical working about the time the first remarks on imagisme were published. The first use of the word "Imagiste" was in my note to T.E. Hulme's[5] five poems, printed at the end of my "Ripostes" in the autumn of 1912. I reprint my cautions from *Poetry* for March, 1913.

A FEW DON'TS

An "Image" is that which presents an intellectual and emotional complex in an instant of time. I use the term "complex" rather in the technical sense employed by the newer psychologists, such as Hart,[6] though we might not agree absolutely in our application.

1. H.D. and the British poet Richard Aldington (1892–1962), who married H.D. in 1913, were among the first poets designated "Imagistes" by Pound.
2. Scottish poet and critic Harold Munro founded the *Poetry Review* in 1911. The British poet and translator Frank Stuart Flint (1885–1960) was a friend of Pound's and another Imagist.
3. Free verse (French); poetry without a fixed pattern of rhyme or meter.
4. The British Victorian poet Algernon Swinburne (1837–1909) was famous for using elaborate poetic forms.
5. Thomas Ernest Hulme (1883–1917), British poet and critic who, with Pound, formulated early statements of Imagism.
6. British psychologist Bernard Hart (1879–1960), influenced by the theories of Sigmund Freud, popularized the idea of the "complex" as an "emotional system of ideas."

It is the presentation of such a "complex" instantaneously which gives that sense of sudden liberation; that sense of freedom from time limits and space limits; that sense of sudden growth, which we experience in the presence of the greatest works of art.

It is better to present one Image in a lifetime than to produce voluminous works.

All this, however, some may consider open to debate. The immediate necessity is to tabulate A LIST OF DON'TS for those beginning to write verses. I can not put all of them into Mosaic[7] negative.

To begin with, consider the three propositions (demanding direct treatment, economy of words, and the sequence of the musical phrase), not as dogma—never consider anything as dogma—but as the result of long contemplation, which, even if it is some one else's contemplation, may be worth consideration.

Pay no attention to the criticism of men who have never themselves written a notable work. Consider the discrepancies between the actual writing of the Greek poets and dramatists, and the theories of the Graeco-Roman grammarians, concocted to explain their metres.

LANGUAGE

Use no superfluous word, no adjective which does not reveal something.

Don't use such an expression as "dim lands *of peace*." It dulls the image. It mixes an abstraction with the concrete. It comes from the writer's not realizing that the natural object is always the *adequate* symbol.

Go in fear of abstractions. Do not retell in mediocre verse what has already been done in good prose. Don't think any intelligent person is going to be deceived when you try to shirk all the difficulties of the unspeakably difficult art of good prose by chopping your composition into line lengths.

What the expert is tired of today the public will be tired of tomorrow.

Don't imagine that the art of poetry is any simpler than the art of music, or that you can please the expert before you have spent at least as much effort on the art of verse as the average piano teacher spends on the art of music.

Be influenced by as many great artists as you can, but have the decency either to acknowledge the debt outright, or to try to conceal it.

Don't allow "influence" to mean merely that you mop up the particular decorative vocabulary of some one or two poets whom you happen to admire. A Turkish war correspondent was recently caught red-handed babbling in his despatches of "dove-grey" hills, or else it was "pearl-pale," I can not remember.

Use either no ornament or good ornament.

1918

7. Referring to the "Thou shalt not . . ." formula of the Ten Commandments of Moses (Exodus 20.1–17).

WILLA CATHER

"The Novel Démeublé" strikes many familiar high modernist themes: distrust of mass production, the importance of distinguishing popular entertainment from serious art, and disdain for nineteenth-century realism with its consumerist catalogs of material objects. In this essay, however, Cather (1873–1947) sifts through the nineteenth-century heritage rather than rejecting it wholesale; she finds a precursor for her own ideal of the "unfurnished" modernist novel in Hawthorne's *The Scarlet Letter.*

From The Novel Démeublé

The novel, for a long while, has been over-furnished. The property-man has been so busy on its pages, the importance of material objects and their vivid presentation have been so stressed, that we take it for granted whoever can observe, and can write the English language, can write a novel. Often the latter qualification is considered unnecessary.

In any discussion of the novel, one must make it clear whether one is talking about the novel as a form of amusement, or as a form of art; since they serve very different purposes and in very different ways. One does not wish the egg one eats for breakfast, or the morning paper, to be made of the stuff of immortality. The novel manufactured to entertain great multitudes of people must be considered exactly like a cheap soap or a cheap perfume, or cheap furniture. Fine quality is a distinct disadvantage in articles made for great numbers of people who do not want quality but quantity, who do not want a thing that "wears," but who want change,—a succession of new things that are quickly thread-bare and can be lightly thrown away. Does anyone pretend that if the Woolworth store windows were piled high with Tanagra figurines at ten cents, they could for a moment compete with Kewpie brides[1] in the popular esteem? Amusement is one thing; enjoyment of art is another.

* * *

There is a popular superstition that "realism" asserts itself in the cataloguing of a great number of material objects, in explaining mechanical processes, the methods of operating manufactories and trades, and in minutely and unsparingly describing physical sensations. But is not realism, more than it is anything else, an attitude of mind on the part of the writer toward his material, a vague indication of the sympathy and candour with which he accepts, rather than chooses, his theme? Is the story of a

1. Kewpie dolls, enormously popular from their introduction in the 1910s, were manufactured in ceramic and, later, plastic. Named for their resemblance to images of Cupid, they were often distributed in bride and groom sets. "Woolworth's": American chain store founded in the late 19th century and noted for inexpensive merchandise. "Tanagra figurines": miniature terra-cotta statues, usually of fashionably dressed women, mass produced in Greece at the end of the 4th century B.C.E.

banker who is unfaithful to his wife and who ruins himself by speculation in trying to gratify the caprices of his mistresses, at all reinforced by a masterly exposition of banking, our whole system of credits, the methods of the Stock Exchange? Of course, if the story is thin, these things do reinforce it in a sense,—any amount of red meat thrown into the scale to make the beam dip. But are the banking system and the Stock Exchange worth being written about at all? Have such things any proper place in imaginative art?

* * *

If the novel is a form of imaginative art, it cannot be at the same time a vivid and brilliant form of journalism. Out of the teeming, gleaming stream of the present it must select the eternal material of art. There are hopeful signs that some of the younger writers are trying to break away from mere verisimilitude, and, following the development of modern painting, to interpret imaginatively the material and social investiture of their characters; to present their scene by suggestion rather than by enumeration. The higher processes of art are all processes of simplification. The novelist must learn to write, and then he must unlearn it; just as the modern painter learns to draw, and then learns when utterly to disregard his accomplishment, when to subordinate it to a higher and truer effect. In this direction only, it seems to me, can the novel develop into anything more varied and perfect than all the many novels that have gone before.

One of the very earliest American romances might well serve as a suggestion to later writers. In *The Scarlet Letter* how truly in the spirit of art is the mise-en-scène[2] presented. That drudge, the theme-writing high-school student, could scarcely be sent there for information regarding the manners and dress and interiors of Puritan society. The material investiture of the story is presented as if unconsciously; by the reserved, fastidious hand of an artist, not by the gaudy fingers of a showman or the mechanical industry of a department-store window-dresser. As I remember it, in the twilight melancholy of that book, in its consistent mood, one can scarcely ever see the actual surroundings of the people; one feels them, rather, in the dusk.

Whatever is felt upon the page without being specifically named there—that, one might say, is created. It is the inexplicable presence of the thing not named, of the overtone divined by the ear but not heard by it, the verbal mood, the emotional aura of the fact or the thing or the deed, that gives high quality to the novel or the drama, as well as to poetry itself.

* * *

How wonderful it would be if we could throw all the furniture out of the window; and along with it, all the meaningless reiterations concerning physical sensations, all the tiresome old patterns, and leave the room as bare as the stage of a Greek theatre, or as that house into which the glory of Pentecost[3] descended; leave the scene bare for the play of emotions, great and little—for the nursery tale, no less than the tragedy, is killed by tasteless

2. Stage setting (French). *The Scarlet Letter* (1850), by American novelist Nathaniel Hawthorne (1804–1864).
3. Christian festival marking the descent of the Holy Spirit to Christ's disciples after his death and resurrection (Acts 2.1–4); often painted as described in the Bible, with the disciples at a table in a closed room.

amplitude. The elder Dumas[4] enunciated a great principle when he said that to make a drama, a man needed one passion, and four walls.

1922

4. Alexandre Dumas (1802–1870), popular French novelist, author of *The Three Musketeers* (1844).

WILLIAM CARLOS WILLIAMS

Williams's 1923 *Spring and All* interspersed untitled short poems (many of them, like "Spring and All" and "The Red Wheelbarrow," now familiar to readers as free-standing lyrics) with sections of manifesto-style prose. *Spring and All* dramatizes repeatedly what Williams (1883–1963) calls "the leap from prose to the process of imagination," charting the rhythmic ebb and flow of imagination's force. Although the poems in *Spring and All* are numbered consecutively, the headings of the prose interludes frequently, as here, play with typographical conventions of numbering.

From Spring and All

CHAPTER VI

Now, in the imagination, all flesh, all human flesh has been dead upon the earth for ten million, billion years. The bird has turned into a stone within whose heart an egg, unlaid, remained hidden.

It is spring! but miracle of miracles a miraculous miracle has gradually taken place during these seemingly wasted eons. Through the orderly sequences of unmentionable time EVOLUTION HAS REPEATED ITSELF FROM THE BEGINNING.

Good God!

Every step once taken in the first advance of the human race, from the amoeba to the highest type of intelligence, has been duplicated, every step exactly paralleling the one that preceded in the dead ages gone by. A perfect plagiarism results. Everything is and is new. Only the imagination is undeceived.

At this point the entire complicated and laborious process begins to near a new day. (More of this in Chapter XIX) But for the moment everything is fresh, perfect, recreated.

In fact now, for the first time, everything IS new. Now at last the perfect effect is being witlessly discovered. The terms "veracity" "actuality" "real" "natural" "sincere" are being discussed at length, every word in the discussion being evolved from an identical discussion which took place the day before yesterday.

Yes, the imagination, drunk with prohibitions, has destroyed and recreated everything afresh in the likeness of that which it was. Now indeed men look about in amazement at each other with a full realization of the meaning of "art."

CHAPTER 2

It is spring: life again begins to assume its normal appearance as of "today." Only the imagination is undeceived. The volcanos are extinct. Coal is beginning to be dug again where the fern forests stood last night. (If an error is noted here, pay no attention to it.)

CHAPTER XIX

I realize that the chapters are rather quick in their sequence and that nothing much is contained in any one of them but no one should be surprised at this today.

THE TRADITIONALISTS OF PLAGIARISM

It is spring. That is to say, it is approaching THE BEGINNING.

In that huge and microscopic career of time, as it were a wild horse racing in an illimitable pampa[1] under the stars, describing immense and microscopic circles with his hoofs on the solid turf, running without a stop for the millionth part of a second until he is aged and worn to a heap of skin, bones and ragged hoofs—In that majestic progress of life, that gives the exact impression of Phidias' frieze,[2] the men and beasts of which, though they seem of the rigidity of marble are not so but move, with blinding rapidity, though we do not have the time to notice it, their legs advancing a millionth part of an inch every fifty thousand years—In that progress of life which seems stillness itself in the mass of its movements—at last SPRING is approaching.

In that colossal surge toward the finite and the capable life has now arrived for the second time at that exact moment when in the ages past the destruction of the species *Homo sapiens* occurred.

Now at last that process of miraculous verisimilitude, that great copying which evolution has followed, repeating move for move every move that it made in the past—is approaching the end.

Suddenly it is at an end. THE WORLD IS NEW.[3]

1923

1. Extensive grassy plains of central Argentina (Spanish, *la pampa*).
2. The most important sculptor of classical Athens, Phidias (c. 500–c. 432 B.C.E.) or his students executed the frieze (a long band of relief sculpture surmounting columns) decorating the Parthenon in Athens. The frieze depicts a festival procession of men and horses.
3. In the original publication, the poem "Spring and All" ("By the road to the contagious hospital"; see p. 286) directly followed this section.

LANGSTON HUGHES

Where Willa Cather, along with many other modernists, sought to divide high art from popular entertainment, Langston Hughes (1902–1967) urged African American artists to embrace black popular culture, epitomized for Hughes and many other observers of the 1920s by the innovations of jazz. "The Negro Artist and the Racial Mountain," published at the height of the Harlem Renaissance, takes aim at white audiences who looked to black artists for easy, stereotypical entertainment. Hughes's essay reserves most of its anger, however, for black elites who—he charged—preferred their artists to imitate white standards.

From The Negro Artist and the Racial Mountain

One of the most promising of the young Negro poets said to me once, "I want to be a poet—not a Negro poet," meaning, I believe, "I want to write like a white poet"; meaning subconsciously, "I would like to be a white poet"; meaning behind that, "I would like to be white." And I was sorry the young man said that, for no great poet has ever been afraid of being himself. And I doubted then that, with his desire to run away spiritually from his race, this boy would ever be a great poet. But this is the mountain standing in the way of any true Negro art in America—this urge within the race toward whiteness, the desire to pour racial individuality into the mold of American standardization, and to be as little Negro and as much American as possible.

* * *

The Negro artist works against an undertow of sharp criticism and misunderstanding from his own group and unintentional bribes from the whites. "O, be respectable, write about nice people, show how good we are," say the Negroes. "Be stereotyped, don't go too far, don't shatter our illusions about you, don't amuse us too seriously. We will pay you," say the whites. Both would have told Jean Toomer not to write "Cane."[1] The colored people did not praise it. The white people did not buy it. Most of the colored people who did read "Cane" hate it. They are afraid of it. Although the critics gave it good reviews the public remained indifferent. Yet (excepting the work of Du Bois[2]) "Cane" contains the finest prose written by a Negro in America. And like the singing of Robeson,[3] it is truly racial.

* * *

1. Jean Toomer's *Cane* combines prose and poems in a modernist dual portrait of rural Georgia and the urban black community of Washington, D.C.; see p. 618.
2. W. E. B. Du Bois (1868–1963), author of *The Souls of Black Folk* (1903) and other works on African American life and history.
3. Paul Robeson (1898–1976), African American actor and singer; in 1925 he made his concert debut in New York City with a program of black spirituals.

Most of my own poems are racial in theme and treatment, derived from the life I know. In many of them I try to grasp and hold some of the meanings and rhythms of jazz. I am sincere as I know how to be in these poems and yet after every reading I answer questions like these from my own people: Do you think Negroes should always write about Negroes? I wish you wouldn't read some of your poems to white folks. How do you find anything interesting in a place like a cabaret? Why do you write about black people? You aren't black. What makes you do so many jazz poems?

But jazz to me is one of the inherent expressions of Negro life in America: the eternal tom-tom beating in the Negro soul—the tom-tom of revolt against weariness in a white world, a world of subway trains, and work, work, work; the tom-tom of joy and laughter, and pain swallowed in a smile. Yet the Philadelphia clubwoman is ashamed to say that her race created it and she does not like me to write about it. The old subconscious "white is best" runs through her mind. Years of study under white teachers, a lifetime of white books, pictures, and papers, and white manners, morals, and Puritan standards made her dislike the spirituals. And now she turns up her nose at jazz and all its manifestations—likewise almost everything else distinctly racial. She doesn't care for the Winold Reiss[4] portraits of Negroes because they are "too Negro." She does not want a true picture of herself from anybody. She wants the artist to flatter her, to make the white world believe that all Negroes are as smug and as near white in soul as she wants to be. But, to my mind, it is the duty of the younger Negro artist, if he accepts any duties at all from outsiders, to change through the force of his art that old whispering "I want to be white," hidden in the aspirations of his people, to "Why should I want to be white? I am a Negro—and beautiful!"

So I am ashamed for the black poet who says, "I want to be a poet, not a Negro poet," as though his own racial world were not as interesting as any other world. I am ashamed, too, for the colored artist who runs from the painting of Negro faces to the painting of sunsets after the manner of the academicians because he fears the strange un-whiteness of his own features. An artist must be free to choose what he does, certainly, but he must also never be afraid to do what he might choose.

Let the blare of Negro Jazz bands and the bellowing voice of Bessie Smith singing Blues penetrate the closed ears of the colored near-intellectuals until they listen and perhaps understand. Let Paul Robeson singing Water Boy, and Rudolph Fisher writing about the streets of Harlem, and Jean Toomer holding the heart of Georgia in his hands, and Aaron Douglas[5] drawing strange black fantasies cause the smug Negro middle class to turn from their white, respectable, ordinary books and papers to catch a glimmer of their own beauty. We younger Negro artists who create now intend to express our individual dark-skinned selves without fear or shame. If white people are pleased we are glad. If they are not, it doesn't matter. We know we are beautiful. And ugly too. The tom-tom cries and the tom-tom laughs. If colored people are pleased we are glad. If they are not, their displeasure

4. German-born artist (1886–1953), known for his portraits of figures from the Harlem Renaissance.

5. Painter and muralist (1899–1979), who studied with Reiss and who became the first head of the Harlem Artists' Guild. Bessie Smith (1894?–1937), noted blues singer at the height of her fame in the 1920s. Rudolph Fisher (1897–1934), Harlem Renaissance author and musician who arranged songs for Robeson's 1925 New York concert debut.

doesn't matter either. We build our temples for tomorrow, strong as we know how, and we stand on top of the mountain, free within ourselves.

1926

H.D. (HILDA DOOLITTLE)
1886–1961

In January 1913, Harriet Monroe's influential little magazine, *Poetry,* printed three vivid poems by an unknown "H.D., Imagiste." These spare, elegant lyrics were among the first important products of the "Imagist" movement: poems devoid of explanation and declamation, unrhymed and lacking regular beat, depending on the power of an image to arrest attention and convey emotion. The poet's pen name, the movement's name, and the submission to the magazine were all the work of Ezra Pound, poet and tireless publicist for anything new in the world of poetry. The poems themselves had been written by his friend Hilda Doolittle. In later years, H.D. would look back at these events as epitomizing her dilemma: how to be a woman poet speaking in a world where women were spoken for and about by men. It is, perhaps, a symbol of her sense of difficulty that, though she strove for a voice that could be recognized as clearly feminine, she continued to publish under the name that Pound had devised for her.

She was born in Bethlehem, Pennsylvania, one girl in a family of five boys. Her mother was a musician and music teacher, active in the Moravian church to which many in Bethlehem belonged. The symbols and rituals of this group, along with its tradition of secrecy created in response to centuries of oppression, had much to do with H.D.'s interest in images and her attraction in later life to occult and other symbol systems: the cabala, numerology, the tarot, and psychoanalysis.

When her father, an astronomer and mathematician, was appointed director of the observatory at the University of Pennsylvania, the family moved to a suburb of Philadelphia. There, when she was fifteen years old, H.D. met Ezra Pound, a student at the university, already dedicated to poetry and acting the poet's role with dramatic intensity. The two were engaged for a while, but Pound's influence continued long after each had gone on to other partners. H.D. attended college at Bryn Mawr for two years; in 1911 she made a bold move to London, where Pound had gone some years earlier. She married a member of his circle, the English poet Richard Aldington, in 1913. With Aldington she studied Greek and read the classics, but the marriage was not a success and was destroyed by their separation during World War I when Aldington went into the army and served in France.

The years 1918–19 were terrible for H.D.: her brother Gilbert was killed in the fighting in France, her father died soon thereafter, her marriage broke up, close friendships with Pound and with D. H. Lawrence came to an end, she had a nearly fatal case of flu, and amid all this gave birth to a daughter who Aldington said was not his child. But she was rescued from the worst of her emotional and financial troubles by Winifred Ellerman, whose father, a shipping magnate, was one of the wealthiest men in England. Ellerman, a writer who had adopted the pen name

Bryher, had initially been attracted by H.D.'s poetry; their relationship developed first as a love affair and then into a lifelong friendship.

In 1923, H.D. settled in Switzerland. With Bryher's financial help she raised her daughter and cared for her ailing mother, who had joined her household. During 1933 and 1934 she spent time in Vienna, where she underwent analysis by Sigmund Freud, hoping to understand both her writer's block and what she called her "two loves" of women and men. Freud's theory of the unconscious and the disguised ways in which it reaches expression accorded well with H.D.'s understanding of how the unexplained images in a poem could be significant; the images were coded personal meanings. H.D.'s religious mysticism clashed with Freud's materialism, however, and she had mixed reactions to Freud's developing theory that women's unhappiness was determined by their sense of biological inferiority to men. But H.D. was instrumental (with Bryher's help) in getting Freud, who was Jewish, safely to London when the Nazi regime took over in Austria. When World War II broke out H.D. went back to London to share England's fate in crisis.

During the 1930s she worked mostly in prose forms and composed several autobiographical pieces (some of which remain unpublished). Like many major poets of the era, H.D. came in time to feel the need to write longer works; the bombardment of London inspired three long related poems about World War II, *The Walls Do Not Fall* (1944), *Tribute to the Angels* (1945), and *The Flowering of the Rod* (1946), which appeared together as *Trilogy*. In them she combined layers of historical and personal experience; wars going back to the Trojan War all fused in one image of humankind forever imposing and enduring violence.

The personal and the historical had always been one to her, and she became increasingly attracted to the image of Helen, the so-called cause of the Trojan War, as an image of herself. According to Homer's *Iliad,* Helen's beauty led Paris, a Trojan prince, to steal her from her Greek husband, Menelaus; and all the Greek warriors made common cause to get her back. After ten years' encampment before the walls of Troy, they found a devious way to enter the city and destroy it. H.D. was struck by the fact that the legend was related entirely from the male point of view; Helen never had a chance to speak. The object of man's acts and the subject of their poems, she was herself always silent. If Helen tried to speak, would she even have a voice or a point of view? Out of these broodings, and helped by her study of symbols, H.D. wrote her meditative epic of more than fourteen hundred lines, *Helen in Egypt*. The poem, composed between 1951 and 1955, consists of three books of interspersed verse and prose commentary, which follow Helen's quest. "She herself is the writing" that she seeks to understand, the poet observes.

H.D.'s Imagist poetry, for which she was known during her lifetime, represents the Imagist credo with its vivid phrasing, compelling imagery, free verse, short poetic line, and avoidance of abstraction and generalization. She followed Pound's example in producing many translations of poetry from older literature, especially from her favorite Greek poets. Her natural images are influenced by her early immersion in astronomy as well as by Greek poetry's Mediterranean settings. Austere landscapes of sea, wind, stars, and sand are contrasted with sensual figures of jewels, honey, and shells. Traditional metaphorical resources of earlier women's poetry, such as flowers and birds, are absorbed into modernism's aesthetic of "fiery tempered steel." As when her "Oread" calls upon the sea to "splash your great pines / on our rocks," H.D.'s best-known poems embody high modernism's goal of condensing forces at once lush and shattering, violent and creative, into a single arresting image.

The texts of the poems included here are those of *Collected Poems 1912–1944,* edited by Louis L. Martz (1983).

Mid-day

The light beats upon me.
I am startled—
a split leaf crackles on the paved floor—
I am anguished—defeated.

A slight wind shakes the seed-pods—
my thoughts are spent
as the black seeds.
My thoughts tear me,
I dread their fever.
I am scattered in its whirl.
I am scattered like
the hot shrivelled seeds.

The shrivelled seeds
are split on the path—
the grass bends with dust,
the grape slips
under its crackled leaf:
yet far beyond the spent seed-pods,
and the blackened stalks of mint,
the poplar is bright on the hill,
the poplar spreads out,
deep-rooted among trees.

O poplar, you are great
among the hill-stones,
while I perish on the path
among the crevices of the rocks.

1916

Oread[1]

Whirl up, sea—
whirl your pointed pines,
splash your great pines
on our rocks,
hurl your green over us,
cover us with your pools of fir.

1914, 1924

1. A nymph of mountains and hills.

Leda[1]

Where the slow river
meets the tide,
a red swan lifts red wings
and darker beak,
and underneath the purple down
of his soft breast
uncurls his coral feet.

Through the deep purple
of the dying heat
of sun and mist,
the level ray of sun-beam
has caressed
the lily with dark breast,
and flecked with richer gold
its golden crest.

Where the slow lifting
of the tide,
floats into the river
and slowly drifts
among the reeds,
and lifts the yellow flags,
he floats
where tide and river meet.

Ah kingly kiss—
no more regret
nor old deep memories
to mar the bliss;
where the low sedge is thick,
the gold day-lily
outspreads and rests
beneath soft fluttering
of red swan wings
and the warm quivering
of the red swan's breast.

1919, 1921

1. In Greek mythology, Leda is the mortal raped by Zeus, in the guise of a swan. Helen of Troy was her daughter.

Fragment 113

"Neither honey nor bee for me."
—Sappho.[1]

Not honey,
not the plunder of the bee
from meadow or sand-flower
or mountain bush;
from winter-flower or shoot
born of the later heat:
not honey, not the sweet
stain on the lips and teeth:
not honey, not the deep
plunge of soft belly
and the clinging of the gold-edged
pollen-dusted feet;

not so—
though rapture blind my eyes,
and hunger crisp
dark and inert my mouth,
not honey, not the south,
not the tall stalk
of red twin-lilies,
nor light branch of fruit tree
caught in flexible light branch;

not honey, not the south;
ah flower of purple iris,
flower of white,
or of the iris, withering the grass—
for fleck of the sun's fire,
gathers such heat and power,
that shadow-print is light,
cast through the petals
of the yellow iris flower;

not iris—old desire—old passion—
old forgetfulness—old pain—
not this, nor any flower,
but if you turn again,
seek strength of arm and throat,
touch as the god;
neglect the lyre-note;
knowing that you shall feel,
about the frame,
no trembling of the string
but heat, more passionate

1. Greek woman lyric poet of Lesbos in the 7th century B.C.E.

of bone and the white shell
and fiery tempered steel.

1922

Helen[1]

All Greece hates
the still eyes in the white face,
the lustre as of olives
where she stands,
and the white hands.

All Greece reviles
the wan face when she smiles,
hating it deeper still
when it grows wan and white,
remembering past enchantments
and past ills.

Greece sees unmoved,
God's daughter, born of love,
the beauty of cool feet
and slenderest knees,
could love indeed the maid,
only if she were laid,
white ash amid funereal cypresses.

1924

From The Walls Do Not Fall

To Bryher
FOR KARNAK 1923
FROM LONDON 1942

1

An incident here and there,
and rails gone (for guns)
from your (and my) old town square:

mist and mist-grey, no colour,
still the Luxor bee, chick and hare[1]
pursue unalterable purpose

1. In Greek legend, the wife of Menelaus. Her kidnapping by the Trojan prince Paris started the Trojan War. She was the daughter of the god Zeus, the product of his rape, when disguised as a swan, of the mortal Leda.

1. Luxor is a town on the Nile River in Egypt, close to the ruins of the ancient city of Thebes, where the Temple of Karnak is located. The bee, chick, and hare are carved symbols that appear on the temple.

in green, rose-red, lapis;
they continue to prophesy
from the stone papyrus:

there, as here, ruin opens
the tomb, the temple; enter,
there as here, there are no doors:

the shrine lies open to the sky,
the rain falls, here, there
sand drifts; eternity endures:

ruin everywhere, yet as the fallen roof
leaves the sealed room
open to the air,

so, through our desolation,
thoughts stir, inspiration stalks us
through gloom:

unaware, Spirit announces the Presence;
shivering overtakes us,
as of old, Samuel:[2]

trembling at a known street-corner,
we know not nor are known;
the Pythian[3] pronounces—we pass on

to another cellar, to another sliced wall
where poor utensils show
like rare objects in a museum;

Pompeii[4] has nothing to teach us,
we know crack of volcanic fissure,
slow flow of terrible lava,

pressure on heart, lungs, the brain
about to burst its brittle case
(what the skull can endure!):

over us, Apocryphal[5] fire,
under us, the earth sway, dip of a floor,
slope of a pavement

where men roll, drunk
with a new bewilderment,
sorcery, bedevilment:

2. A biblical seer and prophet.
3. Pythia is another name for Delphi, a Greek town famous because the Oracle of Apollo was located there. The Pythian is the high priestess of that oracle, who was possessed by the Delphic spirit and prophesied.
4. Ancient Italian city near Naples, burned and buried in a few hours by the eruption of Mount Vesuvius in 79 C.E.
5. The Apocrypha are books rejected from the Bible because of doubtful authenticity.

the bone-frame was made for
no such shock knit within terror,
yet the skeleton stood up to it:

the flesh? it was melted away,
the heart burnt out, dead ember,
tendons, muscles shattered, outer husk dismembered,

yet the frame held:
we passed the flame: we wonder
what saved us? what for?

1944

MARIANNE MOORE
1887–1972

Marianne Moore was a radically inventive modernist, greatly admired by other poets of her generation, and a powerful influence on such later writers as Robert Lowell, Randall Jarrell, and Richard Wilbur. Like her forerunner Emily Dickinson, she made of the traditional and constraining "woman's place" a protected space to do her own work, but unlike Dickinson, she was a deliberate professional, publishing her poems regularly, in touch with the movements and artists of her time. She was famous for the statement that poetry, though departing from the real world, re-created that world within its forms: poems were "imaginary gardens with real toads in them." Her earlier work is distinguished by great precision of observation and language, ornate diction, and complex stanza and prosodic patterns. Her later work is much less ornate; and in revising her poetry, she tended to simplify and shorten.

She was born in Kirkwood, Missouri, a suburb of St. Louis. In her childhood, the family was abandoned by her father; they moved to Carlisle, Pennsylvania, where—in a pattern common among both men and women writers of this period—her mother supported them by teaching school. She went to Bryn Mawr College, graduating in 1909; traveled with her mother in England and France in 1911; and returned to Carlisle to teach at the U.S. Indian School between 1911 and 1915. Having begun to write poetry in college, she was first published in 1915 and 1916 in such little magazines as the *Egoist* (an English magazine with which Ezra Pound was associated), *Poetry,* and *Others* (a journal for experimental writing with which William Carlos Williams was associated, founded by Alfred Kreymbourg, a New York poet and playwright). Through these magazines she entered the avant-garde and modernist world. She never married; in 1916 she and her mother merged their household with that of Moore's brother, a Presbyterian minister, and they moved with him to a parish in Brooklyn, New York. There Moore was close to literary circles and Ebbets Field, where the Dodgers, then a Brooklyn baseball team, had their home stadium. Moore was a lifelong fan.

While holding jobs in schools and libraries, Moore worked at her poetry. A volume called simply *Poems* was brought out in London in 1921 without her knowledge through the efforts of two women friends who were writers, H.D. (whom she had met at Bryn Mawr) and Bryher. A long and ambitious poem, "Marriage," appeared in the little magazine *Manikan* in 1923. Another book, *Observations*, appeared in 1924 and won the Dial Award; William Carlos Williams praised it as "a break *through* all preconceptions of poetic form and mood and pace." In 1925 she began to work as editor of the *Dial*, continuing in this influential position until the magazine was disbanded in 1929. Her reviews and editorial judgments were greatly respected, although her preference for elegance and decorum over sexual frankness was not shared by some of the writers—Hart Crane and James Joyce among them—whose work she rejected or published only after they revised it. As a critic, Moore was prolific; her collected prose makes a larger book than her collected poetry.

Moore believed that poets usually undervalued prose; "precision, economy of statement, logic" were features of good prose that could "liberate" the imagination, she wrote, and she often found these qualities in scientific and historical description. Her poems were an amalgam of her own observation and her wide reading, which she acknowledged by quotation marks and often by footnotes as well. Many of her quotations are obscure or inexact, and some have no identifiable sources. Moore's poetry rarely incorporates direct quotations from or allusions to other poets, the kinds of reference by which poets conventionally invoke a great tradition and assert their own place in it. She prefers to juxtapose disparate areas of human knowledge and to combine the elevated with the ordinary. Moore's notebooks suggest, for example, that the image of the kiwi bird in "The Mind Is an Enchanting Thing" emerged from a sketch Moore made of a shoe-polish tin; she praises the human mind both for its capacity to be mesmerized by the small facets of its environment and for its changeful, self-undoing freedom.

Against the exactitude and "unbearable accuracy" (as she put it) of her language, Moore counterpointed a complex texture of stanza form and versification. Pound worked with the clause, Williams with the line, H.D. with the image, Stevens and Stein with the word; Moore, unlike these modernist contemporaries, for the most part used the entire stanza as the unit of her poetry. Her stanzas are composed of regular lines counted by syllables, instead of by stress, and rhymes often occur at unaccented syllables and in the middle of a line or even a word. The effects she achieves are complex and subtle; she was often called the "poet's poet" of her day because the reader needed to pay close attention to appreciate the audacity of her formal experiments.

Nevertheless, her poetry also had a thematic, declarative edge, which the outbreak of World War II led her to expand. In "The Paper Nautilus," she drew on her characteristic vein of natural observation in order to will that a threatened civilization be protected by love. At the same time, Moore was keenly aware of her distance, as a civilian and a woman, from direct experience of combat; "In Distrust of Merits," her most famous poem of the war, reflects Moore's struggle (like Dickinson's during the Civil War) to adopt an ethically responsible relationship toward the fighting she could know only through newsreels and photographs.

Moore received the Bollingen, National Book, and Pulitzer awards for *Collected Poems* in 1951. Throughout her lifetime she continued to revise, expand, cut, and select, so that from volume to volume a poem with the same name may be a very different work. Her *Complete Poems* of 1967 represented her poetry as she wanted it remembered, but a full understanding of Moore calls for reading all of the versions of her changing work.

Poetry[1]

I, too, dislike it: there are things that are important beyond all
this fiddle.
Reading it, however, with a perfect contempt for it, one
discovers in
it after all, a place for the genuine.
Hands that can grasp, eyes
that can dilate, hair that can rise
if it must, these things are important not because a

high-sounding interpretation can be put upon them but because
they are
useful. When they become so derivative as to become
unintelligible,
the same thing may be said for all of us, that we
do not admire what
we cannot understand: the bat
holding on upside down or in quest of something to

eat, elephants pushing, a wild horse taking a roll, a tireless wolf
under
a tree, the immovable critic twitching his skin like a horse
that feels a flea, the base-
ball fan, the statistician—
nor is it valid
to discriminate against "business documents and

school-books";[2] all these phenomena are important. One must
make a distinction
however: when dragged into prominence by half poets, the
result is not poetry,
nor till the poets among us can be
"literalists of
the imagination"[3]—above
insolence and triviality and can present

for inspection, "imaginary gardens with real toads in them," shall
we have
it. In the meantime, if you demand on the one hand,
the raw material of poetry in
all its rawness and
that which is on the other hand
genuine, then you are interested in poetry.

1921, 1935

1. The version printed here follows the text and format of *Selected Poems* (1935).
2. Diary of Tolstoy (Dutton), p. 84. "Where the boundary between prose and poetry lies, I shall never be able to understand. The question is raised in manuals of style, yet the answer to it lies beyond me. Poetry is verse; prose is not verse. Or else poetry is everything with the exception of business documents and school books" [Moore's note].
3. Yeats's *Ideas of Good and Evil* (A.H. Bullen), p. 182. "The limitation of his view was from the very intensity of his vision; he was a too literal realist of imagination, as others are of nature; and because he believed that the figures seen by the mind's eye, when exalted by inspiration, were 'eternal existences,' symbols of divine essences, he hated every grace of style that might obscure their lineaments" [Moore's note].

Marriage[1]

This institution,
perhaps one should say enterprise
out of respect for which
one says one need not change one's mind
about a thing one has believed in,
requiring public promises
of one's intention
to fulfil a private obligation:
I wonder what Adam and Eve
think of it by this time,
this fire-gilt steel
alive with goldenness;
how bright it shows—
"of circular traditions and impostures,
committing many spoils,"[2]
requiring all one's criminal ingenuity
to avoid!
Psychology which explains everything
explains nothing,
and we are still in doubt.
Eve: beautiful woman—
I have seen her
when she was so handsome
she gave me a start,
able to write simultaneously
in three languages—
English, German and French—
and talk in the meantime;[3]
equally positive in demanding a commotion
and in stipulating quiet:
"*I* should like to be alone";
to which the visitor replies,
"I should like to be alone;
why not be alone together?"
Below the incandescent stars
below the incandescent fruit,
the strange experience of beauty;
its existence is too much;

1. The text here is from *Complete Poems* (1967), where Moore describes "Marriage" as "Statements that took my fancy which I tried to arrange plausibly."
2. "*Of circular traditions . . .*" Francis Bacon [Moore's note]. From a letter by the English philosopher, scientist, and statesman (1561–1626).
3. *Write simultaneously.* "Miss A——will write simultaneously in three languages, English, German, and French, talking in the meantime. [She] takes advantage of her abilities in everyday life, writing her letters simultaneously with both hands; namely, the first, third, and fifth words with her left and the second, fourth, and sixth with her right hand. While generally writing outward, she is able as well to write inward with both hands." "Multiple consciousness or Reflex Action of Unaccustomed Range," *Scientific American*, January 1922 [Moore's note].

it tears one to pieces
and each fresh wave of consciousness
is poison.
"See her, see her in this common world,"[4]
the central flaw
in that first crystal-fine experiment,
this amalgamation which can never be more
than an interesting impossibility,
describing it
as "that strange paradise
unlike flesh, stones,
gold or stately buildings,
the choicest piece of my life:
the heart rising
in its estate of peace
as a boat rises
with the rising of the water";[5]
constrained in speaking of the serpent—
shed snakeskin in the history of politeness
not to be returned to again—
that invaluable accident
exonerating Adam.[6]
And he has beauty also;
it's distressing—the O thou
to whom from whom,
without whom nothing—Adam;
"something feline,
something colubrine"[7]—how true!
a crouching mythological monster
in that Persian miniature of emerald mines,
raw silk—ivory white, snow white,
oyster white and six others—
that paddock full of leopards and giraffes—
long lemon-yellow bodies
sown with trapezoids of blue.
Alive with words,
vibrating like a cymbal
touched before it has been struck,
he has prophesied correctly—

4. *"See her, see her in this common world."* George Shock. [Moore's note]. Shock is not otherwise identified.
5. "That strange paradise, unlike flesh, stones . . ." Richard Baxter, *The Saints' Everlasting Rest* [Moore's note]. Moore's quotation does not exactly recall any single passage in this much-reprinted 1649 devotional treatise by Baxter (1615–1691), an English Puritan minister.
6. In the Bible, Eve yields to the serpent's temptation to eat the fruit of the tree forbidden by God, and passes it along to Adam: "she gave me of the tree, and I did eat" (Genesis 3.12).
7. "We were puzzled and we were fascinated, as if by something feline, by something colubrine." Philip Littell, reviewing Santayana's *Poems* in *The New Republic*, March 21, 1923 [Moore's note]. George Santayana (1863–1952) was better known as a philosopher whose students at Harvard included T. S. Eliot, Robert Frost, Gertrude Stein, and W. E. B. Du Bois. "Colubrine": snakelike.

the industrious waterfall,
"the speedy stream
which violently bears all before it,
at one time silent as the air
and now as powerful as the wind."[8]
"Treading chasms
on the uncertain footing of a spear,"[9]
forgetting that there is in woman
a quality of mind
which as an instinctive manifestation
is unsafe,
he goes on speaking
in a formal customary strain,
of "past states, the present state,
seals, promises,
the evil one suffered,
the good one enjoys,
hell, heaven,
everything convenient
to promote one's joy."[1]
In him a state of mind
perceives what it was not
intended that he should;
"he experiences a solemn joy
in seeing that he has become an idol."[2]
Plagued by the nightingale
in the new leaves,
with its silence—
not its silence but its silences,
he says of it:
"It clothes me with a shirt of fire."[3]
"He dares not clap his hands
to make it go on
lest it should fly off;
if he does nothing, it will sleep;

8. Unannotated by Moore but quoted almost directly from Baxter, *The Saints' Everlasting Rest*.

9. "*Treading chasms . . .*" Hazlitt: Essay on Burke's Style [Moore's note]. Quoted inexactly from "On the Prose Style of Poets" (1822), in which the essayist William Hazlitt (1778–1830) praises the English statesman Edmund Burke (1729–1797) for a prose style that went "nearest to the verge of poetry, and yet never fell over" and that "loses no particle of the exact, characteristic, extreme impression of the thing he writes about." Hazlitt takes "the unsteadfast footing of a spear" from Shakespeare's 1 *Henry IV* 1.3.524.

1. "*Past states . . .*" Richard Baxter [Moore's note].

2. "*He experiences a solemn joy.*" "A Travers Champs," by Anatole France in *Filles et Garçons* (Hachette): "*Le Petit Jean comprend qu'el est beau et cette idée le pénétre d'un respect profound de lui-même . . . Il goûte une joie pieuse à se sentir devenu une idole.*" [Moore's note]. *Filles et Garçons* (literally, Daughters and Sons [French]), a collection of illustrated children's stories by novelist and poet Anatole France (1844–1942), appeared in 1887. The first sentence, not translated by Moore, may be rendered as "Little John understood that he was handsome and this idea filled him with deep self-respect."

3. "*It clothes me with a shirt of fire.*" Hagop Boghossian in a poem, "The Nightingale" [Moore's note]. In *Observations* (1924), where "Marriage" appeared first in book form, Moore added that Boghossian was a teacher of philosophy at Worcester College in Massachusetts and his poem originally written in Armenian. In Greek myth, the hero Heracles puts on a poisoned shirt, sent by an enemy; it burns so painfully that he builds and walks into his own funeral pyre.

if he cries out, it will not understand."[4]
Unnerved by the nightingale
and dazzled by the apple,
impelled by "the illusion of a fire
effectual to extinguish fire,"
compared with which
the shining of the earth
is but deformity—a fire
"as high as deep
as bright as broad
as long as life itself,"[5]
he stumbles over marriage,
"a very trivial object indeed"[6]
to have destroyed the attitude
in which he stood—
the ease of the philosopher
unfathered by a woman.
Unhelpful Hymen![7]
a kind of overgrown cupid
reduced to insignificance
by the mechanical advertising
parading as involuntary comment,
by that experiment of Adam's
with ways out but no way in—
the ritual of marriage,
augmenting all its lavishness;
its fiddle-head ferns,
lotus flowers, opuntias, white dromedaries,
its hippopotamus—
nose and mouth combined
in one magnificent hopper—
its snake and the potent apple.
He tells us
that "for love that will
gaze an eagle blind,
that is with Hercules
climbing the trees
in the garden of the Hesperides,
from forty-five to seventy
is the best age,"[8]
commending it
as a fine art, as an experiment,

4. *"He dares not clap his hands . . ."* Edward Thomas, *Feminine Influence on the Poets* (Martin Secker, 1910) [Moore's note]. From Thomas's summary of a poem by King James I of Scotland (1394–1437), in which the speaker is listening to a nightingale and looking at a lovely, inaccessible woman.

5. *"Illusion of a fire . . . ," "as high as deep . . ."* Richard Baxter [Moore's note].

6. "Marriage is a law, and the worst of all laws . . . a very trivial object indeed." Godwin [Moore's note]. From *An Enquiry Concerning Political Justice* (1793) by the radical English journalist, novelist, and philosopher William Godwin (1756–1836), husband of the pioneering feminist Mary Wollstonecraft and father of Mary Wollstonecraft Shelley, the author of *Frankenstein* (1818).

7. In Greek myth, the god of marriage.

8. *"For love that will gaze an eagle blind . . ."* Anthony Trollope, *Barchester Towers* [Moore's note]. This novel by Trollope (1815–1882) appeared in 1857.

a duty or as merely recreation.
One must not call him ruffian
nor friction a calamity—
the fight to be affectionate:
"no truth can be fully known
until it has been tried
by the tooth of disputation."[9]
The blue panther with black eyes,
the basalt panther with blue eyes,
entirely graceful—
one must give them the path—
the black obsidian Diana
who "darkeneth her countenance
as a bear doth,"[1]
the spiked hand
that has an affection for one
and proves it to the bone,
impatient to assure you
that impatience is the mark of independence,
not of bondage.
"Married people often look that way"[2]—
"seldom and cold, up and down,
mixed and malarial
with a good day and a bad."[3]
We Occidentals are so unemotional,
self lost, the irony preserved
in "the Ahasuerus *tête-à-tête* banquet"[4]
with its small orchids like snakes' tongues,
with its "good monster, lead the way,"[5]
with little laughter
and munificence of humor
in that quixotic atmosphere of frankness
in which "four o'clock does not exist,
but at five o'clock
the ladies in their imperious humility

9. "*No truth can be fully known* . . ." Robert of Sorbonne [Moore's note]. Sorbonne (1201–1274), theologian and chaplain to the king of France, founded the Sorbonne, now the University of Paris, in 1257. Moore's quotation is from his rules for students.

1. "Darkeneth her countenance as a bear doth." Ecclesiasticus [Moore's note]. From Sirach (also known as Ecclesiasticus) 25.24 in the Douay-Rheims translation of the Bible (1582–1610), which begins, "The wickedness of a woman changeth her face."

2. "*Married people often look that way.*" C. Bertram Hartmann [Moore's note]. The modernist painter Hartman (1882–1960) was an acquaintance of Moore's.

3. "Seldom and cold . . ." Richard Baxter [Moore's note].

4. "Ahasuerus' *tête-à-tête* banquet." George Adam Smith, *Expositor's Bible* [Moore's note]. "*Tête-à-tête*": private, between two people (French); literally, head to head. Ahasuerus is the biblical Persian king who first insults his wife and queen, Vashti, then replaces her with Esther, unaware that Esther is a Jew. When one of the king's ministers, Haman, persecutes the kingdom's Jews, Esther invites him to a private dinner with herself and Ahasuerus; Haman brags of being singled out (Esther 5.12) but pays for it with his life when Esther persuades Ahasuerus to take her part. The commentary on Esther in the *Expositor's Bible* (authored by Walter Frederic Adeney, rather than George Adam Smith, and published in 1893) casts it as a modern battle of the sexes, chastising the despotic male egotism that sees the world "always through the medium of his own vastly magnified shadow" and asserting that "The first of a woman's rights is her right to her own person."

5. "Good monster, lead the way." *The Tempest* [Moore's note]. From Shakespeare's play (2.2), referring to Caliban.

are ready to receive you";[6]
in which experience attests
that men have power
and sometimes one is made to feel it.
He says, "What monarch would not blush
to have a wife
with hair like a shaving-brush?"[7]
The fact of woman
is "not the sound of the flute
but very poison."[8]
She says, "Men are monopolists
of 'stars, garters, buttons
and other shining baubles'—
unfit to be the guardians
of another person's happiness."[9]
He says, "These mummies
must be handled carefully—
'the crumbs from a lion's meal,
a couple of shins and the bit of an ear';[1]
turn to the letter M
and you will find
that 'a wife is a coffin,'[2]
that severe object
with the pleasing geometry
stipulating space not people,
refusing to be buried
and uniquely disappointing,
revengefully wrought in the attitude
of an adoring child
to a distinguished parent."
She says, "This butterfly,
this waterfly, this nomad
that has 'proposed
to settle on my hand for life'[3]—
What can one do with it?
There must have been more time

6. *"Four o'clock does not exist . . ."* Comtesse de Noailles, "Le Thé," *Femina*, December 1921. *"Dans leur impérieuse humilité elles jouent leurs rôles sur le globe"* [Moore's note]. *Femina* was a fashionable French women's magazine. "Le Thé": "Tea-time." The French sentence may be translated as "The ladies play their roles on earth with imperious humility."
7. *"What monarch . . ."* From "The Rape of the Lock," a parody by Mary Frances Nearing, with suggestions by M. Moore [Moore's note]. Nearing was a friend of Moore's. The object of her parody is the mock-heroic poem "The Rape of the Lock" (1712) by Alexander Pope (1688–1744).
8. *"The sound of the flute . . ."* A. Mitram Rihbany, *The Syrian Christ* (Houghton, Mifflin, 1916). Silence of women—"to an Oriental, this is as poetry set to music" [Moore's note]. Like Adeney's commentary on the book of Esther, this quotation stereotypically links male domination in marriage to "Oriental" cultures.
9. *"Men are monopolists . . ."* Miss M. Carey Thomas, Founder's address, Mount Holyoke, 1921: "Men practically reserve for themselves stately funerals, splendid monuments, memorial statues, membership in academies, medals, titles, honorary degrees, stars, garters, ribbons, buttons and other shining baubles, so valueless in themselves and yet so infinitely desirable because they are symbols of recognition by their fellow-craftsmen of difficult work well done" [Moore's note]. Thomas was president of Bryn Mawr College from 1894 to 1922.
1. *"The crumbs from a lion's meal . . ."*: Amos iii, 12. Translation by George Adam Smith, *Expositor's Bible* [Moore's note].
2. *"A wife is a coffin."* Ezra Pound [Moore's note].
3. *"Settle on my hand."* Charles Reade, *Christie Johnston* [Moore's note]. This popular romantic novel by Reade (1814–1884) was made into a silent film in 1921.

in Shakespeare's day
to sit and watch a play.
You know so many artists who are fools."
He says, "You know so many fools
who are not artists."
The fact forgot
that "some have merely rights
while some have obligations,"[4]
he loves himself so much,
he can permit himself
no rival in that love.
She loves herself so much,
she cannot see herself enough—
a statuette of ivory on ivory,
the logical last touch
to an expansive splendor
earned as wages for work done:
one is not rich but poor
when one can always seem so right.
What can one do for them—
these savages
condemned to disaffect
all those who are not visionaries
alert to undertake the silly task
of making people noble?
This model of petrine[5] fidelity
who "leaves her peaceful husband
only because she has seen enough of him"[6]—
that orator reminding you,
"I am yours to command."
"Everything to do with love is mystery;
it is more than a day's work
to investigate this science."[7]
One sees that it is rare—
that striking grasp of opposites
opposed each to the other, not to unity,
which in cycloid inclusiveness
has dwarfed the demonstration
of Columbus with the egg[8]—
a triumph of simplicity—

4. "Asiatics have rights; Europeans have obligations." Edmund Burke [Moore's note]. This summary of Burke's views comes from one of his biographers, the British author, editor, and statesman John Morley (1838–1923).
5. Related to or recalling Saint Peter, the chief of Christ's disciples, who after Christ's arrest denied knowing him (Matthew 26.69–75).
6. "*Leaves her peaceful husband* . . ." Simone Puget, advertisement entitled "Change of Fashion," *English Review*, June 1914: "Thus proceed pretty dolls when they leave their old home to renovate their frame, and dear others who may abandon their peaceful husband only because they have seen enough of him" [Moore's note].
7. "Everything to do with love is mystery . . ." F. C. Tilney, *Fables of La Fontaine*, "Love and Folly," Book XII, No. 14 [Moore's note]. Jean de La Fontaine (1621–1695) adapted his *Fables* (1668–94) from the literatures of many eras and languages.
8. According to legend, Christopher Columbus (1450/51–1506) replied to those who scoffed that sooner or later anyone would have found a way to the New World by wagering that they could not find a way to stand an egg on its tip; when they failed, he cracked the shell lightly at the egg's end and succeeded, making the point that once the way was shown it seemed obvious.

that charitive Euroclydon[9]
of frightening disinterestedness
which the world hates,
admitting:

"I am such a cow,
if I had a sorrow
I should feel it a long time;
I am not one of those
who have a great sorrow
in the morning
and a great joy at noon";

which says: "I have encountered it
among those unpretentious
protégés of wisdom,
where seeming to parade
as the debater and the Roman,
the statesmanship
of an archaic Daniel Webster[1]
persists to their simplicity of temper
as the essence of the matter:

'Liberty and union
now and forever';

the Book on the writing-table;
the hand in the breast-pocket."[2]

1923, 1967

To a Snail[1]

If "compression is the first grace of style,"[2]
you have it. Contractility is a virtue
as modesty is a virtue.
It is not the acquisition of any one thing
that is able to adorn,
or the incidental quality that occurs
as a concomitant of something well said,
that we value in style,
but the principle that is hid:
in the absence of feet, "a method of conclusions";

9. A stormy Mediterranean wind, identified in the Bible with the wind that led to the wreck of a ship carrying Saint Paul (Acts 27.14).
1. American statesman, lawyer and orator (1782–1852); as a member of Congress for New Hampshire (1813–17) and Massachusetts (1823–41, 1845–50) he vigorously opposed efforts to dissolve or diminish the constitutional powers of the federal government of the United States.
2. "*Liberty and Union* . . ." Daniel Webster (statue with inscription, Central Park, New York City) [Moore's note]. The inscription quotes from Webster's famous Senate speech of January 27, 1824, affirming the "glorious Union" against South Carolina's efforts to nullify the U.S. Constitution.
1. The text is from *Complete Poems* (1967).
2. "The very first grace of style is that which comes from compression." *Demetrius on Style* translated by W. Hamilton Fyfe. Heinemann, 1932 [Moore's note].

"a knowledge of principles,"
in the curious phenomenon of your occipital horn.

1924

The Paper Nautilus[1]

For authorities whose hopes
are shaped by mercenaries?
Writers entrapped by
teatime fame and by
commuters' comforts? Not for these
the paper nautilus
constructs her thin glass shell.

Giving her perishable
souvenir of hope, a dull
white outside and smooth
edged inner surface
glossy as the sea, the watchful
maker of it guards it
day and night; she scarcely

eats until the eggs are hatched.
Buried eight-fold in her eight
arms, for she is in
a sense a devil
fish, her glass ram'shorn-cradled freight
is hid but is not crushed;
as Hercules,[2] bitten

by a crab loyal to the hydra,
was hindered to succeed,
the intensively
watched eggs coming from
the shell free it when they are freed,—
leaving its wasp-nest flaws
of white on white, and close

laid Ionic[3] chiton-folds
like the lines in the mane of
a Parthenon[4] horse,
round which the arms had
wound themselves as if they knew love
is the only fortress
strong enough to trust to.

1941, 1967

1. The text is from *Complete Poems* (1967).
2. Hero of Greek myth, who performed numerous exploits including battle with the hydra, a many-headed monster.
3. Classical Greek, specifically Athenian.
4. Temple in Athens decorated by a carved marble band of sculptures, including processions of horses.

The Mind Is an Enchanting Thing[1]

is an enchanted thing
    like the glaze on a
katydid-wing
        subdivided by sun
        till the nettings are legion.
Like Gieseking playing Scarlatti;[2]

like the apteryx[3] awl
    as a beak, or the
kiwi's rain-shawl
        of haired feathers, the mind
        feeling its way as though blind,
walks along with its eyes on the ground.

It has memory's ear
    that can hear without
having to hear.
        Like the gyroscope's fall,
        truly unequivocal
because trued by regnant certainty,

it is a power of
    strong enchantment. It
is like the dove
        neck animated by
        sun; it is memory's eye;
it's conscientious inconsistency.

It tears off the veil; tears
    the temptation, the
mist the heart wears,
        from its eye—if the heart
        has a face; it takes apart
dejection. It's fire in the dove-neck's

iridescence; in the
    inconsistencies
of Scarlatti.
        Unconfusion submits
        its confusion to proof; it's
not a Herod's[4] oath that cannot change.

1944

1. The text is from *Complete Poems* (1967).
2. Walter Wilhelm Gieseking (1895–1956), French-born German pianist, known for his renditions of compositions by the Italian composer Domenico Scarlatti (1685–1757).
3. A flightless New Zealand bird, related to the kiwi, with a beak shaped like an awl.
4. Herod Antipas (d. 39 C.E.), ruler of Judea under the Romans. He had John the Baptist beheaded to fulfill a promise to Salome (Mark 6.22–27).

In Distrust of Merits[1]

Strengthened to live, strengthened to die for
medals and positioned victories?
They're fighting, fighting, fighting the blind
man who thinks he sees,—
who cannot see that the enslaver is
enslaved; the hater, harmed. O shining O
firm star, O tumultuous
ocean lashed till small things go
as they will, the mountainous
wave makes us who look, know

depth. Lost at sea before they fought! O
star of David, star of Bethlehem,[2]
O black imperial lion[3]
of the Lord—emblem
of a risen world—be joined at last, be
joined. There is hate's crown beneath which all is
death; there's love's without which none
is king; the blessed deeds bless
the halo. As contagion
of sickness makes sickness,

contagion of trust can make trust. They're
fighting in deserts and caves, one by
one, in battalions and squadrons;
they're fighting that I
may yet recover from the disease, My
Self; some have it lightly; some will die. "Man's
wolf to man" and we devour
ourselves. The enemy could not
have made a greater breach in our
defenses. One pilot-

ing a blind man can escape him, but
Job disheartened by false comfort[4] knew
that nothing can be so defeating
as a blind man who
can see. O alive who are dead, who are
proud not to see, O small dust of the earth
that walks so arrogantly
trust begets power and faith is
an affectionate thing. We
vow, we make this promise

1. The text is from *Complete Poems* (1967).
2. A symbol of christianity. "Star of David": a symbol of Judaism.
3. Emperor Haile Selassie of Ethiopia, leader of his country's resistance against Italian occupation during World War II. After Mussolini's fall in 1943, Selassie declared Ethiopia "less interested in vengeance for the past than in justice for the future."
4. When undergoing Jehovah's test of his fidelity, Job rejected the attempts of friends to comfort him.

to the fighting—it's a promise—"We'll
never hate black, white, red, yellow, Jew,
Gentile, Untouchable."[5] We are
not competent to
make our vows. With set jaw they are fighting,
fighting, fighting,—some we love whom we know,
some we love but know not—that
hearts may feel and not be numb.
It cures me; or am I what
I can't believe in? Some

in snow, some on crags, some in quicksands,
little by little, much by much, they
are fighting fighting fighting that where
there was death there may
be life. "When a man is prey to anger,
he is moved by outside things; when he holds
his ground in patience patience
patience, that is action or
beauty," the soldier's defense
and hardest armor for

the fight. The world's an orphans' home. Shall
we never have peace without sorrow?
without pleas of the dying for
help that won't come? O
quiet form upon the dust, I cannot
look and yet I must. If these great patient
dyings—all these agonies
and wound bearings and bloodshed—
can teach us how to live, these
dyings were not wasted.

Hate-hardened heart, O heart of iron,
iron is iron till it is rust.
There never was a war that was
not inward; I must
fight till I have conquered in myself what
causes war, but I would not believe it.
I inwardly did nothing.
O Iscariot[6]-like crime!
Beauty is everlasting
and dust is for a time.

1944

5. The lowest hereditary caste in India.
6. Judas Iscariot was the apostle who betrayed Jesus Christ.

T. S. ELIOT
1888–1965

The publication in 1922 of *The Waste Land* in the British little magazine *Criterion* and the American *Dial* was a cultural and literary event. The poem's title and the view it incorporated of modern civilization seemed, to many, to catch precisely the state of culture and society after World War I. The war, supposedly fought to save European civilization, had been the most brutal and destructive in Western history: what kind of civilization could have allowed it to take place? The long, fragmented structure of *The Waste Land*, too, contained so many technical innovations that ideas of what poetry was and how it worked seemed fundamentally changed. A generation of poets either imitated or resisted it.

The author of this poem was an American living in London, T. S. Eliot. Eliot had a comfortable upbringing in St. Louis: his mother was involved in cultural and charitable activities and wrote poetry; his father was a successful businessman. His grandfather Eliot had been a New England Unitarian minister who, moving to St. Louis, had founded Washington University. Eliot was thus a product of that New England–based "genteel tradition" that shaped the nation's cultural life after the Civil War. He attended Harvard for both undergraduate (1906–10) and graduate (1911–14) work. He studied at the Sorbonne in Paris from 1910 to 1911 and at Oxford from 1915 to 1916, writing a dissertation on the idealistic philosophy of the English logician and metaphysician F. H. Bradley (1846–1924). The war prevented Eliot from returning to Harvard for the oral defense of his doctoral degree, and this delay became the occasion of his turning to a life in poetry and letters rather than in academics.

Eliot had begun writing traditional poetry as a college student. In 1908, however, he read Arthur Symons's *The Symbolist Movement in Literature* (1899) and learned about Jules LaForgue and other French Symbolist poets. Symons's book altered Eliot's view of poetry, as "The Love Song of J. Alfred Prufrock" (published in *Poetry* in 1915) and "Preludes" (published in *Blast* in the same year) showed; in these poems Eliot took Symons's "revolt against exteriority, against rhetoric" in the direction of associative, oblique free verse. His fellow expatriate and poet Ezra Pound, reading this work, began enthusiastically introducing Eliot in literary circles as a young American who had "trained himself *and* modernized himself *on his own*." Pound helped Eliot over several years to get financially established. In addition, he was a perceptive reader and critic of Eliot's draft poems.

Eliot settled in England, marrying Vivian Haigh-Wood in 1915. Separated in 1932, they never divorced; Haigh-Wood died in a mental institution in 1947. After marrying, Eliot worked in London, first as a teacher and then from 1917 to 1925 in the foreign department of Lloyd's Bank, hoping to find time to write poetry and literary essays. His criticism was published in the *Egoist* and then in the little magazine that he founded, *Criterion*, which was published from 1922 to 1939. His persuasive style, a mixture of advocacy and judiciousness, effectively counterpointed Pound's aggressive, confrontational approach; the two together had a tremendous effect on how the poetry of the day was written and how the poetry of the past was evaluated. More than any other Americans they defined what is now thought of as "high" modernism.

Eliot began working on *The Waste Land* in 1921 and finished it in a Swiss sanatorium while recovering from a mental collapse brought on by overwork, marital problems, and general depression. He accepted some alterations suggested by his wife and cut huge chunks out of the poem on Pound's advice. Although Pound's work on the poem was all excision, so different was the manuscript before and after Pound's suggestions were incorporated that some critics suggest we should think of *The Waste Land* as jointly authored. The poem as published in *Criterion* and the *Dial* had no footnotes; these were appended for its publication in book form and added yet another layer (possibly self-mocking) to the complex texture of the poem.

The Waste Land consists of five discontinuous segments, each composed of fragments incorporating multiple voices and characters, literary and historical allusions and quotations, vignettes of contemporary life, surrealistic images, myths and legends. "These fragments I have shored against my ruins," the poet writes, asking whether he can form any coherent structure from the splinters of civilization. The poem's discontinuous elements are organized by recurrent allusions to the myth of seasonal death, burial, and rebirth that, according to much anthropological thinking of the time, underlay all religions. In Sir James Frazer's multivolume *The Golden Bough* (1890–1915) and Jessie Weston's *From Ritual to Romance* (1920), Eliot found a repertory of myths through which he could invoke, without specifically naming any religion, the story of a desert land brought to life by a king's sacrifice. Although it gestures toward religious belief, *The Waste Land* concludes with the outcome of the quest for regeneration uncertain in a cacophonous, desolate landscape.

Many readers saw *The Waste Land* as the definitive cultural statement of its time, but it was not definitive for Eliot. The poem may have been Eliot's indirect confession of personal discord, for which he sought resolution in social orders beyond those of poetry. In 1927 he became a British citizen; in a preface to the collection of essays *For Lancelot Andrewes* (1928), he declared himself a "classicist in literature, royalist in politics, and anglo-catholic in religion." After "The Hollow Men" and the "Sweeney" poems, which continue *The Waste Land*'s critique of modern civilization, he turned increasingly to poems of religious doubt and reconciliation. "The Journey of the Magi" and "Ash Wednesday" are poems about the search for a faith desperately needed, yet difficult to sustain. The *Four Quartets*, begun with "Burnt Norton" in 1934 and completed in 1943, are not so much reports of secure faith as dramatizations of the difficult process of arriving at belief. The *Four Quartets* move away from the fragmentary quotation and collage techniques of *The Waste Land* in favor of plainer expository statement grounded in particular times and places—the England of Eliot's chosen citizenship and the America of his origins—while aspiring to a timeless religious faith.

An emphasis on order, hierarchy, and racial homogeneity emerged in Eliot's social essays of the later 1920s and 1930s; a strain of crude anti-Semitism had appeared in the earlier Sweeney poems. As European politics became increasingly turbulent, the stability promised by totalitarian regimes appealed to some observers, Eliot included. The Communist rejection of all religion also tended to drive the more traditionally religious modernists into the opposing camp of fascism. Pound's and Eliot's Fascist sympathies in the 1930s, together with their immense influence on poetry, linked high modernism with reactionary politics in the public's perception, even while individual modernists in these years embraced political movements ranging from the far left to the extreme right, maintained centrist or liberal allegiances, or despised politics completely.

During the 1930s and 1940s, Eliot's criticism and poetry became increasingly important to the group of writers—many of them poets and academics in the United States—whose work became known collectively as the "New Criticism." In his influential essay "Tradition and the Individual Talent," Eliot had defined the English and European poetic tradition as a self-sufficient organic whole, an elastic equilibrium

Eliot inspecting manuscripts at his desk.

that constantly reformed itself to accommodate new poets. What makes poems matter, in Eliot's definition of tradition, is their effect on other poems, not their capacity to act upon the world outside of poetry. Poets contribute to the tradition, he argued, not through the direct expression of individual emotion but through a difficult process of distancing "the man who suffers" from "the mind which creates"; readers, therefore, should focus on the feeling embodied in the poem itself rather than reading the poem through the life of the poet. In other essays, Eliot denigrated didactic, expository, or narrative poets like Milton and the Victorians while applauding the verbally complex, paradoxical, indirect, symbolic work of seventeenth-century Metaphysical poets like John Donne and George Herbert. Through the New Criticism, Eliot's "impersonal" approach to poetry had a powerful role in shaping the literary curriculum in American colleges and universities, especially following World War II.

For the New Criticism, which analyzed poems for imagery, allusion, ambiguity, and irony, Eliot's essays provided theory, his poetry opportunities for practical criticism. But when critics used Eliot's preference for difficult indirection to judge literary quality and made interpretation the main task of readers, they often overlooked the lyricism, obvious didacticism, and humor of Eliot's own poetry. And they minimized the poems' cultural, historical, and autobiographical content.

However elitist his pronouncements, however hostile to modernity he claimed to be, Eliot drew heavily on popular forms and longed to have wide cultural influence. There are vaudeville turns throughout *The Waste Land*. He admired Charlie Chaplin and wanted "as large and miscellaneous an audience as possible." He pursued this ambition by writing verse plays. *Murder in the Cathedral* (1935) was a church pageant; *The Family Reunion* (1939), *The Cocktail Party* (1949), *The Confidential Clerk* (1953), and *The Elder Statesman* (1959), all religious in theme, were successfully produced in London and on Broadway. He never became a popular poet, however, despite his tremendous impact on the teaching and writing of poetry. Although Eliot remained a resident of England, he returned to the United States frequently to lecture and to give readings of his poems. He married his assistant, Valerie Fletcher, in 1957. By the time of his death he had become a social and cultural institution.

The text of the poems is that of *The Complete Poems and Plays of T. S. Eliot* (1969).

The Love Song of J. Alfred Prufrock

S'io credessi che mia risposta fosse
a persona che mai tornasse al mondo,
questa fiamma staria senza più scosse.
Ma per ciò che giammai di questo fondo
non tornò vivo alcun, s'i'odo il vero,
senza tema d'infamia ti rispondo.[1]

Let us go then, you and I,
When the evening is spread out against the sky
Like a patient etherised upon a table;
Let us go, through certain half-deserted streets,
The muttering retreats
Of restless nights in one-night cheap hotels
And sawdust restaurants with oyster-shells:
Streets that follow like a tedious argument
Of insidious intent
To lead you to an overwhelming question . . .
Oh, do not ask, 'What is it?'
Let us go and make our visit.

In the room the women come and go
Talking of Michelangelo.

The yellow fog that rubs its back upon the window-panes,
The yellow smoke that rubs its muzzle on the window-panes,
Licked its tongue into the corners of the evening,

Lingered upon the pools that stand in drains,
Let fall upon its back the soot that falls from chimneys,
Slipped by the terrace, made a sudden leap,
And seeing that it was a soft October night,
Curled once about the house, and fell asleep.

And indeed there will be time[2]
For the yellow smoke that slides along the street
Rubbing its back upon the window-panes;
There will be time, there will be time
To prepare a face to meet the faces that you meet;
There will be time to murder and create,
And time for all the works and days[3] of hands
That lift and drop a question on your plate;
Time for you and time for me,
And time yet for a hundred indecisions,

1. If I thought that my reply would be to one who would ever return to the world, this flame would stay without further movement; but since none has ever returned alive from this depth, if what I hear is true, I answer you without fear of infamy (Italian; Dante's *Inferno* 27.61–66). The speaker, Guido da Montefeltro, consumed in flame as punishment for giving false counsel, confesses his shame without fear of its being reported since he believes Dante cannot return to earth.

2. An echo of Andrew Marvell, "To His Coy Mistress" (1681): "Had we but world enough and time."

3. *Works and Days* is a didactic poem about farming by the Greek poet Hesiod (8th century B.C.E.).

And for a hundred visions and revisions,
Before the taking of a toast and tea.

In the room the women come and go
Talking of Michelangelo.

And indeed there will be time
To wonder, 'Do I dare?' and, 'Do I dare?'
Time to turn back and descend the stair,
With a bald spot in the middle of my hair—
(They will say: 'How his hair is growing thin!')
My morning coat, my collar mounting firmly to the chin,
My necktie rich and modest, but asserted by a simple pin—
(They will say: 'But how his arms and legs are thin!')
Do I dare
Disturb the universe?
In a minute there is time
For decisions and revisions which a minute will reverse.

For I have known them all already, known them all—
Have known the evenings, mornings, afternoons,
I have measured out my life with coffee spoons;
I know the voices dying with a dying fall[4]
Beneath the music from a farther room.
  So how should I presume?

And I have known the eyes already, known them all—
The eyes that fix you in a formulated phrase,
And when I am formulated, sprawling on a pin,
When I am pinned and wriggling on the wall,
Then how should I begin
To spit out all the butt-ends of my days and ways?
  And how should I presume?
And I have known the arms already, known them all—
Arms that are braceleted and white and bare
(But in the lamplight, downed with light brown hair!)
Is it perfume from a dress
That makes me so digress?
Arms that lie along a table, or wrap about a shawl.
  And should I then presume?
  And how should I begin?

. . . .

Shall I say, I have gone at dusk through narrow streets
And watched the smoke that rises from the pipes
Of lonely men in shirt-sleeves, leaning out of windows? . . .

I should have been a pair of ragged claws
Scuttling across the floors of silent seas.

. . . .

4. Echo of Duke Orsino's invocation of music in Shakespeare's *Twelfth Night* 1.1.4: "If music be the food of love, play on. . . . That strain again! It had a dying fall."

And the afternoon, the evening, sleeps so peacefully!
Smoothed by long fingers,
Asleep . . . tired . . . or it malingers,
Stretched on the floor, here beside you and me.
Should I, after tea and cakes and ices,
Have the strength to force the moment to its crisis?
But though I have wept and fasted, wept and prayed,
Though I have seen my head (grown slightly bald) brought in
upon a platter,[5]
I am no prophet—and here's no great matter;
I have seen the moment of my greatness flicker,
And I have seen the eternal Footman hold my coat, and snicker,
And in short, I was afraid.

And would it have been worth it, after all,
After the cups, the marmalade, the tea,
Among the porcelain, among some talk of you and me,
Would it have been worth while,
To have bitten off the matter with a smile,
To have squeezed the universe into a ball
To roll it towards some overwhelming question,
To say: 'I am Lazarus,[6] come from the dead,
Come back to tell you all, I shall tell you all'—
If one, settling a pillow by her head,
Should say: 'That is not what I meant at all.
That is not it, at all.'

And would it have been worth it, after all,
Would it have been worth while,
After the sunsets and the dooryards and the sprinkled streets,
After the novels, after the teacups, after the skirts that trail
along the floor—
And this, and so much more?—
It is impossible to say just what I mean!
But as if a magic lantern threw the nerves in patterns on a screen:
Would it have been worth while
If one, settling a pillow or throwing off a shawl,
And turning toward the window, should say:
'That is not it at all,
That is not what I meant, at all.'

. . . . . .

No! I am not Prince Hamlet, nor was meant to be;
Am an attendant lord, one that will do
To swell a progress,[7] start a scene or two,
Advise the prince; no doubt, an easy tool,
Deferential, glad to be of use,
Politic, cautious, and meticulous;

5. The head of the prophet John the Baptist, who was killed at the behest of Princess Salome, was brought to her on a platter (see Mark 6.17–20, Matthew 14.3–11).

6. The resurrection of Lazarus is recounted in John 11.1–44; see also Luke 16.19–31.

7. A journey or procession made by royal courts and often portrayed on Elizabethan stages.

Full of high sentence,[8] but a bit obtuse;
At times, indeed, almost ridiculous—
Almost, at times, the Fool.

I grow old . . . I grow old . . .
I shall wear the bottoms of my trousers rolled.

Shall I part my hair behind? Do I dare to eat a peach?
I shall wear white flannel trousers, and walk upon the beach.
I have heard the mermaids singing, each to each.

I do not think that they will sing to me.

I have seen them riding seaward on the waves
Combing the white hair of the waves blown back
When the wind blows the water white and black.

We have lingered in the chambers of the sea
By sea-girls wreathed with seaweed red and brown
Till human voices wake us, and we drown.

1915, 1917

Sweeney among the Nightingales[1]

ὤμοι, πέπληγμαι καιρίαν πληγὴν ἔσω.[2]

Apeneck Sweeney spreads his knees
Letting his arms hang down to laugh,
The zebra stripes along his jaw
Swelling to maculate giraffe.

The circles of the stormy moon
Slide westward toward the River Plate,[3]
Death and the Raven drift above
And Sweeney guards the hornèd gate.[4]

Gloomy Orion and the Dog[5]
Are veiled; and hushed the shrunken seas;
The person in the Spanish cape
Tries to sit on Sweeney's knees

8. Opinions, sententiousness.

1. The poem juxtaposes the imminent death of Sweeney in a nonheroic present, the ritual sacrifice of Christ enacted in a convent, the murder (by his wife and her lover) of Agamemnon in Aeschylus's tragedy, and the tragedy of Philomela in Greek mythology. Raped by her sister's husband, who then cut out her tongue, Philomela was transformed into a nightingale whose song springs from the violation she has suffered but cannot report.

2. Alas, I am struck a mortal blow within (Greek; Aeschylus's *Agamemnon*); this is Agamemnon's cry when he is murdered.

3. Estuary between Argentina and Uruguay.

4. The Gates of Horn, in the Greek underworld; dreams pass through them to the upper world.

5. Sirius, also called the Dog Star, is the brightest star in the sky. "Orion": a constellation representing the mythical hunter. Sirius is said to be his dog.

Slips and pulls the table cloth
Overturns a coffee-cup,
Reorganised upon the floor
She yawns and draws a stocking up;

The silent man in mocha brown
Sprawls at the window-sill and gapes;
The waiter brings in oranges
Bananas figs and hothouse grapes;

The silent vertebrate in brown
Contracts and concentrates, withdraws;
Rachel *née* Rabinovitch
Tears at the grapes with murderous paws;

She and the lady in the cape
Are suspect, thought to be in league;
Therefore the man with heavy eyes
Declines the gambit, shows fatigue,

Leaves the room and reappears
Outside the window, leaning in,
Branches of wistaria
Circumscribe a golden grin;

The host with someone indistinct
Converses at the door apart,
The nightingales are singing near
The Convent of the Sacred Heart,

And sang within the bloody wood
When Agamemnon cried aloud
And let their liquid siftings fall
To stain the stiff dishonoured shroud.

1918, 1919

From Tradition and the Individual Talent[1]

In English writing we seldom speak of tradition, though we occasionally apply its name in deploring its absence. We cannot refer to "the tradition" or to "a tradition"; at most, we employ the adjective in saying that the poetry of So-and-so is "traditional" or even "too traditional." Seldom, perhaps, does the word appear except in a phrase of censure. If otherwise, it is vaguely approbative, with the implication, as to the work approved, of some pleasing

1. From *The Sacred Wood* (1920), first published in the *Egoist* (1919). The text is that of *Selected Essays* (1951).

archaeological reconstruction. You can hardly make the word agreeable to English ears without this comfortable reference to the reassuring science of archaeology.

Certainly the word is not likely to appear in our appreciations of living or dead writers. Every nation, every race, has not only its own creative, but its own critical turn of mind; and is even more oblivious of the shortcomings and limitations of its critical habits than of those of its creative genius. We know, or think we know, from the enormous mass of critical writing that has appeared in the French language the critical method or habit of the French; we only conclude (we are such unconscious people) that the French are "more critical" than we, and sometimes even plume ourselves a little with the fact, as if the French were the less spontaneous. Perhaps they are; but we might remind ourselves that criticism is as inevitable as breathing, and that we should be none the worse for articulating what passes in our minds when we read a book and feel an emotion about it, for criticizing our own minds in their work of criticism. One of the facts that might come to light in this process is our tendency to insist, when we praise a poet, upon those aspects of his work in which he least resembles anyone else. In these aspects or parts of his work we pretend to find what is individual, what is the peculiar essence of the man. We dwell with satisfaction upon the poet's difference from his predecessors, especially his immediate predecessors; we endeavour to find something that can be isolated in order to be enjoyed. Whereas if we approach a poet without this prejudice we shall often find that not only the best, but the most individual parts of his work may be those in which the dead poets, his ancestors, assert their immortality most vigorously. And I do not mean the impressionable period of adolescence, but the period of full maturity.

Yet if the only form of tradition, of handing down, consisted in following the ways of the immediate generation before us in a blind or timid adherence to its successes, "tradition" should positively be discouraged. We have seen many such simple currents soon lost in the sand; and novelty is better than repetition. Tradition is a matter of much wider significance. It cannot be inherited, and if you want it you must obtain it by great labor. It involves, in the first place, the historical sense, which we may call nearly indispensable to anyone who would continue to be a poet beyond his twenty-fifth year; and the historical sense involves a perception, not only of the pastness of the past, but of its presence; the historical sense compels a man to write not merely with his own generation in his bones, but with a feeling that the whole of the literature of Europe from Homer and within it the whole of the literature of his own country has a simultaneous existence and composes a simultaneous order. This historical sense, which is a sense of the timeless as well as of the temporal and of the timeless and of the temporal together, is what makes a writer traditional. And it is at the same time what makes a writer most acutely conscious of his place in time, of his own contemporaneity.

No poet, no artist of any art, has his complete meaning alone. His significance, his appreciation is the appreciation of his relation to the dead poets and artists. You cannot value him alone; you must set him, for contrast and comparison, among the dead. I mean this as a principle of aesthetic, not merely historical, criticism. The necessity that he shall conform, that he shall cohere, is not onesided; what happens when a new work of art is created is something that happens simultaneously to all the works of art which preceded it. The existing monuments form an ideal order among themselves, which is modified by the introduction of the new (the really new) work of art among them. The existing order is complete before the new work arrives; for order to persist after the supervention of novelty, the *whole* existing order must be, if ever so slightly, altered; and so the relations, proportions, values of each work of art toward the whole are readjusted; and this is conformity between the old and the new. Whoever has approved this idea of order, of the form of European, of English literature will not find it preposterous that the past should be altered by the present as much as the present is directed by the past. And the poet who is aware of this will be aware of great difficulties and responsibilities.

* * *

II

Honest criticism and sensitive appreciation are directed not upon the poet but upon the poetry. If we attend to the confused cries of the newspaper critics and the susurrus of popular repetition that follows, we shall hear the names of poets in great numbers; if we seek not Blue-book[2] knowledge but the enjoyment of poetry, and ask for a poem, we shall seldom find it. I have tried to point out the importance of the relation of the poem to other poems by other authors, and suggested the conception of poetry as a living whole of all the poetry that has ever been written. The other aspect of this Impersonal theory of poetry is the relation of the poem to its author. And I hinted, by an analogy, that the mind of the mature poet differs from that of the immature one not precisely in any valuation of "personality," not being necessarily more interesting, or having "more to say," but rather by being a more finely perfected medium in which special, or very varied, feelings are at liberty to enter into new combinations.

The analogy was that of the catalyst. When the two gases previously mentioned are mixed in the presence of a filament of platinum, they form sulfurous acid. This combination takes place only if the platinum is present; nevertheless the newly formed acid contains no trace of platinum, and the platinum itself is apparently unaffected: has remained inert, neutral, and unchanged. The mind of the poet is the shred of platinum. It may partly or exclusively operate upon the experience of the man himself; but, the more perfect the artist, the more completely separate in him will be the man who suffers and the mind which creates; the more perfectly will the mind digest and transmute the passions which are its material.

* * *

It is not in his personal emotions, the emotions provoked by particular events in his life, that the poet is in any way remarkable or interesting. His particular emotions may be simple, or crude, or flat. The emotion in his poetry will be a very complex thing, but not with the complexity of the emotions of people who have very complex or unusual emotions in life. One error, in fact, of

2. Official guidebooks. "Susurrus": murmuring, buzzing (Latin).

eccentricity in poetry is to seek for new human emotions to express, and in this search for novelty in the wrong place it discovers the perverse. The business of the poet is not to find new emotions, but to use the ordinary ones and, in working them up into poetry, to express feelings which are not in actual emotions at all. And emotions which he has never experienced will serve his turn as well as those familiar to him. Consequently, we must believe that "emotion recollected in tranquillity"[3] is an inexact formula. For it is neither emotion, nor recollection, nor, without distortion of meaning, tranquillity. It is a concentration, and a new thing resulting from the concentration, of a very great number of experiences which to the practical and active person would not seem to be experiences at all; it is a concentration which does not happen consciously or of deliberation. These experiences are not "recollected," and they finally unite in an atmosphere which is "tranquil" only in that it is a passive attending upon the event. Of course this is not quite the whole story. There is a great deal, in the writing of poetry, which must be conscious and deliberate. In fact, the bad poet is usually unconscious where he ought to be conscious, and conscious where he ought to be unconscious. Both errors tend to make him "personal." Poetry is not a turning loose of emotion, but an escape from emotion; it is not the expression of personality, but an escape from personality. But, of course, only those who have personality and emotions know what it means to want to escape from these things.

III

ὁ δὲ νοῦς ἴσως Θειότερόν τι χαὶ ἀπαθές ἐατιν.[4]

This essay proposes to halt at the frontiers of metaphysics or mysticism, and confine itself to such practical conclusions as can be applied by the responsible person interested in poetry. To divert interest from the poet to the poetry is a laudable aim: for it would conduce to a juster estimation of actual poetry, good and bad. There are many people who appreciate the expression of sincere emotion in verse, and there is a smaller number of people who can appreciate technical excellence. But very few know when there is an expression of *significant* emotion, emotion which has its life in the poem and not in the history of the poet. The emotion of art is impersonal. And the poet cannot reach this impersonality without surrendering himself wholly to the work to be done. And he is not likely to know what is to be done unless he lives in what is not merely the present, but the present moment of the past, unless he is conscious, not of what is dead, but of what is already living.

1919, 1920

3. From Wordsworth's "Preface" to *Lyrical Ballads* (2nd ed., 1800): "poetry takes its origin from emotion recollected in tranquillity."

4. No doubt the mind is something divine and not subject to external impressions (Greek; Aristotle's *De Anima* [On the soul] 1.4).

Gerontion[1]

Thou hast nor youth nor age
But as it were an after dinner sleep
Dreaming of both.[2]

Here I am, an old man in a dry month,
Being read to by a boy, waiting for rain.
I was neither at the hot gates[3]
Nor fought in the warm rain
Nor knee deep in the salt-marsh, heaving a cutlass,
Bitten by flies, fought.
My house is a decayed house,
And the Jew squats on the window sill, the owner,
Spawned in some estaminet[4] of Antwerp,
Blistered in Brussels, patched and peeled in London.[5]
The goat coughs at night in the field overhead;
Rocks, moss, stonecrop, iron, merds.[6]
The woman keeps the kitchen, makes tea,
Sneezes at evening, poking the peevish gutter.
                                        I an old man,
A dull head among windy spaces.

Signs are taken for wonders. 'We would see a sign!'[7]
The word within a word, unable to speak a word,
Swaddled with darkness. In the juvescence of the year
Came Christ the tiger

In depraved May,[8] dogwood and chestnut, flowering judas,
To be eaten, to be divided, to be drunk
Among whispers;[9] by Mr. Silvero
With caressing hands, at Limoges
Who walked all night in the next room;
By Hakagawa, bowing among the Titians;
By Madame de Tornquist, in the dark room
Shifting the candles; Fräulein von Kulp
Who turned in the hall, one hand on the door.
        Vacant shuttles
Weave the wind. I have no ghosts,
An old man in a draughty house
Under a windy knob.

1. Eliot intended to reprint this dramatic monologue as a prelude to *The Waste Land* until persuaded not to by Ezra Pound. The title is derived from the Greek word meaning "an old man."
2. Lines spoken by the duke of Vienna to describe death in Shakespeare's *Measure for Measure* 3.1.32–34.
3. An allusion to Thermopylae, the mountain pass where the Spartans heroically resisted the Persians (480 B.C.E.).
4. Café. The anti-Semitic passage identifies the landlord with urban decay.
5. Allusions to symptoms of and cures for venereal disease.
6. Dung.
7. Echoes of the "signs and wonders" expected as testimony to Christ's divinity in John 4.48 and the demand "Master, we would see a sign from thee" in Matthew 12.38.
8. Cf. *The Education of Henry Adams* (1918), chap. 18: the "passionate depravity that marked the Maryland May."
9. In lines 18–22, Gerontion imagines Christ as a powerful beast, like "the Lion of the tribe of Juda" (Revelation 5.5). Line 22 alludes to dividing and eating the bread, and drinking the wine, in Christian Communion.

After such knowledge, what forgiveness? Think now
History has many cunning passages, contrived corridors
And issues, deceives with whispering ambitions,
Guides us by vanities. Think now
She gives when our attention is distracted
And what she gives, gives with such supple confusions
That the giving famishes the craving. Gives too late
What's not believed in, or is still believed,
In memory only, reconsidered passion. Gives too soon
Into weak hands, what's thought can be dispensed with
Till the refusal propagates a fear. Think
Neither fear nor courage saves us. Unnatural vices
Are fathered by our heroism. Virtues
Are forced upon us by our impudent crimes.
These tears are shaken from the wrath-bearing tree.

The tiger springs in the new year. Us he devours. Think at last
We have not reached conclusion, when I
Stiffen in a rented house. Think at last
I have not made this show purposelessly
And it is not by any concitation
Of the backward devils.
I would meet you upon this honestly.
I that was near your heart was removed therefrom
To lose beauty in terror, terror in inquisition.
I have lost my passion: why should I need to keep it
Since what is kept must be adulterated?
I have lost my sight, smell, hearing, taste and touch:
How should I use them for your closer contact?

These with a thousand small deliberations
Protract the profit of their chilled delirium,
Excite the membrane, when the sense has cooled,
With pungent sauces, multiply variety
In a wilderness of mirrors. What will the spider do,
Suspend its operations, will the weevil
Delay? De Bailhache, Fresca, Mrs. Cammel, whirled
Beyond the circuit of the shuddering Bear[1]
In fractured atoms. Gull against the wind, in the windy straits
Of Belle Isle, or running on the Horn.
White feathers in the snow, the Gulf claims,
And an old man driven by the Trades[2]
To a sleepy corner.

Tenants of the house,
Thoughts of a dry brain in a dry season.

1920

1. The polestar in the constellation the Bear.
2. Trade winds.

The Waste Land[1]

"Nam Sibyllam quidem Cumis ego ipse oculis meis vidi in ampulla pendere, et cum illi pueri dicerent: Σίβυλα τί θέλεις *respondebat illa:* ἀποθανεῖν θέλω."[2]

FOR EZRA POUND
IL MIGLIOR FABBRO.[3]

I. The Burial of the Dead[4]

April is the cruellest month, breeding
Lilacs out of the dead land, mixing
Memory and desire, stirring
Dull roots with spring rain.
Winter kept us warm, covering
Earth in forgetful snow, feeding
A little life with dried tubers.
Summer surprised us, coming over the Starnbergersee[5]
With a shower of rain; we stopped in the colonnade,
And went on in sunlight, into the Hofgarten,[6]
And drank coffee, and talked for an hour.
Bin gar keine Russin, stamm' aus Litauen, echt deutsch.[7]
And when we were children, staying at the arch-duke's,
My cousin's, he took me out on a sled,
And I was frightened. He said, Marie,
Marie, hold on tight. And down we went.
In the mountains, there you feel free.
I read, much of the night, and go south in the winter.

What are the roots that clutch, what branches grow
Out of this stony rubbish? Son of man,[8]
You cannot say, or guess, for you know only
A heap of broken images, where the sun beats,
And the dead tree gives no shelter, the cricket no relief,[9]

1. Eliot's notes for the first hardcover edition of *The Waste Land* opened with his acknowledgment that "not only the title, but the plan and a good deal of the incidental symbolism of the poem" were suggested by Jessie L. Weston's book on the Grail Legend, *From Ritual to Romance* (1920), and that he was indebted also to James G. Frazer's *The Golden Bough* (1890–1915), "especially the two volumes *Adonis, Attis, Osiris,*" which deal with vegetation myths and fertility rites. Eliot's notes are incorporated in the footnotes to this text. Many critics believe that the notes were added in a spirit of parody. The numerous and extensive literary quotations add to the multivocal effect of the poem.
2. A quotation from Petronius's *Satyricon* (1st century C.E.) about the Sibyl (prophetess) of Cumae, blessed with eternal life by Apollo but doomed to perpetual old age, who guided Aeneas through Hades in Virgil's *Aeneid:* "For once I myself saw with my own eyes the Sibyl at Cumae hanging in a cage, and when the boys said to her 'Sibyl, what do you want?' she replied, 'I want to die.'"
3. "The better maker," the tribute in Dante's *Purgatorio* 26.117 to the Provençal poet Arnaut Daniel.
4. The title of the Anglican burial service.
5. A lake near Munich. Lines 8–16 were suggested by the Countess Marie Larisch's memoir, *My Past* (1913).
6. A public park in Munich, with cafés; former grounds of a Bavarian palace.
7. I am certainly not Russian; I come from Lithuania, a true German (German).
8. "Cf. Ezekiel II, i" [Eliot's note]. There God addresses the prophet Ezekiel as "Son of man" and declares: "stand upon thy feet, and I will speak unto thee."
9. "Cf. Ecclesiastes XII, v" [Eliot's note]. There the preacher describes the bleakness of old age when "the grasshopper shall be a burden, and desire shall fail."

And the dry stone no sound of water. Only
There is shadow under this red rock,[1]
(Come in under the shadow of this red rock),
And I will show you something different from either
Your shadow at morning striding behind you
Or your shadow at evening rising to meet you;
I will show you fear in a handful of dust.
Frisch weht der Wind
Der Heimat zu
Mein Irisch Kind,
Wo weilest du?[2]
'You gave me hyacinths first a year ago;
'They called me the hyacinth girl.'
—Yet when we came back, late, from the hyacinth[3] garden,
Your arms full, and your hair wet, I could not
Speak, and my eyes failed, I was neither
Living nor dead, and I knew nothing,
Looking into the heart of light, the silence.
Oed' und leer das Meer.[4]

Madame Sosostris,[5] famous clairvoyante,
Had a bad cold, nevertheless
Is known to be the wisest woman in Europe,
With a wicked pack of cards.[6] Here, said she,
Is your card, the drowned Phoenician Sailor,[7]
(Those are pearls that were his eyes.[8] Look!)
Here is Belladonna,[9] the Lady of the Rocks,
The lady of situations.
Here is the man with three staves, and here the Wheel,
And here is the one-eyed merchant,[1] and this card,
Which is blank, is something he carries on his back,

1. Cf. Isaiah 32.1–2 and the prophecy that the reign of the Messiah "shall be . . . as rivers of water in a dry place, as the shadow of a great rock in a weary land."
2. "V. [see] *Tristan und Isolde,* I, verses 5–8" [Eliot's note]. In Wagner's opera, a sailor aboard Tristan's ship recalls his love back in Ireland: "Fresh blows the wind to the homeland; my Irish child, where are you waiting?"
3. The boy in Ovid's *Metamorphoses* 10, who was beloved by Apollo but slain by a jealous rival. The Greeks celebrated his festival in May.
4. "III, verse 24" [Eliot's note]. In *Tristan,* III, verse 24, the dying Tristan, awaiting the ship that carries his beloved Isolde, is told that "Empty and barren is the sea."
5. Eliot derived the name from "Sesostris, the Sorceress of Ectabana," the pseudo-Egyptian name assumed by a woman who tells fortunes in Aldous Huxley's novel *Chrome Yellow* (1921). Sesostris was a 12th-dynasty Egyptian king.
6. The tarot deck of cards. Eliot's note to this passage reads: "I am not familiar with the exact constitution of the Tarot pack of cards, from which I have obviously departed to suit my own convenience. The Hanged Man, a member of the traditional pack, fits my purpose in two ways: because he is associated in my mind with the Hanged God of Frazer, and because I associate him with the hooded figure in the passage of the disciples to Emmaus in Part V. The Phoenician Sailor and the Merchant appear later; also the 'crowds of people,' and Death by Water is executed in Part IV. The Man with Three Staves (an authentic member of the Tarot pack) I associate, quite arbitrarily, with the Fisher King himself."
7. A symbolic figure that includes "Mr. Eugenides, the Smyrna merchant" in Part III and "Phlebas the Phoenician" in Part IV. The ancient Phoenicians were seagoing merchants who spread Egyptian fertility cults throughout the Mediterranean.
8. The line is a quotation from Ariel's song in Shakespeare's *Tempest* 1.2.398. Prince Ferdinand, disconsolate because he thinks his father has drowned in the storm, is consoled when Ariel sings of a miraculous sea change that has transformed death into "something rich and strange."
9. Literally "beautiful lady"; the name of both the poisonous plant deadly nightshade and a cosmetic.
1. These three figures are from the Tarot deck.

Which I am forbidden to see. I do not find
The Hanged Man. Fear death by water.
I see crowds of people, walking round in a ring.
Thank you. If you see dear Mrs. Equitone,
Tell her I bring the horoscope myself:
One must be so careful these days.

Unreal City,[2]
Under the brown fog of a winter dawn,
A crowd flowed over London Bridge, so many,
I had not thought death had undone so many.[3]
Sighs, short and infrequent, were exhaled,[4]
And each man fixed his eyes before his feet.
Flowed up the hill and down King William Street,
To where Saint Mary Woolnoth kept the hours
With a dead sound on the final stroke of nine.[5]
There I saw one I knew, and stopped him, crying: 'Stetson![6]
'You who were with me in the ships at Mylae![7]
'That corpse you planted last year in your garden,
'Has it begun to sprout? Will it bloom this year?
'Or has the sudden frost disturbed its bed?
'O keep the Dog far hence, that's friend to men,
'Or with his nails he'll dig it up again![8]
'You! hypocrite lecteur!—mon semblable,—mon frère!'[9]

II. A Game of Chess[1]

The Chair she sat in, like a burnished throne,[2]
Glowed on the marble, where the glass

2. "Cf. Baudelaire: 'Fourmillante cité, cité pleine de rêves, / Où le spectre en plein jour raccroche le passant'" [Eliot's note]. The lines are quoted from "Les Sept Vieillards" (The seven old men), poem 93 of *Les Fleurs du Mal* (The flowers of evil, 1857) by the French Symbolist Charles Baudelaire (1821–1867), and may be translated from the French: "Swarming city, city full of dreams, / Where the specter in broad daylight accosts the passerby."
3. "*Cf. Inferno* III, 55–57" [Eliot's note]. The note continues to quote Dante's lines, which may be translated: "So long a train of people, / That I should never have believed / That death had undone so many."
4. "Cf. *Inferno* IV, 25–27" [Eliot's note]. Dante describes, in Limbo, the virtuous pagan dead, who, living before Christ, could not hope for salvation. The lines read: "Here, so far as I could tell by listening, / There was no lamentation except sighs, / which caused the eternal air to tremble."
5. "A phenomenon which I have often noticed" [Eliot's note]. The church named is in the financial district of London.
6. A hat manufacturer.
7. The battle of Mylae (260 B.C.E.) was a victory for Rome against Carthage.
8. "Cf. the dirge in Webster's *White Devil*" [Eliot's note]. In the play by John Webster (d. 1625), a crazed woman fears that the corpses of her decadent and murdered relatives might be disinterred: "But keep the wolf far thence, that's foe to men, / For with his nails he'll dig them up again." In echoing the lines Eliot altered "foe" to "friend" and the "wolf" to "Dog," invoking the brilliant Dog Star, Sirius, whose rise in the heavens accompanied the flooding of the Nile and promised the return of fertility to Egypt.
9. "V. Baudelaire, Preface to *Fleurs du Mal*" [Eliot's note]. The last line of the introductory poem to *Les Fleurs du Mal*. "Au Lecteur" (To the reader) may be translated from the French: "Hypocrite reader!—my likeness—my brother!
1. The title suggests two plays by Thomas Middleton: *A Game of Chess* (1627), about a marriage of political expediency, and *Women Beware Women* (1657), containing a scene in which a mother-in-law is engrossed in a chess game while her daughter-in-law is seduced nearby. Eliot's note to line 118 refers readers to this play. It is now believed that much of this section reflects Eliot's disintegrating marriage.
2. "Cf. *Antony and Cleopatra*, II, ii. 190" [Eliot's note]. In Shakespeare's play, Enobarbus's description of Cleopatra begins: "The barge she sat in, like a burnish'd throne, / Burn'd on the water."

Held up by standards wrought with fruited vines
From which a golden Cupidon peeped out
(Another hid his eyes behind his wing)
Doubled the flames of sevenbranched candelabra
Reflecting light upon the table as
The glitter of her jewels rose to meet it,
From satin cases poured in rich profusion.
In vials of ivory and coloured glass
Unstoppered, lurked her strange synthetic perfumes,
Unguent, powdered, or liquid—troubled, confused
And drowned the sense in odours; stirred by the air
That freshened from the window, these ascended
In fattening the prolonged candle-flames,
Flung their smoke into the laquearia,[3]
Stirring the pattern on the coffered ceiling.
Huge sea-wood fed with copper
Burned green and orange, framed by the coloured stone,
In which sad light a carvèd dolphin swam.
Above the antique mantel was displayed
As though a window gave upon the sylvan scene[4]
The change of Philomel, by the barbarous king
So rudely forced; yet there the nightingale
Filled all the desert with inviolable voice
And still she cried, and still the world pursues,
'Jug Jug'[5] to dirty ears.
And other withered stumps of time
Were told upon the walls; staring forms
Leaned out, leaning, hushing the room enclosed.
Footsteps shuffled on the stair.
Under the firelight, under the brush, her hair
Spread out in fiery points
Glowed into words, then would be savagely still.

'My nerves are bad to-night. Yes, bad. Stay with me.
'Speak to me. Why do you never speak. Speak.
  'What are you thinking of? What thinking? What?
'I never know what you are thinking. Think.'

I think we are in rats' alley[6]
Where the dead men lost their bones.

3. "Laquearia, V. *Aeneid*, I, 726" [Eliot's note]. Eliot quotes the passage containing the term *laquearia* ("paneled ceiling") and describing the banquet hall where Queen Dido welcomed Aeneas to Carthage. It reads: "Blazing torches hang from the gilded paneled ceiling, and torches conquer the night with flames." Aeneas became Dido's lover but abandoned her to continue his journey to found Rome, and she committed suicide.

4. Eliot's notes for lines 98–99 refer the reader to "Milton, *Paradise Lost*, IV, 140" for the phrase "sylvan scene" and to "Ovid, *Metamorphoses*, VI, Philomela." The lines splice the setting of Eve's temptation in the Garden of Eden, first described through Satan's eyes, with the rape of Philomela by her sister's husband, King Tereus, and her transformation into the nightingale. Eliot's note for line 100 refers the reader ahead to the nightingale's song in Part III, line 204, of his own poem.

5. The conventional rendering of the nightingale's song in Elizabethan poetry.

6. Eliot's note refers readers to "Part III, l. 195."

'What is that noise?'
                                        The wind under the door.[7]
'What is that noise now? What is the wind doing?'
                                        Nothing again nothing.
                                                                'Do
'You know nothing? Do you see nothing? Do you remember
'Nothing?'

        I remember
Those are pearls that were his eyes.
'Are you alive, or not? Is there nothing in your head?'
                                                                But
O O O O that Shakespeherian Rag—
It's so elegant
So intelligent
'What shall I do now? What shall I do?'
'I shall rush out as I am, and walk the street
'With my hair down, so. What shall we do tomorrow?
'What shall we ever do?'
                                        The hot water at ten.
And if it rains, a closed car at four.
And we shall play a game of chess,
Pressing lidless eyes and waiting for a knock upon the door.

When Lil's husband got demobbed,[8] I said—
I didn't mince my words, I said to her myself,
HURRY UP PLEASE ITS TIME[9]
Now Albert's coming back, make yourself a bit smart.
He'll want to know what you done with that money he gave you
To get yourself some teeth. He did, I was there.
You have them all out, Lil, and get a nice set,
He said, I swear, I can't bear to look at you.
And no more can't I, I said, and think of poor Albert,
He's been in the army four years, he wants a good time,
And if you don't give it him, there's others will, I said.
Oh is there, she said. Something o' that, I said.
Then I'll know who to thank, she said, and give me a straight look.
HURRY UP PLEASE ITS TIME
If you don't like it you can get on with it, I said.
Others can pick and choose if you can't.
But if Albert makes off, it won't be for lack of telling.
You ought to be ashamed, I said, to look so antique.
(And her only thirty-one.)
I can't help it, she said, pulling a long face,
It's them pills I took, to bring it off, she said.

7. "Cf. Webster: 'Is the wind in that door still?'" [Eliot's note]. In John Webster's *The Devil's Law Case* (1623) 3.2.162, a duke is cured of an infection by a wound intended to kill him; a surprised surgeon asks the quoted question, meaning, "Is he still alive?"
8. Slang for "demobilized," discharged from the army.
9. Routine call of British bartenders to clear the pub at closing time.

(She's had five already, and nearly died of young George.)
The chemist[1] said it would be all right, but I've never been the same.
You *are* a proper fool, I said.
Well, if Albert won't leave you alone, there it is, I said,
What you get married for if you don't want children?
HURRY UP PLEASE ITS TIME
Well, that Sunday Albert was home, they had a hot gammon,[2]
And they asked me in to dinner, to get the beauty of it hot—
HURRY UP PLEASE ITS TIME
HURRY UP PLEASE ITS TIME
Goonight Bill, Goonight Lou. Goonight May. Goonight.
Ta ta. Goonight. Goonight.
Good night, ladies, good night, sweet ladies, good night, good night.[3]

III. The Fire Sermon[4]

The river's tent is broken; the last fingers of leaf
Clutch and sink into the wet bank. The wind
Crosses the brown land, unheard. The nymphs are departed.
Sweet Thames, run softly, till I end my song.[5]
The river bears no empty bottles, sandwich papers,
Silk handkerchiefs, cardboard boxes, cigarette ends
Or other testimony of summer nights. The nymphs are departed.
And their friends, the loitering heirs of City directors;
Departed, have left no addresses.
By the waters of Leman I sat down and wept[6] . . .
Sweet Thames, run softly till I end my song,
Sweet Thames, run softly, for I speak not loud or long.
But at my back in a cold blast I hear[7]
The rattle of the bones, and chuckle spread from ear to ear.

A rat crept softly through the vegetation
Dragging its slimy belly on the bank
While I was fishing in the dull canal
On a winter evening round behind the gashouse
Musing upon the king my brother's wreck[8]
And on the king my father's death before him.

1. Pharmacist.
2. Ham or bacon.
3. A double echo of the popular song "Good night ladies, we're going to leave you now" and mad Ophelia's farewell before drowning, in Shakespeare, *Hamlet* 4.5.72.
4. I.e., Buddha's Fire Sermon. See p. 374, n. 8.
5. "V. Spenser, *Prothalamion*" [Eliot's note]. The line is the refrain of the marriage song by Edmund Spenser (1552–1599), a pastoral celebration of marriage set along the Thames River near London.
6. The phrasing recalls Psalms 137.1, in which the exiled Jews mourn for their homeland: "By the rivers of Babylon, there we sat down, yea, we wept, when we remembered Zion." Lake Leman is another name for Lake Geneva, location of the sanatorium where Eliot wrote the bulk of *The Waste Land*. The archaic term *leman*, for "illicit mistress," led to the phrase "waters of leman" signifying lusts.
7. This line and line 196 echo Andrew Marvell (1621–1678), *To His Coy Mistress*, lines 21–24: "But at my back I always hear / Time's wingèd chariot hurrying near; / And yonder all before us lie / Deserts of vast eternity."
8. "Cf. *The Tempest*, I, ii" [Eliot's note]. Another allusion to Shakespeare's play, 1.2.389–90, where Prince Ferdinand, thinking his father dead, describes himself as "Sitting on a bank, / Weeping again the King my father's wrack."

White bodies naked on the low damp ground
And bones cast in a little low dry garret,
Rattled by the rat's foot only, year to year.
But at my back from time to time I hear
The sound of horns and motors, which shall bring
Sweeney to Mrs. Porter in the spring.[9]
O the moon shone bright on Mrs. Porter
And on her daughter
They wash their feet in soda water[1]
Et, O ces voix d'enfants, chantant dans la coupole!;[2]

Twit twit twit
Jug jug jug jug jug jug

So rudely forc'd.
Tereu[3]

Unreal City
Under the brown fog of a winter noon
Mr. Eugenides, the Smyrna merchant
Unshaven, with a pocket full of currants
C.i.f.[4] London: documents at sight,
Asked me in demotic French
To luncheon at the Cannon Street Hotel
Followed by a weekend at the Metropole.

At the violet hour, when the eyes and back
Turn upward from the desk, when the human engine waits
Like a taxi throbbing waiting,
I Tiresias,[5] though blind, throbbing between two lives,

9. "Cf. Day, *Parliament of Bees*: 'When of the sudden, listening, you shall hear, / A noise of horns and hunting, which shall bring / Actaeon to Diana in the spring, / Where all shall see her naked skin'" [Eliot's note]. Actaeon was changed into a stag and hunted to death as punishment for seeing Diana, goddess of chastity, bathing. John Day (1574–c. 1640), English poet.

1. "I do not know the origin of the ballad from which these lines are taken: it was reported to me from Sydney, Australia" [Eliot's note]. The bawdy song was popular among World War I troops.

2. "V. Verlaine, *Parsifal*" [Eliot's note]. The last line of the sonnet "Parsifal" by the French Symbolist Paul Verlaine (1844–1896) reads: "And O those children's voices singing in the cupola." In Wagner's opera, the feet of Parsifal, the questing knight, are washed before he enters the sanctuary of the Grail.

3. Alludes to Tereus, who raped Philomela, and like *jug* is a conventional Elizabethan term for the nightingale's song; also a slang pronunciation of *true*.

4. "The currants were quoted at a price 'carriage and insurance free to London'; and the Bill of Lading, etc. were to be handed to the buyer upon payment of the sight draft" [Eliot's note]. Some have suggested another possibility for the phrase "carriage and insurance free": "cost, insurance and freight."

5. Eliot's note reads: "Tiresias, although a mere spectator and not indeed a 'character,' is yet the most important personage in the poem, uniting all the rest. Just as the one-eyed merchant, seller of currants, melts into the Phoenician Sailor, and the latter is not wholly distinct from Ferdinand Prince of Naples, so all the women are one woman, and the two sexes meet in Tiresias. What Tiresias *sees,* in fact, is the substance of the poem. The whole passage from Ovid is of great anthropological interest." The note quotes the Latin passage from Ovid, *Metamorphoses* 2.421–43, which may be translated: "Jove [very drunk] said jokingly to Juno: 'You women have greater pleasure in love than that enjoyed by men.' She denied it. So they decided to refer the question to wise Tiresias who knew love from both points of view. For once, with a blow of his staff, he had separated two huge snakes who were copulating in the forest, and miraculously was changed instantly from a man into a woman and remained so for seven years. In the eighth year he saw the snakes again and said: 'If a blow against you is so powerful that it changes the sex of the author of it, now I shall strike you again.' With these words he struck them, and his former shape and masculinity were restored. As

Old man with wrinkled female breasts, can see
At the violet hour, the evening hour that strives
Homeward, and brings the sailor home from sea,[6]
The typist home at teatime, clears her breakfast, lights
Her stove, and lays out food in tins.
Out of the window perilously spread
Her drying combinations touched by the sun's last rays,
On the divan are piled (at night her bed)
Stockings, slippers, camisoles, and stays.
I Tiresias, old man with wrinkled dugs
Perceived the scene, and foretold the rest—
I too awaited the expected guest.
He, the young man carbuncular, arrives,
A small house agent's clerk, with one bold stare,
One of the low on whom assurance sits
As a silk hat on a Bradford[7] millionaire.
The time is now propitious, as he guesses,
The meal is ended, she is bored and tired,
Endeavours to engage her in caresses
Which still are unreproved, if undesired.
Flushed and decided, he assaults at once;
Exploring hands encounter no defence;
His vanity requires no response,
And makes a welcome of indifference.
(And I Tiresias have foresuffered all
Enacted on this same divan or bed;
I who have sat by Thebes below the wall[8]
And walked among the lowest of the dead.)
Bestows one final patronising kiss,
And gropes his way, finding the stairs unlit . . .

She turns and looks a moment in the glass,
Hardly aware of her departed lover;
Her brain allows one half-formed thought to pass:
'Well now that's done: and I'm glad it's over.'
When lovely woman stoops to folly and
Paces about her room again, alone,
She smoothes her hair with automatic hand,
And puts a record on the gramophone.[9]

referee in the sportive quarrel, he supported Jove's claim. Juno, overly upset by the decision, condemned the arbitrator to eternal blindness. But the all-powerful father (inasmuch as no god can undo what has been done by another god) gave him the power of prophecy, with this honor compensating him for the loss of sight."

6. "This may not appear as exact as Sappho's lines, but I had in mind the 'longshore' or 'dory' fisherman, who returns at nightfall" [Eliot's note]. Fragment 149, by the female Greek poet Sappho (fl. 600 B.C.E.), celebrates the Evening Star who "brings homeward all those / Scattered by the dawn, / The sheep to fold . . . / The children to their mother's side." A more familiar echo is "Home is the sailor, home from sea" in "Requiem" by Robert Louis Stevenson (1850–1894).

7. A Yorkshire, England, manufacturing town where fortunes were made during World War I.

8. Tiresias prophesied in the marketplace below the wall of Thebes, witnessed the tragedies of Oedipus and Creon in that city, and retained his prophetic powers in the underworld.

9. Eliot's note refers to the novel *The Vicar of Wakefield* (1766) by Oliver Goldsmith (1728–1774) and the song sung by Olivia when she revisits the scene of her seduction: "When lovely woman stoops to folly / And finds too late that men betray / What charm can soothe her melancholy, / What art can wash her guilt away? / The only art her guilt to cover, / To hide her shame from every eye, / To give repentance to her lover / And wring his bosom—is to die."

'This music crept by me upon the waters'[1]
And along the Strand, up Queen Victoria Street.
O City city, I can sometimes hear
Beside a public bar in Lower Thames Street,
The pleasant whining of a mandoline
And a clatter and a chatter from within
Where fishmen lounge at noon: where the walls
Of Magnus Martyr[2] hold
Inexplicable splendour of Ionian white and gold.

The river sweats[3]
Oil and tar
The barges drift
With the turning tide
Red sails
Wide
To leeward, swing on the heavy spar.
The barges wash
Drifting logs
Down Greenwich reach
Past the Isle of Dogs.[4]
Weialala leia
Wallala leialala

Elizabeth and Leicester[5]
Beating oars
The stern was formed
A gilded shell
Red and gold
The brisk swell
Rippled both shores
Southwest wind
Carried down stream
The peal of bells
White towers
Weialala leia
Wallala leialala

1. Eliot's note refers to Shakespeare's *The Tempest,* the scene where Ferdinand listens to Ariel's song telling of his father's miraculous sea change: "This music crept by me on the waters, / Allaying both their fury and my passion / With its sweet air" (1.2.391–93).
2. "The interior of St. Magnus Martyr is to my mind one of the finest among [Christopher] Wren's interiors" [Eliot's note].
3. "The Song of the (three) Thames-daughters begins here. From line 292 to 306 inclusive they speak in turn. V. *Götterdämmerung,* III, i: the Rhine-daughters" [Eliot's note]. Lines 277–78 and 290–91 are from the lament of the Rhine maidens for the lost beauty of the Rhine River in the opera by Richard Wagner (1813–1883), *Götterdämmerung* (The twilight of the gods, 1876).
4. A peninsula in the Thames opposite Greenwich, a borough of London and the birthplace of Queen Elizabeth I. Throughout this section Eliot has named places along the Thames River.
5. Reference to the romance between Queen Elizabeth I and the earl of Leicester. Eliot's note refers to the historian James A. Froude, "*Elizabeth,* Vol. I. ch. iv, letter of [bishop] De Quadra [the ambassador] to Philip of Spain: 'In the afternoon we were in a barge, watching the games on the river. (The queen) was alone with Lord Robert and myself on the poop, when they began to talk nonsense, and went so far that Lord Robert at last said, as I was on the spot there was no reason why they should not be married if the queen pleased.'"

Trams and dusty trees.
Highbury bore me. Richmond and Kew
Undid me.[6] By Richmond I raised my knees
Supine on the floor of a narrow canoe.'
'My feet are at Moorgate, and my heart
Under my feet. After the event
He wept. He promised "a new start."
I made no comment. What should I resent?'

'On Margate Sands,
I can connect
Nothing with nothing.
The broken fingernails of dirty hands.
My people humble people who expect
Nothing.'
                    la la

To Carthage then I came[7]

Burning burning burning burning[8]
O Lord Thou pluckest me out[9]
O Lord Thou pluckest

burning

IV. Death by Water

Phlebas the Phoenician, a fortnight dead,
Forgot the cry of gulls, and the deep sea swell
And the profit and loss.
                                    A current under sea
Picked his bones in whispers. As he rose and fell
He passed the stages of his age and youth
Entering the whirlpool.
                                    Gentile or Jew
O you who turn the wheel and look to windward,
Consider Phlebas, who was once handsome and tall as you.

V. What the Thunder Said[1]

After the torchlight red on sweaty faces
After the frosty silence in the gardens

6. "Cf. *Purgatorio,* V, 133" [Eliot's note]. Eliot parodies Dante's lines, which may be translated: "Remember me, who am La Pia. / Siena made me, Maremma undid me."
7. "V. St. Augustine's *Confessions:* 'to Carthage then I came, where a cauldron of unholy loves sang all about mine ears'" [Eliot's note]. Augustine here recounts his licentious youth.
8. Eliot's note to lines 307–09 refers to "Buddha's Fire Sermon (which corresponds in importance to the Sermon on the Mount)" and "St. Augustine's Confessions." The "collocation of these two representatives of eastern and western asceticism, as the culmination of this part of the poem, is not an accident."
9. The line is from Augustine's *Confessions* and echoes also Zechariah 3.2, where Jehovah, rebuking Satan, calls the high priest Joshua "a brand plucked out of the fire."
1. "In the first part of Part V three themes are employed: the journey to Emmaus, the approach to the Chapel Perilous (see Miss Weston's book) and the present decay of eastern Europe" [Eliot's note]. During his disciples' journey to Emmaus,

After the agony in stony places
The shouting and the crying
Prison and palace and reverberation
Of thunder of spring over distant mountains
He who was living is now dead
We who were living are now dying
With a little patience[2]

Here is no water but only rock
Rock and no water and the sandy road
The road winding above among the mountains
Which are mountains of rock without water
If there were water we should stop and drink
Amongst the rock one cannot stop or think
Sweat is dry and feet are in the sand
If there were only water amongst the rock
Dead mountain mouth of carious teeth that cannot spit
Here one can neither stand nor lie nor sit
There is not even silence in the mountains
But dry sterile thunder without rain
There is not even solitude in the mountains
But red sullen faces sneer and snarl
From doors of mudcracked houses
If there were water

And no rock
If there were rock
And also water
And water
A spring
A pool among the rock
If there were the sound of water only
Not the cicada[3]
And dry grass singing
But sound of water over a rock
Where the hermit-thrush[4] sings in the pine trees
Drip drop drip drop drop drop drop
But there is no water

Who is the third who walks always beside you?[5]
When I count, there are only you and I together

---

after his Crucifixion and Resurrection, Jesus walked alongside and conversed with them, but they did not recognize him (Luke 24.13–34).

2. The opening nine lines allude to Christ's imprisonment and trial, to his agony in the garden of Gethsemane, and to his Crucifixion on Golgotha (Calvary) and burial.

3. Grasshopper. Cf. line 23 and see p. 365, n. 9.

4. "This is . . . the hermit-thrush which I have heard in Quebec Province. Chapman says (*Handbook of Birds of Eastern North America*) 'it is most at home in secluded woodland and thickety retreats.' . . . Its 'water dripping song' is justly celebrated" [Eliot's note].

5. "The following lines were stimulated by the account of one of the Antarctic expeditions (I forget which, but I think one of Shackleton's): it was related that the party of explorers, at the extremity of their strength, had the constant delusion that there was *one more member* than could actually be counted" [Eliot's note].

But when I look ahead up the white road
There is always another one walking beside you
Gliding wrapt in a brown mantle, hooded
I do not know whether a man or a woman
—But who is that on the other side of you?

What is that sound high in the air[6]
Murmur of maternal lamentation
Who are those hooded hordes swarming
Over endless plains, stumbling in cracked earth
Ringed by the flat horizon only
What is the city over the mountains
Cracks and reforms and bursts in the violet air
Falling towers
Jerusalem Athens Alexandria
Vienna London
Unreal

A woman drew her long black hair out tight
And fiddled whisper music on those strings
And bats with baby faces in the violet light
Whistled, and beat their wings
And crawled head downward down a blackened wall
And upside down in air were towers
Tolling reminiscent bells, that kept the hours
And voices singing out of empty cisterns and exhausted wells.

In this decayed hole among the mountains
In the faint moonlight, the grass is singing
Over the tumbled graves, about the chapel
There is the empty chapel, only the wind's home.
It has no windows, and the door swings,
Dry bones can harm no one.
Only a cock stood on the rooftree
Co co rico co co rico[7]
In a flash of lightning. Then a damp gust
Bringing rain

Ganga[8] was sunken, and the limp leaves
Waited for rain, while the black clouds
Gathered far distant, over Himavant.[9]
The jungle crouched, humped in silence.
Then spoke the thunder

6. Eliot's note quotes a passage in German from *Blick ins Chaos* (1920) by Hermann Hesse (1877–1962), which may be translated: "Already half of Europe, already at least half of Eastern Europe, on the way to Chaos, drives drunk in sacred infatuation along the edge of the precipice, since drunkenly, as though hymn-singing, as Dimitri Karamazov sang in [the novel] *The Brothers Karamazov* [1882] by Feodor Dostoevsky [1821–1881]. The offended bourgeois laughs at the songs; the saint and the seer hear them with tears."

7. A cock's crow in folklore signaled the departure of ghosts (as in Shakespeare's *Hamlet* 1.1.157ff.); in Matthew 26.34 and 74, a cock crowed, as Christ predicted, when Peter denied him three times.

8. The Indian river Ganges.

9. A mountain in the Himalayas.

DA[1]
Datta: what have we given?
My friend, blood shaking my heart
The awful daring of a moment's surrender
Which an age of prudence can never retract
By this, and this only, we have existed
Which is not to be found in our obituaries
Or in memories draped by the beneficent spider[2]
Or under seals broken by the lean solicitor
In our empty rooms
DA
Dayadhvam: I have heard the key[3]
Turn in the door once and turn once only
We think of the key, each in his prison
Thinking of the key, each confirms a prison
Only at nightfall, aethereal rumours
Revive for a moment a broken Coriolanus[4]
DA
Damyata: The boat responded
Gaily, to the hand expert with sail and oar
The sea was calm, your heart would have responded
Gaily, when invited, beating obedient
To controlling hands

I sat upon the shore
Fishing,[5] with the arid plain behind me
Shall I at least set my lands in order?[6]
London Bridge is falling down falling down falling down
Poi s'ascose nel foco che gli affina[7]
Quando fiam uti chelidon[8]—O swallow swallow

1. "'Datta, dayadhvam, damyata' (Give, sympathise, control). The fable of the meaning of the Thunder is found in the *Brihadaranyaka—Upanishad,* 5, 1" [Eliot's note]. In the Hindu legend, the injunction of Prajapati (supreme deity) is *Da,* which is interpreted in three different ways by gods, men, and demons, to mean "control ourselves," "give alms," and "have compassion." Prajapati assures them that when "the divine voice, The Thunder," repeats the syllable it means all three things and that therefore "one should practice . . . Self-Control, Alms-giving, and Compassion."
2. Eliot's note refers to Webster's *The White Devil* 5.6: "they'll remarry / Ere the worm pierce your winding-sheet, ere the spider / Make a thin curtain for your epitaphs."
3. "Cf. *Inferno,* XXXIII, 46" [Eliot's note]. At this point Ugolino recalls his imprisonment with his children, where they starved to death: "And I heard below the door of the horrible tower being locked up." Eliot's note continues: "Also F. H. Bradley, *Appearance and Reality,* p.346. 'My external sensations are no less private to myself than are my thoughts or my feelings. In either case my experience falls within my own circle, a circle closed on the outside; and, with all its elements alike, every sphere is opaque to the others which surround it. . . . In brief, regarded as an existence which appears in a soul, the whole world for each is peculiar and private to that soul.'"
4. Roman patrician who defiantly chose self-exile when threatened with banishment by the leaders of the populace. He is the tragic protagonist in Shakespeare's *Coriolanus* (1608).
5. "V. Weston: *From Ritual to Romance;* chapter on the Fisher King" [Eliot's note].
6. Cf. Isaiah 38.1: "Thus saith the Lord, Set thine house in order: for thou shalt die, and not live."
7. Eliot's note to *Purgatorio* 26 quotes in Italian the passage (lines 145–48) where the Provençal poet Arnaut Daniel, recalling his lusts, addresses Dante: "I pray you now, by the Goodness that guides you to the summit of this staircase, reflect in due season on my suffering." Then, in the line quoted in *The Waste Land,* "he hid himself in the fire that refines them."
8. Eliot's note refers to the *Pervigilium Veneris* (The Vigil of Venus), an anonymous Latin poem, and suggests a comparison with "Philomela in Parts II and III" of *The Waste Land.* The last stanzas of the *Pervigilium* recreate the myth of the nightingale in the image of a swallow, and the poet listening to the bird speaks the quoted line, "When shall I be as the swallow," and adds: "that I may cease to be silent." "O Swallow, Swallow" are the opening words of one of the songs interspersed in Tennyson's narrative poem *The Princess* (1847).

Le Prince d'Aquitaine à la tour abolie[9]
These fragments I have shored against my ruins
Why then Ile fit you. Hieronymo's mad againe.[1]
Datta. Dayadhvam. Damyata.
Shantih shantih shantih[2]

1921 1922

The Hollow Men

Mistah Kurtz—he dead.[1]
A penny for the Old Guy[2]

I

We are the hollow men
We are the stuffed men
Leaning together
Headpiece filled with straw. Alas!
Our dried voices, when
We whisper together
Are quiet and meaningless
As wind in dry grass
Or rats' feet over broken glass
In our dry cellar

Shape without form, shade without colour,
Paralysed force, gesture without motion;

Those who have crossed
With direct eyes, to death's other Kingdom
Remember us—if at all—not as lost
Violent souls, but only
As the hollow men
The stuffed men.

9. "V. Gerard de Nerval, Sonnet *El Desdichado*" [Eliot's note]. The line reads: "The Prince of Aquitaine in the ruined tower."
1. Eliot's note refers to Thomas Kyd's revenge play, *The Spanish Tragedy,* subtitled *Hieronymo's Mad Againe* (1594). In it Hieronymo is asked to write a court play and he answers, "I'll fit you," in the double sense of "oblige" and "get even." He manages, although mad, to kill the murderers of his son by acting in the play and assigning parts appropriately, then commits suicide.
2. "Shantih. Repeated as here, a formal ending to an Upanishad. 'The peace which passeth understanding' is our equivalent to this word" [Eliot's note]. The Upanishad is a Vedic treatise, a sacred Hindu text.

1. Quotation from *Heart of Darkness,* by Joseph Conrad (1857–1924). Kurtz went into the African jungle as an official of a trading company and degenerated into an evil, tyrannical man. His dying words were "the horror!"
2. Guy Fawkes led a group of conspirators who planned to blow up the English House of Commons in 1605; he was caught and executed before the plan was carried out. On the day of his execution (November 5) children make straw effigies of the "guy" and beg for pennies for fireworks.

II

Eyes I dare not meet in dreams
In death's dream kingdom
These do not appear:
There, the eyes are
Sunlight on a broken column
There, is a tree swinging
And voices are
In the wind's singing
More distant and more solemn
Than a fading star.

Let me be no nearer
In death's dream kingdom
Let me also wear
Such deliberate disguises
Rat's coat, crowskin, crossed staves
In a field
Behaving as the wind behaves
No nearer—

Not that final meeting
In the twilight kingdom

III

This is the dead land
This is cactus land
Here the stone images
Are raised, here they receive
The supplication of a dead man's hand
Under the twinkle of a fading star.

Is it like this
In death's other kingdom
Waking alone
At the hour when we are
Trembling with tenderness
Lips that would kiss
Form prayers to broken stone.

IV

The eyes are not here
There are no eyes here
In this valley of dying stars
In this hollow valley
This broken jaw of our lost kingdoms

In this last of meeting places
We grope together

And avoid speech
Gathered on this beach of the tumid river

Sightless, unless
The eyes reappear
As the perpetual star
Multifoliate rose[3]
Of death's twilight kingdom
The hope only
Of empty men.

V

Here we go round the prickly pear
Prickly pear prickly pear
Here we go round the prickly pear
At five o'clock in the morning.[4]

Between the idea
And the reality
Between the motion
And the act
Falls the Shadow

For Thine is the Kingdom[5]

Between the conception
And the creation
Between the emotion
And the response
Falls the Shadow

Life is very long

Between the desire
And the spasm
Between the potency
And the existence
Between the essence
And the descent
Falls the Shadow

For Thine is the Kingdom

For Thine is
Life is
For Thine is the

3. Part 3 of *The Divine Comedy,* by Dante Alighieri (1265–1321), is a vision of Paradise. The souls of the saved in heaven range themselves around the deity in the figure of a "multifoliate rose" (*Paradiso* 28.30).

4. Allusion to a children's rhyming game, "Here we go round the mulberry bush," substituting a prickly pear cactus for the mulberry bush.

5. Part of a line from the Lord's Prayer.

This is the way the world ends
This is the way the world ends
This is the way the world ends
Not with a bang but a whimper.

1925

Journey of the Magi[1]

'A cold coming we had of it,
Just the worst time of the year
For a journey, and such a long journey:
The ways deep and the weather sharp,
The very dead of winter.'[2]
And the camels galled, sore-footed, refractory,
Lying down in the melting snow.
There were times we regretted
The summer palaces on slopes, the terraces,
And the silken girls bringing sherbet.
Then the camel men cursing and grumbling
And running away, and wanting their liquor and women,
And the night-fires going out, and the lack of shelters,
And the cities hostile and the towns unfriendly
And the villages dirty and charging high prices:
A hard time we had of it.
At the end we preferred to travel all night,
Sleeping in snatches,
With the voices singing in our ears, saying
That this was all folly.

Then at dawn we came down to a temperate valley,
Wet, below the snow line, smelling of vegetation,
With a running stream and a water-mill beating the darkness,
And three trees on the low sky.
And an old white horse galloped away in the meadow.
Then we came to a tavern with vine-leaves over the lintel,
Six hands at an open door dicing for pieces of silver,
And feet kicking the empty wine-skins.
But there was no information, and so we continued
And arrived at evening, not a moment too soon
Finding the place; it was (you may say) satisfactory.

All this was a long time ago, I remember,
And I would do it again, but set down
This set down
This: were we led all that way for

1. The three wise men, or kings, who followed the star of Bethlehem, bringing gifts to the newly born Christ.

2. These lines are adapted from the sermon preached at Christmas, in 1622, by Bishop Lancelot Andrewes.

Birth or Death? There was a Birth, certainly,
We had evidence and no doubt. I had seen birth and death,
But had thought they were different; this Birth was
Hard and bitter agony for us, like Death, our death.
We returned to our places, these Kingdoms,
But no longer at ease here, in the old dispensation,
With an alien people clutching their gods.
I should be glad of another death.

1935

From Four Quartets

Burnt Norton[1]

τοῦ λόγου δ'εόντος ξυνοῦ ζώουσιν οἱ πολλοί
ὡς ἰδίαν ἔχοντες φρόνησιν.
I. p.77. Fr. 2.
ὁδὸς ἄνω κάτω μία καί ὡυτή.
I. p.89. Fr. 60.[2]
—Diels: *Die Fragmente der Vorsokratiker*
(Herakleitos)

I

Time present and time past
Are both perhaps present in time future,
And time future contained in time past.[3]
If all time is eternally present
All time is unredeemable.
What might have been is an abstraction
Remaining a perpetual possibility
Only in a world of speculation.
What might have been and what has been
Point to one end, which is always present.
Footfalls echo in the memory

1. Eliot made "Burnt Norton," published originally as a separate poem, the basis and formal model for "East Coker" (1940), "The Dry Salvages" (1941), and "Little Gidding" (1942). Together they make up *Four Quartets* (1943). The *Quartets* seeks to capture those rare moments when eternity "intersects" the temporal continuum, while treating also the relations between those moments and the flux of time. Central to "Burnt Norton" is the idea of the Spanish mystic St. John of the Cross (1542–1591) that the ascent of a soul to union with God is facilitated by memory and disciplined meditation but that meditation is superseded by a "dark night of the soul" that deepens paradoxically the nearer one approaches the light of God. Burnt Norton is a manor house in Gloucestershire, England.

2. The Greek epigraphs are from the pre-Socratic philosopher Heraclitus (540?–475 B.C.E.) and may be translated: "But although the Word is common to all, the majority of people live as though they had each an understanding peculiarly his own" and "The way up and the way down are one and the same."

3. The opening lines echo Ecclesiastes 3.15: "That which hath been is now; and that which is to be hath already been."

Down the passage which we did not take
Towards the door we never opened
Into the rose-garden.[4] My words echo
Thus, in your mind.
                              But to what purpose
Disturbing the dust on a bowl of rose-leaves
I do not know.
                        Other echoes
Inhabit the garden. Shall we follow?
Quick, said the bird, find them, find them,
Round the corner. Through the first gate,
Into our first world, shall we follow
The deception of the thrush? Into our first world.
There they were, dignified, invisible,
Moving without pressure, over the dead leaves,
In the autumn heat, through the vibrant air,
And the bird called, in response to
The unheard music hidden in the shrubbery,
And the unseen eyebeam crossed, for the roses
Had the look of flowers that are looked at.
There they were as our guests, accepted and accepting.
So we moved, and they, in a formal pattern,
Along the empty alley, into the box circle,[5]
To look down into the drained pool.
Dry the pool, dry concrete, brown edged,
And the pool was filled with water out of sunlight,
And the lotos rose, quietly, quietly,
The surface glittered out of heart of light,[6]
And they were behind us, reflected in the pool.
Then a cloud passed, and the pool was empty.
Go, said the bird, for the leaves were full of children,
Hidden excitedly, containing laughter.
Go, go, go, said the bird: human kind
Cannot bear very much reality.
Time past and time future
What might have been and what has been.
Point to one end, which is always present.

II

Garlic and sapphires in the mud
Clot the bedded axle-tree.
The trilling wire in the blood
Sings below inveterate scars
Appeasing long forgotten wars.
The dance along the artery
The circulation of the lymph

4. The rose is a symbol of sexual and spiritual love; in Christian traditions it is associated with the harmony of religious truth and with the Virgin Mary. The memory may be personal as well.

5. Evergreen boxwood shrubs, planted in a circle.

6. An echo of Dante, *Paradiso* 12.28–29: "From out of the heart of one of the new lights there moved a voice."

Are figured in the drift of stars
Ascend to summer in the tree
We move above the moving tree
In light upon the figured leaf[7]
And hear upon the sodden floor
Below, the boarhound and the boar
Pursue their pattern as before
But reconciled among the stars.

At the still point of the turning world. Neither flesh nor fleshless;
Neither from nor towards; at the still point, there the dance is,
But neither arrest nor movement. And do not call it fixity,
Where past and future are gathered. Neither movement from nor towards,
Neither ascent nor decline. Except for the point, the still point,
There would be no dance and there is only the dance.
I can only say, *there* we have been: but I cannot say where.
And I cannot say, how long, for that is to place it in time.
The inner freedom from the practical desire,
The release from action and suffering, release from the inner
And the outer compulsion, yet surrounded
By a grace of sense, a white light still and moving,
Erhebung[8] without motion, concentration
Without elimination, both a new world
And the old made explicit, understood
In the completion of its partial ecstasy,
The resolution of its partial horror.
Yet the enchainment of past and future
Woven in the weakness of the changing body,
Protects mankind from heaven and damnation
Which flesh cannot endure.
                                        Time past and time future
Allow but a little consciousness.
To be conscious is not to be in time
But only in time can the moment in the rose-garden,
The moment in the arbour where the rain beat,
The moment in the draughty church at smokefall
Be remembered; involved with past and future.
Only through time time is conquered.

III

Here is a place of disaffection
Time before and time after
In a dim light: neither daylight
Investing form with lucid stillness
Turning shadow into transient beauty
With slow rotation suggesting permanence

7. An echo of the description of death in Tennyson, *In Memoriam* (1850) 43.10–12: "So that still garden of the souls / In many a figured leaf enrolls / The total world since life began."
8. Exaltation (German).

Nor darkness to purify the soul
Emptying the sensual with deprivation
Cleansing affection from the temporal.
Neither plenitude nor vacancy. Only a flicker
Over the strained time-ridden faces
Distracted from distraction by distraction
Filled with fancies and empty of meaning
Tumid apathy with no concentration
Men and bits of paper, whirled by the cold wind
That blows before and after time,
Wind in and out of unwholesome lungs
Time before and time after.
Eructation of unhealthy souls
Into the faded air, the torpid
Driven on the wind that sweeps the gloomy hills of London,
Hampstead and Clerkenwell, Campden and Putney,
Highgate, Primrose and Ludgate.[9] Not here
Not here the darkness, in this twittering world.

Descend lower, descend only
Into the world of perpetual solitude,
World not world, but that which is not world,
Internal darkness, deprivation
And destitution of all property,
Desiccation of the world of sense,
Evacuation of the world of fancy,
Inoperancy of the world of spirit;
This is the one way, and the other
Is the same, not in movement
But abstention from movement; while the world moves
In appetency, on its metalled ways
Of time past and time future.

IV

Time and the bell have buried the day,
The black cloud carries the sun away.
Will the sunflower turn to us, will the clematis
Stray down, bend to us; tendril and spray
Clutch and cling?
Chill
Fingers of yew be curled
Down on us? After the kingfisher's wing
Has answered light to light, and is silent, the light is still
At the still point of the turning world.

9. Districts and neighborhoods in London.

V

Words move, music moves
Only in time; but that which is only living
Can only die. Words, after speech, reach
Into the silence. Only by the form, the pattern,
Can words or music reach
The stillness, as a Chinese jar still
Moves perpetually in its stillness.
Not the stillness of the violin, while the note lasts,
Not that only, but the co-existence,
Or say that the end precedes the beginning,
And the end and the beginning were always there
Before the beginning and after the end.
And all is always now. Words strain,
Crack and sometimes break, under the burden,
Under the tension, slip, slide, perish,
Decay with imprecision, will not stay in place,
Will not stay still. Shrieking voices
Scolding, mocking, or merely chattering,
Always assail them. The Word in the desert[1]
Is most attacked by voices of temptation,
The crying shadow in the funeral dance,
The loud lament of the disconsolate chimera.[2]
The detail of the pattern is movement,
As in the figure of the ten stairs.[3]
Desire itself is movement
Not in itself desirable;
Love is itself unmoving,
Only the cause and end of movement,
Timeless, and undesiring
Except in the aspect of time
Caught in the form of limitation
Between un-being and being.
Sudden in a shaft of sunlight
Even while the dust moves
There rises the hidden laughter
Of children in the foliage
Quick, now, here, now always—
Ridiculous the waste sad time
Stretching before and after.

1936, 1943

1. An allusion to Christ's temptation in the wilderness (Luke 4.1–4).
2. A monster in Greek mythology and a symbol of fantasies and delusions.
3. An allusion to St. John of the Cross's figure for the soul's ascent to God: "The Ten Degrees of the Mystical Ladder of Divine Love."

EUGENE O'NEILL
1888–1953

Eugene O'Neill, the nation's first major playwright, was born in a New York City hotel on Broadway on October 16, 1888. His father was James O'Neill, an actor who abandoned his early success in Shakespearean roles to make a fortune playing the lead role in a dramatization of Alexander Dumas's swashbuckling novel *The Count of Monte Cristo* (1844–45), which he performed on tour more than five thousand times. O'Neill's mother, Ella Quinlan, the daughter of a successful Irish immigrant businessman in Cincinnati, hated backstage life and became addicted to morphine. An older brother, James Jr., had been born in 1878 and during most of Eugene's childhood was away at various boarding schools. Later "Jamie," Eugene's idol, became an actor and an alcoholic.

During O'Neill's childhood, his parents toured for part of every year, lived in New York City hotels for another part, and spent summers at their home in New London, Connecticut. O'Neill went to good preparatory schools and started college at Princeton in 1906. Suspended after his freshman year for missing classes and exams, O'Neill found work in New York City, where he met Kathleen Jenkins; when she became pregnant, the two eloped. With his father's help, he shipped out to sea and went searching for gold in South America, leaving his wife behind; it would be eleven years before he met their son, Eugene Jr., born in 1910. O'Neill drank and drifted, alternating sea voyages with sojourns in Greenwich Village, an area of lower Manhattan that was becoming home to artists and political radicals. After nearly dying of tuberculosis in 1912, O'Neill decided to curtail his drinking and write plays. In 1914 his father subsidized the publication of *Thirst*, a collection of five one-act plays; fortified by this accomplishment, O'Neill applied and was accepted as a special student at Harvard in the playwriting class of Professor George Pierce Baker—the first such class offered at an American university. O'Neill's real entry into the contemporary theater, though, came through his Greenwich Village friends: he joined a new experimental theater group called the Provincetown Players—in the summer its members staged plays on a wharf in Provincetown, Massachusetts. For the rest of the year they used a small theater in the Village. They produced O'Neill's one-act play *Bound East for Cardiff* in the summer of 1916.

The Provincetown group gave O'Neill his forum, and—working closely with playwright Susan Glaspell—he gave them a place in American theater history. Play followed play in these early years: five of his plays were staged in 1917, and he wrote another six in 1918. The works with likely appeal for general audiences were moved uptown from the Village to Broadway, making O'Neill both famous and financially successful. Many of these early plays, with crude and slangy dialogue that departed strikingly from the stage rhetoric of the day, were grim one-acts based on his experiences at sea. Instead of the elegant witticisms of drawing-room comedy or the flowery eloquence of historical drama, audiences were faced with ships' holds and sailors' bars. An exaggerated realism, veering toward expressionism, was the mode of these earliest works.

Around 1920, O'Neill's plays became longer and less realistic, and his aims more ambitious. He began to experiment with techniques to convey inner emotions not expressible in dramatic action—the world of the mind, of memories and fears. He ignored standard play divisions of scenes and acts; made his characters wear masks; split one character between two actors; and reintroduced ghosts, choruses, and

Shakespearean-style monologues and direct addresses to the audience. The political radicalism of his Greenwich Village circles was reflected in the themes of many of these plays, although O'Neill would always be more drawn to the deep-lived emotions of social conflicts than to organized political movements aimed at resolving them. In *The Emperor Jones* (1920), a former Pullman porter uses the lessons of Wall Street ("Dere's little stealin' like you does, and dere's big stealin' like I does") to oppress the inhabitants of a Caribbean island; their revolt sends Jones into flight, pursued by the ghosts of New World slavery. In *The Hairy Ape* (1922), a sailor, becoming aware of how he is viewed by the upper class, degenerates into what he is perceived to be. *Desire under the Elms* (1924) links family conflict to lust after property and control as well as to erotic desire; *The Great God Brown* (1926) drew on O'Neill's full array of experimental techniques to expose the inner life of a business magnate. Centered on the turbulent emotional life of a beautiful woman, *Strange Interlude* (1928), despite its audacious nine-act length, won the Pulitzer Prize, was made into a Hollywood film, and became O'Neill's greatest commercial success.

O'Neill's father had died in 1920, his mother in 1921, his brother in 1923. During the mid-1920s, O'Neill became interested in dramatizing the complicated pattern of his family's life. He was influenced by the popularization of Sigmund Freud's ideas: the power of irrational drives; the existence of a subconscious; the roles of repression and inhibition in the formation of personality and in adult suffering; the importance of sex; and above all the lifelong influence of parents. With Freud, he saw the family as a locus of intense and irresolvable conflicting feelings: as Edmund observes of his mother in *Long Day's Journey into Night*, "it's as if, in spite of loving us, she hated us." But where Freud's famous case histories explore the conflicts of an individual, O'Neill's dramatic method came to focus on the family, rather than the person, as the fundamental human unit. He found inspiration and confirmation for this approach in classical Greek drama, which had always centered on families. His 1931 *Mourning Becomes Electra*, based on the *Oresteia* cycle of the classical Greek playwright Aeschylus, situated the ancient story of family murder and divine retribution in Civil War America with great success.

Twice married after the annulment of his early elopement, O'Neill began to suffer from a series of health problems in the 1930s, was diagnosed with Parkinson's disease in 1941, and lived in relative seclusion for the last twenty years of his life. Following the production of *Mourning Becomes Electra* in 1931, his output slowed. Much of his work from the 1930s and 1940s remained in manuscript until after his death, and there was a twelve-year gap in the staging of his plays between *Days without End* (1934), which failed on Broadway, and *The Iceman Cometh*, in 1946, which also did poorly. During this interval O'Neill set out and revised increasingly ambitious plans for cycles of plays that would encompass American history through the stories of several families. Recalling the conflicting immigrant experiences of his own parents—the prosperous assimilation of his mother's family contrasted with his Irish-born father's famine-driven economic insecurity and greed—sharpened O'Neill's sense of American history as a family drama of possession and dispossession.

Three years after O'Neill's death, *Iceman* was successfully revived, and O'Neill's work reattained prominence. His widow, the former actress Carlotta Monterey, whom O'Neill had married in 1929, released other plays, which were widely acclaimed in posthumous productions. Among such stagings were parts of a projected nine- or eleven-play sequence (critics differ in the interpretation of the surviving manuscript material) about an Irish family in America named the Melody family and some obviously autobiographical dramas about a family named the Tyrones. The Melody plays produced after O'Neill's death include *A Touch of the Poet*, produced in 1957, and *More Stately Mansions*, which was staged in 1967; the Tyrone plays include *Long Day's Journey into Night*, produced in 1956, and *A Moon for the Misbegotten*, produced in 1957.

In inscribing the manuscript of *Long Day's Journey* to Carlotta, O'Neill wrote that he had faced his dead in this play, writing "with deep pity and understanding and forgiveness for *all* the four haunted Tyrones." His treatment made it impossible to blame any of the characters for the suffering they inflicted on the others; each Tyrone was both a victim and an oppressor. The Tyrones are at the mercy of the past, and the word *ghosts* recurs throughout the play: ghosts of those they remember, those who influenced them, their younger selves, their dreams and ambitions, and their disappointments. O'Neill handled the emotionalism of his theme with rigorous dramatic formalism, designing the play as a series of encounters—each character is placed with one, two, or three of the others, until every combination is worked through. *Long Day's Journey* observes the classical dramatic unities of time and space, following the family's various configurations through one day, from the pretense of conventional family life in the morning to the tragic truth of their night. The audience thus witnesses a literal day in the lives of the Tyrones, as well as the journey through life toward death.

Romantic, realistic, naturalistic, melodramatic, sentimental, cynical, poetic—O'Neill's work in general is all of these. Even while he made his characters espouse philosophical positions, O'Neill was not trying to write philosophical drama. He wanted to make plays conveying emotions of such intensity and complexity that the theater would become a vital force in American life. In all his works, the spectacle of emotional intensity was meant to produce emotional response in an audience—what Aristotle, in his *Poetics*, had called "catharsis." O'Neill's plays have been translated and staged all over the world; he won the Pulitzer Prize four times and the Nobel Prize in 1936, the first and so far only American dramatist to do so.

The text is that of the Yale University Press Edition (1956).

Long Day's Journey into Night

Characters

JAMES TYRONE
MARY CAVAN TYRONE, *his wife*
JAMES TYRONE, JR., *their elder son*
EDMUND TYRONE, *their younger son*
CATHLEEN, *second girl*[1]

Scenes

ACT 1 *Living room of the Tyrones' summer home* 8:30 A.M. *of a day in August,* 1912
ACT 2 SCENE 1 *The same, around* 12:45
SCENE 2 *The same, about a half hour later*
ACT 3 *The same, around* 6:30 *that evening*
ACT 4 *The same, around midnight*

Act 1

SCENE—*Living room of* JAMES TYRONE*'s summer home on a morning in August, 1912.*

1. A servant.

At rear are two double doorways with portieres. The one at right leads into a front parlor with the formally arranged, set appearance of a room rarely occupied. The other opens on a dark, windowless back parlor, never used except as a passage from living room to dining room. Against the wall between the doorways is a small bookcase, with a picture of Shakespeare above it, containing novels by Balzac, Zola, Stendhal, philosophical and sociological works by Schopenhauer, Nietzsche, Marx, Engels, Kropotkin, Max Sterner, plays by Ibsen, Shaw, Strindberg, poetry by Swinburne, Rossetti, Wilde, Ernest Dowson, Kipling, etc.[2]

In the right wall, rear, is a screen door leading out on the porch which extends halfway around the house. Farther forward, a series of three windows looks over the front lawn to the harbor and the avenue that runs along the water front. A small wicker table and an ordinary oak desk are against the wall, flanking the windows.

In the left wall, a similar series of windows looks out on the grounds in back of the house. Beneath them is a wicker couch with cushions, its head toward rear. Farther back is a large, glassed-in bookcase with sets of Dumas, Victor Hugo, Charles Lever, three sets of Shakespeare, The World's Best Literature in fifty large volumes, Hume's History of England, Thiers' History of the Consulate and Empire, Smollett's History of England, Gibbon's Roman Empire and miscellaneous volumes of old plays, poetry, and several histories of Ireland. The astonishing thing about these sets is that all the volumes have the look of having been read and reread.

The hardwood floor is nearly covered by a rug, inoffensive in design and color. At center is a round table with a green shaded reading lamp, the cord plugged in one of the four sockets in the chandelier above. Around the table within reading-light range are four chairs, three of them wicker armchairs, the fourth (at right front of table) a varnished oak rocker with leather bottom.

It is around 8:30. Sunshine comes through the windows at right.

As the curtain rises, the family have just finished breakfast. MARY TYRONE *and her husband enter together from the back parlor, coming from the dining room.*

MARY *is fifty-four, about medium height. She still has a young, graceful figure, a trifle plump, but showing little evidence of middle-aged waist and hips, although she is not tightly corseted. Her face is distinctly Irish in type. It must once have been extremely pretty, and is still striking. It does not match her healthy figure but is thin and pale with the bone structure prominent. Her nose is long and straight, her mouth wide with full, sensitive lips. She uses no rouge or any sort of make-up. Her high forehead is framed by thick, pure white hair. Accentuated by her pallor and white hair, her dark brown eyes appear black. They are unusually large and beautiful, with black brows and long curling lashes.*

What strikes one immediately is her extreme nervousness. Her hands are never still. They were once beautiful hands, with long, tapering fingers, but rheumatism has knotted the joints and warped the fingers, so that now they have an ugly crippled look. One avoids looking at them, the more so because one is conscious she is sensitive about their appearance and humiliated by her inability to control the nervousness which draws attention to them.

2. A variety of 19th-century (especially late-19th-century) authors are cited. Nobody in the audience would be able to read the titles and authors on these books—an example of O'Neill's novelistic approach to theatrical detail, also seen in the minute physical descriptions he provides of the characters' appearance and behavior throughout.

She is dressed simply but with a sure sense of what becomes her. Her hair is arranged with fastidious care. Her voice is soft and attractive. When she is merry, there is a touch of Irish lilt in it.

Her most appealing quality is the simple, unaffected charm of a shy convent-girl youthfulness she has never lost—an innate unworldly innocence.

JAMES TYRONE *is sixty-five but looks ten years younger. About five feet eight, broad-shouldered and deep-chested, he seems taller and slenderer because of his bearing, which has a soldierly quality of head up, chest out, stomach in, shoulders squared. His face has begun to break down but he is still remarkably good looking—a big, finely shaped head, a handsome profile, deep-set light-brown eyes. His grey hair is thin with a bald spot like a monk's tonsure.*

The stamp of his profession is unmistakably on him. Not that he indulges in any of the deliberate temperamental posturings of the stage star. He is by nature and preference a simple, unpretentious man, whose inclinations are still close to his humble beginnings and his Irish farmer forebears. But the actor shows in all his unconscious habits of speech, movement and gesture. These have the quality of belonging to a studied technique. His voice is remarkably fine, resonant and flexible, and he takes great pride in it.

His clothes, assuredly, do not costume any romantic part. He wears a threadbare, ready-made, grey sack suit and shineless black shoes, a collar-less shirt with a thick white handkerchief knotted loosely around his throat. There is nothing picturesquely careless about this get-up. It is commonplace shabby. He believes in wearing his clothes to the limit of usefulness, is dressed now for gardening, and doesn't give a damn how he looks.

He has never been really sick a day in his life. He has no nerves. There is a lot of stolid, earthy peasant in him, mixed with streaks of sentimental melancholy and rare flashes of intuitive sensibility.

TYRONE*'s arm is around his wife's waist as they appear from the back parlor. Entering the living room he gives her a playful hug.*

TYRONE You're a fine armful now, Mary, with those twenty pounds you've gained.

MARY [*smiles affectionately*] I've gotten too fat, you mean, dear. I really ought to reduce.

TYRONE None of that, my lady! You're just right. We'll have no talk of reducing. Is that why you ate so little breakfast?

MARY So little? I thought I ate a lot.

TYRONE You didn't. Not as much as I'd like to see, anyway.

MARY [*teasingly*] Oh you! You expect everyone to eat the enormous breakfast you do. No one else in the world could without dying of indigestion. [*She comes forward to stand by the right of table.*]

TYRONE [*following her*] I hope I'm not as big a glutton as that sounds. [*with hearty satisfaction*] But thank God, I've kept my appetite and I've the digestion of a young man of twenty, if I am sixty-five.

MARY You surely have, James. No one could deny that.

[*She laughs and sits in the wicker armchair at right rear of table. He comes around in back of her and selects a cigar from a box on the table and cuts off the end with a little clipper. From the dining room* JAMIE*'s and* EDMUND*'s voices are heard. Mary turns her head that way.*]

Why did the boys stay in the dining room, I wonder? Cathleen must be waiting to clear the table.

TYRONE [*jokingly but with an undercurrent of resentment*] It's a secret confab they don't want me to hear, I suppose. I'll bet they're cooking up some new scheme to touch the Old Man.

[*She is silent on this, keeping her head turned toward their voices. Her hands appear on the table top, moving restlessly. He lights his cigar and sits down in the rocker at right of table, which is his chair, and puffs contentedly.*]

There's nothing like the first after-breakfast cigar, if it's a good one, and this new lot have the right mellow flavor. They're a great bargain, too. I got them dead cheap. It was McGuire put me on to them.

MARY [*a trifle acidly*] I hope he didn't put you on to any new piece of property at the same time. His real estate bargains don't work out so well.

TYRONE [*defensively*] I wouldn't say that, Mary. After all, he was the one who advised me to buy that place on Chestnut Street and I made a quick turnover on it for a fine profit.

MARY [*smiles now with teasing affection*] I know. The famous one stroke of good luck. I'm sure McGuire never dreamed—[*Then she pats his hand.*] Never mind, James. I know it's a waste of breath trying to convince you you're not a cunning real estate speculator.

TYRONE [*huffily*] I've no such idea. But land is land, and it's safer than the stocks and bonds of Wall Street swindlers. [*then placatingly*] But let's not argue about business this early in the morning.

[*A pause. The boys' voices are again heard and one of them has a fit of coughing.* MARY *listens worriedly. Her fingers play nervously on the table top.*]

MARY James, it's Edmund you ought to scold for not eating enough. He hardly touched anything except coffee. He needs to eat to keep up his strength. I keep telling him that but he says he simply has no appetite. Of course, there's nothing takes away your appetite like a bad summer cold.

TYRONE Yes, it's only natural. So don't let yourself get worried—

MARY [*quickly*] Oh, I'm not. I know he'll be all right in a few days if he takes care of himself. [*as if she wanted to dismiss the subject but can't*] But it does seem a shame he should have to be sick right now.

TYRONE Yes, it is bad luck. [*He gives her a quick, worried look.*] But you mustn't let it upset you, Mary. Remember, you've got to take care of yourself, too.

MARY [*quickly*] I'm not upset. There's nothing to be upset about. What makes you think I'm upset?

TYRONE Why, nothing, except you've seemed a bit high-strung the past few days.

MARY [*forcing a smile*] I have? Nonsense, dear. It's your imagination. [*with sudden tenseness*] You really must not watch me all the time, James. I mean, it makes me self-conscious.

TYRONE [*putting a hand over one of her nervously playing ones*] Now, now, Mary. That's your imagination. If I've watched you it was to admire how fat and beautiful you looked. [*His voice is suddenly moved by deep feeling.*] I can't tell you the deep happiness it gives me, darling, to see you as you've been since you came back to us, your dear old self again.

[*He leans over and kisses her cheek impulsively—then turning back adds with a constrained air*] So keep up the good work, Mary.

MARY [*has turned her head away*] I will, dear. [*She gets up restlessly and goes to the windows at right.*] Thank heavens, the fog is gone. [*She turns back.*] I do feel out of sorts this morning. I wasn't able to get much sleep with that awful foghorn going all night long.

TYRONE Yes, it's like having a sick whale in the back yard. It kept me awake, too.

MARY [*affectionately amused*] Did it? You had a strange way of showing your restlessness. You were snoring so hard I couldn't tell which was the foghorn! [*She comes to him, laughing, and pats his cheek playfully.*] Ten foghorns couldn't disturb you. You haven't a nerve in you. You've never had.

TYRONE [*his vanity piqued—testily*] Nonsense. You always exaggerate about my snoring.

MARY I couldn't. If you could only hear yourself once—

[*A burst of laughter comes from the dining room. She turns her head, smiling.*]

What's the joke, I wonder?

TYRONE [*grumpily*] It's on me. I'll bet that much. It's always on the Old Man.

MARY [*teasingly*] Yes, it's terrible the way we all pick on you, isn't it? You're so abused! [*She laughs—then with a pleased, relieved air*] Well, no matter what the joke is about, it's a relief to hear Edmund laugh. He's been so down in the mouth lately.

TYRONE [*ignoring this—resentfully*] Some joke of Jamie's, I'll wager. He's forever making sneering fun of somebody, that one.

MARY Now don't start in on poor Jamie, dear. [*without conviction*] He'll turn out all right in the end, you wait and see.

TYRONE He'd better start soon, then. He's nearly thirty-four.

MARY [*ignoring this*] Good heavens, are they going to stay in the dining room all day? [*She goes to the back parlor doorway and calls*] Jamie! Edmund! Come in the living room and give Cathleen a chance to clear the table.

[EDMUND *calls back,* "We're coming, Mama." *She goes back to the table.*]

TYRONE [*grumbling*] You'd find excuses for him no matter what he did.

MARY [*sitting down beside him, pats his hand*] Shush.

Their sons JAMES, JR., *and* EDMUND *enter together from the back parlor. They are both grinning, still chuckling over what had caused their laughter, and as they come forward they glance at their father and their grins grow broader.*

JAMIE, *the elder, is thirty-three. He has his father's broad-shouldered, deep-chested physique, is an inch taller and weighs less, but appears shorter and stouter because he lacks* TYRONE'S *bearing and graceful carriage. He also lacks his father's vitality. The signs of premature disintegration are on him. His face is still good looking, despite marks of dissipation, but it has never been handsome like* TYRONE'S, *although* JAMIE *resembles him rather than his mother. He has fine brown eyes, their color midway between his father's lighter and his mother's darker ones. His hair is thinning and already there is indication of a bald spot like* TYRONE'S. *His nose is unlike that of any other member of the family, pro-*

nouncedly aquiline. Combined with his habitual expression of cynicism it gives his countenance a Mephistophelian cast. But on the rare occasions when he smiles without sneering, his personality possesses the remnant of a humorous, romantic, irresponsible Irish charm—that of the beguiling ne'er-do-well, with a strain of the sentimentally poetic, attractive to women and popular with men.

He is dressed in an old sack suit, not as shabby as TYRONE*'s, and wears a collar and tie. His fair skin is sunburned a reddish, freckled tan.*

EDMUND *is ten years younger than his brother, a couple of inches taller, thin and wiry. Where* JAMIE *takes after his father, with little resemblance to his mother,* EDMUND *looks like both his parents, but is more like his mother. Her big, dark eyes are the dominant feature in his long, narrow Irish face. His mouth has the same quality of hypersensitiveness hers possesses. His high fore-head is hers accentuated, with dark brown hair, sunbleached to red at the ends, brushed straight back from it. But his nose is his father's and his face in profile recalls* TYRONE*'s.* EDMUND*'s hands are noticeably like his mother's, with the same exceptionally long fingers. They even have to a minor degree the same nervousness. It is in the quality of extreme nervous sensibility that the likeness of* EDMUND *to his mother is most marked.*

He is plainly in bad health. Much thinner than he should be, his eyes appear feverish and his cheeks are sunken. His skin, in spite of being sunburned a deep brown, has a parched sallowness. He wears a shirt, collar and tie, no coat, old flannel trousers, brown sneakers.

MARY [*turns smilingly to them, in a merry tone that is a bit forced*] I've been teasing your father about his snoring. [*to* TYRONE] I'll leave it to the boys, James. They must have heard you. No, not you, Jamie. I could hear you down the hall almost as bad as your father. You're like him. As soon as your head touches the pillow you're off and ten foghorns couldn't wake you. [*She stops abruptly, catching* JAMIE*'s eyes regarding her with an uneasy, probing look. Her smile vanishes and her manner becomes self-conscious.*] Why are you staring, Jamie? [*Her hands flutter up to her hair.*] Is my hair coming down? It's hard for me to do it up properly now. My eyes are getting so bad and I never can find my glasses.

JAMIE [*looks away guiltily*] Your hair's all right, Mama. I was only thinking how well you look.

TYRONE [*heartily*] Just what I've been telling her, Jamie. She's so fat and sassy, there'll soon be no holding her.

EDMUND Yes, you certainly look grand, Mama. [*She is reassured and smiles at him lovingly. He winks with a kidding grin.*] I'll back you up about Papa's snoring. Gosh, what a racket!

JAMIE I heard him, too. [*He quotes, putting on a ham-actor manner*] "The Moor, I know his trumpet."[3]

[*His mother and brother laugh.*]

TYRONE [*scathingly*] If it takes my snoring to make you remember Shakespeare instead of the dope sheet on the ponies, I hope I'll keep on with it.

MARY Now, James! You mustn't be so touchy.

[JAMIE *shrugs his shoulders and sits down in the chair on her right.*]

3. Shakespeare's *Othello* 2.1.180.

EDMUND [*irritably*] Yes, for Pete's sake, Papa! The first thing after breakfast! Give it a rest, can't you? [*He slumps down in the chair at left of table next to his brother. His father ignores him.*]

MARY [*reprovingly*] Your father wasn't finding fault with you. You don't have to always take Jamie's part. You'd think you were the one ten years older.

JAMIE [*boredly*] What's all the fuss about? Let's forget it.

TYRONE [*contemptuously*] Yes, forget! Forget everything and face nothing! It's a convenient philosophy if you've no ambition in life except to—

MARY James, do be quiet. [*She puts an arm around his shoulder—coaxingly*] You must have gotten out of the wrong side of the bed this morning. [*to the boys, changing the subject*] What were you two grinning about like Cheshire cats when you came in? What was the joke?

TYRONE [*with a painful effort to be a good sport*] Yes, let us in on it, lads. I told your mother I knew damned well it would be one on me, but never mind that, I'm used to it.

JAMIE [*dryly*] Don't look at me. This is the Kid's story.

EDMUND [*grins*] I meant to tell you last night, Papa, and forgot it. Yesterday when I went for a walk I dropped in at the Inn—

MARY [*worriedly*] You shouldn't drink now, Edmund.

EDMUND [*ignoring this*] And who do you think I met there, with a beautiful bun on,[4] but Shaughnessy, the tenant on that farm of yours.

MARY [*smiling*] That dreadful man! But he is funny.

TYRONE [*scowling*] He's not so funny when you're his landlord. He's a wily Shanty Mick, that one. He could hide behind a corkscrew. What's he complaining about now, Edmund—for I'm damned sure he's complaining. I suppose he wants his rent lowered. I let him have the place for almost nothing, just to keep someone on it, and he never pays that till I threaten to evict him.

EDMUND No, he didn't beef about anything. He was so pleased with life he even bought a drink, and that's practically unheard of. He was delighted because he'd had a fight with your friend, Harker, the Standard Oil millionaire, and won a glorious victory.

MARY [*with amused dismay*] Oh, Lord! James, you'll really have to do something—

TYRONE Bad luck to Shaughnessy, anyway!

JAMIE [*maliciously*] I'll bet the next time you see Harker at the Club and give him the old respectful bow, he won't see you.

EDMUND Yes. Harker will think you're no gentleman for harboring a tenant who isn't humble in the presence of a king of America.

TYRONE Never mind the Socialist gabble. I don't care to listen—

MARY [*tactfully*] Go on with your story, Edmund.

EDMUND [*grins at his father provocatively*] Well, you remember, Papa, the ice pond on Harker's estate is right next to the farm, and you remember Shaughnessy keeps pigs. Well, it seems there's a break in the fence and the pigs have been bathing in the millionaire's ice pond, and Harker's foreman told him he was sure Shaughnessy had broken the fence on purpose to give his pigs a free wallow.

4. I.e., drunk.

MARY [*shocked and amused*] Good heavens!

TYRONE [*sourly, but with a trace of admiration*] I'm sure he did, too, the dirty scallywag. It's like him.

EDMUND So Harker came in person to rebuke Shaughnessy. [*He chuckles.*] A very bonehead play! If I needed any further proof that our ruling plutocrats, especially the ones who inherited their boodle, are not mental giants, that would clinch it.

TYRONE [*with appreciation, before he thinks*] Yes, he'd be no match for Shaughnessy. [*then he growls*] Keep your damned anarchist remarks to yourself. I won't have them in my house. [*But he is full of eager anticipation.*] What happened?

EDMUND Harker had as much chance as I would with Jack Johnson.[5] Shaughnessy got a few drinks under his belt and was waiting at the gate to welcome him. He told me he never gave Harker a chance to open his mouth. He began by shouting that he was no slave Standard Oil could trample on. He was a King of Ireland, if he had his rights, and scum was scum to him, no matter how much money it had stolen from the poor.

MARY Oh, Lord! [*But she can't help laughing.*]

EDMUND Then he accused Harker of making his foreman break down the fence to entice the pigs into the ice pond in order to destroy them. The poor pigs, Shaughnessy yelled, had caught their death of cold. Many of them were dying of pneumonia, and several others had been taken down with cholera from drinking the poisoned water. He told Harker he was hiring a lawyer to sue him for damages. And he wound up by saying that he had to put up with poison ivy, ticks, potato bugs, snakes and skunks on his farm, but he was an honest man who drew the line somewhere, and he'd be damned if he'd stand for a Standard Oil thief trespassing. So would Harker kindly remove his dirty feet from the premises before he sicked the dog on him. And Harker did! [*He and* JAMIE *laugh.*]

MARY [*shocked but giggling*] Heavens, what a terrible tongue that man has!

TYRONE [*admiringly before he thinks*] The damned old scoundrel! By God, you can't beat him! [*He laughs—then stops abruptly and scowls.*] The dirty blackguard! He'll get me in serious trouble yet. I hope you told him I'd be mad as hell—

EDMUND I told him you'd be tickled to death over the great Irish victory, and so you are. Stop faking, Papa.

TYRONE Well, I'm not tickled to death.

MARY [*teasingly*] You are, too, James. You're simply delighted!

TYRONE No, Mary, a joke is a joke, but—

EDMUND I told Shaughnessy he should have reminded Harker that a Standard Oil millionaire ought to welcome the flavor of hog in his ice water as an appropriate touch.

TYRONE The devil you did! [*frowning*] Keep your damned Socialist anarchist sentiments out of my affairs!

EDMUND Shaughnessy almost wept because he hadn't thought of that one, but he said he'd include it in a letter he's writing to Harker, along with a few other insults he'd overlooked. [*He and* JAMIE *laugh.*]

5. Famous prizefighter, the first African American heavyweight boxing champion of the world.

TYRONE What are you laughing at? There's nothing funny—A fine son you are to help that blackguard get me into a lawsuit!

MARY Now, James, don't lose your temper.

TYRONE [*turns on* JAMIE] And you're worse than he is, encouraging him. I suppose you're regretting you weren't there to prompt Shaughnessy with a few nastier insults. You've a fine talent for that, if for nothing else.

MARY James! There's no reason to scold Jamie.

[JAMIE *is about to make some sneering remark to his father, but he shrugs his shoulders.*]

EDMUND [*with sudden nervous exasperation*] Oh, for God's sake, Papa! If you're starting that stuff again, I'll beat it. [*He jumps up.*] I left my book upstairs, anyway. [*He goes to the front parlor, saying disgustedly*] God, Papa, I should think you'd get sick of hearing yourself—

[*He disappears.* TYRONE *looks after him angrily.*]

MARY You musn't mind Edmund, James. Remember he isn't well.

[EDMUND *can be heard coughing as he goes upstairs. She adds nervously*] A summer cold makes anyone irritable.

JAMIE [*genuinely concerned*] It's not just a cold he's got. The Kid is damned sick.

[*His father gives him a sharp warning look but he doesn't see it.*]

MARY [*turns on him resentfully*] Why do you say that? It *is* just a cold! Anyone can tell that! You always imagine things!

TYRONE [*with another warning glance at* JAMIE—*easily*] All Jamie meant was Edmund might have a touch of something else, too, which makes his cold worse.

JAMIE Sure, Mama. That's all I meant.

TYRONE Doctor Hardy thinks it might be a bit of malarial fever he caught when he was in the tropics. If it is, quinine will soon cure it.

MARY [*a look of contemptuous hostility flashes across her face*] Doctor Hardy! I wouldn't believe a thing he said, if he swore on a stack of Bibles! I know what doctors are. They're all alike. Anything, they don't care what, to keep you coming to them. [*She stops short, overcome by a fit of acute self-consciousness as she catches their eyes fixed on her. Her hands jerk nervously to her hair. She forces a smile.*] What is it? What are you looking at? Is my hair—?

TYRONE [*puts his arm around her—with guilty heartiness, giving her a playful hug*] There's nothing wrong with your hair. The healthier and fatter you get, the vainer you become. You'll soon spend half the day primping before the mirror.

MARY [*half reassured*] I really should have new glasses. My eyes are so bad now.

TYRONE [*with Irish blarney*] Your eyes are beautiful, and well you know it.

[*He gives her a kiss. Her face lights up with a charming, shy embarrassment. Suddenly and startlingly one sees in her face the girl she had once been, not a ghost of the dead, but still a living part of her.*]

MARY You mustn't be so silly, James. Right in front of Jamie!

TYRONE Oh, he's on to you, too. He knows this fuss about eyes and hair is only fishing for compliments. Eh, Jamie?

JAMIE [*his face has cleared, too, and there is an old boyish charm in his loving smile at his mother*] Yes. You can't kid us, Mama.

MARY [*laughs and an Irish lilt comes into her voice*] Go along with both of you! [*then she speaks with a girlish gravity*] But I did truly have beautiful hair once, didn't I, James?

TYRONE The most beautiful in the world!

MARY It was a rare shade of reddish brown and so long it came down below my knees. You ought to remember it, too, Jamie. It wasn't until after Edmund was born that I had a single grey hair. Then it began to turn white. [*The girlishness fades from her face.*]

TYRONE [*quickly*] And that made it prettier than ever.

MARY [*again embarrassed and pleased*] Will you listen to your father, Jamie—after thirty-five years of marriage! He isn't a great actor for nothing, is he? What's come over you, James? Are you pouring coals of fire on my head for teasing you about snoring? Well, then, I take it all back. It must have been only the foghorn I heard. [*She laughs, and they laugh with her. Then she changes to a brisk businesslike air.*] But I can't stay with you any longer, even to hear compliments. I must see the cook about dinner and the day's marketing. [*She gets up and sighs with humorous exaggeration.*] Bridget is so lazy. And so sly. She begins telling me about her relatives so I can't get a word in edgeways and scold her. Well, I might as well get it over. [*She goes to the back-parlor doorway, then turns, her face worried again.*] You mustn't make Edmund work on the grounds with you, James, remember. [*again with the strange obstinate set to her face*] Not that he isn't strong enough, but he'd perspire and he might catch more cold.

[*She disappears through the back parlor.* TYRONE *turns on* JAMIE *condemningly.*]

TYRONE You're a fine lunkhead! Haven't you any sense? The one thing to avoid is saying anything that would get her more upset over Edmund.

JAMIE [*shrugging his shoulders*] All right. Have it your way. I think it's the wrong idea to let Mama go on kidding yourself. It will only make the shock worse when she has to face it. Anyway, you can see she's deliberately fooling herself with that summer cold talk. She knows better.

TYRONE Knows? Nobody knows yet.

JAMIE Well, I do. I was with Edmund when he went to Doc Hardy on Monday. I heard him pull that touch of malaria stuff. He was stalling. That isn't what he thinks any more. You know it as well as I do. You talked to him when you went uptown yesterday, didn't you?

TYRONE He couldn't say anything for sure yet. He's to phone me today before Edmund goes to him.

JAMIE [*slowly*] He thinks it's consumption,[6] doesn't he, Papa?

TYRONE [*reluctantly*] He said it might be.

JAMIE [*moved, his love for his brother coming out*] Poor kid! God damn it! [*He turns on his father accusingly.*] It might never have happened if you'd sent him to a real doctor when he first got sick.

TYRONE What's the matter with Hardy? He's always been our doctor up here.

JAMIE Everything's the matter with him! Even in this hick burg he's rated third class! He's a cheap old quack!

6. Tuberculosis.

TYRONE That's right! Run him down! Run down everybody! Everyone is a fake to you!

JAMIE [*contemptuously*] Hardy only charges a dollar. That's what makes you think he's a fine doctor!

TYRONE [*stung*] That's enough! You're not drunk now! There's no excuse— [*He controls himself—a bit defensively*] If you mean I can't afford one of the fine society doctors who prey on the rich summer people—

JAMIE Can't afford? You're one of the biggest property owners around here.

TYRONE That doesn't mean I'm rich. It's all mortgaged—

JAMIE Because you always buy more instead of paying off mortgages. If Edmund was a lousy acre of land you wanted, the sky would be the limit!

TYRONE That's a lie! And your sneers against Doctor Hardy are lies! He doesn't put on frills, or have an office in a fashionable location, or drive around in an expensive automobile. That's what you pay for with those other five-dollars-to-look-at-your-tongue fellows, not their skill.

JAMIE [*with a scornful shrug of his shoulders*] Oh, all right. I'm a fool to argue. You can't change the leopard's spots.

TYRONE [*with rising anger*] No, you can't. You've taught me that lesson only too well. I've lost all hope you will ever change yours. You dare tell me what I can afford? You've never known the value of a dollar and never will! You've never saved a dollar in your life! At the end of each season you're penniless! You've thrown your salary away every week on whores and whiskey!

JAMIE My salary! Christ!

TYRONE It's more than you're worth, and you couldn't get that if it wasn't for me. If you weren't my son, there isn't a manager in the business who would give you a part, your reputation stinks so. As it is, I have to humble my pride and beg for you, saying you've turned over a new leaf, although I know it's a lie!

JAMIE I never wanted to be an actor. You forced me on the stage.

TYRONE That's a lie! You made no effort to find anything else to do. You left it to me to get you a job and I have no influence except in the theater. Forced you! You never wanted to do anything except loaf in barrooms! You'd have been content to sit back like a lazy lunk and sponge on me for the rest of your life! After all the money I'd wasted on your education, and all you did was get fired in disgrace from every college you went to!

JAMIE Oh, for God's sake, don't drag up that ancient history!

TYRONE It's not ancient history that you have to come home every summer to live on me.

JAMIE I earn my board and lodging working on the grounds. It saves you hiring a man.

TYRONE Bah! You have to be driven to do even that much! [*His anger ebbs into a weary complaint.*] I wouldn't give a damn if you ever displayed the slightest sign of gratitude. The only thanks is to have you sneer at me for a dirty miser, sneer at my profession, sneer at every damned thing in the world—except yourself.

JAMIE [*wryly*] That's not true, Papa. You can't hear me talking to myself, that's all.

TYRONE [*stares at him puzzledly, then quotes mechanically*] "Ingratitude, the vilest weed that grows"![7]

JAMIE I could see that line coming! God, how many thousand times—! [*He stops, bored with their quarrel, and shrugs his shoulders.*] All right, Papa. I'm a bum. Anything you like, so long as it stops the argument.

TYRONE [*with indignant appeal now*] If you'd get ambition in your head instead of folly! You're young yet. You could still make your mark. You had the talent to become a fine actor! You have it still. You're my son—!

JAMIE [*boredly*] Let's forget me. I'm not interested in the subject. Neither are you. [TYRONE *gives up.* JAMIE *goes on casually.*] What started us on this? Oh, Doc Hardy. When is he going to call you up about Edmund?

TYRONE Around lunch time. [*He pauses—then defensively*] I couldn't have sent Edmund to a better doctor. Hardy's treated him whenever he was sick up here, since he was knee high. He knows his constitution as no other doctor could. It's not a question of my being miserly, as you'd like to make out. [*bitterly*] And what could the finest specialist in America do for Edmund, after he's deliberately ruined his health by the mad life he's led ever since he was fired from college? Even before that when he was in prep school, he began dissipating and playing the Broadway sport to imitate you, when he's never had your constitution to stand it. You're a healthy hulk like me—or you were at his age—but he's always been a bundle of nerves like his mother. I've warned him for years his body couldn't stand it, but he wouldn't heed me, and now it's too late.

JAMIE [*sharply*] What do you mean, too late? You talk as if you thought—

TYRONE [*guiltily explosive*] Don't be a damned fool! I meant nothing but what's plain to anyone! His health has broken down and he may be an invalid for a long time.

JAMIE [*stares at his father, ignoring his explanation*] I know it's an Irish peasant idea consumption is fatal. It probably is when you live in a hovel on a bog, but over here, with modern treatment—

TYRONE Don't I know that! What are you gabbing about, anyway? And keep your dirty tongue off Ireland, with your sneers about peasants and bogs and hovels! [*accusingly*] The less you say about Edmund's sickness, the better for your conscience! You're more responsible than anyone!

JAMIE [*stung*] That's a lie! I won't stand for that, Papa!

TYRONE It's the truth! You've been the worst influence for him. He grew up admiring you as a hero! A fine example you set him! If you ever gave him advice except in the ways of rottenness, I've never heard of it! You made him old before his time, pumping him full of what you consider worldly wisdom, when he was too young to see that your mind was so poisoned by your own failure in life, you wanted to believe every man was a knave with his soul for sale, and every woman who wasn't a whore was a fool!

JAMIE [*with a defensive air of weary indifference again*] All right. I did put Edmund wise to things, but not until I saw he'd started to raise hell, and knew he'd laugh at me if I tried the good advice, older brother stuff. All I did was make a pal of him and be absolutely frank so he'd learn

7. Shakespeare's *King Lear* 1.4.

from my mistakes that—[*He shrugs his shoulders—cynically*] Well, that if you can't be good you can at least be careful.

[*His father snorts contemptuously. Suddenly* JAMIE *becomes really moved.*]

That's a rotten accusation, Papa. You know how much the Kid means to me, and how close we've always been—not like the usual brothers! I'd do anything for him.

TYRONE [*impressed—mollifyingly*] I know you may have thought it was for the best, Jamie. I didn't say you did it deliberately to harm him.

JAMIE Besides it's damned rot! I'd like to see anyone influence Edmund more than he wants to be. His quietness fools people into thinking they can do what they like with him. But he's stubborn as hell inside and what he does is what he wants to do, and to hell with anyone else! What had I to do with all the crazy stunts he's pulled in the last few years—working his way all over the map as a sailor and all that stuff. I thought that was a damned fool idea, and I told him so. You can't imagine me getting fun out of being on the beach in South America, or living in filthy dives, drinking rotgut, can you? No, thanks! I'll stick to Broadway, and a room with a bath, and bars that serve bonded Bourbon.

TYRONE You and Broadway! It's made you what you are! [*with a touch of pride*] Whatever Edmund's done, he's had the guts to go off on his own, where he couldn't come whining to me the minute he was broke.

JAMIE [*stung into sneering jealousy*] He's always come home broke finally, hasn't he? And what did his going away get him? Look at him now! [*He is suddenly shamefaced.*] Christ! That's a lousy thing to say. I don't mean that.

TYRONE [*decides to ignore this*] He's been doing well on the paper. I was hoping he'd found the work he wants to do at last.

JAMIE [*sneering jealously again*] A hick town rag! Whatever bull they hand you, they tell me he's a pretty bum reporter. If he weren't your son—[*ashamed again*] No, that's not true! They're glad to have him, but it's the special stuff that gets him by. Some of the poems and parodies he's written are damned good. [*grudgingly again*] Not that they'd ever get him anywhere on the big time. [*hastily*] But he's certainly made a damned good start.

TYRONE Yes. He's made a start. You used to talk about wanting to become a newspaper man but you were never willing to start at the bottom. You expected—

JAMIE Oh, for Christ's sake, Papa! Can't you lay off me!

TYRONE [*stares at him—then looks away—after a pause*] It's damnable luck Edmund should be sick right now. It couldn't have come at a worse time for him. [*He adds, unable to conceal an almost furtive uneasiness*] Or for your mother. It's damnable she should have this to upset her, just when she needs peace and freedom from worry. She's been so well in the two months since she came home. [*His voice grows husky and trembles a little.*] It's been heaven to me. This home has been a home again. But I needn't tell you, Jamie.

[*His son looks at him, for the first time with an understanding sympathy. It is as if suddenly a deep bond of common feeling existed between them in which their antagonisms could be forgotten.*]

JAMIE [*almost gently*] I've felt the same way, Papa.

TYRONE Yes, this time you can see how strong and sure of herself she is. She's a different woman entirely from the other times. She has control of her nerves—or she had until Edmund got sick. Now you can feel her growing tense and frightened underneath. I wish to God we could keep the truth from her, but we can't if he has to be sent to a sanatorium. What makes it worse is her father died of consumption. She worshiped him and she's never forgotten. Yes, it will be hard for her. But she can do it! She has the will power now! We must help her, Jamie, in every way we can!

JAMIE [*moved*] Of course, Papa. [*hesitantly*] Outside of nerves, she seems perfectly all right this morning.

TYRONE [*with hearty confidence now*] Never better. She's full of fun and mischief. [*Suddenly he frowns at* JAMIE *suspiciously.*] Why do you say, seems? Why shouldn't she be all right? What the hell do you mean?

JAMIE Don't start jumping down my throat! God, Papa, this ought to be one thing we can talk over frankly without a battle.

TYRONE I'm sorry, Jamie. [*tensely*] But go on and tell me—

JAMIE There's nothing to tell. I was all wrong. It's just that last night—Well, you know how it is, I can't forget the past. I can't help being suspicious. Any more than you can. [*bitterly*] That's the hell of it. And it makes it hell for Mama! She watches us watching her—

TYRONE [*sadly*] I know. [*tensely*] Well, what was it! Can't you speak out!

JAMIE Nothing, I tell you. Just my damned foolishness. Around three o'clock this morning, I woke up and heard her moving around in the spare room. Then she went to the bathroom. I pretended to be asleep. She stopped in the hall to listen, as if she wanted to make sure I was.

TYRONE [*with forced scorn*] For God's sake, is that all? She told me herself the foghorn kept her awake all night, and every night since Edmund's been sick she's been up and down, going to his room to see how he was.

JAMIE [*eagerly*] Yes, that's right, she did stop to listen outside his room. [*hesitantly again*] It was her being in the spare room that scared me. I couldn't help remembering that when she starts sleeping alone in there, it has always been a sign—

TYRONE It isn't this time! It's easily explained. Where else could she go last night to get away from my snoring? [*He gives way to a burst of resentful anger.*] By God, how you can live with a mind that sees nothing but the worst motives behind everything is beyond me!

JAMIE [*stung*] Don't pull that! I've just said I was all wrong. Don't you suppose I'm as glad of that as you are!

TYRONE [*mollifyingly*] I'm sure you are, Jamie. [*A pause. His expression becomes somber. He speaks slowly with a superstitious dread.*] It would be like a curse she can't escape if worry over Edmund—It was her long sickness after bringing him into the world that she first—

JAMIE She didn't have anything to do with it!

TYRONE I'm not blaming her.

JAMIE [*bitingly*] Then who are you blaming? Edmund, for being born?

TYRONE You damned fool! No one was to blame.

JAMIE The bastard of a doctor was! From what Mama's said, he was another cheap quack like Hardy! You wouldn't pay for a first-rate—

TYRONE That's a lie! [*furiously*] So I'm to blame! That's what you're driving at, is it? You evil-minded loafer!

JAMIE [*warningly as he hears his mother in the dining room*] Ssh!

[TYRONE *gets hastily to his feet and goes to look out the windows at right.* JAMIE *speaks with a complete change of tone.*]

Well, if we're going to cut the front hedge today, we'd better go to work.

[MARY *comes in from the back parlor. She gives a quick, suspicious glance from one to the other, her manner nervously self-conscious.*]

TYRONE [*turns from the window—with an actor's heartiness*] Yes, it's too fine a morning to waste indoors arguing. Take a look out the window, Mary. There's no fog in the harbor. I'm sure the spell of it we've had is over now.

MARY [*going to him*] I hope so, dear. [*to* JAMIE, *forcing a smile*] Did I actually hear you suggesting work on the front hedge, Jamie? Wonders will never cease! You must want pocket money badly.

JAMIE [*kiddingly*] When don't I? [*He winks at her, with a derisive glance at his father.*] I expect a salary of at least one large iron man[8] at the end of the week—to carouse on!

MARY [*does not respond to his humor—her hands fluttering over the front of her dress*] What were you two arguing about?

JAMIE [*shrugs his shoulders*] The same old stuff.

MARY I heard you say something about a doctor, and your father accusing you of being evil-minded.

JAMIE [*quickly*] Oh, that. I was saying again Doc Hardy isn't my idea of the world's greatest physician.

MARY [*knows he is lying—vaguely*] Oh. No, I wouldn't say he was either. [*changing the subject—forcing a smile*] That Bridget! I thought I'd never get away. She told me about her second cousin on the police force in St. Louis. [*then with nervous irritation*] Well, if you're going to work on the hedge why don't you go? [*hastily*] I mean, take advantage of the sunshine before the fog comes back. [*strangely, as if talking aloud to herself*] Because I know it will. [*Suddenly she is self-consciously aware that they are both staring fixedly at her—flurriedly, raising her hands*] Or I should say, the rheumatism in my hands knows. It's a better weather prophet than you are, James. [*She stares at her hands with fascinated repulsion.*] Ugh! How ugly they are! Who'd ever believe they were once beautiful?

[*They stare at her with a growing dread.*]

TYRONE [*takes her hands and gently pushes them down*] Now, now, Mary. None of that foolishness. They're the sweetest hands in the world.

[*She smiles, her face lighting up, and kisses him gratefully. He turns to his son.*]

Come on Jamie. Your mother's right to scold us. The way to start work is to start work. The hot sun will sweat some of that booze fat off your middle.

[*He opens the screen door and goes out on the porch and disappears down a flight of steps leading to the ground.* JAMIE *rises from his chair and, taking off his coat, goes to the door. At the door he turns back but avoids looking at her, and she does not look at him.*]

8. Dollar (slang).

JAMIE [*with an awkward, uneasy tenderness*] We're all so proud of you, Mama, so darned happy.

[*She stiffens and stares at him with a frightened defiance. He flounders on.*]

But you've still got to be careful. You mustn't worry so much about Edmund. He'll be all right.

MARY [*with a stubborn, bitterly resentful look*] Of course, he'll be all right. And I don't know what you mean, warning me to be careful.

JAMIE [*rebuffed and hurt, shrugs his shoulders*] All right, Mama. I'm sorry I spoke.

[*He goes out on the porch. She waits rigidly until he disappears down the steps. Then she sinks down in the chair he had occupied, her face betraying a frightened, furtive desperation, her hands roving over the table top, aimlessly moving objects around. She hears* EDMUND *descending the stairs in the front hall. As he nears the bottom he has a fit of coughing. She springs to her feet, as if she wanted to run away from the sound, and goes quickly to the windows at right. She is looking out, apparently calm, as he enters from the front parlor, a book in one hand. She turns to him, her lips set in a welcoming, motherly smile.*]

MARY Here you are. I was just going upstairs to look for you.

EDMUND I waited until they went out. I don't want to mix up in any arguments. I feel too rotten.

MARY [*almost resentfully*] Oh, I'm sure you don't feel half as badly as you make out. You're such a baby. You like to get us worried so we'll make a fuss over you. [*hastily*] I'm only teasing, dear. I know how miserably uncomfortable you must be. But you feel better today, don't you? [*worriedly, taking his arm*] All the same, you've grown much too thin. You need to rest all you can. Sit down and I'll make you comfortable.

[*He sits down in the rocking chair and she puts a pillow behind his back.*]

There, How's that?

EDMUND Grand. Thanks, Mama.

MARY [*kisses him—tenderly*] All you need is your mother to nurse you. Big as you are, you're still the baby of the family to me, you know.

EDMUND [*takes her hand—with deep seriousness*] Never mind me. You take care of yourself. That's all that counts.

MARY [*evading his eyes*] But I am, dear. [*forcing a laugh*] Heavens, don't you see how fat I've grown! I'll have to have all my dresses let out. [*She turns away and goes to the windows at right. She attempts a light, amused tone.*] They've started clipping the hedge. Poor Jamie! How he hates working in front where everyone passing can see him. There go the Chatfields in their new Mercedes. It's a beautiful car, isn't it? Not like our secondhand Packard. Poor Jamie! He bent almost under the hedge so they wouldn't notice him. They bowed to your father and he bowed back as if he were taking a curtain call. In that filthy old suit I've tried to make him throw away. [*Her voice has grown bitter.*] Really, he ought to have more pride than to make such a show of himself.

EDMUND He's right not to give a damn what anyone thinks. Jamie's a fool to care about the Chatfields. For Pete's sake, who ever heard of them outside this hick burg?

MARY [*with satisfaction*] No one. You're quite right, Edmund. Big frogs in a small puddle. It is stupid of Jamie. [*She pauses, looking out the window—then with an undercurrent of lonely yearning*] Still, the Chatfields and people like them stand for something. I mean they have decent, presentable homes they don't have to be ashamed of. They have friends who entertain them and whom they entertain. They're not cut off from everyone. [*She turns back from the window.*] Not that I want anything to do with them. I've always hated this town and everyone in it. You know that. I never wanted to live here in the first place, but your father liked it and insisted on building this house, and I've had to come here every summer.

EDMUND Well, it's better than spending the summer in a New York hotel, isn't it? And this town's not so bad. I like it well enough. I suppose because it's the only home we've had.

MARY I've never felt it was my home. It was wrong from the start. Everything was done in the cheapest way. Your father would never spend the money to make it right. It's just as well we haven't any friends here. I'd be ashamed to have them step in the door. But he's never wanted family friends. He hates calling on people, or receiving them. All he likes is to hobnob with men at the Club or in a barroom. Jamie and you are the same way, but you're not to blame. You've never had a chance to meet decent people here. I know you both would have been so different if you'd been able to associate with nice girls instead of—You'd never have disgraced yourselves as you have, so that now no respectable parents will let their daughters be seen with you.

EDMUND [*irritably*] Oh, Mama, forget it! Who cares? Jamie and I would be bored stiff. And about the Old Man, what's the use of talking? You can't change him.

MARY [*mechanically rebuking*] Don't call your father the Old Man. You should have more respect. [*then dully*] I know it's useless to talk. But sometimes I feel so lonely. [*Her lips quiver and she keeps her head turned away.*]

EDMUND Anyway, you've got to be fair, Mama. It may have been all his fault in the beginning, but you know that later on, even if he'd wanted to, we couldn't have had people here—[*He flounders guiltily.*] I mean, you wouldn't have wanted them.

MARY [*wincing—her lips quivering pitifully*] Don't. I can't bear having you remind me.

EDMUND Don't take it that way! Please, Mama! I'm trying to help. Because it's bad for you to forget. The right way is to remember. So you'll always be on your guard. You know what's happened before. [*miserably*] God, Mama, you know I hate to remind you. I'm doing it because it's been so wonderful having you home the way you've been, and it would be terrible—

MARY [*strickenly*] Please, dear. I know you mean it for the best, but—[*A defensive uneasiness comes into her voice again.*] I don't understand why you should suddenly say such things. What put it in your mind this morning?

EDMUND [*evasively*] Nothing. Just because I feel rotten and blue, I suppose.

MARY Tell me the truth. Why are you so suspicious all of a sudden?

EDMUND I'm not!

MARY Oh, yes you are. I can feel it. Your father and Jamie, too—particularly Jamie.

EDMUND Now don't start imagining things, Mama.

MARY [*her hands fluttering*] It makes it so much harder, living in this atmosphere of constant suspicion, knowing everyone is spying on me, and none of you believe in me, or trust me.

EDMUND That's crazy, Mama. We do trust you.

MARY If there was only some place I could go to get away for a day, or even an afternoon, some woman friend I could talk to—not about anything serious, simply laugh and gossip and forget for a while—someone besides the servants—that stupid Cathleen!

EDMUND [*gets up worriedly and puts his arm around her*] Stop it, Mama. You're getting yourself worked up over nothing.

MARY Your father goes out. He meets his friends in barrooms or at the Club. You and Jamie have the boys you know. You go out. But I am alone. I've always been alone.

EDMUND [*soothingly*] Come now! You know that's a fib. One of us always stays around to keep you company, or goes with you in the automobile when you take a drive.

MARY [*bitterly*] Because you're afraid to trust me alone! [*She turns on him—sharply.*] I insist you tell me why you act so differently this morning—why you felt you had to remind me—

EDMUND [*hesitates—then blurts out guiltily*] It's stupid. It's just that I wasn't asleep when you came in my room last night. You didn't go back to your and Papa's room. You went in the spare room for the rest of the night.

MARY Because your father's snoring was driving me crazy! For heaven's sake, haven't I often used the spare room as my bedroom? [*bitterly*] But I see what you thought. That was when—

EDMUND [*too vehemently*] I didn't think anything!

MARY So you pretended to be asleep in order to spy on me!

EDMUND No! I did it because I knew if you found out I was feverish and couldn't sleep, it would upset you.

MARY Jamie was pretending to be asleep, too, I'm sure, and I suppose your father—

EDMUND Stop it, Mama!

MARY Oh, I can't bear it, Edmund, when even you—! [*Her hands flutter up to pat her hair in their aimless, distracted way. Suddenly a strange undercurrent of revengefulness comes into her voice.*] It would serve all of you right if it was true!

EDMUND Mama! Don't say that! That's the way you talk when—

MARY Stop suspecting me! Please, dear! You hurt me! I couldn't sleep because I was thinking about you. That's the real reason! I've been so worried ever since you've been sick. [*She puts her arms around him and hugs him with a frightened, protective tenderness.*]

EDMUND [*soothingly*] That's foolishness. You know it's only a bad cold.

MARY Yes, of course, I know that!

EDMUND But listen, Mama. I want you to promise me that even if it should turn out to be something worse, you'll know I'll soon be all right again, anyway, and you won't worry yourself sick, and you'll keep on taking care of yourself—

MARY [*frightenedly*] I won't listen when you're so silly! There's absolutely no reason to talk as if you expected something dreadful! Of course, I promise you. I give you my sacred word of honor! [*then with a sad bitterness*] But I suppose you're remembering I've promised before on my word of honor.

EDMUND No!

MARY [*her bitterness receding into a resigned helplessness*] I'm not blaming you, dear. How can you help it? How can any one of us forget? [*strangely*] That's what makes it so hard—for all of us. We can't forget.

EDMUND [*grabs her shoulder*] Mama! Stop it!

MARY [*forcing a smile*] All right, dear. I didn't mean to be so gloomy. Don't mind me. Here. Let me feel your head. Why, it's nice and cool. You certainly haven't any fever now.

EDMUND Forget! It's you—

MARY But I'm quite all right, dear. [*with a quick, strange, calculating, almost sly glance at him*] Except I naturally feel tired and nervous this morning, after such a bad night. I really ought to go upstairs and lie down until lunch time and take a nap.

[*He gives her an instinctive look of suspicion—then, ashamed of himself, looks quickly away. She hurries on nervously.*]

What are you going to do? Read here? It would be much better for you to go out in the fresh air and sunshine. But don't get overheated, remember. Be sure and wear a hat.

[*She stops, looking straight at him now. He avoids her eyes. There is a tense pause. Then she speaks jeeringly.*]

Or are you afraid to trust me alone?

EDMUND [*tormentedly*] No! Can't you stop talking like that! I think you ought to take a nap. [*He goes to the screen door—forcing a joking tone*] I'll go down and help Jamie bear up. I love to lie in the shade and watch him work.

[*He forces a laugh in which she makes herself join. Then he goes out on the porch and disappears down the steps. Her first reaction is one of relief. She appears to relax. She sinks down in one of the wicker armchairs at rear of table and leans her head back, closing her eyes. But suddenly she grows terribly tense again. Her eyes open and she strains forward, seized by a fit of nervous panic. She begins a desperate battle with herself. Her long fingers, warped and knotted by rheumatism, drum on the arms of the chair, driven by an insistent life of their own, without her consent.*]

CURTAIN

Act 2

SCENE 1

SCENE—*The same. It is around quarter to one. No sunlight comes into the room now through the windows at right. Outside the day is still fine but increasingly sultry, with a faint haziness in the air which softens the glare of the sun.*

EDMUND *sits in the armchair at left of table, reading a book. Or rather he is trying to concentrate on it but cannot. He seems to be listening for some sound from upstairs. His manner is nervously apprehensive and he looks more sickly than in the previous act.*

The second girl, CATHLEEN, *enters from the back parlor. She carries a tray on which is a bottle of bonded Bourbon, several whiskey glasses and a pitcher of ice water. She is a buxom Irish peasant, in her early twenties, with a red-cheeked comely face, black hair and blue eyes—amiable, ignorant, clumsy, and possessed by a dense, well-meaning stupidity. She puts the tray on the table.* EDMUND *pretends to be so absorbed in his book he does not notice her, but she ignores this.*

CATHLEEN [*with garrulous familiarity*] Here's the whiskey. It'll be lunch time soon. Will I call your father and Mister Jamie, or will you?

EDMUND [*without looking up from his book*] You do it.

CATHLEEN It's a wonder your father wouldn't look at his watch once in a while. He's a divil for making the meals late, and then Bridget curses me as if I was to blame. But he's a grand handsome man, if he is old. You'll never see the day you're as good looking—nor Mister Jamie, either. [*She chuckles.*] I'll wager Mister Jamie wouldn't miss the time to stop work and have his drop of whiskey if he had a watch to his name!

EDMUND [*gives up trying to ignore her and grins*] You win that one.

CATHLEEN And here's another I'd win, that you're making me call them so you can sneak a drink before they come.

EDMUND Well, I hadn't thought of that—

CATHLEEN Oh no, not you! Butter wouldn't melt in your mouth, I suppose.

EDMUND But now you suggest it—

CATHLEEN [*suddenly primly virtuous*] I'd never suggest a man or a woman touch drink, Mister Edmund. Sure, didn't it kill an uncle of mine in the old country. [*relenting*] Still, a drop now and then is no harm when you're in low spirits, or have a bad cold.

EDMUND Thanks for handing me a good excuse. [*then with forced casualness*] You'd better call my mother, too.

CATHLEEN What for? She's always on time without any calling. God bless her, she has some consideration for the help.

EDMUND She's been taking a nap.

CATHLEEN She wasn't asleep when I finished my work upstairs a while back. She was lying down in the spare room with her eyes wide open. She'd a terrible headache, she said.

EDMUND [*his casualness more forced*] Oh well then, just call my father.

CATHLEEN [*goes to the screen door, grumbling good-naturedly*] No wonder my feet kill me each night. I won't walk out in this heat and get sunstroke. I'll call from the porch.

[*She goes out on the side porch, letting the screen door slam behind her, and disappears on her way to the front porch. A moment later she is heard shouting.*]

Mister Tyrone! Mister Jamie! It's time!

[EDMUND, *who has been staring frightenedly before him, forgetting his book, springs to his feet nervously.*]

EDMUND God, what a wench!

[He grabs the bottle and pours a drink, adds ice water and drinks. As he does so, he hears someone coming in the front door. He puts the glass hastily on the tray and sits down again, opening his book. JAMIE *comes in from the front parlor, his coat over his arm. He has taken off collar and tie and carries them in his hand. He is wiping sweat from his forehead with a handkerchief.* EDMUND *looks up as if his reading was interrupted.* JAMIE *takes one look at the bottle and glasses and smiles cynically.]*

JAMIE Sneaking one, eh? Cut out the bluff, Kid. You're a rottener actor than I am.

EDMUND [*grins*] Yes, I grabbed one while the going was good.

JAMIE [*puts a hand affectionately on his shoulder*] That's better. Why kid me? We're pals, aren't we?

EDMUND I wasn't sure it was you coming.

JAMIE I made the Old Man look at his watch. I was halfway up the walk when Cathleen burst into song. Our wild Irish lark! She ought to be a train announcer.

EDMUND That's what drove me to drink. Why don't you sneak one while you've got a chance?

JAMIE I was thinking of that little thing. [*He goes quickly to the window at right.*] The Old Man was talking to old Captain Turner. Yes, he's still at it. [*He comes back and takes a drink.*] And now to cover up from his eagle eye. [*He measures two drinks of water and pours them in the whiskey bottle and shakes it up.*] There. That fixes it. [*He pours water in the glass and sets it on the table by* EDMUND.] And here's the water you've been drinking.

EDMUND Fine! You don't think it will fool him, do you?

JAMIE Maybe not, but he can't prove it. [*Putting on his collar and tie.*] I hope he doesn't forget lunch listening to himself talk. I'm hungry. [*He sits across the table from* EDMUND*—irritably*] That's what I hate about working down in front. He puts on an act for every damned fool that comes along.

EDMUND [*gloomily*] You're in luck to be hungry. The way I feel I don't care if I ever eat again.

JAMIE [*gives him a glance of concern*] Listen, Kid. You know me. I've never lectured you, but Doctor Hardy was right when he told you to cut out the redeye.

EDMUND Oh, I'm going to after he hands me the bad news this afternoon. A few before then won't make any difference.

JAMIE [*hesitates—then slowly*] I'm glad you've got your mind prepared for bad news. It won't be such a jolt. [*He catches* EDMUND *staring at him.*] I mean, it's a cinch you're really sick, and it would be wrong dope to kid yourself.

EDMUND [*disturbed*] I'm not. I know how rotten I feel, and the fever and chills I get at night are no joke. I think Doctor Hardy's last guess was right. It must be the damned malaria come back on me.

JAMIE Maybe, but don't be too sure.

EDMUND Why? What do you think it is?

JAMIE Hell, how would I know? I'm no Doc. [*abruptly*] Where's Mama?

EDMUND Upstairs.

JAMIE [*looks at him sharply*] When did she go up?

EDMUND Oh, about the time I came down to the hedge, I guess. She said she was going to take a nap.

JAMIE You didn't tell me—

EDMUND [*defensively*] Why should I? What about it? She was tired out. She didn't get much sleep last night.

JAMIE I know she didn't.

[*A pause. The brothers avoid looking at each other.*]

EDMUND That damned foghorn kept me awake, too.

[*Another pause.*]

JAMIE She's been upstairs alone all morning, eh? You haven't seen her?

EDMUND No. I've been reading here. I wanted to give her a chance to sleep.

JAMIE Is she coming down to lunch?

EDMUND Of course.

JAMIE [*dryly*] No of course about it. She might not want any lunch. Or she might start having most of her meals alone upstairs. That's happened, hasn't it?

EDMUND [*with frightened resentment*] Cut it out, Jamie! Can't you think anything but—? [*persuasively*] You're all wrong to suspect anything. Cathleen saw her not long ago. Mama didn't tell her she wouldn't be down to lunch.

JAMIE Then she wasn't taking a nap?

EDMUND Not right then, but she was lying down, Cathleen said.

JAMIE In the spare room?

EDMUND Yes. For Pete's sake, what of it?

JAMIE [*bursts out*] You damned fool! Why did you leave her alone so long? Why didn't you stick around?

EDMUND Because she accused me—and you and Papa—of spying on her all the time and not trusting her. She made me feel ashamed. I know how rotten it must be for her. And she promised on her sacred word of honor—

JAMIE [*with a bitter weariness*] You ought to know that doesn't mean anything.

EDMUND It does this time!

JAMIE That's what we thought the other times. [*He leans over the table to give his brother's arm an affectionate grasp.*] Listen, Kid, I know you think I'm a cynical bastard, but remember I've seen a lot more of this game than you have. You never knew what was really wrong until you were in prep-school. Papa and I kept it from you. But I was wise ten years or more before we had to tell you. I know the game backwards and I've been thinking all morning of the way she acted last night when she thought we were asleep. I haven't been able to think of anything else. And now you tell me she got you to leave her alone upstairs all morning.

EDMUND She didn't! You're crazy!

JAMIE [*placatingly*] All right, Kid. Don't start a battle with me. I hope as much as you do I'm crazy. I've been as happy as hell because I'd really begun to believe that this time—[*He stops—looking through the front parlor toward the hall—lowering his voice, hurriedly*] She's coming downstairs. You win on that. I guess I'm a damned suspicious louse.

[*They grow tense with a hopeful, fearful expectancy.* JAMIE *mutters*] Damn! I wish I'd grabbed another drink.

EDMUND Me, too.

[*He coughs nervously and this brings on a real fit of coughing.* JAMIE *glances at him with worried pity.* MARY *enters from the front parlor. At first one notices no change except that she appears to be less nervous, to be more as she was when we first saw her after breakfast, but then one becomes aware that her eyes are brighter, and there is a peculiar detachment in her voice and manner, as if she were a little withdrawn from her words and actions.*]

MARY [*goes worriedly to* EDMUND *and puts her arm around him*] You mustn't cough like that. It's bad for your throat. You don't want to get a sore throat on top of your cold.

[*She kisses him. He stops coughing and gives her a quick apprehensive glance, but if his suspicions are aroused her tenderness makes him renounce them and he believes what he wants to believe for the moment. On the other hand,* JAMIE *knows after one probing look at her that his suspicions are justified. His eyes fall to stare at the floor, his face sets in an expression of embittered, defensive cynicism.* MARY *goes on, half sitting on the arm of* EDMUND'*s chair, her arm around him, so her face is above and behind his and he cannot look into her eyes.*]

But I seem to be always picking on you, telling you don't do this and don't do that. Forgive me, dear. It's just that I want to take care of you.

EDMUND I know, Mama. How about you? Do you feel rested?

MARY Yes, ever so much better. I've been lying down ever since you went out. It's what I needed after such a restless night. I don't feel nervous now.

EDMUND That's fine.

[*He pats her hand on his shoulder.* JAMIE *gives him a strange, almost contemptuous glance, wondering if his brother can really mean this.* EDMUND *does not notice but his mother does.*]

MARY [*in a forced teasing tone*] Good heavens, how down in the mouth you look, Jamie. What's the matter now?

JAMIE [*without looking at her*] Nothing.

MARY Oh, I'd forgotten you've been working on the front hedge. That accounts for your sinking into the dumps, doesn't it?

JAMIE If you want to think so, Mama.

MARY [*keeping her tone*] Well, that's the effect it always has, isn't it? What a big baby you are! Isn't he, Edmund?

EDMUND He's certainly a fool to care what anyone thinks.

MARY [*strangely*] Yes, the only way is to make yourself not care.

[*She catches* JAMIE *giving her a bitter glance and changes the subject.*]

Where is your father? I heard Cathleen call him.

EDMUND Gabbing with old Captain Turner, Jamie says. He'll be late, as usual.

[JAMIE *gets up and goes to the windows at right, glad of an excuse to turn his back.*]

MARY I've told Cathleen time and again she must go wherever he is and tell him. The idea of screaming as if this were a cheap boardinghouse!

JAMIE [*looking out the window*] She's down there now. [*sneeringly*] Interrupting the famous Beautiful Voice! She should have more respect.

MARY [*sharply—letting her resentment toward him come out*] It's you who should have more respect. Stop sneering at your father! I won't have it! You ought to be proud you're his son! He may have his faults. Who hasn't? But he's worked hard all his life. He made his way up from ignorance and poverty to the top of his profession! Everyone else admires him and you should be the last one to sneer—you, who, thanks to him, have never had to work hard in your life!

[*Stung,* JAMIE *has turned to stare at her with accusing antagonism. Her eyes waver guiltily and she adds in a tone which begins to placate*]

Remember your father is getting old, Jamie. You really ought to show more consideration.

JAMIE *I* ought to?

EDMUND [*uneasily*] Oh, dry up, Jamie!

[JAMIE *looks out the window again.*]

And, for Pete's sake, Mama, why jump on Jamie all of a sudden?

MARY [*bitterly*] Because he's always sneering at someone else, always looking for the worst weakness in everyone. [*then with a strange, abrupt change to a detached, impersonal tone*] But I suppose life has made him like that, and he can't help it. None of us can help the things life has done to us. They're done before you realize it, and once they're done they make you do other things until at last everything comes between you and what you'd like to be, and you've lost your true self forever.

[EDMUND *is made apprehensive by her strangeness. He tries to look up in her eyes but she keeps them averted.* JAMIE *turns to her—then looks quickly out of the window again.*]

JAMIE [*dully*] I'm hungry. I wish the Old Man would get a move on. It's a rotten trick the way he keeps meals waiting, and then beefs because they're spoiled.

MARY [*with a resentment that has a quality of being automatic and on the surface while inwardly she is indifferent*] Yes, it's very trying, Jamie. You don't know how trying. You don't have to keep house with summer servants who don't care because they know it isn't a permanent position. The really good servants are all with people who have homes and not merely summer places. And your father won't even pay the wages the best summer help ask. So every year I have stupid, lazy greenhorns to deal with. But you've heard me say this a thousand times. So has he, but it goes in one ear and out the other. He thinks money spent on a home is money wasted. He's lived too much in hotels. Never the best hotels, of course. Second-rate hotels. He doesn't understand a home. He doesn't feel at home in it. And yet, he wants a home. He's even proud of having this shabby place. He loves it here. [*She laughs—a hopeless and yet amused laugh.*] It's really funny, when you come to think of it. He's a peculiar man.

EDMUND [*again attempting uneasily to look up in her eyes*] What makes you ramble on like that, Mama?

MARY [*quickly casual—patting his cheek*] Why, nothing in particular, dear. It *is* foolish.

[*As she speaks,* CATHLEEN *enters from the back parlor.*]

CATHLEEN [*volubly*] Lunch is ready, Ma'am, I went down to Mister Tyrone, like you ordered, and he said he'd come right away, but he kept on talking to that man, telling him of the time when—

MARY [*indifferently*] All right, Cathleen. Tell Bridget I'm sorry but she'll have to wait a few minutes until Mister Tyrone is here.

[CATHLEEN *mutters,* "Yes, Ma'am," *and goes off through the back parlor, grumbling to herself.*]

JAMIE Damn it! Why don't you go ahead without him? He told us to.

MARY [*with a remote, amused smile*] He doesn't mean it. Don't you know your father yet? He'd be so terribly hurt.

EDMUND [*jumps up—as if he was glad of an excuse to leave*] I'll make him get a move on.

[*He goes out on the side porch. A moment later he is heard calling from the porch exasperatedly.*]

Hey! Papa! Come on! We can't wait all day!

[MARY *has risen from the arm of the chair. Her hands play restlessly over the table top. She does not look at* JAMIE *but she feels the cynically appraising glance he gives her face and hands.*]

MARY [*tensely*] Why do you stare like that?

JAMIE You know. [*He turns back to the window.*]

MARY I don't know.

JAMIE Oh, for God's sake, do you think you can fool me, Mama? I'm not blind.

MARY [*looks directly at him now, her face set again in an expression of blank, stubborn denial*] I don't know what you're talking about.

JAMIE No? Take a look at your eyes in the mirror!

EDMUND [*coming in from the porch*] I got Papa moving. He'll be here in a minute. [*with a glance from one to the other, which his mother avoids—uneasily*] What happened? What's the matter, Mama?

MARY [*disturbed by his coming, gives way to a flurry of guilty, nervous excitement*] Your brother ought to be ashamed of himself. He's been insinuating I don't know what.

EDMUND [*turns on* JAMIE] God damn you!

[*He takes a threatening step toward him.* JAMIE *turns his back with a shrug and looks out the window.*]

MARY [*more upset, grabs* EDMUND's *arm—excitedly*] Stop this at once, do you hear me? How dare you use such language before me! [*Abruptly her tone and manner change to the strange detachment she has shown before.*] It's wrong to blame your brother. He can't help being what the past has made him. Any more than your father can. Or you. Or I.

EDMUND [*frightenedly—with a desperate hoping against hope*] He's a liar! It's a lie, isn't it, Mama?

MARY [*keeping her eyes averted*] What is a lie? Now you're talking in riddles like Jamie. [*Then her eyes meet his stricken, accusing look. She stammers*] Edmund! Don't! [*She looks away and her manner instantly regains the quality of strange detachment—calmly*] There's your father coming up the steps now. I must tell Bridget.

[*She goes through the back parlor.* EDMUND *moves slowly to his chair. He looks sick and hopeless.*]

JAMIE [*from the window, without looking around*] Well?

EDMUND [*refusing to admit anything to his brother yet—weakly defiant*] Well, what? You're a liar.

[JAMIE *again shrugs his shoulders. The screen door on the front porch is heard closing.* EDMUND *says dully*]

Here's Papa. I hope he loosens up with the old bottle.

[TYRONE *comes in through the front parlor. He is putting on his coat.*]

TYRONE Sorry I'm late. Captain Turner stopped to talk and once he starts gabbing you can't get away from him.

JAMIE [*without turning—dryly*] You mean once he starts listening.

[*His father regards him with dislike. He comes to the table with a quick measuring look at the bottle of whiskey. Without turning,* JAMIE *senses this.*]

It's all right. The level in the bottle hasn't changed.

TYRONE I wasn't noticing that. [*He adds caustically*] As if it proved anything with you around. I'm on to your tricks.

EDMUND [*dully*] Did I hear you say, let's all have a drink?

TYRONE [*frowns at him*] Jamie is welcome after his hard morning's work, but I won't invite you. Doctor Hardy—

EDMUND To hell with Doctor Hardy! One isn't going to kill me. I feel—all in, Papa.

TYRONE [*with a worried look at him—putting on a fake heartiness*] Come along, then. It's before a meal and I've always found that good whiskey, taken in moderation as an appetizer, is the best of tonics.

[EDMUND *gets up as his father passes the bottle to him. He pours a big drink.* TYRONE *frowns admonishingly.*]

I said, in moderation.

[*He pours his own drink and passes the bottle to* JAMIE, *grumbling.*]

It'd be a waste of breath mentioning moderation to you.

[*Ignoring the hint,* JAMIE *pours a big drink. His father scowls—then, giving it up, resumes his hearty air, raising his glass.*]

Well, here's health and happiness!

[EDMUND *gives a bitter laugh.*]

EDMUND That's a joke!

TYRONE What is?

EDMUND Nothing. Here's how. [*They drink.*]

TYRONE [*becoming aware of the atmosphere*] What's the matter here? There's gloom in the air you could cut with a knife. [*turns on* JAMIE *resentfully*] You got the drink you were after, didn't you? Why are you wearing that gloomy look on your mug?

JAMIE [*shrugging his shoulders*] You won't be singing a song yourself soon.

EDMUND Shut up, Jamie.

TYRONE [*uneasy now—changing the subject*] I thought lunch was ready. I'm hungry as a hunter. Where is your mother?

MARY [*returning through the back parlor, calls*] Here I am.

[*She comes in. She is excited and self-conscious. As she talks, she glances everywhere except at any of their faces.*]

I've had to calm down Bridget. She's in a tantrum over your being late again, and I don't blame her. If your lunch is dried up from waiting in the oven, she said it served you right, you could like it or leave it for all she cared. [*with increasing excitement*] Oh, I'm so sick and tired of pretending this is a home! You won't help me! You won't put yourself out the least bit! You don't know how to act in a home! You don't really want one! You never have wanted one—never since the day we were married! You should have remained a bachelor and lived in second-rate hotels and entertained your friends in barrooms! [*She adds strangely, as if she were now talking aloud to herself rather than to* TYRONE] Then nothing would ever have happened.

[*They stare at her.* TYRONE *knows now. He suddenly looks a tired, bitterly sad old man.* EDMUND *glances at his father and sees that he knows, but he still cannot help trying to warn his mother.*]

EDMUND Mama! Stop talking. Why don't we go in to lunch.

MARY [*Starts and at once the quality of unnatural detachment settles on her face again. She even smiles with an ironical amusement to herself.*] Yes, it is inconsiderate of me to dig up the past, when I know your father and Jamie must be hungry. [*putting her arm around* EDMUND*'s shoulder—with a fond solicitude which is at the same time remote*] I do hope you have an appetite, dear. You really must eat more [*Her eyes become fixed on the whiskey glass on the table beside him—sharply*] Why is that glass there? Did you take a drink? Oh, how can you be such a fool? Don't you know it's the worst thing? [*She turns on* TYRONE.] You're to blame, James. How could you let him? Do you want to kill him? Don't you remember my father? He wouldn't stop after he was stricken. He said doctors were fools! He thought, like you, that whiskey is a good tonic! [*A look of terror comes into her eyes and she stammers*] But, of course, there's no comparison at all. I don't know why I—Forgive me for scolding you, James. One small drink won't hurt Edmund. It might be good for him, if it gives him an appetite.

[*She pats* EDMUND*'s cheek playfully, the strange detachment again in her manner. He jerks his head away. She seems not to notice, but she moves instinctively away.*]

JAMIE [*roughly, to hide his tense nerves*] For God's sake, let's eat. I've been working in the damned dirt under the hedge all morning. I've earned my grub.

[*He comes around in back of his father, not looking at his mother, and grabs* EDMUND*'s shoulder.*]

Come on, Kid. Let's put on the feed bag.

[EDMUND *gets up, keeping his eyes averted from his mother. They pass her, heading for the back parlor.*]

TYRONE [*dully*] Yes, you go in with your mother, lads. I'll join you in a second.

[*But they keep on without waiting for her. She looks at their backs with a helpless hurt and, as they enter the back parlor, starts to follow them.* TYRONE*'s eyes are on her, sad and condemning. She feels them and turns sharply without meeting his stare.*]

MARY Why do you look at me like that? [*Her hands flutter up to pat her hair.*] Is it my hair coming down? I was so worn out from last night, I thought I'd better lie down this morning. I drowsed off and had a nice refreshing nap. But I'm sure I fixed my hair again when I woke up. [*forcing a laugh*] Although, as usual, I couldn't find my glasses. [*sharply*] Please stop staring! One would think you were accusing me—[*then pleadingly*] James! You don't understand!

TYRONE [*with dull anger*] I understand that I've been a God-damned fool to believe in you!

[*He walks away from her to pour himself a big drink.*]

MARY [*her face again sets in stubborn defiance*] I don't know what you mean by "believing in me." All I've felt was distrust and spying and suspicion. [*then accusingly*] Why are you having another drink? You never have more than one before lunch. [*bitterly*] I know what to expect. You will be drunk tonight. Well, it won't be the first time, will it—or the thousandth? [*again she bursts out pleadingly*] Oh, James, please! You don't understand! I'm worried about Edmund! I'm so afraid he—

TYRONE I don't want to listen to excuses, Mary.

MARY [*strickenly*] Excuses? You mean—? Oh, you can't believe that of me! You mustn't believe that, James! [*then slipping away into her strange detachment—quite casually*] Shall we not go into lunch dear? I don't want anything but I know you're hungry.

[*He walks slowly to where she stands in the doorway. He walks like an old man. As he reaches her she bursts out piteously.*]

James! I tried so hard! I tried so hard! Please believe—!

TYRONE [*moved in spite of himself—helplessly*] I suppose you did, Mary. [*then grief-strickenly*] For the love of God, why couldn't you have the strength to keep on?

MARY [*her face setting into that stubborn denial again*] I don't know what you're talking about. Have the strength to keep on what?

TYRONE [*hopelessly*] Never mind. It's no use now.

[*He moves on and she keeps beside him as they disappear in the back parlor.*]

CURTAIN

Act 2

SCENE 2

SCENE—*The same, about a half hour later. The tray with the bottle of whiskey has been removed from the table. The family are returning from lunch as the curtain rises.* MARY *is the first to enter from the back parlor. Her husband follows. He is not with her as he was in the similar entrance after breakfast at the opening of Act One. He avoids touching her or looking at her. There is condemnation in his face, mingled now with the beginning of an old weary, helpless resignation.* JAMIE *and* EDMUND *follow their father.* JAMIE*'s face is hard with defensive cynicism.* EDMUND *tries to copy this defense but without success. He plainly shows he is heartsick as well as physically ill.*

MARY *is terribly nervous again, as if the strain of sitting through lunch with them had been too much for her. Yet at the same time, in contrast to this, her expression shows more of that strange aloofness which seems to stand apart from her nerves and the anxieties which harry them.*

She is talking as she enters—a stream of words that issues casually, in a routine of family conversation, from her mouth. She appears indifferent to the fact that their thoughts are not on what she is saying any more than her own are. As she talks, she comes to the left of the table and stands, facing front, one hand fumbling with the bosom of her dress, the other playing over the table top. TYRONE *lights a cigar and goes to the screen door, staring out.* JAMIE *fills a pipe from a jar on top of the bookcase at rear. He lights it as he goes to look out the window at right.* EDMUND *sits in a chair by the table, turned half away from his mother so he does not have to watch her.*

MARY It's no use finding fault with Bridget. She doesn't listen. I can't threaten her, or she'd threaten she'd leave. And she does do her best at times. It's too bad they seem to be just the times you're sure to be late, James. Well, there's this consolation: it's difficult to tell from her cooking whether she's doing her best or her worst. [*She gives a little laugh of detached amusement—indifferently*] Never mind. The summer will soon be over, thank goodness. Your season will open again and we can go back to second-rate hotels and trains. I hate them, too, but at least I don't expect them to be like a home, and there's no housekeeping to worry about. It's unreasonable to expect Bridget or Cathleen to act as if this was a home. They know it isn't as well as we know it. It never has been and it never will be.

TYRONE [*bitterly without turning around*] No, it never can be now. But it was once, before you—

MARY [*her face instantly set in blank denial*] Before I what? [*There is dead silence. She goes on with a return of her detached air.*] No, no. Whatever you mean, it isn't true, dear. It was never a home. You've always preferred the Club or barroom. And for me it's always been as lonely as a dirty room in a one-night stand hotel. In a real home one is never lonely. You forget I know from experience what a home is like. I gave up one to marry you—my father's home. [*At once, through an association of ideas she turns to* EDMUND. *Her manner becomes tenderly solicitous, but there is the strange quality of detachment in it.*] I'm worried about you, Edmund. You hardly touched a thing at lunch. That's no way to take care of yourself. It's all right for me not to have an appetite. I've been growing too fat. But you must eat. [*coaxingly maternal*] Promise me you will, dear, for my sake.

EDMUND [*dully*] Yes, Mama.

MARY [*pats his cheek as he tries not to shrink away*] That's a good boy.

[*There is another pause of dead silence. Then the telephone in the front hall rings and all of them stiffen startledly.*]

TYRONE [*hastily*] I'll answer. McGuire said he'd call me. [*He goes out through the front parlor.*]

MARY [*indifferently*] McGuire. He must have another piece of property on his list that no one would think of buying except your father. It doesn't matter any more, but it's always seemed to me your father could afford to keep on buying property but never to give me a home.

[*She stops to listen as* TYRONE'*s voice is heard from the hall.*]

TYRONE Hello. [*with forced heartiness*] Oh, how are you, Doctor?

[JAMIE *turns from the window.* MARY'*s fingers play more rapidly on the table top.* TYRONE'*s voice, trying to conceal, reveals that he is hearing bad news.*]

I see—[*hurriedly*] Well, you'll explain all about it when you see him this afternoon. Yes, he'll be in without fail. Four o'clock. I'll drop in myself and have a talk with you before that. I have to go uptown on business, anyway. Goodbye, Doctor.

EDMUND [*dully*] That didn't sound like glad tidings.

[JAMIE *gives him a pitying glance—then looks out the window again.* MARY'S *face is terrified and her hands flutter distractedly.* TYRONE *comes in. The strain is obvious in his casualness as he addresses* EDMUND.]

TYRONE It was Doctor Hardy. He wants you to be sure and see him at four.

EDMUND [*dully*] What did he say? Not that I give a damn now.

MARY [*bursts out excitedly*] I wouldn't believe him if he swore on a stack of Bibles. You mustn't pay attention to a word he says, Edmund.

TYRONE [*sharply*] Mary!

MARY [*more excitedly*] Oh, we all realize why you like him, James! Because he's cheap! But please don't try to tell me! I know all about Doctor Hardy. Heaven knows I ought to after all these years. He's an ignorant fool! There should be a law to keep men like him from practicing. He hasn't the slightest idea—When you're in agony and half insane, he sits and holds your hand and delivers sermons on will power! [*Her face is drawn in an expression of intense suffering by the memory. For the moment, she loses all caution. With bitter hatred*] He deliberately humiliates you! He makes you beg and plead! He treats you like a criminal! He understands nothing! And yet it was exactly the same type of cheap quack who first gave you the medicine—and you never knew what it was until too late! [*passionately*] I hate doctors! They'll sell their souls! What's worse, they'll sell yours, and you never know it till one day you find yourself in hell!

EDMUND Mama! For God's sake, stop talking.

TYRONE [*shakily*] Yes, Mary, it's no time—

MARY [*suddenly is overcome by guilty confusion—stammers*] I—Forgive me, dear. You're right. It's useless to be angry now. [*There is again a pause of dead silence. When she speaks again, her face has cleared and is calm, and the quality of uncanny detachment is in her voice and manner.*] I'm going upstairs for a moment, if you'll excuse me. I have to fix my hair. [*she adds smilingly*] That is if I can find my glasses. I'll be right down.

TYRONE [*as she starts through the doorway—pleading and rebuking*] Mary!

MARY [*turns to stare at him calmly*] Yes, dear? What is it?

TYRONE [*helplessly*] Nothing.

MARY [*with a strange derisive smile*] You're welcome to come up and watch me if you're so suspicious.

TYRONE As if that could do any good! You'd only postpone it. And I'm not your jailor. This isn't a prison.

MARY No. I know you can't help thinking it's a home. [*She adds quickly with a detached contrition*] I'm sorry, dear. I don't mean to be bitter. It's not your fault.

[*She turns and disappears through the back parlor. The three in the room remain silent. It is as if they were waiting until she got upstairs before speaking.*]

JAMIE [*cynically brutal*] Another shot in the arm!

EDMUND [*angrily*] Cut out that kind of talk!

TYRONE Yes! Hold your foul tongue and your rotten Broadway loafer's lingo! Have you no pity or decency? [*losing his temper*] You ought to be kicked out in the gutter! But if I did it, you know damned well who'd weep and plead for you, and excuse you and complain till I let you come back.

JAMIE [*a spasm of pain crosses his face*] Christ, don't I know that? No pity? I have all the pity in the world for her. I understand what a hard game to beat she's up against—which is more than you ever have! My lingo didn't mean I had no feeling. I was merely putting bluntly what we all know, and have to live with now, again. [*bitterly*] The cures are no damned good except for a while. The truth is there is no cure and we've been saps to hope—[*cynically*] They never come back!

EDMUND [*scornfully parodying his brother's cynicism*] They never come back! Everything is in the bag! It's all a frame-up! We're all fall guys and suckers and we can't beat the game! [*disdainfully*] Christ, if I felt the way you do—!

JAMIE [*stung for a moment—then shrugging his shoulders, dryly*] I thought you did. Your poetry isn't very cheery. Nor the stuff you read and claim to admire. [*He indicates the small bookcase at rear.*] Your pet with the unpronounceable name, for example.

EDMUND Nietzsche. You don't know what you're talking about. You haven't read him.

JAMIE Enough to know it's a lot of bunk!

TYRONE Shut up, both of you! There's little choice between the philosophy you learned from Broadway loafers, and the one Edmund got from his books. They're both rotten to the core. You've both flouted the faith you were born and brought up in—the one true faith of the Catholic Church—and your denial has brought nothing but self-destruction!

[*His two sons stare at him contemptuously. They forget their quarrel and are as one against him on this issue.*]

EDMUND That's the bunk, Papa!

JAMIE We don't pretend, at any rate. [*caustically*] I don't notice you've worn any holes in the knees of your pants going to Mass.

TYRONE It's true I'm a bad Catholic in the observance, God forgive me. But I believe! [*angrily*] And you're a liar! I may not go to church but every night and morning of my life I get on my knees and pray!

EDMUND [*bitingly*] Did you pray for Mama?

TYRONE I did. I've prayed to God these many years for her.

EDMUND Then Nietzsche must be right. [*He quotes from* Thus Spake Zarathustra.] "God is dead: of His pity for man hath God died."

TYRONE [*ignores this*] If your mother had prayed, too—She hasn't denied her faith, but she's forgotten it, until now there's no strength of the spirit left in her to fight against her curse. [*then dully resigned*] But what's the good of talk? We've lived with this before and now we must again. There's no help for it. [*bitterly*] Only I wish she hadn't led me to hope this time. By God, I never will again!

EDMUND That's a rotten thing to say, Papa! [*defiantly*] Well, I'll hope! She's just started. It can't have got a hold on her yet. She can still stop. I'm going to talk to her.

JAMIE [*shrugs his shoulders*] You can't talk to her now. She'll listen but she won't listen. She'll be here but she won't be here. You know the way she gets.

TYRONE Yes, that's the way the poison acts on her always. Every day from now on, there'll be the same drifting away from us until by the end of each night—

EDMUND [*miserably*] Cut it out, Papa! [*He jumps up from his chair.*] I'm going to get dressed. [*bitterly, as he goes*] I'll make so much noise she can't suspect I've come to spy on her.

[*He disappears through the front parlor and can be heard stamping noisily upstairs.*]

JAMIE [*after a pause*] What did Doc Hardy say about the Kid?

TYRONE [*dully*] It's what you thought. He's got consumption.

JAMIE God damn it!

TYRONE There is no possible doubt, he said.

JAMIE He'll have to go to a sanatorium.

TYRONE Yes, and the sooner the better, Hardy said, for him and everyone around him. He claims that in six months to a year Edmund will be cured, if he obeys orders. [*He sighs—gloomily and resentfully*] I never thought a child of mine—It doesn't come from my side of the family. There wasn't one of us that didn't have lungs as strong as an ox.

JAMIE Who gives a damn about that part of it! Where does Hardy want to send him?

TYRONE That's what I'm to see him about.

JAMIE Well, for God's sake, pick out a good place and not some cheap dump!

TYRONE [*stung*] I'll send him wherever Hardy thinks best!

JAMIE Well, don't give Hardy your old over-the-hills-to-the-poorhouse song about taxes and mortgages.

TYRONE I'm no millionaire who can throw money away! Why shouldn't I tell Hardy the truth?

JAMIE Because he'll think you want him to pick a cheap dump, and because he'll know it isn't the truth—especially if he hears afterwards you've seen McGuire and let that flannel-mouth, gold-brick merchant sting you with another piece of bum property!

TYRONE Keep your nose out of my business!

JAMIE This is Edmund's business. What I'm afraid of is, with your Irish bog trotter idea that consumption is fatal, you'll figure it would be a waste of money to spend any more than you can help.

TYRONE You liar!

JAMIE All right. Prove I'm a liar. That's what I want. That's why I brought it up.

TYRONE [*his rage still smoldering*] I have every hope Edmund will be cured. And keep your dirty tongue off Ireland! You're a fine one to sneer, with the map of it on your face!

JAMIE Not after I wash my face. [*Then before his father can react to this insult to the Old Sod he adds dryly, shrugging his shoulders*] Well, I've said all I have to say. It's up to you. [*abruptly*] What do you want me to do this afternoon, now you're going uptown? I've done all I can do on the hedge until you cut more of it. You don't want me to go ahead with your clipping, I know that.

TYRONE No. You'd get it crooked, as you get everything else.

JAMIE Then I'd better go uptown with Edmund. The bad news coming on top of what's happened to Mama may hit him hard.

TYRONE [*forgetting his quarrel*] Yes, go with him, Jamie. Keep up his spirits, if you can. [*He adds caustically*] If you can without making it an excuse to get drunk!

JAMIE What would I use for money? The last I heard they were still selling booze, not giving it away. [*He starts for the front-parlor doorway.*] I'll get dressed.

[*He stops in the doorway as he sees his mother approaching from the hall, and moves aside to let her come in. Her eyes look brighter, and her manner is more detached. This change becomes more marked as the scene goes on.*]

MARY [*vaguely*] You haven't seen my glasses anywhere, have you, Jamie?

[*She doesn't look at him. He glances away, ignoring her question but she doesn't seem to expect an answer. She comes forward, addressing her husband without looking at him.*]

You haven't seen them, have you, James?

[*Behind her* JAMIE *disappears through the front parlor.*]

TYRONE [*turns to look out the screen door*] No, Mary.

MARY What's the matter with Jamie? Have you been nagging at him again? You shouldn't treat him with such contempt all the time. He's not to blame. If he'd been brought up in a real home, I'm sure he would have been different. [*She comes to the windows at right—lightly*] You're not much of a weather prophet, dear. See how hazy it's getting. I can hardly see the other shore.

TYRONE [*trying to speak naturally*] Yes, I spoke too soon. We're in for another night of fog, I'm afraid.

MARY Oh, well, I won't mind it tonight.

TYRONE No, I don't imagine you will, Mary.

MARY [*flashes a glance at him—after a pause*] I don't see Jamie going down to the hedge. Where did he go?

TYRONE He's going with Edmund to the Doctor's. He went up to change his clothes. [*then, glad of an excuse to leave her*] I'd better do the same or I'll be late for my appointment at the Club.

[*He makes a move toward the front-parlor doorway, but with a swift impulsive movement she reaches out and clasps his arm.*]

MARY [*a note of pleading in her voice*] Don't go yet, dear. I don't want to be alone. [*hastily*] I mean, you have plenty of time. You know you boast you can dress in one-tenth the time it takes the boys. [*vaguely*] There is something I wanted to say. What is it? I've forgotten. I'm glad Jamie is going uptown. You didn't give him any money, I hope.

TYRONE I did not.

MARY He'd only spend it on drink and you know what a vile, poisonous tongue he has when he's drunk. Not that I would mind anything he said tonight, but he always manages to drive you into a rage, especially if you're drunk, too, as you will be.

TYRONE [*resentfully*] I won't. I never get drunk.

MARY [*teasing indifferently*] Oh, I'm sure you'll hold it well. You always have. It's hard for a stranger to tell, but after thirty-five years of marriage—

TYRONE I've never missed a performance in my life. That's the proof! [*then bitterly*] If I did get drunk it is not you who should blame me. No man has ever had a better reason.

MARY Reason? What reason? You always drink too much when you go to the Club, don't you? Particularly when you meet McGuire. He sees to that. Don't think I'm finding fault, dear. You must do as you please. I won't mind.

TYRONE I know you won't. [*He turns toward the front parlor, anxious to escape.*] I've got to get dressed.

MARY [*again she reaches out and grasps his arm—pleadingly*] No, please wait a little while, dear. At least, until one of the boys comes down. You will all be leaving me so soon.

TYRONE [*with bitter sadness*] It's you who are leaving us, Mary.

MARY I? That's a silly thing to say, James. How could I leave? There is nowhere I could go. Who would I go to see? I have no friends.

TYRONE It's your own fault—[*He stops and sighs helplessly—persuasively*] There's surely one thing you can do this afternoon that will be good for you, Mary. Take a drive in the automobile. Get away from the house. Get a little sun and fresh air. [*injuredly*] I bought the automobile for you. You know I don't like the damned things. I'd rather walk any day, or take a trolley. [*with growing resentment*] I had it here waiting for you when you came back from the sanatorium. I hoped it would give you pleasure and distract your mind. You used to ride in it every day, but you've hardly used it at all lately. I paid a lot of money I couldn't afford, and there's the chauffeur I have to board and lodge and pay high wages whether he drives you or not. [*bitterly*] Waste! The same old waste that will land me in the poorhouse in my old age! What good did it do you? I might as well have thrown the money out the window.

MARY [*with detached calm*] Yes, it was a waste of money, James. You shouldn't have bought a secondhand automobile. You were swindled again as you always are, because you insist on secondhand bargains in everything.

TYRONE It's one of the best makes! Everyone says it's better than any of the new ones!

MARY [*ignoring this*] It was another waste to hire Smythe, who was only a helper in a garage and had never been a chauffeur. Oh, I realize his wages are less than a real chauffeur's, but he more than makes up for that, I'm sure, by the graft he gets from the garage on repair bills. Something is always wrong. Smythe sees to that, I'm afraid.

TYRONE I don't believe it! He may not be a fancy millionaire's flunky but he's honest! You're as bad as Jamie, suspecting everyone!

MARY You mustn't be offended, dear. I wasn't offended when you gave me the automobile. I knew you didn't mean to humiliate me. I knew that was the way you had to do everything. I was grateful and touched. I knew buying the car was a hard thing for you to do, and it proved how much you loved me, in your way, especially when you couldn't really believe it would do me any good.

TYRONE Mary! [*He suddenly hugs her to him—brokenly*] Dear Mary! For the love of God, for my sake and the boys' sake and your own, won't you stop now?

MARY [*stammers in guilty confusion for a second*] I—James! Please! [*Her strange, stubborn defense comes back instantly.*] Stop what? What are you talking about?

[*He lets his arm fall to his side brokenly. She impulsively puts her arm around him.*]

James! We've loved each other! We always will! Let's remember only that, and not try to understand what we cannot understand, or help things that cannot be helped—the things life has done to us we cannot excuse or explain.

TYRONE [*as if he hadn't heard—bitterly*] You won't even try?

MARY [*her arms drop hopelessly and she turns away—with detachment*] Try to go for a drive this afternoon, you mean? Why, yes, if you wish me to, although it makes me feel lonelier than if I stayed here. There is no one I can invite to drive with me, and I never know where to tell Smythe to go. If there was a friend's house where I could drop in and laugh and gossip awhile. But, of course, there isn't. There never has been. [*her manner becoming more and more remote*] At the Convent I had so many friends. Girls whose families lived in lovely homes. I used to visit them and they'd visit me in my father's home. But, naturally, after I married an actor—you know how actors were considered in those days—a lot of them gave me the cold shoulder. And then, right after we were married, there was the scandal of that woman who had been your mistress, suing you. From then on, all my old friends either pitied me or cut me dead. I hated the ones who cut me much less than the pitiers.

TYRONE [*with guilty resentment*] For God's sake, don't dig up what's long forgotten. If you're that far gone in the past already, when it's only the beginning of the afternoon, what will you be tonight?

MARY [*stares at him defiantly now*] Come to think of it, I do have to drive uptown. There's something I must get at the drugstore.

TYRONE [*bitterly scornful*] Leave it to you to have some of the stuff hidden, and prescriptions for more! I hope you'll lay in a good stock ahead so we'll never have another night like the one when you screamed for it, and ran out of the house in your nightdress half crazy, to try and throw yourself off the dock!

MARY [*tries to ignore this*] I have to get tooth powder and toilet soap and cold cream—[*She breaks down pitiably.*] James! You mustn't remember! You mustn't humiliate me so!

TYRONE [*ashamed*] I'm sorry. Forgive me, Mary!

MARY [*defensively detached again*] It doesn't matter. Nothing like that ever happened. You must have dreamed it.

[*He stares at her hopelessly. Her voice seems to drift farther and farther away.*]

I was so healthy before Edmund was born. You remember, James. There wasn't a nerve in my body. Even traveling with you season after season, with week after week of one-night stands, in trains without Pullmans, in dirty rooms of filthy hotels, eating bad food, bearing children in hotel rooms, I still kept healthy. But bearing Edmund was the last straw. I was so sick afterwards, and that ignorant quack of a cheap hotel doctor—All he knew was I was in pain. It was easy for him to stop the pain.

TYRONE Mary! For God's sake, forget the past!

MARY [*with strange objective calm*] Why? How can I? The past is the present, isn't it? It's the future, too. We all try to lie out of that but life won't let us. [*going on*] I blame only myself. I swore after Eugene died I would never have another baby. I was to blame for his death. If I hadn't left him with my mother to join you on the road, because you wrote telling me you missed me and were so lonely, Jamie would never have been allowed, when he still had measles, to go in the baby's room. [*her face hardening*] I've always believed Jamie did it on purpose. He was jealous of the baby. He hated him. [*as* TYRONE *starts to protest*] Oh, I know Jamie was only seven, but he was never stupid. He'd been warned it might kill the baby. He knew. I've never been able to forgive him for that.

TYRONE [*with bitter sadness*] Are you back with Eugene now? Can't you let our dead baby rest in peace?

MARY [*as if she hadn't heard him*] It was my fault. I should have insisted on staying with Eugene and not have let you persuade me to join you, just because I loved you. Above all, I shouldn't have let you insist I have another baby to take Eugene's place, because you thought that would make me forget his death. I knew from experience by then that children should have homes to be born in, if they are to be good children, and women need homes, if they are to be good mothers. I was afraid all the time I carried Edmund. I knew something terrible would happen. I knew I'd proved by the way I'd left Eugene that I wasn't worthy to have another baby, and that God would punish me if I did. I never should have borne Edmund.

TYRONE [*with an uneasy glance through the front parlor*] Mary! Be careful with your talk. If he heard you he might think you never wanted him. He's feeling bad enough already without—

MARY [*violently*] It's a lie! I did want him! More than anything in the world! You don't understand! I meant, for his sake. He has never been happy. He never will be. Nor healthy. He was born nervous and too sensitive, and that's my fault. And now, ever since he's been so sick I've kept remembering Eugene and my father and I've been so frightened and guilty—[*then, catching herself, with an instant change to stubborn denial*] Oh, I know it's foolish to imagine dreadful things when there's no reason for it. After all, everyone has colds and gets over them.

[TYRONE *stares at her and sighs helplessly. He turns away toward the front parlor and sees* EDMUND *coming down the stairs in the hall.*]

TYRONE [*sharply, in a low voice*] Here's Edmund. For God's sake try and be yourself—at least until he goes! You can do that much for him!

[*He waits, forcing his face into a pleasantly paternal expression. She waits frightenedly, seized again by a nervous panic, her hands fluttering over the bosom of her dress, up to her throat and hair, with a distracted aimlessness. Then, as* EDMUND *approaches the doorway, she cannot face him. She goes swiftly away to the windows at left and stares out with her back to the front parlor.* EDMUND *enters. He has changed to a ready-made blue serge suit, high stiff collar and tie, black shoes. With an actor's heartiness*]

Well! You look spic and span. I'm on my way up to change, too. [*He starts to pass him.*]

EDMUND [*dryly*] Wait a minute, Papa. I hate to bring up disagreeable topics, but there's the matter of carfare. I'm broke.

TYRONE [*starts automatically on a customary lecture*] You'll always be broke until you learn the value—[*checks himself guiltily, looking at his son's sick face with worried pity*] But you've been learning, lad. You worked hard before you took ill. You've done splendidly. I'm proud of you.

[*He pulls out a small roll of bills from his pants pocket and carefully selects one.* EDMUND *takes it. He glances at it and his face expresses astonishment. His father again reacts customarily—sarcastically*]

Thank you. [*He quotes*] "How sharper than a serpent's tooth it is—"

EDMUND "To have a thankless child."[9] I know. Give me a chance, Papa. I'm knocked speechless. This isn't a dollar. It's a ten spot.

TYRONE [*embarrassed by his generosity*] Put it in your pocket. You'll probably meet some of your friends uptown and you can't hold your end up and be sociable with nothing in your jeans.

EDMUND You meant it? Gosh, thank you, Papa. [*He is genuinely pleased and grateful for a moment—then he stares at his father's face with uneasy suspicion.*] But why all of a sudden—? [*cynically*] Did Doc Hardy tell you I was going to die? [*Then he sees his father is bitterly hurt.*] No! That's a rotten crack. I was only kidding, Papa. [*He puts an arm around his father impulsively and gives him an affectionate hug.*] I'm very grateful. Honest, Papa.

TYRONE [*touched, returns his hug*] You're welcome, lad.

MARY [*suddenly turns to them in a confused panic of frightened anger*] I won't have it! [*She stamps her foot.*] Do you hear, Edmund! Such morbid nonsense! Saying you're going to die! It's the books you read! Nothing but sadness and death! Your father shouldn't allow you to have them. And some of the poems you've written yourself are even worse! You'd think you didn't want to live! A boy of your age with everything before him! It's just a pose you get out of books! You're not really sick at all!

TYRONE Mary! Hold your tongue!

MARY [*instantly changing to a detached tone*] But, James, it's absurd of Edmund to be so gloomy and make such a great to-do about nothing. [*turning to* EDMUND *but avoiding his eyes—teasingly affectionate*] Never mind, dear. I'm on to you. [*She comes to him.*] You want to be petted and spoiled and made a fuss over, isn't that it? You're still such a baby. [*She puts her arm around him and hugs him. He remains rigid and unyielding. Her voice begins to tremble.*] But please don't carry it too far, dear. Don't say horrible things. I know it's foolish to take them seriously but I can't help it. You've got me—so frightened.

[*She breaks and hides her face on his shoulder, sobbing.* EDMUND *is moved in spite of himself. He pats her shoulder with an awkward tenderness.*]

EDMUND Don't, mother. [*His eyes meet his father's.*]

9. Shakespeare's *King Lear* 1.4.312.

TYRONE [*huskily—clutching at hopeless hope*] Maybe if you asked your mother now what you said you were going to—[*He fumbles with his watch.*] By God, look at the time! I'll have to shake a leg.

[*He hurries away through the front parlor.* MARY *lifts her head. Her manner is again one of detached motherly solicitude. She seems to have forgotten the tears which are still in her eyes.*]

MARY How do you feel, dear? [*She feels his forehead.*] Your head is a little hot, but that's just from going out in the sun. You look ever so much better than you did this morning. [*taking his hand*] Come and sit down. You mustn't stand on your feet so much. You must learn to husband your strength.

[*She gets him to sit and she sits sideways on the arm of his chair, an arm around his shoulder, so he cannot meet her eyes.*]

EDMUND [*starts to blurt out the appeal he now feels is quite hopeless*] Listen, Mama—

MARY [*interrupting quickly*] Now, now! Don't talk. Lean back and rest. [*persuasively*] You know, I think it would be much better for you if you stayed home this afternoon and let me take care of you. It's such a tiring trip uptown in the dirty old trolley on a hot day like this. I'm sure you'd be much better off here with me.

EDMUND [*dully*] You forget I have an appointment with Hardy. [*trying again to get his appeal started*] Listen, Mama—

MARY [*quickly*] You can telephone and say you don't feel well enough. [*excitedly*] It's simply a waste of time and money seeing him. He'll only tell you some lie. He'll pretend he's found something serious the matter because that's his bread and butter. [*She gives a hard sneering little laugh.*] The old idiot! All he knows about medicine is to look solemn and preach will power!

EDMUND [*trying to catch her eyes*] Mama! Please listen! I want to ask you something! You—You're only just started. You can still stop. You've got the will power! We'll all help you. I'll do anything! Won't you, Mama?

MARY [*stammers pleadingly*] Please don't—talk about things you don't understand!

EDMUND [*dully*] All right, I give up. I knew it was no use.

MARY [*in blank denial now*] Anyway, I don't know what you're referring to. But I do know you should be the last one—Right after I returned from the sanatorium, you began to be ill. The doctor there had warned me I must have peace at home with nothing to upset me, and all I've done is worry about you. [*then distractedly*] But that's no excuse! I'm only trying to explain. It's not an excuse! [*She hugs him to her—pleadingly*] Promise me, dear, you won't believe I made you an excuse.

EDMUND [*bitterly*] What else can I believe?

MARY [*slowly takes her arm away—her manner remote and objective again*] Yes, I suppose you can't help suspecting that.

EDMUND [*ashamed but still bitter*] What do you expect?

MARY Nothing, I don't blame you. How could you believe me—when I can't believe myself? I've become such a liar. I never lied about anything once upon a time. Now I have to lie, especially to myself. But how can you understand, when I don't myself. I've never understood anything about it, except that one day long ago I found I could no longer call my soul my own. [*She pauses—then lowering her voice to a strange tone of whispered confidence*] But some day, dear, I will find it again—some day when you're all well, and I see you healthy and happy and successful, and I don't have to feel guilty any more—some day when the Blessed Virgin Mary forgives me and gives me back the faith in Her love and pity I used to have in my convent days, and I can pray to Her again—when She sees no one in the world can believe in me even for a moment any more, then She will believe in me, and with Her help it will be so easy. I will hear myself scream with agony, and at the same time I will laugh because I will be so sure of myself. [*then as* EDMUND *remains hopelessly silent, she adds sadly*] Of course, you can't believe that, either. [*She rises from the arm of his chair and goes to stare out the windows at right with her back to him—casually*] Now I think of it, you might as well go uptown. I forgot I'm taking a drive. I have to go to the drugstore. You would hardly want to go there with me. You'd be so ashamed.

EDMUND [*brokenly*] Mama! Don't!

MARY I suppose you'll divide that ten dollars your father gave you with Jamie. You always divide with each other, don't you? Like good sports. Well, I know what he'll do with his share. Get drunk someplace where he can be with the only kind of woman he understands or likes. [*She turns to him, pleading frightenedly*] Edmund! Promise me you won't drink! It's so dangerous! You know Doctor Hardy told you—

EDMUND [*bitterly*] I thought he was an old idiot. Anyway, by tonight, what will you care?

MARY [*pitifully*] Edmund!

[JAMIE'*s voice is heard from the front hall,* "Come on, Kid, let's beat it." MARY'*s manner at once becomes detached again.*]

Go on, Edmund. Jamie's waiting. [*She goes to the front-parlor doorway.*] There comes your father downstairs, too.

[TYRONE'*s voice calls,* "Come on, Edmund."]

EDMUND [*jumping up from his chair*] I'm coming.

[*He stops beside her—without looking at her.*]

Goodbye, Mama.

MARY [*kisses him with detached affection*] Goodbye, dear. If you're coming home for dinner, try not to be late. And tell your father. You know what Bridget is.

[*He turns and hurries away.* TYRONE *calls from the hall,* "Goodbye, Mary," *and then* JAMIE, "Goodbye, Mama." *She calls back*]

Goodbye. [*The front screen door is heard closing after them. She comes and stands by the table, one hand drumming on it, the other fluttering up to pat her hair. She stares about the room with frightened, forsaken eyes and whispers to herself.*] It's so lonely here. [*Then her face hardens into bitter self-contempt.*] You're lying to yourself again. You wanted to get rid of them. Their contempt and disgust aren't pleasant company. You're glad they're gone. [*She gives a little despairing laugh.*] Then Mother of God, why do I feel so lonely?

CURTAIN

Act 3

SCENE—*The same. It is around half past six in the evening. Dusk is gathering in the living room, an early dusk due to the fog which has rolled in from the Sound and is like a white curtain drawn down outside the windows. From a lighthouse beyond the harbor's mouth, a foghorn is heard at regular intervals, moaning like a mournful whale in labor, and from the harbor itself, intermittently, comes the warning ringing of bells on yachts at anchor.*

The tray with the bottle of whiskey, glasses, and pitcher of ice water is on the table, as it was in the pre-luncheon scene of the previous act. MARY *and the second girl,* CATHLEEN, *are discovered. The latter is standing at left of table. She holds an empty whiskey glass in her hand as if she'd forgotten she had it. She shows the effects of drink. Her stupid, good-humored face wears a pleased and flattered simper.*

MARY *is paler than before and her eyes shine with unnatural brilliance. The strange detachment in her manner has intensified. She has hidden deeper within herself and found refuge and release in a dream where present reality is but an appearance to be accepted and dismissed unfeelingly—even with a hard cynicism—or entirely ignored. There is at times an uncanny gay, free youthfulness in her manner, as if in spirit she were released to become again, simply and without self-consciousness, the naive, happy, chattering schoolgirl of her convent days. She wears the dress into which she had changed for her drive to town, a simple, fairly expensive affair, which would be extremely becoming if it were not for the careless, almost slovenly way she wears it. Her hair is no longer fastidiously in place. It has a slightly disheveled, lopsided look. She talks to* CATHLEEN *with a confiding familiarity, as if the second girl were an old, intimate friend. As the curtain rises, she is standing by the screen door looking out. A moan of the foghorn is heard.*

MARY [*amused—girlishly*] That foghorn! Isn't it awful, Cathleen?

CATHLEEN [*talks more familiarly than usual but never with intentional impertinence because she sincerely likes her mistress*] It is indeed, Ma'am. It's like a banshee.

MARY [*Goes on as if she hadn't heard. In nearly all the following dialogue there is the feeling that she has* CATHLEEN *with her merely as an excuse to keep talking.*] I don't mind it tonight. Last night it drove me crazy. I lay awake worrying until I couldn't stand it any more.

CATHLEEN Bad cess to it.[1] I was scared out of my wits riding back from town. I thought that ugly monkey, Smythe, would drive us in a ditch or against a tree. You couldn't see your hand in front of you. I'm glad you had me sit in back with you, Ma'am. If I'd been in front with that monkey—He can't keep his dirty hands to himself. Give him half a chance and he's pinching me on the leg or you-know-where—asking your pardon, Ma'am, but it's true.

MARY [*dreamily*] It wasn't the fog I minded, Cathleen, I really love fog.

CATHLEEN They say it's good for the complexion.

1. Bad luck to it (Irish).

MARY It hides you from the world and the world from you. You feel that everything has changed, and nothing is what it seemed to be. No one can find or touch you any more.

CATHLEEN I wouldn't care so much if Smythe was a fine, handsome man like some chauffeurs I've seen—I mean, if it was all in fun, for I'm a decent girl. But for a shriveled runt like Smythe—! I've told him, you must think I'm hard up that I'd notice a monkey like you. I've warned him, one day I'll give a clout that'll knock him into next week. And so I will!

MARY It's the foghorn I hate. It won't let you alone. It keeps reminding you, and warning you, and calling you back. [*She smiles strangely.*] But it can't tonight. It's just an ugly sound. It doesn't remind me of anything. [*She gives a teasing, girlish laugh.*] Except, perhaps, Mr. Tyrone's snores. I've always had such fun teasing him about it. He has snored ever since I can remember, especially when he's had too much to drink, and yet he's like a child, he hates to admit it. [*She laughs, coming to the table.*] Well, I suppose I snore at times, too, and I don't like to admit it. So I have no right to make fun of him, have I? [*She sits in the rocker at right of table.*]

CATHLEEN Ah, sure, everybody healthy snores. It's a sign of sanity, they say. [*then, worriedly*] What time is it, Ma'am? I ought to go back in the kitchen. The damp is in Bridget's rheumatism and she's like a raging divil. She'll bite my head off.

[*She puts her glass on the table and makes a movement toward the back parlor.*]

MARY [*with a flash of apprehension*] No, don't go, Cathleen. I don't want to be alone, yet.

CATHLEEN You won't be for long. The Master and the boys will be home soon.

MARY I doubt if they'll come back for dinner. They have too good an excuse to remain in the barrooms where they feel at home.

[CATHLEEN *stares at her, stupidly puzzled.* MARY *goes on smilingly*]

Don't worry about Bridget. I'll tell her I kept you with me, and you can take a big drink of whiskey to her when you go. She won't mind then.

CATHLEEN [*grins—at her ease again*] No, Ma'am. That's the one thing can make her cheerful. She loves her drop.

MARY Have another drink yourself, if you wish, Cathleen.

CATHLEEN I don't know if I'd better, Ma'am. I can feel what I've had already. [*reaching for the bottle*] Well, maybe one more won't harm. [*She pours a drink.*] Here's your good health, Ma'am. [*She drinks without bothering about a chaser.*]

MARY [*dreamily*] I really did have good health once, Cathleen. But that was long ago.

CATHLEEN [*worried again*] The Master's sure to notice what's gone from the bottle. He has the eye of a hawk for that.

MARY [*amusedly*] Oh, we'll play Jamie's trick on him. Just measure a few drinks of water and pour them in.

CATHLEEN [*does this—with a silly giggle*] God save me, it'll be half water. He'll know by the taste.

MARY [*indifferently*] No, by the time he comes home he'll be too drunk to tell the difference. He has such a good excuse, he believes, to drown his sorrows.

CATHLEEN [*philosophically*] Well, it's a good man's failing. I wouldn't give a trauneen[2] for a teetotaler. They've no high spirits. [*then, stupidly puzzled*] Good excuse? You mean Master Edmund, Ma'am? I can tell the Master is worried about him.

MARY [*stiffens defensively—but in a strange way the reaction has a mechanical quality, as if it did not penetrate to real emotion*] Don't be silly, Cathleen. Why should he be? A touch of grippe is nothing. And Mr. Tyrone never is worried about anything, except money and property and the fear he'll end his days in poverty. I mean, deeply worried. Because he cannot really understand anything else. [*She gives a little laugh of detached, affectionate amusement.*] My husband is a very peculiar man, Cathleen.

CATHLEEN [*vaguely resentful*] Well, he's a fine, handsome, kind gentleman just the same, Ma'am. Never mind his weakness.

MARY Oh, I don't mind. I've loved him dearly for thirty-six years. That proves I know he's lovable at heart and can't help being what he is, doesn't it?

CATHLEEN [*hazily reassured*] That's right. Ma'am. Love him dearly, for any fool can see he worships the ground you walk on. [*fighting the effect of her last drink and trying to be soberly conversational*] Speaking of acting, Ma'am, how is it you never went on the stage?

MARY [*resentfully*] I? What put that absurd notion in your head? I was brought up in a respectable home and educated in the best convent in the Middle West. Before I met Mr. Tyrone I hardly knew there was such a thing as a theater. I was a very pious girl. I even dreamed of becoming a nun. I've never had the slightest desire to be an actress.

CATHLEEN [*bluntly*] Well, I can't imagine you a holy nun, Ma'am. Sure, you never darken the door of a church, God forgive you.

MARY [*ignores this*] I've never felt at home in the theater. Even though Mr. Tyrone has made me go with him on all his tours, I've had little to do with the people in his company, or with anyone on the stage. Not that I have anything against them. They have always been kind to me, and I to them. But I've never felt at home with them. Their life is not my life. It has always stood between me and—[*She gets up—abruptly*] But let's not talk of old things that couldn't be helped. [*She goes to the porch door and stares out.*] How thick the fog is. I can't see the road. All the people in the world could pass by and I would never know. I wish it was always that way. It's getting dark already. It will soon be night, thank goodness. [*She turns back—vaguely*] It was kind of you to keep me company this afternoon, Cathleen. I would have been lonely driving uptown alone.

CATHLEEN Sure, wouldn't I rather ride in a fine automobile than stay here and listen to Bridget's lies about her relations? It was like a vacation, Ma'am. [*She pauses—then stupidly*] There was only one thing I didn't like.

MARY [*vaguely*] What was that, Cathleen?

CATHLEEN The way the man in the drugstore acted when I took in the prescription for you. [*indignantly*] The impidence[3] of him!

MARY [*with stubborn blankness*] What are you talking about? What drugstore? What prescription? [*then hastily, as* CATHLEEN *stares in stupid amazement*] Oh, of course, I'd forgotten. The medicine for the rheumatism in

2. Coin of very low value (Irish).

3. Impudence.

my hands. What did the man say? [*then with indifference*] Not that it matters, as long as he filled the prescription.

CATHLEEN It mattered to me, then! I'm not used to being treated like a thief. He gave me a long look and says insultingly, "Where did you get hold of this?" and I says, "It's none of your damned business, but if you must know, it's for the lady I work for, Mrs. Tyrone, who's sitting out in the automobile." That shut him up quick. He gave a look out at you and said, "Oh," and went to get the medicine.

MARY [*vaguely*] Yes, he knows me. [*She sits in the armchair at right rear of table. She adds in a calm, detached voice*] It's a special kind of medicine. I have to take it because there is no other that can stop the pain—*all* the pain—I mean, in my hands. [*She raises her hands and regards them with melancholy sympathy. There is no tremor in them now.*] Poor hands! You'd never believe it, but they were once one of my good points, along with my hair and eyes, and I had a fine figure, too. [*Her tone has become more and more far-off and dreamy.*] They were a musician's hands. I used to love the piano. I worked so hard at my music in the Convent—if you can call it work when you do something you love. Mother Elizabeth and my music teacher both said I had more talent than any student they remembered. My father paid for special lessons. He spoiled me. He would do anything I asked. He would have sent me to Europe to study after I graduated from the Convent. I might have gone—if I hadn't fallen in love with Mr. Tyrone. Or I might have become a nun. I had two dreams. To be a nun, that was the more beautiful one. To become a concert pianist, that was the other. [*She pauses, regarding her hands fixedly.* CATHLEEN *blinks her eyes to fight off drowsiness and a tipsy feeling.*] I haven't touched a piano in so many years. I couldn't play with such crippled fingers, even if I wanted to. For a time after my marriage I tried to keep up my music. But it was hopeless. One-night stands, cheap hotels, dirty trains, leaving children, never having a home—[*She stares at her hands with fascinated disgust.*] See, Cathleen, how ugly they are! So maimed and crippled! You would think they'd been through some horrible accident! [*She gives a strange little laugh.*] So they have, come to think of it. [*She suddenly thrusts her hands behind her back.*] I won't look at them. They're worse than the foghorn for reminding me—[*then with defiant self-assurance*] But even they can't touch me now. [*She brings her hands from behind her back and deliberately stares at them—calmly*] They're far away. I see them, but the pain has gone.

CATHLEEN [*stupidly puzzled*] You've taken some of the medicine? It made you act funny, Ma'am. If I didn't know better, I'd think you'd a drop taken.

MARY [*dreamily*] It kills the pain. You go back until at last you are beyond its reach. Only the past when you were happy is real. [*She pauses—then as if her words had been an evocation which called back happiness she changes in her whole manner and facial expression. She looks younger. There is a quality of an innocent convent girl about her, and she smiles shyly.*] If you think Mr. Tyrone is handsome now, Cathleen, you should have seen him when I first met him. He had the reputation of being one of the best looking men in the country. The girls in the Convent who had seen him act, or seen his photographs, used to rave about him. He was a great matinee idol then, you know. Women used to wait at the stage door just to see him come out. You can imagine how excited I was when my father wrote me he and James Tyrone had become friends, and that I was to meet him when I came home for Easter vacation. I showed the letter to all the girls, and how envious they were! My father took me to see him act first. It was a play about the French Revolution and the leading part was a nobleman. I couldn't take my eyes off him. I wept when he was thrown in prison—and then was so mad at myself because I was afraid my eyes and nose would be red. My father had said we'd go backstage to his dressing room right after the play, and so we did. [*She gives a little excited, shy laugh.*] I was so bashful all I could do was stammer and blush like a little fool. But he didn't seem to think I was a fool. I know he liked me the first moment we were introduced. [*coquettishly*] I guess my eyes and nose couldn't have been red, after all. I was really very pretty then, Cathleen. And he was handsomer than my wildest dream, in his make-up and his nobleman's costume that was so becoming to him. He was different from all ordinary men, like someone from another world. At the same time he was simple, and kind, and unassuming, not a bit stuck-up or vain. I fell in love right then. So did he, he told me afterwards. I forgot all about becoming a nun or a concert pianist. All I wanted was to be his wife. [*She pauses, staring before her with unnaturally bright, dreamy eyes, and a rapt, tender, girlish smile.*] Thirty-six years ago, but I can see it as clearly as if it were tonight! We've loved each other ever since. And in all those thirty-six years, there has never been a breath of scandal about him. I mean, with any other woman. Never since he met me. That has made me very happy, Cathleen. It has made me forgive so many other things.

CATHLEEN [*fighting tipsy drowsiness—sentimentally*] He's a fine gentleman and you're a lucky woman. [*then, fidgeting*] Can I take the drink to Bridget, Ma'am? It must be near dinnertime and I ought to be in the kitchen helping her. If she don't get something to quiet her temper, she'll be after me with the cleaver.

MARY [*with a vague exasperation at being brought back from her dream*] Yes, yes, go. I don't need you now.

CATHLEEN [*with relief*] Thank you, Ma'am. [*She pours out a big drink and starts for the back parlor with it.*] You won't be alone long. The Master and the boys—

MARY [*impatiently*] No, no, they won't come. Tell Bridget I won't wait. You can serve dinner promptly at half past six. I'm not hungry but I'll sit at the table and we'll get it over with.

CATHLEEN You ought to eat something, Ma'am. It's a queer medicine if it takes away your appetite.

MARY [*has begun to drift into dreams again—reacts mechanically*] What medicine? I don't know what you mean. [*in dismissal*] You better take the drink to Bridget.

CATHLEEN Yes, Ma'am.

[*She disappears through the back parlor.* MARY *waits until she hears the pantry door close behind her. Then she settles back in relaxed dreaminess, staring fixedly at nothing. Her arms rest limply along the arms of the chair, her hands with long, warped, swollen-knuckled, sensitive fingers drooping in complete calm. It is growing dark in the room. There is a pause of dead quiet. Then from the world outside comes the melancholy moan of the foghorn, followed by a chorus of bells, muffled by the fog, from the anchored craft in the harbor.* MARY'S *face gives no sign she has heard, but her hands jerk and the fingers automatically play for a moment on the air. She frowns and shakes her head mechanically as if a fly had walked across her mind. She suddenly loses all the girlish quality and is an aging, cynically sad, embittered woman.*]

MARY [*bitterly*] You're a sentimental fool. What is so wonderful about that first meeting between a silly romantic schoolgirl and a matinee idol? You were much happier before you knew he existed, in the Convent when you used to pray to the Blessed Virgin. [*longingly*] If I could only find the faith I lost, so I could pray again! [*She pauses—then begins to recite the Hail Mary in a flat, empty tone.*] "Hail, Mary, full of grace! The Lord is with Thee; blessed art Thou among women." [*sneeringly*] You expect the Blessed Virgin to be fooled by a lying dope fiend reciting words! You can't hide from her! [*She springs to her feet. Her hands fly up to pat her hair distractedly.*] I must go upstairs. I haven't taken enough. When you start again you never know exactly how much you need. [*She goes toward the front parlor—then stops in the doorway as she hears the sound of voices from the front path. She starts guiltily.*] That must be them—[*She hurries back to sit down. Her face sets in stubborn defensiveness—resentfully*] Why are they coming back? They don't want to. And I'd much rather be alone. [*Suddenly her whole manner changes. She becomes pathetically relieved and eager.*] Oh, I'm so glad they've come! I've been so horribly lonely!

[*The front door is heard closing and* TYRONE *calls uneasily from the hall.*]

TYRONE Are you there, Mary?

[*The light in the hall is turned on and shines through the front parlor to fall on* MARY.]

MARY [*rises from her chair, her face lighting up lovingly—with excited eagerness*] I'm here, dear. In the living room. I've been waiting for you.

[TYRONE *comes in through the front parlor.* EDMUND *is behind him.* TYRONE *has had a lot to drink but beyond a slightly glazed look in his eyes and a trace of blur in his speech, he does not show it.* EDMUND *has also had more than a few drinks without much apparent effect, except that his sunken cheeks are flushed and his eyes look bright and feverish. They stop in the doorway to stare appraisingly at her. What they see fulfills their worst expectations. But for the moment* MARY *is unconscious of their condemning eyes. She kisses her husband and then* EDMUND. *Her manner is unnaturally effusive. They submit shrinkingly. She talks excitedly.*]

I'm so happy you've come. I had given up hope. I was afraid you wouldn't come home. It's such a dismal, foggy evening. It must be much more cheerful in the barrooms uptown, where there are people you can talk and joke with. No, don't deny it. I know how you feel. I don't blame you a bit. I'm all the more grateful to you for coming home. I was sitting here so lonely and blue. Come and sit down.

[*She sits at left rear of table,* EDMUND *at left of table, and* TYRONE *in the rocker at right of it.*]

Dinner won't be ready for a minute. You're actually a little early. Will wonders never cease. Here's the whiskey, dear. Shall I pour a drink for you? [*Without waiting for a reply she does so.*] And you, Edmund? I don't want to encourage you, but one before dinner, as an appetizer, can't do any harm.

[*She pours a drink for him. They make no move to take the drinks. She talks on as if unaware of their silence.*]

Where's Jamie? But, of course, he'll never come home so long as he has the price of a drink left. [*She reaches out and clasps her husband's hand—sadly*] I'm afraid Jamie has been lost to us for a long time, dear. [*Her face hardens.*] But we mustn't allow him to drag Edmund down with him, as he'd like to do. He's jealous because Edmund has always been the baby—just as he used to be of Eugene. He'll never be content until he makes Edmund as hopeless a failure as he is.

EDMUND [*miserably*] Stop talking, Mama.

TYRONE [*dully*] Yes, Mary, the less you say now—[*then to Edmund, a bit tipsily*] All the same there's truth in your mother's warning. Beware of that brother of yours, or he'll poison life for you with his damned sneering serpent's tongue!

EDMUND [*as before*] Oh, cut it out, Papa.

MARY [*goes on as if nothing had been said*] It's hard to believe, seeing Jamie as he is now, that he was ever my baby. Do you remember what a healthy, happy baby he was, James? The one-night stands and filthy trains and cheap hotels and bad food never made him cross or sick. He was always smiling or laughing. He hardly ever cried. Eugene was the same, too, happy and healthy, during the two years he lived before I let him die through my neglect.

TYRONE Oh, for the love of God! I'm a fool for coming home!

EDMUND Papa! Shut up!

MARY [*smiles with detached tenderness at* EDMUND] It was Edmund who was the crosspatch when he was little, always getting upset and frightened about nothing at all. [*She pats his hand—teasingly*] Everyone used to say, dear, you'd cry at the drop of a hat.

EDMUND [*cannot control his bitterness*] Maybe I guessed there was a good reason not to laugh.

TYRONE [*reproving and pitying*] Now, now, lad. You know better than to pay attention—

MARY [*as if she hadn't heard—sadly again*] Who would have thought Jamie would grow up to disgrace us. You remember, James, for years after he went to boarding school, we received such glowing reports. Everyone liked him. All his teachers told us what a fine brain he had, and how easily he learned his lessons. Even after he began to drink and they had to expel him, they wrote us how sorry they were, because he was so likable and such a brilliant student. They predicted a wonderful future for him if he would only learn to take life seriously. [*She pauses—then adds with a strange, sad detachment*] It's such a pity. Poor Jamie! It's hard to understand—[*Abruptly a change comes over her. Her face hardens and she stares at her husband with accusing hostility.*] No, it isn't at all. You brought him up to be a boozer. Since he first opened his eyes, he's seen you drinking. Always a bottle on the bureau in the cheap hotel rooms! And if he had a nightmare when he was little, or a stomach-ache, your remedy was to give him a teaspoonful of whiskey to quiet him.

TYRONE [*stung*] So I'm to blame because that lazy hulk has made a drunken loafer of himself? Is that what I came home to listen to? I might have known! When you have the poison in you, you want to blame everyone but yourself!

EDMUND Papa! You told me not to pay attention. [*then, resentfully*] Anyway it's true. You did the same thing with me. I can remember that teaspoonful of booze every time I woke up with a nightmare.

MARY [*in a detached reminiscent tone*] Yes, you were continually having nightmares as a child. You were born afraid. Because I was so afraid to bring you into the world. [*She pauses—then goes on with the same detachment*] Please don't think I blame your father, Edmund. He didn't know any better. He never went to school after he was ten. His people were the most ignorant kind of poverty-stricken Irish. I'm sure they honestly believed whiskey is the healthiest medicine for a child who is sick or frightened.

[TYRONE *is about to burst out in angry defense of his family but* EDMUND *intervenes.*]

EDMUND [*sharply*] Papa! [*changing the subject*] Are we going to have this drink, or aren't we?

TYRONE [*controlling himself—dully*] You're right. I'm a fool to take notice. [*He picks up his glass listlessly.*] Drink hearty, lad.

[EDMUND *drinks but* TYRONE *remains staring at the glass in his hand.* EDMUND *at once realizes how much the whiskey has been watered. He frowns, glancing from the bottle to his mother—starts to say something but stops.*]

MARY [*in a changed tone—repentantly*] I'm sorry if I sounded bitter, James. I'm not. It's all so far away. But I did feel a little hurt when you wished you hadn't come home. I was so relieved and happy when you came, and grateful to you. It's very dreary and sad to be here alone in the fog with night falling.

TYRONE [*moved*] I'm glad I came, Mary, when you act like your real self.

MARY I was so lonesome I kept Cathleen with me just to have someone to talk to. [*Her manner and quality drift back to the shy convent girl again.*] Do you know what I was telling her, dear? About the night my father took me to your dressing room and I first fell in love with you. Do you remember?

TYRONE [*deeply moved—his voice husky*] Can you think I'd ever forget, Mary?

[EDMUND *looks away from them, sad and embarrassed.*]

MARY [*tenderly*] No. I know you still love me, James, in spite of everything.

TYRONE [*His face works and he blinks back tears—with quiet intensity*] Yes! As God is my judge! Always and forever, Mary!

MARY And I love you, dear, in spite of everything.

[*There is a pause in which* EDMUND *moves embarrassedly. The strange detachment comes over her manner again as if she were speaking impersonally of people seen from a distance.*]

But I must confess, James, although I couldn't help loving you, I would never have married you if I'd known you drank so much. I remember the first night your barroom friends had to help you up to the door of our hotel room, and knocked and then ran away before I came to the door. We were still on our honeymoon, do you remember?

TYRONE [*with guilty vehemence*] I don't remember! It wasn't on our honeymoon! And I never in my life had to be helped to bed, or missed a performance!

MARY [*as though he hadn't spoken*] I had waited in that ugly hotel room hour after hour. I kept making excuses for you. I told myself it must be some business connected with the theater. I knew so little about the theater. Then I became terrified. I imagined all sorts of horrible accidents. I got on my knees and prayed that nothing had happened to you—and then they brought you up and left you outside the door. [*She gives a little, sad sigh.*] I didn't know how often that was to happen in the years to come, how many times I was to wait in ugly hotel rooms. I became quite used to it.

EDMUND [*bursts out with a look of accusing hate at his father*] Christ! No wonder—! [*He controls himself—gruffly*] When is dinner, Mama? It must be time.

TYRONE [*overwhelmed by shame which he tries to hide, fumbles with his watch*] Yes. It must be. Let's see. [*He stares at his watch without seeing it—pleadingly*] Mary! Can't you forget—?

MARY [*with detached pity*] No, dear. But I forgive. I always forgive you. So don't look so guilty. I'm sorry I remembered out loud. I don't want to be sad, or to make you sad. I want to remember only the happy part of the past. [*Her manner drifts back to the shy, gay convent girl.*] Do you remember our wedding, dear? I'm sure you've completely forgotten what my wedding gown looked like. Men don't notice such things. They don't think they're important. But it was important to me, I can tell you! How I fussed and worried! I was so excited and happy! My father told me to buy anything I wanted and never mind what it cost. The best is none too good, he said. I'm afraid he spoiled me dreadfully. My mother didn't. She was very pious and strict. I think she was a little jealous. She didn't approve of my marrying—especially an actor. I think she hoped I would become a nun. She used to scold my father. She'd grumble, "You never tell me, never mind what it costs, when I buy anything! You've spoiled that girl so, I pity her husband if she ever marries. She'll expect him to give her the moon. She'll never make a good wife." [*She laughs affectionately.*] Poor mother! [*She smiles at* TYRONE *with a strange, incongruous coquetry.*] But she was mistaken, wasn't she, James? I haven't been such a bad wife, have I?

TYRONE [*huskily, trying to force a smile*] I'm not complaining, Mary.

MARY [*a shadow of vague guilt crosses her face*] At least, I've loved you dearly, and done the best I could—under the circumstances. [*The shadow vanishes and her shy, girlish expression returns.*] That wedding gown was nearly the death of me and the dressmaker, too! [*She laughs.*] I was so particular. It was never quite good enough. At last she said she refused to touch it any more or she might spoil it, and I made her leave so I could be alone to examine myself in the mirror. I was so pleased and vain. I thought to myself, "Even if your nose and mouth and ears are a trifle too large, your eyes and hair and figure, and your hands, make up for it. You're just as pretty as any actress he's ever met, and you don't have to use paint." [*She pauses, wrinkling her brow in an effort of memory.*] Where is my wedding gown now, I wonder? I kept it wrapped up in tissue paper in my trunk. I used to hope I would have a daughter and when it came time for her to marry—She couldn't have bought a lovelier gown, and I knew, James, you'd never tell her, never mind the cost. You'd want her to pick up something at a bargain. It was made of soft, shimmering satin, trimmed with wonderful old duchesse lace, in tiny ruffles around the neck and sleeves, and worked in with the folds that were draped round in a bustle effect at the back. The basque[4] was boned and very tight. I remember I held my breath when it was fitted, so my waist would be as small as possible. My father even let me have duchesse lace on my white satin slippers, and lace with orange blossoms in my veil. Oh, how I loved that gown! It was so beautiful! Where is it now, I wonder? I used to take it out from time to time when I was lonely, but it always made me cry, so finally a long while ago—[*She wrinkles her forehead again.*] I wonder where I hid it? Probably in one of the old trunks in the attic. Some day I'll have to look.

[*She stops, staring before her.* TYRONE *sighs, shaking his head hopelessly, and attempts to catch his son's eye, looking for sympathy, but* EDMUND *is staring at the floor.*]

TYRONE [*forces a casual tone*] Isn't it dinner time, dear? [*with a feeble attempt at teasing*] You're forever scolding me for being late, but now I'm on time for once, it's dinner that's late.

[*She doesn't appear to hear him. He adds, still pleasantly*]

Well, if I can't eat yet, I can drink. I'd forgotten I had this.

[*He drinks his drink.* EDMUND *watches him.* TYRONE *scowls and looks at his wife with sharp suspicion—roughly*]

Who's been tampering with my whiskey? The damned stuff is half water! Jamie's been away and he wouldn't overdo his trick like this, anyway. Any fool could tell—Mary, answer me! [*with angry disgust*] I hope to God you haven't taken to drink on top of—

EDMUND Shut up, Papa! [*to his mother, without looking at her*] You treated Cathleen and Bridget, isn't that it, Mama?

MARY [*with indifferent casualness*] Yes, of course. They work hard for poor wages. And I'm the housekeeper, I have to keep them from leaving. Besides, I wanted to treat Cathleen because I had her drive uptown with me, and sent her to get my prescription filled.

EDMUND For God's sake, Mama! You can't trust her! Do you want everyone on earth to know?

MARY [*her face hardening stubbornly*] Know what? That I suffer from rheumatism in my hands and have to take medicine to kill the pain? Why should I be ashamed of that? [*turns on* EDMUND *with a hard, accusing antagonism—almost a revengeful enmity*] I never knew what rheumatism was before you were born! Ask your father!

[EDMUND *looks away, shrinking into himself.*]

TYRONE Don't mind her, lad. It doesn't mean anything. When she gets to the stage where she gives the old crazy excuse about her hands she's gone far away from us.

4. Tight-fitting bodice.

MARY [*turns on him—with a strangely triumphant, taunting smile*] I'm glad you realize that, James! Now perhaps you'll give up trying to remind me, you and Edmund! [*abruptly, in a detached, matter-of-fact tone*] Why don't you light the light, James? It's getting dark. I know you hate to, but Edmund has proved to you that one bulb burning doesn't cost much. There's no sense letting your fear of the poorhouse make you too stingy.

TYRONE [*reacts mechanically*] I never claimed one bulb cost much! It's having them on, one here and one there, that makes the Electric Light Company rich. [*He gets up and turns on the reading lamp—roughly*] But I'm a fool to talk reason to you. [*to* EDMUND] I'll get a fresh bottle of whiskey, lad, and we'll have a real drink. [*He goes through the back parlor.*]

MARY [*with detached amusement*] He'll sneak around to the outside cellar door so the servants won't see him. He's really ashamed of keeping his whiskey padlocked in the cellar. Your father is a strange man, Edmund. It took many years before I understood him. You must try to understand and forgive him, too, and not feel contempt because he's close-fisted. His father deserted his mother and their six children a year or so after they came to America. He told them he had a premonition he would die soon, and he was homesick for Ireland, and wanted to go back there to die. So he went and he did die. He must have been a peculiar man, too. Your father had to go to work in a machine shop when he was only ten years old.

EDMUND [*protests dully*] Oh, for Pete's sake, Mama. I've heard Papa tell that machine shop story ten thousand times.

MARY Yes, dear, you've had to listen, but I don't think you've ever tried to understand.

EDMUND [*ignoring this—miserably*] Listen, Mama! You're not so far gone yet you've forgotten everything. You haven't asked me what I found out this afternoon. Don't you care a damn?

MARY [*shakenly*] Don't say that! You hurt me, dear!

EDMUND What I've got is serious, Mama. Doc Hardy knows for sure now.

MARY [*stiffens into scornful, defensive stubbornness*] That lying old quack! I warned you he'd invent—!

EDMUND [*miserably dogged*] He called in a specialist to examine me, so he'd be absolutely sure.

MARY [*ignoring this*] Don't tell me about Hardy! If you heard what the doctor at the sanatorium, who really knows something, said about how he'd treated me! He said he ought to be locked up! He said it was a wonder I hadn't gone mad! I told him I had once, that time I ran down in my nightdress to throw myself off the dock. You remember that, don't you? And yet you want me to pay attention to what Doctor Hardy says. Oh, no!

EDMUND [*bitterly*] I remember, all right. It was right after that Papa and Jamie decided they couldn't hide it from me any more. Jamie told me. I called him a liar! I tried to punch him in the nose. But I knew he wasn't lying. [*His voice trembles, his eyes begin to fill with tears.*] God, it made everything in life seem rotten!

MARY [*pitiably*] Oh, don't. My baby! You hurt me so dreadfully!

EDMUND [*dully*] I'm sorry, Mama. It was you who brought it up. [*then with a bitter, stubborn persistence*] Listen, Mama. I'm going to tell you whether you want to hear or not. I've got to go to a sanatorium.

MARY [*dazedly, as if this was something that had never occurred to her*] Go away? [*violently*] No! I won't have it! How dare Doctor Hardy advise such a thing without consulting me! How dare your father allow him! What right has he? You are my baby! Let him attend to Jamie! [*more and more excited and bitter*] I know why he wants you sent to a sanatorium. To take you from me! He's always tried to do that. He's been jealous of every one of my babies! He kept finding ways to make me leave them. That's what caused Eugene's death. He's been jealous of you most of all. He knew I loved you most because—

EDMUND [*miserably*] Oh, stop talking crazy, can't you, Mama! Stop trying to blame him. And why are you so against my going away now? I've been away a lot, and I've never noticed it broke your heart!

MARY [*bitterly*] I'm afraid you're not very sensitive, after all. [*sadly*] You might have guessed, dear, that after I knew you knew—about me—I had to be glad whenever you were where you couldn't see me.

EDMUND [*brokenly*] Mama! Don't! [*He reaches out blindly and takes her hand—but he drops it immediately, overcome by bitterness again.*] All this talk about loving me—and you won't even listen when I try to tell you how sick—

MARY [*with an abrupt transformation into a detached bullying motherliness*] Now, now. That's enough! I don't care to hear because I know it's nothing but Hardy's ignorant lies.

[*He shrinks back into himself. She keeps on in a forced, teasing tone but with an increasing undercurrent of resentment.*]

You're so like your father, dear. You love to make a scene out of nothing so you can be dramatic and tragic. [*with a belittling laugh*] If I gave you the slightest encouragement, you'd tell me next you were going to die—

EDMUND People do die of it. Your own father—

MARY [*sharply*] Why do you mention him? There's no comparison at all with you. He had consumption. [*angrily*] I hate you when you become gloomy and morbid! I forbid you to remind me of my father's death, do you hear me?

EDMUND [*his face hard—grimly*] Yes, I hear you, Mama. I wish to God I didn't! [*He gets up from his chair and stands staring condemningly at her—bitterly*] It's pretty hard to take at times, having a dope fiend for a mother!

[*She winces—all life seeming to drain from her face, leaving it with the appearance of a plaster cast. Instantly* EDMUND *wishes he could take back what he has said. He stammers miserably.*]

Forgive me, Mama. I was angry. You hurt me.

[*There is a pause in which the foghorn and the ships' bells are heard.*]

MARY [*goes slowly to the windows at right like an automaton—looking out, a blank, far-off quality in her voice*] Just listen to that awful foghorn. And the bells. Why is it fog makes everything sound so sad and lost, I wonder?

EDMUND [*brokenly*] I—I can't stay here. I don't want any dinner.

[*He hurries away through the front parlor. She keeps staring out the window until she hears the front door close behind him. Then she comes back and sits in her chair, the same blank look on her face.*]

MARY [*vaguely*] I must go upstairs. I haven't taken enough. [*She pauses—then longingly*] I hope, sometime, without meaning it, I will take an overdose. I never could do it deliberately. The Blessed Virgin would never forgive me, then.

[*She hears* TYRONE *returning and turns as he comes in, through the back parlor, with a bottle of whiskey he has just uncorked. He is fuming.*]

TYRONE [*wrathfully*] The padlock is all scratched. That drunken loafer has tried to pick the lock with a piece of wire, the way he's done before. [*with satisfaction, as if this was a perpetual battle of wits with his elder son*] But I've fooled him this time. It's a special padlock a professional burglar couldn't pick. [*He puts the bottle on the tray and suddenly is aware of* EDMUND*'s absence.*] Where's Edmund?

MARY [*with a vague far-away air*] He went out. Perhaps he's going uptown again to find Jamie. He still has some money left, I suppose, and it's burning a hole in his pocket. He said he didn't want any dinner. He doesn't seem to have any appetite these days. [*then stubbornly*] But it's just a summer cold.

[TYRONE *stares at her and shakes his head helplessly and pours himself a big drink and drinks it. Suddenly it is too much for her and she breaks out and sobs.*]

Oh, James, I'm so frightened! [*She gets up and throws her arms around him and hides her face on his shoulder—sobbingly*] I know he's going to die!

TYRONE Don't say that! It's not true! They promised me in six months he'd be cured.

MARY You don't believe that! I can tell when you're acting! And it will be my fault. I should never have borne him. It would have been better for his sake. I could never hurt him then. He wouldn't have had to know his mother was a dope fiend—and hate her!

TYRONE [*his voice quivering*] Hush, Mary, for the love of God! He loves you. He knows it was a curse put on you without your knowing or willing it. He's proud you're his mother! [*abruptly as he hears the pantry door opening*] Hush, now! Here comes Cathleen. You don't want her to see you crying.

[*She turns quickly away from him to the windows at right, hastily wiping her eyes. A moment later* CATHLEEN *appears in the back-parlor doorway. She is uncertain in her walk and grinning woozily.*]

CATHLEEN [*starts guiltily when she sees* TYRONE*—with dignity*] Dinner is served, Sir. [*raising her voice unnecessarily*] Dinner is served, Ma'am. [*She forgets her dignity and addresses* TYRONE *with good-natured familiarity*] So you're here, are you? Well, well. Won't Bridget be in a rage! I told her the Madame said you wouldn't be home. [*then reading accusation in his eye*] Don't be looking at me that way. If I've a drop taken, I didn't steal it. I was invited.

[*She turns with huffy dignity and disappears through the back parlor.*]

TYRONE [*sighs—then summoning his actor's heartiness*] Come along, dear. Let's have our dinner. I'm hungry as a hunter.

MARY [*comes to him—her face is composed in plaster again and her tone is remote*] I'm afraid you'll have to excuse me, James. I couldn't possibly eat anything. My hands pain me dreadfully. I think the best thing for me is to go to bed and rest. Good night dear.

[*She kisses him mechanically and turns toward the front parlor.*]

TYRONE [*harshly*] Up to take more of that God-damned poison, is that it? You'll be like a mad ghost before the night's over!

MARY [*starts to walk away—blankly*] I don't know what you're talking about, James. You say such mean, bitter things when you've drunk too much. You're as bad as Jamie or Edmund.

[*She moves off through the front parlor. He stands a second as if not knowing what to do. He is a sad, bewildered, broken old man. He walks wearily off through the back parlor toward the dining room.*]

CURTAIN

Act 4

SCENE—*The same. It is around midnight. The lamp in the front hall has been turned out, so that now no light shines through the front parlor. In the living room only the reading lamp on the table is lighted. Outside the windows the wall of fog appears denser than ever. As the curtain rises, the foghorn is heard, followed by the ships' bells from the harbor.*

TYRONE *is seated at the table. He wears his pince-nez*[5] *and is playing solitaire. He has taken off his coat and has on an old brown dressing gown. The whiskey bottle on the tray is three-quarters empty. There is a fresh full bottle on the table, which he has brought from the cellar so there will be an ample reserve on hand. He is drunk and shows it by the owlish, deliberate manner in which he peers at each card to make certain of its identity, and then plays it as if he wasn't certain of his aim. His eyes have a misted, oily look and his mouth is slack. But despite all the whiskey in him, he has not escaped, and he looks as he appeared at the close of the preceding act, a sad, defeated old man, possessed by hopeless resignation.*

As the curtain rises, he finishes a game and sweeps the cards together. He shuffles them clumsily, dropping a couple on the floor. He retrieves them with difficulty, and starts to shuffle again, when he hears someone entering the front door. He peers over his pince-nez through the front parlor.

TYRONE [*his voice thick*] Who's that? Is it you, Edmund?

[EDMUND'*s voice answers curtly, "Yes." Then he evidently collides with something in the dark hall and can be heard cursing. A moment later the hall lamp is turned on.* TYRONE *frowns and calls.*]

Turn that light out before you come in.

[*But* EDMUND *doesn't. He comes in through the front parlor. He is drunk now, too, but like his father he carries it well, and gives little physical sign of it except in his eyes and a chip-on-the-shoulder aggressiveness in his manner.* TYRONE *speaks, at first with a warm, relieved welcome.*]

I'm glad you've come, lad. I've been damned lonely. [*then resentfully*] You're a fine one to run away and leave me to sit alone here all night when you know—[*with sharp irritation*] I told you to turn out that light! We're

5. Eyeglasses clipped to the nose.

not giving a ball. There's no reason to have the house ablaze with electricity at this time of night, burning up money!

EDMUND [*angrily*] Ablaze with electricity! One bulb! Hell, everyone keeps a light on in the front hall until they go to bed. [*He rubs his knee.*] I damned near busted my knee on the hat stand.

TYRONE The light from here shows in the hall. You could see your way well enough if you were sober.

EDMUND If *I* was sober? I like that!

TYRONE I don't give a damn what other people do. If they want to be wasteful fools, for the sake of show, let them be!

EDMUND One bulb! Christ, don't be such a cheap skate! I've proved by figures if you left the light bulb on all night it wouldn't be as much as one drink!

TYRONE To hell with your figures! The proof is in the bills I have to pay!

EDMUND [*sits down opposite his father—contemptuously*] Yes, facts don't mean a thing, do they? What you want to believe, that's the only truth! [*derisively*] Shakespeare was an Irish Catholic, for example.

TYRONE [*stubbornly*] So he was. The proof is in his plays.

EDMUND Well he wasn't, and there's no proof of it in his plays, except to you! [*jeeringly*] The Duke of Wellington, there was another good Irish Catholic!

TYRONE I never said he was a good one. He was a renegade but a Catholic just the same.

EDMUND Well, he wasn't. You just want to believe no one but an Irish Catholic general could beat Napoleon.

TYRONE I'm not going to argue with you. I asked you to turn out that light in the hall.

EDMUND I heard you, and as far as I'm concerned it stays on.

TYRONE None of your damned insolence! Are you going to obey me or not?

EDMUND Not! If you want to be a crazy miser put it out yourself!

TYRONE [*with threatening anger*] Listen to me! I've put up with a lot from you because from the mad things you've done at times I've thought you weren't quite right in your head. I've excused you and never lifted my hand to you. But there's a straw that breaks the camel's back. You'll obey me and put out that light or, big as you are, I'll give you a thrashing that'll teach you—! [*Suddenly he remembers* EDMUND*'s illness and instantly becomes guilty and shamefaced.*] Forgive me, lad. I forgot—You shouldn't goad me into losing my temper.

EDMUND [*ashamed himself now*] Forget it, Papa. I apologize, too. I had no right being nasty about nothing. I am a bit soused, I guess. I'll put out the damned light. [*He starts to get up.*]

TYRONE No, stay where you are. Let it burn.

[*He stands up abruptly—and a bit drunkenly—and begins turning on the three bulbs in the chandelier, with a childish, bitterly dramatic self-pity.*]

We'll have them all on! Let them burn! To hell with them! The poorhouse is the end of the road, and it might as well be sooner as later! [*He finishes turning on the lights.*]

EDMUND [*has watched this proceeding with an awakened sense of humor—now he grins, teasing affectionately*] That's a grand curtain. [*He laughs.*] You're a wonder, Papa.

TYRONE [*sits down sheepishly—grumbles pathetically*] That's right, laugh at the old fool! The poor old ham! But the final curtain will be in the poorhouse just the same, and that's not comedy! [*Then as* EDMUND *is still grinning, he changes the subject.*] Well, well, let's not argue. You've got brains in that head of yours, though you do your best to deny them. You'll live to learn the value of a dollar. You're not like your damned tramp of a brother. I've given up hope he'll ever get sense. Where is he, by the way?

EDMUND How would I know?

TYRONE I thought you'd gone back uptown to meet him.

EDMUND No. I walked out to the beach. I haven't seen him since this afternoon.

TYRONE Well, if you split the money I gave you with him, like a fool—

EDMUND Sure I did. He's always staked me when he had anything.

TYRONE Then it doesn't take a soothsayer to tell he's probably in the whorehouse.

EDMUND What of it if he is? Why not?

TYRONE [*contemptuously*] Why not, indeed. It's the fit place for him. If he's ever had a loftier dream than whores and whiskey, he's never shown it.

EDMUND Oh, for Pete's sake, Papa! If you're going to start that stuff, I'll beat it. [*He starts to get up.*]

TYRONE [*placatingly*] All right, all right, I'll stop. God knows, I don't like the subject either. Will you join me in a drink?

EDMUND Ah! Now you're talking!

TYRONE [*passes the bottle to him—mechanically*] I'm wrong to treat you. You've had enough already.

EDMUND [*pouring a big drink—a bit drunkenly*] Enough is *not* as good as a feast. [*He hands back the bottle.*]

TYRONE It's too much in your condition.

EDMUND Forget my condition! [*He raises his glass.*] Here's how.

TYRONE Drink hearty. [*They drink.*] If you walked all the way to the beach you must be damp and chilled.

EDMUND Oh, I dropped in at the Inn on the way out and back.

TYRONE It's not a night I'd pick for a long walk.

EDMUND I loved the fog. It was what I needed. [*He sounds more tipsy and looks it.*]

TYRONE You should have more sense than to risk—

EDMUND To hell with sense! We're all crazy. What do we want with sense? [*He quotes from Dowson*[6] *sardonically.*]

> "They are not long, the weeping and the laughter,
> Love and desire and hate:
> I think they have no portion in us after
> We pass the gate.

6. Ernest Dowson (1867–1900), English poet.

They are not long, the days of wine and roses:
Out of a misty dream
Our path emerges for a while, then closes
Within a dream."

[*staring before him*] The fog was where I wanted to be. Halfway down the path you can't see this house. You'd never know it was here. Or any of the other places down the avenue. I couldn't see but a few feet ahead. I didn't meet a soul. Everything looked and sounded unreal. Nothing was what it is. That's what I wanted—to be alone with myself in another world where truth is untrue and life can hide from itself. Out beyond the harbor, where the road runs along the beach, I even lost the feeling of being on land. The fog and the sea seemed part of each other. It was like walking on the bottom of the sea. As if I had drowned long ago. As if I was a ghost belonging to the fog, and the fog was the ghost of the sea. It felt damned peaceful to be nothing more than a ghost within a ghost. [*He sees his father staring at him with mingled worry and irritated disapproval. He grins mockingly.*] Don't look at me as if I'd gone nutty. I'm talking sense. Who wants to see life as it is, if they can help it? It's the three Gorgons[7] in one. You look in their faces and turn to stone. Or it's Pan.[8] You see him and you die—that is, inside you—and have to go on living as a ghost.

TYRONE [*impressed and at the same time revolted*] You have a poet in you but it's a damned morbid one! [*forcing a smile*] Devil take your pessimism. I feel low-spirited enough. [*He sighs.*] Why can't you remember your Shakespeare and forget the third-raters. You'll find what you're trying to say in him—as you'll find everything else worth saying. [*He quotes, using his fine voice*] "We are such stuff as dreams are made on, and our little life is rounded with a sleep."[9]

EDMUND [*ironically*] Fine! That's beautiful. But I wasn't trying to say that. We are such stuff as manure is made on, so let's drink up and forget it. That's more my idea.

TYRONE [*disgustedly*] Ach! Keep such sentiments to yourself. I shouldn't have given you that drink.

EDMUND It did pack a wallop, all right. On you, too. [*He grins with affectionate teasing.*] Even if you've never missed a performance! [*aggressively*] Well, what's wrong with being drunk? It's what we're after, isn't it? Let's not kid each other, Papa. Not tonight. We know what we're trying to forget. [*hurriedly*] But let's not talk about it. It's no use now.

TYRONE [*dully*] No. All we can do is try to be resigned—again.

EDMUND Or be so drunk you can forget. [*He recites, and recites well, with bitter, ironical passion, the Symons' translation of Baudelaire's*[1] prose poem.] "Be always drunken. Nothing else matters: that is the only question. If you would not feel the horrible burden of Time weighing on your shoulders and crushing you to the earth, be drunken continually.

7. In Greek mythology, three monstrous sisters so ugly that the sight of them turned one to stone.
8. Greek god of woods, fields, and flocks, half man and half goat, associated with wildness.
9. Shakespeare's *The Tempest* 4.1.156–58.
1. Charles Baudelaire (1821–1867), French poet. Arthur Symons (1865–1945), English poet and literary critic.

"Drunken with what? With wine, with poetry, or with virtue, as you will. But be drunken.

"And if sometimes, on the stairs of a palace, or on the green side of a ditch, or in the dreary solitude of your own room, you should awaken and the drunkenness be half or wholly slipped away from you, ask of the wind, or of the wave, or of the star, or of the bird, or of the clock, of whatever flies, or sighs, or rocks, or sings, or speaks, ask what hour it is; and the wind, wave, star, bird, clock, will answer you: 'It is the hour to be drunken! Be drunken, if you would not be martyred slaves of Time; be drunken continually! With wine, with poetry, or with virtue, as you will.'" [*He grins at his father provocatively.*]

TYRONE [*thickly humorous*] I wouldn't worry about the virtue part of it, if I were you. [*then disgustedly*] Pah! It's morbid nonsense! What little truth is in it you'll find nobly said in Shakespeare. [*then appreciatively*] But you recited it well, lad. Who wrote it?

EDMUND Baudelaire.

TYRONE Never heard of him.

EDMUND [*grins provocatively*] He also wrote a poem about Jamie and the Great White Way.

TYRONE That loafer! I hope to God he misses the last car and has to stay uptown!

EDMUND [*goes on, ignoring this*] Although he was French and never saw Broadway and died before Jamie was born, he knew him and Little Old New York just the same. [*He recites the Symons' translation of Baudelaire's "Epilogue."*]

"With heart at rest I climbed the citadel's
Steep height, and saw the city as from a tower,
Hospital, brothel, prison, and such hells,

Where evil comes up softly like a flower.
Thou knowest, O Satan, patron of my pain,
Not for vain tears I went up at that hour;

But like an old sad faithful lecher, fain
To drink delight of that enormous trull
Whose hellish beauty makes me young again.

Whether thou sleep, with heavy vapours full,
Sodden with day, or, new apparelled, stand
In gold-laced veils of evening beautiful,

I love thee, infamous city! Harlots and
Hunted have pleasures of their own to give,
The vulgar herd can never understand."

TYRONE [*with irritable disgust*] Morbid filth! Where the hell do you get your taste in literature? Filth and despair and pessimism! Another atheist, I suppose. When you deny God, you deny hope. That's the trouble with you. If you'd get down on your knees—

EDMUND [*as if he hadn't heard—sardonically*] It's a good likeness of Jamie, don't you think, hunted by himself and whiskey, hiding in a Broadway hotel room with some fat tart—he likes them fat—reciting Dowson's Cynara to her. [*He recites derisively, but with deep feeling*]

"All night upon mine heart I felt her warm heart beat,
Night-long within mine arms in love and sleep she lay;
Surely the kisses of her bought red mouth were sweet;
But I was desolate and sick of an old passion,
When I awoke and found the dawn was gray:
I have been faithful to thee, Cynara! in my fashion."

[*jeeringly*] And the poor fat burlesque queen doesn't get a word of it, but suspects she's being insulted! And Jamie never loved any Cynara, and was never faithful to a woman in his life, even in his fashion! But he lies there, kidding himself he is superior and enjoys pleasures "the vulgar herd can never understand"! [*He laughs.*] It's nuts—completely nuts!

TYRONE [*vaguely—his voice thick*] It's madness, yes. If you'd get on your knees and pray. When you deny God, you deny sanity.

EDMUND [*ignoring this*] But who am I to feel superior? I've done the same damned thing. And it's no more crazy than Dowson himself, inspired by an absinthe hangover, writing it to a dumb barmaid, who thought he was a poor crazy souse, and gave him the gate to marry a waiter! [*He laughs—then soberly, with genuine sympathy*] Poor Dowson. Booze and consumption got him. [*He starts and for a second looks miserable and frightened. Then with defensive irony*] Perhaps it would be tactful of me to change the subject.

TYRONE [*thickly*] Where you get your taste in authors—That damned library of yours! [*He indicates the small bookcase at rear.*] Voltaire, Rousseau, Schopenhauer, Nietzsche, Ibsen! Atheists, fools, and madmen! And your poets! This Dowson, and this Baudelaire, and Swinburne and Oscar Wilde, and Whitman and Poe! Whore-mongers and degenerates! Pah! When I've three good sets of Shakespeare there [*he nods at the large bookcase*] you could read.

EDMUND [*provocatively*] They say he was a souse, too.

TYRONE They lie! I don't doubt he liked his glass—it's a good man's failing—but he knew how to drink so it didn't poison his brain with morbidness and filth. Don't compare him with the pack you've got in there. [*He indicates the small bookcase again.*] Your dirty Zola! And your Dante Gabriel Rossetti who was a dope fiend! [*He starts and looks guilty.*]

EDMUND [*with defensive dryness*] Perhaps it would be wise to change the subject. [*a pause*] You can't accuse me of not knowing Shakespeare. Didn't I win five dollars from you once when you bet me I couldn't learn a leading part of his in a week, as you used to do in stock in the old days. I learned Macbeth and recited it letter perfect, with you giving me the cues.

TYRONE [*approvingly*] That's true. So you did. [*He smiles teasingly and sighs.*] It was a terrible ordeal, I remember, hearing you murder the lines. I kept wishing I'd paid over the bet without making you prove it.

[*He chuckles and* EDMUND *grins. Then he starts as he hears a sound from upstairs—with dread*]

Did you hear? She's moving around. I was hoping she'd gone to sleep.

EDMUND Forget it! How about another drink?

[*He reaches out and gets the bottle, pours a drink and hands it back. Then with a strained casualness, as his father pours a drink*]

When did Mama go to bed?

TYRONE Right after you left. She wouldn't eat any dinner. What made you run away?

EDMUND Nothing. [*Abruptly raising his glass.*] Well, here's how.

TYRONE [*mechanically*] Drink hearty, lad. [*They drink.* TYRONE *again listens to sounds upstairs—with dread*] She's moving around a lot. I hope to God she doesn't come down.

EDMUND [*dully*] Yes. She'll be nothing but a ghost haunting the past by this time. [*He pauses—then miserably*] Back before I was born—

TYRONE Doesn't she do the same with me? Back before she ever knew me. You'd think the only happy days she's ever known were in her father's home, or at the Convent, praying and playing the piano. [*jealous resentment in his bitterness*] As I've told you before, you must take her memories with a grain of salt. Her wonderful home was ordinary enough. Her father wasn't the great, generous, noble Irish gentleman she makes out. He was a nice enough man, good company and a good talker. I liked him and he liked me. He was prosperous enough, too, in his wholesale grocery business, an able man. But he had his weakness. She condemns my drinking but she forgets his. It's true he never touched a drop till he was forty, but after that he made up for lost time. He became a steady champagne drinker, the worst kind. That was his grand pose, to drink only champagne. Well, it finished him quick—that and the consumption—[*He stops with a guilty glance at his son.*]

EDMUND [*sardonically*] We don't seem able to avoid unpleasant topics, do we?

TYRONE [*sighs sadly*] No. [*then with a pathetic attempt at heartiness*] What do you say to a game or two of Casino, lad?

EDMUND All right.

TYRONE [*shuffling the cards clumsily*] We can't lock up and go to bed till Jamie comes on the last trolley—which I hope he won't—and I don't want to go upstairs, anyway, till she's asleep.

EDMUND Neither do I.

TYRONE [*keeps shuffling the cards fumblingly, forgetting to deal them*] As I was saying, you must take her tales of the past with a grain of salt. The piano playing and her dream of becoming a concert pianist. That was put in her head by the nuns flattering her. She was their pet. They loved her for being so devout. They're innocent women, anyway, when it comes to the world. They don't know that not one in a million who shows promise ever rises to concert playing. Not that your mother didn't play well for a schoolgirl, but that's no reason to take it for granted she could have—

EDMUND [*sharply*] Why don't you deal, if we're going to play.

TYRONE Eh? I am. [*dealing with very uncertain judgment of distance*] And the idea she might have become a nun. That's the worst. Your mother was one of the most beautiful girls you could ever see. She knew it, too. She was a bit of a rogue and a coquette, God bless her, behind all her shyness and blushes. She was never made to renounce the world. She was bursting with health and high spirits and the love of loving.

EDMUND For God's sake, Papa! Why don't you pick up your hand?

TYRONE [*picks it up—dully*] Yes, let's see what I have here.

[*They both stare at their cards unseeingly. Then they both start.* TYRONE *whispers*]

Listen!

EDMUND She's coming downstairs.

TYRONE [*hurriedly*] We'll play our game. Pretend not to notice and she'll soon go up again.

EDMUND [*staring through the front parlor—with relief*] I don't see her. She must have started down and then turned back.

TYRONE Thank God.

EDMUND Yes. It's pretty horrible to see her the way she must be now. [*with bitter misery*] The hardest thing to take is the blank wall she builds around her. Or it's more like a bank of fog in which she hides and loses herself. Deliberately, that's the hell of it! You know something in her does it deliberately—to get beyond our reach, to be rid of us, to forget we're alive! It's as if, in spite of loving us, she hated us!

TYRONE [*remonstrates gently*] Now, now, lad. It's not her. It's the damned poison.

EDMUND [*bitterly*] She takes it to get that effect. At least, I know she did this time! [*abruptly*] My play, isn't it? Here. [*He plays a card.*]

TYRONE [*plays mechanically—gently reproachful*] She's been terribly frightened about your illness, for all her pretending. Don't be too hard on her, lad. Remember she's not responsible. Once that cursed poison gets a hold on anyone—

EDMUND [*his face grows hard and he stares at his father with bitter accusation*] It never should have gotten a hold on her! I know damned well she's not to blame! And I know who is! You are! Your damned stinginess! If you'd spent money for a decent doctor when she was so sick after I was born, she'd never have known morphine existed! Instead you put her in the hands of a hotel quack who wouldn't admit his ignorance and took the easiest way out, not giving a damn what happened to her afterwards! All because his fee was cheap! Another one of your bargains!

TYRONE [*stung—angrily*] Be quiet! How dare you talk of something you know nothing about! [*trying to control his temper*] You must try to see my side of it, too, lad. How was I to know he was that kind of a doctor? He had a good reputation—

EDMUND Among the souses in the hotel bar, I suppose!

TYRONE That's a lie! I asked the hotel proprietor to recommend the best—

EDMUND Yes! At the same time crying poorhouse and making it plain you wanted a cheap one! I know your system! By God, I ought to after this afternoon!

TYRONE [*guiltily defensive*] What about this afternoon?

EDMUND Never mind now. We're talking about Mama! I'm saying no matter how you excuse yourself you know damned well your stinginess is to blame—

TYRONE And I say you're a liar! Shut your mouth right now, or—

EDMUND [*ignoring this*] After you found out she'd been made a morphine addict, why didn't you send her to a cure then, at the start, while she still had a chance? No, that would have meant spending some money! I'll bet you told her all she had to do was use a little will power! That's what you still believe in your heart, in spite of what doctors, who really know something about it, have told you!

TYRONE You lie again! I know better than that now! But how was I to know then? What did I know of morphine? It was years before I discovered what was wrong. I thought she'd never got over her sickness, that's all. Why didn't I send her to a cure, you say? [*bitterly*] Haven't I? I've spent thousands upon thousands in cures! A waste. What good have they done her? She always started again.

EDMUND Because you've never given her anything that would help her want to stay off it! No home except this summer dump in a place she hates and you've refused even to spend money to make this look decent, while you keep buying more property, and playing sucker for every con man with a gold mine, or a silver mine, or any kind of get-rich-quick swindle! You've dragged her around on the road, season after season, on one-night stands, with no one she could talk to, waiting night after night in dirty hotel rooms for you to come back with a bun on after the bars closed! Christ, is it any wonder she didn't want to be cured. Jesus, when I think of it I hate your guts!

TYRONE [*strickenly*] Edmund! [*then in a rage*] How dare you talk to your father like that, you insolent young cub! After all I've done for you.

EDMUND We'll come to that, what you're doing for me!

TYRONE [*looking guilty again—ignores this*] Will you stop repeating your mother's crazy accusations, which she never makes unless it's the poison talking? I never dragged her on the road against her will. Naturally, I wanted her with me. I loved her. And she came because she loved me and wanted to be with me. That's the truth, no matter what she says when she's not herself. And she needn't have been lonely. There was always the members of my company to talk to, if she'd wanted. She had her children, too, and I insisted, in spite of the expense, on having a nurse to travel with her.

EDMUND [*bitterly*] Yes, your one generosity, and that because you were jealous of her paying too much attention to us, and wanted us out of your way! It was another mistake, too! If she'd had to take care of me all by herself, and had that to occupy her mind, maybe she'd have been able—

TYRONE [*goaded into vindictiveness*] Or for that matter, if you insist in judging things by what she says when she's not in her right mind, if you hadn't been born she'd never—[*He stops ashamed.*]

EDMUND [*suddenly spent and miserable*] Sure. I know that's what she feels, Papa.

TYRONE [*protests penitently*] She doesn't! She loves you as dearly as ever mother loved a son! I only said that because you put me in such a God-damned rage, raking up the past, and saying you hate me—

EDMUND [*dully*] I didn't mean it, Papa. [*He suddenly smiles—kidding a bit drunkenly*] I'm like Mama, I can't help liking you, in spite of everything.

TYRONE [*grins a bit drunkenly in return*] I might say the same of you. You're no great shakes as a son. It's a case of "A poor thing but mine own."[2] [*They both chuckle with real, if alcoholic, affection.* TYRONE *changes the subject.*] What's happened to our game? Whose play is it?

EDMUND Yours, I guess.

[TYRONE *plays a card which* EDMUND *takes and the game gets forgotten again.*]

TYRONE You mustn't let yourself be too downhearted, lad, by the bad news you had today. Both the doctors promised me, if you obey orders at this place you're going, you'll be cured in six months, or a year at most.

EDMUND [*his face hard again*] Don't kid me. You don't believe that.

TYRONE [*too vehemently*] Of course I believe it! Why shouldn't I believe it when both Hardy and the specialist—?

EDMUND You think I'm going to die.

TYRONE That's a lie! You're crazy!

EDMUND [*more bitterly*] So why waste money? That's why you're sending me to a state farm—

TYRONE [*in guilty confusion*] What state farm? It's the Hilltown Sanatorium, that's all I know, and both doctors said it was the best place for you.

EDMUND [*scathingly*] For the money! That is, for nothing, or practically nothing. Don't lie, Papa! You know damned well Hilltown Sanatorium is a state institution! Jamie suspected you'd cry poorhouse to Hardy and he wormed the truth out of him.

TYRONE [*furiously*] That drunken loafer! I'll kick him out in the gutter! He's poisoned your mind against me ever since you were old enough to listen!

EDMUND You can't deny it's the truth about the state farm, can you?

TYRONE It's not true the way you look at it! What if it is run by the state? That's nothing against it. The state has the money to make a better place than any private sanatorium. And why shouldn't I take advantage of it? It's my right—and yours. We're residents. I'm a property owner. I help to support it. I'm taxed to death—

EDMUND [*with bitter irony*] Yes, on property valued at a quarter of a million.

TYRONE Lies! It's all mortgaged!

EDMUND Hardy and the specialist know what you're worth. I wonder what they thought of you when they heard you moaning poorhouse and showing you wanted to wish me on charity!

TYRONE It's a lie! All I told them was I couldn't afford any millionaire's sanatorium because I was land poor. That's the truth!

EDMUND And then you went to the Club to meet McGuire and let him stick you with another bum piece of property! [*as* TYRONE *starts to deny*] Don't lie about it! We met McGuire in the hotel bar after he left you. Jamie kidded him about hooking you, and he winked and laughed!

TYRONE [*lying feebly*] He's a liar if he said—

EDMUND Don't lie about it! [*with gathering intensity*] God, Papa, ever since I went to sea and was on my own, and found out what hard work

2. Shakespeare's *As You Like It* 5.4.60.

for little pay was, and what it felt like to be broke, and starve, and camp on park benches because I had no place to sleep, I've tried to be fair to you because I knew what you'd been up against as a kid. I've tried to make allowances. Christ, you have to make allowances in this damned family or go nuts! I have tried to make allowances for myself when I remember all the rotten stuff I've pulled! I've tried to feel like Mama that you can't help being what you are where money is concerned. But God Almighty, this last stunt of yours is too much! It makes me want to puke! Not because of the rotten way you're treating me. To hell with that! I've treated you rottenly, in my way, more than once. But to think when it's a question of your son having consumption, you can show yourself up before the whole town as such a stinking old tightwad! Don't you know Hardy will talk and the whole damned town will know! Jesus, Papa, haven't you any pride or shame? [*bursting with rage*] And don't think I'll let you get away with it! I won't go to any damned state farm just to save you a few lousy dollars to buy more bum property with! You stinking old miser—! [*He chokes huskily, his voice trembling with rage, and then is shaken by a fit of coughing.*]

TYRONE [*has shrunk back in his chair under this attack, his guilty contrition greater than his anger—he stammers*] Be quiet! Don't say that to me! You're drunk! I won't mind you. Stop coughing, lad. You've got yourself worked up over nothing. Who said you had to go to this Hilltown place? You can go anywhere you like. I don't give a damn what it costs. All I care about is to have you get well. Don't call me a stinking miser, just because I don't want doctors to think I'm a millionaire they can swindle.

[EDMUND *has stopped coughing. He looks sick and weak. His father stares at him frightenedly.*]

You look weak, lad. You'd better take a bracer.

EDMUND [*grabs the bottle and pours his glass brimfull—weakly*] Thanks. [*He gulps down the whiskey.*]

TYRONE [*pours himself a big drink, which empties the bottle, and drinks it; his head bows and he stares dully at the cards on the table—vaguely*] Whose play is it? [*He goes on dully, without resentment.*] A stinking old miser. Well, maybe you're right. Maybe I can't help being, although all my life since I had anything I've thrown money over the bar to buy drinks for everyone in the house, or loaned money to sponges I knew would never pay it back—[*with a loose-mouthed sneer of self-contempt*] But, of course, that was in barrooms, when I was full of whiskey. I can't feel that way about it when I'm sober in my home. It was at home I first learned the value of a dollar and the fear of the poorhouse. I've never been able to believe in my luck since. I've always feared it would change and everything I had would be taken away. But still, the more property you own, the safer you think you are. That may not be logical, but it's the way I have to feel. Banks fail, and your money's gone, but you think you can keep land beneath your feet. [*Abruptly his tone becomes scornfully superior.*] You said you realized what I'd been up against as a boy. The hell you do! How could you? You've had everything—nurses, schools, college, though you didn't stay there. You've had food, clothing. Oh, I know you had a fling of hard work with your back and hands, a bit of being homeless and penniless in a foreign land, and I respect you for it. But it was a game of romance and adventure to you. It was play.

EDMUND [*dully sarcastic*] Yes, particularly the time I tried to commit suicide at Jimmie the Priest's, and almost did.

TYRONE You weren't in your right mind. No son of mine would ever—You were drunk.

EDMUND I was stone cold sober. That was the trouble. I'd stopped to think too long.

TYRONE [*with drunken peevishness*] Don't start your damned atheist morbidness again! I don't care to listen. I was trying to make plain to you—[*scornfully*] What do you know of the value of a dollar? When I was ten my father deserted my mother and went back to Ireland to die. Which he did soon enough, and deserved to, and I hope he's roasting in hell. He mistook rat poison for flour, or sugar, or something. There was gossip it wasn't by mistake but that's a lie. No one in my family ever—

EDMUND My bet is, it wasn't by mistake.

TYRONE More morbidness! Your brother put that in your head. The worst he can suspect is the only truth for him. But never mind. My mother was left, a stranger in a strange land, with four small children, me and a sister a little older and two younger than me. My two older brothers had moved to other parts. They couldn't help. They were hard put to it to keep themselves alive. There was no damned romance in our poverty. Twice we were evicted from the miserable hovel we called home, with my mother's few sticks of furniture thrown out in the street, and my mother and sisters crying. I cried, too, though I tried hard not to, because I was the man of the family. At ten years old! There was no more school for me. I worked twelve hours a day in a machine shop, learning to make files. A dirty barn of a place where rain dripped through the roof, where you roasted in summer, and there was no stove in winter, and your hands got numb with cold, where the only light came through two small filthy windows, so on grey days I'd have to sit bent over with my eyes almost touching the files in order to see! You talk of work! And what do you think I got for it? Fifty cents a week! It's the truth! Fifty cents a week! And my poor mother washed and scrubbed for the Yanks by the day, and my older sister sewed, and my two younger stayed at home to keep the house. We never had clothes enough to wear, nor enough food to eat. Well I remember one Thanksgiving, or maybe it was Christmas, when some Yank in whose house mother had been scrubbing gave her a dollar extra for a present, and on the way home she spent it all on food. I can remember her hugging and kissing us and saying with tears of joy running down her tired face: "Glory be to God, for once in our lives we'll have enough for each of us!" [*He wipes tears from his eyes.*] A fine, brave, sweet woman. There never was a braver or finer.

EDMUND [*moved*] Yes, she must have been.

TYRONE Her one fear was she'd get old and sick and have to die in the poorhouse. [*He pauses—then adds with grim humor*] It was in those days I learned to be a miser. A dollar was worth so much then. And once you've learned a lesson, it's hard to unlearn it. You have to look for bargains. If I took this state farm sanatorium for a good bargain, you'll have to forgive me. The doctors did tell me it's a good place. You must believe that,

Edmund. And I swear I never meant you to go there if you didn't want to. [*vehemently*] You can choose any place you like! Never mind what it costs! Any place I can afford. Any place you like—within reason.

[*At this qualification, a grin twitches* EDMUND*'s lips. His resentment has gone. His father goes on with an elaborately offhand, casual air.*]

There was another sanatorium the specialist recommended. He said it had a record as good as any place in the country. It's endowed by a group of millionaire factory owners, for the benefit of their workers principally, but you're eligible to go there because you're a resident. There's such a pile of money behind it, they don't have to charge much. It's only seven dollars a week but you get ten times that value. [*hastily*] I don't want to persuade you to anything, understand. I'm simply repeating what I was told.

EDMUND [*concealing his smile—casually*] Oh, I know that. It sounds like a good bargain to me. I'd like to go there. So that settles that. [*Abruptly he is miserably desperate again—dully*] It doesn't matter a damn now, anyway. Let's forget it! [*changing the subject*] How about our game? Whose play is it?

TYRONE [*mechanically*] I don't know. Mine, I guess. No, it's yours.

[EDMUND *plays a card. His father takes it. Then about to play from his hand, he again forgets the game.*]

Yes, maybe life overdid the lesson for me, and made a dollar worth too much, and the time came when that mistake ruined my career as a fine actor. [*sadly*] I've never admitted this to anyone before, lad, but tonight I'm so heartsick I feel at the end of everything, and what's the use of fake pride and pretense. That God-damned play I bought for a song and made such a great success in—a great money success—it ruined me with its promise of an easy fortune. I didn't want to do anything else, and by the time I woke up to the fact I'd become a slave to the damned thing and did try other plays, it was too late. They had identified me with that one part, and didn't want me in anything else. They were right, too. I'd lost the great talent I once had through years of easy repetition, never learning a new part, never really working hard. Thirty-five to forty thousand dollars net profit a season like snapping your fingers! It was too great a temptation. Yet before I bought the damned thing I was considered one of the three or four young actors with the greatest artistic promise in America. I'd worked like hell. I'd left a good job as a machinist to take supers'[3] parts because I loved the theater. I was wild with ambition. I read all the plays ever written. I studied Shakespeare as you'd study the Bible. I educated myself. I got rid of an Irish brogue you could cut with a knife. I loved Shakespeare. I would have acted in any of his plays for nothing, for the joy of being alive in his great poetry. And I acted well in him. I felt inspired by him. I could have been a great Shakespearean actor, if I'd kept on. I know that! In 1874 when Edwin Booth[4] came to the theater in Chicago where I was leading man, I played Cassius to his Brutus one night, Brutus to his Cassius the next, Othello to his Iago, and so on. The first night I played Othello, he said to our manager. "That young man is playing Othello better than I ever did!" [*proudly*] That from Booth, the

3. Supernumeraries, extras.
4. Edwin Booth (1833–1893), American actor and theatrical manager.

greatest actor of his day or any other! And it was true! And I was only twenty-seven years old! As I look back on it now, that night was the high spot in my career. I had life where I wanted it! And for a time after that I kept on upward with ambition high. Married your mother. Ask her what I was like in those days. Her love was an added incentive to ambition. But a few years later my good bad luck made me find the big money-maker. It wasn't that in my eyes at first. It was a great romantic part I knew I could play better than anyone. But it was a great box office success from the start—and then life had me where it wanted me—at from thirty-five to forty thousand net profit a season! A fortune in those days—or even in these. [*bitterly*] What the hell was it I wanted to buy, I wonder, that was worth—Well, no matter. It's a late day for regrets. [*He glances vaguely at his cards.*] My play, isn't it?

EDMUND [*moved, stares at his father with understanding—slowly*] I'm glad you've told me this, Papa. I know you a lot better now.

TYRONE [*with a loose, twisted smile*] Maybe I shouldn't have told you. Maybe you'll only feel more contempt for me. And it's a poor way to convince you of the value of a dollar. [*Then as if this phrase automatically aroused an habitual association in his mind, he glances up at the chandelier disapprovingly.*] The glare from those extra lights hurts my eyes. You don't mind if I turn them out, do you? We don't need them, and there's no use making the Electric Company rich.

EDMUND [*controlling a wild impulse to laugh—agreeably*] No, sure not. Turn them out.

TYRONE [*gets heavily and a bit waveringly to his feet and gropes uncertainly for the lights—his mind going back to its line of thought*] No, I don't know what the hell it was I wanted to buy. [*He clicks out one bulb.*] On my solemn oath, Edmund, I'd gladly face not having an acre of land to call my own, nor a penny in the bank—[*He clicks out another bulb.*] I'd be willing to have no home but the poorhouse in my old age if I could look back now on having been the fine artist I might have been.

[*He turns out the third bulb, so only the reading lamp is on, and sits down again heavily.* EDMUND *suddenly cannot hold back a burst of strained, ironical laughter.* TYRONE *is hurt.*]

What the devil are you laughing at?

EDMUND Not at you, Papa. At life. It's so damned crazy.

TYRONE [*growls*] More of your morbidness! There's nothing wrong with life. It's we who—[*He quotes*] "The fault, dear Brutus, is not in our stars, but in ourselves that we are underlings."[5] [*He pauses—then sadly*] The praise Edwin Booth gave my Othello. I made the manager put down his exact words in writing. I kept it in my wallet for years. I used to read it every once in a while until finally it made me feel so bad I didn't want to face it any more. Where is it now, I wonder? Somewhere in this house. I remember I put it away carefully—

EDMUND [*with a wry ironical sadness*] It might be in an old trunk in the attic, along with Mama's wedding dress. [*Then as his father stares at him, he adds quickly*] For Pete's sake, if we're going to play cards, let's play.

5. Shakespeare's *Julius Caesar* 1.2.134.

[*He takes the card his father had played and leads. For a moment, they play the game, like mechanical chess players. Then* TYRONE *stops, listening to a sound upstairs.*]

TYRONE She's still moving around. God knows when she'll go to sleep.

EDMUND [*pleads tensely*] For Christ's sake, Papa, forget it!

[*He reaches out and pours a drink.* TYRONE *starts to protest, then gives it up.* EDMUND *drinks. He puts down the glass. His expression changes. When he speaks it is as if he were deliberately giving way to drunkenness and seeking to hide behind a maudlin manner.*]

Yes, she moves above and beyond us, a ghost haunting the past, and here we sit pretending to forget, but straining our ears listening for the slightest sound, hearing the fog drip from the eaves like the uneven tick of a rundown, crazy clock—or like the dreary tears of a trollop spattering in a puddle of stale beer on a honky-tonk table top! [*He laughs with maudlin appreciation.*] Not so bad, that last, eh? Original, not Baudelaire. Give me credit! [*then with alcoholic talkativeness*] You've just told me some high spots in your memories. Want to hear mine? They're all connected with the sea. Here's one. When I was on the Squarehead square rigger, bound for Buenos Aires. Full moon in the Trades. The old hooker driving fourteen knots. I lay on the bowsprit, facing astern, with the water foaming into spume under me, the masts with every sail white in the moonlight, towering high above me. I became drunk with the beauty and singing rhythm of it, and for a moment I lost myself—actually lost my life. I was set free! I dissolved in the sea, became white sails and flying spray, became beauty and rhythm, became moonlight and the ship and the high dim-starred sky! I belonged, without past or future, within peace and unity and a wild joy, within something greater than my own life, or the life of Man, to Life itself! To God, if you want to put it that way. Then another time, on the American Line, when I was lookout on the crow's nest in the dawn watch. A calm sea, that time. Only a lazy ground swell and a slow drowsy roll of the ship. The passengers asleep and none of the crew in sight. No sound of man. Black smoke pouring from the funnels behind and beneath me. Dreaming, not keeping lookout, feeling alone, and above, and apart, watching the dawn creep like a painted dream over the sky and sea which slept together. Then the moment of ecstatic freedom came. The peace, the end of the quest, the last harbor, the joy of belonging to a fulfillment beyond men's lousy, pitiful, greedy fears and hopes and dreams! And several other times in my life, when I was swimming far out, or lying alone on a beach, I have had the same experience. Became the sun, the hot sand, green seaweed anchored to a rock, swaying in the tide. Like a saint's vision of beatitude. Like the veil of things as they seem drawn back by an unseen hand. For a second you see—and seeing the secret, are the secret. For a second there is meaning! Then the hand lets the veil fall and you are alone, lost in the fog again, and you stumble on toward nowhere, for no good reason! [*He grins wryly.*] It was a great mistake, my being born a man, I would have been much more successful as a sea gull or a fish. As it is, I will always be a stranger who never feels at home, who does not really want and is not really wanted, who can never belong, who must always be a little in love with death!

TYRONE [*stares at him—impressed*] Yes, there's the makings of a poet in you all right. [*then protesting uneasily*] But that's morbid craziness about not being wanted and loving death.

EDMUND [*sardonically*] The *makings* of a poet. No, I'm afraid I'm like the guy who is always panhandling for a smoke. He hasn't even got the makings. He's got only the habit. I couldn't touch what I tried to tell you just now. I just stammered. That's the best I'll ever do. I mean, if I live. Well, it will be faithful realism, at least. Stammering is the native eloquence of us fog people.

[*A pause. Then they both jump startledly as there is a noise from outside the house, as if someone had stumbled and fallen on the front steps.* EDMUND *grins.*]

Well, that sounds like the absent brother. He must have a peach of a bun on.

TYRONE [*scowling*] That loafer! He caught the last car, bad luck to it. [*He gets to his feet.*] Get him to bed, Edmund. I'll go out on the porch. He has a tongue like an adder when he's drunk. I'd only lose my temper.

[*He goes out the door to the side porch as the front door in the hall bangs shut behind* JAMIE. EDMUND *watches with amusement* JAMIE'*s wavering progress through the front parlor.* JAMIE *comes in. He is very drunk and woozy on his legs. His eyes are glassy, his face bloated, his speech blurred, his mouth slack like his father's, a leer on his lips.*]

JAMIE [*swaying and blinking in the doorway—in a loud voice*] What ho! What ho!

EDMUND [*sharply*] Nix on the loud noise!

JAMIE [*blinks at him*] Oh, hello, Kid. [*with great seriousness*] I'm as drunk as a fiddler's bitch.

EDMUND [*dryly*] Thanks for telling me your great secret.

JAMIE [*grins foolishly*] Yes. Unneshesary information Number One, eh? [*He bends and slaps at the knees of his trousers.*] Had serious accident. The front steps tried to trample on me. Took advantage of fog to waylay me. Ought to be a lighthouse out there. Dark in here, too. [*scowling*] What the hell is this, the morgue? Lesh have some light on subject. [*He sways forward to the table, reciting Kipling*[6]]

"Ford, ford, ford o' Kabul river,
Ford o' Kabul river in the dark!
Keep the crossing-stakes beside you, an' they
  will surely guide you
'Cross the ford o' Kabul river in the dark."

[*He fumbles at the chandelier and manages to turn on the three bulbs.*] Thash more like it. The hell with old Gaspard.[7] Where is the old tightwad?

EDMUND Out on the porch.

JAMIE Can't expect us to live in the Black Hole of Calcutta.[8] [*His eyes fix on the full bottle of whiskey.*] Say! Have I got the d.t.'s?[9] [*He reaches out*

6. Rudyard Kipling (1865–1936), English author.
7. Jamie's contemptuous name for his father, drawn from a character in the popular drama *The Bells*.
8. Small dungeon in Calcutta, India, where, on June 20, 1756, 123 of 146 British prisoners died of suffocation. Hence, any small, cramped space.
9. Delirium tremens.

fumblingly and grabs it.] By God, it's real. What's matter with the Old Man tonight? Must be ossified to forget he left this out. Grab opportunity by the forelock. Key to my success. [*He slops a big drink into a glass.*]

EDMUND You're stinking now. That will knock you stiff.

JAMIE Wisdom from the mouth of babes. Can the wise stuff, Kid. You're still wet behind the ears. [*He lowers himself into a chair, holding the drink carefully aloft.*]

EDMUND All right. Pass out if you want to.

JAMIE Can't, that's trouble. Had enough to sink a ship, but can't sink. Well, here's hoping. [*He drinks.*]

EDMUND Shove over the bottle. I'll have one, too.

JAMIE [*with sudden, big-brotherly solicitude, grabbing the bottle*] No, you don't. Not while I'm around. Remember doctor's orders. Maybe no one else gives a damn if you die, but I do. My kid brother. I love your guts, Kid. Everything else is gone. You're all I've got left. [*pulling bottle closer to him*] So no booze for you, if I can help it. [*Beneath his drunken sentimentality there is a genuine sincerity.*]

EDMUND [*irritably*] Oh, lay off it.

JAMIE [*is hurt and his face hardens*] You don't believe I care, eh? Just drunken bull. [*He shoves the bottle over.*] All right. Go ahead and kill yourself.

EDMUND [*seeing he is hurt—affectionately*] Sure I know you care, Jamie, and I'm going on the wagon. But tonight doesn't count. Too many damned things have happened today. [*He pours a drink.*] Here's how. [*He drinks.*]

JAMIE [*sobers up momentarily and with a pitying look*] I know, Kid. It's been a lousy day for you. [*then with sneering cynicism*] I'll bet old Gaspard hasn't tried to keep you off booze. Probably give you a case to take with you to the state farm for pauper patients. The sooner you kick the bucket, the less expense. [*with contemptuous hatred*] What a bastard to have for a father! Christ, if you put him in a book, no one would believe it!

EDMUND [*defensively*] Oh, Papa's all right, if you try to understand him—and keep your sense of humor.

JAMIE [*cynically*] He's been putting on the old sob act for you, eh? He can always kid you. But not me. Never again. [*then slowly*] Although, in a way, I do feel sorry for him about one thing. But he has even that coming to him. He's to blame. [*hurriedly*] But to hell with that. [*He grabs the bottle and pours another drink, appearing very drunk again.*] That lash drink's getting me. This one ought to put the lights out. Did you tell Gaspard I got it out of Doc Hardy this sanatorium is a charity dump?

EDMUND [*reluctantly*] Yes. I told him I wouldn't go there. It's all settled now. He said I can go anywhere I want. [*He adds, smiling without resentment*] Within reason, of course.

JAMIE [*drunkenly imitating his father*] Of course, lad. Anything within reason. [*sneering*] That means another cheap dump. Old Gaspard, the miser in "The Bells," that's a part he can play without make-up.

EDMUND [*irritably*] Oh, shut up, will you. I've heard that Gaspard stuff a million times.

JAMIE [*shrugs his shoulders—thickly*] Aw right, if you're shatisfied—let him get away with it. It's your funeral—I mean, I hope it won't be.

EDMUND [*changing the subject*] What did you do uptown tonight? Go to Mamie Burns?

JAMIE [*very drunk, his head nodding*] Sure thing. Where else could I find suitable feminine companionship? And love. Don't forget love. What is a man without a good woman's love? A God-damned hollow shell.

EDMUND [*chuckles tipsily, letting himself go now and be drunk*] You're a nut.

JAMIE [*quotes with gusto from Oscar Wilde's*[1] "The Harlot's House"]

"Then, turning to my love, I said,
'The dead are dancing with the dead,
The dust is whirling with the dust.'

But she—she heard the violin,
And left my side and entered in:
Love passed into the house of lust.

Then suddenly the tune went false,
The dancers wearied of the waltz . . ."

[*He breaks off, thickly*] Not strictly accurate. If my love was with me, I didn't notice it. She must have been a ghost. [*He pauses.*] Guess which one of Mamie's charmers I picked to bless me with her woman's love. It'll hand you a laugh, Kid. I picked Fat Violet.

EDMUND [*laughs drunkenly*] No, honest? Some pick! God, she weighs a ton. What the hell for, a joke?

JAMIE No joke. Very serious. By the time I hit Mamie's dump I felt very sad about myself and all the other poor bums in the world. Ready for a weep on any old womanly bosom. You know how you get when John Barleycorn turns on the soft music inside you. Then, soon as I got in the door, Mamie began telling me all her troubles. Beefed how rotten business was, and she was going to give Fat Violet the gate. Customers didn't fall for Vi. Only reason she'd kept her was she could play the piano. Lately Vi's gone on drunks and been too boiled to play, and was eating her out of house and home, and although Vi was a goodhearted dumbbell, and she felt sorry for her because she didn't know how the hell she'd make a living, still business was business, and she couldn't afford to run a house for fat tarts. Well, that made me feel sorry for Fat Violet, so I squandered two bucks of your dough to escort her upstairs. With no dishonorable intentions whatever. I like them fat, but not that fat. All I wanted was a little heart-to-heart talk concerning the infinite sorrow of life.

EDMUND [*chuckles drunkenly*] Poor Vi! I'll bet you recited Kipling and Swinburne and Dowson and gave her "I have been faithful to thee, Cynara, in my fashion."

JAMIE [*grins loosely*] Sure—with the Old Master, John Barleycorn, playing soft music. She stood it for a while. Then she got good and sore. Got the idea I took her upstairs for a joke. Gave me a grand bawling out. Said she was better than a drunken bum who recited poetry. Then she began to cry. So I had to say I loved her because she was fat, and she wanted to believe that, and I stayed with her to prove it, and that

1. Irish author (1854–1900).

cheered her up, and she kissed me when I left, and said she'd fallen hard for me, and we both cried a little more in the hallway, and everything was fine, except Mamie Burns thought I'd gone bughouse.

EDMUND [*quotes derisively*]

"Harlots and
Hunted have pleasures of their own to give,
The vulgar herd can never understand."

JAMIE [*nods his head drunkenly*] Egzactly! Hell of a good time, at that. You should have stuck around with me, Kid. Mamie Burns inquired after you. Sorry to hear you were sick. She meant it, too. [*He pauses—then with maudlin humor, in a ham-actor tone*] This night has opened my eyes to a great career in store for me, my boy! I shall give the art of acting back to the performing seals, which are its most perfect expression. By applying my natural God-given talents in their proper sphere, I shall attain the pinnacle of success! I'll be the lover of the fat woman in Barnum and Bailey's circus! [EDMUND *laughs.* JAMIE'*s mood changes to arrogant disdain.*] Pah! Imagine me sunk to the fat girl in a hick town hooker shop! Me! Who have made some of the best-lookers on Broadway sit up and beg! [*He quotes from Kipling's "Sestina of the Tramp-Royal"*]

"Speakin' in general, I 'ave tried 'em all,
The 'appy roads that take you o'er the world."

[*with sodden melancholy*] Not so apt. Happy roads is bunk. Weary roads is right. Get you nowhere fast. That's where I've got—nowhere. Where everyone lands in the end, even if most of the suckers won't admit it.

EDMUND [*derisively*] Can it! You'll be crying in a minute.

JAMIE [*starts and stares at his brother for a second with bitter hostility—thickly*] Don't get—too damned fresh. [*then abruptly*] But you're right. To hell with repining! Fat Violet's a good kid. Glad I stayed with her. Christian act. Cured her blues. Hell of a good time. You should have stuck with me, Kid. Taken your mind off your troubles. What's the use coming home to get the blues over what can't be helped. All over—finished now—not a hope! [*He stops, his head nodding drunkenly, his eyes closing—then suddenly he looks up, his face hard, and quotes jeeringly.*]

"If I were hanged on the highest hill,
Mother o' mine, O mother o' mine!
I know whose love would follow me still . . ."

EDMUND [*violently*] Shut up!

JAMIE [*in a cruel, sneering tone with hatred in it*] Where's the hophead? Gone to sleep?

[EDMUND *jerks as if he'd been struck. There is a tense silence.* EDMUND'*s face looks stricken and sick. Then in a burst of rage he springs from his chair.*]

EDMUND You dirty bastard!

[*He punches his brother in the face, a blow that glances off the cheekbone. For a second* JAMIE *reacts pugnaciously and half rises from his chair to do battle, but suddenly he seems to sober up to a shocked realization of what he has said and he sinks back limply.*]

JAMIE [*miserably*] Thanks, Kid. I certainly had that coming. Don't know what made me—booze talking—You know me, Kid.

EDMUND [*his anger ebbing*] I know you'd never say that unless—But God, Jamie, no matter how drunk you are, it's no excuse! [*He pauses—miserably*] I'm sorry I hit you. You and I never scrap—that bad. [*He sinks back on his chair.*]

JAMIE [*huskily*] It's all right. Glad you did. My dirty tongue. Like to cut it out. [*He hides his face in his hands—dully*] I suppose it's because I feel so damned sunk. Because this time Mama had me fooled. I really believed she had it licked. She thinks I always believe the worst, but this time I believed the best. [*His voice flutters.*] I suppose I can't forgive her—yet. It meant so much. I'd begun to hope, if she'd beaten the game, I could, too. [*He begins to sob, and the horrible part of his weeping is that it appears sober, not the maudlin tears of drunkenness.*]

EDMUND [*blinking back tears himself*] God, don't I know how you feel! Stop it, Jamie!

JAMIE [*trying to control his sobs*] I've known about Mama so much longer than you. Never forget the first time I got wise. Caught her in the act with a hypo. Christ, I'd never dreamed before that any women but whores took dope! [*He pauses.*] And then this stuff of you getting consumption. It's got me licked. We've been more than brothers. You're the only pal I've ever had. I love your guts. I'd do anything for you.

EDMUND [*reaches out and pats his arm*] I know that, Jamie.

JAMIE [*his crying over—drops his hands from his face—with a strange bitterness*] Yet I'll bet you've heard Mama and old Gaspard spill so much bunk about my hoping for the worst, you suspect right now I'm thinking to myself that Papa is old and can't last much longer, and if you were to die, Mama and I would get all he's got, and so I'm probably hoping—

EDMUND [*indignantly*] Shut up, you damned fool! What the hell put that in your nut? [*He stares at his brother accusingly.*] Yes, that's what I'd like to know. What put that in your mind?

JAMIE [*confusedly—appearing drunk again*] Don't be a dumbbell! What I said! Always suspected of hoping for the worst. I've got so I can't help—[*then drunkenly resentful*] What are you trying to do, accuse me? Don't play the wise guy with me! I've learned more of life than you'll ever know! Just because you've read a lot of highbrow junk, don't think you can fool me! You're only an overgrown kid! Mama's baby and Papa's pet! The family White Hope! You've been getting a swelled head lately. About nothing! About a few poems in a hick town newspaper! Hell, I used to write better stuff for the Lit magazine in college! You better wake up! You're setting no rivers on fire! You let hick town boobs flatter you with bunk about your future—

[*Abruptly his tone changes to disgusted contrition.* EDMUND *has looked away from him, trying to ignore this tirade.*]

Hell, Kid, forget it. That goes for Sweeny. You know I don't mean it. No one hopes more than I do you'll knock 'em all dead. No one is prouder you've started to make good. [*drunkenly assertive*] Why shouldn't I be proud? Hell, it's purely selfish. You reflect credit on me. I've had more to do with bringing you up than anyone. I wised you up about women, so you'd never be a fall guy, or make any mistakes you didn't want to make!

And who steered you on to reading poetry first? Swinburne,[2] for example? I did! And because I once wanted to write, I planted it in your mind that someday you'd write! Hell, you're more than my brother. I made you! You're my Frankenstein![3]

[*He has risen to a note of drunken arrogance.* EDMUND *is grinning with amusement now.*]

EDMUND All right, I'm your Frankenstein. So let's have a drink. [*He laughs.*] You crazy nut!

JAMIE [*thickly*] I'll have a drink. Not you. Got to take care of you. [*He reaches out with a foolish grin of doting affection and grabs his brother's hand.*] Don't be scared of this sanatorium business. Hell, you can beat that standing on your head. Six months and you'll be in the pink. Probably haven't got consumption at all. Doctors lot of fakers. Told me years ago to cut out booze or I'd soon be dead—and here I am. They're all con men. Anything to grab your dough. I'll bet this state farm stuff is political graft game. Doctors get a cut for every patient they send.

EDMUND [*disgustedly amused*] You're the limit! At the Last Judgment, you'll be around telling everyone it's in the bag.

JAMIE And I'll be right. Slip a piece of change to the Judge and be saved, but if you're broke you can go to hell!

[*He grins at this blasphemy and* EDMUND *has to laugh.* JAMIE *goes on.*]

"Therefore put money in thy purse."[4] That's the only dope. [*mockingly*] The secret of my success! Look what it's got me!

[*He lets* EDMUND*'s hand go to pour a big drink, and gulps it down. He stares at his brother with bleary affection—takes his hand again and begins to talk thickly but with a strange, convincing sincerity.*]

Listen, Kid, you'll be going away. May not get another chance to talk. Or might not be drunk enough to tell you truth. So got to tell you now. Something I ought to have told you long ago—for your own good.

[*He pauses—struggling with himself.* EDMUND *stares, impressed and uneasy. Jamie blurts out*]

Not drunken bull, but "in vino veritas"[5] stuff. You better take it seriously. Want to warn you—against me. Mama and Papa are right. I've been rotten bad influence. And worst of it is, I did it on purpose.

EDMUND [*uneasily*] Shut up! I don't want to hear—

JAMIE Nix, Kid! You listen! Did it on purpose to make a bum of you. Or part of me did. A big part. That part that's been dead so long. That hates life. My putting you wise so you'd learn from my mistakes. Believed that myself at times, but it's a fake. Made my mistakes look good. Made getting drunk romantic. Made whores fascinating vampires instead of poor, stupid, diseased slobs they really are. Made fun of work as sucker's game. Never wanted you to succeed and make me look even worse by comparison. Wanted you to fail. Always jealous of you. Mama's baby, Papa's pet! [*He stares at* EDMUND *with increasing enmity.*] And it

2. Algernon Charles Swinburne (1837–1909), English poet and critic.

3. In the novel *Frankenstein* by the English author Mary Shelley (1797–1851), the scientist Dr. Frankenstein creates a monster. Jamie confuses the scientist with his creation, although it is possible that the mistake is O'Neill's.

4. Shakespeare's *Othello* 1.3.354.

5. In wine there is truth (Latin).

was your being born that started Mama on dope. I know that's not your fault, but all the same, God damn you, I can't help hating your guts—!

EDMUND [*almost frightenedly*] Jamie! Cut it out! You're crazy!

JAMIE But don't get wrong idea, Kid. I love you more than I hate you. My saying what I'm telling you now proves it. I run the risk you'll hate me—and you're all I've got left. But I didn't mean to tell you that last stuff—go that far back. Don't know what made me. What I wanted to say is, I'd like to see you become the greatest success in the world. But you'd better be on your guard. Because I'll do my damnedest to make you fail. Can't help it. I hate myself. Got to take revenge. On everyone else. Especially you. Oscar Wilde's "Reading Gaol" has the dope twisted. The man was dead and so he had to kill the thing he loved. That's what it ought to be. The dead part of me hopes you won't get well. Maybe he's even glad the game has got Mama again! He wants company, he doesn't want to be the only corpse around the house! [*He gives a hard, tortured laugh.*]

EDMUND Jesus, Jamie! You really have gone crazy!

JAMIE Think it over and you'll see I'm right. Think it over when you're away from me in the sanatorium. Make up your mind you've got to tie a can to me—get me out of your life—think of me as dead—tell people, "I had a brother, but he's dead." And when you come back, look out for me. I'll be waiting to welcome you with that "my old pal" stuff, and give you the glad hand, and at the first good chance I get stab you in the back.

EDMUND Shut up! I'll be God-damned if I'll listen to you any more—

JAMIE [*as if he hadn't heard*] Only don't forget me. Remember I warned you—for your sake. Give me credit. Greater love hath no man than this, that he saveth his brother from himself. [*very drunkenly, his head bobbing*] That's all. Feel better now. Gone to confession. Know you absolve me, don't you, Kid? You understand. You're a damned fine kid. Ought to be. I made you. So go and get well. Don't die on me. You're all I've got left. God bless you, Kid. [*His eyes close. He mumbles*] That last drink—the old K.O.

[*He falls into a drunken doze, not completely asleep.* EDMUND *buries his face in his hands miserably.* TYRONE *comes in quietly through the screen door from the porch, his dressing gown wet with fog, the collar turned up around his throat. His face is stern and disgusted but at the same time pitying.* EDMUND *does not notice his entrance.*]

TYRONE [*in a low voice*] Thank God he's asleep.

[EDMUND *looks up with a start.*]

I thought he'd never stop talking. [*He turns down the collar of his dressing gown.*] We'd better let him stay where he is and sleep it off.

[EDMUND *remains silent.* TYRONE *regards him—then goes on*]

I heard the last part of his talk. It's what I've warned you. I hope you'll heed the warning, now it comes from his own mouth.

[EDMUND *gives no sign of having heard.* TYRONE *adds pityingly*]

But don't take it too much to heart, lad. He loves to exaggerate the worst of himself when he's drunk. He's devoted to you. It's the one good thing left in him. [*He looks down on* JAMIE *with a bitter sadness.*] A sweet spectacle for me! My first-born, who I hoped would bear my name in honor and dignity, who showed such brilliant promise!

EDMUND [*miserably*] Keep quiet, can't you, Papa?

TYRONE [*pours a drink*] A waste! A wreck, a drunken hulk, done with and finished!

[*He drinks.* JAMIE *has become restless, sensing his father's presence, struggling up from his stupor. Now he gets his eyes open to blink up at* TYRONE. *The latter moves back a step defensively, his face growing hard.*]

JAMIE [*suddenly points a finger at him and recites with dramatic emphasis*]

"Clarence is come, false, fleeting, perjured Clarence,
That stabbed me in the field by Tewksbury.
Seize on him, Furies, take him into torment."[6]

[*then resentfully*] What the hell are you staring at? [*He recites sardonically from Rossetti*[7]]

"Look in my face. My name is Might-Have-Been;
I am also called No More, Too Late, Farewell."

TYRONE I'm well aware of that, and God knows I don't want to look at it.

EDMUND Papa! Quit it!

JAMIE [*derisively*] Got a great idea for you, Papa. Put on revival of "The Bells" this season. Great part in it you can play without make-up. Old Gaspard, the miser!

[TYRONE *turns away, trying to control his temper.*]

EDMUND Shut up, Jamie!

JAMIE [*jeeringly*] I claim Edwin Booth never saw the day when he could give as good a performance as a trained seal. Seals are intelligent and honest. They don't put up any bluffs about the Art of Acting. They admit they're just hams earning their daily fish.

TYRONE [*stung, turns on him in a rage*] You loafer!

EDMUND Papa! Do you want to start a row that will bring Mama down? Jamie, go back to sleep! You've shot off your mouth too much already.

[TYRONE *turns away.*]

JAMIE [*thickly*] All right, Kid. Not looking for argument. Too damned sleepy.

[*He closes his eyes, his head nodding.* TYRONE *comes to the table and sits down, turning his chair so he won't look at* JAMIE. *At once he becomes sleepy, too.*]

TYRONE [*heavily*] I wish to God she'd go to bed so that I could, too. [*drowsily*] I'm dog tired. I can't stay up all night like I used to. Getting old—old and finished. [*with a bone-cracking yawn*] Can't keep my eyes open. I think I'll catch a few winks. Why don't you do the same, Edmund? It'll pass the time until she—

[*His voice trails off. His eyes close, his chin sags, and he begins to breathe heavily through his mouth.* EDMUND *sits tensely. He hears something and jerks nervously forward in his chair, staring through the front parlor into the hall. He jumps up with a hunted, distracted expression. It seems for a second he is going to hide in the back parlor. Then he sits down again and waits, his eyes averted, his hands gripping the arms of his chair. Suddenly all five bulbs of the chandelier in the front parlor are turned*

6. Shakespeare's *Richard III* 1.4.55–57.
7. Dante Gabriel Rossetti (1821–1882), English poet and painter.

on from a wall switch, and a moment later someone starts playing the piano in there—the opening of one of Chopin's[8] simpler waltzes, done with a forgetful, stiff-fingered groping, as if an awkward schoolgirl were practicing it for the first time. TYRONE *starts to wide-awakeness and sober dread, and* JAMIE'*s head jerks back and his eyes open. For a moment they listen frozenly. The playing stops as abruptly as it began, and* MARY *appears in the doorway. She wears a sky-blue dressing gown over her nightdress, dainty slippers and pompons on her bare feet. Her face is paler than ever. Her eyes look enormous. They glisten like polished black jewels. The uncanny thing is that her face now appears so youthful. Experience seems ironed out of it. It is a marble mask of girlish innocence, the mouth caught in a shy smile. Her white hair is braided in two pigtails which hang over her breast. Over one arm, carried neglectfully, trailing on the floor, as if she had forgotten she held it, is an old-fashioned white satin wedding gown, trimmed with duchesse lace. She hesitates in the doorway, glancing round the room, her forehead puckered puzzledly, like someone who has come to a room to get something but has become absent-minded on the way and forgotten what it was. They stare at her. She seems aware of them merely as she is aware of other objects in the room, the furniture, the windows, familiar things she accepts automatically as naturally belonging there but which she is too preoccupied to notice.*]

JAMIE [*breaks the cracking silence—bitterly, self-defensively sardonic*] The Mad Scene. Enter Ophelia![9]

[*His father and brother both turn on him fiercely.* EDMUND *is quicker. He slaps* JAMIE *across the mouth with the back of his hand.*]

TYRONE [*his voice trembling with suppressed fury*] Good boy, Edmund. The dirty blackguard! His own mother!

JAMIE [*mumbles guiltily, without resentment*] All right, Kid. Had it coming. But I told you how much I'd hoped—[*He puts his hands over his face and begins to sob.*]

TYRONE I'll kick you out in the gutter tomorrow, so help me God. [*But* JAMIE'*s sobbing breaks his anger, and he turns and shakes his shoulder, pleading*] Jamie, for the love of God, stop it!

[*Then* MARY *speaks, and they freeze into silence again, staring at her. She has paid no attention whatever to the incident. It is simply a part of the familiar atmosphere of the room, a background which does not touch her preoccupation; and she speaks aloud to herself, not to them.*]

MARY I play so badly now. I'm all out of practice. Sister Theresa will give me a dreadful scolding. She'll tell me it isn't fair to my father when he spends so much money for extra lessons. She's quite right, it isn't fair, when he's so good and generous, and so proud of me. I'll practice every day from now on. But something horrible has happened to my hands. The fingers have gotten so stiff—[*She lifts her hands to examine them with a frightened puzzlement.*] The knuckles are all swollen. They're so ugly. I'll have to go to the Infirmary and show Sister Martha. [*with a sweet smile of affectionate trust*] She's old and a little cranky, but I love her just the same, and she has things in her medicine chest that'll cure

8. Frederic Chopin (1810–1849), Polish composer famous for works for the piano.

9. An allusion to Shakespeare's *Hamlet*.

anything. She'll give me something to rub on my hands, and tell me to pray to the Blessed Virgin, and they'll be well again in no time. [*She forgets her hands and comes into the room, the wedding gown trailing on the floor. She glances around vaguely, her forehead puckered again.*] Let me see. What did I come here to find? It's terrible, how absent-minded I've become. I'm always dreaming and forgetting.

TYRONE [*in a stifled voice*] What's that she's carrying, Edmund?

EDMUND [*dully*] Her wedding gown, I suppose.

TYRONE Christ! [*He gets to his feet and stands directly in her path—in anguish*] Mary! Isn't it bad enough—? [*controlling himself—gently persuasive*] Here, let me take it, dear. You'll only step on it and tear it and get it dirty dragging it on the floor. Then you'd be sorry afterwards.

[*She lets him take it, regarding him from somewhere far away within herself, without recognition, without either affection or animosity.*]

MARY [*with the shy politeness of a well-bred young girl toward an elderly gentleman who relieves her of a bundle*] Thank you. You are very kind. [*She regards the wedding gown with a puzzled interest.*] It's a wedding gown. It's very lovely, isn't it? [*A shadow crosses her face and she looks vaguely uneasy.*] I remember now. I found it in the attic hidden in a trunk. But I don't know what I wanted it for. I'm going to be a nun—that is, if I can only find—[*She looks around the room, her forehead puckered again.*] What is it I'm looking for? I know it's something I lost. [*She moves back from* TYRONE, *aware of him now only as some obstacle in her path.*]

TYRONE [*in hopeless appeal*] Mary!

[*But it cannot penetrate her preoccupation. She doesn't seem to hear him. He gives up helplessly, shrinking into himself, even his defensive drunkenness taken from him, leaving him sick and sober. He sinks back on his chair, holding the wedding gown in his arms with an unconscious clumsy, protective gentleness.*]

JAMIE [*drops his hand from his face, his eyes on the table top. He has suddenly sobered up, too—dully*] It's no good, Papa. [*He recites from Swinburne's "A Leave-taking" and does it well, simply but with a bitter sadness.*]

"Let us rise up and part; she will not know.
Let us go seaward as the great winds go,
Full of blown sand and foam; what help is here?
There is no help, for all these things are so,
And all the world is bitter as a tear.
And how these things are, though ye strove to show,
She would not know."

MARY [*looking around her*] Something I miss terribly. It can't be altogether lost. [*She starts to move around in back of* JAMIE*'s chair.*]

JAMIE [*turns to look up into her face—and cannot help appealing pleadingly in his turn*] Mama!

[*She does not seem to hear. He looks away hopelessly.*]

Hell! What's the use? It's no good. [*He recites from "A Leave-taking" again with increased bitterness.*]

"Let us go hence, my songs; she will not hear.
Let us go hence together without fear;
Keep silence now, for singing-time is over,
And over all old things and all things dear.
She loves not you nor me as all we love her.
Yea, though we sang as angels in her ear,
She would not hear."

MARY [*looking around her*] Something I need terribly. I remember when I had it I was never lonely nor afraid. I can't have lost it forever, I would die if I thought that. Because then there would be no hope.

[*She moves like a sleepwalker, around the back of* JAMIE*'s chair, then forward toward left front, passing behind* EDMUND.]

EDMUND [*turns impulsively and grabs her arm. As he pleads he has the quality of a bewilderedly hurt little boy.*] Mama! It isn't a summer cold! I've got consumption!

MARY [*For a second he seems to have broken through to her. She trembles and her expression becomes terrified. She calls distractedly, as if giving a command to herself.*] No! [*And instantly she is far away again. She murmurs gently but impersonally*] You must not try to touch me. You must not try to hold me. It isn't right, when I am hoping to be a nun.

[*He lets his hand drop from her arm. She moves left to the front end of the sofa beneath the windows and sits down, facing front, her hands folded in her lap, in a demure school-girlish pose.*]

JAMIE [*gives Edmund a strange look of mingled pity and jealous gloating*] You damned fool. It's no good. [*He recites again from the Swinburne poem.*]

"Let us go hence, go hence; she will not see.
Sing all once more together; surely she,
She too, remembering days and words that were,
Will turn a little toward us, sighing; but we,
We are hence, we are gone, as though we had not been there.
Nay, and though all men seeing had pity on me,
She would not see."

TYRONE [*trying to shake off his hopeless stupor*] Oh, we're fools to pay any attention. It's the damned poison. But I've never known her to drown herself in it as deep as this. [*gruffly*] Pass me that bottle, Jamie. And stop reciting that damned morbid poetry. I won't have it in my house!

[JAMIE *pushes the bottle toward him. He pours a drink without disarranging the wedding gown he holds carefully over his other arm and on his lap, and shoves the bottle back.* JAMIE *pours his and passes the bottle to* EDMUND, *who, in turn, pours one.* TYRONE *lifts his glass and his sons follow suit mechanically, but before they can drink* MARY *speaks and they slowly lower their drinks to the table, forgetting them.*]

MARY [*staring dreamily before her. Her face looks extraordinarily youthful and innocent. The shyly eager, trusting smile is on her lips as she talks aloud to herself.*] I had a talk with Mother Elizabeth. She is so sweet and good. A saint on earth. I love her dearly. It may be sinful of me but I love her better than my own mother. Because she always understands, even before you say a word. Her kind blue eyes look right into your heart. You can't keep any secrets from her. You couldn't deceive her, even if you were mean enough to want to. [*She gives a little rebellious toss of her head—with girlish pique*] All the same, I don't think she was so understanding this time. I told her I wanted to be a nun. I explained how sure I was of my vocation, that I had prayed to the Blessed Virgin to make me sure, and to find me worthy. I told Mother I had had a true vision when I was praying in the shrine of Our Lady of Lourdes, on the little island in the lake. I said I knew, as surely as I knew I was kneeling there, that the Blessed Virgin had smiled and blessed me with her consent. But Mother Elizabeth told me I must be more sure than that, even, that I must prove it wasn't simply my imagination. She said, if I was so sure, then I wouldn't mind putting myself to a test by going home after I graduated, and living as other girls lived, going out to parties and dances and enjoying myself; and then if after a year or two I still felt sure, I could come back to see her and we would talk it over again. [*She tosses her head—indignantly*] I never dreamed Holy Mother would give me such advice! I was really shocked. I said, of course, I would do anything she suggested, but I knew it was simply a waste of time. After I left her, I felt all mixed up, so I went to the shrine and prayed to the Blessed Virgin and found peace again because I knew she heard my prayer and would always love me and see no harm ever came to me so long as I never lost my faith in her. [*She pauses and a look of growing uneasiness comes over her face. She passes a hand over her forehead as if brushing cobwebs from her brain—vaguely*] That was in the winter of senior year. Then in the spring something happened to me. Yes, I remember. I fell in love with James Tyrone and was so happy for a time. [*She stares before her in a sad dream.* TYRONE *stirs in his chair.* EDMUND *and* JAMIE *remain motionless.*]

CURTAIN

1940

CLAUDE McKAY
1889–1948

One of his biographers aptly calls Claude McKay a lifelong wanderer, a "sojourner" in the Harlem Renaissance. A Jamaican by birth, he did not become an American citizen until 1940; he left Harlem just when the Renaissance was getting started; he criticized leading black intellectuals like W. E. B. Du Bois and Alain Locke (who, in turn, criticized him). Nevertheless, *Harlem Shadows,* his 1922 book of poetry, is generally considered the book that initiated the Harlem Renaissance; his *Home to Harlem* (1928) was the only best-selling African American novel of the decade. Whether the Harlem Renaissance was a unified movement or a resonant label encompassing artists with diverse aims, whether McKay was an American Harlemite or a man of the world, he was unquestionably one of the most important black writers of the 1920s. As well as influencing African American literature, he has had a major impact on writing by West Indians and Africans.

Claude McKay (Festus Claudius McKay) was born in Sunny Ville, a rural village in central Jamaica. This village, with its setting of spectacular natural beauty, became in later years his symbol of a lost golden age. McKay's grandfather, a West African Ashanti, had been brought to the island as a slave, and McKay's father passed on to his son what he remembered of Ashanti values and rituals. Economic necessity led the young McKay to Kingston (Jamaica's principal city) in 1909, where he was apprenticed to a cabinetmaker and wheelwright. Combining his emerging literary ambitions with an interest in Jamaican folkways, McKay published two ground-breaking books of dialect poetry—*Songs of Jamaica* and *Constab Ballads*—in 1912. Prize money from these books took him to the United States to study agriculture, but his literary ambitions drew him to New York City after two years in school (first at the Tuskegee Institute, then at Kansas State College). He married his Jamaican sweetheart, Eulalie Imelda Lewars, in 1914; the couple had a daughter, but the marriage did not last. Supporting himself in jobs like restaurant kitchen helper and Pullman railroad waiter, he began to publish in avant-garde journals; by 1917 he was appearing in *The Seven Arts, Pearson's,* and the prominent left-wing *Liberator,* edited by Max Eastman. *The Liberator* published his famous poem "If We Must Die" in 1919. His poetry, much of it written in strict sonnet form, braided racial subject matter, radical politics, and poetic technique into compelling statements that were also good poetry according to traditional standards.

McKay's radical politics, already formed in Jamaica, rose from his belief that racism was inseparable from capitalism, which he saw as a structure designed to perpetuate economic inequality. To him, attacking capitalism was attacking racial injustice. Before the publication of *Harlem Shadows,* McKay had spent 1919–21 in England; in 1923 he went to Moscow, where he was welcomed as a celebrity. His connections to the Communist regime in Russia made him a target for the FBI, which issued orders to keep him from returning to the United States. He stayed in Europe until 1934, living mainly in France but also in Spain and Morocco. *Home to Harlem* (1928), written mostly in France, was an episodic guide to Harlem's artistic, popular, and intellectual life. Later events turned it into one of the movement's last statements; retrenchment in the publishing industry after the stock market crash of 1929, the emergence of younger African American writers with different values, and dissension among Harlem artists themselves combined to bring an end to the Harlem Renaissance and altered the character of life in Harlem itself.

When McKay was finally able to return to the United States in 1934, the nation was deep in the Great Depression. With general unemployment at over 25 percent, paid literary work was extremely hard to come by. In 1935 he joined the New York City branch of the Federal Writers' Project, a New Deal organization giving work to unemployed writers. Except for his important autobiography, *A Long Way from Home* (1937), he did little creative work, and his health failed. Through his friendship with Ellen Tarry, a young African American writer who was a Catholic, he received medical care from Friendship House, a Catholic lay organization in Harlem. In the later years of his life, appalled by Stalin's purges, McKay repudiated his earlier Communist sympathies. He began to work at Friendship House and, after moving to Chicago, worked for the Catholic Youth Organization. He converted to Catholicism in 1944 and died in Chicago four years later.

All texts are from *Harlem Shadows* (1922).

The Harlem Dancer

Applauding youths laughed with young prostitutes
And watched her perfect, half-clothed body sway;
Her voice was like the sound of blended flutes
Blown by black players upon a picnic day.
She sang and danced on gracefully and calm,
The light gauze hanging loose about her form;
To me she seemed a proudly-swaying palm
Grown lovelier for passing through a storm.
Upon her swarthy neck black shiny curls
Luxuriant fell; and tossing coins in praise,
The wine-flushed, bold-eyed boys, and even the girls,
Devoured her shape with eager, passionate gaze;
But looking at her falsely-smiling face,
I knew her self was not in that strange place.

1917, 1922

Harlem Shadows

I hear the halting footsteps of a lass
  In Negro Harlem when the night lets fall
Its veil. I see the shapes of girls who pass
  To bend and barter at desire's call.
Ah, little dark girls who in slippered feet
Go prowling through the night from street to street!

Through the long night until the silver break
  Of day the little gray feet know no rest;
Through the lone night until the last snow-flake
  Has dropped from heaven upon the earth's white breast,
The dusky, half-clad girls of tired feet
Are trudging, thinly shod, from street to street.

Ah, stern harsh world, that in the wretched way
  Of poverty, dishonor and disgrace,
Has pushed the timid little feet of clay,
  The sacred brown feet of my fallen race!
Ah, heart of me, the weary, weary feet
In Harlem wandering from street to street.

1918, 1922

The Lynching

His Spirit in smoke ascended to high heaven.
His father, by the cruelest way of pain,
Had bidden him to his bosom once again;
The awful sin remained still unforgiven.
All night a bright and solitary star
(Perchance the one that ever guided him,
Yet gave him up at last to Fate's wild whim)
Hung pitifully o'er the swinging char.
Day dawned, and soon the mixed crowds came to view
The ghastly body swaying in the sun
The women thronged to look, but never a one
Showed sorrow in her eyes of steely blue;
And little lads, lynchers that were to be,
Danced round the dreadful thing in fiendish glee.

1919, 1922

If We Must Die

If we must die, let it not be like hogs
Hunted and penned in an inglorious spot,
While round us bark the mad and hungry dogs,
Making their mock at our accursèd lot.
If we must die, O let us nobly die,
So that our precious blood may not be shed
In vain; then even the monsters we defy
Shall be constrained to honor us though dead!
O kinsmen! we must meet the common foe!
Though far outnumbered let us show us brave,
And for their thousand blows deal one deathblow!
What though before us lies the open grave?
Like men we'll face the murderous, cowardly pack,
Pressed to the wall, dying, but fighting back!

1919, 1922

Africa

The sun sought thy dim bed and brought forth light,
The sciences were sucklings at thy breast;
When all the world was young in pregnant night
Thy slaves toiled at thy monumental best.
Thou ancient treasure-land, thou modern prize,
New peoples marvel at thy pyramids!
The years roll on, thy sphinx of riddle eyes

Watches the mad world with immobile lids.
The Hebrews humbled them at Pharaoh's name.
Cradle of Power! Yet all things were in vain!
Honor and Glory, Arrogance and Fame!
They went. The darkness swallowed thee again.
Thou art the harlot, now thy time is done,
Of all the mighty nations of the sun.

1921, 1922

America

Although she feeds me bread of bitterness,
And sinks into my throat her tiger's tooth,
Stealing my breath of life, I will confess
I love this cultured hell that tests my youth!
Her vigor flows like tides into my blood,
Giving me strength erect against her hate.
Her bigness sweeps my being like a flood.
Yet as a rebel fronts a king in state,
I stand within her walls with not a shred
Of terror, malice, not a word of jeer.
Darkly I gaze into the days ahead,
And see her might and granite wonders there,
Beneath the touch of Time's unerring hand,
Like priceless treasures sinking in the sand.

1921, 1922

KATHERINE ANNE PORTER
1890–1980

Over a long writing life Katherine Anne Porter produced only four books of stories and one novel, *Ship of Fools,* which did not appear until she was over seventy. Her reputation as a prose writer did not depend on quantity; each story was technically skilled, emotionally powerful, combining traditional narration with new symbolic techniques and contemporary subject matter.

Callie Porter—she changed the name to Katherine Anne when she became a writer—was born in the small settlement of Indian Creek, Texas; her mother died soon after giving birth to her fourth child, when Porter was not quite two years old. Her father moved them all to his mother's home in Kyle, Texas, where the paternal grandmother raised the family in extreme poverty. The father gave up all attempts to support them either financially or emotionally; the security provided by the strong, loving, but pious and stern grandmother ended with her death when Porter was eleven. Porter married to leave home immediately after her sixteenth birthday, only to find that rooted domesticity was not for her. Long before her divorce in 1915, she had separated from her first husband and begun a life of travel, activity, and changes of jobs.

She started writing in 1916 as a reporter for a Dallas newspaper. In 1917 she moved to Denver, the next year to New York City's Greenwich Village. Between 1918 and 1924 she lived mainly in Mexico, freelancing, meeting artists and intellectuals, and becoming involved in revolutionary politics. In Mexico she found the resources of journalism inadequate to her ambitions; using an anecdote she had heard from an archaeologist as a kernel, she wrote her first story, "María Concepción," which was published in the prestigious *Century* magazine in 1922. Like all her stories, it dealt with powerful emotions and had a strong sense of locale. Critics praised her as a major talent.

Although she considered herself a serious writer from this time on, Porter was distracted from fiction by many crosscurrents. A self-supporting woman with expensive tastes, she hesitated to give up lucrative freelance offers. She enjoyed travel and gladly took on jobs that sent her abroad. She became involved in political causes, including the Sacco-Vanzetti case. She was married four times.

Porter planned each story meticulously—taking extensive notes, devising scenarios, roughing out dialogue, and revising many times, sometimes over a period of years. She did not write confessional or simple autobiographical fiction, but each story originated in an important experience of her life. Although not a feminist, Porter devoted much of her work to exploring the tensions in women's lives in the modern era. The story that made her famous for life, so that everything else she published thereafter was looked on as a literary event, was "Flowering Judas" (1929), set in Mexico and dealing with revolutionary politics, lust, and betrayal. The reality of mixed motives and the difference between pure idealism and egotistical opportunism as they are encountered in revolutionary politics are among the themes in this deceptively simple narrative. It appeared in the little magazine *Hound and Horn.* The collections *Flowering Judas* and *Noon Wine* came out in 1930 and 1937. In 1930 Porter went back to Mexico and the following year to Europe on a Guggenheim fellowship; she lived in Berlin, Paris, and Basel before returning to the United States in 1936. Two more collections of stories and novellas appeared in 1939 (*Pale Horse, Pale Rider*) and in 1944 (*The Leaning Tower*). These later collections feature several stories about Miranda Gay, a character who is partly autobiographical and partly an idealized image of the southern belle facing the modern world. *Pale Horse, Pale Rider* narrates Miranda's World War I romance with a soldier in the highly charged political climate of the American home front.

Soon after arriving in Europe in 1931 Porter began working on a novel, but it was not until 1962 that *Ship of Fools,* which runs to almost five hundred pages, appeared. Set on an ocean liner crossing the Atlantic to Germany in August 1931, it explores the characters and developing relationships of a large number of passengers; the ship, as Porter wrote in a preface, stands for "this world on its voyage to eternity." As in "Flowering Judas" and *Pale Horse, Pale Rider* the personal and the political intersect in *Ship of Fools,* since the coming of Nazism in Germany frames the interlinked stories of the travelers. In its film version, *Ship of Fools* brought Porter a great deal of money. Capitalizing on the publicity, her publishers brought out the *Collected Stories* in 1965, from which followed the National Book Award, the Pulitzer Prize, the Gold Medal for fiction of the National Institute of Arts and Letters, and election to the American Academy of Letters, all in the next two years. The happiest occasions in her later years—she lived to be ninety—were connected with endowing and establishing the Katherine Anne Porter Room at the University of Maryland, not far from her last home near Washington, D.C.

The texts are from the *Collected Stories* (1965).

Flowering Judas[1]

Braggioni sits heaped upon the edge of a straight-backed chair much too small for him, and sings to Laura in a furry, mournful voice. Laura has begun to find reasons for avoiding her own house until the latest possible moment, for Braggioni is there almost every night. No matter how late she is, he will be sitting there with a surly, waiting expression, pulling at his kinky yellow hair, thumbing the strings of his guitar, snarling a tune under his breath. Lupe the Indian maid meets Laura at the door, and says with a flicker of a glance towards the upper room, "He waits."

Laura wishes to lie down, she is tired of her hairpins and the feel of her long tight sleeves, but she says to him, "Have you a new song for me this evening?" If he says yes, she asks him to sing it. If he says no, she remembers his favorite one, and asks him to sing it again. Lupe brings her a cup of chocolate and a plate of rice, and Laura eats at the small table under the lamp, first inviting Braggioni, whose answer is always the same: "I have eaten, and besides, chocolate thickens the voice."

Laura says, "Sing, then," and Braggioni heaves himself into song. He scratches the guitar familiarly as though it were a pet animal, and sings passionately off key, taking the high notes in a prolonged painful squeal. Laura, who haunts the markets listening to the ballad singers, and stops every day to hear the blind boy playing his reed-flute in Sixteenth of September Street,[2] listens to Braggioni with pitiless courtesy, because she dares not smile at his miserable performance. Nobody dares to smile at him. Braggioni is cruel to everyone, with a kind of specialized insolence, but he is so vain of his talents, and so sensitive to slights, it would require a cruelty and vanity greater than his own to lay a finger on the vast cureless wound of his self-esteem. It would require courage, too, for it is dangerous to offend him, and nobody has this courage.

Braggioni loves himself with such tenderness and amplitude and eternal charity that his followers—for he is a leader of men, a skilled revolutionist, and his skin has been punctured in honorable warfare—warm themselves in the reflected glow, and say to each other: "He has a real nobility, a love of humanity raised above mere personal affections." The excess of this self-love has flowed out, inconveniently for her, over Laura, who, with so many others, owes her comfortable situation and her salary to him. When he is in a very good humor, he tells her, "I am tempted to forgive you for being a *gringa. Gringita!*"[3] and Laura, burning, imagines herself leaning forward suddenly, and with a sound back-handed slap wiping the suety smile from his face. If he notices her eyes at these moments he gives no sign.

She knows what Braggioni would offer her, and she must resist tenaciously without appearing to resist, and if she could avoid it she would not admit even to herself the slow drift of his intention. During these long evenings which have spoiled a long month for her, she sits in her deep chair

1. One of a genus of trees and shrubs with purplish rosy flowers. According to legend, Judas Iscariot, betrayer of Jesus, hanged himself from such a tree.
2. A street in Morelia, a city in western Mexico where the story is set.
3. A young female foreigner, non-Mexican girl; a patronizing term meaning "cute little foreign girl." Diminutive of *gringa,* which is used pejoratively, especially for an American.

with an open book on her knees, resting her eyes on the consoling rigidity of the printed page when the sight and sound of Braggioni singing threaten to identify themselves with all her remembered afflictions and to add their weight to her uneasy premonitions of the future. The gluttonous bulk of Braggioni has become a symbol of her many disillusions, for a revolutionist should be lean, animated by heroic faith, a vessel of abstract virtues. This is nonsense, she knows it now and is ashamed of it. Revolution must have leaders, and leadership is a career for energetic men. She is, her comrades tell her, full of romantic error, for what she defines as cynicism in them is merely "a developed sense of reality." She is almost too willing to say, "I am wrong, I suppose I don't really understand the principles," and afterward she makes a secret truce with herself, determined not to surrender her will to such expedient logic. But she cannot help feeling that she has been betrayed irreparably by the disunion between her way of living and her feeling of what life should be, and at times she is almost contented to rest in this sense of grievance as a private store of consolation. Sometimes she wishes to run away, but she stays. Now she longs to fly out of this room, down the narrow stairs, and into the street where the houses lean together like conspirators under a single mottled lamp, and leave Braggioni singing to himself.

Instead she looks at Braggioni, frankly and clearly, like a good child who understands the rules of behavior. Her knees cling together under sound blue serge, and her round white collar is not purposely nun-like. She wears the uniform of an idea, and has renounced vanities. She was born Roman Catholic, and in spite of her fear of being seen by someone who might make a scandal of it, she slips now and again into some crumbling little church, kneels on the chilly stone, and says a Hail Mary on the gold rosary she bought in Tehuantepec. It is no good and she ends by examining the altar with its tinsel flowers and ragged brocades, and feels tender about the battered doll-shape of some male saint whose white, lace-trimmed drawers hang limply around his ankles below the hieratic dignity of his velvet robe. She has encased herself in a set of principles derived from her early training, leaving no detail of gesture or of personal taste untouched, and for this reason she will not wear lace made on machines. This is her private heresy, for in her special group the machine is sacred, and will be the salvation of the workers. She loves fine lace, and there is a tiny edge of fluted cobweb on this collar, which is one of twenty precisely alike, folded in blue tissue paper in the upper drawer of her clothes chest.

Braggioni catches her glance solidly as if he had been waiting for it, leans forward, balancing his paunch between his spread knees, and sings with tremendous emphasis, weighing his words. He has, the song relates, no father and no mother, nor even a friend to console him; lonely as a wave of the sea he comes and goes, lonely as a wave. His mouth opens round and yearns sideways, his balloon cheeks grow oily with the labor of song. He bulges marvelously in his expensive garments. Over his lavender collar, crushed upon a purple necktie, held by a diamond hoop: over his ammunition belt of tooled leather worked in silver, buckled cruelly around his gasping middle: over the tops of his glossy yellow shoes Braggioni swells with ominous ripeness, his mauve silk hose stretched taut, his ankles bound with the stout leather thongs of his shoes.

When he stretches his eyelids at Laura she notes again that his eyes are the true tawny yellow cat's eyes. He is rich, not in money, he tells her, but in power, and this power brings with it the blameless ownership of things, and the right to indulge his love of small luxuries. "I have a taste for the elegant refinements," he said once, flourishing a yellow silk handkerchief before her nose. "Smell that? It is Jockey Club, imported from New York." Nonetheless he is wounded by life. He will say so presently. "It is true everything turns to dust in the hand, to gall on the tongue." He sighs and his leather belt creaks like a saddle girth. "I am disappointed in everything as it comes. Everything." He shakes his head. "You, poor thing, you will be disappointed too. You are born for it. We are more alike than you realize in some things. Wait and see. Some day you will remember what I have told you, you will know that Braggioni was your friend."

Laura feels a slow chill, a purely physical sense of danger, a warning in her blood that violence, mutilation, a shocking death, wait for her with lessening patience. She has translated this fear into something homely, immediate, and sometimes hesitates before crossing the street. "My personal fate is nothing, except as the testimony of a mental attitude," she reminds herself, quoting from some forgotten philosophic primer, and is sensible enough to add, "Anyhow, I shall not be killed by an automobile if I can help it."

"It may be true I am as corrupt, in another way, as Braggioni," she thinks in spite of herself, "as callous, as incomplete," and if this is so, any kind of death seems preferable. Still she sits quietly, she does not run. Where could she go? Uninvited she has promised herself to this place; she can no longer imagine herself as living in another country, and there is no pleasure in remembering her life before she came here.

Precisely what is the nature of this devotion, its true motives, and what are its obligations? Laura cannot say. She spends part of her days in Xochimilco, near by, teaching Indian children to say in English, "The cat is on the mat." When she appears in the classroom they crowd about her with smiles on their wise, innocent, clay-colored faces, crying, "Good morning, my titcher!" in immaculate voices, and they make of her desk a fresh garden of flowers every day.

During her leisure she goes to union meetings and listens to busy important voices quarreling over tactics, methods, internal politics. She visits the prisoners of her own political faith in their cells, where they entertain themselves with counting cockroaches, repenting of their indiscretions, composing their memoirs, writing out manifestoes and plans for their comrades who are still walking about free, hands in pockets, sniffing fresh air. Laura brings them food and cigarettes and a little money, and she brings messages disguised in equivocal phrases from the men outside who dare not set foot in the prison for fear of disappearing into the cells kept empty for them. If the prisoners confuse night and day, and complain, "Dear little Laura, time doesn't pass in this infernal hole, and I won't know when it is time to sleep unless I have a reminder," she brings them their favorite narcotics, and says in a tone that does not wound them with pity, "Tonight will really be night for you," and though her Spanish amuses them, they find her comforting, useful. If they lose patience and all faith, and curse the slowness of their friends in coming to their rescue with money and influence, they trust her not to repeat everything, and if she inquires, "Where do you think we can find money, or influence?" they are certain to answer, "Well, there is Braggioni, why doesn't he do something?"

She smuggles letters from headquarters to men hiding from firing squads in back streets in mildewed houses, where they sit in tumbled beds and talk bitterly as if all Mexico were at their heels, when Laura knows positively they might appear at the band concert in the Alameda[4] on Sunday morning, and no one would notice them. But Braggioni says, "Let them sweat a little. The next time they may be careful. It is very restful to have them out of the way for a while." She is not afraid to knock on any door in any street after midnight, and enter in the darkness, and say to one of these men who is really in danger: "They will be looking for you—seriously—tomorrow morning after six. Here is some money from Vicente. Go to Vera Cruz and wait."

She borrows money from the Roumanian agitator to give to his bitter enemy the Polish agitator. The favor of Braggioni is their disputed territory, and Braggioni holds the balance nicely, for he can use them both. The Polish agitator talks love to her over café tables, hoping to exploit what he believes is her secret sentimental preference for him, and he gives her misinformation which he begs her to repeat as the solemn truth to certain persons. The Roumanian is more adroit. He is generous with his money in all good causes, and lies to her with an air of ingenuous candor, as if he were her good friend and confidant. She never repeats anything they may say. Braggioni never asks questions. He has other ways to discover all that he wishes to know about them.

Nobody touches her, but all praise her gray eyes, and the soft, round under lip which promises gayety, yet is always grave, nearly always firmly closed: and they cannot understand why she is in Mexico. She walks back and forth on her errands, with puzzled eyebrows, carrying her little folder of drawings and music and school papers. No dancer dances more beautifully than Laura walks, and she inspires some amusing, unexpected ardors, which cause little gossip, because nothing comes of them. A young captain who had been a soldier in Zapata's[5] army attempted, during a horseback ride near Cuernavaca, to express his desire for her with the noble simplicity befitting a rude folk-hero: but gently, because he was gentle. This gentleness was his defeat, for when he alighted, and removed her foot from the stirrup, and essayed to draw her down into his arms, her horse, ordinarily a tame one, shied fiercely, reared and plunged away. The young hero's horse careered blindly after his stable-mate, and the hero did not return to the hotel until rather late that evening. At breakfast he came to her table in full charro dress,[6] gray buckskin jacket and trousers with strings of silver buttons down the leg, and he was in a humorous, careless mood. "May I sit with you?" and "You are a wonderful rider. I was terrified that you might be thrown and dragged. I should never have forgiven myself. But I cannot admire you enough for your riding!"

"I learned to ride in Arizona," said Laura.

4. Public promenade bordered with trees.
5. Emiliano Zapata (c. 1879–1919), Mexican peasant revolutionary general whose movement, *zapatismo*, combined agrarian and Mexican Indian cultural aspirations; one of the most significant figures in Mexico from 1910 to 1919, when he was murdered.
6. Costume worn by a peasant horseman of special status.

"If you will ride with me again this morning, I promise you a horse that will not shy with you," he said. But Laura remembered that she must return to Mexico City at noon.

Next morning the children made a celebration and spent their playtime writing on the blackboard, "We lov ar ticher," and with tinted chalks they drew wreaths of flowers around the words. The young hero wrote her a letter: "I am a very foolish, wasteful, impulsive man. I should have first said I love you, and then you would not have run away. But you shall see me again." Laura thought, "I must send him a box of colored crayons," but she was trying to forgive herself for having spurred her horse at the wrong moment.

A brown, shock-haired youth came and stood in her patio one night and sang like a lost soul for two hours, but Laura could think of nothing to do about it. The moonlight spread a wash of gauzy silver over the clear spaces of the garden, and the shadows were cobalt blue. The scarlet blossoms of the Judas tree were dull purple, and the names of the colors repeated themselves automatically in her mind, while she watched not the boy, but his shadow, fallen like a dark garment across the fountain rim, trailing in the water. Lupe came silently and whispered expert counsel in her ear: "If you will throw him one little flower, he will sing another song or two and go away." Laura threw the flower, and he sang a last song and went away with the flower tucked in the band of his hat. Lupe said, "He is one of the organizers of the Typographers Union, and before that he sold corridos[7] in the Merced market, and before that, he came from Guanajuato, where I was born. I would not trust any man, but I trust least those from Guanajuato."

She did not tell Laura that he would be back again the next night, and the next, nor that he would follow her at a certain fixed distance around the Merced market, through the Zócolo, up Francisco I. Madero Avenue, and so along the Paseo de la Reforma to Chapultepec Park, and into the Philosopher's Footpath, still with that flower withering in his hat, and an indivisible attention in his eyes.

Now Laura is accustomed to him, it means nothing except that he is nineteen years old and is observing a convention with all propriety, as though it were founded on a law of nature, which in the end it might well prove to be. He is beginning to write poems which he prints on a wooden press, and he leaves them stuck like handbills in her door. She is pleasantly disturbed by the abstract, unhurried watchfulness of his black eyes which will in time turn easily towards another object. She tells herself that throwing the flower was a mistake, for she is twenty-two years old and knows better; but she refuses to regret it, and persuades herself that her negation of all external events as they occur is a sign that she is gradually perfecting herself in the stoicism she strives to cultivate against that disaster she fears, though she cannot name it.

She is not at home in the world. Every day she teaches children who remain strangers to her, though she loves their tender round hands and their charming opportunist savagery. She knocks at unfamiliar doors not knowing whether a friend or a stranger shall answer, and even if a known face emerges from the sour gloom of that unknown interior, still it is the face of a stranger. No matter what this stranger says to her, nor what her message to him, the

7. Popular ballads.

very cells of her flesh reject knowledge and kinship in one monotonous word. No. No. No. She draws her strength from this one holy talismanic word which does not suffer her to be led into evil. Denying everything, she may walk anywhere in safety, she looks at everything without amazement.

No, repeats this firm unchanging voice of her blood; and she looks at Braggioni without amazement. He is a great man, he wishes to impress this simple girl who covers her great round breasts with thick dark cloth, and who hides long, invaluably beautiful legs under a heavy skirt. She is almost thin except for the incomprehensible fullness of her breasts, like a nursing mother's, and Braggioni, who considers himself a judge of women, speculates again on the puzzle of her notorious virginity, and takes the liberty of speech which she permits without a sign of modesty, indeed, without any sort of sign, which is disconcerting.

"You think you are so cold, *gringita!* Wait and see. You will surprise yourself some day! May I be there to advise you!" He stretches his eyelids at her, and his ill-humored cat's eyes waver in a separate glance for the two points of light marking the opposite ends of a smoothly drawn path between the swollen curve of her breasts. He is not put off by that blue serge, nor by her resolutely fixed gaze. There is all the time in the world. His cheeks are bellying with the wind of song. "O girl with the dark eyes," he sings, and reconsiders. "But yours are not dark. I can change all that. O girl with the green eyes, you have stolen my heart away!" then his mind wanders to the song, and Laura feels the weight of his attention being shifted elsewhere. Singing thus, he seems harmless, he is quite harmless, there is nothing to do but sit patiently and say "No," when the moment comes. She draws a full breath, and her mind wanders also, but not far. She dares not wander too far.

Not for nothing has Braggioni taken pains to be a good revolutionist and a professional lover of humanity. He will never die of it. He has the malice, the cleverness, the wickedness, the sharpness of wit, the hardness of heart, stipulated for loving the world profitably. *He will never die of it.* He will live to see himself kicked out from his feeding trough by other hungry world-saviors. Traditionally he must sing in spite of his life which drives him to bloodshed, he tells Laura, for his father was a Tuscany[8] peasant who drifted to Yucatan and married a Maya woman: a woman of race, an aristocrat. They gave him the love and knowledge of music, thus: and under the rip of his thumbnail, the strings of the instrument complain like exposed nerves.

Once he was called Delgadito by all the girls and married women who ran after him; he was so scrawny all his bones showed under his thin cotton clothing, and he could squeeze his emptiness to the very backbone with his two hands. He was a poet and the revolution was only a dream then; too many women loved him and sapped away his youth, and he could never find enough to eat anywhere, anywhere! Now he is a leader of men, crafty men who whisper in his ear, hungry men who wait for hours outside his office for a word with him, emaciated men with wild faces who waylay him at the street gate with a timid, "Comrade, let me tell you . . ." and they blow the foul breath from their empty stomachs in his face.

He is always sympathetic. He gives them handfuls of small coins from his own pocket, he promises them work, there will be demonstrations, they

8. A region in north-central Italy.

must join the unions and attend the meetings, above all they must be on the watch for spies. They are closer to him than his own brothers, without them he can do nothing—until tomorrow, comrade!

Until tomorrow. "They are stupid, they are lazy, they are treacherous, they would cut my throat for nothing," he says to Laura. He has good food and abundant drink, he hires an automobile and drives in the Paseo on Sunday morning, and enjoys plenty of sleep in a soft bed beside a wife who dares not disturb him; and he sits pampering his bones in easy billows of fat, singing to Laura, who knows and thinks these things about him. When he was fifteen, he tried to drown himself because he loved a girl, his first love, and she laughed at him. "A thousand women have paid for that," and his tight little mouth turns down at the corners. Now he perfumes his hair with Jockey Club, and confides to Laura: "One woman is really as good as another for me, in the dark. I prefer them all."

His wife organizes unions among the girls in the cigarette factories, and walks in picket lines, and even speaks at meetings in the evening. But she cannot be brought to acknowledge the benefits of true liberty. "I tell her I must have my freedom, net. She does not understand my point of view." Laura has heard this many times. Braggioni scratches the guitar and meditates. "She is an instinctively virtuous woman, pure gold, no doubt of that. If she were not, I should lock her up, and she knows it."

His wife, who works so hard for the good of the factory girls, employs part of her leisure lying on the floor weeping because there are so many women in the world, and only one husband for her, and she never knows where nor when to look for him. He told her: "Unless you can learn to cry when I am not here, I must go away for good." That day he went away and took a room at the Hotel Madrid.

It is this month of separation for the sake of higher principles that has been spoiled not only for Mrs. Braggioni, whose sense of reality is beyond criticism, but for Laura, who feels herself bogged in a nightmare. Tonight Laura envies Mrs. Braggioni, who is alone, and free to weep as much as she pleases about a concrete wrong. Laura has just come from a visit to the prison, and she is waiting for tomorrow with a bitter anxiety as if tomorrow may not come, but time may be caught immovably in this hour, with herself transfixed, Braggioni singing on forever, and Eugenio's body not yet discovered by the guard.

Braggioni says: "Are you going to sleep?" Almost before she can shake her head, he begins telling her about the May-day disturbances coming on in Morelia, for the Catholics hold a festival in honor of the Blessed Virgin, and the Socialists celebrate their martyrs on that day. "There will be two independent processions, starting from either end of town, and they will march until they meet, and the rest depends . . ." He asks her to oil and load his pistols. Standing up, he unbuckles his ammunition belt, and spreads it laden across her knees. Laura sits with the shells slipping through the cleaning cloth dipped in oil, and he says again he cannot understand why she works so hard for the revolutionary idea unless she loves some man who is in it. "Are you not in love with someone?" "No," says Laura. "And no one is in love with you?" "No." "Then it is your own fault. No woman need go begging. Why, what is the matter with you? The legless beggar woman in the Alameda has a perfectly faithful lover. Did you know that?"

Laura peers down the pistol barrel and says nothing, but a long, slow faintness rises and subsides in her; Braggioni curves his swollen fingers around the throat of the guitar and softly smothers the music out of it, and when she hears him again he seems to have forgotten her, and is speaking in the hypnotic voice he uses when talking in small rooms to a listening, close-gathered crowd. Some day this world, now seemingly so composed and eternal, to the edges of every sea shall be merely a tangle of gaping trenches, of crashing walls and broken bodies. Everything must be torn from its accustomed place where it has rotted for centuries, hurled skyward and distributed, cast down again clean as rain, without separate identity. Nothing shall survive that the stiffened hands of poverty have created for the rich and no one shall be left alive except the elect spirits destined to procreate a new world cleansed of cruelty and injustice, ruled by benevolent anarchy: "Pistols are good, I love them, cannon are even better, but in the end I pin my faith to good dynamite," he concludes, and strokes the pistol lying in her hands. "Once I dreamed of destroying this city, in case it offered resistance to General Ortíz, but it fell into his hands like an overripe pear."

He is made restless by his own words, rises and stands waiting. Laura holds up the belt to him: "Put that on, and go kill somebody in Morelia, and you will be happier," she says softly. The presence of death in the room makes her bold. "Today, I found Eugenio going into a stupor. He refused to allow me to call the prison doctor. He had taken all the tablets I brought him yesterday. He said he took them because he was bored."

"He is a fool, and his death is his own business," says Braggioni, fastening his belt carefully.

"I told him if he had waited only a little while longer, you would have got him set free," says Laura. "He said he did not want to wait."

"He is a fool and we are well rid of him," says Braggioni, reaching for his hat.

He goes away. Laura knows his mood has changed, she will not see him any more for a while. He will send word when he needs her to go on errands into strange streets, to speak to the strange faces that will appear, like clay masks with the power of human speech, to mutter their thanks to Braggioni for his help. Now she is free, and she thinks, I must run while there is time. But she does not go.

Braggioni enters his own house where for a month his wife has spent many hours every night weeping and tangling her hair upon her pillow. She is weeping now, and she weeps more at the sight of him, the cause of all her sorrows. He looks about the room. Nothing is changed, the smells are good and familiar, he is well acquainted with the woman who comes toward him with no reproach except grief on her face. He says to her tenderly: "You are so good, please don't cry any more, you dear good creature." She says, "Are you tired, my angel? Sit here and I will wash your feet." She brings a bowl of water, and kneeling, unlaces his shoes, and when from her knees she raises her sad eyes under her blackened lids, he is sorry for everything, and bursts into tears. "Ah, yes, I am hungry, I am tired, let us eat something together," he says, between sobs. His wife leans her head on his arm and says, "Forgive me!" and this time he is refreshed by the solemn, endless rain of her tears.

Laura takes off her serge dress and puts on a white linen nightgown and goes to bed. She turns her head a little to one side, and lying still, reminds herself that it is time to sleep. Numbers tick in her brain like little clocks, soundless doors close of themselves around her. If you would sleep, you must not remember anything, the children will say tomorrow, good morning, my teacher, the poor prisoners who come every day bringing flowers to their jailor. 1-2-3-4-5—it is monstrous to confuse love with revolution, night with day, life with death—ah, Eugenio!

The tolling of the midnight bell is a signal, but what does it mean? Get up, Laura, and follow me: come out of your sleep, out of your bed, out of this strange house. What are you doing in this house? Without a word, without fear she rose and reached for Eugenio's hand, but he eluded her with a sharp, sly smile and drifted away. This is not all, you shall see—Murderer, he said, follow me, I will show you a new country, but it is far away and we must hurry. No, said Laura, not unless you take my hand, no; and she clung first to the stair rail, and then to the topmost branch of the Judas tree that bent down slowly and set her upon the earth, and then to the rocky ledge of a cliff, and then to the jagged wave of a sea that was not water but a desert of crumbling stone. Where are you taking me, she asked in wonder but without fear. To death, and it is a long way off, and we must hurry, said Eugenio. No, said Laura, not unless you take my hand. Then eat these flowers, poor prisoner, said Eugenio in a voice of pity, take and eat: and from the Judas tree he stripped the warm bleeding flowers, and held them to her lips. She saw that his hand was fleshless, a cluster of small white petrified branches, and his eye sockets were without light, but she ate the flowers greedily for they satisfied both hunger and thirst. Murderer! said Eugenio, and Cannibal! This is my body and my blood. Laura cried No! and at the sound of her own voice, she awoke trembling, and was afraid to sleep again.

1929, 1930

Pale Horse, Pale Rider[1]

In sleep she knew she was in her bed, but not the bed she had lain down in a few hours since, and the room was not the same but it was a room she had known somewhere. Her heart was a stone lying upon her breast outside of her; her pulses lagged and paused, and she knew that something strange was going to happen, even as the early morning winds were cool through the lattice, the streaks of light were dark blue and the whole house was snoring in its sleep.

Now I must get up and go while they are all quiet. Where are my things? Things have a will of their own in this place and hide where they like. Daylight will strike a sudden blow on the roof startling them all up to their feet; faces will beam asking, Where are you going, What are you doing, What are you thinking, How do you feel, Why do you say such things, What do you

1. First words of an African American spiritual, based on Revelation 6, in which four horses and their riders associated with the Apocalypse appear: "power was given unto them over the fourth part of the earth, to kill with sword, and with hunger, and with death, and with the beasts of the earth" (verse 8). The last of these figures is a "pale horse: and his name that sat on him was Death, and Hell followed with him" (verse 8).

mean? No more sleep. Where are my boots and what horse shall I ride? Fiddler or Graylie or Miss Lucy with the long nose and the wicked eye? How I have loved this house in the morning before we are all awake and tangled together like badly cast fishing lines. Too many people have been born here, and have wept too much here, and have laughed too much, and have been too angry and outrageous with each other here. Too many have died in this bed already, there are far too many ancestral bones propped up on the mantel-pieces, there have been too damned many antimacassars in this house, she said loudly, and oh, what accumulation of storied dust never allowed to settle in peace for one moment.

And the stranger? Where is that lank greenish stranger I remember hanging about the place, welcomed by my grandfather, my great-aunt, my five times removed cousin, my decrepit hound and my silver kitten? Why did they take to him, I wonder? And where are they now? Yet I saw him pass the window in the evening. What else besides them did I have in the world? Nothing. Nothing is mine, I have only nothing but it is enough, it is beautiful and it is all mine. Do I even walk about in my own skin or is it something I have borrowed to spare my modesty? Now what horse shall I borrow for this journey I do not mean to take, Graylie or Miss Lucy or Fiddler who can jump ditches in the dark and knows how to get the bit between his teeth? Early morning is best for me because trees are trees in one stroke, stones are stones set in shades known to be grass, there are no false shapes or surmises, the road is still asleep with the crust of dew unbroken. I'll take Graylie because he is not afraid of bridges.

Come now, Graylie, she said, taking his bridle, we must outrun Death and the Devil. You are no good for it, she told the other horses standing saddled before the stable gate, among them the horse of the stranger, gray also, with tarnished nose and ears. The stranger swung into his saddle beside her, leaned far towards her and regarded her without meaning, the blank still stare of mindless malice that makes no threats and can bide its time. She drew Graylie around sharply, urged him to run. He leaped the low rose hedge and the narrow ditch beyond, and the dust of the lane flew heavily under his beating hoofs. The stranger rode beside her, easily, lightly, his reins loose in his half-closed hand, straight and elegant in dark shabby garments that flapped upon his bones; his pale face smiled in an evil trance, he did not glance at her. Ah, I have seen this fellow before, I know this man if I could place him. He is no stranger to me.

She pulled Graylie up, rose in her stirrups and shouted, I'm not going with you this time—ride on! Without pausing or turning his head the stranger rode on. Graylie's ribs heaved under her, her own ribs rose and fell, Oh, why am I so tired, I must wake up. "But let me get a fine yawn first," she said, opening her eyes and stretching, "a slap of cold water in my face, for I've been talking in my sleep again, I heard myself but what was I saying?"

Slowly, unwillingly, Miranda drew herself up inch by inch out of the pit of sleep, waited in a daze for life to begin again. A single word struck in her mind, a gong of warning, reminding her for the day long what she forgot happily in sleep, and only in sleep. The war, said the gong, and she shook her head. Dangling her feet idly with their slippers hanging, she was reminded of the way all sorts of persons sat upon her desk at the newspaper office. Every day she found someone there, sitting upon her desk instead of the

Black Belt, Archibald J. Motley, 1934

Motley attended the School of the Art Institute of Chicago and later studied European art on a Guggenheim fellowship in Paris, where he was drawn to Renaissance and nineteenth-century realistic portraiture. During the 1930s his painting was supported by the federal Works Progress Administration. *Black Belt* captures the social breadth and vitality of Chicago's South Side and other emerging African American urban centers, using a stylized realism of vivid colors and flat perspective. His men and women include well-dressed couples; a matronly, homeward-bound woman; and the stoic, downcast worker in the foreground. In the middle background a man in a suit and hat glances warily over his shoulder toward the viewer; in his poem about the South Side (p. 839), Langston Hughes explicitly challenged outsiders looking in on black life. Chicago's diverse African American community was an important setting for Nella Larsen's novel *Passing* (p. 538).

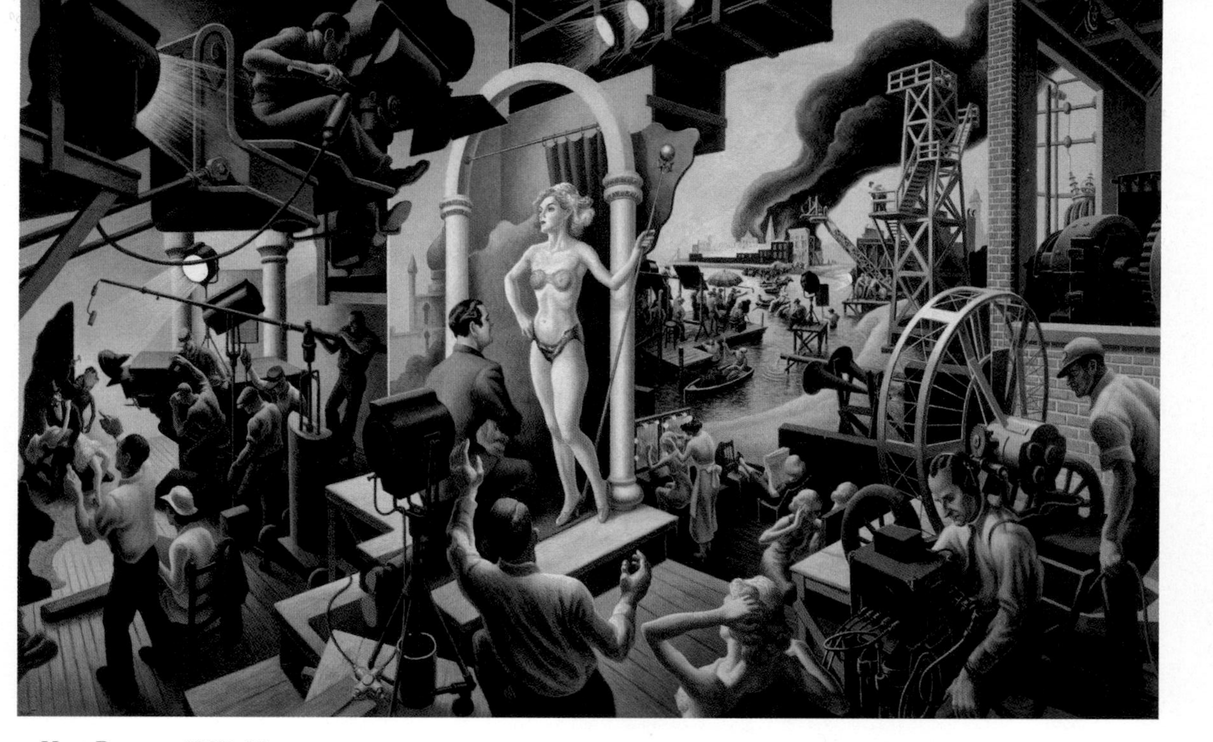

Hollywood, Thomas Hart Benton, 1937–38

The Missouri-born painter Thomas Hart Benton studied at the Art Institute of Chicago and then, like other American artists of his generation, traveled to Paris for further education and immersion in avant-garde circles. On returning to the United States, Benton worked as a painter of backdrops for early silent movies being filmed in Fort Lee, New Jersey. His service in the U.S. Navy during World War I introduced him to still another use for painting, as camouflage for warships. But after the war, Benton declared himself "an enemy of modernism" and turned toward a more realistic style. During the Great Depression, he earned a national reputation by producing several series of murals on subjects from American regional life and history, including controversial topics like slavery and the Ku Klux Klan. In 1937 *Life* magazine sent Benton to Los Angeles to cover the film industry; his large canvas *Hollywood* was the result. Like many famous paintings in Western art, *Hollywood* centers the viewer's gaze on a nearly nude female body, a modern-day goddess in the process of creation. Surrounding this body are not cupids and angels but managers and technicians of an industrial workplace—one of many American work settings that Benton painted. Like Nathanael West in *The Day of the Locust,* Benton in *Hollywood* focuses on the unnamed and invisible laborers supporting the film industry.

Portrait of a German Officer, Marsden Hartley, 1914

Born in Lewiston, Maine, Hartley immersed himself in European modernist painting at Gertrude Stein's Paris salon during a 1912 trip financed by the photographer Alfred Stieglitz. Hartley's abstract "portrait," completed on his second European trip to Berlin and before the United States entered World War I, represents its wartime subject in fragments of ribbons, uniforms, and flags. The painting memorializes Hartley's friend Karl von Freyburg, a German cavalry officer who had been killed in combat. Hartley's *Portrait* is deliberately far removed from the kind of traditional memorial art that might have idealized an officer on his horse. Among the elements incorporated into the painting are Freyburg's initials (K v. F) and the age at which he died (24). Like T. S. Eliot's *The Waste Land* (p. 365), this work registers a world blown to pieces.

1914–1945

Nude Descending a Staircase, No. 2, Marcel Duchamp, 1912

Rejected by Duchamp's fellow French modernists when he submitted it to the annual Salon des Indépendants (the annual exhibition of France's Society of Independent Artists) in 1912, *Nude Descending a Staircase* went on to become the most controversial work shown at the 1913 International Exhibition of Modern Art in New York City—the Armory Show, as it became known, after its site in a National Guard armory. Featuring paintings and sculpture by European avant-garde artists as well as a scattering of Americans, including Edward Hopper and Charles Sheeler, the Armory Show brought modernist art to the attention of a broad American public. *Nude Descending a Staircase* links Cubism's technique of representing objects in multiple perspectives with the innovations of late nineteenth-century multiple-exposure photography, the precursor to motion pictures.

River Rouge Plant, Charles Sheeler, 1932

This painting of a Ford Motor Company factory near Detroit grew out of a series of photographs that Sheeler took for an advertising agency. Along with other "precisionist" painters of the 1920s and 1930s, Sheeler was influenced by Futurism's celebration of the machine and by Cubism's breaking of traditional unified perspective into multiple flat planes. Sheeler's painterly style, however, remained realistic; he sought the broken planes and angles of Cubism in the objects themselves (here, the multiple white planes of the factory and its reflection) and avoided calling attention to the medium of paint—its texture and brushwork, the surface of the canvas—over what it represented. Like the poet Hart Crane, Sheeler found the materials for a modernist art in the American industrial landscape.

From the Faraway, Nearby, Georgia O'Keeffe, 1937

O'Keeffe found inspiration in the landscapes of the American Southwest. Noted in the 1920s for her large, vivid paintings of flowers "with great sexy involutions" (as *Life* magazine observed), O'Keeffe in the 1930s began painting the bones she found scattered about the New Mexico desert. In this almost surrealist image, the sharp lines of the elk antlers floating in the foreground are echoed in softer form by the hills; the painting's perspective collapses the middle distance to put the faraway and the nearby on top of one another. O'Keeffe's paintings became modernist icons of the American landscape; the bones of the Southwest, she wrote, opened her work up to "the wideness and wonder of the world as I live in it."

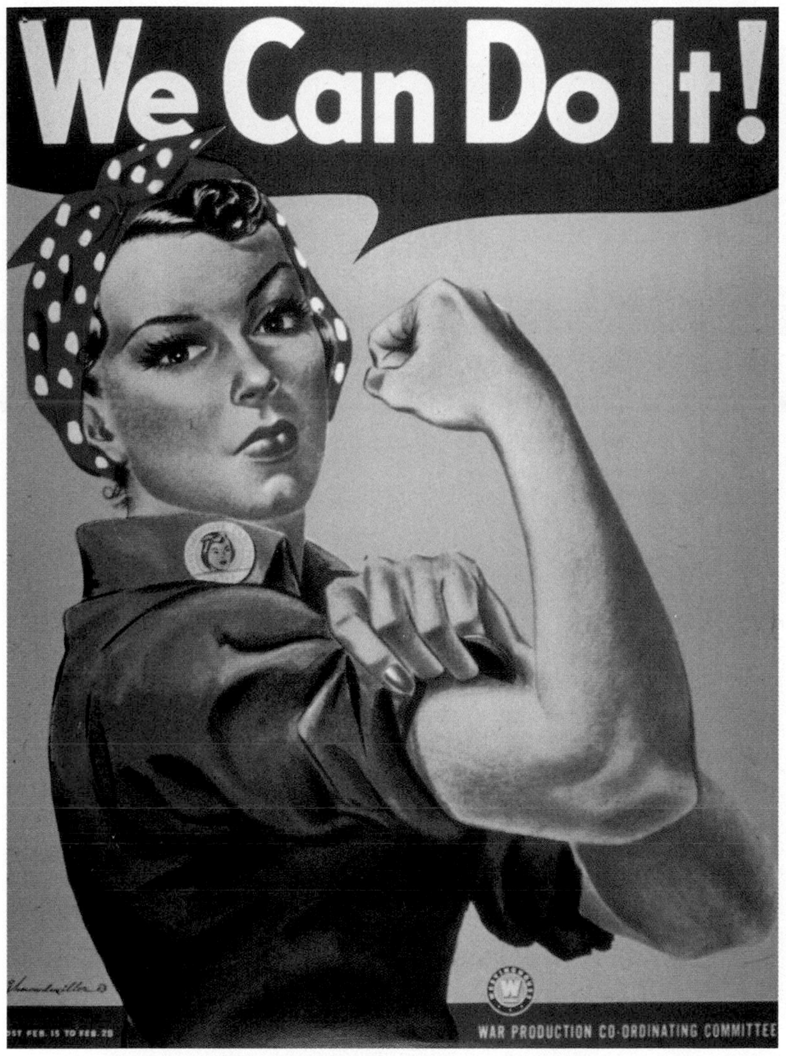

We Can Do It! ("Rosie the Riveter"), J. Howard Miller, c. 1942

World War II drew many women out of traditional roles in the home and into the industrial labor force and various forms of war-related work. Miller's poster *We Can Do It!,* produced by the defense contractor Westinghouse for the War Production Co-ordinating Committee, uses the bright colors and clean, simple lines of advertising to make the dislocations of traditional gender patterns familiar and acceptable, at least for the duration of the war. The worker's pert face and feminine grooming balance her assertively flexed bicep. A popular wartime song, "Rosie the Riveter," gave Miller's anonymous heroine her familiar nickname.

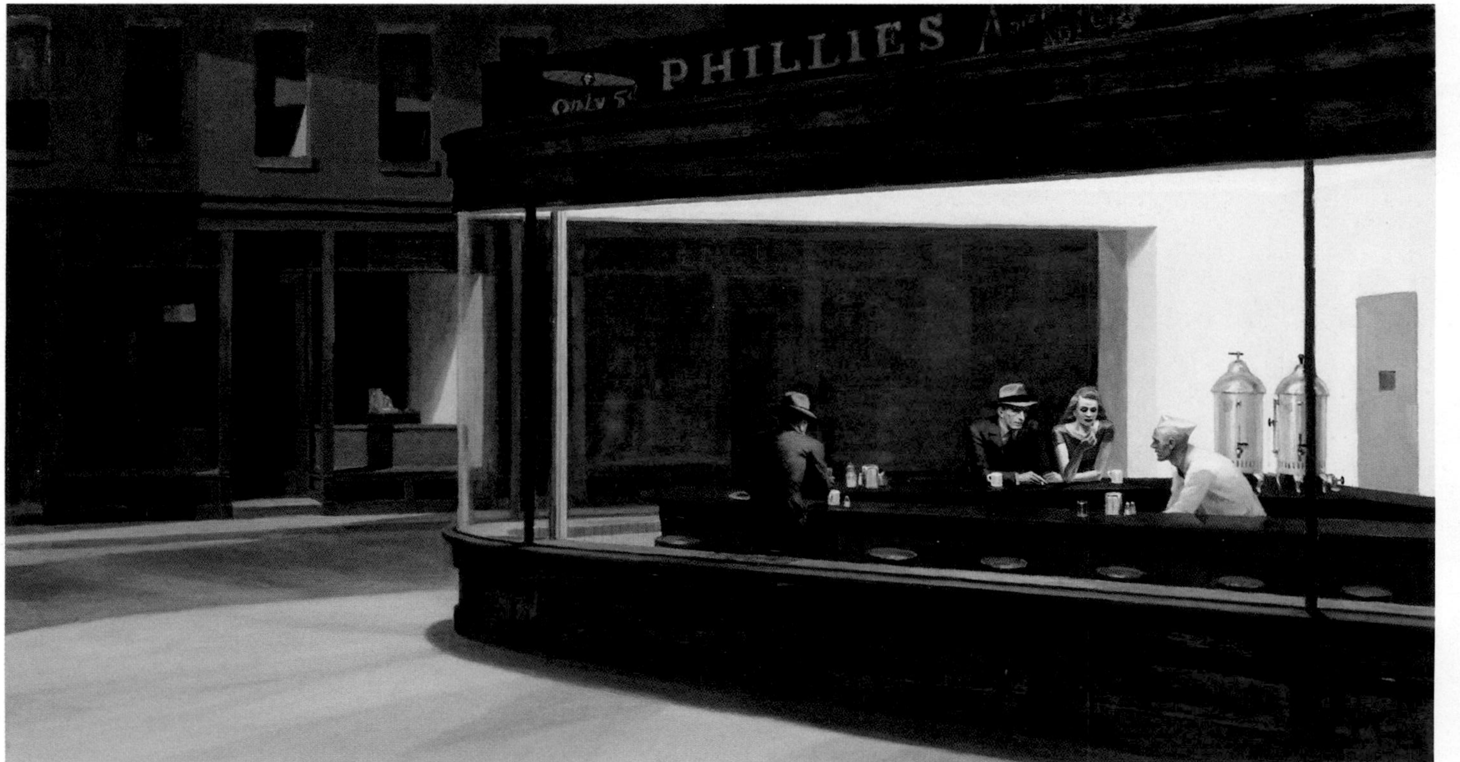

Night Hawks, Edward Hopper, 1942

Born in Nyack, New York, and trained at the New York Institute of Design, Hopper sold his first painting at the 1913 Armory show and lived in New York's Greenwich Village for most of his career. Hopper's painting represents the night life of loners in the city. Its stylized realism preserves traditional perspective, accentuated by the deep view through the restaurant's large plate-glass window, but simplifies both realistic detail and painterly brushwork. In both style and subject, Hopper's painting is often compared to the work of writers like Ernest Hemingway and to the visual style of 1940s *film noir* (literally, "dark film"). *Night Hawks* depicts a clean, well-lighted restaurant against a dark urban background of uncertain danger or promise. The customer with his back to the viewer, like one of the "private eye" characters of *film noir,* keeps to himself but stands in for the chair provided, dangling his legs, eyes roving, full of his important affairs, waiting to pounce about something or other. "*Why* won't they sit in the chair? Should I put a sign on it, saying, 'For God's sake, sit here'?"

Far from putting up a sign, she did not even frown at her visitors. Usually she did not notice them at all until their determination to be seen was greater than her determination not to see them. Saturday, she thought, lying comfortably in her tub of hot water, will be pay day, as always. Or I hope always. Her thoughts roved hazily in a continual effort to bring together and unite firmly the disturbing oppositions in her day-to-day existence, where survival, she could see clearly, had become a series of feats of sleight of hand. I owe—let me see, I wish I had pencil and paper—well, suppose I *did* pay five dollars now on a Liberty Bond,[2] I couldn't possibly keep it up. Or maybe. Eighteen dollars a week. So much for rent, so much for food, and I mean to have a few things besides. About five dollars' worth. Will leave me twenty-seven cents. I suppose I can make it. I suppose I should be worried. I am worried. Very well, now I am worried and what next? Twenty-seven cents. That's not so bad. Pure profit, really. Imagine if they should suddenly raise me to twenty I should then have two dollars and twenty-seven cents left over. But they aren't going to raise me to twenty. They are in fact going to throw me out if I don't buy a Liberty Bond. I hardly believe that. I'll ask Bill. (Bill was the city editor.) I wonder if a threat like that isn't a kind of blackmail. I don't believe even a Lusk Committeeman[3] can get away with that.

Yesterday there had been two pairs of legs dangling, on either side of her typewriter, both pairs stuffed thickly into funnels of dark expensive-looking material. She noticed at a distance that one of them was oldish and one was youngish, and they both of them had a stale air of borrowed importance which apparently they had got from the same source. They were both much too well nourished and the younger one wore a square little mustache. Being what they were, no matter what their business was it would be something unpleasant. Miranda had nodded them at them, pulled out her chair and without removing her cap or gloves had reached into a pile of letters and sheets from the copy desk as if she had not a moment to spare. They did not move, or take off their hats. At last she had said "Good morning" to them, and asked if they were, perhaps, waiting for her?

The two men slid off the desk, leaving some of her papers rumpled, and the oldish man had inquired why she had not bought a Liberty Bond. Miranda had looked at him then, and got a poor impression. He was a pursy-faced man, gross-mouthed, with little lightless eyes, and Miranda wondered why nearly all of those selected to do the war work at home were of his sort. He might be anything at all, she thought; advance agent for a road show, promoter of a wildcat oil company, a former saloon keeper announcing the opening of a new cabaret, an automobile salesman—any follower of any one of the crafty, haphazard callings. But he was now all Patriot, working for

2. Equivalent of a U.S. Savings Bond, established to finance the war effort during World War I.

3. Member of a committee established in 1919 by the New York State Legislature, chaired by state senator Clayton Lusk, to investigate subversive activities: pacifism, left-wing labor activism, socialism, communism; it was one of several undertakings associated with the "red scare" of 1919–21. Porter's dating is in error, because the narrative—set in a small city named Blue Mountain—takes place immediately before and during the war's end, i.e., autumn 1918.

the government. "Look here," he asked her, "do you know there's a war, or don't you?"

Did he expect an answer to that? Be quiet, Miranda told herself, this was bound to happen. Sooner or later it happens. Keep your head. The man wagged his finger at her, "Do you?" he persisted, as if he were prompting an obstinate child.

"Oh, the war," Miranda had echoed on a rising note and she almost smiled at him. It was habitual, automatic, to give that solemn, mystically uplifted grin when you spoke the words or heard them spoken. *"C'est la guerre,"*[4] whether you could pronounce it or not, was even better, and always, always, you shrugged.

"Yeah," said the younger man in a nasty way, "the war." Miranda, startled by the tone, met his eye; his stare was really stony, really viciously cold, the kind of thing you might expect to meet behind a pistol on a deserted corner. This expression gave temporary meaning to a set of features otherwise nondescript, the face of those men who have no business of their own. "We're having a war, and some people are buying Liberty Bonds and others just don't seem to get around to it," he said. "That's what we mean."

Miranda frowned with nervousness, the sharp beginnings of fear. "Are you selling them?" she asked, taking the cover off her typewriter and putting it back again.

"No, we're not selling them," said the older man. "We're just asking you why you haven't bought one." The voice was persuasive and ominous.

Miranda began to explain that she had no money, and did not know where to find any, when the older man interrupted: "That's no excuse, no excuse at all, and you know it, with the Huns[5] overrunning martyred Belgium."

"With our American boys fighting and dying in Belleau Wood," said the younger man, "anybody can raise fifty dollars to help beat the Boche."[6]

Miranda said hastily, "I have eighteen dollars a week and not another cent in the world. I simply cannot buy anything."

"You can pay for it five dollars a week," said the older man (they had stood there cawing back and forth over her head), "like a lot of other people in this office, and a lot of other offices besides are doing."

Miranda, desperately silent, had thought, "Suppose I were not a coward, but said what I really thought? Suppose I said to hell with this filthy war? Suppose I asked that little thug, What's the matter with you, why aren't you rotting in Belleau Wood? I wish you were . . ."

She began to arrange her letters and notes, her fingers refusing to pick up things properly. The older man went on making his little set speech. It was hard, of course. Everybody was suffering, naturally. Everybody had to do his share. But as to that, a Liberty Bond was the safest investment you could make. It was just like having the money in the bank. Of course. The government was back of it and where better could you invest?

4. It is war (French, literal trans.); used colloquially to mean "what else can you expect?"
5. Disparaging term for German soldiers fighting against the combined armies of France, England, and the United States.
6. Another disparaging term for German soldiers. Belleau Wood is a forested area in northeastern France, which was the scene of a hard-won victory over German troops by a force composed chiefly of Americans in a battle waged on June 6–25, 1918.

"I agree with you about that," said Miranda, "but I haven't any money to invest."

And of course, the man had gone on, it wasn't so much her fifty dollars that was going to make any difference. It was just a pledge of good faith on her part. A pledge of good faith that she was a loyal American doing her duty. And the thing was safe as a church. Why, if he had a million dollars he'd be glad to put every last cent of it in these Bonds. . . . "You can't lose by it," he said, almost benevolently, "and you can lose a lot if you don't. Think it over. You're the only one in this whole newspaper office that hasn't come in. And every firm in this city has come in one hundred per cent. Over at the *Daily Clarion* nobody had to be asked twice."

"They pay better over there," said Miranda. "But next week, if I can. Not now, next week."

"See that you do," said the younger man. "This ain't any laughing matter."

They lolled away, past the Society Editor's desk, past Bill the City Editor's desk, past the long copy desk where old man Gibbons sat all night shouting at intervals, "Jarge! Jarge!" and the copy boy would come flying. "Never say *people* when you mean *persons*," old man Gibbons had instructed Miranda, "and never say *practically*, say *virtually*, and don't for God's sake ever so long as I am at this desk use the barbarism *inasmuch* under any circumstances whatsoever. Now you're educated, you may go." At the head of the stairs her inquisitors had stopped in their fussy pride and vainglory, lighting cigars and wedging their hats more firmly over their eyes.

Miranda turned over in the soothing water, and wished she might fall asleep there, to wake up only when it was time to sleep again. She had a burning slow headache, and noticed it now, remembering she had waked up with it and it had in fact begun the evening before. While she dressed she tried to trace the insidious career of her headache, and it seemed reasonable to suppose it had started with the war. "It's been a headache, all right, but not quite like this." After the Committeemen had left, yesterday, she had gone to the cloakroom and had found Mary Townsend, the Society Editor, quietly hysterical about something. She was perched on the edge of the shabby wicker couch with ridges down the center, knitting on something rose-colored. Now and then she would put down her knitting, seize her head with both hands and rock, saying, "My *God*," in a surprised, inquiring voice. Her column was called Ye Towne Gossyp, so of course everybody called her Towney. Miranda and Towney had a great deal in common, and liked each other. They had both been real reporters once, and had been sent together to "cover" a scandalous elopement, in which no marriage had taken place, after all, and the recaptured girl, her face swollen, had sat with her mother, who was moaning steadily under a mound of blankets. They had both wept painfully and implored the young reporters to suppress the worst of the story. They had suppressed it, and the rival newspaper printed it all the next day. Miranda and Towney had then taken their punishment together, and had been degraded publicly to routine female jobs, one to the theaters, the other to society. They had this in common, that neither of them could see what else they could possibly have done, and they knew they were considered fools by the rest of the staff—nice girls, but fools. At sight of Miranda,

Towney had broken out in a rage. "I can't do it, I'll never be able to raise the money, I told them, I can't, I can't, but they wouldn't listen."

Miranda said, "I knew I wasn't the only person in this office who couldn't raise five dollars. I told them I couldn't, too, and I can't."

"My *God*," said Towney, in the same voice, "they told me I'd lose my job—"

"I'm going to ask Bill," Miranda said; "I don't believe Bill would do that."

"It's not up to Bill," said Towney. "He'd have to if they got after him. Do you suppose they could put us in jail?"

"I don't know," said Miranda. "If they do, we won't be lonesome." She sat down beside Towney and held her own head. "What kind of soldier are you knitting that for? It's a sprightly color, it ought to cheer him up."

"Like hell," said Towney, her needles going again. "I'm making this for myself. That's that."

"Well," said Miranda, "we won't be lonesome and we'll catch up on our sleep." She washed her face and put on fresh make-up. Taking clean gray gloves out of her pocket she went out to join a group of young women fresh from the country club dances, the morning bridge, the charity bazaar, the Red Cross workrooms, who were wallowing in good works. They gave tea dances and raised money, and with the money they bought quantities of sweets, fruit, cigarettes, and magazines for the men in the cantonment hospitals. With this loot they were now setting out, a gay procession of high-powered cars and brightly tinted faces to cheer the brave boys who already, you might very well say, had fallen in defense of their country. It must be frightfully hard on them, the dears, to be floored like this when they're all crazy to get overseas and into the trenches as quickly as possible. Yes, and some of them are the cutest things you ever saw, I didn't know there were so many good-looking men in this country, good heavens, I said, where do they come from? Well, my dear, you may ask yourself that question, who knows where they did come from? You're quite right, the way I feel about it is this, we must do everything we can to make them contented, but I draw the line at talking to them. I told the chaperons at those dances for enlisted men, I'll dance with them, every dumbbell who asks me, but I will NOT talk to them, I said, even if there is a war. So I danced hundreds of miles without opening my mouth except to say, Please keep your knees to yourself. I'm glad we gave those dances up. Yes, and the men stopped coming, anyway. But listen, I've heard that a great many of the enlisted men come from very good families; I'm not good at catching names, and those I did catch I'd never heard before, so I don't know . . . but it seems to me if they were from good families, you'd know it, wouldn't you? I mean, if a man is well bred he doesn't step on your feet, does he? At least not that. I used to have a pair of sandals ruined at every one of those dances. Well, I think any kind of social life is in very poor taste just now, I think we should all put on our Red Cross head dresses and wear them for the duration of the war—

Miranda, carrying her basket and her flowers, moved in among the young women, who scattered out and rushed upon the ward uttering girlish laughter meant to be refreshingly gay, but there was a grim determined clang in it calculated to freeze the blood. Miserably embarrassed at the idiocy of her errand, she walked rapidly between the long rows of high beds, set foot to foot with a narrow aisle between. The men, a selected presentable lot, sheets drawn up to their chins, not seriously ill, were bored and restless, most of them willing to be amused at anything. They were for the most part picturesquely bandaged as to arm or head, and those who were not visibly wounded invariably replied "Rheumatism" if some tactless girl, who had been solemnly warned never to ask this question, still forgot and asked a man what his illness was. The good-natured, eager ones, laughing and calling out from their hard narrow beds, were soon surrounded. Miranda, with her wilting bouquet and her basket of sweets and cigarettes, looking about, caught the unfriendly bitter eye of a young fellow lying on his back, his right leg in a cast and pulley. She stopped at the foot of his bed and continued to look at him, and he looked back with an unchanged, hostile face. Not having any, thank you and be damned to the whole business, his eyes said plainly to her, and will you be so good as to take your trash off my bed? For Miranda had set it down, leaning over to place it where he might be able to reach it if he would. Having set it down, she was incapable of taking it up again, but hurried away, her face burning, down the long aisle and out into the cool October sunshine, where the dreary raw barracks swarmed and worked with an aimless life of scurrying, dun-colored insects; and going around to a window near where he lay, she looked in, spying upon her soldier. He was lying with his eyes closed, his eyebrows in a sad bitter frown. She could not place him at all, she could not imagine where he came from nor what sort of being he might have been "in life," she said to herself. His face was young and the features sharp and plain, the hands were not laborer's hands but not well-cared-for hands either. They were good useful properly shaped hands, lying there on the coverlet. It occurred to her that it would be her luck to find him, instead of a jolly hungry puppy glad of a bite to eat and a little chatter. It is like turning a corner absorbed in your painful thoughts and meeting your state of mind embodied, face to face, she said. "My own feelings about this whole thing, made flesh. Never again will I come here, this is no sort of thing to be doing. This is disgusting," she told herself plainly. "Of course I would pick him out," she thought, getting into the back seat of the car she came in, "serves me right, I know better."

Another girl came out looking very tired and climbed in beside her. After a short silence, the girl said in a puzzled way, "I don't know what good it does, really. Some of them wouldn't take anything at all. I don't like this, do you?"

"I hate it," said Miranda.

"I suppose it's all right, though," said the girl, cautiously.

"Perhaps," said Miranda, turning cautious also.

That was for yesterday. At this point Miranda decided there was no good in thinking of yesterday, except for the hour after midnight she had spent dancing with Adam. He was in her mind so much, she hardly knew when she was thinking about him directly. His image was simply always present in more or less degree, he was sometimes nearer the surface of her thoughts, the pleasantest, the only really pleasant thought she had. She examined her face in the mirror between the windows and decided that her uneasiness was not all imagination. For three days at least she had felt odd and her expression was unfamiliar. She would have to raise that fifty dollars somehow, she supposed, or who knows what can happen? She was hardened to stories of personal disaster, of outrageous accusations and extraordinarily bitter penalties that had grown monstrously out of incidents very little more important than her failure—her refusal—to buy a Bond. No, she did not find herself a pleasing sight, flushed and shiny, and even her hair felt as if it had decided to grow in the other direction. I must do something about this, I can't let Adam see me like this, she told herself, knowing that even now at that moment he was listening for the turn of her door knob, and he would be in the hallway, or on the porch when she came out, as if by sheerest coincidence. The noon sunlight cast cold slanting shadows in the room where, she said, I suppose I live, and this day is beginning badly, but they all do now, for one reason or another. In a drowse, she sprayed perfume on her hair, put on her moleskin cap and jacket, now in their second winter, but still good, still nice to wear, again being glad she had paid a frightening price for them. She had enjoyed them all this time, and in no case would she have had the money now. Maybe she could manage for that Bond. She could not find the lock without leaning to search for it, then stood undecided a moment possessed by the notion that she had forgotten something she would miss seriously later on.

Adam was in the hallway, a step outside his own door; he swung about as if quite startled to see her, and said, "Hello. I don't have to go back to camp today after all—isn't that luck?"

Miranda smiled at him gaily because she was always delighted at the sight of him. He was wearing his new uniform, and he was all olive and tan and tawny, hay colored and sand colored from hair to boots. She half noticed again that he always began by smiling at her; that his smile faded gradually; that his eyes became fixed and thoughtful as if he were reading in a poor light.

They walked out together into the fine fall day, scuffling bright ragged leaves under their feet, turning their faces up to a generous sky really blue and spotless. At the first corner they waited for a funeral to pass, the mourners seated straight and firm as if proud in their sorrow.

"I imagine I'm late," said Miranda, "as usual. What time is it?"

"Nearly half past one," he said, slipping back his sleeve with an exaggerated thrust of his arm upward. The young soldiers were still self-conscious about their wrist watches. Such of them as Miranda knew were boys from southern and southwestern towns, far off the Atlantic seaboard, and they had always believed that only sissies wore wrist watches. "I'll slap you on the wrist watch," one vaudeville comedian would simper to another, and it was always a good joke, never stale.

"I think it's a most sensible way to carry a watch," said Miranda. "You needn't blush."

"I'm nearly used to it," said Adam, who was from Texas. "We've been told time and again how all the he-manly regular army men wear them. It's the horrors of war," he said; "are we downhearted? I'll say we are."

It was the kind of patter going the rounds. "You look it," said Miranda.

He was tall and heavily muscled in the shoulders, narrow in the waist and flanks, and he was infinitely buttoned, strapped, harnessed into a uniform as tough and unyielding in cut as a strait jacket, though the cloth was fine and supple. He had his uniforms made by the best tailor he could find, he confided to Miranda one day when she told him how squish he was looking in his new soldier suit. "Hard enough to make anything of the outfit, anyhow," he told her. "It's the least I can do for my beloved country, not to go around looking like a tramp." He was twenty-four years old and a Second

Lieutenant in an Engineers Corps, on leave because his outfit expected to be sent over shortly. "Came in to make my will," he told Miranda, "and get a supply of toothbrushes and razor blades. By what gorgeous luck do you suppose," he asked her, "I happened to pick on your rooming house? How did I know you were there?"

Strolling, keeping step, his stout polished well-made boots setting themselves down firmly beside her thin-soled black suède, they put off as long as they could the end of their moment together, and kept up as well as they could their small talk that flew back and forth over little grooves worn in the thin upper surface of the brain, things you could say and hear clink reassuringly at once without disturbing the radiance which played and darted about the simple and lovely miracle of being two persons named Adam and Miranda, twenty-four years old each, alive and on the earth at the same moment: "Are you in the mood for dancing, Miranda?" and "I'm always in the mood for dancing, Adam!" but there were things in the way, the day that ended with dancing was a long way to go.

He really did look, Miranda thought, like a fine healthy apple this morning. One time or another in their talking, he had boasted that he had never had a pain in his life that he could remember. Instead of being horrified at this monster, she approved his monstrous uniqueness. As for herself, she had had too many pains to mention, so she did not mention them. After working for three years on a morning newspaper she had an illusion of maturity and experience; but it was fatigue merely, she decided, from keeping what she had been brought up to believe were unnatural hours, eating casually at dirty little restaurants, drinking bad coffee all night, and smoking too much. When she said something of her way of living to Adam, he studied her face a few seconds as if he had never seen it before, and said in a forthright way, "Why, it hasn't hurt you a bit, I think you're beautiful," and left her dangling there, wondering if he had thought she wished to be praised. She did wish to be praised, but not at that moment. Adam kept unwholesome hours too, or had in the ten days they had known each other, staying awake until one o'clock to take her out for supper; he smoked also continually, though if she did not stop him he was apt to explain to her exactly what smoking did to the lungs. "But," he said, "does it matter so much if you're going to war, anyway?"

"No," said Miranda, "and it matters even less if you're staying at home knitting socks. Give me a cigarette, will you?" They paused at another corner, under a half-foliaged maple, and hardly glanced at a funeral procession approaching. His eyes were pale tan with orange flecks in them, and his hair was the color of a haystack when you turn the weathered top back to the clear straw beneath. He fished out his cigarette case and snapped his silver lighter at her, snapped it several times in his own face, and they moved on, smoking.

"I can see you knitting socks," he said. "That would be just your speed. You know perfectly well you can't knit."

"I do worse," she said, soberly; "I write pieces advising other young women to knit and roll bandages and do without sugar and help win the war."

"Oh, well," said Adam, with the easy masculine morals in such questions, "that's merely your job, that doesn't count."

"I wonder," said Miranda. "How did you manage to get an extension of leave?"

"They just gave it," said Adam, "for no reason. The men are dying like flies out there, anyway. This funny new disease.[7] Simply knocks you into a cocked hat."

"It seems to be a plague," said Miranda, "something out of the Middle Ages. Did you ever see so many funerals, ever?"

"Never did. Well, let's be strong minded and not have any of it. I've got four days more straight from the blue and not a blade of grass must grow under our feet. What about tonight?"

"Same thing," she told him, "but make it about half past one. I've got a special job beside my usual run of the mill."

"What a job you've got," said Adam, "nothing to do but run from one dizzy amusement to another and then write a piece about it."

"Yes, it's too dizzy for words," said Miranda. They stood while a funeral passed, and this time they watched it in silence. Miranda pulled her cap to an angle and winked in the sunlight, her head swimming slowly "like goldfish," she told Adam, "my head swims. I'm only half awake, I must have some coffee."

They lounged on their elbows over the counter of a drug store. "No more cream for the stay-at-homes," she said, "and only one lump of sugar. I'll have two or none; that's the kind of martyr I'm being. I mean to live on boiled cabbage and wear shoddy from now on and get in good shape for the next round. No war is going to sneak up on me again."

"Oh, there won't be any more wars, don't you read the newspapers?" asked Adam. "We're going to mop 'em up this time, and they're going to stay mopped, and this is going to be all."

"So they told me," said Miranda, tasting her bitter lukewarm brew and making a rueful face. Their smiles approved of each other, they felt they had got the right tone, they were taking the war properly. Above all, thought Miranda, no tooth-gnashing, no hair-tearing, it's noisy and unbecoming and it doesn't get you anywhere.

"Swill," said Adam rudely, pushing back his cup. "Is that all you're having for breakfast?"

"It's more than I want," said Miranda.

"I had buckwheat cakes, with sausage and maple syrup, and two bananas, and two cups of coffee, at eight o'clock, and right now, again, I feel like a famished orphan left in the ashcan. I'm all set," said Adam, "for broiled steak and fried potatoes and—"

"Don't go on with it," said Miranda, "it sounds delirious to me. Do all that after I'm gone." She slipped from the high seat, leaned against it slightly, glanced at her face in her round mirror, rubbed rouge on her lips and decided that she was past praying for.

"There's something terribly wrong," she told Adam. "I feel too rotten. It can't just be the weather, and the war."

"The weather is perfect," said Adam, "and the war is simply too good to be true. But since when? You were all right yesterday."

7. A global influenza epidemic, lasting from 1918 to 1919, affected at least half a billion people, killing about half a million in the United States and at least 50 million worldwide. The influenza seems to have arrived in the United States via ships bringing wounded soldiers back from Europe. Soldiers in crowded conditions were especially vulnerable—more military people died in the pandemic than were killed in battle during the entire war.

"I don't know," she said slowly, her voice sounding small and thin. They stopped as always at the open door before the flight of littered steps leading up to the newspaper loft. Miranda listened for a moment to the rattle of typewriters above, the steady rumble of presses below. "I wish we were going to spend the whole afternoon on a park bench," she said, "or drive to the mountains."

"I do too," he said; "let's do that tomorrow."

"Yes, tomorrow, unless something else happens. I'd like to run away," she told him; "let's both."

"Me?" said Adam. "Where I'm going there's no running to speak of. You mostly crawl about on your stomach here and there among the debris. You know, barbed wire and such stuff. It's going to be the kind of thing that happens once in a lifetime." He reflected a moment, and went on, "I don't know a darned thing about it, really, but they make it sound awfully messy. I've heard so much about it I feel as if I had been there and back. It's going to be an anticlimax," he said, "like seeing the pictures of a place so often you can't see it at all when you actually get there. Seems to me I've been in the army all my life."

Six months, he meant. Eternity. He looked so clear and fresh, and he had never had a pain in his life. She had seen them when they had been there and back and they never looked like this again. "Already the returned hero," she said, "and don't I wish you were."

"When I learned the use of the bayonet in my first training camp," said Adam, "I gouged the vitals out of more sandbags and sacks of hay than I could keep track of. They kept bawling at us, 'Get him, get that Boche, stick him before he sticks you'—and we'd go for those sandbags like wildfire, and honestly, sometimes I felt a perfect fool for getting so worked up when I saw the sand trickling out. I used to wake up in the night sometimes feeling silly about it."

"I can imagine," said Miranda. "It's perfect nonsense." They lingered, unwilling to say good-by. After a little pause, Adam, as if keeping up the conversation, asked, "Do you know what the average life expectation of a sapping party[8] is after it hits the job?"

"Something speedy, I suppose."

"Just nine minutes," said Adam; "I read that in your own newspaper not a week ago."

"Make it ten and I'll come along," said Miranda.

"Not another second," said Adam, "exactly nine minutes, take it or leave it."

"Stop bragging," said Miranda. "Who figured that out?"

"A noncombatant," said Adam, "a fellow with rickets."

This seemed very comic, they laughed and leaned towards each other and Miranda heard herself being a little shrill. She wiped the tears from her eyes. "My, it's a funny war," she said; "isn't it? I laugh every time I think about it."

Adam took her hand in both of his and pulled a little at the tips of her gloves and sniffed them. "What nice perfume you have," he said, "and such

8. Group of soldiers skilled in explosives who dig trenches to approach or undermine enemy positions.

a lot of it, too. I like a lot of perfume on gloves and hair," he said, sniffing again.

"I've got probably too much," she said. "I can't smell or see or hear today. I must have a fearful cold."

"Don't catch cold," said Adam; "my leave is nearly up and it will be the last, the very last." She moved her fingers in her gloves as he pulled at the fingers and turned her hands as if they were something new and curious and of great value, and she turned shy and quiet. She liked him, she liked him, and there was more than this but it was no good even imagining, because he was not for her nor for any woman, being beyond experience already, committed without any knowledge or act of his own to death. She took back her hands. "Good-by," she said finally, "until tonight."

She ran upstairs and looked back from the top. He was still watching her, and raised his hand without smiling. Miranda hardly ever saw anyone look back after he had said good-by. She could not help turning sometimes for one glimpse more of the person she had been talking with, as if that would save too rude and too sudden a snapping of even the lightest bond. But people hurried away, their faces already changed, fixed, in their straining towards their next stopping place, already absorbed in planning their next act or encounter. Adam was waiting as if he expected her to turn, and under his brows fixed in a strained frown, his eyes were very black.

At her desk she sat without taking off jacket or cap, slitting envelopes and pretending to read the letters. Only Chuck Rouncivale, the sports reporter, and Ye Towne Gossyp were sitting on her desk today, and them she liked having there. She sat on theirs when she pleased. Towney and Chuck were talking and they went on with it.

"They say," said Towney, "that it is really caused by germs brought by a German ship to Boston, a camouflaged ship, naturally, it didn't come in under its own colors. Isn't that ridiculous?"

"Maybe it was a submarine," said Chuck, "sneaking in from the bottom of the sea in the dead of night. Now that sounds better."

"Yes, it does," said Towney; "they always slip up somewhere in these details . . . and they think the germs were sprayed over the city—it started in Boston, you know—and somebody reported seeing a strange, thick, greasy-looking cloud float up out of Boston Harbor and spread slowly all over that end of town. I think it was an old woman who saw it."

"Should have been," said Chuck.

"I read it in a New York newspaper," said Towney; "so it's bound to be true."

Chuck and Miranda laughed so loudly at this that Bill stood up and glared at them. "Towney still reads the newspapers," explained Chuck.

"Well, what's funny about that?" asked Bill, sitting down again and frowning into the clutter before him.

"It was a noncombatant saw that cloud," said Miranda.

"Naturally," said Towney.

"Member of the Lusk Committee, maybe," said Miranda.

"The Angel of Mons," said Chuck, "or a dollar-a-year man."

Miranda wished to stop hearing, and talking, she wished to think for just five minutes of her own about Adam, really to think about him, but there was no time. She had seen him first ten days ago, and since then they had been crossing streets together, darting between trucks and limousines and push-carts and farm wagons; he had waited for her in doorways and in little restaurants that smelled of stale frying fat; they had eaten and danced to the urgent whine and bray of jazz orchestras, they had sat in dull theaters because Miranda was there to write a piece about the play. Once they had gone to the mountains and, leaving the car, had climbed a stony trail, and had come out on a ledge upon a flat stone, where they sat and watched the lights change on a valley landscape that was, no doubt, Miranda said, quite apocryphal—"We need not believe it, but it is fine poetry," she told him; they had leaned their shoulders together there, and had sat quite still, watching. On two Sundays they had gone to the geological museum, and had pored in shared fascination over bits of meteors, rock formations, fossilized tusks and trees, Indian arrows, grottoes from the silver and gold lodes. "Think of those old miners washing out their fortunes in little pans beside the streams," said Adam, "and inside the earth there was this—" and he had told her he liked better those things that took long to make; he loved airplanes too, all sorts of machinery, things carved out of wood or stone. He knew nothing much about them, but he recognized them when he saw them. He had confessed that he simply could not get through a book, any kind of book except textbooks on engineering; reading bored him to crumbs; he regretted now he hadn't brought his roadster, but he hadn't thought he would need a car; he loved driving, he wouldn't expect her to believe how many hundreds of miles he could get over in a day . . . he had showed her snapshots of himself at the wheel of his roadster; of himself sailing a boat, looking very free and windblown, all angles, hauling on the ropes; he would have joined the air force, but his mother had hysterics every time he mentioned it. She didn't seem to realize that dog fighting in the air was a good deal safer than sapping parties on the ground at night. But he hadn't argued, because of course she did not realize about sapping parties. And here he was, stuck, on a plateau a mile high with no water for a boat and his car at home, otherwise they could really have had a good time. Miranda knew he was trying to tell her what kind of person he was when he had his machinery with him. She felt she knew pretty well what kind of person he was, and would have liked to tell him that if he thought he had left himself at home in a boat or an automobile, he was much mistaken. The telephones were ringing, Bill was shouting at somebody who kept saying, "Well, but listen, well, but listen—" but nobody was going to listen, of course, nobody. Old man Gibbons bellowed in despair, "Jarge, Jarge—"

"Just the same," Towney was saying in her most complacent patriotic voice. "Hut Service[9] is a fine idea, and we should all volunteer even if they don't want us." Towney does well at this, thought Miranda, look at her; remembering the rose-colored sweater and the tight rebellious face in the cloakroom. Towney was now all open-faced glory and goodness, willing to sacrifice herself for her country. "After all," said Towney, "I *can* sing and dance well enough for the Little Theater, and I could write their letters for them, and at a pinch I might drive an ambulance. I have driven a Ford for years."

Miranda joined in: "Well, I can sing and dance too, but who's going to do the bed-making and the scrubbing up? Those huts are hard to keep, and it

9. Civilian aid provided for soldiers abroad.

would be a dirty job and we'd be perfectly miserable; and as I've got a hard dirty job and am perfectly miserable, I'm going to stay at home."

"I think the women should keep out of it," said Chuck Rouncivale. "They just add skirts to the horrors of war." Chuck had bad lungs and fretted a good deal about missing the show. "I could have been there and back with a leg off by now; it would have served the old man right. Then he'd either have to buy his own hooch or sober up."

Miranda had seen Chuck on pay day giving the old man money for hooch. He was a good-humored ingratiating old scoundrel, too, that was the worst of him. He slapped his son on the back and beamed upon him with the bleared eye of paternal affection while he took his last nickel.

"It was Florence Nightingale[1] ruined wars," Chuck went on.

"What's the idea of petting soldiers and binding up their wounds and soothing their fevered brows? That's not war. Let 'em perish where they fall. That's what they're there for."

"You can talk," said Towney, with a slantwise glint at him.

"What's the idea?" asked Chuck, flushing and hunching his shoulders. "You know I've got this lung, or maybe half of it anyway by now."

"You're much too sensitive," said Towney. "I didn't mean a thing."

Bill had been raging about, chewing his half-smoked cigar, his hair standing up in a brush, his eyes soft and lambent but wild, like a stag's. He would never, thought Miranda, be more than fourteen years old if he lived for a century, which he would not, at the rate he was going. He behaved exactly like city editors in the moving pictures, even to the chewed cigar. Had he formed his style on the films, or had scenario writers seized once for all on the type Bill in its inarguable purity? Bill was shouting to Chuck: "*And* if he comes back here take him up the alley and saw his head off *by hand*!"

Chuck said, "He'll be back, don't worry." Bill said mildly, already off on another track, "Well, saw him off." Towney went to her own desk, but Chuck sat waiting amiably to be taken to the new vaudeville show. Miranda, with two tickets, always invited one of the reporters to go with her on Monday. Chuck was lavishly hardboiled and professional in his sports writing, but he had told Miranda that he didn't give a damn about sports, really; the job kept him out in the open, and paid him enough to buy the old man's hooch. He preferred shows and didn't see why women always had the job.

"Who does Bill want sawed today?" asked Miranda.

"That hoofer you panned in this morning's," said Chuck. "He was up here bright and early asking for the guy that writes up show business. He said he was going to take the goof who wrote that piece up the alley and bop him in the nose. He said . . ."

"I hope he's gone," said Miranda; "I do hope he had to catch a train."

Chuck stood up and arranged his maroon-colored turtle-necked sweater, glanced down at the peasoup tweed plus fours and the hobnailed tan boots which he hoped would help to disguise the fact that he had a bad lung and didn't care for sports, and said, "He's long gone by now, don't worry. Let's get going; you're late as usual."

1. English woman (1820–1910) who founded modern nursing and in 1854 organized a unit of thirty-eight female nurses to serve in the Crimean War.

Miranda, facing about, almost stepped on the toes of a little drab man in a derby hat. He might have been a pretty fellow once, but now his mouth drooped where he had lost his side teeth, and his sad red-rimmed eyes had given up coquetry. A thin brown wave of hair was combed out with brilliantine and curled against the rim of the derby. He didn't move his feet, but stood planted with a kind of inert resistance, and asked Miranda: "Are you the so-called dramatic critic on this hick newspaper?"

"I'm afraid I am," said Miranda.

"Well," said the little man, "I'm just asking for one minute of your valuable time." His underlip shot out, he began with shaking hands to fish about in his waistcoat pocket. "I just hate to let you get away with it, that's all." He riffled through a collection of shabby newspaper clippings. "Just give these the once-over, will you? And then let me ask you if you think I'm gonna stand for being knocked by a tanktown critic," he said, in a toneless voice; "look here, here's Buffalo, Chicago, Saint Looey, Philadelphia, Frisco, besides New York. Here's the best publications in the business, *Variety*, the *Billboard*, they all broke down and admitted that Danny Dickerson knows his stuff. So you don't think so, hey? That's all I wanta ask you."

"No, I don't," said Miranda, as bluntly as she could, "and I can't stop to talk about it,"

The little man leaned nearer, his voice shook as if he had been nervous for a long time. "Look here, what was there you didn't like about me? Tell me that."

Miranda said, "You shouldn't pay any attention at all. What does it matter what I think?"

"I don't care what you think, it ain't that," said the little man, "but these things get round and booking agencies back East don't know how it is out here. We get panned in the sticks and they think it's the same as getting panned in Chicago, see? They don't know the difference. They don't know that the more high class an act is the more the hick critics pan it. But I've been called the best in the business by the best in the business and I wanta know what you think is wrong with me."

Chuck said, "Come on, Miranda, curtain's going up." Miranda handed the little man his clippings, they were mostly ten years old, and tried to edge past him. He stepped before her again and said without much conviction, "If you was a man I'd knock your block off." Chuck got up at that and lounged over, taking his hands out of his pockets, and said, "Now you've done your song and dance you'd better get out. Get the hell out now before I throw you downstairs."

The little man pulled at the top of his tie, a small blue tie with red polka dots, slightly frayed at the knot. He pulled it straight and repeated as if he had rehearsed it, "Come out in the alley." The tears filled his thickened red lids. Chuck said, "Ah, shut up," and followed Miranda, who was running towards the stairs. He overtook her on the sidewalk. "I left him sniveling and shuffling his publicity trying to find the joker," said Chuck, "the poor old heel."

Miranda said, "There's too much of everything in this world just now. I'd like to sit down here on the curb, Chuck, and die, and never again see—I wish I could lose my memory and forget my own name . . . I wish—"

Chuck said, "Toughen up, Miranda. This is no time to cave in. Forget that fellow. For every hundred people in show business, there are ninety-nine like him. But you don't manage right, anyway. You bring it on yourself. All you have to do is play up the headliners, and you needn't even mention the also-rans. Try to keep in mind that Rypinsky has got show business cornered in this town; please Rypinsky and you'll please the advertising department, please them and you'll get a raise. Hand-in-glove, my poor dumb child, will you never learn?"

"I seem to keep learning all the wrong things," said Miranda, hopelessly.

"You do for a fact," Chuck told her cheerfully. "You are as good at it as I ever saw. Now do you feel better?"

"This is a rotten show you've invited me to," said Chuck. "Now what are you going to do about it? If I were writing it up, I'd—"

"Do write it up," said Miranda. "You write it up this time. I'm getting ready to leave, anyway, but don't tell anybody yet."

"You mean it? All my life," said Chuck, "I've yearned to be a so-called dramatic critic on a hick newspaper, and this is positively my first chance."

"Better take it," Miranda told him. "It may be your last." She thought, This is the beginning of the end of something. Something terrible is going to happen to me. I shan't need bread and butter where I'm going. I'll will it to Chuck, he has a venerable father to buy hooch for. I hope they let him have it. Oh, Adam, I hope I see you once more before I go under with whatever is the matter with me. "I wish the war were over," she said to Chuck, as if they had been talking about that. "I wish it were over and I wish it had never begun."

Chuck had got out his pad and pencil and was already writing his review. What she had said seemed sage enough but how would he take it? "I don't care how it started or when it ends," said Chuck, scribbling away, "I'm not going to be there."

All the rejected men talked like that, thought Miranda. War was the one thing they wanted, now they couldn't have it. Maybe they had wanted badly to go, some of them. All of them had a sidelong eye for the women they talked with about it, a guarded resentment which said, "Don't pin a white feather[2] on me, you bloodthirsty female. I've offered my meat to the crows and they won't have it." The worst thing about war for the stay-at-homes is there isn't anyone to talk to any more. The Lusk Committee will get you if you don't watch out. Bread will win the war. Work will win, sugar will win, peach pits will win the war. Nonsense. *Not* nonsense, I tell you, there's some kind of valuable high explosive to be got out of peach pits. So all the happy housewives hurry during the canning season to lay their baskets of peach pits on the altar of their country. It keeps them busy and makes them feel useful, and all these women running wild with the men away are dangerous, if they aren't given something to keep their little minds out of mischief. So rows of young girls, the intact cradles of the future, with their pure serious faces framed becomingly in Red Cross wimples,[3] roll cockeyed bandages that will never reach a base hospital, and knit sweaters that will never warm a manly chest, their minds dwelling lovingly on all the blood and mud and the next dance at the Acanthus Club for the officers of the flying corps. Keeping still and quiet will win the war.

2. Sign of cowardice.
3. Headcoverings surrounding the entire face and chin.

"I'm simply not going to be there," said Chuck, absorbed in his review. No, Adam will be there, thought Miranda. She slipped down in the chair and leaned her head against the dusty plush, closed her eyes and faced for one instant that was a lifetime the certain, the overwhelming and awful knowledge that there was nothing at all ahead for Adam and for her. Nothing. She opened her eyes and held her hands together palms up, gazing at them and trying to understand oblivion.

"Now look at this," said Chuck, for the lights had come on and the audience was rustling and talking again. "I've got it all done, even before the headliner comes on. It's old Stella Mayhew, and she's always good, she's been good for forty years, and she's going to sing 'O the blues ain't nothin' but the easy-going heart disease.' That's all you need to know about her. Now just glance over this. Would you be willing to sign it?"

Miranda took the pages and stared at them conscientiously, turning them over, she hoped, at the right moment, and gave them back. "Yes, Chuck, yes, I'd sign that. But I won't. We must tell Bill you wrote it, because it's your start, maybe."

"You don't half appreciate it," said Chuck. "You read it too fast. Here, listen to this—" and he began to mutter excitedly. While he was reading she watched his face. It was a pleasant face with some kind of spark of life in it, and a good severity in the modeling of the brow above the nose. For the first time since she had known him she wondered what Chuck was thinking about. He looked preoccupied and unhappy, he wasn't so frivolous as he sounded. The people were crowding into the aisle, bringing out their cigarette cases ready to strike a match the instant they reached the lobby; women with waved hair clutched at their wraps, men stretched their chins to ease them of their stiff collars, and Chuck said, "We might as well go now." Miranda, buttoning her jacket, stepped into the moving crowd, thinking, What did I ever know about them? There must be a great many of them here who think as I do, and we dare not say a word to each other of our desperation, we are speechless animals letting ourselves be destroyed, and why? Does anybody here believe the things we say to each other?

Stretched in unease on the ridge of the wicker couch in the cloakroom, Miranda waited for time to pass and leave Adam with her. Time seemed to proceed with more than usual eccentricity, leaving twilight gaps in her mind for thirty minutes which seemed like a second, and then hard flashes of light that shone clearly on her watch proving that three minutes is an intolerable stretch of waiting, as if she were hanging by her thumbs. At last it was reasonable to imagine Adam stepping out of the house in the early darkness into the blue mist that might soon be rain, he would be on the way, and there was nothing to think about him, after all. There was only the wish to see him and the fear, the present threat, of not seeing him again; for every step they took towards each other seemed perilous, drawing them apart instead of together, as a swimmer in spite of his most determined strokes is yet drawn slowly backward by the tide. "I don't want to love," she would think in spite of herself, "not Adam, there is no time and we are not ready for it and yet this is all we have—"

And there he was on the sidewalk, with his foot on the first step, and Miranda almost ran down to meet him. Adam, holding her hands, asked,

"Do you feel well now? Are you hungry? Are you tired? Will you feel like dancing after the show?"

"Yes to everything," said Miranda, "yes, yes. . . ." Her head was like a feather, and she steadied herself on his arm. The mist was still mist that might be rain later, and though the air was sharp and clean in her mouth, it did not, she decided, make breathing any easier. "I hope the show is good, or at least funny," she told him, "but I promise nothing."

It was a long, dreary play, but Adam and Miranda sat very quietly together waiting patiently for it to be over. Adam carefully and seriously pulled off her glove and held her hand as if he were accustomed to holding her hand in theaters. Once they turned and their eyes met, but only once, and the two pairs of eyes were equally steady and noncommittal. A deep tremor set up in Miranda, and she set about resisting herself methodically as if she were closing windows and doors and fastening down curtains against a rising storm. Adam sat watching the monotonous play with a strange shining excitement, his face quite fixed and still.

When the curtain rose for the third act, the third act did not take place at once. There was instead disclosed a backdrop almost covered with an American flag improperly and disrespectfully exposed, nailed at each upper corner, gathered in the middle and nailed again, sagging dustily. Before it posed a local dollar-a-year man, now doing his bit as a Liberty Bond salesman. He was an ordinary man past middle life, with a neat little melon buttoned into his trousers and waistcoat, an opinionated tight mouth, a face and figure in which nothing could be read save the inept sensual record of fifty years. But for once in his life he was an important fellow in an impressive situation, and he reveled, rolling his words in an actorish tone.

"Looks like a penguin," said Adam. They moved, smiled at each other, Miranda reclaimed her hand, Adam folded his together and they prepared to wear their way again through the same old moldy speech with the same old dusty backdrop. Miranda tried not to listen, but she heard. These vile Huns—glorious Belleau Wood—our keyword is Sacrifice—Martyred Belgium—give till it hurts—our noble boys Over There—Big Berthas[4]—the death of civilization—the Boche—

"My head aches," whispered Miranda. "Oh, why won't he hush?"

"He won't," whispered Adam. "I'll get you some aspirin."

"In Flanders Field the poppies grow, Between the crosses row on row"[5]—"He's getting into the home stretch," whispered Adam—atrocities, innocent babes hoisted on Boche bayonets—your child and my child—if our children are spared these things, then let us say with all reverence that these dead have not died in vain—the war, the *war*, the WAR to end WAR, war for Democracy, for humanity, a safe world forever and ever—and to prove our faith in Democracy to each other, and to the world, let everybody get together and buy Liberty Bonds and do without sugar and wool socks—was that it? Miranda asked herself, Say that over, I didn't catch the last line. Did you mention Adam? If you didn't I'm not interested. What about Adam, you little pig? And what are

4. Powerful, long-range mounted artillery guns used by the Germans; named for Bertha Krupp, daughter of German armaments manufacturer Alfred Krupp.

5. First two lines of a famous World War I poem by the Canadian army doctor John McCrea (1872–1918), first published in the English magazine *Punch* on December 8, 1915, and then in McCrea's posthumous volume *In Flanders Fields and Other Poems* (1919).

we going to sing this time, "Tipperary" or "There's a Long, Long Trail"?[6] Oh, please do let the show go on and get over with. I must write a piece about it before I can go dancing with Adam and we have no time. Coal, oil, iron, gold, international finance, why don't you tell us about them, you little liar?

The audience rose and sang, "There's a Long, Long Trail A-winding," their opened mouths black and faces pallid in the reflected footlights; some of the faces grimaced and wept and had shining streaks like snail's tracks on them. Adam and Miranda joined in at the tops of their voices, grinning shamefacedly at each other once or twice.

In the street, they lit their cigarettes and walked slowly as always. "Just another nasty old man who would like to see the young ones killed," said Miranda in a low voice; "the tom-cats try to eat the little tom-kittens, you know. They don't fool you really, do they, Adam?"

The young people were talking like that about the business by then. They felt they were seeing pretty clearly through that game. She went on, "I hate these potbellied baldheads, too fat, too old, too cowardly, to go to war themselves, they know they're safe; it's you they are sending instead—"

Adam turned eyes of genuine surprise upon her. "Oh, *that* one," he said. "Now what could the poor sap do if they did take him? It's not his fault," he explained, "he can't do anything but talk." His pride in his youth, his forbearance and tolerance and contempt for that unlucky being breathed out of his very pores as he strolled, straight and relaxed in his strength. "What *could* you expect of him, Miranda?"

She spoke his name often, and he spoke hers rarely. The little shock of pleasure the sound of her name in his mouth gave her stopped her answer. For a moment she hesitated, and began at another point of attack. "Adam," she said, "the worst of war is the fear and suspicion and the awful expression in all the eyes you meet . . . as if they had pulled down the shutters over their minds and their hearts and were peering out at you, ready to leap if you make one gesture or say one word they do not understand instantly. It frightens me; I live in fear too, and no one should have to live in fear. It's the skulking about, and the lying. It's what war does to the mind and the heart, Adam, and you can't separate these two—what it does to them is worse than what it can do to the body."

Adam said soberly, after a moment, "Oh, yes, but suppose one comes back whole? The mind and the heart sometimes get another chance, but if anything happens to the poor old human frame, why, it's just out of luck, that's all."

"Oh, yes," mimicked Miranda. "It's just out of luck, that's all."

"If I didn't go," said Adam, in a matter-of-fact voice, "I couldn't look myself in the face."

So that's all settled. With her fingers flattened on his arm, Miranda was silent, thinking about Adam. No, there was no resentment or revolt in him. Pure, she thought, all the way through, flawless, complete, as the sacrificial lamb must be. The sacrificial lamb strode along casually, accommodating his long pace to hers, keeping her on the inside of the walk in the good American style, helping her across street corners as if she were a cripple—"I hope we don't come to a mud puddle, he'll carry me over it"—giving off

6. Popular war songs.

whiffs of tobacco smoke, a manly smell of scentless soap, freshly cleaned leather and freshly washed skin, breathing through his nose and carrying his chest easily. He threw back his head and smiled into the sky which still misted, promising rain. "Oh, boy," he said, "what a night. Can't you hurry that review of yours so we can get started?"

He waited for her before a cup of coffee in the restaurant next to the pressroom, nicknamed The Greasy Spoon. When she came down at last, freshly washed and combed and powdered, she saw Adam first, sitting near the dingy big window, face turned to the street, but looking down. It was an extraordinary face, smooth and fine and golden in the shabby light, but now set in a blind melancholy, a look of pained suspense and disillusion. For just one split second she got a glimpse of Adam when he would have been older, the face of the man he would not live to be. He saw her then, rose, and the bright glow was there.

Adam pulled their chairs together at their table; they drank hot tea and listened to the orchestra jazzing "Pack Up Your Troubles."

"In an old kit bag, and smoil, smoil, smoil," shouted half a dozen boys under the draft age, gathered around a table near the orchestra. They yelled incoherently, laughed in great hysterical bursts of something that appeared to be merriment, and passed around under the tablecloth flat bottles containing a clear liquid—for in this western city founded and built by roaring drunken miners, no one was allowed to take his alcohol openly—splashed it into their tumblers of ginger ale, and went on singing, "It's a Long Way to Tipperary." When the tune changed to "Madelon," Adam said, "Let's dance." It was a tawdry little place, crowded and hot and full of smoke, but there was nothing better. The music was gay; and life is completely crazy anyway, thought Miranda, so what does it matter? This is what we have, Adam and I, this is all we're going to get, this is the way it is with us. She wanted to say, "Adam, come out of your dream and listen to me. I have pains in my chest and my head and my heart and they're real. I am in pain all over, and you are in such danger as I can't bear to think about, and why can we not save each other?" When her hand tightened on his shoulder his arm tightened about her waist instantly, and stayed there, holding firmly. They said nothing but smiled continually at each other, odd changing smiles as though they had found a new language. Miranda, her face near Adam's shoulder, noticed a dark young pair sitting at a corner table, each with an arm around the waist of the other, their heads together, their eyes staring at the same thing, whatever it was, that hovered in space before them. Her right hand lay on the table, his hand over it, and her face was a blur with weeping. Now and then he raised her hand and kissed it, and set it down and held it, and her eyes would fill again. They were not shameless, they had merely forgotten where they were, or they had no other place to go, perhaps. They said not a word, and the small pantomime repeated itself, like a melancholy short film running monotonously over and over again. Miranda envied them. She envied that girl. At least she can weep if that helps, and he does not even have to ask, What is the matter? Tell me. They had cups of coffee before them, and after a long while—Miranda and Adam had danced and sat down again twice—when the coffee was quite cold, they drank it suddenly, then embraced as before, without a word and scarcely a glance at each other. Something was done and settled between them, at least; it was enviable, enviable, that they could sit quietly together and have the same expression on their faces while they looked into the hell they shared, no matter what kind of hell, it was theirs, they were together.

At the table nearest Adam and Miranda a young woman was leaning on her elbow, telling her young man a story. "And I don't like him because he's too fresh. He kept on asking me to take a drink and I kept telling him, I don't drink and he said, Now look here, I want a drink the worst way and I think it's mean of you not to drink with me, I can't sit up here and drink by myself, he said. I told him, You're not by yourself in the first place; I like that, I said, and if you want a drink go ahead and have it, I told him, why drag *me* in? So he called the waiter and ordered ginger ale and two glasses and I drank straight ginger ale like I always do but he poured a shot of hooch in his. He was awfully proud of that hooch, said he made it himself out of potatoes. Nice homemade likker, warm from the pipe, he told me, three drops of this and your ginger ale will taste like Mumm's Extry.[7] But I said, No, and I mean no, can't you get that through your bean? He took another drink and said, Ah, come on, honey, don't be so stubborn, this'll make your shimmy shake. So I just got tired of the argument, and I said, I don't need to drink, to shake my shimmy, I can strut my stuff on tea, I said. Well, why don't you then, he wanted to know, and I just told him—"

She knew she had been asleep for a long time when all at once without even a warning footstep or creak of the door hinge, Adam was in the room turning on the light, and she knew it was he, though at first she was blinded and turned her head away. He came over at once and sat on the side of the bed and began to talk as if he were going on with something they had been talking about before. He crumpled a square of paper and tossed it in the fireplace.

"You didn't get my note," he said. "I left it under the door. I was called back suddenly to camp for a lot of inoculations. They kept me longer than I expected, I was late. I called the office and they told me you were not coming in today. I called Miss Hobbe here and she said you were in bed and couldn't come to the telephone. Did she give you my message?"

"No," said Miranda drowsily, "but I think I have been asleep all day. Oh, I do remember. There was a doctor here. Bill sent him. I was at the telephone once, for Bill told me he would send an ambulance and have me taken to the hospital. The doctor tapped my chest and left a prescription and said he would be back, but he hasn't come."

"Where is it, the prescription?" asked Adam.

"I don't know. He left it, though, I saw him."

Adam moved about searching the tables and the mantelpiece.

"Here it is," he said. "I'll be back in a few minutes. I must look for an all-night drug store. It's after one o'clock. Good-by."

Good-by, good-by. Miranda watched the door where he had disappeared for quite a while, then closed her eyes, and thought, When I am not here I cannot remember anything about this room where I have lived for nearly a year, except that the curtains are too thin and there was never any way of

7. Brand of champagne.

shutting out the morning light. Miss Hobbe had promised heavier curtains, but they had never appeared. When Miranda in her dressing gown had been at the telephone that morning, Miss Hobbe had passed through, carrying a tray. She was a little red-haired nervously friendly creature, and her manner said all too plainly that the place was not paying and she was on the ragged edge.

"My dear *child*," she said sharply, with a glance at Miranda's attire, "what is the matter?"

Miranda, with the receiver to her ear, said, "Influenza, I think."

"*Horrors*," said Miss Hobbe, in a whisper, and the tray wavered in her hands. "Go back to bed at once . . . go at *once*!"

"I must talk to Bill first," Miranda had told her, and Miss Hobbe had hurried on and had not returned. Bill had shouted directions at her, promising everything, doctor, nurse, ambulance, hospital, her check every week as usual, everything, but she was to get back to bed and stay there. She dropped into bed, thinking that Bill was the only person she had ever seen who actually tore his own hair when he was excited enough . . . I suppose I should ask to be sent home, she thought, it's a respectable old custom to inflict your death on the family if you can manage it. No, I'll stay here, this is my business, but not in this room, I hope . . . I wish I were in the cold mountains in the snow, that's what I should like best; and all about her rose the measured ranges of the Rockies wearing their perpetual snow, their majestic blue laurels of cloud, chilling her to the bone with their sharp breath. Oh, no, I must have warmth—and her memory turned and roved after another place she had known first and loved best, that now she could see only in drifting fragments of palm and cedar, dark shadows and a sky that warmed without dazzling, as this strange sky had dazzled without warming her; there was the long slow wavering of gray moss in the drowsy oak shade, the spacious hovering of buzzards overhead, the smell of crushed water herbs along a bank, and without warning a broad tranquil river into which flowed all the rivers she had known. The walls shelved away in one deliberate silent movement on either side, and a tall sailing ship was moored near by, with a gangplank weathered to blackness touching the foot of her bed. Back of the ship was jungle, and even as it appeared before her, she knew it was all she had ever read or had been told or felt or thought about jungles; a writhing terribly alive and secret place of death, creeping with tangles of spotted serpents, rainbow-colored birds with malign eyes, leopards with humanly wise faces and extravagantly crested lions; screaming long-armed monkeys tumbling among broad fleshy leaves that glowed with sulphur-colored light and exuded the ichor of death, and rotting trunks of unfamiliar trees sprawled in crawling slime. Without surprise, watching from her pillow, she saw herself run swiftly down this gangplank to the slanting deck, and standing there, she leaned on the rail and waved gaily to herself in bed, and the slender ship spread its wings and sailed away into the jungle. The air trembled with the shattering scream and the hoarse bellow of voices all crying together, rolling and colliding above her like ragged storm-clouds, and the words became two words only rising and falling and clamoring about her head. Danger, danger, danger, the voices said, and War, war, war. There was her door half open, Adam standing with his hand on the knob, and Miss Hobbe with her face all out of shape with terror was crying shrilly, "I tell you, they must come for her *now*, or I'll put her on the sidewalk . . . I tell you, this is a plague, a plague, my God, and I've got a houseful of people to think about!"

Adam said, "I know that. They'll come for her tomorrow morning."

"Tomorrow morning, my God, they'd better come now!"

"They can't get an ambulance," said Adam, "and there aren't any beds. And we can't find a doctor or a nurse. They're all busy. That's all there is to it. You stay out of the room, and I'll look after her."

"Yes, you'll look after her, I can see that," said Miss Hobbe, in a particularly unpleasant tone.

"Yes, that's what I said," answered Adam, drily, "and you keep out."

He closed the door carefully. He was carrying an assortment of misshapen packages, and his face was astonishingly impassive.

"Did you hear that?" he asked, leaning over and speaking very quietly.

"Most of it," said Miranda, "it's a nice prospect, isn't it?"

"I've got your medicine," said Adam, "and you're to begin with it this minute. She can't put you out."

"So it's really as bad as that," said Miranda.

"It's as bad as anything can be," said Adam, "all the theaters and nearly all the shops and restaurants are closed, and the streets have been full of funerals all day and ambulances all night—"

"But not one for me," said Miranda, feeling hilarious and light-headed. She sat up and beat her pillow into shape and reached for her robe. "I'm glad you're here, I've been having a nightmare. Give me a cigarette, will you, and light one for yourself and open all the windows and sit near one of them. You're running a risk," she told him, "don't you know that? Why do you do it?"

"Never mind," said Adam, "take your medicine," and offered her two large cherry-colored pills. She swallowed them promptly and instantly vomited them up. "*Do* excuse me," she said, beginning to laugh. "I'm so sorry." Adam without a word and with a very concerned expression washed her face with a wet towel, gave her some cracked ice from one of the packages, and firmly offered her two more pills. "That's what they always did at home," she explained to him, "and it worked." Crushed with humiliation, she put her hands over her face and laughed again, painfully.

"There are two more kinds yet," said Adam, pulling her hands from her face and lifting her chin. "You've hardly begun. And I've got other things, like orange juice and ice cream—they told me to feed you ice cream—and coffee in a thermos bottle, and a thermometer. You have to work through the whole lot so you'd better take it easy."

"This time last night we were dancing," said Miranda, and drank something from a spoon. Her eyes followed him about the room, as he did things for her with an absent-minded face, like a man alone; now and again he would come back, and slipping his hand under her head, would hold a cup or a tumbler to her mouth, and she drank, and followed him with her eyes again, without a clear notion of what was happening.

"Adam," she said, "I've just thought of something. Maybe they forgot St. Luke's Hospital. Call the sisters there and ask them not to be so selfish with their silly old rooms. Tell them I only want a very small dark ugly one for three days, or less. Do try them, Adam."

He believed, apparently, that she was still more or less in her right mind, for she heard him at the telephone explaining in his deliberate voice. He was back again almost at once, saying, "This seems to be my day for getting mixed up with peevish old maids. The sister said that even if they had a room you couldn't have it without doctor's orders. But they didn't have one, anyway. She was pretty sour about it."

"Well," said Miranda in a thick voice, "I think that's abominably rude and mean, don't you?" She sat up with a wild gesture of both arms, and began to retch again, violently.

"Hold it, as you were," called Adam, fetching the basin. He held her head, washed her face and hands with ice water, put her head straight on the pillow, and went over and looked out of the window. "Well," he said at last, sitting beside her again, "they haven't got a room. They haven't got a bed. They haven't even got a baby crib, the way she talked. So I think that's straight enough, and we may as well dig in."

"Isn't the ambulance coming?"

"Tomorrow, maybe."

He took off his tunic and hung it on the back of a chair. Kneeling before the fireplace, he began carefully to set kindling sticks in the shape of an Indian tepee, with a little paper in the center for them to lean upon. He lighted this and placed other sticks upon them, and larger bits of wood. When they were going nicely he added still heavier wood, and coal a few lumps at a time, until there was a good blaze, and a fire that would not need rekindling. He rose and dusted his hands together, the fire illuminated him from the back and his hair shone.

"Adam," said Miranda, "I think you're very beautiful." He laughed out at this, and shook his head at her. "What a hell of a word," he said, "for me." "It was the first that occurred to me," she said, drawing up on her elbow to catch the warmth of the blaze. "That's a good job, that fire."

He sat on the bed again, dragging up a chair and putting his feet on the rungs. They smiled at each other for the first time since he had come in that night. "How do you feel now?" he asked.

"Better, much better," she told him. "Let's talk. Let's tell each other what we meant to do."

"You tell me first," said Adam. "I want to know about you."

"You'd get the notion I had a very sad life," she said, "and perhaps it was, but I'd be glad enough to have it now. If I could have it back, it could be easy to be happy about almost anything at all. That's not true, but that's the way I feel now." After a pause, she said, "There's nothing to tell, after all, if it ends now, for all this time I was getting ready for something that was going to happen later, when the time came. So now it's nothing much."

"But it must have been worth having until now, wasn't it?" he asked seriously as if it were something important to know.

"Not if this is all," she repeated obstinately.

"Weren't you ever—happy?" asked Adam, and he was plainly afraid of the word; he was shy of it as he was of the word *love*, he seemed never to have spoken it before, and was uncertain of its sound or meaning.

"I don't know," she said, "I just lived and never thought about it. I remember things I liked, though, and things I hoped for."

"I was going to be an electrical engineer," said Adam. He stopped short. "And I shall finish up when I get back," he added, after a moment.

"Don't you love being alive?" asked Miranda. "Don't you love weather and the colors at different times of the day, and all the sounds and noises like children screaming in the next lot, and automobile horns and little bands playing in the street and the smell of food cooking?"

"I love to swim, too," said Adam.

"So do I," said Miranda; "we never did swim together."

"Do you remember any prayers?" she asked him suddenly. "Did you ever learn anything at Sunday School?"

"Not much," confessed Adam without contrition. "Well, the Lord's Prayer."

"Yes, and there's Hail Mary," she said, "and the really useful one beginning, I confess to Almighty God and to blessed Mary ever virgin and to the holy Apostles Peter and Paul—"

"Catholic," he commented.

"Prayers just the same, you big Methodist. I'll bet you *are* a Methodist."

"No, Presbyterian."

"Well, what others do you remember?"

"Now I lay me down to sleep—" said Adam.

"Yes, that one, and Blessed Jesus meek and mild—you see that my religious education wasn't neglected either. I even know a prayer beginning O Apollo. Want to hear it?"

"No," said Adam, "you're making fun."

"I'm not," said Miranda, "I'm trying to keep from going to sleep. I'm afraid to go to sleep, I may not wake up. Don't let me go to sleep, Adam. Do you know Matthew, Mark, Luke and John? Bless the bed I lie upon?"

"If I should die before I wake, I pray the Lord my soul to take. Is that it?" asked Adam. "It doesn't sound right, somehow."

"Light me a cigarette, please, and move over and sit near the window. We keep forgetting about fresh air. You must have it." He lighted the cigarette and held it to her lips. She took it between her fingers and dropped it under the edge of her pillow. He found it and crushed it out in the saucer under the water tumbler. Her head swam in darkness for an instant, cleared, and she sat up in panic, throwing off the covers and breaking into a sweat. Adam leaped up with an alarmed face, and almost at once was holding a cup of hot coffee to her mouth.

"You must have some too," she told him, quiet again, and they sat huddled together on the edge of the bed, drinking coffee in silence.

Adam said, "You must lie down again. You're awake now."

"Let's sing," said Miranda. "I know an old spiritual, I can remember some of the words." She spoke in a natural voice. "I'm fine now." She began in a hoarse whisper, "'Pale horse, pale rider, done taken my lover away . . .' Do you know that song?"

'Yes," said Adam, "I heard Negroes in Texas sing it, in an oil field."

"I heard them sing it in a cotton field," she said; "it's a good song."

They sang that line together. "But I can't remember what comes next," said Adam.

"'Pale horse, pale rider,'" said Miranda, "(We really need a good banjo) 'done taken my lover away—'" Her voice cleared and she said, "But we ought to get on with it. What's the next line?"

"There's a lot more to it than that," said Adam, "about forty verses, the rider done taken away mammy, pappy, brother, sister, the whole family besides the lover—"

"But not the singer, not yet," said Miranda. "Death always leaves one singer to mourn. 'Death,'" she sang, "'oh, leave one singer to mourn—'"

"'Pale horse, pale rider,'" chanted Adam, coming in on the beat, "'done taken my lover away!' (I think we're good, I think we ought to get up an act—)"

"Go in Hut Service," said Miranda, "entertain the poor defenseless heroes Over There."

"We'll play banjos," said Adam; "I always wanted to play the banjo."

Miranda sighed, and lay back on the pillow and thought, I must give up, I can't hold out any longer. There was only that pain, only that room, and only Adam. There were no longer any multiple planes of living, no tough filaments of memory and hope pulling taut backwards and forwards holding her upright between them. There was only this one moment and it was a dream of time, and Adam's face, very near hers, eyes still and intent, was a shadow, and there was to be nothing more. . . .

"Adam," she said out of the heavy soft darkness that drew her down, down, "I love you, and I was hoping you would say that to me, too."

He lay down beside her with his arm under her shoulder, and pressed his smooth face against hers, his mouth moved towards her mouth and stopped. "Can you hear what I am saying? . . . What do you think I have been trying to tell you all this time?"

She turned towards him, the cloud cleared and she saw his face for an instant. He pulled the covers about her and held her, and said, "Go to sleep, darling, darling, if you will go to sleep now for one hour I will wake you up and bring you hot coffee and tomorrow we will find somebody to help. I love you, go to sleep—"

Almost with no warning at all, she floated into the darkness, holding his hand, in sleep that was not sleep but clear evening light in a small green wood, an angry dangerous wood full of inhuman concealed voices singing sharply like the whine of arrows and she saw Adam transfixed by a flight of these singing arrows that struck him in the heart and passed shrilly cutting their path through the leaves. Adam fell straight back before her eyes, and rose again unwounded and alive; another flight of arrows loosed from the invisible bow struck him again and he fell, and yet he was there before her untouched in a perpetual death and resurrection. She threw herself before him, angrily and selfishly she interposed between him and the track of the arrow, crying, No, no, like a child cheated in a game, It's my turn now, why must you always be the one to die? and the arrows struck her cleanly through the heart and through his body and he lay dead, and she still lived, and the wood whistled and sang and shouted, every branch and leaf and blade of grass had its own terrible accusing voice. She ran then, and Adam caught her in the middle of the room, running, and said, "Darling, I must have been asleep too. What happened, you screamed terribly?"

After he had helped her to settle again, she sat with her knees drawn up under her chin, resting her head on her folded arms and began carefully searching for her words because it was important to explain clearly. "It was a very odd sort of dream, I don't know why it could have frightened me.

There was something about an old-fashioned valentine. There were two hearts carved on a tree, pierced by the same arrow—you know, Adam—"

"Yes, I know, honey," he said in the gentlest sort of way, and sat kissing her on the cheek and forehead with a kind of accustomedness, as if he had been kissing her for years, "one of those lace paper things."

"Yes, and yet they were alive, and were us, you understand—this doesn't seem to be quite the way it was, but it was something like that. It was in a wood—"

"Yes," said Adam. He got up and put on his tunic and gathered up the thermos bottle. "I'm going back to that little stand and get us some ice cream and hot coffee," he told her, "and I'll be back in five minutes, and you keep quiet. Good-by for five minutes," he said, holding her chin in the palm of his hand and trying to catch her eye, "and you be very quiet."

"Good-by," she said. "I'm awake again." But she was not, and the two alert young internes from the County hospital who had arrived, after frantic urgings from the noisy city editor of the Blue Mountain *News*, to carry her away in a police ambulance, decided that they had better go down and get the stretcher. Their voices roused her, she sat up, got out of bed at once and stood glancing about brightly. "Why, you're all right," said the darker and stouter of the two young men, both extremely fit and competent-looking in their white clothes, each with a flower in his buttonhole. "I'll just carry you." He unfolded a white blanket and wrapped it around her. She gathered up the folds and asked, "But where is Adam?" taking hold of the doctor's arm. He laid a hand on her drenched forehead, shook his head, and gave her a shrewd look. "Adam?"

"Yes," Miranda told him, lowering her voice confidentially, "he was here and now he is gone."

"Oh, he'll be back," the interne told her easily, "he's just gone round the block to get cigarettes. Don't worry about Adam. He's the least of your troubles."

"Will he know where to find me?" she asked, still holding back.

"We'll leave him a note," said the interne. "Come now, it's time we got out of here."

He lifted and swung her up to his shoulder. "I feel very badly," she told him; "I don't know why."

"I'll bet you do," said he, stepping out carefully, the other doctor going before them, and feeling for the first step of the stairs. "Put your arms around my neck," he instructed her. "It won't do you any harm and it's a great help to me."

"What's your name?" Miranda asked as the other doctor opened the front door and they stepped out into the frosty sweet air.

"Hildesheim," he said, in the tone of one humoring a child.

"Well, Dr. Hildesheim, aren't we in a pretty mess?"

"We certainly are," said Dr. Hildesheim.

The second young interne, still quite fresh and dapper in his white coat, though his carnation was withering at the edges, was leaning over listening to her breathing through a stethoscope, whistling thinly, "There's a Long, Long Trail—" From time to time he tapped her ribs smartly with two fingers, whistling. Miranda observed him for a few moments until she fixed his bright busy hazel eye not four inches from hers. "I'm not unconscious," she explained, "I know what I want to say." Then to her horror she heard herself babbling nonsense, knowing it was nonsense though she could not hear what she was saying. The flicker of attention in the eye near her vanished, the second interne went on tapping and listening, hissing softly under his breath.

"I wish you'd stop whistling," she said clearly. The sound stopped. "It's a beastly tune," she added. Anything, anything at all to keep her small hold on the life of human beings, a clear line of communication, no matter what, between her and the receding world. "Please let me see Dr. Hildesheim," she said, "I have something important to say to him. I must say it now." The second interne vanished. He did not walk away, he fled into the air without a sound, and Dr. Hildesheim's face appeared in his stead.

"Dr. Hildesheim, I want to ask you about Adam."

"That young man? He's been here, and left you a note, and has gone again," said Dr. Hildesheim, "and he'll be back tomorrow and the day after." His tone was altogether too merry and flippant.

"I don't believe you," said Miranda, bitterly, closing her lips and eyes and hoping she might not weep.

"Miss Tanner," called the doctor, "have you got that note?"

Miss Tanner appeared beside her, handed her an unsealed envelope, took it back, unfolded the note and gave it to her.

"I can't see it," said Miranda, after a pained search of the page full of hasty scratches in black ink.

"Here, I'll read it," said Miss Tanner. "It says, 'They came and took you while I was away and now they will not let me see you. Maybe tomorrow they will, with my love, Adam,'" read Miss Tanner in a firm dry voice, pronouncing the words distinctly. "Now, do you see?" she asked soothingly.

Miranda, hearing the words one by one, forgot them one by one. "Oh, read it again, what does it say?" she called out over the silence that pressed upon her, reaching towards the dancing words that just escaped as she almost touched them. "That will do," said Dr. Hildesheim, calmly authoritarian. "Where is that bed?"

"There is no bed yet," said Miss Tanner, as if she said, We are short of oranges. Dr. Hildesheim said, "Well, we'll manage something," and Miss Tanner drew the narrow trestle with bright crossed metal supports and small rubbery wheels into a deep jut of the corridor, out of the way of the swift white figures darting about, whirling and skimming like water flies all in silence. The white walls rose sheer as cliffs, a dozen frosted moons followed each other in perfect self-possession down a white lane and dropped mutely one by one into a snowy abyss.

What is this whiteness and silence but the absence of pain? Miranda lay lifting the nap of her white blanket softly between eased fingers, watching a dance of tall deliberate shadows moving behind a wide screen of sheets spread upon a frame. It was there, near her, on her side of the wall where she could see it clearly and enjoy it, and it was so beautiful she had no curiosity as to its meaning. Two dark figures nodded, bent, curtsied to each other, retreated and bowed again, lifted long arms and spread great hands against the white shadow of the screen; then with a single round movement, the sheets were folded back, disclosing two speechless men in white, standing, and another speechless man in white, lying on the bare springs of a white iron bed. The man on the springs was swathed smoothly from head to foot in white, with folded bands across the face, and a large stiff bow like merry rabbit ears dangled at the crown of his head.

The two living men lifted a mattress standing hunched against the wall, spread it tenderly and exactly over the dead man. Wordless and white they vanished down the corridor, pushing the wheeled bed before them. It had been an entrancing and leisurely spectacle, but now it was over. A pallid white fog rose in their wake insinuatingly and floated before Miranda's eyes, a fog in which was concealed all terror and all weariness, all the wrung faces and twisted backs and broken feet of abused, outraged living things, all the shapes of their confused pain and their estranged hearts; the fog might part at any moment and loose the horde of human torments. She put up her hands and said, Not yet, not yet, but it was too late. The fog parted and two executioners, white clad, moved towards her pushing between them with marvelously deft and practiced hands the misshapen figure of an old man in filthy rags whose scanty beard waggled under his opened mouth as he bowed his back and braced his feet to resist and delay the fate they had prepared for him. In a high weeping voice he was trying to explain to them that the crime of which he was accused did not merit the punishment he was about to receive; and except for this whining cry there was silence as they advanced. The soiled cracked bowls of the old man's hands were held before him beseechingly as a beggar's as he said, "Before God I am not guilty," but they held his arms and drew him onward, passed, and were gone.

The road to death is a long march beset with all evils, and the heart fails little by little at each new terror, the bones rebel at each step, the mind sets up its own bitter resistance and to what end? The barriers sink one by one, and no covering of the eyes shuts out the landscape of disaster, nor the sight of crimes committed there. Across the field came Dr. Hildesheim, his face a skull beneath his German helmet, carrying a naked infant writhing on the point of his bayonet, and a huge stone pot marked Poison in Gothic letters. He stopped before the well that Miranda remembered in a pasture on her father's farm, a well once dry but now bubbling with living water, and into its pure depths he threw the child and the poison, and the violated water sank back soundlessly into the earth. Miranda, screaming, ran with her arms above her head; her voice echoed and came back to her like a wolf's howl, Hildesheim is a Boche, a spy, a Hun, kill him, kill him before he kills you. . . . She woke howling, she heard the foul words accusing Dr. Hildesheim tumbling from her mouth; opened her eyes and knew she was in a bed in a small white room, with Dr. Hildesheim sitting beside her, two firm fingers on her pulse. His hair was brushed sleekly and his buttonhole flower was fresh. Stars gleamed through the window, and Dr. Hildesheim seemed to be gazing at them with no particular expression, his stethoscope dangling around his neck. Miss Tanner stood at the foot of the bed writing something on a chart.

"Hello," said Dr. Hildesheim, "at least you take it out in shouting. You don't try to get out of bed and go running around." Miranda held her eyes open with a terrible effort, saw his rather heavy, patient face clearly even as her mind tottered and slithered again, broke from its foundation and spun like a cast wheel in a ditch. "I didn't mean it, I never believed it, Dr. Hildesheim, you musn't remember it—" and was gone again, not being able to wait for an answer.

The wrong she had done followed her and haunted her dream: this wrong took vague shapes of horror she could not recognize or name, though her heart cringed at sight of them. Her mind, split in two, acknowledged and denied what she saw in the one instant, for across an abyss of complaining darkness her reasoning coherent self watched the strange frenzy of the other coldly, reluctant to admit the truth of its visions, its tenacious remorses and despairs.

"I know those are your hands," she told Miss Tanner, "I know it, but to me they are white tarantulas, don't touch me."

"Shut your eyes," said Miss Tanner.

"Oh, no," said Miranda, "for then I see worse things," but her eyes closed in spite of her will, and the midnight of her internal torment closed about her.

Oblivion, thought Miranda, her mind feeling among her memories of words she had been taught to describe the unseen, the unknowable, is a whirlpool of gray water turning upon itself for all eternity . . . eternity is perhaps more than the distance to the farthest star. She lay on a narrow ledge over a pit that she knew to be bottomless, though she could not comprehend it; the ledge was her childhood dream of danger, and she strained back against a reassuring wall of granite at her shoulders, staring into the pit, thinking, There it is, there it is at last, it is very simple; and soft carefully shaped words like oblivion and eternity are curtains hung before nothing at all. I shall not know when it happens, I shall not feel or remember, why can't I consent now, I am lost, there is no hope for me. Look, she told herself, there it is, that is death and there is nothing to fear. But she could not consent, still shrinking stiffly against the granite wall that was her childhood dream of safety, breathing slowly for fear of squandering breath, saying desperately, Look, don't be afraid, it is nothing, it is only eternity.

Granite walls, whirlpools, stars are things. None of them is death, nor the image of it. Death is death, said Miranda, and for the dead it has no attributes. Silenced she sank easily through deeps under deeps of darkness until she lay like a stone at the farthest bottom of life, knowing herself to be blind, deaf, speechless, no longer aware of the members of her own body, entirely withdrawn from all human concerns, yet alive with a peculiar lucidity and coherence; all notions of the mind, the reasonable inquiries of doubt, all ties of blood and the desires of the heart, dissolved and fell away from her, and there remained of her only a minute fiercely burning particle of being that knew itself alone, that relied upon nothing beyond itself for its strength; not susceptible to any appeal or inducement, being itself composed entirely of one single motive, the stubborn will to live. This fiery motionless particle set itself unaided to resist destruction, to survive and to be in its own madness of being, motiveless and planless beyond that one essential end. Trust me, the hard unwinking angry point of light said. Trust me. I stay.

At once it grew, flattened, thinned to a fine radiance, spread like a great fan and curved out into a rainbow through which Miranda, enchanted, altogether believing, looked upon a deep clear landscape of sea and sand, of soft meadow and sky, freshly washed and glistening with transparencies of blue. Why, of course, of course, said Miranda, without surprise but with serene rapture as if some promise made to her had been kept long after she had ceased to hope for it. She rose from her narrow ledge and ran lightly through the tall portals of the great bow that arched in its splendor over the burning blue of the sea and the cool green of the meadow on either hand.

The small waves rolled in and over unhurriedly, lapped upon the sand in silence and retreated; the grasses flurried before a breeze that made no sound. Moving towards her leisurely as clouds through the shimmering air came a great company of human beings, and Miranda saw in an amazement of joy that they were all the living she had known. Their faces were transfigured, each in its own beauty, beyond what she remembered of them, their eyes were clear and untroubled as good weather, and they cast no shadows. They were pure identities and she knew them every one without calling their names or remembering what relation she bore to them. They surrounded her smoothly on silent feet, then turned their entranced faces again towards the sea, and she moved among them easily as a wave among waves. The drifting circle widened, separated, and each figure was alone but not solitary; Miranda, alone too, questioning nothing, desiring nothing, in the quietude of her ecstasy, stayed where she was, eyes fixed on the overwhelming deep sky where it was always morning.

Lying at ease, arms under her head, in the prodigal warmth which flowed evenly from sea and sky and meadow, within touch but not touching the serenely smiling familiar beings about her, Miranda felt without warning a vague tremor of apprehension, some small flick of distrust in her joy; a thin frost touched the edges of this confident tranquillity; something, somebody, was missing, she had lost something, she had left something valuable in another country, oh, what could it be? There are no trees, no trees here, she said in fright, I have left something unfinished. A thought struggled at the back of her mind, came clearly as a voice in her ear. Where are the dead? We have forgotten the dead, oh, the dead, where are they? At once as if a curtain had fallen, the bright landscape faded, she was alone in a strange stony place of bitter cold, picking her way along a steep path of slippery snow, calling out, Oh, I must go back! But in what direction? Pain returned, a terrible compelling pain running through her veins like heavy fire, the stench of corruption filled her nostrils, the sweetish sickening smell of rotting flesh and pus; she opened her eyes and saw pale light through a coarse white cloth over her face, knew that the smell of death was in her own body, and struggled to lift her hand. The cloth was drawn away; she saw Miss Tanner filling a hypodermic needle in her methodical expert way, and heard Dr. Hildesheim saying, "I think that will do the trick. Try another." Miss Tanner plucked firmly at Miranda's arm near the shoulder, and the unbelievable current of agony ran burning through her veins again. She struggled to cry out, saying, Let me go, let me go; but heard only incoherent sounds of animal suffering. She saw doctor and nurse glance at each other with the glance of initiates at a mystery, nodding in silence, their eyes alive with knowledgeable pride. They looked briefly at their handiwork and hurried away.

Bells screamed all off key, wrangling together as they collided in mid air, horns and whistles mingled shrilly with cries of human distress; sulphur colored light exploded through the black window pane and flashed away in darkness. Miranda waking from a dreamless sleep asked without expecting an answer, "What is happening?" for there was a bustle of voices and footsteps in the corridor, and a sharpness in the air; the far clamor went on, a furious exasperated shrieking like a mob in revolt.

The light came on, and Miss Tanner said in a furry voice, "Hear that? They're celebrating. It's the Armistice. The war is over, my dear." Her hands trembled. She rattled a spoon in a cup, stopped to listen, held the cup out to Miranda. From the ward for old bedridden women down the hall floated a ragged chorus of cracked voices singing, "My country, 'tis of thee . . ."

Sweet land . . . oh, terrible land of this bitter world where the sound of rejoicing was a clamor of pain, where ragged tuneless old women, sitting up waiting for their evening bowl of cocoa, were singing, "Sweet land of Liberty—"

"Oh, say, can you see?" their hopeless voices were asking next, the hammer strokes of metal tongues drowning them out. "The war is over," said Miss Tanner, her underlip held firmly, her eyes blurred. Miranda said, "Please open the window, please, I smell death in here."

Now if real daylight such as I remember having seen in this world would only come again, but it is always twilight or just before morning, a promise of day that is never kept. What has become of the sun? That was the longest and loneliest night and yet it will not end and let the day come. Shall I ever see light again?

Sitting in a long chair, near a window, it was in itself a melancholy wonder to see the colorless sunlight slanting on the snow, under a sky drained of its blue. "Can this be my face?" Miranda asked her mirror. "Are these my own hands?" she asked Miss Tanner, holding them up to show the yellow tint like melted wax glimmering between the closed fingers. The body is a curious monster, no place to live in, how could anyone feel at home there? Is it possible I can ever accustom myself to this place? she asked herself. The human faces around her seemed dulled and tired, with no radiance of skin and eyes as Miranda remembered radiance; the once white walls of her room were now a soiled gray. Breathing slowly, falling asleep and waking again, feeling the splash of water on her flesh, taking food, talking in bare phrases with Dr. Hildesheim and Miss Tanner, Miranda looked about her with the covertly hostile eyes of an alien who does not like the country in which he finds himself, does not understand the language nor wish to learn it, does not mean to live there and yet is helpless, unable to leave it at his will.

"It is morning," Miss Tanner would say, with a sigh, for she had grown old and weary once for all in the past month, "morning again, my dear," showing Miranda the same monotonous landscape of dulled evergreens and leaden snow. She would rustle about in her starched skirts, her face bravely powdered, her spirit unbreakable as good steel, saying, "Look, my dear, what a heavenly morning, like a crystal," for she had an affection for the salvaged creature before her, the silent ungrateful human being whom she, Cornelia Tanner, a nurse who knew her business, had snatched back from death with her own hands. "Nursing is nine-tenths, just the same," Miss Tanner would tell the other nurses; "keep that in mind." Even the sunshine was Miss Tanner's own prescription for the further recovery of Miranda, this patient the doctors had given up for lost, and who yet sat here, visible proof of Miss Tanner's theory. She said, "Look at the sunshine, now," as she might be saying, "I ordered this for you, my dear, do sit up and take it."

"It's beautiful," Miranda would answer, even turning her head to look, thanking Miss Tanner for her goodness, most of all her goodness about the weather, "beautiful, I always loved it." And I might love it again if I saw it, she thought, but truth was, she could not see it. There was no light, there might never be light again, compared as it must always be with the light she had seen beside the blue sea that lay so tranquilly along the shore of her paradise. That was a child's dream of the heavenly meadow, the vision of repose that comes to a tired body in sleep, she thought, but I have seen it when I did not know it was a dream. Closing her eyes she would rest for a moment remembering that bliss which had repaid all the pain of the journey to reach it; opening them again she saw with a new anguish the dull world to which she was condemned, where the light seemed filmed over with cobwebs, all the bright surfaces corroded, the sharp planes melted and formless, all objects and beings meaningless, ah, dead and withered things that believed themselves alive!

At night, after the long effort of lying in her chair, in her extremity of grief for what she had so briefly won, she folded her painful body together and wept silently, shamelessly, in pity for herself and her lost rapture. There was no escape. Dr. Hildesheim, Miss Tanner, the nurses in the diet kitchen, the chemist, the surgeon, the precise machine of the hospital, the whole humane conviction and custom of society, conspired to pull her inseparable rack of bones and wasted flesh to its feet, to put in order her disordered mind, and to set her once more safely in the road that would lead her again to death.

Chuck Rouncivale and Mary Townsend came to see her, bringing her a bundle of letters they had guarded for her. They brought a basket of delicate small hothouse flowers, lilies of the valley with sweet peas and feathery fern, and above these blooms their faces were merry and haggard.

Mary said, "You *have* had a tussle, haven't you?" and Chuck said, "Well, you made it back, didn't you?" Then after an uneasy pause, they told her that everybody was waiting to see her again at her desk. "They've put me back on sports already, Miranda," said Chuck. For ten minutes Miranda smiled and told them how gay and what a pleasant surprise it was to find herself alive. For it will not do to betray the conspiracy and tamper with the courage of the living; there is nothing better than to be alive, everyone has agreed on that; it is past argument, and who attempts to deny it is justly outlawed. "I'll be back in no time at all," she said; "this is almost over."

Her letters lay in a heap in her lap and beside her chair. Now and then she turned one over to read the inscription, recognized this handwriting or that, examined the blotted stamps and the post-marks, and let them drop again. For two or three days they lay upon the table beside her, and she continued to shrink from them. "They will all be telling me again how good it is to be alive, they will say again they love me, they are glad I am living too, and what can I answer to that?" and her hardened, indifferent heart shuddered in despair at itself, because before it had been tender and capable of love.

Dr. Hildesheim said, "What, all these letters not opened yet?" and Miss Tanner said, "Read your letters, my dear, I'll open them for you." Standing beside the bed, she slit them cleanly with a paper knife. Miranda, cornered, picked and chose until she found a thin one in an unfamiliar handwriting. "Oh, no, now," said Miss Tanner, "take them as they come. Here, I'll hand them to you." She sat down, prepared to be helpful to the end.

What a victory, what triumph, what happiness to be alive, sang the letters in a chorus. The names were signed with flourishes like the circles in air of bugle notes, and they were the names of those she had loved best; some of those she had known well and pleasantly; and a few who meant nothing to her, then or now. The thin letter in the unfamiliar handwriting was from a strange man at the camp where Adam had been, telling her that Adam had died of influenza in the camp hospital. Adam had asked him, in case anything happened, to be sure to let her know.

If anything happened. To be sure to let her know. If anything happened. "Your friend, Adam Barclay," wrote the strange man. It had happened—she looked at the date—more than a month ago.

"I've been here a long time, haven't I?" she asked Miss Tanner, who was folding letters and putting them back in their proper envelopes.

"Oh, quite a while," said Miss Tanner, "but you'll be ready to go soon now. But you must be careful of yourself and not overdo, and you should come back now and then and let us look at you, because sometimes the aftereffects are very—"

Miranda, sitting up before the mirror, wrote carefully: "One lipstick, medium, one ounce flask Bois d'Hiver perfume, one pair of gray suède gauntlets[8] without straps, two pairs gray sheer stockings without clocks—"

Towney, reading after her, said, "Everything without something so that it will be almost impossible to get?"

"Try it, though," said Miranda, "they're nicer without. One walking stick of silvery wood with a silver knob."

"That's going to be expensive," warned Towney. "Walking is hardly worth it."

"You're right," said Miranda, and wrote in the margin, "a nice one to match my other things. Ask Chuck to look for this, Mary. Good looking and not too heavy." Lazarus, come forth. Not unless you bring me my top hat and stick. Stay where you are then, you snob. Not at all. I'm coming forth. "A jar of cold cream," wrote Miranda, "a box of apricot powder—and, Mary, I don't need eye shadow, do I?" She glanced at her face in the mirror and away again. "Still, no one need pity this corpse if we look properly to the art of the thing."

Mary Townsend said, "You won't recognize yourself in a week."

"Do you suppose, Mary," asked Miranda, "I could have my old room back again?"

"That should be easy," said Mary. "We stored away all your things there with Miss Hobbe." Miranda wondered again at the time and trouble the living took to be helpful to the dead. But not quite dead now, she reassured herself, one foot in either world now; soon I shall cross back and be at home again. The light will seem real and I shall be glad when I hear that someone I know has escaped from death. I shall visit the escaped ones and help them dress and tell them how lucky they are, and how lucky I am still to have them. Mary will be back soon with my gloves and my walking stick, I must go now, I must begin saying good-by to Miss Tanner and Dr. Hildesheim. Adam, she said, now you need not die again, but still I wish you were here; I wish you had come back, what do you think I came back for, Adam, to be deceived like this?

8. Gloves with a cuff covering part of the arm. "Bois d'Hiver": winter wood (French).

At once he was there beside her, invisible but urgently present, a ghost but more alive than she was, the last intolerable cheat of her heart; for knowing it was false she still clung to the lie, the unpardonable lie of her bitter desire. She said, "I love you," and stood up trembling, trying by the mere act of her will to bring him to sight before her. If I could call you up from the grave I would, she said, if I could see your ghost I would say, I believe . . . "I believe," she said aloud. "Oh, let me see you once more." The room was silent, empty, the shade was gone from it, struck away by the sudden violence of her rising and speaking aloud. She came to herself as if out of sleep. Oh, no, that is not the way, I must never do that, she warned herself. Miss Tanner said, "Your taxicab is waiting, my dear," and there was Mary. Ready to go.

No more war, no more plague, only the dazed silence that follows the ceasing of the heavy guns; noiseless houses with the shades drawn, empty streets, the dead cold light of tomorrow. Now there would be time for everything.

1937, 1939

ZORA NEALE HURSTON
1891–1960

Zora Neale Hurston was born in 1891 in Notasulga, Alabama, and moved with her family in 1892 to Eatonville, Florida, an all-black town. Her father, a Baptist preacher of considerable eloquence, was not a family man and made life difficult for his wife and eight children. The tie between mother and daughter was strong; Lucy Hurston was a driving force and strong support for all her children. But her death when Zora Hurston was about eleven left the child with little home life. Hitherto, the town of Eatonville had been like an extended family to her, and her early childhood was protected from racism because she encountered no white people. With her mother's death, Hurston's wanderings and her initiation into American racism began. The early security had given her the core of self-confidence she needed to survive. She moved from one relative's home to another until she was old enough to support herself, and with her earnings she began slowly to pursue an education. Although she had never finished grade school in Eatonville she was able to enter and complete college. In the early 1920s at Howard University in Washington, D.C. (the nation's leading African American university at that time), she studied with the great black educator Alain Locke, who was to make history with his anthology *The New Negro* in 1925. After a short story, "Drenched in Light," appeared in the New York African American magazine *Opportunity,* she decided to move to Harlem and pursue a literary career there.

As her biographer, Robert Hemenway, writes, "Zora Hurston was an extraordinarily witty woman, and she acquired an instant reputation in New York for her high spirits and side-splitting tales of Eatonville life. She could walk into a room of strangers . . . and almost immediately gather people, charm, amuse, and impress them." The Eatonville vignettes printed here convey the flavor of this discourse. Generous, outspoken, high spirited, an interesting conversationalist, she worked as

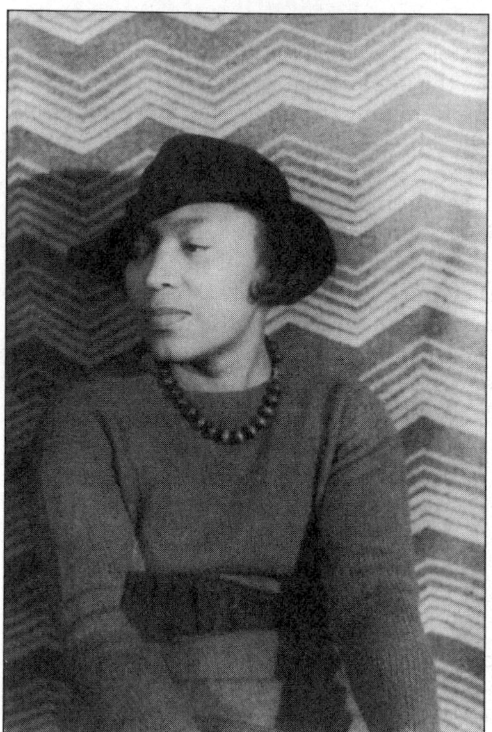

Zora Neale Hurston, as photographed by Carl Van Vechten in 1938.

a personal secretary for the politically liberal novelist Fannie Hurst and entered Barnard College. Her career took two simultaneous directions: at Barnard she studied with the famous anthropologist Franz Boas and developed an interest in black folk traditions, and in Harlem she became well known as a storyteller, an informal performing artist. Thus she was doubly committed to oral narrative, and her work excels in its representation of people talking.

When she graduated from Barnard in 1927 she received a fellowship to return to Florida and study the oral traditions of Eatonville. From then on, she strove to achieve a balance between focusing on the folk and her origins and focusing on herself as an individual. After the fellowship money ran out, Hurston was supported by Mrs. R. Osgood Mason, an elderly white patron of the arts. Mason had firm ideas about what she wanted her protégés to produce; she required them all to get her permission before publishing any of the work that she had subsidized. In this relationship, Hurston experienced a difficulty that all the black artists of the Harlem Renaissance had to face—the fact that well-off white people were the sponsors of, and often expected to be the chief audience for, their work.

Hurston's work was not entirely popular with the male intellectual leaders of the Harlem community. She quarreled especially with Langston Hughes; she rejected the idea that a black writer's chief concern should be how blacks were being portrayed to the white reader. She did not write to "uplift her race," either; because in her view it was already uplifted, she (like Claude McKay) was not embarrassed to present her characters as mixtures of good and bad, strong and weak. Some of the other Harlem writers thought her either naive or egotistical, but Hurston argued that freedom could only mean freedom from all coercion, no matter what the source.

The Great Depression brought an end to the structure that had undergirded Hurston's fieldwork, and she turned fully to writing. Unfortunately her most important work appeared in the mid-1930s when there was little interest in it, or in African American writing in general. She published *Jonah's Gourd Vine* in 1934 (a novel whose main character is based on her father); *Mules and Men* in 1935 (based on material from her field trips in Florida—this was her best-selling book, but it earned a total of only $943.75); and *Their Eyes Were Watching God,* in 1937. This novel about an African American woman's quest for selfhood has become a popular and critical favorite, both a woman's story, and a descriptive critique of southern African American folk society, showing its divisions and diversity. Technically, it is a loosely organized, highly metaphorical novel, with passages of broad folk humor and of extreme artistic compression. Other books followed in 1938 and 1939, and she wrote an autobiography—*Dust Tracks on a Road*—which appeared in 1942, with its occasional expression of antiwhite sentiments removed by her editors. At this point, however, Hurston had no audience. For the last decade of her life she lived in Florida, working from time to time as a maid.

Sweat[1]

It was eleven o'clock of a Spring night in Florida. It was Sunday. Any other night, Delia Jones would have been in bed for two hours by this time. But she was a washwoman, and Monday morning meant a great deal to her. So she collected the soiled clothes on Saturday when she returned the clean things. Sunday night after church, she sorted them and put the white things to soak. It saved her almost a half day's start. A great hamper in the bedroom held the clothes that she brought home. It was so much neater than a number of bundles lying around.

She squatted in the kitchen floor beside the great pile of clothes, sorting them into small heaps according to color, and humming a song in a mournful key, but wondering through it all where Sykes, her husband, had gone with her horse and buckboard.

Just then something long, round, limp and black fell upon her shoulders and slithered to the floor beside her. A great terror took hold of her. It softened her knees and dried her mouth so that it was a full minute before she could cry out or move. Then she saw that it was the big bull whip her husband liked to carry when he drove.

She lifted her eyes to the door and saw him standing there bent over with laughter at her fright. She screamed at him.

"Sykes, what you throw dat whip on me like dat? You know it would skeer me—looks just like a snake, an' you knows how skeered Ah is of snakes."

"Course Ah knowed it! That's how come Ah done it." He slapped his leg with his hand and almost rolled on the ground in his mirth. "If you such a big fool dat you got to have a fit over a earth worm or a string, Ah don't keer how bad Ah skeer you."

"You aint got no business doing it. Gawd knows it's a sin. Some day Ah'm gointuh drop dead from some of yo' foolishness. 'Nother thing, where you been wid mah rig? Ah feeds dat pony. He aint fuh you to be drivin' wid no bull whip."

"You sho is one aggravatin' nigger woman!" he declared and stepped into the room. She resumed her work and did not answer him at once. "Ah done tole you time and again to keep them white folks' clothes outa dis house."

He picked up the whip and glared down at her. Delia went on with her work. She went out into the yard and returned with a galvanized tub and sat it on the washbench. She saw that Sykes had kicked all of the clothes together again, and now stood in her way truculently, his whole manner hoping, *praying*, for an argument. But she walked calmly around him and commenced to re-sort the things.

"Next time, Ah'm gointer kick 'em outdoors," he threatened as he struck a match along the leg of his corduroy breeches.

1. The text is that of the first printing in *Fire!!* (1926).

Delia never looked up from her work, and her thin, stooped shoulders sagged further.

"Ah aint for no fuss t'night, Sykes. Ah just come from taking sacrament at the church house."

He snorted scornfully. "Yeah, you just come from de church house on a Sunday night, but heah you is gone to work on them clothes. You ain't nothing but a hypocrite. One of them amen-corner Christians—sing, whoop, and shout, then come home and wash white folks clothes on the Sabbath."

He stepped roughly upon the whitest pile of things, kicking them helter-skelter as he crossed the room. His wife gave a little scream of dismay, and quickly gathered them together again.

"Sykes, you quit grindin' dirt into these clothes! How can Ah git through by Sat'day if Ah don't start on Sunday?"

"Ah don't keer if you never git through. Anyhow, Ah done promised Gawd and a couple of other men, Ah aint gointer have it in mah house. Don't gimme no lip neither, else Ah'll throw 'em out and put mah fist up side yo' head to boot."

Delia's habitual meekness seemed to slip from her shoulders like a blown scarf. She was on her feet; her poor little body, her bare knuckly hands bravely defying the strapping hulk before her.

"Looka heah, Sykes, you done gone too fur. Ah been married to you fur fifteen years, and Ah been takin' in washin' fur fifteen years. Sweat, sweat, sweat! Work and sweat, cry and sweat, pray and sweat!"

"What's that got to do with me?" he asked brutally.

"What's it got to do with you, Sykes? Mah tub of suds is filled yo' belly with vittles more times than yo' hands is filled it. Mah sweat is done paid for this house and Ah reckon Ah kin keep on sweatin' in it."

She seized the iron skillet from the stove and struck a defensive pose, which act surprised him greatly, coming from her. It cowed him and he did not strike her as he usually did.

"Naw you won't," she panted, "that ole snaggle-toothed black woman you runnin' with aint comin' heah to pile up on *mah* sweat and blood. You aint paid for nothin' on this place, and Ah'm gointer stay right heah till Ah'm toted out foot foremost."

"Well, you better quit gittin' me riled up, else they'll be totin' you out sooner than you expect. Ah'm so tired of you Ah don't know whut to do. Gawd! how Ah hates skinny wimmen!"

A little awed by this new Delia, he sidled out of the door and slammed the back gate after him. He did not say where he had gone, but she knew too well. She knew very well that he would not return until nearly daybreak also. Her work over, she went on to bed but not to sleep at once. Things had come to a pretty pass!

She lay awake, gazing upon the debris that cluttered their matrimonial trail. Not an image left standing along the way. Anything like flowers had long ago been drowned in the salty stream that had been pressed from her heart. Her tears, her sweat, her blood. She had brought love to the union and he had brought a longing after the flesh. Two months after the wedding, he had given her the first brutal beating. She had the memory of his numerous trips to Orlando with all of his wages when he had returned to her penniless, even before the first year had passed. She was young and soft then, but now she thought of her knotty, muscled limbs, her harsh knuckly hands, and drew herself up into an unhappy little ball in the middle of the big feather bed. Too late now to hope for love, even if it were not Bertha it would be someone else. This case differed from the others only in that she was bolder than the others. Too late for everything except her little home. She had built it for her old days, and planted one by one the trees and flowers there. It was lovely to her, lovely.

Somehow, before sleep came, she found herself saying aloud: "Oh well, whatever goes over the Devil's back, is got to come under his belly. Sometime or ruther, Sykes, like everybody else, is gointer reap his sowing." After that she was able to build a spiritual earthworks against her husband. His shells could no longer reach her. *Amen.* She went to sleep and slept until he announced his presence in bed by kicking her feet and rudely snatching the cover away.

"Gimme some kivah heah, an' git yo' damn foots over on yo' own side! Ah oughter mash you in yo' mouf fuh drawing dat skillet on me."

Delia went clear to the rail without answering him. A triumphant indifference to all that he was or did.

The week was as full of work for Delia as all other weeks, and Saturday found her behind her little pony, collecting and delivering clothes.

It was a hot, hot day near the end of July. The village men on Joe Clarke's porch even chewed cane listlessly. They did not hurl the cane-knots as usual. They let them dribble over the edge of the porch. Even conversation had collapsed under the heat.

"Heah come Delia Jones," Jim Merchant said, as the shaggy pony came 'round the bend of the road toward them. The rusty buckboard was heaped with baskets of crisp, clean laundry.

"Yep," Joe Lindsay agreed. "Hot or col', rain or shine, jes ez reg'lar ez de weeks roll roun' Delia carries 'em an' fetches 'em on Sat'day."

"She better if she wanter eat," said Moss. "Sykes Jones aint wuth de shot an' powder hit would tek tuh kill 'em. Not to *huh* he aint."

"He sho' aint," Walter Thomas chimed in. "It's too bad, too, cause she wuz a right pritty li'l trick when he got huh. Ah'd uh mah'ied huh mahseff if he hadnter beat me to it."

Delia nodded briefly at the men as she drove past.

"Too much knockin' will ruin *any* 'oman. He done beat huh 'nough tuh kill three women, let 'lone change they looks," said Elijah Moseley. "How Sykes kin stommuck dat big black greasy Mogul he's layin' roun' wid, gits me. Ah swear dat eight-rock couldn't kiss a sardine can Ah done thowed out de back do' 'way las' yeah."

"Aw, she's fat, thass how come. He's allus been crazy 'bout fat women," put in Merchant. "He'd a' been tied up wid one long time ago if he could a' found one tuh have him. Did Ah tell yuh 'bout him come sidlin' roun' *mah* wife—bringin' her a basket uh pee-cans outa his yard fuh a present? Yessir, mah wife! She tol' him tuh take 'em right straight back home, cause Delia works so hard ovah dat washtub she reckon everything on de place taste lak sweat an' soapsuds. Ah jus' wisht Ah'd a' caught 'im 'roun' dere! Ah'd a' made his hips ketch on fiah down dat shell road."

"Ah know he done it, too. Ah sees 'im grinnin' at every 'oman dat passes," Walter Thomas said. "But even so, he useter eat some mighty big hunks uh humble pie tuh git dat lil' 'oman he got. She wuz ez pritty ez a speckled pup! Dat wuz fifteen yeahs ago. He useter be so skeered uh losin' huh, she could make him do some parts of a husband's duty. Dey never wuz de same in de mind."

"There oughter be a law about him," said Lindsay. "He aint fit tuh carry guts tuh a bear."

Clarke spoke for the first time. "Taint no law on earth dat kin make a man be decent if it aint in 'im. There's plenty men dat takes a wife lak dey do a joint uh sugar-cane. It's round, juicy an' sweet when dey gits it. But dey squeeze an' grind, squeeze an' grind an' wring tell dey wring every drop uh pleasure dat's in 'em out. When dey's satisfied dat dey is wrung dry, dey treats 'em jes lak dey do a cane-chew. Dey thows 'em away. Dey knows whut dey is doin' while dey is at it, an' hates theirselves fuh it but they keeps on hangin' after huh tell she's empty. Den dey hates huh fuh bein' a cane-chew an' in de way."

"We oughter take Sykes an' dat stray 'oman uh his'n down in Lake Howell swamp an' lay on de rawhide till they cain't say 'Lawd a' mussy.' He allus wuz uh ovahbearin' niggah, but since dat white 'oman from up north done teached 'im how to run a automobile, he done got too biggety to live—an' we oughter kill 'im," Old Man Anderson advised.

A grunt of approval went around the porch. But the heat was melting their civic virtue and Elijah Moseley began to bait Joe Clarke.

"Come on, Joe, git a melon outa dere an' slice it up for yo' customers. We'se all sufferin' wid de heat. De bear's done got *me!*"

"Thass right, Joe, a watermelon is jes' whut Ah needs tuh cure de eppizudicks." Walter Thomas joined forces with Moseley. "Come on dere, Joe. We all is steady customers an' you aint set us up in a long time. Ah chooses dat long, bowlegged Floridy favorite."

"A god, an' be dough. You all gimme twenty cents and slice away," Clarke retorted. "Ah needs a col' slice m'self. Heah, everybody chip in. Ah'll lend y'all mah meat knife."

The money was quickly subscribed and the huge melon brought forth. At that moment, Sykes and Bertha arrived. A determined silence fell on the porch and the melon was put away again.

Merchant snapped down the blade of his jack-knife and moved toward the store door.

"Come on in, Joe, an' gimme a slab uh sow belly an' uh pound uh coffee—almost fuhgot 'twas Sat'day. Got to git on home." Most of the men left also.

Just then Delia drove past on her way home, as Sykes was ordering magnificently for Bertha. It pleased him for Delia to see.

"Git whutsoever yo' heart desires, Honey. Wait a minute, Joe. Give huh two botles uh strawberry soda-water, uh quart uh parched ground-peas, an a block uh chewin' gum."

With all this they left the store, with Sykes reminding Bertha that this was his town and she could have it if she wanted it.

The men returned soon after they left, and held their watermelon feast.

"Where did Sykes Jones git dat 'oman from nohow?" Lindsay asked.

"Ovah Apopka. Guess dey musta been cleanin' out de town when she lef'. She don't look lak a thing but a hunk uh liver wid hair on it."

"Well, she sho' kin squall," Dave Carter contributed. "When she gits ready tuh laff, she jes' opens huh mouf an' latches it back tuh de las' notch. No ole grandpa alligator down in Lake Bell aint got nothin' on huh."

Bertha had been in town three months now. Sykes was still paying her room rent at Della Lewis'—the only house in town that would have taken her in. Sykes took her frequently to Winter Park to "stomps." He still assured her that he was the swellest man in the state.

"Sho' you kin have dat lil' ole house soon's Ah kin git dat 'oman outa dere. Everything b'longs tuh me an' you sho' kin have it. Ah sho' 'bominates uh skinny 'oman. Lawdy, you sho' is got one portly shape on you! You kin git *anything* you wants. Dis is *mah* town an' you sho' kin have it."

Delia's work-worn knees crawled over the earth in Gethsemane and up the rocks of Calvary many, many times during these months. She avoided the villagers and meeting places in her efforts to be blind and deaf. But Bertha nullified this to a degree, by coming to Delia's house to call Sykes out to her at the gate.

Delia and Sykes fought all the time now with no peaceful interludes. They slept and ate in silence. Two or three times Delia had attempted a timid friendliness, but she was repulsed each time. It was plain that the breaches must remain agape.

The sun had burned July to August. The heat streamed down like a million hot arrows, smiting all things living upon the earth. Grass withered, leaves browned, snakes went blind in shedding and men and dogs went mad. Dog days!

Delia came home one day and found Sykes there before her. She wondered, but started to go on into the house without speaking, even though he was standing in the kitchen door and she must either stoop under his arm or ask him to move. He made no room for her. She noticed a soap box beside the steps, but paid no particular attention to it, knowing that he must have brought it there. As she was stooping to pass under his outstretched arm, he suddenly pushed her backward, laughingly.

"Look in de box dere Delia, Ah done brung yuh somethin'!"

She nearly fell upon the box in her stumbling, and when she saw what it held, she all but fainted outright.

"Sykes! Sykes, mah Gawd! You take dat rattlesnake 'way from heah! You *gottuh*. Oh, Jesus, have mussy!"

"Ah aint gut tuh do nuthin' uh de kin'—fact is Ah aint got tuh do nothin' but die. Taint no use uh you puttin' on airs makin' out lak you skeered uh dat snake—he's gointer stay right heah tell he die. He wouldn't bite me cause Ah knows how tuh handle 'im. Nohow he wouldn't risk breakin' out his fangs 'gin *yo'* skinny laigs."

"Naw, now Sykes, don't keep dat thing 'roun' heah tuh skeer me tuh death. You knows Ah'm even feared uh earth worms. Thass de biggest snake Ah evah did see. Kill 'im Sykes, please."

"Doan ast me tuh do nothin' fuh yuh. Goin' 'roun' tryin' tuh be so damn astorperious. Naw, Ah aint gonna kill it. Ah think uh damn sight mo' uh him dan you! Dat's a nice snake an' anybody doan lak 'im kin jes' hit de grit."

The village soon heard that Sykes had the snake, and came to see and ask questions.

"How de hen-fire did you ketch dat six-foot rattler, Sykes?" Thomas asked.

"He's full uh frogs so he caint hardly move, thass how Ah eased up on 'm. But Ah'm a snake charmer an' knows how tuh handle 'em. Shux, dat aint nothin'. Ah could ketch one eve'y day if Ah so wanted tuh."

"Whut he needs is a heavy hick'ry club leaned real heavy on his head. Dat's de bes 'way tuh charm a rattlesnake."

"Naw, Walt, y'all jes' don't understand dese diamon' backs lak Ah do," said Sykes in a superior tone of voice.

The village agreed with Walter, but the snake stayed on. His box remained by the kitchen door with its screen wire covering. Two or three days later it had digested its meal of frogs and literally came to life. It rattled at every movement in the kitchen or the yard. One day as Delia came down the kitchen steps she saw his chalky-white fangs curved like scimitars hung in the wire meshes. This time she did not run away with averted eyes as usual. She stood for a long time in the doorway in a red fury that grew bloodier for every second that she regarded the creature that was her torment.

That night she broached the subject as soon as Sykes sat down to the table.

"Sykes, Ah wants you tuh take dat snake 'way fum heah. You done starved me an' Ah put up widcher, you done beat me an Ah took dat, but you done kilt all mah insides bringin' dat varmint heah."

Sykes poured out a saucer full of coffee and drank it deliberately before he answered her.

"A whole lot Ah keer 'bout how you feels inside uh out. Dat snake aint goin' no damn wheah till Ah gits ready fuh 'im tuh go. So fur as beatin' is concerned, yuh aint took near all dat you gointer take ef yuh stay 'roun' *me*."

Delia pushed back her plate and got up from the table. "Ah hates you, Sykes," she said calmly. "Ah hates you tuh de same degree dat Ah useter love yuh. Ah done took an' took till mah belly is full up tuh mah neck. Dat's de reason Ah got mah letter fum de church an' moved mah membership tuh Woodbridge—so Ah don't haftuh take no sacrament wid yuh. Ah don't wantuh see yuh 'roun' me a-tall. Lay 'roun' wid dat 'oman all yuh wants tuh, but gwan 'way fum me an' mah house. Ah hates yuh lak uh suck-egg dog."

Sykes almost let the huge wad of corn bread and collard greens he was chewing fall out of his mouth in amazement. He had a hard time whipping himself up to the proper fury to try to answer Delia.

"Well, Ah'm glad you does hate me. Ah'm sho' tiahed uh you hangin' ontuh me. Ah don't want yuh. Look at yuh stringey ole neck! Yo' rawbony laigs an' arms is enough tuh cut uh man tuh death. You looks jes' lak de devvul's doll-baby tuh *me*. You cain't hate me no worse dan Ah hates you. Ah been hatin' *you* fuh years."

"Yo' ole black hide don't look lak nothin' tuh me, but uh passel uh wrinkled up rubber, wid yo' big ole yeahs flappin' on each side lak uh paih uh buzzard wings. Don't think Ah'm gointuh be run way fum mah house neither. Ah'm goin' tuh de white folks bout *you*, mah young man, de very nex' time you lay yo' han's on me. Mah cup is done run ovah." Delia said this with no signs of fear and Sykes departed from the house, threatening her, but made not the slightest move to carry out any of them.

That night he did not return at all, and the next day being Sunday, Delia was glad that she did not have to quarrel before she hitched up her pony and drove the four miles to Woodbridge.

She stayed to the night service—"love feast"—which was very warm and full of spirit. In the emotional winds her domestic trials were borne far and wide so that she sang as she drove homeward,

Jurden water, black an' col'
Chills de body, not de soul
An' Ah wantah cross Jurden in uh calm time.

She came from the barn to the kitchen door and stopped.

"Whut's de mattah, ol' satan, you aint kickin' up yo' racket?" She addressed the snake's box. Complete silence. She went on into the house with a new hope in its birth struggles. Perhaps her threat to go to the white folks had frightened Sykes! Perhaps he was sorry! Fifteen years of misery and suppression had brought Delia to the place where she would hope *anything* that looked towards a way over or through her wall of inhibitions.

She felt in the match safe behind the stove at once for a match. There was only one there.

"Dat niggah wouldn't fetch nothin' heah tuh save his rotten neck, but he kin run thew whut Ah brings quick enough. Now he done toted off nigh on tuh haff uh box uh matches. He done had dat 'oman heah in mah house, too."

Nobody but a woman could tell how she knew this even before she struck the match. But she did and it put her into a new fury.

Presently she brought in the tubs to put the white things to soak. This time she decided she need not bring the hamper out of the bedroom; she would go in there and do the sorting. She picked up the pot-bellied lamp and went in. The room was small and the hamper stood hard by the foot of the white iron bed. She could sit and reach through the bedposts—resting as she worked.

"Ah wantah cross Jurden in uh calm time." She was singing again. The mood of the "love feast" had returned. She threw back the lid of the basket almost gaily. Then, moved by both horror and terror, she sprung back toward the door. *There lay the snake in the basket!* He moved sluggishly at first, but even as she turned round and round, jumped up and down in an insanity of fear, he began to stir vigorously. She saw him pouring his awful beauty from the basket upon the bed, then she seized the lamp and ran as fast as she could to the kitchen. The wind from the open door blew out the light and the darkness added to her terror. She sped to the darkness of the yard, slamming the door after her before she thought to set down the lamp. She did not feel safe even on the ground, so she climbed up in the hay barn.

There for an hour or more she lay sprawled upon the hay a gibbering wreck.

Finally she grew quiet, and after that, coherent thought. With this, stalked through her a cold, bloody rage. Hours of this. A period of introspection, a space of retrospection, then a mixture of both. Out of this an awful calm.

"Well, Ah done de bes' Ah could. If things aint right, Gawd knows taint mah fault."

She went to sleep—a twitchy sleep—and woke up to a faint gray sky. There was a loud hollow sound below. She peered out. Sykes was at the wood-pile, demolishing a wire-covered box.

He hurried to the kitchen door, but hung outside there some minutes before he entered, and stood some minutes more inside before he closed it after him.

The gray in the sky was spreading. Delia descended without fear now, and crouched beneath the low bedroom window. The drawn shade shut out the dawn, shut in the night. But the thin walls held back no sound.

"Dat ol' scratch is woke up now!" She mused at the tremendous whirr inside, which every woodsman knows, is one of the sound illusions. The rattler is a ventriloquist. His whirr sounds to the right, to the left, straight ahead, behind, close under foot—everywhere but where it is. Woe to him who guesses wrong unless he is prepared to hold up his end of the argument! Sometimes he strikes without rattling at all.

Inside, Skyes heard nothing until he knocked a pot lid off the stove while trying to reach the match safe in the dark. He had emptied his pockets at Bertha's.

The snake seemed to wake up under the stove and Skyes made a quick leap into the bedroom. In spite of the gin he had had, his head was clearing now.

"Mah Gawd!" he chattered, "ef Ah could on'y strack uh light!"

The rattling ceased for a moment as he stood paralyzed. He waited. It seemed that the snake waited also.

"Oh fuh de light! Ah thought he'd be too sick"—Skyes was muttering to himself when the whirr began again, closer, right underfoot this time. Long before this, Skyes' ability to think had been flattened down to primitive instinct and he leaped—onto the bed.

Outside Delia heard a cry that might have come from a maddened chimpanzee, a stricken gorilla. All the terror, all the horror, all the rage that man possibly could express, without a recognizable human sound.

A tremendous stir inside there, another series of animal screams, the intermittent whirr of the reptile. The shade torn violently down from the window, letting in the red dawn, a huge brown hand seizing the window stick, great dull blows upon the wooden floor punctuating the gibberish of sound long after the rattle of the snake had abruptly subsided. All this Delia could see and hear from her place beneath the window, and it made her ill. She crept over to the four-o'clocks and stretched herself on the cool earth to recover.

She lay there. "Delia, Delia!" She could hear Skyes calling in a most despairing tone as one who expected no answer. The sun crept on up, and he called. Delia could not move—her legs were gone flabby. She never moved, he called, and the sun kept rising.

"Mah Gawd!" she heard him moan. "Mah Gawd fum Heben!" She heard him stumbling about and got up from her flower-bed. The sun was growing warm. As she approached the door she heard him call out hopefully, "Delia, is dat you Ah heah?"

She saw him on his hands and knees as soon as she reached the door. He crept an inch or two toward her—all that he was able, and she saw his horribly swollen neck and his one open eye shining with hope. A surge of pity too strong to support bore her away from that eye that must, could not, fail to see the tubs. He would see the lamp. Orlando with its doctors was too far. She could scarcely reach the Chinaberry tree, where she waited in the growing heat while inside she knew the cold river was creeping up and up to extinguish that eye which must know by now that she knew.

1926

The Eatonville Anthology[1]

I. The Pleading Woman

Mrs. Tony Roberts is the pleading woman. She just loves to ask for things. Her husband gives her all he can take and scrape, which is considerably more than most wives get for their housekeeping, but she goes from door to door begging for things.

She starts at the store. "Mist' Clarke," she sing-songs in a high keening voice, "gimme lil' piece uh meat tuh boil a pot uh greens wid. Lawd knows me an' mah chillen is so hongry! Hits uh SHAME! Tony don't fee-ee-eee-ed me!"

Mr. Clarke knows that she has money and that her larder is well stocked, for Tony Roberts is the best provider on his list. But her keening annoys him and he rises heavily. The pleader at his elbow shows all the joy of a starving man being seated at a feast.

"Thass right Mist' Clarke. De Lawd loveth de cheerful giver. Gimme jes' a lil' piece 'bout dis big (indicating the width of her hand) an' de Lawd'll bless yuh."

She follows this angel-on-earth to his meat tub and superintends the cutting, crying out in pain when he refuses to move the knife over just a teeny bit mo'.

Finally, meat in hand, she departs, remarking on the meanness of some people who give a piece of salt meat only two-fingers wide when they were plainly asked for a hand-wide piece. Clarke puts it down to Tony's account and resumes his reading.

With the slab of salt pork as a foundation, she visits various homes until she has collected all she wants for the day. At the Piersons for instance: "Sister Pierson, plee-ee-ease gimme uh han'full uh collard greens fuh me an' mah po' chillen! 'Deed, me an' mah chillen is so hongry. Tony doan' fee-ee-eed me!"

Mrs. Pierson picks a bunch of greens for her, but she springs away from them as if they were poison. "Lawd a mussy, Mis' Pierson, you ain't gonna gimme dat lil' eye-full uh greens fuh me an' mah chillen, is you? Don't be so graspin'; Gawd won't bless yuh. Gimme uh han'full mo'. Lawd, some folks is got everything, an' theys jes' as gripin' an stingy!"

Mrs. Pierson raises the ante, and the pleading woman moves on to the next place, and on and on. The next day, it commences all over.

1. The text is that of *I Love Myself When I Am Laughing . . . and Then Again When I Am Looking Mean and Impressive* (1979), edited by Alice Walker. Eatonville was Hurston's hometown; here she brings together many of the stories about its residents that she told at parties in Harlem. The stories are cast in the forms of traditional African American tales.

II. Turpentine Love

Jim Merchant is always in good humor—even with his wife. He says he fell in love with her at first sight. That was some years ago. She has had all her teeth pulled out, but they still get along splendidly.

He says the first time he called on her he found out that she was subject to fits. This didn't cool his love, however. She had several in his presence.

One Sunday, while he was there, she had one, and her mother tried to give her a dose of turpentine to stop it. Accidentally, she spilled it in her eye and it cured her. She never had another fit, so they got married and have kept each other in good humor ever since.

III.

Becky Moore has eleven children of assorted colors and sizes. She has never been married, but that is not her fault. She has never stopped any of the fathers of her children from proposing, so if she has no father for her children it's not her fault. The men round about are entirely to blame.

The other mothers of the town are afraid that it is catching. They won't let their children play with hers.

IV. Tippy

Sykes Jones' family all shoot craps. The most interesting member of the family—also fond of bones, but another kind—is Tippy, the Jones' dog.

He is so thin, that it amazes one that he lives at all. He sneaks into village kitchens if the housewives are careless about the doors and steals meats, even off the stoves. He also sucks eggs.

For these offenses he has been sentenced to death dozens of times, and the sentences executed upon him, only they didn't work. He has been fed bluestone, strychnine, nux vomica, even an entire Peruna[2] bottle beaten up. It didn't fatten him, but it didn't kill him. So Eatonville has resigned itself to the plague of Tippy, reflecting that it has erred in certain matters and is being chastened.

In spite of all the attempts upon his life, Tippy is still willing to be friendly with anyone who will let him.

V. The Way of a Man with a Train

Old Man Anderson lived seven or eight miles out in the country from Eatonville. Over by Lake Apopka. He raised feed-corn and cassava and went to market with it two or three times a year. He bought all of his victuals wholesale so he wouldn't have to come to town for several months more.

He was different from citybred folks. He had never seen a train. Everybody laughed at him for even the smallest child in Eatonville had either been to Maitland or Orlando and watched a train go by. On Sunday afternoons all of the young people of the village would go over to Maitland, a

2. A patent medicine cure-all.

mile away, to see Number 35 whizz southward on its way to Tampa and wave at the passengers. So we looked down on him a little. Even we children felt superior in the presence of a person so lacking in worldly knowledge.

The grown-ups kept telling him he ought to go see a train. He always said he didn't have time to wait so long. Only two trains a day passed through Maitland. But patronage and ridicule finally had its effect and Old Man Anderson drove in one morning early. Number 78 went north to Jacksonville at 10:20. He drove his light wagon over in the woods beside the railroad below Maitland, and sat down to wait. He began to fear that his horse would get frightened and run away with the wagon. So he took him out and led him deeper into the grove and tied him securely. Then he returned to his wagon and waited some more. Then he remembered that some of the train-wise villagers had said the engine belched fire and smoke. He had better move his wagon out of danger. It might catch fire. He climbed down from the seat and placed himself between the shafts to draw it away. Just then 78 came thundering over the trestle spouting smoke, and suddenly began blowing for Maitland. Old Man Anderson became so frightened he ran away with the wagon through the woods and tore it up worse than the horse ever could have done. He doesn't know yet what a train looks like, and says he doesn't care.

VI. Coon Taylor

Coon Taylor never did any real stealing. Of course, if he saw a chicken or a watermelon he'd take it. The people used to get mad but they never could catch him. He took so many melons from Joe Clarke that he set up in the melon patch one night with his shotgun loaded with rock-salt. He was going to fix Coon. But he was tired. It is hard work being a mayor, postmaster, storekeeper and everything. He dropped asleep sitting on a stump in the middle of the patch. So he didn't see Coon when he came. Coon didn't see him either, that is, not at first. He knew the stump was there, however. He had opened many of Clarke's juicy Florida Favorite on it. He selected his fruit, walked over to the stump and burst the melon on it. This is, he thought it was the stump until it fell over with a yell. Then he knew it was no stump and departed hastily from those parts. He had cleared the fence when Clarke came to, as it were. So the charge of rock-salt was wasted on the desert air.

During the sugar-cane season, he found he couldn't resist Clarke's soft green cane, but Clarke did not go to sleep this time. So after he had cut six or eight stalks by the moonlight, Clarke rose up out of the cane strippings with his shotgun and made Coon sit right down and chew up the last one of them on the spot. And the next day he made Coon leave his town for three months.

VII. Village Fiction

Joe Lindsay is said by Lum Boger to be the largest manufacturer of prevarications in Eatonville; Brazzle (late owner of the world's leanest and meanest mule) contends that his business is the largest in the state and his wife holds that he is the biggest liar in the world.

Exhibit A—He claims that while he was in Orlando one day he saw a doctor cut open a woman, remove everything—liver, lights and heart included—

clean each of them separately; the doctor then washed out the empty woman, dried her out neatly with a towel and replaced the organs so expertly that she was up and about her work in a couple of weeks.

VIII.

Sewell is a man who lives all to himself. He moves a great deal. So often, that 'Lige Moseley says his chickens are so used to moving that every time he comes out into his backyard the chickens lie down and cross their legs, ready to be tied up again.

He is baldheaded; but he says he doesn't mind that, because he wants as little as possible between him and God.

IX.

Mrs. Clarke is Joe Clarke's wife. She is a soft-looking, middle-aged woman, whose bust and stomach are always holding a get-together.

She waits on the store sometimes and cries every time he yells at her which he does every time she makes a mistake, which is quite often. She calls her husband "Jody." They say he used to beat her in the store when he was a young man, but he is not so impatient now. He can wait until he goes home.

She shouts in Church every Sunday and shakes the hand of fellowship with everybody in the Church with her eyes closed, but somehow always misses her husband.

X.

Mrs. McDuffy goes to Church every Sunday and always shouts and tells her "determination." Her husband always sits in the back row and beats her as soon as they get home. He says there's no sense in her shouting, as big a devil as she is. She just does it to slur him. Elijah Moseley asked her why she didn't stop shouting, seeing she always got a beating about it. She says she can't "squinch the sperrit." Then Elijah asked Mr. McDuffy to stop beating her, seeing that she was going to shout anyway. He answered that she just did it for spite and that his fist was just as hard as her head. He could last just as long as she. So the village let the matter rest.

XI. Double-Shuffle

Back in the good old days before the World War, things were very simple in Eatonville. People didn't fox-trot. When the town wanted to put on its Sunday clothes and wash behind the ears, it put on a "breakdown." The daring younger set would two-step and waltz, but the good church members and the elders stuck to the grand march. By rural canons dancing is wicked, but one is not held to have danced until the feet have been crossed. Feet don't get crossed when one grand marches.

At elaborate affairs the organ from the Methodist church was moved up to the hall and Lizzimore, the blind man, presided. When informal gatherings were held, he merely played his guitar assisted by any volunteer with mouth organs or accordions.

Among white people the march is as mild as if it had been passed on by Volstead.[3] But it still has a kick in Eatonville. Everybody happy, shining eyes, gleaming teeth. Feet dragged 'shhlap, shhlap! to beat out the time. No orchestra needed. Round and round! Back again, parse-me-la! shlap! shlap! Strut! Strut! Seaboard! Shlap! Shalp! Tiddy bumm! Mr. Clarke in the lead with Mrs. Moseley.

It's too much for some of the young folks. Double shuffling commences. Buck and wing. Lizzimore about to break his guitar. Accordion doing contortions. People fall back against the walls, and let the soloist have it, shouting as they clap the old, old double-shuffle songs.

'Me an' mah honey got two mo' days
Two mo' days tuh do de buck'

Sweating bodies, laughing mouths, grotesque faces, feet drumming fiercely. Deacons clapping as hard as the rest.

"Great big nigger, black as tar
Trying tuh git tuh hebben on uh 'lectric car."

"Some love cabbage, some love kale
But I love a gal wid a short skirt tail."
Long tall angel—steppin' down,
Long white robe an' starry crown.

'Ah would not marry uh black gal (bumm bumm!)
Tell yuh de reason why
Every time she comb her hair
She make de goo-goo eye.

Would not marry a yaller gal (bumm bumm!)
Tell yuh de reason why
Her neck so long an' stringy
Ahm 'fraid she'd never die.

Would not marry uh preacher
Tell yuh de reason why
Every time he comes tuh town
He makes de chicken fly.

When the buck dance[4] was over, the boys would give the floor to the girls and they would parse-me-la with a sly eye out of the corner to see if anybody was looking who might "have them up in church" on conference night.[5] Then there would be more dancing. Then Mr. Clarke would call for everybody's best attention and announce that *'freshments was served! Every gent'man would please take his lady by the arm and scorch*[6] her right up to de table fur a treat!

Then the men would stick their arms out with a flourish and ask their ladies: "You lak chicken? Well, then, take a wing." And the ladies would take the proferred "wings" and parade up to the long table and be served.

3. Andrew J. Volstead (1860–1947), congressman who introduced the Prohibition Amendment.
4. All-male dance.
5. A formal meeting of church officials. The girls are afraid they might be accused of loose behavior.
6. Escort (dialect).

Of course most of them had brought baskets in which were heaps of jointed and fried chicken, two or three kinds of pies, cakes, potato pone and chicken purlo.[7] The hall would separate into happy groups about the baskets until time for more dancing.

But the boys and girls got scattered about during the war, and now they dance the fox-trot by a brand new piano. They do waltz and two-step still, but no one now considers it good form to lock his chin over his partner's shoulder and stick out behind. One night just for fun and to humor the old folks, they danced, that is, they grand marched, but everyone picked up their feet. *Bah!!*

XII. The Head of the Nail

Daisy Taylor was the town vamp. Not that she was pretty. But sirens were all but non-existent in the town. Perhaps she was forced to it by circumstances. She was quite dark, with little bushy patches of hair squatting over her head. These were held down by shingle-nails often. No one knows whether she did this for artistic effect or for lack of hairpins, but there they were shining in the little patches of hair when she got all dressed for the afternoon and came up to Clarke's store to see if there was any mail for her.

It was seldom that anyone wrote to Daisy, but she knew that the men of the town would be assembled there by five o'clock, and some one could usually be induced to buy her some soda water or peanuts.

Daisy flirted with married men. There were only two single men in town. Lum Boger, who was engaged to the assistant school-teacher, and Hiram Lester, who had been off to school at Tuskegee and wouldn't look at a person like Daisy. In addition to other drawbacks, she was pigeon-toed and her petticoat was always showing so perhaps he was justified. There was nothing else to do except flirt with married men.

This went on for a long time. First one wife and then another complained of her, or drove her from the preserves by threat.

But the affair with Crooms was the most prolonged and serious. He was even known to have bought her a pair of shoes.

Mrs. Laura Crooms was a meek little woman who took all of her troubles crying, and talked a great deal of leaving things in the hands of God.

The affair came to a head one night in orange picking time. Crooms was over at Oneido picking oranges. Many fruit pickers move from one town to the other during the season.

The *town* was collected at the store-postoffice as is customary on Saturday nights. The *town* has had its bath and with its week's pay in pocket fares forth to be merry. The men tell stories and treat the ladies to soda water, peanuts and peppermint candy.

Daisy was trying to get treats, but the porch was cold to her that night.

"Ah don't keer if you don't treat me. What's a dirty lil nickel?" She flung this at Walter Thomas. "The everloving Mister Crooms will gimme anything atall Ah wants."

7. I.e., pilaf; a stew of rice, vegetables, and chicken.

"You better shet up yo' mouf talking 'bout Albert Crooms. Heah his wife comes right now."

Daisy went akimbo. "Who? Me! Ah don't keer whut Laura Crooms think. If she ain't a heavy hip-ted Mama enough to keep him, she don't need to come crying to me."

She stood making goo-goo eyes as Mrs. Crooms walked upon the porch. Daisy laughed loud, made several references to Albert Crooms, and when she saw the mail-bag come in from Maitland she said, "Ah better go in an' see if Ah ain't got a letter from Oneido."

The more Daisy played the game of getting Mrs. Crooms' goat, the better she liked it. She ran in and out of the store laughing until she could scarcely stand. Some of the people present began to talk to Mrs. Crooms—to egg her on to halt Daisy's boasting, but she was for leaving it all in the hands of God. Walter Thomas kept on after Mrs. Crooms until she stiffened and resolved to fight. Daisy was inside when she came to this resolve and never dreamed anything of the kind could happen. She had gotten hold of an envelope and came laughing and shouting, "Oh, Ah can't stand to see Oneido lose!"

There was a box of ax-handles on display on the porch, propped up against the door jamb. As Daisy stepped upon the porch, Mrs. Crooms leaned the heavy end of one of those handles heavily upon her head. She staggered from the porch to the ground and the timid Laura, fearful of a counter-attack, struck again and Daisy toppled into the town ditch. There was not enough water in there to do more than muss her up. Every time she tried to rise, down would come that ax-handle again. Laura was fighting a scared fight. With Daisy thoroughly licked, she retired to the store porch and left her fallen enemy in the ditch. But Elijah Moseley, who was some distance down the street when the trouble began, arrived as the victor was withdrawing. He rushed up and picked Daisy out of the mud and began feeling her head.

"Is she hurt much?" Joe Clarke asked from the doorway.

"I don't know," Elijah answered. "I was just looking to see if Laura had been lucky enough to hit one of those nails on the head and drive it in."

Before a week was up, Daisy moved to Orlando. There in a wider sphere, perhaps, her talents as a vamp were appreciated.

XIII. Pants and Cal'line

Sister Cal'line Potts was a silent woman. Did all of her laughing down inside, but did the thing that kept the town in an uproar of laughter. It was the general opinion of the village that Cal'line would do anything she had a mind to. And she had a mind to do several things.

Mitchell Potts, her husband, had a weakness for women. No one ever believed that she was jealous. She did things to the women, surely. But most any townsman would have said that she did them because she liked the novel situation and the queer things she could bring out of it.

Once he took up with Delphine—called Mis' Pheeny by the town. She lived on the outskirts on the edge of the piney woods. The town winked and talked. People don't make secrets of such things in villages. Cal'line went about her business with her thin black lips pursed tight as ever, and her shiny black eyes unchanged.

"Dat devil of a Cal'line's got somethin' up her sleeve!" The town smiled in anticipation.

"Delphine is too big a cigar for her to smoke. She ain't crazy," said some as the weeks went on and nothing happened. Even Pheeny herself would give an extra flirt to her over-starched petticoats as she rustled into church past her of Sundays.

Mitch Potts said furthermore, that he was tired of Cal'line's foolishness. She had to stay where he put her. His African soup-bone (arm) was too strong to let a woman run over him. 'Nough was 'nough. And he did some fancy cussing, and he was the fanciest cusser in the county.

So the town waited and the longer it waited, the odds changed slowly from the wife to the husband.

One Saturday, Mitch knocked off work at two o'clock and went over to Maitland. He came back with a rectangular box under his arm and kept straight on out to the barn to put it away. He ducked around the corner of the house quickly, but even so, his wife glimpsed the package. Very much like a shoe box. So!

He put on the kettle and took a bath. She stood in her bare feet at the ironing board and kept on ironing. He dressed. It was about five o'clock but still very light. He fiddled around outside. She kept on with her ironing. As soon as the sun got red, he sauntered out to the barn, got the parcel and walked away down the road, past the store and out into the piney woods. As soon as he left the house, Cal'line slipped on her shoes without taking time to don stockings, put on one of her husband's old Stetsons, worn and floppy, slung the axe over her shoulder and followed in his wake. He was hailed cheerily as he passed the sitters on the store porch and answered smiling sheepishly and passed on. Two minutes later passed his wife, silently, unsmilingly, and set the porch to giggling and betting.

An hour passed perhaps. It was dark. Clarke had long ago lighted the swinging kerosene lamp inside.

XIV.

Once 'way back yonder before the stars fell all the animals used to talk just like people. In them days dogs and rabbits was the best of friends—even tho both of them was stuck on the same gal—which was Miss Nancy Coon. She had the sweetest smile and the prettiest striped and bushy tail to be found anywhere.

They both run their legs nigh off trying to win her for themselves—fetching nice ripe persimmons and such. But she never give one or the other no satisfaction.

Finally one night Mr. Dog popped the question right out. "Miss Coon," he says, "Ma'am, also Ma'am which would you ruther be—a lark flyin' or a dove a settin'?"

Course Miss Nancy she blushed and laughed a little and hid her face behind her bushy tail for a spell. Then she said sorter shy like, "I does love yo' sweet voice, brother dawg—but—I ain't jes' exactly set my mind yit."

Her and Mr. Dog set on a spell, when up comes hopping Mr. Rabbit wid his tail fresh washed and his whiskers shining. He got right down to business and asked Miss Coon to marry him, too.

"Oh, Miss Nancy," he says, "Ma'am, also Ma'am, if you'd see me settin' straddle of a mud-cat[8] leadin' a minnow, what would you think? Ma'am also Ma'am?" Which is a out and out proposal as everybody knows.

"Youse awful nice, Brother Rabbit and a beautiful dancer, but you cannot sing like Brother Dog. Both you uns come back next week to gimme time for to decide."

They both left arm-in-arm. Finally Mr. Rabbit says to Mr. Dog. "Taint no use in me going back—she ain't gwinter have me. So I mought as well give up. She loves singing, and I ain't got nothing but a squeak."

"Oh, don't talk that a way," says Mr. Dog, tho' he is glad Mr. Rabbit can't sing none.

"Thass all right, Brer Dog. But if I had a sweet voice like you got, I'd have it worked on and make it sweeter."

"How! How! How!" Mr. Dog cried, jumping up and down.

"Lemme fix it for you, like I do for Sister Lark and Sister Mockingbird."

"When? Where?" asked Mr. Dog, all excited. He was figuring that if he could sing just a little better Miss Coon would be bound to have him.

"Just you meet me t'morrer in de huckleberry patch," says the rabbit and off they both goes to bed.

The dog is there on time next day and after a while the rabbit comes loping up.

"Mawnin', Brer Dawg," he says kinder chippy like. "Ready to git yo' voice sweetened?"

"Sholy, sholy, Brer Rabbit. Let's we all hurry about it. I wants tuh serenade Miss Nancy from the piney woods tuh night."

"Well, den, open yo' mouf and poke out yo' tongue," says the rabbit.

No sooner did Mr. Dog poke out his tongue than Mr. Rabbit split it with a knife and ran for all he was worth to a hollow stump and hid hisself.

The dog has been mad at the rabbit ever since.

Anybody who don't believe it happened, just look at the dog's tongue and he can see for himself where the rabbit slit it right up the middle.

Stepped on a tin, mah story ends.

1927

How It Feels to Be Colored Me[1]

I am colored but I offer nothing in the way of extenuating circumstances except the fact that I am the only Negro in the United States whose grandfather on the mother's side was *not* an Indian chief.

I remember the very day that I became colored. Up to my thirteenth year I lived in the little Negro town of Eatonville, Florida. It is exclusively a colored town. The only white people I knew passed through the town going to or coming from Orlando. The native whites rode dusty horses, the Northern tourists chugged down the sandy village road in automobiles. The town

8. Catfish.
1. The text is that of *I Love Myself When I Am Laughing . . . and Then Again When I Am Looking Mean and Impressive* (1979), edited by Alice Walker.

knew the Southerners and never stopped cane chewing when they passed. But the Northerners were something else again. They were peered at cautiously from behind the curtains by the timid. The more venturesome would come out on the porch to watch them go past and got just as much pleasure out of the tourists as the tourists got out of the village.

The front porch might seem a daring place for the rest of the town, but it was a gallery seat for me. My favorite place was atop the gate-post. Proscenium box[2] for a born first-nighter. Not only did I enjoy the show, but I didn't mind the actors knowing that I liked it. I usually spoke to them in passing. I'd wave at them and when they returned my salute, I would say something like this: "Howdy-do-well-I-thank-you-where-you-goin'?" Usually automobile or the horse paused at this, and after a queer exchange of compliments, I would probably "go a piece of the way" with them, as we say in farthest Florida. If one of my family happened to come to the front in time to see me, of course negotiations would be rudely broken off. But even so, it is clear that I was the first "welcome-to-our-state" Floridian, and I hope the Miami Chamber of Commerce will please take notice.

During this period, white people differed from colored to me only in that they rode through town and never lived there. They liked to hear me "speak pieces" and sing and wanted to see me dance the parse-me-la, and gave me generously of their small silver for doing these things, which seemed strange to me for I wanted to do them so much that I needed bribing to stop. Only they didn't know it. The colored people gave no dimes. They deplored any joyful tendencies in me, but I was their Zora nevertheless. I belonged to them, to the nearby hotels, to the county—everybody's Zora.

But changes came in the family when I was thirteen, and I was sent to school in Jacksonville. I left Eatonville, the town of the oleanders, as Zora. When I disembarked from the river-boat at Jacksonville, she was no more. It seemed that I had suffered a sea change. I was not Zora of Orange County any more, I was now a little colored girl. I found it out in certain ways. In my heart as well as in the mirror, I became a fast brown—warranted not to rub nor run.

But I am not tragically colored. There is no great sorrow dammed up in my soul, nor lurking behind my eyes. I do not mind at all. I do not belong to the sobbing school of Negrohood who hold that nature somehow has given them a lowdown dirty deal and whose feelings are all hurt about it. Even in the helter-skelter skirmish that is my life, I have seen that the world is to the strong regardless of a little pigmentation more or less. No, I do not weep at the world—I am too busy sharpening my oyster knife.

Someone is always at my elbow reminding me that I am the granddaughter of slaves. It fails to register depression with me. Slavery is sixty years in the past. The operation was successful and the patient is doing well, thank you. The terrible struggle that made me an American out of a potential slave said "On the line!" The Reconstruction said "Get set!"; and the generation before said "Go!" I am off to a flying start and I must not halt in the stretch to look behind and weep. Slavery is the price I paid for civilization, and the choice was not with me. It is a bully adventure and worth all that I have paid

2. Box at the front of the auditorium, closest to the stage.

through my ancestors for it. No one on earth ever had a greater chance for glory. The world to be won and nothing to be lost. It is thrilling to think—to know that for any act of mine, I shall get twice as much praise or twice as much blame. It is quite exciting to hold the center of the national stage, with the spectators not knowing whether to laugh or to weep.

The position of my white neighbor is much more difficult. No brown specter pulls up a chair beside me when I sit down to eat. No dark ghost thrusts its leg against mine in bed. The game of keeping what one has is never so exciting as the game of getting.

I do not always feel colored. Even now I often achieve the unconscious Zora of Eatonville before the Hegira.[3] I feel most colored when I am thrown against a sharp white background.

For instance at Barnard. "Besides the waters of the Hudson" I feel my race. Among the thousand white persons, I am a dark rock surged upon, and overswept, but through it all, I remain myself. When covered by the waters, I am; and the ebb but reveals me again.

Sometimes it is the other way around. A white person is set down in our midst, but the contrast is just as sharp for me. For instance, when I sit in the drafty basement that is The New World Cabaret[4] with a white person, my color comes. We enter chatting about any little nothing that we have in common and are seated by the jazz waiters. In the abrupt way that jazz orchestras have, this one plunges into a number. It loses no time in circumlocutions, but gets right down to business. It constricts the thorax and splits the heart with its tempo and narcotic harmonies. This orchestra grows rambunctious, rears on its hind legs and attacks the tonal veil with primitive fury, rending it, clawing it until it breaks through to the jungle beyond. I follow those heathen—follow them exultingly. I dance wildly inside myself; I yell within, I whoop; I shake my assegai[5] above my head, I hurl it true to the mark *yeeeeooww!* I am in the jungle and living in the jungle way. My face is painted red and yellow and my body is painted blue. My pulse is throbbing like a war drum. I want to slaughter something—give pain, give death to what, I do not know. But the piece ends. The men of the orchestra wipe their lips and rest their fingers. I creep back slowly to the veneer we call civilization with the last tone and find the white friend sitting motionless in his seat smoking calmly.

"Good music they have here," he remarks, drumming the table with his fingertips.

Music. The great blobs of purple and red emotion have not touched him. He has only heard what I felt. He is far away and I see him but dimly across the ocean and the continent that have fallen between us. He is so pale with his whiteness then and I am *so* colored.

At certain times I have no race, I am *me*. When I set my hat at a certain angle and saunter down Seventh Avenue, Harlem City, feeling as snooty as the lions in front of the Forty-Second Street Library, for instance. So far as

3. Forced march of Muhammad from Mecca to Medina in 622 C.E.; hence any forced flight or journey for safety.

4. Popular Harlem nightclub in the 1920s.

5. A slender spear used by some South African peoples.

my feelings are concerned, Peggy Hopkins Joyce on the Boule Mich[6] with her gorgeous raiment, stately carriage, knees knocking together in a most aristocratic manner, has nothing on me. The cosmic Zora emerges. I belong to no race nor time. I am the eternal feminine with its string of beads.

I have no separate feeling about being an American citizen and colored. I am merely a fragment of the Great Soul that surges within the boundaries. My country, right or wrong.

Sometimes, I feel discriminated against, but it does not make me angry. It merely astonishes me. How *can* any deny themselves the pleasure of my company? It's beyond me.

But in the main, I feel like a brown bag of miscellany propped against a wall. Against a wall in company with other bags, white, red and yellow. Pour out the contents, and there is discovered a jumble of small things priceless and worthless. A first-water diamond, an empty spool, bits of broken glass, lengths of string, a key to a door long since crumbled away, a rusty knife-blade, old shoes saved for a road that never was and never will be, a nail bent under the weight of things too heavy for any nail, a dried flower or two still a little fragrant. In your hand is the brown bag. On the ground before you is the jumble it held—so much like the jumble in the bags, could they be emptied, that all might be dumped in a single heap and the bags refilled without altering the content of any greatly. A bit of colored glass more or less would not matter. Perhaps that is how the Great Stuffer of Bags filled them in the first place—who knows?

1928

6. Boulevard St. Michel, a street on the Left Bank of Paris running through the Latin Quarter. It is lined with cafés that were—and still are—frequented by Americans. Joyce was a much-photographed socialite and heiress.

NELLA LARSEN
1891–1964

Harlem Renaissance leaders proposed that African American artists and intellectuals should uplift their race. In the famous phrase of W. E. B. Du Bois, it was the duty of the "talented tenth" to educate the masses of black Americans while at the same time leading the struggle against white prejudice. This ideology inspired many writers but produced divisive arguments: should African American writing be anchored in authentic popular black culture—whether found in the folkways of the rural South or in the jazz scene of urban communities—or should it represent the deliberately cosmopolitan, educated cultural style of the "New Negroes"? Modernist writers' interest in the "primitive" accentuated these debates. Writers of the Harlem Renaissance were well aware of how African Americans had been stereotypically demeaned as primitive, uncultured, indeed barely human; given that history, was it possible to celebrate an African American identity authentically rooted in black folk culture?

Nella Larsen's writings showed how uplift's demand for racial allegiance could tear apart the inner lives of African Americans. Her own mixed-race background enabled her to see that already in the 1920s the majority of Americans socially categorized as "Negroes" were in fact people of mixed racial ancestry, and this led her to ask how there could be such a thing as racial authenticity if there was no such thing as "pure" race. Nevertheless, she saw that even if race was an artificial construct, it had powerfully real effects—effects that to her were always destructive of African American selfhood.

Larsen was born in Chicago, of a white mother—a Danish immigrant—and a black West Indian father. He died when she was two, and her mother then married a white man. Larsen, a visibly dark child, was viewed by her visibly light family as an embarrassment. At the age of sixteen she attended a high school connected to Fisk University in Nashville, Tennessee. This, her first experience in an all-black environment, lasted for only a year (1907–8). She moved to Copenhagen, Denmark, where she stayed from 1909 to 1912, visiting relatives and auditing classes at the university. Up to this point—but not beyond it—her life story resembles that of Helga Crane, protagonist of Larsen's first novel, *Quicksand*.

Returning to the United States after three years abroad, Larsen studied and then practiced nursing for several years. In 1919 she married Elmer Samuel Imes, a black research physicist who later became chair of Fisk University's Physics Department. In 1922, now residing in Harlem, she left nursing and began to work for the New York Public Library system. By 1926 she and her husband were involved in the Harlem Renaissance scene, and she decided to become a writer.

Carl Van Vechten, wealthy white patron of Harlem Renaissance writers, helped get *Quicksand* (1928) and *Passing* (1929)—her two completed novels—published by the prestigious house of Alfred A. Knopf. Both books sold well and were praised by reviewers across the critical spectrum. Larsen won a Guggenheim fellowship in 1930 for creative writing—the first "black" woman to receive such an award—and went to Spain to work on a third novel, which never materialized. In fact, except for one controversial short story (she was accused of having plagiarized it) and her subsequent published defense of her integrity (in the African American journal *Forum*, in 1930), she seems to have published only the two novels.

Her retreat from literature may have been caused by the painful plagiarism incident; by a lengthy divorce proceeding; or as the result of sharply falling book sales, which affected all Harlem Renaissance authors after the stock market crashed in 1929. Whatever the explanation, she stopped writing, returned to nursing for self-support, moved from Harlem to Brooklyn, and cut her ties with former literary friends and colleagues. At the time of her death, her work had been forgotten. After the 1986 reissue of the two novels in one volume, with an introduction by Deborah E. McDowell, she quickly became recognized as an important Harlem Renaissance figure, perhaps the movement's best novelist.

Passing looks at black characters who are able to pass as white, and do so to enjoy privileges that white people take for granted. Like *Quicksand*, it represents the erotic fascination that such mixed or passing characters—especially women—inspire in both black and white observers. *Passing* is narrated from the point of view of Irene Redfield, a married, middle-class black woman drawn into an ambivalent friendship with Clare Kendry, a childhood acquaintance who lives her adult life on the boundary between black and white social worlds. Like the paintings of Archibald Motley (see the color insert to this volume), *Passing* presents a vivid picture of urban black life, including its professional and artistic elites; Larsen's sardonic perspective further encompasses the white intellectuals

Girls waiting for Episcopal Church to end so they can see the processional, South Side of Chicago, Illinois, Russell Lee, 1941. Lee's photographs of the South Side neighborhood were inspired by Richard Wright's bestselling novel *Native Son* (1940).

who come to Harlem in search of excitement and exoticism. Following Irene and Clare's contacts from Chicago to New York City, Larsen traces the complicated urban geographies of pleasure and danger that each woman navigates. Although Irene disapproves of Clare's racial fluidity, she herself passes for brief periods of time; although she participates dutifully in the politics of uplift, racial identity never provides Irene with the "security of place and substance" that she longs for.

The text of *Passing* is the first edition of 1929.

Passing

One three centuries removed
From the scenes his fathers loved,
Spicy grove, cinnamon tree,
What is Africa to me?
—Countee Cullen[1]

Part One. Encounter

ONE

It was the last letter in Irene Redfield's little pile of morning mail. After her other ordinary and clearly directed letters the long envelope of thin

1. From Countee Cullen's poem "Heritage"; see p. 855.

Italian paper with its almost illegible scrawl seemed out of place and alien. And there was, too, something mysterious and slightly furtive about it. A thin sly thing which bore no return address to betray the sender. Not that she hadn't immediately known who its sender was. Some two years ago she had one very like it in outward appearance. Furtive, but yet in some peculiar, determined way a little flaunting. Purple ink. Foreign paper of extraordinary size.

It had been, Irene noted, postmarked in New York the day before. Her brows came together in a tiny frown. The frown, however, was more from perplexity than from annoyance; though there was in her thoughts an element of both. She was wholly unable to comprehend such an attitude towards danger as she was sure the letter's contents would reveal; and she disliked the idea of opening and reading it.

This, she reflected, was of a piece with all that she knew of Clare Kendry. Stepping always on the edge of danger. Always aware, but not drawing back or turning aside. Certainly not because of any alarms or feeling of outrage on the part of others.

And for a swift moment Irene Redfield seemed to see a pale small girl sitting on a ragged blue sofa, sewing pieces of bright red cloth together, while her drunken father, a tall, powerfully built man, raged threateningly up and down the shabby room, bellowing curses and making spasmodic lunges at her which were not the less frightening because they were, for the most part, ineffectual. Sometimes he did manage to reach her. But only the fact that the child had edged herself and her poor sewing over to the farthermost corner of the sofa suggested that she was in any way perturbed by this menace to herself and her work.

Clare had known well enough that it was unsafe to take a portion of the dollar that was her weekly wage for the doing of many errands for the dressmaker who lived on the top floor of the building of which Bob Kendry was janitor. But that knowledge had not deterred her. She wanted to go to her Sunday school's picnic, and she had made up her mind to wear a new dress. So, in spite of certain unpleasantness and possible danger, she had taken the money to buy the material for that pathetic little red frock.

There had been, even in those days, nothing sacrificial in Clare Kendry's idea of life, no allegiance beyond her own immediate desire. She was selfish, and cold, and hard. And yet she had, too, a strange capacity of transforming warmth and passion, verging sometimes almost on theatrical heroics.

Irene, who was a year or more older than Clare, remembered the day that Bob Kendry had been brought home dead, killed in a silly saloon-fight. Clare, who was at that time a scant fifteen years old, had just stood there with her lips pressed together, her thin arms folded across her narrow chest, staring down at the familiar pasty-white face of her parent with a sort of disdain in her slanting black eyes. For a very long time she had stood like that, silent and staring. Then, quite suddenly, she had given way to a torrent of weeping, swaying her thin body, tearing at her bright hair, and stamping her small feet. The outburst had ceased as suddenly as it had begun. She glanced quickly about the bare room, taking everyone in, even the two policemen, in a sharp look of flashing scorn. And, in the next instant, she had turned and vanished through the door.

Seen across the long stretch of years, the thing had more the appearance of an outpouring of pent-up fury than of an overflow of grief for her dead father; though she had been, Irene admitted, fond enough of him in her own rather catlike way.

Catlike. Certainly that was the word which best described Clare Kendry, if any single word could describe her. Sometimes she was hard and apparently without feeling at all; sometimes she was affectionate and rashly impulsive. And there was about her an amazing soft malice, hidden well away until provoked. Then she was capable of scratching, and very effectively too. Or, driven to anger, she would fight with a ferocity and impetuousness that disregarded or forgot any danger; superior strength, numbers, or other unfavourable circumstances. How savagely she had clawed those boys the day they had hooted her parent and sung a derisive rhyme, of their own composing, which pointed out certain eccentricities in his careening gait! And how deliberately she had—

Irene brought her thoughts back to the present, to the letter from Clare Kendry that she still held unopened in her hand. With a little feeling of apprehension, she very slowly cut the envelope, drew out the folded sheets, spread them, and began to read.

It was, she saw at once, what she had expected since learning from the postmark that Clare was in the city. An extravagantly phrased wish to see her again. Well, she needn't and wouldn't, Irene told herself, accede to that. Nor would she assist Clare to realize her foolish desire to return for a moment to that life which long ago, and of her own choice, she had left behind her.

She ran through the letter, puzzling out, as best she could, the carelessly formed words or making instinctive guesses at them.

". . . For I am lonely, so lonely . . . cannot help longing to be with you again, as I have never longed for anything before; and I have wanted many things in my life. . . . You can't know how in this pale life of mine I am all the time seeing the bright pictures of that other that I once thought I was glad to be free of. . . . It's like an ache, a pain that never ceases. . . ." Sheets upon thin sheets of it. And ending finally with, "and it's your fault, 'Rene dear. At least partly. For I wouldn't now, perhaps, have this terrible, this wild desire if I hadn't seen you that time in Chicago. . . ."

Brilliant red patches flamed in Irene Redfield's warm olive cheeks.

"That time in Chicago." The words stood out from among the many paragraphs of other words, bringing with them a clear, sharp remembrance, in which even now, after two years, humiliation, resentment, and rage were mingled.

TWO

This is what Irene Redfield remembered.

Chicago. August. A brilliant day, hot, with a brutal staring sun pouring down rays that were like molten rain. A day on which the very outlines of the buildings shuddered as if in protest at the heat. Quivering lines sprang up from baked pavements and wriggled along the shining car-tracks. The automobiles parked at the kerbs were a dancing blaze, and the glass of the shop-windows threw out a blinding radiance. Sharp particles of dust rose from the burning sidewalks, stinging the seared or dripping skins of wilting pedestrians. What small breeze there was seemed like the breath of a flame fanned by slow bellows.

It was on that day of all others that Irene set out to shop for the things which she had promised to take home from Chicago to her two small sons, Brian junior and Theodore. Characteristically, she had put it off until only a few crowded days remained of her long visit. And only this sweltering one was free of engagements till the evening.

Without too much trouble she had got the mechanical aeroplane for Junior. But the drawing-book, for which Ted had so gravely and insistently given her precise directions, had sent her in and out of five shops without success.

It was while she was on her way to a sixth place that right before her smarting eyes a man toppled over and became an inert crumpled heap on the scorching cement. About the lifeless figure a little crowd gathered. Was the man dead, or only faint? someone asked her. But Irene didn't know and didn't try to discover. She edged her way out of the increasing crowd, feeling disagreeably damp and sticky and soiled from contact with so many sweating bodies.

For a moment she stood fanning herself and dabbing at her moist face with an inadequate scrap of handkerchief. Suddenly she was aware that the whole street had a wobbly look, and realized that she was about to faint. With a quick perception of the need for immediate safety, she lifted a wavering hand in the direction of a cab parked directly in front of her. The perspiring driver jumped out and guided her to his car. He helped, almost lifted her in. She sank down on the hot leather seat.

For a minute her thoughts were nebulous. They cleared.

"I guess," she told her Samaritan, "it's tea I need. On a roof somewhere."

"The Drayton,[2] ma'am?" he suggested. "They do say as how it's always a breeze up there."

"Thank you. I think the Drayton'll do nicely," she told him.

There was that little grating sound of the clutch being slipped in as the man put the car in gear and slid deftly out into the boiling traffic. Reviving under the warm breeze stirred up by the moving cab, Irene made some small attempts to repair the damage that the heat and crowds had done to her appearance.

All too soon the rattling vehicle shot towards the sidewalk and stood still. The driver sprang out and opened the door before the hotel's decorated attendant could reach it. She got out, and thanking him smilingly as well as in a more substantial manner for his kind helpfulness and understanding, went in through the Drayton's wide doors.

Stepping out of the elevator that had brought her to the roof, she was led to a table just in front of a long window whose gently moving curtains suggested a cool breeze. It was, she thought, like being wafted upward on a magic carpet to another world, pleasant, quiet, and strangely remote from the sizzling one that she had left below.

2. The fictional hotel's lakeside location and elegance link it to Chicago's Drake Hotel, opened in 1920.

The tea, when it came, was all that she had desired and expected. In fact, so much was it what she had desired and expected that after the first deep cooling drink she was able to forget it, only now and then sipping, a little absently, from the tall green glass, while she surveyed the room about her or looked out over some lower buildings at the bright unstirred blue of the lake reaching away to an undetected horizon.

She had been gazing down for some time at the specks of cars and people creeping about in streets, and thinking how silly they looked, when on taking up her glass she was surprised to find it empty at last. She asked for more tea and while she waited, began to recall the happenings of the day and to wonder what she was to do about Ted and his book. Why was it that almost invariably he wanted something that was difficult or impossible to get? Like his father. For ever wanting something that he couldn't have.

Presently there were voices, a man's booming one and a woman's slightly husky. A waiter passed her, followed by a sweetly scented woman in a fluttering dress of green chiffon[3] whose mingled pattern of narcissuses, jonquils, and hyacinths[4] was a reminder of pleasantly chill spring days. Behind her there was a man, very red in the face, who was mopping his neck and forehead with a big crumpled handkerchief.

"Oh dear!" Irene groaned, rasped by annoyance, for after a little discussion and commotion they had stopped at the very next table. She had been alone there at the window and it had been so satisfyingly quiet. Now, of course, they would chatter.

But no. Only the woman sat down. The man remained standing, abstractedly pinching the knot of his bright blue tie. Across the small space that separated the two tables his voice carried clearly.

"See you later, then," he declared, looking down at the woman. There was pleasure in his tones and a smile on his face.

His companion's lips parted in some answer, but her words were blurred by the little intervening distance and the medley of noises floating up from the streets below. They didn't reach Irene. But she noted the peculiar caressing smile that accompanied them.

The man said: "Well, I suppose I'd better," and smiled again, and said good-bye, and left.

An attractive-looking woman, was Irene's opinion, with those dark, almost black, eyes and that wide mouth like a scarlet flower against the ivory of her skin. Nice clothes too, just right for the weather, thin and cool without being mussy, as summer things were so apt to be.

A waiter was taking her order. Irene saw her smile up at him as she murmured something—thanks, maybe. It was an odd sort of smile. Irene couldn't quite define it, but she was sure that she would have classed it, coming from another woman, as being just a shade too provocative for a waiter. About this one, however, there was something that made her hesitate to name it that. A certain impression of assurance, perhaps.

The waiter came back with the order. Irene watched her spread out her napkin, saw the silver spoon in the white hand slit the dull gold of the melon. Then, conscious that she had been staring, she looked quickly away.

3. A smooth, shiny lightweight fabric, typically of silk or cotton.
4. All bloom in early spring.

Her mind returned to her own affairs. She had settled, definitely, the problem of the proper one of two frocks for the bridge party that night, in rooms whose atmosphere would be so thick and hot that every breath would be like breathing soup. The dress decided, her thoughts had gone back to the snag of Ted's book, her unseeing eyes far away on the lake, when by some sixth sense she was acutely aware that someone was watching her.

Very slowly she looked around, and into the dark eyes of the woman in the green frock at the next table. But she evidently failed to realize that such intense interest as she was showing might be embarrassing, and continued to stare. Her demeanour was that of one who with utmost singleness of mind and purpose was determined to impress firmly and accurately each detail of Irene's features upon her memory for all time, nor showed the slightest trace of disconcertment at having been detected in her steady scrutiny.

Instead, it was Irene who was put out. Feeling her colour heighten under the continued inspection, she slid her eyes down. What, she wondered, could be the reason for such persistent attention? Had she, in her haste in the taxi, put her hat on backwards? Guardedly she felt at it. No. Perhaps there was a streak of powder somewhere on her face. She made a quick pass over it with her handkerchief. Something wrong with her dress? She shot a glance over it. Perfectly all right. *What* was it?

Again she looked up, and for a moment her brown eyes politely returned the stare of the other's black ones, which never for an instant fell or wavered. Irene made a little mental shrug. Oh well, let her look! She tried to treat the woman and her watching with indifference, but she couldn't. All her efforts to ignore her, it, were futile. She stole another glance. Still looking. What strange languorous eyes she had!

And gradually there rose in Irene a small inner disturbance, odious and hatefully familiar. She laughed softly, but her eyes flashed.

Did that woman, could that woman, somehow know that here before her very eyes on the roof of the Drayton sat a Negro?[5]

Absurd! Impossible! White people were so stupid about such things for all that they usually asserted that they were able to tell; and by the most ridiculous means, finger-nails, palms of hands, shapes of ears, teeth, and other equally silly rot. They always took her for an Italian, a Spaniard, a Mexican, or a gipsy. Never, when she was alone, had they even remotely seemed to suspect that she was a Negro. No, the woman sitting there staring at her couldn't possibly know.

Nevertheless, Irene felt, in turn, anger, scorn, and fear slide over her. It wasn't that she was ashamed of being a Negro, or even of having it declared. It was the idea of being ejected from any place, even in the polite and tactful way in which the Drayton would probably do it, that disturbed her.

But she looked, boldly this time, back into the eyes still frankly intent upon her. They did not seem to her hostile or resentful. Rather, Irene had the feeling that they were ready to smile if she would. Nonsense, of course. The feeling passed, and she turned away with the firm intention of keeping her gaze on the lake, the roofs of the buildings across the way, the sky,

5. Public accommodations in Chicago in the 1920s were desegregated by law but not necessarily in practice.

anywhere but on that annoying woman. Almost immediately, however, her eyes were back again. In the midst of her fog of uneasiness she had been seized by a desire to outstare the rude observer. Suppose the woman did know or suspect her race. She couldn't prove it.

Suddenly her small fright increased. Her neighbour had risen and was coming towards her. What was going to happen now?

"Pardon me," the woman said pleasantly, "but I think I know you." Her slightly husky voice held a dubious note.

Looking up at her, Irene's suspicions and fears vanished. There was no mistaking the friendliness of that smile or resisting its charm. Instantly she surrendered to it and smiled too, as she said: "I'm afraid you're mistaken."

"Why, of course, I know you!" the other exclaimed. "Don't tell me you're not Irene Westover. Or do they still call you 'Rene?"

In the brief second before her answer, Irene tried vainly to recall where and when this woman could have known her. There, in Chicago. And before her marriage. That much was plain. High school? College? Y. W. C. A.[6] committees? High school, most likely. What white girls had she known well enough to have been familiarly addressed as 'Rene by them? The woman before her didn't fit her memory of any of them. Who was she?

"Yes, I'm Irene Westover. And though nobody calls me 'Rene any more, it's good to hear the name again. And you—" She hesitated, ashamed that she could not remember, and hoping that the sentence would be finished for her.

"Don't you know me? Not really, 'Rene?"

"I'm sorry, but just at the minute I can't seem to place you."

Irene studied the lovely creature standing beside her for some clue to her identity. Who could she be? Where and when had they met? And through her perplexity there came the thought that the trick which her memory had played her was for some reason more gratifying than disappointing to her old acquaintance, that she didn't mind not being recognized.

And, too, Irene felt that she was just about to remember her. For about the woman was some quality, an intangible something, too vague to define, too remote to seize, but which was, to Irene Redfield, very familiar. And that voice. Surely she'd heard those husky tones somewhere before. Perhaps before time, contact, or something had been at them, making them into a voice remotely suggesting England. Ah! Could it have been in Europe that they had met? 'Rene. No.

"Perhaps," Irene began, "you—"

The woman laughed, a lovely laugh, a small sequence of notes that was like a trill and also like the ringing of a delicate bell fashioned of a precious metal, a tinkling.

Irene drew a quick sharp breath. "Clare!" she exclaimed, "not really Clare Kendry?"

So great was her astonishment that she had started to rise.

"No, no, don't get up," Clare Kendry commanded, and sat down herself. "You've simply got to stay and talk. We'll have something more. Tea? Fancy meeting you here! It's simply too, too lucky!"

6. Young Women's Christian Association, founded in 1855 in London to improve the lives of young working women in the city. By the 1920s it had chapters in cities throughout the United States.

"It's awfully surprising," Irene told her, and, seeing the change in Clare's smile, knew that she had revealed a corner of her own thoughts. But she only said: "I'd never in this world have known you if you hadn't laughed. You are changed, you know. And yet, in a way, you're just the same."

"Perhaps," Clare replied. "Oh, just a second."

She gave her attention to the waiter at her side. "M-mm, let's see. Two teas. And bring some cigarettes. Y-es, they'll be all right. Thanks." Again that odd upward smile. Now, Irene was sure that it was too provocative for a waiter.

While Clare had been giving the order, Irene made a rapid mental calculation. It must be, she figured, all of twelve years since she, or anybody that she knew, had laid eyes on Clare Kendry.

After her father's death she'd gone to live with some relatives, aunts or cousins two or three times removed, over on the west side: relatives that nobody had known the Kendry's possessed until they had turned up at the funeral and taken Clare away with them.

For about a year or more afterwards she would appear occasionally among her old friends and acquaintances on the south side for short little visits that were, they understood, always stolen from the endless domestic tasks in her new home. With each succeeding one she was taller, shabbier, and more belligerently sensitive. And each time the look on her face was more resentful and brooding. "I'm worried about Clare, she seems so unhappy," Irene remembered her mother saying. The visits dwindled, becoming shorter, fewer, and further apart until at last they ceased.

Irene's father, who had been fond of Bob Kendry, made a special trip over to the west side about two months after the last time Clare had been to see them and returned with the bare information that he had seen the relatives and that Clare had disappeared. What else he had confided to her mother, in the privacy of their own room, Irene didn't know.

But she had had something more than a vague suspicion of its nature. For there had been rumours. Rumours that were, to girls of eighteen and nineteen years, interesting and exciting.

There was the one about Clare Kendry's having been seen at the dinner hour in a fashionable hotel in company with another woman and two men, all of them white. And *dressed!* And there was another which told of her driving in Lincoln Park[7] with a man, unmistakably white, and evidently rich. Packard[8] limousine, chauffeur in livery, and all that. There had been others whose context Irene could no longer recollect, but all pointing in the same glamorous direction.

And she could remember quite vividly how, when they used to repeat and discuss these tantalizing stories about Clare, the girls would always look knowingly at one another and then, with little excited giggles, drag away their eager shining eyes and say with lurking undertones of regret or disbelief some such thing as: "Oh, well, maybe she's got a job or something," or "After all, it mayn't have been Clare," or "You can't believe all you hear."

And always some girl, more matter-of-fact or more frankly malicious than the rest, would declare: "Of course it was Clare! Ruth said it was and so did Frank, and they certainly know her when they see her as well as we do."

7. Chicago's largest public park, fronting Lake Michigan.
8. A U.S. auto company known for luxury cars.

And someone else would say: "Yes, you can bet it was Clare all right." And then they would all join in asserting that there could be no mistake about it's having been Clare, and that such circumstances could mean only one thing. Working indeed! People didn't take their servants to the Shelby for dinner. Certainly not all dressed up like that. There would follow insincere regrets, and somebody would say: "Poor girl, I suppose it's true enough, but what can you expect. Look at her father. And her mother, they say, would have run away if she hadn't died. Besides, Clare always had a—a—having way with her."

Precisely that! The words came to Irene as she sat there on the Drayton roof, facing Clare Kendry. "A having way." Well, Irene acknowledged, judging from her appearance and manner, Clare seemed certainly to have succeeded in having a few of the things that she wanted.

It was, Irene repeated, after the interval of the waiter, a great surprise and a very pleasant one to see Clare again after all those years, twelve at least.

"Why, Clare, you're the last person in the world I'd have expected to run into. I guess that's why I didn't know you."

Clare answered gravely: "Yes. It is twelve years. But I'm not surprised to see you, 'Rene. That is, not so very. In fact, ever since I've been here, I've more or less hoped that I should, or someone. Preferably you, though. Still, I imagine that's because I've thought of you often and often, while you—I'll wager you've never given me a thought."

It was true, of course. After the first speculations and indictments, Clare had gone completely from Irene's thoughts. And from the thoughts of others too—if their conversation was any indication of their thoughts.

Besides, Clare had never been exactly one of the group, just as she'd never been merely the janitor's daughter, but the daughter of Mr. Bob Kendry, who, it was true, was a janitor, but who also, it seemed, had been in college with some of their fathers. Just how or why he happened to be a janitor, and a very inefficient one at that, they none of them quite knew. One of Irene's brothers, who had put the question to their father, had been told: "That's something that doesn't concern you," and given him the advice to be careful not to end in the same manner as "poor Bob."

No, Irene hadn't thought of Clare Kendry. Her own life had been too crowded. So, she supposed, had the lives of other people. She defended her—their—forgetfulness. "You know how it is. Everybody's so busy. People leave, drop out, maybe for a little while there's talk about them, or questions; then, gradually they're forgotten."

"Yes, that's natural," Clare agreed. And what, she inquired, had they said of her for that little while at the beginning before they'd forgotten her altogether?

Irene looked away. She felt the tell-tale colour rising in her cheeks. "You can't," she evaded, "expect me to remember trifles like that over twelve years of marriages, births, deaths, and the war."

There followed that trill of notes that was Clare Kendry's laugh, small and clear and the very essence of mockery.

"Oh, 'Rene!" she cried, "of course you remember! But I won't make you tell me, because I know just as well as if I'd been there and heard every unkind word. Oh, I know, I know. Frank Danton saw me in the Shelby one night.

Don't tell me he didn't broadcast that, and with embroidery. Others may have seen me at other times. I don't know. But once I met Margaret Hammer in Marshall Field's.[9] I'd have spoken, was on the very point of doing it, but she cut me dead. My dear 'Rene, I assure you that from the way she looked through me, even I was uncertain whether I was actually there in the flesh or not. I remember it clearly, too clearly. It was that very thing which, in a way, finally decided me not to go out and see you one last time before I went away to stay. Somehow, good as all of you, the whole family, had always been to the poor forlorn child that was me, I felt I shouldn't be able to bear that. I mean if any of you, your mother or the boys or—Oh, well, I just felt I'd rather not know it if you did. And so I stayed away. Silly, I suppose. Sometimes I've been sorry I didn't go."

Irene wondered if it was tears that made Clare's eyes so luminous.

"And now 'Rene, I want to hear all about you and everybody and everything. You're married, I s'pose?"

Irene nodded.

"Yes," Clare said knowingly, "you would be. Tell me about it."

And so for an hour or more they had sat there smoking and drinking tea and filling in the gap of twelve years with talk. That is, Irene did. She told Clare about her marriage and removal to New York, about her husband, and about her two sons, who were having their first experience of being separated from their parents at a summer camp, about her mother's death, about the marriages of her two brothers. She told of the marriages, births and deaths in other families that Clare had known, opening up, for her, new vistas on the lives of old friends and acquaintances.

Clare drank it all in, these things which for so long she had wanted to know and hadn't been able to learn. She sat motionless, her bright lips slightly parted, her whole face lit by the radiance of her happy eyes. Now and then she put a question, but for the most part she was silent.

Somewhere outside, a clock struck. Brought back to the present, Irene looked down at her watch and exclaimed: "Oh, I must go, Clare!"

A moment passed during which she was the prey of uneasiness. It had suddenly occurred to her that she hadn't asked Clare anything about her own life and that she had a very definite unwillingness to do so. And she was quite well aware of the reason for that reluctance. But, she asked herself, wouldn't it, all things considered, be the kindest thing not to ask? If things with Clare were as she—as they all—had suspected, wouldn't it be more tactful to seem to forget to inquire how she had spent those twelve years?

If? It was that "if" which bothered her. It might be, it might just be, in spite of all gossip and even appearances to the contrary, that there was nothing, had been nothing, that couldn't be simply and innocently explained. Appearances, she knew now, had a way sometimes of not fitting facts, and if Clare hadn't—Well, if they had all been wrong, then certainly she ought to express some interest in what had happened to her. It would seem queer and rude if she didn't. But how was she to know? There was, she at last decided, no way; so she merely said again. "I must go, Clare."

9. Chicago's largest department store in the 1920s.

"Please, not so soon, 'Rene," Clare begged, not moving.

Irene thought: "She's really almost too good-looking. It's hardly any wonder that she—"

"And now, 'Rene dear, that I've found you, I mean to see lots and lots of you. We're here for a month at least. Jack, that's my husband, is here on business. Poor dear! in this heat. Isn't it beastly? Come to dinner with us tonight, won't you?" And she gave Irene a curious little sidelong glance and a sly, ironical smile peeped out on her full red lips, as if she had been in the secret of the other's thoughts and was mocking her.

Irene was conscious of a sharp intake of breath, but whether it was relief or chagrin that she felt, she herself could not have told. She said hastily: "I'm afraid I can't, Clare. I'm filled up. Dinner and bridge. I'm so sorry."

"Come tomorrow instead, to tea," Clare insisted. "Then you'll see Margery—she's just ten—and Jack too, maybe, if he hasn't got an appointment or something."

From Irene came an uneasy little laugh. She had an engagement for tomorrow also and she was afraid that Clare would not believe it. Suddenly, now, that possibility disturbed her. Therefore it was with a half-vexed feeling at the sense of undeserved guilt that had come upon her that she explained that it wouldn't be possible because she wouldn't be free for tea, or for luncheon or dinner either. "And the next day's Friday when I'll be going away for the week-end, Idlewild,[1] you know. It's quite the thing now." And then she had an inspiration.

"Clare!" she exclaimed, "why don't you come up with me? Our place is probably full up—Jim's wife has a way of collecting mobs of the most impossible people—but we can always manage to find room for one more. And you'll see absolutely everybody."

In the very moment of giving the invitation she regretted it. What a foolish, what an idiotic impulse to have given way to! She groaned inwardly as she thought of the endless explanations in which it would involve her, of the curiosity, and the talk, and the lifted eyebrows. It wasn't she assured herself, that she was a snob, that she cared greatly for the petty restrictions and distinctions with which what called itself Negro society chose to hedge itself about; but that she had a natural and deeply rooted aversion to the kind of front-page notoriety that Clare Kendry's presence in Idlewild, as her guest, would expose her to. And here she was, perversely and against all reason, inviting her.

But Clare shook her head. "Really, I'd love to, 'Rene," she said, a little mournfully. "There's nothing I'd like better. But I couldn't. I mustn't, you see. It wouldn't do at all. I'm sure you understand. I'm simply crazy to go, but I can't." The dark eyes glistened and there was a suspicion of a quaver in the husky voice. "And believe me, 'Rene, I do thank you for asking me. Don't think I've entirely forgotten just what it would mean for you if I went. That is, if you still care about such things."

All indication of tears had gone from her eyes and voice, and Irene Redfield, searching her face, had an offended feeling that behind what was now

1. Vacation community in western Michigan, founded in 1912 by white developers and marketed to African Americans, who were excluded from other resorts. Notable property owners in the 1920s included W. E. B. Du Bois and other black intellectuals.

only an ivory mask lurked a scornful amusement. She looked away, at the wall far beyond Clare. Well, she deserved it, for, as she acknowledged to herself, she *was* relieved. And for the very reason at which Clare had hinted. The fact that Clare had guesssed her perturbation did not, however, in any degree lessen that relief. She was annoyed at having been detected in what might seem to be an insincerity; but that was all.

The waiter came with Clare's change. Irene reminded herself that she ought immediately to go. But she didn't move.

The truth was, she was curious. There were things that she wanted to ask Clare Kendry. She wished to find out about this hazardous business of "passing," this breaking away from all that was familiar and friendly to take one's chance in another environment, not entirely strange, perhaps, but certainly not entirely friendly. What, for example, one did about background, how one accounted for oneself. And how one felt when one came into contact with other Negroes. But she couldn't. She was unable to think of a single question that in its context or its phrasing was not too frankly curious, if not actually impertinent.

As if aware of her desire and her hesitation, Clare remarked, thoughtfully: "You know, 'Rene, I've often wondered why more coloured girls, girls like you and Margaret Hammer and Esther Dawson and—oh, lots of others—never 'passed' over. It's such a frightfully easy thing to do. If one's the type, all that's needed is a little nerve."

"What about background? Family, I mean. Surely you can't just drop down on people from nowhere and expect them to receive you with open arms, can you?"

"Almost," Clare asserted. "You'd be surprised, 'Rene, how much easier that is with white people than with us. Maybe because there are so many more of them, or maybe because they are secure and so don't have to bother. I've never quite decided."

Irene was inclined to be incredulous. "You mean that you didn't have to explain where you came from? It seems impossible."

Clare cast a glance of repressed amusement across the table at her. "As a matter of fact, I didn't. Though I suppose under any other circumstances I might have had to provide some plausible tale to account for myself. I've a good imagination, so I'm sure I could have done it quite creditably, and credibly. But it wasn't necessary. There were my aunts, you see, respectable and authentic enough for anything or anybody."

"I see. They were 'passing' too."

"No. They weren't. They were white."

"Oh!" And in the next instant it came back to Irene that she had heard this mentioned before; by her father, or, more likely, her mother. They were Bob Kendry's aunts. He had been a son of their brother's, on the left hand.[2] A wild oat.

"They were nice old ladies," Clare explained, "very religious and as poor as church mice. That adored brother of theirs, my grandfather, got through every penny they had after he'd finished his own little bit."

Clare paused in her narrative to light another cigarette. Her smile, her expression, Irene noticed, was faintly resentful.

2. Outside of marriage.

"Being good Christians," she continued, "when dad came to his tipsy end, they did their duty and gave me a home of sorts. I was, it was true, expected to earn my keep by doing all the housework and most of the washing. But do you realize, 'Rene, that if it hadn't been for them, I shouldn't have had a home in the world?"

Irene's nod and little murmur were comprehensive, understanding.

Clare made a small mischievous grimace and proceeded. "Besides, to their notion, hard labour was good for me. I had Negro blood and they belonged to the generation that had written and read long articles headed: 'Will the Blacks Work?' Too, they weren't quite sure that the good God hadn't intended the sons and daughters of Ham to sweat because he had poked fun at old man Noah once when he had taken a drop too much. I remember the aunts telling me that that old drunkard had cursed Ham and his sons for all time."[3]

Irene laughed. But Clare remained quite serious.

"It was more than a joke, I assure you, 'Rene. It was a hard life for a girl of sixteen. Still, I had a roof over my head, and food, and clothes—such as they were. And there were the Scriptures, and talks on morals and thrift and industry and the loving-kindness of the good Lord."

"Have you ever stopped to think, Clare," Irene demanded, "how much unhappiness and downright cruelty are laid to the loving-kindness of the Lord? And always by His most ardent followers, it seems."

"Have I?" Clare exclaimed. "It, they, made me what I am today. For, of course, I was determined to get away, to be a person and not a charity or a problem, or even a daughter of the indiscreet Ham. Then, too, I wanted things. I knew I wasn't bad-looking and that I could 'pass.' You can't know, 'Rene, how, when I used to go over to the south side, I used almost to hate all of you. You had all the things I wanted and never had had. It made me all the more determined to get them, and others. Do you, can you understand what I felt?"

She looked up with a pointed and appealing effect, and, evidently finding the sympathetic expression on Irene's face sufficient answer, went on. "The aunts were queer. For all their Bibles and praying and ranting about honesty, they didn't want anyone to know that their darling brother had seduced—ruined, they called it—a Negro girl. They could excuse the ruin, but they couldn't forgive the tar-brush.[4] They forbade me to mention Negroes to the neighbours, or even to mention the south side. You may be sure that I didn't. I'll bet they were good and sorry afterwards."

She laughed and the ringing bells in her laugh had a hard metallic sound.

"When the chance to get away came, that omission was of great value to me. When Jack, a schoolboy acquaintance of some people in the neighbour-

3. Noah's son Ham, seeing his drunken father naked in his tent, told his two brothers, who covered their father's nakedness while averting their eyes. On waking, Noah "knew what his younger son had done unto him" and cursed Ham, vowing that "a servant of servants shall he be unto his brethren" (Genesis 9.24–25). Noah's curse was frequently cited in the pre–Civil War United States as justifying the enslavement of Africans, who were thought to be descended from Ham.

4. Derogatory reference to African descent. The south side of Chicago, especially between Thirty-Fifth and Forty-Seventh Streets, emerged in the 1920s as "Bronzeville," the center of African American community and culture in an increasingly segregated city. For later representations in art and literature, see Archibald Motley's *Black Belt* (in this volume's color insert) and Langston Hughes's "Visitors to the Black Belt" (p. 839).

hood, turned up from South America with untold gold, there was no one to tell him that I was coloured, and many to tell him about the severity and the religiousness of Aunt Grace and Aunt Edna. You can guess the rest. After he came, stopped slipping off to the south side and slipped off to meet him instead. I couldn't manage both. In the end I had no great difficulty in convincing him that it was useless to talk marriage to the aunts. So on the day that I was eighteen, we went off and were married. So that's that. Nothing could have been easier."

"Yes, I do see that for you it was easy enough. By the way! I wonder why they didn't tell father that you were married. He went over to find out about you when you stopped coming over to see us. I'm sure they didn't tell him. Not that you were married."

Clare Kendry's eyes were bright with tears that didn't fall. "Oh, how lovely! To have cared enough about me to do that. The dear sweet man! Well, they couldn't tell him because they didn't know it. I took care of that, for I couldn't be sure that those consciences of theirs wouldn't begin to work on them afterwards and make them let the cat out of the bag. The old things probably thought I was living in sin, wherever I was. And it would be about what they expected."

An amused smile lit the lovely face for the smallest fraction of a second. After a little silence she said soberly: "But I'm sorry if they told your father so. That was something I hadn't counted on."

"I'm not sure that they did," Irene told her. "He didn't say so, anyway."

"He wouldn't, 'Rene dear. Not your father."

"Thanks. I'm sure he wouldn't."

"But you've never answered my question. Tell me, honestly, haven't you ever thought of 'passing'?"

Irene answered promptly: "No. Why should I?" And so disdainful was her voice and manner that Clare's face flushed and her eyes glinted. Irene hastened to add: "You see, Clare, I've everything I want. Except, perhaps, a little more money."

At that Clare laughed, her spark of anger vanished as quickly as it had appeared. "Of course," she declared, "that's what everybody wants, just a little more money, even the people who have it. And I must say I don't blame them. Money's awfully nice to have. In fact, all things considered, I think, 'Rene, that it's even worth the price."

Irene could only shrug her shoulders. Her reason partly agreed, her instinct wholly rebelled. And she could not say why. And though conscious that if she didn't hurry away, she was going to be late to dinner, she still lingered. It was as if the woman sitting on the other side of the table, a girl that she had known, who had done this rather dangerous and, to Irene Redfield, abhorrent thing successfully and had announced herself well satisfied, had for her a fascination, strange and compelling.

Clare Kendry was still leaning back in the tall chair, her sloping shoulders against the carved top. She sat with an air of indifferent assurance, as if arranged for, desired. About her clung that dim suggestion of polite insolence with which a few women are born and which some acquire with the coming of riches or importance.

Clare, it gave Irene a little prick of satisfaction to recall, hadn't got that by passing herself off as white. She herself had always had it.

Just as she'd always had that pale gold hair, which, unsheared still, was drawn loosely back from a broad brow, partly hidden by the small close hat. Her lips, painted a brilliant geranium-red, were sweet and sensitive and a little obstinate. A tempting mouth. The face across the forehead and cheeks was a trifle too wide, but the ivory skin had a peculiar soft lustre. And the eyes were magnificent! dark, sometimes absolutely black, always luminous, and set in long, black lashes. Arresting eyes, slow and mesmeric, and with, for all their warmth, something withdrawn and secret about them.

Ah! Surely! They were Negro eyes! mysterious and concealing. And set in that ivory face under that bright hair, there was about them something exotic.

Yes, Clare Kendry's loveliness was absolute, beyond challenge, thanks to those eyes which her grandmother and later her mother and father had given her.

Into those eyes there came a smile and over Irene the sense of being petted and caressed. She smiled back.

"Maybe," Clare suggested, "you can come Monday, if you're back. Or, if you're not, then Tuesday."

With a small regretful sigh, Irene informed Clare that she was afraid she wouldn't be back by Monday and that she was sure she had dozens of things for Tuesday, and that she was leaving Wednesday. It might be, however, that she could get out of something Tuesday.

"Oh, do try. Do put somebody else off. The others can see you any time, while I—Why, I may never see you again! Think of that, 'Rene! You'll have to come. You'll simply have to! I'll never forgive you if you don't."

At that moment it seemed a dreadful thing to think of never seeing Clare Kendry again. Standing there under the appeal, the caress, of her eyes, Irene had the desire, the hope, that this parting wouldn't be the last.

"I'll try, Clare," she promised gently. "I'll call you—or will you call me?"

"I think, perhaps, I'd better call you. Your father's in the book, I know, and the address is the same. Sixty-four eighteen. Some memory, what? Now remember, I'm going to expect you. You've got to be able to come."

Again that peculiar mellowing smile.

"I'll do my best, Clare."

Irene gathered up her gloves and bag. They stood up. She put out her hand. Clare took and held it.

"It has been nice seeing you again, Clare. How pleased and glad father'll be to hear about you!"

"Until Tuesday, then," Clare Kendry replied. "I'll spend every minute of the time from now on looking forward to seeing you again. Good-bye, 'Rene dear. My love to your father, and this kiss for him."

The sun had gone from overhead, but the streets were still like fiery furnaces. The languid breeze was still hot. And the scurrying people looked even more wilted than before Irene had fled from their contact.

Crossing the avenue in the heat, far from the coolness of the Drayton's roof, away from the seduction of Clare Kendry's smile, she was aware of a sense of irritation with herself because she had been pleased and a little flattered at the other's obvious gladness at their meeting.

With her perspiring progress homeward this irritation grew, and she began to wonder just what had possessed her to make her promise to find time, in the crowded days that remained of her visit, to spend another afternoon with a woman whose life had so definitely and deliberately diverged from hers; and whom, as had been pointed out, she might never see again.

Why in the world had she made such a promise?

As she went up the steps to her father's house, thinking with what interest and amazement he would listen to her story of the afternoon's encounter, it came to her that Clare had omitted to mention her marriage name. She had referred to her husband as Jack. That was all. Had that, Irene asked herself, been intentional?

Clare had only to pick up the telephone to communicate with her, or to drop her a card, or to jump into a taxi. But she couldn't reach Clare in any way. Nor could anyone else to whom she might speak of their meeting.

"As if I should!"

Her key turned in the lock. She went in. Her father, it seemed, hadn't come in yet.

Irene decided that she wouldn't, after all, say anything to him about Clare Kendry. She had, she told herself, no inclination to speak of a person who held so low an opinion of her loyalty, or her discretion. And certainly she had no desire or intention of making the slightest effort about Tuesday. Nor any other day for that matter.

She was through with Clare Kendry.

THREE

On Tuesday morning a dome of grey sky rose over the parched city, but the stifling air was not relieved by the silvery mist that seemed to hold a promise of rain, which did not fall.

To Irene Redfield this soft foreboding fog was another reason for doing nothing about seeing Clare Kendry that afternoon.

But she did see her.

The telephone. For hours it had rung like something possessed. Since nine o'clock she had been hearing its insistent jangle. Awhile she was resolute, saying firmly each time: "Not in, Liza, take the message." And each time the servant returned with the information: "It's the same lady, ma'am; she says she'll call again."

But at noon, her nerves frayed and her conscience smiting her at the reproachful look on Liza's ebony face as she withdrew for another denial, Irene weakened.

"Oh, never mind. I'll answer this time, Liza."

"It's her again."

"Hello. . . . Yes."

"It's Clare, 'Rene. . . . Where *have* you been? . . . Can you be here around four? . . . What? . . . But, 'Rene, you promised! Just for a little while. . . . You can if you want to. . . . I am *so* disappointed. I had counted so on seeing you. . . . Please be nice and come. Only for a minute. I'm sure you can manage it if you try. . . . I won't beg you to stay. . . . Yes. . . . I'm going to expect you . . . It's the Morgan . . . Oh, yes! The name's Bellew, Mrs. John Bellew. . . . About four, then. . . . I'll be so happy to see you! . . . Goodbye."

"Damn!"

Irene hung up the receiver with an emphatic bang, her thoughts immediately filled with self-reproach. She'd done it again. Allowed Clare Kendry to persuade her into promising to do something for which she had neither time nor any special desire. What was it about Clare's voice that was so appealing, so very seductive?

Clare met her in the hall with a kiss. She said: "You're good to come, 'Rene. But, then, you always were nice to me." And under her potent smile a part of Irene's annoyance with herself fled. She was even a little glad that she had come.

Clare led the way, stepping lightly, towards a room whose door was standing partly open, saying: "There's a surprise. It's a real party. See."

Entering, Irene found herself in a sitting-room, large and high, at whose windows hung startling blue draperies which triumphantly dragged attention from the gloomy chocolate-coloured furniture. And Clare was wearing a thin floating dress of the same shade of blue, which suited her and the rather difficult room to perfection.

For a minute Irene thought the room was empty, but turning her head, she discovered, sunk deep in the cushions of a huge sofa, a woman staring up at her with such intense concentration that her eyelids were drawn as though the strain of that upward glance had paralysed them. At first Irene took her to be a stranger, but in the next instant she said in an unsympathetic, almost harsh voice: "And how are you, Gertrude?"

The woman nodded and forced a smile to her pouting lips. "I'm all right," she replied. "And you're just the same, Irene. Not changed a bit."

"Thank you." Irene responded, as she chose a seat. She was thinking: "Great goodness! Two of them."

For Gertrude too had married a white man, though it couldn't be truthfully said that she was "passing." Her husband—what was his name?—had been in school with her and had been quite well aware, as had his family and most of his friends, that she was a Negro. It hadn't, Irene knew, seemed to matter to him then. Did it now, she wondered? Had Fred—Fred Martin, that was it—had he ever regretted his marriage because of Gertrude's race? Had Gertrude?

Turning to Gertrude, Irene asked: "And Fred, how is he? It's unmentionable years since I've seen him."

"Oh, he's all right," Gertrude answered briefly.

For a full minute no one spoke. Finally out of the oppressive little silence Clare's voice came pleasantly, conversationally: "We'll have tea right away. I know that you can't stay long, 'Rene. And I'm so sorry you won't see Margery. We went up the lake over the week end to see some of Jack's people, just out of Milwaukee. Margery wanted to stay with the children. It seemed a shame not to let her, especially since it's so hot in town. But I'm expecting Jack any second."

Irene said briefly: "That's nice."

Gertrude remained silent. She was, it was plain, a little ill at ease. And her presence there annoyed Irene, roused in her a defensive and resentful feeling for which she had at the moment no explanation. But it did seem to her odd that the woman that Clare was now should have invited the woman that Gertrude was. Still, of course, Clare couldn't have known. Twelve years since they had met.

Later, when she examined her feeling of annoyance, Irene admitted, a shade reluctantly, that it arose from a feeling of being outnumbered, a sense of aloneness, in her adherence to her own class and kind; not merely in the great thing of marriage, but in the whole pattern of her life as well.

Clare spoke again, this time at length. Her talk was of the change that Chicago presented to her after her long absence in European cities. Yes, she said in reply to some question from Gertrude, she'd been back to America a time or two, but only as far as New York and Philadelphia, and once she had spent a few days in Washington. John Bellew, who, it appeared, was some sort of international banking agent, hadn't particularly wanted her to come with him on this trip, but as soon as she had learned that it would probably take him as far as Chicago, she made up her mind to come anyway.

"I simply had to. And after I once got here, I was determined to see someone I knew and find out what had happened to everybody. I didn't quite see how I was going to manage it, but I meant to. Somehow. I'd just about decided to take a chance and go out to your house, 'Rene, or call up and arrange a meeting, when I ran into you. What luck!"

Irene agreed that it was luck. "It's the first time I've been home for five years, and now I'm about to leave. A week later and I'd have been gone. And how in the world did you find Gertrude?"

"In the book. I remembered about Fred. His father still has the meat market."

"Oh, yes," said Irene, who had only remembered it as Clare had spoken, "on Cottage Grove near—"

Gertrude broke in. "No. It's moved. We're on Maryland Avenue—used to be Jackson—now. Near Sixty-third Street.[5] And the market's Fred's. His name's the same as his father's."

Gertrude, Irene thought, looked as if her husband might be a butcher. There was left of her youthful prettiness, which had been so much admired in their high-school days, no trace. She had grown broad, fat almost, and though there were no lines on her large white face, its very smoothness was somehow prematurely ageing. Her black hair was clipt, and by some unfortunate means all the live curliness had gone from it. Her over-trimmed Georgette *crêpe*[6] dress was too short and showed an appalling amount of leg, stout legs in sleazy stockings of a vivid rose-beige shade. Her plump hands were newly and not too competently manicured—for the occasion, probably. And she wasn't smoking.

Clare said—and Irene fancied that her husky voice held a slight edge—"Before you came, Irene, Gertrude was telling me about her two boys. Twins. Think of it! Isn't it too marvellous for words?"

5. In the 1920s the junction of Maryland Avenue and Sixty-Third Street lay at the far end of Chicago's black South Side, where it adjoined the then predominantly white neighborhoods of Hyde Park and Woodlawn.

6. Lightweight textured fabric, usually of silk.

Irene felt a warmness creeping into her cheeks. Uncanny, the way Clare could divine what one was thinking. She was a little put out, but her manner was entirely easy as she said: "That is nice. I've two boys myself, Gertrude. Not twins, though. It seems that Clare's rather behind, doesn't it?"

Gertrude, however, wasn't sure that Clare hadn't the best of it. "She's got a girl. I wanted a girl. So did Fred."

"Isn't that a bit unusual?" Irene asked. "Most men want sons. Egotism, I suppose."

"Well, Fred didn't."

The tea-things had been placed on a low table at Clare's side. She gave them her attention now, pouring the rich amber fluid from the tall glass pitcher into stately slim glasses, which she handed to her guests, and then offered them lemon or cream and tiny sandwiches or cakes.

After taking up her own glass she informed them: "No, I have no boys and I don't think I'll ever have any. I'm afraid. I nearly died of terror the whole nine months before Margery was born for fear that she might be dark. Thank goodness, she turned out all right. But I'll never risk it again. Never! The strain is simply too—too hellish."

Gertrude Martin nodded in complete comprehension.

This time it was Irene who said nothing.

"You don't have to tell me!" Gertrude said fervently. "I know what it is all right. Maybe you don't think I wasn't scared to death too. Fred said I was silly, and so did his mother. But, of course, they thought it was just a notion I'd gotten into my head and they blamed it on my condition. They don't know like we do, how it might go way back, and turn out dark no matter what colour the father and mother are."

Perspiration stood out on her forehead. Her narrow eyes rolled first in Clare's, then in Irene's direction. As she talked she waved her heavy hands about.

"No," she went on, "no more for me either. Not even a girl. It's awful the way it skips generations and then pops out. Why, he actually said he didn't care what colour it turned out, if I would only stop worrying about it. But, of course, nobody wants a dark child." Her voice was earnest and she took for granted that her audience was in entire agreement with her.

Irene, whose head had gone up with a quick little jerk, now said in a voice of whose even tones she was proud: "One of my boys is dark."

Gertrude jumped as if she had been shot at. Her eyes goggled. Her mouth flew open. She tried to speak, but could not immediately get the words out. Finally she managed to stammer: "Oh! And your husband, is he—is he—er—dark, too?"

Irene, who was struggling with a flood of feelings, resentment, anger, and contempt, was, however, still able to answer as coolly as if she had not that sense of not belonging to and of despising the company in which she found herself drinking iced tea from tall amber glasses on that hot August afternoon. Her husband, she informed them quietly, couldn't exactly "pass."

At that reply Clare turned on Irene her seductive caressing smile and remarked a little scoffingly: "I do think that coloured people—we—are too silly about some things. After all, the thing's not important to Irene or hundreds of others. Not awfully, even to you, Gertrude. It's only deserters like me who have to be afraid of freaks of the nature. As my inestimable dad used to say, 'Everything must be paid for.' Now, please one of you tell me what ever happened to Claude Jones. You know, the tall, lanky specimen who used to wear that comical little moustache that the girls used to laugh at so. Like a thin streak of soot. The moustache, I mean."

At that Gertrude shrieked with laughter. "Claude Jones!" and launched into the story of how he was no longer a Negro or a Christian but had become a Jew.

"A Jew!" Clare exclaimed.

"Yes, a Jew. A black Jew, he calls himself. He won't eat ham and goes to the synagogue on Saturday. He's got a beard now as well as a moustache. You'd die laughing if you saw him. He's really too funny for words. Fred says he's crazy and I guess he is. Oh, he's a scream all right, a regular scream!" And she shrieked again.

Clare's laugh tinkled out. "It certainly sounds funny enough. Still, it's his own business. If he gets along better by turning—"

At that, Irene, who was still hugging her unhappy don't-care feeling of rightness, broke in, saying bitingly: "It evidently doesn't occur to either you or Gertrude that he might possibly be sincere in changing his religion. Surely everyone doesn't do everything for gain."

Clare Kendry had no need to search for the full meaning of that utterance. She reddened slightly and retorted seriously: "Yes, I admit that might be possible—his being sincere, I mean. It just didn't happen to occur to me, that's all. I'm surprised," and the seriousness changed to mockery, "that you should have expected it to. Or did you really?"

"You don't, I'm sure, imagine that that is a question that I can answer," Irene told her. "Not here and now."

Gertrude's face expressed complete bewilderment. However, seeing that little smiles had come out on the faces of the two other women and not recognizing them for the smiles of mutual reservations which they were, she smiled too.

Clare began to talk, steering carefully away from anything that might lead towards race or other thorny subjects. It was the most brilliant exhibition of conversational weight-lifting that Irene had ever seen. Her words swept over them in charming well-modulated streams. Her laughs tinkled and pealed. Her little stories sparkled.

Irene contributed a bare "Yes" or "No" here and there. Gertrude, a "You don't say!" less frequently.

For a while the illusion of general conversation was nearly perfect. Irene felt her resentment changing gradually to a silent, somewhat grudging admiration.

Clare talked on, her voice, her gestures, colouring all she said of wartime in France, of after-the-wartime in Germany, of the excitement at the time of the general strike in England, of dressmaker's openings in Paris, of the new gaiety of Budapest.[7]

But it couldn't last, this verbal feat. Gertrude shifted in her seat and fell to fidgeting with her fingers. Irene, bored at last by all this repetition of the

7. World War I ended in 1918; in its aftermath Budapest, formerly part of the Austria-Hungarian Empire, became the capital of an independent Hungary. "General Strike": in May 1926 a nine-day general strike idled much of Great Britain's transportation and industry.

selfsame things that she had read all too often in papers, magazines, and books, set down her glass and collected her bag and handkerchief. She was smoothing out the tan fingers of her gloves preparatory to putting them on when she heard the sound of the outer door being opened and saw Clare spring up with an expression of relief saying: "How lovely! Here's Jack at exactly the right minute. You can't go now, 'Rene dear."

John Bellew came into the room. The first thing that Irene noticed about him was that he was not the man that she had seen with Clare Kendry on the Drayton roof. This man, Clare's husband, was a tallish person, broadly made. His age she guessed to be somewhere between thirty-five and forty. His hair was dark brown and waving, and he had a soft mouth, somewhat womanish, set in an unhealthy-looking dough-coloured face. His steel-grey opaque eyes were very much alive, moving ceaselessly between thick bluish lids. But there was, Irene decided, nothing unusual about him, unless it was an impression of latent physical power.

"Hello, Nig," was his greeting to Clare.

Gertrude who had started slightly, settled back and looked covertly towards Irene, who had caught her lip between her teeth and sat gazing at husband and wife. It was hard to believe that even Clare Kendry would permit this ridiculing of her race by an outsider, though he chanced to be her husband. So he knew, then, that Clare was a Negro? From her talk the other day Irene had understood that he didn't. But how rude, how positively insulting, for him to address her in that way in the presence of guests!

In Clare's eyes, as she presented her husband, was a queer gleam, a jeer, it might be. Irene couldn't define it.

The mechanical professions that attend an introduction over, she inquired: "Did you hear what Jack called me?"

"Yes," Gertrude answered, laughing with a dutiful eagerness.

Irene didn't speak. Her gaze remained level on Clare's smiling face.

The black eyes fluttered down. "Tell them, dear, why you call me that."

The man chuckled, crinkling up his eyes, not, Irene was compelled to acknowledge, unpleasantly. He explained: "Well, you see, it's like this. When we were first married, she was as white as—as—well as white as a lily. But I declare she's gettin' darker and darker. I tell her if she don't look out, she'll wake up one of these days and find she's turned into a nigger."

He roared with laughter. Clare's ringing bell-like laugh joined his. Gertrude after another uneasy shift in her seat added her shrill one. Irene, who had been sitting with lips tightly compressed, cried out: "That's good!" and gave way to gales of laughter. She laughed and laughed and laughed. Tears ran down her cheeks. Her sides ached. Her throat hurt. She laughed on and on and on, long after the others had subsided. Until, catching sight of Clare's face, the need for a more quiet enjoyment of this priceless joke, and for caution, struck her. At once she stopped.

Clare handed her husband his tea and laid her hand on his arm with an affectionate little gesture. Speaking with confidence as well as with amusement, she said: "My goodness, Jack! What difference would it make if, after all these years, you were to find out that I was one or two per cent coloured?"

Bellew put out his hand in a repudiating fling, definite and final. "Oh, no, Nig," he declared, "nothing like that with me. I know you're no nigger, so it's all right. You can get as black as you please as far as I'm concerned, since I know you're no nigger. I draw the line at that. No niggers in my family. Never have been and never will be."

Irene's lips trembled almost uncontrollably, but she made a desperate effort to fight back her disastrous desire to laugh again, and succeeded. Carefully selecting a cigarette from the lacquered box on the tea-table before her, she turned an oblique look on Clare and encountered her peculiar eyes fixed on her with an expression so dark and deep and unfathomable that she had for a short moment the sensation of gazing into the eyes of some creature utterly strange and apart. A faint sense of danger brushed her, like the breath of a cold fog. Absurd, her reason told her, as she accepted Bellew's proffered light for her cigarette. Another glance at Clare showed her smiling. So, as one always ready to oblige, was Gertrude.

An on-looker, Irene reflected, would have thought it a most congenial tea-party, all smiles and jokes and hilarious laughter. She said humorously: "So you dislike Negroes, Mr. Bellew?" But her amusement was at her thought, rather than her words.

John Bellew gave a short denying laugh. "You got me wrong there, Mrs. Redfield. Nothing like that at all. I don't dislike them, I hate them. And so does Nig, for all she's trying to turn into one. She wouldn't have a nigger maid around her for love nor money. Not that I'd want her to. They give me the creeps. The black scrimy devils."

This wasn't funny. Had Bellew, Irene inquired, ever known any Negroes? The defensive tone of her voice brought another start from the uncomfortable Gertrude, and, for all her appearance of serenity, a quick apprehensive look from Clare.

Bellew answered: "Thank the Lord, no! And never expect to! But I know people who've known them, better than they know their black selves. And I read in the papers about them. Always robbing and killing people. And," he added darkly, "worse."

From Gertrude's direction came a queer little suppressed sound, a snort or a giggle. Irene couldn't tell which. There was a brief silence, during which she feared that her self-control was about to prove too frail a bridge to support her mounting anger and indignation. She had a leaping desire to shout at the man beside her: "And you're sitting here surrounded by three black devils, drinking tea."

The impulse passed, obliterated by her consciousness of the danger in which such rashness would involve Clare, who remarked with a gentle reprovingness: "Jack dear, I'm sure 'Rene doesn't care to hear all about your pet aversions. Nor Gertrude either. Maybe they read the papers too, you know." She smiled on him, and her smile seemed to transform him, to soften and mellow him, as the rays of the sun does a fruit.

"All right, Nig, old girl. I'm sorry," he apologized. Reaching over, he playfully touched his wife's pale hands, then turned back to Irene. "Didn't mean to bore you, Mrs. Redfield. Hope you'll excuse me," he said sheepishly. "Clare tells me you're living in New York. Great city, New York. The city of the future."

In Irene, rage had not retreated, but was held by some dam of caution and allegiance to Clare. So, in the best casual voice she could muster, she agreed with Bellew. Though, she reminded him, it was exactly what Chicagoans were apt to say of their city. And all the while she was speaking, she was thinking how amazing it was that her voice did not tremble, that outwardly she was calm. Only her hands shook slightly. She drew them inward from their rest in her lap and pressed the tips of her fingers together to still them.

"Husband's a doctor, I understand. Manhattan, or one of the other boroughs?"

Manhattan, Irene informed him, and explained the need for Brian to be within easy reach of certain hospitals and clinics.

"Interesting life, a doctor's."

"Ye-es. Hard, though. And, in a way, monotonous. Nerve-racking too."

"Hard on the wife's nerves at least, eh? So many lady patients." He laughed, enjoying, with a boyish heartiness, the hoary joke.

Irene managed a momentary smile, but her voice was sober as she said: "Brian doesn't care for ladies, especially sick ones. I sometimes wish he did. It's South America that attracts him."

"Coming place, South America, if they ever get the niggers out of it. It's run over—"

"Really, Jack!" Clare's voice was on the edge of temper.

"Honestly, Nig, I forgot." To the others he said: "You see how henpecked I am." And to Gertrude: "You're still in Chicago, Mrs.—er—Mrs. Martin?"

He was, it was plain, doing his best to be agreeable to these old friends of Clare's. Irene had to concede that under other conditions she might have liked him. A fairly good-looking man of amiable disposition, evidently, and in easy circumstances. Plain and with no nonsense about him.

Gertrude replied that Chicago was good enough for her. She'd never been out of it and didn't think she ever should. Her husband's business was there.

"Of course, of course. Can't jump up and leave a business."

There followed a smooth surface of talk about Chicago, New York, their differences and their recent spectacular changes.

It was, Irene, thought, unbelievable and astonishing that four people could sit so unruffled, so ostensibly friendly, while they were in reality seething with anger, mortification, shame. But no, on second thought she was forced to amend her opinion. John Bellew, most certainly, was as undisturbed within as without. So, perhaps, was Gertrude Martin. At least she hadn't the mortification and shame that Clare Kendry must be feeling, or, in such full measure, the rage and rebellion that she, Irene, was repressing.

"More tea, 'Rene," Clare offered.

"Thanks, no. And I must be going. I'm leaving tomorrow, you know, and I've still got packing to do."

She stood up. So did Gertrude, and Clare, and John Bellew.

"How do you like the Drayton, Mrs. Redfield?" the latter asked.

"The Drayton? Oh, very much. Very much indeed," Irene answered, her scornful eyes on Clare's unrevealing face.

"Nice place, all right. Stayed there a time or two myself," the man informed her.

"Yes, it is nice," Irene agreed. "Almost as good as our best New York places." She had withdrawn her look from Clare and was searching in her bag for some non-existent something. Her understanding was rapidly increasing, as was her pity and her contempt. Clare was so daring, so lovely, and so "having."

They gave their hands to Clare with appropriate murmurs. "So good to have seen you." . . . "I do hope I'll see you again soon."

"Good-bye," Clare returned. "It was good of you to come, 'Rene dear. And you too, Gertrude."

"Good-bye, Mr. Bellew." . . . "So glad to have met you." It was Gertrude who had said that. Irene couldn't, she absolutely couldn't bring herself to utter the polite fiction or anything approaching it.

He accompanied them out into the hall, summoned the elevator.

"Good-bye," they said again, stepping in.

Plunging downward they were silent.

They made their way through the lobby without speaking.

But as soon as they had reached the street Gertrude, in the manner of one unable to keep bottled up for another minute that which for the last hour she had had to retain, burst out: "My God! What an awful chance! She must be plumb crazy."

"Yes, it certainly seems risky," Irene admitted.

"Risky! I should say it was. Risky! My God! What a word! And the mess she's liable to get herself into!"

"Still, I imagine she's pretty safe. They don't live here, you know. And there's a child. That's a certain security."

"It's an awful chance, just the same," Gertrude insisted. "I'd never in the world have married Fred without him knowing. You can't tell what will turn up."

"Yes, I do agree that it's safer to tell. But then Bellew wouldn't have married her. And, after all, that's what she wanted."

Gertrude shook her head. "I wouldn't be in her shoes for all the money she's getting out of it, when he finds out. Not with him feeling the way he does. Gee! Wasn't it awful? For a minute I was so mad I could have slapped him."

It had been, Irene acknowledged, a distinctly trying experience, as well as a very unpleasant one. "I was more than a little angry myself."

"And imagine her not telling us about him feeling that way! Anything might have happened. We might have said something."

That, Irene pointed out, was exactly like Clare Kendry. Taking a chance, and not at all considering anyone else's feelings.

Gertrude said: "Maybe she thought we'd think it a good joke. And I guess you did. The way you laughed. My land! I was scared to death he might catch on."

"Well, it was rather a joke," Irene told her, "on him and us and maybe on her."

"All the same, it's an awful chance. I'd hate to be her."

"She seems satisfied enough. She's got what she wanted, and the other day she told me it was worth it."

But about that Gertrude was sceptical. "She'll find out different," was her verdict. "She'll find out different all right."

Rain had begun to fall, a few scattered large drops.

The end-of-the-day crowds were scurrying in the directions of street-cars and elevated roads.

Irene said: "You're going south? I'm sorry. I've got an errand. If you don't mind, I'll just say good-bye here. It has been nice seeing you, Gertrude. Say hello to Fred for me, and to your mother if she remembers me. Good-bye."

She had wanted to be free of the other woman, to be alone; for she was still sore and angry.

What right, she kept demanding of herself, had Clare Kendry to expose her, or even Gertrude Martin, to such humiliation, such downright insult?

And all the while, on the rushing ride out to her father's house, Irene Redfield was trying to understand the look on Clare's face as she had said good-bye. Partly mocking, it had seemed, and partly menacing. And something else for which she could find no name. For an instant a recrudescence of that sensation of fear which she had had while looking into Clare's eyes that afternoon touched her. A slight shiver ran over her.

"It's nothing," she told herself. "Just somebody walking over my grave, as the children say." She tried a tiny laugh and was annoyed to find that it was close to tears.

What a state she had allowed that horrible Bellew to get her into!

And late that night, even, long after the last guest had gone and the old house was quiet, she stood at her window frowning out into the dark rain and puzzling again over that look on Clare's incredibly beautiful face. She couldn't, however, come to any conclusion about its meaning, try as she might. It was unfathomable, utterly beyond any experience or comprehension of hers.

She turned away from the window, at last, with a still deeper frown. Why, after all, worry about Clare Kendry? She was well able to take care of herself, had always been able. And there were, for Irene, other things, more personal and more important to worry about.

Besides, her reason told her, she had only herself to blame for her disagreeable afternoon and its attendant fears and questions. She ought never to have gone.

FOUR

The next morning, the day of her departure for New York, had brought a letter, which, at first glance, she had instinctively known came from Clare Kendry, though she couldn't remember ever having had a letter from her before. Ripping it open and looking at the signature, she saw that she had been right in her guess. She wouldn't, she told herself, read it. She hadn't the time. And, besides, she had no wish to be reminded of the afternoon before. As it was, she felt none too fresh for her journey; she had had a wretched night. And all because of Clare's innate lack of consideration for the feelings of others.

But she did read it. After father and friends had waved good-bye, and she was being hurled eastward, she became possessed of an uncontrollable curiosity to see what Clare had said about yesterday. For what, she asked, as she took it out of her bag and opened it, could she, what could anyone, say about a thing like that?

Clare Kendry had said:

'RENE DEAR:

However am I to thank you for your visit? I know you are feeling that under the circumstances I ought not to have asked you to come, or, rather, insisted. But if you could know how glad, how excitingly happy, I was to meet you and how I ached to see more of you (to see everybody and couldn't), you would understand my wanting to see you again, and maybe forgive me a little.

My love to you always and always and to your dear father, and all my poor thanks.

CLARE.

And there was a postcript which said:

It may be, 'Rene dear, it may just be, that, after all, your way may be the wiser and infinitely happier one. I'm not sure just now. At least not so sure as I have been.

C.

But the letter hadn't conciliated Irene. Her indignation was not lessened by Clare's flattering reference to her wiseness. As if, she thought wrathfully, anything could take away the humiliation, or any part of it, of what she had gone through yesterday afternoon for Clare Kendry.

With an unusual methodicalness she tore the offending letter into tiny ragged squares that fluttered down and made a small heap in her black *crêpe de Chine*[8] lap. The destruction completed, she gathered them up, rose, and moved to the train's end. Standing there, she dropped them over the railing and watched them scatter, on tracks, on cinders, on forlorn grass, in rills of dirty water.

And that, she told herself, was that. The chances were one in a million that she would ever again lay eyes on Clare Kendry. If, however, that millionth chance should turn up, she had only to turn away her eyes, to refuse her recognition.

She dropped Clare out of her mind and turned her thoughts to her own affairs. To home, to the boys, to Brian. Brian, who in the morning would be waiting for her in the great clamourous station. She hoped that he had been comfortable and not too lonely without her and the boys. Not so lonely that that old, queer, unhappy restlessness had begun again within him; that craving for some place strange and different, which at the beginning of her marriage she had had to make such strenuous efforts to repress, and which yet faintly alarmed her, though it now sprang up at gradually lessening intervals.

8. A lightweight textured fabric, usually of silk, and therefore named by association with China (*Chine*, French).

Part Two. Re-Encounter

ONE

Such were Irene Redfield's memories as she sat there in her room, a flood of October sunlight streaming in upon her, holding that second letter of Clare Kendry's.

Laying it aside, she regarded with an astonishment that had in it a mild degree of amusement the violence of the feelings which it stirred in her.

It wasn't the great measure of anger that surprised and slightly amused her. That, she was certain, was justified and reasonable, as was the fact that it could hold, still strong and unabated, across the stretch of two years' time entirely removed from any sight or sound of John Bellew, or of Clare. That even at this remote date the memory of the man's words and manner had power to set her hands to trembling and to send the blood pounding against her temples did not seem to her extraordinary. But that she should retain that dim sense of fear, of panic, was surprising, silly.

That Clare should have written, should, even all things considered, have expressed a desire to see her again, did not so much amaze her. To count as nothing the annoyances, the bitterness, or the suffering of others, that was Clare.

Well—Irene's shoulders went up—one thing was sure: that she needn't, and didn't intend to, lay herself open to any repetition of a humiliation as galling and outrageous as that which, for Clare Kendry's sake, she had borne "that time in Chicago." Once was enough.

If, at the time of choosing, Clare hadn't precisely reckoned the cost, she had, nevertheless, no right to expect others to help make up the reckoning. The trouble with Clare was, not only that she wanted to have her cake and eat it too, but that she wanted to nibble at the cakes of other folk as well.

Irene Redfield found it hard to sympathize with this new tenderness, this avowed yearning of Clare's for "my own people."

The letter which she just put out of her hand was, to her taste, a bit too lavish in its wordiness, a shade too unreserved in the manner of its expression. It roused again that old suspicion that Clare was acting, not consciously, perhaps—that is, not too consciously—but, none the less, acting. Nor was Irene inclined to excuse what she termed Clare's downright selfishness.

And mingled with her disbelief and resentment was another feeling, a question. Why hadn't she spoken that day? Why, in the face of Bellew's ignorant hate and aversion, had she concealed her own origin? Why had she allowed him to make his assertions and express his misconceptions undisputed? Why, simply because of Clare Kendry, who had exposed her to such torment, had she failed to take up the defence of the race to which she belonged?

Irene asked these questions, felt them. They were, however, merely rhetorical, as she herself was well aware. She knew their answers, every one, and it was the same for them all. The sardony[9] of it! She couldn't betray Clare, couldn't even run the risk of appearing to defend a people that were

9. Larsen's coinage, from "sardonic" (in parallel with "irony"/"ironic").

being maligned, for fear that that defence might in some infinitesimal degree lead the way to final discovery of her secret. She had to Clare Kendry a duty. She was bound to her by those very ties of race, which, for all her repudiation of them, Clare had been unable to completely sever.

And it wasn't, as Irene knew, that Clare cared at all about the race or what was to become of it. She didn't. Or that she had for any of its members great, or even real, affection, though she professed undying gratitude for the small kindnesses which the Westover family had shown her when she was a child. Irene doubted the genuineness of it, seeing herself only as a means to an end where Clare was concerned. Nor could it be said that she had even the slight artistic or sociological interest in the race that some members of other races displayed. She hadn't. No, Clare Kendry cared nothing for the race. She only belonged to it.

"Not another damned thing!" Irene declared aloud as she drew a fragile stocking over a pale beige-coloured foot.

"Aha! Swearing again, are you, madam? Caught you in the act that time."

Brian Redfield had come into the room in that noiseless way which, in spite, of the years of their life together, still had the power to disconcert her. He stood looking down on her with that amused smile of his, which was just the faintest bit supercilious and yet was somehow very becoming to him.

Hastily Irene pulled on the other stocking and slipped her feet into the slippers beside her chair.

"And what brought on this particular outburst of profanity? That is, if an indulgent but perturbed husband may inquire. The mother of sons too! The times, alas, the times!"

"I've had this letter," Irene told him. "And I'm sure that anybody'll admit it's enough to make a saint swear. The nerve of her!"

She passed the letter to him, and in the act made a little mental frown. For, with a nicety of perception, she saw that she was doing it instead of answering his question with words, so that he might be occupied while she hurried through her dressing. For she was late again, and Brian, she well knew, detested that. Why, oh why, couldn't she ever manage to be on time? Brian had been up for ages, had made some calls for all she knew, besides having taken the boys downtown to school. And she wasn't dressed yet; had only begun. Damn Clare! This morning it was her fault.

Brian sat down and bent his head over the letter, puckering his brows slightly in his effort to make out Clare's scrawl.

Irene, who had risen and was standing before the mirror, ran a comb through her black hair, then tossed her head with a light characteristic gesture, in order to disarrange a little the set locks. She touched a powder-puff to her warm olive skin, and then put on her frock with a motion so hasty that it was with some difficulty properly adjusted. At last she was ready, though she didn't immediately say so, but stood, instead, looking with a sort of curious detachment at her husband across the room.

Brian, she was thinking, was extremely good-looking. Not, of course, pretty or effeminate; the slight irregularity of his nose saved him from the prettiness, and the rather marked heaviness of his chin saved him from the effeminacy. But he was, in a pleasant masculine way, rather handsome. And yet, wouldn't he, perhaps, have been merely ordinarily good-looking but for the richness, the beauty of his skin, which was of an exquisitely fine texture and deep copper colour.

He looked up and said: "Clare? That must be the girl you told me about meeting the last time you were out home. The one you went to tea with?"

Irene's answer to that was an inclination of the head.

"I'm ready," she said.

They were going downstairs, Brian deftly, unnecessarily, piloting her round the two short curved steps, just before the centre landing.

"You're not," he asked, "going to see her?"

His words, however, were in reality not a question, but, as Irene was aware, an admonition.

Her front teeth just touched. She spoke through them, and her tones held a thin sarcasm. "Brian, darling, I'm really not such an idiot that I don't realize that if a man calls me a nigger, it's his fault the first time, but mine if he has the opportunity to do it again."

They went into the dining-room. He drew back her chair and she sat down behind the fat-bellied German coffee-pot, which sent out its morning fragrance, mingled with the smell of crisp toast and savoury bacon, in the distance. With his long, nervous fingers he picked up the morning paper from his own chair and sat down.

Zulena, a small mahogany-coloured creature, brought in the grapefruit.

They took up their spoons.

Out of the silence Brian spoke. Blandly. "My dear, you misunderstand me entirely. I simply meant that I hope you're not going to let her pester you. She will, you know, if you give her half a chance and she's anything at all like your description of her. Anyway, they always do. Besides," he corrected, "the man, her husband, didn't call you a nigger. There's a difference, you know."

"No, certainly he didn't. Not actually. He couldn't, not very well, since he didn't know. But he would have. It amounts to the same thing. And I'm sure it was just as unpleasant."

"U-mm, I don't know. But it seems to me," he pointed out, "that you, my dear, had all the advantage. You knew what his opinion of you was, while he—Well, 'twas ever thus. We know, always have. They don't. Not quite. It has, you will admit, it's humorous side, and, sometimes, its conveniences."

She poured the coffee.

"I can't see it. I'm going to write Clare. Today, if I can find a minute. It's a thing we might as well settle definitely, and immediately. Curious, isn't it, that knowing, as she does, his unqualified attitude, she still—"

Brian interrupted: "It's always that way. Never known it to fail. Remember Albert Hammond, how he used to be forever haunting Seventh Avenue, and Lenox Avenue, and the dancing-places, until some 'shine'[1] took a shot at him for casting an eye towards his 'sheba?'[2] They always come back. I've seen it happen time and time again."

"But why?" Irene wanted to know. "Why?"

1. Derogatory slang for an African American man.
2. Derogatory slang for an African American woman, after the biblical queen of Sheba (1 Kings 10).

"If I knew that, I'd know what race is."

"But wouldn't you think that having got the thing, or things, they were after, and at such risk, they'd be satisfied? Or afraid?"

"Yes," Brian agreed, "you certainly would think so. But, the fact remains, they aren't. Not satisfied, I mean. I think they're scared enough most of the time, when they give way to the urge and slip back. Not scared enough to stop them, though. Why, the good God only knows."

Irene leaned forward, speaking, she was aware, with a vehemence absolutely unnecessary, but which she could not control.

"Well, Clare can just count me out. I've no intention of being the link between her and her poorer darker brethren. After that scene in Chicago too! To calmly expect me—" She stopped short, suddenly too wrathful for words.

"Quite right. The only sensible thing to do. Let her miss you. It's an unhealthy business, the whole affair. Always is."

Irene nodded. "More coffee," she offered.

"Thanks, no." He took up his paper again, spreading it open with a little rattling noise.

Zulena came in bringing more toast. Brian took a slice and bit into it with that audible crunching sound that Irene disliked so intensely, and turned back to his paper.

She said: "It's funny about 'passing.' We disapprove of it and at the same time condone it. It excites our contempt and yet we rather admire it. We shy away from it with an odd kind of revulsion, but we protect it."

"Instinct of the race to survive and expand."

"Rot! Everything can't be explained by some general biological phrase."

"Absolutely everything can. Look at the so-called whites, who've left bastards all over the known earth. Same thing in them. Instinct of the race to survive and expand."[3]

With that Irene didn't at all agree, but many arguments in the past had taught her the futility of attempting to combat Brian on ground where he was more nearly at home than she. Ignoring his unqualified assertion, she slid away from the subject entirely.

"I wonder," she asked, "if you'll have time to run me down to the printing-office. It's on a Hundred and Sixteenth Street. I've got to see about some handbills and some more tickets for the dance."

"Yes, of course. How's it going? Everything all set?"

"Ye-es. I guess so. The boxes are all sold and nearly all the first batch of tickets. And we expect to take in almost as much again at the door. Then, there's all that cake to sell. It's a terrible lot of work, though."

"I'll bet it is. Uplifting the brother's no easy job. I'm as busy as a cat with fleas, myself." And over his face there came a shadow. "Lord! how I hate sick people, and their stupid, meddling families, and smelly, dirty rooms, and climbing filthy steps in dark hallways."

"Surely," Irene began, fighting back the fear and irritation that she felt, "surely—"

3. Brian echoes the evolutionary theory of the survival of the fittest, as articulated by Charles Darwin (1809–1882) in *On the Origin of Species* (1859).

Her husband silenced her, saying sharply: "Let's not talk about it, please." And immediately, in his usual, slightly mocking tone he asked: "Are you ready to go now? I haven't a great deal of time to wait."

He got up. She followed him out into the hall without replying. He picked up his soft brown hat from the small table and stood a moment whirling it round on his long tea-coloured fingers.

Irene, watching him, was thinking: "It isn't fair, it isn't fair." After all these years to still blame her like this. Hadn't his success proved that she'd been right in insisting that he stick to his profession right there in New York? Couldn't he see, even now, that it *had* been best? Not for her, oh no, not for her—she had never really considered herself—but for him and the boys. Was she never to be free of it, that fear which crouched, always, deep down within her, stealing away the sense of security, the feeling of permanence, from the life which she had so admirably arranged for them all, and desired so ardently to have remain as it was? That strange, and to her fantastic, notion of Brian's of going off to Brazil, which, though unmentioned, yet lived within him; how it frightened her, and—yes, angered her!

"Well?" he asked lightly.

"I'll just get my things. One minute," she promised and turned upstairs.

Her voice had been even and her step was firm, but in her there was no slackening of the agitation, of the alarms, which Brian's expression of discontent had raised. He had never spoken of his desire since that long-ago time of storm and strain, of hateful and nearly disastrous quarrelling, when she had so firmly opposed him, so sensibly pointed out its utter impossibility and its probable consequences to her and the boys, and had even hinted at a dissolution of their marriage in the event of his persistence in his idea. No, there had been, in all the years that they had lived together since then, no other talk of it, no more than there had been any other quarrelling or any other threats. But because, so she insisted, the bond of flesh and spirit between them was so strong, she knew, had always known, that his dissatisfaction had continued, as had his dislike and disgust for his profession and his country.

A feeling of uneasiness stole upon her at the inconceivable suspicion that she might have been wrong in her estimate of her husband's character. But she squirmed away from it. Impossible! She couldn't have been wrong. Everything proved that she had been right. More than right, if such a thing could be. And all, she assured herself, because she understood him so well, because she had, actually, a special talent for understanding him. It was, as she saw it, the one thing that had been the basis of the success which she had made of a marriage that had threatened to fail. She knew him as well as he knew himself, or better.

Then why worry? The thing, this discontent which had exploded into words, would surely die, flicker out, at last. True, she had in the past often been tempted to believe that it had died, only to become conscious, in some instinctive, subtle way, that she had been merely deceiving herself for a while and that it still lived. But it *would* die. Of that she was certain. She had only to direct and guide her man, to keep him going in the right direction.

She put on her coat and adjusted her hat.

Yes, it would die, as long ago she had made up her mind that it should. But in the meantime, while it was still living and still had the power to flare up and alarm her, it would have to be banked, smothered, and something offered in its stead. She would have to make some plan, some decision, at once. She frowned, for it annoyed her intensely. For, though temporary, it would be important and perhaps disturbing. Irene didn't like changes, particularly changes that affected the smooth routine of her household. Well, it couldn't be helped. Something would have to be done. And immediately.

She took up her purse and drawing on her gloves, ran down the steps and out through the door which Brian held open for her and stepped into the waiting car.

"You know," she said, settling herself into the seat beside him, "I'm awfuly glad to get this minute alone with you. It does seem that we're always so busy—I do hate that—but what can we do? I've had something on my mind for ever so long, something that needs talking over and really serious consideration."

The car's engine rumbled as it moved out from the kerb and into the scant traffic of the street under Brian's expert guidance.

She studied his profile.

They turned into Seventh Avenue. Then he said: "Well, let's have it. No time like the present for the settling of weighty matters."

"It's about Junior. I wonder if he isn't going too fast in school? We do forget that he's not eleven yet. Surely it can't be good for him to—well, if he is, I mean. Going too fast, you know. Of course, you know more about these things than I do. You're better able to judge. That is, if you've noticed or thought about it at all."

"I do wish, Irene, you wouldn't be for ever fretting about those kids. They're all right. Perfectly all right. Good, strong, healthy boys, especially Junior. Most especially Junior."

"We-ll, I s'pose you're right. You're expected to know about things like that, and I'm sure you wouldn't make a mistake about your own boy." (Now, why had she said that?) "But that isn't all. I'm terribly afraid he's picked up some queer ideas about things—some things—from the older boys, you know."

Her manner was consciously light. Apparently she was intent of the maze of traffic, but she was still watching Brian's face closely. On it was a peculiar expression. Was it, could it possibly be, a mixture of scorn and distaste?

"Queer ideas?" he repeated. "D'you mean ideas about sex, Irene?"

"Ye-es. Not quite nice ones. Dreadful jokes, and things like that."

"Oh, I see," he threw at her. For a while there was silence between them. After a moment he demanded bluntly: "Well, what of it? If sex isn't a joke, what is it? And what is a joke?"

"As you please, Brian. He's your son, you know." Her voice was clear, level, disapproving.

"Exactly! And you're trying to make a molly-coddle out of him. Well, just let me tell you, I won't have it. And you needn't think I'm going to let you change him to some nice kindergarten kind of a school because he's getting a little necessary education. I won't! He'll stay right where he is. The sooner and the more he learns about sex, the better for him. And most certainly if he learns that it's a grand joke, the greatest in the world. It'll keep him from lots of disappointments later on."

Irene didn't answer.

They reached the printing-shop. She got out, emphatically slamming the car's door behind her. There was a piercing agony of misery in her heart. She hadn't intended to behave like this, but her extreme resentment at his attitude, the sense of having been wilfully misunderstood and reproved, drove her to fury.

Inside the shop, she stilled the trembling of her lips and drove back her rising anger. Her business transacted, she came back to the car in a chastened mood. But against the armour of Brian's stubborn silence she heard herself saying in a calm, metallic voice: "I don't believe I'll go back just now. I've remembered that I've got to do something about getting something decent to wear. I haven't a rag that's fit to be seen. I'll take the bus downtown."

Brian merely doffed his hat in that maddening polite way which so successfully curbed and yet revealed his temper.

"Good-bye," she said bitingly. "Thanks for the lift," and turned towards the avenue.

What, she wondered contritely, was she to do next? She was vexed with herself for having chosen, as it had turned out, so clumsy an opening for what she had intended to suggest: some European school for Junior next year, and Brian to take him over. If she had been able to present her plan, and he had accepted it, as she was sure that he would have done, with other more favourable opening methods, he would have had that to look forward to as a break in the easy monotony that seemed, for some reason she was wholly unable to grasp, so hateful to him.

She was even more vexed at her own explosion of anger. What could have got into her to give way to it in such a moment?

Gradually her mood passed. She drew back from the failure her first attempt at substitution, not so much discouraged as disappointed and ashamed. It might be, she reflected, that, in addition to her ill-timed loss of temper, she had been too hasty in her eagerness to distract him, had rushed too closely on the heels of his outburst, and had thus aroused his suspicions and his obstinacy. She had but to wait. Another more appropriate time would come, tomorrow, next week, next month. It wasn't now, as it had been once, that she was afraid that he would throw everything aside and rush off to that remote place of his heart's desire. He wouldn't, she knew. He was fond of her, loved her, in his slightly undemonstrative way.

And there were the boys.

It was only that she wanted him to be happy, resenting, however, his inability to be so with things as they were, and never acknowledging that though she did want him to be happy, it was only in her own way and by some plan of hers for him that she truly desired him to be so. Nor did she admit that all other plans, all other ways, she regarded as menaces, more or less indirect, to that security of place and substance which she insisted upon for her sons and in a lesser degree for herself.

TWO

Five days had gone by since Clare Kendry's appealing letter. Irene Redfield had not replied to it. Nor had she had any other word from Clare.

She had not carried out her first intention of writing at once because on going back to the letter for Clare's address, she had come upon something which, in the rigour of her determination to maintain unbroken between them the wall that Clare herself had raised, she had forgotten, or not fully noted. It was the fact that Clare had requested her to direct her answer to the post office's general delivery.[4]

That had angered Irene, and increased her disdain and contempt for the other.

Tearing the letter across, she had flung it into the scrap-basket. It wasn't so much Clare's carefulness and her desire for secrecy in their relations—Irene understood the need for that—as that Clare should have doubted her discretion, implied that she might not be cautious in the wording of her reply and the choice of a posting-box. Having always had complete confidence in her own good judgment and tact, Irene couldn't bear to have anyone seem to question them. Certainly not Clare Kendry.

In another, calmer moment she decided that it was, after all, better to answer nothing, to explain nothing, to refuse nothing; to dispose of the matter simply by not writing at all. Clare, of whom it couldn't be said that she was stupid, would not mistake the implication of that silence. She might—and Irene was sure that she would—choose to ignore it and write again, but that didn't matter. The whole thing would be very easy. The basket for all letters, silence for their answers.

Most likely she and Clare would never meet again. Well, she, for one, could endure that. Since childhood their lives had never really touched. Actually they were strangers. Strangers in their ways and means of living. Strangers in their desires and ambitions. Strangers even in their racial consciousness. Between them the barrier was just as high, just as broad, and just as firm as if in Clare did not run that strain of black blood. In truth, it was higher, broader, and firmer; because for her there were perils, not known, or imagined, by those others who had no such secrets to alarm or endanger them.

The day was getting on toward evening. It was past the middle of October. There had been a week of cold rain, drenching the rotting leaves which had fallen from the poor trees that lined the street on which the Redfields' house was located, and sending a damp air of penetrating chill into the house, with a hint of cold days to come. In Irene's room a low fire was burning. Outside, only a dull grey light was left of the day. Inside, lamps had already been lighted.

From the floor above there was the sound of young voices. Sometimes Junior's serious and positive; again, Ted's deceptively gracious one. Often there was laughter, or the noise of commotion, tussling, or toys being slammed down.

Junior, tall for his age, was almost incredibly like his father in feature and colouring; but his temperament was hers, practical and determined, rather than Brian's. Ted, speculative and withdrawn, was, apparently, less positive in his ideas and desires. About him there was a deceiving air of candour

4. Mail held at the post office for pickup rather than delivered to an address.

that was, Irene knew, like his father's show of reasonable acquiescence. If, for the time being, and with a charming appearance of artlessness, he submitted to the force of superior strength, or some other immovable condition or circumstance, it was because of his intense dislike of scenes and unpleasant argument. Brian over again.

Gradually Irene's thought slipped away from Junior and Ted, to become wholly absorbed in their father.

The old fear, with strength increased, the fear for the future, had again laid its hand on her. And, try as she might, she could not shake it off. It was as if she had admitted to herself that against that easy surface of her husband's concordance with her wishes, which had, since the war had given him back to her physically unimpaired, covered an increasing inclination to tear himself and his possessions loose from their proper setting, she was helpless.

The chagrin which she had felt at her first failure to subvert this latest manifestation of his discontent had receded, leaving in its wake an uneasy depression. Were all her efforts, all her labours, to make up to him that one loss, all her silent striving to prove to him that her way had been best, all her ministrations to him, all her outward sinking of self, to count for nothing in some unperceived sudden moment? And if so, what, then, would be the consequences to the boys? To her? To Brian himself? Endless searching had brought no answer to these questions. There was only an intense weariness from their shuttle-like procession in her brain.

The noise and commotion from above grew increasingly louder. Irene was about to go to the stairway and request the boys to be quieter in their play when she heard the doorbell ringing.

Now, who was that likely to be? She listened to Zulena's heels, faintly tapping on their way to the door, then to the shifting sound of her feet on the steps, then to her light knock on the bedroom door.

"Yes. Come in," Irene told her.

Zulena stood in the doorway. She said: "Someone to see you, Mrs. Redfield." Her tone was discreetly regretful, as if to convey that she was reluctant to disturb her mistress at that hour, and for a stranger. "A Mrs. Bellew."

Clare!

"Oh dear! Tell her, Zulena," Irene began, "that I can't—No. I'll see her. Please bring her up here."

She heard Zulena pass down the hall, down the stairs, then stood up, smoothing out the tumbled green and ivory draperies of her dress with light stroking pats. At the mirror she dusted a little powder on her nose and brushed out her hair.

She meant to tell Clare Kendry at once, and definitely, that it was of no use, her coming, that she couldn't be responsible, that she'd talked it over with Brian, who had agreed with her that it was wiser, for Clare's own sake, to refrain—

But that was as far as she got in her rehearsal. For Clare had come softly into the room without knocking, and before Irene could greet her, had dropped a kiss on her dark curls.

Looking at the woman before her, Irene Redfield had a sudden inexplicable onrush of affectionate feeling. Reaching out, she grasped Clare's two hand in her own and cried with something like awe in her voice: "Dear God! But aren't you lovely, Clare!"

Clare tossed that aside. Like the furs and small blue hat which she threw on the bed before seating herself slantwise in Irene's favourite chair, with one foot curled under her.

"Didn't you mean to answer my letter, 'Rene?" she asked gravely.

Irene looked away. She had that uncomfortable feeling that one has when one has not been wholly kind or wholly true.

Clare went on: "Every day I went to that nasty little post-office place. I'm sure they were all beginning to think that I'd been carrying on an illicit love-affair and that the man had thrown me over. Every morning the same answer: 'Nothing for you.' I got into an awful fright, thinking that something might have happened to your letter, or to mine. And half the nights I would lie awake looking out at the watery stars—hopeless things, the stars—worrying and wondering. But at last it soaked in, that you hadn't written and didn't intend to. And then—well, as soon as ever I'd seen Jack off for Florida, I came straight here. And now, 'Rene, please tell me quite frankly why you didn't answer my letter."

"Because, you see—" Irene broke off and kept Clare waiting while she lit a cigarette, blew out the match, and dropped it into a tray. She was trying to collect her arguments, for some sixth sense warned her that it was going to be harder than she thought to convince Clare Kendry of the folly of Harlem for her. Finally she proceeded: "I can't help thinking that you ought not to come up here, ought not to run the risk of knowing Negroes."

"You mean you don't want me, 'Rene?"

Irene hadn't supposed that anyone could look so hurt. She said, quite gently, "No, Clare, it's not that. But even you must see that it's terribly foolish, and not just the right thing."

The tinkle of Clare's laugh rang out, while she passed her hands over the bright sweep of her hair. "Oh, 'Rene!" she cried, "you're priceless! And you haven't changed a bit. The right thing!" Leaning forward, she looked curiously into Irene's disapproving brown eyes. "You don't, you really can't mean exactly that! Nobody could. It's simply unbelievable."

Irene was on her feet before she realized that she had risen. "What I really mean," she retorted, "is that it's dangerous and that you ought not to run such silly risks. No one ought to. You least of all."

Her voice was brittle. For into her mind had come a thought, strange and irrelevant, a suspicion, that had surprised and shocked her and driven her to her feet. It was that in spite of her determined selfishness the woman before her was yet capable of heights and depths of feeling that she, Irene Redfield, had never known. Indeed, never cared to know. The thought, the suspicion, was gone as quickly as it had come.

Clare said: "Oh, me!"

Irene touched her arm caressingly, as if in contrition for that flashing thought. "Yes, Clare, you. It's not safe. Not safe at all."

"Safe!"

It seemed to Irene that Clare had snapped her teeth down on the word and then flung it from her. And for another flying second she had that suspicion of Clare's ability for a quality of feeling that was to her strange, and even repugnant. She was aware, too, of a dim premonition of some impending disaster. It was as if Clare Kendry had said to her, for whom safety, security, were all-important: "Safe! Damn being safe!" and meant it.

With a gesture of impatience she sat down. In a voice of cool formality, she said: "Brian and I have talked the whole thing over carefully and decided that it isn't wise. He says it's always a dangerous business, this coming back. He's seen more than one come to grief because of it. And, Clare, considering everything—Mr. Bellew's attitude and all that—don't you think you ought to be as careful as you can?"

Clare's deep voice broke the small silence that had followed Irene's speech. She said, speaking almost plaintively: "I ought to have known. It's Jack. I don't blame you for being angry, though I must say you behaved beautifully that day. But I did think you'd understand, 'Rene. It was that, partly, that has made me want to see other people. It just swooped down and changed everything. If it hadn't been for that, I'd have gone on to the end, never seeing any of you. But that did something to me, and I've been so lonely since! You can't know. Not close to a single soul. Never anyone to really talk to."

Irene pressed out her cigarette. While doing so, she saw again the vision of Clare Kendry staring disdainfully down at the face of her father, and thought that it would be like that that she would look at her husband if he lay dead before her.

Her own resentment was swept aside and her voice held an accent of pity as she exclaimed: "Why, Clare! I didn't know. Forgive me. I feel like seven beasts.[5] It was stupid of me not to realize."

"No. Not at all. You couldn't. Nobody, none of you, could," Clare moaned. The black eyes filled with tears that ran down her cheeks and spilled into her lap, ruining the priceless velvet of her dress. Her long hands were a little uplifted and clasped tightly together. Her effort to speak moderately was obvious, but not successful. "How could you know? How could you? You're free. You're happy. And," with faint derision, "safe."

Irene passed over that touch of derision, for the poignant rebellion of the other's words had brought the tears to her own eyes, though she didn't allow them to fall. The truth was that she knew weeping did not become her. Few women, she imagined, wept as attractively as Clare. "I'm beginning to believe," she murmured, "that no one is ever completely happy, or free, or safe."

"Well, then, what does it matter? One risk more or less, if we're not safe anyway, if even you're not, it can't make all the difference in the world. It can't to me. Besides, I'm used to risks. And this isn't such a big one as you're trying to make it."

"Oh, but it is. And it can make all the difference in the world. There's your little girl, Clare. Think of the consequences to her."

Clare's face took on a startled look, as though she were totally unprepared for this new weapon with which Irene had assailed her. Seconds passed, during which she sat with stricken eyes and compressed lips. "I think," she said at last, "that being a mother is the cruellest thing in the world." Her clasped hands swayed forward and back again, and her scarlet mouth trembled irrepressibly.

5. After the seven-headed monster described in the Book of Revelation (13.1).

"Yes," Irene softly agreed. For a moment she was unable to say more, so accurately had Clare put into words that which, not so definitely defined, was so often in her own heart of late. At the same time she was conscious that here, to her hand, was a reason which could not be lightly brushed aside. "Yes," she repeated, "and the most responsible, Clare. We mothers are all responsible for the security and happiness of our children. Think what it would mean to your Margery if Mr. Bellew should find out. You'd probably lose her. And even if you didn't, nothing that concerned her would ever be the same again. He'd never forget that she had Negro blood. And if she should learn—Well, I believe that after twelve it is too late to learn a thing like that. She'd never forgive you. You may be used to risks, but this is one you mustn't take, Clare. It's a selfish whim, an unnecessary and—

"Yes, Zulena, what is it?" she inquired, a trifle tartly, of the servant who had silently materialized in the doorway.

"The telephone's for you, Mrs. Redfield. It's Mr. Wentworth."

"All right. Thank you. I'll take it here." And, with a muttered apology to Clare, she took up the instrument.

"Hello. . . . Yes, Hugh. . . . Oh, quite. . . . And you? . . . I'm sorry, every single thing's gone. . . . Oh, too bad. . . . Ye-es, I s'pose you could. Not very pleasant, though. . . . Yes, of course, in a pinch everything goes. . . . Wait! I've got it! I'll change mine with whoever's next to you, and you can have that. . . . No. . . . I mean it. . . . I'll be so busy I shan't know whether I'm sitting or standing. . . . As long as Brian has a place to drop down now and then. . . . Not a single soul. . . . No, don't. . . . That's nice. . . . My love to Bianca. . . . I'll see to it right away and call you back. . . . Goodbye."

She hung up and turned back to Clare, a little frown on her softly chiselled features. "It's the N. W. L. dance," she explained, "the Negro Welfare League,[6] you know. I'm on the ticket committee, or, rather, I *am* the committee. Thank heaven it comes off tomorrow night and doesn't happen again for a year. I'm about crazy, and now I've got to persuade somebody to change boxes with me."

"That wasn't," Clare asked, "Hugh Wentworth? Not *the* Hugh Wentworth?"[7]

Irene inclined her head. On her face was a tiny triumphant smile. "Yes, *the* Hugh Wentworth. D'you know him?"

"No. How should I? But I do know about him. And I've read a book or two of his."

"Awfully good, aren't they?"

"U-umm, I s'pose so. Sort of contemptuous, I thought. As if he more or less despised everything and everybody."

"I shouldn't be a bit surprised if he did. Still, he's about earned the right to. Lived on the edges of nowhere in at least three continents. Been through every danger in all kinds of savage places. It's no wonder he thinks the rest

6. An organization dedicated to racial uplift. A number of U.S. cities in the early 20th century had local chapters; in the 1920s, many of these and other local uplift organizations merged with the New York–based National Urban League.

7. Hugh and Bianca Wentworth may be modeled on Carl Van Vechten (1880–1964), the famous white patron and publicist of the Harlem Renaissance, and his wife, Fania Marinoff (1890–1971), to both of whom Larsen dedicated *Passing*.

of us are a lazy self-pampering lot. Hugh's a dear, though, generous as one of the twelve disciples; give you the shirt off his back. Bianca—that's his wife—is nice too."

"And he's coming up here to your dance?"

Irene asked why not.

"It seems rather curious, a man like that, going to a Negro dance."

This, Irene told her, was the year 1927 in the city of New York, and hundreds of white people of Hugh Wentworth's type came to affairs in Harlem, more all the time. So many that Brian had said: "Pretty soon the coloured people won't be allowed in at all, or will have to sit in Jim Crowed[8] sections."

"What do they come for?"

"Same reason you're here, to see Negroes."

"But why?"

"Various motives," Irene explained. "A few purely and frankly to enjoy themselves. Others to get material to turn into shekels.[9] More, to gaze on these great and near great while they gaze on the Negroes."

Clare clapped her hand. " 'Rene, suppose I come too! It sounds terribly interesting and amusing. And I don't see why I shouldn't."

Irene, who was regarding her through narrowed eyelids, had the same thought that she had had two years ago on the roof of the Drayton, that Clare Kendry was just a shade too good-looking. Her tone was on the edge of irony as she said: "You mean because so many other white people go?"

A pale rose-colour came into Clare's ivory cheeks. She lifted a hand in protest. "Don't be silly! Certainly not! I mean that in a crowd of that kind I shouldn't be noticed."

On the contrary, was Irene's opinion. It might be even doubly dangerous. Some friend or acquaintance of John Bellew or herself might see and recognize her.

At that, Clare laughed for a long time, little musical trills following one another in sequence after sequence. It was as if the thought of any friend of John Bellew's going to a Negro dance was to her the most amusing thing in the world.

"I don't think," she said, when she had done laughing, "we need worry about that."

Irene, however, wasn't so sure. But all her efforts to dissuade Clare were useless. To her, "You never can tell whom you're likely to meet there," Clare's rejoinder was: "I'll take my chance on getting by."

"Besides, you won't know a soul and I shall be too busy to look after you. You'll be bored stiff."

"I won't, I won't. If nobody asks me to dance, not even Dr. Redfield, I'll just sit and gaze on the great and the near great, too. Do, 'Rene, be polite and invite me."

Irene turned away from the caress of Clare's smile, saying promptly and positively: "I will not."

"I mean to go anyway," Clare retorted, and her voice was no less positive than Irene's.

8. Segregated.
9. Money (slang), from the currency of ancient Israel and with anti-Semitic connotations.

"Oh, no. You couldn't possibly go there alone. It's a public thing. All sorts of people go, anybody who can pay a dollar, even ladies of easy virtue looking for trade.[1] If you were to go there alone, you might be mistaken for one of them, and that wouldn't be too pleasant."

Clare laughed again. "Thanks. I never have been. It might be amusing. I'm warning you, 'Rene, that if you're not going to be nice and take me, I'll still be among those present. I suppose, my dollar's as good as anyone's."

"Oh, the dollar! Don't be a fool, Claire. I don't care where you go, or what you do. All I'm concerned with is the unpleasantness and possible danger which your going might incur, because of your situation. To put it frankly, I shouldn't like to be mixed up in any row of the kind." She had risen again as she spoke and was standing at the window lifting and spreading the small yellow chrysanthemums in the grey stone jar on the sill. Her hands shook slightly, for she was in a near rage of impatience and exasperation.

Claire's face looked strange, as if she wanted to cry again. One of her satin-covered feet swung restlessly back and forth. She said vehemently, violently almost: "Damn Jack! He keeps me out of everything. Everything I want. I could kill him! I expect I shall, some day."

"I wouldn't," Irene advised her, "you see, there's still capital punishment, in this state at least. And really, Clare, after everything's said, I can't see that you've a right to put all the blame on him. You've got to admit that there's his side to the thing. You didn't tell him you were coloured, so he's got no way of knowing about this hankering of yours after Negroes, or that it galls you to fury to hear them called niggers and black devils. As far as I can see, you'll just have to endure some things and give up others. As we've said before, everything must be paid for. Do, please, be reasonable."

But Clare, it was plain, had shut away reason as well as caution. She shook her head. "I can't, I can't," she said. "I would if I could, but I can't. You don't know, you can't realize how I want to see Negroes, to be with them again, to talk with them, to hear them laugh."

And in the look she gave Irene, there was something groping, and hopeless, and yet so absolutely determined that it was like an image of the futile searching and the firm resolution in Irene's own soul, and increased the feeling of doubt and compunction that had been growing within her about Clare Kendry.

She gave in.

"Oh, come if you want to. I s'pose you're right. Once can't do such a terrible lot of harm."

Pushing aside Clare's extravagant thanks, for immediately she was sorry that she had consented, she said briskly: "Should you like to come up and see my boys?"

"I'd love to."

They went up, Irene thinking that Brian would consider that she'd behaved like a spineless fool. And he would be right. She certainly had.

Clare was smiling. She stood in the doorway of the boys' playroom, her shadowy eyes looking down on Junior and Ted, who had sprung apart from their tusselling. Junior's face had a funny little look of resentment. Ted's was blank.

1. Prostitutes seeking customers.

Clare said: "Please don't be cross. Of course, I know I've gone and spoiled everything. But maybe, if I promise not to get too much in the way, you'll let me come in, just the same."

"Sure, come in if you want to," Ted told her. "We can't stop you, you know." He smiled and made her a little bow and then turned away to a shelf that held his favourite books. Taking one down, he settled himself in a chair and began to read.

Junior said nothing, did nothing, merely stood there waiting.

"Get up, Ted! That's rude. This is Theodore, Mrs. Bellew. Please excuse his bad manners. He does know better. And this is Brian junior. Mrs. Bellew is an old friend of mother's. We used to play together when we were little girls."

Clare had gone and Brian had telephoned that he'd been detained and would have his dinner downtown. Irene was a little glad for that. She was going out later herself, and that meant she wouldn't, probably, see Brian until morning and so could put off for a few more hours speaking of Clare and the N. W. L. dance.

She was angry with herself and with Clare. But more with herself, for having permitted Clare to tease her into doing something that Brian had, all but expressly, asked her not to do. She didn't want him ruffled, not just then, not while he was possessed of that unreasonable restless feeling.

She was annoyed, too, because she was aware that she had consented to something which, if it went beyond the dance, would involve her in numerous petty inconveniences and evasions. And not only at home with Brian, but outside with friends and acquaintances. The disagreeable possibilities in connection with Clare Kendry's coming among them loomed before her in endless irritating array.

Clare, it seemed, still retained her ability to secure the thing that she wanted in the face of any opposition, and in utter disregard of the convenience and desire of others. About her there was some quality, hard and persistent, with the strength and endurance of rock, that would not be beaten or ignored. She couldn't, Irene thought, have had an entirely serene life. Not with that dark secret for ever crouching in the background of her consciousness. And yet she hadn't the air of a woman whose life had been touched by uncertainty or suffering. Pain, fear, and grief were things that left their mark on people. Even love, that exquisite torturing emotion, left its subtle traces on the countenance.

But Clare—she had remained almost what she had always been, an attractive, somewhat lonely child—selfish, wilful, and disturbing.

THREE

The things which Irene Redfield remembered afterward about the Negro Welfare League dance seemed, to her, unimportant and unrelated.

She remembered the not quite derisive smile with which Brian had cloaked his vexation when she informed him—oh, so apologetically—that she had promised to take Clare, and related the conversation of her visit.

She remembered her own little choked exclamation of admiration, when, on coming downstairs a few minutes later than she had intended, she had rushed into the living-room where Brian was waiting and had found Clare there too. Clare, exquisite, golden, fragrant, flaunting, in a stately gown of shining black taffeta,[2] whose long, full skirt lay in graceful folds about her slim golden feet; her glistening hair drawn smoothly back into a small twist at the nape of her neck; her eyes sparkling like dark jewels. Irene, with her new rose-coloured chiffon frock ending at the knees, and her cropped curls, felt dowdy and commonplace. She regretted that she hadn't counselled Clare to wear something ordinary and inconspicuous. What on earth would Brian think of deliberate courting of attention? But if Clare Kendry's appearance had in it anything that was, to Brian Redfield, annoying or displeasing, the fact was not discernible to his wife as, with an uneasy feeling of guilt, she stood there looking into his face while Clare explained that she and he had made their own introductions, accompanying her words with a little deferential smile for Brian, and receiving in return one of his amused, slightly mocking smiles.

She remembered Clare's saying, as they sped northward: "You know, I feel exactly as I used to on the Sunday we went to the Christmas-tree celebration. I knew there was to be a surprise for me and couldn't quite guess what it was to be. I am *so* excited. You can't possibly imagine! It's marvellous to be really on the way! I can hardly believe it!"

At her words and tone a chilly wave of scorn had crept through Irene. All those superlatives! She said, taking care to speak indifferently: "Well, maybe in some ways you will be surprised, more, probably, than you anticipate."

Brian, at the wheel, had thrown back: "And then again, she won't be so very surprised after all, for it'll no doubt be about what she expects. Like the Christmas-tree."

She remembered rushing around here and there, consulting with this person and that one, and now and then snatching a part of a dance with some man whose dancing she particularly liked.

She remembered catching glimpses of Clare in the whirling crowd, dancing, sometimes with a white man, more often with a Negro, frequently with Brian. Irene was glad that he was being nice to Clare, and glad that Clare was having the opportunity to discover that some coloured men were superior to some white men.

She remembered a conversation she had with Hugh Wentworth in a free half-hour when she had dropped into a chair in an emptied box and let her gaze wander over the bright crowd below.

Young men, old men, white men, black men; youthful women, older women, pink women, golden women; fat men, thin men, tall men, short men; stout women, slim women, stately women, small women moved by. An old nursery rhyme popped into her head. She turned to Wentworth, who had just taken a seat beside her, and recited it:

> "Rich man, poor man,
> Beggar man, thief,
> Doctor, lawyer,
> Indian chief."

2. A smooth fabric, often made of silk, typically used in formal women's clothing.

"Yes," Wentworth said, "that's it. Everybody seems to be here and a few more. But what I'm trying to find out is the name, status, and race of the blonde beauty out of the fairy-tale. She's dancing with Ralph Hazelton at the moment. Nice study in contrasts, that."

It was. Clare fair and golden, like a sunlit day. Hazelton dark, with gleaming eyes, like a moonlit night.

"She's a girl I used to know a long time ago in Chicago. And she wanted especially to meet you."

" 'S awfully good of her, I'm sure. And now, alas! the usual thing's happened. All these others, these—er—'gentlemen of colour' have driven a mere Nordic from her mind."

"Stuff!"

" 'S a fact, and what happens to all the ladies of my superior race who're lured up here. Look at Bianca. Have I laid eyes on her tonight except in spots, here and there, being twirled about by some Ethiopian? I have not."

"But, Hugh, you've got to admit that the average coloured man is a better dancer than the average white man—that is, if the celebrities and 'butter and egg' men[3] who find their way up here are fair specimens of white Terpsichorean[4] art."

"Not having tripped the light fantastic[5] with any of the males, I'm not in a position to argue the point. But I don't think it's merely that. 'S something else, some other attraction. They're always raving about the good looks of some Negro, preferably an unusually dark one. Take Hazelton there, for example. Dozens of women have declared him to be fascinatingly handsome. How about you, Irene? Do you think he's—er—ravishingly beautiful?"

"I do not! And I don't think the others do either. Not honestly, I mean. I think that what they feel is—well, a kind of emotional excitement. You know, the sort of thing you feel in the presence of something strange, and even, perhaps, a bit repugnant to you; something so different that it's really at the opposite end of the pole from all your accustomed notions of beauty."

"Damned if I don't think you're halfway right!"

"I'm sure I am. Completely. (Except, of course, when it's just patronizing kindness on their part.) And I know coloured girls who've experienced the same thing—the other way round, naturally."

"And the men? You don't subscribe to the general opinion about their reason for coming up here. Purely predatory. Or, do you?"

"N-no. More curious, I should say."

Wentworth, whose eyes were a clouded amber colour, had given her a long, searching look that was really a stare. He said: "All this is awfully interestin', Irene. We've got to have a long talk about it some time soon. There's your friend from Chicago, first time up here and all that. A case in point."

Irene's smile had only just lifted the corners of her painted lips. A match blazed in Wentworth's broad hands as he lighted her cigarette and his own, and flickered out before he asked: "Or isn't she?"

3. Big spenders.
4. From Terpsichore, the classical Greek Muse of dancing and song.
5. Danced; the phrase goes back at least as far as John Milton's poem "L'Allegro" (1645).

Her smile changed to a laugh. "Oh, Hugh! You're so clever. You usually know everything. Even how to tell the sheep from the goats. What do you think? Is she?"

He blew a long contemplative wreath of smoke. "Damned if I know! I'll be as sure as anything that I've learned the trick. And then in the next minute I'll find I couldn't pick some of 'em if my life depended on it."

"Well, don't let that worry you. Nobody can. Not by looking."

"Not by looking, eh? Meaning?"

"I'm afraid I can't explain. Not clearly. There are ways. But they're not definite or tangible."

"Feeling of kinship, or something like that?"

"Good heavens, no! Nobody has that, except for their in-laws."

"Right again! But go on about the sheep and the goats."

"Well, take my own experience with Dorothy Thompkins. I'd met her four or five times, in groups and crowds of people, before I knew she wasn't a Negro. One day I went to an awful tea, terribly dicty.[6] Dorothy was there. We got talking. In less than five minutes, I knew she was 'fay.'[7] Not from anything she did or said or anything in her appearance. Just—just something. A thing that couldn't be registered."

"Yes, I understand what you mean. Yet lots of people 'pass' all the time."

"Not on our side, Hugh. It's easy for a Negro to 'pass' for white. But I don't think it would be so simple for a white person to 'pass' for coloured."

"Never thought of that."

"No, you wouldn't. Why should you?"

He regarded her critically through mists of smoke. "Slippin' me, Irene?"

She said soberly: "Not you, Hugh. I'm too fond of you. And you're too sincere."

And she remembered that towards the end of the dance Brian had come to her and said: "I'll drop you first and then run Clare down." And that he had been doubtful of her discretion when she had explained to him that he wouldn't have to bother because she had asked Bianca Wentworth to take her down with them. Did she, he had asked, think it had been wise to tell them about Clare?

"I told them nothing," she said sharply, for she was unbearably tired, "except that she was at the Walsingham. It's on their way, And, really, I haven't thought anything about the wisdom of it, but now that I do, I'd say it's much better for them to take her than you."

"As you please. She's your friend, you know," he had answered, with a disclaiming shrug of his shoulders.

Except for these few unconnected things the dance faded to a blurred memory, its outlines mingling with those of other dances of its kind that she had attended in the past and would attend in the future.

FOUR

But undistinctive as the dance had seemed, it was, nevertheless, important. For it marked the beginning of a new factor in Irene Redfield's life, some-

6. Pretentious.

7. From "ofay," derogatory slang term for a white person.

thing that left its trace on all the future years of her existence. It was the beginning of a new friendship with Clare Kendry.

She came to them frequently after that. Always with a touching gladness that welled up and overflowed on all the Redfield household. Yet Irene could never be sure whether her comings were a joy or a vexation.

Certainly she was no trouble. She had not to be entertained, or even noticed—if anyone could ever avoid noticing Clare. If Irene happened to be out or occupied, Clare could very happily amuse herself with Ted and Junior, who had conceived for her an admiration that verged on adoration, especially Ted. Or, lacking the boys, she would descend to the kitchen and, with—to Irene—an exasperating childlike lack of perception, spend her visit in talk and merriment with Zulena and Sadie.

Irene, while secretly resenting these visits to the playroom and kitchen, for some obscure reason which she shied away from putting into words, never requested that Clare make an end of them, or hinted that she wouldn't have spoiled her own Margery so outrageously, nor been so friendly with white servants.

Brian looked on these things with the same tolerant amusement that marked his entire attitude toward Clare. Never since his faintly derisive surprise at Irene's information that she was to go with them the night of the dance, had he shown any disapproval of Clare's presence. On the other hand, it couldn't be said that her presence seemed to please him. It didn't annoy or disturb him, so far as Irene could judge. That was all.

Didn't he, she once asked him, think Clare was extraordinarily beautiful?

"No," he had answered. "That is, not particularly."

"Brian, you're fooling!"

"No, honestly. Maybe I'm fussy. I s'pose she'd be an unusually good-looking white woman. I like my ladies darker. Beside an A-number-one sheba, she simply hasn't got 'em."

Clare went, sometimes with Irene and Brian, to parties and dances, and on a few occasions when Irene hadn't been able or inclined to go out, she had gone alone with Brian to some bridge party or benefit dance.

Once in a while she came formally to dine with them. She wasn't, however, in spite of her poise and air of worldliness, the ideal dinner-party guest. Beyond the æsthetic pleasure one got from watching her, she contributed little, sitting for the most part silent, an odd dreaming look in her hypnotic eyes. Though she could for some purpose of her own—the desire to be included in some party being made up to go cabareting, or an invitation to a dance or a tea—talk fluently and entertainingly.

She was generally liked. She was so friendly and responsive, and so ready to press the sweet food of flattery on all. Nor did she object to appearing a bit pathetic and ill-used, so that people could feel sorry for her. And, no matter how often she came among them, she still remained someone apart, a little mysterious and strange, someone to wonder about and to admire and to pity.

Her visits were undecided and uncertain, being, as they were, dependent on the presence or absence of John Bellew in the city. But she did, once in a while, manage to steal uptown for an afternoon even when he was not away. As time went on without any apparent danger of discovery, even Irene ceased to be perturbed about the possibility of Clare's husband's stumbling on her racial identity.

The daughter, Margery, had been left in Switzerland in school, for Clare and Bellew would be going back in the early spring. In March, Clare thought. "And how I do hate to think of it!" she would say, always with a suggestion of leashed rebellion; "but I can't see how I'm going to get out of it. Jack won't hear of my staying behind. If I could have just a couple of months more in New York, alone I mean, I'd be the happiest thing in the world."

"I imagine you'll be happy enough, once you get away," Irene told her one day when she was bewailing her approaching departure. "Remember, there's Margery. Think how glad you'll be to see her after all this time."

"Children aren't everything," was Clare Kendry's answer to that. "There are other things in the world, though I admit some people don't seem to suspect it." And she laughed, more, it seemed, at some secret joke of her own than at her words.

Irene replied: "You know you don't mean that, Clare. You're only trying to tease me. I know very well that I take being a mother rather seriously. I *am* wrapped up in my boys and the running of my house. I can't help it. And, really, I don't think it's anything to laugh at." And though she was aware of the slight primness in her words and attitude, she had neither power nor wish to efface it.

Clare, suddenly very sober and sweet, said: "You're right. It's no laughing matter. It's shameful of me to tease you, 'Rene. You are so good." And she reached out and gave Irene's hand an affectionate little squeeze. "Don't think," she added, "whatever happens, that I'll ever forget how good you've been to me."

"Nonsense!"

"Oh, but you have, you have. It's just that I haven't any proper morals or sense of duty, as you have, that makes me act as I do."

"Now you are talking nonsense."

"But it's true, 'Rene. Can't you realize that I'm not like you a bit? Why, to get the things I want badly enough, I'd do anything, hurt anybody, throw anything away. Really, 'Rene, I'm not safe." Her voice as well as the look on her face had a beseeching earnestness that made Irene vaguely uncomfortable.

She said: "I don't believe it. In the first place what you're saying is so utterly, so wickedly wrong. And as for your giving up things—" She stopped, at a loss for an acceptable term to express her opinion of Clare's "having" nature.

But Clare Kendry had begun to cry, audibly, with no effort at restraint, and for no reason that Irene could discover.

Part Three. Finale

ONE

The year was getting on towards its end. October, November had gone. December had come and brought with it a little snow and then a freeze and after that a thaw and some soft pleasant days that had in them a feeling of spring.

It wasn't, this mild weather, a bit Christmasy, Irene Redfield was thinking, as she turned out of Seventh Avenue into her own street. She didn't like it to be warm and springy when it should have been cold and crisp, or grey and cloudy as if snow was about to fall. The weather, like people, ought to enter into the spirit of the season. Here the holidays were almost upon them, and the streets through which she had come were streaked with rills of muddy water and the sun shone so warmly that children had taken off their hats and scarfs. It was all as soft, as like April, as possible. The kind of weather for Easter. Certainly not for Christmas.

Though, she admitted, reluctantly, she herself didn't feel the proper Christmas spirit this year, either. But that couldn't be helped, it seemed, any more than the weather. She was weary and depressed. And for all her trying, she couldn't be free of that dull, indefinite misery which with increasing tenaciousness had laid hold of her. The morning's aimless wandering through the teeming Harlem streets, long after she had ordered the flowers which had been her excuse for setting out, was but another effort to tear herself loose from it.

She went up the cream stone steps, into the house, and down to the kitchen. There were to be people in to tea. But that, she found, after a few words with Sadie and Zulena, need give her no concern. She was thankful. She didn't want to be bothered. She went upstairs and took off her things and got into bed.

She thought: "Bother those people coming to tea!"

She thought: "If I could only be sure that at bottom it's just Brazil."

She thought: "Whatever it is, if I only knew what it was, I could manage it."

Brian again. Unhappy, restless, withdrawn. And she, who had prided herself on knowing his moods, their causes and their remedies, had found it first unthinkable, and then intolerable, that this, so like and yet so unlike those other spasmodic restlessnesses of his, should be to her incomprehensible and elusive.

He was restless and he was not restless. He was discontented, yet there were times when she felt he was possessed of some intense secret satisfaction, like a cat who had stolen the cream. He was irritable with the boys, especially Junior, for Ted, who seemed to have an uncanny knowledge of his father's periods of off moods, kept out of his way when possible. They got on his nerves, drove him to violent outbursts of temper, very different from his usual gently sarcastic remarks that constituted his idea of discipline for them. On the other hand, with her he was more than customarily considerate and abstemious. And it had been weeks since she had felt the keen edge of his irony.

He was like a man marking time, waiting. But what was he waiting for? It was extraordinary that, after all these years of accurate perception, she now lacked the talent to discover what that appearance of waiting meant. It was the knowledge that, for all her watching, all her patient study, the reason for his humour still eluded her which filled her with foreboding dread. That guarded reserve of his seemed to her unjust, inconsiderate, and alarming. It was as if he had stepped out beyond her reach into some section, strange and walled, where she could not get at him.

She closed her eyes, thinking what a blessing it would be if she could get a little sleep before the boys came in from school. She couldn't, of course, though she was so tired, having had, of late, so many sleepless nights. Nights filled with questionings and premonitions.

But she did sleep—several hours.

She wakened to find Brian standing at her bedside looking down at her, an unfathomable expression in his eyes.

She said: "I must have dropped off to sleep," and watched a slender ghost of his old amused smile pass over his face.

"It's getting on to four," he told her, meaning, she knew, that she was going to be late again.

She fought back the quick answer that rose to her lips and said instead: "I'm getting right up. It was good of you to think to call me." She sat up.

He bowed. "Always the attentive husband, you see."

"Yes indeed. Thank goodness, everything's ready."

"Except you. Oh, and Clare's downstairs."

"Clare! What a nuisance! I didn't ask her. Purposely."

"I see. Might a mere man ask why? Or is the reason so subtly feminine that it wouldn't be understood by him?"

A little of his smile had come back. Irene, who was beginning to shake off some of her depression under his familiar banter, said, almost gaily: "Not at all. It just happens that this party happens to be for Hugh, and that Hugh happens not to care a great deal for Clare; therefore I, who happen to be giving the party, didn't happen to ask her. Nothing could be simpler. Could it?"

"Nothing. It's so simple that I can easily see beyond your simple explanation and surmise that Clare, probably, just never happened to pay Hugh the admiring attention that he happens to consider no more than his just due. Simplest thing in the world."

Irene exclaimed in amazement: "Why, I thought you liked Hugh! You don't, you can't, believe anything so idiotic!"

"Well, Hugh does think he's God, you know."

"That," Irene declared, getting out of bed, "is absolutely not true. He thinks ever so much better of himself than that, as you, who know and have read him, ought to be able to guess. If you remember what a low opinion he has of God, you won't make such a silly mistake."

She went into the closet for her things and, coming back, hung her frock over the back of a chair and placed her shoes on the floor beside it. Then she sat down before her dressing-table.

Brian didn't speak. He continued to stand beside the bed, seeming to look at nothing in particular. Certainly not at her. True, his gaze was on her, but in it there was some quality that made her feel that at that moment she was no more to him than a pane of glass through which he stared. At what? She didn't know, couldn't guess. And this made her uncomfortable. Piqued her.

She said: "It just happens that Hugh prefers intelligent women."

Plainly he was startled. "D'you mean that you think Clare is stupid?" he asked, regarding her with lifted eyebrows, which emphasized the disbelief of his voice.

She wiped the cold cream from her face, before she said: "No, I don't. She isn't stupid. She's intelligent enough in a purely feminine way. Eighteenth-century France would have been a marvellous setting for her, or the old South if she hadn't made the mistake of being born a Negro."

"I see. Intelligent enough to wear a tight bodice and keep bowing swains whispering compliments and retrieving dropped fans. Rather a pretty picture. I take it, though, as slightly feline in its implication."

"Well, then, all I can say is that you take it wrongly. Nobody admires Clare more than I do, for the kind of intelligence she has, as well as for her decorative qualities. But she's not—She isn't—She hasn't—Oh, I can't explain it. Take Bianca, for example, or, to keep to the race, Felise Freeland. Looks *and* brains. Real brains that can hold their own with anybody. Clare has got brains of a sort, the kind that are useful too. Acquisitive, you know. But she'd bore a man like Hugh to suicide. Still, I never thought that even Clare would come to a private party to which she hadn't been asked. But, it's like her."

For a minute there was silence. She completed the bright red arch of her full lips. Brian moved towards the door. His hand was on the knob. He said: "I'm sorry, Irene. It's my fault entirely. She seemed so hurt at being left out that I told her I was sure you'd forgotten and to just come along."

Irene cried out: "But, Brian, I—" and stopped, amazed at the fierce anger that had blazed up in her.

Brian's head came round with a jerk. His brows lifted in an odd surprise.

Her voice, she realized, *had* gone queer. But she had an instinctive feeling that it hadn't been the whole cause of his attitude. And that little straightening motion of the shoulders. Hadn't it been like that of a man drawing himself up to receive a blow? Her fright was like a scarlet spear of terror leaping at her heart.

Clare Kendry! So that was it! Impossible. It couldn't be.

In the mirror before her she saw that he was still regarding her with that air of slight amazement. She dropped her eyes to the jars and bottles on the table and began to fumble among them with hands whose fingers shook slightly.

"Of course," she said carefully, "I'm glad you did. And in spite of my recent remarks, Clare does add to any party. She's so easy on the eyes."

When she looked again, the surprise had gone from his face and the expectancy from his bearing.

"Yes," he agreed. "Well, I guess I'll run along. One of us ought to be down, I s'pose."

"You're right. One of us ought to." She was surprised that it was in her normal tones she spoke, caught as she was by the heart since that dull indefinite fear had grown suddenly into sharp panic. "I'll be down before you know it," she promised.

"All right." But he still lingered. "You're quite certain. You don't mind my asking her? Not awfully, I mean? I see now that I ought to have spoken to you. Trust women to have their reasons for everything."

She made a little pretence at looking at him, managed a tiny smile, and turned away. Clare! How sickening!

"Yes, don't they?" she said, striving to keep her voice casual. Within her she felt a hardness from feeling, not absent, but repressed. And that hardness was rising, swelling. Why didn't he go? Why didn't he?

He had opened the door at last. "You won't be long?" he asked, admonished.

She shook her head, unable to speak, for there was a choking in her throat, and the confusion in her mind was like the beating of wings. Behind her she heard the gentle impact of the door as it closed behind him, and knew that he had gone. Down to Clare.

For a long minute she sat in strained stiffness. The face in the mirror vanished from her sight, blotted out by this thing which had so suddenly flashed across her groping mind. Impossible for her to put it immediately into words or give it outline, for, prompted by some impulse of self-protection, she recoiled from exact expression.

She closed her unseeing eyes and clenched her fists. She tried not to cry. But her lips tightened and no effort could check the hot tears of rage and shame that sprang into her eyes and flowed down her cheeks; so she laid her face in her arms and wept silently.

When she was sure that she had done crying, she wiped away the warm remaining tears and got up. After bathing her swollen face in cold, refreshing water and carefully applying a stinging splash of toilet water, she went back to the mirror and regarded herself gravely. Satisfied that there lingered no betraying evidence of weeping, she dusted a little powder on her dark-white face and again examined it carefully, and with a kind of ridiculing contempt.

"I do think," she confided to it, "that you've been something—oh, very much—of a damned fool."

Downstairs the ritual of tea gave her some busy moments, and that, she decided, was a blessing. She wanted no empty spaces of time in which her mind would immediately return to that horror which she had not yet gathered sufficient courage to face. Pouring tea properly and nicely was an occupation that required a kind of well-balanced attention.

In the room beyond, a clock chimed. A single sound. Fifteen minutes past five o'clock. That was all! And yet in the short space of half an hour all of life had changed, lost its colour, its vividness, its whole meaning. No, she reflected, it wasn't that that had happened. Life about her, apparently, went on exactly as before.

"Oh, Mrs. Runyon. . . . So nice to see you. . . . Two? . . . Really? . . . How exciting! . . . Yes, I think Tuesday's all right. . . ."

Yes, life went on precisely as before. It was only she that had changed. Knowing, stumbling on this thing, had changed her. It was as if in a house long dim, a match had been struck, showing ghastly shapes where had been only blurred shadows.

Chatter, chatter, chatter. Someone asked her a question. She glanced up with what she felt was a rigid smile.

"Yes . . . Brian picked it up last winter in Haiti. Terribly weird, isn't it? . . . It *is* rather marvellous in its own hideous way. . . . Practically nothing, I believe. A few cents. . . ."

Hideous. A great weariness came over her. Even the small exertion of pouring golden tea into thin old cups seemed almost too much for her. She went on pouring. Made repetitions of her smile. Answered questions. Manufactured conversation. She thought: "I feel like the oldest person in the world with the longest stretch of life before me."

"Josephine Baker?[8] . . . No. I've never seen her. . . . Well, she might have been in *Shuffle Along*[9] when I saw it, but if she was, I don't remember her. . . . Oh, but you're wrong! . . . I do think Ethel Waters[1] is awfully good. . . ."

There were the familiar little tinkling sounds of spoons striking against frail cups, the soft running sounds of inconsequential talk, punctuated now and then with laughter. In irregular small groups, disintegrating, coalescing, striking just the right note of disharmony, disorder in the big room, which Irene had furnished with a sparingness that was almost chaste, moved the guests with that slight familiarity that makes a party a success. On the floor and the walls the sinking sun threw long, fantastic shadows.

So like many other tea-parties she had had. So unlike any of those others. But she mustn't think yet. Time enough for that after. All the time in the world. She had a second's flashing knowledge of what those words might portend. Time with Brian. Time without him. It was gone, leaving in its place an almost uncontrollable impulse to laugh, to scream, to hurl things about. She wanted, suddenly, to shock people, to hurt them, to make them notice her, to be aware of her suffering.

"Hello, Dave. . . . Felise. . . . Really your clothes are the despair of half the women in Harlem. . . . How do you do it? . . . Lovely, is it Worth or Lanvin?[2] . . . Oh, a mere Babani.[3] . . ."

"Merely that," Felise Freeland acknowledged. "Come out of it, Irene, whatever it is. You look like the second grave-digger."[4]

"Thanks, for the hint, Felise. I'm not feeling quite up to par. The weather, I guess."

"Buy yourself an expensive new frock, child. It always helps. Any time this child gets the blues, it means money out of Dave's pocket. How're those boys of yours?"

The boys! For once she'd forgotten them.

They were, she told Felise, very well. Felise mumbled something about that being awfully nice, and said she'd have to fly, because for a wonder she saw Mrs. Bellew sitting by herself, "and I've been trying to get her alone all afternoon. I want her for a party. Isn't she stunning today?"

Clare was. Irene couldn't remember ever having seen her look better. She was wearing a superlatively simple cinnamon-brown frock which brought out all her vivid beauty, and a little golden bowl of a hat. Around her neck hung a string of amber beads that would easily have made six or eight like one Irene owned. Yes, she was stunning.

The ripple of talk flowed on. The fire roared. The shadows stretched longer.

Across the room was Hugh. He wasn't, Irene hoped, being too bored. He seemed as he always did, a bit aloof, a little amused, and somewhat weary. And as usual he was hovering before the book-shelves. But he was not, she noticed, looking at the book he had taken down. Instead, his dull amber eyes were held by something across the room. They were a little scornful. Well, Hugh had never cared for Clare Kendry. For a minute Irene hesitated, then

8. Singer and dancer (1906–1975), whose fame flowered when she moved from the United States to Paris.
9. An all-black musical that was a Broadway hit in the early 1920s and launched Baker's career.
1. Blues singer (1896–1977), who was one of the most celebrated performers to emerge from the Harlem Renaissance.
2. Classic Parisian houses of high fashion.
3. A fashion house known for exotic designs imported to Paris from China, Japan, the Middle East, Africa, and London.
4. The second of two unnamed minor characters in Shakespeare's *Hamlet* (5.1).

turned her head, though she knew what it was that held Hugh's gaze. Clare, who had suddenly clouded all her days. Brian, the father of Ted and Junior.

Clare's ivory face was what it always was, beautiful and caressing. Or maybe today a little masked. Unrevealing. Unaltered and undisturbed by any emotion within or without. Brian's seemed to Irene to be pitiably bare. Or was it too as it always was? That half-effaced seeking look, did he always have that? Queer, that now she didn't know, couldn't recall. Then she saw him smile, and the smile made his face all eager and shining. Impelled by some inner urge of loyalty to herself, she glanced away. But only for a moment. And when she turned towards them again, she thought that the look on his face was the most melancholy and yet the most scoffing that she had ever seen upon it.

In the next quarter of an hour she promised herself to Bianca Wentworth in Sixty-second Street, Jane Tenant at Seventh Avenue and a Hundred and Fiftieth Street, and the Dashields in Brooklyn[5] for dinner all on the same evening and at almost the same hour.

Oh well, what did it matter? She had no thoughts at all now, and all she felt was a great fatigue. Before her tired eyes Clare Kendry was talking to Dave Freeland. Scraps of their conversation, in Clare's husky voice, floated over to her: ". . . always admired you . . . so much about you long ago . . . everybody says so . . . no one but you. . . ." And more of the same. The man hung rapt on her words, though he was the husband of Felise Freeland, and the author of novels that revealed a man of perception and a devastating irony. And he fell for such pish-posh! And all because Clare had a trick of sliding down ivory lids over astonishing black eyes and then lifting them suddenly and turning on a caressing smile. Men like Dave Freeland fell for it. And Brian.

Her mental and physical languor receded. Brian. What did it mean? How would it affect her and the boys? The boys! She had a surge of relief. It ebbed, vanished. A feeling of absolute unimportance followed. Actually, she didn't count. She was, to him, only the mother of his sons. That was all. Alone she was nothing. Worse. An obstacle.

Rage boiled up in her.

There was a slight crash. On the floor at her feet lay the shattered cup. Dark stains dotted the bright rug. Spread. The chatter stopped. Went on. Before her, Zulena gathered up the white fragments.

As from a distance Hugh Wentworth's clipt voice came to her, though he was, she was aware, somehow miraculously at her side. "Sorry," he apologized. "Must have pushed you. Clumsy of me. Don't tell me it's priceless and irreplaceable."

It hurt. Dear God! How the thing hurt! But she couldn't think of that now. Not with Hugh sitting there mumbling apologies and lies. The significance of his words, the power of his discernment, stirred in her a sense of caution. Her pride revolted. Damn Hugh! Something would have to be done about him. Now. She couldn't, it seemed, help his knowing. It was too late for that. But she could and would keep him from knowing that she knew. She could, she would bear it. She'd have to. There were the boys. Her whole

5. The fast-growing, ethnically diverse industrial city had become a borough of Manhattan in 1898. Sixty-second Street traverses the Upper West and Upper East Side neighborhoods of Manhattan. One Hundred Fiftieth Street lies in Harlem.

body went taut. In that second she saw that she could bear anything, but only if no one knew that she had anything to bear. It hurt. It frightened her, but she could bear it.

She turned to Hugh. Shook her head. Raised innocent dark eyes to his concerned pale ones. "Oh, no," she protested, "you didn't push me. Cross your heart, hope to die, and I'll tell you how it happened."

"Done!"

"Did you notice that cup? Well, you're lucky. It was the ugliest thing that your ancestors, the charming Confederates ever owned. I've forgotten how many thousands of years ago it was that Brian's great-great-grand-uncle owned it. But it has, or had, a good old hoary history. It was brought North by way of the subway. Oh, all right! Be English if you want to and call it the underground. What I'm coming to is the fact that I've never figured out a way of getting rid of it until about five minutes ago. I had an inspiration. I had only to break it, and I was rid of it for ever. So simple! And I'd never thought of it before."

Hugh nodded and his frosty smile spread over his features. Had she convinced him?

"Still," she went on with a little laugh that didn't, she was sure, sound the least bit forced, "I'm perfectly willing for you to take the blame and admit that you pushed me at the wrong moment. What are friends for, if not to help bear our sins? Brian will certainly be told that it was your fault.

"More tea, Clare? . . . I haven't had a minute with you. . . . Yes, it is a nice party. . . . You'll stay to dinner, I hope. . . . Oh, too bad! . . . I'll be alone with the boys. . . . They'll be sorry. Brian's got a medical meeting, or something. . . . Nice frock you're wearing. . . . Thanks. . . . Well, good-bye; see you soon, I hope."

The clock chimed. One. Two, Three. Four. Five. Six. Was it, could it be, only a little over an hour since she had come down to tea? One little hour.

"Must you go? . . . Good-bye. . . . Thank you so much. . . . So nice to see you. . . . Yes, Wednesday. . . . My love to Madge. . . . Sorry, but I'm filled up for Tuesday. . . . Oh, really? . . . Yes. . . . Good-bye. . . . Good-bye. . . ."

It hurt. It hurt like hell. But it didn't matter, if no one knew. If everything could go on as before. If the boys were safe.

It did hurt.

But it didn't matter.

TWO

But it did matter. It mattered more than anything had ever mattered before.

What bitterness! That the one fear, the one uncertainty, that she had felt, Brian's ache to go somewhere else, should have dwindled to a childish triviality! And with it the quality of the courage and resolution with which she had met it. From the visions and dangers which she now perceived she shrank away. For them she had no remedy or courage. Desperately she tried to shut out the knowledge from which had risen this turmoil, which she had no power to moderate or still, within her. And half succeeded.

For, she reasoned, what was there, what had there been, to show that she was even half correct in her tormenting notion? Nothing. She had seen nothing, heard nothing. She had no facts or proofs. She was only making herself unutterably wretched by an unfounded suspicion. It had been a case of looking for trouble and finding it in good measure. Merely that.

With this self-assurance that she had no real knowledge, she redoubled her efforts to drive out of her mind the distressing thought of faiths broken and trusts betrayed which every mental vision of Clare, of Brian, brought with them. She could not, she would not, go again through the tearing agony that lay just behind her.

She must, she told herself, be fair. In all their married life she had had no slightest cause to suspect her husband of any infidelity, of any serious flirtation even. If—and she doubted it—he had had his hours of outside erratic conduct, they were unknown to her. Why begin now to assume them? And on nothing more concrete than an idea that had leapt into her mind because he had told her that he had invited a friend, a friend of hers, to a party in his own house. And at a time when she had been, it was likely, more asleep than awake. How could she without anything done or said, or left undone or unsaid, so easily believe him guilty? How be so ready to renounce all confidence in the worth of their life together?

And if, perchance, there were some small something—well, what could it mean? Nothing. There were the boys. There was John Bellew. The thought of these three gave her some slight relief. But she did not look the future in the face. She wanted to feel nothing, to think nothing; simply to believe that it was all silly invention on her part. Yet she could not. Not quite.

Christmas, with its unreality, its hectic rush, its false gaiety, came and went. Irene was thankful for the confused unrest of the season. Its irksomeness, its crowds, its inane and insincere repetitions of genialities, pushed between her and the contemplation of her growing unhappiness.

She was thankful, too, for the continued absence of Clare, who, John Bellew having returned from a long stay in Canada, had withdrawn to that other life of hers, remote and inaccessible. But beating against the walled prison of Irene's thoughts was the shunned fancy that, though absent, Clare Kendry was still present, that she was close.

Brian, too, had withdrawn. The house contained his outward self and his belongings. He came and went with his usual noiseless irregularity. He sat across from her at table. He slept in his room next to hers at night. But he was remote and inaccessible. No use pretending that he was happy, that things were the same as they had always been. He wasn't and they weren't. However, she assured herself, it needn't necessarily be because of anything that involved Clare. It was, it must be, another manifestation of the old longing.

But she did wish it were spring, March, so that Clare would be sailing, out of her life and Brian's. Though she had come almost to believe that there was nothing but generous friendship between those two, she was very tired of Clare Kendry. She wanted to be free of her, and of her furtive comings and goings. If something would only happen, something that would make John Bellew decide on an earlier departure, or that would remove Clare. Anything. She didn't care what. Not even if it were that Clare's Margery were ill, or dying. Not even if Bellew should discover—

She drew a quick, sharp breath. And for a long time sat staring down at the hands in her lap. Strange, she had not before realized how easily she could put Clare out of her life! She had only to tell John Bellew that his wife—No. Not that! But if he should somehow learn of these Harlem visits—Why should she hesitate? Why spare Clare?

But she shrank away from the idea of telling that man, Clare Kendry's white husband, anything that would lead him to suspect that his wife was a Negro. Nor could she write it, or telephone it, or tell it to someone else who would tell him.

She was caught between two allegiances, different, yet the same. Herself. Her race. Race! The thing that bound and suffocated her. Whatever steps she took, or if she took none at all, something would be crushed. A person or the race. Clare, herself, or the race. Or, it might be, all three. Nothing, she imagined, was ever more completely sardonic.

Sitting alone in the quiet living-room in the pleasant fire-light, Irene Redfield wished, for the first time in her life, that she had not been born a Negro. For the first time she suffered and rebelled because she was unable to disregard the burden of race. It was, she cried silently, enough to suffer as a woman, an individual, on one's own account, without having to suffer for the race as well. It was a brutality, and undeserved. Surely, no other people so cursed as Ham's dark children.

Nevertheless, her weakness, her shrinking, her own inability to compass the thing, did not prevent her from wishing fervently that, in some way with which she had no concern, John Bellew would discover, not that his wife had a touch of the tar-brush—Irene didn't want that—but that she was spending all the time that he was out of the city in black Harlem. Only that. It would be enough to rid her forever of Clare Kendry.

THREE

As if in answer to her wish, the very next day Irene came face to face with Bellew.

She had gone downtown with Felise Freeland to shop. The day was an exceptionally cold one, with a strong wind that had whipped a dusky red into Felise's smooth golden cheeks and driven moisture into Irene's soft brown eyes.

Clinging to each other, with heads bent against the wind, they turned out of the Avenue into Fifty-seventh Street.[6] A sudden bluster flung them around the corner with unexpected quickness and they collided with a man.

"Pardon," Irene begged laughingly, and looked up into the face of Clare Kendry's husband.

"Mrs. Redfield!"

His hat came off. He held out his hand, smiling genially.

6. In the shopping district of midtown Manhattan.

But the smile faded at once. Surprise, incredulity, and—was it understanding?—passed over his features.

He had, Irene knew, become conscious of Felise, golden, with curly black Negro hair, whose arm was still linked in her own. She was sure, now, of the understanding in his face, as he looked at her again and then back at Felise. And displeasure.

He didn't, however, withdraw his outstretched hand. Not at once.

But Irene didn't take it. Instinctively, in the first glance of recognition, her face had become a mask. Now she turned on him a totally uncomprehending look, a bit questioning. Seeing that he still stood with hand outstretched, she gave him the cool appraising stare which she reserved for mashers, and drew Felise on.

Felise drawled: "Aha! Been 'passing,' have you? Well, I've queered that."

"Yes, I'm afraid you have."

"Why, Irene Redfield! You sound as if you cared terribly. I'm sorry."

"I do, but not for the reason you think. I don't believe I've ever gone native[7] in my life except for the sake of convenience, restaurants, theatre tickets, and things like that. Never socially I mean, except once. You've just passed the only person that I've ever met disguised as a white woman."

"Awfully sorry. Be sure your sin will find you out and all that. Tell me about it."

"I'd like to. It would amuse you. But I can't."

Felise's laughter was as languidly nonchalant as her cool voice. "Can it possible that the honest Irene has—Oh, do look at that coat! There. The red one. Isn't it a dream?"

Irene was thinking: "I had my chance and didn't take it. I had only to speak and to introduce him to Felise with the casual remark that he was Clare's husband. Only that. Fool. Fool." That instinctive loyalty to a race. Why couldn't she get free of it? Why should it include Clare? Clare, who'd shown little enough consideration for her, and hers. What she felt was not so much resentment as a dull despair because she could not change herself in this respect, could not separate individuals from the race, herself from Clare Kendry.

"Let's go home, Felise. I'm so tired I could drop."

"Why, we haven't done half the things we planned."

"I know, but it's too cold to be running all over town. But you stay down if you want to."

"I think I'll do that, if you don't mind."

And now another problem confronted Irene. She must tell Clare of this meeting. Warn her. But how? She hadn't seen her for days. Writing and telephoning were equally unsafe. And even if it was possible to get in touch with her, what good would it do? If Bellew hadn't concluded that he'd made a mistake, if he was certain of her identity—and he was nobody's fool—telling Clare wouldn't avert the results of the encounter. Besides, it was too late. Whatever was in store for Clare Kendry had already overtaken her.

7. Passed for white; an ironic reversal of the phrase's usual sense of a white person adopting "native" ways of life.

Irene was conscious of a feeling of relieved thankfulness at the thought that she was probably rid of Clare, and without having lifted a finger or uttered one word.

But she did mean to tell Brian about meeting John Bellew.

But that, it seemed, was impossible. Strange. Something held her back. Each time she was on the verge of saying: "I ran into Clare's husband on the street downtown today. I'm sure he recognized me, and Felise was with me," she failed to speak. It sounded too much like the warning she wanted it to be. Not even in the presence of the boys at dinner could she make the bare statement.

The evening dragged. At last she said good-night and went upstairs, the words unsaid.

She thought: "Why didn't I tell him? Why didn't I? If trouble comes from this, I'll never forgive myself. I'll tell him when he comes up."

She took up a book, but she could not read, so oppressed was she by a nameless foreboding.

What if Bellew should divorce Clare? Could he? There was the Rhinelander case.[8] But in France, in Paris, such things were very easy. If he divorced her—If Clare were free—But of all the things that could happen, that was the one she did not want. She must get her mind away from that possibility. She must.

Then came a thought which she tried to drive away. If Clare should die! Then—Oh, it was vile! To think, yes, to wish that! She felt faint and sick. But the thought stayed with her. She could not get rid of it.

She heard the outer door open. Close. Brian had gone out. She turned her face into her pillow to cry. But no tears came.

She lay there awake, thinking of things past. Of her courtship and marriage and Junior's birth. Of the time they had bought the house in which they had lived so long and so happily. Of the time Ted had passed his pneumonia crisis and they knew he would live. And of other sweet painful memories that would never come again.

Above everything else she had wanted, had striven, to keep undisturbed the pleasant routine of her life. And now Clare Kendry had come into it, and with her the menace of impermanence.

"Dear God," she prayed, "make March come quickly."

By and by she slept.

FOUR

The next morning brought with it a snow-storm lasted throughout the day.

After a breakfast, which had been eaten almost in silence and which she was relieved to have done with, Irene Redfield lingered for a little while in the downstairs hall, looking out at the soft flakes fluttering down. She was

8. *Rhinelander v. Rhinelander* was a notorious case of 1925 in which Leonard Rhinelander, a member of a wealthy New York family, sued his wife, Alice Jones Rhinelander, for an annulment of their marriage on the grounds that she had concealed from him her mixed-race ancestry. After a trial that included examining parts of her body in private—her arms, shoulders, and lower legs—the jury found in Alice's favor, concluding that she had not hidden her race and that Leonard had married her knowing that she was "colored."

watching them immediately fill some ugly irregular gaps left by the feet of hurrying pedestrians when Zulena came to her, saying: "The telephone, Mrs. Redfield. It's Mrs. Bellew."

"Take the message, Zulena, please."

Though she continued to stare out of the window, Irene saw nothing now, stabbed as she was by fear—and hope. Had anything happened between Clare and Bellew? And if so, what? And was she to be freed at last from the aching anxiety of the past weeks? Or was there to be more, and worse? She had a wrestling moment, in which it seemed that she must rush after Zulena and hear for herself what it was that Clare had to say. But she waited.

Zulena, when she came back, said: "She says, ma'am, that she'll be able to go to Mrs. Freeland's tonight. She'll be here some time between eight and nine."

"Thank you, Zulena."

The day dragged on to its end.

At dinner Brian spoke bitterly of a lynching that he had been reading about in the evening paper.

"Dad, why is it that they only lynch coloured people?"[9] Ted asked.

"Because they hate 'em, son."

"Brian!" Irene's voice was a plea and a rebuke.

Ted said: "Oh! And why do they hate 'em?"

"Because they are afraid of them."

"But what makes them afraid of 'em?"

"Because—"

"Brian!"

"It seems, son, that is a subject we can't go into at the moment without distressing the ladies of our family," he told the boy with mock seriousness, "but we'll take it up some time when we're alone together."

Ted nodded in his engaging grave way. "I see. Maybe we can talk about it tomorrow on the way to school."

"That'll be fine."

"Brian!"

"Mother," Junior remarked, "that's the third time you've said 'Brian' like that."

"But not the last, Junior, never you fear," his father told him.

After the boys had gone up to their own floor, Irene said suavely: "I do wish, Brian, that you wouldn't talk about lynching before Ted and Junior. It was really inexcusable for you to bring up a thing like that at dinner. There'll be time enough for them to learn about such horrible things when they're older."

"You're absolutely wrong! If, as you're so determined, they've got to live in this damned country, they'd better find out what sort of thing they're up

9. Murder by mob, mostly of black men, remained widespread in the United States during the early 20th century, in the North as well as the South. Major anti-lynching campaigns were mounted during this period by the National Association for the Advancement of Colored People and networks of African American women's clubs.

against as soon as possible. The earlier they learn it, the better prepared they'll be."

"I don't agree. I want their childhood to be happy and as free from the knowledge of such things as it possibly can be."

"Very laudable," was Brian's sarcastic answer. "Very laudable indeed, all things considered. But can it?"

"Certainly it can. If you'll only do your part."

"Stuff! You know as well as I do, Irene, that it can't. What was the use of our trying to keep them from learning the word 'nigger' and its connotation? They found out, didn't they? And how? Because somebody called Junior a dirty nigger."

"Just the same you're not to talk to them about the race problem. I won't have it."

They glared at each other.

"I tell you, Irene, they've got to know these things, and it might as well be now as later."

"They do not!" she insisted, forcing back the tears of anger that were threatening to fall.

Brian growled: "I can't understand how anybody as intelligent as you like to think you are can show evidences of such stupidity." He looked at her in a puzzled harassed way.

"Stupid!" she cried. "Is it stupid to want my children to be happy?" Her lips were quivering.

"At the expense of proper preparation for life and their future happiness, yes. And I'd feel I hadn't done my duty by them if I didn't give them some inkling of what's before them. It's the least I can do. I wanted to get them out of this hellish place years ago. You wouldn't let me. I gave up the idea, because you objected. Don't expect me to give up everything."

Under the lash of his words she was silent. Before any answer came to her, he had turned and gone from the room.

Sitting there alone in the forsaken dining-room, unconsciously pressing the hands lying in her lap, tightly together, she was seized by a convulsion of shivering. For, to her, there had been something ominous in the scene that she had just had with her husband. Over and over in her mind his last words: "Don't expect me to give up everything," repeated themselves. What had they meant? What could they mean? Clare Kendry?

Surely, she was going mad with fear and suspicion. She must not work herself up. She must not! Where were all the self-control, the common sense, that she was so proud of? Now, if ever, was the time for it.

Clare would soon be there. She must hurry or she would be late again, and those two would wait for her downstairs together, as they had done so often since that first time, which now seemed so long ago. Had it been really only last October? Why, she felt years, not months, older.

Drearily she rose from her chair and went upstairs to set about the business of dressing to go out when she would far rather have remained at home. During the process she wondered, for the hundredth time, why she hadn't told Brian about herself and Felise running into Bellew the day before, and for the hundredth time she turned away from acknowledging to herself the real reason for keeping back the information.

When Clare arrived, radiant in a shining red gown, Irene had not finished dressing. But her smile scarcely hesitated as she greeted her, saying: "I always seem to keep C. P. time,[1] don't I? We hardly expected you to be able to come. Felise will be pleased. How nice you look."

Clare kissed a bare shoulder, seeming not to notice a slight shrinking.

"I hadn't an idea in the world, myself, that I'd be able to make it; but Jack had to run down to Philadelphia unexpectedly. So here I am."

Irene looked up, a flood of speech on her lips. "Philadelphia. That's not very far, is it? Clare, I—?"

She stopped, one of her hands clutching the side of her stool, the other lying clenched on the dressing-table. Why didn't she go on and tell Clare about meeting Bellew? Why couldn't she?

But Clare didn't notice the unfinished sentence. She laughed and said lightly: "It's far enough for me. Anywhere, away from me, is far enough. I'm not particular."

Irene passed a hand over her eyes to shut out the accusing face in the glass before her. With one corner of her mind she wondered how long she had looked like that, drawn and haggard and—yes, frightened. Or was it only imagination?

"Clare," she asked, "have you ever seriously thought what it would mean if he should find you out?"

"Yes."

"Oh! You have! And what you'd do in that case?"

"Yes." And having said it, Clare Kendry smiled quickly, a smile that came and went like a flash, leaving untouched the gravity of her face.

That smile and the quiet resolution of that one word, "yes," filled Irene with a primitive paralysing dread. Her hands were numb, her feet like ice, her heart like a stone weight. Even her tongue was like a heavy dying thing. There were long spaces between the words as she asked: "And what should you do?"

Clare, who was sunk in a deep chair, her eyes far away, seemed wrapped in some pleasant impenetrable reflection. To Irene, sitting expectantly upright, it was an interminable time before she dragged herself back to the present to say calmly: "I'd do what I want to do more than anything else right now. I'd come up here to live. Harlem, I mean. Then I'd be able to do as I please, when I please."

Irene leaned forward, cold and tense. "And what about Margery?" Her voice was a strained whisper.

"Margery?" Clare repeated, letting her eyes flutter over Irene's concerned face. "Just this, 'Rene. If it wasn't for her, I'd do it anyway. She's all that holds me back. But if Jack finds out, if our marriage is broken, that lets me out. Doesn't it?"

Her gentle resigned tone, her air of innocent candour, appeared, to her listener, spurious. A conviction that the words were intended as a warning took possession of Irene. She remembered that Clare Kendry had always seemed to know what other people were thinking. Her compressed lips grew firm and obdurate. Well, she wouldn't know this time.

1. I.e., colored people's time, an idiom stereotyping African Americans as habitually late.

She said: "Do go downstairs and talk to Brian. He's got a mad on."

Though she had determined that Clare should not get at her thoughts and fears, the words had sprung, unthought of, to her lips. It was as if they had come from some outer layer of callousness that had no relation to her tortured heart. And they had been, she realized, precisely the right words for her purpose.

For as Clare got up and went out, she saw that that arrangement was as good as her first plan of keeping her waiting up there while she dressed—or better. She would only have hindered and rasped her. And what matter if those two spent one hour, more or less, alone together, one or many, now that everything had happened between them?

Ah! The first time that she had allowed herself to admit to herself that everything had happened, had not forced herself to believe, to hope, that nothing irrevocable had been consummated! Well, it had happened. She knew it, and knew that she knew it.

She was surprised that, having thought the thought, conceded the fact, she was no more hurt, cared no more, than during her previous frenzied endeavours to escape it. And this absence of acute, unbearable pain seemed to her unjust, as if she had been denied some exquisite solace of suffering which the full acknowledgment should have given her.

Was it, perhaps, that she had endured all that a woman could endure of tormenting humiliation and fear? Or was it that she lacked the capacity for the acme of suffering? "No, no!" she denied fiercely. "I'm human like everybody else. It's just that I'm so tired, so worn out, I can't feel any more." But she did not really believe that.

Security. Was it just a word? If not, then was it only by the sacrifice of other things, happiness, love, or some wild ecstasy that she had never known, that it could be obtained? And did too much striving, too much faith in safety and permanence, unfit one for these other things?

Irene didn't know, couldn't decide, though for a long time she sat questioning and trying to understand. Yet all the while, in spite of her searchings and feeling of frustration, she was aware that, to her, security was the most important and desired thing in life. Not for any of the others, or for all of them, would she exchange it. She wanted only to be tranquil. Only, unmolested, to be allowed to direct for their own best good the lives of her sons and her husband.

Now that she had relieved herself of what was almost like a guilty knowledge, admitted that which by some sixth sense she had long known, she could again reach out for plans. Could think again of ways to keep Brian by her side, and in New York. For she would not go to Brazil. She belonged in this land of rising towers. She was an American. She grew from this soil, and she would not be uprooted. Not even because of Clare Kendry, or a hundred Clare Kendrys.

Brian, too, belonged here. His duty was to her and to his boys.

Strange, that she couldn't now be sure that she had ever truly known love. Not even for Brian. He was her husband and the father of her sons. But was he anything more? Had she ever wanted or tried for more? In that hour she thought not.

Nevertheless, she meant to keep him. Her freshly painted lips narrowed to a thin straight line. True, she had left off trying to believe that he and

Clare loved and yet did not love, but she still intended to hold fast to the outer shell of her marriage, to keep her life fixed, certain. Brought to the edge of distasteful reality, her fastidious nature did not recoil. Better, far better, to share him than to lose him completely. Oh, she could close her eyes, if need be. She could bear it. She could bear anything. And there was March ahead. March and the departure of Clare.

Horribly clear, she could now see the reason for her instinct to withhold—omit, rather—her news of the encounter with Bellew. If Clare was freed, anything might happen.

She paused in her dressing, seeing with perfect clearness that dark truth which she had from that first October afternoon felt about Clare Kendry and of which Clare herself had once warned her—that she got the things she wanted because she met the great condition of conquest, sacrifice. If she wanted Brian, Clare wouldn't revolt from the lack of money or place. It was as she had said, only Margery kept her from throwing all that away. And if things were taken out of her hands—Even if she was only alarmed, only suspected that such a thing was about to occur, anything might happen. Anything.

No! At all costs, Clare was not to know of that meeting with Bellew. Nor was Brian. It would only weaken her own power to keep him.

They would never know from her that he was on his way to suspecting the truth about his wife. And she would do anything, risk anything, to prevent him from finding out that truth. How fortunate that she had obeyed her instinct and omitted to recognize Bellew!

"Ever go up to the sixth floor, Clare?" Brian asked as he stopped the car and got out to open the door for them.

"Why, of course! We're on the seventeenth."

"I mean, did you ever go up by nigger-power?"[2]

"That's good!" Clare laughed. "Ask 'Rene. My father was a janitor, you know, in the good old days before every ramshackle flat had its elevator. But you can't mean we've got to walk up? Not here!"

"Yes, here. And Felise lives at the very top," Irene told her.

"What on earth for?"

"I believe she claims it discourages the casual visitor."

"And she's probably right. Hard on herself, though."

Brian said "Yes, a bit. But she says she'd rather be dead than bored."

"Oh, a garden! And how lovely with that undisturbed snow!"

"Yes, isn't it? But keep to the walk with those foolish thin shoes. You too, Irene."

Irene walked beside them on the cleared cement path that split the whiteness of the courtyard garden. She felt a something in the air, something that had been between those two and would be again. It was like a live thing pressing against her. In a quick furtive glance she saw Clare clinging to Brian's other arm. She was looking at him with that provocative upward glance of hers, and his eyes were fastened on her face with what seemed to Irene an expression of wistful eagerness.

2. On foot.

"It's this entrance, I believe," she informed them in quite her ordinary voice.

"Mind," Brian told Clare, "you don't fall by the wayside before the fourth floor. They absolutely refuse to carry anyone up more than the last two flights."

"Don't be silly!" Irene snapped.

The party began gaily.

Dave Freeland was at his best, brilliant, crystal clear, and sparkling. Felise, too, was amusing, and not so sarcastic as usual, because she liked the dozen or so guests that dotted the long, untidy living-room. Brian was witty, though, Irene noted, his remarks were somewhat more barbed than was customary even with him. And there was Ralph Hazelton, throwing nonsensical shining things into the pool of talk, which the others, even Clare, picked up and flung back with fresh adornment.

Only Irene wasn't merry. She sat almost silent, smiling now and then, that she might appear amused.

"What's the matter, Irene?" someone asked. "Taken a vow never to laugh, or something? You're as sober as a judge."

"No. It's simply that the rest of you are so clever that I'm speechless, absolutely stunned."

"No wonder," Dave Freeland remarked, "that you're on the verge of tears. You haven't a drink. What'll you take?"

"Thanks. If I must take something, make it a glass of ginger-ale and three drops of Scotch. The Scotch first, please. Then the ice, then the ginger ale."

"Heavens! Don't attempt to mix that yourself, Dave darling. Have the butler in," Felise mocked.

"Yes, do. And the footman." Irene laughed a little, then said: "It seems dreadfully warm in here. Mind if I open this window?" With that she pushed open one of the long casement-windows[3] of which the Freelands were so proud.

It had stopped snowing some two or three hours back. The moon was just rising, and far behind the tall buildings a few stars were creeping out. Irene finished her cigarette and threw it out, watching the tiny spark drop slowly down to the white ground below.

Someone in the room had turned on the phonograph. Or was it the radio? She didn't know which she disliked more. And nobody was listening to its blare. The talking, the laughter never for a minute ceased. Why must they have more noise?

Dave came with her drink. "You ought not," he told her, "to stand there like that. You'll take cold. Come along and talk to me, or listen to me gabble." Taking her arm, he led her across the room. They had just found seats when the door-bell rang and Felise called over to him to go and answer it.

In the next moment Irene heard his voice in the hall, carelessly polite: "Your wife? Sorry. I'm afraid you're wrong. Perhaps next—"

3. Hinged windows that typically open outward.

Then the roar of John Bellew's voice above all the other noises of the room: "I'm *not* wrong! I've been to the Redfields and I know she's with them. You'd better stand out of my way and save yourself trouble in the end."

"What is it, Dave?" Felise ran out to the door.

And so did Brian. Irene heard him saying: "I'm Redfield. What the devil's the matter with you?"

But Bellew didn't heed him. He pushed past them all into the room and strode towards Clare. They all looked at her as she got up from her chair, backing a little from his approach.

"So you're a nigger, a damned dirty nigger!" His voice was a snarl and a moan, an expression of rage and of pain.

Everything was in confusion. The men had sprung forward. Felise had leapt between them and Bellew. She said quickly: "Careful. You're the only white man here." And the silver chill of her voice, as well as her words, was a warning.

Clare stood at the window, as composed as if everyone were not staring at her in curiosity and wonder, as if the whole structure of her life were not lying in fragments before her. She seemed unaware of any danger or uncaring. There was even a faint smile on her full, red lips, and in her shining eyes.

It was that smile that maddened Irene. She ran across the room, her terror tinged with ferocity, and laid a hand on Clare's bare arm. One thought possessed her. She couldn't have Clare Kendry cast aside by Bellew. She couldn't have her free.

Before them stood John Bellew, speechless now in his hurt and anger. Beyond them the little huddle of other people, and Brian stepping out from among them.

What happened next, Irene Redfield never afterwards allowed herself to remember. Never clearly.

One moment Clare had been there, a vital glowing thing, like a flame of red and gold. The next she was gone.

There was a gasp of horror, and above it a sound not quite human, like a beast in agony. "Nig! My God! Nig!"

A frenzied rush of feet down long flights of stairs. The slamming of distant doors. Voices.

Irene stayed behind. She sat down and remained quite still, staring at a ridiculous Japanese print on the wall across the room.

Gone! The soft white face, the bright hair, the disturbing scarlet mouth, the dreaming eyes, the caressing smile, the whole torturing loveliness that had been Clare Kendry. That beauty that had torn at Irene's placid life. Gone! The mocking daring, the gallantry of her pose, the ringing bells of her laughter.

Irene wasn't sorry. She was amazed, incredulous almost.

What would the others think? That Clare had fallen? That she had deliberately leaned backward? Certainly one or the other. Not—

But she mustn't, she warned herself, think of that. She was too tired, and too shocked. And, indeed, both were true. She was utterly weary, and she was violently staggered. But her thoughts reeled on. If only she could be as free of mental as she was of bodily vigour; could only put from her memory the vision of her hand on Clare's arm!

"It was an accident, a terrible accident," she muttered fiercely. "It *was*."

People were coming up the stairs. Through the still open door their steps and talk sounded nearer, nearer.

Quickly she stood up and went noiselessly into the bedroom and closed the door softly behind her.

Her thoughts raced. Ought she to have stayed? Should she go back out there to them? But there would be questions. She hadn't thought of them, of afterwards, of this. She had thought of nothing in that sudden moment of action.

It was cold. Icy chills ran up her spine and over her bare neck and shoulders.

In the room outside there were voices. Dave Freeland's and others that she did not recognize.

Should she put on her coat? Felise had rushed down without any wrap. So had all the others. So had Brian. Brian! He mustn't take cold. She took up his coat and left her own. At the door she paused for a moment, listening fearfully. She heard nothing. No voices. No footsteps. Very slowly she opened the door. The room was empty. She went out.

In the hall below she heard dimly the sound of feet going down the steps, of a door being opened and closed, and of voices far away.

Down, down, down, she went, Brian's great coat clutched in her shivering arms and trailing a little on each step behind her.

What was she to say to them when at last she had finished going down those endless stairs? She should have rushed out when they did. What reason could she give for her dallying behind? Even she didn't know why she had done that. And what else would she be asked? There had been her hand reaching out towards Clare. What about that?

In the midst of her wonderings and questionings came a thought so terrifying, so horrible, that she had had to grasp hold of the banister to save herself from pitching downwards. A cold perspiration drenched her shaking body. Her breath came short in sharp and painful gasps.

What if Clare was not dead?

She felt nauseated, as much at the idea of the glorious body mutilated as from fear.

How she managed to make the rest of the journey without fainting she never knew. But at last she was down. Just at the bottom she came on the others, surrounded by a little circle of strangers. They were all speaking in whispers, or in the awed, discreetly lowered tones adapted to the presence of disaster. In the first instant she wanted to turn and rush back up the way she had come. Then a calm desperation came over her. She braced herself, physically and mentally.

"Here's Irene now," Dave Freeland announced, and told her that, having only just missed her, they had concluded that she had fainted or something like that, and were on the way to find out about her. Felise, she saw, was holding on to his arm, all the insolent nonchalance gone out of her, and the golden brown of her handsome face changed to a queer mauve colour.

Irene made no indication that she had heard Freeland, but went straight to Brian. His face looked aged and altered, and his lips were purple and trembling. She had a great longing to comfort him, to charm away his suffering and horror. But she was helpless, having so completely lost control of his mind and heart.

She stammered: "Is she—is she—?"

It was Felise who answered. "Instantly, we think."

Irene struggled against the sob of thankfulness that rose in her throat. Choked down, it turned to a whimper, like a hurt child's. Someone laid a hand on her shoulder in a soothing gesture. Brian wrapped his coat about her. She began to cry rackingly, her entire body heaving with convulsive sobs. He made a slight perfunctory attempt to comfort her.

"There, there, Irene. You mustn't. You'll make yourself sick. She's—" His voice broke suddenly.

As from a long distance she heard Ralph Hazelton's voice saying: "I was looking right at her. She just tumbled over and was gone before you could say 'Jack Robinson.' Fainted, I guess. Lord! It was quick. Quickest thing I ever saw in all my life."

"It's impossible, I tell you! Absolutely impossible!"

It was Brian who spoke in that frenzied hoarse voice, which Irene had never heard before. Her knees quaked under her.

Dave Freeland said: "Just a minute, Brian. Irene was there beside her. Let's hear what she has to say."

She had a moment of stark craven fear. "Oh God," she thought, prayed, "help me."

A strange man, official and authoritative, addressed her. "You're sure she fell? Her husband didn't give her a shove or anything like that, as Dr. Redfield seems to think?"

For the first time she was aware that Bellew was not in the little group shivering in the small hallway. What did that mean? As she began to work it out in her numbed mind, she was shaken with another hideous trembling. Not that! Oh, not that!

"No, no!" she protested. "I'm quite certain that he didn't. I was there, too. As close as he was. She just fell, before anybody could stop her. I—"

Her quaking knees gave way under her. She moaned and sank down, moaned again. Through the great heaviness that submerged and drowned her she was dimly conscious of strong arms lifting her up. Then everything was dark.

Centuries after, she heard the strange man saying: "Death by misadventure, I'm inclined to believe. Let's go up and have another look at that window."

1929

EDNA ST. VINCENT MILLAY
1892–1950

Edna St. Vincent Millay's output ranged from Elizabethan sonnets through plays and sketches to political speeches. In the 1920s she became a kind of national symbol of the modern woman—liberated from Victorian mores, independent, self-supporting, full of energy and talent. She was raised in a small town on the coast of Maine by her divorced mother, who supported herself and three daughters through work as a practical nurse. The mother provided her children with books and music lessons and encouraged ambition and independence. Millay began to write poetry in high school and published her first book of poetry, *Renascence and Other Poems,* in 1917, when she was twenty-five. She went to Vassar College from 1913 to 1917 through the generosity of a benefactor impressed by her writing. At Vassar she studied languages, wrote songs and verse plays, and became interested in acting. After graduation she went to New York City, settling in the Greenwich Village section of the city and becoming associated with the unconventional life of the literary and political rebels who lived there. A member of the Provincetown Players group, she acted and also wrote two plays for them. *The Ballad of the Harp-Weaver* (1923, later retitled *The Harp-Weaver and Other Poems*) was awarded a Pulitzer Prize.

Millay lived in Europe from 1921 to 1923 and, upon her return, married and moved with her businessman husband Eugene Boissevain to a farm in upstate New York. She participated in the protests against the executions of Sacco and Vanzetti in 1927 and during the 1930s wrote anti-fascist newspaper verse, radio plays, and speeches. She was an early advocate of U.S. entrance into World War II.

Although as a young woman Millay achieved notoriety mainly for love poetry that described free, guiltless sexuality, her poems are more founded in the failure of love than in the joy of sex. The tone of her earliest work was flippantly cynical; she often wrote in elevated diction and traditional forms, only to bring her poems to mocking conclusions. Later work became more muted and lyrical. Working with closed stanza forms and regular metrical lines, she displayed a high degree of technical virtuosity within chosen limits: "I will put chaos into fourteen lines," she wrote in one sonnet. Her anti-fascist writing explored freer poetic forms and a more direct public voice.

The text of the poems included here is that of *Collected Poems: Edna St. Vincent Millay* (1956).

Recuerdo[1]

We were very tired, we were very merry—
We had gone back and forth all night on the ferry.
It was bare and bright, and smelled like a stable—
But we looked into a fire, we leaned across a table,
We lay on a hill-top underneath the moon;
And the whistles kept blowing, and the dawn came soon.

1. Remembrance, souvenir.

We were very tired, we were very merry—
We had gone back and forth all night on the ferry;
And you ate an apple, and I ate a pear,
From a dozen of each we had bought somewhere;
And the sky went wan, and the wind came cold,
And the sun rose dripping, a bucketful of gold.

We were very tired, we were very merry,
We had gone back and forth all night on the ferry.
We hailed, "Good morrow, mother!" to a shawl-covered head,
And bought a morning paper, which neither of us read;
And she wept, "God bless you!" for the apples and pears,
And we gave her all our money but our subway fares.

1922

I Think I Should Have Loved You Presently

I think I should have loved you presently,
And given in earnest words I flung in jest;
And lifted honest eyes for you to see,
And caught your hand against my cheek and breast;
And all my pretty follies flung aside
That won you to me, and beneath your gaze,
Naked of reticence and shorn of pride,
Spread like a chart my little wicked ways.
I, that had been to you, had you remained,
But one more waking from a recurrent dream,
Cherish no less the certain stakes I gained,
And walk your memory's halls, austere, supreme,
A ghost in marble of a girl you knew
Who would have loved you in a day or two.

1922

[I, being born a woman]

I, being born a woman and distressed
By all the needs and notions of my kind,
Am urged by your propinquity to find
Your person fair, and feel a certain zest
To bear your body's weight upon my breast:
So subtly is the fume of life designed,
To clarify the pulse and cloud the mind,
And leave me once again undone, possessed.
Think not for this, however, the poor treason
Of my stout blood against my staggering brain,
I shall remember you with love, or season

My scorn with pity,—let me make it plain:
I find this frenzy insufficient reason
For conversation when we meet again.

1923

Apostrophe to Man

(On reflecting that the world is ready to go to war again)

Detestable race, continue to expunge yourself, die out.
Breed faster, crowd, encroach, sing hymns, build bombing airplanes;
Make speeches, unveil statues, issue bonds, parade;
Convert again into explosives the bewildered ammonia and the distracted cellulose;
Convert again into putrescent matter drawing flies
The hopeful bodies of the young; exhort,
Pray, pull long faces, be earnest, be all but overcome, be photographed;
Confer, perfect your formulae, commercialize
Bacteria harmful to human tissue,
Put death on the market;
Breed, crowd, encroach, expand, expunge yourself, die out,
Homo called *sapiens.*

1934

I Too beneath Your Moon, Almighty Sex

I too beneath your moon, almighty Sex,
Go forth at nightfall crying like a cat,
Leaving the lofty tower I laboured at
For birds to foul and boys and girls to vex
With tittering chalk; and you, and the long necks
Of neighbours sitting where their mothers sat
Are well aware of shadowy this and that
In me, that's neither noble nor complex.
Such as I am, however, I have brought
To what it is, this tower; it is my own;
Though it was reared To Beauty, it was wrought
From what I had to build with: honest bone
Is there, and anguish; pride; and burning thought;
And lust is there, and nights not spent alone.

1939

I Forgot for a Moment

July 1940

I forgot for a moment France; I forgot England; I forgot my care:
I lived for a moment in a world where I was free to be
With the things and people that I love, and I was happy there.
I forgot for a moment Holland, I forgot my heavy care.

I lived for a moment in a world so lovely, so inept
At twisted words and crookèd deeds, it was as if I slept and dreamt.

It seemed that all was well with Holland—not a tank had crushed
The tulips there.
Mile after mile the level lowlands blossomed—yellow square,
    white square,
Scarlet strip and mauve strip bright beneath the brightly clouded sky,
    the round clouds and the gentle air.
Along the straight canals between striped fields of tulips in the
    morning sailed
Broad ships, their hulls by tulip-beds concealed, only the sails showing.

It seemed that all was well with England—the harsh foreign voice
    hysterically vowing,
Once more, to keep its word, at length was disbelieved, and hushed.

It seemed that all was well with France, with her straight roads
Lined with slender poplars, and the peasants on the skyline ploughing.

1940

E. E. CUMMINGS
1894–1962

Beginning in the 1920s and 1930s, Edward Estlin Cummings built a reputation as author of a particularly agreeable kind of modernist poetry, distinguished by clever formal innovation, a tender lyricism, and the thematic celebration of individuals against mass society. These qualities were evident in his first literary success, a zesty prose account of his experience in a French prison camp during World War I, *The Enormous Room* (1922; see p. 206). He and a friend had joined the ambulance corps in France the day after the United States entered the war; their disdain for the bureaucracy, expressed in outspoken letters home, aroused antagonism among French officials and they were imprisoned. To be made a prisoner by one's own side struck Cummings as outrageous and yet funny; from the experience he produced an ironic, profane celebration of the ordinary soldier and an attack on

E. E. Cummings, self-portrait, 1939. Cummings showed his early abstract paintings at modernist exhibitions like that of New York's Society of Independent Artists; his later work, like this self-portrait, became more realistic and figurative.

bureaucracy. His poetry continued the attack on depersonalized, commercial, exploitative mass culture and celebrated loners, lovers, and nonconformists.

He was born in Cambridge, Massachusetts. His father was a Congregationalist minister and teacher at Harvard; the family was close knit and Cummings, a much-loved son. While a student at Harvard (he graduated in 1915 and took an M.A. in 1916) he began to write poetry based on the intricate stanza patterns of the pre-Raphaelite and Metaphysical writers he was reading in English literature classes. When he began to innovate—as he did after discovering the poetry of Ezra Pound—he was able to build (like Pound himself) from a firm apprenticeship in traditional techniques.

After the war, Cummings established a life that included a studio in Greenwich Village, travel and sojourns in France, and summers at the family home in New Hampshire. He was a painter as well as a poet; simple living and careful management of a small allowance from his mother, along with prizes, royalties, and commissions, enabled him to work full time as an artist. He published four volumes of well-received poetry in the 1920s and a book of collected poems toward the end of the 1930s. In the 1950s he visited and read at many college campuses, where students enjoyed his tricks of verse and vocabulary and appreciated his tender yet earthy poetry. He received a special citation by the National Book Award committee in 1955 and the Bollingen Prize in 1957.

In his attempts to reshape poetry Cummings was also concerned with being widely accessible. Cummings's verse is characterized by common speech and attention to the visual form of the poem—that is, the poem as it appears on the page as distinguished from its sound when read aloud. Experiments with capitalization or lack of it, punctuation, line breaks, hyphenation, and verse shapes were all carried out for the reader's eyes as well as ears. To express his sense that life was always in process, he wrote untitled poems without beginnings and endings, consisting of fragmentary lines. There is always humor in his poetry, and his outrage at cruelty and exploitation is balanced with gusto and celebration of the body.

The text of the poems included here is that of *Complete Poems* (1991).

Thy fingers make early flowers of

Thy fingers make early flowers of
all things.
thy hair mostly the hours love:
a smoothness which
sings,saying
(though love be a day)
do not fear,we will go amaying.

thy whitest feet crisply are straying.
Always
thy moist eyes are at kisses playing,
whose strangeness much
says;singing
(though love be a day)
for which girl art thou flowers bringing?

To be thy lips is a sweet thing
and small.
Death,Thee i call rich beyond wishing
if this thou catch,
else missing.
(though love be a day
and life be nothing,it shall not stop kissing).

1923

in Just-

in Just-
spring   when the world is mud-
luscious the little
lame balloonman

whistles   far   and wee

and eddieandbill come
running from marbles and
piracies and it's
spring

when the world is puddle-wonderful

the queer
old balloonman whistles
far   and   wee
and bettyandisbel come dancing

from hop-scotch and jump-rope and

it's
spring
and
 the

 goat-footed

balloonMan whistles
far
and
wee

1920, 1923

O sweet spontaneous

O sweet spontaneous
earth how often have
the
doting

 fingers of
prurient philosophers pinched
and
poked

thee
,has the naughty thumb
of science prodded
thy

 beauty .how
often have religions taken
thee upon their scraggy knees
squeezing and

buffeting thee that thou mightest conceive
gods
 (but
true

to the incomparable
couch of death thy
rhythmic
lover

 thou answerest

them only with

spring)

1920, 1923

Buffalo Bill 's

Buffalo Bill 's[1]
defunct
who used to
ride a watersmooth-silver
stallion
and break onetwothreefourfive pigeonsjustlikethat
Jesus

he was a handsome man
and what i want to know is
how do you like your blueeyed boy
Mister Death

1920, 1923

the Cambridge ladies who live in furnished souls

the Cambridge ladies who live in furnished souls
are unbeautiful and have comfortable minds
(also,with the church's protestant blessings
daughters,unscented shapeless spirited)
they believe in Christ and Longfellow,[1] both dead,
are invariably interested in so many things—
at the present writing one still finds
delighted fingers knitting for the is it Poles?
perhaps. While permanent faces coyly bandy
scandal of Mrs. N and Professor D
. . . . the Cambridge ladies do not care,above
Cambridge if sometimes in its box of
sky lavender and cornerless,the
moon rattles like a fragment of angry candy

1923

1. William F. Cody (1846–1917), American scout and Wild West showman.

1. Henry Wadsworth Longfellow (1807–1882), American poet often used as a symbol for traditionalist writing and values. He was a professor of romance languages at Harvard University in Cambridge.

"next to of course god america i

"next to of course god america i
love you land of the pilgrims' and so forth oh
say can you see by the dawn's early my
country 'tis of centuries come and go
and are no more what of it we should worry
in every language even deafanddumb
thy sons acclaim your glorious name by gorry
by jingo by gee by gosh by gum
why talk of beauty what could be more beautiful than these heroic happy dead
who rushed like lions to the roaring slaughter
they did not stop to think they died instead
then shall the voice of liberty be mute?"

He spoke. And drank rapidly a glass of water

1926

i sing of Olaf glad and big

i sing of Olaf glad and big
whose warmest heart recoiled at war:
a conscientious object-or

his wellbelovéd colonel(trig
westpointer[1] most succinctly bred)
took erring Olaf soon in hand;
but—though an host of overjoyed
noncoms[2](first knocking on the head
him)do through icy waters roll
that helplessness which others stroke
with brushes recently employed
anent this muddy toiletbowl,
while kindred intellects evoke
allegiance per blunt instruments—
Olaf(being to all intents
a corpse and wanting any rag
upon what God unto him gave)
responds,without getting annoyed
"I will not kiss your fucking flag"

straightway the silver bird[3] looked grave
(departing hurriedly to shave)

1. Graduate of the U.S. Military Academy at West Point, New York.
2. Noncommissioned officers.
3. Insignia of a colonel.

but—though all kinds of officers
(a yearning nation's blueeyed pride)
their passive prey did kick and curse
until for wear their clarion
voices and boots were much the worse,
and egged the firstclassprivates on
his rectum wickedly to tease
by means of skilfully applied
bayonets roasted hot with heat—
Olaf(upon what were once knees)
does almost ceaselessly repeat
"there is some shit I will not eat"

our president,being of which
assertions duly notified
threw the yellowsonofabitch
into a dungeon,where he died

Christ(of His mercy infinite)
i pray to see; and Olaf,too

preponderatingly because
unless statistics lie he was
more brave than me:more blond than you.

1931

somewhere i have never travelled,gladly beyond

somewhere i have never travelled,gladly beyond
any experience,your eyes have their silence:
in your most frail gesture are things which enclose me,
or which i cannot touch because they are too near

your slightest look easily will unclose me
though i have closed myself as fingers,
you open always petal by petal myself as Spring opens
(touching skilfully,mysteriously)her first rose

or if your wish be to close me,iand
my life will shut very beautifully,suddenly,
as when the heart of this flower imagines
the snow carefully everywhere descending;

nothing which we are to perceive in this world equals
the power of your intense fragility:whose texture
compels me with the colour of its countries,
rendering death and forever with each breathing

(i do not know what it is about you that closes
and opens;only something in me understands
the voice of your eyes is deeper than all roses)
nobody,not even the rain,has such small hands

1931

anyone lived in a pretty how town

anyone lived in a pretty how town
(with up so floating many bells down)
spring summer autumn winter
he sang his didn't he danced his did.

Women and men(both little and small)
cared for anyone not at all
they sowed their isn't they reaped their same
sun moon stars rain

children guessed(but only a few
and down they forgot as up they grew
autumn winter spring summer)
that noone loved him more by more

when by now and tree by leaf
she laughed his joy she cried his grief
bird by snow and stir by still
anyone's any was all to her

someones married their everyones
laughed their cryings and did their dance
(sleep wake hope and then)they
said their nevers they slept their dream

stars rain sun moon
(and only the snow can begin to explain
how children are apt to forget to remember
with up so floating many bells down)

one day anyone died i guess
(and noone stooped to kiss his face)
busy folk buried them side by side
little by little and was by was

all by all and deep by deep
and more by more they dream their sleep
noone and anyone earth by april
wish by spirit and if by yes.

Women and men(both dong and ding)
summer autumn winter spring
reaped their sowing and went their came
sun moon stars rain

1940

my father moved through dooms of love

my father moved through dooms of love
through sames of am through haves of give,
singing each morning out of each night
my father moved through depths of height

this motionless forgetful where
turned at his glance to shining here;
that if(so timid air is firm)
under his eyes would stir and squirm

newly as from unburied which
floats the first who,his april touch
drove sleeping selves to swarm their fates
woke dreamers to their ghostly roots

and should some why completely weep
my father's fingers brought her sleep:
vainly no smallest voice might cry
for he could feel the mountains grow.

Lifting the valleys of the sea
my father moved through griefs of joy;
praising a forehead called the moon
singing desire into begin

joy was his song and joy so pure
a heart of star by him could steer
and pure so now and now so yes
the wrists of twilight would rejoice

keen as midsummer's keen beyond
conceiving mind of sun will stand,
so strictly(over utmost him
so hugely)stood my father's dream

his flesh was flesh his blood was blood:
no hungry man but wished him food;
no cripple wouldn't creep one mile
uphill to only see him smile.

Scorning the pomp of must and shall
my father moved through dooms of feel;
his anger was as right as rain
his pity was as green as grain

septembering arms of year extend
less humbly wealth to foe and friend
than he to foolish and to wise
offered immeasurable is

proudly and(by octobering flame
beckoned)as earth will downward climb,
so naked for immortal work
his shoulders marched against the dark

his sorrow was as true as bread:
no liar looked him in the head;
if every friend became his foe
he'd laugh and build a world with snow.

My father moved through theys of we,
singing each new leaf out of each tree
(and every child was sure that spring
danced when she heard my father sing)

then let men kill which cannot share,
let blood and flesh be mud and mire,
scheming imagine,passion willed,
freedom a drug that's bought and sold

giving to steal and cruel kind,
a heart to fear,to doubt a mind,
to differ a disease of same,
conform the pinnacle of am

though dull were all we taste as bright,
bitter all utterly things sweet,
maggoty minus and dumb death
all we inherit,all bequeath

and nothing quite so least as truth
—i say though hate were why men breathe—
because my father lived his soul
love is the whole and more than all

1940

pity this busy monster,manunkind

pity this busy monster,manunkind,

not. Progress is a comfortable disease:
your victim(death and life safely beyond)

plays with the bigness of his littleness
—electrons deify one razorblade
into a mountainrange;lenses extend

unwish through curving wherewhen till unwish
returns on its unself.
A world of made
is not a world of born—pity poor flesh

and trees,poor stars and stones,but never this
fine specimen of hypermagical

ultraomnipotence. We doctors know

a hopeless case if—listen:there's a hell
of a good universe next door;let's go

1944

JEAN TOOMER
1894–1967

Jean Toomer's *Cane*, the author's contribution to Harlem Renaissance literature, received immediate acclaim when it appeared in 1923. Toomer described African American communities from Chicago and Washington, D.C., to small-town Georgia through the analytic filter of a modernist, urban literary style. William Stanley Braithwaite, in the NAACP-sponsored *Crisis*, praised him as the first to "write about the Negro without the surrender or the compromise of the author's vision." Sherwood Anderson recognized *Cane* as the work of an artistic peer, and other readers compared it favorably to Anderson's *Winesburg, Ohio*.

Born in Washington, D.C., Toomer never knew his father. He grew up with his grandfather, who had been an important Louisiana politician during the Reconstruction era, and his mother. After high school graduation, he attended several colleges—the University of Wisconsin, the Massachusetts College of Agriculture, the American College of Physical Training in Chicago, the University of Chicago, and the City College of New York—without completing a degree. He held numerous short-term jobs in various parts of the country, including four months in 1921 as superintendent of a small black school in Sparta, Georgia. This encounter with black Americans in the rural South formed the basis of *Cane*.

Toomer began writing when he was in his middle twenties, publishing poems and stories in avant-garde magazines such as *Broom*, the *Little Review*, and *Prairie*. He also published in the major political and artistic journals of the Harlem Renaissance such as the *Liberator, Crisis*, and *Opportunity*. Composed as an assemblage of short stories, sketches, poems, and even a play, *Cane* brought together many of Toomer's published magazine pieces.

Part I of *Cane*, set in rural Georgia, depicts a black community based in the rhythms of cotton culture, charged with sexual desire, and menaced by white violence. Part II shows black life in Washington, D.C., and Chicago, the fast-paced urban hives of money and ambition. The autobiographical third part describes an African American intellectual teaching in the South, trying to put down roots in an unfamiliar setting that he struggles to recognize as the source of his own artistic ambitions. This three-part structure is held together by a narrator who alternately steps forward in a first-person voice and recedes into third-person narration, poetry, or drama. *Cane*'s shifting voices explore whether a northern, urban African American can understand himself and his vocation by immersion in a black folk heritage that he has never known. The work is distinguished by its poetic, imagistic, evocative prose; its linguistic innovativeness; and its experimental construction.

Toomer spent much of the last forty years of his life looking for a spiritual community; he had difficulty finding publishers for the writing he produced during these decades. For a while he was a disciple of the Russian mystic George I. Gurdjieff. In the late 1940s he became a committed Quaker. At his death he left many unpublished short stories, as well as novels, plays, and an autobiography.

The text is that of the first edition (1923) as corrected in 1973.

From Cane[1]

Georgia Dusk

The sky, lazily disdaining to pursue
   The setting sun, too indolent to hold
   A lengthened tournament for flashing gold,
Passively darkens for night's barbecue,

A feast of moon and men and barking hounds,
   An orgy for some genius of the South
   With blood-hot eyes and cane-lipped scented mouth,
Surprised in making folk-songs from soul sounds.

The sawmill blows its whistle, buzz-saws stop,
   And silence breaks the bud of knoll and hill,
   Soft settling pollen where plowed lands fulfill
Their early promise of a bumper crop.

Smoke from the pyramidal sawdust pile
   Curls up, blue ghosts of trees, tarrying low

1. Of the book's three sections, the first and the last are Georgia scenes. "Fern" appears in the first section after the poem "Georgia Dusk." "Portrait in Georgia" followed by "Blood-Burning Moon" conclude the first section. "Seventh Street" is the first sketch in the second section, which is devoted to Washington, D.C., and Chicago.

Where only chips and stumps are left to show
The solid proof of former domicile.

Meanwhile, the men, with vestiges of pomp,
Race memories of king and caravan,
High-priests, an ostrich, and a juju-man,[2]
Go singing through the footpaths of the swamp.

Their voices rise . . the pine trees are guitars,
Strumming, pine-needles fall like sheets of rain . .
Their voices rise . . the chorus of the cane
Is caroling a vesper to the stars . .

O singers, resinous and soft your songs
Above the sacred whisper of the pines,
Give virgin lips to cornfield concubines,
Bring dreams of Christ to dusky cane-lipped throngs.

Fern

Face flowed into her eyes. Flowed in soft cream foam and plaintive ripples, in such a way that wherever your glance may momentarily have rested, it immediately thereafter wavered in the direction of her eyes. The soft suggestion of down slightly darkened, like the shadow of a bird's wing might, the creamy brown color of her upper lip. Why, after noticing it, you sought her eyes, I cannot tell you. Her nose was aquiline, Semitic. If you have heard a Jewish cantor[3] sing, if he has touched you and made your own sorrow seem trivial when compared with his, you will know my feeling when I follow the curves of her profile, like mobile rivers, to their common delta. They were strange eyes. In this, that they sought nothing—that is, nothing that was obvious and tangible and that one could see, and they gave the impression that nothing was to be denied. When a woman seeks, you will have observed, her eyes deny. Fern's eyes desired nothing that you could give her; there was no reason why they should withhold. Men saw her eyes and fooled themselves. Fern's eyes said to them that she was easy. When she was young, a few men took her, but got no joy from it. And then, once done, they felt bound to her (quite unlike their hit and run with other girls), felt as though it would take them a lifetime to fulfill an obligation which they could find no name for. They became attached to her, and hungered after finding the barest trace of what she might desire. As she grew up, new men who came to town felt as almost everyone did who ever saw her: that they would not be denied. Men were everlastingly bringing her their bodies. Something inside of her got tired of them, I guess, for I am certain that for the life of her she could not tell why or how she began to turn them off. A man in fever is no trifling thing to send away. They began to leave her, baffled and ashamed, yet vowing to themselves that some day they would do some fine thing for her: send her candy every week and not let her know whom it came from, watch out for her

2. West African tribesman who controls the magical fetish or charm, or "juju."
3. Singer in religious services.

wedding-day and give her a magnificent something with no name on it, buy a house and deed it to her, rescue her from some unworthy fellow who had tricked her into marrying him. As you know, men are apt to idolize or fear that which they cannot understand, especially if it be a woman. She did not deny them, yet the fact was that they were denied. A sort of superstition crept into their consciousness of her being somehow above them. Being above them meant that she was not to be approached by anyone. She became a virgin. Now a virgin in a small southern town is by no means the usual thing, if you will believe me. That the sexes were made to mate is the practice of the South. Particularly, black folks were made to mate. And it is black folks whom I have been talking about thus far. What white men thought of Fern I can arrive at only by analogy. They let her alone.

Anyone, of course, could see her, could see her eyes. If you walked up the Dixie Pike most any time of day, you'd be most like to see her resting listless-like on the railing of her porch, back propped against a post, head tilted a little forward because there was a nail in the porch post just where her head came which for some reason or other she never took the trouble to pull out. Her eyes, if it were sunset, rested idly where the sun, molten and glorious, was pouring down between the fringe of pines. Or maybe they gazed at the gray cabin on the knoll from which an evening folk-song was coming. Perhaps they followed a cow that had been turned loose to roam and feed on cotton-stalks and corn leaves. Like as not they'd settle on some vague spot above the horizon, though hardly a trace of wistfulness would come to them. If it were dusk, then they'd wait for the search-light of the evening train which you could see miles up the track before it flared across the Dixie Pike, close to her home. Wherever they looked, you'd follow them and then waver back. Like her face, the whole countryside seemed to flow into her eyes. Flowed into them with the soft listless cadence of Georgia's South. A young Negro, once, was looking at her, spellbound, from the road. A white man passing in a buggy had to flick him with his whip if he was to get by without running him over. I first saw her on her porch. I was passing with a fellow whose crusty numbness (I was from the North and suspected of being prejudiced and stuck-up) was melting as he found me warm. I asked him who she was. "That's Fern," was all that I could get from him. Some folks already thought that I was given to nosing around; I let it go at that, so far as questions were concerned. But at first sight of her I felt as if I heard a Jewish cantor sing. As if his singing rose above the unheard chorus of a folk-song. And I felt bound to her. I too had my dreams: something I would do for her. I have knocked about from town to town too much not to know the futility of mere change of place. Besides, picture if you can, this cream-colored solitary girl sitting at a tenement window looking down on the indifferent throngs of Harlem. Better that she listen to folk-songs at dusk in Georgia, you would say, and so would I. Or, suppose she came up North and married. Even a doctor or a lawyer, say, one who would be sure to get along—that is, make money. You and I know, who have had experience in such things, that love is not a thing like prejudice which can be bettered by changes of town. Could men in Washington, Chicago, or New York, more than the men of Georgia, bring her something left vacant by the bestowal of their bodies? You and I who know men in these cities will have to say, they could not. See her out and out a prostitute along State Street in Chicago. See her move into a southern town where white men are more aggressive. See her become a white man's concubine . . . Something I must do for her. There was myself. What could I do for her? Talk, of course. Push back the fringe of pines upon new horizons. To what purpose? and what for? Her? Myself? Men in her case seem to lose their selfishness. I lost mine before I touched her. I ask you, friend (it makes no difference if you sit in the Pullman or the Jim Crow[4] as the train crosses her road), what thoughts would come to you—that is, after you'd finished with the thoughts that leap into men's minds at the sight of a pretty woman who will not deny them; what thoughts would come to you, had you seen her in a quick flash, keen and intuitively, as she sat there on her porch when your train thundered by? Would you have got off at the next station and come back for her to take her where? Would you have completely forgotten her as soon as you reached Macon, Atlanta, Augusta, Pasadena, Madison, Chicago, Boston, or New Orleans? Would you tell your wife or sweetheart about a girl you saw? Your thoughts can help me, and I would like to know. Something I would do for her . . .

One evening I walked up the Pike on purpose, and stopped to say hello. Some of her family were about, but they moved away to make room for me. Damn if I knew how to begin. Would you? Mr. and Miss So-and-So, people, the weather, the crops, the new preacher, the frolic, the church benefit, rabbit and possum hunting, the new soft drink they had at old Pap's store, the schedule of the trains, what kind of town Macon was, Negro's migration north, bollweevils, syrup, the Bible—to all these things she gave a yassur or nassur, without further comment. I began to wonder if perhaps my own emotional sensibility had played one of its tricks on me. "Lets take a walk," I at last ventured. The suggestion, coming after so long an isolation, was novel enough, I guess, to surprise. But it wasnt that. Something told me that men before me had said just that as a prelude to the offering of their bodies. I tried to tell her with my eyes. I think she understood. The thing from her that made my throat catch, vanished. Its passing left her visible in a way I'd thought, but never seen. We walked down the Pike with people on all the porches gaping at us. "Doesnt it make you mad?" She meant the row of petty gossiping people. She meant the world. Through a canebrake that was ripe for cutting, the branch was reached. Under a sweet-gum tree, and where reddish leaves had dammed the creek a little, we sat down. Dusk, suggesting the almost imperceptible procession of giant trees, settled with a purple haze about the cane. I felt strange, as I always do in Georgia, particularly at dusk. I felt that things unseen to men were tangibly immediate. It would not have surprised me had I had vision. People have them in Georgia more often than you would suppose. A black woman once saw the mother of Christ and drew her in charcoal on the courthouse wall . . . When one is on the soil of one's ancestors, most anything can come to one . . . From force of habit, I suppose, I held Fern in my arms—that is, without at first noticing it. Then my mind came back to her. Her eyes, unusually weird and open, held me. Held God. He flowed in as I've seen the countryside flow in. Seen men. I

4. In the segregated South, black persons were required to sit in the "Jim Crow" section of railway cars and were not allowed as passengers in the first-class "Pullman" lounges, or sleeping cars.

must have done something—what, I don't know, in the confusion of my emotion. She sprang up. Rushed some distance from me. Fell to her knees, and began swaying, swaying. Her body was tortured with something it could not let out. Like boiling sap it flooded arms and fingers till she shook them as if they burned her. It found her throat, and spattered inarticulately in plaintive, convulsive sounds, mingled with calls to Christ Jesus. And then she sang, brokenly. A Jewish cantor singing with a broken voice. A child's voice, uncertain, or an old man's. Dusk hid her; I could hear only her song. It seemed to me as though she were pounding her head in anguish upon the ground. I rushed at her. She fainted in my arms.

There was talk about her fainting with me in the canefield. And I got one or two ugly looks from town men who'd set themselves up to protect her. In fact, there was talk of making me leave town. But they never did. They kept a watch-out for me, though. Shortly after, I came back North. From the train window I saw her as I crossed her road. Saw her on her porch, head tilted a little forward where the nail was, eyes vaguely focused on the sunset. Saw her face flow into them, the countryside and something that I call God, flowing into them . . . Nothing ever really happened. Nothing ever came to Fern, not even I. Something I would do for her. Some fine unnamed thing . . . And, friend, you? She is still living, I have reason to know. Her name, against the chance that you might happen down that way, is Fernie May Rosen.

* * *

Portrait in Georgia

Hair—braided chestnut,
        coiled like a lyncher's rope,
Eyes—fagots,
Lips—old scars, or the first red blisters,
Breath—the last sweet scent of cane,
And her slim body, white as the ash
   of black flesh after flame.

* * *

Blood-Burning Moon

I

Up from the skeleton stone walls, up from the rotting floor boards and the solid hand-hewn beams of oak of the pre-war cotton factory, dusk came. Up from the dusk the full moon came, Glowing like a fired pine-knot, it illumined the great door and soft showered the Negro shanties aligned along the single street of factory town. The full moon in the great door was an omen. Negro women improvised songs against its spell.

Louisa sang as she came over the crest of the hill from the white folks' kitchen. Her skin was the color of oak leaves on young trees in fall. Her breasts, firm and up-pointed like ripe acorns. And her singing had the low murmur of winds in fig trees. Bob Stone, younger son of the people she worked for, loved her. By the way the world reckons things, he had won her. By measure of that warm glow which came into her mind at thought of him, he had won her. Tom Burwell, whom the whole town called Big Boy, also loved her. But working in the fields all day, and far away from her, gave him no chance to show it. Though often enough of evenings he had tried to. Somehow, he never got along. Strong as he was with hands upon the ax or plow, he found it difficult to hold her. Or so he thought. But the fact was that he held her to factory town more firmly than he thought for. His black balanced, and pulled against, the white of Stone, when she thought of them. And her mind was vaguely upon them as she came over the crest of the hill, coming from the white folks' kitchen. As she sang softly at the evil face of the full moon.

A strange stir was in her. Indolently, she tried to fix upon Bob or Tom as the cause of it. To meet Bob in the canebrake, as she was going to do an hour or so later, was nothing new. And Tom's proposal which she felt on its way to her could be indefinitely put off. Separately, there was no unusual significance to either one. But for some reason, they jumbled when her eyes gazed vacantly at the rising moon. And from the jumble came the stir that was strangely within her. Her lips trembled. The slow rhythm of her song grew agitant and restless. Rusty black and tan spotted hounds, lying in the dark corners of porches or prowling around back yards, put their noses in the air and caught its tremor. They began plaintively to yelp and howl. Chickens woke up and cackled. Intermittently, all over the countryside dogs barked and roosters crowed as if heralding a weird dawn or some ungodly awakening. The women sang lustily. Their songs were cotton-wads to stop their ears. Louisa came down into factory town and sank wearily upon the step before her home. The moon was rising towards a thick cloud-bank which soon would hide it.

Red nigger moon. Sinner!
Blood-burning moon. Sinner!
Come out that fact'ry door.

2

Up from the deep dusk of a cleared spot on the edge of the forest a mellow glow arose and spread fan-wise into the low-hanging heavens. And all around the air was heavy with the scent of boiling cane. A large pile of cane-stalks lay like ribboned shadows upon the ground. A mule, harnessed to a pole, trudged lazily round and round the pivot of the grinder. Beneath a swaying oil lamp, a Negro alternately whipped out at the mule, and fed cane-stalks to the grinder. A fat boy waddled pails of fresh ground juice between the grinder and the boiling stove. Steam came from the copper boiling pan. The scent of cane came from the copper pan and drenched the forest and the hill that sloped to factory town, beneath its fragrance. It drenched the men in circle seated around the stove. Some of them chewed at the white pulp of stalks, but there was no need for them to, if all they wanted was to taste the cane. One tasted it in factory town. And from factory town one could see the soft haze thrown by the glowing stove upon the low-hanging heavens.

Old David Georgia stirred the thickening syrup with a long ladle, and ever so often drew it off. Old David Georgia tended his stove and told tales about the white folks, about moonshining and cotton picking, and about sweet nigger gals, to the men who sat there about his stove to listen to him. Tom Burwell chewed cane-stalk and laughed with the others till some one mentioned Louisa. Till some one said something about Louisa and Bob Stone, about the silk stockings she must have gotten from him. Blood ran up Tom's neck hotter than the glow that flooded from the stove. He sprang up. Glared at the men and said, "She's my gal." Will Manning laughed. Tom strode over to him. Yanked him up and knocked him to the ground. Several of Manning's friends got up to fight for him. Tom whipped out a long knife and would have cut them to shreds if they hadnt ducked into the woods. Tom had had enough. He nodded to Old David Georgia and swung down the path to factory town. Just then, the dogs started barking and the roosters began to crow. Tom felt funny. Away from the fight, away from the stove, chill got to him. He shivered. He shuddered when he saw the full moon rising towards the cloud-bank. He who didnt give a godam for the fears of old women. He forced his mind to fasten on Louisa. Bob Stone. Better not be. He turned into the street and saw Louisa sitting before her home. He went towards her, ambling, touched the brim of a marvelously shaped, spotted, felt hat, said he wanted to say something to her, and then found that he didnt know what he had to say, or if he did, that he couldnt say it. He shoved his big fists in his overalls, grinned, and started to move off.

"Youall want me, Tom?"

"That's what us wants, sho, Louisa."

"Well, here I am—"

"An here I is, but that aint ahelpin none, all th same."

"You wanted to say something? . ."

"I did that, sho. But words is like th spots on dice: no matter how y fumbles em, there's times when they jes wont come. I dunno why. Seems like th love I feels fo yo done stole m tongue. I got it now. Whee! Louisa, honey, I oughtnt tell y, I feel I oughtnt cause yo is young an goes t church an I has had other gals, but Louisa I sho do love y. Lil gal, Ise watched y from them first days when youall sat right here befo yo door befo th well an sang sometimes in a way that like t broke m heart. Ise carried y with me into th fields, day after day, an after that, an I sho can plow when yo is there, an I can pick cotton. Yassur! Come near beatin Barlo yesterday. I sho did. Yassur! An next year if ole Stone'll trust me, I'll have a farm. My own. My bales will buy yo what y gets from white folks now. Silk stockings an purple dresses—course I dont believe what some folks been whisperin as t how y gets them things now. White folks always did do for niggers what they likes. An they jes cant help alikin yo, Louisa. Bob Stone likes y. Course he does. But not th way folks is awhisperin. Does he, hon?"

"I dont know what you mean, Tom."

"Course y dont. Ise already cut two niggers. Had t hon, t tell em so. Niggers always tryin t make somethin out a nothin. An then besides, white folks aint up t them tricks so much nowadays. Godam better not be. Leastawise not with yo. Cause I wouldnt stand f it. Nassur."

"What would you do, Tom?"

"Cut him jes like I cut a nigger."

"No, Tom—"

"I said I would an there aint no mo to it. But that aint th talk f now. Sing, honey Louisa, an while I'm listenin t y I'll be makin love."

Tom took her hand in his. Against the tough thickness of his own, hers felt soft and small. His huge body slipped down to the step beside her. The full moon sank upward into the deep purple of the cloud-bank. An old woman brought a lighted lamp and hung it on the common well whose bulky shadow squatted in the middle of the road, opposite Tom and Louisa. The old woman lifted the well-lid, took hold the chain, and began drawing up the heavy bucket. As she did so, she sang. Figures shifted, restlesslike, between lamp and window in the front rooms of the shanties. Shadows of the figures fought each other on the gray dust of the road. Figures raised the windows and joined the old woman in song. Louisa and Tom, the whole street, singing:

Red nigger moon. Sinner!
Blood-burning moon. Sinner!
Come out that fact'ry door.

3

Bob Stone sauntered from his veranda out into the gloom of fir trees and magnolias. The clear white of his skin paled, and the flush of his cheeks turned purple. As if to balance this outer change, his mind became consciously a white man's. He passed the house with its huge open hearth which, in the days of slavery, was the plantation cookery. He saw Louisa bent over that hearth. He went in as a master should and took her. Direct, honest, bold. None of this sneaking that he had to go through now. The contrast was repulsive to him. His family had lost ground. Hell no, his family still owned the niggers, practically. Damned if they did, or he wouldnt have to duck around so. What would they think if they knew? His mother? His sister? He shouldnt mention them, shouldnt think of them in this connection. There in the dusk he blushed at doing so. Fellows about town were all right, but how about his friends up North? He could see them incredible, repulsed. They didnt know. The thought first made him laugh. Then, with their eyes still upon him, he began to feel embarrassed. He felt the need of explaining things to them. Explain hell. They wouldnt understand, and moreover, who ever-heard of a Southerner getting on his knees to any Yankee, or anyone. No sir. He was going to see Louisa to-night, and love her. She was lovely—in her way. Nigger way. What way was that? Damned if he knew. Must know. He'd known her long enough to know. Was there something about niggers that you couldnt know? Listening to them at church didnt tell you anything. Looking at them didnt tell you anything. Talking to them didnt tell you anything—unless it was gossip, unless they wanted to talk. Of course, about farming, and licker, and craps—but those werent nigger. Nigger was something more. How much more? Something to be afraid of, more? Hell no. Who ever heard of being afraid of a nigger? Tom Burwell. Cartwell had told him that Tom went with Louisa after she reached home. No sir. No nigger had ever been with his girl. He'd like to see one try. Some position for him to be in. Him, Bob Stone, of the old Stone family, in a scrap with a nigger over a nigger girl. In the good old days . . . Ha! Those were the days. His family had lost ground. Not so much, though. Enough for him to have to cut through old Lemon's canefield by way of the woods, that he might meet her. She was worth it. Beautiful nigger gal. Why nigger? Why not, just gal? No, it was because she was nigger that he went to her. Sweet . . . The scent of boiling cane came to him. Then he saw the rich glow of the stove. He heard the voices of the men circled around it. He was about to skirt the clearing when he heard his own name mentioned. He stopped. Quivering. Leaning against a tree, he listened.

"Bad nigger. Yassur, he sho is one bad nigger when he gets started."

"Tom Burwell's been on th gang three times fo cutting men."

"What y think he's agwine t do t Bob Stone?"

"Dunno yet. He aint found out. When he does— Baby!"

"Aint no tellin."

"Young Stone aint no quitter an I ken tell y that. Blood of th old uns in his veins."

"Thats right. He'll scrap, sho."

"Be gettin too hot f niggers round this away."

"Shut up, nigger. Y dont know what y talkin bout."

Bob Stone's ears burned as though he had been holding them over the stove. Sizzling heat welled up within him. His feet felt as if they rested on red-hot coals. They stung him to quick movement. He circled the fringe of the glowing. Not a twig cracked beneath his feet. He reached the path that led to factory town. Plunged furiously down it. Haltway along, a blindness within him veered him aside. He crashed into the bordering canebrake. Cane leaves cut his face and lips. He tasted blood. He threw himself down and dug his fingers in the ground. The earth was cool. Cane-roots took the fever from his hands. After a long while, or so it seemed to him, the thought came to him that it must be time to see Louisa. He got to his feet and walked calmly to their meeting place. No Louisa. Tom Burwell had her. Veins in his forehead bulged and distended. Saliva moistened the dried blood on his lips. He bit down on his lips. He tasted blood. Not his own blood; Tom Burwell's blood. Bob drove through the cane and out again upon the road. A hound swung down the path before him towards factory town. Bob couldnt see it. The dog loped aside to let him pass. Bob's blind rushing made him stumble over it. He fell with a thud that dazed him. The hound yelped. Answering yelps came from all over the countryside. Chickens cackled. Roosters crowed, heralding the bloodshot eyes of southern awakening. Singers in the town were silenced. They shut their windows down. Palpitant between the rooster crows, a chill hush settled upon the huddled forms of Tom and Louisa. A figure rushed from the shadow and stood before them. Tom popped to his feet.

"Whats y want?"

"I'm Bob Stone."

"Yassur—an I'm Tom Burwell. Whats y want?"

Bob lunged at him. Tom side-stepped, caught him by the shoulder, and flung him to the ground. Straddled him.

"Let me up."

"Yassur—but watch yo doins, Bob Stone."

A few dark figures, drawn by the sound of scuffle, stood about them. Bob sprang to his feet.

"Fight like a man, Tom Burwell, an I'll lick y."

Again he lunged. Tom side-stepped and flung him to the ground. Straddled him.

"Get off me, you godam nigger you."

"Yo sho has started somethin now. Get up."

Tom yanked him up and began hammering at him. Each blow sounded as if it smashed into a precious, irreplaceable soft something. Beneath them, Bob staggered back. He reached in his pocket and whipped out a knife.

"Thats my game, sho."

Blue flash, a steel blade slashed across Bob Stone's throat. He had a sweetish sick feeling. Blood began to flow. Then he felt a sharp twitch of pain. He let his knife drop. He slapped one hand against his neck. He pressed the other on top of his head as if to hold it down. He groaned. He turned, and staggered towards the crest of the hill in the direction of white town. Negroes who had seen the fight slunk into their homes and blew the lamps out. Louisa, dazed, hysterical, refused to go indoors. She slipped, crumbled, her body loosely propped against the woodwork of the well. Tom Burwell leaned against it. He seemed rooted there.

Bob reached Broad Street. White men rushed up to him. He collapsed in their arms.

"Tom Burwell. . . ."

White men like ants upon a forage rushed about. Except for the taut hum of their moving, all was silent. Shotguns, revolvers, rope, kerosene, torches. Two high-powered cars with glaring search-lights. They came together. The taut hum rose to a low roar. Then nothing could be heard but the flop of their feet in the thick dust of the road. The moving body of their silence preceded them over the crest of the hill into factory town. It flattened the Negroes beneath it. It rolled to the wall of the factory, where it stopped. Tom knew that they were coming. He couldnt move. And then he saw the search-lights of the two cars glaring down on him. A quick shock went through him. He stiffened. He started to run. A yell went up from the mob. Tom wheeled about and faced them. They poured down on him. They swarmed. A large man with dead-white face and flabby cheeks came to him and almost jabbed a gun-barrel through his guts.

"Hands behind y, nigger."

Tom's wrists were bound. The big man shoved him to the well. Burn him over it, and when the woodwork caved in, his body would drop to the bottom. Two deaths for a godam nigger. Louisa was driven back. The mob pushed in. Its pressure, its momentum was too great. Drag him to the factory. Wood and stakes already there. Tom moved in the direction indicated. But they had to drag him. They reached the great door. Too many to get in there. The mob divided and flowed around the walls to either side. The big man shoved him through the door. The mob pressed in from the sides. Taut humming. No words. A stake was sunk into the ground. Rotting floor boards piled around it. Kerosene poured on the rotting floor boards. Tom bound to the stake. His breast was bare. Nails' scratches let little lines of blood trickle down and mat into the hair. His face, his eyes were set and stony. Except for irregular breathing, one would have thought him already dead. Torches were flung onto the pile. A great flare muffled in black smoke shot upward. The mob yelled. The mob was silent. Now Tom could be seen within the flames. Only his head, erect, lean, like a blackened stone. Stench of burning flesh soaked the air. Tom's eyes popped. His head settled downward. The mob yelled. Its yell echoed against the skeleton stone walls and sounded like a hundred yells. Like a hundred mobs yelling. Its yell thudded against the thick front wall and fell back. Ghost of a yell slipped through the flames and out the great door of the factory. It fluttered like a dying thing down the single street of factory town. Louisa, upon the step before her home, did not hear it, but her eyes opened slowly. They saw the full moon glowing in the great door. The full moon, an evil thing, an omen, soft showering the homes of folks she knew. Where were they, these people? She'd sing, and perhaps they'd come out and join her. Perhaps Tom Burwell would come. At any rate, the full moon in the great door was an omen which she must sing to:

Red nigger moon. Sinner!
Blood-burning moon. Sinner!
Come out that fact'ry door.

Seventh Street

Money burns the pocket, pocket hurts,
Bootleggers in silken shirts,
Ballooned, zooming Cadillacs,
Whizzing, whizzing down the street-car tracks.

Seventh Street is a bastard of Prohibition and the War.[5] A crude-boned, soft-skinned wedge of nigger life breathing its loafer air, jazz songs and love, thrusting unconscious rhythms, black reddish blood into the white and whitewashed wood of Washington. Stale soggy wood of Washington. Wedges rust in soggy wood . . . Split it! In two! Again! Shred it! . . the sun. Wedges are brilliant in the sun; ribbons of wet wood dry and blow away. Black reddish blood. Pouring for crude-boned soft-skinned life, who set you flowing? Blood suckers of the War would spin in a frenzy of dizziness if they drank your blood. Prohibition would put a stop to it. Who set you flowing? White and whitewash disappear in blood. Who set you flowing? Flowing down the smooth asphalt of Seventh Street, in shanties, brick office buildings, theaters, drug stores, restaurants, and cabarets? Eddying on the corners? Swirling like a blood-red smoke up where the buzzards fly in heaven? God would not dare to suck black red blood. A Nigger God! He would duck his head in shame and call for the Judgment Day. Who set you flowing?

Money burns the pocket, pocket hurts,
Bootleggers in silken shirts,
Ballooned, zooming Cadillacs,
Whizzing, whizzing down the street-car tracks.

1923

5. World War I.

F. SCOTT FITZGERALD
1896–1940

In the 1920s and 1930s F. Scott Fitzgerald was equally famous as a writer and as a celebrity author whose lifestyle seemed to symbolize the two decades; in the 1920s he stood for all-night partying, drinking, and the pursuit of pleasure, while in the 1930s he stood for the gloomy aftermath of excess. "Babylon Revisited," written immediately after the stock market crash, is simultaneously a personal and a national story.

Fitzgerald was born in a middle-class neighborhood in St. Paul, Minnesota, descended on his father's side from southern colonial landowners and legislators, on his mother's from Irish immigrants. Much of his boyhood was spent in Buffalo and Syracuse, New York. The family was not prosperous and it took an aunt's support to send him to a Catholic boarding school in New Jersey in 1911. Two years later he entered Princeton University, where he participated in extracurricular literary and dramatic activities, forming friendships with campus intellectuals, like the prominent critic Edmund Wilson, who were to help him in later years. But he failed to make the football team and felt the disappointment for years. After three years of college Fitzgerald quit to join the army, but the war ended before he saw active service. Stationed in Montgomery, Alabama, he met and courted Zelda Sayre, a local belle who rejected him. In 1919 he went to New York City, determined to make a fortune and win Zelda. Amazingly, he succeeded. A novel he had begun in college, revised, and published in 1920 as *This Side of Paradise* became an immediate bestseller, making its author rich and famous at the age of twenty-four. As one of the earliest examples of a novel about college life, *This Side of Paradise* was accepted as the voice of the younger generation in a society increasingly oriented toward youth. He combined the traditional narrative and rhetorical gifts of a good fiction writer, it appeared, with a thoroughly modern sensibility. A week after the novel appeared, Scott and Zelda were married. Living extravagantly in New York City and St. Paul, and on Long Island, they more than spent the money Fitzgerald made from two collections of short stories—*Flappers and Philosophers* (1920) and *Tales of the Jazz Age* (1922)—and a second novel, *The Beautiful and Damned* (1922). Their only child, a daughter, was born in 1921.

In 1924, the Fitzgeralds moved to Europe to live more cheaply. They made friends with American expatriates: Hemingway, Stein, and Pound among others. During this time Fitzgerald published his best-known and most successful novel, *The Great Gatsby* (1925), and another book of short stories, *All the Sad Young Men* (1926). *The Great Gatsby* tells the story of a self-made young man whose dream of success, personified in a rich and beautiful young woman named Daisy, turns out to be a fantasy in every sense: Daisy belongs to a corrupt society, Gatsby corrupts himself in the quest for her, and above all, the rich have no intention of sharing their privileges. The novel is narrated from the point of view of Nick Carraway, an onlooker who is both moved and repelled by the tale he tells and whose responses form a sort of subplot: this experiment in narrative point of view was widely imitated. The structure of *The Great Gatsby* is compact; the style dazzling; and its images of automobiles, parties, and garbage heaps seem to capture the contradictions of a consumer society. The novel became an instant classic and remains so to this day.

Fitzgerald wrote dozens of short stories during the twenties; many were published in the mass-circulation weekly the *Saturday Evening Post,* which paid extremely well. Despite the pace at which he worked—in all he wrote 178 short stories—the Fitzgeralds could not get out of debt. Scott became an alcoholic, and Zelda had a mental breakdown in 1930 and spent most of the rest of her life institutionalized. In 1931 Fitzgerald reestablished himself permanently in the United States, living at first near Baltimore, where his wife was hospitalized. A fourth novel, *Tender Is the Night,* appeared in 1934. The novel follows the emotional decline of a young American psychiatrist whose personal energies are sapped and his career corroded equally by his marriage to a beautiful and wealthy patient and his own weakness of character ("character" was one of Fitzgerald's favorite concepts). As in *The Great Gatsby,* the character begins as a disciple of the work ethic and turns into a pursuer of wealth, and the American Dream accordingly turns into a nightmare. Unlike *Gatsby,* whose characters never really connect with each other, *Tender Is the Night* shows a range of intimacies, none of them successful. The novel did not sell well. In 1937 Fitzgerald turned to Hollywood screenwriting; toward the end of the decade things were looking up for him, and he planned to revive his career as a fiction writer. But his health had been ruined by heavy drinking; he died of a heart attack in Hollywood at the age of forty-four, leaving an unfinished novel about a film mogul, *The Last Tycoon,* which was brought out by Edmund Wilson in 1941. Wilson also successfully promoted Fitzgerald's posthumous reputation by editing a collection of his writings, which he called *The Crack-Up,* in 1945.

The text of "Winter Dreams" is from *Metropolitan* magazine (1922); that of "Babylon Revisited" is from *Stories of F. Scott Fitzgerald* (1951).

Winter Dreams

Some of the caddies were poor as sin and lived in one-room houses with a neurasthenic cow in the front yard, but Dexter Green's father owned the second best grocery store in Dillard—the best one was "The Hub," patronized by the wealthy people from Lake Erminie—and Dexter caddied only for pocket-money.

In the fall when the days became crisp and grey and the long Minnesota winter shut down like the white lid of a box, Dexter's skis moved over the snow that hid the fairways of the golf course. At these times the country gave him a feeling of profound melancholy—it offended him that the links should lie in enforced fallowness, haunted by ragged sparrows for the long season. It was dreary, too, that on the tees where the gay colors fluttered in summer there were now only the desolate sand-boxes knee-deep in crusted ice. When he crossed the hills the wind blew cold as misery, and if the sun was out he tramped with his eyes squinted up against the hard dimensionless glare.

In April the winter ceased abruptly. The snow ran down into Lake Erminie scarcely tarrying for the early golfers to brave the season with red and black balls. Without elation, without an interval of moist glory the cold was gone.

Dexter knew that there was something dismal about this northern spring, just as he knew there was something gorgeous about the fall. Fall made him clench his hands and tremble and repeat idiotic sentences to himself and make brisk abrupt gestures of command to imaginary audiences and armies. October filled him with hope which November raised to a sort of ecstatic triumph, and in this wood the fleeting brilliant impressions of the summer at Lake Erminie were ready grist to his will. He became a golf champion and defeated Mr. T. A. Hedrick in a marvelous match played over a hundred times in the fairways of his imagination, a match each detail of which he changed about untiringly—sometimes winning with almost laughable ease, sometimes coming up magnificently from behind. Again, stepping from a Pierce-Arrow automobile, like Mr. Mortimer Jones, he strolled frigidly into the lounge of the Erminie Golf Club—or perhaps, surrounded by an admiring crowd, he gave an exhibition of fancy diving from the springboard of the Erminie Club raft. . . . Among those most impressed was Mr. Mortimer Jones.

And one day it came to pass that Mr. Jones, himself and not his ghost, came up to Dexter, almost with tears in his eyes and said that Dexter was the —— best caddy in the club and wouldn't he decide not to quit if Mr. Jones made it worth his while, because every other —— caddy in the club lost one ball a hole for him—regularly—

"No, sir," said Dexter, decisively, "I don't want to caddy any more." Then, after a pause, "I'm too old."

"You're—why, you're not more than fourteen. Why did you decide just this morning that you wanted to quit? You promised that next week you'd go over to the state tournament with me."

"I decided I was too old."

Dexter handed in his "A Class" badge, collected what money was due him from the caddy master and caught the train for Dillard.

"The best —— caddy I ever saw," shouted Mr. Mortimer Jones over a drink that afternoon. "Never lost a ball! Willing! Intelligent! Quiet! Honest! Grateful!—"

The little girl who had done this was eleven—beautifully ugly as little girls are apt to be who are destined after a few years to be inexpressably lovely and bring no end of misery to a great number of men. The spark, however, was perceptible. There was a general ungodliness in the way her lips twisted down at the corners when she smiled and in the—Heaven help us!—in the almost passionate quality of her eyes. Vitality is born early in such women. It was utterly in evidence now, shining through her thin frame in a sort of glow.

She had come eagerly out on to the course at nine o'clock with a white linen nurse and five small new golf clubs in a white canvas bag which the nurse was carrying. When Dexter first saw her she was standing by the caddy house, rather ill-at-ease and trying to conceal the fact by engaging her nurse in an obviously unnatural conversation illumined by startling and irrevelant smiles from herself.

"Well, it's certainly a nice day, Hilda," Dexter heard her say, then she drew down the corners of her mouth, smiled and glanced furtively around, her eyes in transit falling for an instant on Dexter.

Then to the nurse:

"Well, I guess there aren't very many people out here this morning, are there?"

The smile again radiant, blatantly artificial—convincing.

"I don't know what we're supposed to do now," said the nurse, looking nowhere in particular.

"Oh, that's all right"—the smile—"I'll fix it up."

Dexter stood perfectly still, his mouth faintly ajar. He knew that if he moved forward a step his stare would be in her line of vision—if he moved backward he would lose his full view of her face—For a moment he had not realized how young she was. Now he remembered having seen her several times the year before—in bloomers.

Suddenly, involuntarily, he laughed, a short abrupt laugh—then, startled by himself, he turned and began to walk quickly away.

"Boy!"

Dexter stopped.

"Boy—"

Beyond question he was addressed. Not only that, but he was treated to that absurd smile, that preposterous smile—the memory of which at least half a dozen men were to carry to the grave.

"Boy, do you know where the golf teacher is?"

"He's giving a lesson."

"Well, do you know where the caddy-master is?"

"He's not here yet this morning."

"Oh." For a moment this baffled her. She stood alternately on her right and left foot.

"We'd like to get a caddy," said the nurse. "Mrs. Mortimer Jones sent us out to play golf and we don't know how without we get a caddy."

Here she was stopped by an ominous glance from Miss Jones, followed immediately by the smile.

"There aren't any caddies here except me," said Dexter to the nurse. "And I got to stay here in charge until the caddy-master gets here."

"Oh."

Miss Jones and her retinue now withdrew and at a proper distance from Dexter became involved in a heated conversation. The conversation was concluded by Miss Jones taking one of the clubs and hitting it on the ground with violence. For further emphasis she raised it again and was about to bring it down smartly upon the nurse's bosom, when the nurse seized the club and twisted it from her hands.

"You darn *fool!*" cried Miss Jones wildly.

Another argument ensued. Realizing that the elements of the comedy were implied in the scene, Dexter several times began to smile but each time slew the smile before it reached maturity. He could not resist the monstrous conviction that the little girl was justified in beating the nurse.

The situation was resolved by the fortuitous appearance of the caddy-master who was appealed to immediately by the nurse.

"Miss Jones is to have a little caddy and this one says he can't go."

"Mr. McKenna said I was to wait here till you came," said Dexter quickly.

"Well, he's here now." Miss Jones smiled cheerfully at the caddy-master. Then she dropped her bag and set off at a haughty mince toward the first tee.

"Well?" The caddy-master turned to Dexter. "What you standing there like a dummy for? Go pick up the young lady's clubs."

"I don't think I'll go out today," said Dexter.

"You don't—"

"I think I'll quit."

The enormity of his decision frightened him. He was a favorite caddy and the thirty dollars a month he earned through the summer were not to be made elsewhere in Dillard. But he had received a strong emotional shock and his perturbation required a violent and immediate outlet.

It is not so simple as that, either. As so frequently would be the case in the future, Dexter was unconsciously dictated to by his winter dreams.

Now, of course, the quality and the seasonability of these winter dreams varied, but the stuff of them remained. They persuaded Dexter several years later to pass up a business course at the State University—his father, prospering now, would have paid his way—for the precarious advantage of attending an older and more famous university in the East, where he was bothered by his scanty funds. But do not get the impression, because his winter dreams happened to be concerned at first with musings on the rich, that there was anything shoddy in the boy. He wanted not association with glittering things and glittering people—he wanted the glittering things themselves. Often he reached out for the best without knowing why he wanted it—and sometimes he ran up against the mysterious denials and prohibitions in which life indulges. It is with one of those denials and not with his career as a whole that this story deals.

He made money. It was rather amazing. After college he went to the city from which Lake Erminie draws its wealthy patrons. When he was only twenty-three and had been there not quite two years, there were already people who liked to say, "Now *there's* a boy—" All about him rich men's sons were peddling bonds precariously, or investing patrimonies precariously, or plodding through the two dozen volumes of canned rubbish in the "George Washington Commercial Course," but Dexter borrowed a thousand dollars on his college degree and his steady eyes, and bought a partnership in a *laundry*.

It was a small laundry when he went into it. Dexter made a specialty of learning how the English washed fine woolen golf stockings without shrinking them. Inside of a year he was catering to the trade who wore knickerbockers. Men were insisting that their shetland hose and sweaters go to his laundry just as they had insisted on a caddy who could find golf balls. A little later he was doing their wives' lingerie as well—and running five branches in different parts of the city. Before he was twenty-seven he owned the largest string of laundries in his section of the country. It was then that he sold out and went to New York. But the part of his story that concerns us here goes back to when he was making his first big success.

When he was twenty-three Mr. W. L. Hart, one of the grey-haired men who like to say "Now there's a boy"—gave him a guest card to the Lake Erminie Club for over a week-end. So he signed his name one day on the register, and that afternoon played golf in a foursome with Mr. Hart and Mr. Sandwood and Mr. T. A. Hedrick. He did not consider it necessary to remark that he had once carried Mr. Hart's bag over this same links and that he knew every trap and gully with his eyes shut—but he found himself glancing at the four caddies who trailed them, trying to catch a gleam or gesture that would remind him of himself, that would lessen the gap which lay between his past and his future.

It was a curious day, slashed abruptly with fleeting, familiar impressions. One minute he had the sense of being a trespasser—in the next he was impressed by the tremendous superiority he felt toward Mr. T. A. Hedrick, who was a bore and not even a good golfer any more.

Then, because of a ball Mr. Hart lost near the fifteenth green an enormous thing happened. While they were searching the stiff grasses of the rough there was a clear call of "Fore!" from behind a hill in their rear. And as they all turned abruptly from their search a bright new ball sliced abruptly over the hill and caught Mr. T. A. Hedrick rather neatly in the stomach.

Mr. T. A. Hedrick grunted and cursed.

"By Gad!" cried Mr. Hedrick, "they ought to put some of these crazy women off the course. It's getting to be outrageous."

A head and a voice came up together over the hill:

"Do you mind if we go through?"

"You hit me in the stomach!" thundered Mr. Hedrick.

"Did I?" The girl approached the group of men. "I'm sorry. I yelled 'Fore!'"

Her glance fell casually on each of the men. She nodded to Sandwood and then scanned the fairway for her ball.

"Did I bounce off into the rough?"

It was impossible to determine whether this question was ingenuous or malicious. In a moment, however, she left no doubt, for as her partner came up over the hill she called cheerfully.

"Here I am! I'd have gone on the green except that I hit something."

As she took her stance for a short mashie shot, Dexter looked at her closely. She wore a blue gingham dress, rimmed at throat and shoulders with a white edging that accentuated her tan. The quality of exaggeration, of thinness that had made her passionate eyes and down turning mouth absurd at eleven was gone now. She was arrestingly beautiful. The color in her cheeks was centered like the color in a picture—it was not a "high" color, but a sort of fluctuating and feverish warmth, so shaded that it seemed at any moment it would recede and disappear. This color and the mobility of her mouth gave a continual impression of flux, of intense life, of passionate vitality—balanced only partially by the sad luxury of her eyes.

She swung her mashie impatiently and without interest, pitching the ball into a sandpit on the other side of the green. With a quick insincere smile and a careless "Thank you!" she went on after it.

"That Judy Jones!" remarked Mr. Hedrick on the next tee, as they waited—some moments—for her to play on ahead. "All she needs is to be turned up and spanked for six months and then to be married off to an old-fashioned cavalry captain."

"Gosh, she's good looking!" said Mr. Sandwood, who was just over thirty.

"Good-looking!" cried Mr. Hedrick contemptuously. "She always looks as if she wanted to be kissed! Turning those big cow-eyes on every young calf in town!"

It is doubtful if Mr. Hedrick intended a reference to the maternal instinct.

"She'd play pretty good golf if she'd try," said Mr. Sandwood.

"She has no form," said Mr. Hedrick solemnly.

"She has a nice figure," said Mr. Sandwood.

"Better thank the Lord she doesn't drive a swifter ball," said Mr. Hart, winking at Dexter. "Come on. Let's go."

Later in the afternoon the sun went down with a riotous swirl of gold and varying blues and scarlets, and left the dry rustling night of western summer. Dexter watched from the verandah of the Erminie Club, watched the even overlap of the waters in the little wind, silver molasses under the harvest moon. Then the moon held a finger to her lips and the lake became a clear pool, pale and quiet. Dexter put on his bathing suit and swam out to the farthest raft, where he stretched dripping on the wet canvas of the spring board.

There was a fish jumping and a star shining and the lights around the lake were gleaming. Over on a dark peninsula a piano was playing the songs of last summer and of summers before that—songs from "The Pink Lady" and "The Chocolate Soldier" and "Mlle. Modiste"—and because the sound of a piano over a stretch of water had always seemed beautiful to Dexter he lay perfectly quiet and listened.

The tune the piano was playing at that moment had been gay and new five years before when Dexter was a sophomore at college. They had played it at a prom once and because he could not afford the luxury of proms in those days he had stood outside the gymnasium and listened. The sound of the tune and the splash of the fish jumping precipitated in him a sort of ecstasy and it was with that ecstasy he viewed what happened to him now. The ecstasy was a gorgeous appreciation. It was his sense that, for once, he was magnificently atune to life and that everything about him was radiating a brightness and a glamor he might never know again.

A low pale oblong detached itself suddenly from the darkness of the peninsula, spitting forth the reverberate sound of a racing motorboat. Two white streamers of cleft water rolled themselves out behind it and almost immediately the boat was beside him, drowning out the hot tinkle of the piano in the drone of its spray. Dexter raising himself on his arms was aware of a figure standing at the wheel, of two dark eyes regarding him over the lengthening space of water—then the boat had gone by and was sweeping in an immense and purposeless circle of spray round and round in the middle of the lake. With equal eccentricity one of the circles flattened out and headed back toward the raft.

"Who's that?" she called, shutting off the motor. She was so near now that Dexter could see her bathing suit, which consisted apparently of pink rompers. "Oh—you're one of the men I hit in the stomach."

The nose of the boat bumped the raft. After an inexpert struggle, Dexter managed to twist the line around a two-by-four. Then the raft tilted rakishly as she sprung on.

"Well, kiddo," she said huskily, "do you"—she broke off. She had sat herself upon the springboard, found it damp and jumped up quickly,—"do you want to go surf-board riding?"

He indicated that he would be delighted.

"The name is Judy Jones. Ghastly reputation but enormously popular." She favored him with an absurd smirk—rather, what tried to be a smirk, for, twist her mouth as she might, it was not grotesque, it was merely beautiful. "See that house over on the peninsula?"

"No."

"Well, there's a house there that I live in only you can't see it because it's too dark. And in that house there is a fella waiting for me. When he drove up by the door I drove out by the dock because he has watery eyes and asks me if I have an ideal."

There was a fish jumping and a star shining and the lights around the lake were gleaming. Dexter sat beside Judy Jones and she explained how her boat was driven. Then she was in the water, swimming to the floating surf-board with exquisite crawl. Watching her was as without effort to the eye as watching a branch waving or a sea-gull flying. Her arms, burned to butternut, moved sinuously among the dull platinum ripples, elbow appearing first, casting the forearm back with a cadence of falling water, then reaching out and down stabbing a path ahead.

They moved out into the lake and, turning, Dexter saw that she was kneeling on the low rear of the now up-tilted surf-board.

"Go faster," she called, "fast as it'll go."

Obediently he jammed the lever forward and the white spray mounted at the bow. When he looked around again the girl was standing up on the rushing board, her arms spread ecstatically, her eyes lifted toward the moon.

"It's awful cold, kiddo," she shouted. "What's your name anyways?"

"The name is Dexter Green. Would it amuse you to know how good you look back there?"

"Yes," she shouted, "it would amuse me. Except that I'm too cold. Come to dinner tomorrow night."

He kept thinking how glad he was that he had never caddied for this girl. The damp gingham clinging made her like a statue and turned her intense mobility to immobility at last.

"—At seven o'clock," she shouted, "Judy Jones, Girl, who hit man in stomach. Better write it down,"—and then, "Faster—oh, faster!"

Had he been as calm inwardly as he was in appearance, Dexter would have had time to examine his surroundings in detail. He received, however, an enduring impression that the house was the most elaborate he had ever seen. He had known for a long time that it was the finest on Lake Erminie, with a Pompeiian swimming pool and twelve acres of lawn and garden. But what gave it an air of breathless intensity was the sense that it was inhabited by Judy Jones—that it was as casual a thing to her as the little house in the village had once been to Dexter. There was a feeling of mystery in it, of bedrooms upstairs more beautiful and strange than other bedrooms, of gay and radiant activities taking place through these deep corridors and of romances that were not musty and laid already in lavender, but were fresh and breathing and set forth in rich motor cars and in great dances whose flowers were scarcely withered. They were more real because he could feel them all about him, pervading the air with the shades and echoes of still vibrant emotion.

And so while he waited for her to appear he peopled the soft deep summer room and the sun porch that opened from it with the men who had already loved Judy Jones. He knew the sort of men they were—the men who when he first went to college had entered from the great prep-schools with graceful clothes and the deep tan of healthy summer, who did nothing or anything with the same debonaire ease.

Dexter had seen that, in one sense, he was better than these men. He was newer and stronger. Yet in acknowledging to himself that he wished his children to be like them he was admitting that he was but the rough, strong stuff from which this graceful aristocracy eternally sprang.

When, a year before, the time had come when he could wear good clothes, he had known who were the best tailors in America, and the best tailor in America had made him the suit he wore this evening. He had acquired that particular reserve peculiar to his university, that set it off from other universities. He recognized the value to him of such a mannerism and he had adopted it; he knew that to be careless in dress and manner required more confidence than to be careful. But carelessness was for his children. His mother's name had been Krimslich. She was a Bohemian[1] of the peasant class and she had talked broken English to the end of her days. Her son must keep to the set patterns.

He waited for Judy Jones in her house, and he saw these other young men around him. It excited him that many men had loved her. It increased her value in his eyes.

At a little after seven Judy Jones came downstairs. She wore a blue silk afternoon dress. He was disappointed at first that she had not put on something more elaborate, and this feeling was accentuated when, after a brief greeting, she went to the door of a butler's pantry and pushing it open called: "You can have dinner, Martha." He had rather expected that a butler would announce dinner, that there would be a cocktail perhaps. It even offended him that she should know the maid's name.

Then he put these thoughts behind him as they sat down together on a chintz-covered lounge.

"Father and mother won't be here," she said.

"Ought I to be sorry?"

"They're really quite nice," she confessed, as if it had just occurred to her. "I think my father's the best looking man of his age I've ever seen. And mother looks about thirty."

He remembered the last time he had seen her father, and found he was glad the parents were not to be here tonight. They would wonder who he was. He had been born in Keeble, a Minnesota village fifty miles farther north and he always gave Keeble as his home instead of Dillard. Country towns were well enough to come from if they weren't inconveniently in sight and used as foot-stools by fashionable lakes.

Before dinner he found the conversation unsatisfactory. The beautiful Judy seemed faintly irritable—as much so as it was possible to be with a comparative stranger. They discussed Lake Erminie and its golf course, the surf-board riding of the night before and the cold she had caught, which made her voice more husky and charming than ever. They talked of his university which she had visited frequently during the past two years, and of the nearby city which supplied Lake Erminie with its patrons and whither Dexter would return next day to his prospering laundries.

During dinner she slipped into a moody depression which gave Dexter a feeling of guilt. Whatever petulance she uttered in her throaty voice worried him. Whatever she smiled at—at him, at a silver fork, at nothing—, it disturbed him that her smile could have no root in mirth, or even in amusement. When the red corners of her lips curved down, it was less a smile than an invitation to a kiss.

Then, after dinner, she led him out on the dark sun-porch and deliberately changed the atmosphere.

"Do I seem gloomy?" she demanded.

"No, but I'm afraid I'm boring you," he answered quickly.

1. Native of Bohemia, in the Czech Republic.

"You're not. I like you. But I've just had rather an unpleasant afternoon. There was a—man I cared about. He told me out of a clear sky that he was poor as a church-mouse. He'd never even hinted it before. Does this sound horribly mundane?"

"Perhaps he was afraid to tell you."

"I suppose he was," she answered thoughtfully. "He didn't start right. You see, if I'd thought of him as poor—well, I've been mad about loads of poor men, and fully intended to marry them all. But in this case, I hadn't thought of him that way and my interest in him wasn't strong enough to survive the shock."

"I know. As if a girl calmly informed her fiancé that she was a widow. He might not object to widows, but——"

"Let's start right," she suggested suddenly. "Who are you, anyhow?"

For a moment Dexter hesitated. There were two versions of his life that he could tell. There was Dillard and his caddying and his struggle through college, or——

"I'm nobody," he announced. "My career is largely a matter of futures."

"Are you poor?"

"No," he said frankly, "I'm probably making more money than any man my age in the northwest. I know that's an obnoxious remark, but you advised me to start right."

There was a pause. She smiled, and with a touch of amusement.

"You sound like a man in a play."

"It's your fault. You tempted me into being assertive."

Suddenly she turned her dark eyes directly upon him and the corners of her mouth drooped until her face seemed to open like a flower. He dared scarcely to breathe, he had the sense that she was exerting some force upon him; making him overwhelmingly conscious of the youth and mystery that wealth imprisons and preserves, the freshness of many clothes, of cool rooms and gleaming things, safe and proud above the hot struggles of the poor.

The porch was bright with the bought luxury of starshine. The wicker of the settee squeaked fashionably when he put his arm around her, commanded by her eyes. He kissed her curious and lovely mouth and committed himself to the following of a grail.

It began like that—and continued, with varying shades of intensity, on such a note right up to the dénouement. Dexter surrendered a part of himself to the most direct and unprincipled personality with which he had ever come in contact. Whatever the beautiful Judy Jones desired, she went after with the full pressure of her charm. There was no divergence of method, no jockeying for position or premeditation of effects—there was very little mental quality in any of her affairs. She simply made men conscious to the highest degree of her physical loveliness.

Dexter had no desire to change her. Her deficiencies were knit up with a passionate energy that transcended and justified them.

When, as Judy's head lay against his shoulder that first night, she whispered:

"I don't know what's the matter with me. Last night I thought I was in love with a man and tonight I think I'm in love with you—"

—it seemed to him a beautiful and romantic thing to say. It was the exquisite excitability that for the moment he controlled and owned. But a week later he was compelled to view this same quality in a different light. She took him in her roadster to a picnic supper and after supper she disappeared, likewise in her roadster, with another man. Dexter became enormously upset and was scarcely able to be decently civil to the other people present. When she assured him that she had not kissed the other man he knew she was lying—yet he was glad that she had taken the trouble to lie to him.

He was, as he found before the summer ended, one of a dozen, a varying dozen, who circulated about her. Each of them had at one time been favored above all others—about half of them still basked in the solace of occasional sentimental revivals. Whenever one showed signs of dropping out through long neglect she granted him a brief honeyed hour which encouraged him to tag along for a year or so longer. Judy made these forays upon the helpless and defeated without malice, indeed half unconscious that there was anything mischievous in what she did.

When a new man came to town everyone dropped out—dates were automatically cancelled.

The helpless part of trying to do anything about it was that she did it all herself. She was not a girl who could be "won" in the kinetic sense—she was proof against cleverness, she was proof against charm, if any of these assailed her too strongly she would immediately resolve the affair to a physical basis and under the magic of her physical splendor the strong as well as the brilliant played her game and not their own. She was entertained only by the gratification of her desires and by the direct exercise of her own charm. Perhaps from so much youthful love, so many youthful lovers she had come, in self defense, to nourish herself wholly from within.

Succeeding Dexter's first exhilaration came restlessness and dissatisfaction. The helpless ecstasy of losing himself in her charm was a powerful opiate rather than a tonic. It was fortunate for his work during the winter that those moments of ecstasy came infrequently. Early in their acquaintance it had seemed for a while that there was a deep and spontaneous mutual attraction—that first August for example—three days of long evenings on her dusky verandah, of strange wan kisses through the late afternoon, in shadowy alcoves or behind the protecting trellises of the garden arbors, of mornings when she was fresh as a dream and almost shy at meeting him in the clarity of the rising day. There was all the ecstasy of an engagement about it, sharpened by his realization that there was no engagement. It was during those three days that, for the first time, he had asked her to marry him. She said "maybe some day," she said "kiss me," she said "I'd like to marry you," she said "I love you,"—she said—nothing.

The three days were interrupted by the arrival of a New York man who visited the Jones' for half September. To Dexter's agony, rumor engaged them. The man was the son of the president of a great trust company. But at the end of a month it was reported that Judy was yawning. At a dance one night she sat all evening in a motor boat with an old beau, while the New Yorker searched the club for her frantically. She told the old beau that she was bored with her visitor and two days later he left. She was seen with him at the station and it was reported that he looked very mournful indeed.

On this note the summer ended. Dexter was twenty-four and he found himself increasingly in a position to do as he wished. He joined two clubs in the city and lived at one of them. Though he was by no means an integral part of the stag-lines at these clubs he managed to be on hand at dances where Judy Jones was likely to appear. He could have gone out socially as much as he liked—he was an eligible young man, now, and popular with downtown fathers. His confessed devotion to Judy Jones had rather solidified his position. But he had no social aspirations and rather despised the dancing men who were always on tap for the Thursday or Saturday parties and who filled in at dinners with the younger married set. Already he was playing with the idea of going East to New York. He wanted to take Judy Jones with him. No disillusion as to the world in which she had grown up could cure his illusion as to her desirability.

Remember that—for only in the light of it can what he did for her be understood.

Eighteen months after he first met Judy Jones he became engaged to another girl. Her name was Irene Scheerer and her father was one of the men who had always believed in Dexter. Irene was light haired and sweet and honorable and a little stout and she had two beaus whom she pleasantly relinquished when Dexter formally asked her to marry him.

Summer, fall, winter, spring, another summer, another fall—so much he had given of his active life to the curved lips of Judy Jones. She had treated him with interest, with encouragement, with malice, with indifference, with contempt. She had inflicted on him the innumerable little slights and indignities possible in such a case—as if in revenge for having ever cared for him at all. She had beckoned him and yawned at him and beckoned him again and he had responded often with bitterness and narrowed eyes. She had brought him ecstatic happiness and intolerable agony of spirit. She had caused him untold inconvenience and not a little trouble. She had insulted him and she had ridden over him and she had played his interest in her against his interest in his work—for fun. She had done everything to him except to criticize him—this she had not done—it seemed to him only because it might have sullied the utter indifference she manifested and sincerely felt toward him.

When autumn had come and gone again it occurred to him that he could not have Judy Jones. He had to beat this into his mind but he convinced himself at last. He lay awake at night for a while and argued it over. He told himself the trouble and the pain she had caused him, he enumerated her glaring deficiencies as a wife. Then he said to himself that he loved her and after a while he fell asleep. For a week, lest he imagine her husky voice over the telephone or her eyes opposite him at lunch, he worked hard and late and at night he went to his office and plotted out his years.

At the end of a week he went to a dance and cut in on her once. For almost the first time since they had met he did not ask her to sit out with him or tell her that she was lovely. It hurt him that she did not miss these things—that was all. He was not jealous when he saw that there was a new man tonight. He had been hardened against jealousy long before.

He stayed late at the dance. He sat for an hour with Irene Scheerer and talked about books and about music. He knew very little about either. But he was beginning to be master of his own time now and he had a rather priggish notion that he—the young and already fabulously successful Dexter Green—should know more about such things.

That was in October when he was twenty-five. In January Dexter and Irene became engaged. It was to be announced in June and they were to be married three months later.

The Minnesota winter prolonged itself interminably and it was almost May when the winds came soft and the snow ran down into Lake Erminie at last. For the first time in over a year Dexter was enjoying a certain tranquility of spirit. Judy Jones had been in Florida and afterwards in Hot Springs and somewhere she had been engaged and somewhere she had broken it off. At first, when Dexter had definitely given her up, it had made him sad that people still linked them together and asked for news of her, but when he began to be placed at dinner next to Irene Scheerer people didn't ask him about her any more—they told him about her. He ceased to be an authority on her.

May at last. Dexter walked the streets at night when the darkness was damp as rain, wondering that so soon, with so little done, so much of ecstasy had gone from him. May one year back had been marked by Judy's poignant, unforgivable, yet forgiven turbulence—it had been one of those rare times when he fancied she had grown to care for him. That old penny's worth of happiness he had spent for this bushel of content. He knew that Irene would be no more than a curtain spread behind him, a hand moving among gleaming tea cups, a voice calling to children . . . fire and loveliness were gone, magic of night and the hushed wonder of the hours and seasons . . . slender lips, down turning, dropping to his lips like poppy petals, bearing him up into a heaven of eyes . . . a haunting gesture, light of a warm lamp on her hair. The thing was deep in him. He was too strong, too alive for it to die lightly.

In the middle of May when the weather balanced for a few days on the thin bridge that led to deep summer he turned in one night at Irene's house. Their engagement was to be announced in a week now—no one would be surprised at it. And tonight they would sit together on the lounge at the College Club and look on for an hour at the dancers. It gave him a sense of solidity to go with her—. She was so sturdily popular, so intensely a "good egg."

He mounted the steps of the brown stone house and stepped inside.

"Irene," he called.

Mrs. Scheerer came out of the living room to meet him.

"Dexter," she said. "Irene's gone upstairs with a splitting headache. She wanted to go with you but I made her go to bed."

"Nothing serious I—"

"Oh, no. She's going to play golf with you in the morning. You can spare her for just one night, can't you, Dexter?"

Her smile was kind. She and Dexter liked each other. In the living room he talked for a moment before he said goodnight.

Returning to the College Club, where he had rooms, he stood in the doorway for a moment and watched the dancers. He leaned against the door post, nodded at a man or two—yawned.

"Hello, kiddo."

The familiar voice at his elbow startled him. Judy Jones had left a man and crossed the room to him—Judy Jones, a slender enamelled doll in cloth of gold, gold in a band at her head, gold in two slipper points at her dress's hem. The fragile glow of her face seemed to blossom as she smiled at him. A breeze of warmth and light blew through the room. His hands in the pockets of his dinner jacket tightened spasmodically. He was filled with a sudden excitement.

"When did you get back?" he asked casually.

"Come here and I'll tell you about it."

She turned and he followed her. She had been away—he could have wept at the wonder of her return. She had passed through enchanted streets, doing young things that were like plaintive music. All mysterious happenings, all fresh and quickening hopes, had gone away with her, come back with her now.

She turned in the doorway.

"Have you a car here? If you haven't I have."

"I have a coupé."

In then, with a rustle of golden cloth. He slammed the door. Into so many cars she had stepped—like this—like that—her back against the leather, so—her elbow resting on the door—waiting. She would have been soiled long since had there been anything to soil her,—except herself—but these things were all her own outpouring.

With an effort he forced himself to start the car and avoiding her surprised glance backed into the street. This was nothing, he must remember. She had done this before and he had put her behind him, as he would have slashed a bad account from his books.

He drove slowly downtown and affecting a disinterested abstraction traversed the deserted streets of the business section, peopled here and there, where a movie was giving out its crowd or where consumptive or pugilistic youth lounged in front of pool halls. The clink of glasses and the slap of hands on the bars issued from saloons, cloisters of glazed glass and dirty yellow light.

She was watching him closely and the silence was embarrassing yet in this crisis he could find no casual word with which to profane the hour. At a convenient turning he began to zig-zag back toward the College Club.

"Have you missed me?" she asked suddenly.

"Everybody missed you."

He wondered if she knew of Irene Scheerer. She had been back only a day—her absence had been almost contemporaneous with his engagement.

"What a remark!" Judy laughed sadly—without sadness. She looked at him searchingly. He became absorbed for a moment in the dashboard.

"You're handsomer than you used to be," she said thoughtfully. "Dexter, you have the most rememberable eyes."

He could have laughed at this, but he did not laugh. It was the sort of thing that was said to sophomores. Yet it stabbed at him.

"I'm awfully tired of everything, kiddo." She called everyone kiddo, endowing the obsolete slang with careless, individual camaraderie. "I wish you'd marry me."

The directness of this confused him. He should have told her now that he was going to marry another girl but he could not tell her. He could as easily have sworn that he had never loved her.

"I think we'd get along," she continued, on the same note, "unless probably you've forgotten me and fallen in love with another girl."

Her confidence was obviously enormous. She had said, in effect, that she found such a thing impossible to believe, that if it were true he had merely committed a childish indiscretion—and probably to show off. She would forgive him, because it was not a matter of any moment but rather something to be brushed aside lightly.

"Of course you could never love anybody but me," she continued. "I like the way you love me. Oh, Dexter, have you forgotten last year?"

"No, I haven't forgotten."

"Neither have I!"

Was she sincerely moved—or was she carried along by the wave of her own acting?

"I wish we could be like that again," she said, and he forced himself to answer:

"I don't think we can."

"I suppose not. . . . I hear you're giving Irene Scheerer a violent rush."

There was not the faintest emphasis on the name, yet Dexter was suddenly ashamed.

"Oh, take me home," cried Judy suddenly. "I don't want to go back to that idiotic dance—with those children."

Then, as he turned up the street that led to the residence district, Judy began to cry quietly to herself. He had never seen her cry before.

The dark street lightened, the dwellings of the rich loomed up around them, he stopped his coupé in front of the great white bulk of the Mortimer Jones' house, somnolent, gorgeous, drenched with the splendor of the damp moonlight. Its solidity startled him. The strong walls, the fine steel of the girders, the breadth and beam and pomp of it were there only to bring out the contrast with the young beauty beside him. It was sturdy to accentuate her slightness—as if to show what a breeze could be generated by a butterfly's wing.

He sat perfectly quiet, his nerves in wild clamor, afraid that if he moved he would find her irresistibly in his arms. Two tears had rolled down her wet face and trembled on her upper lip.

"I'm more beautiful than anybody else," she said brokenly, "why can't I be happy?" Her moist eyes tore at his stability—mouth turned slowly downward with an exquisite sadness. "I'd like to marry you if you'll have me, Dexter. I suppose you think I'm not worth having but I'll be so beautiful for you, Dexter."

A million phrases of anger, of pride, of passion, of hatred, of tenderness fought on his lips. Then a perfect wave of emotion washed over him, carrying off with it a sediment of wisdom, of convention, of doubt, of honor. This was his girl who was speaking, his own, his beautiful, his pride.

"Won't you come in?" he heard her draw in her breath sharply.

Waiting.

"All right," his voice was trembling, "I'll come in."

It seems strange to say that neither when it was over nor a long time afterward did he regret that night. Looking at it from the perspective of ten years, the fact that Judy's flare for him endured just one month seemed of little importance. Nor did it matter that by his yielding he subjected himself to a deeper agony in the end and gave serious hurt to Irene Scheerer and to

Irene's parents who had befriended him. There was nothing sufficiently pictorial about Irene's grief to stamp itself on his mind.

Dexter was at bottom hard-minded. The attitude of the city on his action was of no importance to him, not because he was going to leave the city, but because any outside attitude on the situation seemed superficial. He was completely indifferent to popular opinion. Nor, when he had seen that it was no use, that he did not possess in himself the power to move fundamentally or to hold Judy Jones, did he bear any malice toward her. He loved her and he would love her until the day he was too old for loving—but he could not have her. So he tasted the deep pain that is reserved only for the strong, just as he had tasted for a little while the deep happiness.

Even the ultimate falsity of the grounds upon which Judy terminated the engagement—that she did not want to "take him away" from Irene, that it—was on her conscience—did not revolt him. He was beyond any revulsion or any amusement.

He went east in February with the intention of selling out his laundries and settling in New York—but the war[2] came to America in March and changed his plans. He returned to the west, handed over the management of the business to his partner and went into the first officers' training camp in late April. He was one of those young thousands who greeted the war with a certain amount of relief, welcoming the liberation from webs of tangled emotion.

This story is not his biography, remember, although things creep into it which have nothing to do with those dreams he had when he was young. We are almost done with them and with him now. There is only one more incident to be related here and it happens seven years farther on.

It took place in New York, where he had done well—so well that there were no barriers too high for him now. He was thirty-two years old, and, except for one flying trip immediately after the war, he had not been west in seven years. A man named Devlin from Detroit came into his office to see him in a business way, and then and there this incident occurred, and closed out, so to speak, this particular side of his life.

"So you're from the middle west," said the man Devlin with careless curiosity. "That's funny—I thought men like you were probably born and raised on Wall Street. You know—wife of one of my best friends in Detroit came from your city. I was an usher at the wedding."

Dexter waited with no apprehension of what was coming. There was a magic that his city would never lose for him. Just as Judy's house had always seemed to him more mysterious and gay than other houses, so his dream of the city itself, now that he had gone from it, was pervaded with a melancholy beauty.

"Judy Simms," said Devlin with no particular interest, "Judy Jones she was once."

"Yes. I knew her." A dull impatience spread over him. He had heard, of course, that she was married,—perhaps deliberately he had heard no more.

"Awfully nice girl," brooded Devlin, meaninglessly, "I'm sort of sorry for her."

"Why?" Something in Dexter was alert, receptive, at once.

2. World War I, which the United States entered in 1917.

"Oh, Joe Simms has gone to pieces in a way. I don't mean he beats her, you understand, or anything like that. But he drinks and runs around—"

"Doesn't she run around?"

"No. Stays at home with her kids."

"Oh."

"She's a little too old for him," said Devlin.

"Too old!" cried Dexter, "why man, she's only twenty-seven."

He was possessed with a wild notion of rushing out into the streets and taking a train to Detroit. He rose to his feet, spasmodically, involuntarily.

"I guess you're busy," Devlin apologized quickly. "I didn't realize—"

"No, I'm not busy," said Dexter, steadying his voice. "I'm not busy at all. Not busy at all. Did you say she was—twenty-seven. No, I said she was twenty-seven."

"Yes, you did," agreed Devlin drily.

"Go on, then. Go on."

"What do you mean?"

"About Judy Jones."

Devlin looked at him helplessly.

"Well, that's—I told you all there is to it. He treats her like the devil. Oh, they're not going to get divorced or anything. When he's particularly outrageous she forgives him. In fact, I'm inclined to think she loves him. She was a pretty girl when she first came to Detroit."

A pretty girl! The phrase struck Dexter as ludicrous.

"Isn't she—a pretty girl any more?"

"Oh, she's all right."

"Look here," said Dexter, sitting down suddenly, "I don't understand. You say she was a 'pretty girl' and now you say she's 'all right.' I don't understand what you mean—Judy Jones wasn't a pretty girl, at all. She was a great beauty. Why, I knew her, I knew her. She was—"

Devlin laughed pleasantly.

"I'm not trying to start a row," he said. "I think Judy's a nice girl and I like her. I can't understand how a man like Joe Simms could fall madly in love with her, but he did." Then he added, "Most of the women like her."

Dexter looked closely at Devlin, thinking wildly that there must be a reason for this, some insensitivity in the man or some private malice.

"Lots of women fade just-like-*that*." Devlin snapped his fingers. "You must have seen it happen. Perhaps I've forgotten how pretty she was at her wedding. I've seen her so much since then, you see. She has nice eyes."

A sort of dullness settled down upon Dexter. For the first time in his life he felt like getting very drunk. He knew that he was laughing loudly at something Devlin had said but he did not know what it was or why it was funny. When Devlin went, in a few minutes, he lay down on his lounge and looked out the window at the New York skyline into which the sun was sinking in dully lovely shades of pink and gold.

He had thought that having nothing else to lose he was invulnerable at last—but he knew that he had just lost something more, as surely as if he had married Judy Jones and seen her fade away before his eyes.

The dream was gone. Something had been taken from him. In a sort of panic he pushed the palms of his hands into his eyes and tried to bring up a picture of the waters lapping at Lake Erminie and the moonlit verandah, and gingham on the golf links and the dry sun and the gold color of her neck's soft down. And her mouth damp to his kisses and her eyes plaintive with melancholy and her freshness like new fine linen in the morning. Why these things were no longer in the world. They had existed and they existed no more.

For the first time in years the tears were streaming down his face. But they were for himself now. He did not care about mouth and eyes and moving hands. He wanted to care and he could not care. For he had gone away and he could never go back any more. The gates were closed, the sun was gone down and there was no beauty but the grey beauty of steel that withstands all time. Even the grief he could have borne was left behind in the country of illusion, of youth, of the richness of life, where his winter dreams had flourished.

"Long ago," he said, "long ago, there was something in me, but now that thing is gone. Now that thing is gone, that thing is gone. I cannot cry. I cannot care. That thing will come back no more."

1922

Babylon Revisited[1]

"And where's Mr. Campbell?" Charlie asked.

"Gone to Switzerland. Mr. Campbell's a pretty sick man, Mr. Wales."

"I'm sorry to hear that. And George Hardt?" Charlie inquired.

"Back in America, gone to work."

"And where is the Snow Bird?"

"He was in here last week. Anyway, his friend, Mr. Schaeffer, is in Paris."

Two familiar names from the long list of a year and a half ago. Charlie scribbled an address in his notebook and tore out the page.

"If you see Mr. Schaeffer, give him this," he said. "It's my brother-in-law's address. I haven't settled on a hotel yet."

He was not really disappointed to find Paris was so empty. But the stillness in the Ritz bar was strange and portentous. It was not an American bar any more—he felt polite in it, and not as if he owned it. It had gone back into France. He felt the stillness from the moment he got out of the taxi and saw the doorman, usually in a frenzy of activity at this hour, gossiping with a *chasseur*[2] by the servants' entrance.

Passing through the corridor, he heard only a single, bored voice in the once-clamorous women's room. When he turned into the bar he traveled the twenty feet of green carpet with his eyes fixed straight ahead by old habit; and then, with his foot firmly on the rail, he turned and surveyed the room, encountering only a single pair of eyes that fluttered up from a newspaper in the corner. Charlie asked for the head barman, Paul, who in the latter days of the bull market had come to work in his own custom-built

1. Babylon was an ancient, prosperous city in Mesopotamia, associated by the Hebrews and Greeks with materialism and sensual pleasure; here, the reference is to Paris, where the story is set in the aftermath of the stock market crash of 1929.

2. Messenger-boy, errand runner (French).

car—disembarking, however, with due nicety at the nearest corner. But Paul was at his country house today and Alix giving him information.

"No, no more," Charlie said, "I'm going slow these days."

Alix congratulated him: "You were going pretty strong a couple of years ago."

"I'll stick to it all right," Charlie assured him. "I've stuck to it for over a year and a half now."

"How do you find conditions in America?"

"I haven't been to America for months. I'm in business in Prague, representing a couple of concerns there. They don't know about me down there."

Alix smiled.

"Remember the night of George Hardt's bachelor dinner here?" said Charlie. "By the way, what's become of Claude Fessenden?"

Alix lowered his voice confidentially: "He's in Paris, but he doesn't come here any more. Paul doesn't allow it. He ran up a bill of thirty thousand francs, charging all his drinks and his lunches, and usually his dinner, for more than a year. And when Paul finally told him he had to pay, he gave him a bad check."

Alix shook his head sadly.

"I don't understand it, such a dandy fellow. Now he's all bloated up—" He made a plump apple of his hands.

Charlie watched a group of strident queens installing themselves in a corner.

"Nothing affects them," he thought. "Stocks rise and fall, people loaf or work, but they go on forever." The place oppressed him. He called for the dice and shook with Alix for the drink.

"Here for long, Mr. Wales?"

"I'm here for four or five days to see my little girl."

"Oh-h! You have a little girl?"

Outside, the fire-red, gas-blue, ghost-green signs shone smokily through the tranquil rain. It was late afternoon and the streets were in movement; the *bistros*[3] gleamed. At the corner of the Boulevard des Capucines he took a taxi. The Place de la Concorde moved by in pink majesty; they crossed the logical Seine, and Charlie felt the sudden provincial quality of the left bank.[4]

Charlie directed his taxi to the Avenue de l'Opera, which was out of his way. But he wanted to see the blue hour spread over the magnificent façade, and imagine that the cab horns, playing endlessly the first few bars of *Le Plus que Lent,*[5] were the trumpets of the Second Empire. They were closing the iron grill in front of Brentano's Book-store, and people were already at dinner behind the trim little bourgeois hedge of Duval's. He had never eaten at a really cheap restaurant in Paris. Five-course dinner, four francs fifty, eighteen cents, wine included. For some odd reason he wished that he had.

As they rolled on to the Left Bank and he felt its sudden provincialism, he thought, "I spoiled this city for myself. I didn't realize it, but the days came along one after another, and then two years were gone, and everything was gone, and I was gone."

3. Small, informal restaurants.

4. Paris is divided by the Seine River; the grander buildings and broader streets are on the Right Bank. To Charlie, the Left Bank is more like a town than a city.

5. I.e., *La Plus que Lente* (More than slow), piano composition by French composer Claude Debussy (1862–1918).

He was thirty-five, and good to look at. The Irish mobility of his face was sobered by a deep wrinkle between his eyes. As he rang his brother-in-law's bell in the Rue Palatine, the wrinkle deepened till it pulled down his brows; he felt a cramping sensation in his belly. From behind the maid who opened the door darted a lovely little girl of nine who shrieked "Daddy!" and flew up, struggling like a fish, into his arms. She pulled his head around by one ear and set her cheek against his.

"My old pie," he said.

"Oh, daddy, daddy, daddy, daddy, dads, dads, dads!"

She drew him into the salon, where the family waited, a boy and a girl his daughter's age, his sister-in-law and her husband. He greeted Marion with his voice pitched carefully to avoid either feigned enthusiasm or dislike, but her response was more frankly tepid, though she minimized her expression of unalterable distrust by directing her regard toward his child. The two men clasped hands in a friendly way and Lincoln Peters rested his for a moment on Charlie's shoulder.

The room was warm and comfortably American. The three children moved intimately about, playing through the yellow oblongs that led to other rooms; the cheer of six o'clock spoke in the eager smacks of the fire and the sounds of French activity in the kitchen. But Charlie did not relax; his heart sat up rigidly in his body and he drew confidence from his daughter, who from time to time came close to him, holding in her arms the doll he had brought.

"Really extremely well," he declared in answer to Lincoln's question. "There's a lot of business there that isn't moving at all, but we're doing even better than ever. In fact, damn well. I'm bringing my sister over from America next month to keep house for me. My income last year was bigger than it was when I had money. You see, the Czechs—"

His boasting was for a specific purpose; but after a moment, seeing a faint restiveness in Lincoln's eye, he changed the subject:

"Those are fine children of yours, well brought up, good manners."

"We think Honoria's a great little girl too."

Marion Peters came back from the kitchen. She was a tall woman with worried eyes, who had once possessed a fresh American loveliness. Charlie had never been sensitive to it and was always surprised when people spoke of how pretty she had been. From the first there had been an instinctive antipathy between them.

"Well, how do you find Honoria?" she asked.

"Wonderful. I was astonished how much she's grown in ten months. All the children are looking well."

"We haven't had a doctor for a year. How do you like being back in Paris?"

"It seems very funny to see so few Americans around."

"I'm delighted," Marion said vehemently. "Now at least you can go into a store without their assuming you're a millionaire. We've suffered like everybody, but on the whole it's a good deal pleasanter."

"But it was nice while it lasted," Charlie said. "We were a sort of royalty, almost infallible, with a sort of magic around us. In the bar this afternoon"—he stumbled, seeing his mistake—"there wasn't a man I knew."

She looked at him keenly. "I should think you'd have had enough of bars."

"I only stayed a minute. I take one drink every afternoon, and no more."

"Don't you want a cocktail before dinner?" Lincoln asked.

"I take only one drink every afternoon, and I've had that."

"I hope you keep to it," said Marion.

Her dislike was evident in the coldness with which she spoke, but Charlie only smiled; he had larger plans. Her very aggressiveness gave him an advantage, and he knew enough to wait. He wanted them to initiate the discussion of what they knew had brought him to Paris.

At dinner he couldn't decide whether Honoria was most like him or her mother. Fortunate if she didn't combine the traits of both that had brought them to disaster. A great wave of protectiveness went over him. He thought he knew what to do for her. He believed in character; he wanted to jump back a whole generation and trust in character again as the eternally valuable element. Everything else wore out.

He left soon after dinner, but not to go home. He was curious to see Paris by night with clearer and more judicious eyes than those of other days. He bought a *strapontin* for the Casino and watched Josephine Baker[6] go through her chocolate arabesques.

After an hour he left and strolled toward Montmartre, up the Rue Pigalle into the Place Blanche. The rain had stopped and there were a few people in evening clothes disembarking from taxis in front of cabarets, and *cocottes*[7] prowling singly or in pairs, and many Negroes. He passed a lighted door from which issued music, and stopped with the sense of familiarity; it was Bricktop's, where he had parted with so many hours and so much money. A few doors farther on he found another ancient rendezvous and incautiously put his head inside. Immediately an eager orchestra burst into sound, a pair of professional dancers leaped to their feet and a maître d'hôtel swooped toward him, crying, "Crowd just arriving, sir!" But he withdrew quickly.

"You have to be damn drunk," he thought.

Zelli's was closed, the bleak and sinister cheap hotels surrounding it were dark; up in the Rue Blanche there was more light and a local, colloquial French crowd. The Poet's Cave had disappeared, but the two great mouths of the Café of Heaven and the Café of Hell still yawned—even devoured, as he watched, the meager contents of a tourist bus—a German, a Japanese, and an American couple who glanced at him with frightened eyes.

So much for the effort and ingenuity of Montmartre. All the catering to vice and waste was on an utterly childish scale, and he suddenly realized the meaning of the word "dissipate"—to dissipate into thin air; to make nothing out of something. In the little hours of the night every move from place to place was an enormous human jump, an increase of paying for the privilege of slower and slower motion.

He remembered thousand-franc notes given to an orchestra for playing a single number, hundred-franc notes tossed to a doorman for calling a cab.

But it hadn't been given for nothing.

It had been given, even the most wildly squandered sum, as an offering to destiny that he might not remember the things most worth remembering, the things that now he would always remember—his child taken from his control, his wife escaped to a grave in Vermont.

6. African American jazz singer and dancer (1906–1975) who arrived in Paris with a vaudeville troupe in 1925 and remained as a star entertainer. "*Strapontin*": folding seat.

7. Coquettes (French, literal trans.); prostitutes.

In the glare of a *brasserie*[8] a woman spoke to him. He bought her some eggs and coffee, and then, eluding her encouraging stare, gave her a twenty-franc note and took a taxi to his hotel.

II

He woke upon a fine fall day—football weather. The depression of yesterday was gone and he liked the people on the streets. At noon he sat opposite Honoria at Le Grand Vatel, the only restaurant he could think of not reminiscent of champagne dinners and long luncheons that began at two and ended in a blurred and vague twilight.

"Now, how about vegetables? Oughtn't you to have some vegetables?"

"Well, yes."

"Here's *épinards* and *chou-fleur* and carrots and *haricots*."[9]

"I'd like *chou-fleur*."

"Wouldn't you like to have two vegetables?"

"I usually only have one at lunch."

The waiter was pretending to be inordinately fond of children. *"Qu'elle est mignonne la petite! Elle parle exactement comme une Française."*[1]

"How about dessert? Shall we wait and see?"

The waiter disappeared. Honoria looked at her father expectantly.

"What are we going to do?"

"First, we're going to that toy store in the Rue Saint-Honoré and buy you anything you like. And then we're going to the vaudeville at the Empire."

She hesitated. "I like it about the vaudeville, but not the toy store."

"Why not?"

"Well, you brought me this doll." She had it with her. "And I've got lots of things. And we're not rich any more, are we?"

"We never were. But today you are to have anything you want."

"All right," she agreed resignedly.

When there had been her mother and a French nurse he had been inclined to be strict; now he extended himself, reached out for a new tolerance; he must be both parents to her and not shut any of her out of communication.

"I want to get to know you," he said gravely. "First let me introduce myself. My name is Charles J. Wales, of Prague."

"Oh, daddy!" her voice cracked with laughter.

"And who are you, please?" he persisted, and she accepted a rôle immediately: "Honoria Wales, Rue Palatine, Paris."

"Married or single?"

"No, not married. Single."

He indicated the doll. "But I see you have a child, madame."

Unwilling to disinherit it, she took it to her heart and thought quickly: "Yes, I've been married, but I'm not married now. My husband is dead."

He went on quickly, "And the child's name?"

"Simone. That's after my best friend at school."

8. Large, plain restaurant specializing in simple meals and beer.

9. Green beans (French). *"Épinards"*: spinach. *"Chou-fleur"*: cauliflower.

1. How cute she is! She speaks exactly like a French girl (French).

"I'm very pleased that you're doing so well at school."

"I'm third this month," she boasted. "Elsie"—that was her cousin—"is only about eighteenth, and Richard is about at the bottom."

"You like Richard and Elsie, don't you?"

"Oh, yes. I like Richard quite well and I like her all right."

Cautiously and casually he asked: "And Aunt Marion and Uncle Lincoln—which do you like best?"

"Oh, Uncle Lincoln, I guess."

He was increasingly aware of her presence. As they came in, a murmur of ". . . adorable" followed them, and now the people at the next table bent all their silences upon her, staring as if she were something no more conscious than a flower.

"Why don't I live with you?" she asked suddenly. "Because mamma's dead?"

"You must stay here and learn more French. It would have been hard for daddy to take care of you so well."

"I don't really need much taking care of any more. I do everything for myself."

Going out of the restaurant, a man and a woman unexpectedly hailed him.

"Well, the old Wales!"

"Hello there, Lorraine. . . . Dunc."

Sudden ghosts out of the past: Duncan Schaeffer, a friend from college. Lorraine Quarrles, a lovely, pale blonde of thirty; one of a crowd who had helped them make months into days in the lavish times of three years ago.

"My husband couldn't come this year," she said, in answer to his question. "We're poor as hell. So he gave me two hundred a month and told me I could do my worst on that. . . . This your little girl?"

"What about coming back and sitting down?" Duncan asked.

"Can't do it." He was glad for an excuse. As always, he felt Lorraine's passionate, provocative attraction, but his own rhythm was different now.

"Well, how about dinner?" she asked.

"I'm not free. Give me your address and let me call you."

"Charlie, I believe you're sober," she said judicially. "I honestly believe he's sober, Dunc. Pinch him and see if he's sober."

Charlie indicated Honoria with his head. They both laughed.

"What's your address?" said Duncan skeptically.

He hesitated, unwilling to give the name of his hotel.

"I'm not settled yet. I'd better call you. We're going to see the vaudeville at the Empire."

"There! That's what I want to do," Lorraine said. "I want to see some clowns and acrobats and jugglers. That's just what we'll do, Dunc."

"We've got to do an errand first," said Charlie. "Perhaps we'll see you there."

"All right, you snob. . . . Good-by, beautiful little girl."

"Good-by."

Honoria bobbed politely.

Somehow, an unwelcome encounter. They liked him because he was functioning, because he was serious; they wanted to see him, because he was stronger than they were now, because they wanted to draw a certain sustenance from his strength.

At the Empire, Honoria proudly refused to sit upon her father's folded coat. She was already an individual with a code of her own, and Charlie was more and more absorbed by the desire of putting a little of himself into her before she crystallized utterly. It was hopeless to try to know her in so short a time.

Between the acts they came upon Duncan and Lorraine in the lobby where the band was playing.

"Have a drink?"

"All right, but not up at the bar. We'll take a table."

"The perfect father."

Listening abstractedly to Lorraine, Charlie watched Honoria's eyes leave their table, and he followed them wistfully about the room, wondering what they saw. He met her glance and she smiled.

"I liked that lemonade," she said.

What had she said? What had he expected? Going home in a taxi afterward, he pulled her over until her head rested against his chest.

"Darling, do you ever think about your mother?"

"Yes, sometimes," she answered vaguely.

"I don't want you to forget her. Have you got a picture of her?"

"Yes, I think so. Anyhow, Aunt Marion has. Why don't you want me to forget her?"

"She loved you very much."

"I loved her too."

They were silent for a moment.

"Daddy, I want to come and live with you," she said suddenly.

His heart leaped; he had wanted it to come like this.

"Aren't you perfectly happy?"

"Yes, but I love you better than anybody. And you love me better than anybody, don't you, now that mummy's dead?"

"Of course I do. But you won't always like me best, honey. You'll grow up and meet somebody your own age and go marry him and forget you ever had a daddy."

"Yes, that's true," she agreed tranquilly.

He didn't go in. He was coming back at nine o'clock and he wanted to keep himself fresh and new for the thing he must say then.

"When you're safe inside, just show yourself in that window."

"All right. Good-by, dads, dads, dads, dads."

He waited in the dark street until she appeared, all warm and glowing, in the window above and kissed her fingers out into the night.

III

They were waiting. Marion sat behind the coffee service in a dignified black dinner dress that just faintly suggested mourning. Lincoln was walking up and down with the animation of one who had already been talking. They were as anxious as he was to get into the question. He opened it almost immediately:

"I suppose you know what I want to see you about—why I really came to Paris."

Marion played with the black stars on her necklace and frowned.

"I'm awfully anxious to have a home," he continued. "And I'm awfully anxious to have Honoria in it. I appreciate your taking in Honoria for her mother's sake, but things have changed now"—he hesitated and then continued more forcibly—"changed radically with me, and I want to ask you to reconsider the matter. It would be silly for me to deny that about three years ago I was acting badly—"

Marion looked up at him with hard eyes.

"—but all that's over. As I told you, I haven't had more than a drink a day for over a year, and I take that drink deliberately, so that the idea of alcohol won't get too big in my imagination. You see the idea?"

"No," said Marion succinctly.

"It's a sort of stunt I set myself. It keeps the matter in proportion."

"I get you," said Lincoln. "You don't want to admit it's got any attraction for you."

"Something like that. Sometimes I forget and don't take it. But I try to take it. Anyhow, I couldn't afford to drink in my position. The people I represent are more than satisfied with what I've done, and I'm bringing my sister over from Burlington to keep house for me, and I want awfully to have Honoria too. You know that even when her mother and I weren't getting along well we never let anything that happened touch Honoria. I know she's fond of me and I know I'm able to take care of her and—well, there you are. How do you feel about it?"

He knew that now he would have to take a beating. It would last an hour or two hours, and it would be difficult, but if he modulated his inevitable resentment to the chastened attitude of the reformed sinner, he might win his point in the end.

Keep your temper, he told himself. You don't want to be justified. You want Honoria.

Lincoln spoke first: "We've been talking it over ever since we got your letter last month. We're happy to have Honoria here. She's a dear little thing, and we're glad to be able to help her, but of course that isn't the question—"

Marion interrupted suddenly. "How long are you going to stay sober, Charlie?" she asked.

"Permanently, I hope."

"How can anybody count on that?"

"You know I never did drink heavily until I gave up business and came over here with nothing to do. Then Helen and I began to run around with—"

"Please leave Helen out of it. I can't bear to hear you talk about her like that."

He stared at her grimly; he had never been certain how fond of each other the sisters were in life.

"My drinking only lasted about a year and a half—from the time we came over until I—collapsed."

"It was time enough."

"It was time enough," he agreed.

"My duty is entirely to Helen," she said. "I try to think what she would have wanted me to do. Frankly, from the night you did that terrible thing you haven't really existed for me. I can't help that. She was my sister."

"Yes."

"When she was dying she asked me to look out for Honoria. If you hadn't been in a sanitarium then, it might have helped matters."

He had no answer.

"I'll never in my life be able to forget the morning when Helen knocked at my door, soaked to the skin and shivering and said you'd locked her out."

Charlie gripped the sides of the chair. This was more difficult than he expected; he wanted to launch out into a long expostulation and explanation, but he only said: "The night I locked her out—" and she interrupted, "I don't feel up to going over that again."

After a moment's silence Lincoln said: "We're getting off the subject. You want Marion to set aside her legal guardianship and give you Honoria. I think the main point for her is whether she has confidence in you or not."

"I don't blame Marion," Charlie said slowly, "but I think she can have entire confidence in me. I had a good record up to three years ago. Of course, it's within human possibilities I might go wrong any time. But if we wait much longer I'll lose Honoria's childhood and my chance for a home." He shook his head, "I'll simply lose her, don't you see?"

"Yes, I see," said Lincoln.

"Why didn't you think of all this before?" Marion asked.

"I suppose I did, from time to time, but Helen and I were getting along badly. When I consented to the guardianship, I was flat on my back in a sanitarium and the market had cleaned me out. I knew I'd acted badly, and I thought if it would bring any peace to Helen, I'd agree to anything. But now it's different. I'm functioning, I'm behaving damn well, so far as—"

"Please don't swear at me," Marion said.

He looked at her, startled. With each remark the force of her dislike became more and more apparent. She had built up all her fear of life into one wall and faced it toward him. This trivial reproof was possibly the result of some trouble with the cook several hours before. Charlie became increasingly alarmed at leaving Honoria in this atmosphere of hostility against himself; sooner or later it would come out, in a word here, a shake of the head there, and some of that distrust would be irrevocably implanted in Honoria. But he pulled his temper down out of his face and shut it up inside him; he had won a point, for Lincoln realized the absurdity of Marion's remark and asked her lightly since when she had objected to the word "damn."

"Another thing," Charlie said: "I'm able to give her certain advantages now. I'm going to take a French governess to Prague with me. I've got a lease on a new apartment—"

He stopped, realizing that he was blundering. They couldn't be expected to accept with equanimity the fact that his income was again twice as large as their own.

"I suppose you can give her more luxuries than we can," said Marion. "When you were throwing away money we were living along watching every ten francs. . . . I suppose you'll start doing it again."

"Oh, no," he said. "I've learned. I worked hard for ten years, you know—until I got lucky in the market, like so many people. Terribly lucky. It won't happen again."

There was a long silence. All of them felt their nerves straining, and for the first time in a year Charlie wanted a drink. He was sure now that Lincoln Peters wanted him to have his child.

Marion shuddered suddenly; part of her saw that Charlie's feet were planted on the earth now, and her own maternal feeling recognized the naturalness of his desire; but she had lived for a long time with a prejudice—a prejudice founded on a curious disbelief in her sister's happiness, and which, in the shock of one terrible night, had turned to hatred for him. It had all happened at a point in her life where the discouragement of ill health and adverse circumstances made it necessary for her to believe in tangible villainy and a tangible villain.

"I can't help what I think!" she cried out suddenly. "How much you were responsible for Helen's death, I don't know. It's something you'll have to square with your own conscience."

An electric current of agony surged through him; for a moment he was almost on his feet, an unuttered sound echoing in his throat. He hung on to himself for a moment, another moment.

"Hold on there," said Lincoln uncomfortably. "I never thought you were responsible for that."

"Helen died of heart trouble," Charlie said dully.

"Yes, heart trouble." Marion spoke as if the phrase had another meaning for her.

Then, in the flatness that followed her outburst, she saw him plainly and she knew he had somehow arrived at control over the situation. Glancing at her husband, she found no help from him, and as abruptly as if it were a matter of no importance, she threw up the sponge.

"Do what you like!" she cried, springing up from her chair. "She's your child. I'm not the person to stand in your way. I think if it were my child I'd rather see her—" She managed to check herself. "You two decide it. I can't stand this. I'm sick. I'm going to bed."

She hurried from the room; after a moment Lincoln said:

"This has been a hard day for her. You know how strongly she feels—" His voice was almost apologetic: "When a woman gets an idea in her head."

"Of course."

"It's going to be all right. I think she sees now that you—can provide for the child, and so we can't very well stand in your way or Honoria's way."

"Thank you, Lincoln."

"I'd better go along and see how she is."

"I'm going."

He was still trembling when he reached the street, but a walk down the Rue Bonaparte to the *quais*[2] set him up, and as he crossed the Seine, fresh and new by the *quai* lamps, he felt exultant. But back in his room he couldn't sleep. The image of Helen haunted him. Helen whom he had loved so until they had senselessly begun to abuse each other's love, tear it into shreds. On that terrible February night that Marion remembered so vividly, a slow quarrel had gone on for hours. There was a scene at the Florida, and then he attempted to take her home, and then she kissed young Webb at a table; after that there was what she had hysterically said. When he arrived home alone he turned the key in the lock in wild anger. How could he know she would arrive an hour later alone, that there would be a snowstorm in which she wandered about in slippers, too confused to find a taxi? Then the

2. Quays (French); a section of the Left Bank is lined with quays, or walking places along the river.

aftermath, her escaping pneumonia by a miracle, and all the attendant horror. They were "reconciled," but that was the beginning of the end, and Marion, who had seen with her own eyes and who imagined it to be one of many scenes from her sister's martyrdom, never forgot.

Going over it again brought Helen nearer, and in the white, soft light that steals upon half sleep near morning he found himself talking to her again. She said that he was perfectly right about Honoria and that she wanted Honoria to be with him. She said she was glad he was being good and doing better. She said a lot of other things—very friendly things—but she was in a swing in a white dress, and swinging faster and faster all the time, so that at the end he could not hear clearly all that she said.

IV

He woke up feeling happy. The door of the world was open again. He made plans, vistas, futures for Honoria and himself, but suddenly he grew sad, remembering all the plans he and Helen had made. She had not planned to die. The present was the thing—work to do and someone to love. But not to love too much, for he knew the injury that a father can do to a daughter or a mother to a son by attaching them too closely: afterward, out in the world, the child would seek in the marriage partner the same blind tenderness and, failing probably to find it, turn against love and life.

It was another bright, crisp day. He called Lincoln Peters at the bank where he worked and asked if he could count on taking Honoria when he left for Prague. Lincoln agreed that there was no reason for delay. One thing—the legal guardianship. Marion wanted to retain that a while longer. She was upset by the whole matter, and it would oil things if she felt that the situation was still in her control for another year. Charlie agreed, wanting only the tangible, visible child.

Then the question of a governess. Charles sat in a gloomy agency and talked to a cross Béarnaise and to a buxom Breton peasant,[3] neither of whom he could have endured. There were others whom he would see tomorrow.

He lunched with Lincoln Peters at Griffons, trying to keep down his exultation.

"There's nothing quite like your own child," Lincoln said. "But you understand how Marion feels too."

"She's forgotten how hard I worked for seven years there," Charlie said. "She just remembers one night."

"There's another thing." Lincoln hesitated. "While you and Helen were tearing around Europe throwing money away, we were just getting along. I didn't touch any of the prosperity because I never got ahead enough to carry anything but my insurance. I think Marion felt there was some kind of injustice in it—you not even working toward the end, and getting richer and richer."

"It went just as quick as it came," said Charlie.

3. Béarn and Breton are two French provincial regions. The implication is that Charlie wants a higher-class (preferably Parisian) governess.

"Yes, a lot of it stayed in the hands of *chasseurs* and saxophone players and maîtres d'hôtel—well, the big party's over now. I just said that to explain Marion's feeling about those crazy years. If you drop in about six o'clock tonight before Marion's too tired, we'll settle the details on the spot."

Back at his hotel, Charlie found a *pneumatique* that had been redirected from the Ritz bar where Charlie had left his address for the purpose of finding a certain man.

> "DEAR CHARLIE: You were so strange when we saw you the other day that I wondered if I did something to offend you. If so, I'm not conscious of it. In fact, I have thought about you too much for the last year, and it's always been in the back of my mind that I might see you if I came over here. We *did* have such good times that crazy spring, like the night you and I stole the butcher's tricycle, and the time we tried to call on the president and you had the old derby rim and the wire cane. Everybody seems so old lately, but I don't feel old a bit. Couldn't we get together some time today for old time's sake? I've got a vile hang-over for the moment, but will be feeling better this afternoon and will look for you about five in the sweatshop at the Ritz.
>
> "Always devotedly,
> LORRAINE."

His first feeling was one of awe that he had actually, in his mature years, stolen a tricycle and pedaled Lorraine all over the Étoile between the small hours and dawn. In retrospect it was a nightmare. Locking out Helen didn't fit in with any other act of his life, but the tricycle incident did—it was one of many. How many weeks or months of dissipation to arrive at that condition of utter irresponsibility?

He tried to picture how Lorraine had appeared to him then—very attractive; Helen was unhappy about it, though she said nothing. Yesterday, in the restaurant, Lorraine had seemed trite, blurred, worn away. He emphatically did not want to see her, and he was glad Alix had not given away his hotel address. It was a relief to think, instead, of Honoria, to think of Sundays spent with her and of saying good morning to her and of knowing she was there in his house at night, drawing her breath in the darkness.

At five he took a taxi and bought presents for all the Peters—a piquant cloth doll, a box of Roman soldiers, flowers for Marion, big linen handkerchiefs for Lincoln.

He saw, when he arrived in the apartment, that Marion had accepted the inevitable. She greeted him now as though he were a recalcitrant member of the family, rather than a menacing outsider. Honoria had been told she was going; Charlie was glad to see that her tact made her conceal her excessive happiness. Only on his lap did she whisper her delight and the question "When?" before she slipped away with the other children.

He and Marion were alone for a minute in the room, and on an impulse he spoke out boldly:

"Family quarrels are bitter things. They don't go according to any rules. They're not like aches or wounds; they're more like splits in the skin that won't heal because there's not enough material. I wish you and I could be on better terms."

"Some things are hard to forget," she answered. "It's a question of confidence." There was no answer to this and presently she asked, "When do you propose to take her?"

"As soon as I can get a governess. I hoped the day after tomorrow."

"That's impossible. I've got to get her things in shape. Not before Saturday."

He yielded. Coming back into the room, Lincoln offered him a drink.

"I'll take my daily whisky," he said.

It was warm here, it was a home, people together by a fire. The children felt very safe and important; the mother and father were serious, watchful. They had things to do for the children more important than his visit here. A spoonful of medicine was, after all, more important than the strained relations between Marion and himself. They were not dull people, but they were very much in the grip of life and circumstances. He wondered if he couldn't do something to get Lincoln out of his rut at the bank.

A long peal at the door-bell; the *bonne à tout faire*[4] passed through and went down the corridor. The door opened upon another long ring, and then voices, and the three in the salon looked up expectantly; Richard moved to bring the corridor within his range of vision, and Marion rose. Then the maid came back along the corridor, closely followed by the voices, which developed under the light into Duncan Schaeffer and Lorraine Quarrles.

They were gay, they were hilarious, they were roaring with laughter. For a moment Charlie was astounded; unable to understand how they ferreted out the Peters' address.

"Ah-h-h!" Duncan wagged his finger roguishly at Charlie. "Ah-h-h!"

They both slid down another cascade of laughter. Anxious and at a loss, Charlie shook hands with them quickly and presented them to Lincoln and Marion. Marion nodded, scarcely speaking. She had drawn back a step toward the fire; her little girl stood beside her, and Marion put an arm about her shoulder.

With growing annoyance at the intrusion, Charlie waited for them to explain themselves. After some concentration Duncan said:

"We came to invite you out to dinner. Lorraine and I insist that all this shishi, cagy business 'bout your address got to stop."

Charlie came closer to them, as if to force them backward down the corridor.

"Sorry, but I can't. Tell me where you'll be and I'll phone you in half an hour."

This made no impression. Lorraine sat down suddenly on the side of a chair, and focusing her eyes on Richard, cried, "Oh, what a nice little boy! Come here, little boy." Richard glanced at his mother, but did not move. With a perceptible shrug of her shoulders, Lorraine turned back to Charlie:

"Come and dine. Sure your cousins won' mine. See you so sel'om. Or solemn."

"I can't," said Charlie sharply. "You two have dinner and I'll phone you."

4. Maid of all work (French). The Peters family cannot afford to hire several servants with specialized tasks.

Her voice became suddenly unpleasant. "All right, we'll go. But I remember once when you hammered on my door at four A.M. I was enough of a good sport to give you a drink. Come on, Dunc."

Still in slow motion, with blurred, angry faces, with uncertain feet, they retired along the corridor.

"Good night," Charlie said.

"Good night!" responded Lorraine emphatically.

When he went back into the salon Marion had not moved, only now her son was standing in the circle of her other arm. Lincoln was still swinging Honoria back and forth like a pendulum from side to side.

"What an outrage!" Charlie broke out. "What an absolute outrage!"

Neither of them answered. Charlie dropped into an armchair, picked up his drink, set it down again and said:

"People I haven't seen for two years having the colossal nerve—"

He broke off. Marion had made the sound "Oh!" in one swift, furious breath, turned her body from him with a jerk and left the room.

Lincoln set down Honoria carefully.

"You children go in and start your soup," he said, and when they obeyed, he said to Charlie:

"Marion's not well and she can't stand shocks. That kind of people make her really physically sick."

"I didn't tell them to come here. They wormed your name out of somebody. They deliberately—"

"Well, it's too bad. It doesn't help matters. Excuse me a minute."

Left alone, Charlie sat tense in his chair. In the next room he could hear the children eating, talking in monosyllables, already oblivious to the scene between their elders. He heard a murmur of conversation from a farther room and then the ticking bell of a telephone receiver picked up, and in a panic he moved to the other side of the room and out of earshot.

In a minute Lincoln came back. "Look here, Charlie. I think we'd better call off dinner for tonight. Marion's in bad shape."

"Is she angry with me?"

"Sort of," he said, almost roughly. "She's not strong and—"

"You mean she's changed her mind about Honoria?"

"She's pretty bitter right now. I don't know. You phone me at the bank tomorrow."

"I wish you'd explain to her I never dreamed these people would come here. I'm just as sore as you are."

"I couldn't explain anything to her now."

Charlie got up. He took his coat and hat and started down the corridor. Then he opened the door of the dining room and said in a strange voice, "Good night, children."

Honoria rose and ran around the table to hug him.

"Good night, sweetheart," he said vaguely, and then trying to make his voice more tender, trying to conciliate something, "Good night, dear children."

V

Charlie went directly to the Ritz bar with the furious idea of finding Lorraine and Duncan, but they were not there, and he realized that in any case there was nothing he could do. He had not touched his drink at the Peters, and now he ordered a whisky-and-soda. Paul came over to say hello.

"It's a great change," he said sadly. "We do about half the business we did. So many fellows I hear about back in the States lost everything, maybe not in the first crash, but then in the second. Your friend George Hardt lost every cent, I hear. Are you back in the States?"

"No, I'm in business in Prague."

"I heard that you lost a lot in the crash."

"I did," and he added grimly, "but I lost everything I wanted in the boom."

"Selling short."

"Something like that."

Again the memory of those days swept over him like a nightmare—the people they had met travelling; then people who couldn't add a row of figures or speak a coherent sentence. The little man Helen had consented to dance with at the ship's party, who had insulted her ten feet from the table; the women and girls carried screaming with drink or drugs out of public places—

—The men who locked their wives out in the snow, because the snow of twenty-nine wasn't real snow. If you didn't want it to be snow, you just paid some money.

He went to the phone and called the Peters' apartment; Lincoln answered.

"I called up because this thing is on my mind. Has Marion said anything definite?"

"Marion's sick," Lincoln answered shortly. "I know this thing isn't altogether your fault, but I can't have her go to pieces about it. I'm afraid we'll have to let it slide for six months; I can't take the chance of working her up to this state again."

"I see."

"I'm sorry, Charlie."

He went back to his table. His whisky glass was empty, but he shook his head when Alix looked at it questioningly. There wasn't much he could do now except send Honoria some things; he would send her a lot of things tomorrow. He thought rather angrily that this was just money—he had given so many people money. . . .

"No, no more," he said to another waiter. "What do I owe you?"

He would come back some day; they couldn't make him pay forever. But he wanted his child, and nothing was much good now, beside that fact. He wasn't young any more, with a lot of nice thoughts and dreams to have by himself. He was absolutely sure Helen wouldn't have wanted him to be so alone.

1931

JOHN DOS PASSOS
1896–1970

John Dos Passos's trilogy *U.S.A.* (1938) ranks with John Steinbeck's *The Grapes of Wrath* (1939) as a major piece of post-Depression leftist fiction. Always politically committed to the rights of the individual, Dos Passos migrated from social radicalism in the 1930s to social conservatism in the 1950s. He was born in Chicago of well-to-do Portuguese-American parents who were unmarried, and lived with his mother. He went to the exclusive Choate School and then to Harvard, graduating in 1916. At first he followed his father's wishes and studied architecture in Spain, but in 1917, like many young men impatient at the United States' delay in entering World War I, he joined the famous Norton-Harjes volunteer ambulance corps. After the United States entered the war, he became a medical corpsman in the U.S. Army.

After the war he married and spent a decade as a freelance journalist, traveling in Spain and Europe, and writing poetry, travel essays, plays, and fiction on the side. His novel *Three Soldiers* (1921) showed three young men from different backgrounds—a factory worker from San Francisco, a Harvard-educated composer, and a farm youth from Indiana—destroyed by their own bureaucratic army. Another novel, *Manhattan Transfer* (1925), experimented with kaleidoscopic and cinematic techniques to present the depersonalization of contemporary urban life.

Like many of the liberal and radical writers of the day, Dos Passos supported the accused anarchists Sacco and Vanzetti. In 1926 he joined the executive board of the Communist journal *The New Masses*. For the next eight years he took part in Communist activities but never joined the party, for he rejected the Communist demand that all writers in the party express only the party line. In 1934 the Communists broke up a Socialist rally at New York City's Madison Square Garden; this event persuaded Dos Passos that the Communists were more interested in power than social justice. Soon after he severed his Communist ties.

The three novels making up *U.S.A.*—*The 42nd Parallel, 1919,* and *The Big Money*—appeared between 1930 and 1936. Its subject is twentieth-century America from coast to coast and at every social level; its portrayal is savagely satirical. It has a cast of eleven major characters, followed separately, whose lives occasionally intersect. Even the idealistic left-wing characters have a moral flabbiness and superficiality that, Dos Passos believed, was the effect of American materialism and its encouragement of personal greed. At that point in his life, Dos Passos believed that capitalism led to a division between rich and poor that could be remedied only by social change. And yet, because change could be produced only by individuals, and individuals were corrupted by their society, the source of change seemed elusive.

Dos Passos's blending of fiction with nonfiction in *U.S.A.* and his adaptation of cinematic strategies to written work were early uses of techniques that became commonplace in post–World War II fiction. Fiction alternated with other kinds of material—notably the "Newsreel" sections, in which newspaper excerpts and headlines, snippets from popular songs, and quotations from speeches and documents are brought together in an imitation of the weekly feature one saw at the movie house before television took over visual newscasting; the "Camera Eye" sections, which are impressionistic, emotional, lyrical fragments; and biographies of American notables like the dancer Isadora Duncan, the film star Rudolph Valentino, the inventors

Thomas Edison and the Wright brothers, the financier J. P. Morgan, the labor leader Eugene Debs, the architect Frank Lloyd Wright, and the sociologist Thorstein Veblen.

Beginning with Franklin D. Roosevelt's second term in 1936, Dos Passos supported the president. But after the war his concern for personal liberty and his fear of institutions and of concentrated power led him to reconceive the threat to America as coming from the left rather than the right. He wrote a number of novels from this vantage point, including a trilogy called *District of Columbia* (1952), and *Midcentury* (1961), which returned to the format of *U.S.A.*

The text is that of the first complete edition of *U.S.A.* (1938).

From U.S.A.

The Big Money[1]

Newsreel LXVIII

WALL STREET STUNNED

This is not Thirtyeight, but it's old Ninetyseven[2]
You must put her in Center on time

MARKET SURE TO RECOVER FROM SLUMP

DECLINE IN CONTRACTS

POLICE TURN MACHINE GUNS ON COLORADO
MINE STRIKERS KILL 5 WOUND 40

sympathizers appeared on the scene just as thousands of office workers were pouring out of the buildings at the lunch hour. As they raised their placard high and started an indefinite march from one side to the other, they were jeered and hooted not only by the office workers but also by workmen on a building under construction

NEW METHODS OF SELLING SEEN
RESCUE CREWS TRY TO UPEND ILL-FATED CRAFT
WHILE WAITING FOR PONTOONS

He looked 'round an' said to his black greasy fireman
Jus' shovel in a little more coal
And when we cross that White Oak Mountain
You can watch your Ninety-seven roll

I find your column interesting and need advice. I have saved four thousand dollars which I want to invest for a better income. Do you think I might buy stocks?

1. The following sections come at the end of *The Big Money*.
2. The 1903 wreck of the "old Ninetyseven" train between Washington, D.C., and Atlanta, Georgia, gave rise to several popular railroad ballads. A 1924 recording of one of these sold over a million copies.

POLICE KILLER FLICKS CIGARETTE AS HE GOES TREMBLING TO DOOM

PLAY AGENCIES IN RING OF SLAVE GIRL MARTS

MAKER OF LOVE DISBARRED AS LAWYER

Oh the right wing clothesmakers
And the Socialist fakers
They make by the workers . . .
Double cross

They preach Social-ism
But practice Fasc-ism
To keep capitalism
By the boss[3]

MOSCOW CONGRESS OUSTS OPPOSITION[4]

It's a mighty rough road from Lynchburg to Danville
An' a line on a three mile grade
It was on that grade he lost his average
An' you see what a jump he made

MILL THUGS IN MURDER RAID

here is the most dangerous example of how at the decisive moment the bourgeois ideology liquidates class solidarity and turns a friend of the workingclass of yesterday into a most miserable propagandist for imperialism today

RED PICKETS FINED FOR PROTEST HERE

We leave our home in the morning
We kiss our children goodbye

OFFICIALS STILL HOPE FOR RESCUE OF MEN

He was goin' downgrade makin' ninety miles an hour
When his whistle broke into a scream
He was found in the wreck with his hand on the throttle
An' was scalded to death with the steam

RADICALS FIGHT WITH CHAIRS AT UNITY MEETING

PATROLMEN PROTECT REDS

U.S. CHAMBER OF COMMERCE URGES CONFIDENCE

REAL VALUES UNHARMED

While we slave for the bosses
Our children scream an' cry
But when we draw our money
Our grocery bills to pay

PRESIDENT SEES PROSPERITY NEAR

3. Excerpts from this Socialist labor-union protest song are also interspersed in this "newsreel."

4. Probably the Seventh Congress of the Third International held in Moscow in 1935.

Not a cent to spend for clothing
Not a cent to lay away

STEAMROLLER IN ACTION AGAINST MILITANTS

MINERS BATTLE SCABS

But we cannot buy for our children
Our wages are too low
Now listen to me you workers
Both you women and men
Let us win for them the victory
I'm sure it ain't no sin

CARILLON PEALS IN SINGING TOWER[5]

the President[6] declared it was impossible to view the increased advantages for the many without smiling at those who a short time ago expressed so much fear lest our country might come under the control of a few individuals of great wealth.

HAPPY CROWDS THRONG CEREMONY

on a tiny island nestling like a green jewel in the lake that mirrors the singing tower, the President today participated in the dedication of a bird sanctuary and its pealing carillon, fulfilling the dream of an immigrant boy

The Camera Eye (51)

at the head of the valley in the dark of the hills on the broken floor of a lurchedover cabin a man halfsits halflies propped up by an old woman two wrinkled girls that might be young chunks of coal flare in the hearth flicker in his face white and sagging as dough blacken the cavedin mouth the taut throat the belly swelled enormous with the wound he got working on the minetipple[7]

the barefoot girl brings him a tincup of water the woman wipes sweat off his streaming face with a dirty denim sleeve the firelight flares in his eyes stretched big with fever in the women's scared eyes and in the blanched faces of the foreigners

without help in the valley hemmed by dark strike-silent hills the man will die (my father died we know what it is like to see a man die) the women will lay him out on the rickety cot the miners will bury him

in the jail it's light too hot the steamheat hisses we talk through the greenpainted iron bars to a tall white mustachioed old man some smiling miners in shirtsleeves a boy faces white from mining have already the tallowy look of jailfaces

foreigners what can we say to the dead? foreigners what can we say to the jailed? the representative of the political party talks fast through the bars join up with us and no other union we'll send you tobacco candy solidarity

5. The Singing Tower was erected in Florida through the efforts of Edward W. Bok (1863–1930), Dutch-born editor and philanthropist.
6. President Calvin Coolidge, who spoke at the tower's dedication in 1929.
7. The apparatus at a coal mine that tips cars to unload the coal.

our lawyers will write briefs speakers will shout your names at meetings they'll carry your names on cardboard on picketlines the men in jail shrug their shoulders smile thinly our eyes look in their eyes through the bars

what can I say? (in another continent I have seen the faces looking out through the barred basement windows behind the ragged sentry's boots I have seen before day the straggling footsore prisoners herded through the streets limping between bayonets heard the volley

I have seen the dead lying out in those distant deeper valleys) what can we say to the jailed?

in the law's office we stand against the wall the law is a big man with eyes angry in a big pumpkinface who sits and stares at us meddling foreigners through the door the deputies crane with their guns they stand guard at the mines they blockade the miners' soupkitchens they've cut off the road up the valley the hiredmen with guns stand ready to shoot (they have made us foreigners in the land where we were born they are the conquering army that has filtered into the country unnoticed they have taken the hilltops by stealth they levy toll they stand at the minehead they stand at the polls they stand by when the bailiffs carry the furniture of the family evicted from the city tenement out on the sidewalk they are there when the bankers foreclose on a farm they are ambushed and ready to shoot down the strikers marching behind the flag up the switchback road to the mine those that the guns spare they jail)

the law stares across the desk out of angry eyes his face reddens in splotches like a gobbler's neck with the strut of the power of submachine-guns sawedoffshotguns teargas and vomitinggas the power that can feed you or leave you to starve

sits easy at his desk his back is covered he feels strong behind him he feels the prosecutingattorney the judge an owner himself the political boss the minesuperintendent the board of directors the president of the utility the manipulator of the holdingcompany

he lifts his hand towards the telephone
the deputies crowd in the door
we have only words against

* * *

1936

WILLIAM FAULKNER
1897–1962

Between 1929 and 1936 William Faulkner published novels about childhood, families, sex, race, obsessions, time, the past, his native South, and the modern world. He invented voices for characters ranging from sages to children, criminals, the insane, even the dead—sometimes all within one book. He developed, beyond this ventriloquism, his own unmistakable narrative voice: urgent, intense, highly rhetorical. He experimented with narrative chronology and with techniques for representing mind and memory. He invented an entire southern county and wrote its history.

He was a native Mississippian, born near Oxford, where his parents moved when he was about five. His great-grandfather had been a local legend: a colonel in the Civil War, lawyer, railroad builder, financier, politician, writer, and public figure who was shot and killed by a business and political rival in 1889. Faulkner's grandfather carried on some of the family enterprises, and his father worked first for the railroad (the Gulf and Chicago) and later as business manager of the University of Mississippi. His father was a reclusive man who loved to hunt, drink, and swap stories with his hunting friends; the mother, ambitious, sensitive, and literary, was a more profound influence on Faulkner, her favorite of four sons. In Faulkner's childhood his maternal grandmother also lived with them; she was a high-spirited, independent, and imaginative old lady whose death in 1907 seems to have affected Faulkner deeply.

Faulkner dropped out of high school in 1915 and had no further formal education beyond a year (1919–20) as a special student at the University of Mississippi. Through family connections, various jobs were made for him, but he was unhappy in all of them. In 1918 Estelle Oldham, his high school love, married someone else; Faulkner briefly left Oxford. First he went to New Haven, where his best friend and informal tutor, Phil Stone, was attending law school at Yale; then he enlisted in the British Royal Flying Corps and was sent to Canada to train. World War I ended before he saw active service; nevertheless, when he returned to Oxford in 1919 he was limping from what he claimed was a war wound.

Back at home, Faulkner drifted from one job to another and wrote poetry that was a mélange of Shakespearean, pastoral, Victorian, and Edwardian modes, with an overlay of French Symbolism, which he published in *The Marble Faun*, in 1924. In 1925 he went to New Orleans where, for the first time, he met and mingled with literary people, including Sherwood Anderson, who encouraged Faulkner to develop his own style, to concentrate on prose, and to use his region for material.

Faulkner wrote his first novel, *Soldier's Pay*, in New Orleans, and Anderson recommended it to his own publisher, Liveright; it appeared in 1926. He also published in the New Orleans magazine *The Double Dealer* and the newspaper *The Times Picayune*. He learned about the experimental writing of James Joyce and the ideas of Sigmund Freud. After a trip to Europe at the end of the same year, he returned to Oxford. In 1929 he married Estelle Oldham, who had been divorced and had returned to Oxford with her two children. They bought a ruined mansion, Rowan Oak, in 1930 and began to restore it to its antebellum appearance. A daughter born in 1931 died in infancy; a second daughter, Jill, was born in 1933.

Faulkner's second novel was a satire on New Orleans intellectuals called *Mosquitos* (1927). His more typical subject matter emerged with his rejected novel *Flags in the Dust*, and the shortened version of it that appeared in 1929 as *Sartoris*. In this work Faulkner focused on the interconnections between a prominent southern family and the local community: the Sartoris family as well as many other characters appeared in later works, and the region, renamed Yoknapatawpha County, was to become the locale of Faulkner's imaginative world.

The social and historical emphasis in *Sartoris* was not directly followed up in the works Faulkner wrote next. *The Sound and the Fury* (1929)—Faulkner's favorite novel—and *As I Lay Dying* (1930) were dramatically experimental attempts to articulate the inexpressible aspects of individual psychology. *The Sound and the Fury* has four sections, each with a different narrator, each supplying a different piece of the plot. Three of the narrators are brothers: Benjy, the idiot; Quentin, the suicide; and Jason, the business failure. Each of them, for different reasons, mourns the loss of their sister, Caddie. While the story moves out to the disintegration of the old southern family to which these brothers belong, its focus is on the private obsessions of the brothers, and it invents an entirely different style for each narrator. Only the last section, told from a traditionally omniscient point of view, provides a sequential narration; the other three jump freely in time and space. The structure of *As I Lay Dying*, included here in its entirety, is even more complex. Like *The Sound and the Fury*, it is organized around the loss of a beloved woman. The precipitating event in the novel is the death of a mother. The story moves forward in chronological time as the "poor white" Bundren family takes her body to the town of Jefferson for burial. Its narration is divided into fifty-nine sections of interior monologue by fifteen characters, each with a different perception of the action and a different way of relating to reality. The family's adventures and misadventures on the road are comic, tragic, grotesque, absurd, and deeply moving.

Neither these books nor Faulkner's early short stories were very popular. *Sanctuary*, a sensational work about sex, gangsters, official corruption, and urban violence, attracted considerable attention, however. Published in 1931, it took its place in the large amount of hard-boiled fiction that appeared in the decade, notably by such authors as Dashiell Hammett and Raymond Chandler. During four different intervals—1932–37, 1942–45, 1951, and 1954—Faulkner spent time in Hollywood or on contract as a scriptwriter. He worked well with the director Howard Hawks and wrote the scripts for two famous movies, an adaptation of Ernest Hemingway's *To Have and Have Not* and

***To Have and Have Not*,** movie poster, 1944. Faulkner coauthored the screenplay that adapted Hemingway's 1937 novel as a romantic vehicle for Humphrey Bogart and the newcomer Lauren Bacall.

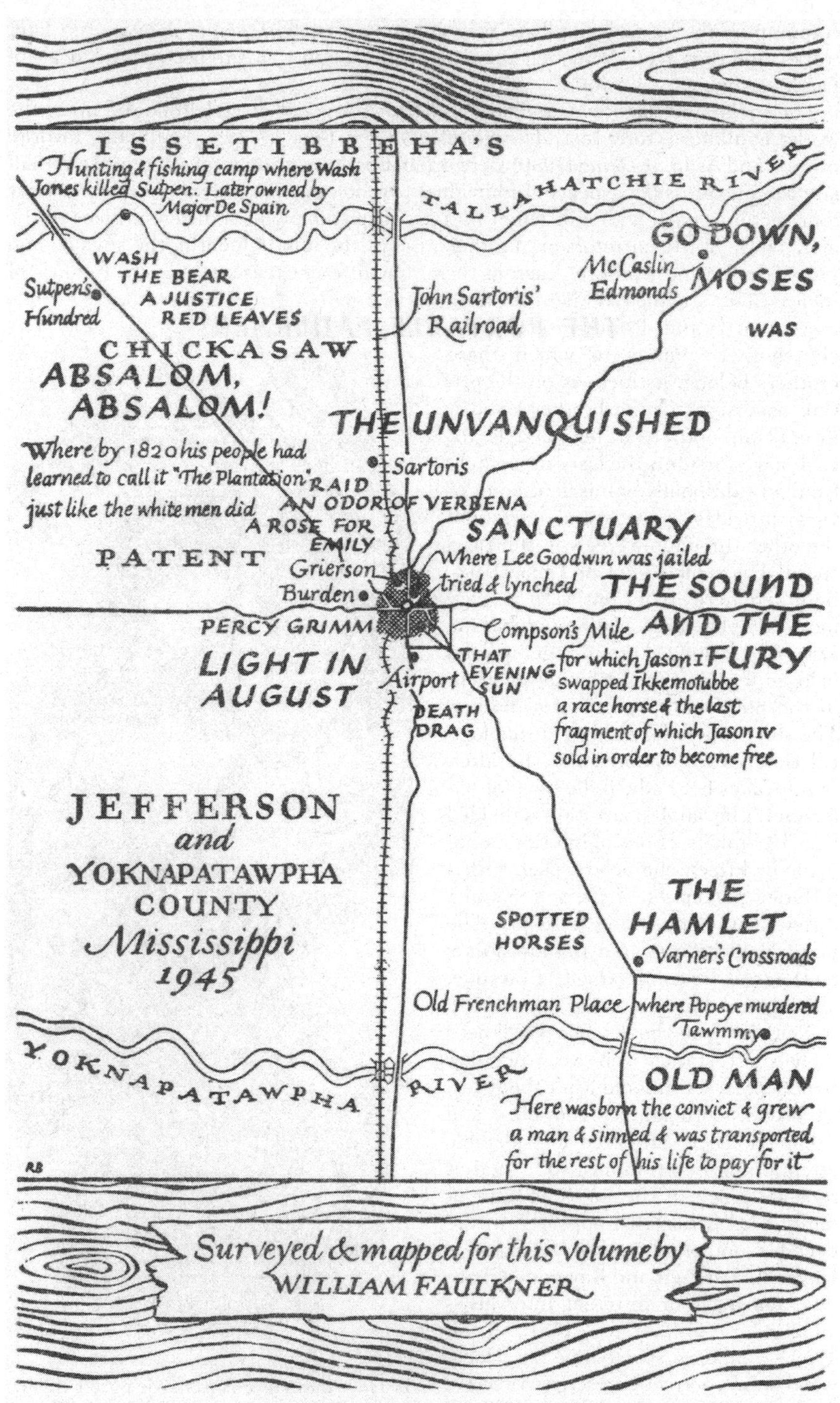

Yoknapatawpha County. Faulkner drew this map of his fictional world for Malcolm Cowley's 1946 collection *The Portable Faulkner.*

an adaptation of Raymond Chandler's *The Big Sleep,* both starring Humphrey Bogart and Lauren Bacall.

He continued to produce brilliant and inventive novels during these years. *Light in August* (1932) counterpointed a comic pastoral about the pregnant earth-mother figure Lena Grove with a grim tragedy about the embittered outcast Joe Christmas, who may or may not be racially mixed; it interrelated individual psychology and cultural pathology. *Absalom, Absalom!*, which followed in 1936, is thought by many to be Faulkner's masterpiece. The story of Thomas Sutpen, the ruthless would-be founder of a southern dynasty after the Civil War, is related by four different speakers, each trying to find "the meaning" of the story. The reader, observing how the story changes in each telling, comes to see that making stories is the human way of making meaning. Like Faulkner's earlier novels, *Absalom* is thus simultaneously about an individual, about the South, and about itself as a work of fiction. But its emphasis shifts from the private psychology that dominated in earlier work to social psychology: to the collective mind of the South.

With World War II, Faulkner's work became more traditional and less difficult. He began to write about the rise, in Yoknapatawpha County, of the poor white family named Snopes—this family had appeared in earlier works (like "Barn Burning")—and the simultaneous decline of the region's "aristocratic" families. *The Hamlet* (1940) was the first of three novels devoted to the Snopeses. Because all his works had been set in Yoknapatawpha County and were interconnected, the region and its people began to take on an existence independent of any one book in which they appeared.

Faulkner's national reputation soared after the publication in 1946 of an anthology of his writings, *The Portable Faulkner,* edited by the critic Malcolm Cowley. He already had a major reputation abroad, especially in France, where his work in translation was a powerful influence on the French so-called new novel and its practitioners such as Michel Butor and Alain Robbe-Grillet. His antiracist *Intruder in the Dust* (1948) occasioned the award of the Nobel Prize in 1950. In the 1950s Faulkner visited many college campuses. His writing took on more of the air of an old-fashioned yarn; he dealt with more legendary and local color materials; he rounded out the Snopes saga with *The Town* (1957) and *The Mansion* (1959). At the age of sixty-five he died of a heart attack.

The text of *As I Lay Dying* is that established by Noel Polk (1985). The texts of "A Rose for Emily" and "Barn Burning" are those of *Collected Stories* (1950).

As I Lay Dying[1]

Darl

Jewel and I come up from the field, following the path in single file. Although I am fifteen feet ahead of him, anyone watching us from the cottonhouse can see Jewel's frayed and broken straw hat a full head above my own.

The path runs straight as a plumb-line, worn smooth by feet and baked brick-hard by July, between the green rows of laid-by cotton,[2] to the cottonhouse in the center of the field, where it turns and circles the cottonhouse at four soft right angles and goes on across the field again, worn so by feet in fading precision.

The cottonhouse is of rough logs, from between which the chinking has long fallen. Square, with a broken roof set at a single pitch, it leans in empty

1. For assistance with the footnotes, we are indebted to Joseph Blotner's notes in William Faulkner, *Novels 1930–1935* (1985).

2. Cultivated cotton crop, waiting to be picked.

and shimmering dilapidation in the sunlight, a single broad window in two opposite walls giving onto the approaches of the path. When we reach it I turn and follow the path which circles the house. Jewel, fifteen feet behind me, looking straight ahead, steps in a single stride through the window. Still staring straight ahead, his pale eyes like wood set into his wooden face, he crosses the floor in four strides with the rigid gravity of a cigar store Indian dressed in patched overalls and endued with life from the hips down, and steps in a single stride through the opposite window and into the path again just as I come around the corner. In single file and five feet apart and Jewel now in front, we go on up the path toward the foot of the bluff.

Tull's wagon stands beside the spring, hitched to the rail, the reins wrapped about the seat stanchion. In the wagon bed are two chairs. Jewel stops at the spring and takes the gourd from the willow branch and drinks. I pass him and mount the path, beginning to hear Cash's saw.

When I reach the top he has quit sawing. Standing in a litter of chips, he is fitting two of the boards together. Between the shadow spaces they are yellow as gold, like soft gold, bearing on their flanks in smooth undulations the marks of the adze blade: a good carpenter, Cash is. He holds the two planks on the trestle, fitted along the edges in a quarter of the finished box. He kneels and squints along the edge of them, then he lowers them and takes up the adze. A good carpenter. Addie Bundren could not want a better one, a better box to lie in. It will give her confidence and comfort. I go on to the house, followed by the

Chuck. Chuck. Chuck.

of the adze.

Cora

So I saved out the eggs and baked yesterday. The cakes turned out right well. We depend a lot on our chickens. They are good layers, what few we have left after the possums and such. Snakes too, in the summer. A snake will break up a hen-house quicker than anything. So after they were going to cost so much more than Mr Tull thought, and after I promised that the difference in the number of eggs would make it up, I had to be more careful than ever because it was on my final say-so we took them. We could have stocked cheaper chickens, but I gave my promise as Miss Lawington said when she advised me to get a good breed, because Mr Tull himself admits that a good breed of cows or hogs pays in the long run. So when we lost so many of them we couldn't afford to use the eggs ourselves, because I could not have had Mr Tull chide me when it was on my say-so we took them. So when Miss Lawington told me about the cakes I thought that I could bake them and earn enough at one time to increase the net value of the flock the equivalent of two head. And that by saving the eggs out one at a time, even the eggs wouldn't be costing anything. And that week they laid so well that I not only saved out enough eggs above what we had engaged to sell, to bake the cakes with, I had saved enough so that the flour and the sugar and the stove wood would not be costing anything. So I baked yesterday, more careful than ever I baked in my life, and the cakes turned out right well. But when we got to town this morning Miss Lawington told me the lady had changed her mind and was not going to have the party after all.

"She ought to taken those cakes anyway," Kate says.

"Well," I say, "I reckon she never had no use for them now."

"She ought to taken them," Kate says. "But those rich town ladies can change their minds. Poor folks cant."

Riches is nothing in the face of the Lord, for He can see into the heart. "Maybe I can sell them at the bazaar Saturday," I say. They turned out real well.

"You cant get two dollars a piece for them," Kate says.

"Well, it isn't like they cost me anything," I say. I saved them out and swapped a dozen of them for the sugar and flour. It isn't like the cakes cost me anything, as Mr Tull himself realises that the eggs I saved were over and beyond what we had engaged to sell, so it was like we had found the eggs or they had been given to us.

"She ought to taken those cakes when she same as gave you her word," Kate says. The Lord can see into the heart. If it is His will that some folks has different ideas of honesty from other folks, it is not my place to question His decree.

"I reckon she never had any use for them," I say. They turned out real well, too.

The quilt is drawn up to her chin, hot as it is, with only her two hands and her face outside. She is propped on the pillow, with her head raised so she can see out the window, and we can hear him every time he takes up the adze or the saw. If we were deaf we could almost watch her face and hear him, see him. Her face is wasted away so that the bones draw just under the skin in white lines. Her eyes are like two candles when you watch them gutter down into the sockets of iron candle-sticks. But the eternal and the everlasting salvation and grace is not upon her.

"They turned out real nice," I say. "But not like the cakes Addie used to bake." You can see that girl's washing and ironing in the pillow-slip, if ironed it ever was. Maybe it will reveal her blindness to her, laying there at the mercy and the ministration of four men and a tom-boy girl. "There's not a woman in this section could ever bake with Addie Bundren," I say. "First thing we know she'll be up and baking again, and then we wont have any sale for ours at all." Under the quilt she makes no more of a hump than a rail would, and the only way you can tell she is breathing is by the sound of the mattress shucks. Even the hair at her cheek does not move, even with that girl standing right over her, fanning her with the fan. While we watch she swaps the fan to the other hand without stopping it.

"Is she sleeping?" Kate whispers.

"She's just watching Cash yonder," the girl says. We can hear the saw in the board. It sounds like snoring. Eula turns on the trunk and looks out the window. Her necklace looks real nice with her red hat. You wouldn't think it only cost twenty-five cents.

"She ought to taken those cakes," Kate says.

I could have used the money real well. But it's not like they cost me anything except the baking. I can tell him that anybody is likely to make a miscue, but it's not all of them that can get out of it without loss, I can tell him. It's not everybody can eat their mistakes, I can tell him.

Someone comes through the hall. It is Darl. He does not look in as he passes the door. Eula watches him as he goes on and passes from sight again toward the back. Her hand rises and touches her beads lightly, and then her hair. When she finds me watching her, her eyes go blank.

Darl

Pa and Vernon are sitting on the back porch. Pa is tilting snuff from the lid of his snuff-box into his lower lip, holding the lip outdrawn between thumb and finger. They look around as I cross the porch and dip the gourd into the water bucket and drink.

"Where's Jewel?" pa says. When I was a boy I first learned how much better water tastes when it has set a while in a cedar bucket. Warmish-cool, with a faint taste like the hot July wind in cedar trees smells. It has to set at least six hours, and be drunk from a gourd. Water should never be drunk from metal.

And at night it is better still. I used to lie on the pallet in the hall, waiting until I could hear them all asleep, so I could get up and go back to the bucket. It would be black, the shelf black, the still surface of the water a round orifice in nothingness, where before I stirred it awake with the dipper I could see maybe a star or two in the bucket, and maybe in the dipper a star or two before I drank. After that I was bigger, older. Then I would wait until they all went to sleep so I could lie with my shirt-tail up, hearing them asleep, feeling myself without touching myself, feeling the cool silence blowing upon my parts and wondering if Cash was yonder in the darkness doing it too, had been doing it perhaps for the last two years before I could have wanted to or could have.

Pa's feet are badly splayed, his toes cramped and bent and warped, with no toenail at all on his little toes, from working so hard in the wet in homemade shoes when he was a boy. Beside his chair his brogans sit. They look as though they had been hacked with a blunt axe out of pig-iron. Vernon has been to town. I have never seen him go to town in overalls. His wife, they say. She taught school too, once.

I fling the dipper dregs to the ground and wipe my mouth on my sleeve. It is going to rain before morning. Maybe before dark. "Down to the barn," I say. "Harnessing the team."

Down there fooling with that horse. He will go on through the barn, into the pasture. The horse will not be in sight: he is up there among the pine seedlings, in the cool. Jewel whistles, once and shrill. The horse snorts, then Jewel sees him, glinting for a gaudy instant among the blue shadows. Jewel whistles again; the horse comes dropping down the slope, stiff-legged, his ears cocking and flicking, his mis-matched eyes rolling, and fetches up twenty feet away, broadside on, watching Jewel over his shoulder in an attitude kittenish and alert.

"Come here, sir," Jewel says. He moves. Moving that quick his coat, bunching, tongues swirling like so many flames. With tossing mane and tail and rolling eye the horse makes another short curvetting rush and stops again, feet bunched, watching Jewel. Jewel walks steadily toward him, his hands at his sides. Save for Jewel's legs they are like two figures carved for a tableau savage in the sun.

When Jewel can almost touch him, the horse stands on his hind legs and slashes down at Jewel. Then Jewel is enclosed by a glittering maze of hooves as by an illusion of wings; among them, beneath the upreared chest, he moves with the flashing limberness of a snake. For an instant before the jerk comes onto his arms he sees his whole body earth-free, horizontal, whipping snake-limber, until he finds the horse's nostrils and touches earth again. Then they are rigid, motionless, terrific, the horse back-thrust on stiffened, quivering legs, with lowered head; Jewel with dug heels, shutting off the horse's wind with one hand, with the other patting the horse's neck in short strokes myriad and caressing, cursing the horse with obscene ferocity.

They stand in rigid terrific hiatus, the horse trembling and groaning. Then Jewel is on the horse's back. He flows upward in a stooping swirl like the lash of a whip, his body in midair shaped to the horse. For another moment the horse stands spraddled, with lowered head, before it bursts into motion. They descend the hill in a series of spine-jolting jumps, Jewel high, leech-like on the withers, to the fence where the horse bunches to a scuttering halt again.

"Well," Jewel says, "you can quit now, if you got a-plenty."

Inside the barn Jewel slides running to the ground before the horse stops. The horse enters the stall, Jewel following. Without looking back the horse kicks at him, slamming a single hoof into the wall with a pistol-like report. Jewel kicks him in the stomach; the horse arches his neck back, crop-toothed; Jewel strikes him across the face with his fist and slides on to the trough and mounts upon it. Clinging to the hay-rack he lowers his head and peers out across the stall tops and through the doorway. The path is empty; from here he cannot even hear Cash sawing. He reaches up and drags down hay in hurried armsful and crams it into the rack.

"Eat," he says. "Get the goddamn stuff out of sight while you got a chance, you pussel-gutted[3] bastard. You sweet son of a bitch," he says.

Jewel

It's because he stays out there, right under the window, hammering and sawing on that goddamn box. Where she's got to see him. Where every breath she draws is full of his knocking and sawing where she can see him saying See. See what a good one I am making for you. I told him to go somewhere else. I said Good God do you want to see her in it. It's like when he was a little boy and she says if she had some fertilizer she would try to raise some flowers and he taken the bread pan and brought it back from the barn full of dung.

And now them others sitting there, like buzzards. Waiting, fanning themselves. Because I said If you wouldn't keep on sawing and nailing at it until a man cant sleep even and her hands laying on the quilt like two of them roots dug up and tried to wash and you couldn't get them clean. I can see the fan and Dewey Dell's arm. I said if you'd just let her alone. Sawing and knocking, and keeping the air always moving so fast on her face that when you're tired you cant breathe it, and that goddamn adze going One lick less. One lick less. One lick less until everybody that passes in the road will have to stop and see it and say what a fine carpenter he is. If it had just been me when Cash fell off of that church and if it had just been me when pa laid sick with that load of wood fell on him, it would not be happening with every bastard in the county coming in to stare at her because if there is a God what the hell is He for. It would just be me and her on a high hill and me rolling the rocks down the hill at their faces, picking them up and throwing them down the hill faces

3. Fat.

and teeth and all by God until she was quiet and not that goddamn adze going One lick less. One lick less and we could be quiet.

Darl

We watch him come around the corner and mount the steps. He does not look at us. "You ready?" he says.

"If you're hitched up," I say. I say "Wait." He stops, looking at pa. Vernon spits, without moving. He spits with decorous and deliberate precision into the pocked dust below the porch. Pa rubs his hands slowly on his knees. He is gazing out beyond the crest of the bluff, out across the land. Jewel watches him a moment, then he goes on to the pail and drinks again.

"I mislike undecision as much as ere a man," pa says.

"It means three dollars," I say. The shirt across pa's hump is faded lighter than the rest of it. There is no sweat stain on his shirt. I have never seen a sweat stain on his shirt. He was sick once from working in the sun when he was twenty-two years old, and he tells people that if he ever sweats, he will die. I suppose he believes it.

"But if she dont last until you get back," he says. "She will be disappointed."

Vernon spits into the dust. But it will rain before morning.

"She's counted on it," pa says. "She'll want to start right away. I know her. I promised her I'd keep the team here and ready, and she's counting on it."

"We'll need that three dollars then, sure," I say. He gazes out over the land, rubbing his hands on his knees. Since he lost his teeth his mouth collapses in slow repetition when he dips. The stubble gives his lower face that appearance that old dogs have. "You'd better make up your mind soon, so we can get there and get a load on before dark," I say.

"Ma aint that sick," Jewel says. "Shut up, Darl."

"That's right," Vernon says. "She seems more like herself today than she has in a week. Time you and Jewel get back, she'll be setting up."

"You ought to know," Jewel says. "You been here often enough looking at her. You or your folks." Vernon looks at him. Jewel's eyes look like pale wood in his high-blooded face. He is a head taller than any of the rest of us, always was. I told them that's why ma always whipped him and petted him more. Because he was peakling around the house more. That's why she named him Jewel I told them.

"Shut up, Jewel," pa says, but as though he is not listening much. He gazes out across the land, rubbing his knees.

"You could borrow the loan of Vernon's team and we could catch up with you," I say. "If she didn't wait for us."

"Ah, shut your goddamn mouth," Jewel says.

"She'll want to go in ourn," pa says. He rubs his knees. "Dont ere a man mislike it more."

"It's laying there, watching Cash whittle on that damn . . ." Jewel says. He says it harshly, savagely, but he does not say the word. Like a little boy in the dark to flail his courage and suddenly aghast into silence by his own noise.

"She wanted that like she wants to go in our own wagon," pa says. "She'll rest easier for knowing it's a good one, and private. She was ever a private woman. You know it well."

"Then let it be private," Jewel says. "But how the hell can you expect it to be—" he looks at the back of pa's head, his eyes like pale wooden eyes.

"Sho," Vernon says, "she'll hold on till it's finished. She'll hold on till everything's ready, till her own good time. And with the roads like they are now, it wont take you no time to get her to town."

"It's fixing up to rain," pa says. "I am a luckless man. I have ever been." He rubs his hands on his knees. "It's that durn doctor, liable to come at any time. I couldn't get word to him till so late. If he was to come tomorrow and tell her the time was nigh, she wouldn't wait. I know her. Wagon or no wagon, she wouldn't wait. Then she'd be upset, and I wouldn't upset her for the living world. With that family burying-ground in Jefferson and them of her blood waiting for her there, she'll be impatient. I promised my word me and the boys would get her there quick as mules could walk it, so she could rest quiet." He rubs his hands on his knees. "No man ever misliked it more."

"If everybody wasn't burning hell to get her there," Jewel says in that harsh, savage voice. "With Cash all day long right under the window, hammering and sawing at that—"

"It was her wish," pa says. "You got no affection nor gentleness for her. You never had. We would be beholden to no man," he says, "me and her. We have never yet been, and she will rest quieter for knowing it and that it was her own blood sawed out the boards and drove the nails. She was ever one to clean up after herself."

"It means three dollars," I say. "Do you want us to go, or not?" Pa rubs his knees. "We'll be back by tomorrow sundown."

"Well . . ." pa says. He looks out over the land, awry-haired, mouthing the snuff slowly against his gums.

"Come on," Jewel says. He goes down the steps. Vernon spits neatly into the dust.

"By sundown, now," pa says. "I would not keep her waiting."

Jewel glances back, then he goes on around the house. I enter the hall, hearing the voices before I reach the door. Tilting a little down the hill, as our house does, a breeze draws through the hall all the time, upslanting. A feather dropped near the front door will rise and brush along the ceiling, slanting backward, until it reaches the down-turning current at the back door: so with voices. As you enter the hall, they sound as though they were speaking out of the air about your head.

Cora

It was the sweetest thing I ever saw. It was like he knew he would never see her again, that Anse Bundren was driving him from his mother's death bed, never to see her in this world again. I always said Darl was different from those others. I always said he was the only one of them that had his mother's nature, had any natural affection. Not that Jewel, the one she labored so to bear and coddled and petted so and him flinging into tantrums or sulking spells, inventing devilment to devil her until I would have frailed[4] him time and time. Not him to come and tell her goodbye. Not him to miss a chance to make that extra three dollars at the price of his mother's goodbye kiss. A Bundren through and

4. I.e., "flailed"; beaten.

through, loving nobody, caring for nothing except how to get something with the least amount of work. Mr Tull says Darl asked them to wait. He said Darl almost begged them on his knees not to force him to leave her in her condition. But nothing would do but Anse and Jewel must make that three dollars. Nobody that knows Anse could have expected different, but to think of that boy, that Jewel, selling all those years of self-denial and down-right partiality—they couldn't fool me: Mr Tull says Mrs Bundren liked Jewel the least of all, but I knew better. I knew she was partial to him, to the same quality in him that let her put up with Anse Bundren when Mr Tull said she ought to poisoned him—for three dollars, denying his dying mother the goodbye kiss.

Why, for the last three weeks I have been coming over every time I could, coming sometimes when I shouldn't have, neglecting my own family and duties so that somebody would be with her in her last moments and she would not have to face the Great Unknown without one familiar face to give her courage. Not that I deserve credit for it: I will expect the same for myself. But thank God it will be the faces of my loved kin, my blood and flesh, for in my husband and children I have been more blessed than most, trials though they have been at times.

She lived, a lonely woman, lonely with her pride, trying to make folks believe different, hiding the fact that they just suffered her, because she was not cold in the coffin before they were carting her forty miles away to bury her, flouting the will of God to do it. Refusing to let her lie in the same earth with those Bundrens.

"But she wanted to go," Mr Tull said. "It was her own wish to lie among her own people."

"Then why didn't she go alive?" I said. "Not one of them would have stopped her, with even that little one almost old enough now to be selfish and stone-hearted like the rest of them."

"It was her own wish," Mr Tull said. "I heard Anse say it was."

"And you would believe Anse, of course," I said. "A man like you would. Dont tell me."

"I'd believe him about something he couldn't expect to make anything off of me by not telling," Mr Tull said.

"Dont tell me," I said. "A woman's place is with her husband and children, alive or dead. Would you expect me to want to go back to Alabama and leave you and the girls when my time comes, that I left of my own will to cast my lot with yours for better and worse, until death and after?"

"Well, folks are different," he said.

I should hope so. I have tried to live right in the sight of God and man, for the honor and comfort of my Christian husband and the love and respect of my Christian children. So that when I lay me down in the consciousness of my duty and reward I will be surrounded by loving faces, carrying the farewell kiss of each of my loved ones into my reward. Not like Addie Bundren dying alone, hiding her pride and her broken heart. Glad to go. Lying there with her head propped up so she could watch Cash building the coffin, having to watch him so he would not skimp on it, like as not, with those men not worrying about anything except if there was time to earn another three dollars before the rain come and the river got too high to get across it. Like as not, if they hadn't decided to make that last load, they would have loaded her into the wagon on a quilt and crossed the river first and then stopped and give her time to die what Christian death they would let her.

Except Darl. It was the sweetest thing I ever saw. Sometimes I lose faith in human nature for a time; I am assailed by doubt. But always the Lord restores my faith and reveals to me His bounteous love for His creatures. Not Jewel, the one she had always cherished, not him. He was after that three extra dollars. It was Darl, the one that folks say is queer, lazy, pottering about the place no better than Anse, with Cash a good carpenter and always more building than he can get around to, and Jewel always doing something that made him some money or got him talked about, and that near-naked girl always standing over Addie with a fan so that every time a body tried to talk to her and cheer her up, would answer for her right quick, like she was trying to keep anybody from coming near her at all.

It was Darl. He come to the door and stood there, looking at his dying mother. He just looked at her, and I felt the bounteous love of the Lord again and His mercy. I saw that with Jewel she had just been pretending, but that it was between her and Darl that the understanding and the true love was. He just looked at her, not even coming in where she could see him and get upset, knowing that Anse was driving him away and he would never see her again. He said nothing, just looking at her.

"What you want, Darl?" Dewey Dell said, not stopping the fan, speaking up quick, keeping even him from her. He didn't answer. He just stood and looked at his dying mother, his heart too full for words.

Dewey Dell

The first time me and Lafe picked on down the row. Pa dassent[5] sweat because he will catch his death from the sickness so that everybody that comes to help us. And Jewel dont care about anything he is not kin to us in caring, not care-kin. And Cash like sawing the long hot sad yellow days up into planks and nailing them to something. And pa thinks because neighbors will always treat one another that way because he has always been too busy letting neighbors do for him to find out. And I did not think that Darl would, that sits at the supper table with his eyes gone further than the food and the lamp, full of the land dug out of his skull and the holes filled with distance beyond the land.

We picked on down the row, the woods getting closer and closer and the secret shade, picking on into the secret shade with my sack and Lafe's sack. Because I said will I or wont I when the sack was half full because I said if the sack is full when we get to the woods it wont be me. I said if it dont mean for me to do it the sack will not be full and I will turn up the next row but if the sack is full, I cannot help it. It will be that I had to do it all the time and I cannot help it. And we picked on toward the secret shade and our eyes would drown together touching on his hands and my hands and I didn't say anything. I said "What are you doing?" and he said "I am picking into your sack." And so it was full when we came to the end of the row and I could not help it.

And so it was because I could not help it. It was then, and then I saw Darl and he knew. He said he knew without the words like he told me that ma is going to die without words, and I knew he knew because if he had said he knew with the words I would not have believed that he had been there and saw us. But he said he did know and I said "Are you going to tell pa are you going to kill

5. Dares not.

him?" without the words I said it and he said "Why?" without the words. And that's why I can talk to him with knowing with hating because he knows.

He stands in the door, looking at her.

"What you want, Darl?" I say.

"She is going to die," he says. And old turkey-buzzard Tull coming to watch her die but I can fool them.

"When is she going to die?" I say.

"Before we get back," he says.

"Then why are you taking Jewel?" I say.

"I want him to help me load," he says.

Tull

Anse keeps on rubbing his knees. His overalls are faded; on one knee a serge patch cut out of a pair of Sunday pants, wore iron-slick. "No man mislikes it more than me," he says.

"A fellow's got to guess ahead now and then," I say. "But, come long and short, it wont be no harm done neither way."

"She'll want to get started right off," he says. "It's far enough to Jefferson at best."

"But the roads is good now," I say. It's fixing to rain tonight, too. His folks buries at New Hope, too, not three miles away. But it's just like him to marry a woman born a day's hard ride away and have her die on him.

He looks out over the land, rubbing his knees. "No man so mislikes it," he says.

"They'll get back in plenty of time," I say. "I wouldn't worry none."

"It means three dollars," he says.

"Might be it wont be no need for them to rush back, noways," I say. "I hope it."

"She's a-going," he says. "Her mind is set on it."

It's a hard life on women, for a fact. Some women. I mind my mammy lived to be seventy and more. Worked every day, rain or shine; never a sick day since her last chap was born until one day she kind of looked around her and then she went and taken that lace-trimmed night gown she had had forty-five years and never wore out of the chest and put it on and laid down on the bed and pulled the covers up and shut her eyes. "You all will have to look out for pa the best you can," she said. "I'm tired."

Anse rubs his hands on his knees. "The Lord giveth," he says. We can hear Cash a-hammering and sawing beyond the corner.

It's true. Never a truer breath was ever breathed. "The Lord giveth," I say.

That boy comes up the hill. He is carrying a fish nigh long as he is. He slings it to the ground and grunts "Hah" and spits over his shoulder like a man. Durn nigh long as he is.

"What's that?" I say. "A hog? Where'd you get it?"

"Down to the bridge," he says. He turns it over, the under side caked over with dust where it is wet, the eye coated over, humped under the dirt.

"Are you aiming to leave it laying there?" Anse says.

"I aim to show it to ma," Vardaman says. He looks toward the door. We can hear the talking, coming out on the draft. Cash too, knocking and hammering at the boards. "There's company in there," he says.

"Just my folks," I say. "They'd enjoy to see it too."

He says nothing, watching the door. Then he looks down at the fish laying in the dust. He turns it over with his foot and prods at the eye-bump with his toe, gouging at it. Anse is looking out over the land. Vardaman looks at Anse's face, then at the door. He turns, going toward the corner of the house, when Anse calls him without looking around.

"You clean that fish," Anse says.

Vardaman stops. "Why cant Dewey Dell clean it?" he says.

"You clean that fish," Anse says.

"Aw, pa," Vardaman says.

"You clean it," Anse says. He dont look around. Vardaman comes back and picks up the fish. It slides out of his hands, smearing wet dirt onto him, and flops down, dirtying itself again, gapmouthed, goggle-eyed, hiding into the dust like it was ashamed of being dead, like it was in a hurry to get back hid again. Vardaman cusses it. He cusses it like a grown man, standing a-straddle of it. Anse dont look around. Vardaman picks it up again. He goes on around the house, toting it in both arms like a armful of wood, it overlapping him on both ends, head and tail. Durn nigh big as he is.

Anse's wrists dangle out of his sleeves: I never see him with a shirt on that looked like it was his in all my life. They all looked like Jewel might have give him his old ones. Not Jewel, though. He's long-armed, even if he is spindling. Except for the lack of sweat. You could tell they aint been nobody else's but Anse's that way without no mistake. His eyes look like pieces of burnt-out cinder fixed in his face, looking out over the land.

When the shadow touches the steps he says "It's five oclock."

Just as I get up Cora comes to the door and says it's time to get on. Anse reaches for his shoes. "Now, Mr Bundren," Cora says, "dont you get up now." He puts his shoes on, stomping into them, like he does everything, like he is hoping all the time he really cant do it and can quit trying to. When we go up the hall we can hear them clumping on the floor like they was iron shoes. He comes toward the door where she is, blinking his eyes, kind of looking ahead of hisself before he sees, like he is hoping to find her setting up, in a chair maybe or maybe sweeping, and looks into the door in that surprised way like he looks in and finds her still in bed every time and Dewey Dell still a-fanning her with the fan. He stands there, like he dont aim to move again nor nothing else.

"Well, I reckon we better get on," Cora says. "I got to feed the chickens." It's fixing to rain, too. Clouds like that dont lie, and the cotton making every day the Lord sends. That'll be something else for him. Cash is still trimming at the boards. "If there's ere a thing we can do," Cora says.

"Anse'll let us know," I say.

Anse dont look at us. He looks around, blinking, in that surprised way, like he had wore hisself down being surprised and was even surprised at that. If Cash just works that careful on my barn.

"I told Anse it likely wont be no need," I say. "I so hope it."

"Her mind is set on it," he says. "I reckon she's bound to go."

"It comes to all of us," Cora says. "Let the Lord comfort you."

"About that corn," I say. I tell him again I will help him out if he gets into a tight, with her sick and all. Like most folks around here, I done holp him so much already I cant quit now.

"I aimed to get to it today," he says. "Seems like I cant get my mind on nothing."

"Maybe she'll hold out till you are laid-by," I say.

"If God wills it," he says.

"Let Him comfort you," Cora says.

If Cash just works that careful on my barn. He looks up when we pass. "Dont reckon I'll get to you this week," he says.

"'Taint no rush," I say. "Whenever you get around to it."

We get into the wagon. Cora sets the cake box on her lap. It's fixing to rain, sho.

"I dont know what he'll do," Cora says. "I just dont know."

"Poor Anse," I say. "She kept him at work for thirty-odd years. I reckon she is tired."

"And I reckon she'll be behind him for thirty years more," Kate says. "Or if it aint her, he'll get another one before cotton-picking."

"I reckon Cash and Darl can get married now," Eula says.

"That poor boy," Cora says. "The poor little tyke."

"What about Jewel?" Kate says.

"He can, too," Eula says.

"Hmph," Kate says. "I reckon he will. I reckon so. I reckon there's more gals than one around here that dont want to see Jewel tied down. Well, they needn't to worry."

"Why, Kate!" Cora says. The wagon begins to rattle. "The poor little tyke," Cora says.

It's fixing to rain this night. Yes, sir. A rattling wagon is mighty dry weather, for a Birdsell. But that'll be cured. It will for a fact.

"She ought to taken them cakes after she said she would," Kate says.

Anse

Durn that road. And it fixing to rain, too. I can stand here and same as see it with second-sight, a-shutting down behind them like a wall, shutting down betwixt them and my given promise. I do the best I can, much as I can get my mind on anything, but durn them boys.

A-laying there, right up to my door, where every bad luck that comes and goes is bound to find it. I told Addie it want[6] any luck living on a road when it come by here, and she said, for the world like a woman, "Get up and move, then." But I told her it want no luck in it, because the Lord put roads for travelling: why He laid them down flat on the earth. When He aims for something to be always a-moving, He makes it longways, like a road or a horse or a wagon, but when He aims for something to stay put, He makes it up-and-down ways, like a tree or a man. And so He never aimed for folks to live on a road, because which gets there first, I says, the road or the house? Did you ever know Him to set a road down by a house? I says. No you never, I says, because it's always men cant rest till they gets the house set where everybody that passes in a wagon can spit in the doorway, keeping the folks restless and wanting to get up and go somewheres else when He aimed for them to stay put like a tree or a stand of corn. Because if He'd a aimed for man to be always a-moving and going somewheres else, wouldn't He a put him longways on his belly, like a snake? It stands to reason He would.

6. Wasn't.

Putting it where every bad luck prowling can find it and come straight to my door, charging me taxes on top of it. Making me pay for Cash having to get them carpenter notions when if it hadn't been no road come there, he wouldn't a got them; falling off of churches and lifting no hand in six months and me and Addie slaving and a-slaving, when there's plenty of sawing on this place he could do if he's got to saw.

And Darl too. Talking me out of him, durn them. It aint that I am afraid of work; I always is fed me and mine and kept a roof above us: it's that they would short-hand me just because he tends to his own business, just because he's got his eyes full of the land all the time. I says to them, he was alright at first, with his eyes full of the land, because the land laid up-and-down ways then; it wasn't till that ere road come and switched the land around longways and his eyes still full of the land, they begun to threaten me out of him, trying to short-hand me with the law.

Making me pay for it. She was well and hale as ere a woman ever were, except for that road. Just laying down, resting herself in her own bed, asking naught of none. "Are you sick, Addie?" I said.

"I am not sick," she said.

"You lay you down and rest you," I said. "I knowed you are not sick. You're just tired. You lay you down and rest."

"I am not sick," she said. "I will get up."

"Lay still and rest," I said. "You are just tired. You can get up tomorrow." And she was laying there, well and hale as ere a woman ever were, except for that road.

"I never sent for you," I said. "I take you to witness I never sent for you."

"I know you didn't," Peabody said. "I bound that. Where is she?"

"She's a-laying down," I said. "She's just a little tired, but she'll—"

"Get outen here, Anse," he said. "Go set on the porch a while."

And now I got to pay for it, me without a tooth in my head, hoping to get ahead enough so I could get my mouth fixed where I could eat God's own victuals as a man should, and her hale and well as ere a woman in the land until that day. Got to pay for being put to the need of that three dollars. Got to pay for the way for them boys to have to go away to earn it. And now I can see same as second sight the rain shutting down betwixt us, a-coming up that road like a durn man, like it want ere a other house to rain on in all the living land.

I have heard men cuss their luck, and right, for they were sinful men. But I do not say it's a curse on me, because I have done no wrong to be cussed by. I am not religious, I reckon. But peace is my heart: I know it is. I have done things but neither better nor worse than them that pretend otherlike, and I know that Old Marster will care for me as for ere a sparrow that falls.[7] But it seems hard that a man in his need could be so flouted by a road.

Vardaman comes around the house, bloody as a hog to his knees, and that ere fish chopped up with the axe like as not, or maybe throwed away for him to lie about the dogs et it. Well, I reckon I aint no call to expect no more of him than of his man-growed brothers. He comes along, watching the house, quiet, and sits on the steps. "Whew," he says, "I'm pure tired."

"Go wash them hands," I say. But couldn't no woman strove harder than Addie to make them right, man and boy: I'll say that for her.

7. "As for every sparrow that falls." Cf. Matthew 10.29: "Are not two sparrows sold for a farthing? and one of them shall not fall on the ground without your Father."

"It was full of blood and guts as a hog," he says. But I just cant seem to get no heart into anything, with this here weather sapping me, too. "Pa," he says, "is ma sick some more?"

"Go wash them hands," I say. But I just cant seem to get no heart into it.

Darl

He has been to town this week: the back of his neck is trimmed close, with a white line between hair and sunburn like a joint of white bone. He has not once looked back.

"Jewel," I say. Back running, tunnelled between the two sets of bobbing mule ears, the road vanishes beneath the wagon as though it were a ribbon and the front axle were a spool. "Do you know she is going to die, Jewel?"

It takes two people to make you, and one people to die. That's how the world is going to end.

I said to Dewey Dell: "You want her to die so you can get to town: is that it?" She wouldn't say what we both knew. "The reason you will not say it is, when you say it, even to yourself, you will know it is true: is that it? But you know it is true now. I can almost tell you the day when you knew it is true. Why wont you say it, even to yourself?" She will not say it. She just keeps on saying Are you going to tell pa? Are you going to kill him? "You cannot believe it is true because you cannot believe that Dewey Dell, Dewey Dell Bundren, could have such bad luck: is that it?"

The sun, an hour above the horizon, is poised like a bloody egg upon a crest of thunderheads; the light has turned copper: in the eye portentous, in the nose sulphurous, smelling of lightning. When Peabody comes, they will have to use the rope. He has pussel-gutted himself eating cold greens. With the rope they will haul him up the path, balloon-like up the sulphurous air.

"Jewel," I say, "do you know that Addie Bundren is going to die? Addie Bundren is going to die?"

Peabody

When Anse finally sent for me of his own accord, I said "He has wore her out at last." And I said a damn good thing, and at first I would not go because there might be something I could do and I would have to haul her back, by God. I thought maybe they have the same sort of fool ethics in heaven they have in the Medical College and that it was maybe Vernon Tull sending for me again, getting me there in the nick of time, as Vernon always does things, getting the most for Anse's money like he does for his own. But when it got far enough into the day for me to read weather sign I knew it couldn't have been anybody but Anse that sent. I knew that nobody but a luckless man could ever need a doctor in the face of a cyclone. And I knew that if it had finally occurred to Anse himself that he needed one, it was already too late.

When I reach the spring and get down and hitch the team, the sun has gone down behind a bank of black cloud like a topheavy mountain range, like a load of cinders dumped over there, and there is no wind. I could hear Cash sawing for a mile before I got there. Anse is standing at the top of the bluff above the path.

"Where's the horse?" I say.

"Jewel's taken and gone," he says. "Cant nobody else ketch hit. You'll have to walk up, I reckon."

"Me, walk up, weighing two hundred and twenty-five pounds?" I say. "Walk up that durn wall?" He stands there beside a tree. Too bad the Lord made the mistake of giving trees roots and giving the Anse Bundrens He makes feet and legs. If He'd just swapped them, there wouldn't ever be a worry about this country being deforested someday. Or any other country. "What do you aim for me to do?" I say. "Stay here and get blowed clean out of the country when that cloud breaks?" Even with the horse it would take me fifteen minutes to ride up across the pasture to the top of the ridge and reach the house. The path looks like a crooked limb blown against the bluff. Anse has not been in town in twelve years. And how his mother ever got up there to bear him, he being his mother's son.

"Vardaman's gittin the rope," he says.

After a while Vardaman appears with the plowline. He gives the end of it to Anse and comes down the path, uncoiling it.

"You hold it tight," I say. "I done already wrote this visit onto my books, so I'm going to charge you just the same, whether I get there or not."

"I got hit," Anse says. "You kin come on up."

I'll be damned if I can see why I dont quit. A man seventy years old, weighing two hundred and odd pounds, being hauled up and down a damn mountain on a rope. I reckon it's because I must reach the fifty thousand dollar mark of dead accounts on my books before I can quit. "What the hell does your wife mean," I say, "taking sick on top of a durn mountain?"

"I'm right sorry," he says. He let the rope go, just dropped it, and he has turned toward the house. There is a little daylight up here still, of the color of sulphur matches. The boards look like strips of sulphur. Cash does not look back. Vernon Tull says he brings each board up to the window for her to see it and say it is all right. The boy overtakes us. Anse looks back at him. "Wher's the rope?" he says.

"It's where you left it," I say. "But never you mind that rope. I got to get back down that bluff. I dont aim for that storm to catch me up here. I'd blow too durn far once I got started."

The girl is standing by the bed, fanning her. When we enter she turns her head and looks at us. She has been dead these ten days. I suppose it's having been a part of Anse for so long that she cannot even make that change, if change it be. I can remember how when I was young I believed death to be a phenomenon of the body; now I know it to be merely a function of the mind—and that of the minds of the ones who suffer the bereavement. The nihilists say it is the end; the fundamentalists, the beginning; when in reality it is no more than a single tenant or family moving out of a tenement or a town.

She looks at us. Only her eyes seem to move. It's like they touch us, not with sight or sense, but like the stream from a hose touches you, the stream at the instant of impact as dissociated from the nozzle as though it had never been there. She does not look at Anse at all. She looks at me, then at the boy. Beneath the quilt she is no more than a bundle of rotten sticks.

"Well, Miss Addie," I say. The girl does not stop the fan. "How are you, sister?" I say. Her head lies gaunt on the pillow, looking at the boy. "You picked out a fine time to get me out here and bring up a storm." Then I send Anse and the boy out. She watches the boy as he leaves the room. She has not moved save her eyes.

He and Anse are on the porch when I come out, the boy sitting on the steps, Anse standing by a post, not even leaning against it, his arms dangling, the hair pushed and matted up on his head like a dipped rooster. He turns his head, blinking at me.

"Why didn't you send for me sooner?" I say.

"Hit was jest one thing and then another," he says. "That ere corn me and the boys was aimin to git up with, and Dewey Dell a-takin good keer of her, and folks comin in, a-offerin to help and sich, till I jest thought . . ."

"Damn the money," I say. "Did you ever hear of me worrying a fellow before he was ready to pay?"

"Hit aint begrudgin the money," he says. "I jest kept a-thinking . . . She's goin, is she?" The durn little tyke is sitting on the top step, looking smaller than ever in the sulphur-colored light. That's the one trouble with this country: everything, weather, all, hangs on too long. Like our rivers, our land: opaque, slow, violent; shaping and creating the life of man in its implacable and brooding image. "I knowed hit," Anse says. "All the while I made sho. Her mind is sot on hit."

"And a damn good thing, too," I say. "With a trifling—" He sits on the top step, small, motionless in faded overalls. When I came out he looked up at me, then at Anse. But now he has stopped looking at us. He just sits there.

"Have you told her yit?" Anse says.

"What for?" I say. "What the devil for?"

"She'll know hit. I knowed that when she see you she would know hit, same as writing. You wouldn't need to tell her. Her mind—"

Behind us the girl says, "Paw." I look at her, at her face.

"You better go quick," I say.

When we enter the room she is watching the door. She looks at me. Her eyes look like lamps blaring up just before the oil is gone. "She wants you to go out," the girl says.

"Now, Addie," Anse says, "when he come all the way from Jefferson to git you well?" She watches me: I can feel her eyes. It's like she was shoving at me with them. I have seen it before in women. Seen them drive from the room them coming with sympathy and pity, with actual help, and clinging to some trifling animal to whom they never were more than pack-horses. That's what they mean by the love that passeth understanding: that pride, that furious desire to hide that abject nakedness which we bring here with us, carry with us into operating rooms, carry stubbornly and furiously with us into the earth again. I leave the room. Beyond the porch Cash's saw snores steadily into the board. A minute later she calls his name, her voice harsh and strong.

"Cash," she says; "you, Cash!"

Darl

Pa stands beside the bed. From behind his leg Vardaman peers, with his round head and his eyes round and his mouth beginning to open. She looks at pa; all her failing life appears to drain into her eyes, urgent, irremediable. "It's Jewel she wants," Dewey Dell says.

"Why, Addie," pa says, "him and Darl went to make one more load. They thought there was time. That you would wait for them, and that three dollars and all . . ." He stoops laying his hand on hers. For a while yet she looks at him, without reproach, without anything at all, as if her eyes alone are listening to the irrevocable cessation of his voice. Then she raises herself, who has not moved in ten days. Dewey Dell leans down, trying to press her back.

"Ma," she says; "ma."

She is looking out the window, at Cash stooping steadily at the board in the failing light, laboring on toward darkness and into it as though the stroking of the saw illumined its own motion, board and saw engendered.

"You, Cash," she shouts, her voice harsh, strong, and unimpaired. "You, Cash!"

He looks up at the gaunt face framed by the window in the twilight. It is a composite picture of all time since he was a child. He drops the saw and lifts the board for her to see, watching the window in which the face has not moved. He drags a second plank into position and slants the two of them into their final juxtaposition, gesturing toward the ones yet on the ground, shaping with his empty hand in pantomime the finished box. For a while still she looks down at him from the composite picture, neither with censure nor approbation. Then the face disappears.

She lies back and turns her head without so much as glancing at pa. She looks at Vardaman; her eyes, the life in them, rushing suddenly upon them; the two flames glare up for a steady instant. Then they go out as though someone had leaned down and blown upon them.

"Ma," Dewey Dell says; "ma!" Leaning above the bed, her hands lifted a little, the fan still moving like it has for ten days, she begins to keen. Her voice is strong, young, tremulous and clear, rapt with its own timbre and volume, the fan still moving steadily up and down, whispering the useless air. Then she flings herself across Addie Bundren's knees, clutching her, shaking her with the furious strength of the young before sprawling suddenly across the handful of rotten bones that Addie Bundren left, jarring the whole bed into a chattering sibilance of mattress shucks, her arms outflung and the fan in one hand still beating with expiring breath into the quilt.

From behind pa's leg Vardaman peers, his mouth full open all color draining from his face into his mouth, as though he has by some means fleshed his own teeth in himself, sucking. He begins to move slowly backward from the bed, his eyes round, his pale face fading into the dusk like a piece of paper pasted on a failing wall, and so out of the door.

Pa leans above the bed in the twilight, his humped silhouette partaking of that owl-like quality of awry-feathered, disgruntled outrage within which lurks a wisdom too profound or too inert for even thought.

"Durn them boys," he says.

Jewel, I say. Overhead the day drives level and gray, hiding the sun by a flight of gray spears. In the rain the mules smoke a little, splashed yellow with mud, the off[8] *one clinging in sliding lunges to the side of the road above the ditch. The tilted lumber gleams dull yellow, water-soaked and heavy as lead, tilted at a steep angle into the ditch above the broken wheel; about the shattered spokes and about Jewel's ankles a runnel of yellow neither water nor earth swirls, curving with the yellow road neither of earth nor water, down the hill dissolving into a streaming mass of dark green neither of earth nor sky, Jewel, I say*

8. Right.

Cash comes to the door, carrying the saw. Pa stands beside the bed, humped, his arms dangling. He turns his head, his shabby profile, his chin collapsing slowly as he works the snuff against his gums.

"She's gone," Cash says.

"She taken and left us," pa says. Cash does not look at him. "How nigh are you done?" pa says. Cash does not answer. He enters, carrying the saw. "I reckon you better get at it," pa says. "You'll have to do the best you can, with them boys gone off that-a-way." Cash looks down at her face. He is not listening to pa at all. He does not approach the bed. He stops in the middle of the floor, the saw against his leg, his sweating arms powdered lightly with sawdust, his face composed. "If you get in a tight, maybe some of them'll get here tomorrow and help you," pa says. "Vernon could." Cash is not listening. He is looking down at her peaceful, rigid face fading into the dusk as though darkness were a precursor of the ultimate earth, until at last the face seems to float detached upon it, lightly as the reflection of a dead leaf. "There is Christians enough to help you," pa says. Cash is not listening. After a while he turns without looking at pa and leaves the room. Then the saw begins to snore again. "They will help us in our sorrow," pa says.

The sound of the saw is steady, competent, unhurried, stirring the dying light so that at each stroke her face seems to wake a little into an expression of listening and of waiting, as though she were counting the strokes. Pa looks down at the face, at the black sprawl of Dewey Dell's hair, the outflung arms, the clutched fan now motionless on the fading quilt. "I reckon you better get supper on," he says.

Dewey Dell does not move.

"Git up, now, and put supper on," pa says. "We got to keep our strength up. I reckon Doctor Peabody's right hungry, coming all this way. And Cash'll need to eat quick and get back to work so he can finish it in time."

Dewey Dell rises, heaving to her feet. She looks down at the face. It is like a casting of fading bronze upon the pillow, the hands alone still with any semblance of life: a curled, gnarled inertness; a spent yet alert quality from which weariness, exhaustion, travail has not yet departed, as though they doubted even yet the actuality of rest, guarding with horned and penurious alertness the cessation which they know cannot last.

Dewey Dell stoops and slides the quilt from beneath them and draws it up over them to the chin, smoothing it down, drawing it smooth. Then without looking at pa she goes around the bed and leaves the room.

She will go out where Peabody is, where she can stand in the twilight and look at his back with such an expression that, feeling her eyes and turning, he will say: I would not let it grieve me, now. She was old, and sick too. Suffering more than we knew. She couldn't have got well. Vardaman's getting big now, and with you to take good care of them all. I would try not to let it grieve me. I expect you'd better go and get some supper ready. It dont have to be much. But they'll need to eat, and she looking at him, saying You could do so much for me if you just would. If you just knew. I am I and you are you and I know it and you dont know it and you could do so much for me if you just would and if you just would then I could tell you and then nobody would have to know it except you and me and Darl

Pa stands over the bed, dangle-armed, humped, motionless. He raises his hand to his head, scouring his hair, listening to the saw. He comes nearer and rubs his hand, palm and back, on his thigh and lays it on her face and then on the hump of quilt where her hands are. He touches the quilt as he saw Dewey Dell do, trying to smoothe it up to the chin, but disarranging it instead. He tries to smoothe it again, clumsily, his hand awkward as a claw, smoothing at the wrinkles which he made and which continue to emerge beneath his hand with perverse ubiquity, so that at last he desists, his hand falling to his side and stroking itself again, palm and back, on his thigh. The sound of the saw snores steadily into the room. Pa breathes with a quiet, rasping sound, mouthing the snuff against his gums. "God's will be done," he says. "Now I can get them teeth."

Jewel's hat droops limp about his neck, channelling water onto the soaked towsack tied about his shoulders as, ankle-deep in the running ditch, he pries with a slipping two-by-four, with a piece of rotting log for fulcrum, at the axle. Jewel, I say, she is dead, Jewel. Addie Bundren is dead

Vardaman

Then I begin to run. I run toward the back and come to the edge of the porch and stop. Then I begin to cry. I can feel where the fish was in the dust. It is cut up into pieces of not-fish now, not-blood on my hands and overalls. Then it wasn't so. It hadn't happened then. And now she is getting so far ahead I cannot catch her.

The trees look like chickens when they ruffle out into the cool dust on the hot days. If I jump off the porch I will be where the fish was, and it all cut up into not-fish now. I can hear the bed and her face and them and I can feel the floor shake when he walks on it that came and did it. That came and did it when she was all right but he came and did it.

"The fat son of a bitch."

I jump from the porch, running. The top of the barn comes swooping up out of the twilight. If I jump I can go through it like the pink lady in the circus, into the warm smelling, without having to wait. My hands grab at the bushes; beneath my feet the rocks and dirt go rubbling down.

Then I can breathe again, in the warm smelling. I enter the stall, trying to touch him, and then I can cry then I vomit the crying. As soon as he gets through kicking I can and then I can cry, the crying can.

"He kilt her. He kilt her."

The life in him runs under the skin, under my hand, running through the splotches, smelling up into my nose where the sickness is beginning to cry, vomiting the crying, and then I can breathe, vomiting it. It makes a lot of noise. I can smell the life running up from under my hands, up my arms, and then I can leave the stall.

I cannot find it. In the dark, along the dust, the walls I cannot find it. The crying makes a lot of noise. I wish it wouldn't make so much noise. Then I find it in the wagon shed, in the dust, and I run across the lot and into the road, the stick jouncing on my shoulder.

They watch me as I run up, beginning to jerk back, their eyes rolling, snorting, jerking back on the hitch-rein. I strike. I can hear the stick striking; I can see it hitting their heads, the breast-yoke, missing altogether sometimes as they rear and plunge, but I am glad.

"You kilt my maw!"

The stick breaks, they rearing and snorting, their feet popping loud on the ground; loud because it is going to rain and the air is empty for the rain. But it is still long enough. I run this way and that as they rear and jerk at the hitch-rein, striking.

"You kilt her!"

I strike at them, striking, they wheeling in a long lunge, the buggy wheeling onto two wheels and motionless like it is nailed to the ground and the horses motionless like they are nailed by the hind feet to the center of a whirling plate.

I run in the dust. I cannot see, running in the sucking dust where the buggy vanishes tilted on two wheels. I strike, the stick hitting into the ground, bouncing, striking into the dust and then into the air again and the dust sucking on down the road faster than if a car was in it. And then I can cry, looking at the stick. It is broken down to my hand, not longer than stove wood that was a long stick. I throw it away and I can cry. It does not make so much noise now.

The cow is standing in the barn door, chewing. When she sees me come into the lot she lows, her mouth full of flopping green, her tongue flopping.

"I aint a-goin to milk you. I aint a-goin to do nothing for them."

I hear her turn when I pass. When I turn she is just behind me with her sweet, hot, hard breath.

"Didn't I tell you I wouldn't?"

She nudges me, snuffing. She moans deep inside, her mouth closed. I jerk my hand, cursing her like Jewel does.

"Git, now."

I stoop my hand to the ground and run at her. She jumps back and whirls away and stops, watching me. She moans. She goes on to the path and stands there, looking up the path.

It is dark in the barn, warm, smelling, silent. I can cry quietly, watching the top of the hill.

Cash comes to the hill, limping where he fell off of the church. He looks down at the spring, then up the road and back toward the barn. He comes down the path stiffly and looks at the broken hitch-rein and at the dust in the road and then up the road, where the dust is gone.

"I hope they've got clean past Tull's by now. I so hope hit."

Cash turns and limps up the path.

"Durn him. I showed him. Durn him."

I am not crying now. I am not anything. Dewey Dell comes to the hill and calls me. Vardaman. I am not anything. I am quiet. You, Vardaman. I can cry quiet now, feeling and hearing my tears.

"Then hit want. Hit hadn't happened then. Hit was a-layin right there on the ground. And now she's gittin ready to cook hit."

It is dark. I can hear wood, silence: I know them. But not living sounds, not even him. It is as though the dark were resolving him out of his integrity, into an unrelated scattering of components—snuffings and stampings; smells of cooling flesh and ammoniac hair; an illusion of a co-ordinated whole of splotched hide and strong bones within which, detached and secret and familiar, an *is* different from my *is*. I see him dissolve—legs, a rolling eye, a gaudy splotching like cold flames—and float upon the dark in fading solution; all one yet neither; all either yet none. I can see hearing coil toward him, caressing, shaping his hard shape—fetlock, hip, shoulder and head; smell and sound. I am not afraid.

"Cooked and et. Cooked and et."

Dewey Dell

He could do so much for me if he just would. He could do everything for me. It's like everything in the world for me is inside a tub full of guts, so that you wonder how there can be any room in it for anything else very important. He is a big tub of guts and I am a little tub of guts and if there is not any room for anything else important in a big tub of guts, how can it be room in a little tub of guts. But I know it is there because God gave women a sign when something has happened bad.

It's because I am alone. If I could just feel it, it would be different, because I would not be alone. But if I were not alone, everybody would know it. And he could do so much for me, and then I would not be alone. Then I could be all right alone.

I would let him come in between me and Lafe, like Darl came in between me and Lafe, and so Lafe is alone too. He is Lafe and I am Dewey Dell, and when mother died I had to go beyond and outside of me and Lafe and Darl to grieve because he could do so much for me and he dont know it. He dont even know it.

From the back porch I cannot see the barn. Then the sound of Cash's sawing comes in from that way. It is like a dog outside the house, going back and forth around the house to whatever door you come to, waiting to come in. He said I worry more than you do and I said You dont know what worry is so I cant worry. I try to but I cant think long enough to worry.

I light the kitchen lamp. The fish, cut into jagged pieces, bleeds quietly in the pan. I put it into the cupboard quick, listening into the hall, hearing. It took her ten days to die; maybe she dont know it is yet. Maybe she wont go until Cash. Or maybe until Jewel. I take the dish of greens from the cupboard and the bread pan from the cold stove, and I stop, watching the door.

"Where's Vardaman?" Cash says. In the lamp his sawdusted arms look like sand.

"I dont know. I aint seen him."

"Peabody's team run away. See if you can find Vardaman. The horse will let him catch him."

"Well. Tell them to come to supper."

I cannot see the barn. I said, I dont know how to worry. I dont know how to cry. I tried, but I cant. After a while the sound of the saw comes around, coming dark along the ground in the dust-dark. Then I can see him, going up and down above the plank.

"You come in to supper," I say. "Tell him." He could do everything for me. And he dont know it. He is his guts and I am my guts. And I am Lafe's guts. That's it. I dont see why he didn't stay in town. We are country people, not as good as town people. I dont see why he didn't. Then I can see the top of the barn. The cow stands at the foot of the path, lowing. When I turn back, Cash is gone.

I carry the buttermilk in. Pa and Cash and he are at the table.

"Where's that big fish Bud caught, sister?" he says.

I set the milk on the table. "I never had no time to cook it."

"Plain turnip greens is mighty spindling eating for a man my size," he says. Cash is eating. About his head the print of his hat is sweated into his hair. His shirt is blotched with sweat. He has not washed his hands and arms.

"You ought to took time," pa says. "Where's Vardaman?"

I go toward the door. "I cant find him."

"Here, sister," he says; "never mind about the fish. It'll save, I reckon. Come on and sit down."

"I aint minding it," I say. "I'm going to milk before it sets in to rain."

Pa helps himself and pushes the dish on. But he does not begin to eat. His hands are halfclosed on either side of his plate, his head bowed a little, his awry hair standing into the lamplight. He looks like right after the maul hits the steer and it no longer alive and dont yet know that it is dead.

But Cash is eating, and he is too. "You better eat something," he says. He is looking at pa. "Like Cash and me. You'll need it."

"Ay," pa says. He rouses up, like a steer that's been kneeling in a pond and you run at it. "She would not begrudge me it."

When I am out of sight of the house, I go fast. The cow lows at the foot of the bluff. She nuzzles at me, snuffing, blowing her breath in a sweet, hot blast, through my dress, against my hot nakedness, moaning. "You got to wait a little while. Then I'll tend to you." She follows me into the barn where I set the bucket down. She breathes into the bucket, moaning. "I told you. You just got to wait, now. I got more to do than I can tend to." The barn is dark. When I pass, he kicks the wall a single blow. I go on. The broken plank is like a pale plank standing on end. Then I can see the slope, feel the air moving on my face again, slow, pale with lesser dark and with empty seeing, the pine clumps blotched up the tilted slope, secret and waiting.

The cow in silhouette against the door nuzzles at the silhouette of the bucket, moaning.

Then I pass the stall. I have almost passed it. I listen to it saying for a long time before it can say the word and the listening part is afraid that there may not be time to say it. I feel my body, my bones and flesh beginning to part and open upon the alone, and the process of coming unalone is terrible. Lafe. Lafe. "Lafe" Lafe. Lafe. I lean a little forward, one foot advanced with dead walking. I feel the darkness rushing past my breast, past the cow; I begin to rush upon the darkness but the cow stops me and the darkness rushes on upon the sweet blast of her moaning breath, filled with wood and with silence.

"Vardaman. You, Vardaman."

He comes out of the stall. "You durn little sneak! You durn little sneak!"

He does not resist; the last of rushing darkness flees whistling away. "What? I aint done nothing."

"You durn little sneak!" My hands shake him, hard. Maybe I couldn't stop them. I didn't know they could shake so hard. They shake both of us, shaking.

"I never done it," he says. "I never touched them."

My hands stop shaking him, but I still hold him. "What are you doing here? Why didn't you answer when I called you?"

"I aint doing nothing."

"You go on to the house and get your supper."

He draws back. I hold him. "You quit now. You leave me be."

"What are you doing down here? You didn't come down here to sneak after me?"

"I never. I never. You quit, now. I didn't even know you was down here. You leave me be."

I hold him, leaning down to see his face, feel it with my eyes. He is about to cry. "Go on, now. I done put supper on and I'll be there soon as I milk. You better go on before he eats everything up. I hope that team runs clean back to Jefferson."

"He kilt her," he says. He begins to cry.

"Hush."

"She never hurt him and he come and kilt her."

"Hush." He struggles. I hold him. "Hush."

"He kilt her." The cow comes up behind us, moaning. I shake him again.

"You stop it, now. Right this minute. You're fixing to make yourself sick and then you cant go to town. You go on to the house and eat your supper."

"I dont want no supper. I dont want to go to town."

"We'll leave you here, then. Lessen you behave, we will leave you. Go on, now, before that old green-eating tub of guts eats everything up from you." He goes on, disappearing slowly into the hill. The crest, the trees, the roof of the house stand against the sky. The cow nuzzles at me, moaning. "You'll just have to wait. What you got in you aint nothing to what I got in me, even if you are a woman too." She follows me, moaning. Then the dead, hot, pale air breathes on my face again. He could fix it all right, if he just would. And he dont even know it. He could do everything for me if he just knowed it. The cow breathes upon my hips and back, her breath warm, sweet, stertorous, moaning. The sky lies flat down the slope, upon the secret clumps. Beyond the hill sheet-lightning stains upward and fades. The dead air shapes the dead earth in the dead darkness, further away than seeing shapes the dead earth. It lies dead and warm upon me, touching me naked through my clothes. I said You dont know what worry is. I dont know what it is. I dont know whether I am worrying or not. Whether I can or not. I dont know whether I can cry or not, I dont know whether I have tried to or not. I feel like a wet seed wild in the hot blind earth.

Vardaman

When they get it finished they are going to put her in it and then for a long time I couldn't say it. I saw the dark stand up and go whirling away and I said "Are you going to nail her up in it, Cash? Cash? Cash?" I got shut up in the crib the new door it was too heavy for me it went shut I couldn't breathe because the rat was breathing up all the air, I said "Are you going to nail it shut, Cash? Nail it? *Nail* it?"

Pa walks around. His shadow walks around, over Cash going up and down above the saw, at the bleeding plank.

Dewey Dell said we will get some bananas. The train is behind the glass, red on the track. When it runs the track shines on and off. Pa said flour and sugar and coffee costs so much. Because I am a country boy because boys in town. Bicycles. Why do flour and sugar and coffee cost so much when he is a country boy. "Wouldn't you ruther have some bananas instead?" Bananas are gone, eaten. Gone. When it runs on the track shines again. "Why aint I a town boy, pa?" I said. God made me. I did not said to God to made me in the country. If He can make the train, why cant He make them all in the town because flour and sugar and coffee. "Wouldn't you ruther have bananas?"

He walks around. His shadow walks around.

It was not her. I was there, looking. I saw. I thought it was her, but it was not. It was not my mother. She went away when the other one laid down in her bed and drew the quilt up. She went away. "Did she go as far as town?" "She went further than town." "Did all those rabbits and possums go further than town?" God made the rabbits and possums. He made the train. Why must He make a different place for them to go if she is just like the rabbit.

Pa walks around. His shadow does. The saw sounds like it is asleep.

And so if Cash nails the box up, she is not a rabbit. And so if she is not a rabbit I couldn't breathe in the crib and Cash is going to nail it up. And so if she lets him it is not her. I know. I was there. I saw when it did not be her. I saw. They think it is and Cash is going to nail it up.

It was not her because it was laying right yonder in the dirt. And now it's all chopped up. I chopped it up. It's laying in the kitchen in the bleeding pan, waiting to be cooked and et. Then it wasn't and she was, and now it is and she wasn't. And tomorrow it will be cooked and et and she will be him and pa and Cash and Dewey Dell and there wont be anything in the box and so she can breathe. It was laying right yonder on the ground. I can get Vernon. He was there and he seen it, and with both of us it will be and then it will not be.

Tull

It was nigh to midnight and it had set in to rain when he woke us. It had been a misdoubtful night, with the storm making; a night when a fellow looks for most anything to happen before he can get the stock fed and himself to the house and supper et and in bed with the rain starting, and when Peabody's team come up, lathered, with the broke harness dragging and the neck-yoke betwixt the off critter's legs, Cora says "It's Addie Bundren. She's gone at last."

"Peabody mought have been to ere a one of a dozen houses hereabouts," I says. "Besides, how do you know it's Peabody's team?"

"Well, aint it?" she says. "You hitch up, now."

"What for?" I says. "If she is gone, we cant do nothing till morning. And it fixing to storm, too."

"It's my duty," she says. "You put the team in."

But I wouldn't do it. "It stands to reason they'd send for us if they needed us. You dont even know she's gone yet."

"Why, dont you know that's Peabody's team? Do you claim it aint? Well, then." But I wouldn't go. When folks wants a fellow, it's best to wait till they sends for him, I've found. "It's my Christian duty," Cora says. "Will you stand between me and my Christian duty?"

"You can stay there all day tomorrow, if you want," I says.

So when Cora waked me it had set in to rain. Even while I was going to the door with the lamp and it shining on the glass so he could see I am coming, it kept on knocking. Not loud, but steady, like he might have gone to sleep thumping, but I never noticed how low down on the door the knocking was till I opened it and never seen nothing. I held the lamp up, with the rain sparkling across it and Cora back in the hall saying "Who is it, Vernon?" but I couldn't see nobody a-tall at first until I looked down and around the door, lowering the lamp.

He looked like a drownded puppy, in them overalls, without no hat, splashed up to his knees where he had walked them four miles in the mud. "Well, I'll be durned," I says.

"Who is it, Vernon?" Cora says.

He looked at me, his eyes round and black in the middle like when you throw a light in a owl's face. "You mind[9] that ere fish," he says.

"Come in the house," I says. "What is it? Is your maw—"

"Vernon," Cora says.

He stood kind of around behind the door, in the dark. The rain was blowing onto the lamp, hissing on it so I am scared every minute it'll break. "You was there," he says. "You seen it."

Then Cora come to the door. "You come right in outen the rain," she says, pulling him in and him watching me. He looked just like a drownded puppy. "I told you," Cora says. "I told you it was a-happening. You go and hitch."

"But he aint said—" I says.

He looked at me, dripping onto the floor. "He's a-ruining the rug," Cora says. "You go get the team while I take him to the kitchen."

But he hung back, dripping, watching me with them eyes. "You was there. You seen it laying there. Cash is fixing to nail her up, and it was a-laying right there on the ground. You seen it. You seen the mark in the dirt. The rain never come up till after I was a-coming here. So we can get back in time."

I be durn if it didn't give me the creeps, even when I didn't know yet. But Cora did. "You get that team quick as you can," she says. "He's outen his head with grief and worry."

I be durn if it didn't give me the creeps. Now and then a fellow gets to thinking. About all the sorrow and afflictions in this world; how it's liable to strike anywhere, like lightning. I reckon it does take a powerful trust in the Lord to guard a fellow, though sometimes I think that Cora's a mite overcautious, like she was trying to crowd the other folks away and get in closer than anybody else. But then, when something like this happens, I reckon she is right and you got to keep after it and I reckon I am blessed in having a wife that ever strives for sanctity and well-doing like she says I am.

Now and then a fellow gets to thinking about it. Not often, though. Which is a good thing. For the Lord aimed for him to do and not to spend too much time thinking, because his brain it's like a piece of machinery: it wont stand a whole lot of racking. It's best when it all runs along the same, doing the day's work and not no one part used no more than needful. I have said and I say again, that's ever living thing the matter with Darl: he just thinks by himself too much. Cora's right when she says all he needs is a wife to straighten him out. And when I think about that, I think that if nothing but being married will help a man, he's durn nigh hopeless. But I reckon Cora's right when she says the reason the Lord had to create women is because man dont know his own good when he sees it.

9. Remember.

When I come back to the house with the team, they was in the kitchen. She was dressed on top of her nightgown, with a shawl over her head and her umbrella and her bible wrapped up in the oilcloth, and him sitting on a up-turned bucket on the stove-zinc where she had put him, dripping onto the floor. "I cant get nothing outen him except about a fish," she says. "It's a judgment on them. I see the hand of the Lord upon this boy for Anse Bundren's judgment and warning."

"The rain never come up till after I left," he says. "I had done left. I was on the way. And so it was there in the dust. You seen it. Cash is fixing to nail her, but you seen it."

When we got there it was raining hard, and him sitting on the seat between us, wrapped up in Cora's shawl. He hadn't said nothing else, just sitting there with Cora holding the umbrella over him. Now and then Cora would stop singing long enough to say "It's a judgment on Anse Bundren. May it show him the path of sin he is a-trodding." Then she would sing again, and him sitting there between us, leaning forward a little like the mules couldn't go fast enough to suit him.

"It was laying right yonder," he says, "but the rain come up after I taken and left. So I can go and open the windows, because Cash aint nailed her yet."

It was long a-past midnight when we drove the last nail, and almost dust-dawn when I got back home and taken the team out and got back in bed, with Cora's nightcap laying on the other pillow. And be durned if even then it wasn't like I could still hear Cora singing and feel that boy leaning forward between us like he was ahead of the mules, and still see Cash going up and down with that saw, and Anse standing there like a scarecrow, like he was a steer standing knee-deep in a pond and somebody come by and set the pond up on edge and he aint missed it yet.

It was nigh toward daybreak when we drove the last nail and toted it into the house, where she was laying on the bed with the window open and the rain blowing on her again. Twice he did it, and him so dead for sleep that Cora says his face looked like one of these here Christmas masts[1] that had done been buried a while and then dug up, until at last they put her into it and nailed it down so he couldn't open the window on her no more. And the next morning they found him in his shirt tail, laying asleep on the floor like a felled steer, and the top of the box bored clean full of holes and Cash's new auger broke off in the last one. When they taken the lid off they found that two of them had bored on into her face.

If it's a judgment, it aint right. Because the Lord's got more to do than that. He's bound to have. Because the only burden Anse Bundren's ever had is himself. And when folks talks him low, I think to myself he aint that less of a man or he couldn't a bore himself this long.

It aint right. I be durn if it is. Because He said Suffer little children to come unto Me dont make it right, neither. Cora said, "I have bore you what the Lord God sent me. I faced it without fear nor terror because my faith was strong in the Lord, a-bolstering and sustaining me. If you have no son, it's because the Lord has decreed otherwise in His wisdom. And my life is and has ever been a open book to ere a man or woman among His creatures because I trust in my God and my reward."

1. Masks.

I reckon she's right. I reckon if there's ere a man or woman anywhere that He could turn it all over to and go away with His mind at rest, it would be Cora. And I reckon she would make a few changes, no matter how He was running it. And I reckon they would be for man's good. Leastways, we would have to like them. Leastways, we might as well go on and make like we did.

Darl

The lantern sits on a stump. Rusted, grease-fouled, its cracked chimney smeared on one side with a soaring smudge of soot, it sheds a feeble and sultry glare upon the trestles and the boards and the adjacent earth. Upon the dark ground the chips look like random smears of soft pale paint on a black canvas. The boards look like long smooth tatters torn from the flat darkness and turned backside out.

Cash labors about the trestles, moving back and forth, lifting and placing the planks with long clattering reverberations in the dead air as though he were lifting and dropping them at the bottom of an invisible well, the sounds ceasing without departing, as if any movement might dislodge them from the immediate air in reverberant repetition. He saws again, his elbow flashing slowly, a thin thread of fire running along the edge of the saw, lost and recovered at the top and bottom of each stroke in unbroken elongation, so that the saw appears to be six feet long, into and out of pa's shabby and aimless silhouette. "Give me that plank," Cash says. "No; the other one." He puts the saw down and comes and picks up the plank he wants, sweeping pa away with the long swinging gleam of the balanced board.

The air smells like sulphur. Upon the impalpable plane of it their shadows form as upon a wall, as though like sound they had not gone very far away in falling but had merely congealed for a moment, immediate and musing. Cash works on, half turned into the feeble light, one thigh and one pole-thin arm braced, his face sloped into the light with a rapt, dynamic immobility above his tireless elbow. Below the sky sheet-lightning slumbers lightly; against it the trees, motionless, are ruffled out to the last twig, swollen, increased as though quick with young.

It begins to rain. The first harsh, sparse, swift drops rush through the leaves and across the ground in a long sigh, as though of relief from intolerable suspense. They are big as buckshot, warm as though fired from a gun; they sweep across the lantern in a vicious hissing. Pa lifts his face, slack-mouthed, the wet black rim of snuff plastered close along the base of his gums; from behind his slack-faced astonishment he muses as though from beyond time, upon the ultimate outrage. Cash looks once at the sky, then at the lantern. The saw has not faltered, the running gleam of its pistoning edge unbroken. "Get something to cover the lantern," he says.

Pa goes to the house. The rain rushes suddenly down, without thunder, without warning of any sort; he is swept onto the porch upon the edge of it and in an instant Cash is wet to the skin. Yet the motion of the saw has not faltered, as though it and the arm functioned in a tranquil conviction that rain was an illusion of the mind. Then he puts down the saw and goes and crouches above the lantern, shielding it with his body, his back shaped lean and scrawny by his wet shirt as though he had been abruptly turned wrong-side out, shirt and all.

Pa returns. He is wearing Jewel's raincoat and carrying Dewey Dell's. Squatting over the lantern, Cash reaches back and picks up four sticks and drives them into the earth and takes Dewey Dell's raincoat from pa and spreads it over the sticks, forming a roof above the lantern. Pa watches him. "I dont know what you'll do," he says. "Darl taken his coat with him."

"Get wet," Cash says. He takes up the saw again; again it moves up and down, in and out of that unhurried imperviousness as a piston moves in the oil; soaked, scrawny, tireless, with the lean light body of a boy or an old man. Pa watches him, blinking, his face streaming; again he looks up at the sky with that expression of dumb and brooding outrage and yet of vindication, as though he had expected no less; now and then he stirs; moves, gaunt and streaming, picking up a board or a tool and then laying it down. Vernon Tull is there now, and Cash is wearing Mrs Tull's raincoat and he and Vernon are hunting the saw. After a while they find it in pa's hand.

"Why don't you go on to the house, out of the rain?" Cash says. Pa looks at him, his face streaming slowly. It is as though upon a face carved by a savage caricaturist a monstrous burlesque of all bereavement flowed. "You go on in," Cash says. "Me and Vernon can finish it."

Pa looks at them. The sleeves of Jewel's coat are too short for him. Upon his face the rain streams, slow as cold glycerin. "I dont begrudge her the wetting," he says. He moves again and falls to shifting the planks, picking them up, laying them down again carefully, as though they are glass. He goes to the lantern and pulls at the propped raincoat until he knocks it down and Cash comes and fixes it back.

"You get on to the house," Cash says. He leads pa to the house and returns with the raincoat and folds it and places it beneath the shelter where the lantern sits. Vernon has not stopped. He looks up, still sawing.

"You ought to done that at first," he says. "You knowed it was fixing to rain."

"It's his fever," Cash says. He looks at the board.

"Ay," Vernon says. "He'd a come, anyway."

Cash squints at the board. On the long flank of it the rain crashed steadily, myriad, fluctuant. "I'm going to bevel it," he says.

"It'll take more time," Vernon says. Cash sets the plank on edge; a moment longer Vernon watches him, then he hands him the plane.

Vernon holds the board steady while Cash bevels the edge of it with the tedious and minute care of a jeweler. Mrs Tull comes to the edge of the porch and calls Vernon. "How near are you done?" she says.

Vernon does not look up. "Not long. Some, yet."

She watches Cash stooping at the plank, the turgid savage gleam of the lantern slicking on the raincoat as he moves. "You go down and get some planks off the barn and finish it and come in out of the rain," she says. "You'll both catch your death." Vernon does not move. "Vernon," she says.

"We wont be long," he says. "We'll be done after a spell." Mrs Tull watches them a while. Then she reenters the house.

"If we git in a tight, we could take some of them planks," Vernon says. "I'll help you put them back."

Cash ceases the plane and squints along the plank, wiping it with his palm. "Give me the next one," he says.

Some time toward dawn the rain ceases. But it is not yet day when Cash drives the last nail and stands stiffly up and looks down at the finished coffin, the others watching him. In the lantern light his face is calm, musing; slowly he strokes his hands on his raincoated thighs in a gesture deliberate, final and composed. Then the four of them—Cash and pa and Vernon and Peabody—raise the coffin to their shoulders and turn toward the house. It is light, yet they move slowly; empty, yet they carry it carefully; lifeless, yet they move with hushed precautionary words to one another, speaking of it as though, complete, it now slumbered lightly alive, waiting to come awake. On the dark floor their feet clump awkwardly, as though for a long time they have not walked on floors.

They set it down by the bed. Peabody says quietly: "Let's eat a snack. It's almost daylight. Where's Cash?"

He has returned to the trestles, stooped again in the lantern's feeble glare as he gathers up his tools and wipes them on a cloth carefully and puts them into the box with its leather sling to go over the shoulder. Then he takes up box, lantern and raincoat and returns to the house, mounting the steps into faint silhouette against the paling east.

In a strange room you must empty yourself for sleep. And before you are emptied for sleep, what are you. And when you are emptied for sleep, you are not. And when you are filled with sleep, you never were. I dont know what I am. I dont know if I am or not. Jewel knows he is, because he does not know that he does not know whether he is or not. He cannot empty himself for sleep because he is not what he is and he is what he is not. Beyond the unlamped wall I can hear the rain shaping the wagon that is ours, the load that is no longer theirs that felled and sawed it nor yet theirs that bought it and which is not ours either, lie on our wagon though it does, since only the wind and the rain shape it only to Jewel and me, that are not asleep. And since sleep is is-not and rain and wind are *was,* it is not. Yet the wagon *is,* because when the wagon is *was,* Addie Bundren will not be. And Jewel *is,* so Addie Bundren must be. And then I must be, or I could not empty myself for sleep in a strange room. And so if I am not emptied yet, I am *is.*

How often have I lain beneath rain on a strange roof, thinking of home.

Cash

I made it on the bevel.

1. There is more surface for the nails to grip.
2. There is twice the gripping-surface to each seam.
3. The water will have to seep into it on a slant. Water moves easiest up and down or straight across.
4. In a house people are upright two thirds of the time. So the seams and joints are made up-and-down. Because the stress is up-and-down.
5. In a bed where people lie down all the time, the joints and seams are made sideways, because the stress is sideways.
6. Except.
7. A body is not square like a crosstie.
8. Animal magnetism.
9. The animal magnetism of a dead body makes the stress come slanting, so the seams and joints of a coffin are made on the bevel.
10. You can see by an old grave that the earth sinks down on the bevel.

11. While in a natural hole it sinks by the center, the stress being up-and-down.
12. So I made it on the bevel.
13. It makes a neater job.

Vardaman

My mother is a fish.

Tull

It was ten oclock when I got back, with Peabody's team hitched on to the back of the wagon. They had already dragged the buckboard back from where Quick found it upside down straddle of the ditch about a mile from the spring. It was pulled out of the road at the spring, and about a dozen wagons was already there. It was Quick found it. He said the river was up and still rising. He said it had already covered the highest water-mark on the bridge-piling he had ever seen. "That bridge wont stand a whole lot of water," I said. "Has somebody told Anse about it?"

"I told him," Quick said. "He says he reckons them boys has heard and unloaded and are on the way back by now. He says they can load up and get across."

"He better go on and bury her at New Hope," Armstid said. "That bridge is old. I wouldn't monkey with it."

"His mind is set on taking her to Jefferson," Quick said.

"Then he better get at it soon as he can," Armstid said.

Anse meets us at the door. He has shaved, but not good. There is a long cut on his jaw, and he is wearing his Sunday pants and a white shirt with the neckband buttoned. It is drawn smooth over his hump, making it look bigger than ever, like a white shirt will, and his face is different too. He looks folks in the eye now, dignified, his face tragic and composed, shaking us by the hand as we walk up onto the porch and scrape our shoes, a little stiff in our Sunday clothes, our Sunday clothes rustling, not looking full at him as he meets us.

"The Lord giveth," we say.

"The Lord giveth."

That boy is not there. Peabody told about how he come into the kitchen, hollering, swarming and clawing at Cora when he found her cooking that fish, and how Dewey Dell taken him down to the barn. "My team all right?" Peabody says.

"All right," I tell him. "I give them a bait this morning. Your buggy seems all right too. It aint hurt."

"And no fault of somebody's," he says. "I'd give a nickel to know where that boy was when that team broke away."

"If it's broke anywhere, I'll fix it," I say.

The women folks go on into the house. We can hear them, talking and fanning. The fans go whish. whish. whish and them talking, the talking sounding kind of like bees murmuring in a water bucket. The men stop on the porch, talking some, not looking at one another.

"Howdy, Vernon," they say. "Howdy, Tull."

"Looks like more rain."

"It does for a fact."

"Yes, sir. It will rain some more."

"It come up quick."

"And going away slow. It dont fail."

I go around to the back. Cash is filling up the holes he bored in the top of it. He is trimming out plugs for them, one at a time, the wood wet and hard to work. He could cut up a tin can and hide the holes and nobody wouldn't know the difference. Wouldn't mind, anyway. I have seen him spend a hour trimming out a wedge like it was glass he was working, when he could have reached around and picked up a dozen sticks and drove them into the joint and made it do.

When we finished I go back to the front. The men have gone a little piece from the house, sitting on the ends of the boards and on the sawhorses where we made it last night, some sitting and some squatting. Whitfield aint come yet.

They look up at me, their eyes asking.

"It's about," I say. "He's ready to nail."

While they are getting up Anse comes to the door and looks at us and we return to the porch. We scrape our shoes again, careful, waiting for one another to go in first, milling a little at the door. Anse stands inside the door, dignified, composed. He waves us in and leads the way into the room.

They had laid her in it reversed. Cash made it clock-shape, like this

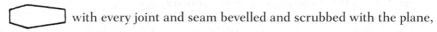

 with every joint and seam bevelled and scrubbed with the plane, tight as a drum and neat as a sewing basket, and they had laid her in it head to foot so it wouldn't crush her dress. It was her wedding dress and it had a flare-out bottom, and they had laid her head to foot in it so the dress could spread out, and they had made her a veil out of a mosquito bar so the auger holes in her face wouldn't show.

When we are going out, Whitfield comes. He is wet and muddy to the waist, coming in. "The Lord comfort this house," he says. "I was late because the bridge has gone. I went down to the old ford and swum my horse over, the Lord protecting me. His grace be upon this house."

We go back to the trestles and plank-ends and sit or squat.

"I knowed it would go," Armstid says.

"It's been there a long time, that ere bridge," Quick says.

"The Lord has kept it there, you mean," Uncle Billy says. "I dont know ere a man that's touched hammer to it in twenty-five years."

"How long has it been there, Uncle Billy?" Quick says.

"It was built in . . . let me see . . . It was in the year 1888," Uncle Billy says. "I mind it because the first man to cross it was Peabody coming to my house when Jody was born."

"If I'd a crossed it every time your wife littered since, it'd a been wore out long before this, Billy," Peabody says.

We laugh, suddenly loud, then suddenly quiet again. We look a little aside at one another.

"Lots of folks has crossed it that wont cross no more bridges," Houston says.

"It's a fact," Littlejohn says. "It's so."

"One more aint, no ways," Armstid says. "It'd taken them two-three days to get her to town in the wagon. They'd be gone a week, getting her to Jefferson and back."

"What's Anse so itching to take her to Jefferson for, anyway?" Houston says.

"He promised her," I say. "She wanted it. She come from there. Her mind was set on it."

"And Anse is set on it, too," Quick says.

"Ay," Uncle Billy says. "It's like a man that's let everything slide all his life to get set on something that will make the most trouble for everybody he knows."

"Well, it'll take the Lord to get her over that river now," Peabody says. "Anse cant do it."

"And I reckon He will," Quick says. "He's took care of Anse a long time, now."

"It's a fact," Littlejohn says.

"Too long to quit now," Armstid says.

"I reckon He's like everybody else around here," Uncle Billy says. "He's done it so long now He cant quit."

Cash comes out. He has put on a clean shirt; his hair, wet, is combed smooth down on his brow, smooth and black as if he had painted it onto his head. He squats stiffly among us, we watching him.

"You feeling this weather, aint you?" Armstid says.

Cash says nothing.

"A broke bone always feels it," Littlejohn says. "A fellow with a broke bone can tell it a-coming."

"Lucky Cash got off with just a broke leg," Armstid says. "He might have hurt himself bed-rid. How far'd you fall, Cash?"

"Twenty-eight foot, four and a half inches, about," Cash says. I move over beside him.

"A fellow can sho slip quick on wet planks," Quick says.

"It's too bad," I say. "But you couldn't a holp it."

"It's them durn women," he says. "I made it to balance with her. I made it to her measure and weight."

If it takes wet boards for folks to fall, it's fixing to be lots of falling before this spell is done.

"You couldn't have holp it," I say.

I dont mind the folks falling. It's the cotton and corn I mind.

Neither does Peabody mind the folks falling. How bout it, Doc?

It's a fact. Washed clean outen the ground it will be. Seems like something is always happening to it.

Course it does. That's why it's worth anything. If nothing didn't happen and everybody made a big crop, do you reckon it would be worth the raising?

Well, I be durn if I like to see my work washed outen the ground, work I sweat over.

It's a fact. A fellow wouldn't mind seeing it washed up if he could just turn on the rain himself.

Who is that man can do that? Where is the color of his eyes?

Ay. The Lord made it to grow. It's Hisn to wash up if He sees it fitten so.

"You couldn't have holp it," I say.

"It's them durn women," he says.

In the house the women begin to sing. We hear the first line commence, beginning to swell as they take hold, and we rise and move toward the door, taking off our hats and throwing our chews away. We do not go in. We stop at the steps, clumped, holding our hats between our lax hands in front or behind, standing with one foot advanced and our heads lowered, looking aside, down at our hats in our hands and at the earth or now and then at the sky and at one another's grave, composed face.

The song ends; the voices quaver away with a rich and dying fall. Whitfield begins. His voice is bigger than him. It's like they are not the same. It's like he is one, and his voice is one, swimming on two horses side by side across the ford and coming into the house, the mud-splashed one and the one that never even got wet, triumphant and sad. Somebody in the house begins to cry. It sounds like her eyes and her voice were turned back inside her, listening; we move, shifting to the other leg, meeting one another's eye and making like they hadn't touched.

Whitfield stops at last. The women sing again. In the thick air it's like their voices come out of the air, flowing together and on in the sad, comforting tunes. When they cease it's like they hadn't gone away. It's like they had just disappeared into the air and when we moved we would loose them again out of the air around us, sad and comforting. Then they finish and we put on our hats, our movements stiff, like we hadn't never wore hats before.

On the way home Cora is still singing. "I am bounding toward my God and my reward," she sings, sitting on the wagon, the shawl around her shoulders and the umbrella open over her, though it is not raining.

"She has hern," I say. "Wherever she went, she has her reward in being free of Anse Bundren." *She laid there three days in that box, waiting for Darl and Jewel to come clean back home and get a new wheel and go back to where the wagon was in the ditch. Take my team, Anse, I said.*

We'll wait for ourn, he said. She'll want it so. She was ever a particular woman.

On the third day they got back and they loaded her into the wagon and started and it already too late. You'll have to go all the way round by Samson's bridge. It'll take you a day to get there. Then you'll be forty miles from Jefferson. Take my team, Anse.

We'll wait for ourn. She'll want it so.

It was about a mile from the house we saw him, sitting on the edge of the slough. It hadn't had a fish in it never that I knowed. He looked around at us, his eyes round and calm, his face dirty, the pole across his knees. Cora was still singing.

"This aint no good day to fish," I said. "You come on home with us and me and you'll go down to the river first thing in the morning and catch some fish."

"It's one in here," he said. "Dewey Dell seen it."

"You come on with us. The river's the best place."

"It's in here," he said. "Dewey Dell seen it."

"I'm bounding toward my God and my reward," Cora sung.

Darl

"It's not your horse that's dead, Jewel," I say. He sits erect on the seat, leaning a little forward, wooden-backed. The brim of his hat has soaked free of the crown in two places, dropping across his wooden face so that, head lowered, he looks through it like through the visor of a helmet, looking long across the valley to where the barn leans against the bluff, shaping the invisible horse. "See them?" I say. High above the house, against the quick thick sky, they hang in narrowing circles. From here they are no more than specks, implacable, patient, portentous. "But it's not your horse that's dead."

"Goddamn you," he says. "Goddamn you."

I cannot love my mother because I have no mother. Jewel's mother is a horse.

Motionless, the tall buzzards hang in soaring circles, the clouds giving them an illusion of retrograde.

Motionless, wooden-backed, wooden-faced, he shapes the horse in a rigid stoop like a hawk, hook-winged. They are waiting for us, ready for the moving of it, waiting for him. He enters the stall and waits until it kicks at him so that he can slip past and mount onto the trough and pause, peering out across the intervening stall-tops toward the empty path, before he reaches into the loft.

"Goddamn him. Goddamn him."

Cash

"It wont balance. If you want it to tote and ride on a balance, we will have—"

"Pick up. Goddamn you, pick up."

"I'm telling you it wont tote and it wont ride on a balance unless—"

"Pick up! Pick up, goddamn your thick-nosed soul to hell, pick up!"

It wont balance. If they want it to tote and ride on a balance, they will have

Darl

He stoops among us above it, two of the eight hands. In his face the blood goes in waves. In between them his flesh is greenish looking, about that smooth, thick, pale green of cow's cud; his face suffocated, furious, his lip lifted upon his teeth. "Pick up!" he says. "Pick up, goddamn your thick-nosed soul!"

He heaves, lifting one whole side so suddenly that we all spring into the lift to catch and balance it before he hurls it completely over. For an instant it resists, as though volitional, as though within it her pole-thin body clings furiously, even though dead, to a sort of modesty, as she would have tried to conceal a soiled garment that she could not prevent her body soiling. Then it breaks free, rising suddenly as though the emaciation of her body had added buoyancy to the planks or as though, seeing that the garment was about to be torn from her, she rushes suddenly after it in a passionate reversal that flouts its own desire and need. Jewel's face goes completely green and I can hear teeth in his breath.

We carry it down the hall, our feet harsh and clumsy on the floor, moving with shuffling steps, and through the door.

"Steady it a minute, now," pa says, letting go. He turns back to shut and lock the door, but Jewel will not wait.

"Come on," he says in that suffocating voice. "Come on."

We lower it carefully down the steps. We move, balancing it as though it were something infinitely precious, our faces averted, breathing through our teeth to keep our nostrils closed. We go down the path, toward the slope.

"We better wait," Cash says. "I tell you it aint balanced now. We'll need another hand on the hill."

"Then turn loose," Jewel says. He will not stop. Cash begins to fall behind, hobbling to keep up, breathing harshly; then he is distanced and Jewel carries the entire front end alone, so that, tilting as the path begins to slant, it begins to rush away from one and slip down the air like a sled upon invisible snow, smoothly evacuating atmosphere in which the sense of it is still shaped.

"Wait, Jewel," I say. But he will not wait. He is almost running now and Cash is left behind. It seems to me that the end which I now carry alone has no weight, as though it coasts like a rushing straw upon the furious tide of Jewel's despair. I am not even touching it when, turning, he lets it overshoot him, swinging, and stops it and sloughs it into the wagon bed in the same motion and looks back at me, his face suffused with fury and despair.

"Goddamn you. Goddamn you."

Vardaman

We are going to town. Dewey Dell says it wont be sold because it belongs to Santa Claus and he taken it back with him until next Christmas. Then it will be behind the glass again, shining with waiting.

Pa and Cash are coming down the hill, but Jewel is going to the barn. "Jewel," pa says. Jewel does not stop. "Where you going?" pa says. But Jewel does not stop. "You leave that horse here," pa says. Jewel stops and looks at pa. Jewel's eyes look like marbles. "You leave that horse here," pa says. "We'll all go in the wagon with ma, like she wanted."

But my mother is a fish. Vernon seen it. He was there.

"Jewel's mother is a horse," Darl said.

"Then mine can be a fish, cant it, Darl?" I said.

Jewel is my brother.

"Then mine will have to be a horse, too," I said.

"Why?" Darl said. "If pa is your pa, why does your ma have to be a horse just because Jewel's is?"

"Why does it?" I said. "Why does it, Darl?"

Darl is my brother.

"Then what is your ma, Darl?" I said.

"I haven't got ere one," Darl said. "Because if I had one, it is *was*. And if it is was, it cant be *is*. Can it?"

"No," I said.

"Then I am not," Darl said. "Am I?"

"No," I said.

I am. Darl is my brother.

"But you *are,* Darl," I said.

"I know it," Darl said. "That's why I am not *is. Are* is too many for one woman to foal."

Cash is carrying his tool box. Pa looks at him. "I'll stop at Tull's on the way back," Cash says. "Get on that barn roof."

"It aint respectful," pa says. "It's a deliberate flouting of her and of me."

"Do you want him to come all the way back here and carry them up to Tull's afoot?" Darl says. Pa looks at Darl, his mouth chewing. Pa shaves every day now because my mother is a fish.

"It aint right," pa says.

Dewey Dell has the package in her hand. She has the basket with our dinner too.

"What's that?" pa says.

"Mrs Tull's cakes," Dewey Dell says, getting into the wagon. "I'm taking them to town for her."

"It aint right," pa says. "It's a flouting of the dead."

It'll be there. It'll be there come Christmas, she says, shining on the track. She says he wont sell it to no town boys.

Darl

He goes on toward the barn, entering the lot, woodenbacked.

Dewey Dell carries the basket on one arm, in the other hand something wrapped square in a newspaper. Her face is calm and sullen, her eyes brooding and alert; within them I can see Peabody's back like two round peas in two thimbles: perhaps in Peabody's back two of those worms which work surreptitious and steady through you and out the other side and you waking suddenly from sleep or from waking, with on your face an expression sudden, intent, and concerned. She sets the basket into the wagon and climbs in, her leg coming long from beneath her tightening dress: that lever which moves the world; one of that caliper which measures the length and breadth of life. She sits on the seat beside Vardaman and sets the parcel on her lap.

Then he enters the barn. He has not looked back.

"It aint right," pa says. "It's little enough for him to do for her."

"Go on," Cash says. "Leave him stay if he wants. He'll be all right here. Maybe he'll go up to Tull's and stay."

"He'll catch us," I say. "He'll cut across and meet us at Tull's lane."

"He would have rid that horse, too," pa says, "if I hadn't a stopped him. A durn spotted critter wilder than a cattymount.[2] A deliberate flouting of her and of me."

The wagon moves; the mules' ears begin to bob. Behind us, above the house, motionless in tall and soaring circles, they diminish and disappear.

Anse

I told him not to bring that horse out of respect for his dead ma, because it wouldn't look right, him prancing along on a durn circus animal and her wanting us all to be in the wagon with her that sprung from her flesh and blood,

2. Mountain lion.

but we hadn't no more than passed Tull's lane when Darl begun to laugh. Setting back there on the plank seat with Cash, with his dead ma laying in her coffin at his feet, laughing. How many times I told him it's doing such things as that that makes folks talk about him, I dont know. I says I got some regard for what folks says about my flesh and blood even if you haven't, even if I have raised such a durn passel of boys, and when you fixes it so folks can say such about you, it's a reflection on your ma, I says, not me: I am a man and I can stand it; it's on your womenfolks, your ma and sister that you should care for, and I turned and looked back at him and him setting there, laughing.

"I dont expect you to have no respect for me," I says. "But with your own ma not cold in her coffin yet."

"Yonder," Cash says, jerking his head toward the lane. The horse is still a right smart piece away, coming up at a good pace, but I dont have to be told who it is. I just looked back at Darl, setting there laughing.

"I done my best," I says. "I tried to do as she would wish it. The Lord will pardon me and excuse the conduct of them He sent me." And Darl setting on the plank seat right above her where she was laying, laughing.

Darl

He comes up the lane fast, yet we are three hundred yards beyond the mouth of it when he turns into the road, the mud flying beneath the flicking drive of the hooves. Then he slows a little, light and erect in the saddle, the horse mincing through the mud.

Tull is in his lot. He looks at us, lifts his hand. We go on, the wagon creaking, the mud whispering on the wheels. Vernon still stands there. He watches Jewel as he passes, the horse moving with a light, high-kneed driving gait, three hundred yards back. We go on, with a motion so soporific, so dreamlike as to be uninferant of progress, as though time and not space were decreasing between us and it.

It turns off at right angles, the wheel-marks of last Sunday healed away now: a smooth, red scoriation curving away into the pines; a white signboard with faded lettering: New Hope Church. 3 mi. It wheels up like a motionless hand lifted above the profound desolation of the ocean; beyond it the red road lies like a spoke of which Addie Bundren is the rim. It wheels past, empty, unscarred, the white signboard turns away its fading and tranquil assertion. Cash looks up the road quietly, his head turning as we pass it like an owl's head, his face composed. Pa looks straight ahead, humped. Dewey Dell looks at the road too, then she looks back at me, her eyes watchful and repudiant, not like that question which was in those of Cash, for a smoldering while. The signboard passes; the unscarred road wheels on. Then Dewey Dell turns her head. The wagon creaks on.

Cash spits over the wheel. "In a couple of days now it'll be smelling," he says.

"You might tell Jewel that," I say.

He is motionless now, sitting the horse at the junction, upright, watching us, no less still than the signboard that lifts its fading capitulation opposite him.

"It aint balanced right for no long ride," Cash says.

"Tell him that, too," I say. The wagon creaks on.

A mile further along he passes us, the horse, archnecked, reined back to a swift singlefoot. He sits lightly, poised, upright, wooden-faced in the saddle, the broken hat raked at a swaggering angle. He passes us swiftly, without looking at us, the horse driving, its hooves hissing in the mud. A gout of mud, backflung, plops onto the box. Cash leans forward and takes a tool from his box and removes it carefully. When the road crosses Whiteleaf, the willows leaning near enough, he breaks off a branch and scours at the stain with the wet leaves.

Anse

It's a hard country on man; it's hard. Eight miles of the sweat of his body washed up outen the Lord's earth, where the Lord Himself told him to put it.[3] Nowhere in this sinful world can a honest, hardworking man profit. It takes them that runs the stores in the towns, doing no sweating, living off of them that sweats. It ain't the hardworking man, the farmer. Sometimes I wonder why we keep at it. It's because there is a reward for us above, where they cant take their autos and such. Every man will be equal there and it will be taken from them that have and give to them that have not by the Lord.[4]

But it's a long wait, seems like. It's bad that a fellow must earn the reward of his right-doing by flouting hisself and his dead. We drove all the rest of the day and got to Samson's at dusk-dark and then that bridge was gone, too. They hadn't never see the river so high, and it not done raining yet. There was old men that hadn't never see nor hear of it being so in the memory of man. I am the chosen of the Lord, for who He loveth, so doeth He chastiseth.[5] But I be durn if He dont take some curious ways to show it, seems like.

But now I can get them teeth. That will be a comfort. It will.

Samson

It was just before sundown. We were sitting on the porch when the wagon came up the road with the five of them in it and the other one on the horse behind. One of them raised his hand, but they were going on past the store without stopping.

"Who's that?" MacCallum says: I cant think of his name: Rafe's twin; that one it was.

"It's Bundren, from down beyond New Hope," Quick says. "There's one of them Snopes horses Jewel's riding."

"I didn't know there was ere a one of them horses left," MacCallum says. "I thought you folks down there finally contrived to give them all away."

"Try and get that one," Quick says. The wagon went on.

"I bet old man Lon never gave it to him," I says.

"No," Quick says. "He bought it from pappy." The wagon went on. "They must not a heard about the bridge," he says.

"What're they doing up here, anyway?" MacCallum says.

3. Cf. Genesis 3.19: "In the sweat of thy face shalt thou eat bread, till thou return unto the ground."
4. Cf. Matthew 13.12: "For whosoever hath, to him shall be given, and he shall have more abundance: but whosoever hath not, from him shall be taken away even that he hath."
5. Cf. Hebrews 12.6: "For whom the Lord loveth he chasteneth, and scourgeth every son whom he receiveth."

"Taking a holiday since he got his wife buried, I reckon," Quick says. "Heading for town, I reckon, with Tull's bridge gone too. I wonder if they aint heard about the bridge."

"They'll have to fly, then," I says. "I dont reckon there's ere a bridge between here and Mouth of Ishatawa."

They had something in the wagon. But Quick had been to the funeral three days ago and we naturally never thought anything about it except that they were heading away from home mighty late and that they hadn't heard about the bridge. "You better holler at them," MacCallum says. Durn it, the name is right on the tip of my tongue. So Quick hollered and they stopped and he went to the wagon and told them.

He come back with them. "They're going to Jefferson," he says. "The bridge at Tull's is gone, too." Like we didn't know it, and his face looked funny, around the nostrils, but they just sat there, Bundren and the girl and the chap on the seat, and Cash and the second one, the one folks talks about, on a plank across the tail-gate, and the other one on that spotted horse. But I reckon they was used to it by then, because when I said to Cash that they'd have to pass by New Hope again and what they'd better do, he just says,

"I reckon we can get there."

I aint much for meddling. Let every man run his own business to suit himself, I say. But after I talked to Rachel about them not having a regular man to fix her and it being July and all, I went back down to the barn and tried to talk to Bundren about it.

"I give her my promise," he says. "Her mind was set on it."

I notice how it takes a lazy man, a man that hates moving, to get set on moving once he does get started off, the same as he was set on staying still, like it aint the moving he hates so much as the starting and the stopping. And like he would be kind of proud of whatever come up to make the moving or the setting still look hard. He set there on the wagon, hunched up, blinking, listening to us tell about how quick the bridge went and how high the water was, and I be durn if he didn't act like he was proud of it, like he had made the river rise himself.

"You say it's higher than you ever see it before?" he says. "God's will be done," he says. "I reckon it wont go down much by morning, neither," he says.

"You better stay here tonight," I says, "and get a early start for New Hope tomorrow morning." I was just sorry for them bone-gaunted mules. I told Rachel, I says, "Well, would you have had me turn them away at dark, eight miles from home? What else could I do," I says. "It wont be but one night, and they'll keep it in the barn, and they'll sholy get started by daylight." And so I says, "You stay here tonight and early tomorrow you can go back to New Hope. I got tools enough, and the boys can go on right after supper and have it dug and ready if they want" and then I found that girl watching me. If her eyes had a been pistols, I wouldn't be talking now. I be dog[6] if they didn't blaze at me. And so when I went down to the barn I come on them, her talking so she never noticed when I come up.

"You promised her," she says. "She wouldn't go until you promised. She thought she could depend on you. If you dont do it, it will be a curse on you."

6. Doggone or darned.

"Cant no man say I dont aim to keep my word," Bundren says. "My heart is open to ere a man."

"I dont care what your heart is," she says. She was whispering, kind of, talking fast. "You promised her. You've got to. You—" then she seen me and quit, standing there. If they'd been pistols, I wouldn't be talking now. So when I talked to him about it, he says,

"I give her my promise. Her mind is set on it."

"But seems to me she'd rather have her ma buried close by, so she could—"

"It's Addie I give the promise to," he says. "Her mind is set on it."

So I told them to drive it into the barn, because it was threatening rain again, and that supper was about ready. Only they didn't want to come in.

"I thank you," Bundren says. "We wouldn't discommode you. We got a little something in the basket. We can make out."

"Well," I says, "since you are so particular about your womenfolks, I am too. And when folks stops with us at meal time and wont come to the table, my wife takes it as a insult."

So the girl went on to the kitchen to help Rachel. And then Jewel come to me.

"Sho," I says. "Help yourself outen the loft. Feed him when you bait the mules."

"I rather pay you for him," he says.

"What for?" I says. "I wouldn't begrudge no man a bait for his horse."

"I rather pay you," he says; I thought he said extra.

"Extra for what?" I says. "Wont he eat hay and corn?"

"Extra feed," he says. "I feed him a little extra and I dont want him beholden to no man."

"You cant buy no feed from me, boy," I says. "And if he can eat that loft clean, I'll help you load the barn onto the wagon in the morning."

"He aint never been beholden to no man," he says. "I rather pay you for it."

And if I had my rathers, you wouldn't be here a-tall, I wanted to say. But I just says, "Then it's high time he commenced. You cant buy no feed from me."

When Rachel put supper on, her and the girl went and fixed some beds. But wouldn't any of them come in. "She's been dead long enough to get over that sort of foolishness," I says. Because I got just as much respect for the dead as ere a man, but you've got to respect the dead themselves, and a woman that's been dead in a box four days, the best way to respect her is to get her into the ground as quick as you can. But they wouldn't do it.

"It wouldn't be right," Bundren says. "Course, if the boys wants to go to bed, I reckon I can set up with her. I dont begrudge her it."

So when I went back down there they were squatting on the ground around the wagon, all of them. "Let that chap come to the house and get some sleep, anyway," I says. "And you better come too," I says to the girl. I wasn't aiming to interfere with them. And I sholy hadn't done nothing to her that I knowed.

"He's done already asleep," Bundren says. They had done put him to bed in the trough in a empty stall.

"Well, you come on, then," I says to her. But still she never said nothing. They just squatted there. You couldn't hardly see them. "How about you boys?" I says. "You got a full day tomorrow." After a while Cash says,

"I thank you. We can make out."

"We wouldn't be beholden," Bundren says. "I thank you kindly."

So I left them squatting there. I reckon after four days they was used to it. But Rachel wasn't.

"It's a outrage," she says. "A outrage."

"What could he a done?" I says. "He give her his promised word."

"Who's talking about him?" she says. "Who cares about him?" she says, crying. "I just wish that you and him and all the men in the world that torture us alive and flout us dead, dragging us up and down the country—"

"Now, now," I says. "You're upset."

"Dont you touch me!" she says. "Dont you touch me!"

A man cant tell nothing about them. I lived with the same one fifteen years and I be durn if I can. And I imagined a lot of things coming up between us, but I be durn if I ever thought it would be a body four days dead and that a woman. But they make life hard on them, not taking it as it comes up, like a man does.

So I laid there, hearing it commence to rain, thinking about them down there, squatting around the wagon and the rain on the roof, and thinking about Rachel crying there until after a while it was like I could still hear her crying even after she was asleep, and smelling it even when I knowed I couldn't. I couldn't decide even then whether I could or not, or if it wasn't just knowing it was what it was.

So next morning I never went down there. I heard them hitching up and then when I knowed they must be about ready to take out, I went out the front and went down the road toward the bridge until I heard the wagon come out of the lot and go back toward New Hope. And then when I come back to the house, Rachel jumped on me because I wasn't there to make them come in to breakfast. You cant tell about them. Just about when you decide they mean one thing, I be durn if you not only haven't got to change your mind, like as not you got to take a rawhiding for thinking they meant it.

But it was still like I could smell it. And so I decided then that it wasn't smelling it, but it was just knowing it was there, like you will get fooled now and then. But when I went to the barn I knew different. When I walked into the hallway I saw something. It kind of hunkered up when I come in and I thought at first it was one of them got left, then I saw what it was. It was a buzzard. It looked around and saw me and went on down the hall, spraddle-legged, with its wings kind of hunkered out, watching me first over one shoulder and then over the other, like a old baldheaded man. When it got outdoors it begun to fly. It had to fly a long time before it ever got up into the air, with it thick and heavy and full of rain like it was.

If they was bent on going to Jefferson, I reckon they could have gone around up by Mount Vernon, like MacCallum did. He'll get home about day after tomorrow, horseback. Then they'd be just eighteen miles from town. But maybe this bridge being gone too has learned him the Lord's sense and judgment.

That MacCallum. He's been trading with me off and on for twelve years. I have known him from a boy up; know his name as well as I do my own. But be durn if I can say it.

Dewey Dell

The signboard comes in sight. It is looking out at the road now, because it can wait. New Hope. 3 mi. it will say. New Hope. 3 mi. New Hope. 3 mi. And then the road will begin, curving away into the trees, empty with waiting, saying New Hope three miles.

I heard that my mother is dead. I wish I had time to let her die. I wish I had time to wish I had. It is because in the wild and outraged earth too soon too soon too soon. It's not that I wouldn't and will not it's that it is too soon too soon too soon.

Now it begins to say it. New Hope three miles. New Hope three miles. *That's what they mean by the womb of time: the agony and the despair of spreading bones, the hard girdle in which lie the outraged entrails of events*

Cash's head turns slowly as we approach, his pale empty sad composed and questioning face following the red and empty curve; beside the back wheel Jewel sits the horse, gazing straight ahead.

The land runs out of Darl's eyes; they swim to pinpoints. They begin at my feet and rise along my body to my face, and then my dress is gone: I sit naked on the seat above the unhurrying mules, above the travail. *Suppose I tell him to turn. He will do what I say. Dont you know he will do what I say?* Once I waked with a black void rushing under me. I could not see. I saw Vardaman rise and go to the window and strike the knife into the fish, the blood gushing, hissing like steam but I could not see. *He'll do as I say. He always does. I can persuade him to anything. You know I can. Suppose I say Turn here.* That was when I died that time. *Suppose I do. We'll go to New Hope. We wont have to go to town.* I rose and took the knife from the streaming fish still hissing and I killed Darl.

When I used to sleep with Vardaman I had a nightmare once I thought I was awake but I couldn't see and couldn't feel I couldn't feel the bed under me and I couldn't think what I was I couldn't think of my name I couldn't even think I am a girl I couldn't even think I nor even think I want to wake up nor remember what was opposite to awake so I could do that I knew that something was passing but I couldn't even think of time then all of a sudden I knew that something was it was wind blowing over me it was like the wind came and blew me back from where it was I was not blowing the room and Vardaman asleep and all of them back under me again and going on like a piece of cool silk dragging across my naked legs

It blows cool out of the pines, a sad steady sound. New Hope. Was 3 mi. Was 3 mi. I believe in God I believe in God.

"Why didn't we go to New Hope, pa?" Vardaman says. "Mr Samson said we was, but we done passed the road."

Darl says, "Look, Jewel." But he is not looking at me. He is looking at the sky. The buzzard is as still as if he were nailed to it.

We turn into Tull's lane. We pass the barn and go on, the wheels whispering in the mud, passing the green rows of cotton in the wild earth, and Vernon little across the field behind the plow. He lifts his hand as we pass and stands there looking after us for a long while.

"Look, Jewel," Darl says. Jewel sits on his horse like they were both made out of wood, looking straight ahead.

I believe in God, God. God, I believe in God.

Tull

After they passed I taken the mule out and looped up the trace chains and followed. They was setting in the wagon at the end of the levee when I caught up with them. Anse was setting there, looking at the bridge where it was swagged down into the river with just the two ends in sight. He was looking at it like he had believed all the time that folks had been lying to him about it being gone, but like he was hoping all the time it really was. Kind of pleased astonishment he looked, setting on the wagon in his Sunday pants, mumbling his mouth. Looking like a uncurried horse dressed up: I dont know.

The boy was watching the bridge where it was mid-sunk and logs and such drifted up over it and it swagging and shivering like the whole thing would go any minute, big-eyed he was watching it, like he was to a circus. And the gal too. When I come up she looked around at me, her eyes kind of blaring up and going hard like I had made to touch her. Then she looked at Anse again and then back at the water again.

It was nigh up to the levee on both sides, the earth hid except for the tongue of it we was on going out to the bridge and then down into the water, and except for knowing how the road and the bridge used to look, a fellow couldn't tell where was the river and where the land. It was just a tangle of yellow and the levee not less wider than a knife-back kind of, with us setting in the wagon and on the horse and the mule.

Darl was looking at me, and then Cash turned and looked at me with that look in his eyes like when he was figuring on whether the planks would fit her that night, like he was measuring them inside of him and not asking you to say what you thought and not even letting on he was listening if you did say it, but listening all right. Jewel hadn't moved. He sat there on the horse, leaning a little forward, with that same look on his face when him and Darl passed the house yesterday, coming back to get her.

"If it was just up, we could drive across," Anse says. "We could drive right on across it."

Sometimes a log would get shoved over the jam and float on, rolling and turning, and we could watch it go on to where the ford used to be. It would slow up and whirl crossways and hang out of water for a minute, and you could tell by that that the ford used to be there.

"But that dont show nothing," I say. "It could be a bar of quicksand built up there." We watch the log. Then the gal is looking at me again.

"Mr Whitfield crossed it," she says.

"He was a-horseback," I say. "And three days ago. It's a riz five foot since."

"If the bridge was just up," Anse says.

The log bobs up and goes on again. There is a lot of trash and foam, and you can hear the water.

"But it's down," Anse says.

Cash says, "A careful fellow could walk across yonder on the planks and logs."

"But you couldn't tote nothing," I say. "Likely time you set foot on that mess, it'll all go, too. What you think, Darl?"

He is looking at me. He dont say nothing; just looks at me with them queer eyes of hisn that makes folks talk. I always say it aint never been what he done so much or said or anything so much as how he looks at you. It's like he had got into the inside of you, someway. Like somehow you was looking at yourself and your doings outen his eyes. Then I can feel that gal watching me like I had made to touch her. She says something to Anse. ". . . Mr Whitfield. . . ." she says.

"I give her my promised word in the presence of the Lord," Anse says. "I reckon it aint no need to worry."

But still he does not start the mules. We set there above the water. Another log bobs up over the jam and goes on; we watch it check up and swing slow for a minute where the ford used to be. Then it goes on.

"It might start falling tonight," I say. "You could lay over one more day."

Then Jewel turns sideways on the horse. He has not moved until then, and he turns and looks at me. His face is kind of green, then it would go red and then green again. "Get to hell on back to your damn plowing," he says. "Who the hell asked you to follow us here?"

"I never meant no harm," I say.

"Shut up, Jewel," Cash says. Jewel looks back at the water, his face gritted, going red and green and then red. "Well," Cash says after a while, "what you want to do?"

Anse dont say nothing. He sets humped up, mumbling his mouth. "If it was just up, we could drive across it," he says.

"Come on," Jewel says, moving the horse.

"Wait," Cash says. He looks at the bridge. We look at him, except Anse and the gal. They are looking at the water. "Dewey Dell and Vardaman and pa better walk across on the bridge," Cash says.

"Vernon can help them," Jewel says. "And we can hitch his mule ahead of ourn."

"You ain't going to take my mule into that water," I say.

Jewel looks at me. His eyes look like pieces of a broken plate. "I'll pay for your damn mule. I'll buy it from you right now."

"My mule aint going into that water," I say.

"Jewel's going to use his horse," Darl says. "Why wont you risk your mule, Vernon?"

"Shut up, Darl," Cash says. "You and Jewel both."

"My mule aint going into that water," I say.

Darl

He sits the horse, glaring at Vernon, his lean face suffused up to and beyond the pale rigidity of his eyes. The summer when he was fifteen, he took a spell of sleeping. One morning when I went to feed the mules the cows were still in the tie-up and then I heard pa go back to the house and call him. When we came on back to the house for breakfast he passed us, carrying the milk buckets, stumbling along like he was drunk, and he was milking when we put the mules in and went on to the field without him. We had been there an hour and still he never showed up. When Dewey Dell came with our lunch, pa sent her back to find Jewel. They found him in the tie-up, sitting on the stool, asleep.

After that, every morning pa would go in and wake him. He would go to sleep at the supper table and soon as supper was finished he would go to bed, and when I came in to bed he would be lying there like a dead man. Yet still pa would have to wake him in the morning. He would get up, but he wouldn't hardly have half sense: he would stand for pa's jawing and complaining without a word and take the milk buckets and go to the barn, and once I found him asleep at the cow, the bucket in place and half full and his hands up to the wrists in the milk and his head against the cow's flank.

After that Dewey Dell had to do the milking. He still got up when pa waked him, going about what we told him to do in that dazed way. It was like he was trying hard to do them; that he was as puzzled as anyone else.

"Are you sick?" ma said. "Dont you feel all right?"

"Yes," Jewel said. "I feel all right."

"He's just lazy, trying me," pa said, and Jewel standing there, asleep on his feet like as not. "Ain't you?" he said, waking Jewel up again to answer.

"No," Jewel said.

"You take off and stay in the house today," ma said.

"With that whole bottom piece to be busted out?"[7] pa said. "If you aint sick, what's the matter with you?"

"Nothing," Jewel said. "I'm all right."

"All right?" pa said. "You're asleep on your feet this minute."

"No," Jewel said. "I'm all right."

"I want him to stay at home today," ma said.

"I'll need him," pa said. "It's tight enough, with all of us to do it."

"You'll just have to do the best you can with Cash and Darl," ma said. "I want him to stay in today."

But he wouldn't do it. "I'm all right," he said, going on. But he wasn't all right. Anybody could see it. He was losing flesh, and I have seen him go to sleep chopping; watched the hoe going slower and slower up and down, with less and less of an arc, until it stopped and he leaning on it motionless in the hot shimmer of the sun.

Ma wanted to get the doctor, but pa didn't want to spend the money without it was needful, and Jewel did seem all right except for his thinness and his way of dropping off to sleep at any moment. He ate hearty enough, except for his way of going to sleep in his plate, with a piece of bread halfway to his mouth and his jaws still chewing. But he swore he was all right.

It was ma that got Dewey Dell to do his milking, paid her somehow, and the other jobs around the house that Jewel had been doing before supper she found some way for Dewey Dell and Vardaman to do them. And doing them herself when pa wasn't there. She would fix him special things to eat and hide them for him. And that may have been when I first found it out, that Addie Bundren should be hiding anything she did, who had tried to teach us that deceit was such that, in a world where it was, nothing else could be very bad or very important, not even poverty. And at times when I went in to go to bed she would be sitting in the dark by Jewel where he was asleep. And I knew that she was hating herself for that deceit and hating Jewel because she had to love him so that she had to act the deceit.

One night she was taken sick and when I went to the barn to put the team in and drive to Tull's, I couldn't find the lantern. I remembered noticing it on the nail the night before, but it wasn't there now at midnight. So I hitched in the dark and went on and came back with Mrs Tull just after daylight.

7. Plowed.

And there the lantern was, hanging on the nail where I remembered it and couldn't find it before. And then one morning while Dewey Dell was milking just before the sunup, Jewel came into the barn from the back, through the hole in the back wall, with the lantern in his hand.

I told Cash, and Cash and I looked at one another.

"Rutting," Cash said.

"Yes," I said. "But why the lantern? And every night, too. No wonder he's losing flesh. Are you going to say anything to him?"

"Wont do any good," Cash said.

"What he's doing now wont do any good, either."

"I know. But he'll have to learn that himself. Give him time to realise that it'll save, that there'll be just as much more tomorrow, and he'll be all right. I wouldn't tell anybody, I reckon."

"No," I said. "I told Dewey Dell not to. Not ma, anyway."

"No. Not ma."

After that I thought it was right comical: he acting so bewildered and willing and dead for sleep and gaunt as a bean-pole, and thinking he was so smart with it. And I wondered who the girl was. I thought of all I knew that it might be, but I couldn't say for sure.

"'Taint any girl," Cash said. "It's a married woman somewhere. Aint any young girl got that much daring and staying power. That's what I dont like about it."

"Why?" I said. "She'll be safer for him than a girl would. More judgment."

He looked at me, his eyes fumbling, the words fumbling at what he was trying to say. "It ain't always the safe things in this world that a fellow . . ."

"You mean, the safe things are not always the best things?"

"Ay; best," he said, fumbling again. "It aint the best things, the things that are good for him. . . . A young boy. A fellow kind of hates to see . . . wallowing in somebody else's mire . . ." That's what he was trying to say. When something is new and hard and bright, there ought to be something a little better for it than just being safe, since the safe things are just the things that folks have been doing so long they have worn the edges off and there's nothing to the doing of them that leaves a man to say, That was not done before and it cannot be done again.

So we didn't tell, not even when after a while he'd appear suddenly in the field beside us and go to work, without having had time to get home and make out he had been in bed all night. He would tell ma that he hadn't been hungry at breakfast or that he had eaten a piece of bread while he was hitching up the team. But Cash and I knew that he hadn't been home at all on those nights and he had come up out of the woods when we got to the field. But we didn't tell. Summer was almost over then; we knew that when the nights began to get cool, she would be done if he wasn't.

But when fall came and the nights began to get longer, the only difference was that he would always be in bed for pa to wake him, getting him up at last in that first state of semi-idiocy like when it first started, worse than when he had stayed out all night.

"She's sure a stayer," I told Cash. "I used to admire her, but I downright respect her now."

"It aint a woman," he said.

"You know," I said. But he was watching me. "What is it, then?"

"That's what I aim to find out," he said.

"You can trail him through the woods all night if you want to," I said. "I'm not."

"I aint trailing him," he said.

"What do you call it, then?"

"I aint trailing him," he said. "I dont mean it that way."

And so a few nights later I heard Jewel get up and climb out the window, and then I heard Cash get up and follow him. The next morning when I went to the barn, Cash was already there, the mules fed, and he was helping Dewey Dell milk. And when I saw him I knew that he knew what it was. Now and then I would catch him watching Jewel with a queer look, like having found out where Jewel went and what he was doing had given him something to really think about at last. But it was not a worried look; it was the kind of look I would see on him when I would find him doing some of Jewel's work around the house, work that pa still thought Jewel was doing and that ma thought Dewey Dell was doing. So I said nothing to him, believing that when he got done digesting it in his mind, he would tell me. But he never did.

One morning—it was November then, five months since it started—Jewel was not in bed and he didn't join us in the field. That was the first time ma learned anything about what had been going on. She sent Vardaman down to find where Jewel was, and after a while she came down too. It was as though, so long as the deceit ran along quiet and monotonous, all of us let ourselves be deceived, abetting it unawares or maybe through cowardice, since all people are cowards and naturally prefer any kind of treachery because it has a bland outside. But now it was like we had all—and by a kind of telepathic agreement of admitted fear—flung the whole thing back like covers on the bed and we all sitting bolt upright in our nakedness, staring at one another and saying "Now is the truth. He hasn't come home. Something has happened to him. We let something happen to him."

Then we saw him. He came up along the ditch and then turned straight across the field, riding the horse. Its mane and tail were going, as though in motion they were carrying out the splotchy pattern of its coat: he looked like he was riding on a big pinwheel, barebacked, with a rope bridle, and no hat on his head. It was a descendant of those Texas ponies Flem Snopes brought here twenty-five years ago and auctioned off for two dollars a head and nobody but old Lon Quick ever caught his and still owned some of the blood because he could never give it away.

He galloped up and stopped, his heels in the horse's ribs and it dancing and swirling like the shape of its mane and tail and the splotches of its coat had nothing whatever to do with the flesh-and-bone horse inside them, and he sat there, looking at us.

"Where did you get that horse?" pa said.

"Bought it," Jewel said. "From Mr. Quick."

"Bought it?" pa said. "With what? Did you buy that thing on my word?"

"It was my money," Jewel said. "I earned it. You wont need to worry about it."

"Jewel," ma said; "Jewel."

"It's all right," Cash said. "He earned the money. He cleaned up that forty acres of new ground Quick laid out last spring. He did it single handed, working at night by lantern. I saw him. So I dont reckon that horse cost anybody anything except Jewel. I dont reckon we need worry."

"Jewel," ma said. "Jewel . . ." Then she said: "You come right to the house and go to bed."

"Not yet," Jewel said. "I aint got time. I got to get me a saddle and bridle. Mr. Quick says he . . ."

"Jewel," ma said, looking at him. "I'll give—I'll give . . . give . . ." Then she began to cry. She cried hard, not hiding her face, standing there in her faded wrapper, looking at him and him on the horse, looking down at her, his face growing cold and a little sick looking, until he looked away quick and Cash came and touched her.

"You go on to the house," Cash said. "This here ground is too wet for you. You go on, now." She put her hands to her face then and after a while she went on, stumbling a little on the plow-marks. But pretty soon she straightened up and went on. She didn't look back. When she reached the ditch she stopped and called Vardaman. He was looking at the horse, kind of dancing up and down by it.

"Let me ride, Jewel," he said. "Let me ride, Jewel."

Jewel looked at him, then he looked away again, holding the horse reined back. Pa watched him, mumbling his lip.

"So you bought a horse," he said. "You went behind my back and bought a horse. You never consulted me; you know how tight it is for us to make by, yet you bought a horse for me to feed. Taken the work from your flesh and blood and bought a horse with it."

Jewel looked at pa, his eyes paler than ever. "He wont never eat a mouthful of yours," he said. "Not a mouthful. I'll kill him first. Dont you never think it. Dont you never."

"Let me ride, Jewel," Vardaman said. "Let me ride, Jewel." He sounded like a cricket in the grass, a little one. "Let me ride, Jewel."

That night I found ma sitting beside the bed where he was sleeping, in the dark. She cried hard, maybe because she had to cry so quiet; maybe because she felt the same way about tears she did about deceit, hating herself for doing it, hating him because she had to. And then I knew that I knew. I knew that as plain on that day as I knew about Dewey Dell on that day.

Tull

So they finally got Anse to say what he wanted to do, and him and the gal and the boy got out of the wagon. But even when we were on the bridge Anse kept on looking back, like he thought maybe, once he was outen the wagon, the whole thing would kind of blow up and he would find himself back yonder in the field again and her laying up there in the house, waiting to die and it to do all over again.

"You ought to let them taken your mule," he says, and the bridge shaking and swaying under us, going down into the moiling water like it went clean through to the other side of the earth, and the other end coming up outen the water like it wasn't the same bridge a-tall and that them that would walk up outen the water on that side must come from the bottom of the earth. But it was still whole; you could tell that by the way when this end swagged, it didn't look like the other end swagged at all: just like the other trees and the bank yonder were swinging back and forth slow like on a big clock. And them logs scraping and bumping at the sunk part and tilting end-up and shooting clean outen the water and tumbling on toward the ford and the waiting, slick, whirling, and foamy.

"What good would that a done?" I says. "If your team cant find the ford and haul it across, what good would three mules or even ten mules do?"

"I aint asking it of you," he says. "I can always do for me and mine. I aint asking you to risk your mule. It aint your dead; I am not blaming you."

"They ought to went back and laid over until tomorrow," I says. The water was cold. It was thick, like slush ice. Only it kind of lived. One part of you knowed it was just water, the same thing that had been running under this same bridge for a long time, yet when them logs would come spewing up outen it, you were not surprised, like they was a part of water, of the waiting and the threat.

It was like when we was across, up out of the water again and the hard earth under us, that I was surprised. It was like we hadn't expected the bridge to end on the other bank, on something tame like the hard earth again that we had tromped on before this time and knowed well. Like it couldn't be me here, because I'd have had better sense than to done what I just done. And when I looked back and saw the other bank and saw my mule standing there where I used to be and knew that I'd have to get back there someway, I knew it couldn't be, because I just couldn't think of anything that could make me cross that bridge ever even once. Yet here I was, and the fellow that could make himself cross it twice, couldn't be me, not even if Cora told him to.

It was that boy. I said "Here; you better take a holt of my hand" and he waited and held to me. I be durn if it wasn't like he come back and got me; like he was saying They wont nothing hurt you. Like he was saying about a fine place he knowed where Christmas come twice with Thanksgiving and lasts on through the winter and the spring and the summer, and if I just stayed with him I'd be all right too.

When I looked back at my mule it was like he was one of these here spy-glasses and I could look at him standing there and see all the broad land and my house sweated outen it like it was the more the sweat, the broader the land; the more the sweat, the tighter the house because it would take a tight house for Cora, to hold Cora like a jar of milk in the spring: you've got to have a tight jar or you'll need a powerful spring, so if you have a big spring, why then you have the incentive to have tight, wellmade jars, because it is your milk, sour or not, because you would rather have milk that will sour than to have milk that wont, because you are a man.

And him holding to my hand, his hand that hot and confident, so that I was like to say: Look-a-here. Cant you see that mule yonder? He never had no business over here, so he never come, not being nothing but a mule. Because a fellow can see ever now and then that children have more sense than him. But he dont like to admit it to them until they have beards. After they have a beard, they are too busy because they dont know if they'll ever quite make it back to where they were in sense before they was haired, so you dont mind admitting then to folks that are worrying about the same thing that aint worth the worry that you are yourself.

Then we was over and we stood there, looking at Cash turning the wagon around. We watched them drive back down the road to where the trail turned off into the bottom. After a while the wagon was out of sight.

"We better get on down to the ford and git ready to help," I said.

"I give her my word," Anse says. "It is sacred on me. I know you begrudge it, but she will bless you in heaven."

"Well, they got to finish circumventing the land before they can dare the water," I said. "Come on."

"It's the turning back," he said. "It ain't no luck in turning back."

He was standing there, humped, mournful, looking at the empty road beyond the swagging and swaying bridge. And that gal, too, with the lunch basket on one arm and that package under the other. Just going to town. Bent on it. They would risk the fire and the earth and the water and all just to eat a sack of bananas. "You ought to laid over a day," I said. "It would a fell some by morning. It mought not a rained tonight. And it cant get no higher."

"I give my promise," he says. "She is counting on it."

Darl

Before us the thick dark current runs. It talks up to us in a murmur become ceaseless and myriad, the yellow surface dimpled monstrously into fading swirls travelling along the surface for an instant, silent, impermanent and profoundly significant, as though just beneath the surface something huge and alive waked for a moment of lazy alertness out of and into light slumber again.

It clucks and murmurs among the spokes and about the mules' knees, yellow, skummed with flotsam and with thick soiled gouts of foam as though it had sweat, lathering, like a driven horse. Through the undergrowth it goes with a plaintive sound, a musing sound; in it the unwinded cane and saplings lean as before a little gale, swaying without reflections as though suspended on invisible wires from the branches overhead. Above the ceaseless surface they stand—trees, cane, vines—rootless, severed from the earth, spectral above a scene of immense yet circumscribed desolation filled with the voice of the waste and mournful water.

Cash and I sit in the wagon; Jewel sits the horse at the off rear wheel. The horse is trembling, its eye rolling wild and baby-blue in its long pink face, its breathing stertorous like groaning. He sits erect, poised, looking quietly and steadily and quickly this way and that, his face calm, a little pale, alert. Cash's face is also gravely composed; he and I look at one another with long probing looks, looks that plunge unimpeded through one another's eyes and into the ultimate secret place where for an instant Cash and Darl crouch flagrant and unabashed in all the old terror and the old foreboding, alert and secret and without shame. When we speak our voices are quiet, detached.

"I reckon we're still in the road, all right."

"Tull taken and cut them two big whiteoaks. I heard tell how at high water in the old days they used to line up the ford by them trees."

"I reckon he did that two years ago when he was logging down here. I reckon he never thought that anybody would ever use this ford again."

"I reckon not. Yes, it must have been then. He cut a sight of timber outen here then. Payed off that mortgage with it, I hear tell."

"Yes. Yes, I reckon so. I reckon Vernon could have done that."

"That's a fact. Most folks that logs in this here country, they need a durn good farm to support the sawmill. Or maybe a store. But I reckon Vernon could."

"I reckon so. He's a sight."

"Ay. Vernon is. Yes, it must still be here. He never would have got that timber out of here if he hadn't cleaned out that old road. I reckon we are still on it." He looks about quietly, at the position of the trees, leaning this way and that, looking back along the floorless road shaped vaguely high in air by the position of the lopped and felled trees, as if the road too had been soaked free of earth and floated upward, to leave in its spectral tracing a monument to a still more profound desolation than this above which we now sit, talking quietly of old security and old trivial things. Jewel looks at him, then at me, then his face turns in in that quiet, constant, questing about the scene, the horse trembling quietly and steadily between his knees.

"He could go on ahead slow and sort of feel it out," I say.

"Yes," Cash says, not looking at me. His face is in profile as he looks forward where Jewel has moved on ahead.

"He cant miss the river," I say. "He couldn't miss seeing it fifty yards ahead."

Cash does not look at me, his face in profile. "If I'd just suspicioned it, I could a come down last week and taken a sight on it."

"The bridge was up then," I say. He does not look at me. "Whitfield crossed it a-horseback."

Jewel looks at us again, his expression sober and alert and subdued. His voice is quiet. "What you want me to do?"

"I ought to come down last week and taken a sight on it," Cash says.

"We couldn't have known," I say. "There wasn't any way for us to know."

"I'll ride on ahead," Jewel says. "You can follow where I am." He lifts the horse. It shrinks, bowed; he leans to it, speaking to it, lifting it forward almost bodily, it setting its feet down with gingerly splashings, trembling, breathing harshly. He speaks to it, murmurs to it. "Go on," he says. "I aint going to let nothing hurt you. Go on, now."

"Jewel," Cash says. Jewel does not look back. He lifts the horse on.

"He can swim," I say. "If he'll just give the horse time, anyhow . . ." When he was born, he had a bad time of it. Ma would sit in the lamp-light, holding him on a pillow on her lap. We would wake and find her so. There would be no sound from them.

"That pillow was longer than him," Cash says. He is leaning a little forward. "I ought to come down last week and sighted. I ought to done it."

"That's right," I say. "Neither his feet nor his head would reach the end of it. You couldn't have known," I say.

"I ought to done it," he says. He lifts the reins. The mules move, into the traces; the wheels murmur alive in the water. He looks back and down at Addie. "It aint on a balance," he says.

At last the trees open; against the open river Jewel sits the horse, half turned, it belly deep now. Across the river we can see Vernon and pa and Vardaman and Dewey Dell. Vernon is waving at us, waving us further downstream.

"We are too high up," Cash says. Vernon is shouting too, but we cannot make out what he says for the noise of the water. It runs steady and deep now, unbroken, without sense of motion until a log comes along, turning slowly. "Watch it," Cash says. We watch it and see it falter and hang for a moment, the current building up behind it in a thick wave, submerging it for an instant before it shoots up and tumbles on.

"There it is," I say.

"Ay," Cash says. "It's there." We look at Vernon again. He is now flapping his arms up and down. We move on downstream, slowly and carefully, watching Vernon. He drops his hands. "This is the place," Cash says.

"Well, goddamn it, let's get across, then," Jewel says. He moves the horse on.

"You wait," Cash says. Jewel stops again.

"Well, by God—" he says. Cash looks at the water, then he looks back at Addie. "It aint on a balance," he says.

"Then go on back to the goddamn bridge and walk across," Jewel says. "You and Darl both. Let me on that wagon."

Cash does not pay him any attention. "It aint on a balance," he says. "Yes, sir. We got to watch it."

"Watch it, hell," Jewel says. "You get out of that wagon and let me have it. By God, if you're afraid to drive it over . . ." His eyes are pale as two bleached chips in his face. Cash is looking at him.

"We'll get it over," he says. "I tell you what you do. You ride on back and walk across the bridge and come down the other bank and meet us with the rope. Vernon'll take your horse home with him and keep it till we get back."

"You go to hell," Jewel says.

"You take the rope and come down the bank and be ready with it," Cash says. "Three cant do no more than two can—one to drive and one to steady it."

"Goddamn you," Jewel says.

"Let Jewel take the end of the rope and cross upstream of us and brace it," I say. "Will you do that, Jewel?"

Jewel watches me, hard. He looks quick at Cash, then back at me, his eyes alert and hard. "I dont give a damn. Just so we do something. Setting here, not lifting a goddamn hand . . ."

"Let's do that, Cash," I say.

"I reckon we'll have to," Cash says.

The river itself is not a hundred yards across, and pa and Vernon and Vardaman and Dewey Dell are the only things in sight not of that single monotony of desolation leaning with that terrific quality a little from right to left, as though we had reached the place where the motion of the wasted world accelerates just before the final precipice. Yet they appear dwarfed. It is as though the space between us were time: an irrevocable quality. It is as though time, no longer running straight before us in a diminishing line, now runs parallel between us like a looping string, the distance between the doubling accretion of the thread and not the interval between. The mules stand, their fore quarters already sloped a little, their rumps high. They too are breathing now with a deep groaning sound; looking back once, their gaze sweeps across us with in their eyes a wild, sad, profound and despairing quality as though they had already seen in the thick water the shape of the disaster which they could not speak and we could not see.

Cash turns back into the wagon. He lays his hands flat on Addie, rocking her a little. His face is calm, down-sloped, calculant, concerned. He lifts his box of tools and wedges it forward under the seat; together we shove Addie forward, wedging her between the tools and the wagon bed. Then he looks at me.

"No," I say. "I reckon I'll stay. Might take both of us."

From the tool box he takes his coiled rope and carries the end twice around the seat stanchion and passes the end to me without tying it. The other end he pays out to Jewel, who takes a turn about his saddle horn.

He must force the horse down into the current. It moves, highkneed, archnecked, boring and chafing. Jewel sits lightly forward, his knees lifted a little; again his swift alert calm gaze sweeps upon us and on. He lowers the horse into the stream, speaking to it in a soothing murmur. The horse slips, goes under to the saddle, surges to its feet again, the current building up against Jewel's thighs.

"Watch yourself," Cash says.

"I'm on it now," Jewel says. "You can come ahead now."

Cash takes the reins and lowers the team carefully and skillfully into the stream.

I felt the current take us and I knew we were on the ford by that reason, since it was only by means of that slipping contact that we could tell that we were in motion at all. What had once been a flat surface was now a succession of troughs and hillocks lifting and falling about us, shoving at us, teasing at us with light lazy touches in the vain instants of solidity underfoot. Cash looked back at me, and then I knew that we were gone. But I did not realise the reason for the rope until I saw the log. It surged up out of the water and stood for an instant upright upon that surging and heaving desolation like Christ. Get out and let the current take you down to the bend, Cash said, You can make it all right. No, I said, I'd get just as wet that way as this

The log appears suddenly between two hills, as if it had rocketed suddenly from the bottom of the river. Upon the end of it a long gout of foam hangs like the beard of an old man or a goat. When Cash speaks to me I know that he has been watching it all the time, watching it and watching Jewel ten feet ahead of us. "Let the rope go," he says. With his other hand he reaches down and reeves the two turns from the stanchion. "Ride on, Jewel," he says; "see if you can pull us ahead of the log."

Jewel shouts at the horse; again he appears to lift it bodily between his knees. He is just above the top of the ford and the horse has a purchase of some sort for it surges forward, shining wetly half out of water, crashing on in a succession of lunges. It moves unbelievably fast; by that token Jewel realises at last that the rope is free, for I can see him sawing back on the reins, his head turned, as the log rears in a long sluggish lunge between us, bearing down upon the team. They see it too; for a moment they also shine black out of water. Then the downstream one vanishes, dragging the other with him; the wagon sheers crosswise, poised on the crest of the ford as the log strikes it, tilting it up and on. Cash is half turned, the reins running taut from his hand and disappearing into the water, the other hand reached back upon Addie, holding her jammed over against the high side of the wagon. "Jump clear," he says quietly. "Stay away from the team and dont try to fight it. It'll swing you into the bend all right."

"You come too," I say. Vernon and Vardaman are running along the bank, pa and Dewey Dell stand watching us, Dewey Dell with the basket and the package in her arms. Jewel is trying to fight the horse back. The head of one mule appears, its eyes wide; it looks back at us for an instant, making a sound almost human. The head vanishes again.

"Back, Jewel," Cash shouts. "Back, Jewel." For another instant I see him leaning to the tilting wagon, his arm braced back against Addie and his tools; I see the bearded head of the rearing log strike up again, and beyond it Jewel holding the horse upreared, its head wrenched around, hammering its head with his fist. I jump from the wagon on the downstream side. Between two hills I see the mules once more. They roll up out of the water in succession, turning completely over, their legs stiffly extended as when they had lost contact with the earth.

Vardaman

Cash tried but she fell off and Darl jumped going under he went under and Cash hollering to catch her and I hollering running and hollering and Dewey Dell hollering at me Vardaman you vardaman you vardaman and Vernon passed me because he was seeing her come up and she jumped into the water again and Darl hadn't caught her yet

He came up to see and I hollering catch her Darl catch her and he didn't come back because she was too heavy he had to go on catching at her and I hollering catch her darl catch her darl because in the water she could go faster than a man and Darl had to grabble for her so I knew he could catch her because he is the best grabber even with the mules in the way again they dived up rolling their feet stiff rolling down again and their backs up now and Darl had to again because in the water she could go faster than a man or a woman and I passed Vernon and he wouldn't get in the water and help Darl he wouldn't grabble for her with Darl he knew but he wouldn't help.

The mules dived up again diving their legs stiff their stiff legs rolling slow and then Darl again and I hollering catch her darl catch her head her into the bank darl and Vernon wouldn't help and then Darl dodged past the mules where he could he had her under the water coming in to the bank coming in slow because in the water she fought to stay under the water but Darl is strong and he was coming in slow and so I knew he had her because he came slow and I ran down into the water to help and I couldn't stop hollering because Darl was strong and steady holding her under the water even if she did fight he would not let her go he was seeing me and he would hold her and it was all right now it was all right now it was all right

Then he comes up out of the water. He comes a long way up slow before his hands do but he's got to have her got to so I can bear it. Then his hands come up and all of him above the water. I cant stop. I have not got time to try. I will try to when I can but his hands came empty out of the water emptying the water emptying away

"Where is ma, Darl?" I said. "You never got her. You knew she is a fish but you let her get away. You never got her. Darl. Darl. Darl." I began to run along the bank, watching the mules dive up slow again and then down again.

Tull

When I told Cora how Darl jumped out of the wagon and left Cash sitting there trying to save it and the wagon turning over, and Jewel that was almost to the bank fighting that horse back where it had more sense than to go, she says "And you're one of the folks that says Darl is the queer one, the one that aint bright, and him the only one of them that had sense enough to get off that wagon. I notice Anse was too smart to been on it a-tall."

"He couldn't a done no good, if he'd been there," I said. "They was going about it right and they would have made it if it hadn't a been for that log."

"Log, fiddlesticks," Cora said. "It was the hand of God."

"Then how can you say it was foolish?" I said. "Nobody cant guard against the hand of God. It would be sacrilege to try to."

"Then why dare it?" Cora says. "Tell me that."

"Anse didn't," I said. "That's just what you faulted him for."

"His place was there," Cora said. "If he had been a man, he would a been there instead of making his sons do what he dursn't."

"I dont know what you want, then," I said. "One breath you say they was daring the hand of God to try it, and the next breath you jump on Anse because he wasn't with them." Then she begun to sing again, working at the washtub, with that singing look in her face like she had done give up folks and all their foolishness and had done went on ahead of them, marching up the sky, singing.

The wagon hung for a long time while the current built up under it, shoving it off the ford, and Cash leaning more and more, trying to keep the coffin braced so it wouldn't slip down and finish tilting the wagon over. Soon as the wagon got tilted good, to where the current could finish it, the log went on. It headed around the wagon and went on good as a swimming man could have done. It was like it had been sent there to do a job and done it and went on.

When the mules finally kicked loose, it looked for a minute like maybe Cash would get the wagon back. It looked like him and the wagon wasn't moving at all, and just Jewel fighting that horse back to the wagon. Then that boy passed me, running and hollering at Darl and the gal trying to catch him, and then I see the mules come rolling slow up out of the water, their legs spraddled stiff like they had balked upside down, and roll on into the water again.

Then the wagon tilted over and then it and Jewel and the horse was all mixed up together. Cash went outen sight, still holding the coffin braced, and then I couldn't tell anything for the horse lunging and splashing. I thought that Cash had give up then and was swimming for it and I was yelling at Jewel to come on back and then all of a sudden him and the horse went under too and I thought they was all going. I knew that the horse had got dragged off the ford too, and with that wild drowning horse and that wagon and that loose box, it was going to be pretty bad, and there I was, standing knee-deep in the water, yelling at Anse behind me: "See what you done now? See what you done now?"

The horse come up again. It was headed for the bank now, throwing its head up, and then I saw one of them holding to the saddle on the downstream side, so I started running along the bank, trying to catch sight of Cash because he couldn't swim, yelling at Jewel where Cash was like a durn fool, bad as that boy that was on down the bank still hollering at Darl.

So I went down into the water so I could still keep some kind of a grip in the mud, when I saw Jewel. He was middle deep, so I knew he was on the ford, anyway, leaning hard upstream, and then I see the rope, and then I see the water building up where he was holding the wagon snubbed just below the ford.

So it was Cash holding to the horse when it come splashing and scrambling up the bank, moaning and groaning like a natural man. When I come to it it was just kicking Cash loose from his holt on the saddle. His face turned up a second when he was sliding back into the water. It was gray, with his eyes closed and a long swipe of mud across his face. Then he let go and turned over in the water. He looked just like a old bundle of clothes kind of washing up and down against the bank. He looked like he was laying there in the water on his face, rocking up and down a little, looking at something on the bottom.

We could watch the rope cutting down into the water, and we could feel the weight of the wagon kind of blump and lunge lazy like, like it just as soon as not, and that rope cutting down into the water hard as a iron bar. We could hear the water hissing on it like it was red hot. Like it was a straight iron bar stuck into the bottom and us holding the end of it, and the wagon lazing up and down, kind of pushing and prodding at us like it had come around and got behind us, lazy like, like it just as soon as not when it made up its mind. There was a shoat come by, blowed up like a balloon: one of them spotted shoats of Lon Quick's. It bumped against the rope like it was a iron bar and bumped off and went on, and us watching that rope slanting down into the water. We watched it.

Darl

Cash lies on his back on the earth, his head raised on a rolled garment. His eyes are closed, his face is gray, his hair plastered in a smooth smear across his forehead as though done with a paint brush. His face appears sunken a little, sagging from the bony ridges of eye sockets, nose, gums, as though the wetting had slacked the firmness which had held the skin full; his teeth, set in pale gums, are parted a little as if he had been laughing quietly. He lies pole-thin in his wet clothes, a little pool of vomit at his head and a thread of it running from the corner of his mouth and down his cheek where he couldn't turn his head quick or far enough, until Dewey Dell stoops and wipes it away with the hem of her dress.

Jewel approaches. He has the plane. "Vernon just found the square," he says. He looks down at Cash, dripping too. "Aint he talked none yet?"

"He had his saw and hammer and chalk-line and rule," I say. "I know that."

Jewel lays the square down. Pa watches him. "They cant be far away," pa says. "It all went together. Was there ere a such misfortunate man."

Jewel does not look at Pa. "You better call Vardaman back here," he says. He looks at Cash. Then he turns and goes away. "Get him to talk soon as he can," he says, "so he can tell us what else there was."

We return to the river. The wagon is hauled clear, the wheels chocked (carefully: we all helped; it is as though upon the shabby, familiar, inert shape of the wagon there lingered somehow, latent yet still immediate, that violence which had slain the mules that drew it not an hour since) above the edge of the flood. In the wagon bed it lies profoundly, the long pale planks hushed a little with wetting yet still yellow, like gold seen through water, save for two long muddy smears. We pass it and go on to the bank.

One end of the rope is made fast to a tree. At the edge of the stream, knee-deep, Vardaman stands, bent forward a little, watching Vernon with rapt absorption. He has stopped yelling and he is wet to the armpits. Vernon is at the other end of the rope, shoulder-deep in the river, looking back at Vardaman. "Further back than that," he says. "You git back by the tree and hold the rope for me, so it cant slip."

Vardaman backs along the rope, to the tree, moving blindly, watching Vernon. When we come up he looks at us once, his eyes round and a little dazed. Then he looks at Vernon again in that posture of rapt alertness.

"I got the hammer too," Vernon says. "Looks like we ought to done already got that chalk-line. It ought to floated."

"Floated clean away," Jewel says. "We wont get it. We ought to find the saw, though."

"I reckon so," Vernon says. He looks at the water. "That chalk-line, too. What else did he have?"

"He aint talked yet," Jewel says, entering the water. He looks back at me. "You go back and get him roused up to talk," he says.

"Pa's there," I say. I follow Jewel into the water, along the rope. It feels alive in my hand, bellied faintly in a prolonged and resonant arc. Vernon is watching me.

"You better go," he says. "You better be there."

"Let's see what else we can get before it washes on down," I say.

We hold to the rope, the current curling and dimpling about our shoulders. But beneath that false blandness the true force of it leans against us lazily. I had not thought that water in July could be so cold. It is like hands molding and prodding at the very bones. Vernon is still looking back toward the bank.

"Reckon it'll hold us all?" he says. We too look back, following the rigid bar of the rope as it rises from the water to the tree and Vardaman crouched a little beside it, watching us. "Wish my mule wouldn't strike out for home," Vernon says.

"Come on," Jewel says. "Let's get outen here."

We submerge in turn, holding to the rope, being clutched by one another while the cold wall of the water sucks the slanting mud backward and upstream from beneath our feet and we are suspended so, groping along the cold bottom. Even the mud there is not still. It has a chill, scouring quality, as though the earth under us were in motion too. We touch and fumble at one another's extended arms, letting ourselves go cautiously against the rope; or, erect in turn, watch the water suck and boil where one of the other two gropes beneath the surface. Pa has come down to the shore, watching us.

Vernon comes up, streaming, his face sloped down into his pursed blowing mouth. His mouth is bluish, like a circle of weathered rubber. He has the rule.

"He'll be glad of that," I say. "It's right new. He bought it just last month out of the catalogue."

"If we just knowed for sho what else," Vernon says, looking over his shoulder and then turning to face where Jewel had disappeared. "Didn't he go down fore me?" Vernon says.

"I dont know," I say. "I think so. Yes. Yes, he did."

We watch the thick curling surface, streaming away from us in slow whorls.

"Give him a pull on the rope," Vernon says.

"He's on your end of it," I say.

"Aint nobody on my end of it," he says.

"Pull it in," I say. But he has already done that, holding the end above the water; and then we see Jewel. He is ten yards away; he comes up, blowing, and looks at us, tossing his long hair back with a jerk of his head, then he looks toward the bank; we can see him filling his lungs.

"Jewel," Vernon says, not loud, but his voice going full and clear along the water, peremptory yet tactful. "It'll be back here. Better come back."

Jewel dives again. We stand there, leaning back against the current, watching the water where he disappeared, holding the dead rope between us like two men holding the nozzle of a fire hose, waiting for the water. Suddenly Dewey Dell is behind us in the water. "You make him come back," she says. "Jewel!" she says. He comes up again, tossing his hair back from his eyes. He is swimming now, toward the bank, the current sweeping him downstream quartering. "You, Jewel!" Dewey Dell says. We stand holding the rope and see him gain the bank and climb out. As he rises from the water, he stoops and picks up something. He comes back along the bank. He has found the chalk-line. He comes opposite us and stands there, looking about as if he were seeking something. Pa goes on down the bank. He is going back to look at the mules again where their round bodies float and rub quietly together in the slack water within the bend.

"What did you do with the hammer, Vernon?" Jewel says.

"I give it to him," Vernon says, jerking his head at Vardaman. Vardaman is looking after pa. Then he looks at Jewel. "With the square." Vernon is watching Jewel. He moves toward the bank, passing Dewey Dell and me.

"You get on out of here," I say. She says nothing, looking at Jewel and Vernon.

"Where's the hammer?" Jewel says. Vardaman scuttles up the bank and fetches it.

"It's heavier than the saw," Vernon says. Jewel is tying the end of the chalk-line about the hammer shaft.

"Hammer's got the most wood in it," Jewel says. He and Vernon face one another, watching Jewel's hands.

"And flatter, too," Vernon says, "It'd float three to one, almost. Try the plane."

Jewel looks at Vernon. Vernon is tall, too; long and lean, eye to eye they stand in their close wet clothes. Lon Quick could look even at a cloudy sky and tell the time to ten minutes. Big Lon I mean, not little Lon.

"Why dont you get out of the water?" I say.

"It wont float like a saw," Jewel says.

"It'll float nigher to a saw than a hammer will," Vernon says.

"Bet you," Jewel says.

"I wont bet," Vernon says.

They stand there, watching Jewel's still hands.

"Hell," Jewel says. "Get the plane, then."

So they get the plane and tie it to the chalk-line and enter the water again. Pa comes back along the bank. He stops for a while and looks at us, hunched, mournful, like a failing steer or an old tall bird.

Vernon and Jewel return, leaning against the current. "Get out of the way," Jewel says to Dewey Dell. "Get out of the water."

She crowds against me a little so they can pass, Jewel holding the plane high as though it were perishable, the blue string trailing back over his shoulder. They pass us and stop; they fall to arguing quietly about just where the wagon went over.

"Darl ought to know," Vernon says. They look at me.

"I dont know," I says. "I wasn't there that long."

"Hell," Jewel says. They move on, gingerly, leaning against the current, reading the ford with their feet.

"Have you got a holt of the rope?" Vernon says. Jewel does not answer. He glances back at the shore, calculant, then at the water. He flings the plane outward, letting the string run through his fingers, his fingers turning blue where it runs over them. When the line stops, he hands it back to Vernon.

"Better let me go this time," Vernon says. Again Jewel does not answer; we watch him duck beneath the surface.

"Jewel," Dewey Dell whimpers.

"It aint so deep there," Vernon says. He does not look back. He is watching the water where Jewel went under.

When Jewel comes up he has the saw.

When we pass the wagon pa is standing beside it, scrubbing at the two mud smears with a handful of leaves. Against the jungle Jewel's horse looks like a patchwork quilt hung on a line.

Cash has not moved. We stand above him, holding the plane, the saw, the hammer, the square, the rule, the chalk-line, while Dewey Dell squats and lifts Cash's head. "Cash," she says; "Cash."

He opens his eyes, staring profoundly up at our inverted faces.

"If ever was such a misfortunate man," pa says.

"Look, Cash," we say, holding the tools up so he can see; "what else did you have?"

He tries to speak, rolling his head, shutting his eyes.

"Cash," we say; "Cash."

It is to vomit he is turning his head. Dewey Dell wipes his mouth on the wet hem of her dress; then he can speak.

"It's his saw-set," Jewel says. "The new one he bought when he bought the rule." He moves, turning away. Vernon looks up after him, still squatting. Then he rises and follows Jewel down to the water.

"If ever was such a misfortunate man," pa says. He looms tall above us as we squat; he looks like a figure carved clumsily from tough wood by a drunken caricaturist. "It's a trial," he says. "But I dont begrudge her it. No man can say I begrudge her it." Dewey Dell has laid Cash's head back on the folded coat, twisting his head a little to avoid the vomit. Beside him his tools lie. "A fellow might call it lucky it was the same leg he broke when he fell offen that church," pa says. "But I dont begrudge her it."

Jewel and Vernon are in the river again. From here they do not appear to violate the surface at all; it is as though it had severed them both at a single blow, the two torsos moving with infinitesimal and ludicrous care upon the surface. It looks peaceful, like machinery does after you have watched it and listened to it for a long time. As though the clotting which is you had dissolved into the myriad original motion, and seeing and hearing in themselves blind and deaf; fury in itself quiet with stagnation. Squatting, Dewey Dell's wet dress shapes for the dead eyes of three blind men those mammalian ludicrosities which are the horizons and the valleys of the earth.

Cash

It wasn't on a balance. I told them that if they wanted it to tote and ride on a balance, they would have to

Cora

One day we were talking. She had never been pure religious, not even after that summer at the camp meeting when Brother Whitfield wrestled with her spirit, singled her out and strove with the vanity in her mortal heart, and I said to her many a time, "God gave you children to comfort your hard human lot and for a token of His own suffering and love, for in love you conceived and bore them." I said that because she took God's love and her duty to Him too much as a matter of course, and such conduct is not pleasing to Him. I said, "He gave us the gift to raise our voices in His undying praise" because I said there is more rejoicing in heaven over one sinner than over a hundred that never sinned.[8] And she said "My daily life is an acknowledgment and expiation of my sin" and I said "Who are you, to say what is sin and what is not sin? It is the Lord's part to judge; ours to praise His mercy and His holy name in the hearing of our fellow mortals" because He alone can see into the heart, and just because a woman's life is right in the sight of man, she cant know if there is no sin in her heart without she opens her heart to the Lord and receives His grace. I said, "Just because you have been a faithful wife is no sign that there is no sin in your heart, and just because your life is hard is no sign that the Lord's grace is absolving you." And she said, "I know my own sin. I know that I deserve my punishment. I do not begrudge it." And I said, "It is out of your vanity that you would judge sin and salvation in the Lord's place. It is our mortal lot to suffer and to raise our voices in praise of Him who judges the sin and offers the salvation through our trials and tribulations time out of mind amen. Not even after Brother Whitfield, a godly man if ever one breathed God's breath, prayed for you and strove as never a man could except him," I said.

Because it is not us that can judge our sins or know what is sin in the Lord's eyes. She has had a hard life, but so does every woman. But you'd think from the way she talked that she knew more about sin and salvation than the Lord God Himself, than them who have strove and labored with the sin

8. Cf. Luke 15.7: "I say unto you, that likewise joy shall be in heaven over one sinner that repenteth, more than over ninety and nine just persons, which need no repentance."

in this human world. When the only sin she ever committed was being partial to Jewel that never loved her and was its own punishment, in preference to Darl that was touched by God Himself and considered queer by us mortals and that did love her. I said, "There is your sin. And your punishment too. Jewel is your punishment. But where is your salvation? And life is short enough," I said, "to win eternal grace in. And God is a jealous God. It is His to judge and to mete; not yours."

"I know," she said. "I—" Then she stopped, and I said,

"Know what?"

"Nothing," she said. "He is my cross and he will be my salvation. He will save me from the water and from the fire. Even though I have laid down my life, he will save me."

"How do you know, without you open your heart to Him and lift your voice in His praise?" I said. Then I realised that she did not mean God. I realised that out of the vanity of her heart she had spoken sacrilege. And I went down on my knees right there. I begged her to kneel and open her heart and cast from it the devil of vanity and cast herself upon the mercy of the Lord. But she wouldn't. She just sat there, lost in her vanity and her pride, that had closed her heart to God and set that selfish mortal boy in His place. Kneeling there I prayed for her. I prayed for that poor blind woman as I had never prayed for me and mine.

Addie

In the afternoon when school was out and the last one had left with his little dirty snuffling nose, instead of going home I would go down the hill to the spring where I could be quiet and hate them. It would be quiet there then, with the water bubbling up and away and the sun slanting quiet in the trees and the quiet smelling of damp and rotting leaves and new earth; especially in the early spring, for it was worst then.

I could just remember how my father used to say that the reason for living was to get ready to stay dead a long time. And when I would have to look at them day after day, each with his and her secret and selfish thought, and blood strange to each other blood and strange to mine, and think that this seemed to be the only way I could get ready to stay dead, I would hate my father for having ever planted me. I would look forward to the times when they faulted, so I could whip them. When the switch fell I could feel it upon my flesh; when it welted and ridged it was my blood that ran, and I would think with each blow of the switch: Now you are aware of me! Now I am something in your secret and selfish life, who have marked your blood with my own for ever and ever.

And so I took Anse. I saw him pass the school house three or four times before I learned that he was driving four miles out of his way to do it. I noticed then how he was beginning to hump—a tall man and young—so that he looked already like a tall bird hunched in the cold weather, on the wagon seat. He would pass the school house, the wagon creaking slow, his head turning slow to watch the door of the school house as the wagon passed, until he went on around the curve and out of sight. One day I went to the door and stood there when he passed. When he saw me he looked quickly away and did not look back again.

In the early spring it was worst. Sometimes I thought that I could not bear it, lying in bed at night, with the wild geese going north and their honking coming faint and high and wild out of the wild darkness, and during the day it would seem as though I couldn't wait for the last one to go so I could go down to the spring. And so when I looked up that day and saw Anse standing there in his Sunday clothes, turning his hat round and round in his hands, I said:

"If you've got any womenfolks, why in the world dont they make you get your hair cut?"

"I aint got none," he said. Then he said suddenly, driving his eyes at me like two hounds in a strange yard: "That's what I come to see you about."

"And make you hold your shoulders up," I said. "You haven't got any? But you've got a house. They tell me you've got a house and a good farm. And you live there alone, doing for yourself, do you?" He just looked at me, turning the hat in his hands. "A new house," I said. "Are you going to get married?"

And he said again, holding his eyes to mine: "That's what I come to see you about."

Later he told me, "I aint got no people. So that wont be no worry to you. I dont reckon you can say the same."

"No. I have people. In Jefferson."

His face fell a little. "Well, I got a little property. I'm forehanded; I got a good honest name. I know how town folks are, but maybe when they talk to me . . ."

"They might listen," I said. "But they'll be hard to talk to." He was watching my face. "They're in the cemetery."

"But your living kin," he said. "They'll be different."

"Will they?" I said. "I dont know. I never had any other kind."

So I took Anse. And when I knew that I had Cash, I knew that living was terrible and that this was the answer to it. That was when I learned that words are no good; that words dont ever fit even what they are trying to say at. When he was born I knew that motherhood was invented by someone who had to have a word for it because the ones that had the children didn't care whether there was a word for it or not. I knew that fear was invented by someone that had never had the fear; pride, who never had the pride. I knew that it had been, not that they had dirty noses, but that we had had to use one another by words like spiders dangling by their mouths from a beam, swinging and twisting and never touching, and that only through the blows of the switch could my blood and their blood flow as one stream. I knew that it had been, not that my aloneness had to be violated over and over each day, but that it had never been violated until Cash came. Not even by Anse in the nights.

He had a word, too. Love, he called it. But I had been used to words for a long time. I knew that that word was like the others: just a shape to fill a lack; that when the right time came, you wouldn't need a word for that anymore than for pride or fear. Cash did not need to say it to me nor I to him, and I would say, Let Anse use it, if he wants to. So that it was Anse or love; love or Anse: it didn't matter.

I would think that even while I lay with him in the dark and Cash asleep in the cradle within the swing of my hand. I would think that if he were to wake and cry, I would suckle him, too. Anse or love: it didn't matter. My aloneness had been violated and then made whole again by the violation: time, Anse, love, and what you will, outside the circle.

Then I found that I had Darl. At first I would not believe it. Then I believed that I would kill Anse. It was as though he had tricked me, hidden within a word like within a paper screen and struck me in the back through it. But then I realised that I had been tricked by words older than Anse or love, and that the same word had tricked Anse too, and that my revenge would be that he would never know I was taking revenge. And when Darl was born I asked Anse to promise to take me back to Jefferson when I died, because I knew that father had been right, even when he couldn't have known he was right anymore than I could have known I was wrong.

"Nonsense," Anse said; "you and me aint nigh done chapping yet, with just two."

He did not know that he was dead, then. Sometimes I would lie by him in the dark, hearing the land that was now of my blood and flesh, and I would think: Anse. Why Anse. Why are you Anse. I would think about his name until after a while I could see the word as a shape, a vessel, and I would watch him liquify and flow into it like cold molasses flowing out of the darkness into the vessel, until the jar stood full and motionless: a significant shape profoundly without life like an empty door frame; and then I would find that I had forgotten the name of the jar. I would think: The shape of my body where I used to be a virgin is in the shape of a   and I couldn't think *Anse,* couldn't remember *Anse.* It was not that I could think of myself as no longer unvirgin, because I was three now. And when I would think *Cash* and *Darl* that way until their names would die and solidify into a shape and then fade away, I would say, All right. It doesn't matter. It doesn't matter what they call them.

And so when Cora Tull would tell me I was not a true mother, I would think how words go straight up in a thin line, quick and harmless, and how terribly doing goes along the earth, clinging to it, so that after a while the two lines are too far apart for the same person to straddle from one to the other; and that sin and love and fear are just sounds that people who never sinned nor loved nor feared have for what they never had and cannot have until they forget the words. Like Cora, who could never even cook.

She would tell me what I owed to my children and to Anse and to God. I gave Anse the children. I did not ask for them. I did not even ask him for what he could have given me: not-Anse. That was my duty to him, to not ask that, and that duty I fulfilled. I would be I; I would let him be the shape and echo of his word. That was more than he asked, because he could not have asked for that and been Anse, using himself so with a word.

And then he died. He did not know he was dead. I would lie by him in the dark, hearing the dark land talking of God's love and His beauty and His sin; hearing the dark voicelessness in which the words are the deeds, and the other words that are not deeds, that are just the gaps in peoples' lacks, coming down like the cries of the geese out of the wild darkness in the old terrible nights, fumbling at the deeds like orphans to whom are pointed out in a crowd two faces and told, That is your father, your mother.

I believed that I had found it. I believed that the reason was the duty to the alive, to the terrible blood, the red bitter flood boiling through the land. I would think of sin as I would think of the clothes we both wore in the world's face, of the circumspection necessary because he was he and I was I; the sin the more utter and terrible since he was the instrument ordained by God who created the sin, to sanctify that sin He had created. While I waited for him in the woods, waiting for him before he saw me, I would think of him as dressed in sin. I would think of him as thinking of me as dressed also in sin, he the more beautiful since the garment which he had exchanged for sin was sanctified. I would think of the sin as garments which we would remove in order to shape and coerce the terrible blood to the forlorn echo of the dead word high in the air. Then I would lay with Anse again—I did not lie to him: I just refused, just as I refused my breast to Cash and Darl after their time was up—hearing the dark land talking the voiceless speech.

I hid nothing. I tried to deceive no one. I would not have cared. I merely took the precautions that he thought necessary for his sake, not for my safety, but just as I wore clothes in the world's face. And I would think then when Cora talked to me, of how the high dead words in time seemed to lose even the significance of their dead sound.

Then it was over. Over in the sense that he was gone and I knew that, see him again though I would, I would never again see him coming swift and secret to me in the woods dressed in sin like a gallant garment already blowing aside with the speed of his secret coming.

But for me it was not over. I mean, over in the sense of beginning and ending, because to me there was no beginning nor ending to anything then. I even held Anse refraining still, not that I was holding him recessional, but as though nothing else had ever been. My children were of me alone, of the wild blood boiling along the earth, of me and of all that lived; of none and of all. Then I found that I had Jewel. When I waked to remember to discover it, he was two months gone.

My father said that the reason for living is getting ready to stay dead. I knew at last what he meant and that he could not have known what he meant himself, because a man cannot know anything about cleaning up the house afterward. And so I have cleaned my house. With Jewel—I lay by the lamp, holding up my own head, watching him cap and suture it before he breathed—the wild blood boiled away and the sound of it ceased. Then there was only the milk, warm and calm, and I lying calm in the slow silence, getting ready to clean my house.

I gave Anse Dewey Dell to negative Jewel. Then I gave him Vardaman to replace the child I had robbed him of. And now he has three children that are his and not mine. And then I could get ready to die.

One day I was talking to Cora. She prayed for me because she believed I was blind to sin, wanting me to kneel and pray too, because people to whom sin is just a matter of words, to them salvation is just words too.

Whitfield

When they told me she was dying, all that night I wrestled with Satan, and I emerged victorious. I woke to the enormity of my sin; I saw the true light at last, and I fell on my knees and confessed to God and asked His guidance and received it. "Rise," He said; "repair to that home in which you have put a living lie, among those people with whom you have outraged My Word; confess your sin aloud. It is for them, for that deceived husband, to forgive you: not I."

So I went. I heard that Tull's bridge was gone; I said "Thanks, O Lord, O Mighty Ruler of all;" for by those dangers and difficulties which I should have to surmount I saw that He had not abandoned me; that my reception again into His holy peace and love would be the sweeter for it. "Just let me not perish before I have begged the forgiveness of the man whom I betrayed," I prayed; "let me not be too late; let not the tale of mine and her transgression come from her lips instead of mine. She had sworn then that she would never tell it, but eternity is a fearsome thing to face: have I not wrestled thigh to thigh with Satan myself? let me not have also the sin of her broken vow upon my soul. Let not the waters of Thy Mighty Wrath encompass me until I have cleansed my soul in the presence of them whom I injured."

It was His hand that bore me safely above the flood, that fended from me the dangers of the waters. My horse was frightened, and my own heart failed me as the logs and the uprooted trees bore down upon my littleness. But not my soul: time after time I saw them averted at destruction's final instant, and I lifted my voice above the noise of the flood: "Praise to Thee, O Mighty Lord and King. By this token shall I cleanse my soul and gain again into the fold of Thy undying love."

I knew then that forgiveness was mine. The flood, the danger, behind, and as I rode on across the firm earth again and the scene of my Gethsemane drew closer and closer, I framed the words which I should use. I would enter the house; I would stop her before she had spoken; I would say to her husband: "Anse, I have sinned. Do with me as you will."

It was already as though it were done. My soul felt freer, quieter than it had in years; already I seemed to dwell in abiding peace again as I rode on. To either side I saw His hand; in my heart I could hear His voice: "Courage. I am with thee."

Then I reached Tull's house. His youngest girl came out and called to me as I was passing. She told me that she was already dead.

I have sinned, O Lord. Thou knowest the extent of my remorse and the will of my spirit. But He is merciful; He will accept the will for the deed, Who knew that when I framed the words of my confession it was to Anse I spoke them, even though he was not there. It was He in His infinite wisdom that restrained the tale from her dying lips as she lay surrounded by those who loved and trusted her; mine the travail by water which I sustained by the strength of His hand. Praise to Thee in Thy bounteous and omnipotent love; O praise.

I entered the house of bereavement, the lowly dwelling where another erring mortal lay while her soul faced the awful and irrevocable judgment, peace to her ashes.

"God's grace upon this house," I said.

Darl

On the horse he rode up to Armstid's and *came back on the horse,* leading Armstid's team. We hitched up and laid Cash on top of Addie. When we laid him down he vomited again, but he got his head over the wagon bed in time.

"He taken a lick in the stomach, too," Vernon said.

"The horse may have kicked him in the stomach too," I said. "Did he kick you in the stomach, Cash?"

He tried to say something. Dewey Dell wiped his mouth again.

"What's he say?" Vernon said.

"What is it, Cash?" Dewey Dell said. She leaned down. "His tools," she said. Vernon got them and put them into the wagon. Dewey Dell lifted Cash's head so he could see. We drove on, Dewey Dell and I sitting beside Cash to steady him *and he riding on ahead on the horse*. Vernon stood watching us for a while. Then he turned and went back toward the bridge. He walked gingerly, beginning to flap the wet sleeves of his shirt as though he had just got wet.

He was sitting the horse before the gate. Armstid was waiting at the gate. We stopped *and he got down* and we lifted Cash down and carried him into the house, where Mrs Armstid had the bed ready. We left her and Dewey Dell undressing him.

We followed pa out to the wagon. He went back and got into the wagon and drove on, we following on foot, into the lot. The wetting had helped, because Armstid said, "You're welcome to the house. You can put it there." *He followed, leading the horse, and stood beside the wagon, the reins in his hand.*

"I thank you," pa said. "We'll use in the shed yonder. I know it's a imposition on you."

"You're welcome to the house," Armstid said. *He had that wooden look on his face again; that bold, surly, high-colored rigid look like his face and eyes were two colors of wood, the wrong one pale and the wrong one dark. His shirt was beginning to dry, but it still clung close upon him when he moved.*

"She would appreciate it," pa said.

We took the team out and rolled the wagon back under the shed. One side of the shed was open.

"It wont rain under," Armstid said. "But if you'd rather . . ."

Back of the barn was some rusted sheets of tin roofing. We took two of them and propped them against the open side.

"You're welcome to the house," Armstid said.

"I thank you," pa said. "I'd take it right kind if you'd give them a litttle snack."

"Sho," Armstid said. "Lula'll have supper ready soon as she gets Cash comfortable." *He had gone back to the horse and he was taking the saddle off, his damp shirt lapping flat to him when he moved.*

Pa wouldn't come in the house.

"Come in and eat," Armstid said. "It's nigh ready."

"I wouldn't crave nothing," pa said. "I thank you."

"You come in and dry and eat," Armstid said. "It'll be all right here."

"It's for her," pa said. "It's for her sake I am taking the food. I got no team, no nothing. But she will be grateful to ere a one of you."

"Sho," Armstid said. "You folks come in and dry."

But after Armstid gave pa a drink, he felt better, and when we went in to see about Cash *he hadn't come in with us. When I looked back he was leading the horse into the barn* he was already talking about getting another team, and by supper time he had good as bought it. *He is down there in the barn, sliding fluidly past the gaudy lunging swirl, into the stall with it. He climbs onto the manger and drags the hay down and leaves the stall and seeks and finds the curry-comb. Then he returns and slips quickly past the single crashing thump and up against the horse, where it cannot overreach. He applies the curry-comb, holding himself within the horse's striking radius with the agility of an acrobat, cursing the horse in a whisper of obscene caress. Its head flashes back, tooth-cropped; its eyes roll in the dusk like marbles on a gaudy velvet cloth as he strikes it upon the face with the back of the curry-comb.*

Armstid

But time I give him another sup of whiskey and supper was about ready, he had done already bought a team from somebody, on a credit. Picking and choosing he were by then, saying how he didn't like this span and wouldn't put his money in nothing so-and-so owned, not even a hen coop.

"You might try Snopes," I said. "He's got three-four span. Maybe one of them would suit you."

Then he begun to mumble his mouth, looking at me like it was me that owned the only span of mules in the county and wouldn't sell them to him, when I knew that like as not it would be my team that would ever get them out of the lot at all. Only I dont know what they would do with them, if they had a team. Littlejohn had told me that the levee through Haley bottom had done gone for two miles and that the only way to get to Jefferson would be to go around by Mottson. But that was Anse's business.

"He's a close man to trade with," he says, mumbling his mouth. But when I give him another sup after supper, he cheered up some. He was aiming to go back to the barn and set up with her. Maybe he thought that if he just stayed down there ready to take out, Santa Claus would maybe bring him a span of mules. "But I reckon I can talk him around," he says. "A man'll always help a fellow in a tight, if he's got ere a drop of Christian blood in him."

"Of course you're welcome to the use of mine," I said, me knowing how much he believed that was the reason.

"I thank you," he said. "She'll want to go in ourn," and him knowing how much I believed that was the reason.

After supper Jewel rode over to the Bend to get Peabody. I heard he was to be there today at Varner's. Jewel come back about midnight. Peabody had gone down below Inverness somewhere, but Uncle Billy come back with him, with his satchel of horse-physic. Like he says, a man aint so different from a horse or a mule, come long come short, except a mule or a horse has got a little more sense. "What you been into now, boy?" he says, looking at Cash. "Get me a mattress and a chair and a glass of whisky," he says.

He made Cash drink the whiskey, then he run Anse out of the room. "Lucky it was the same leg he broke last summer," Anse says, mournful, mumbling and blinking. "That's something."

We folded the mattress across Cash's legs and set the chair on the mattress and me and Jewel set on the chair and the gal held the lamp and Uncle Billy taken a chew of tobacco and went to work. Cash fought pretty hard for a while, until he fainted. Then he laid still, with big balls of sweat standing on his face like they had started to roll down and then stopped to wait for him.

When he waked up, Uncle Billy had done packed up and left. He kept on trying to say something until the gal leaned down and wiped his mouth. "It's his tools," she said.

"I brought them in," Darl said. "I got them."

He tried to talk again; she leaned down. "He wants to see them," she said. So Darl brought them in where he could see them. They shoved them under the side of the bed, where he could reach his hand and touch them when he felt better. Next morning Anse taken that horse and rode over to the Bend to see Snopes. Him and Jewel stood in the lot talking a while, then Anse got on the horse and rode off. I reckon that was the first time Jewel ever let anybody ride that horse, and until Anse come back he hung around in that swole-up way, watching the road like he was half a mind to take out after Anse and get the horse back.

Along toward nine oclock it begun to get hot. That was when I see the first buzzard. Because of the wetting, I reckon. Anyway it wasn't until well into the day that I see them. Lucky the breeze was setting away from the house, so it wasn't until well into the morning. But soon as I see them it was like I could smell it in the field a mile away from just watching them, and them circling and circling for everybody in the county to see what was in my barn.

I was still a good half a mile from the house when I heard that boy yelling. I thought maybe he might have fell into the well or something, so I whipped up and come into the lot on the lope.

There must have been a dozen of them setting along the ridge-pole of the barn, and that boy was chasing another one around the lot like it was a turkey and it just lifting enough to dodge him and go flopping back to the roof of the shed again where he had found it setting on the coffin. It had got hot then, right, and the breeze had dropped or changed or something, so I went and found Jewel, but Lulu come out.

"You got to do something," she said. "It's a outrage."

"That's what I aim to do," I said.

"It's a outrage," she said. "He should be lawed for treating her so."

"He's getting her into the ground the best he can," I said. So I found Jewel and asked him if he didn't want to take one of the mules and go over to the Bend and see about Anse. He didn't say nothing. He just looked at me with his jaws going bone-white and them bone-white eyes of hisn, then he went and begun to call Darl.

"What you fixing to do?" I said.

He didn't answer. Darl come out. "Come on," Jewel said.

"What you aim to do?" Darl said.

"Going to move the wagon," Jewel said over his shoulder.

"Dont be a fool," I said. "I never meant nothing. You couldn't help it." And Darl hung back too, but nothing wouldn't suit Jewel.

"Shut your goddamn mouth," he says.

"It's got to be somewhere," Darl said. "We'll take out soon as pa gets back."

"You wont help me?" Jewel says, them white eyes of hisn kind of blaring and his face shaking like he had a aguer.[9]

"No," Darl said. "I wont. Wait till pa gets back."

So I stood in the door and watched him push and haul at that wagon. It was on a downhill, and once I thought he was fixing to beat out the back end of the shed. Then the dinner bell rung. I called him, but he didn't look around. "Come on to dinner," I said. "Tell that boy." But he didn't answer, so

9. Ague or fever.

I went on to dinner. The gal went down to get that boy, but she come back without him. About half through dinner we heard him yelling again, running that buzzard out.

"It's a outrage," Lula said; "a outrage."

"He's doing the best he can," I said. "A fellow dont trade with Snopes in thirty minutes. They'll set in the shade all afternoon to dicker."

"Do?" she says. "Do? He's done too much, already."

And I reckon he had. Trouble is, his quitting was just about to start our doing. He couldn't buy no team from nobody, let alone Snopes, withouten he had something to mortgage he didn't know would mortgage yet. And so when I went back to the field I looked at my mules and same as told them goodbye for a spell. And when I come back that evening and the sun shining all day on that shed, I wasn't so sho I would regret it.

He come riding up just as I went out to the porch, where they all was. He looked kind of funny: kind of more hang-dog than common, and kind of proud too. Like he had done something he thought was cute but wasn't so sho now how other folks would take it.

"I got a team," he said.

"You bought a team from Snopes?" I said.

"I reckon Snopes aint the only man in this country that can drive a trade," he said.

"Sho," I said. He was looking at Jewel, with that funny look, but Jewel had done got down from the porch and was going toward the horse. To see what Anse had done to it, I reckon.

"Jewel," Anse says. Jewel looked back. "Come here," Anse says. Jewel come back a little and stopped again.

"What you want?" he said.

"So you got a team from Snopes," I said. "He'll send them over tonight, I reckon? You'll want a early start tomorrow, long as you'll have to go by Mottson."

Then he quit looking like he had been for a while. He got that badgered look like he used to have, mumbling his mouth.

"I do the best I can," he said. "Fore God, if there were ere a man in the living world suffered the trials and floutings I have suffered."

"A fellow that just beat Snopes in a trade ought to feel pretty good," I said. "What did you give him, Anse?"

He didn't look at me. "I give a chattel mortgage on my cultivator and seeder," he said.

"But they aint worth forty dollars. How far do you aim to get with a forty dollar team?"

They were all watching him now, quiet and steady. Jewel was stopped, halfway back, waiting to go on to the horse. "I give other things," Anse said. He begun to mumble his mouth again, standing there like he was waiting for somebody to hit him and him with his mind already made up not to do nothing about it.

"What other things?" Darl said.

"Hell," I said. "You take my team. You can bring them back. I'll get along someway."

"So that's what you were doing in Cash's clothes last night," Darl said. He said it just like he was reading it outen the paper. Like he never give a durn himself one way or the other. Jewel had come back now, standing there, looking at Anse with them marble eyes of hisn. "Cash aimed to buy that talking machine from Suratt with that money," Darl said.

Anse stood there, mumbling his mouth. Jewel watched him. He aint never blinked yet.

"But that's just eight dollars more," Darl said, in that voice like he was just listening and never give a durn himself. "That still wont buy a team."

Anse looked at Jewel, quick, kind of sliding his eyes that way, then he looked down again. "God knows, if there were ere a man," he says. Still they didn't say nothing. They just watched him, waiting, and him sliding his eyes toward their feet and up their legs but no higher. "And the horse," he says.

"What horse?" Jewel said. Anse just stood there. I be durn, if a man cant keep the upper hand of his sons, he ought to run them away from home, no matter how big they are. And if he cant do that, I be durn if he oughtn't to leave himself. I be durn if I wouldn't. "You mean, you tried to swap my horse?" Jewel says.

Anse stands there, dangle-armed. "For fifteen years I aint had a tooth in my head," he says. "God knows it. He knows in fifteen years I aint et the victuals He aimed for man to eat to keep his strength up, and me saving a nickel here and nickel there so my family wouldn't suffer it, to buy them teeth so I could eat God's appointed food. I give that money. I thought that if I could do without eating, my sons could do without riding. God knows I did."

Jewel stands with his hands on his hips, looking at Anse. Then he looks away. He looked out across the field, his face still as a rock. Like it was somebody else talking about somebody else's horse and him not even listening. Then he spit, slow, and said "Hell" and he turned and went on to the gate and unhitched the horse and got on it. It was moving when he come into the saddle and by the time he was on it they was tearing down the road like the Law might have been behind them. They went out of sight that way, the two of them looking like some kind of a spotted cyclone.

"Well," I says. "You take my team," I said. But he wouldn't do it. And they wouldn't even stay, and that boy chasing them buzzards all day in the hot sun until he was nigh as crazy as the rest of them. "Leave Cash here, anyway," I said. But they wouldn't do that. They made a pallet for him with quilts on top of the coffin and laid him on it and set his tools by him, and we put my team in and hauled the wagon about a mile down the road.

"If we'll bother you here," Anse says, "just say so."

"Sho," I said. "It'll be fine here. Safe, too. Now let's go back and eat supper."

"I thank you," Anse said. "We got a little something in the basket. We can make out."

"Where'd you get it?" I said.

"We brought it from home."

"But it'll be stale now," I said. "Come and get some hot victuals."

But they wouldn't come. "I reckon we can make out," Anse said. So I went home and et and taken a basket back to them and tried again to make them come back to the house.

"I thank you," he said. "I reckon we can make out." So I left them there, squatting around a little fire, waiting; God knows what for.

I come on home. I kept thinking about them there, and about that fellow tearing away on that horse. And that would be the last they would see of him. And I be durn if I could blame him. Not for wanting to not give up his horse, but for getting shut of such a durn fool as Anse.

Or that's what I thought then. Because be durn if there aint something about a durn fellow like Anse that seems to make a man have to help him, even when he knows he'll be wanting to kick himself next minute. Because about a hour after breakfast next morning Eustace Grimm that works Snopes' place come up with a span of mules, hunting Anse.

"I thought him and Anse never traded," I said.

"Sho," Eustace said. "All they liked was the horse. Like I said to Mr Snopes, he was letting this team go for fifty dollars, because if his uncle Flem had a just kept them Texas horses when he owned them, Anse wouldn't a never—"

"The horse?" I said. "Anse's boy taken that horse and cleared out last night, probably halfway to Texas by now, and Anse—"

"I didn't know who brung it," Eustace said. "I never see them. I just found the horse in the barn this morning when I went to feed, and I told Mr Snopes and he said to bring the team on over here."

Well, that'll be the last they'll ever see of him now, sho enough. Come Christmas time they'll maybe get a postal card from him in Texas, I reckon. And if it hadn't been Jewel, I reckon it'd a been me; I owe him that much, myself. I be durn if Anse dont conjure a man, some way. I be durn if he aint a sight.

Vardaman

Now there are seven of them, in little tall black circles.

"Look, Darl," I say; "see?"

He looks up. We watch them in little tall black circles of not-moving.

"Yesterday there were just four," I say.

There were more than four on the barn.

"Do you know what I would do if he tries to light on the wagon again?" I say.

"What would you do?" Darl says.

"I wouldn't let him light on her," I say. "I wouldn't let him light on Cash, either."

Cash is sick. He is sick on the box. But my mother is a fish.

"We got to get some medicine in Mottson," pa says. "I reckon we'll just have to."

"How do you feel, Cash?" Darl says.

"It dont bother none," Cash says.

"Do you want it propped a little higher?" Darl says.

Cash has a broken leg. He has had two broken legs. He lies on the box with a quilt rolled under his head and a piece of wood under his knee.

"I reckon we ought to left him at Armstid's," pa says.

I haven't got a broken leg and pa hasn't and Darl hasn't and "It's just the bumps," Cash says. "It kind of grinds together a little on a bump. It dont bother none." Jewel *has gone away. He and his horse went away one supper time*

"It's because she wouldn't have us beholden," pa says. "Fore God, I do the best that ere a man" *Is it because Jewel's mother is a horse Darl? I said.*

"Maybe I can draw the ropes a little tighter," Darl says. *That's why Jewel and I were both in the shed and she was in the wagon because the horse lives in the barn and I had to keep on running the buzzard away from*

"If you just would," Cash says. And Dewey Dell hasn't got a broken leg and I haven't. Cash is my brother.

We stop. When Darl loosens the rope Cash begins to sweat again. His teeth look out.

"Hurt?" Darl says.

"I reckon you better put it back," Cash says.

Darl puts the rope back, pulling hard. Cash's teeth look out.

"Hurt?" Darl says.

"It dont bother none," Cash says.

"Do you want pa to drive slower?" Darl says.

"No," Cash says. "Aint no time to hang back. It dont bother none."

"We'll have to get some medicine at Mottson," pa says. "I reckon we'll have to."

"Tell him to go on," Cash says. We go on. Dewey Dell leans back and wipes Cash's face. Cash is my brother. *But Jewel's mother is a horse. My mother is a fish. Darl says that when we come to the water again I might see her and Dewey Dell said, She's in the box; how could she have got out? She got out through the holes I bored, into the water I said, and when we come to the water again I am going to see her. My mother is not in the box. My mother does not smell like that. My mother is a fish*

"Those cakes will be in fine shape by the time we get to Jefferson," Darl says.

Dewey Dell does not look around.

"You better try to sell them in Mottson," Darl says.

"When will we get to Mottson, Darl?" I say.

"Tomorrow," Darl says. "If this team dont rack to pieces. Snopes must have fed them on sawdust."

"Why did he feed them on sawdust, Darl?" I say.

"Look," Darl says. "See?"

Now there are nine of them, tall in little tall black circles.

When we come to the foot of the hill pa stops and Darl and Dewey Dell and I get out. Cash cant walk because he has a broken leg. "Come up, mules," pa says. The mules walk hard; the wagon creaks. Darl and Dewey Dell and I walk behind the wagon, up the hill. When we come to the top of the hill pa stops and we get back into the wagon.

Now there are ten of them, tall in little tall black circles on the sky.

Moseley

I happened to look up, and saw her outside the window, looking in. Not close to the glass, and not looking at anything in particular; just standing there with her head turned this way and her eyes full on me and kind of blank too, like she was waiting for a sign. When I looked up again she was moving toward the door.

She kind of bumbled at the screen door a minute, like they do, and came in. She had on a stiff-brimmed straw hat setting on the top of her head and she was carrying a package wrapped in newspaper: I thought that she had a quarter or a dollar at the most, and that after she stood around a while she would maybe buy a cheap comb or a bottle of nigger toilet water, so I never disturbed her for a minute or so except to notice that she was pretty in a kind of sullen, awkward way, and that she looked a sight better in her gingham dress and her own complexion than she would after she bought whatever she would finally decide on. Or tell that she wanted. I knew that she had already decided before she came in. But you have to let them take their time. So I went on with what I was doing, figuring to let Albert wait on her when he caught up at the fountain, when he came back to me.

"That woman," he said. "You better see what she wants."

"What does she want?" I said.

"I dont know. I cant get anything out of her. You better wait on her."

So I went around the counter. I saw that she was barefooted, standing with her feet flat and easy on the floor, like she was used to it. She was looking at me, hard, holding the package; I saw she had about as black a pair of eyes as ever I saw, and she was a stranger. I never remembered seeing her in Mottson before. "What can I do for you?" I said.

Still she didn't say anything. She stared at me without winking. Then she looked back at the folks at the fountain. Then she looked past me, toward the back of the store.

"Do you want to look at some toilet things?" I said. "Or is it medicine you want?"

"That's it," she said. She looked quick back at the fountain again. So I thought maybe her ma or somebody had sent her in for some of this female dope and she was ashamed to ask for it. I knew she couldn't have a complexion like hers and use it herself, let alone not being much more than old enough to barely know what it was for. It's a shame, the way they poison themselves with it. But a man's got to stock it or go out of business in this country.

"Oh," I said. "What do you use? We have—" She looked at me again, almost like she had said hush, and looked toward the back of the store again.

"I'd liefer go back there," she said.

"All right," I said. You have to humor them. You save time by it. I followed her to the back. She put her hand on the gate. "There's nothing back there but the prescription case," I said. "What do you want?" She stopped and looked at me. It was like she had taken some kind of a lid off her face, her eyes. It was her eyes: kind of dumb and hopeful and sullenly willing to be disappointed all at the same time. But she was in trouble of some sort; I could see that. "What's your trouble?" I said. "Tell me what it is you want. I'm pretty busy." I wasn't meaning to hurry her, but a man just hasn't got the time they have out there.

"It's the female trouble," she said.

"Oh," I said. "Is that all?" I thought maybe she was younger than she looked, and her first one had scared her, or maybe one had been a little abnormal as it will in young women. "Where's your ma?" I said. "Haven't you got one?"

"She's out yonder in the wagon," she said.

"Why not talk to her about it before you take any medicine," I said. "Any woman would have told you about it." She looked at me, and I looked at her again and said, "How old are you?"

"Seventeen," she said.

"Oh," I said. "I thought maybe you were . . ." She was watching me. But then, in the eyes all of them look like they had no age and knew everything in the world, anyhow. "Are you too regular, or not regular enough?"

She quit looking at me but she didn't move. "Yes," she said. "I reckon so. Yes."

"Well, which?" I said. "Dont you know?" It's a crime and a shame; but after all, they'll buy it from somebody. She stood there, not looking at me. "You want something to stop it?" I said. "Is that it?"

"No," she said. "That's it. It's already stopped."

"Well, what—" Her face was lowered a little, still, like they do in all their dealings with a man so he dont ever know just where the lightning will strike next. "You are not married, are you?" I said.

"No."

"Oh," I said. "And how long has it been since it stopped? about five months maybe?"

"It aint been but two," she said.

"Well, I haven't got anything in my store you want to buy," I said, "unless it's a nipple. And I'd advise you to buy that and go back home and tell your pa, if you have one, and let him make somebody buy you a wedding license. Was that all you wanted?"

But she just stood there, not looking at me.

"I got the money to pay you," she said.

"Is it your own, or did he act enough of a man to give you the money?"

"He give it to me. Ten dollars. He said that would be enough."

"A thousand dollars wouldn't be enough in my store and ten cents wouldn't be enough," I said. "You take my advice and go home and tell your pa or your brothers if you have any or the first man you come to in the road."

But she didn't move. "Lafe said I could get it at the drugstore. He said to tell you me and him wouldn't never tell nobody you sold it to us."

"And I just wish your precious Lafe had come for it himself; that's what I wish. I dont know: I'd have had a little respect for him then. And you can go back and tell him I said so—if he aint halfway to Texas by now, which I dont doubt. Me, a respectable druggist, that's kept store and raised a family and been a church-member for fifty-six years in this town. I'm a good mind to tell your folks myself, if I can just find who they are."

She looked at me now, her eyes and face kind of blank again like when I first saw her through the window. "I didn't know," she said. "He told me I could get something at the drugstore. He said they might not want to sell it to me, but if I had ten dollars and told them I wouldn't never tell nobody . . ."

"He never said this drugstore," I said. "If he did or mentioned my name, I defy him to prove it. I defy him to repeat it or I'll prosecute him to the full extent of the law, and you can tell him so."

"But maybe another drugstore would," she said.

"Then I dont want to know it. Me, that's—" Then I looked at her. But it's a hard life they have; sometimes a man . . . if there can ever be any excuse for sin, which it cant be. And then, life wasn't made to be easy on folks: they wouldn't ever have any reason to be good and die. "Look here," I said. "You get that notion out of your head. The Lord gave you what you have, even if He did use the devil to do it; you let Him take it away from you if it's His will to do so. You go on back to Lafe and you and him take that ten dollars and get married with it."

"Lafe said I could get something at the drugstore," she said.

"Then go and get it," I said. "You wont get it here."

She went out, carrying the package, her feet making a little hissing on the floor. She bumbled again at the door and went out. I could see her through the glass going on down the street.

It was Albert told me about the rest of it. He said the wagon was stopped in front of Grummet's hardware store, with the ladies all scattering up and down the street with handkerchiefs to their noses, and a crowd of hard-nosed men and boys standing around the wagon, listening to the marshal arguing with the man. He was a kind of tall, gaunted man sitting on the wagon, saying it was a public street and he reckoned he had as much right there as anybody, and the marshal telling him he would have to move on; folks couldn't stand it. It had been dead eight days, Albert said. They came from some place out in Yoknapatawpha county, trying to get to Jefferson with it. It must have been like a piece of rotten cheese coming into an ant-hill, in that ramshackle wagon that Albert said folks were scared would fall all to pieces before they could get it out of town, with that home-made box and another fellow with a broken leg lying on a quilt on top of it, and the father and a little boy sitting in the seat and the marshal trying to make them get out of town.

"It's a public street," the man says. "I reckon we can stop to buy something same as airy other man. We got the money to pay for hit, and hit aint airy law that says a man cant spend his money where he wants."

They had stopped to buy some cement. The other son was in Grummet's, trying to make Grummet break a sack and let him have ten cents' worth, and finally Grummet broke the sack to get him out. They wanted the cement to fix the fellow's broken leg, someway.

"Why, you'll kill him," the marshal said. "You'll cause him to lose his leg. You take him on to the doctor, and you get this thing buried soon as you can. Dont you know you're liable to jail for endangering the public health?"

"We're doing the best we can," the father said. Then he told a long tale about how they had to wait for the wagon to come back and how the bridge was washed away and how they went eight miles to another bridge and it was gone too so they came back and swum the ford and the mules got drowned and how they got another team and found that the road was washed out and they had to come clean around by Mottson, and then the one with the cement came back and told him to shut up.

"We'll be gone in a minute," he told the marshal.

"We never aimed to bother nobody," the father said.

"You take that fellow to a doctor," the marshal told the one with the cement.

"I reckon he's all right," he said.

"It aint that we're hard-hearted," the marshal said. "But I reckon you can tell yourself how it is."

"Sho," the other said. "We'll take out soon as Dewey Dell comes back. She went to deliver a package."

So they stood there with the folks backed off with handkerchiefs to their faces, until in a minute the girl came up with that newspaper package.

"Come on," the one with the cement said, "we've lost too much time." So they got in the wagon and went on. And when I went to supper it still seemed like I could smell it. And the next day I met the marshal and I begun to sniff and said,

"Smell anything?"

"I reckon they're in Jefferson by now," he said.

"Or in jail. Well, thank the Lord it's not our jail."

"That's a fact," he said.

Darl

"Here's a place," pa says. He pulls the team up and sits looking at the house. "We could get some water over yonder."

"All right," I say. "You'll have to borrow a bucket from them, Dewey Dell."

"God knows," pa says. "I wouldn't be beholden, God knows."

"If you see a good-sized can, you might bring it," I say. Dewey Dell gets down from the wagon, carrying the package. "You had more trouble than you expected, selling those cakes in Mottson," I say. How do our lives ravel out into the no-wind, no-sound, the weary gestures wearily recapitulant: echoes of old compulsions with no-hand on no-strings: in sunset we fall into furious attitudes, dead gestures of dolls. Cash broke his leg and now the sawdust is running out. He is bleeding to death is Cash.

"I wouldn't be beholden," pa says. "God knows."

"Then make some water yourself," I say. "We can use Cash's hat."

When Dewey Dell comes back the man comes with her. Then he stops and she comes on and he stands there and after a while he goes back to the house and stands on the porch, watching us.

"We better not try to lift him down," pa says. "We can fix it here."

"Do you want to be lifted down, Cash?" I say.

"Wont we get to Jefferson tomorrow?" he says. He is watching us, his eyes interrogatory, intent, and sad. "I can last it out."

"It'll be easier on you," pa says. "It'll keep it from rubbing together."

"I can last it," Cash says. "We'll lose time stopping."

"We done bought the cement now," pa says.

"I could last it," Cash says. "It aint but one more day. It dont bother to speak of." He looks at us, his eyes wide in his thin gray face, questioning. "It sets up so," he says.

"We done bought it now," pa says.

I mix the cement in the can, stirring the slow water into the pale green thick coils. I bring the can to the wagon where Cash can see. He lies on his back, his thin profile in silhouette, ascetic and profound against the sky. "Does that look about right?" I say.

"You dont want too much water, or it wont work right," he says.

"Is this too much?"

"Maybe if you could get a little sand," he says. "It aint but one more day," he says. "It dont bother me none."

Vardaman goes back down the road to where we crossed the branch and returns with sand. He pours it slowly into the thick coiling in the can. I go to the wagon again.

"Does that look all right?"

"Yes," Cash says. "I could have lasted. It dont bother me none."

We loosen the splints and pour the cement over his leg, slow.

"Watch out for it," Cash says. "Dont get none on it if you can help."

"Yes," I say. Dewey Dell tears a piece of paper from the package and wipes the cement from the top of it as it drips from Cash's leg.

"How does that feel?"

"It feels fine," he says. "It's cold. It feels fine."

"If it'll just help you," pa says. "I asks your forgiveness. I never foreseen it no more than you."

"It feels fine," Cash says.

If you could just ravel out into time. That would be nice. It would be nice if you could just ravel out into time.

We replace the splints, the cords, drawing them tight, the cement in thick pale green slow surges among the cords, Cash watching us quietly with that profound questioning look.

"That'll steady it," I say.

"Ay," Cash says. "I'm obliged."

Then we all turn on the wagon and watch him. He is coming up the road behind us, wooden-backed, wooden-faced, moving only from his hips down. He comes up without a word, with his pale rigid eyes in his high sullen face, and gets into the wagon.

"Here's a hill," pa says. "I reckon you'll have to get out and walk."

Vardaman

Darl and Jewel and Dewey Dell and I are walking up the hill, behind the wagon. Jewel came back. He came up the road and got into the wagon. He was walking. Jewel hasn't got a horse anymore. Jewel is my brother. Cash is my brother. Cash has a broken leg. We fixed Cash's leg so it doesn't hurt. Cash is my brother. Jewel is my brother too, but he hasn't got a broken leg.

Now there are five of them, tall in little tall black circles.

"Where do they stay at night, Darl?" I say. "When we stop at night in the barn, where do they stay?"

The hill goes off into the sky. Then the sun comes up from behind the hill and the mules and the wagon and pa walk on the sun. You cannot watch them, walking slow on the sun. In Jefferson it is red on the track behind the glass. The track goes shining round and round. Dewey Dell says so.

Tonight I am going to see where they stay while we are in the barn.

Darl

"Jewel" I say, "whose son are you?"

The breeze was setting up from the barn, so we put her under the apple tree, where the moonlight can dapple the apple tree upon the long slumbering flanks within which now and then she talks in little trickling bursts of secret and murmurous bubbling. I took Vardaman to listen. When we came up the cat leaped down from it and flicked away with silver claw and silver eye into the shadow.

"Your mother was a horse, but who was your father, Jewel?"

"You goddamn lying son of a bitch."

"Dont call me that," I say.

"You goddamn lying son of a bitch."

"Dont you call me that, Jewel." In the tall moonlight his eyes look like spots of white paper pasted on a high small football.

After supper Cash began to sweat a little. "It's getting a little hot," he said. "It was the sun shining on it all day, I reckon."

"You want some water poured on it?" we say. "Maybe that will ease it some."

"I'd be obliged," Cash said. "It was the sun shining on it, I reckon. I ought to thought and kept it covered."

"We ought to thought," we said. "You couldn't have suspicioned."

"I never noticed it getting hot," Cash said. "I ought to minded it."

So we poured the water over it. His leg and foot below the cement looked like they had been boiled. "Does that feel better?" we said.

"I'm obliged," Cash said. "It feels fine."

Dewey Dell wipes his face with the hem of her dress.

"See if you can get some sleep," we say.

"Sho," Cash says. "I'm right obliged. It feels fine now."

Jewel, I say, Who was your father, Jewel?

Goddamn you. Goddamn you.

Vardaman

She was under the apple tree and Darl and I go across the moon and the cat jumps down and runs and we can hear her inside the wood.

"Hear?" Darl says. "Put your ear close."

I put my ear close and I can hear her. Only I cant tell what she is saying.

"What is she saying, Darl?" I say. "Who is she talking to?"

"She's talking to God," Darl says. "She is calling on Him to help her."

"What does she want Him to do?" I say.

"She wants Him to hide her away from the sight of man," Darl says.

"Why does she want to hide her away from the sight of man, Darl?"

"So she can lay down her life," Darl says.

"Why does she want to lay down her life, Darl?"

"Listen," Darl says. We hear her. We hear her turn over on her side. "Listen," Darl says.

"She's turned over," I say. "She's looking at me through the wood."

"Yes," Darl says.

"How can she see through the wood, Darl?"

"Come," Darl says. "We must let her be quiet. Come."

"She cant see out there, because the holes are in the top," I say. "How can she see, Darl?"

"Let's go see about Cash," Darl says.

And I saw something Dewey Dell told me not to tell nobody

Cash is sick in his leg. We fixed his leg this afternoon, but he is sick in it again, lying on the bed. We pour water on his leg and then he feels fine.

"I feel fine," Cash says. "I'm obliged to you."

"Try to get some sleep," we say.

"I feel fine," Cash says. "I'm obliged to you."

And I saw something Dewey Dell told me not to tell nobody. It is not about pa and it is not about Cash and it is not about Jewel and it is not about Dewey Dell and it is not about me

Dewey Dell and I are going to sleep on the pallet. It is on the back porch, where we can see the barn, and the moon shines on half of the pallet and we will lie half in the white and half in the black, with the moonlight on our legs. And then I am going to see where they stay at night while we are in the barn. We are not in the barn tonight but I can see the barn and so I am going to find where they stay at night.

We lie on the pallet, with our legs in the moon.

"Look," I say, "my legs look black. Your legs look black, too."

"Go to sleep," Dewey Dell says.

Jefferson is a far piece.

"Dewey Dell."

"What."

"If it's not Christmas now, how will it be there?"

It goes round and round on the shining track. Then the track goes shining round and round.

"Will what be there?"

"That train. In the window."

"You go to sleep. You can see tomorrow if it's there."

Maybe Santa Claus wont know they are town boys.

"Dewey Dell."

"You go to sleep. He aint going to let none of them town boys have it."

It was behind the window, red on the track, the track shining round and round. It made my heart hurt. And then it was pa and Jewel and Darl and Mr Gillespie's boy. Mr Gillespie's boy's legs come down under his nightshirt. When he goes into the moon, his legs fuzz. They go on around the house toward the apple tree.

"What are they going to do, Dewey Dell?"

They went around the house toward the apple tree.

"I can smell her," I say. "Can you smell her, too?"

"Hush," Dewey Dell says. "The wind's changed. Go to sleep."

And so I am going to know where they stay at night soon. They come around the house, going across the yard in the moon, carrying her on their shoulders. They carry her down to the barn, the moon shining flat and quiet on her. Then they come back and go into the house again. While they were in the moon, Mr Gillespie's boy's legs fuzzed. And then I waited and I said Dewey Dell? and then I waited and then I went to find where they stay at night and I saw something that Dewey Dell told me not to tell nobody.

Darl

Against the dark doorway he seems to materialise out of darkness, lean as a race horse in his underclothes in the beginning of the glare. He leaps to the ground with on his face an expression of furious unbelief. He has seen me without even turning his head or his eyes in which the glare swims like two small torches. "Come on," he says, leaping down the slope toward the barn.

For an instant longer he runs silver in the moonlight, then he springs out like a flat figure cut leanly from tin against an abrupt and soundless explosion as the whole loft of the barn takes fire at once, as though it had been stuffed with powder. The front, the conical façade with the square orifice of doorway broken only by the square squat shape of the coffin on the sawhorses like a cubistic bug, comes into relief. Behind me pa and Gillespie and Mack and Dewey Dell and Vardaman emerge from the house.

He pauses at the coffin, stooping, looking at me, his face furious. Overhead the flames sound like thunder; across us rushes a cool draft: there is no heat in it at all yet, and a handful of chaff lifts suddenly and sucks swiftly along the stalls where a horse is screaming. "Quick," I say; "the horses."

He glares a moment longer at me, then at the roof overhead, then he leaps toward the stall where the horse screams. It plunges and kicks, the sound of the crashing blows sucking up into the sound of the flames. They sound like an interminable train crossing an endless trestle. Gillespie and Mack pass me, in knee-length nightshirts, shouting, their voices thin and high and meaningless and at the same time profoundly wild and sad: ". . . cow . . . stall . . ." Gillespie's nightshirt rushes ahead of him on the draft, ballooning about his hairy thighs.

The stall door has swung shut. Jewel thrusts it back with his buttocks and he appears, his back arched, the muscles ridged through his garment as he drags the horse out by its head. In the glare its eyes roll with soft, fleet, wild opaline fire; its muscles bunch and run as it flings its head about, lifting Jewel clear of the ground. He drags it on, slowly, terrifically; again he gives me across his shoulder a single glare furious and brief. Even when they are clear of the barn the horse continues to fight and lash backward toward the doorway until Gillespie passes me, stark-naked, his nightshirt wrapped about the mule's head, and beats the maddened horse on out of the door.

Jewel returns, running; again he looks down at the coffin. But he comes on. "Where's cow?" he cries, passing me. I follow him. In the stall Mack is struggling with the other mule. When its head turns into the glare I can see the wild rolling of its eye too, but it makes no sound. It just stands there, watching Mack over its shoulder, swinging its hind quarters toward him whenever he approaches. He looks back at us, his eyes and mouth three round holes in his face on which the freckles look like English peas on a plate. His voice is thin, high, faraway.

"I cant do nothing . . ." It is as though the sound had been swept from his lips and up and away, speaking back to us from an immense distance of exhaustion. Jewel slides past us; the mule whirls and lashes out, but he has already gained its head. I lean to Mack's ear:

"Nightshirt. Around his head."

Mack stares at me. Then he rips the nightshirt off and flings it over the mule's head, and it becomes docile at once. Jewel is yelling at him: "Cow? Cow?"

"Back," Mack cries. "Last stall."

The cow watches us as we enter. She is backed into the corner, head lowered, still chewing though rapidly. But she makes no move. Jewel has paused, looking up, and suddenly we watch the entire floor to the loft dissolve. It just turns to fire; a faint litter of sparks rains down. He glances about. Back under the trough is a three-legged milking stool. He catches it up and swings it into the planking of the rear wall. He splinters a plank, then another, a third; we tear the fragments away. While we are stooping at the opening something charges into us from behind. It is the cow; with a single whistling breath she rushes between us and through the gap and into the outer glare, her tail erect and rigid as a broom nailed upright to the end of her spine.

Jewel turns back into the barn. "Here," I say; "Jewel!" I grasp at him; he strikes my hand down. "You fool," I say, "dont you see you cant make it back yonder?" The hallway looks like a searchlight turned into rain. "Come on," I say, "around this way."

When we are through the gap he begins to run. "Jewel," I say, running. He darts around the corner. When I reach it he has almost reached the next one, running against the glare like that figure cut from tin. Pa and Gillespie and Mack are some distance away, watching the barn, pink against the darkness where for the time the moonlight has been vanquished. "Catch him!" I cry; "stop him!"

When I reach the front, he is struggling with Gillespie; the one lean in underclothes, the other stark naked. They are like two figures in a Greek frieze, isolated out of all reality by the red glare. Before I can reach them he has struck Gillespie to the ground and turned and run back into the barn.

The sound of it has become quite peaceful now, like the sound of the river did. We watch through the dissolving proscenium of the doorway as Jewel runs crouching to the far end of the coffin and stoops to it. For an instant he looks up and out at us through the rain of burning hay like a portiere of flaming beads, and I can see his mouth shape as he calls my name.

"Jewel!" Dewey Dell cries; "Jewel!" It seems to me that I now hear the accumulation of her voice through the last five minutes, and I hear her scuffling and struggling as pa and Mack hold her, screaming "Jewel! Jewel!" But he is no longer looking at us. We see his shoulders strain as he upends the coffin and slides it single-handed from the sawhorses. It looms unbelievably tall, hiding him: I would not have believed that Addie Bundren would have needed that much room to lie comfortable in; for another instant it stands upright while the sparks rain on it in scattering bursts as though they engendered other sparks from the contact. Then it topples forward, gaining momentum, revealing Jewel and the sparks raining on him too in engendering gusts, so that he appears to be enclosed in a thin nimbus of fire. Without stopping it overends and rears again, pauses, then crashes slowly forward and through the curtain. This time Jewel is riding upon it, clinging to it, until it crashes down and flings him forward and clear and Mack leaps forward into the thin smell of scorching meat and slaps at the widening crimson-edged holes that bloom like flowers in his undershirt.

Vardaman

When I went to find where they stay at night, I saw something They said, "Where is Darl? Where did Darl go?"

They carried her back under the apple tree.

The barn was still red, but it wasn't a barn now. It was sunk down, and the red went swirling up. The barn went swirling up in little red pieces, against the sky and the stars so that the stars moved backward.

And then Cash was still awake. He turned his head from side to side, with sweat on his face.

"Do you want some more water on it, Cash?" Dewey Dell said.

Cash's leg and foot turned black. We held the lamp and looked at Cash's foot and leg where it was black.

"Your foot looks like a nigger's foot, Cash," I said.

"I reckon we'll have to bust it off," pa said.

"What in the tarnation you put it on there for," Mr Gillespie said.

"I thought it would steady it some," pa said. "I just aimed to help him."

They got the flat iron and the hammer. Dewey Dell held the lamp. They had to hit it hard. And then Cash went to sleep.

"He's asleep now," I said. "It cant hurt him while he's asleep."

It just cracked. It wouldn't come off.

"It'll take the hide, too," Mr Gillespie said. "Why in the tarnation you put it on there. Didn't none of you think to grease his leg first?"

"I just aimed to help him," pa said. "It was Darl put it on."

"Where is Darl?" they said.

"Didn't none of you have more sense than that?" Mr Gillespie said. "I'd a thought he would, anyway."

Jewel was lying on his face. His back was red. Dewey Dell put the medicine on it. The medicine was made out of butter and soot, to draw out the fire. Then his back was black.

"Does it hurt, Jewel?" I said. "Your back looks like a nigger's, Jewel," I said. Cash's foot and leg looked like a nigger's. Then they broke it off. Cash's leg bled.

"You go on back and lay down," Dewey Dell said. "You ought to be asleep."

"Where is Darl?" they said.

He is out there under the apple tree with her, lying on her. He is there so the cat wont come back. I said, "Are you going to keep the cat away, Darl?"

The moonlight dappled on him too. On her it was still, but on Darl it dappled up and down.

"You needn't to cry," I said. "Jewel got her out. You needn't to cry, Darl."

The barn is still red. It used to be redder than this. Then it went swirling, making the stars run backward without falling. It hurt my heart like the train did.

When I went to find where they stay at night, I saw something that Dewey Dell says I mustn't never tell nobody

Darl

We have been passing the signs for some time now: the drug stores, the clothing stores, the patent medicine and the garages and cafes, and the mile-boards diminishing, becoming more starkly reaccruent: 3 mi. 2 mi. From the crest of a hill, as we get into the wagon again, we can see the smoke low and flat, seemingly unmoving in the unwinded afternoon.

"Is that it, Darl?" Vardaman says. "Is that Jefferson?" He too has lost flesh; like ours, his face has an expression strained, dreamy, and gaunt.

"Yes," I say. He lifts his head and looks at the sky. High against it they hang in narrowing circles, like the smoke, with an outward semblance of form and purpose, but with no inference of motion, progress or retrograde. We mount the wagon again where Cash lies on the box, the jagged shards of cement cracked about his leg. The shabby mules droop rattling and clanking down the hill.

"We'll have to take him to the doctor," pa says. "I reckon it aint no way around it." The back of Jewel's shirt, where it touches him, stains slow and black with grease. Life was created in the valleys. It blew up onto the hills on the old terrors, the old lusts, the old despairs. That's why you must walk up the hills so you can ride down.

Dewey Dell sits on the seat, the newspaper package on her lap. When we reach the foot of the hill where the road flattens between close walls of trees, she begins to look about quietly from one side of the road to the other. At last she says,

"I got to stop."

Pa looks at her, his shabby profile that of anticipant and disgruntled annoyance. He does not check the team. "What for?"

"I got to go to the bushes," Dewey Dell says.

Pa does not check the team. "Cant you wait till we get to town? It aint over a mile now."

"Stop," Dewey Dell says. "I got to go to the bushes."

Pa stops in the middle of the road and we watch Dewey Dell descend, carrying the package. She does not look back.

"Why not leave your cakes here?" I say. "We'll watch them."

She descends steadily, not looking at us.

"How would she know where to go if she waited till we get to town?" Vardaman says. "Where would you go to do it in town, Dewey Dell?"

She lifts the package down and turns and disappears among the trees and undergrowth.

"Dont be no longer than you can help," pa says. "We aint got no time to waste." She does not answer. After a while we cannot hear her even. "We ought to done like Armstid and Gillespie said and sent word to town and had it dug and ready," he says.

"Why didn't you?" I say. "You could have telephoned."

"What for?" Jewel says. "Who the hell cant dig a hole in the ground?"

A car comes over the hill. It begins to sound the horn, slowing. It runs along the roadside in low gear, the outside wheels in the ditch, and passes us and goes on. Vardaman watches it until it is out of sight.

"How far is it now, Darl?" he says.

"Not far," I say.

"We ought to done it," pa says. "I just never wanted to be beholden to none except her flesh and blood."

"Who the hell cant dig a damn hole in the ground?" Jewel says.

"It aint respectful, talking that way about her grave," pa says. "You all dont know what it is. You never pure loved her, none of you." Jewel does not answer. He sits a little stiffly erect, his body arched away from his shirt. His high-colored jaw juts.

Dewey Dell returns. We watch her emerge from the bushes, carrying the package, and climb into the wagon. She now wears her Sunday dress, her beads, her shoes and stockings.

"I thought I told you to leave them clothes to home," pa says. She does not answer, does not look at us. She sets the package in the wagon and gets in. The wagon moves on.

"How many more hills now, Darl?" Vardaman says.

"Just one," I say. "The next one goes right up into town."

This hill is red sand, bordered on either hand by negro cabins; against the sky ahead the massed telephone lines run, and the clock on the courthouse lifts among the trees. In the sand the wheels whisper, as though the very earth would hush our entry. We descend as the hill commences to rise.

We follow the wagon, the whispering wheels, passing the cabins where faces come suddenly to the doors, white-eyed. We hear sudden voices, ejaculant. Jewel has been looking from side to side; now his head turns forward and I can see his ears taking on a still deeper tone of furious red. Three negroes walk beside the road ahead of us; ten feet ahead of them a white man walks. When we pass the negroes their heads turn suddenly with that expression of shock and instinctive outrage. "Great God," one says; "what they got in that wagon?"

Jewel whirls. "Son of a bitches," he says. As he does so he is abreast of the white man, who has paused. It is as though Jewel had gone blind for the moment, for it is the white man toward whom he whirls.

"Darl!" Cash says from the wagon. I grasp at Jewel. The white man has fallen back a pace, his face still slack-jawed; then his jaw tightens, claps to. Jewel leans above him, his jaw muscles gone white.

"What did you say?" he says.

"Here," I say. "He dont mean anything, mister. Jewel," I say. When I touch him he swings at the man. I grasp his arm; we struggle. Jewel has never looked at me. He is trying to free his arm. When I see the man again he has an open knife in his hand.

"Hold on, mister," I say; "I've got him. Jewel," I say.

"Thinks because he's a goddamn town fellow," Jewel says, panting, wrenching at me. "Son of a bitch," he says.

The man moves. He begins to edge around me, watching Jewel, the knife low against his flank. "Cant no man call me that," he says. Pa has got down, and Dewey Dell is holding Jewel, pushing at him. I release him and face the man.

"Wait," I say. "He dont mean nothing. He's sick; got burned in a fire last night, and he aint himself."

"Fire or no fire," the man says, "cant no man call me that."

"He thought you said something to him," I say.

"I never said nothing to him. I never see him before."

"Fore God," pa says; "fore God."

"I know," I say. "He never meant anything. He'll take it back."

"Let him take it back, then."

"Put up your knife, and he will."

The man looks at me. He looks at Jewel. Jewel is quiet now.

"Put up your knife," I say.

The man shuts the knife.

"Fore God," pa says. "Fore God."

"Tell him you didn't mean anything, Jewel," I say.

"I thought he said something," Jewel says. "Just because he's—"

"Hush," I say. "Tell him you didn't mean it."

"I didn't mean it," Jewel says.

"He better not," the man says. "Calling me a—"

"Do you think he's afraid to call you that?" I say.

The man looks at me. "I never said that," he said.

"Don't think it, neither," Jewel says.

"Shut up," I say. "Come on. Drive on, pa."

The wagon moves. The man stands watching us. Jewel does not look back. "Jewel would a whipped him," Vardaman says.

We approach the crest, where the street runs, where cars go back and forth; the mules haul the wagon up and onto the crest and the street. Pa stops them. The street runs on ahead, where the square opens and the monument stands before the courthouse. We mount again while the heads turn with that expression which we know; save Jewel. He does not get on, even though the wagon has started again. "Get in, Jewel," I say. "Come on. Let's get away from here." But he does not get in. Instead he sets his foot on the turning hub of the rear wheel, one hand grasping the stanchion, and with the hub turning smoothly under his sole he lifts the other foot and squats there, staring straight ahead, motionless, lean, wooden-backed, as though carved squatting out of the lean wood.

Cash

It wasn't nothing else to do. It was either send him to Jackson, or have Gillespie sue us, because he knowed some way that Darl set fire to it. I dont know how he knowed, but he did. Vardaman see him do it, but he swore he never told nobody but Dewey Dell and that she told him not to tell nobody. But Gillespie knowed it. But he would a suspicioned it sooner or later. He could have done it that night just watching the way Darl acted.

And so pa said, "I reckon there aint nothing else to do," and Jewel said,

"You want to fix him now?"

"Fix him?" pa said.

"Catch him and tie him up," Jewel said. "Goddamn it, do you want to wait until he sets fire to the goddamn team and wagon?"

But there wasn't no use in that. "There aint no use in that," I said. "We can wait till she is underground." A fellow that's going to spend the rest of his life locked up, he ought to be let to have what pleasure he can have before he goes.

"I reckon he ought to be there," pa says. "God knows, it's a trial on me. Seems like it aint no end to bad luck when once it starts."

Sometimes I aint so sho who's got ere a right to say when a man is crazy and when he aint. Sometimes I think it aint none of us pure crazy and aint none of us pure sane until the balance of us talks him that-a-way. It's like it aint so much what a fellow does, but it's the way the majority of folks is looking at him when he does it.

Because Jewel is too hard on him. Of course it was Jewel's horse was traded to get her that nigh to town, and in a sense it was the value of his horse Darl tried to burn up. But I thought more than once before we crossed the river and after, how it would be God's blessing if He did take her outen our hands and get shut of her in some clean way, and it seemed to me that when Jewel worked so to get her outen the river, he was going against God in a way, and then when Darl seen that it looked like one of us would have to do something, I can almost believe he done right in a way. But I dont reckon nothing excuses setting fire to a man's barn and endangering his stock and destroying his property. That's how I reckon a man is crazy. That's how he cant see eye to eye with other folks. And I reckon they aint nothing else to do with him but what the most folks says is right.

But it's a shame, in a way. Folks seems to get away from the olden right teaching that says to drive the nails down and trim the edges well always like it was for your own use and comfort you were making it. It's like some folks has the smooth, pretty boards to build a courthouse with and others dont have no more than rough lumber fitten to build a chicken coop. But it's better to build a tight chicken coop than a shoddy courthouse, and when they both build shoddy or build well, neither because it's one or tother is going to make a man feel the better nor the worse.

So we went up the street, toward the square, and he said, "We better take Cash to the doctor first. We can leave him there and come back for him." That's it. It's because me and him was born close together, and it nigh ten years before Jewel and Dewey Dell and Vardaman begun to come along. I feel kin to them, all right, but I dont know. And me being the oldest, and thinking already the very thing that he done: I dont know.

Pa was looking at me, then at him, mumbling his mouth.

"Go on," I said. "We'll get it done first."

"She would want us all there," pa says.

"Let's take Cash to the doctor first," Darl said. "She'll wait. She's already waited nine days."

"You all dont know," pa says. "The somebody you was young with and you growed old in her and she growed old in you, seeing the old coming on and it was the one somebody you could hear say it dont matter and know it was the truth outen the hard world and all a man's grief and trials. You all dont know."

"We got the digging to do, too," I said.

"Armstid and Gillespie both told you to send word ahead," Darl said. "Dont you want to go to Peabody's now, Cash?"

"Go on," I said. "It feels right easy now. It's best to get things done in the right place."

"If it was just dug," pa says. "We forgot our spade, too."

"Yes," Darl said. "I'll go to the hardware store. We'll have to buy one."

"It'll cost money," pa says.

"Do you begrudge her it?" Darl says.

"Go on and get a spade," Jewel said. "Here. Give me the money."

But pa didn't stop. "I reckon we can get a spade," he said. "I reckon there are Christians here." So Darl set still and we went on, with Jewel squatting on the tail-gate, watching the back of Darl's head. He looked like one of these bull dogs, one of these dogs that dont bark none, squatting against the rope, watching the thing he was waiting to jump at.

He set that way all the time we was in front of Mrs Bundren's house, hearing the music, watching the back of Darl's head with them hard white eyes of hisn.

The music was playing in the house. It was one of them graphophones.[1] It was natural as a music-band.

"Do you want to go to Peabody's?" Darl said. "They can wait here and tell pa, and I'll drive you to Peabody's and come back for them."

1. Trademark of an early machine for playing recorded music using wax platters.

"No," I said. It was better to get her underground, now we was this close, just waiting until pa borrowed the shovel. He drove along the street until we could hear the music.

"Maybe they got one here," he said. He pulled up at Mrs Bundren's. It was like he knowed. Sometimes I think that if a working man could see work as far ahead as a lazy man can see laziness. So he stopped there like he knowed, before that little new house, where the music was. We waited there, hearing it. I believe I could have dickered Suratt down to five dollars on that one of his. It's a comfortable thing, music is. "Maybe they got one here," pa says.

"You want Jewel to go," Darl says, "or do you reckon I better?"

"I reckon I better," pa says. He got down and went up the path and around the house to the back. The music stopped, then it started again.

"He'll get it, too," Darl said.

"Ay," I said. It was just like he knowed, like he could see through the walls and into the next ten minutes.

Only it was more than ten minutes. The music stopped and never commenced again for a good spell, where her and pa was talking at the back. We waited in the wagon.

"You let me take you back to Peabody's," Darl said.

"No," I said. "We'll get her underground."

"If he ever gets back," Jewel said. He begun to cuss. He started to get down from the wagon. "I'm going," he said.

Then we saw pa coming back. He had two spades, coming around the house. He laid them in the wagon and got in and we went on. The music never started again. Pa was looking back at the house. He kind of lifted his hand a little and I saw the shade pulled back a little at the window and her face in it.

But the curiousest thing was Dewey Dell. It surprised me. I see all the while how folks could say he was queer, but that was the very reason couldn't nobody hold it personal. It was like he was outside of it too, same as you, and getting mad at it would be kind of like getting mad at a mud-puddle that splashed you when you stepped in it. And then I always kind of had a idea that him and Dewey Dell kind of knowed things betwixt them. If I'd a said it was ere a one of us she liked better than ere a other, I'd a said it was Darl. But when we got it filled and covered and drove out the gate and turned into the lane where them fellows was waiting, when they come out and come on him and he jerked back, it was Dewey Dell that was on him before even Jewel could get at him. And then I believed I knowed how Gillespie knowed about how his barn taken fire.

She hadn't said a word, hadn't even looked at him, but when them fellows told him what they wanted and that they had come to get him and he throwed back, she jumped on him like a wild cat so that one of the fellows had to quit and hold her and her scratching and clawing at him like a wild cat, while the other one and pa and Jewel throwed Darl down and held him lying on his back, looking up at me.

"I thought you would have told me," he said. "I never thought you wouldn't have."

"Darl," I said. But he fought again, him and Jewel and the fellow, and the other one holding Dewey Dell and Vardaman yelling and Jewel saying,

"Kill him. Kill the son of a bitch."

It was bad so. It was bad. A fellow cant get away from a shoddy job. He cant do it. I tried to tell him, but he just said, "I thought you'd a told me. It's not that I," he said, then he begun to laugh. The other fellow pulled Jewel off of him and he sat there on the ground, laughing.

I tried to tell him. If I could have just moved, even set up. But I tried to tell him and he quit laughing, looking up at me.

"Do you want me to go?" he said.

"It'll be better for you," I said. "Down there it'll be quiet, with none of the bothering and such. It'll be better for you, Darl," I said.

"Better," he said. He begun to laugh again. "Better," he said. He couldn't hardly say it for laughing. He sat on the ground and us watching him, laughing and laughing. It was bad. It was bad so. I be durn if I could see anything to laugh at. Because there just aint nothing justifies the deliberate destruction of what a man has built with his own sweat and stored the fruit of his sweat into.

But I aint so sho that ere a man has the right to say what is crazy and what aint. It's like there was a fellow in every man that's done a-past the sanity or the insanity, that watches the sane and the insane doings of that man with the same horror and the same astonishment.

Peabody

I said, "I reckon a man in a tight might let Bill Varner patch him up like a damn mule, but I be damned if the man that'd let Anse Bundren treat him with raw cement aint got more spare legs than I have."

"They just aimed to ease hit some," he said.

"Aimed, hell," I said. "What in hell did Armstid mean by even letting them put you on that wagon again?"

"Hit was gittin right noticeable," he said. "We never had time to wait." I just looked at him. "Hit never bothered me none," he said.

"Dont you lie there and try to tell me you rode six days on a wagon without springs, with a broken leg and it never bothered you."

"It never bothered me much," he said.

"You mean, it never bothered Anse much," I said. "No more than it bothered him to throw that poor devil down in the public street and handcuff him like a damn murderer. Dont tell me. And dont tell me it aint going to bother you to lose sixty-odd square inches of skin to get that concrete off. And dont tell me it aint going to bother you to have to limp around on one short leg for the balance of your life—if you walk at all again. Concrete," I said. "God Amighty, why didn't Anse carry you to the nearest sawmill and stick your leg in the saw? That would have cured it. Then you all could have stuck his head into the saw and cured a whole family . . . Where is Anse, anyway? What's he up to now?"

"He's takin back them spades he borrowed," he said.

"That's right," I said. "Of course he'd have to borrow a spade to bury his wife with. Unless he could borrow a hole in the ground. Too bad you all didn't put him in it too . . . Does that hurt?"

"Not to speak of," he said, and the sweat big as marbles running down his face and his face about the color of blotting paper.

"Course not," I said. "About next summer you can hobble around fine on this leg. Then it wont bother you, not to speak of . . . If you had anything you could call luck, you might say it was lucky this is the same leg you broke before," I said.

"Hit's what paw says," he said.

MacGowan

It happened I am back of the prescription case, pouring up some chocolate sauce, when Jody comes back and says, "Say, Skeet, there's a woman up front that wants to see the doctor and when I said What doctor you want to see, she said she wants to see the doctor that works here and when I said There aint any doctor works here, she just stood there, looking back this way."

"What kind of a woman is it?" I says. "Tell her to go upstairs to Alford's office."

"Country woman," he says.

"Send her to the courthouse," I says. "Tell her all the doctors have gone to Memphis to a Barbers' Convention."

"All right," he says, going away. "She looks pretty good for a country girl," he says.

"Wait," I says. He waited and I went and peeped through the crack. But I couldn't tell nothing except she had a good leg against the light. "Is she young, you say?" I says.

"She looks like a pretty hot mamma, for a country girl," he says.

"Take this," I says, giving him the chocolate. I took off my apron and went up there. She looked pretty good. One of them black eyed ones that look like she'd as soon put a knife in you as not if you two-timed her. She looked pretty good. There wasn't nobody else in the store; it was dinner time.

"What can I do for you?" I says.

"Are you the doctor?" she says.

"Sure," I says. She quit looking at me and was kind of looking around.

"Can we go back yonder?" she says.

It was just a quarter past twelve, but I went and told Jody to kind of watch out and whistle if the old man come in sight, because he never got back before one.

"You better lay off of that," Jody says. "He'll fire your stern out of here so quick you cant wink."

"He dont never get back before one," I says. "You can see him go into the postoffice. You keep your eye peeled, now, and give me a whistle."

"What you going to do?" he says.

"You keep your eye out. I'll tell you later."

"Aint you going to give me no seconds on it?" he says.

"What the hell do you think this is?" I says; "a stud-farm? You watch out for him. I'm going into conference."

So I go on to the back. I stopped at the glass and smoothed my hair, then I went behind the prescription case, where she was waiting. She is looking at the medicine cabinet, then she looks at me.

"Now madam," I says; "what is your trouble?"

"It's the female trouble," she says, watching me. "I got the money," she says.

"Ah," I says. "Have you got female troubles or do you want female troubles? If so, you come to the right doctor." Them country people. Half the time they dont know what they want, and the balance of the time they cant tell it to you. The clock said twenty past twelve.

"No," she says.

"No which?" I says.

"I aint had it," she says. "That's it." She looked at me. "I got the money," she says.

So I knew what she was talking about.

"Oh," I says. "You got something in your belly you wish you didn't have." She looks at me. "You wish you had a little more or a little less, huh?"

"I got the money," she says. "He said I could git something at the drugstore for hit."

"Who said so?" I says.

"He did," she says, looking at me.

"You dont want to call no names," I says. "The one that put the acorn in your belly? He the one that told you?" She dont say nothing. "You aint married, are you?" I says. I never saw no ring. But like as not, they aint heard yet out there that they use rings.

"I got the money," she says. She showed it to me, tied up in her handkerchief: a ten spot.

"I'll swear you have," I says. "He give it to you?"

"Yes," she says.

"Which one?" I says. She looks at me. "Which one of them give it to you?"

"It aint but one," she says. She looks at me.

"Go on," I says. She dont say nothing. The trouble about the cellar is, it aint but one way out and that's back up the inside stairs. The clock says twenty-five to one. "A pretty girl like you," I says.

She looks at me. She begins to tie the money back up in the handkerchief. "Excuse me a minute," I says. I go around the prescription case. "Did you hear about that fellow sprained his ear?" I says. "After that he couldn't even hear a belch."

"You better get her out from back there before the old man comes," Jody says.

"If you'll stay up there in front where he pays you to stay, he wont catch nobody but me," I says.

He goes on, slow, toward the front. "What you doing to her, Skeet?" he says.

"I cant tell you," I says. "It wouldn't be ethical. You go on up there and watch."

"Say, Skeet," he says.

"Ah, go on," I says. "I aint doing nothing but filling a prescription."

"He may not do nothing about that woman back there, but if he finds you monkeying with that prescription case, he'll kick your stern clean down them cellar stairs."

"My stern has been kicked by bigger bastards than him," I says. "Go back and watch out for him, now."

So I come back. The clock said fifteen to one. She is tying the money in the handkerchief. "You aint the doctor," she says.

"Sure I am," I says. She watches me. "Is it because I look too young, or am I too handsome?" I says. "We used to have a bunch of old water-jointed doctors here," I says; "Jefferson used to be a kind of Old Doctors' Home for them. But business started falling off and folks stayed so well until one day they found out that the women wouldn't never get sick at all. So they run all the old doctors out and got us young good-looking ones that the women would like and then the women begun to get sick again and so business picked up. They're doing that all over the country. Hadn't you heard about it? Maybe it's because you aint never needed a doctor."

"I need one now," she says.

"And you come to the right one," I says. "I already told you that."

"Have you got something for it?" she says. "I got the money."

"Well," I says, "of course a doctor has to learn all sorts of things while he's learning to roll calomel; he cant help himself. But I dont know about your trouble."

"He told me I could get something. He told me I could get it at the drugstore."

"Did he tell you the name of it?" I says. "You better go back and ask him."

She quit looking at me, kind of turning the handkerchief in her hands. "I got to do something," she says.

"How bad do you want to do something?" I says. She looks at me. "Of course, a doctor learns all sorts of things folks dont think he knows. But he aint supposed to tell all he knows. It's against the law."

Up front Jody says, "Skeet."

"Excuse me a minute," I says. I went up front. "Do you see him?" I says.

"Aint you done yet?" he says. "Maybe you better come up here and watch and let me do that consulting."

"Maybe you'll lay a egg," I says. I come back. She is looking at me. "Of course you realise that I could be put in the penitentiary for doing what you want," I says. "I would lose my license and then I'd have to go to work. You realise that?"

"I aint got but ten dollars," she says. "I could bring the rest next month, maybe."

"Pooh," I says, "ten dollars? You see, I cant put no price on my knowledge and skill. Certainly not for no little paltry sawbuck."

She looks at me. She dont even blink. "What you want, then?"

The clock said four to one. So I decided I better get her out. "You guess three times and then I'll show you," I says.

She dont even blink her eyes. "I got to do something," she says. She looks behind her and around, then she looks toward the front. "Gimme the medicine first," she says.

"You mean, you're ready to right now?" I says. "Here?"

"Gimme the medicine first," she says.

So I took a graduated glass and kind of turned my back to her and picked out a bottle that looked all right, because a man that would keep poison setting around in a unlabelled bottle ought to be in jail, anyway. It smelled like turpentine. I poured some into the glass and give it to her. She smelled it, looking at me across the glass.

"Hit smells like turpentine," she says.

"Sure," I says. "That's just the beginning of the treatment. You come back at ten oclock tonight and I'll give you the rest of it and perform the operation."

"Operation?" she says.

"It wont hurt you. You've had the same operation before. Ever hear about the hair of the dog?"

She looks at me. "Will it work?" she says.

"Sure it'll work. If you come back and get it."

So she drunk whatever it was without batting a eye, and went out. I went up front.

"Didn't you get it?" Jody says.

"Get what?" I says.

"Ah, come on," he says. "I aint going to try to beat your time."

"Oh, her," I says. "She just wanted a little medicine. She's got a bad case of dysentery and she's a little ashamed about mentioning it with a stranger there."

It was my night, anyway, so I helped the old bastard check up and I got his hat on him and got him out of the store by eight-thirty. I went as far as the corner with him and watched him until he passed under two street lamps and went on out of sight. Then I come back to the store and waited until nine-thirty and turned out the front lights and locked the door and left just one light burning at the back, and I went back and put some talcum powder into six capsules and kind of cleared up the cellar and then I was all ready.

She come in just at ten, before the clock had done striking. I let her in and she come in, walking fast. I looked out the door, but there wasn't nobody but a boy in overalls sitting on the curb. "You want something?" I says. He never said nothing, just looking at me. I locked the door and turned off the light and went on back. She was waiting. She didn't look at me now.

"Where is it?" she said.

I gave her the box of capsules. She held the box in her hand, looking at the capsules.

"Are you sure it'll work?" she says.

"Sure," I says. "When you take the rest of the treatment."

"Where do I take it?" she says.

"Down in the cellar," I says.

Vardaman

Now it is wider and lighter, but the stores are dark because they have all gone home. The stores are dark, but the lights pass on the windows when we pass. The lights are in the trees around the courthouse. They roost in the trees, but the courthouse is dark. The clock on it looks four ways, because it is not dark. The moon is not dark too. Not very dark. *Darl he went to Jackson is my brother Darl is my brother* Only it was over that way, shining on the track.

"Let's go that way, Dewey Dell," I say.

"What for?" Dewey Dell says. The track went shining around the window, it red on the track. But she said he would not sell it to the town boys. "But it will be there Christmas," Dewey Dell says. "You'll have to wait till then, when he brings it back."

Darl went to Jackson. Lots of people didn't go to Jackson. Darl is my brother. My brother is going to Jackson

While we walk the lights go around, roosting in the trees. On all sides it is the same. They go around the courthouse and then you cannot see them. But you can see them in the black windows beyond. They have all gone home to bed except me and Dewey Dell.

Going on the train to Jackson. My brother

There is a light in the store, far back. In the window are two big glasses of soda water, red and green. Two men could not drink them. Two mules could not. Two cows could not. *Darl*

A man comes to the door. He looks at Dewey Dell.

"You wait out here," Dewey Dell says.

"Why cant I come in?" I say. "I want to come in, too."

"You wait out here," she says.

"All right," I say.

Dewey Dell goes in.

Darl is my brother. Darl went crazy

The walk is harder than sitting on the ground. He is in the open door. He looks at me. "You want something?" he says. His head is slick. Jewel's head is slick sometimes. Cash's head is not slick. *Darl he went to Jackson my brother Darl* In the street he ate a banana. *Wouldn't you rather have bananas? Dewey Dell said. You wait till Christmas. It'll be there then. Then you can see it. So we are going to have some bananas. We are going to have a bag full, me and Dewey Dell.* He locks the door. Dewey Dell is inside. Then the light winks out.

He went to Jackson. He went crazy and went to Jackson both. Lots of people didn't go crazy. Pa and Cash and Jewel and Dewey Dell and me didn't go crazy. We never did go crazy. We didn't go to Jackson either. Darl

I hear the cow a long time, clopping on the street. Then she comes into the square. She goes across the square, her head down clopping. She lows. There was nothing in the square before she lowed, but it wasn't empty. Now it is empty after she lowed. She goes on, clopping. She lows. *My brother is Darl. He went to Jackson on the train. He didn't go on the train to go crazy. He went crazy in our wagon. Darl* She has been in there a long time. And the cow is gone too. A long time. She has been in there longer than the cow was. But not as long as empty. *Darl is my brother. My brother Darl*

Dewey Dell comes out. She looks at me.

"Let's go around that way now," I say.

She looks at me. "It aint going to work," she says. "That son of a bitch."

"What aint going to work, Dewey Dell?"

"I just know it wont," she says. She is not looking at anything. "I just know it."

"Let's go that way," I say.

"We got to go back to the hotel. It's late. We got to slip back in."

"Cant we go by and see, anyway?"

"Hadn't you rather have bananas? Hadn't you rather?"

"All right." *My brother he went crazy and he went to Jackson too. Jackson is further away than crazy*

"It wont work," Dewey Dell says. "I just know it wont."

"What wont work?" I say. *He had to get on the train to go to Jackson. I have not been on the train, but Darl has been on the train. Darl. Darl is my brother. Darl. Darl*

Darl

Darl has gone to Jackson. They put him on the train, laughing, down the long car laughing, the heads turning like the heads of owls when he passed. "What are you laughing at?" I said.

"Yes yes yes yes yes."

Two men put him on the train. They wore mismatched coats, bulging behind over their right hip pockets. Their necks were shaved to a hairline, as though the recent and simultaneous barbers had had a chalk-line like Cash's. "Is it the pistols you're laughing at?" I said. "Why do you laugh? I said. "Is it because you hate the sound of laughing?"

They pulled two seats together so Darl could sit by the window to laugh. One of them sat beside him, the other sat on the seat facing him, riding backward. One of them had to ride backward because the state's money has a face to each backside and a backside to each face, and they are riding on the state's money which is incest. A nickel has a woman on one side and a buffalo on the other; two faces and no back. I dont know what that is. Darl had a little spy-glass he got in France at the war. In it it had a woman and a pig with two backs and no face. I know what that is. "Is that why you are laughing, Darl?"

"Yes yes yes yes yes yes."

The wagon stands on the square, hitched, the mules motionless, the reins wrapped about the seat-spring, the back of the wagon toward the courthouse. It looks no different from a hundred other wagons there; Jewel standing beside it and looking up the street like any other man in town that day, yet there is something different, distinctive. There is about it that unmistakable air of definite and imminent departure that trains have, perhaps due to the fact that Dewey Dell and Vardaman on the seat and Cash on a pallet in the wagon bed are eating bananas from a paper bag. "Is that why you are laughing, Darl?"

Darl is our brother, our brother Darl. Our brother Darl in a cage in Jackson where, his grimed hands lying light in the quiet interstices, looking out he foams.

"Yes yes yes yes yes yes yes yes."

Dewey Dell

When he saw the money I said, "It's not my money, it doesn't belong to me."

"Whose is it, then?"

"It's Cora Tull's money. It's Mrs Tull's. I sold the cakes for it."

"Ten dollars for two cakes?"

"Dont you touch it. It's not mine."

"You never had them cakes. It's a lie. It was them Sunday clothes you had in that package."

"Dont you touch it! If you take it you are a thief."

"My own daughter accuses me of being a thief. My own daughter."

"Pa. Pa."

"I have fed you and sheltered you. I give you love and care, yet my own daughter, the daughter of my dead wife, calls me a thief over her mother's grave."

"Its not mine, I tell you. If it was, God knows you could have it."
"Where did you get ten dollars?"
"Pa. Pa."
"You wont tell me. Did you come by it so shameful you dare not?"
"It's not mine, I tell you. Cant you understand it's not mine?"
"It's not like I wouldn't pay it back. But she calls her own father a thief."
"I cant, I tell you. I tell you it's not my money. God knows you could have it."
"I wouldn't take it. My own born daughter that has et my food for seventeen years, begrudges me the loan of ten dollars."
"It's not mine. I cant."
"Whose is it, then?"
"It was give to me. To buy something with."
"To buy what with?"
"Pa. Pa."
"It's just a loan. God knows, I hate for my blooden children to reproach me. But I give them what was mine without stint. Cheerful I give them, without stint. And now they deny me. Addie. It was lucky for you you died, Addie."
"Pa. Pa."
"God knows it is."
He took the money and went out.

Cash

So when we stopped there to borrow the shovels we heard the graphophone playing in the house, and so when we got done with the shovels pa says, "I reckon I better take them back."

So we went back to the house. "We better take Cash on to Peabody's," Jewel said.

"It wont take but a minute," pa said. He got down from the wagon. The music was not playing now.

"Let Vardaman do it," Jewel said. "He can do it in half the time you can. Or here, you let me—"

"I reckon I better do it," pa says. "Long as it was me that borrowed them."

So we set in the wagon, but the music wasn't playing now. I reckon it's a good thing we aint got ere a one of them. I reckon I wouldn't never get no work done a-tall for listening to it. I dont know if a little music aint about the nicest thing a fellow can have. Seems like when he comes in tired of a night, it aint nothing could rest him like having a little music played and him resting. I have see them that shuts up like a hand-grip, with a handle and all, so a fellow can carry it with him wherever he wants.

"What you reckon he's doing?" Jewel says. "I could a toted them shovels back and forth ten times by now."

"Let him take his time," I said. "He aint as spry as you, remember."

"Why didn't he let me take them back, then? We got to get your leg fixed up so we can start home tomorrow."

"We got plenty of time," I said. "I wonder what them machines costs on the installment."

"Installment of what?" Jewel said. "What you got to buy it with?"

"A fellow cant tell," I said. "I could a bought that one from Suratt for five dollars, I believe."

And so pa come back and we went to Peabody's. While we was there pa said he was going to the barbershop and get a shave. And so that night he said he had some business to tend to, kind of looking away from us while he said it, with his hair combed wet and slick and smelling sweet with perfume, but I said leave him be; I wouldn't mind hearing a little more of that music myself.

And so next morning he was gone again, then he come back and told us to get hitched up and ready to take out and he would meet us and when they was gone he said,

"I dont reckon you got no more money."

"Peabody just give me enough to pay the hotel with," I said. "We dont need nothing else, do we?"

"No," pa said; "no. We dont need nothing." He stood there, not looking at me.

"If it is something we got to have, I reckon maybe Peabody," I said.

"No," he said; "it aint nothing else. You all wait for me at the corner."

So Jewel got the team and come for me and they fixed me a pallet in the wagon and we drove across the square to the corner where pa said, and we was waiting there in the wagon, with Dewey Dell and Vardaman eating bananas, when we see them coming up the street. Pa was coming along with that kind of daresome and hangdog look all at once like when he has been up to something he knows ma aint going to like, carrying a grip in his hand, and Jewel says,

"Who's that?"

Then we see it wasn't the grip that made him look different; it was his face, and Jewel says, "He got them teeth."

It was a fact. It made him look a foot taller, kind of holding his head up, hangdog and proud too, and then we see her behind him, carrying the other grip—a kind of duck-shaped woman all dressed up, with them kind of hard-looking pop eyes like she was daring ere a man to say nothing. And there we set watching them, with Dewey Dell's and Vardaman's mouth half open and half-et bananas in their hands and her coming around from behind pa, looking at us like she dared ere a man. And then I see that the grip she was carrying was one of them little graphophones. It was for a fact, all shut up as pretty as a picture, and everytime a new record would come from the mail order and us setting in the house in the winter, listening to it, I would think what a shame Darl couldn't be to enjoy it too. But it is better so for him. This world is not his world; this life his life.

"It's Cash and Jewel and Vardaman and Dewey Dell," pa says, kind of hangdog and proud too, with his teeth and all, even if he wouldn't look at us. "Meet Mrs Bundren," he says.

1930

A Rose for Emily

I

When Miss Emily Grierson died, our whole town went to her funeral: the men through a sort of respectful affection for a fallen monument, the women mostly out of curiosity to see the inside of her house, which no one save an old manservant—a combined gardener and cook—had seen in at least ten years.

It was a big, squarish frame house that had once been white, decorated with cupolas and spires and scrolled balconies in the heavily lightsome style of the seventies, set on what had once been our most select street. But garages and cotton gins had encroached and obliterated even the august names of that neighborhood; only Miss Emily's house was left, lifting its stubborn and coquettish decay above the cotton wagons and the gasoline pumps—an eyesore among eyesores. And now Miss Emily had gone to join the representatives of those august names where they lay in the cedar-bemused cemetery among the ranked and anonymous graves of Union and Confederate soldiers who fell at the battle of Jefferson.

Alive, Miss Emily had been a tradition, a duty, and a care; a sort of hereditary obligation upon the town, dating from that day in 1894 when Colonel Sartoris, the mayor—he who fathered the edict that no Negro woman should appear on the streets without an apron—remitted her taxes, the dispensation dating from the death of her father on into perpetuity. Not that Miss Emily would have accepted charity. Colonel Sartoris invented an involved tale to the effect that Miss Emily's father had loaned money to the town, which the town, as a matter of business, preferred this way of repaying. Only a man of Colonel Sartoris' generation and thought could have invented it, and only a woman could have believed it.

When the next generation, with its more modern ideas, became mayors and aldermen, this arrangement created some little dissatisfaction. On the first of the year they mailed her a tax notice. February came, and there was no reply. They wrote her a formal letter, asking her to call at the sheriff's office at her convenience. A week later the mayor wrote her himself, offering to call or to send his car for her, and received in reply a note on paper of an archaic shape, in a thin, flowing calligraphy in faded ink, to the effect that she no longer went out at all. The tax notice was also enclosed, without comment.

They called a special meeting of the Board of Aldermen. A deputation waited upon her, knocked at the door through which no visitor had passed since she ceased giving china-painting lessons eight or ten years earlier. They were admitted by the old Negro into a dim hall from which a stairway mounted into still more shadow. It smelled of dust and disuse—a close, dank smell. The Negro led them into the parlor. It was furnished in heavy, leather-covered furniture. When the Negro opened the blinds of one window, they could see that the leather was cracked; and when they sat down, a faint dust rose sluggishly about their thighs, spinning with slow motes in the single sunray. On a tarnished gilt easel before the fireplace stood a crayon portrait of Miss Emily's father.

They rose when she entered—a small, fat woman in black, with a thin gold chain descending to her waist and vanishing into her belt, leaning on an ebony cane with a tarnished gold head. Her skeleton was small and spare; perhaps that was why what would have been merely plumpness in another was obesity in her. She looked bloated, like a body long submerged in motionless water, and of that pallid hue. Her eyes, lost in the fatty ridges of her face, looked like two small pieces of coal pressed into a lump of dough as they moved from one face to another while the visitors stated their errand.

She did not ask them to sit. She just stood in the door and listened quietly until the spokesman came to a stumbling halt. Then they could hear the invisible watch ticking at the end of the gold chain.

Her voice was dry and cold. "I have no taxes in Jefferson. Colonel Sartoris explained it to me. Perhaps one of you can gain access to the city records and satisfy yourselves."

"But we have. We are the city authorities, Miss Emily. Didn't you get a notice from the sheriff, signed by him?"

"I received a paper, yes," Miss Emily said. "Perhaps he considers himself the sheriff . . . . . . I have no taxes in Jefferson."

"But there is nothing on the books to show that, you see. We must go by the—"

"See Colonel Sartoris. I have no taxes in Jefferson."

"But, Miss Emily—"

"See Colonel Sartoris." (Colonel Sartoris had been dead almost ten years.) "I have no taxes in Jefferson. Tobe!" The Negro appeared. "Show these gentlemen out."

II

So she vanquished them, horse and foot, just as she had vanquished their fathers thirty years before about the smell. That was two years after her father's death and a short time after her sweetheart—the one we believed would marry her—had deserted her. After her father's death she went out very little; after her sweetheart went away, people hardly saw her at all. A few of the ladies had the temerity to call, but were not received, and the only sign of life about the place was the Negro man—a young man then—going in and out with a market basket.

"Just as if a man—any man—could keep a kitchen properly," the ladies said; so they were not surprised when the smell developed. It was another link between the gross, teeming world and the high and mighty Griersons.

A neighbor, a woman, complained to the mayor, Judge Stevens, eighty years old.

"But what will you have me do about it, madam?" he said.

"Why, send her word to stop it," the woman said. "Isn't there a law?"

"I'm sure that won't be necessary," Judge Stevens said. "It's probably just a snake or a rat that nigger of hers killed in the yard. I'll speak to him about it."

The next day he received two more complaints, one from a man who came in diffident deprecation. "We really must do something about it, Judge. I'd be the last one in the world to bother Miss Emily, but we've got to do something." That night the Board of Aldermen met—three gray-beards and one younger man, a member of the rising generation.

"It's simple enough," he said. "Send her word to have her place cleaned up. Give her a certain time to do it in, and if she don't . . . . . ."

"Dammit, sir," Judge Stevens said, "will you accuse a lady to her face of smelling bad?"

So the next night, after midnight, four men crossed Miss Emily's lawn and slunk about the house like burglars, sniffing along the base of the brickwork and at the cellar openings while one of them performed a regular sowing motion with his hand out of a sack slung from his shoulder. They broke open the cellar door and sprinkled lime there, and in all the outbuildings. As they recrossed the lawn, a window that had been dark was lighted and Miss Emily sat in it, the light behind her, and her upright torso motionless as that of an idol. They crept quietly across the lawn and into the shadow of the locusts that lined the street. After a week or two the smell went away.

That was when people had begun to feel really sorry for her. People in our town, remembering how old lady Wyatt, her great-aunt, had gone completely crazy at last, believed that the Griersons held themselves a little too high for what they really were. None of the young men were quite good enough for Miss Emily and such. We had long thought of them as a tableau; Miss Emily a slender figure in white in the background, her father a spraddled silhouette in the foreground, his back to her and clutching a horsewhip, the two of them framed by the back-flung front door. So when she got to be thirty and was still single, we were not pleased exactly, but vindicated; even with insanity in the family she wouldn't have turned down all of her chances if they had really materialized.

When her father died, it got about that the house was all that was left to her; and in a way, people were glad. At last they could pity Miss Emily. Being left alone, and a pauper, she had become humanized. Now she too would know the old thrill and the old despair of a penny more or less.

The day after his death all the ladies prepared to call at the house and offer condolence and aid, as is our custom. Miss Emily met them at the door, dressed as usual and with no trace of grief on her face. She told them that her father was not dead. She did that for three days, with the ministers calling on her, and the doctors, trying to persuade her to let them dispose of the body. Just as they were about to resort to law and force, she broke down, and they buried her father quickly.

We did not say she was crazy then. We believed she had to do that. We remembered all the young men her father had driven away, and we knew that with nothing left, she would have to cling to that which had robbed her, as people will.

III

She was sick for a long time. When we saw her again, her hair was cut short, making her look like a girl, with a vague resemblance to those angels in colored church windows—sort of tragic and serene.

The town had just let the contracts for paving the sidewalks, and in the summer after her father's death they began to work. The construction company came with niggers and mules and machinery, and a foreman named Homer Barron, a Yankee—a big, dark, ready man, with a big voice and eyes lighter than his face. The little boys would follow in groups to hear him cuss the niggers, and the niggers singing in time to the rise and fall of picks. Pretty soon he knew everybody in town. Whenever you heard a lot of laughing anywhere about the square, Homer Barron would be in the center of the group. Presently we began to see him and Miss Emily on Sunday afternoons driving in the yellow-wheeled buggy and the matched team of bays from the livery stable.

At first we were glad that Miss Emily would have an interest, because the ladies all said, "Of course a Grierson would not think seriously of a Northerner, a day laborer." But there were still others, older people, who said that even grief could not cause a real lady to forget *noblesse oblige*—without calling it *noblesse oblige*. They just said, "Poor Emily. Her kinsfolk should come to her." She had some kin in Alabama; but years ago her father had fallen out with them over the estate of old lady Wyatt, the crazy woman, and there was no communication between the two families. They had not even been represented at the funeral.

And as soon as the old people said, "Poor Emily," the whispering began. "Do you suppose it's really so?" they said to one another. "Of course it is. What else could . . . . . ." This behind their hands; rustling of craned silk and satin behind jalousies closed upon the sun of Sunday afternoon as the thin, swift clop-clop-clop of the matched team passed: "Poor Emily."

She carried her head high enough—even when we believed that she was fallen. It was as if she demanded more than ever the recognition of her dignity as the last Grierson; as if it had wanted that touch of earthiness to reaffirm her imperviousness. Like when she bought the rat poison, the arsenic. That was over a year after they had begun to say "Poor Emily," and while the two female cousins were visiting her.

"I want some poison," she said to the druggist. She was over thirty then, still a slight woman, though thinner than usual, with cold, haughty black eyes in a face the flesh of which was strained across the temples and about the eyesockets as you imagine a lighthouse-keeper's face ought to look. "I want some poison," she said.

"Yes, Miss Emily. What kind? For rats and such? I'd recom—"

"I want the best you have. I don't care what kind."

The druggist named several. "They'll kill anything up to an elephant. But what you want is—"

"Arsenic," Miss Emily said. "Is that a good one?"

"Is . . . . . . arsenic? Yes ma'am. But what you want—"

"I want arsenic."

The druggist looked down at her. She looked back at him, erect, her face like a strained flag. "Why, of course," the druggist said. "If that's what you want. But the law requires you to tell what you are going to use it for."

Miss Emily just stared at him, her head tilted back in order to look him eye for eye, until he looked away and went and got the arsenic and wrapped it up. The Negro delivery boy brought her the package; the druggist didn't come back. When she opened the package at home there was written on the box, under the skull and bones: "For rats."

IV

So the next day we all said, "She will kill herself"; and we said it would be the best thing. When she had first begun to be seen with Homer Barron, we had said, "She will marry him." Then we said, "She will persuade him yet," because Homer himself had remarked—he liked men, and it was known that he drank with the younger men in the Elks' Club—that he was not a marrying man. Later we said, "Poor Emily," behind the jalousies as they passed on Sunday afternoon in the glittering buggy, Miss Emily with her head high and Homer Barron with his hat cocked and a cigar in his teeth, reins and whip in a yellow glove.

Then some of the ladies began to say that it was a disgrace to the town and a bad example to the young people. The men did not want to interfere, but at last the ladies forced the Baptist minister—Miss Emily's people were Episcopal—to call upon her. He would never divulge what happened during that interview, but he refused to go back again. The next Sunday they again drove about the streets, and the following day the minister's wife wrote to Miss Emily's relations in Alabama.

So she had blood-kin under her roof again and we sat back to watch developments. At first nothing happened. Then we were sure that they were to be married. We learned that Miss Emily had been to the jeweler's and ordered a man's toilet set in silver, with the letters H. B. on each piece. Two days later we learned that she had bought a complete outfit of men's clothing, including a nightshirt, and we said, "They are married." We were really glad. We were glad because the two female cousins were even more Grierson than Miss Emily had ever been.

So we were not surprised when Homer Barron—the streets had been finished some time since—was gone. We were a little disappointed that there was not a public blowing-off, but we believed that he had gone on to prepare for Miss Emily's coming, or to give her a chance to get rid of the cousins. (By that time it was a cabal, and we were all Miss Emily's allies to help circumvent the cousins.) Sure enough, after another week they departed. And, as we had expected all along, within three days Homer Barron was back in town. A neighbor saw the Negro man admit him at the kitchen door at dusk one evening.

And that was the last we saw of Homer Barron. And of Miss Emily for some time. The Negro man went in and out with the market basket, but the front door remained closed. Now and then we would see her at a window for a moment, as the men did that night when they sprinkled the lime, but for almost six months she did not appear on the streets. Then we knew that this was to be expected too; as if that quality of her father which had thwarted her woman's life so many times had been too virulent and too furious to die.

When we next saw Miss Emily, she had grown fat and her hair was turning gray. During the next few years it grew grayer and grayer until it attained an even pepper-and-salt iron-gray, when it ceased turning. Up to the day of her death at seventy-four it was still that vigorous iron-gray, like the hair of an active man.

From that time on her front door remained closed, save for a period of six or seven years, when she was about forty, during which she gave lessons in china-painting. She fitted up a studio in one of the downstairs rooms, where the daughters and granddaughters of Colonel Sartoris' contemporaries were sent to her with the same regularity and in the same spirit that they were sent on Sundays with a twenty-five-cent piece for the collection plate. Meanwhile her taxes had been remitted.

Then the newer generation became the backbone and the spirit of the town, and the painting pupils grew up and fell away and did not send their children to her with boxes of color and tedious brushes and pictures cut from the ladies' magazines. The front door closed upon the last one and remained closed for good. When the town got free postal delivery Miss Emily alone refused to let them fasten the metal numbers above her door and attach a mailbox to it. She would not listen to them.

Daily, monthly, yearly we watched the Negro grow grayer and more stooped, going in and out with the market basket. Each December we sent her a tax notice, which would be returned by the post office a week later, unclaimed. Now and then we would see her in one of the downstairs windows—she had evidently shut up the top floor of the house—like the carven torso of an idol in a niche, looking or not looking at us, we could never tell which. Thus she passed from generation to generation—dear, inescapable, impervious, tranquil, and perverse.

And so she died. Fell ill in the house filled with dust and shadows, with only a doddering Negro man to wait on her. We did not even know she was sick; we had long since given up trying to get any information from the Negro. He talked to no one, probably not even to her, for his voice had grown harsh and rusty, as if from disuse.

She died in one of the downstairs rooms, in a heavy walnut bed with a curtain, her gray head propped on a pillow yellow and moldy with age and lack of sunlight.

V

The Negro met the first of the ladies at the front door and let them in, with their hushed, sibilant voices and their quick, curious glances, and then he disappeared. He walked right through the house and out the back and was not seen again.

The two female cousins came at once. They held the funeral on the second day, with the town coming to look at Miss Emily beneath a mass of bought flowers, with the crayon face of her father musing profoundly above the bier and the ladies sibilant and macabre; and the very old men—some in their brushed Confederate uniforms—on the porch and the lawn, talking of Miss Emily as if she had been a contemporary of theirs, believing that they had danced with her and courted her perhaps, confusing time with its mathematical progression, as the old do, to whom all the past is not a diminishing road, but, instead, a huge meadow which no winter ever quite touches, divided from them now by the narrow bottle-neck of the most recent decade of years.

Already we knew that there was one room in that region above stairs which no one had seen in forty years, and which would have to be forced. They waited until Miss Emily was decently in the ground before they opened it.

The violence of breaking down the door seemed to fill this room with pervading dust. A thin, acrid pall as of the tomb seemed to lie everywhere upon this room decked and furnished as for a bridal: upon the valance curtains of faded rose color, upon the rose-shaded lights, upon the dressing table, upon the delicate array of crystal and the man's toilet things backed with tarnished silver, silver so tarnished that the monogram was obscured. Among them lay a collar and tie, as if they had just been removed, which, lifted, left upon the surface a pale crescent in the dust. Upon a chair hung the suit, carefully folded; beneath it the two mute shoes and the discarded socks.

The man himself lay in the bed.

For a long while we just stood there, looking down at the profound and fleshless grin. The body had apparently once lain in the attitude of an embrace, but now the long sleep that outlasts love, that conquers even the grimace of love, had cuckolded him. What was left of him, rotted beneath what was left of the nightshirt, had become inextricable from the bed in which he lay; and upon him and upon the pillow beside him lay that even coating of the patient and biding dust.

Then we noticed that in the second pillow was the indentation of a head. One of us lifted something from it, and leaning forward, that faint and invisible dust dry and acrid in the nostrils, we saw a long strand of iron-gray hair.

1931

Barn Burning

The store in which the Justice of the Peace's court was sitting smelled of cheese. The boy, crouched on his nail keg at the back of the crowded room, knew he smelled cheese, and more: from where he sat he could see the ranked shelves close-packed with the solid, squat, dynamic shapes of tin cans whose labels his stomach read, not from the lettering which meant nothing to his mind but from the scarlet devils and the silver curve of fish—this, the cheese which he knew he smelled and the hermetic meat which his intestines believed he smelled coming in intermittent gusts momentary and brief between the other constant one, the smell and sense just a little of fear because mostly of despair and grief, the old fierce pull of blood. He could not see the table where the Justice sat and before which his father and his father's enemy (*our enemy* he thought in that despair; *ourn! mine and hisn both! He's my father!*) stood, but he could hear them, the two of them that is, because his father had said no word yet:

"But what proof have you, Mr. Harris?"

"I told you. The hog got into my corn. I caught it up and sent it back to him. He had no fence that would hold it. I told him so, warned him. The next time I put the hog in my pen. When he came to get it I gave him enough wire to patch up his pen. The next time I put the hog up and kept it. I rode down to his house and saw the wire I gave him still rolled on to the spool in his yard. I told him he could have the hog when he paid me a dollar pound fee. That evening a nigger came with the dollar and got the hog. He was a strange nigger. He said, 'He say to tell you wood and hay kin burn.' I said, 'What?' 'That whut he say to tell you,' the nigger said. 'Wood and hay kin burn.' That night my barn burned. I got the stock out but I lost the barn."

"Where is the nigger? Have you got him?"

"He was a strange nigger, I tell you. I don't know what became of him."

"But that's not proof. Don't you see that's not proof?"

"Get that boy up here. He knows." For a moment the boy thought too that the man meant his older brother until Harris said, "Not him. The little one.

The boy," and, crouching, small for his age, small and wiry like his father, in patched and faded jeans even too small for him, with straight, uncombed, brown hair and eyes gray and wild as storm scud, he saw the men between himself and the table part and become a lane of grim faces, at the end of which he saw the Justice, a shabby, collarless, graying man in spectacles, beckoning him. He felt no floor under his bare feet; he seemed to walk beneath the palpable weight of the grim turning faces. His father, stiff in his black Sunday coat donned not for the trial but for the moving, did not even look at him. *He aims for me to lie,* he thought, again with that frantic grief and despair. *And I will have to do hit.*

"What's your name, boy?" the Justice said.

"Colonel Sartoris Snopes,"[1] the boy whispered.

"Hey?" the Justice said. "Talk louder. Colonel Sartoris? I reckon anybody named for Colonel Sartoris in this country can't help but tell the truth, can they?" The boy said nothing. *Enemy! Enemy!* he thought; for a moment he could not even see, could not see that the Justice's face was kindly nor discern that his voice was troubled when he spoke to the man named Harris: "Do you want me to question this boy?" But he could hear, and during those subsequent long seconds while there was absolutely no sound in the crowded little room save that of quiet and intent breathing it was as if he had swung outward at the end of a grape vine, over a ravine, and at the top of the swing had been caught in a prolonged instant of mesmerized gravity, weightless in time.

"No!" Harris said violently, explosively. "Damnation! Send him out of here!" Now time, the fluid world, rushed beneath him again, the voices coming to him again through the smell of cheese and sealed meat, the fear and despair and the old grief of blood:

"This case is closed. I can't find against you, Snopes, but I can give you advice. Leave this country and don't come back to it."

His father spoke for the first time, his voice cold and harsh, level, without emphasis: "I aim to. I don't figure to stay in a country among people who . . ." he said something unprintable and vile, addressed to no one.

"That'll do," the Justice said. "Take your wagon and get out of this country before dark. Case dismissed."

His father turned, and he followed the stiff black coat, the wiry figure walking a little stiffly from where a Confederate provost's man's musket ball had taken him in the heel on a stolen horse thirty years ago, followed the two backs now, since his older brother had appeared from somewhere in the crowd, no taller than the father but thicker, chewing tobacco steadily, between the two lines of grim-faced men and out of the store and across the worn gallery and down the sagging steps and among the dogs and half-grown boys in the mild May dust, where as he passed a voice hissed:

"Barn burner!"

Again he could not see, whirling; there was a face in a red haze, moonlike, bigger than the full moon, the owner of it half again his size, he leaping in

1. The boy is named for Colonel Sartoris, a leading citizen of Jefferson (the fictional town that Faulkner based on his hometown of Oxford, Mississippi) and an officer in the Confederate Army. The Snopeses are a poor white family from the same area. Both families appear in other works by Faulkner.

the red haze toward the face, feeling no blow, feeling no shock when his head struck the earth, scrabbling up and leaping again, feeling no blow this time either and tasting no blood, scrabbling up to see the other boy in full flight and himself already leaping into pursuit as his father's hand jerked him back, the harsh, cold voice speaking above him: "Go get in the wagon."

It stood in a grove of locusts and mulberries across the road. His two hulking sisters in their Sunday dresses and his mother and her sister in calico and sunbonnets were already in it, sitting on and among the sorry residue of the dozen and more movings which even the boy could remember—the battered stove, the broken beds and chairs, the clock inlaid with mother-of-pearl, which would not run, stopped at some fourteen minutes past two o'clock of a dead and forgotten day and time, which had been his mother's dowry. She was crying, though when she saw him she drew her sleeve across her face and began to descend from the wagon. "Get back," the father said.

"He's hurt. I got to get some water and wash his . . ."

"Get back in the wagon," his father said. He got in too, over the tail-gate. His father mounted to the seat where the older brother already sat and struck the gaunt mules two savage blows with the peeled willow, but without heat. It was not even sadistic; it was exactly that same quality which in later years would cause his descendants to over-run the engine before putting a motor car into motion, striking and reining back in the same movement. The wagon went on, the store with its quiet crowd of grimly watching men dropped behind; a curve in the road hid it. *Forever* he thought. *Maybe he's done satisfied now, now that he has* . . . stopping himself, not to say it aloud even to himself. His mother's hand touched his shoulder.

"Does hit hurt?" she said.

"Naw," he said. "Hit don't hurt. Lemme be."

"Can't you wipe some of the blood off before hit dries?"

"I'll wash to-night," he said. "Lemme be, I tell you."

The wagon went on. He did not know where they were going. None of them ever did or ever asked, because it was always somewhere, always a house of sorts waiting for them a day or two days or even three days away. Likely his father had already arranged to make a crop on another farm before he . . . Again he had to stop himself. He (the father) always did. There was something about his wolflike independence and even courage when the advantage was at least neutral which impressed strangers, as if they got from his latent ravening ferocity not so much a sense of dependability as a feeling that his ferocious conviction in the rightness of his own actions would be of advantage to all whose interest lay with his.

That night they camped, in a grove of oaks and beeches where a spring ran. The nights were still cool and they had a fire against it, of a rail lifted from a nearby fence and cut into lengths—a small fire, neat, niggard almost, a shrewd fire; such fires were his father's habit and custom always, even in freezing weather. Older, the boy might have remarked this and wondered why not a big one; why should not a man who had not only seen the waste and extravagance of war, but who had in his blood an inherent voracious prodigality with material not his own, have burned everything in sight? Then he might have gone a step farther and thought that that was the reason: that niggard blaze was the living fruit of nights passed during those four years in the woods hiding from all men, blue or gray, with his strings of horses (captured horses, he called them). And older still, he might have divined the true reason: that the element of fire spoke to some deep mainspring of his father's being, as the element of steel or of powder spoke to other men, as the one weapon for the preservation of integrity, else breath were not worth the breathing, and hence to be regarded with respect and used with discretion.

But he did not think this now and he had seen those same niggard blazes all his life. He merely ate his supper beside it and was already half asleep over his iron plate when his father called him, and once more he followed the stiff back, the stiff and ruthless limp, up the slope and on to the starlit road where, turning, he could see his father against the stars but without face or depth—a shape black, flat, and bloodless as though cut from tin in the iron folds of the frockcoat which had not been made for him, the voice harsh like tin and without heat like tin:

"You were fixing to tell them. You would have told him." He didn't answer. His father struck him with the flat of his hand on the side of the head, hard but without heat, exactly as he had struck the two mules at the store, exactly as he would strike either of them with any stick in order to kill a horse fly, his voice still without heat or anger: "You're getting to be a man. You got to learn. You got to learn to stick to your own blood or you ain't going to have any blood to stick to you. Do you think either of them, any man there this morning, would? Don't you know all they wanted was a chance to get at me because they knew I had them beat? Eh?" Later, twenty years later, he was to tell himself, "If I had said they wanted only truth, justice, he would have hit me again." But now he said nothing. He was not crying. He just stood there. "Answer me," his father said.

"Yes," he whispered. His father turned.

"Get on to bed. We'll be there to-morrow."

To-morrow they were there. In the early afternoon the wagon stopped before a paintless two-room house identical almost with the dozen others it had stopped before even in the boy's ten years, and again, as on the other dozen occasions, his mother and aunt got down and began to unload the wagon, although his two sisters and his father and brother had not moved.

"Likely hit ain't fitten for hawgs," one of the sisters said.

"Nevertheless, fit it will and you'll hog it and like it," his father said. "Get out of them chairs and help your Ma unload."

The two sisters got down, big, bovine, in a flutter of cheap ribbons; one of them drew from the jumbled wagon bed a battered lantern, the other a worn broom. His father handed the reins to the older son and began to climb stiffly over the wheel. "When they get unloaded, take the team to the barn and feed them." Then he said, and at first the boy thought he was still speaking to his brother: "Come with me."

"Me?" he said.

"Yes," his father said. "You."

"Abner," his mother said. His father paused and looked back—the harsh level stare beneath the shaggy, graying, irascible brows.

"I reckon I'll have a word with the man that aims to begin to-morrow owning me body and soul for the next eight months."

They went back up the road. A week ago—or before last night, that is—he would have asked where they were going, but not now. His father had struck him before last night but never before had he paused afterward to explain why; it was as if the blow and the following calm, outrageous voice still rang, repercussed, divulging nothing to him save the terrible handicap of being young, the light weight of his few years, just heavy enough to prevent his soaring free of the world as it seemed to be ordered but not heavy enough to keep him footed solid in it, to resist it and try to change the course of its events.

Presently he could see the grove of oaks and cedars and the other flowering trees and shrubs where the house would be, though not the house yet. They walked beside a fence massed with honeysuckle and Cherokee roses and came to a gate swinging open between two brick pillars, and now, beyond a sweep of drive, he saw the house for the first time and at that instant he forgot his father and the terror and despair both, and even when he remembered his father again (who had not stopped) the terror and despair did not return. Because, for all the twelve movings, they had sojourned until now in a poor country, a land of small farms and fields and houses, and he had never seen a house like this before. *Hit's big as a courthouse* he thought quietly, with a surge of peace and joy whose reason he could not have thought into words, being too young for that: *They are safe from him. People whose lives are a part of this peace and dignity are beyond his touch, he no more to them than a buzzing wasp: capable of stinging for a little moment but that's all; the spell of this peace and dignity rendering even the barns and stable and cribs which belong to it impervious to the puny flames he might contrive* . . . this, the peace and joy, ebbing for an instant as he looked again at the stiff black back, the stiff and implacable limp of the figure which was not dwarfed by the house, for the reason that it had never looked big anywhere and which now, against the serene columned backdrop, had more than ever that impervious quality of something cut ruthlessly from tin, depthless, as though, sidewise to the sun, it would cast no shadow. Watching him, the boy remarked the absolutely undeviating course which his father held and saw the stiff foot come squarely down in a pile of fresh droppings where a horse had stood in the drive and which his father could have avoided by a simple change of stride. But it ebbed only for a moment, though he could not have thought this into words either, walking on in the spell of the house, which he could even want but without envy, without sorrow, certainly never with that ravening and jealous rage which unknown to him walked in the ironlike black coat before him: *Maybe he will feel it too. Maybe it will even change him now from what maybe he couldn't help but be.*

They crossed the portico. Now he could hear his father's stiff foot as it came down on the boards with clocklike finality, a sound out of all proportion to the displacement of the body it bore and which was not dwarfed either by the white door before it, as though it had attained to a sort of vicious and ravening minimum not to be dwarfed by anything—the flat, wide, black hat, the formal coat of broadcloth which had once been black but which had now that friction-glazed greenish cast of the bodies of old house flies, the lifted sleeve which was too large, the lifted hand like a curled claw. The door opened so promptly that the boy knew the Negro must have been watching them all the time, an old man with neat grizzled hair, in a linen jacket, who stood barring the door with his body, saying, "Wipe yo foots, white man, fo you come in here. Major ain't home nohow."

"Get out of my way, nigger," his father said, without heat too, flinging the door back and the Negro also and entering, his hat still on his head. And now the boy saw the prints of the stiff foot on the doorjamb and saw them appear on the pale rug behind the machinelike deliberation of the foot which seemed to bear (or transmit) twice the weight which the body compassed. The Negro was shouting "Miss Lula! Miss Lula!" somewhere behind them, then the boy, deluged as though by a warm wave by a suave turn of carpeted stair and a pendant glitter of chandeliers and a mute gleam of gold frames, heard the swift feet and saw her too, a lady—perhaps he had never seen her like before either—in a gray, smooth gown with lace at the throat and an apron tied at the waist and the sleeves turned back, wiping cake or biscuit dough from her hands with a towel as she came up the hall, looking not at his father at all but at the tracks on the blond rug with an expression of incredulous amazement.

"I tried," the Negro cried. "I tole him to . . ."

"Will you please go away?" she said in a shaking voice. "Major de Spain is not at home. Will you please go away?"

His father had not spoken again. He did not speak again. He did not even look at her. He just stood stiff in the center of the rug, in his hat, the shaggy iron-gray brows twitching slightly above the pebble-colored eyes as he appeared to examine the house with brief deliberation. Then with the same deliberation he turned; the boy watched him pivot on the good leg and saw the stiff foot drag round the arc of the turning, leaving a final long and fading smear. His father never looked at it, he never once looked down at the rug. The Negro held the door. It closed behind them, upon the hysteric and indistinguishable woman-wail. His father stopped at the top of the steps and scraped his boot clean on the edge of it. At the gate he stopped again. He stood for a moment, planted stiffly on the stiff foot, looking back at the house. "Pretty and white, ain't it?" he said. "That's sweat. Nigger sweat. Maybe it ain't white enough yet to suit him. Maybe he wants to mix some white sweat with it."

Two hours later the boy was chopping wood behind the house within which his mother and aunt and the two sisters (the mother and aunt, not the two girls, he knew that; even at this distance and muffled by walls the flat loud voices of the two girls emanated an incorrigible idle inertia) were setting up the stove to prepare a meal, when he heard the hooves and saw the linen-clad man on a fine sorrel mare, whom he recognized even before he saw the rolled rug in front of the Negro youth following on a fat bay carriage horse—a suffused, angry face vanishing, still at full gallop, beyond the corner of the house where his father and brother were sitting in the two tilted chairs; and a moment later, almost before he could have put the axe down, he heard the hooves again and watched the sorrel mare go back out of the yard, already galloping again. Then his father began to shout one of the sisters' names, who presently emerged backward from the kitchen door dragging the rolled rug along the ground by one end while the other sister walked behind it.

"If you ain't going to tote, go on and set up the wash pot," the first said.

"You, Sarty!" the second shouted. "Set up the wash pot!" His father appeared at the door, framed against that shabbiness, as he had been against that other bland perfection, impervious to either, the mother's anxious face at his shoulder.

"Go on," the father said. "Pick it up." The two sisters stooped, broad, lethargic; stooping, they presented an incredible expanse of pale cloth and a flutter of tawdry ribbons.

"If I thought enough of a rug to have to git hit all the way from France I wouldn't keep hit where folks coming in would have to tromp on hit," the first said. They raised the rug.

"Abner," the mother said. "Let me do it."

"You go back and git dinner," his father said. "I'll tend to this."

From the woodpile through the rest of the afternoon the boy watched them, the rug spread flat in the dust beside the bubbling wash-pot, the two sisters stooping over it with that profound and lethargic reluctance, while the father stood over them in turn, implacable and grim, driving them though never raising his voice again. He could smell the harsh homemade lye they were using; he saw his mother come to the door once and look toward them with an expression not anxious now but very like despair; he saw his father turn, and he fell to with the axe and saw from the corner of his eye his father raise from the ground a flattish fragment of field stone and examine it and return to the pot, and this time his mother actually spoke: "Abner. Abner. Please don't. Please, Abner."

Then he was done too. It was dusk; the whippoorwills had already begun. He could smell coffee from the room where they would presently eat the cold food remaining from the mid-afternoon meal, though when he entered the house he realized they were having coffee again probably because there was a fire on the hearth, before which the rug now lay spread over the backs of the two chairs. The tracks of his father's foot were gone. Where they had been were now long, water-cloudy scoriations resembling the sporadic course of a lilliputian mowing machine.

It still hung there while they ate the cold food and then went to bed, scattered without order or claim up and down the two rooms, his mother in one bed, where his father would later lie, the older brother in the other, himself, the aunt, and the two sisters on pallets on the floor. But his father was not in bed yet. The last thing the boy remembered was the depthless, harsh silhouette of the hat and coat bending over the rug and it seemed to him that he had not even closed his eyes when the silhouette was standing over him, the fire almost dead behind it, the stiff foot prodding him awake. "Catch up the mule," his father said.

When he returned with the mule his father was standing in the black door, the rolled rug over his shoulder. "Ain't you going to ride?" he said.

"No. Give me your foot."

He bent his knee into his father's hand, the wiry, surprising power flowed smoothly, rising, he rising with it, on to the mule's bare back (they had owned a saddle once; the boy could remember it though not when or where) and with the same effortlessness his father swung the rug up in front of him. Now in the starlight they retraced the afternoon's path, up the dusty road rife with honeysuckle, through the gate and up the black tunnel of the drive to the lightless house, where he sat on the mule and felt the rough warp of the rug drag across his thighs and vanish.

"Don't you want me to help?" he whispered. His father did not answer and now he heard again that stiff foot striking the hollow portico with that wooden and clocklike deliberation, that outrageous overstatement of the weight it carried. The rug, hunched, not flung (the boy could tell that even in the darkness) from his father's shoulder, struck the angle of wall and floor with a sound unbelievably loud, thunderous, then the foot again, unhurried and enormous; a light came on in the house and the boy sat, tense, breathing steadily and quietly and just a little fast, though the foot itself did not increase its beat at all, descending the steps now; now the boy could see him.

"Don't you want to ride now?" he whispered. "We kin both ride now," the light within the house altering now, flaring up and sinking. *He's coming down the stairs now,* he thought. He had already ridden the mule up beside the horse block; presently his father was up behind him and he doubled the reins over and slashed the mule across the neck, but before the animal could begin to trot the hard, thin arm came round him, the hard, knotted hand jerking the mule back to a walk.

In the first red rays of the sun they were in the lot, putting plow gear on the mules. This time the sorrel mare was in the lot before he heard it at all, the rider collarless and even bareheaded, trembling, speaking in a shaking voice as the woman in the house had done, his father merely looking up once before stooping again to the hame he was buckling, so that the man on the mare spoke to his stooping back:

"You must realize you have ruined that rug. Wasn't there anybody here, any of your women . . ." he ceased, shaking, the boy watching him, the older brother leaning now in the stable door, chewing, blinking slowly and steadily at nothing apparently. "It cost a hundred dollars. But you never had a hundred dollars. You never will. So I'm going to charge you twenty bushels of corn against your crop. I'll add it in your contract and when you come to the commissary you can sign it. That won't keep Mrs. de Spain quiet but maybe it will teach you to wipe your feet off before you enter her house again."

Then he was gone. The boy looked at his father, who still had not spoken or even looked up again, who was now adjusting the logger-head in the hame.

"Pap," he said. His father looked at him—the inscrutable face, the shaggy brows beneath which the gray eyes glinted coldly. Suddenly the boy went toward him, fast, stopping as suddenly. "You done the best you could!" he cried. "If he wanted hit done different why didn't he wait and tell you how? He won't git no twenty bushels! He won't git none! We'll gether hit and hide hit! I kin watch . . ."

"Did you put the cutter back in that straight stock like I told you?"

"No, sir," he said.

"Then go do it."

That was Wednesday. During the rest of that week he worked steadily, at what was within his scope and some which was beyond it, with an industry that did not need to be driven nor even commanded twice; he had this from his mother, with the difference that some at least of what he did he liked to do, such as splitting wood with the half-size axe which his mother and aunt had earned, or saved money somehow, to present him with at Christmas. In company with the two older women (and on one afternoon, even one of the sisters), he built pens for the shoat and the cow which were a part of his father's contract with the landlord, and one afternoon, his father being absent, gone somewhere on one of the mules, he went to the field.

They were running a middle buster now, his brother holding the plow straight while he handled the reins, and walking beside the straining mule, the rich black soil shearing cool and damp against his bare ankles, he thought *Maybe this is the end of it. Maybe even that twenty bushels that seems hard to have to pay for just a rug will be a cheap price for him to stop forever and always from being what he used to be;* thinking, dreaming now, so that his brother had to speak sharply to him to mind the mule: *Maybe he even won't collect the twenty bushels. Maybe it will all add up and balance and vanish—corn, rug, fire; the terror and grief, the being pulled two ways like between two teams of horses—gone, done with for ever and ever.*

Then it was Saturday; he looked up from beneath the mule he was harnessing and saw his father in the black coat and hat. "Not that," his father said. "The wagon gear." And then, two hours later, sitting in the wagon bed behind his father and brother on the seat, the wagon accomplished a final curve, and he saw the weathered paintless store with its tattered tobacco- and patent-medicine posters and the tethered wagons and saddle animals below the gallery. He mounted the gnawed steps behind his father and brother, and there again was the lane of quiet, watching faces for the three of them to walk through. He saw the man in spectacles sitting at the plank table and he did not need to be told this was a Justice of the Peace; he sent one glare of fierce, exultant, partisan defiance at the man in collar and cravat now, whom he had seen but twice before in his life, and that on a galloping horse, who now wore on his face an expression not of rage but of amazed unbelief which the boy could not have known was at the incredible circumstance of being sued by one of his own tenants, and came and stood against his father and cried at the Justice: "He ain't done it! He ain't burnt . . ."

"Go back to the wagon," his father said.

"Burnt?" the Justice said. "Do I understand this rug was burned too?"

"Does anybody here claim it was?" his father said. "Go back to the wagon." But he did not, he merely retreated to the rear of the room, crowded as that other had been, but not to sit down this time, instead, to stand pressing among the motionless bodies, listening to the voices:

"And you claim twenty bushels of corn is too high for the damage you did to the rug?"

"He brought the rug to me and said he wanted the tracks washed out of it. I washed the tracks out and took the rug back to him."

"But you didn't carry the rug back to him in the same condition it was in before you made the tracks on it."

His father did not answer, and now for perhaps half a minute there was no sound at all save that of breathing, the faint, steady suspiration of complete and intent listening.

"You decline to answer that, Mr. Snopes?" Again his father did not answer. "I'm going to find against you, Mr. Snopes. I'm going to find that you were responsible for the injury to Major de Spain's rug and hold you liable for it. But twenty bushels of corn seems a little high for a man in your circumstances to have to pay. Major de Spain claims it cost a hundred dollars. October corn will be worth about fifty cents. I figure that if Major de Spain can stand a ninety-five-dollar loss on something he paid cash for, you can stand a five-dollar loss you haven't earned yet. I hold you in damages to Major de

Spain to the amount of ten bushels of corn over and above your contract with him, to be paid to him out of your crop at gathering time. Court adjourned."

It had taken no time hardly, the morning was but half begun. He thought they would return home and perhaps back to the field, since they were late, far behind all other farmers. But instead his father passed on behind the wagon, merely indicating with his hand for the older brother to follow with it, and crossed the road toward the blacksmith shop opposite, pressing on after his father, overtaking him, speaking, whispering up at the harsh, calm face beneath the weathered hat: "He won't git no ten bushels neither. He won't git one. We'll . . ." until his father glanced for an instant down at him, the face absolutely calm, the grizzled eyebrows tangled above the cold eyes, the voice almost pleasant, almost gentle:

"You think so? Well, we'll wait till October anyway."

The matter of the wagon—the setting of a spoke or two and the tightening of the tires—did not take long either, the business of the tires accomplished by driving the wagon into the spring branch behind the shop and letting it stand there, the mules nuzzling into the water from time to time, and the boy on the seat with the idle reins, looking up the slope and through the sooty tunnel of the shed where the slow hammer rang and where his father sat on an upended cypress bolt, easily, either talking or listening, still sitting there when the boy brought the dripping wagon up out of the branch and halted it before the door.

"Take them on to the shade and hitch," his father said. He did so and returned. His father and the smith and a third man squatting on his heels inside the door were talking, about crops and animals; the boy, squatting too in the ammoniac dust and hoof-parings and scales of rust, heard his father tell a long and unhurried story out of the time before the birth of the older brother even when he had been a professional horsetrader. And then his father came up beside him where he stood before a tattered last year's circus poster on the other side of the store, gazing rapt and quiet at the scarlet horses, the incredible poisings and convolutions of tulle and tights and the painted leers of comedians, and said "It's time to eat."

But not at home. Squatting beside his brother against the front wall, he watched his father emerge from the store and produce from a paper sack a segment of cheese and divide it carefully and deliberately into three with his pocket knife and produce crackers from the same sack. They all three squatted on the gallery and ate, slowly, without talking; then in the store again, they drank from a tin dipper tepid water smelling of the cedar bucket and of living beech trees. And still they did not go home. It was a horse lot this time, a tall rail fence upon and along which men stood and sat and out of which one by one horses were led, to be walked and trotted and then cantered back and forth along the road while the slow swapping and buying went on and the sun began to slant westward, they—the three of them—watching and listening, the older brother with his muddy eyes and his steady, inevitable tobacco, the father commenting now and then on certain of the animals, to no one in particular.

It was after sundown when they reached home. They ate supper by lamplight, then, sitting on the doorstep, the boy watched the night fully accomplish, listening to the whippoorwills and the frogs, when he heard his mother's voice: "Abner! No! No! Oh, God. Oh, God. Abner!" and he rose, whirled, and saw the altered light through the door where a candle stub now burned in a bottle neck on the table and his father, still in the hat and coat, at once formal and burlesque as though dressed carefully for some shabby and ceremonial violence, emptying the reservoir of the lamp back into the five-gallon kerosene can from which it had been filled, while the mother tugged at his arm until he shifted the lamp to the other hand and flung her back, not savagely or viciously, just hard, into the wall, her hands flung out against the wall for balance, her mouth open and in her face the same quality of hopeless despair as had been in her voice. Then his father saw him standing in the door.

"Go to the barn and get that can of oil we were oiling the wagon with," he said. The boy did not move. Then he could speak.

"What . . ." he cried. "What are you . . ."

"Go get that oil," his father said. "Go."

Then he was moving, running, outside the house, toward the stable: this is the old habit, the old blood which he had not been permitted to choose for himself, which had been bequeathed him willy nilly and which had run for so long (and who knew where, battening on what of outrage and savagery and lust) before it came to him. *I could keep on,* he thought. *I could run on and on and never look back, never need to see his face again. Only I can't. I can't,* the rusted can in his hand now, the liquid sploshing in it as he ran back to the house and into it, into the sound of his mother's weeping in the next room, and handed the can to his father.

"Ain't you going to even send a nigger?" he cried. "At least you sent a nigger before!"

This time his father didn't strike him. The hand came even faster than the blow had, the same hand which had set the can on the table with almost excruciating care flashing from the can toward him too quick for him to follow it, gripping him by the back of his shirt and on to tiptoe before he had seen it quit the can, the face stooping at him in breathless and frozen ferocity, the cold, dead voice speaking over him to the older brother who leaned against the table, chewing with that steady, curious, sidewise motion of cows:

"Empty the can into the big one and go on. I'll catch up with you."

"Better tie him up to the bedpost," the brother said.

"Do like I told you," the father said. Then the boy was moving, his bunched shirt and the hard, bony hand between his shoulder-blades, his toes just touching the floor, across the room and into the other one, past the sisters sitting with spread heavy thighs in the two chairs over the cold hearth, and to where his mother and aunt sat side by side on the bed, the aunt's arms about his mother's shoulders.

"Hold him," the father said. The aunt made a startled movement. "Not you," the father said. "Lennie. Take hold of him. I want to see you do it." His mother took him by the wrist. "You'll hold him better than that. If he gets loose don't you know what he is going to do? He will go up yonder." He jerked his head toward the road. "Maybe I'd better tie him."

"I'll hold him," his mother whispered.

"See you do then." Then his father was gone, the stiff foot heavy and measured upon the boards, ceasing at last.

Then he began to struggle. His mother caught him in both arms, he jerking and wrenching at them. He would be stronger in the end, he knew that.

But he had no time to wait for it. "Lemme go!" he cried. "I don't want to have to hit you!"

"Let him go!" the aunt said. "If he don't go, before God, I am going there myself!"

"Don't you see I can't!" his mother cried. "Sarty! Sarty! No! No! Help me, Lizzie!"

Then he was free. His aunt grasped at him but it was too late. He whirled, running, his mother stumbled forward on to her knees behind him, crying to the nearer sister: "Catch him, Net! Catch him!" But that was too late too, the sister (the sisters were twins, born at the same time, yet either of them now gave the impression of being, encompassing as much living meat and volume and weight as any other two of the family) not yet having begun to rise from the chair, her head, face, alone merely turned, presenting to him in the flying instant an astonishing expanse of young female features untroubled by any surprise even, wearing only an expression of bovine interest. Then he was out of the room, out of the house, in the mild dust of the starlit road and the heavy rifeness of honeysuckle, the pale ribbon unspooling with terrific slowness under his running feet, reaching the gate at last and turning in, running, his heart and lungs drumming, on up the drive toward the lighted house, the lighted door. He did not knock, he burst in, sobbing for breath, incapable for the moment of speech; he saw the astonished face of the Negro in the linen jacket without knowing when the Negro had appeared.

"De Spain!" he cried, panted. "Where's . . ." then he saw the white man too emerging from a white door down the hall. "Barn!" he cried. "Barn!"

"What?" the white man said. "Barn?"

"Yes!" the boy cried. "Barn!"

"Catch him!" the white man shouted.

But it was too late this time too. The Negro grasped his shirt, but the entire sleeve, rotten with washing, carried away, and he was out that door too and in the drive again, and had actually never ceased to run even while he was screaming into the white man's face.

Behind him the white man was shouting, "My horse! Fetch my horse!" and he thought for an instant of cutting across the park and climbing the fence into the road, but he did not know the park nor how high the vine-massed fence might be and he dared not risk it. So he ran on down the drive, blood and breath roaring; presently he was in the road again though he could not see it. He could not hear either: the galloping mare was almost upon him before he heard her, and even then he held his course, as if the very urgency of his wild grief and need must in a moment more find him wings, waiting until the ultimate instant to hurl himself aside and into the weed-choked roadside ditch as the horse thundered past and on, for an instant in furious silhouette against the stars, the tranquil early summer night sky which, even before the shape of the horse and rider vanished, stained abruptly and violently upward: a long, swirling roar incredible and soundless, blotting the stars, and he springing up and into the road again, running again, knowing it was too late yet still running even after he heard the shot and, an instant later, two shots, pausing now without knowing he had ceased to run, crying "Pap! Pap!", running again before he knew he had begun to run, stumbling, tripping over something and scrabbling up again without ceasing to run, looking backward over his shoulder at the glare as he got up, running on among the invisible trees, panting, sobbing, "Father! Father!"

At midnight he was sitting on the crest of a hill. He did not know it was midnight and he did not know how far he had come. But there was no glare behind him now and he sat now, his back toward what he had called home for four days anyhow, his face toward the dark woods which he would enter when breath was strong again, small, shaking steadily in the chill darkness, hugging himself into the remainder of his thin, rotten shirt, the grief and despair now no longer terror and fear but just grief and despair. *Father. My father,* he thought. "He was brave!" he cried suddenly, aloud but not loud, no more than a whisper: "He was! He was in the war! He was in Colonel Sartoris' cav'ry!" not knowing that his father had gone to that war a private in the fine old European sense, wearing no uniform, admitting the authority of and giving fidelity to no man or army or flag, going to war as Malbrouck[2] himself did: for booty—it meant nothing and less than nothing to him if it were enemy booty or his own.

The slow constellations wheeled on. It would be dawn and then sun-up after a while and he would be hungry. But that would be to-morrow and now he was only cold, and walking would cure that. His breathing was easier now and he decided to get up and go on, and then he found that he had been asleep because he knew it was almost dawn, the night almost over. He could tell that from the whippoorwills. They were everywhere now among the dark trees below him, constant and inflectioned and ceaseless, so that, as the instant for giving over to the day birds drew nearer and nearer, there was no interval at all between them. He got up. He was a little stiff, but walking would cure that too as it would the cold, and soon there would be the sun. He went on down the hill, toward the dark woods within which the liquid silver voices of the birds called unceasing—the rapid and urgent beating of the urgent and quiring heart of the late spring night. He did not look back.

1938

2. Figure in an 18th-century French ballad, "Malbrouck Has Gone to the War," popularly identified with John Churchill, First Duke of Marlborough (1650–1722), who rose through the ranks from private to become a famous commander. Despite his military genius, he was often accused of greed and disloyalty.

HART CRANE
1899–1932

Before his suicide at the age of thirty-two, Hart Crane led a life of extremes: he wrote poetry of frequently ecstatic intensity, drank uncontrollably, had bitterly ambivalent relations with his quarreling parents; he relished the comparative erotic freedom of post–World War I Greenwich Village while enduring his literary friends' disapproval of his homosexuality. Born and raised in Ohio, Crane went to New York

City in 1917, ostensibly to prepare for college but in fact to investigate the possibility of a literary career. Returning to Cleveland for four years (1919–23), he tried unsuccessfully to enter business as a means of financing an after-hours literary life. During these years he read widely and developed a large circle of intellectual friends and correspondents. He also published some of the poems that made his early reputation: "My Grandmother's Love Letters" in 1920, "Chaplinesque" in 1921, and "For the Marriage of Faustus and Helen" in 1922. He also began work on the love sequence *Voyages*. By 1923, believing himself ready to succeed as a writer, he moved back to New York City.

His most productive years came between 1923 and 1927. He completed *Voyages* in 1924, published his first collection, *White Buildings,* in 1926, and composed ten of the fifteen poems that were to make up *The Bridge* in 1926. He held occasional jobs, but received most of his support from his parents, friends, and above all from the patronage of a banker, Otto Kahn. Crane defined himself as a follower of Walt Whitman in the visionary, prophetic, affirmative American tradition, aiming at nothing less than to master the techniques of modernism while reversing its direction—to make it positive, celebratory, and deeply meshed with contemporary American life without sacrificing technical complexity or richness. For him as for the somewhat older William Carlos Williams, T. S. Eliot's *The Waste Land* was both threat and model. That poem could become an "absolute impasse," he wrote, unless one could "go *through* it to a different goal," leaving its negations behind. This was the task he attempted in *The Bridge*.

Crane's practice centered on metaphor—the device that, in his view, represented the difference between poetry and expository prose. He believed that metaphor had preceded logic in the development of human thought and that it still remained the primary mode in which human knowledge was acquired and through which experience was connected to mind. The center of *The Bridge,* for example, is the Brooklyn Bridge—a tangible object transformed metaphorically into the sign of connection, technology, America, history, and the future. The poem, published in 1930, was not particularly well received by the critics; this was a great disappointment to Crane, and even though *Poetry* magazine awarded it a prize and the Guggenheim Foundation gave him a fellowship in the same year, he was perplexed about his future. In Mexico he completed work for a third book, *Key West,* but on the return trip to New York City he jumped overboard and drowned.

The Bridge is a visionary poem made up of fifteen individual sections of varying lengths. It encapsulates a heroic quest, at once personal and epic, to find and enunciate "America." Like Walt Whitman's "Song of the Open Road," which also focused on a symbol of expansion and dynamism, *The Bridge* moves westward in imagination from Brooklyn to California. It also goes back into the American past, dwelling on historical or legendary figures such as Columbus, Pocahontas, and Rip Van Winkle. It moves upward under the guidance of Whitman; down in "The Tunnel" it meets the wandering spirit of Edgar Allan Poe. The material bridge stands at the center of all this motion and stands, finally, for the poem and poetry itself. The separate lyrics making up *The Bridge* are arranged like music, with recurring, modulated themes rather than a narrative or an expository line. As in most modernist poems, the verse is open and varied, the syntax complicated and often ambiguous, the references often dependent on a personal, sometimes inaccessible train of thought. Like his model Whitman, Crane wrote from the paradoxical, conflicted position of the outsider claiming to speak from and for the very center of America.

The text of the poems included here is that of *Complete Poems of Hart Crane,* edited by Marc Simon (1993).

Chaplinesque[1]

We make our meek adjustments,
Contented with such random consolations
As the wind deposits
In slithered and too ample pockets.

For we can still love the world, who find
A famished kitten on the step, and know
Recesses for it from the fury of the street,
Or warm torn elbow coverts.

We will sidestep, and to the final smirk
Dally the doom of that inevitable thumb
That slowly chafes its puckered index toward us,
Facing the dull squint with what innocence
And what surprise!

And yet these fine collapses are not lies
More than the pirouettes of any pliant cane;
Our obsequies[2] are, in a way, no enterprise.
We can evade you, and all else but the heart:
What blame to us if the heart live on.

The game enforces smirks; but we have seen
The moon in lonely alleys make
A grail of laughter of an empty ash can,
And through all sound of gaiety and quest
Have heard a kitten in the wilderness.

1921, 1926

At Melville's Tomb[1]

Often beneath the wave, wide from this ledge
The dice of drowned men's bones he saw bequeath
An embassy. Their numbers as he watched,
Beat on the dusty shore and were obscured.[2]

1. Crane wrote of seeing Charlie Chaplin's film *The Kid* (1921) and said that he aimed "to put in words some of the Chaplin pantomime, so beautiful, and so full of eloquence, and so modern." The film "made me feel myself, as a poet, as being 'in the same boat' with him," Crane wrote.
2. In the double sense of "funeral rites" and "obsequiousness."
1. This poem was published in *Poetry* magazine only after Crane provided the editor, Harriet Monroe, with a detailed explanation of its images. His letter and Monroe's inquiries and comments were published with the poem. Crane's detailed comments in the letter are incorporated in the notes to the poem. Herman Melville (1819–1891), American author.
2. "Dice bequeath an embassy, in the first place, by being ground (in this connection only, of course) in little cubes from the bones of drowned men by the action of the sea, and are finally thrown up on the sand, having 'numbers' but no identification. These being the bones of dead men who never completed their voyage, it seems legitimate to refer to them as the only surviving evidence of certain messages undelivered, mute evidence of certain things. . . . Dice as a symbol of chance and circumstance is also implied" [Crane's note].

And wrecks passed without sound of bells,
The calyx of death's bounty giving back
A scattered chapter, livid hieroglyph,
The portent wound in corridors of shells.[3]

Then in the circuit calm of one vast coil,
Its lashings charmed and malice reconciled,
Frosted eyes there were that lifted altars;[4]
And silent answers crept across the stars.

Compass, quadrant and sextant contrive
No farther tides[5] . . . High in the azure steeps
Monody shall not wake the mariner.
This fabulous shadow only the sea keeps.

1926

From The Bridge

From going to and fro in the earth,
and from walking up and down in it.
—The Book of Job[1]

To Brooklyn Bridge

How many dawns, chill from his rippling rest
The seagull's wings shall dip and pivot him,
Shedding white rings of tumult, building high
Over the chained bay waters Liberty—

Then, with inviolate curve, forsake our eyes
As apparitional as sails that cross
Some page of figures to be filed away;
—Till elevators drop us from our day . . .

3. "This calyx refers in a double ironic sense both to a cornucopia and the vortex made by a sinking vessel. As soon as the water has closed over a ship this whirlpool sends up broken spars, wreckage, etc., which can be alluded to as livid *hieroglyphs,* making a *scattered chapter* so far as any complete record of the recent ship and crew is concerned. In fact, about as much definite knowledge might come from all this as anyone might gain from the roar of his own veins, which is easily heard (haven't you ever done it?) by holding a shell close to one's ear" [Crane's note]. A calyx is a whorl of leaves forming the outer casing of the bud of a plant.

4. "Refers simply to a conviction that a man, not knowing perhaps a definite god yet being endowed with a reverence for deity—such a man naturally postulates a deity somehow, and the altar of that deity by the very *action* of the eyes *lifted* in searching" [Crane's note].

5. "Hasn't it often occurred that instruments originally invented for record and computation have inadvertently so extended the concepts of the entity they were invented to measure (concepts of space, etc.) in the mind and imagination that employed them, that they may metaphorically be said to have extended the original boundaries of the entity measured? This little bit of 'relativity' ought not to be discredited in poetry now that scientists are proceeding to measure the universe on principles of pure *ratio,* quite as metaphorical, so far as previous standards of scientific methods extended, as some of the axioms in *Job*" [Crane's note].

1. Satan's answer to Jehovah when asked where he has been (Job 1.7).

I think of cinemas, panoramic sleights
With multitudes bent toward some flashing scene
Never disclosed, but hastened to again,
Foretold to other eyes on the same screen;

And Thee, across the harbor, silver-paced
As though the sun took step of thee, yet left
Some motion ever unspent in thy stride,—
Implicitly thy freedom staying thee!

Out of some subway scuttle, cell or loft
A bedlamite[2] *speeds to thy parapets,*
Tilting there momently, shrill shirt ballooning,
A jest falls from the speechless caravan.

Down Wall, from girder into street noon leaks,
A rip-tooth of the sky's acetylene;
All afternoon the cloud-flown derricks turn . . .
Thy cables breathe the North Atlantic still.

And obscure as that heaven of the Jews,
Thy guerdon . . . Accolade thou dost bestow
Of anonymity time cannot raise:
Vibrant reprieve and pardon thou dost show.

O harp and altar, of the fury fused,
(How could mere toil align thy choiring strings!)
Terrific threshold of the prophet's pledge,
Prayer of pariah, and the lover's cry,—

Again the traffic lights that skim thy swift
Unfractioned idiom, immaculate sigh of stars,
Beading thy path—condense eternity:
And we have seen night lifted in thine arms.

Under thy shadow by the piers I waited;
Only in darkness is thy shadow clear.
The City's fiery parcels all undone,
Already snow submerges an iron year . . .

O Sleepless as the river under thee,
Vaulting the sea, the prairies' dreaming sod,
Unto us lowliest sometime sweep, descend
And of the curveship lend a myth to God.

1927, 1930

2. Insane person, patient in a hospital for the mentally ill.

From II. Powhatan's Daughter[1]

* * *

The River[2]

. . . and past the din and slogans of the year—

Stick your patent name on a signboard
brother—all over—going west—young man
Tintex—Japalac—Certain-teed Overalls ads[3]
and lands sakes! under the new playbill ripped
in the guaranteed corner—see Bert Williams[4] what?
Minstrels when you steal a chicken just
save me the wing for if it isn't
Erie it ain't for miles around a
Mazda—and the telegraphic night coming on Thomas

a Ediford[5]—and whistling down the tracks
a headlight rushing with the sound—can you
imagine—while an EXpress makes time like
SCIENCE—COMMERCE AND THE HOLYGHOST
RADIO ROARS IN EVERY HOME WE HAVE THE NORTHPOLE
WALLSTREET AND VIRGINBIRTH WITHOUT STONES OR
WIRES OR EVEN RUNning brooks connecting ears
and no more sermons windows flashing roar
breathtaking—as you like it[6] . . . eh?

So the 20th Century—so
whizzed the Limited—roared by and left
three men, still hungry on the tracks, ploddingly
watching the tail lights wizen and converge, slipping gimleted and neatly out of sight.

• • • • • • •

to those whose addresses are never near

The last bear, shot drinking in the Dakotas
Loped under wires that span the mountain stream.
Keen instruments,[7] strung to a vast precision
Bind town to town and dream to ticking dream.
But some men take their liquor slow—and count
—Though they'll confess no rosary nor clue—

1. Powhatan was the Native American chief with whom English settlers in Virginia (1607) had to deal. Pocahontas (1595–1617) was his daughter, whom Crane associated with the American "continent," a "nature symbol" comparable to the "traditional Hertha of ancient Teutonic mythology."
2. Crane wrote the following in a letter: "I'm trying in this part of the poem to chart the pioneer experience of our forefathers—and to tell the story backwards . . . on the 'backs' of hoboes. These hoboes are simply 'psychological ponies' to carry the reader across the country and back to the Mississippi, which you will notice is described as a great River of Time. I also unlatch the door to the pure Indian world which opens out in 'The Dance' section, so the reader is gradually led back in time to the pure savage world, while existing at the same time in the present." In the opening lines the image of a subway is translated into an image of a luxury express train, the Twentieth Century Limited, traveling from New York City to Chicago.
3. Advertising slogans: trade names of a dye, a varnish, and a brand of overalls.
4. Egbert A. Williams (1876–1922), popular black minstrel show performer.
5. A combined reference to Thomas Edison (1847–1931), inventor of the electric lightbulb (trade name "Mazda"), and Henry Ford (1863–1947), automobile manufacturer.
6. An echo of Shakespeare's *As You Like It* 2.1.16–17: "Books in the running brooks, / Sermons in stones."
7. The telephone and telegraph.

The river's minute by the far brook's year.
Under a world of whistles, wires and steam
Caboose-like they go ruminating through
Ohio, Indiana—blind baggage—
To Cheyenne tagging . . . Maybe Kalamazoo.

Time's rendings, time's blendings they construe
As final reckonings of fire and snow;
Strange bird-wit, like the elemental gist
Of unwalled winds they offer, singing low
My Old Kentucky Home and *Casey Jones,*
Some Sunny Day. I heard a road-gang chanting so.

And afterwards, who had a colt's eyes—one said,
"Jesus! Oh I remember watermelon days!" And sped
High in a cloud of merriment, recalled
"—And when my Aunt Sally Simpson smiled," he drawled—
"It was almost Louisiana, long ago."
"There's no place like Booneville though, Buddy,"
One said, excising a last burr from his vest,
"—For early trouting." Then peering in the can,
"—But I kept on the tracks." Possessed, resigned,
He trod the fire down pensively and grinned,
Spreading dry shingles of a beard. . . .

Behind
My father's cannery works I used to see
Rail-squatters ranged in nomad raillery,
The ancient men—wifeless or runaway
Hobo-trekkers that forever search
An empire wilderness of freight and rails.
Each seemed a child, like me, on a loose perch,
Holding to childhood like some termless play.
John, Jake or Charley, hopping the slow freight
—Memphis to Tallahassee—riding the rods,
Blind fists of nothing, humpty-dumpty clods.

Yet they touch something like a key perhaps.
From pole to pole across the hills, the states
—They know a body under the wide rain;
Youngsters with eyes like fjords, old reprobates
With racetrack jargon,—dotting immensity
They lurk across her, knowing her yonder breast
Snow-silvered, sumac-stained or smoky blue—
Is past the valley-sleepers, south or west.
—As I have trod the rumorous midnights, too,

but who have touched her, knowing her without name

And past the circuit of the lamp's thin flame
(O Nights that brought me to her body bare!)
Have dreamed beyond the print that bound her name.
Trains sounding the long blizzards out—I heard
Wail into distances I knew were hers.

Papooses crying on the wind's long mane
Screamed redskin dynasties that fled the brain,
—Dead echoes! But I knew her body there,
Time like a serpent down her shoulder, dark,
And space, an eaglet's wing, laid on her hair.

Under the Ozarks, domed by Iron Mountain,
The old gods of the rain lie wrapped in pools
Where eyeless fish curvet a sunken fountain
And re-descend with corn from querulous crows.
Such pilferings make up their timeless eatage,
Propitiate them for their timber torn
By iron, iron—always the iron dealt cleavage!
They doze now, below axe and powder horn.

nor the myths of her fathers . . .

And Pullman breakfasters glide glistening steel
From tunnel into field—iron strides the dew—
Straddles the hill, a dance of wheel on wheel.
You have a half-hour's wait at Siskiyou,
Or stay the night and take the next train through.
Southward, near Cairo passing, you can see
The Ohio merging,—borne down Tennessee;
And if it's summer and the sun's in dusk
Maybe the breeze will lift the River's musk
—As though the waters breathed that you might know
Memphis Johnny, Steamboat Bill, Missouri Joe.
Oh, lean from the window, if the train slows down,
As though you touched hands with some ancient clown,
—A little while gaze absently below
And hum *Deep River* with them while they go.

Yes, turn again and sniff once more—look see,
O Sheriff, Brakeman and Authority—
Hitch up your pants and crunch another quid,[8]
For you, too, feed the River timelessly.

And few evade full measure of their fate;
Always they smile out eerily what they seem.
I could believe he joked at heaven's gate—
Dan Midland—jolted from the cold brake-beam.[9]

Down, down—born pioneers in time's despite,
Grimed tributaries to an ancient flow—
They win no frontier by their wayward plight,
But drift in stillness, as from Jordan's[1] brow.

You will not hear it as the sea; even stone
Is not more hushed by gravity . . . But slow,
As loth to take more tribute—sliding prone

8. Chunk of chewing tobacco.
9. Structure on a railroad car where hoboes ride. Dan Midland was a legendary hobo who fell to his death from a train.
1. River mentioned frequently in the Bible.

Like one whose eyes were buried long ago
The River, spreading, flows—and spends your dream.
What are you, lost within this tideless spell?
You are your father's father, and the stream—
A liquid theme that floating niggers swell.

Damp tonnage and alluvial march of days—
Nights turbid, vascular with silted shale
And roots surrendered down of moraine clays:
The Mississippi drinks the farthest dale.

O quarrying passion, undertowed sunlight!
The basalt surface drags a jungle grace
Ochreous and lynx-barred in lengthening might;
Patience! and you shall reach the biding place!

Over De Soto's bones the freighted floors
Throb past the City storied of three thrones.[2]
Down two more turns the Mississippi pours
(Anon tall ironsides[3] up from salt lagoons)

And flows within itself, heaps itself free.
All fades but one thin skyline 'round . . . Ahead
No embrace opens but the stinging sea;
The River lifts itself from its long bed,

Poised wholly on its dream, a mustard glow
Tortured with history, its one will—flow!
—The Passion spreads in wide tongues, choked and slow,
Meeting the Gulf, hosannas silently below.

1930

VII. The Tunnel

To Find the Western path
Right thro' the Gates of Wrath.
—Blake[1]

Performances, assortments, résumés—
Up Times Square to Columbus Circle lights
Channel the congresses, nightly sessions,
Refractions of the thousand theatres, faces—
Mysterious kitchens. . . . You shall search them all.
Someday by heart you'll learn each famous sight
And watch the curtain lift in hell's despite;
You'll find the garden in the third act dead,

2. New Orleans, at various times under Spanish, French, and English rule. The body of the Spanish explorer Hernándo de Soto (1500–1542) was consigned to the Mississippi River. In 1862 Admiral David G. Farragut (1801–1870) led a Union fleet up the Mississippi from the Gulf and captured New Orleans.

3. Warships.

1. The opening lines of "Morning," by the visionary English poet William Blake (1757–1827).

Finger your knees—and wish yourself in bed
With tabloid crime-sheets perched in easy sight.

Then let you reach your hat
and go.
As usual, let you—also
walking down—exclaim
to twelve upward leaving
a subscription praise
for what time slays.

Or can't you quite make up your mind to ride;
A walk is better underneath the L[2] a brisk
Ten blocks or so before? But you find yourself
Preparing penguin flexions of the arms,—
As usual you will meet the scuttle yawn:
The subway yawns the quickest promise home.

Be minimum, then, to swim the hiving swarms
Out of the Square, the Circle burning bright[3]—
Avoid the glass doors gyring at your right,
Where boxed alone a second, eyes take fright
—Quite unprepared rush naked back to light:
And down beside the turnstile press the coin
Into the slot. The gongs already rattle.

And so
of cities you bespeak
subways, rivered under streets
and rivers. . . . In the car
the overtone of motion
underground, the monotone
of motion is the sound
of other faces, also underground—

"Let's have a pencil Jimmy—living now
at Floral Park
Flatbush—on the fourth of July—
like a pigeon's muddy dream—potatoes
to dig in the field—travlin the town—too—
night after night—the Culver line—the
girls all shaping up—it used to be—"

Our tongues recant like beaten weather vanes.
This answer lives like verdigris,[4] like hair
Beyond extinction, surcease of the bone;
And repetition freezes—"What
"what do you want? getting weak on the links?
fandaddle daddy don't ask for change—IS THIS
FOURTEENTH? it's half past six she said—if

2. Elevated railway.
3. An echo of Blake's poem "The Tyger"; also the lighted sign indicating a subway station.
4. Green coating or stain on copper.

you don't like my gate why did you
swing on it, why *didja*
swing on it
anyhow—"

And somehow anyhow swing—

The phonographs of hades in the brain
Are tunnels that re-wind themselves, and love
A burnt match skating in a urinal—
Somewhere above Fourteenth TAKE THE EXPRESS
To brush some new presentiment of pain—
"But I want service in this office SERVICE
I said—after
the show she cried a little afterwards but—"

Whose head is swinging from the swollen strap?
Whose body smokes along the bitten rails,
Bursts from a smoldering bundle far behind
In back forks of the chasms of the brain,—
Puffs from a riven stump far out behind
In interborough fissures of the mind . . . ?

And why do I often meet your visage here,
Your eyes like agate lanterns—on and on
Below the toothpaste and the dandruff ads?
—And did their riding eyes right through your side,
And did their eyes like unwashed platters ride?
And Death, aloft,—gigantically down
Probing through you—toward me, O evermore![5]
And when they dragged your retching flesh,
Your trembling hands that night through Baltimore—
That last night on the ballot rounds, did you,
Shaking, did you deny the ticket, Poe?

For Gravesend Manor change at Chambers Street.
The platform hurries along to a dead stop.

The intent escalator lifts a serenade
Stilly
Of shoes, umbrellas, each eye attending its shoe, then
Bolting outright somewhere above where streets
Burst suddenly in rain. . . . The gongs recur:
Elbows and levers, guard and hissing door.
Thunder is galvothermic[6] here below. . . . The car
Wheels off. The train rounds, bending to a scream,
Taking the final level for the dive
Under the river—

5. Echoes of "the agate lamp within thy hand" from "To Helen," "Death looks gigantically down" from "The City in the Sea," and the refrain "Nevermore" in "The Raven" —poems by Edgar Allan Poe (1809–1849).

6. I.e., galvanothermic, producing heat by electricity.

And somewhat emptier than before,
Demented, for a hitching second, humps; then
Lets go. . . . Toward corners of the floor
Newspapers wing, revolve and wing.
Blank windows gargle signals through the roar.

And does the Daemon take you home, also,
Wop washerwoman, with the bandaged hair?
After the corridors are swept, the cuspidors—
The gaunt sky-barracks cleanly now, and bare,
O Genoese, do you bring mother eyes and hands
Back home to children and to golden hair?

Daemon, demurring and eventful yawn!
Whose hideous laughter is a bellows mirth
—Or the muffled slaughter of a day in birth—
O cruelly to inoculate the brinking dawn
With antennae toward worlds that glow and sink;—
To spoon us out more liquid than the dim
Locution of the eldest star, and pack
The conscience navelled in the plunging wind,
Umbilical to call—and straightway die!

O caught like pennies beneath soot and steam,
Kiss of our agony thou gatherest;
Condensed, thou takest all—shrill ganglia
Impassioned with some song we fail to keep.
And yet, like Lazarus,[7] to feel the slope,
The sod and billow breaking,—lifting ground,
—A sound of waters bending astride the sky
Unceasing with some Word that will not die . . . !

• • • • • •

A tugboat, wheezing wreaths of steam,
Lunged past, with one galvanic blare stove up the River.
I counted the echoes assembling, one after one,
Searching, thumbing the midnight on the piers.
Lights, coasting, left the oily tympanum of waters;
The blackness somewhere gouged glass on a sky.
And this thy harbor, O my City, I have driven under,
Tossed from the coil of ticking towers. . . . Tomorrow,
And to be. . . . Here by the River that is East—
Here at the waters' edge the hands drop memory;
Shadowless in that abyss they unaccounting lie.
How far away the star has pooled the sea—
Or shall the hands be drawn away, to die?
Kiss of our agony Thou gatherest,
O Hand of Fire
gatherest—

1927, 1930

7. He was resurrected from the grave by Jesus in John 11.43–44.

ERNEST HEMINGWAY
1899–1961

The narrator in Ernest Hemingway's *A Farewell to Arms,* reflecting on his war experiences, observes at one point, "I was always embarrassed by the words sacred, glorious, and sacrifice and the expression in vain. . . . I had seen nothing sacred, and the things that were glorious had no glory and the sacrifices were like the stockyards at Chicago if nothing was done with the meat except to bury it. There were many words that you could not stand to hear." Hemingway's aim and achievement as a novelist and short-story writer were to convey his concerns in a prose style built from what was left after eliminating all the words one "could not stand to hear." As flamboyant in his personal style as he was severe in his writing, Hemingway became an international celebrity after the publication in 1926 of his first novel, *The Sun Also Rises.* At the time of his death, he was probably the most famous writer in the world.

He was born and raised in Oak Park, Illinois, one of six children. His mother was a music teacher, director of the church choir, and a lover of high culture who had contemplated a career as an opera singer. His father was a successful physician, prone to depression, who enjoyed hunting, fishing, and cooking and who shared in household responsibilities more than most men of his era. The family spent summers at their cottage in northern Michigan, where many of Hemingway's stories are set. After high school, Hemingway took a job on the *Kansas City Star.* When the United States entered the war in 1917, Hemingway was eager to go. An eye problem barred him from the army, so he joined the ambulance corps. Within three weeks he was wounded by shrapnel. After six months in the hospital Hemingway went home as a decorated hero: when wounded, he had carried a comrade more badly hurt than he to safety (see p. 204). He found readjustment difficult and became increasingly estranged from his family, especially his mother. Years later, when his father committed suicide, Hemingway blamed his mother for that death.

In 1920 he married Hadley Richardson and went to Paris. Supported partly by her money and partly by his journalism, Hemingway worked at becoming a writer. He came to know Gertrude Stein, Sherwood Anderson, Ezra Pound, F. Scott Fitzgerald, and others in the large community of expatriate artistic and literary Americans. Besides reading his manuscripts and advising him, Fitzgerald and Anderson, better known than he, used their influence to get his book of short stories *In Our Time* published in the United States in 1925. In this book, stories about the adolescent Nick Adams as he grows up in northern Michigan alternate with very brief, powerful vignettes of war and crime.

In 1926 his novel *The Sun Also Rises* appeared; it presents the stripped-down "Hemingway style" at its finest. "I always try to write on the principle of the iceberg," he told an interviewer. "There is seven-eighths of it under water for every part that shows." Narrated by Jake Barnes, whose World War I wounds have left him sexually impotent, *The Sun Also Rises* depicts Jake's efforts to live according to a self-conscious code of dignity, of "grace under pressure," in the midst of a circle of self-seeking American and English expatriates in Paris—the "lost generation," as Gertrude Stein dubbed them. He finds an ideal in the rich tradition of Spanish peasant life, especially as epitomized in bullfighting and the bullfighter. *The Sun Also Rises* was directly responsible for a surge of American tourism to Pamplona, Spain, where the novel's bullfights are set.

In 1927 Hemingway brought out his second collection of stories, *Men without Women.* Adapting journalistic techniques in telegraphic prose that minimized narrator commentary and depended heavily on uncontextualized dialogue, these stories developed the modern, speeded-up, streamlined style exemplified in "Hills Like White Elephants." His second novel, *A Farewell to Arms,* appeared in 1929. It described a romance between an American army officer, Frederic Henry, and a British nurse, Catherine Barkley. The two run away from war, trying to make "a separate peace," but their idyll is shattered when Catherine dies in childbirth. Hemingway's work has been much criticized for its depictions of women. The wholly good Catherine lives for Frederic Henry alone; and Maria, in his Spanish Civil War novel (*For Whom the Bell Tolls,* 1940), is a fantasy figure of total submissiveness. Characters like Brett Ashley in *The Sun Also Rises* and Pilar in *For Whom the Bell Tolls,* however, are strong, complex figures. Overall, Hemingway identified the rapid change in women's status after World War I and the general blurring of sex roles that accompanied the new sexual freedom as aspects of modernity that men were simultaneously attracted to and found hard to deal with. More recently, especially in light of the themes of some of his posthumously published writings, critics have begun to reinterpret Hemingway's work as preoccupied with the cultural and psychological meanings of masculinity in a way that bespeaks considerable sexual ambivalence.

As Hemingway aged, his interest in exclusively masculine forms of self-assertion and self-definition became more pronounced. War, hunting, and similar pursuits that he had used at first to show men manifesting dignity in the face of certain defeat increasingly became depicted (in his life as well as his writing) as occasions for competitive masculine display and triumph. Soon after the publication of *The Sun Also Rises,* his first marriage broke up; in all he was married four times. In the 1930s and 1940s he adopted the style of life of a celebrity. Some of his best-known work from these years, such as "The Snows of Kilimanjaro" (1936), treats the theme of the successful writer losing his talent in an atmosphere of success, adulation, and wealth.

A political loner distrustful of all ideological abstractions, Hemingway was nevertheless drawn into antifascist politics by the Spanish Civil War. In *To Have and Have Not* (1937), the earliest of his political novels, the good characters are working-class people and the antagonists are idle rich. *For Whom the Bell Tolls* draws on Hemingway's experiences in Spain as a war correspondent, celebrating both the peasant antifascists and the Americans who fought on their behalf. Hemingway's opposition to fascism did not, however, keep him from viewing the pro-Loyalist communists, who were also active in the Spanish Civil War, with considerable skepticism. His one play, *The Fifth Column*—which was printed along with his collected stories in 1938 and staged in 1940—specifically blames the communists for betraying the cause.

Hemingway was fiercely anti-Nazi during World War II. As well as working as a war correspondent, work that sent him often to Europe, he used his fishing boat to keep watch for German submarines off the coast of Cuba, where he had a home. After the war ended, he continued his travels and was badly hurt in Africa in January 1954 in the crash of a small plane. He had already published his allegorical fable *The Old Man and the Sea* (1952), in the mass-circulation weekly magazine *Life;* this, his last major work published during his lifetime, won a Pulitzer Prize in 1953 and was central to his winning the Nobel Prize in 1954. The plane crash had damaged his mental and physical health, and he never fully recovered. Subject increasingly to depression and an incapacitating paranoia—afflictions that seem to have run in his family—he was hospitalized several times before killing himself in 1961. Yet it does appear that some of his suspicions about being watched by U.S. government agents may have been justified. Many writers associated with radical causes had dossiers compiled on them by the FBI. Several books have been published posthumously based on the voluminous manuscript collections he left. These include a book of reminiscences about his life in 1920s Paris, *A Moveable Feast* (1964); a novel about literary fame and sexual ambiguity constructed from several unfinished drafts, *The Garden of Eden* (1986); and *The Nick Adams Stories* (1972), a collection that added eight previously unpublished stories to the group.

From The Sun Also Rises[1]

Chapter III

[IT WAS A WARM SPRING NIGHT]

It was a warm spring night and I sat at a table on the terrace of the Napolitain after Robert[2] had gone, watching it get dark and the electric signs come on, and the red and green stop-and-go traffic-signal, and the crowd going by, and the horse-cabs clippety-clopping along at the edge of the solid taxi traffic, and the *poules*[3] going by, singly and in pairs, looking for the evening meal. I watched a good-looking girl walk past the table and watched her go up the street and lost sight of her, and watched another, and then saw the first one coming back again. She went by once more and I caught her eye, and she came over and sat down at the table. The waiter came up.

"Well, what will you drink?" I asked.

"Pernod."

"That's not good for little girls."

"Little girl yourself. Dites garçon, un pernod."[4]

"A pernod for me, too."

"What's the matter?" she asked. "Going on a party?"

"Sure. Aren't you?"

"I don't know. You never know in this town."

"Don't you like Paris?"

"No."

"Why don't you go somewhere else?"

"Isn't anywhere else."

"You're happy, all right."

"Happy, hell!"

Pernod is greenish imitation absinthe.[5] When you add water it turns milky. It tastes like licorice and it has a good uplift, but it drops you just as far. We sat and drank it, and the girl looked sullen.

"Well," I said, "are you going to buy me a dinner?"

She grinned and I saw why she made a point of not laughing. With her mouth closed she was a rather pretty girl. I paid for the saucers and we walked out to the street. I hailed a horse-cab and the driver pulled up at the curb. Settled back in the slow, smoothly rolling *fiacre* we moved up the Avenue de

1. The text is that of the first edition (1926), published by Charles Scribner's Sons. Hemingway's two epigraphs to the novel cite a remark by Gertrude Stein—"You are all a lost generation"—and Ecclesiastes 1.4–7: "One generation passeth away, and another generation cometh: but the earth abideth for ever. . . . The sun also ariseth, and the sun goeth down, and hasteth to his place where he arose. . . . The wind goeth toward the south, and turneth about unto the north; it whirleth about continually, and the wind returneth again according to his circuits. . . . All the rivers run into the sea; yet the sea is not full; unto the place from whence the rivers come, thither they return again."

2. Robert Cohn, an American expatriate writer with whom the narrator, Jake Barnes, has a barbed, competitive friendship. Barnes like Cohn is an aspiring author, but Cohn has just had his first novel accepted for publication. Cohn also has family money backing his literary career, while Barnes supports himself as a journalist. Cohn has recently become romantically interested in Lady Brett Ashley, a British divorcée whom Barnes met during World War I at a military hospital where she was a volunteer. Although Jake and Brett are intensely attracted to one another, his war wound has left him unable to consummate a sexual relationship. As the chapter begins, Barnes and Cohn have just had a drink together following the end of Barnes's working day, much of which Cohn spent loitering in Barnes's office.

3. Hens (French, literal trans.); slang for *prostitutes*.

4. Tell the waiter, a pernod (French).

5. An anise- and herb-flavored, highly alcoholic spirit.

l'Opéra,[6] passed the locked doors of the shops, their windows lighted, the Avenue broad and shiny and almost deserted. The cab passed the New York *Herald* bureau with the window full of clocks.

"What are all the clocks for?" she asked.

"They show the hour all over America."

"Don't kid me."

We turned off the Avenue up the Rue des Pyramides, through the traffic of the Rue de Rivoli, and through a dark gate into the Tuileries.[7] She cuddled against me and I put my arm around her. She looked up to be kissed. She touched me with one hand and I put her hand away.

"Never mind."

"What's the matter? You sick?"

"Yes."

"Everybody's sick. I'm sick, too."

We came out of the Tuileries into the light and crossed the Seine and then turned up the Rue des Saints Pères.[8]

"You oughtn't to drink pernod if you're sick."

"You neither."

"It doesn't make any difference with me. It doesn't make any difference with a woman."

"What are you called?"

"Georgette. How are you called?"

"Jacob."

"That's a Flemish name."

"American too."

"You're not Flamand?"

"No, American."

"Good, I detest Flamands."

By this time we were at the restaurant. I called to the *cocher*[9] to stop. We got out and Georgette did not like the looks of the place. "This is no great thing of a restaurant."

"No," I said. "Maybe you would rather go to Foyot's.[1] Why don't you keep the cab and go on?"

I had picked her up because of a vague sentimental idea that it would be nice to eat with some one. It was a long time since I had dined with a *poule*, and I had forgotten how dull it could be. We went into the restaurant, passed Madame Lavigne at the desk and into a little room. Georgette cheered up a little under the food.

"It isn't bad here," she said. "It isn't chic, but the food is all right."

"Better than you eat in Liège."

"Brussels,[2] you mean."

We had another bottle of wine and Georgette made a joke. She smiled and showed all her bad teeth, and we touched glasses.

6. Major Parisian thoroughfare running from the Louvre to the Palais Garnier, Paris's central opera house. *"Fiacre"*: a small horse carriage.
7. The large formal garden in the center of Paris. The streets are also in central Paris.
8. St. Peter's Street, on the Left Bank. The Seine divides Paris into the Right Bank, associated with business, wealth, and the state, and the Left Bank, traditionally the neighborhood of artists and students.
9. Coachman.
1. A famous, luxurious restaurant on the Right Bank, frequented by politicians and businessmen.
2. Belgian cities. Liège is historically French speaking; Brussels historically Dutch speaking.

"You're not a bad type," she said. "It's a shame you're sick. We get on well. What's the matter with you, anyway?"

"I got hurt in the war," I said.

"Oh, that dirty war."

We would probably have gone on and discussed the war and agreed that it was in reality a calamity for civilization, and perhaps would have been better avoided. I was bored enough. Just then from the other room some one called: "Barnes! I say, Barnes! Jacob Barnes!"

"It's a friend calling me," I explained, and went out.

There was Braddocks at a big table with a party: Cohn, Frances Clyne,[3] Mrs. Braddocks, several people I did not know.

"You're coming to the dance, aren't you?" Braddocks asked.

"What dance?"

"Why, the dancings. Don't you know we've revived them?" Mrs. Braddocks put in.

"You must come, Jake. We're all going," Frances said from the end of the table. She was tall and had a smile.

"Of course, he's coming," Braddocks said. "Come in and have coffee with us, Barnes."

"Right."

"And bring your friend," said Mrs. Braddocks laughing. She was a Canadian and had all their easy social graces.

"Thanks, we'll be in," I said. I went back to the small room.

"Who are your friends?" Georgette asked.

"Writers and artists."

"There are lots of those on this side of the river."

"Too many."

"I think so. Still, some of them make money."

"Oh, yes."

We finished the meal and the wine. "Come on," I said. "We're going to have coffee with the others."

Georgette opened her bag, made a few passes at her face as she looked in the little mirror, re-defined her lips with the lipstick, and straightened her hat.

"Good," she said.

We went into the room full of people and Braddocks and the men at his table stood up.

"I wish to present my fiancée, Mademoiselle Georgette Leblanc," I said. Georgette smiled that wonderful smile, and we shook hands all round.

"Are you related to Georgette Leblanc,[4] the singer?" Mrs. Braddocks asked.

"Connais pas,"[5] Georgette answered.

"But you have the same name," Mrs. Braddocks insisted cordially.

"No," said Georgette. "Not at all. My name is Hobin."

"But Mr. Barnes introduced you as Mademoiselle Georgette Leblanc. Surely he did," insisted Mrs. Braddocks, who in the excitement of talking French was liable to have no idea what she was saying.

3. Cohn's possessive partner in a fading romantic relationship. Henry Braddocks is another writer in Barnes and Cohn's circle.

4. A noted French opera singer (1869–1941).

5. I don't know (French).

"He's a fool," Georgette said.

"Oh, it was a joke, then," Mrs. Braddocks said.

"Yes," said Georgette. "To laugh at."

"Did you hear that, Henry?" Mrs. Braddocks called down the table to Braddocks. "Mr. Barnes introduced his fiancée as Mademoiselle Leblanc, and her name is actually Hobin."

"Of course, darling. Mademoiselle Hobin, I've known her for a very long time."

"Oh, Mademoiselle Hobin," Frances Clyne called, speaking French very rapidly and not seeming so proud and astonished as Mrs. Braddocks at its coming out really French. "Have you been in Paris long? Do you like it here? You love Paris, do you not?"

"Who's she?" Georgette turned to me. "Do I have to talk to her?"

She turned to Frances, sitting smiling, her hands folded, her head poised on her long neck, her lips pursed ready to start talking again.

"No, I don't like Paris. It's expensive and dirty."

"Really? I find it so extraordinarily clean. One of the cleanest cities in all Europe."

"I find it dirty."

"How strange! But perhaps you have not been here very long."

"I've been here long enough."

"But it does have nice people in it. One must grant that."

Georgette turned to me. "You have nice friends."

Frances was a little drunk and would have liked to have kept it up but the coffee came, and Lavigne with the liqueurs, and after that we all went out and started for Braddocks's dancing-club.

The dancing-club was a *bal musette* in the Rue de la Montagne Sainte Geneviève.[6] Five nights a week the working people of the Pantheon quarter[7] danced there. One night a week it was the dancing-club. On Monday nights it was closed. When we arrived it was quite empty, except for a policeman sitting near the door, the wife of the proprietor back of the zinc bar, and the proprietor himself. The daughter of the house came down-stairs as we went in. There were long benches, and tables ran across the room, and at the far end a dancing-floor.

"I wish people would come earlier," Braddocks said. The daughter came up and wanted to know what we would drink. The proprietor got up on a high stool beside the dancing-floor and began to play the accordion. He had a string of bells around one of his ankles and beat time with his foot as he played. Every one danced. It was hot and we came off the floor perspiring.

"My God," Georgette said. "What a box to sweat in!"

"It's hot."

"Hot, my God!"

"Take off your hat."

"That's a good idea."

Some one asked Georgette to dance, and I went over to the bar. It was really very hot and the accordion music was pleasant in the hot night. I drank

6. Street in the Latin Quarter of the Left Bank, known for its universities and nightlife. "*Bal musette*": a dance hall with an accordion band.

7. The Left Bank neighborhood surrounding the Pantheon. Designed in 1755 as a church, the building was later converted into a secular memorial and burial place for notable French citizens.

a beer, standing in the doorway and getting the cool breath of wind from the street. Two taxis were coming down the steep street. They both stopped in front of the Bal.[8] A crowd of young men, some in jerseys and some in their shirtsleeves, got out. I could see their hands and newly washed, wavy hair in the light from the door. The policeman standing by the door looked at me and smiled. They came in. As they went in, under the light I saw white hands, wavy hair, white faces, grimacing, gesturing, talking. With them was Brett. She looked very lovely and she was very much with them.

One of them saw Georgette and said: "I do declare. There is an actual harlot. I'm going to dance with her, Lett. You watch me."

The tall dark one, called Lett, said: "Don't you be rash."

The wavy blond one answered: "Don't you worry, dear." And with them was Brett.

I was very angry. Somehow they always made me angry. I know they are supposed to be amusing, and you should be tolerant, but I wanted to swing on one, any one, anything to shatter that superior, simpering composure. Instead, I walked down the street and had a beer at the bar at the next Bal. The beer was not good and I had a worse cognac to take the taste out of my mouth. When I came back to the Bal there was a crowd on the floor and Georgette was dancing with the tall blond youth, who danced big-hippily, carrying his head on one side, his eyes lifted as he danced. As soon as the music stopped another one of them asked her to dance. She had been taken up by them. I knew then that they would all dance with her. They are like that.

I sat down at a table. Cohn was sitting there. Frances was dancing. Mrs. Braddocks brought up somebody and introduced him as Robert Prentiss. He was from New York by way of Chicago, and was a rising new novelist. He had some sort of an English accent. I asked him to have a drink.

"Thanks so much," he said, "I've just had one."

"Have another."

"Thanks, I will then."

We got the daughter of the house over and each had a *fine à l'eau*.[9]

"You're from Kansas City, they tell me," he said.

"Yes."

"Do you find Paris amusing?"

"Yes."

"Really?"

I was a little drunk. Not drunk in any positive sense but just enough to be careless.

"For God's sake," I said, "yes. Don't you?"

"Oh, how charmingly you get angry," he said. "I wish I had that faculty."

I got up and walked over toward the dancing-floor. Mrs. Braddocks followed me. "Don't be cross with Robert," she said. "He's still only a child, you know."

"I wasn't cross," I said. "I just thought perhaps I was going to throw up."

"Your fiancée is having a great success," Mrs. Braddocks looked out on the floor where Georgette was dancing in the arms of the tall, dark one, called Lett.

"Isn't she?" I said.

8. I.e., the *bal musette*.

9. Cognac and water.

"Rather," said Mrs. Braddocks.

Cohn came up. "Come on, Jake," he said, "have a drink." We walked over to the bar. "What's the matter with you? You seem all worked up over something?"

"Nothing. This whole show makes me sick is all."

Brett came up to the bar.

"Hello, you chaps."

"Hello, Brett," I said. "Why aren't you tight?"

"Never going to get tight any more. I say, give a chap a brandy and soda."

She stood holding the glass and I saw Robert Cohn looking at her. He looked a great deal as his compatriot must have looked when he saw the promised land.[1] Cohn, of course, was much younger. But he had that look of eager, deserving expectation.

Brett was damned good-looking. She wore a slipover jersey sweater and a tweed skirt, and her hair was brushed back like a boy's. She started all that. She was built with curves like the hull of a racing yacht, and you missed none of it with that wool jersey.

"It's a fine crowd you're with, Brett," I said.

"Aren't they lovely? And you, my dear. Where did you get it?"

"At the Napolitain."

"And have you had a lovely evening?"

"Oh, priceless," I said.

Brett laughed. "It's wrong of you, Jake. It's an insult to all of us. Look at Frances there, and Jo."

This for Cohn's benefit.

"It's in restraint of trade," Brett said. She laughed again.

"You're wonderfully sober," I said.

"Yes. Aren't I? And when one's with the crowd I'm with, one can drink in such safety, too."

The music started and Robert Cohn said: "Will you dance this with me, Lady Brett?"

Brett smiled at him. "I've promised to dance this with Jacob," she laughed. "You've a hell of a biblical name, Jake."

"How about the next?" asked Cohn.

"We're going," Brett said. "We've a date up at Montmartre."[2]

Dancing, I looked over Brett's shoulder, and saw Cohn, standing at the bar, still watching her.

"You've made a new one there," I said to her.

"Don't talk about it. Poor chap. I never knew it till just now."

"Oh, well," I said. "I suppose you like to add them up."

"Don't talk like a fool."

"You do."

"Oh, well. What if I do?"

"Nothing," I said. We were dancing to the accordion and some one was playing the banjo. It was hot and I felt happy. We passed close to Georgette dancing with another one of them.

"What possessed you to bring her?"

"I don't know, I just brought her."

1. I.e., like Moses, who was allowed to see but not to enter the promised land (Deuteronomy 34.4). Barnes here and elsewhere in the novel mocks Cohn's Jewish identity.

2. Parisian neighborhood associated with avant-garde artists.

"You're getting damned romantic."

"No, bored."

"Now?"

"No, not now."

"Let's get out of here. She's well taken care of."

"Do you want to?"

"Would I ask you if I didn't want to?"

We left the floor and I took my coat off a hanger on the wall and put it on. Brett stood by the bar. Cohn was talking to her. I stopped at the bar and asked them for an envelope. The patronne found one. I took a fifty-franc note from my pocket, put it in the envelope, sealed it, and handed it to the patronne.[3]

"If the girl I came with asks for me, will you give her this?" I said. "If she goes out with one of those gentlemen, will you save this for me?"

"C'est entendu, Monsieur,"[4] the patronne said. "You go now? So early?"

"Yes," I said.

We started out the door. Cohn was still talking to Brett. She said good night and took my arm. "Good night, Cohn," I said. Outside in the street we looked for a taxi.

"You're going to lose your fifty francs," Brett said.

"Oh, yes."

"No taxis."

"We could walk up to the Pantheon and get one."

"Come on and we'll get a drink in the pub next door and send for one."

"You wouldn't walk across the street."

"Not if I could help it."

We went into the next bar and I sent a waiter for a taxi.

"Well," I said, "we're out away from them."

We stood against the tall zinc bar and did not talk and looked at each other. The waiter came and said the taxi was outside. Brett pressed my hand hard. I gave the waiter a franc and we went out. "Where should I tell him?" I asked.

"Oh, tell him to drive around."

I told the driver to go to the Parc Montsouris,[5] and got in, and slammed the door. Brett was leaning back in the corner, her eyes closed. I sat beside her. The cab started with a jerk.

"Oh, darling, I've been so miserable," Brett said.

1926

Hills Like White Elephants[1]

The hills across the valley of the Ebro[2] were long and white. On this side there was no shade and no trees and the station was between two lines of rails in the sun. Close against the side of the station there was the warm shadow of the building and a curtain, made of strings of bamboo beads, hung across the open door into the bar, to keep out flies. The American and

3. Landlady, barkeeper (French). In 1925, 50 francs was equivalent to about $2.50 in U.S. dollars, roughly $30.00 in today's money.

4. Understood, sir (French).

5. Large public park on the Left Bank.

1. The text is from *Men without Women* (1927), published by Charles Scribner's Sons.

2. Spain's largest river.

the girl with him sat at a table in the shade, outside the building. It was very hot and the express from Barcelona would come in forty minutes. It stopped at this junction for two minutes and went on to Madrid.

"What should we drink?" the girl asked. She had taken off her hat and put it on the table.

"It's pretty hot," the man said.

"Let's drink beer."

"Dos cervezas,"[3] the man said into the curtain.

"Big ones?" a woman asked from the doorway.

"Yes. Two big ones."

The woman brought two glasses of beer and two felt pads. She put the felt pads and the beer glasses on the table and looked at the man and the girl. The girl was looking off at the line of hills. They were white in the sun and the country was brown and dry.

"They look like white elephants," she said.

"I've never seen one," the man drank his beer.

"No, you wouldn't have."

"I might have," the man said. "Just because you say I wouldn't have doesn't prove anything."

The girl looked at the bead curtain. "They've painted something on it," she said. "What does it say?"

"Anis del Toro.[4] It's a drink."

"Could we try it?"

The man called "Listen" through the curtain. The woman came out from the bar.

"Four reales."[5]

"We want two Anis del Toro."

"With water?"

"Do you want it with water?"

"I don't know," the girl said. "Is it good with water?"

"It's all right."

"You want them with water?" asked the woman.

"Yes, with water."

"It tastes like licorice," the girl said and put the glass down.

"That's the way with everything."

"Yes," said the girl. "Everything tastes of licorice. Especially all the things you've waited so long for, like absinthe."[6]

"Oh, cut it out."

"You started it," the girl said. "I was being amused. I was having a fine time."

"Well, let's try and have a fine time."

"All right. I was trying. I said the mountains looked like white elephants. Wasn't that bright?"

"That was bright."

"I wanted to try this new drink. That's all we do, isn't it—look at things and try new drinks?"

"I guess so."

3. Two beers (Spanish).

4. Bull's anisette (Spanish, literal trans.); a brand of anise-flavored liqueur.

5. Small Spanish coins. In 1925, 4 reales were worth about 15 cents in U.S. money.

6. Anise- and herb-flavored, highly alcoholic spirit, associated with Parisian life and banned in the United States in 1912.

The girl looked across at the hills.

"They're lovely hills," she said. "They don't really look like white elephants. I just meant the coloring of their skin through the trees."

"Should we have another drink?"

"All right."

The warm wind blew the bead curtain against the table.

"The beer's nice and cool," the man said.

"It's lovely," the girl said.

"It's really an awfully simple operation, Jig," the man said. "It's not really an operation at all."

The girl looked at the ground the table legs rested on.

"I know you wouldn't mind it, Jig. It's really not anything. It's just to let the air in."

The girl did not say anything.

"I'll go with you and I'll stay with you all the time. They just let the air in and then it's all perfectly natural."

"Then what will we do afterward?"

"We'll be fine afterward. Just like we were before."

"What makes you think so?"

"That's the only thing that bothers us. It's the only thing that's made us unhappy."

The girl looked at the bead curtain, put her hand out and took hold of two of the strings of beads.

"And you think then we'll be all right and be happy."

"I know we will. You don't have to be afraid. I've known lots of people that have done it."

"So have I," said the girl. "And afterward they were all so happy."

"Well," the man said, "if you don't want to you don't have to. I wouldn't have you do it if you didn't want to. But I know it's perfectly simple."

"And you really want to?"

"I think it's the best thing to do. But I don't want you to do it if you don't really want to."

"And if I do it you'll be happy and things will be like they were and you'll love me?"

"I love you now. You know I love you."

"I know. But if I do it, then it will be nice again if I say things are like white elephants, and you'll like it?"

"I'll love it. I love it now but I just can't think about it. You know how I get when I worry."

"If I do it you won't ever worry?"

"I won't worry about that because it's perfectly simple."

"Then I'll do it. Because I don't care about me."

"What do you mean?"

"I don't care about me."

"Well, I care about you."

"Oh, yes. But I don't care about me. And I'll do it and then everything will be fine."

"I don't want you to do it if you feel that way."

The girl stood up and walked to the end of the station. Across, on the other side, were fields of grain and trees along the banks of the Ebro. Far away, beyond the river, were mountains. The shadow of a cloud moved across the field of grain and she saw the river through the trees.

"And we could have all this," she said. "And we could have everything and every day we make it more impossible."

"What did you say?"

"I said we could have everything."

"We can have everything."

"No, we can't."

"We can have the whole world."

"No, we can't."

"We can go everywhere."

"No, we can't. It isn't ours any more."

"It's ours."

"No, it isn't. And once they take it away, you never get it back."

"But they haven't taken it away."

"We'll wait and see."

"Come on back in the shade," he said. "You mustn't feel that way."

"I don't feel any way," the girl said. "I just know things."

"I don't want you to do anything that you don't want to do——"

"Nor that isn't good for me," she said. "I know. Could we have another beer?"

"All right. But you've got to realize——"

"I realize," the girl said. "Can't we maybe stop talking?"

They sat down at the table and the girl looked across at the hills on the dry side of the valley and the man looked at her and at the table.

"You've got to realize," he said, "that I don't want you to do it if you don't want to. I'm perfectly willing to go through with it if it means anything to you."

"Doesn't it mean anything to you? We could get along."

"Of course it does. But I don't want anybody but you. I don't want any one else. And I know it's perfectly simple."

"Yes, you know it's perfectly simple."

"It's all right for you to say that, but I do know it."

"Would you do something for me now?"

"I'd do anything for you."

"Would you please please please please please please please stop talking?"

He did not say anything but looked at the bags against the wall of the station. There were labels on them from all the hotels where they had spent nights.

"But I don't want you to," he said, "I don't care anything about it."

"I'll scream," the girl said.

The woman came out through the curtains with two glasses of beer and put them down on the damp felt pads. "The train comes in five minutes," she said.

"What did she say?" asked the girl.

"That the train is coming in five minutes."

The girl smiled brightly at the woman, to thank her.

"I'd better take the bags over to the other side of the station," the man said. She smiled at him.

"All right. Then come back and we'll finish the beer."

He picked up the two heavy bags and carried them around the station to the other tracks. He looked up the tracks but could not see the train. Coming back, he walked through the barroom, where people waiting for the train were drinking. He drank an Anis at the bar and looked at the people.

They were all waiting reasonably for the train. He went out through the bead curtain. She was sitting at the table and smiled at him.

"Do you feel better?" he asked.

"I feel fine," she said. "There's nothing wrong with me. I feel fine."

1927

THOMAS WOLFE
1900–1938

Thomas Wolfe's writing was diametrically opposed to the suggestive conciseness of such modernist prose writers as F. Scott Fitzgerald and Ernest Hemingway. He wanted to write about America, he said, "not the government, or the Revolutionary War, or the Monroe Doctrine," but rather "the ten million seconds and moments of your life." Elsewhere he said, "I want to write about everything and say all that can be said about each particular." As a result his manuscripts were vast scrawls that had to be shaped into books by his editors and agents.

Wolfe was born in Asheville, North Carolina, the seventh and youngest child of O. W. and Julia Westall Wolfe. His father, who had been married before, was a stonecutter. His mother came from a Carolina mountain family. When Wolfe was about six years old, she opened a boardinghouse a few blocks from the family home. Thereafter, the family divided its time between these two residences. Later, Julia Wolfe began to invest in real estate, and between the earnings of the two parents, the family was financially comfortable. All its members were highly individualistic, emotional, and self-expressive; the passionate family drama was both Wolfe's inspiration and his burden. His youth was punctuated by loss as well: his brother Grover died when Wolfe was four, his beloved brother Ben when he was eighteen, and his father when he was twenty-two.

There was no tradition of higher education on either side of the family, but some of Wolfe's teachers persuaded his parents to send him to the University of North Carolina at Chapel Hill. After graduating he took a year of additional study at Harvard University, working with George Pierce Baker, who at that time gave one of the very few courses in playwriting in the nation, the famous "47 Workshop," where Eugene O'Neill also studied. In 1924 Wolfe moved to New York City, where he taught composition at New York University while trying to write salable plays.

At about this time, Wolfe met and became involved with Aline Bernstein, a successful scene designer for the Neighborhood Playhouse, a New York theater group. She persuaded the young writer to try writing prose fiction, and with her encouragement he turned to the subject of his own life. A three-hundred-thousand-word manuscript—i.e., about a thousand typed pages—titled *O Lost* made the rounds of several publishers before coming to the attention of Maxwell Perkins at Scribner. Perkins, a leading editor of the day, had made it his life's work to identify major American talents—Fitzgerald and Hemingway were among those he published—and he found in Wolfe a writer who equaled his highest idea of American genius. Reorganized and cut by about a third, the book appeared as *Look Homeward, Angel* in 1929. Despite the fact that book sales were generally down because of the Great Depression, it was a popular success and made Wolfe a celebrity.

Look Homeward, Angel is an extensive fictional re-creation of Wolfe's youth and of the members of his family; the hero, Eugene Gant, is Wolfe himself. Its picture of the mountain South is a substantial contribution to American regional writing. A sequel, *Of Time and the River,* came out in 1935 and was even more popular. Wolfe's autobiographical revelations offended some readers, including residents of Asheville and his own family. Only his mother appeared unperturbed by the merciless way in which he had put living people into print. Pro-German statements that he made in the mid-1930s angered many others, and he made numerous enemies. Maxwell Perkins's role came under critical scrutiny—one reviewer going so far as to suggest that Wolfe was only part author of his own books. In distress, Wolfe changed publishers.

In the summer of 1938 Wolfe, before a visit to the West Coast, delivered a crate of manuscript to his new editor, Edward Aswell of Harper's. The crate, he said, contained his next book. What it really contained were thousands of handwritten pages in no particular order. In Seattle, Wolfe contracted a case of pneumonia that developed serious complications. He died of a brain infection in September, and it was left to Aswell to work up two more books from the manuscript material, *The Web and the Rock,* published in 1939, and *You Can't Go Home Again,* published in 1940. Although these books have a new hero, George Webber, they continue Wolfe's autobiographical saga. Wolfe's reputation suffered after his death for what was deemed his lack of artistry: his formlessness and prolixity in an age where criticism called for tight structure and verbal economy. Those who admire his work point to his treatment of childhood and adolescence, his depiction of the mountain South, and his romantically nostalgic evocations of lost happiness.

"The Lost Boy" is a segment of the Gant saga, with different names for the characters, that was not used in the novels. It was published as a short story in 1937. As noted, Grover Cleveland Wolfe, Thomas Wolfe's brother, died at the age of eleven when the author-to-be was just four. In 1904 Julia Wolfe took some of the children, including Tom and Grover, to St. Louis, where the World's Fair was being held; there she ran a boardinghouse, the Carolina House, for some months. It was in St. Louis that Grover died of typhoid fever. In "The Lost Boy," Grover is called Robert. The story offers a four-angled view of him: (1) an episode involving Robert and his father, (2) a view of Robert through his mother's eyes, (3) an older sister's account of his illness and death, and (4) the attempt of the author-brother to recapture time and his lost brother by returning years later to the house in St. Louis where they had lived.

The text is from *The Complete Short Stories of Thomas Wolfe* (1987).

The Lost Boy[1]

The light came and went, the booming strokes of three o'clock beat out across the town in thronging bronze, light winds of April blew the fountain out in rainbow sheets, until the plume returned and pulsed, as Robert turned into the Square. He was a child dark-eyed and grave, birthmarked upon his neck—a berry of warm brown—and with a gentle face, perhaps too quiet and listening for his years. The scuffed boy's shoes, the thick-ribbed stockings gartered at the knees, the short knee pants cut straight with three small useless buttons at the side, the sailor blouse, the old cap battered out of shape, perched sideways up on top the raven head—these friendly shabby garments, shaped by Robert, uttered him. He turned and passed along the north side of the Square, and in that moment felt the union of Forever and Now.

1. The text reproduces the story as it appeared in *Redbook* magazine in 1937. The story as collected in *The Hills Beyond* (1941) differs in many particulars from the version that appeared in Wolfe's lifetime.

Light came and went and came again; the great plume of the fountain pulsed, and the winds of April sheeted it across the Square in rainbow gossamer of spray. The street-cars ground into the Square from every portion of the town's small compass and halted briefly like wound toys in their old quarter-hourly formula of assembled Eight. The courthouse bell boomed out its solemn warning of immediate Three, and everything was just the same as it had always been.

He saw with quiet eyes that haggis[2] of vexed shapes, that hodge-podge of ill-sorted masonries, and he did not feel lost. For "Here," thought Robert, "here's the Square as it has always been—and Papa's shop, the fire department and the city hall, the fountain pulsing with its plume, the drug-store on the corner there, the row of old brick buildings on this side, the people passing and the cars that come and go, the light that comes and changes and that always will come back again, and everything that comes and goes and changes in the Square, and yet will be the same—here," Robert thought, "here is the Square that never changes; here is Robert almost twelve—and here is Time."

For so it seemed to him: small center of his little universe, itself the accidental masonry of twenty years, the chance agglomerate of time and of disrupted strivings, it was for him earth's pivot and the granite core of changelessness, the eternal Place where all things came and passed, the Place that would abide forever and would never change.

The Square walked past him then with steady steps—plume, pulse, and fountain, and the sheeting spray, the open arches of the fire department doors, the wooden stomp of the great hoofs, the casual whiskings of the dry coarse tails. He passed the firetrap of a wiener stand; and the Singer[3] shop, the steel-bright smartness of the new machines, with their swift evocations of the house, the whir, the treadle, and the mounting hum—the vague monotony of women's work. He passed the music-store, the coffined splendor of piano shapes, the deep-toned richness, and the smell of proud dark wood, the stale yet pleasant memory of parlors.

He passed the grocery store then, the gaunt gray horse, the old head leaning to its hitching block; within, the pickle-barrels, the fans, the sultry coffee and the cloven cheese, the musty compost of cool plenty, the delicious All-Smell, and the buttered unction of the grocer with his straw-cuffed sleeves.

He was going past the hardware store now. He always had to stop by places that had shining perfect things in them, and windows full of geometric tools, of hammers, saws, and planing-boards, and strong new rakes and hoes with unworn handles of white perfect wood, stamped hard and vivid with the maker's seal. Ah, how he loved such things as these, strong perfect shapes and pungent smells, the great integrities of use and need, the certitude of this unchanging pattern, set to the grand assurance of the everlasting Square. He turned a corner, and he *was* caught, held. A waft of air, warm, chocolate-laden, filled his nostrils. He tried to pass the white front of the little eight-foot shop; he paused, struggling with conscience; he could not go on. It was the little candy-shop run by old Crocker and his wife. And Robert could not pass.

"Old stingy Crockers!" he thought scornfully. "I'll not go there again. They're so stingy they stop the clocks at night. But—" The maddening fragrance of rich cooking chocolate touched him once again. "I'll just look in the

2. I.e., pudding.

3. Manufacturer of sewing machines.

window and see what they've got." He paused a moment, looking with his dark and quiet eyes into the window of the candy shop. His dark eyes rested for a moment on a tray of chocolate drops. Unconsciously he licked his lips. Put one of them upon your tongue and it just melted there like honey. And then the trays full of rich home-made fudge. He looked longingly at the deep body of the chocolate fudge, reflectively at the maple walnut, more critically, yet with longing, at the mints, the nougatines, and all the other tempters.

"Old stingy Crockers!" Robert muttered once again, and turned to go. "I wouldn't go in *there* again."

And yet—he did not go away. "Old stingy Crockers," it was true; still, they did make the best candy in town, the best, in fact, that he had ever tasted.

• • •

He looked through the window back into the little shop and saw Mrs. Crocker there. A customer had made a purchase, and as Robert looked, he saw Mrs. Crocker, with her little wrenny[4] face, lean over and peer primly at the scales. She had a piece of fudge in her clean bony fingers—and now she broke it, primly, in her little bony hands. She dropped a morsel down into the scales. They weighted down alarmingly, and her thin lips tightened. She snatched a piece of fudge out of the scales and broke it carefully once again. This time the scale wavered, went down very slowly, and came back again. Mrs. Crocker carefully put the reclaimed piece of fudge back in the tray, put the remainder in a paper bag, folded it and gave it to the customer, counted the money carefully, and doled it out into the till.

Robert stood there, looking scornfully. "Old stingy Crocker—afraid that she might give a crumb away."

He grunted, and again he turned to go. But now Mr. Crocker came out from the little partitioned place behind, bearing a tray of fresh-made candy in his skinny hands. Old man Crocker rocked along the counter to the front and put it down. He was a cripple. One leg was inches shorter than the other, and on this leg there was an enormous thick-soled boot, with a kind of wooden rocker-like arrangement, six inches high at least, to make up for the deficiency of his game right leg. And on this wooden cradle Mr. Crocker rocked along. He was a little pinched and skinny figure of a man with bony hands and meager features, and when he walked, he really rocked along, with a kind of prim and apprehensive little smile, as if he was afraid he was going to lose something.

"Old stingy Crocker," muttered Robert. "Humph! He wouldn't give you *anything.*"

And yet he did not go away. He hung there curiously, peering through the window, with his dark and gentle face now focused and intent, flattening his nose against the glass. Unconsciously he scratched the thick-ribbed fabric of one stockinged leg with the scuffed toe of his old shoe. The fresh warm odor of the new-made fudge had reached him. It was delicious. It was a little maddening. Half-consciously, he began to fumble in one trouser pocket and pulled out his purse, a shabby worn old black one with a twisted clasp. He opened it and prowled about inside.

4. Wrenlike; Wolfe's invented word. The wren is a small, wide-eyed, active bird.

What he found was not inspiring: a nickel and two pennies and—he had forgotten them—the stamps. He took the stamps out and unfolded them. There were five twos, eight ones, all that remained of the dollar and sixty cents' worth which Reed, the pharmacist, had given him for running errands a week or two before.

"Old Crocker," Robert thought, looked somberly at the grotesque little form and—"Well—" indefinitely—"He's had all the rest of them. He might as well take these."

So, soothing conscience with this sop of scorn, he went into the shop, and pointing with a slightly grimy finger at the fresh-made tray of chocolate fudge, he said: "I'll take fifteen cents' worth of this, Mr. Crocker."

He paused a moment, fighting with embarrassment; then he lifted his dark face and said quietly: "And please, I'll have to give you stamps again."

Mr. Crocker made no answer. He pressed his lips together. Then he got the candy scoop, slid open the door of the glass case, put fudge into the scoop, and rocking to the scales, began to weigh the candy out. Robert watched him as he peered and squinted, watched him purse his lips together, saw him take a piece of fudge and break it into two parts. And then old Crocker broke two parts in two. He weighed, he squinted, he hovered, until it seemed to Robert that by calling *Mrs.* Crocker stingy he had been guilty of a rank injustice. But finally the scales hung there, quivering apprehensively, upon the very hairline of nervous balance, as if even the scales were afraid that one more move from old man Crocker and they would be undone.

Mr. Crocker took the candy, dumped it into a paper bag, and rocking back along the counter toward the boy, he said: "Where are the stamps?" Robert gave them to him. Mr. Crocker relinquished his claw-like hold on the bag and set it down upon the counter. Robert took the bag and then remembered. "Mr. Crocker,"—again he felt the old embarrassment that was almost like strong pain,—"I gave you too much," Robert said. "There were eighteen cents in stamps. You—you can just give me three ones back."

Mr. Crocker did not answer for a moment. He was busy unfolding the stamps and flattening them out on top of the glass counter. When he had done so, he peered at them sharply, for a moment, thrusting his scrawny neck forward and running his eye up and down, as a bookkeeper who tots up rows of figures.

Then he said tartly: "I don't like this kind of business. I'm not a post office. The next time you come in here and want anything, you'll have to have the money for it."

Hot anger rose in Robert's throat. His olive face suffused with angry color. His tarry eyes got black and bright. For a moment he was on the verge of saying: "Then why did you take my other stamps? Why do you tell me now, when you have taken all the stamps I had, that you don't want them?"

But he was a quiet, gentle, gravely thoughtful boy, and he had been taught how to respect his elders. So he just stood there looking with his tar-black eyes. Old Man Crocker took the stamps up in his thin, parched fingers, and turning, rocked away down to the till.

He took the twos and laid them in one rounded scallop, then took the ones and folded them and put them in the one next to it. Then he closed the till and started to rock off, down toward the other end. Robert kept looking at him, but Mr. Crocker did not look at Robert. Instead, he began to take some cardboard shapes and fold them into boxes.

In a moment Robert said: "Mr. Crocker, will you give me the three ones, please?"

Mr. Crocker did not answer. But Mrs. Crocker, also folding boxes with her parsley hands, muttered tartly: "Hm! *I'd* give him nothing!"

Mr. Crocker looked at Robert: "What are you waiting for?"

"Will you give me the three ones, please?" Robert said.

"I'll give you nothing," Mr. Crocker said. "Now you get out of here! And don't you come here with any more of those stamps."

"I should like to know where he gets them, that's what *I* should like to know," said Mrs. Crocker.

"You get out of here," said Mr. Crocker. "And don't you come back here with any stamps. . . . Where did you get those stamps?" he said.

"That's just what *I've* been thinking," Mrs. Crocker said.

"You've been coming in here for the last two weeks with stamps," said Mr. Crocker. "I don't like the look of it. Where did you get those stamps?" he said.

"That's what *I've* been thinking all along," said Mrs. Crocker.

Robert had got white underneath his olive skin. His eyes had lost their luster. They looked like dull, stunned balls of tar. "From Mr. Reed," he said. "I got the stamps from Mr. Reed." He burst out desperately: "Mr. Crocker, Mr. Reed will tell you how I got the stamps. I did some work for Mr. Reed; he gave me those stamps two weeks ago."

"Mr. *Reed,*" said Mrs. Crocker acidly. "I call it mighty funny."

"Mr. Crocker," Robert said, "if you'll just let me have the three ones—"

"You get out of here, boy!" cried Mr. Crocker. "Now don't you come in here again! There's something funny about this whole business! If you can't pay as other people do, then I don't want your trade."

"Mr. Crocker," Robert said again, and underneath the olive skin his face was gray, "if you'll just let me have those three—"

"You get out of here," Mr. Crocker cried, and began to rock forward toward the boy. "If you don't get out—"

"I'd call a policeman, that's what I'd do," Mrs. Crocker said.

Mr. Crocker came rocking up to Robert, took the boy and pushed him with his bony little hands. Robert felt sick and gray down to the hollow pit of his stomach.

"You've got to give me those three ones," he said.

"You get out of here!" shrilled Mr. Crocker. He seized the screen door, pulled it open and pushed Robert out. "Don't you come back in here," he said, pausing for a moment, working thinly at the lips. Then he turned and rocked back in the shop again. Robert stood there on the pavement. And light came and went and came again.

The boy stood there for a moment, and a wagon rattled past. There were some people passing by, but Robert did not notice them. He stood there blindly, in the watches of the sun, but something had gone out of the day.

He felt the soul-sickening guilt that all the children, all the good men of the earth, have felt since time began. And even anger had been drowned out, in the swelling tide of guilt. "There is the Square," thought Robert as before.

"This is Now. There is my father's shop. And all of it is as it has always been—save I."

And the Square reeled drunkenly around him, light went in blind gray motes before his eyes, the fountain sheeted out to rainbow iridescence and returned to its proud pulsing plume again. But all the brightness had gone out of day.

The scuffed boots of the lost boy moved and stumbled blindly over. The numb feet crossed the pavement—reached the sidewalk, crossed the plotted central Square—the grass plots, the flower-beds, so soon with red and packed geraniums.

"I want to be alone," thought Robert, "where I can not go near him. Oh, God, I hope he never hears, that no one ever tells him—"

The plume blew out; the iridescent sheet of spray blew over him. He passed through, found the other side and crossed the street. "Oh, God, if Papa ever hears," thought Robert, as his numb feet started up the steps into his father's shop.

He found and felt the steps—the thickness of old lumber twenty feet in length. He saw it all: the iron columns on his father's porch, painted with the dull anomalous black-green that all such columns in this land and weather come to; two angels, fly-specked, and the waiting stones. Beyond and all around, in the stonecutter's shop, cold shapes of white and marble, rounded stone, the limestone base, the languid angel with strong marble hands of love.

He went on down the aisle; the white shapes stood around him. He went on back into the workroom. This he knew—the little cast-iron stove in the left-hand corner, the high, dirty window, looking down across the market square, the rude old shelves, upon the shelves the chisels and a layer of stone dust; an emery wheel with pump tread, and two trestles of coarse wood upon which rested gravestones. At one trestle was a man, at work.

The boy looked numbly, saw the name was *Creasman:* the carved analysis of John, the symmetry of S, the fine finality of *Creasman—November, Nineteen-Three.*

The man looked up and then returned to work. He was a man of fifty-three, immensely long and tall and gaunt. He wore good dark clothes, save he had no coat. He worked in shirt-sleeves with his vest on, a strong watch-chain stretching across his vest; wing collar and black tie, Adam's apple, bony forehead, bony nose, light eyes, gray-green, undeep and cold, and somehow lonely-looking, a striped apron going up around his shoulders, and starched cuffs. And in one hand a tremendous rounded wooden mallet like a butcher's bole; and in his other hand, implacable and cold, the chisel.

"How are you, son?"

He did not look up as he spoke. He spoke quietly, absently. He worked upon the chisel and the wooden mallet as delicately as a jeweler might work upon a watch, except that in the man and the wooden mallet there was power, too.

"What is it, son?" he said.

He moved around the table from the head, and started up on *J* again.

"Papa, I never stole the stamps," said Robert.

The man put down the mallet, laid the chisel down. He came around the trestle.

"What?" he said. And Robert winked his tar-black eyes; they brightened; the hot tears shot out. "I never stole the stamps," he said.

"Hey? What is this?" the man said. "What stamps?"

"That Mr. Reed gave to me, when the other boy was sick and I worked there for three days. . . . And old man Crocker," Robert said, "he took all the stamps. And I told him Mr. Reed had given them to me. And now he owes me three ones—and old man Crocker says—he says—I must have taken them."

"The stamps that Reed gave to you—hey?" the stonecutter said. "The stamps you had—" He wet his great thumb briefly on his lips, strode from his workshop out into the storeroom aisle.

The man came back, cleared his throat, and as he passed the old gray board-partition of his office, he cleared his throat and wet his thumb, and said: "I tell you, now—"

Then he turned and strode up toward the front again and cleared his throat and said: "I tell you, now—" And coming back, along the aisle between the rows of marshaled gravestones, he muttered underneath his breath: "By God, now—"

He took Robert by the hand. They went out flying down along the aisle by all the gravestones, the fly-specked angels waiting there, the wooden steps, across the cobbles and the central plot—across the whole thing, but they did not notice it.

And the fountain pulsed, the plume blew out in sheeted spray and swept across them, and an old gray horse, with a peaceful look about its torn lips, swucked up the cool, the flowing mountain water from the trough as Robert and his father went across the Square.

They went across the Square through the sheeted iridescence of the spray and to the other street and to the candy-shop. The man was dressed in his striped apron still; he was still holding Robert by the hand. He opened the screen door and stepped inside. "Give him the stamps," he said.

Mr. Crocker came rocking forward behind the counter, with a prim and careful look that now was somewhat like a smile. "It was just—" he said.

"Give him the stamps," the man said, and threw some coins down on the counter.

Mr. Crocker rocked away and got the stamps. "I just didn't know—" he said.

The stonecutter took the stamps and gave them to the boy. And Mr. Crocker took the coins.

"It was just that—" Mr. Crocker said, and smiled.

The man in the apron cleared his throat: "You never were a father," the man said. "You never knew the feeling of a child. And that is why you acted as you did. But a judgment is upon you. God has cursed you. He has afflicted you. He has made you lame and childless—and miserable as you are, you will go lame and childless to your grave—and be forgotten!"

And Crocker's wife kept kneading her bony little hands and said imploringly: "Oh, no—oh, don't say that! Please don't say that!"

The stonecutter, the breath still hoarse in him, left the store. Light came again into the day.

"Well, son," he said, and laid his hand on the boy's back. "Now don't you mind."

They walked across the Square, the sheeted spray of iridescent light swept out on them; a horse swizzled at the water-trough.

"Well, son," the gaunt man said again, "now don't you mind."

And he trod his own steps then with his great stride and went back again into his shop.

The lost boy stood upon the Square, close by the porch of his father's shop: light came again into the Square. A car curved in, upon the billboard of the car-end was a poster and some words: *"St. Louis"* and *"Excursion"* and *"The Fair."*

And light came and went into the Square, and Robert stood there thinking quietly: "Here is the Square that never changes; here is Time."

And light came and went and came again into the Square—but now not quite the same as it had done before. He saw that pattern of familiar shapes, and knew that they were just the same as they had always been. But something had gone out of the day, and something had come in again: out of the vision of those quiet eyes some brightness had been lost; into their vision some deeper color come. He could not say, he did not know through what transforming shadows life had passed within that quarter-hour. He only knew that something had been gained forever—something lost.

As we went down through Indiana—you were too young, child, to remember it, but I always think of all of you, the way you looked that morning, when we went down through Indiana, going to the Fair. All of the apple trees were coming out, and it was April; all of the trees were coming out; it was the beginning of the spring in Indiana, and everything was getting green. Of course we don't have farms at home like those in Indiana. The children had never seen such farms as those, and I reckon, kid-like, had to take it in.

So all of them kept running up and down the aisle—well, no, except for you and *Robert—you* were too young; you were just three; I kept you with me. As for Robert: well, I'm going to tell you about that. But the rest of them kept running up and down the aisle and from one window to another. They kept calling out and hollering to each other every time they saw something new. They kept trying to look out on all sides in every way at once, as if they wished they had eyes in the back of their heads. It was the first time any of them had been in Indiana, and I reckon, that, kid-like, it all seemed strange and new.

And so it seemed they couldn't get enough. It seemed they never could be still.

You see, they were excited about going to St. Louis and so curious over everything they saw. They couldn't help it, and they wanted to see everything. But "I'll vow," I said, "if you children don't sit down and rest, you'll be worn to a frazzle before we ever get to see St. Louis and the Fair!"

Except for Robert! He—no sir, not him! Now, boy, I want to tell you—I've raised the lot of you, and if I do say so, there wasn't a numbskull in the lot. But *Robert!* Well, you've all grown up now, all of you have gone away, and none of you are children any more. . . . And of course, I hope that, as the fellow says, you have reached the dignity of man's estate. . . . I suppose you have the judgment of a grown man. . . . But Robert! *Robert* had it, even then!

Oh, even as a child, you know—at a time I was almost afraid to trust the rest of you out of my sight—I could depend on Robert. I could send him anywhere, and I'd always know he'd get back safe, and do exactly what I told him to!

Why, I didn't even have to tell him—you could send that child to market and tell him what you wanted, and he'd come home with *twice* as much as you could get yourself for the same money.

Now you know, I've always been considered a good trader, but *Robert!* Why, it got so finally that your papa said to me: "You'd be better off if you just tell him what you want and leave the rest to him. For," your papa says, "damned if I don't believe he's a better trader than you are. . . . He gets more for the money than anyone I ever saw."

Well, I had to admit it, you know. . . . I had to own up then. . . . Robert, even as a child, was a far better trader than I was. . . . Why, yes, they told it on him all over town, you know. . . . They said all of the market men, all of the farmers, would begin to laugh when they saw him coming. They'd say, "Look out! Here's Robert! Here's one trader you're not going to fool!"

And they were right! . . . *That* child! . . . I'd say: "Robert, suppose you run uptown and see if they've got anything good to *eat* today. Suppose you take this dollar and just see what you can do with it."

Well, sir, that was all that was needed. The minute that you told that child that you depended on his judgment, he'd have gone to the ends of the earth for you—and let me tell you something, he wouldn't *miss,* either!

His eyes would get black as coals—oh, the way that child would look at you, the intelligence and sense in his expression! He'd say, "Yes, *ma'am!* Now don't you worry, Mamma, you leave it all to me—and I'll do *good!"* said Robert.

And he'd be off like a streak of lightning and oh, Lord! As your father said to me, "I've been living in this town for almost thirty years," he said, "and I thought I knew everything there was to know about it—but that child," your papa says, "he knows places that I never heard of!" Oh, he'd go right down there to that place below your papa's shop where the draymen used to park their wagons—or he'd go down there to those old lots on Concord Street where the farmers used to keep their wagons. And child that he was, he'd go right in among them, *sir—Robert* would!—go right in and barter with them like a grown man!

And he'd come home with things he'd bought that would make your eyes stick out. . . . Here he comes one time with another boy, dragging a great bushel basket full of ripe termaters[5] between them. "Why, Robert," I says, "how on earth are we ever going to use them? Why, they'll go bad on us before we're half-way through them." "Well, Mamma," he says, "I know,"—oh, just as solemn as a judge—"but they were the last the man had," he says, "and he wanted to go home, and so I got them for ten cents," he says. "I thought it was a shame to let 'em go, and I figgered what we couldn't eat—why," says Robert, "you could *put up!"* Well, the way he said it, so earnest and so serious, I had to laugh. "But I'll vow," I said, "if you don't beat all!" . . . But that was *Robert* the way he was in *those* days! As everyone said, boy that he was, he had the sense and judgment of a grown man. . . . Child, child, I've seen you all grow up, and all of you were bright enough, but for all-round

5. Tomatoes.

intelligence, judgment, and general ability, Robert surpassed the whole crowd. . . . I've never seen his equal, and everyone who knew him as a child will say the same.

So that's what I tell them now, when they ask me about all of you. I have to tell the truth. I always said that you were smart enough—but when they come around and brag to me about you, and I reckon how you have got on and have a kind of name—I don't let on to them, I never say a word. Why, yes! Why, here, you know—oh, 'long about a month ago, this feller comes. He said he came from New Jersey, or somewhere up in that part of the country—and he began to ask me all sorts of questions, what you were like when you were a boy and all such stuff as that.

I just pretended to study it all over; then I said, "Well, yes," real serious-like, you know. "Well, yes—I reckon I ought to know a little something about him: he was my child, just the same as all the others were; I brought him up just the the way I brought up all the others. And," I says—oh, just as solemn as you please, "he wasn't a *bad* sort of a boy. Why," I says, "up to the time that he was twelve years old he was just about the same as any other boy—a good average normal sort of fellow."

"Oh," he says. "But didn't you notice something? Didn't you notice how brilliant he was? He must have been more brilliant than the rest!"

"Well, now," I says, and pretended to study that all over, too. "Now let me see. . . . Yes," I says—I just looked him in the eye, as solemn as you please. "I guess he was a fairly bright sort of a boy. I never had no complaints to make of him on that score. He was bright enough," I says. "The only trouble with him was that he was lazy."

"Lazy!" he says—oh, you should have seen the look upon his face, you know—he jumped like someone had stuck a pin in him. "Lazy!" he says, "Why, you don't mean to tell me—"

"Yes," I says, "I was telling him the same thing myself the last time that I saw him. I told him it was a mighty lucky thing for him that he had the gift of gab. Of course, he went off to college and read a lot of books, and I reckon that's where he got this flow of language they say he has. . . . But as I said to him, 'Now look a-here,' I said, 'if you can earn your living doing a light easy class of work like this you do,' I says, 'you're mighty lucky, because none of the rest of your people had any such luck as that. They had to work hard for a living.'"

Oh, I told him, you know. I made no bones about it. And I tell you what—I wish you could have seen his face. It was a study.

"Well," he says, at last, "you've got to admit this, haven't you—he was the brightest boy you had, now wasn't he?"

I just looked at him a moment. I had to tell the truth. I couldn't fool him any longer. "No," I says. "He was a good bright boy—I have no complaint to make about him on that score; but the brightest boy I had, the one that surpassed all the rest of them in sense, and in understanding, and in judgment—the best boy that I had, the smartest boy I ever saw, was—well, it wasn't him," I said. "It was another one."

He looked at me a moment; then he said: "Which boy was that?"

Well, I just looked at him, and smiled. I shook my head. I wouldn't tell him. "I never brag about my own," I said. "You'll have to find out for yourself."

But—I'll have to tell *you:* the best one of the whole lot was—*Robert!*

. . . And when I think of Robert as he was long about that time, I always see him sitting there, so grave and earnest-like, with his nose pressed to the window, as we went down through Indiana in the morning, to the Fair.

So Robert sat beside this gentleman and looked out the window. I never knew the man—I never asked his name—but I tell you what! He was certainly a fine-looking, well-dressed, good substantial sort of man, and I could see that he had taken a great liking to Robert, and Robert sat there looking out, and then turned to this gentleman, as grave and earnest as a grown-up man, and says: "What kind of crops grow here, sir?" Well, this gentleman threw his head back and just ha-ha-ed. "Well, I'll see if I can tell you," says this gentleman, and then, you know, he talked to him, and Robert took it all in, as solemn as you please, and asked this gentleman every sort of question—what the trees were, what was growing there, how big the farms were—all sorts of questions, which this gentleman would answer, until I said: "I'll vow, Robert! You'll bother the very life out of this gentleman."

The gentleman threw his head back and laughed right out. "Now you leave that boy alone. He's all right," he said. "He doesn't bother me a bit, and if I know the answers to his questions, I will answer him. And if I don't know, why, then, I'll tell him so. But he's *all right,*" he said, and put his arm around Robert's shoulders. "You leave him alone. He doesn't bother me a bit."

And I can still remember how he looked, that morning, with his black eyes, his black hair, and with the birthmark on his neck—so grave, so serious, so earnest-like—as he looked out the windows at the apple trees, the farms, the barns, the houses, and the orchards, taking it all in because it was, I reckon, strange and new to him.

It was so long ago, but when I think of it, it all comes back, as if it happened yesterday. And all of you have grown up and gone away, and nothing is the same as it was then. But all of you were there with me that morning, and I guess I should remember how the others looked, but every time I think of it, I still see Robert just the way he was, the way he looked that morning when we went down through Indiana, by the river, to the Fair.

Can you remember how Robert used to look? . . . I mean the birthmark, the black eyes, the olive skin—the birthmark always showed because of those open sailor blouses kids used to wear. . . . But I guess you must have been too young. . . . I was looking at that old photograph the other day—that picture showing all of us before the house in Orchard Street? . . . *You* weren't there. . . . *You* hadn't arrived. . . . You remember how mad you used to get when we used to tell you that you were only a dish-rag hanging out in Heaven, when something happened?

I was looking at that old picture just the other day. There we were. . . . And my God, what is it all about? . . . I mean, when you see the way you were—Mary and Dick and Robert, Bill and all of us—and then—look at us now! Do you ever get to feeling funny? You know what I mean—do you ever get to feeling *queer?*—when you try to figure these things out. . . . You've been to college, and you ought to know the answer. . . . And I wish you'd tell me if you know. . . .

My Lord, when I think sometimes of the way I used to be—the dreams I used to have. . . . Taking singing lessons from Aunt Nell because I felt that some day I was going to have a great career in opera. . . . Can you beat it now? . . . Can you imagine it? . . . *Me!* In grand opera! . . . Now I want to ask you. . . . I'd like to know. . . .

My Lord! When I go uptown and look at all these funny-looking little boys and girls hanging around the drug-store—do you suppose any of them have ambitions the way we did? . . . Do you suppose any of these funny-looking little girls are thinking about a big career in opera? . . . Didn't you ever see that picture of us? It was made before the old house down on Orchard Street, with Papa standing there in his swallow-tail,[6] and Mamma there beside him—and Robert and Dick and Jim, and Mary, Bill, and me, with our feet up on our bicycles.

Well, there I was, and my poor old skinny legs and long white dress, and two pigtails hanging down my back. And all the funny-looking clothes we wore, with the doo-lolly[7] business on them. . . . But I guess you can't remember. You weren't born.

But—well, we were a right nice-looking set of people, if I do say so. And there was 86 the way it used to be, with the front porch, the grape-vines, and the flower-beds before the house. And Miss Martha standing there by Papa with a watch-charm pinned to her waist. . . . I shouldn't laugh, but Miss Martha. . . . Well, Mamma was a pretty woman then—and Papa in his swallow-tail was a good-looking man. Do you remember how he used to get dressed up on Sunday? And how grand he thought he was? And how wonderful that dinky little shop on the Square looked to us! . . . Can you beat it now? . . . Why, we thought that Papa was the biggest man in town and—oh, you can't tell me! You can't tell me! He had his faults, but Papa was a wonderful man. You know he was!

And there was Jim and Dick and Robert, Mary, Bill, and me lined up there before the house with one foot on our bicycles. . . . And I got to thinking back about it all. It all came back.

Do you remember anything about St. Louis? You were only three or four years old then, but you must remember something. . . . Do you remember how you used to bawl when I would scrub you? How you'd bawl for Robert? . . . Poor kid, you used to yell for Robert every time I'd get you in the tub. He was a sweet kid, and he was crazy about you: he almost brought you up.

That year Robert was working at the Inside Inn out on the Fair Grounds . . . Do you remember the old Inside Inn? That big old wooden thing inside the Fair? . . . And how I used to take you there to wait for Robert when he got through working? . . . And Billy Pelham at the news-stand, how he used to give you a stick of chewing-gum?

They were all crazy about Robert. . . . Everybody liked him. . . . And how proud Robert was of you! . . . Don't you remember how he used to show you off? . . . How he used to take you around and make you talk to Billy Pelham? . . . And Mr. Curtis at the desk? . . . And how Robert would try to make you talk and get you to say, "Robert"? And you couldn't pronounce the *"r"*—and you'd say *"Wobbut."* Have you forgotten that? . . . You shouldn't forget *that,* because . . . you were a *cute* kid, then . . . Ho-ho-ho-ho-ho. . . . I don't know where it's gone to, but you were a big hit in those days. . . .

6. Formal coat.

7. Dressy, showy (colloquial).

And I was thinking of it all the other day: how we used to go and meet Robert there and how he'd take us to the Midway. . . . Do you remember the Midway? The Snake-Eater and the Living Skeleton, the Fat Woman and the Shoot the Chute, the Scenic Railway and the Ferris Wheel? . . . How you bawled the night we took you up on the Ferris Wheel! You yelled your head off. . . . I tried to laugh it off, but I tell you, I was scared myself . . . And how Robert laughed at us and told us there was no danger. . . . My Lord, poor little Robert! He was only twelve years old at the time, but he seemed so grown-up to us. I was two years older, but I thought he knew it all.

It was always that way with him. . . . Looking back now, it sometimes seems that it was Robert who brought us up. He was always looking after us, telling us what to do, bringing us something—some ice-cream or some candy, something he had bought out of the poor little money he'd got at the Inn. . . .

Then I got to thinking of the afternoon we sneaked away from home. . . . Mamma had gone out somewhere. And Robert and I got on the street-car and came downtown. . . . And my Lord, in those days, that was what we called a *trip.* A ride on the street-car was something to write home about in those days. . . . I hear that it's all built up around there now.

So we got on the car and rode the whole way down into the business section of St. Louis. Robert took me into a drug-store and set me up to[8] soda-water. Then we came out and walked around some, down to the Union Station and clear over to the river. . . . And both of us half scared to death at what we'd done and wondering what Mamma would say if she found out.

We stayed there till it was getting dark, and we passed by a lunch-room—an old joint with one-armed chairs and people eating at the counter. . . . We read all the signs to see what they had to eat and how much it cost, and I guess nothing on the menu was more than fifteen cents, but it couldn't have looked grander to us if it had been Delmonico's.[9] . . . So we stood there with our noses pressed against the window, looking in. . . . Two skinny little kids, both of us scared half to death, getting the thrill of a lifetime out of it. . . . You know what I mean? . . . And smelling everything with all our might and thinking how good it all smelled. . . . Then Robert turned to me and whispered, "Come on, Sue. . . . Let's go in. . . . It says fifteen cents for pork and beans. And I've got money," Robert said. "I've got sixty cents."

I was so scared I couldn't speak. . . . I'd never been in a place like that before. . . . But I kept thinking, "Oh, Lord, if Mamma should find out!" . . . Don't you know how it is when you're a kid? It was the thrill of a lifetime. . . . I couldn't resist. So we both went in and ordered pork and beans and a cup of coffee. . . . I suppose we were too frightened at what we'd done really to enjoy anything. We just gobbled it all up in a hurry, and gulped our coffee down. And I don't know whether it was the excitement—I guess the poor kid was already sick when we came in there and didn't know it. But I turned and looked at him, and he was as white as death. . . . And when I asked him what was the matter, he wouldn't tell me. . . . He was too proud. He said he was all right, but I could see that he was sick as a dog. . . . So

8. Treated me to (slang).
9. A famous and expensive restaurant in New York City.

he paid the bill. . . . It came to forty cents; I'll never forget *that* as long as I live. . . . And sure enough, we no more than got out the door—he'd hardly time to reach the curb—before it all came up. . . .

And the poor kid was so scared and so ashamed. What scared him so was not that he had got sick but that he had spent all that money, and it had come to nothing. And Mamma would find out. . . . Poor kid, he just stood there looking at me and he whispered, "Oh, Sue, don't tell Mamma. She'll be mad if she finds out." Then we hurried home, and he was still white as a sheet when we got there.

Mamma was waiting for us. . . . She looked at us—you know how Miss Martha looks at you, when she thinks you've been doing something that you shouldn't? . . . Mamma said: "Why, where on earth have you two children been?" I guess she was all set to lay us out. Then she took one look at Robert's face. That was enough for her. She said: "Why, child, what in the world—" She was white as a sheet herself. . . . And all that Robert said was "Mamma, I feel sick."

He was sick as a dog. He fell over on the bed, and we undressed him, and Mamma put her hand upon his forehead and came out in the hall—she was so white you could have made a black mark on her face with chalk—and whispered to me:

"Go and get the doctor quick; he's burning up."

And I went running, my pigtails flying, to get Dr. Packer. I brought him back with me. When he came out of Robert's room, he told Mamma what to do, but I don't know if she even heard him.

Her face was white as a sheet. She looked at me and looked right through me. . . . And oh, my Lord, I'll never forget the way she looked, the way my heart stopped and came up in my throat. . . . I was only a skinny little kid of fourteen. But she looked as if she was dying right before my eyes. . . . And I knew that if anything happened to him, she'd never get over it, if she lived to be a hundred.

Poor old Mamma. You know, he always was her eyeballs[1]—you know that, don't you?—Not the rest of us!—No, sir! I know what I'm talking about. It always has been Robert—she always thought more of him than she did of any of the others and—Poor kid! I can see him lying there white as a sheet and remember how sick he was, and how scared I was! . . . I don't know why—all we'd done had been to sneak away from home and go to a lunch-room—but I felt guilty about the whole thing, as if it was my fault. . . .

It all came back to me the other day when I was looking at that picture, and I thought, my God, we were two kids together, and I was only two years older than Robert was. . . . And now I'm forty-six. . . . Can you imagine that—the way we all grow up and change and go away? . . . And my Lord, Robert seemed so grown-up to me even then. He was only a kid; yet he seemed older than the rest of us.

I was thinking of it just the other day, and I wonder what Robert would say now if he could see that picture. For when you look at it, it all comes back—the boarding house, St. Louis and the Fair. . . . And all of it is just the same as it has always been, as if it happened yesterday. . . . And all of us have grown up and gone away. And nothing has turned out the way we thought

1. Favorite (slang).

it would. . . . And all my hopes and dreams and big ambitions have come to nothing.

It's all so long ago, as if it happened in another world. And then it all comes back, as if it happened yesterday. . . . And sometimes I will lie awake at night and think of all the people who have come and gone, and all the things that happened. And hear the trains down by the river, and the whistles and the bell. . . . And how we went to St. Louis back in 1904.

And then I go out into the street and see the faces of the people that I pass. . . . Don't you see something funny in their eyes, as if they were wondering what had happened to them since they were kids—what it was that they had lost? . . . Now am I crazy, or do they look that way to you?

My God, I'd like to find out what is wrong. . . . What has changed since then. . . . And if we have that same queer funny look in our eyes, too. . . . And if it happens to us all, to everyone. . . . Robert and Jim and Dick and me—all standing there before that house on Orchard Street—and then you see the way we were—and how it all gets lost. . . .

The way it all turns out is nothing like the way we thought that it would be. . . . And how it all gets lost, until it seems that it has never happened—that it is something that we dreamed somewhere. . . . You see what I mean now? . . . That it is something that we hear somewhere, that it happened to someone else. . . . And then it all comes back again.

And there you are, two funny, frightened, skinny little kids with their noses pressed against a dirty window thirty years ago. . . . The way it felt, the way it smelled, even the funny smell in that old pantry of our house. And the steps before the house, the way the rooms looked. Those two little boys in sailor suits who used to ride up and down before the house on their tricycles. . . . And the birthmark on Robert's neck. . . . The Inside Inn. . . . St. Louis and the Fair. . . . It all comes back as if it happened yesterday. And then it goes away and seems farther off and stranger than if it happened in a dream.

"This is King's Highway," a man said. I looked and saw that it was just a street. There were some new buildings, and a big hotel; some restaurants, "bar-grill" places of the modern kind, the livid monotone of neon lights, the ceaseless traffic of the motorcars—all this was new, but it was just a street. And I knew that it had always been a street and nothing more. But somehow—I stood there looking at it, wondering what else I had expected to find.

The man kept looking at me, and I asked him if the Fair had been out this way.

"Sure, the Fair was out beyond here," the man said. "Where the park is now. But this street you're looking for? Don't you remember the name of the street or nothing?"

I said I thought the name was Edgemont Street, but that I was not sure. And I said the house was on the corner of this street and another street. And then the man said, "What street was that?" I said I did not know, but that King's Highway was a block or so away and that an interurban line ran past about a block or so from where we lived.

"What line was this?" the man said, and stared at me.

"The interurban line," I said.

Then he stared at me again and finally, "I don't know no interurban line," he said.

I said it was a line that ran behind some houses and that there were board fences there and grass beside the tracks. But somehow I could not say that it was summer in those days and that you could smell the ties, a kind of wooden tarry smell, and feel a kind of absence in the afternoon, after the car had gone. I could not say that King's Highway had not been a street in those days but a kind of road that wound from magic out of some dim land, and that along the way it had got mixed with Tom the Piper's son, with hot cross buns,[2] with all the light that came and went, and with cloud shadows passing on the mountains, with coming down through Indiana in the morning, and the smell of engine smoke, the Union Station, and most of all with voices lost and far and long ago that said, "King's Highway."

I didn't say those things about King's Highway because I looked about me and I saw what King's Highway was. I left him then and went on till I found the place. And again, again, I turned into the street, finding the place where the two corners meet, the huddled block, the turret, and the steps, and paused a moment, looking back, as if the street was Time.

So I waited for a moment for a word, for a door to open, for the child to come. I waited, but no words were spoken; no one came.

Yet all of it was just as it had always been except the steps were lower and the porch less high, the strip of grass less wide than I had thought. A graystone front, St. Louis style, three-storied, with a slant slate roof, the side red brick and windowed, still with the old arched entrance in the center for the doctor's use.

There was a tree in front, a lamp-post, and behind and to the side more trees than I had known there would be. And all the slaty turret gables, all the slaty window gables going into points, the two arched windows, in strong stone, in the front room.

It was all so strong, so solid and so ugly—and so enduring and good, the way I had remembered it, except I did not smell the tar, the hot and caulky dryness of the old cracked ties, the boards of backyard fences and the coarse and sultry grass, and absence in the afternoon when the street-car had gone, and the feel of the hot afternoon, and that everyone was absent at the Fair.

It was a hot day. Darkness had come; the heat hung and sweltered like a sodden blanket in St. Louis. The heat soaked down, and the people sweltered in it; the faces of the people were pale and greasy with the heat. And in their faces was a kind of patient wretchedness, and one felt the kind of desolation that one feels at the end of a hot day in a great city in America—when one's home is far away across the continent, and he thinks of all that distance, all that heat, and feels: "Oh, God, but it's a big country!"

Then he hears the engine and the wheel again, the wailing whistle and the bell, the sound of shifting in the sweltering yard, and walks the street, and walks the street, beneath the clusters of hard lights, and by the people with sagged faces, and is drowned in desolation and no belief.

He feels the way one feels when one comes back, and knows that he should not have come, and when he sees that, after all, King's Highway is—a street;

2. I.e., Mother Goose nursery rhymes.

and St. Louis—the enchanted name—a big hot common town upon the river, sweltering in wet dreary heat, and not quite South, and nothing else enough to make it better.

It had not been like this before. I could remember how it got hot in the afternoons, and how I would feel a sense of absence and vague sadness when everyone had gone away. The house would seem so lonely, and sometimes I would sit inside, on the second step of the hall stairs, and listen to the sound of silence and absence in the afternoon. I could smell the oil upon the floor and on the stairs, and see the sliding doors with their brown varnish and the beady chains across the door, and thrust my hand among the beady chains, and gather them together in my arms, and let them clash, and swish with light beady swishings all round me. I could feel darkness, absence, and stained light, within the house, through the stained glass of the window on the stairs, through the small stained glasses by the door, stained light and absence, and vague sadness in the house in a hot mid-afternoon. And all these things themselves would have a kind of life: would seem to wait attentively, to be most living and most still.

Then I would long for evening and return, the slant of light, and feet along the street, the sharp-faced twins in sailor-suits upon their tricycles, the smell of supper and the sound of voices in the house again, and Robert coming from the Fair.

And again, again, I turned into the street, finding the place where two corners meet, turning at last to see if Time was there. I passed the house; some lights were burning in the house; the door was open, and a woman sat upon the porch. And presently I turned and stopped before the house again. I stood looking at it for a moment, and I put my foot upon the step.

Then I said to the woman who was sitting on the porch: "This house—excuse me, but could you tell me, please, who lives here?"

I know my words were strange and hollow and I had not said what I wished to say. She stared at me a moment, puzzled.

Then she said: "I live here. Who are you looking for?"

I said, "Why, I am looking for—There used to be a house—" I said.

The woman was now staring hard at me.

"I used to live here in this house," I said.

She was silent for a moment; then she said: "When was it that you lived here?"

"In 1904."

Again she was silent, looking at me for a moment. Then presently: "Oh. . . . That was the year of the Fair. You were here then?"

"Yes." I now spoke rapidly, with more confidence: "My mother had the house, and we were here for seven months. . . . And the house belonged to Dr. Packer," I went on. "We rented it from him."

"Yes," the woman said, and nodded now. "This was Dr. Packer's house. He's been dead for many years. But this was the Packer house, all right."

"That entrance on the side," I said, "where the steps go up—that was for Dr. Packer's patients. That was the entrance to his office."

"Oh," the woman said, "I didn't know that. I've often wondered what it was. I didn't know what it was for."

"And this big room here in front," I said, "that was the office. And there were sliding doors, and next to it a kind of alcove for his patients."

"Yes, the alcove is still there, only all of it has been made into one room now—and I never knew just what the alcove was for."

"And there were sliding doors on this side, too, that opened on the hall—and a stairway going up upon this side. And halfway up the stairway, at the landing, a little window of stained glass—and across the sliding doors here in the hall a kind of curtain made of strings of beads."

She nodded, smiling. "Yes, it's just the same—we still have the sliding doors and the stained glass window on the stairs. There's no bead curtain any more," she said, "but I remember when people had them. I know what you mean."

"When we were here," I said, "we used the Doctor's office for a parlor—except later on, the last month or two; and then we used it for a bedroom."

"It is a bedroom now," she said. "I rent rooms—all of the rooms upstairs are rented—but I have two brothers and they sleep in this front room."

And we were silent for a moment; then I said, "My brother stayed there, too."

"In the front room?" the woman said.

I answered: "Yes."

She paused a moment; then she said: "Won't you come in? I don't believe it's changed much. Would you like to see?"

I thanked her and said I would, and I went up the steps. She opened the screen door, and I went in.

And it was just the same—the stairs, the hallway, and the sliding doors, the window of stained glass upon the stairs. All of it was just the same except the stained light of absence in the afternoon, and the child who sat there, waiting on the stairs, and something fading like a dream, something coming like a light, something going, passing, fading like the shadows of a wood. And then it would be gone again, fading like cloud shadows in the hills, coming like the vast, the drowsy rumors of the distant enchanted Fair, and coming, going, coming, being found and lost, possessed and held and never captured, like lost voices in the mountains, long ago, like the dark eyes and the quiet face, the dark lost boy, my brother, who himself like shadows, or like absence in the house, would come, would go, and would return again.

The woman took me into the house and through the hall. I told her of the pantry, and I told her where it was and pointed to the place, but now it was no longer there. And I told her of the back yard, and the old board fence around the yard. But the old board fence was gone. And I told her of the carriage-house, and told her it was painted red. But now there was a small garage. And the back yard was still there, but smaller than I thought, and now there was a tree.

"I did not know there was a tree," I said. "I do not remember any tree."

"Perhaps it wasn't there," she said. "A tree could grow in thirty years." And then we came back through the house and paused a moment at the sliding doors.

"And could I see this room?" I said.

She slid the doors back. They slid open smoothly, with a kind of rolling heaviness, as they used to do. And then I saw the room again. It was the same. There was a window to the side, the two arched windows to the front, the alcove and the sliding doors, the fireplace with the tiles of mottled green, the mantel of dark mission wood, a dresser and a bed, just where the dresser and the bed had been so long ago.

"Is this the room?" the woman said. "It hasn't changed?"

I told her it was the same.

"And your brother slept here where my brothers sleep?"

"This was his room," I said.

And we were silent for a moment. Then I turned to go, and said: "Well, thank you. I appreciate your showing me."

The woman said that she was glad and that it was no trouble. And she said, "And when you see your family, you can tell them that you saw the house," she said. "And my name is Mrs. Bell. You can tell your mother that a Mrs. Bell has got the house. And when you see your brother, you can tell him that you saw the room he slept in, and that you found it just the same."

I told her then that he was dead.

The woman was silent for a moment. Then she looked at me and said: "He died here, didn't he? In this room?"

I told her that he did.

"Well, then," she said, "I knew it. I don't know how. But when you told me he was here, I knew it."

I said nothing. In a moment the woman said: "What did he die of?"

"Typhoid."

She looked shocked and troubled, and began involuntarily:

"My two brothers—"

"That was so long ago," I said. "I don't think you need to worry now."

"Oh, I wasn't thinking about that," she said. . . . "It was just hearing that a little boy—your brother—was—was in this room that my two brothers sleep in now—"

"Well, maybe I shouldn't have told you then. But he was a good boy—and if you'd known him, you wouldn't mind."

She said nothing, and I added quickly: "Besides, he didn't stay here long. This wasn't really his room—but the night he came back with my sister, he was so sick—they didn't move him."

"Oh," the woman said, "I see." And in a moment: "Are you going to tell your mother you were here?"

"I don't think so."

"I—I wonder how she feels about this room."

"I don't know. She never speaks of it."

"Oh. . . . How old was he?"

"He was twelve."

"You must have been pretty young yourself."

"I was four."

"And—you just wanted to see the room, didn't you? Is that why you came back?"

"Yes."

"Well"—indefinitely—"I guess you've seen it now."

"Yes, thank you."

"I guess you don't remember much about him, do you? I shouldn't think you would."

"No, not much."

The years dropped off like fallen leaves: the face came back again—the soft dark oval, the dark eyes, the soft brown berry on the neck, the raven hair, all bending down, approaching—the whole ghost-wise, intent and instant, like faces from a haunted wood.

"Now say it: *Robert!*"

"Wobbut."

"No, not *Wobbut: Robert*. . . . Say it."

"Wobbut."

"Ah-h—you *didn't* say it. . . . You said Wobbut: *Robert!* . . . Now say it."

"Wobbut."

"Look, I'll tell you what I'll do if you say it right. . . . Would you like to go down to King's Highway? Would you like Robert to set you up? All right, then. . . . If you say Robert right, I'll take you to King's Highway and set you up to ice-cream. . . . Now say it right: Say *Robert*."

"Wobbut."

"Ah-h you-u! . . . Old tongue-tie, that's what you are. Some day I'm going to. . . . Well, come on, then. I'll set you up, anyway."

It all came back and faded and was lost again. I turned to go, and thanked the woman, and I said: "Good-bye."

"Well, then, good-bye," the woman said, and we shook hands. "I'm glad if I could show you. I'm glad if—" She did not finish, and at length she said: "Well, then, that was a long time ago. You'll find it all changed now, I guess. It's all built up around here now—way out beyond here, out beyond where the Fair grounds used to be. I guess you'll find it changed," she said.

We could find no more to say. We stood there for a moment on the steps, and shook hands once more.

"Well, then, good-bye."

And again, again, I turned into the street, finding the place where corners meet, turning to look again to see where Time had gone. And all of it was just the same, it seemed that it had never changed since then, except all had been found and caught and captured for forever. And so, finding all, I knew all had been lost.

I knew that I would never come again, and that lost magic would not come again, and that the light that came, that passed and went and that returned again, the memory of lost voices in the hills, cloud shadows passing in the mountains, the voices of our kinsmen long ago, the street, the heat, King's Highway, and the piper's son, the vast and drowsy murmur of the distant Fair—oh, strange and bitter miracle of Time—come back again.

But I knew that it could not come back—the cry of absence in the afternoon, the house that waited and the child that dreamed; and through the thicket of man's memory, from the enchanted wood, the dark eye and the quiet face,—poor child, life's stranger and life's exile, lost, like all of us, a cipher in blind mazes, long ago—my parent, friend, and brother, the lost boy, was gone forever and would not return.

1937, 1987

STERLING BROWN
1901–1989

For much of his long and distinguished career Sterling Brown presented himself to the public mainly as a teacher and scholar of African American folk culture and written literature. During the Harlem Renaissance movement, however, he was also hailed as a technically accomplished and eloquent poet. Rediscovered by younger black poets in the late 1960s, Brown has since been called, to quote the poet Michael S. Harper, "a trustee of consciousness, and a national treasure."

Born in Washington, D.C., and never resident in New York, Brown identified himself with the "New Negro" movement in general rather than with its particular manifestation in Harlem during the 1920s. "The New Negro," he wrote in 1955, "is not to me a group of writers centered in Harlem during the second half of the twenties. Most of the writers were not Harlemites; much of the best writing was not about Harlem, which was the show-window, the cashier's till, but no more Negro America than New York is America." Brown viewed Harlem as the place where African American writing was publicized rather than produced, believing that the cosmopolitan and sophisticated New York writers themselves had not written representatively about, or from the perspective of, ordinary black people. While he himself was well educated and of middle-class background, Brown immersed himself deeply in the full range of African American popular expression—jazz, blues, spirituals, work songs, folk tales—so that his writing could reach beyond his own experience.

Brown's father was the Reverend Sterling Nelson Brown, who had been born a slave but eventually attended Fisk University and Oberlin College and later became professor of religion at Howard University in Washington, D.C. Brown attended the academically oriented Dunbar High School, went to Williams College in 1918, and took a master's degree at Harvard. He won a prize in 1925 for his first nationally published essay—a sketch of the tenor Roland Hayes that appeared in *Opportunity*—and thereby came to the attention of black intellectuals. While teaching at Virginia Seminary and College between 1926 and 1928, he met and married Daisy Turnbull. After brief teaching jobs at Fisk, Lincoln University in Missouri, and Atlanta University, he joined the faculty at Howard University in 1929, where he continued to teach until retirement. His first book, *Outline for the Study of the Poetry of American Negroes* (1931), was a pedagogical supplement to James Weldon Johnson's *Book of American Negro Poetry,* including paper topics, study questions, definitions, and other material. Having published individual poems in magazines and newspapers, Brown brought out a collection of this work called *Southern Road* in 1932. It was highly praised by influential critics, many of whom were especially impressed with Brown's technical virtuosity. Alain Locke, the major theorist of the New Negro movement, believed that the book came very close to his ideal of the "poetic portrayal of Negro folk-life . . . true in both letter and spirit to the idiom of the folk's own way of feeling and thinking." Despite such acclaim, the book did not sell widely—1932 was not a good year for publishing, and the Harlem Renaissance movement had ended abruptly with the onset of the Great Depression in 1929. Brown's planned second book of poems, tentatively called *No Hiding Place* and ready for the press in 1935, was rejected by publishers for economic reasons.

After this setback Brown made little further effort to publish poetry and turned his energies into academic and administrative channels, always retaining his focus on African American culture. From 1936 to 1939 he was Negro affairs editor for the

Federal Writers' Project, a government funding source for writers during the Depression years; he also worked on the staff of the "Carnegie-Myrdal Study of the Negro," the basis of a landmark study of race relations, *An American Dilemma,* written by the Swedish sociologists Gunnar Myrdal and Alva Myrdal and published shortly after the end of World War II. *The Negro in American Fiction,* a book of critical essays, and *Negro Poetry and Drama,* a literary history, both appeared in 1938. Together with Ulysses Lee and Arthur P. Davis, Brown edited the important anthology *Negro Caravan* (1941), collecting important examples of African American literature from its folk foundations to 1940. Over the years he published numerous essays, notes, and commentaries on African American literature, the role of blacks in American writing, black folklore, and black music; he was an acknowledged expert on all of these topics.

The civil rights movement of the 1960s motivated him to conduct lectures and poetry readings that brought him and his poetry back into national view. It became clear at this time that Alain Locke's earlier assessment of Brown was only partly true. Although in some sense Brown strove in his poetry to make a literary form appropriate to authentic black folk voices, he saw these voices not as raw folk data but as already artistically self-conscious. Blues, jazz, and spirituals were complex, expressive, culturally sophisticated forms. In addition, Brown deployed his speakers' voices not for the main purpose of celebrating the black folk tradition—though this was certainly part of his aim—but to expose and criticize racial injustice. Both his scholarly writing and his poetry call attention to African American achievements and deplore American racism.

The text of the poems printed here is from *Collected Poems* (1996).

Mister Samuel and Sam

Mister Samuel, he belong to Rotary,[1]
Sam to de Sons of Rest;[2]
Both wear red hats[3] lak monkey men,
An' you cain't say which is de best.

Mister Samuel ride in a Cadillac,
Sam ride in a Tin Lizzie Fo'd;
Both spend their jack fo' gas an' oil,
An' both git stuck on de road.

Mister Samuel speak in de Chamber of Commerce,
Sam he speak in ch'uch;
Both of 'em talk for a mighty long time,
Widout sayin', Lawd knows, ve'y much.

Mister Samuel deal wid high finance,
Sam deal in a two-bit game;
Mister Samuel crashes, Sam goes broke,
But deys busted jes' de same.

Mister Samuel wife speak sof' an' low,
When dey gits in their weekly fight;

1. The National Association of Rotary Clubs, service clubs founded to bring together businessmen and professionals, was established in the United States in 1910.
2. A social club for industrial workers and retirees that emerged in the United Kingdom and the United States in the early 20th century. Colloquially, any group of idlers or hobos.
3. Associated with the Shriners, a fraternal organization founded in 1870, as well as with the monkeys who often accompanied organ grinders in the streets of U.S. cities.

Sam catches a broomstick crost his rear,
An' both of 'em's henpecked right.

Mister Samuel drinks his Canadian Rye,
Sam drinks his bootleg gin;
Both gits as high as a Georgia pine,
And both calls de doctor in.

Mister Samuel die, an' de folks all know,
Sam die widout no noise;
De worl' go by in de same ol' way,
And dey's both of 'em po' los' boys. . . .

1932, 1980

He Was a Man

It wasn't about no woman,
  It wasn't about no rape,
He wasn't crazy, and he wasn't drunk,
  An' it wasn't no shooting scrape,
    He was a man, and they laid him down.

He wasn't no quarrelsome feller,
  And he let other folks alone,
But he took a life, as a man will do,
  In a fight for to save his own,
    He was a man, and they laid him down.

He worked on his little homeplace
  Down on the Eastern Shore;
He had his family, and he had his friends,
  And he didn't expect much more,
    He was a man, and they laid him down.

He wasn't nobody's great man,
  He wasn't nobody's good,
Was a po' boy tried to get from life
  What happiness he could,
    He was a man, and they laid him down.

He didn't abuse Tom Wickley,
  Said nothing when the white man curst,
But when Tom grabbed his gun, he pulled his own,
  And his bullet got there first,
    He was a man, and they laid him down.

Didn't catch him in no manhunt,
  But they took him from a hospital bed,
Stretched on his back in the nigger ward,
  With a bullet wound in his head,
    He was a man, and they laid him down.

It didn't come off at midnight
  Nor yet at the break of day,
It was in the broad noon daylight,
  When they put po' Will away,
    He was a man, and they laid him down.

Didn't take him to no swampland,
  Didn't take him to no woods,
Didn't hide themselves, didn't have no masks,
  Didn't wear no Ku Klux hoods,
    He was a man, and they laid him down.

They strung him up on Main Street,
  On a tree in the Court House Square,
And people came from miles around
  To enjoy a holiday there,
    He was a man, and they laid him down.

They hung him and they shot him,
  They piled packing cases around,
They burnt up Will's black body,
  'Cause he shot a white man down;
    "He was a man, and we'll lay him down."

It wasn't no solemn business,
  Was more like a barbecue,
The crackers yelled when the fire blazed,
  And the women and the children too—
    "He was a man, and we laid him down."

The Coroner and the Sheriff
  Said "Death by Hands Unknown."
The mob broke up by midnight,
  "Another uppity Nigger gone—
    He was a man, an' we laid him down."

1932, 1980

Master and Man

The yellow ears are crammed in Mr. Cromartie's bin
The wheat is tight sacked in Mr. Cromartie's barn.
The timothy is stuffed in Mr. Cromartie's loft.
The ploughs are lined up in Mr. Cromartie's shed.
The cotton has gone to Mr. Cromartie's factor.
The money is in Mr. Cromartie's bank.
Mr. Cromartie's son made his frat at the college.
Mr. Cromartie's daughter has got her new car.
The veranda is old, but the fireplace is rosy.
Well done, Mr. Cromartie. Time now for rest.

Blackened sticks line the furrows that Uncle Ned laid.
Bits of fluff are in the corners where Uncle Ned ginned.
The mules he ploughed are sleek in Mr. Cromartie's pastures.
The hoes grow dull in Mr. Cromartie's shed.
His winter rations wait on the commissary shelves;
Mr. Cromartie's ledger is there for his service.
Uncle Ned daubs some mortar between the old logs.
His children have traipsed off to God knows where.
His old lady sits patching the old, thin denims;
She's got a new dress, and his young one a doll,
He's got five dollars. The year has come round.
The harvest is over: Uncle Ned's harvesting,
Mr. Cromartie's harvest. Time now for rest.

1936, 1980

Break of Day

Big Jess fired on the Alabama Central,
Man in full, babe, man in full.
Been throwing on coal for Mister Murphy
From times way back, baby, times way back.

Big Jess had a pleasing woman, name of Mamie,
Sweet-hipted Mama, sweet-hipted Mame;
Had a boy growing up for to be a fireman,
Just like his pa, baby, like his pa.

Out by the roundhouse Jess had his cabin,
Longside the tracks, babe, long the tracks,
Jess pulled the whistle when they high-balled past it
"I'm on my way, baby, on my way."

Crackers craved the job what Jess was holding,
Times right tough, babe, times right tough,
Warned Jess to quit his job for a white man,
Jess he laughed, baby, he jes' laughed.

He picked up his lunch-box, kissed his sweet woman,
Sweet-hipted Mama, sweet-hipted Mame,
His son walked with him to the white-washed palings,
"Be seeing you soon, son, see you soon."

Mister Murphy let Big Jess talk on the whistle
"So long sugar baby, so long babe";
Train due back in the early morning
Breakfast time, baby, breakfast time.

Mob stopped the train crossing Black Bear Mountain
Shot rang out, babe, shot rang out.

They left Big Jess on the Black Bear Mountain,
Break of day, baby, break of day.

Sweet Mame sits rocking, waiting for the whistle
Long past due, babe, long past due.
The grits are cold, and the coffee's boiled over,
But Jess done gone, baby he done gone.

1938, 1980

Bitter Fruit of the Tree

They said to my grandmother: "Please do not be bitter,"
When they sold her first-born and let the second die,
When they drove her husband till he took to the swamplands,
And brought him home bloody and beaten at last.
They told her, "It is better you should not be bitter,
Some must work and suffer so that we, who must, can live,
Forgiving is noble, you must not be heathen bitter;
These are your orders: you *are* not to be bitter."
And they left her shack for their porticoed house.

They said to my father: "Please do not be bitter,"
When he ploughed and planted a crop not his,
When he weatherstripped a house that he could not enter,
And stored away a harvest he could not enjoy.
They answered his questions: "It does not concern you,
It is not for you to know, it is past your understanding,
All you need know is: you must not be bitter."

1939, 1980

LANGSTON HUGHES
1902–1967

Langston Hughes was the most popular and versatile of the many writers connected with the Harlem Renaissance. Along with Zora Neale Hurston, and in contrast to Jean Toomer and Countee Cullen (who wanted to work with the patterns of written literary forms, whether traditional or experimental), he wanted to capture the oral and improvisatory traditions of black culture in written form.

Hughes was born in Joplin, Missouri; as a child, since his parents were separated, he lived mainly with his maternal grandmother in Lawrence, Kansas. He did, however, live intermittently both with his mother in Detroit and Cleveland, where he finished high school and began to write poetry, and with his father, who, disgusted with American racism, had gone to Mexico. Like other poets in this era—T. S. Eliot, Hart Crane, Edgar Lee Masters, and Robert Frost—Hughes had a mother sympathetic to his poetic ambitions and a businesslike father with whom he was in deep, scarring conflict.

Hughes entered Columbia University in 1920 but left after a year. Traveling and drifting, he shipped out as a merchant seaman and worked at a nightclub in Paris (France) and as a busboy in Washington, D.C. All this time he was writing and publishing poetry, chiefly in the two important African American periodicals *Opportunity* and the *Crisis*. Eleven of Hughes's poems were published in Alain Locke's pioneering anthology, *The New Negro* (1925), and he was also well represented in Countee Cullen's 1927 anthology, *Caroling Dusk*. Carl Van Vechten, one of the white patrons of African American writing, helped get *The Weary Blues*, Hughes's first volume of poems, published in 1926. It was in this year, too, that his important essay "The Negro Artist and the Racial Mountain" appeared in the *Nation* (see p. 328); in that essay Hughes described the immense challenges to be faced by the serious black artist "who would produce a racial art" but insisted on the need for courageous artists to make the attempt. Other patrons appeared: Amy Spingarn financed his college education at Lincoln University (Pennsylvania), and Charlotte Mason subsidized him in New York City between 1928 and 1930. The publication of his novel *Not without Laughter* in 1930 solidified his reputation and sales, enabling him to support himself. By the 1930s he was being called "the bard of Harlem."

The Great Depression brought an abrupt end to much African American literary activity, but Hughes was already a public figure. In the activist 1930s he was much absorbed in radical politics. Hughes and other blacks were drawn by the American Communist Party, which made racial justice an important plank in its platform, promoting an image of working-class solidarity that nullified racial boundaries. He visited the Soviet Union in 1932 and produced a significant amount of radical writing up to the eve of World War II. He covered the Spanish civil war for the *Baltimore Afro-American* in 1937. By the end of the decade he had also been involved in drama and screenplay writing and had begun an autobiography, all the while publishing poetry. In 1943 he invented the folksy, streetwise character Jesse B. Semple, whose commonsense prose monologues on race were eventually collected in four volumes, and Alberta K. Johnson, Semple's female equivalent, in his series of "Madam" poems.

In the 1950s and 1960s Hughes published a variety of anthologies for children and adults, including *First Book of Negroes* (1952), *The First Book of Jazz* (1955), and *The Book of Negro Folklore* (1958). In 1953 he was called to testify before Senator Joseph McCarthy's committee on subversive activities in connection with his 1930s radicalism. The FBI listed him as a security risk until 1959; and during these years, when he could not travel outside the United States because he would not have been allowed to reenter the country, Hughes worked to rehabilitate his reputation as a good American by producing patriotic poetry. From 1960 to the end of his life he was again on the international circuit.

Within the spectrum of artistic possibilities open to writers of the Harlem Renaissance—drawing on African American rural folk forms; on literary traditions and forms that entered the United States from Europe and Great Britain; or on the new cultural forms of blacks in American cities—Hughes chose to focus his work on modern, urban black life. He modeled his stanza forms on the improvisatory rhythms of jazz music and adapted the vocabulary of everyday black speech to poetry. He also acknowledged finding inspiration for his writing in the work of white American poets who preceded him. Like Walt Whitman he heard America singing, and he asserted his right to sing America back; he also learned from Carl Sandburg's earlier attempts to work jazz into poetry. Hughes did not confuse his pride in African American culture with complacency toward the material deprivations of black life in the United States. He was keenly aware that the modernist "vogue in things Negro" among white Americans was potentially exploitative and voyeuristic; he confronted such racial tourists with the misery as well as the jazz of Chicago's South Side. Early and late, Hughes's poems demanded that African Americans be acknowledged as owners of the culture they gave to the United States and as fully enfranchised American citizens.

The source of the poems printed here is *Collected Poems* (1994).

The Negro Speaks of Rivers

I've known rivers:
I've known rivers ancient as the world and older than the
    flow of human blood in human veins.

My soul has grown deep like the rivers.

I bathed in the Euphrates when dawns were young.
I built my hut near the Congo and it lulled me to sleep.
I looked upon the Nile and raised the pyramids above it.
I heard the singing of the Mississippi when Abe Lincoln
    went down to New Orleans, and I've seen its
    muddy bosom turn all golden in the sunset

I've known rivers:
Ancient, dusky rivers.

My soul has grown deep like the rivers.

1921, 1926

Mother to Son

Well, son, I'll tell you:
Life for me ain't been no crystal stair.
It's had tacks in it,
And splinters,
And boards torn up,
And places with no carpet on the floor—
Bare.
But all the time
I'se been a-climbin' on,
And reachin' landin's,
And turnin' corners,
And sometimes goin' in the dark
Where there ain't been no light.
So boy, don't you turn back.
Don't you set down on the steps
'Cause you finds it's kinder hard.

Don't you fall now—
For I'se still goin', honey,
I'se still climbin',
And life for me ain't been no crystal stair.

1922, 1926

I, Too

I, too, sing America.

I am the darker brother.
They send me to eat in the kitchen
When company comes,
But I laugh,
And eat well,
And grow strong.

Tomorrow,
I'll be at the table
When company comes.
Nobody'll dare
Say to me,
"Eat in the kitchen,"
Then.

Besides,
They'll see how beautiful I am
And be ashamed—

I, too, am America.

1925, 1959

The Weary Blues

Droning a drowsy syncopated tune,
Rocking back and forth to a mellow croon,
    I heard a Negro play.
Down on Lenox Avenue the other night
By the pale dull pallor of an old gas light
    He did a lazy sway. . . .
    He did a lazy sway. . . .
To the tune o' those Weary Blues.
With his ebony hands on each ivory key.
He made that poor piano moan with melody.
    O Blues!
Swaying to and fro on his rickety stool

He played that sad raggy tune like a musical fool.
  Sweet Blues!
Coming from a black man's soul.
  O Blues!
In a deep song voice with a melancholy tone
I heard that Negro sing, that old piano moan—
  "Ain't got nobody in all this world,
  Ain't got nobody but ma self.
  I's gwine to quit ma frownin'
  And put ma troubles on de shelf."
Thump, thump, thump, went his foot on the floor.
He played a few chords then he sang some more—
  "I got de Weary Blues
  And I can't be satisfied.
  Got de Weary Blues
  And can't be satisfied—
  I ain't happy no mo'
  And I wish that I had died."
And far into the night he crooned that tune.
The stars went out and so did the moon.
The singer stopped playing and went to bed.
While the Weary Blues echoed through his head
He slept like a rock or a man that's dead.

1925

Mulatto

I am your son, white man!

Georgia dusk
And the turpentine woods.
One of the pillars of the temple fell.

    You are my son!
    Like hell!

The moon over the turpentine woods.
The Southern night
Full of stars,
Great big yellow stars.
  What's a body but a toy?
    Juicy bodies
    Of nigger wenches
    Blue black
    Against black fences.
    O, you little bastard boy,
    What's a body but a toy?
The scent of pine wood stings the soft night air.

What's the body of your mother?
Silver moonlight everywhere.

What's the body of your mother?
Sharp pine scent in the evening air.
A nigger night,
A nigger joy,
A little yellow
Bastard boy.

Naw, you ain't my brother.
Niggers ain't my brother.
Not ever.
Niggers ain't my brother.
The Southern night is full of stars,
Great big yellow stars.
O, sweet as earth,
Dusk dark bodies
Give sweet birth
To little yellow bastard boys.

Git on back there in the night,
You ain't white.

The bright stars scatter everywhere.
Pine wood scent in the evening air.
A nigger night,
A nigger joy.

I am your son, white man!

A little yellow
Bastard boy.

1927

Song for a Dark Girl

Way Down South in Dixie[1]
(Break the heart of me)
They hung my black young lover
To a cross roads tree.

Way Down South in Dixie
(Bruised body high in air)
I asked the white Lord Jesus
What was the use of prayer.

1. Last line of "Dixie," the popular minstrel song, probably composed by Daniel D. Emmett (1815–1904).

Way Down South in Dixie
(Break the heart of me)
Love is a naked shadow
On a gnarled and naked tree.

1927

Genius Child

This is a song for the genius child.
Sing it softly, for the song is wild.
Sing it softly as ever you can—
Lest the song get out of hand.

Nobody loves a genius child.

Can you love an eagle,
Tame or wild?
Can you love an eagle,
Wild or tame?
Can you love a monster
Of frightening name?

Nobody loves a genius child.

Kill him—and let his soul run wild!

1937, 1947

Visitors to the Black Belt

You can talk about
Across the railroad tracks—
To me it's *here*
On this side of the tracks.

You can talk about
Up in Harlem—
To me it's *here*
In Harlem.

You can say
Jazz on the South Side[1]—
To me it's hell
On the South Side:

1. African American neighborhood in Chicago. See also Archibald J. Motley's 1934 painting, *Black Belt*, in the color insert to this volume.

Kitchenettes
With no heat
And garbage
In the halls.

Who're you, outsider?

Ask me who am I.

1940, 1943

Note on Commercial Theatre

You've taken my blues and gone—
You sing 'em on Broadway
And you sing 'em in Hollywood Bowl,[1]
And you mixed 'em up with symphonies
And you fixed 'em
So they don't sound like me.
Yep, you done taken my blues and gone.

You also took my spirituals and gone.
You put me in *Macbeth* and *Carmen Jones*[2]
And all kinds of *Swing Mikados*[3]
And in everything but what's about me—
But someday somebody'll
Stand up and talk about me,
And write about me—

Black and beautiful—
And sing about me,
And put on plays about me!

I reckon it'll be
Me myself!

Yes, it'll be me.

1940, 1959

1. Outdoor concert amphitheater constructed in the 1920s.
2. An all-black musical (1943), loosely based on the opera *Carmen* by French composer George Bizet (1838–1875), focused on African American life during World War II. An all-black production of Shakespeare's *Macbeth* (1606), set in Haiti, was a Broadway success in 1936.
3. During 1939, two different all-black versions of *The Mikado* (1885), a comic opera by the British team of W. S. Gilbert (1836–1911) and Arthur Sullivan (1842–1900), competed on Broadway: *The Swing Mikado* (which premiered in Chicago in 1938) and *The Hot Mikado*.

Vagabonds

We are the desperate
Who do not care,
The hungry
Who have nowhere
To eat,
No place to sleep,
The tearless
Who cannot
Weep.

1941, 1947

Words Like Freedom[1]

There are words like *Freedom*
Sweet and wonderful to say.
On my heart-strings freedom sings
All day everyday.

There are words like *Liberty*
That almost make me cry.
If you had known what I know
You would know why.

1943, 1967

Madam and Her Madam

I worked for a woman,
She wasn't mean—
But she had a twelve-room
House to clean.

Had to get breakfast,
Dinner, and supper, too—
Then take care of her children
When I got through.

Wash, iron, and scrub,
Walk the dog around—
It was too much,
Nearly broke me down.

1. Originally published under the title "Refugee in America."

I said, Madam,
Can it be
You trying to make a
Pack-horse out of me?

She opened her mouth.
She cried, Oh, no!
You know, Alberta,
I love you so!

I said, Madam,
That may be true—
But I'll be dogged
If I love you!

1943

Freedom [1][1]

Freedom will not come
Today, this year
  Nor ever
Through compromise and fear.

I have as much right
As the other fellow has
  To stand
On my two feet
And own the land.

I tire so of hearing people say,
Let things take their course.
Tomorrow is another day.
I do not need my freedom when I'm dead.
I cannot live on tomorrow's bread.

  Freedom
  Is a strong seed
  Planted
  In a great need.

I live here, too.
I want freedom
Just as you.

1943, 1967

1. Originally published under the title "Democracy."

Madam's Calling Cards

I had some cards printed
The other day.
They cost me more
Than I wanted to pay.

I told the man
I wasn't no mint,
But I hankered to see
My name in print.

MADAM JOHNSON,
ALBERTA K.
He said, Your name looks good
Madam'd that way.

Shall I use Old English
Or a Roman letter?
I said, Use American.
American's better.

There's nothing foreign
To my pedigree:
Alberta K. Johnson—
American that's me.

1943, 1949

Silhouette

Southern gentle lady,
Do not swoon.
They've just hung a black man
In the dark of the moon.

They've hung a black man
To a roadside tree
In the dark of the moon
For the world to see
How Dixie protects
Its white womanhood.

Southern gentle lady,
  Be good!
  Be good!

1944, 1949

Theme for English B

The instructor said,

Go home and write
a page tonight.
And let that page come out of you—
Then, it will be true.

I wonder if it's that simple?
I am twenty-two, colored, born in Winston-Salem.
I went to school there, then Durham, then here
to this college on the hill above Harlem.[1]
I am the only colored student in my class.
The steps from the hill lead down into Harlem,
through a park, then I cross St. Nicholas,
Eighth Avenue, Seventh, and I come to the Y,
the Harlem Branch Y, where I take the elevator
up to my room, sit down, and write this page:

It's not easy to know what is true for you or me
at twenty-two, my age. But I guess I'm what
I feel and see and hear, Harlem, I hear you:
hear you, hear me—we two—you, me, talk on this page.
(I hear New York, too.) Me—who?
Well, I like to eat, sleep, drink, and be in love.
I like to work, read, learn, and understand life.
I like a pipe for a Christmas present,
or records—Bessie, bop, or Bach.[2]
I guess being colored doesn't make me *not* like
the same things other folks like who are other races.
So will my page be colored that I write?
Being me, it will not be white.
But it will be
a part of you, instructor.
You are white—
yet a part of me, as I am a part of you.
That's American.
Sometimes perhaps you don't want to be a part of me.
Nor do I often want to be a part of you.
But we are, that's true!
As I learn from you,
I guess you learn from me—
although you're older—and white—
and somewhat more free.

This is my page for English B.

1949

1. The City College of the City University of New York. Winston-Salem and Durham are cities in North Carolina.
2. Johann Sebastian Bach (1685–1750), German composer of the Baroque era. Bessie Smith (1894–1937), noted blues singer. "Bop": jazz form developed in Harlem during World War II.

JOHN STEINBECK
1902–1968

Most of John Steinbeck's best writing is set in the region of California that he called home, the Salinas Valley and Monterey peninsula of California, where visitors today will find official remembrances of him everywhere. Steinbeck believed in the American promise of opportunity for all, but believed also that social injustices and economic inequalities had put opportunity beyond reach for many. His work merged literary modernism with literary realism, celebrated traditional rural communities along with social outcasts and immigrant cultures, and endorsed conservative values and radical politics at the same time.

Steinbeck's father managed a flour mill and later became treasurer of Monterey County; his mother, who had taught school before marriage, was active in local civic affairs. Their home was full of books, and Steinbeck read avidly from an early age. After graduating from Salinas High School in 1919, he began to study at Stanford University but took time off for a variety of short-term jobs at local mills, farms, and estates. During this period he developed an abiding respect for people who worked on farms and in factories, and committed his literary abilities to their cause. He left college for good in 1925, having completed less than three years of coursework, and continued his roving life.

With financial help from his father, Steinbeck spent most of 1929 writing. He moved to the seaside town of Pacific Grove, on the Monterey coast, and in 1930 was married (the first of three times). In 1935 he achieved commercial success with his third novel, *Tortilla Flat,* a celebration of the Mexican-American culture of the "*paisanos*" who lived in the Monterey hills. Steinbeck's next novel, *In Dubious Battle* (1936), contrasted the decency of striking migratory farm workers both to the cynicism of landowners and their vigilantes, and to the equal cynicism of Communist labor union organizers who exploit the workers' plight for their own purposes. Sympathy for the underdog appears again in *Of Mice and Men* (1937), a best-selling short novel about two itinerant ranch hands, and yet again in *The Grapes of Wrath* (1939), his most famous and most ambitious novel. *The Long Valley* (1938) brought together a number of his stories set in the Salinas Valley, including "The Chrysanthemums."

Inspired by the devastating 1930s drought in the southern plains states and the exodus of thousands of farmers from their homes in the so-called Dust Bowl, *The Grapes of Wrath* told the story of the Joad family, who, after losing their land in Oklahoma, migrated westward to California on U.S. Highway 66 looking for, but not finding, a better life. Because of its supposed radicalism, the novel was banned or burned in several states, but even so, it became the nation's number one best seller and won a Pulitzer Prize in 1940. *Cannery Row* (1945), a local-color novel about workers in the sardine canneries of Monterey, also became a best seller.

During and after World War II, the film industry began paying serious attention to Steinbeck's writing. *Of Mice and Men* was adapted as a film in 1939, and *The Grapes of Wrath* followed in 1940. The family saga *East of Eden* (1952), Steinbeck's longest novel, was filmed in 1955 with the electric young actor James Dean (1931–1955) in a starring role. The qualities that made Steinbeck's fiction so adaptable to the screen were also those for which he won the Nobel Prize in 1962; the prize committee praised his work for "combining sympathetic humour and keen social perception."

The text of "The Chrysanthemums" is that of its first printing, in *Harper's* (1937).

The Chrysanthemums

The high grey-flannel fog of winter closed off the Salinas Valley from the sky and from all the rest of the world. On every side it sat like a lid on the mountains and made of the great valley a closed pot. On the broad, level land floor the gang plows[1] bit deep and left the black earth shining like metal where the shares had cut. On the foothill ranches across the Salinas River, the yellow stubble fields seemed to be bathed in pale cold sunshine, but there was no sunshine in the valley now in December. The thick willow scrub along the river flamed with sharp and positive yellow leaves.

It was a time of quiet and of waiting. The air was cold and tender. A light wind blew up from the southwest so that the farmers were mildly hopeful of a good rain before long; but fog and rain do not go together.

Across the river, on Henry Allen's foothill ranch there was little work to be done, for the hay was cut and stored and the orchards were plowed up to receive the rain deeply when it should come. The cattle on the higher slopes were becoming shaggy and rough-coated.

Elisa Allen, working in her flower garden, looked down across the yard and saw Henry, her husband, talking to two men in business suits. The three of them stood by the tractor shed, each man with one foot on the side of the little Fordson.[2] They smoked cigarettes and studied the machine as they talked.

Elisa watched them for a moment and then went back to her work. She was thirty-five. Her face was lean and strong and her eyes were as clear as water. Her figure looked blocked and heavy in her gardening costume, a man's black hat pulled low down over her eyes, clodhopper shoes, a figured print dress almost completely covered by a big corduroy apron with four big pockets to hold the snips, the trowel and scratcher, the seeds and the knife she worked with. She wore heavy leather gloves to protect her hands while she worked.

She was cutting down the old year's chrysanthemum stalks with a pair of short and powerful scissors. She looked down toward the men by the tractor shed now and then. Her face was eager and mature and handsome; even her work with the scissors was over-eager, over-powerful. The chrysanthemum stems seemed too small and easy for her energy.

She brushed a cloud of hair out of her eyes with the back of her glove, and left a smudge of earth on her cheek in doing it. Behind her stood the neat white farm house with red geraniums close-banked around it as high as the windows. It was a hard-swept looking little house with hard-polished windows, and a clean mud-mat on the front steps.

Elisa cast another glance toward the tractor shed. The strangers were getting into their Ford coupe.[3] She took off a glove and put her strong fingers down into the forest of new green chrysanthemum sprouts that were growing around the old roots. She spread the leaves and looked down among the close-growing stems. No aphids were there, no sowbugs or snails or cutworms. Her terrier fingers destroyed such pests before they could get started.

1. Plows with multiple plowshares, or plowing blades.
2. Brand of tractor made by the Ford Motor Company.
3. Closed-roof, two-door automobile.

Elisa started at the sound of her husband's voice. He had come near quietly, and he leaned over the wire fence that protected her flower garden from cattle and dogs and chickens.

"At it again," he said. "You've got a strong new crop coming."

Elisa straightened her back and pulled on the gardening glove again. "Yes. They'll be strong this coming year." In her tone and on her face there was a little smugness.

"You've got a gift with things," Henry observed. "Some of those yellow chrysanthemums you had this year were ten inches across. I wish you'd work out in the orchard and raise some apples that big."

Her eyes sharpened. "Maybe I could do it, too. I've a gift with things, all right. My mother had it. She could stick anything in the ground and make it grow. She said it was having planters' hands that knew how to do it."

"Well, it sure works with flowers," he said.

"Henry, who were those men you were talking to?"

"Why, sure, that's what I came to tell you. They were from the Western Meat Company. I sold those thirty head of three-year-old steers. Got nearly my own price, too."

"Good," she said. "Good for you."

"And I thought," he continued, "I thought how it's Saturday afternoon, and we might go into Salinas for dinner at a restaurant, and then to a picture show—to celebrate, you see."

"Good," she repeated. "Oh, yes. That will be good."

Henry put on his joking tone. "There's fights tonight. How'd you like to go to the fights?"

"Oh, no," she said breathlessly. "No, I wouldn't like fights."

"Just fooling, Elisa. We'll go to a movie. Let's see. It's two now. I'm going to take Scotty and bring down those steers from the hill. It'll take us maybe two hours. We'll go in town about five and have dinner at the Cominos Hotel. Like that?"

"Of course I'll like it. It's good to eat away from home."

"All right, then. I'll go get up a couple of horses."

She said, "I'll have plenty of time to transplant some of these sets, I guess."

She heard her husband calling Scotty down by the barn. And a little later she saw the two men ride up the pale yellow hillside in search of the steers.

There was a little square sandy bed kept for rooting the chrysanthemums. With her trowel she turned the soil over and over, and smoothed it and patted it firm. Then she dug ten parallel trenches to receive the sets. Back at the chrysanthemum bed she pulled out the little crisp shoots, trimmed off the leaves of each one with her scissors and laid it on a small orderly pile.

A squeak of wheels and plod of hoofs came from the road. Elisa looked up. The country road ran along the dense bank of willows and cottonwoods that bordered the river, and up this road came a curious vehicle, curiously drawn. It was an old spring-wagon, with a round canvas top on it like the cover of a prairie schooner. It was drawn by an old bay horse and a little grey-and-white burro. A big stubble-bearded man sat between the cover flaps and drove the crawling team. Underneath the wagon, between the hind wheels, a lean and rangy mongrel dog walked sedately. Words were painted on the canvas, in clumsy, crooked letters. "Pots, pans, knives, sisors, lawn mores, Fixed." Two rows of articles, and the triumphantly definitive "Fixed" below. The black paint had run down in little sharp points beneath each letter.

Elisa, squatting on the ground, watched to see the crazy, loose-jointed wagon pass by. But it didn't pass. It turned into the farm road in front of her house, crooked old wheels skirling and squeaking. The rangy dog darted from between the wheels and ran ahead. Instantly the two ranch shepherds flew out at him. Then all three stopped, and with stiff and quivering tails, with taut straight legs, with ambassadorial dignity, they slowly circled, sniffing daintily. The caravan pulled up to Elisa's wire fence and stopped. Now the newcomer dog, feeling out-numbered, lowered his tail and retired under the wagon with raised hackles and bared teeth.

The man on the wagon seat called out, "That's a bad dog in a fight when he gets started."

Elisa laughed. "I see he is. How soon does he generally get started?"

The man caught up her laughter and echoed it heartily. "Sometimes not for weeks and weeks," he said. He climbed stiffly down, over the wheel. The horse and the donkey drooped like unwatered flowers.

Elisa saw that he was a very big man. Although his hair and beard were greying, he did not look old. His worn black suit was wrinkled and spotted with grease. The laughter had disappeared from his face and eyes the moment his laughing voice ceased. His eyes were dark, and they were full of the brooding that gets in the eyes of teamsters and of sailors. The calloused hands he rested on the wire fence were cracked, and every crack was a black line. He took off his battered hat.

"I'm off my general road, ma'am," he said. "Does this dirt road cut over across the river to the Los Angeles highway?"

Elisa stood up and shoved the thick scissors in her apron pocket. "Well, yes, it does, but it winds around and then fords the river. I don't think your team could pull through the sand."

He replied with some asperity, "It might surprise you what them beasts can pull through."

"When they get started?" she asked.

He smiled for a second. "Yes. When they get started."

"Well," said Elisa, "I think you'll save time if you go back to the Salinas road and pick up the highway there."

He drew a big finger down the chicken wire and made it sing. "I ain't in any hurry, ma'am. I go from Seattle to San Diego and back every year. Takes all my time. About six months each way. I aim to follow nice weather."

Elisa took off her gloves and stuffed them in the apron pocket with the scissors. She touched the under edge of her man's hat, searching for fugitive hairs. "That sounds like a nice kind of a way to live," she said.

He leaned confidentially over the fence. "Maybe you noticed the writing on my wagon. I mend pots and sharpen knives and scissors. You got any of them things to do?"

"Oh, no," she said quickly. "Nothing like that." Her eyes hardened with resistance.

"Scissors is the worst thing," he explained. "Most people just ruin scissors trying to sharpen 'em, but I know how. I got a special tool. It's a little bobbit kind of thing, and patented. But it sure does the trick."

"No. My scissors are all sharp."

"All right, then. Take a pot," he continued earnestly, "a bent pot, or a pot with a hole. I can make it like new so you don't have to buy no new ones. That's a saving for you."

"No," she said shortly. "I tell you I have nothing like that for you to do."

His face fell to an exaggerated sadness. His voice took on a whining undertone. "I ain't had a thing to do today. Maybe I won't have no supper tonight. You see I'm off my regular road. I know folks on the highway clear from Seattle to San Diego. They save their things for me to sharpen up because they know I do it so good and save them money."

"I'm sorry," Elisa said irritably. "I haven't anything for you to do."

His eyes left her face and fell to searching the ground. They roamed about until they came to the chrysanthemum bed where she had been working. "What's them plants, ma'am?"

The irritation and resistance melted from Elisa's face. "Oh, those are chrysanthemums, giant whites and yellows. I raise them every year, bigger than anybody around here."

"Kind of a long-stemmed flower? Looks like a quick puff of colored smoke?" he asked.

"That's it. What a nice way to describe them."

"They smell kind of nasty till you get used to them," he said.

"It's a good bitter smell," she retorted, "not nasty at all."

He changed his tone quickly. "I like the smell myself."

"I had ten-inch blooms this year," she said.

The man leaned farther over the fence. "Look. I know a lady down the road a piece, has got the nicest garden you ever seen. Got nearly every kind of flower but no chrysantheums. Last time I was mending a copper-bottom washtub for her (that's a hard job but I do it good), she said to me, 'If you ever run acrost some nice chrysantheums I wish you'd try to get me a few seeds.' That's what she told me."

Elisa's eyes grew alert and eager. "She couldn't have known much about chrysanthemums. You *can* raise them from seed, but it's much easier to root the little sprouts you see there."

"Oh," he said. "I s'pose I can't take none to her, then."

"Why yes you can," Elisa cried. "I can put some in damp sand, and you can carry them right along with you. They'll take root in the pot if you keep them damp. And then she can transplant them."

"She'd sure like to have some, ma'am. You say they're nice ones?"

"Beautiful," she said. "Oh, beautiful." Her eyes shone. She tore off the battered hat and shook out her dark pretty hair. "I'll put them in a flower pot, and you can take them right with you. Come into the yard."

While the man came through the picket gate Elisa ran excitedly along the geranium-bordered path to the back of the house. And she returned carrying a big red flower pot. The gloves were forgotten now. She kneeled on the ground by the starting bed and dug up the sandy soil with her fingers and scooped it into the bright new flower pot. Then she picked up the little pile of shoots she had prepared. With her strong fingers she pressed them into the sand and tamped around them with her knuckles. The man stood over her. "I'll tell you what to do," she said. "You remember so you can tell the lady."

"Yes, I'll try to remember."

"Well, look. These will take root in about a month. Then she must set them out, about a foot apart in good rich earth like this, see?" She lifted a handful of dark soil for him to look at. "They'll grow fast and tall. Now remember this: In July tell her to cut them down, about eight inches from the ground."

"Before they bloom?" he asked.

"Yes, before they bloom." Her face was tight with eagerness. "They'll grow right up again. About the last of September the buds will start."

She stopped and seemed perplexed. "It's the budding that takes the most care," she said hesitantly. "I don't know how to tell you." She looked deep into his eyes, searchingly. Her mouth opened a little, and she seemed to be listening. "I'll try to tell you," she said. "Did you ever hear of planting hands?"

"Can't say I have, ma'am."

"Well, I can only tell you what it feels like. It's when you're picking off the buds you don't want. Everything goes right down into your fingertips. You watch your fingers work. They do it themselves. You can feel how it is. They pick and pick the buds. They never make a mistake. They're with the plant. Do you see? Your fingers and the plant. You can feel that, right up your arm. They know. They never make a mistake. You can feel it. When you're like that you can't do anything wrong. Do you see that? Can you understand that?"

She was kneeling on the ground looking up at him. Her breast swelled passionately.

The man's eyes narrowed. He looked away self-consciously. "Maybe I know," he said. "Sometimes in the night in the wagon there—"

Elisa's voice grew husky. She broke in on him, "I've never lived as you do, but I know what you mean. When the night is dark—why, the stars are sharp-pointed, and there's quiet. Why, you rise up and up! Every pointed star gets driven into your body. It's like that. Hot and sharp and—lovely."

Kneeling there, her hand went out toward his legs in the greasy black trousers. Her hesitant fingers almost touched the cloth. Then her hand dropped to the ground. She crouched low like a fawning dog.

He said, "It's nice, just like you say. Only when you don't have no dinner, it ain't."

She stood up then, very straight, and her face was ashamed. She held the flower pot out to him and placed it gently in his arms. "Here. Put it in your wagon, on the seat, where you can watch it. Maybe I can find something for you to do."

At the back of the house she dug in the can pile and found two old and battered aluminum saucepans. She carried them back and gave them to him. "Here, maybe you can fix these."

His manner changed. He became professional. "Good as new I can fix them." At the back of his wagon he set a little anvil, and out of an oily tool box dug a small machine hammer. Elisa came through the gate to watch him while he pounded out the dents in the kettles. His mouth grew sure and knowing. At a difficult part of the work he sucked his under-lip.

"You sleep right in the wagon?" Elisa asked.

"Right in the wagon, ma'am. Rain or shine I'm dry as a cow in there."

"It must be nice," she said. "It must be very nice. I wish women could do such things."

"It ain't the right kind of a life for a woman."

Her upper lip raised a little, showing her teeth. "How do you know? How can you tell?" she said.

"I don't know, ma'am," he protested. "Of course I don't know. Now here's your kettles, done. You don't have to buy no new ones."

"How much?"

"Oh, fifty cents'll do. I keep my prices down and my work good. That's why I have all them satisfied customers up and down the highway."

Elisa brought him a fifty-cent piece from the house and dropped it in his hand. "You might be surprised to have a rival some time. I can sharpen scissors, too. And I can beat the dents out of little pots. I could show you what a woman might do."

He put his hammer back in the oily box and shoved the little anvil out of sight. "It would be a lonely life for a woman, ma'am, and a scary life, too, with animals creeping under the wagon all night." He climbed over the singletree, steadying himself with a hand on the burro's white rump. He settled himself in the seat, picked up the lines. "Thank you kindly, ma'am," he said. "I'll do like you told me; I'll go back and catch the Salinas road."

"Mind," she called, "if you're long in getting there, keep the sand damp."

"Sand, ma'am? . . . Sand? Oh, sure. You mean around the chrysantheums. Sure I will." He clucked his tongue. The beasts leaned luxuriously into their collars. The mongrel dog took his place between the back wheels. The wagon turned and crawled out the entrance road and back the way it had come, along the river.

Elisa stood in front of her wire fence watching the slow progress of the caravan. Her shoulders were straight, her head thrown back, her eyes half-closed, so that the scene came vaguely into them. Her lips moved silently, forming the words "Good-bye—good-bye." Then she whispered, "That's a bright direction. There's a glowing there." The sound of her whisper startled her. She shook herself free and looked about to see whether anyone had been listening. Only the dogs had heard. They lifted their heads toward her from their sleeping in the dust, and then stretched out their chins and settled asleep again. Elisa turned and ran hurriedly into the house.

In the kitchen she reached behind the stove and felt the water tank. It was full of hot water from the noonday cooking. In the bathroom she tore off her soiled clothes and flung them into the corner. And then she scrubbed herself with a little block of pumice, legs and thighs, loins and chest and arms, until her skin was scratched and red. When she had dried herself she stood in front of a mirror in her bedroom and looked at her body. She tightened her stomach and threw out her chest. She turned and looked over her shoulder at her back.

After a while she began to dress, slowly. She put on her newest underclothing and her nicest stockings and the dress which was the symbol of her prettiness. She worked carefully on her hair, penciled her eyebrows and rouged her lips.

Before she was finished she heard the little thunder of hoofs and the shouts of Henry and his helper as they drove the red steers into the corral. She heard the gate bang shut and set herself for Henry's arrival.

His step sounded on the porch. He entered the house calling, "Elisa, where are you?"

"In my room, dressing. I'm not ready. There's hot water for your bath. Hurry up. It's getting late."

When she heard him splashing in the tub, Elisa laid his dark suit on the bed, and shirt and socks and tie beside it. She stood his polished shoes on the floor beside the bed. Then she went to the porch and sat primly and stiffly down. She looked toward the river road where the willow-line was still yellow with frosted leaves so that under the high grey fog they seemed a thin band of sunshine. This was the only color in the grey afternoon. She sat unmoving for a long time. Her eyes blinked rarely.

Henry came banging out of the door, shoving his tie inside his vest as he came. Elisa stiffened and her face grew tight. Henry stopped short and looked at her. "Why—why, Elisa. You look so nice!"

"Nice? You think I look nice? What do you mean by 'nice'?"

Henry blundered on. "I don't know. I mean you look different, strong and happy."

"I am strong? Yes, strong. What do you mean 'strong'?"

He looked bewildered. "You're playing some kind of a game," he said helplessly. "It's a kind of a play. You look strong enough to break a calf over your knee, happy enough to eat it like a watermelon."

For a second she lost her rigidity. "Henry! Don't talk like that. You didn't know what you said." She grew complete again. "I'm strong," she boasted. "I never knew before how strong."

Henry looked down toward the tractor shed, and when he brought his eyes back to her, they were his own again. "I'll get out the car. You can put on your coat while I'm starting."

Elisa went into the house. She heard him drive to the gate and idle down his motor, and then she took a long time to put on her hat. She pulled it here and pressed it there. When Henry turned the motor off she slipped into her coat and went out.

The little roadster bounced along on the dirt road by the river, raising the birds and driving the rabbits into the brush. Two cranes flapped heavily over the willow-line and dropped into the river-bed.

Far ahead on the road Elisa saw a dark speck. She knew.

She tried not to look as they passed it, but her eyes would not obey. She whispered to herself sadly, "He might have thrown them off the road. That wouldn't have been much trouble, not very much. But he kept the pot," she explained. "He had to keep the pot. That's why he couldn't get them off the road."

The roadster turned a bend and she saw the caravan ahead. She swung full around toward her husband so she could not see the little covered wagon and the mismatched team as the car passed them.

In a moment it was over. The thing was done. She did not look back.

She said loudly, to be heard above the motor, "It will be good, tonight, a good dinner."

"Now you've changed again," Henry complained. He took one hand from the wheel and patted her knee. "I ought to take you in to dinner oftener. It would be good for both of us. We get so heavy out on the ranch."

"Henry," she asked, "could we have wine at dinner?"

"Sure we could. Say! That will be fine."

She was silent for a while; then she said, "Henry, at those prize fights, do the men hurt each other very much?"

"Sometimes a little, not often. Why?"

"Well, I've read how they break noses, and blood runs down their chests. I've read how the fighting gloves get heavy and soggy with blood."

He looked around at her. "What's the matter, Elisa? I didn't know you read things like that." He brought the car to a stop, then turned to the right over the Salinas River bridge.

"Do any women ever go to the fights?" she asked.

"Oh, sure, some. What's the matter, Elisa? Do you want to go? I don't think you'd like it, but I'll take you if you really want to go."

She relaxed limply in the seat. "Oh, no. No. I don't want to go. I'm sure I don't." Her face was turned away from him. "It will be enough if we can have wine. It will be plenty." She turned up her coat collar so he could not see that she was crying weakly—like an old woman.

1937

COUNTEE CULLEN
1903–1946

More than most poets of the Harlem Renaissance, Countee Cullen valued traditional poetic forms in English—the sonnet, rhymed couplets, and quatrains—over modernist free verse or rhythms suggested by jazz and popular culture. Never one to shy away from controversy, Cullen prefaced his important anthology of African American poetry, *Caroling Dusk* (1927), with the assertion, "As heretical as it may sound, there is the probability that Negro poets, dependent as they are on the English language, may have more to gain from the rich background of English and American poetry than from any nebulous atavistic yearnings toward an African inheritance." Cullen demanded that black poets be considered as American poets, ultimately without any special racial designation. Nevertheless, the titles of his books of poetry—*Color* (1925), *Copper Sun* (1927), *The Ballad of the Brown Girl* (1928)—showed that, like Claude MacKay and Jean Toomer, he felt a responsibility to write about being black even if he did so in modes outside of black folk traditions. Although he clashed with a number of his contemporaries in the Harlem Renaissance, Cullen could also be generous to black writers whose poetics differed from his. What mattered to Cullen was appreciating the full range of black literary writing, a range as great, he insisted, as that found among white poets in English, and resisting every "attempt to corral the ebony muse into some definite mold" to which all black writers should conform.

Although Cullen's birthplace and early years are obscure, he was adopted at some point in his childhood by a Harlem-based minister and given a good education, first in New York public schools and then at New York University, where he received his B.A. in 1925, and at Harvard, where he took an M.A. in 1926. In high school, Cullen earned a citywide poetry prize for "I Have a Rendezvous with Life," a rejoinder to Alan Seeger's sentimental World War I poem (see p. 203). His first book of poems, *Color*, appeared in his senior year at college; it established him as the "black Keats," a prodigy.

From 1926 to 1928, Cullen was assistant editor at the important black journal *Opportunity*, for which he also wrote a feature column, "The Dark Tower." In 1928 he married Nina Yolande Du Bois, the daughter of W. E. B. Du Bois, and won a Guggenheim fellowship that took him to Paris and enabled him to complete another book of poems, *The Black Christ* (1929). His marriage quickly disintegrated, however, over Cullen's attraction to men, and the couple was divorced in 1930. Neither *The Black Christ* nor the novel that followed, *One Way to Heaven* (1932), earned the acclaim of Cullen's earlier books. He spent the last years of his life teaching at New York's Frederick Douglass Junior High School, where his pupils included the future novelist James Baldwin. With the revival of scholarly interest in the Harlem Renaissance, Cullen's distinctive combination of traditionalist poetic skill with acerbic self-questioning on matters of racism and racial identity has once again brought his poetry to critical attention.

The text of "From the Dark Tower" is that of *Copper Sun* (1927); the text of other poems included here is that of *Color* (1925).

Yet Do I Marvel

I doubt not God is good, well-meaning, kind,
And did He stoop to quibble could tell why
The little buried mole continues blind,
Why flesh that mirrors Him must some day die,
Make plain the reason tortured Tantalus
Is baited by the fickle fruit, declare
If merely brute caprice dooms Sisyphus[1]
To struggle up a never-ending stair.
Inscrutable His ways are, and immune
To catechism by a mind too strewn
With petty cares to slightly understand
What awful brain compels His awful hand.
Yet do I marvel at this curious thing:
To make a poet black, and bid him sing!

1925

Incident

Once riding in old Baltimore,
  Heart-filled, head-filled with glee,
I saw a Baltimorean
  Keep looking straight at me.

Now I was eight and very small,
  And he was no whit bigger,
And so I smiled, but he poked out
  His tongue, and called me, "Nigger."

1. Tantalus and Sisyphus are figures in Greek mythology who were punished in Hades. Tantalus was offered food and water that was then instantly snatched away. Sisyphus had to roll a heavy stone to the top of a hill and, after it rolled back down, repeat the ordeal perpetually.

I saw the whole of Baltimore
From May until December;
Of all the things that happened there
That's all that I remember.

1925

Heritage

What is Africa to me:
Copper sun or scarlet sea,
Jungle star or jungle track,
Strong bronzed men, or regal black
Women from whose loins I sprang
When the birds of Eden sang?
One three centuries removed
From the scenes his fathers loved,
Spicy grove, cinnamon tree,
What is Africa to me?

So I lie, who all day long
Want no sound except the song
Sung by wild barbaric birds
Goading massive jungle herds,
Juggernauts[1] of flesh that pass
Trampling tall defiant grass
Where young forest lovers lie,
Plighting troth beneath the sky.
So I lie, who always hear,
Though I cram against my ear
Both my thumbs, and keep them there,
Great drums throbbing through the air.
So I lie, whose fount of pride,
Dear distress, and joy allied,
Is my somber flesh and skin,
With the dark blood dammed within
Like great pulsing tides of wine
That, I fear, must burst the fine
Channels of the chafing net
Where they surge and foam and fret.

Africa? A book one thumbs
Listlessly, till slumber comes.
Unremembered are her bats
Circling through the night, her cats
Crouching in the river reeds,

1. The juggernaut is a sacred Hindu idol dragged on a huge car in the path of which devotees were believed to throw themselves—hence any power demanding blind sacrifice, here spliced with the image of elephants.

Stalking gentle flesh that feeds
By the river brink; no more
Does the bugle-throated roar
Cry that monarch claws have leapt
From the scabbards where they slept.
Silver snakes that once a year
Doff the lovely coats you wear,
Seek no covert in your fear
Lest a mortal eye should see;
What's your nakedness to me?
Here no leprous flowers rear
Fierce corollas[2] in the air;
Here no bodies sleek and wet,
Dripping mingled rain and sweat,
Tread the savage measures of
Jungle boys and girls in love.
What is last year's snow to me,[3]
Last year's anything? The tree
Budding yearly must forget
How its past arose or set—
Bough and blossom, flower, fruit,
Even what shy bird with mute
Wonder at her travail there,
Meekly labored in its hair.
One three centuries removed
From the scenes his fathers loved,
Spicy grove, cinnamon tree,
What is Africa to me?

So I lie, who find no peace
Night or day, no slight release
From the unremittant beat
Made by cruel padded feet
Walking through my body's street.
Up and down they go, and back,
Treading out a jungle track.
So I lie, who never quite
Safely sleep from rain at night—
I can never rest at all
When the rain begins to fall;
Like a soul gone mad with pain
I must match its weird refrain;
Ever must I twist and squirm,
Writhing like a baited worm,
While its primal measures drip
Through my body, crying, "Strip!
Doff this new exuberance.
Come and dance the Lover's Dance!"

2. The whorl of petals forming the inner envelope of a flower.
3. An echo of the lament "Where are the snows of yesteryear?" from "Grand Testament" by the 15th-century French poet François Villon.

In an old remembered way
Rain works on me night and day.

Quaint, outlandish heathen gods
Black men fashion out of rods,
Clay, and brittle bits of stone,
In a likeness like their own,
My conversion came high-priced;
I belong to Jesus Christ,
Preacher of humility;
Heathen gods are naught to me.

Father, Son, and Holy Ghost,
So I make an idle boast;
Jesus of the twice-turned cheek[4]
Lamb of God, although I speak
With my mouth thus, in my heart
Do I play a double part.
Ever at Thy glowing altar
Must my heart grow sick and falter,
Wishing He I served were black,
Thinking then it would not lack
Precedent of pain to guide it,
Let who would or might deride it;
Surely then this flesh would know
Yours had borne a kindred woe.
Lord, I fashion dark gods, too,
Daring even to give You
Dark despairing features where,
Crowned with dark rebellious hair,
Patience wavers just so much as
Mortal grief compels, while touches
Quick and hot, of anger, rise
To smitten cheek and weary eyes.
Lord, forgive me if my need
Sometimes shapes a human creed.
All day long and all night through,
One thing only must I do:
Quench my pride and cool my blood,
Lest I perish in the flood.
Lest a hidden ember set
Timber that I thought was wet
Burning like the dryest flax,
Melting like the merest wax,
Lest the grave restore its dead.
Not yet has my heart or head
In the least way realized
They and I are civilized.

1925

4. In his Sermon on the Mount (Matthew 5.39), Jesus declared that when struck on the cheek, one should turn the other cheek rather than strike back.

From the Dark Tower[1]

We shall not always plant while others reap
The golden increment of bursting fruit,
Not always countenance, abject and mute,
That lesser men should hold their brothers cheap;
Not everlastingly while others sleep
Shall we beguile their limbs with mellow flute,
Not always bend to some more subtle brute;
We were not made eternally to weep.

The night whose sable breast relieves the stark,
White stars is no less lovely being dark,
And there are buds that cannot bloom at all
In light, but crumple, piteous, and fall;
So in the dark we hide the heart that bleeds,
And wait, and tend our agonizing seeds.

1927

Uncle Jim

"White folks is white," says uncle Jim;
"A platitude," I sneer;
And then I tell him so is milk,
And the froth upon his beer.

His heart walled up with bitterness,
He smokes his pungent pipe,
And nods at me as if to say,
"Young fool, you'll soon be ripe!"

I have a friend who eats his heart
Away with grief of mine,
Who drinks my joy as tipplers drain
Deep goblets filled with wine.

I wonder why here at his side,
Face-in-the-grass with him,
My mind should stray the Grecian urn[1]
To muse on uncle Jim.

1927

1. An allusion to "'Childe Roland to the Dark Tower Came'" by the British Victorian poet Robert Browning (1812–1889). Cullen also titled his *Opportunity* column after Browning's poem.

1. An allusion to "Ode on a Grecian Urn" by the British Romantic poet John Keats (1795–1821). Cullen was particularly fond of Keats's poetry.

NATHANAEL WEST
1903–1940

Born Nathan Weinstein to a prosperous Jewish family living in the Upper East Side neighborhood of New York City, Nathanael West assumed his new legal name in 1926, on the eve of departing for Paris to sample its legendary Bohemian artistic life. It was not his first attempt at self-reinvention. While still in his teens, Weinstein had altered his high school transcript in order to get into Tufts University, where for one brief, giddy semester he made the most of the college's social life—pledging a Jewish fraternity, attending plays in Boston—while meeting none of his academic obligations. Having withdrawn from Tufts, he used the transcript of another student named Nathan Weinstein to apply to Brown University, where he was accepted and from which he managed to graduate in 1924.

Unlike Tufts, Brown at this time had no fraternities open to Jewish men. Weinstein and his friends at Brown created their own social alternatives, based on their appetite for immersion in modern culture in all its forms, both popular and elite. He attended movies; helped found a campus literary magazine, *Casements*, to which he contributed poetry and cover art; acted in plays satirizing college life; and pursued a vigorous reading program outside of the classroom that included writers from the leading edge of American modernism—William Carlos Williams (1883–1963), F. Scott Fitzgerald (1896–1940), E. E. Cummings (1894–1962)—as well as international figures like James Joyce (1882–1941), Oscar Wilde (1854–1900), and Gustave Flaubert (1821–1880).

Nathanael West's brief postgraduate sojourn in Paris bore little immediate fruit. His family could not support his stab at the expatriate artistic life, and he returned to New York in January 1927. There he renewed contacts with college friends such as S. J. Perelman (1904–1979), who was then at the beginning of his prolific career as a contributor to *The New Yorker*, and through them made his way into a range of New York literary circles, including those of John Dos Passos and other writers associated with the Communist publications *New Masses* and *The Daily Worker*. He worked as a manager at residential hotels in the city, a position that allowed him to find rooms for literary friends and that supplied as well the experience of the seamy side of transient city life later reflected in the characters of *The Day of the Locust* (1939).

Unlike his better-established literary friends, however, West still struggled to break into print. His efforts at magazine stories found no buyers. In 1929 he completed revisions to *The Dream Life of Balso Snell*, a surrealistic novelette begun during his time at Brown and in Paris. Its dreaming antihero, an aspiring writer, passes through the anus of the Trojan horse and wends his way through the horse's guts, encountering other authors along the way; through this device, West's narrative becomes a miniature encyclopedia of literary styles and periods. In this respect, in its application of Greek myth to modern life, and in its ending with a sexual coupling, *The Dream Life of Balso Snell* nods to Joyce's *Ulysses* (1918–22). In contrast to Joyce's broad view of modernity, though, West offered a narrower satire on authors in search of an audience; few readers, then or later, found the book's obscene energies rewarding. With the backing of William Carlos Williams, *The Dream of a Balso Snell* finally appeared in 1931 in a limited edition, to little critical fanfare.

In the meantime, however, West had been handed more promising material. His friend Perelman in 1929 introduced him to a woman who contributed an advice column to the *Brooklyn Eagle* under the pseudonym of "Susan Chester"; the letters

Hollywoodland sign, c. 1935. Erected in 1923, the sign originally advertised a housing development.

from her readers that she shared with West became the basis for his next novel, *Miss Lonelyhearts* (1933). Here, what starts out as a purely commercial "stunt"—a young newspaperman writing an advice column intended to increase his paper's circulation—becomes sinister, as the columnist finds himself unable to maintain his ironic distance from the suffering that bombards him. Empathy, cultivated as a primary social virtue in the tradition of classic nineteenth-century realist fiction, comes to a disastrous end in *Miss Lonelyhearts* with the columnist's death at the hands of one of his readers. William Carlos Williams, in a laudatory review, compared the "dreadful logic" of West's plotting to the "classical precedent" set by Greek and Shakespearean tragedy.

Miss Lonelyhearts was a modest critical success, but one that left its author, like its protagonist, faced with the need to make a living. The novel's first publisher went bankrupt just as the book was released, and its rescue and reissue by another firm failed to recapture lost momentum in terms of either sales or publicity. West did, however, sell the movie rights for *Miss Lonelyhearts* to Twentieth Century Pictures (it appeared in late 1933 as *Advice to the Lovelorn*, much altered from the original). In July 1933 West followed the path that William Faulkner before him had taken, and that F. Scott Fitzgerald would take after him: he went to Hollywood to write for the movies, on contract with Columbia Pictures.

West would return to New York several times before the end of his life, but the financial attractions of Hollywood life proved substantial, if not always predictable. The movie rights to *Miss Lonelyhearts* brought him $4,000; by contrast, from 1931 through 1934 West earned a total of only $780 in royalties from his first three novels, including one more that sold poorly and failed to move critics, *A Cool Million* (1934). In 1936 he was able to earn a weekly salary of $250 as a screenwriter from a second-rate studio, Republic Productions; by 1940 he was collaborating on screenplays and adaptations that commanded as much as $25,000 from major studios. A member of the Screen Writers Guild from his earliest years in Hollywood, West was elected to the guild's executive board in 1939.

Hollywood supplied West not only with an income, but also with a memorable subject for fiction, most fully realized in *The Day of the Locust*. West's final novel paints a cruel, raw, and memorable picture of late 1930s American popular culture—its new visual culture, oriented to the movies and stardom, lit by searchlights and neon; its new soundscape, saturated with radio and recordings—and of the multilayered, multiethnic, burgeoning city of Los Angeles, overlaid on an earlier Spanish California. At the center of this panorama hulks the movie industry, vehicle of the hopes and dreams of most of West's characters. Where *The Dream Life of Balso Snell* represents all of Western literary history as living inside the guts of a graffiti-defaced Trojan horse, Tod Hackett, the protagonist of *The Day of the Locust*, encounters a Trojan horse next to a Mayan temple and a Dutch windmill and a thirty-foot-high Buddha—all of them stage sets, sitting in storage on a movie studio's back lot. Although *The Day of the Locust* sold modestly (only 1,164 copies in its first year of publication), West's characterization of Hollywood as a "dream dump," graveyard of both personal and high cultural ambition, remains resonant to this day. So too does the novel's style, modeled in part after the movies West regarded with love and loathing: fast-paced, assembled through cutting and collage, avid for the hard-boiled insider's knowledge of this new modern world.

West died in a car crash, along with his wife, Eileen McKenney, an aspiring actress, in 1940. The text of *The Day of the Locust* printed here is that of the first edition of 1939, published by Random House.

The Day of the Locust[1]

I

Around quitting time, Tod Hackett heard a great din on the road outside his office. The groan of leather mingled with the jangle of iron and over all beat the tattoo of a thousand hooves. He hurried to the window.

An army of cavalry and foot[2] was passing. It moved like a mob; its lines broken, as though fleeing from some terrible defeat. The dolmans of the hussars,[3] the heavy shakos of the guards, Hanoverian[4] light horse, with their flat leather caps and flowing red plumes, were all jumbled together in bobbing disorder. Behind the cavalry came the infantry, a wild sea of waving sabertaches,[5] sloped muskets, crossed shoulder belts and swinging cartridge boxes. Tod recognized the scarlet infantry of England with their white shoulder pads, the black infantry of the Duke of Brunswick,[6] the French grenadiers with their enormous white gaiters, the Scotch with bare knees under plaid skirts.

1. Moses calls a plague of locusts upon Egypt when Pharaoh refuses to let the enslaved Israelites depart: "they covered the face of the whole earth, so that the land was darkened; and they did eat every herb of the land" (Exodus 10.15). In the Book of Revelation (9.4–6), locusts return to torment "those men which have not the seal of God in their foreheads. . . . And in those days shall men seek death, and shall not find it; and shall desire to die, and death shall flee from them."

2. Costumed actors playing extras in a historical movie being filmed about the Battle of Waterloo (1815), which ended the drive of Napoleon (1769–1821) to return to power as emperor of France.

3. Cavalrymen. "Dolmans": short-cut jackets worn as part of the hussars' uniforms.

4. From the German city-state of Hanover, allied with England against Napoleon. "Shakos": high, cylindrical military hats.

5. Flat pouches worn alongside swords.

6. One of the commanders of the multinational army, serving under the general command of the Duke of Wellington of England, that defeated Napoleon's forces.

While he watched, a little fat man, wearing a cork sun-helmet, polo shirt and knickers, darted around the corner of the building in pursuit of the army.

"Stage Nine—you bastards—Stage Nine!" he screamed through a small megaphone.

The cavalry put spur to their horses and the infantry broke into a dog-trot. The little man in the cork hat ran after them, shaking his fist and cursing.

Tod watched until they had disappeared behind half a Mississippi steamboat, then put away his pencils and drawing board, and left the office. On the sidewalk outside the studio he stood for a moment trying to decide whether to walk home or take a streetcar. He had been in Hollywood less than three months and still found it a very exciting place, but he was lazy and didn't like to walk. He decided to take the streetcar as far as Vine Street[7] and walk the rest of the way.

A talent scout for National Films had brought Tod to the Coast after seeing some of his drawings in an exhibit of undergraduate work at the Yale School of Fine Arts. He had been hired by telegram. If the scout had met Tod, he probably wouldn't have sent him to Hollywood to learn set and costume designing. His large, sprawling body, his slow blue eyes and sloppy grin made him seem completely without talent, almost doltish in fact.

Yet, despite his appearance, he was really a very complicated young man with a whole set of personalities, one inside the other like a nest of Chinese boxes. And "The Burning of Los Angeles," a picture he was soon to paint, definitely proved he had talent.

He left the car at Vine Street. As he walked along, he examined the evening crowd. A great many of the people wore sports clothes which were not really sports clothes. Their sweaters, knickers, slacks, blue flannel jackets with brass buttons were fancy dress. The fat lady in the yachting cap was going shopping, not boating; the man in the Norfolk jacket and Tyrolean hat[8] was returning, not from a mountain, but an insurance office; and the girl in slacks and sneaks with a bandanna around her head had just left a switchboard, not a tennis court.

Scattered among these masqueraders were people of a different type. Their clothing was somber and badly cut, bought from mail-order houses. While the others moved rapidly, darting into stores and cocktail bars, they loitered on the corners or stood with their backs to the shop windows and stared at everyone who passed. When their stare was returned, their eyes filled with hatred. At this time Tod knew very little about them except that they had come to California to die.

He was determined to learn much more. They were the people he felt he must paint. He would never again do a fat red barn, old stone wall or sturdy Nantucket fisherman. From the moment he had seen them, he had

7. A major thoroughfare in Hollywood.
8. Items of sports clothing associated, respectively, with the English countryside and the Alps. Norfolk jackets feature pockets and patches for the convenience of hunters and shooters. Tyrolean hats typically feature narrow brims, decorative bands, and a spray of feathers.

known that, despite his race, training and heritage, neither Winslow Homer nor Thomas Ryder could be his masters and he turned to Goya and Daumier.[9]

He had learned this just in time. During his last year in art school, he had begun to think that he might give up painting completely. The pleasures he received from the problems of composition and color had decreased as his facility had increased and he had realized that he was going the way of all his classmates, toward illustration or mere handsomeness. When the Hollywood job had come along, he had grabbed it despite the arguments of his friends who were certain that he was selling out and would never paint again.

He reached the end of Vine Street and began the climb into Pinyon Canyon.[1] Night had started to fall.

The edges of the trees burned with a pale violet light and their centers gradually turned from deep purple to black. The same violet piping, like a Neon tube,[2] outlined the tops of the ugly, humpbacked hills and they were almost beautiful.

But not even the soft wash of dusk could help the houses. Only dynamite would be of any use against the Mexican ranch houses, Samoan huts, Mediterranean villas, Egyptian and Japanese temples, Swiss chalets, Tudor cottages, and every possible combination of these styles that lined the slopes of the canyon.

When he noticed that they were all of plaster, lath and paper, he was charitable and blamed their shape on the materials used. Steel, stone and brick curb a builder's fancy a little, forcing him to distribute his stresses and weights and to keep his corners plumb, but plaster and paper know no law, not even that of gravity.

On the corner of La Huerta Road was a miniature Rhine castle with tarpaper turrets pierced for archers. Next to it was a little highly colored shack with domes and minarets out of the *Arabian Nights.*[3] Again he was charitable. Both houses were comic, but he didn't laugh. Their desire to startle was so eager and guileless.

It is hard to laugh at the need for beauty and romance, no matter how tasteless, even horrible, the results of that need are. But it is easy to sigh. Few things are sadder than the truly monstrous.

2

The house he lived in was a nondescript affair called the San Bernardino Arms. It was an oblong three stories high, the back and sides of which

9. Honoré Daumier (1808–1879), French printmaker and painter known for his scathing caricatures of French life. Franciso Goya (1746–1828), Spanish painter and printmaker whose increasingly dark later work included images of madness and war. Homer (1836–1910), American painter noted for his seascapes. Ryder (1746–1810), English engraver noted for his illustrated Shakespeare and for engraving a famous portrait of Benjamin Franklin. The context also suggests the American painter Albert Pinkham Ryder (1847–1917), noted for his seascapes, who was admired by early modernists.

1. Fictional, modeled after Beachwood Canyon, developed for housing in the 1920s.

2. Pioneered in France in 1910, neon lighting came into wide use in the United States in the 1920s.

3. First English edition (1706) of a famous collection of ancient and medieval Middle Eastern stories and folk tales.

were of plain, unpainted stucco, broken by even rows of unadorned windows. The façade was the color of diluted mustard and its windows, all double, were framed by pink Moorish columns which supported turnip-shaped lintels.

His room was on the third floor, but he paused for a moment on the landing of the second. It was on that floor that Faye Greener lived, in 208. When someone laughed in one of the apartments he started guiltily and continued upstairs.

As he opened his door a card fluttered to the floor. "Honest Abe Kusich," it said in large type, then underneath in smaller italics were several endorsements, printed to look like press notices.

'. . . the Lloyds[4] *of Hollywood' . . . Stanley Rose.*

'Abe's word is better than Morgan's[5] *bonds'—Gail Brenshaw.*

On the other side was a penciled message:

"Kingpin fourth, Solitair sixth. You can make some real dough on those nags."[6]

After opening the window, he took off his jacket and lay down on the bed. Through the window he could see a square of enameled sky and a spray of eucalyptus. A light breeze stirred its long, narrow leaves, making them show first their green side, then their silver one.

He began to think of "Honest Abe Kusich" in order not to think of Faye Greener. He felt comfortable and wanted to remain that way.

Abe was an important figure in a set of lithographs called "The Dancers" on which Tod was working. He was one of the dancers. Faye Greener was another and her father, Harry, still another. They changed with each plate, but the group of uneasy people who formed their audience remained the same. They stood staring at the performers in just the way that they stared at the masqueraders on Vine Street. It was their stare that drove Abe and the others to spin crazily and leap into the air with twisted backs like hooked trout.

Despite the sincere indignation that Abe's grotesque depravity aroused in him, he welcomed his company. The little man excited him and in that way made him feel certain of his need to paint.

He had first met Abe when he was living on Ivar Street,[7] in a hotel called the Chateau Mirabella. Another name for Ivar Street was "Lysol[8] Alley," and the Chateau was mainly inhabited by hustlers, their managers, trainers and advance agents.

In the morning its halls reeked of antiseptic. Tod didn't like this odor. Moreover, the rent was high because it included police protection, a service for which he had no need. He wanted to move, but inertia and the fact that he didn't know where to go kept him in the Chateau until he met Abe. The meeting was accidental.

He was on the way to his room late one night when he saw what he supposed was a pile of soiled laundry lying in front of the door across the hall

4. A famous London-based insurer and banker.
5. J. P. Morgan (1837–1913), the leading American financier at the turn of the 20th century.
6. Advice for betting on a horse race.
7. I.e., Ivar Avenue; runs off Hollywood Boulevard.
8. Brand name of a popular disinfectant, introduced in 1889, that came into widespread use during the 1918 flu pandemic.

from his own. Just as he was passing it, the bundle moved and made a peculiar noise. He struck a match, thinking it might be a dog wrapped in a blanket. When the light flared up, he saw it was a tiny man.

The match went out and he hastily lit another. It was a male dwarf rolled up in a woman's flannel bathrobe. The round thing at the end was his slightly hydrocephalic[9] head. A slow, choked snore bubbled from it.

The hall was cold and draughty. Tod decided to wake the man and stirred him with his toe. He groaned and opened his eyes.

"You oughn't to sleep there."

"The hell you say," said the dwarf, closing his eyes again.

"You'll catch cold."

This friendly observation angered the little man still more.

"I want my clothes!" he bellowed.

The bottom of the door next to which he was lying filled with light. Tod decided to take a chance and knock. A few seconds later a woman opened it part way.

"What the hell do you want?" she demanded.

"There's a friend of yours out here who . . ."

Neither of them let him finish.

"So what!" she barked, slamming the door.

"Give me my clothes, you bitch!" roared the dwarf.

She opened the door again and began to hurl things into the hall. A jacket and trousers, a shirt, socks, shoes and underwear, a tie and hat followed each other through the air in rapid succession. With each article went a special curse.

Tod whistled with amazement.

"Some gal!"

"You bet," said the dwarf. "A lollapalooza—all slut and a yard wide."

He laughed at his own joke, using a high-pitched cackle more dwarflike than anything that had come from him so far, then struggled to his feet and arranged the voluminous robe so that he could walk without tripping. Tod helped him gather his scattered clothing.

"Say, mister," he asked, "could I dress in your place?"

Tod let him into his bathroom. While waiting for him to reappear, he couldn't help imagining what had happened in the woman's apartment. He began to feel sorry for having interfered. But when the dwarf came out wearing his hat, Tod felt better.

The little man's hat fixed almost everything. That year Tyrolean hats were being worn a great deal along Hollywood Boulevard and the dwarf's was a fine specimen. It was the proper magic green color and had a high, conical crown. There should have been a brass buckle on the front, but otherwise it was quite perfect.

The rest of his outfit didn't go well with the hat. Instead of shoes with long points and a leather apron, he wore a blue, double-breasted suit and a black shirt with a yellow tie. Instead of a crooked thorn stick, he carried a rolled copy of the *Daily Running Horse.*

9. Enlarged because of fluid accumulating inside the skull.

"That's what I get for fooling with four-bit broads," he said by way of greeting.

Tod nodded and tried to concentrate on the green hat. His ready acquiescence seemed to irritate the little man.

"No quiff can give Abe Kusich the fingeroo and get away with it," he said bitterly. "Not when I can get her leg broke for twenty bucks and I got twenty."

He took out a thick billfold and shook it at Tod.

"So she thinks she can give me the fingeroo, hah? Well, let me tell . . ."

Tod broke in hastily.

"You're right, Mr. Kusich."

The dwarf came over to where Tod was sitting and for a moment Tod thought he was going to climb into his lap, but he only asked his name and shook hands. The little man had a powerful grip.

"Let me tell you something, Hackett, if you hadn't come along, I'da broke in the door. That dame thinks she can give me the fingeroo, but she's got another thinkola coming. But thanks anyway."

"Forget it."

"I don't forget nothing. I remember. I remember those who do me dirt and those who do me favors."

He wrinkled his brow and was silent for a moment.

"Listen," he finally said, "seeing as you helped me, I got to return it. I don't want anybody going around saying Abe Kusich owes him anything. So I'll tell you what. I'll give you a good one for the fifth at Caliente.[1] You put a fiver on its nose and it'll get you twenty smackeroos. What I'm telling you is strictly correct."

Tod didn't know how to answer and his hesitation offended the little man.

"Would I give you a bum steer?" he demanded, scowling. "Would I?"

Tod walked toward the door to get rid of him.

"No," he said.

"Then why won't you bet, hah?"

"What's the name of the horse?" Tod asked, hoping to calm him.

The dwarf had followed him to the door, pulling the bathrobe after him by one sleeve. Hat and all, he came to a foot below Tod's belt.

"Tragopan. He's a certain, sure winner. I know the guy who owns him and he gave me the office."

"Is he a Greek?" Tod asked.

He was being pleasant in order to hide the attempt he was making to maneuver the dwarf through the door.

"Yeh, he's a Greek. Do you know him?"

"No."

"No?"

"No," said Tod with finality.

"Keep your drawers on," ordered the dwarf, "all I want to know is how you know he's a Greek if you don't know him?"

1. The Agua Caliente racetrack in Baja California, which opened in 1929, was popular with Hollywood celebrities.

His eyes narrowed with suspicion and he clenched his fists.

Tod smiled to placate him.

"I just guessed it."

"You did?"

The dwarf hunched his shoulders as though he were going to pull a gun or throw a punch. Tod backed off and tried to explain.

"I guessed he was a Greek because Tragopan is a Greek word that means pheasant."

The dwarf was far from satisfied.

"How do you know what it means? You ain't a Greek?"

"No, but I know a few Greek words."

"So you're a wise guy, hah, a know-it-all."

He took a short step forward, moving on his toes, and Tod got set to block a punch.

"A college man, hah? Well, let me tell . . ."

His foot caught in the wrapper and he fell forward on his hands. He forgot Tod and cursed the bathrobe, then got started on the woman again.

"So she thinks she can give me the fingeroo."

He kept poking himself in the chest with his thumbs.

"Who gave her forty bucks for an abortion? Who? And another ten to go to the country for a rest that time. To a ranch I sent her. And who got her fiddle out of hock that time in Santa Monica? Who?"

"That's right," Tod said, getting ready to give him a quick shove through the door.

But he didn't have to shove him. The little man suddenly darted out of the room and ran down the hall, dragging the bathrobe after him.

A few days later, Tod went into a stationery store on Vine Street to buy a magazine. While he was looking through the rack, he felt a tug at the bottom of his jacket. It was Abe Kusich, the dwarf, again.

"How's things?" he demanded.

Tod was surprised to find that he was just as truculent as he had been the other night. Later, when he got to know him better, he discovered that Abe's pugnacity was often a joke. When he used it on his friends, they played with him like one does with a growling puppy, staving off his mad rushes and then baiting him to rush again.

"Fair enough," Tod said, "but I think I'll move."

He had spent most of Sunday looking for a place to live and was full of the subject. The moment he mentioned it, however, he knew that he had made a mistake. He tried to end the matter by turning away, but the little man blocked him. He evidently considered himself an expert on the housing situation. After naming and discarding a dozen possibilities without a word from Tod, he finally hit on the San Bernardino Arms.

"That's the place for you, the San Berdoo. I live there, so I ought to know. The owner's strictly from hunger. Come on, I'll get you fixed up swell."

"I don't know, I . . ." Tod began.

The dwarf bridled instantly, and appeared to be mortally offended.

"I suppose it ain't good enough for you. Well, let me tell you something, you . . ."

Tod allowed himself to be bullied and went with the dwarf to Pinyon Canyon. The rooms in the San Berdoo were small and not very clean. He rented one without hesitation, however, when he saw Faye Greener in the hall.

3

Tod had fallen asleep. When he woke again, it was after eight o'clock. He took a bath and shaved, then dressed in front of the bureau mirror. He tried to watch his fingers as he fixed his collar and tie, but his eyes kept straying to the photograph that was pushed into the upper corner of the frame.

It was a picture of Faye Greener, a still from a two-reel farce in which she had worked as an extra. She had given him the photograph willingly enough, had even autographed it in a large, wild hand, "Affectionately yours, Faye Greener," but she refused his friendship, or, rather, insisted on keeping it impersonal. She had told him why. He had nothing to offer her, neither money nor looks, and she could only love a handsome man and would only let a wealthy man love her. Tod was a "good-hearted man," and she liked "good-hearted men," but only as friends. She wasn't hard-boiled. It was just that she put love on a special plane, where a man without money or looks couldn't move.

Tod grunted with annoyance as he turned to the photograph. In it she was wearing a harem costume, full Turkish trousers, breastplates and a monkey jacket, and lay stretched out on a silken divan. One hand held a beer bottle and the other a pewter stein.

He had gone all the way to Glendale to see her in that movie. It was about an American drummer who gets lost in the seraglio[2] of a Damascus merchant and has a lot of fun with the female inmates. Faye played one of the dancing girls. She had only one line to speak, "Oh, Mr. Smith!" and spoke it badly.

She was a tall girl with wide, straight shoulders and long, swordlike legs. Her neck was long, too, and columnar. Her face was much fuller than the rest of her body would lead you to expect and much larger. It was a moon face, wide at the cheek bones and narrow at chin and brow. She wore her "platinum"[3] hair long, letting it fall almost to her shoulders in back, but kept it away from her face and ears with a narrow blue ribbon that went under it and was tied on top of her head with a little bow.

She was supposed to look drunk and she did, but not with alcohol. She lay stretched out on the divan with her arms and legs spread, as though welcoming a lover, and her lips were parted in a heavy, sullen smile. She was supposed to look inviting, but the invitation wasn't to pleasure.

Tod lit a cigarette and inhaled with a nervous gasp. He started to fool with his tie again, but had to go back to the photograph.

Her invitation wasn't to pleasure, but to struggle, hard and sharp, closer to murder than to love. If you threw yourself on her, it would be like throwing yourself from the parapet of a skyscraper. You would do it with a scream. You couldn't expect to rise again. Your teeth would be driven into your skull

2. Harem.
3. Bleached blond. Frank Capra's film *Platinum Blonde* (1931) featured Jean Harlow in the title role and popularized the damaging bleaching process used to achieve her dramatic white-blond hair color.

like nails into a pine board and your back would be broken. You wouldn't even have time to sweat or close your eyes.

He managed to laugh at his language, but it wasn't a real laugh and nothing was destroyed by it.

If she would only let him, he would be glad to throw himself, no matter what the cost. But she wouldn't have him. She didn't love him and he couldn't further her career. She wasn't sentimental and she had no need for tenderness, even if he were capable of it.

When he had finished dressing, he hurried out of the room. He had promised to go to a party at Claude Estee's.

4

Claude was a successful screen writer who lived in a big house that was an exact reproduction of the old Dupuy mansion near Biloxi, Mississippi. When Tod came up the walk between the boxwood hedges, he greeted him from the enormous, two-story porch by doing the impersonation that went with the Southern colonial architecture. He teetered back and forth on his heels like a Civil War colonel and made believe he had a large belly.

He had no belly at all. He was a dried-up little man with the rubbed features and stooped shoulders of a postal clerk. The shiny mohair coat and nondescript trousers of that official would have become him, but he was dressed, as always, elaborately. In the buttonhole of his brown jacket was a lemon flower. His trousers were of reddish Harris tweed with a hound tooth check and on his feet were a pair of magnificent, rust-colored blüchers.[4] His shirt was ivory flannel and his knitted tie[5] a red that was almost black.

While Tod mounted the steps to reach his outstretched hand, he shouted to the butler.

"Here, you black rascal! A mint julep."

A Chinese servant came running with a Scotch and soda.

After talking to Tod for a moment, Claude started him in the direction of Alice, his wife, who was at the other end of the porch.

"Don't run off," he whispered. "We're going to a sporting house."[6]

Alice was sitting in a wicker swing with a woman named Mrs. Joan Schwartzen. When she asked him if he was playing any tennis, Mrs. Schwartzen interrupted her.

"How silly, batting an inoffensive ball across something that ought to be used to catch fish on account of millions are starving for a bite of herring."

"Joan's a female tennis champ," Alice explained.

Mrs. Schwartzen was a big girl with large hands and feet and square, bony shoulders. She had a pretty, eighteen-year-old face and a thirty-five-year-old neck that was veined and sinewy. Her deep sunburn, ruby colored with a slight blue tint, kept the contrast between her face and neck from being too startling.

4. Lace-up men's shoes.
5. Tweed, flannel, and knitted ties are typically associated with casual, cold-weather men's clothing.
6. A brothel.

"Well, I wish we were going to a brothel this minute," she said. "I adore them."

She turned to Tod and fluttered her eyelids.

"Don't you, Mr. Hackett?"

"That's right, Joan darling," Alice answered for him. "Nothing like a bagnio[7] to set a fellow up. Hair of the dog that bit you."

"How dare you insult me!"

She stood up and took Tod's arm.

"Convoy me over there."

She pointed to the group of men with whom Claude was standing.

"For God's sake, convoy her," Alice said. "She thinks they're telling dirty stories."

Mrs. Schwartzen pushed right among them, dragging Tod after her.

"Are you talking smut?" she asked. "I adore smut."

They all laughed politely.

"No, shop," said someone.

"I don't believe it. I can tell from the beast in your voices. Go ahead, do say something obscene."

This time no one laughed.

Tod tried to disengage her arm, but she kept a firm grip on it. There was a moment of awkward silence, then the man she had interrupted tried to make a fresh start.

"The picture business is too humble," he said. "We ought to resent people like Coombes."

"That's right," said another man. "Guys like that come out here, make a lot of money, grouse all the time about the place, flop on their assignments, then go back East and tell dialect stories about producers they've never met."

"My God," Mrs. Schwartzen said to Tod in a loud, stagey whisper, "they *are* talking shop."

"Let's look for the man with the drinks," Tod said.

"No. Take me into the garden. Have you seen what's in the swimming pool?"

She pulled him along.

The air of the garden was heavy with the odor of mimosa and honeysuckle. Through a slit in the blue serge sky poked a grained moon that looked like an enormous bone button. A little flagstone path, made narrow by its border of oleander, led to the edge of the sunken pool. On the bottom, near the deep end, he could see a heavy, black mass of some kind.

"What is it?" he asked.

She kicked a switch that was hidden at the base of a shrub and a row of submerged floodlights illuminated the green water. The thing was a dead horse, or, rather, a life-size, realistic reproduction of one. Its legs stuck up stiff and straight and it had an enormous, distended belly. Its hammerhead lay twisted to one side and from its mouth, which was set in an agonized grin, hung a heavy, black tongue.

7. A brothel.

"Isn't it marvelous!" exclaimed Mrs. Schwartzen, clapping her hands and jumping up and down excitedly like a little girl.

"What's it made of?"

"Then you weren't fooled? How impolite! It's rubber, of course. It cost lots of money."

"But why?"

"To amuse. We were looking at the pool one day and somebody, Jerry Appis, I think, said that it needed a dead horse on the bottom, so Alice got one. Don't you think it looks cute?"

"Very."

"You're just an old meanie. Think how happy the Estees must feel, showing it to people and listening to their merriment and their oh's and ah's of unconfined delight."

She stood on the edge of the pool and "ohed and ahed" rapidly several times in succession.

"Is it still there?" someone called.

Tod turned and saw two women and a man coming down the path.

"I think its belly's going to burst," Mrs. Schwartzen shouted to them gleefully.

"Goody," said the man, hurrying to look.

"But it's only full of air," said one of the women.

Mrs. Schwartzen made believe she was going to cry.

"You're just like that mean Mr. Hackett. You just won't let me cherish my illusions."

Tod was half way to the house when she called after him. He waved but kept going.

The men with Claude were still talking shop.

"But how are you going to get rid of the illiterate mockies[8] that run it? They've got a strangle hold on the industry. Maybe they're intellectual stumblebums, but they're damn good business men. Or at least they know how to go into receivership and come up with a gold watch in their teeth."

"They ought to put some of the millions they make back into the business again. Like Rockefeller does with his Foundation.[9] People used to hate the Rockefellers, but now instead of hollering about their ill-gotten oil dough, everybody praises them for what the Foundation does. It's a swell stunt and pictures could do the same thing. Have a Cinema Foundation and make contributions to Science and Art. You know, give the racket a front."

Tod took Claude to one side to say good night, but he wouldn't let him go. He led him into the library and mixed two double Scotches. They sat down on the couch facing the fireplace.

"You haven't been to Audrey Jenning's place?" Claude asked.

"No, but I've heard tell of it."

"Then you've got to come along."

8. Derogatory slang for Jews.
9. American oil tycoon J. D. Rockefeller (1839–1937) established the Rockefeller Foundation in 1913.

"I don't like pro-sport."

"We won't indulge in any. We're just going to see a movie."

"I get depressed."

"Not at Jenning's you won't. She makes vice attractive by skillful packaging. Her dive's a triumph of industrial design."

Tod liked to hear him talk. He was master of an involved comic rhetoric that permitted him to express his moral indignation and still keep his reputation for worldliness and wit.

Tod fed him another lead. "I don't care how much cellophane she wraps it in," he said—"nautch joints[1] are depressing, like all places for deposit, banks, mail boxes, tombs, vending machines."

"Love is like a vending machine, eh? Not bad. You insert a coin and press home the lever. There's some mechanical activity inside the bowels of the device. You receive a small sweet, frown at yourself in the dirty mirror, adjust your hat, take a firm grip on your umbrella and walk away, trying to look as though nothing had happened. It's good, but it's not for pictures."

Tod played straight again.

"That's not it. I've been chasing a girl and it's like carrying something a little too large to conceal in your pocket, like a briefcase or a small valise. It's uncomfortable."

"I know, I know. It's always uncomfortable. First your right hand gets tired, then your left. You put the valise down and sit on it, but people are surprised and stop to stare at you, so you move on. You hide it behind a tree and hurry away, but someone finds it and runs after you to return it. It's a small valise when you leave home in the morning, cheap and with a bad handle, but by evening it's a trunk with brass corners and many foreign labels. I know. It's good, but it won't film. You've got to remember your audience. What about the barber in Purdue? He's been cutting hair all day and he's tired. He doesn't want to see some dope carrying a valise or fooling with a nickel machine. What the barber wants is armor and glamor."

The last part was for himself and he sighed heavily. He was about to begin again when the Chinese servant came in and said that the others were ready to leave for Mrs. Jenning's.

5

They started out in several cars. Tod rode in the front of the one Claude drove and as they went down Sunset Boulevard he described Mrs. Jenning for him. She had been a fairly prominent actress in the days of silent films, but sound made it impossible for her to get work.[2] Instead of becoming an extra or a bit player like many other old stars, she had shown excellent business sense and had opened a callhouse.[3] She wasn't vicious. Far from it. She ran her business just as other women run lending libraries, shrewdly and with taste.

1. Brothels.
2. The arrival of films with recorded sound, beginning in 1927, ended the careers of many performers who had marked accents or voices otherwise not acceptable in the new medium.
3. Brothel.

None of the girls lived on the premises. You telephoned and she sent a girl over. The charge was thirty dollars for a single night of sport and Mrs. Jenning kept fifteen of it. Some people might think that fifty per cent is a high brokerage fee, but she really earned every cent of it. There was a big overhead. She maintained a beautiful house for the girls to wait in and a car and a chauffeur to deliver them to the clients.

Then, too, she had to move in the kind of society where she could make the right contacts. After all, not every man can afford thirty dollars. She permitted her girls to service only men of wealth and position, not to say taste and discretion. She was so particular that she insisted on meeting the prospective sportsman before servicing him. She had often said, and truthfully, that she would not let a girl of hers go to a man with whom she herself would not be willing to sleep.

And she was really cultured. All the most distinguished visitors considered it quite a lark to meet her. They were disappointed, however, when they discovered how refined she was. They wanted to talk about certain lively matters of universal interest, but she insisted on discussing Gertrude Stein and Juan Gris.[4] No matter how hard the distinguished visitor tried, and some had been known to go to really great lengths, he could never find a flaw in her refinement or make a breach in her culture.

Claude was still using his peculiar rhetoric on Mrs. Jenning when she came to the door of her house to greet them.

"It's so nice to see you again," she said. "I was telling Mrs. Prince at tea only yesterday—the Estees are my favorite couple."

She was a handsome woman, smooth and buttery, with fair hair and a red complexion.

She led them into a small drawing room whose color scheme was violet, gray and rose. The Venetian blinds were rose, as was the ceiling, and the walls were covered with a pale gray paper that had a tiny, widely spaced flower design in violet. On one wall hung a silver screen, the kind that rolls up, and against the opposite wall, on each side of a cherry-wood table, was a row of chairs covered with rose and gray glazed chintz[5] bound in violet piping. There was a small projection machine on the table and a young man in evening dress was fumbling with it.

She waved them to their seats. A waiter then came in and asked what they wanted to drink. When their orders had been taken and filled, she flipped the light switch and the young man started his machine. It whirred merrily, but he had trouble in getting it focused.

"What are we going to see first?" Mrs. Schwartzen asked.

"Le Predicament de Marie."

"That sounds ducky."

"It's charming, utterly charming," said Mrs. Jenning.

"Yes," said the cameraman, who was still having trouble. "I love *Le Predicament de Marie*. It has a marvelous quality that is too exciting."

There was a long delay, during which he fussed desperately with his machine. Mrs. Schwartzen started to whistle and stamp her feet and the

4. Members of the modernist art community of Paris. Gris (1887–1927), Spanish painter. Stein (1874–1946), American writer.

5. Cotton fabric, usually printed in floral patterns, popular in 19th-century clothing and décor.

others joined in. They imitated a rowdy audience in the days of the nickelodeon.[6]

"Get a move on, slow poke."

"What's your hurry? Here's your hat."

"Get a horse!"

"Get out and get under!"

The young man finally found the screen with his light beam and the film began.

LE PREDICAMENT DE MARIE

ou

LA BONNE DISTRAIT[7]

Marie, the "bonne," was a buxom young girl in a tight-fitting black silk uniform with very short skirts. On her head was a tiny lace cap. In the first scene, she was shown serving dinner to a middle-class family in an oak-paneled dining room full of heavy, carved furniture. The family was very respectable and consisted of a bearded, frock-coated father, a mother with a whalebone collar and a cameo brooch, a tall, thin son with a long mustache and almost no chin and a little girl wearing a large bow in her hair and a crucifix on a gold chain around her neck.

After some low comedy with father's beard and the soup, the actors settled down seriously to their theme. It was evident that while the whole family desired Marie, she only desired the young girl. Using his napkin to hide his activities, the old man pinched Marie, the son tried to look down the neck of her dress and the mother patted her knee. Marie, for her part, surreptitiously fondled the child.

The scene changed to Marie's room. She undressed and got into a chiffon negligee, leaving on only her black silk stockings and high-heeled shoes. She was making an elaborate night toilet when the child entered. Marie took her on her lap and started to kiss her. There was a knock on the door. Consternation. She hid the child in the closet and let in the bearded father. He was suspicious and she had to accept his advances. He was embracing her when there was another knock. Again consternation and tableau.[8] This time it was the mustachioed son. Marie hid the father under the bed. No sooner had the son begun to grow warm than there was another knock. Marie made him climb into a large blanket chest. The new caller was the lady of the house. She, too, was just settling down to work when there was another knock.

Who could it be? A telegram? A policeman? Frantically Marie counted the different hiding places. The whole family was present. She tiptoed to the door and listened.

"Who can it be that wishes to enter now?" read the title card.

And there the machine stuck. The young man in evening dress became as frantic as Marie. When he got it running again, there was a flash of light and the film whizzed through the apparatus until it had all run out.

6. In the early years of film, a movie theater charging 5 cents for admission.

7. Marie's Predicament; or the Distracted Maid (French); the correct French feminine form would be "Distraite."

8. Pause in the action during which the performers remain motionless.

"I'm sorry, extremely," he said. "I'll have to rewind."

"It's a frameup," someone yelled.

"Fake!"

"Cheat!"

"The old teaser routine!"

They stamped their feet and whistled.

Under cover of the mock riot, Tod sneaked out. He wanted to get some fresh air. The waiter, whom he found loitering in the hall, showed him to the patio in back of the house.

On his return, he peeked into the different rooms. In one of them he found a large number of miniature dogs in a curio cabinet. There were glass pointers, silver beagles, porcelain schnauzers, stone dachshunds, aluminum bulldogs, onyx whippets, china bassets, wooden spaniels. Every recognized breed was represented and almost every material that could be sculptured, cast or carved.

While he was admiring the little figures, he heard a girl singing. He thought he recognized her voice and peeked into the hall. It was Mary Dove, one of Faye Greener's best friends.

Perhaps Faye also worked for Mrs. Jenning. If so, for thirty dollars . . .

He went back to see the rest of the film.

6

Tod's hope that he could end his trouble by paying a small fee didn't last long. When he got Claude to ask Mrs. Jenning about Faye, that lady said she had never heard of the girl. Claude then asked her to inquire through Mary Dove. A few days later she phoned him to say there was nothing doing. The girl wasn't available.

Tod wasn't really disappointed. He didn't want Faye that way, not at least while he still had a chance some other way. Lately, he had begun to think he had a good one. Harry, her father, was sick and that gave him an excuse for hanging around their apartment. He ran errands and kept the old man company. To repay his kindness, she permitted him the intimacies of a family friend. He hoped to deepen her gratitude and make it serious.

Apart from this purpose, he was interested in Harry and enjoyed visiting him. The old man was a clown and Tod had all the painter's usual love of clowns. But what was more important, he felt that his clownship was a clue to the people who stared (a painter's clue, that is—a clue in the form of a symbol), just as Faye's dreams were another.

He sat near Harry's bed and listened to his stories by the hour. Forty years in vaudeville and burlesque had provided him with an infinite number of them. As he put it, his life had consisted of a lightning series of "nip-ups," "high-gruesomes," "flying-W's" and "hundred-and-eights"[9] done to escape a barrage of "exploding stoves." An "exploding stove" was any catastrophe, natural or human, from a flood in Medicine Hat, Wyoming, to an angry policeman in Moose Factory, Ontario.

When Harry had first begun his stage career, he had probably restricted his clowning to the boards,[1] but now he clowned continuously. It was his

9. Acrobatic maneuvers.

1. I.e., to the stage.

sole method of defense. Most people, he had discovered, won't go out of their way to punish a clown.

He used a set of elegant gestures to accent the comedy of his bent, hopeless figure and wore a special costume, dressing like a banker, a cheap, unconvincing, imitation banker. The costume consisted of a greasy derby with an unusually high crown, a wing collar and polka dot four-in-hand, a shiny double-breasted jacket and gray-striped trousers. His outfit fooled no one, but then he didn't intend it to fool anyone. His slyness was of a different sort.

On the stage he was a complete failure and knew it. Yet he claimed to have once come very close to success. To prove how close, he made Tod read an old clipping from the theatrical section of the Sunday *Times.*

"BEDRAGGLED HARLEQUIN," it was headed.

"The commedia del' arte[2] is not dead, but lives on in Brooklyn, or was living there last week on the stage of the Oglethorpe Theatre in the person of one Harry Greener. Mr. Greener is of a troupe called 'The Flying Lings,' who, by the time this reaches you, have probably moved on to Mystic, Connecticut, or some other place more fitting than the borough of large families. If you have the time and really love the theatre, by all means seek out the Lings wherever they may be.

"Mr. Greener, the bedraggled Harlequin of our caption, is not bedraggled but clean, neat and sweet when he first comes on. By the time the Lings, four muscular Orientals, finish with him, however, he is plenty bedraggled. He is tattered and bloody, but still sweet.

"When Mr. Greener enters the trumpets are properly silent. Mama Ling is spinning a plate on the end of a stick held in her mouth, Papa Ling is doing cartwheels, Sister Ling is juggling fans and Sonny Ling is hanging from the proscenium arch by his pigtail. As he inspects his strenuous colleagues, Mr. Greener tries to hide his confusion under some much too obvious worldliness. He ventures to tickle Sister and receives a powerful kick in the belly in return for this innocent attention. Having been kicked, he is on familiar ground and begins to tell a dull joke. Father Ling sneaks up behind him and tosses him to Brother, who looks the other way. Mr. Greener lands on the back of his neck. He shows his mettle by finishing his dull story from a recumbent position. When he stands up, the audience, which failed to laugh at his joke, laughs at his limp, so he continues lame for the rest of the act.

"Mr. Greener begins another story, even longer and duller than his first. Just before he arrives at the gag line, the orchestra blares loudly and drowns him out. He is very patient and very brave. He begins again, but the orchestra will not let him finish. The pain that almost, not quite, thank God, crumples his stiff little figure would be unbearable if it were not obviously make-believe. It is gloriously funny.

"The finale is superb. While the Ling Family flies through the air, Mr. Greener, held to the ground by his sense of reality and his knowledge of gravitation, tries hard to make the audience think that he is neither surprised nor worried by the rocketing Orientals. It's familiar stuff, his hands signal, but his face denies this. As time goes on and no one is hurt, he

2. Italian popular theater form, originating in the 16th century, in which Harlequin, a comic servant traditionally dressed in a checkered costume, is a stock character.

regains his assurance. The acrobats ignore him, so he ignores the acrobats. His is the final victory; the applause is for him.

"My first thought was that some producer should put Mr. Greener into a big revue against a background of beautiful girls and glittering curtains. But my second was that this would be a mistake. I am afraid that Mr. Greener, like certain humble field plants which die when transferred to richer soil, had better be left to bloom in vaudeville against a background of ventriloquists and lady bicycle riders."

Harry had more than a dozen copies of this article, several on rag paper.[3] After trying to get a job by inserting a small advertisement in *Variety*[4] (". . . 'some producer should put Mr. Greener into a big revue . . .' The *Times*"), he had come to Hollywood, thinking to earn a living playing comedy bits in films. There proved to be little demand for his talents, however. As he himself put it, he "stank from hunger." To supplement his meagre income from the studios, he peddled silver polish which he made in the bathroom of the apartment out of chalk, soap and yellow axle grease. When Faye wasn't at Central Casting, she took him around on his peddling trips in her Model T Ford. It was on their last expedition together that he had fallen sick.

It was on this trip that Faye acquired a new suitor by the name of Homer Simpson. About a week after Harry had taken to his bed, Tod met Homer for the first time. He was keeping the old man company when their conversation was interrupted by a light knock on the apartment door. Tod answered it and found a man standing in the hall with flowers for Faye and a bottle of port wine for her father.

Tod examined him eagerly. He didn't mean to be rude but at first glance this man seemed an exact model for the kind of person who comes to California to die, perfect in every detail down to fever eyes and unruly hands.

"My name is Homer Simpson," the man gasped, then shifted uneasily and patted his perfectly dry forehead with a folded handkerchief.

"Won't you come in?" Tod asked.

He shook his head heavily and thrust the wine and flowers at Tod. Before Tod could say anything, he had lumbered off.

Tod saw that he was mistaken. Homer Simpson was only physically the type. The men he meant were not shy.

He took the gifts in to Harry, who didn't seem at all surprised. He said Homer was one of his grateful customers.

"That Miracle Polish of mine sure does fetch 'em."

Later, when Faye came home and heard the story, she was very much amused. They both told Tod how they had happened to meet Homer, interrupting themselves and each other every few seconds to laugh.

The next night Tod saw Homer staring at the apartment house from the shadow of a date palm on the opposite side of the street. He watched him for a few minutes, then called out a friendly greeting. Without replying, Homer ran away. On the next day and the one after, Tod again saw him lurking near the palm tree. He finally caught him by approaching the tree silently from the rear.

3. Heavy, expensive paper.
4. A major trade journal of the entertainment industry since its launch in 1905.

"Hello, Mr. Simpson," Tod said softly. "The Greeners were very grateful for your gift."

This time Simpson didn't move, perhaps because Tod had him backed against the tree.

"That's fine," he blurted out. "I was passing . . . I live up the street."

Tod managed to keep their conversation going for several minutes before he escaped again.

The next time Tod was able to approach him without the stalk. From then on, he responded very quickly to his advances. Sympathy, even of the most obvious sort, made him articulate, almost garrulous.

7

Tod was right about one thing at least. Like most of the people he was interested in, Homer was a Middle-Westerner. He came from a little town near Des Moines, Iowa, called Wayneville, where he had worked for twenty years in a hotel.

One day, while sitting in the park in the rain, he had caught cold and his cold developed into pneumonia. When he came out of the hospital, he found that the hotel had hired a new bookkeeper. They offered to take him on again, but his doctor advised him to go to California for a rest. The doctor had an authoritative manner, so Homer left Wayneville for the Coast.

After living for a week in a railroad hotel in Los Angeles, he rented a cottage in Pinyon Canyon. It was only the second house the real estate agent showed him, but he took it because he was tired and because the agent was a bully.

He rather liked the way the cottage was located. It was the last house in the canyon and the hills rose directly behind the garage. They were covered with lupines, Canterbury bells, poppies, and several varieties of large yellow daisy. There were also some scrub pines, Joshua and eucalyptus trees. The agent told him that he would see doves and plumed quail, but during all the time he lived there, he saw only a few large, black velvet spiders and a lizard. He grew very fond of the lizard.

The house was cheap because it was hard to rent. Most of the people who took cottages in that neighborhood wanted them to be "Spanish" and this one, so the agent claimed, was "Irish." Homer thought that the place looked kind of queer, but the agent insisted that it was cute.

The house was queer. It had an enormous and very crooked stone chimney, little dormer windows with big hoods and a thatched roof that came down very low on both sides of the front door. This door was of gumwood painted like fumed oak and it hung on enormous hinges. Although made by machine, the hinges had been carefully stamped to appear hand-forged. The same kind of care and skill had been used to make the roof thatching, which was not really straw but heavy fireproof paper colored and ribbed to look like straw.

The prevailing taste had been followed in the living room. It was "Spanish." The walls were pale orange flecked with pink and on them hung several silk armorial banners in red and gold. A big galleon stood on the mantelpiece. Its hull was plaster, its sails paper and its rigging wire. In the fireplace was a variety of cactus in gaily colored Mexican pots. Some of the plants were made of rubber and cork; others were real.

The room was lit by wall fixtures in the shape of galleons with pointed amber bulbs projecting from their decks. The table held a lamp with a paper shade, oiled to look like parchment, that had several more galleons painted on it. On each side of the windows red velvet draperies hung from black, double-headed spears.

The furniture consisted of a heavy couch that had fat monks for legs and was covered with faded red damask, and three swollen armchairs, also red. In the center of the room was a very long mahogany table. It was of the trestle type and studded with large-headed bronze nails. Beside each of the chairs was a small end table, the same color and design as the big one, but with a colored tile let into the top.

In the two small bedrooms still another style had been used. This the agent had called "New England." There was a spool bed made of iron grained like wood, a Windsor chair of the kind frequently seen in tea shops, and a Governor Winthrop dresser[5] painted to look like unpainted pine. On the floor was a small hooked rug. On the wall facing the dresser was a colored etching of a snowbound Connecticut farmhouse, complete with wolf. Both of these rooms were exactly alike in every detail. Even the pictures were duplicates.

There was also a bathroom and a kitchen.

8

It took Homer only a few minutes to get settled in his new home. He unpacked his trunk, hung his two suits, both dark gray, in the closet of one of his bedrooms and put his shirts and underclothes into the dresser drawers. He made no attempt to rearrange the furniture.

After an aimless tour of the house and the yard, he sat down on the couch in the living room. He sat as though waiting for someone in the lobby of a hotel. He remained that way for almost half an hour without moving anything but his hands, then got up and went into the bedroom and sat down on the edge of the bed.

Although it was still early in the afternoon, he felt very sleepy. He was afraid to stretch out and go to sleep. Not because he had bad dreams, but because it was so hard for him to wake again. When he fell asleep, he was always afraid that he would never get up.

But his fear wasn't as strong as his need. He got his alarm clock and set it for seven o'clock, then lay down with it next to his ear. Two hours later, it seemed like seconds to him, the alarm went off. The bell rang for a full minute before he began to work laboriously toward consciousness. The struggle was a hard one. He groaned. His head trembled and his feet shot out. Finally his eyes opened, then widened. Once more the victory was his.

He lay stretched out on the bed, collecting his senses and testing the different parts of his body. Every part was awake but his hands. They still slept. He was not surprised. They demanded special attention, had always demanded it. When he had been a child, he used to stick pins into them and once had even thrust them into a fire. Now he used only cold water.

5. A dresser typically set on short legs and featuring a fold-down desktop, named for John Winthrop (1587/8–1649), first governor of the Massachusetts Bay Colony from 1630 to 1633. "Windsor chair": a wooden chair with a curved bentwood back.

He got out of bed in sections, like a poorly made automaton, and carried his hands into the bathroom. He turned on the cold water. When the basin was full, he plunged his hands in up to the wrists. They lay quietly on the bottom like a pair of strange aquatic animals. When they were thoroughly chilled and began to crawl about, he lifted them out and hid them in a towel.

He was cold. He ran hot water into the tub and began to undress, fumbling with the buttons of his clothing as though he were undressing a stranger. He was naked before the tub was full enough to get in and he sat down on a stool to wait. He kept his enormous hands folded quietly on his belly. Although absolutely still, they seemed curbed rather than resting.

Except for his hands, which belonged on a piece of monumental sculpture, and his small head, he was well proportioned. His muscles were large and round and he had a full, heavy chest. Yet there was something wrong. For all his size and shape, he looked neither strong nor fertile. He was like one of Picasso's great sterile athletes, who brood hopelessly on pink sand, staring at veined marble waves.[6]

When the tub was full, he got in and sank down in the hot water. He grunted his comfort. But in another moment he would begin to remember, in just another moment. He tried to fool his memory by overwhelming it with tears and brought up the sobs that were always lurking uneasily in his chest. He cried softly at first, then harder. The sound he made was like that of a dog lapping gruel. He concentrated on how miserable and lonely he was, but it didn't work. The thing he was trying so desperately to avoid kept crowding into his mind.

One day when he was working in the hotel, a guest called Romola Martin had spoken to him in the elevator.

"Mr. Simpson, you're Mr. Simpson, the bookkeeper?"

"Yes."

"I'm in six-eleven."

She was small and childlike, with a quick, nervous manner. In her arms she coddled a package which obviously contained a square gin bottle.

"Yes," said Homer again, working against his natural instinct to be friendly. He knew that Miss Martin owed several weeks' rent and had heard the room clerk say she was a drunkard.

"Oh! . . ." the girl went on coquettishly, making obvious their difference in size, "I'm sorry you're worried about your bill, I . . ."

The intimacy of her tone embarrassed Homer.

"You'll have to speak to the manager," he rapped out, turning away.

He was trembling when he reached his office.

How bold the creature was! She was drunk, of course, but not so drunk that she didn't know what she was doing. He hurriedly labeled his excitement disgust.

Soon afterwards the manager called and asked him to bring in Miss Martin's credit card. When he went into the manager's office, he found Miss Carlisle, the room clerk, there. Homer listened to what the manager was saying to her.

"You roomed six-eleven?"

6. Suggests figures from the paintings of Pablo Picasso (1881–1973) around the early 1920s.

"I did, yes, sir."

"Why? She's obvious enough, isn't she?"

"Not when she's sober."

"Never mind that. We don't want her kind in this hotel."

"I'm sorry."

The manager turned to Homer and took the credit card he was holding.

"She owes thirty-one dollars," Homer said.

"She'll have to pay up and get out. I don't want her kind around here." He smiled. "Especially when they run up bills. Get her on the phone for me."

Homer asked the telephone operator for six-eleven and after a short time was told that the room didn't answer.

"She's in the house," he said. "I saw her in the elevator."

"I'll have the housekeeper look."

Homer was working on his books some minutes later when his phone rang. It was the manager again. He said that six-eleven had been reported in by the housekeeper and asked Homer to take her a bill.

"Tell her to pay up or get out," he said.

His first thought was to ask that Miss Carlisle be sent because he was busy, but he didn't dare to suggest it. While making out the bill, he began to realize how excited he was. It was terrifying. Little waves of sensation moved along his nerves and the base of his tongue tingled.

When he got off at the sixth floor, he felt almost gay. His step was buoyant and he had completely forgotten his troublesome hands. He stopped at six-eleven and made as though to knock, then suddenly took fright and lowered his fist without touching the door.

He couldn't go through with it. They would have to send Miss Carlisle.

The housekeeper, who had been watching from the end of the hall, came up before he could escape.

"She doesn't answer," Homer said hurriedly.

"Did you knock hard enough? That slut is in there."

Before Homer could reply, she pounded on the door.

"Open up!" she shouted.

Homer heard someone move inside, then the door opened a few inches.

"Who is it, please?" a light voice asked.

"Mr. Simpson, the bookkeeper," he gasped.

"Come in, please."

The door opened a little wider and Homer went in without daring to look around at the housekeeper. He stumbled to the center of the room and stopped. At first he was conscious only of the heavy odor of alcohol and stale tobacco, but then underneath he smelled a metallic perfume. His eyes moved in a slow circle. On the floor was a litter of clothing, newspapers, magazines, and bottles. Miss Martin was huddled up on a corner of the bed. She was wearing a man's black silk dressing gown with light blue cuffs and lapel facings. Her close-cropped hair was the color and texture of straw and she looked like a little boy. Her youthfulness was heightened by her blue button eyes, pink button nose and red button mouth.

Homer was too busy with his growing excitement to speak or even think. He closed his eyes to tend it better, nursing carefully what he felt. He had to be careful, for if he went too fast, it might wither and then he would be cold again. It continued to grow.

"Go away, please, I'm drunk," Miss Martin said.

Homer neither moved nor spoke.

She suddenly began to sob. The coarse, broken sounds she made seemed to come from her stomach. She buried her face in her hands and pounded the floor with her feet.

Homer's feelings were so intense that his head bobbed stiffly on his neck like that of a toy Chinese dragon.

"I'm broke. I haven't any money. I haven't a dime. I'm broke, I tell you."

Homer pulled out his wallet and moved on the girl as though to strike her with it.

She cowered away from him and her sobs grew stronger.

He dropped the wallet in her lap and stood over her, not knowing what else to do. When she saw the wallet, she smiled, but continued sobbing.

"Sit down," she said.

He sat down on the bed beside her.

"You strange man," she said coyly. "I could kiss you for being so nice."

He caught her in his arms and hugged her. His suddenness frightened her and she tried to pull away, but he held on and began awkwardly to caress her. He was completely unconscious of what he was doing. He knew only that what he felt was marvelously sweet and that he had to make the sweetness carry through to the poor, sobbing woman.

Miss Martin's sobs grew less and soon stopped altogether. He could feel her fidget and gather strength.

The telephone rang.

"Don't answer it," she said, beginning to sob once more.

He pushed her away gently and stumbled to the telephone. It was Miss Carlisle.

"Are you all right?" she asked, "or shall we send for the cops?"

"All right," he said, hanging up.

It was all over. He couldn't go back to the bed.

Miss Martin laughed at his look of acute distress.

"Bring the gin, you enormous cow," she shouted gaily. "It's under the table."

He saw her stretch herself out in a way that couldn't be mistaken. He ran out of the room.

Now in California, he was crying because he had never seen Miss Martin again. The next day the manager had told him that he had done a good job and that she had paid up and checked out.

Homer tried to find her. There were two other hotels in Wayneville, small run-down houses, and he inquired at both of them. He also asked in the few rooming places, but with no success. She had left town.

He settled back into his regular routine, working ten hours, eating two, sleeping the rest. Then he caught cold and had been advised to come to California. He could easily afford not to work for a while. His father had left him about six thousand dollars and during the twenty years he had kept books in the hotel, he had saved at least ten more.[7]

7. Homer's assets are worth about $275,000 in current U.S. dollars.

9

He got out of the tub, dried himself hurriedly with a rough towel, then went into the bedroom to dress. He felt even more stupid and washed out than usual. It was always like that. His emotions surged up in an enormous wave, curving and rearing, higher and higher, until it seemed as though the wave must carry everything before it. But the crash never came. Something always happened at the very top of the crest and the wave collapsed to run back like water down a drain, leaving, at the most, only the refuse of feeling.

It took him a long time to get all his clothing on. He stopped to rest after each garment with a desperation far out of proportion to the effort involved.

There was nothing to eat in the house and he had to go down to Hollywood Boulevard for food. He thought of waiting until morning, but then, although he was not hungry, decided against waiting. It was only eight o'clock and the trip would kill some time. If he just sat around, the temptation to go to sleep again would become irresistible.

The night was warm and very still. He started down hill, walking on the outer edge of the pavement. He hurried between lamp-posts, where the shadows were heaviest, and came to a full stop for a moment at every circle of light. By the time he reached the boulevard, he was fighting the desire to run. He stopped for several minutes on the corner to get his bearings. As he stood there, poised for flight, his fear made him seem almost graceful.

When several other people passed without paying any attention to him, he quieted down. He adjusted the collar of his coat and prepared to cross the street. Before he could take two steps someone called to him.

"Hey, you, mister."

It was a beggar who had spotted him from the shadow of a doorway. With the infallible instinct of his kind, he knew that Homer would be easy.

"Can you spare a nickel?"

"No," Homer said without conviction.

The beggar laughed and repeated his question, threateningly.

"A nickel, mister!"

He poked his hand into Homer's face.

Homer fumbled in his change pocket and dropped several coins on the sidewalk. While the man scrambled for them, he made his escape across the street.

The SunGold Market into which he turned was a large, brilliantly lit place. All the fixtures were chromium and the floor and walls were lined with white tile. Colored spotlights played on the showcases and counters, heightening the natural hues of the different foods. The oranges were bathed in red, the lemons in yellow, the fish in pale green, the steaks in rose and the eggs in ivory.

Homer went directly to the canned goods department and bought a can of mushroom soup and another of sardines. These and a half a pound of soda crackers would be enough for his supper.

Out on the street again with his parcel, he started to walk home. When he reached the corner that led to Pinyon Canyon and saw how steep and black the hill looked, he turned back along the lighted boulevard. He thought of waiting until someone else started up the hill, but finally took a taxicab.

10

Although Homer had nothing to do but prepare his scanty meals, he was not bored. Except for the Romola Martin incident and perhaps one or two other widely spaced events, the forty years of his life had been entirely without variety or excitement. As a bookkeeper, he had worked mechanically, totaling figures and making entries with the same impersonal detachment that he now opened cans of soup and made his bed.

Someone watching him go about his little cottage might have thought him sleep-walking or partially blind. His hands seemed to have a life and a will of their own. It was they who pulled the sheets tight and shaped the pillows.

One day, while opening a can of salmon for lunch, his thumb received a nasty cut. Although the wound must have hurt, the calm, slightly querulous expression he usually wore did not change. The wounded hand writhed about on the kitchen table until it was carried to the sink by its mate and bathed tenderly in hot water.

When not keeping house, he sat in the back yard, called the patio by the real estate agent, in an old broken deck chair. He went out to it immediately after breakfast to bake himself in the sun. In one of the closets he had found a tattered book and he held it in his lap without looking at it.

There was a much better view to be had in any direction other than the one he faced. By moving his chair in a quarter circle he could have seen a large part of the canyon twisting down to the city below. He never thought of making this shift. From where he sat, he saw the closed door of the garage and a patch of its shabby, tarpaper roof. In the foreground was a sooty, brick incinerator and a pile of rusty cans. A little to the right of them were the remains of a cactus garden in which a few ragged, tortured plants still survived.

One of these, a clump of thick, paddlelike blades, covered with ugly needles, was in bloom. From the tip of several of its topmost blades protruded a bright yellow flower, somewhat like a thistle blossom but coarser. No matter how hard the wind blew, its petals never trembled.

A lizard lived in a hole near the base of this plant. It was about five inches long and had a wedge-shaped head from which darted a fine, forked tongue. It earned a hard living catching the flies that strayed over to the cactus from the pile of cans.

The lizard was self-conscious and irritable, and Homer found it very amusing to watch. Whenever one of its elaborate stalks was foiled, it would shift about uneasily on its short legs and puff out its throat. Its coloring matched the cactus perfectly, but when it moved over to the cans where the flies were thick, it stood out very plainly. It would sit on the cactus by the hour without moving, then become impatient and start for the cans. The flies would spot it immediately and after several misses, it would sneak back sheepishly to its original post.

Homer was on the side of the flies. Whenever one of them, swinging too widely, would pass the cactus, he prayed silently for it to keep on going or turn back. If it lighted, he watched the lizard begin its stalk and held his breath until it had killed, hoping all the while that something would warn the fly. But no matter how much he wanted the fly to escape, he never thought of interfering, and was careful not to budge or make the slightest noise. Occasionally the lizard would miscalculate. When that happened Homer would laugh happily.

Between the sun, the lizard and the house, he was fairly well occupied. But whether he was happy or not is hard to say. Probably he was neither, just as a plant is neither. He had memories to disturb him and a plant hasn't, but after the first bad night his memories were quiet.

11

He had been living this way for almost a month, when, one day, just as he was about to prepare his lunch, the door bell rang. He opened it and found a man standing on the step with a sample case in one hand and a derby hat in the other. Homer hurriedly shut the door again.

The bell continued to ring. He put his head out of the window nearest the door to order the fellow away, but the man bowed very politely and begged for a drink of water. Homer saw that he was old and tired and thought that he looked harmless. He got a bottle of water from the icebox, then opened the door and asked him in.

"The name, sir, is Harry Greener," the man announced in sing-song, stressing every other syllable.

Homer handed him a glass of water. He swallowed it quickly, then poured himself another.

"Much obliged," he said with an elaborate bow. "That was indeed refreshing."

Homer was astonished when he bowed again, did several quick jig steps, then let his derby hat roll down his arm. It fell to the floor. He stooped to retrieve it, straightening up with a jerk as though he had been kicked, then rubbed the seat of his trousers ruefully.

Homer understood that this was to amuse, so he laughed.

Harry thanked him by bowing again, but something went wrong. The exertion had been too much for him. His face blanched and he fumbled with his collar.

"A momentary indisposition," he murmured, wondering himself whether he was acting or sick.

"Sit down," Homer said.

But Harry wasn't through with his performance. He assumed a gallant smile and took a few unsteady steps toward the couch, then tripped himself. He examined the carpet indignantly, made believe he had found the object that had tripped him and kicked it away. He then limped to the couch and sat down with a whistling sigh like air escaping from a toy balloon.

Homer poured more water. Harry tried to stand up, but Homer pressed him back and made him drink sitting. He drank this glass as he had the other two, in quick gulps, then wiped his mouth with his handkerchief, imitating a man with a big mustache who had just drunk a glass of foamy beer.

"You are indeed kind, sir," he said. "Never fear, some day I'll repay you a thousandfold."

Homer clucked.

From his pocket Harry brought out a small can and held it out for him to take.

"Compliments of the house," he announced. "'Tis a box of Miracle Solvent, the modern polish par excellence, the polish without peer or parallel, used by all the movie stars . . ."

He broke off his spiel with a trilling laugh.

Homer took the can.

"Thank you," he said, trying to appear grateful. "How much is it?"

"The ordinary price, the retail price, is fifty cents, but you can have it for the extraordinary price of a quarter, the wholesale price, the price I pay at the factory."

"A quarter?" asked Homer, habit for the moment having got the better of his timidity. "I can buy one twice that size for a quarter in the store."

Harry knew his man.

"Take it, take it for nothing," he said contemptuously.

Homer was tricked into protesting.

"I guess maybe this is a much better polish."

"No," said Harry, as though he were spurning a bribe. "Keep your money. I don't want it."

He laughed, this time bitterly.

Homer pulled out some change and offered it.

"Take it, please. You need it, I'm sure. I'll have two cans."

Harry had his man where he wanted him. He began to practice a variety of laughs, all of them theatrical, like a musician tuning up before a concert. He finally found the right one and let himself go. It was a victim's laugh.

"Please stop," Homer said.

But Harry couldn't stop. He was really sick. The last block that held him poised over the runway of self-pity had been knocked away and he was sliding down the chute, gaining momentum all the time. He jumped to his feet and began doing Harry Greener, poor Harry, honest Harry, well-meaning, humble, deserving, a good husband, a model father, a faithful Christian, a loyal friend.

Homer didn't appreciate the performance in the least. He was terrified and wondered whether to phone the police. But he did nothing. He just held up his hand for Harry to stop.

At the end of his pantomime, Harry stood with his head thrown back, clutching his throat, as though waiting for the curtain to fall. Homer poured him still another glass of water. But Harry wasn't finished. He bowed, sweeping his hat to his heart, then began again. He didn't get very far this time and had to gasp painfully for breath. Suddenly, like a mechanical toy that had been overwound, something snapped inside of him and he began to spin through his entire repertoire. The effort was purely muscular, like the dance of a paralytic. He jigged, juggled his hat, made believe he had been kicked, tripped, and shook hands with himself. He went through it all in one dizzy spasm, then reeled to the couch and collapsed.

He lay on the couch with his eyes closed and his chest heaving. He was even more surprised than Homer. He had put on his performance four or five times already that day and nothing like this had happened. He was really sick.

"You've had a fit," Homer said when Harry opened his eyes.

As the minutes passed, Harry began to feel better and his confidence returned. He pushed all thought of sickness out of his mind and even went so far as to congratulate himself on having given the finest performance of his career. He should be able to get five dollars out of the big dope who was leaning over him.

"Have you any spirits in the house?" he asked weakly.

The grocer had sent Homer a bottle of port wine on approval and he went to get it. He filled a tumbler half full and handed it to Harry, who drank it in small sips, making the faces that usually go with medicine.

Speaking slowly, as though in great pain, he then asked Homer to bring in his sample case.

"It's on the doorstep. Somebody might steal it. The greater part of my small capital is invested in those cans of polish."

When Homer stepped outside to obey, he saw a girl near the curb. It was Faye Greener. She was looking at the house.

"Is my father in there?" she called out.

"Mr. Greener?"

She stamped her foot.

"Tell him to get a move on, damn it. I don't want to stay here all day."

"He's sick."

The girl turned away without giving any sign that she either heard or cared.

Homer took the sample case back into the house with him. He found Harry pouring himself another drink.

"Pretty fair stuff," he said, smacking his lips over it. "Pretty fair, all right, all right. Might I be so bold as to ask what you pay for a . . ."

Homer cut him short. He didn't approve of people who drank and wanted to get rid of him.

"Your daughter's outside," he said with as much firmness as he could muster. "She wants you."

Harry collapsed on the couch and began to breathe heavily. He was acting again.

"Don't tell her," he gasped. "Don't tell her how sick her old daddy is. She must never know."

Homer was shocked by his hypocrisy.

"You're better," he said as coldly as he could. "Why don't you go home?"

Harry smiled to show how offended and hurt he was by the heartless attitude of his host. When Homer said nothing, his smile became one expressing boundless courage. He got carefully to his feet, stood erect for a minute, then began to sway weakly and tumbled back on the couch.

"I'm faint," he groaned.

Once again he was surprised and frightened. He was faint.

"Get my daughter," he gasped.

Homer found her standing at the curb with her back to the house. When he called her, she whirled and came running toward him. He watched her for a second, then went in, leaving the door unlatched.

Faye burst into the room. She ignored Homer and went straight to the couch.

"Now what in hell's the matter?" she exploded.

"Darling daughter," he said. "I have been badly taken, and this gentleman has been kind enough to let me rest for a moment."

"He had a fit or something," Homer said.

She whirled around on him so suddenly that he was startled.

"How do you do?" she said, holding her hand forward and high up.

He shook it gingerly.

"Charmed," she said, when he mumbled something.

She spun around once more.

"It's my heart," Harry said. "I can't stand up."

The little performance he put on to sell polish was familiar to her and she knew that this wasn't part of it. When she turned to face Homer again, she looked quite tragic. Her head, instead of being held far back, now drooped forward.

"Please let him rest there," she said.

"Yes, of course."

Homer motioned her toward a chair, then got her a match for her cigarette. He tried not to stare at her, but his good manners were wasted. Faye enjoyed being stared at.

He thought her extremely beautiful, but what affected him still more was her vitality. She was taut and vibrant. She was as shiny as a new spoon.

Although she was seventeen, she was dressed like a child of twelve in a white cotton dress with a blue sailor collar. Her long legs were bare and she had blue sandals on her feet.

"I'm so sorry," she said when Homer looked at her father again.

He made a motion with his hand to show that it was nothing.

"He has a vile heart, poor dear," she went on. "I've begged and begged him to go to a specialist, but you men are all alike."

"Yes, he ought to go to a doctor," Homer said.

Her odd mannerisms and artificial voice puzzled him.

"What time is it?" she asked.

"About one o'clock."

She stood up suddenly and buried both her hands in her hair at the sides of her head, making it bunch at the top in a shiny ball.

"Oh," she gasped prettily, "and I had a luncheon date."

Still holding her hair, she turned at the waist without moving her legs, so that her snug dress twisted even tighter and Homer could see her dainty, arched ribs and little, dimpled belly. This elaborate gesture, like all her others, was so completely meaningless, almost formal, that she seemed a dancer rather than an affected actress.

"Do you like salmon salad?" Homer ventured to ask.

"Salmon sal-ahde?"

She seemed to be repeating the question to her stomach. The answer was yes.

"With plenty of mayonnaise, huh? I adore it."

"I was going to have some for lunch. I'll finish making it."

"Let me help."

They looked at Harry, who appeared to be asleep, then went into the kitchen. While he opened a can of salmon, she climbed on a chair and straddled it with her arms folded across the top of its back and rested her chin on her arms. Whenever he looked at her, she smiled intimately and tossed her pale, glittering hair first forward, then back.

Homer was excited and his hands worked quickly. He soon had a large bowl of salad ready. He set the table with his best cloth and his best silver and china.

"It makes me hungry just to look," she said.

The way she said this seemed to mean that it was Homer who made her hungry and he beamed at her. But before he had a chance to sit down, she was already eating. She buttered a slice of bread, covered the butter with sugar and took a big bite. Then she quickly smeared a gob of mayonnaise on the salmon and went to work. Just as he was about to sit down, she asked for something to drink. He poured her a glass of milk and stood watching her like a waiter. He was unaware of her rudeness.

As soon as she had gobbled up her salad, he brought her a large red apple. She ate the fruit more slowly, nibbling daintily, her smallest finger curled away from the rest of her hand. When she had finished it, she went back to the living room and Homer followed her.

Harry still lay as they had left him, stretched out on the sofa. The heavy noon-day sun hit directly on his face, beating down on him like a club. He hardly felt its blows, however. He was busy with the stabbing pain in his chest. He was so busy with himself that he had even stopped trying to plan how to get money out of the big dope.

Homer drew the window curtain to shade his face. Harry didn't even notice. He was thinking about death. Faye bent over him. He saw, from under his partially closed eyelids, that she expected him to make a reassuring gesture. He refused. He examined the tragic expression that she had assumed and didn't like it. In a serious moment like this, her ham sorrow was insulting.

"Speak to me, Daddy," she begged.

She was baiting him without being aware of it.

"What the hell is this," he snarled, "a Tom show?"[8]

His sudden fury scared her and she straightened up with a jerk. He didn't want to laugh, but a short bark escaped before he could stop it. He waited anxiously to see what would happen. When it didn't hurt he laughed again. He kept on, timidly at first, then with growing assurance. He laughed with his eyes closed and the sweat pouring down his brow. Faye knew only one way to stop him and that was to do something he hated as much as she hated his laughter. She began to sing.

"Jeepers Creepers!
Where'd ya get those peepers? . . ."[9]

She trucked, jerking her buttocks and shaking her head from side to side.

Homer was amazed. He felt that the scene he was witnessing had been rehearsed. He was right. Their bitterest quarrels often took this form; he laughing, she singing.

"Jeepers Creepers!
Where'd ya get those eyes?
Gosh, all git up!
How'd they get so lit up?
Gosh all git . . ."

When Harry stopped, she stopped and flung herself into a chair. But Harry was only gathering strength for a final effort. He began again. This

8. Popular performances based on the novel *Uncle Tom's Cabin* (1852) by Harriet Beecher Stowe (1811–1896).

9. Popular song introduced by the jazz trumpeter and singer Louis Armstrong (1901–1971) in the film *Going Places* (1938).

new laugh was not critical; it was horrible. When she was a child, he used to punish her with it. It was his masterpiece. There was a director who always called on him to give it when he was shooting a scene in an insane asylum or a haunted castle.

It began with a sharp, metallic crackle, like burning sticks, then gradually increased in volume until it became a rapid bark, then fell away again to an obscene chuckle. After a slight pause, it climbed until it was the nicker of a horse, then still higher to become a machinelike screech.

Faye listened helplessly with her head cocked on one side. Suddenly, she too laughed, not willingly, but fighting the sound.

"You bastard!" she yelled.

She leaped to the couch, grabbed him by the shoulders and tried to shake him quiet.

He kept laughing.

Homer moved as though he meant to pull her away, but he lost courage and was afraid to touch her. She was so naked under her skimpy dress.

"Miss Greener," he pleaded, making his big hands dance at the end of his arms. "Please, please . . ."

Harry couldn't stop laughing now. He pressed his belly with his hands, but the noise poured out of him. It had begun to hurt again.

Swinging her hand as though it held a hammer, she brought her fist down hard on his mouth. She hit him only once. He relaxed and was quiet.

"I had to do it," she said to Homer when he took her arm and led her away.

He guided her to a chair in the kitchen and shut the door. She continued to sob for a long time. He stood behind her chair, helplessly, watching the rhythmical heave of her shoulders. Several times his hands moved forward to comfort her, but he succeeded in curbing them.

When she was through crying, he handed her a napkin and she dried her face. The cloth was badly stained by her rouge and mascara.

"I've spoilt it," she said, keeping her face averted. "I'm very sorry."

"It was dirty," Homer said.

She took a compact from her pocket and looked at herself in its tiny mirror.

"I'm a fright."

She asked if she could use the bathroom and he showed her where it was. He then tiptoed into the living room to see Harry. The old man's breathing was noisy but regular and he seemed to be sleeping quietly. Homer put a cushion under his head without disturbing him and went back into the kitchen. He lit the stove and put the coffeepot on the flame, then sat down to wait for the girl to return. He heard her go into the living room. A few seconds later she came into the kitchen.

She hesitated apologetically in the doorway.

"Won't you have some coffee?"

Without waiting for her to reply, he poured a cup and moved the sugar and cream so that she could reach them.

"I had to do it," she said. "I just had to."

"That's all right."

To show her that it wasn't necessary to apologize, he busied himself at the sink.

"No, I had to," she insisted. "He laughs that way just to drive me wild. I can't stand it. I simply can't."

"Yes."

"He's crazy. We Greeners are all crazy."

She made this last statement as though there were merit in being crazy.

"He's pretty sick," Homer said, apologizing for her. "Maybe he had a sunstroke."

"No, he's crazy."

He put a plate of gingersnaps on the table and she ate them with her second cup of coffee. The dainty crunching sound she made chewing fascinated him.

When she remained quiet for several minutes, he turned from the sink to see if anything was wrong. She was smoking a cigarette and seemed lost in thought.

He tried to be gay.

"What are you thinking?" he said awkwardly, then felt foolish.

She sighed to show how dark and foreboding her thoughts were, but didn't reply.

"I'll bet you would like some candy," Homer said. "There isn't any in the house, but I could call the drugstore and they'd send it right over. Or some ice cream?"

"No, thanks, please."

"It's no trouble."

"My father isn't really a peddler," she said, abruptly. "He's an actor. I'm an actress. My mother was also an actress, a dancer. The theatre is in our blood."

"I haven't seen many shows. I . . ."

He broke off because he saw that she wasn't interested.

"I'm going to be a star some day," she announced as though daring him to contradict her.

"I'm sure you . . ."

"It's my life. It's the only thing in the whole world that I want."

"It's good to know what you want. I used to be a book-keeper in a hotel, but . . ."

"If I'm not, I'll commit suicide."

She stood up and put her hands to her hair, opened her eyes wide and frowned.

"I don't go to shows very often," he apologized, pushing the gingersnaps toward her. "The lights hurt my eyes."

She laughed and took a cracker.

"I'll get fat."

"Oh, no."

"They say fat women are going to be popular next year. Do you think so? I don't. It's just publicity for Mae West."[1]

He agreed with her.

She talked on and on, endlessly, about herself and about the picture business. He watched her, but didn't listen, and whenever she repeated a question in order to get a reply, he nodded his head without saying anything.

His hands began to bother him. He rubbed them against the edge of the table to relieve their itch, but it only stimulated them. When he clasped them

1. American actress (1893–1980), known for her statuesque figure and racy jokes. Her film career was in decline by 1939.

behind his back, the strain became intolerable. They were hot and swollen. Using the dishes as an excuse, he held them under the cold water tap of the sink.

Faye was still talking when Harry appeared in the doorway. He leaned weakly against the doorjamb. His nose was very red, but the rest of his face was drained white and he seemed to have grown too small for his clothing. He was smiling, however.

To Homer's amazement, they greeted each other as though nothing had happened.

"You okay now, Pop?"

"Fine and dandy, baby. Right as rain, fit as a fiddle and lively as a flea, as the feller says."

The nasal twang he used in imitation of a country yokel made Homer smile.

"Do you want something to eat?" he asked. "A glass of milk, maybe?"

"I could do with a snack."

Faye helped him over to the table. He tried to disguise how weak he was by doing an exaggerated Negro shuffle.

Homer opened a can of sardines and sliced some bread. Harry smacked his lips over the food, but ate slowly and with an effort.

"That hit the spot, all righty right," he said when he had finished.

He leaned back and fished a crumpled cigar butt out of his vest pocket. Faye lit it for him and he playfully blew a puff of smoke in her face.

"We'd better go, Daddy," she said.

"In a jiffy, child."

He turned to Homer.

"Nice place you've got here. Married?"

Faye tried to interfere.

"Dad!"

He ignored her.

"Bachelor, eh?"

"Yes."

"Well, well, a young fellow like you."

"I'm here for my health," Homer found it necessary to say.

"Don't answer his questions," Faye broke in.

"Now, now, daughter, I'm just being friendly like. I don't mean no harm."

He was still using exaggerated backwoods accent. He spat dry into an imaginary spittoon and made believe he was shifting a cud of tobacco from cheek to cheek.

Homer thought his mimicry funny.

"I'd be lonesome and scared living alone in a big house like this," Harry went on. "Don't you ever get lonesome?"

Homer looked at Faye for his answer. She was frowning with annoyance.

"No," he said, to prevent Harry from repeating the uncomfortable question.

"No? Well, that's fine."

He blew several smoke rings at the ceiling and watched their behavior judiciously.

"Did you ever think of taking boarders?" he asked. "Some nice, sociable folks, I mean. It'll bring in a little extra money and make things more homey."

Homer was indignant, but underneath his indignation lurked another idea, a very exciting one. He didn't know what to say.

Faye misunderstood his agitation.

"Cut it out, Dad," she exclaimed before Homer could reply. "You've been a big enough nuisance already."

"Just chinning," he protested innocently. "Just chewing the fat."

"Well, then, let's get going," she snapped.

"There's plenty of time," Homer said.

He wanted to add something stronger, but didn't have the courage. His hands were braver. When Faye shook good-bye, they clutched and refused to let go.

Faye laughed at their warm insistence.

"Thanks a million, Mr. Simpson," she said. "You've been very kind. Thanks for the lunch and for helping Daddy."

"We're very grateful," Harry chimed in. "You've done a Christian deed this day. God will reward you."

He had suddenly become very pious.

"Please look us up," Faye said. "We live close-by in the San Berdoo Apartments, about five blocks down the canyon. It's the big yellow house."

When Harry stood, he had to lean against the table for support. Faye and Homer each took him by the arm and helped him into the street. Homer held him erect, while Faye went to get their Ford which was parked across the street.

"We're forgetting your order of Miracle Salve," Harry said, "the polish without peer or parallel."

Homer found a dollar and slipped it into his hand. He hid the money quickly and tried to become businesslike.

"I'll leave the goods tomorrow."

"Yes, that'll be fine," Homer said. "I really need some silver polish."

Harry was angry because it hurt him to be patronized by a sucker. He made an attempt to re-establish what he considered to be their proper relationship by bowing ironically, but didn't get very far with the gesture and began to fumble with his Adam's apple. Homer helped him into the car and he slumped down in the seat beside Faye.

They drove off. She turned to wave, but Harry didn't even look back.

12

Homer spent the rest of the afternoon in the broken deck chair. The lizard was on the cactus, but he took little interest in its hunting. His hands kept his thoughts busy. They trembled and jerked, as though troubled by dreams. To hold them still, he clasped them together. Their fingers twined like a tangle of thighs in miniature. He snatched them apart and sat on them.

When the days passed and he couldn't forget Faye, he began to grow frightened. He somehow knew that his only defense was chastity, that it served him, like the shell of a tortoise, as both spine and armor. He couldn't shed it even in thought. If he did, he would be destroyed.

He was right. There are men who can lust with parts of themselves. Only their brain or their hearts burn and then not completely. There are others, still more fortunate, who are like the filaments of an incandescent lamp. They burn fiercely, yet nothing is destroyed. But in Homer's case it would be like dropping a spark into a barn full of hay. He had escaped in the

Romola Martin incident, but he wouldn't escape again. Then, for one thing, he had had his job in the hotel, a daily all-day task that protected him by tiring him, but now he had nothing.

His thoughts frightened him and he bolted into the house, hoping to leave them behind like a hat. He ran into his bedroom and threw himself down on the bed. He was simple enough to believe that people don't think while asleep.

In his troubled state, even this delusion was denied him and he was unable to fall asleep. He closed his eyes and tried to make himself drowsy. The approach to sleep which had once been automatic had somehow become a long, shining tunnel. Sleep was at the far end of it, a soft bit of shadow in the hard glare. He couldn't run, only crawl toward the black patch. Just as he was about to give up, habit came to his rescue. It collapsed the shining tunnel and hurled him into the shadow.

When he awoke it was without a struggle. He tried to fall asleep once more, but this time couldn't even find the tunnel. He was thoroughly awake. He tried to think of how very tired he was, but he wasn't tired. He felt more alive than he had at any time since Romola Martin.

Outside a few birds still sang intermittently, starting and breaking off, as though sorry to acknowledge the end of another day. He thought that he heard the lisp of silk against silk, but it was only the wind playing in the trees. How empty the house was! He tried to fill it by singing.

"Oh, say can you see,
By the dawn's early light . . ."

It was the only song he knew. He thought of buying a victrola[2] or a radio. He knew, however, that he would buy neither. This fact made him very sad. It was a pleasant sadness, very sweet and calm.

But he couldn't let well enough alone. He was impatient and began to prod at his sadness, hoping to make it acute and so still more pleasant. He had been getting pamphlets in the mail from a travel bureau and he thought of the trips he would never take. Mexico was only a few hundred miles away. Boats left daily for Hawaii.

His sadness turned to anguish before he knew it and became sour. He was miserable again. He began to cry.

Only those who still have hope can benefit from tears. When they finish, they feel better. But to those without hope, like Homer, whose anguish is basic and permanent, no good comes from crying. Nothing changes for them. They usually know this, but still can't help crying.

Homer was lucky. He cried himself to sleep.

But he awoke again in the morning with Faye uppermost in his mind. He bathed, ate breakfast and sat in his deck chair. In the afternoon, he decided to go for a walk. There was only one way for him to go and that led past the San Bernardino Apartments.

Some time during his long sleep, he had given up the battle. When he came to the apartment house, he peered into the amber-lit hallway and read the Greener card on the letter box, then turned and went home. On the next night, he repeated the trip, carrying a gift of flowers and wine.

2. An early phonograph record player.

13

Harry Greener's condition didn't improve. He remained in bed, staring at the ceiling with his hands folded on his chest.

Tod went to see him almost every night. There were usually other guests. Sometimes Abe Kusich, sometimes Anna and Annabelle Lee, a sister act of the nineteen-tens, more often the four Gingos, a family of performing Eskimos from Point Barrow, Alaska.

If Harry were asleep or there were visitors, Faye usually invited Tod into her room for a talk. His interest in her grew despite the things she said and he continued to find her very exciting. Had any other girl been so affected, he would have thought her intolerable. Faye's affectations, however, were so completely artificial that he found them charming.

Being with her was like being backstage during an amateurish, ridiculous play. From in front, the stupid lines and grotesque situations would have made him squirm with annoyance, but because he saw the perspiring stagehands and the wires that held up the tawdry summerhouse with its tangle of paper flowers, he accepted everything and was anxious for it to succeed.

He found still another way to excuse her. He believed that while she often recognized the falseness of an attitude, she persisted in it because she didn't know how to be simpler or more honest. She was an actress who had learned from bad models in a bad school.

Yet Faye did have some critical ability, almost enough to recognize the ridiculous. He had often seen her laugh at herself. What was more, he had even seen her laugh at her dreams.

One evening they talked about what she did with herself when she wasn't working as an extra. She told him that she often spent the whole day making up stories. She laughed as she said it. When he questioned her, she described her method quite willingly.

She would get some music on the radio, then lie down on her bed and shut her eyes. She had a large assortment of stories to choose from. After getting herself in the right mood, she would go over them in her mind, as though they were a pack of cards, discarding one after another until she found the one that suited. On some days, she would run through the whole pack without making a choice. When that happened, she would either go to Vine Street for an ice cream soda or, if she was broke, thumb over the pack again and force herself to choose.

While she admitted that her method was too mechanical for the best results and that it was better to slip into a dream naturally, she said that any dream was better than no dream and beggars couldn't be choosers. She hadn't exactly said this, but he was able to understand it from what she did say. He thought it important that she smiled while telling him, not with embarrassment, but critically. However, her critical powers ended there. She only smiled at the mechanics.

The first time he had ever heard one of her dreams was late at night in her bedroom. About half an hour earlier, she had knocked on his door and had asked him to come and help her with Harry because she thought he was dying. His noisy breathing, which she had taken for the death rattle, had awakened her and she was badly frightened. Tod put on his bathrobe and followed her downstairs. When he got to the apartment, Harry had managed to clear his throat and his breathing had become quiet again.

She invited him into her room for a smoke. She sat on the bed and he sat beside her. She was wearing an old beach robe of white toweling over her pajamas and it was very becoming.

He wanted to beg her for a kiss but was afraid, not because she would refuse, but because she would insist on making it meaningless. To flatter her, he commented on her appearance. He did a bad job of it. He was incapable of direct flattery and got bogged down in a much too roundabout observation. She didn't listen and he broke off feeling like an idiot.

"I've got a swell idea," she said suddenly. "An idea how we can make some real money."

He made another attempt to flatter her. This time by assuming an attitude of serious interest.

"You're educated," she said. "Well, I've got some swell ideas for pictures. All you got to do is write them up and then we'll sell them to the studios."

He agreed and she described her plan. It was very vague until she came to what she considered would be its results, then she went into concrete details. As soon as they had sold one story, she would give him another. They would make loads and loads of money. Of course she wouldn't give up acting, even if she was a big success as a writer, because acting was her life.

He realized as she went on that she was manufacturing another dream to add to her already very thick pack. When she finally got through spending the money, he asked her to tell him the idea he was to "write up," keeping all trace of irony out of his voice.

On the wall of the room beyond the foot of her bed was a large photograph that must have once been used in the lobby of a theatre to advertise a Tarzan picture.[3] It showed a beautiful young man with magnificent muscles, wearing only a narrow loin cloth, who was ardently squeezing a slim girl in a torn riding habit. They stood in a jungle clearing and all around the pair writhed great vines loaded with fat orchids. When she told her story, he knew that this photograph had a lot to do with inspiring it.

A young girl is cruising on her father's yacht in the South Seas. She is engaged to marry a Russian count, who is tall, thin and old, but with beautiful manners. He is on the yacht, too, and keeps begging her to name the day. But she is spoiled and won't do it. Maybe she became engaged to him in order to spite another man. She becomes interested in a young sailor who is far below her in station, but very handsome. She flirts with him because she is bored. The sailor refuses to be toyed with no matter how much money she's got and tells her that he only takes orders from the captain and to go back to her foreigner. She gets sore as hell and threatens to have him fired, but he only laughs at her. How can he be fired in the middle of the ocean? She falls in love with him, although maybe she doesn't realize it herself, because he is the first man who has ever said no to one of her whims and because he is so handsome. Then there is a big storm and the yacht is wrecked near an island. Everybody is drowned, but she manages to swim to shore. She makes herself

3. Based on the character created by the American novelist Edgar Rice Burroughs (1875–1950) in *Tarzan of the Apes* (1912). Raised by a group of apes as one of them after the death of his parents, Tarzan eventually becomes their king. In the 1930s several Tarzan pictures were made starring the Olympic swimmer Johnny Weissmuller.

a hut of boughs and lives on fish and fruit. It's the tropics. One morning, while she is bathing naked in a brook, a big snake grabs her. She struggles but the snake is too strong for her and it looks like curtains. But the sailor, who has been watching her from behind some bushes, leaps to her rescue. He fights the snake for her and wins.

Tod was to go on from there. He asked her how she thought the picture should end, but she seemed to have lost interest. He insisted on hearing, however.

"Well, he marries her, of course, and they're rescued. First they're rescued and then they're married, I mean. Maybe he turns out to be a rich boy who is being a sailor just for the adventure of it, or something like that. You can work it out easy enough."

"It's sure-fire," Tod said earnestly, staring at her wet lips and the tiny point of her tongue which she kept moving between them.

"I've got just hundreds and hundreds more."

He didn't say anything and her manner changed. While telling the story, she had been full of surface animation and her hands and face were alive with little illustrative grimaces and gestures. But now her excitement narrowed and became deeper and its play internal. He guessed that she must be thumbing over her pack and that she would soon select another card to show him.

He had often seen her like this, but had never before understood it. All these little stories, these little day-dreams of hers, were what gave such extraordinary color and mystery to her movements. She seemed always to be struggling in their soft grasp as though she were trying to run in a swamp. As he watched her, he felt sure that her lips must taste of blood and salt and that there must be a delicious weakness in her legs. His impulse wasn't to aid her to get free, but to throw her down in the soft, warm mud and to keep her there.

He expressed some of his desire by a grunt. If he only had the courage to throw himself on her. Nothing less violent than rape would do. The sensation he felt was like that he got when holding an egg in his hand. Not that she was fragile or even seemed fragile. It wasn't that. It was her completeness, her egglike self-sufficiency, that made him want to crush her.

But he did nothing and she began to talk again.

"I've got another swell idea that I want to tell you. Maybe you had better write this one up first. It's a backstage story and they're making a lot of them this year."

She told him about a young chorus girl who gets her big chance when the star of the show falls sick. It was a familiar version of the Cinderella theme, but her technique was much different from the one she had used for the South Sea tale. Although the events she described were miraculous, her description of them was realistic. The effect was similar to that obtained by the artists of the Middle Ages, who, when doing a subject like the raising of Lazarus from the dead or Christ walking on water,[4] were careful to keep all the details intensely realistic. She, like them, seemed to think that fantasy could be made plausible by a humdrum technique.

"I like that one, too," he said when she had finished.

4. Miracles performed by Jesus Christ; see John 11.1–44 and 6.16–21.

"Think them over and do the one that has the best chance."

She was dismissing him and if he didn't act at once the opportunity would be gone. He started to lean toward her, but she caught his meaning and stood up. She took his arm with affectionate brusqueness—they were now business partners—and guided him to the door.

In the hall, when she thanked him for coming down and apologized for having disturbed him, he tried again. She seemed to melt a little and he reached for her. She kissed him willingly enough, but when he tried to extend the caress, she tore free.

"Whoa there, palsy-walsy," she laughed. "Mama spank."

He started for the stairs.

"Good-bye now," she called after him, then laughed again.

He barely heard her. He was thinking of the drawings he had made of her and of the new one he would do as soon as he got to his room.

In "The Burning of Los Angeles" Faye is the naked girl in the left foreground being chased by the group of men and women who have separated from the main body of the mob. One of the women is about to hurl a rock at her to bring her down. She is running with her eyes closed and a strange half-smile on her lips. Despite the dreamy repose of her face, her body is straining to hurl her along at top speed. The only explanation for this contrast is that she is enjoying the release that wild flight gives in much the same way that a game bird must when, after hiding for several tense minutes, it bursts from cover in complete, unthinking panic.

14

Tod had other and more successful rivals than Homer Simpson. One of the most important was a young man called Earle Shoop.

Earle was a cowboy from a small town in Arizona. He worked occasionally in horse-operas[5] and spent the rest of his time in front of a saddlery store on Sunset Boulevard. In the window of this store was an enormous Mexican saddle covered with carved silver, and around it was arranged a large collection of torture instruments. Among other things there were fancy, braided quirts, spurs with great spiked wheels, and double bits that looked as though they could break a horse's jaw without trouble. Across the back of the window ran a low shelf on which was a row of boots, some black, some red and some a pale yellow. All of the boots had scalloped tops and very high heels.

Earle always stood with his back to the window, his eyes fixed on a sign on the roof of a one-story building across the street that read: "Malted Milks Too Thick For A Straw." Regularly, twice every hour, he pulled a sack of tobacco and a sheaf of papers from his shirt pocket and rolled a cigarette. Then he tightened the cloth of his trousers by lifting his knee and struck a match along the underside of his thigh.

He was over six feet tall. The big Stetson[6] hat he wore added five inches more to his height and the heels of his boots still another three. His pole-like appearance was further exaggerated by the narrowness of his shoulders and by his lack of either hips or buttocks. The years he had spent in the saddle had not made him bowlegged. In fact, his legs were so straight that

5. Western-themed films.

6. A famous brand of cowboy hats.

his dungarees, bleached a very light blue by the sun and much washing, hung down without a wrinkle, as though they were empty.

Tod could see why Faye thought him handsome. He had a two-dimensional face that a talented child might have drawn with a ruler and a compass. His chin was perfectly round and his eyes, which were wide apart, were also round. His thin mouth ran at right angles to his straight, perpendicular nose. His reddish tan complexion was the same color from hairline to throat, as though washed in by an expert, and it completed his resemblance to a mechanical drawing.

Tod had told Faye that Earle was a dull fool. She agreed laughing, but then said that he was "criminally handsome," an expression she had picked up in the chatter column of a trade paper.

Meeting her on the stairs one night, Tod asked if she would go to dinner with him.

"I can't. I've got a date. But you can come along."

"With Earle?"

"Yes, with Earle," she repeated, mimicking his annoyance.

"No, thanks."

She misunderstood, perhaps on purpose, and said, "He'll treat this time."

Earle was always broke and whenever Tod went with them he was the one who paid.

"That isn't it, and you damn well know it."

"Oh, isn't it?" she asked archly, then, absolutely sure of herself, added, "Meet us at Hodge's around five."

Hodge's was the saddlery store. When Tod got there, he found Earle Shoop at his usual post, just standing and just looking at the sign across the street. He had on his ten-gallon hat and his high-heeled boots. Neatly folded over his left arm was a dark gray jacket. His shirt was navy-blue cotton with large polka dots, each the size of a dime. The sleeves of his shirt were not rolled, but pulled to the middle of his forearm and held there by a pair of fancy, rose armbands. His hands were the same clean reddish tan as his face.

"Lo, thar," was the way he returned Tod's salute.

Tod found his Western accent amusing. The first time he had heard it, he had replied, "Lo, thar, stranger," and had been surprised to discover that Earle didn't know he was being kidded. Even when Tod talked about "cayuses," "mean hombres" and "rustlers,"[7] Earle took him seriously.

"Howdy, partner," Tod said.

Next to Earle was another Westerner in a big hat and boots, sitting on his heels and chewing vigorously on a little twig. Close behind him was a battered paper valise held together by heavy rope tied with professional-looking knots.

Soon after Tod arrived a third man came along. He made a thorough examination of the merchandise in the window, then turned and began to stare across the street like the other two.

He was middle-aged and looked like an exercise boy from a racing stable. His face was completely covered with a fine mesh of wrinkles, as though he had been sleeping with it pressed against a roll of rabbit wire. He was very shabby and had probably sold his big hat, but he still had his boots.

7. Cattle thieves. "Cayuses": members of a northwestern American Indian people. "Hombres": men (Spanish).

"Lo, boys," he said.

"Lo, Hink," said the man with the paper valise.

Tod didn't know whether he was included in the greeting, but took a chance and replied.

"Howdy."

Hink prodded the valise with his toe.

"Goin' some place, Calvin?" he asked.

"Azusa,[8] there's a rodeo."

"Who's running it?"

"A fellow calls himself 'Badlands Jack.'"

"That grifter! . . . You goin', Earle?"

"Nope."

"I gotta eat," said Calvin.

Hink carefully considered all the information he had received before speaking again.

"Mono's makin' a new Buck Stevens,"[9] he said. "Will Ferris told me they'd use more than forty riders."

Calvin turned and looked up at Earle.

"Still got the piebald vest?"[1] he asked slyly.

"Why?"

"It'll cinch you a job as a road agent."[2]

Tod understood that this was a joke of some sort because Calvin and Hink chuckled and slapped their thighs loudly while Earle frowned.

There was another long silence, then Calvin spoke again.

"Ain't your old man still got some cows?" he asked Earle.

But Earle was wary this time and refused to answer.

Calvin winked at Tod, slowly and elaborately, contorting one whole side of his face.

"That's right, Earle," Hink said. "Your old man's still got some stock. Why don't you go home?"

They couldn't get a rise out of Earle, so Calvin answered the question.

"He dassint. He got caught in a sheep car with a pair of rubber boots on."

It was another joke. Calvin and Hink slapped their thighs and laughed, but Tod could see that they were waiting for something else. Earle, suddenly, without even shifting his weight, shot his foot out and kicked Calvin solidly in the rump. This was the real point of the joke. They were delighted by Earle's fury. Tod also laughed. The way Earle had gone from apathy to action without the usual transition was funny. The seriousness of his violence was even funnier.

A little while later, Faye drove by in her battered Ford touring car[3] and pulled into the curb some twenty feet away. Calvin and Hink waved, but Earle didn't budge. He took his time, as befitted his dignity. Not until she tooted her horn did he move. Tod followed a short distance behind him.

"Hi, cowboy," said Faye gaily.

8. In 1939, a small city, still surrounded by citrus groves, at the foot of the San Gabriel Mountains northeast of Los Angeles.
9. Suggests Buck Jones (1891–1942), an American actor known for starring in Westerns.
1. Made from the hide of a horse with large patches of color.
2. A stagecoach robber.
3. Open-topped car, like Ford's Model T, out of fashion by the 1930s.

"Lo, honey," he drawled, removing his hat carefully and replacing it with even greater care.

Faye smiled at Tod and motioned for them both to climb in. Tod got in the back. Earle unfolded the jacket he was carrying, slapped it a few times to remove the wrinkles, then put it on and adjusted its collar and shaped the roll of its lapels. He then climbed in beside Faye.

She started the car with a jerk. When she reached LaBrea, she turned right to Hollywood Boulevard and then left along it. Tod could see that she was watching Earle out of the corner of her eye and that he was preparing to speak.

"Get going," she said, trying to hurry him. "What is it?"

"Looka here, honey, I ain't got any dough for supper."

She was very much put out.

"But I told Tod we'd treat him. He's treated us enough times."

"That's all right," Tod interposed. "Next time'll do. I've got plenty of money."

"No, damn it," she said without looking around. "I'm sick of it."

She pulled into the curb and slammed on the brakes.

"It's always the same story," she said to Earle.

He adjusted his hat, his collar and his sleeves, then spoke.

"We've got some grub at camp."

"Beans, I suppose."

"Nope."

She prodded him.

"Well, what've you got?"

"Mig and me's set some traps."

Faye laughed.

"Rat traps, eh? We're going to eat rats."

Earle didn't say anything.

"Listen, you big, strong, silent dope," she said, "either make sense, or God damn it, get out of this car."

"They're quail traps," he said without the slightest change in his wooden, formal manner.

She ignored his explanation.

"Talking to you is like pulling teeth. You wear me out."

Tod knew that there was no hope for him in this quarrel. He had heard it all before.

"I didn't mean nothing," Earle said. "I was only funning. I wouldn't feed you rats."

She slammed off the emergency brake and started the car again. At Zacarias Street, she turned into the hills. After climbing steadily for a quarter of a mile, she reached a dirt road and followed it to its end. They all climbed out, Earle helping Faye.

"Give me a kiss," she said, smiling her forgiveness.

He took his hat off ceremoniously and placed it on the hood of the car, then wrapped his long arms around her. They paid no attention to Tod, who was standing off to one side watching them. He saw Earle close his eyes and pucker up his lips like a little boy. But there was nothing boyish about what he did to her. When she had had as much as she wanted, she pushed him away.

"You, too?" she called gaily to Tod, who had turned his back.

"Oh, some other time," he replied, imitating her casualness.

She laughed, then took out a compact and began to fix her mouth. When she was ready, they started along a little path that was a continuation of the dirt road. Earle led, Faye came next and Tod brought up the rear.

It was full spring. The path ran along the bottom of a narrow canyon and wherever weeds could get a purchase in its steep banks they flowered in purple, blue and yellow. Orange poppies bordered the path. Their petals were wrinkled like crepe and their leaves were heavy with talcumlike dust.

They climbed until they reached another canyon. This one was sterile, but its bare ground and jagged rocks were even more brilliantly colored than the flowers of the first. The path was silver, grained with streaks of rose-gray, and the walls of the canyon were turquoise, mauve, chocolate and lavender. The air itself was vibrant pink.

They stopped to watch a humming bird chase a blue jay. The jay flashed by squawking with its tiny enemy on its tail like a ruby bullet. The gaudy birds burst the colored air into a thousand glittering particles like metal confetti.

When they came out of this canyon, they saw below them a little green valley thick with trees, mostly eucalyptus, with here and there a poplar and one enormous black live-oak. Sliding and stumbling down a dry wash, they made for the valley.

Tod saw a man watching their approach from the edge of the wood. Faye also saw him and waved.

"Hi, Mig!" she shouted.

"Chinita!" he called back.

She ran the last ten yards of the slope and the man caught her in his arms.

He was toffee-colored with large Armenian eyes and pouting black lips. His head was a mass of tight, ordered curls. He wore a long-haired sweater, called a "gorilla" in and around Los Angeles, with nothing under it. His soiled duck trousers were held up by a red bandanna handkerchief. On his feet were a pair of tattered tennis sneakers.

They moved on to the camp which was located in a clearing in the center of the wood. It consisted of little more than a ramshackle hut patched with tin signs that had been stolen from the highway and a stove without legs or bottom set on some rocks. Near the hut was a row of chicken coops.

Earle started a fire under the stove while Faye sat down on a box and watched him. Tod went over to look at the chickens. There was one old hen and half a dozen game cocks. A great deal of pains had been taken in making the coops, which were of grooved boards, carefully matched and joined. Their floors were freshly spread with peat moss.

The Mexican came over and began to talk about the cocks. He was very proud of them.

"That's Hermano, five times winner. He's one of Street's Butcher Boys. Pepe and El Negro are still stags.[4] I fight them next week in San Pedro. That's Villa, he's a blinker,[5] but still good. And that one's Zapata, twice winner, a Tassel Dom[6] he is. And that's Jujutla. My champ."

4. Immature roosters.
5. A gamecock blinded in one eye.
6. A breed of gamecock.

He opened the coop and lifted the bird out for Tod.

"A murderer is what the guy is. Speedy and how!"

The cock's plumage was green, bronze and copper. Its beak was lemon and its legs orange.

"He's beautiful," Tod said.

"I'll say."

Mig tossed the bird back into the coop and they went back to join the others at the fire.

"When do we eat?" Faye asked.

Miguel tested the stove by spitting on it. He next found a large iron skillet and began to scour it with sand. Earle gave Faye a knife and some potatoes to peel, then picked up a burlap sack.

"I'll get the birds," he said.

Tod went along with him. They followed a narrow path that looked as though it had been used by sheep until they came to a tiny field covered with high, tufted grass. Earle stopped behind a gum bush and held up his hand to warn Tod.

A mocking bird was singing near by. Its song was like pebbles being dropped one by one from a height into a pool of water. Then a quail began to call, using two soft guttural notes. Another quail answered and the birds talked back and forth. Their call was not like the cheerful whistle of the Eastern bobwhite. It was full of melancholy and weariness, yet marvelously sweet. Still another quail joined the duet. This one called from near the center of the field. It was a trapped bird, but the sound it made had no anxiety in it, only sadness, impersonal and without hope.

When Earle was satisfied that no one was there to spy on his poaching, he went to the trap. It was a wire basket about the size of a washtub with a small door in the top. He stooped over and began to fumble with the door. Five birds ran wildly along the inner edge and threw themselves at the wire. One of them, a cock, had a dainty plume on his head that curled forward almost to his beak.

Earle caught the birds one at a time and pulled their heads off before dropping them into his sack. Then he started back. As he walked along, he held the sack under his left arm. He lifted the birds out with his right hand and plucked them one at a time. Their feathers fell to the ground, point first, weighed down by the tiny drop of blood that trembled on the tips of their quills.

The sun went down before they reached the camp again. It grew chilly and Tod was glad of the fire. Faye shared her seat on the box with him and they both leaned forward into the heat.

Mig brought a jug of tequila from the hut. He filled a peanut butter jar for Faye and passed the jug to Tod. The liquor smelled like rotten fruit, but he liked the taste. When he had had enough, Earle took it and then Miguel. They continued to pass it from hand to hand.

Earle tried to show Faye how plump the game was, but she wouldn't look. He gutted the birds, then began cutting them into quarters with a pair of heavy tin shears. Faye held her hands over her ears in order not to hear the soft click made by the blades as they cut through flesh and bone. Earle wiped the pieces with a rag and dropped them into the skillet where a large piece of lard was already sputtering.

For all her squeamishness, Faye ate as heartily as the men did. There was no coffee and they finished with tequila. They smoked and kept the jug moving. Faye tossed away the peanut butter jar and drank like the others, throwing her head back and tilting the jug.

Tod could sense her growing excitement. The box on which they were sitting was so small that their backs touched and he could feel how hot she was and how restless. Her neck and face had turned from ivory to rose. She kept reaching for his cigarettes.

Earle's features were hidden in the shadow of his big hat, but the Mexican sat full in the light of the fire. His skin glowed and the oil in his black curls sparkled. He kept smiling at Faye in a manner that Tod didn't like. The more he drank, the less he liked it.

Faye kept crowding Tod, so he left the box to sit on the ground where he could watch her better. She was smiling back at the Mexican. She seemed to know what he was thinking and to be thinking the same thing. Earle, too, became aware of what was passing between them. Tod heard him curse softly and saw him lean forward into the light and pick up a thick piece of firewood.

Mig laughed guiltily and began to sing.

"Las palmeras lloran por tu ausencia,
Las laguna se seco—ay!
La cerca de alambre que estaba en
El patio tambien se cayo!"[7]

His voice was a plaintive tenor and it turned the revolutionary song into a sentimental lament, sweet and cloying. Faye joined in when he began another stanza. She didn't know the words, but she was able to carry the melody and to harmonize.

"Pues mi madre las cuidaba, ay!
Toditito se acabo—ay!"[8]

Their voices touched in the thin, still air to form a minor chord and it was as though their bodies had touched. The song was transformed again. The melody remained the same, but the rhythm broke and its beat became ragged. It was a rumba now.

Earle shifted uneasily and played with his stick. Tod saw her look at him and saw that she was afraid, but instead of becoming wary, she grew still more reckless. She took a long pull at the jug and stood up. She put one hand on each of her buttocks and began to dance.

Mig seemed to have completely forgotten Earle. He clapped his hands, cupping them to make a hollow, drumlike sound, and put all he felt into his voice. He had changed to a more fitting song.

"Tony's wife,
The boys in Havana love Tony's wife . . ."[9]

7. "The palmtrees cry for your absence, / The lake has dried up—ay! / The wire fence that was around / The patio has fallen as well" (Spanish); from "Las cuatro milpas" (The four corn patches), a popular ballad about a farm lost during the Mexican revolution (1910–20), recorded by American singer Lydia Mendoza (1916–2007) in 1934.

8. "Then my mother took care of them, ay! / Everything has come to an end" (Spanish).

9. From "Tony's Wife" (1933), a popular song by Russian-born American songwriter Irving Berlin (1888–1989).

Faye had her hands clasped behind her head now and she rolled her hips to the broken beat. She was doing the "bump."

> *"Tony's wife,*
> *They're fightin' their duels about Tony's wife . . ."*

Perhaps Tod had been mistaken about Earle. He was using his club on the back of the skillet, using it to bang out the rhythm.

The Mexican stood up, still singing, and joined her in the dance. They approached each other with short mincing steps. She held her skirt up and out with her thumbs and forefingers and he did the same with his trousers. They met head on, blue-black against pale-gold, and used their heads to pivot, then danced back to back with their buttocks touching, their knees bent and wide apart. While Faye shook her breasts and her head, holding the rest of her body rigid, he struck the soft ground heavily with his feet and circled her. They faced each other again and made believe they were cradling their behinds in a shawl.

Earle pounded the skillet harder and harder until it rang like an anvil. Suddenly he, too, jumped up and began to dance. He did a crude hoedown. He leaped into the air and knocked his heels together. He whooped. But he couldn't become part of their dance. Its rhythm was like a smooth glass wall between him and the dancers. No matter how loudly he whooped or threw himself around, he was unable to disturb the precision with which they retreated and advanced, separated and came together again.

Tod saw the blow before it fell. He saw Earle raise his stick and bring it down on the Mexican's head. He heard the crack and saw the Mexican go to his knees still dancing, his body unwilling or unable to acknowledge the interruption.

Faye had her back to Mig when he fell, but she didn't turn to look. She ran. She flashed by Tod. He reached for her ankle to pull her down, but missed. He scrambled to his feet and ran after her.

If he caught her now, she wouldn't escape. He could hear her on the hill a little way ahead of him. He shouted to her, a deep, agonized bellow, like that a hound makes when it strikes a fresh line after hours of cold trailing. Already he could feel how it would be when he pulled her to the ground.

But the going was heavy and the stones and sand moved under his feet. He fell prone with his face in a clump of wild mustard that smelled of the rain and sun, clean, fresh and sharp. He rolled over on his back and stared up at the sky. The violent exercise had driven most of the heat out of his blood, but enough remained to make him tingle pleasantly. He felt comfortably relaxed, even happy.

Somewhere farther up the hill a bird began to sing. He listened. At first the low rich music sounded like water dripping on something hollow, the bottom of a silver pot perhaps, then like a stick dragged slowly over the strings of a harp. He lay quietly, listening.

When the bird grew silent, he made an effort to put Faye out of his mind and began to think about the series of cartoons[1] he was making for his canvas of Los Angeles on fire. He was going to show the city burning at high noon, so that the flames would have to compete with the desert sun and

1. Preliminary studies for a painting.

thereby appear less fearful, more like bright flags flying from roofs and windows than a terrible holocaust. He wanted the city to have quite a gala air as it burned, to appear almost gay. And the people who set it on fire would be a holiday crowd.

The bird began to sing again. When it stopped, Faye was forgotten and he only wondered if he weren't exaggerating the importance of the people who come to California to die. Maybe they weren't really desperate enough to set a single city on fire, let alone the whole country. Maybe they were only the pick of America's madmen and not at all typical of the rest of the land.

He told himself that it didn't make any difference because he was an artist, not a prophet. His work would not be judged by the accuracy with which it foretold a future event but by its merit as painting. Nevertheless, he refused to give up the role of Jeremiah.[2] He changed "pick of America's madmen" to "cream" and felt almost certain that the milk from which it had been skimmed was just as rich in violence. The Angelenos[3] would be first, but their comrades all over the country would follow. There would be civil war.

He was amused by the strong feeling of satisfaction this dire conclusion gave him. Were all prophets of doom and destruction such happy men?

He stood up without trying to answer. When he reached the dirt road at the top of the canyon Faye and the car were gone.

15

"She went to the pictures with that Simpson guy," Harry told him when he called to see her the next night.

He sat down to wait for her. The old man was very ill and lay on the bed with extreme care as though it were a narrow shelf from which he might fall if he moved.

"What are they making on your lot?" he asked slowly, rolling his eyes toward Tod without budging his head.

"'Manifest Destiny,' 'Sweet and Low Down,' 'Waterloo,' 'The Great Divide,' 'Begging Your . . .'"

"'The Great Divide'—" Harry said, interrupting eagerly. "I remember that vehicle."[4]

Tod realized he shouldn't have got him started, but there was nothing he could do about it now. He had to let him run down like a clock.

"When it opened I was playing the Irving in a little number called 'Enter Two Gents,' a trifle, but entertainment, real entertainment. I played a Jew comic, a Ben Welch[5] effect, derby and big pants—'Pat, dey hoffered me a chob in de Heagle Laundreh' . . . 'Faith now, Ikey, and did you take it?' . . . 'No, who vants to vash heagles?' Joe Parvos played straight for me in a cop's suit. Well, the night 'The Great Divide' opened, Joe was laying up with a whisker in the old Fifth Avenue when the stove exploded. It was the broad's husband who blew the whistle. He was . . ."

He hadn't run down. He had stopped and was squeezing his left side with both hands.

2. Biblical prophet who foretold the fall of the kingdom of Judah; generically, someone who denounces a corrupt society and predicts its collapse.
3. Residents of Los Angeles.
4. In the entertainment industry, a production designed around the drawing power of its star. None of the titles were in fact being shot in Hollywood in the late 1930s.
5. Comedian (d. 1926) on the early-20th-century American vaudeville circuit.

Tod leaned over anxiously.

"Some water?"

Harry framed the word "no" with his lips, then groaned skillfully. It was a second-act curtain groan, so phony that Tod had to hide a smile. And yet, the old man's pallor hadn't come from a box.

Harry groaned again, modulating from pain to exhaustion, then closed his eyes. Tod saw how skillfully he got the maximum effect out of his agonized profile by using the pillow to set it off. He also noticed that Harry, like many actors, had very little back or top to his head. It was almost all face, like a mask, with deep furrows between the eyes, across the forehead and on either side of the nose and mouth, plowed there by years of broad grinning and heavy frowning. Because of them, he could never express anything either subtly or exactly. They wouldn't permit degrees of feeling, only the furthest degree.

Tod began to wonder if it might not be true that actors suffer less than other people. He thought about this for a while, then decided that he was wrong. Feeling is of the heart and nerves and the crudeness of its expression has nothing to do with its intensity. Harry suffered as keenly as anyone, despite the theatricality of his groans and grimaces.

He seemed to enjoy suffering. But not all kinds, certainly not sickness. Like many people, he only enjoyed the sort that was self-inflicted. His favorite method was to bare his soul to strangers in bar-rooms. He would make believe he was drunk, and stumble over to where some strangers were sitting. He usually began by reciting a poem.

"Let me sit down for a moment,
I have a stone in my shoe.
I was once blithe and happy,
I was once young like you."

If his audience shouted, "scram, bum!" he only smiled humbly and went on with his act.

"Have pity, folks, on my gray hair . . ."

The bartender or someone else had to stop him by force, otherwise he would go on no matter what was said to him. Once he got started everyone in the bar usually listened, for he gave a great performance. He roared and whispered, commanded and cajoled. He imitated the whimper of a little girl crying for her vanished mother, as well as the different dialects of the many cruel managers he had known. He even did the off-stage noises, twittering like birds to herald the dawn of Love and yelping like a pack of bloodhounds when describing how an Evil Fate ever pursued him.

He made his audience see him start out in his youth to play Shakespeare in the auditorium of the Cambridge Latin School,[6] full of glorious dreams, burning with ambition. Follow him, as still a mere stripling, he starved in a Broadway rooming house, an idealist who desires only to share his art with the world. Stand with him, as, in the prime of manhood, he married a beautiful dancer, a headliner on the Gus Sun[7] time. Be close behind him as, one night, he returned

6. Public high school in Cambridge, Massachusetts, named for its classical curriculum.

7. Owner of a chain of theaters and well-known booking agent for minor vaudeville acts (1868–1959).

home unexpectedly to find her in the arms of a head usher. Forgive, as he forgave, out of the goodness of his heart and the greatness of his love. Then laugh, tasting the bitter gall, when the very next night he found her in the arms of a booking agent. Again he forgave her and again she sinned. Even then he didn't cast her out, no, though she jeered, mocked and even struck him repeatedly with an umbrella. But she ran off with a foreigner, a swarthy magician fellow. Behind she left memories and their baby daughter. He made his audience shadow him still as misfortune followed misfortune and, a middle-aged man, he haunted the booking offices, only a ghost of his former self. He who had hoped to play Hamlet, Lear, Othello,[8] must needs become the Co. in an act called Nat Plumstone & Co., light quips and breezy patter. He made them dog his dragging feet as, an aged and trembling old man, he . . .

Faye came in quietly. Tod started to greet her, but she put her finger to her lips for him to be silent and motioned toward the bed.

The old man was asleep. Tod thought his worn, dry skin looked like eroded ground. The few beads of sweat that glistened on his forehead and temples carried no promise of relief. It might rot, like rain that comes too late to a field, but could never refresh.

They both tiptoed out of the room.

In the hall he asked if she had had a good time with Homer.

"That dope!" she exclaimed, making a wry face. "He's strictly home-cooking."

Tod started to ask some more questions, but she dismissed him with a curt, "I'm tired, honey."

16

The next afternoon, Tod was on his way upstairs when he saw a crowd in front of the door to the Greeners' apartment. They were excited and talked in whispers.

"What's happened?" he asked.

"Harry's dead."

He tried the door of the apartment. It wasn't locked, so he went in. The corpse lay stretched out on the bed, completely covered with a blanket. From Faye's room came the sound of crying. He knocked softly on her door. She opened it for him, then turned without saying a word, and stumbled to her bed. She was sobbing into a face towel.

He stood in the doorway, without knowing what to do or say. Finally, he went over to the bed and tried to comfort her. He patted her shoulder.

"You poor kid."

She was wearing a tattered, black lace negligee that had large rents in it. When he leaned over her, he noticed that her skin gave off a warm, sweet odor, like that of buckwheat in flower.

He turned away and lit a cigarette. There was a knock on the door. When he opened it, Mary Dove rushed past him to take Faye in her arms.

Mary also told Faye to be brave. She phrased it differently than he had done, however, and made it sound a lot more convincing.

"Show some guts, kid. Come on now, show some guts."

8. The titular heroes of Shakespeare's major tragedies.

Faye shoved her away and stood up. She took a few wild steps, then sat down on the bed again.

"I killed him," she groaned.

Mary and he both denied this emphatically.

"I killed him, I tell you! I did! I did!"

She began to call herself names. Mary wanted to stop her, but Tod told her not to. Faye had begun to act and he felt that if they didn't interfere she would manage an escape for herself.

"She'll talk herself quiet," he said.

In a voice heavy with self-accusation, she began to tell what had happened. She had come home from the studio and found Harry in bed. She asked him how he was, but didn't wait for an answer. Instead, she turned her back on him to examine herself in the wall mirror. While fixing her face, she told him that she had seen Ben Murphy and that Ben had said that if Harry were feeling better he might be able to use him in a Bowery[9] sequence. She had been surprised when he didn't shout as he always did when Ben's name was mentioned. He was jealous of Ben and always shouted, "To hell with that bastard; I knew him when he cleaned spittoons in a nigger bar-room."

She realized that he must be pretty sick. She didn't turn around because she noticed what looked like the beginning of a pimple. It was only a speck of dirt and she wiped it off, but then she had to do her face all over again. While she was working at it, she told him that she could get a job as a dress extra if she had a new evening gown. Just to kid him, she looked tough and said, "If you can't buy me an evening gown, I'll find someone who can."

When he didn't say anything, she got sore and began to sing, "Jeepers Creepers." He didn't tell her to shut up, so she knew something must be wrong. She ran over to the couch. He was dead.

As soon as she had finished telling all this, she began to sob in a lower key, almost a coo, and rocked herself back and forth.

"Poor papa . . . Poor darling . . ."

The fun they used to have together when she was little. No matter how hard up he was, he always bought her dolls and candy, and no matter how tired, he always played with her. She used to ride piggy-back and they would roll on the floor and laugh and laugh.

Mary's sobs made Faye speed up her own and they both began to get out of hand.

There was a knock on the door. Tod answered it and found Mrs. Johnson, the janitress. Faye shook her head for him not to let her in.

"Come back later," Tod said.

He shut the door in her face. A minute later it opened again and Mrs. Johnson entered boldly. She had used a pass-key.

"Get out," he said.

She tried to push past him, but he held her until Faye told him to let her go.

He disliked Mrs. Johnson intensely. She was an officious, bustling woman with a face like a baked apple, soft and blotched. Later he found out that her hobby was funerals. Her preoccupation with them wasn't morbid; it was formal. She was interested in the arrangement of the flowers, the order of the procession, the clothing and deportment of the mourners.

9. A run-down, disreputable neighborhood in New York.

She went straight to Faye and stopped her sobs with a firm, "Now, Miss Greener."

There was so much authority in her voice and manner that she succeeded where Mary and Tod had failed.

Faye looked up at her respectfully.

"First, my dear," Mrs. Johnson said, counting one with the thumb of her right hand on the index finger of her left, "first, I want you to understand that my sole desire in this matter is to help you."

She looked hard at Mary, then at Tod.

"I don't get anything out of it, and it's just a lot of trouble."

"Yes," Faye said.

"All right. There are several things I have to know, if I'm to help you. Did the deceased leave any money or insurance?"

"No."

"Have you any money?"

"No."

"Can you borrow any?"

"I don't think so."

Mrs. Johnson sighed.

"Then the city will have to bury him."

Faye didn't comment.

"Don't you understand, child, the city will have to bury him in a pauper's grave?"

She put so much contempt into "city" and horror into "pauper" that Faye flushed and began to sob again.

Mrs. Johnson made as though to walk out, even took several steps in the direction of the door, then changed her mind and came back.

"How much does a funeral cost?" Faye asked.

"Two hundred dollars. But you can pay on the installment plan—fifty dollars down and twenty-five a month."

Mary and Tod both spoke together.

"I'll get the money."

"I've got some."

"That's fine," Mrs. Johnson said. "You'll need at least fifty more for incidental expenses. I'll go ahead and take care of everything. Mr. Holsepp will bury your father. He'll do it right."

She shook hands with Faye, as though she were congratulating her, and hurried out of the room.

Mrs. Johnson's little business talk had apparently done Faye some good. Her lips were set and her eyes dry.

"Don't worry," Tod said. "I can raise the money."

"No, thanks," she said.

Mary opened her purse and took out a roll of bills.

"Here's some."

"No," she said, pushing it away.

She sat thinking for a while, then went to the dressing table and began to fix her tear-stained face. She wore a hard smile as she worked. Suddenly she turned, lipstick in air, and spoke to Mary.

"Can you get me into Mrs. Jenning's?"

"What for?" Tod demanded. "I'll get the money."

Both girls ignored him.

"Sure," said Mary, "you ought to done that long ago. It's a soft touch."

Faye laughed.

"I was saving it."

The change that had come over both of them startled Tod. They had suddenly become very tough.

"For a punkola like that Earle. Get smart, girlie, and lay off the cheapies. Let him ride a horse, he's a cowboy, ain't he?"

They laughed shrilly and went into the bathroom with their arms around each other.

Tod thought he understood their sudden change to slang. It made them feel worldly and realistic, and so more able to cope with serious things.

He knocked on the bathroom door.

"What do *you* want?" Faye called out.

"Listen, kid," he said, trying to imitate them. "Why go on the turf?[1] I can get the dough."

"Oh, yeah! No, thanks," Faye said.

"But listen . . ." he began again.

"Go peddle your tripe!" Mary shouted.

17

On the day of Harry's funeral Tod was drunk. He hadn't seen Faye since she went off with Mary Dove, but he knew that he was certain to find her at the undertaking parlor and he wanted to have the courage to quarrel with her. He started drinking at lunch. When he got to Holsepp's in the late afternoon, he had passed the brave state and was well into the ugly one.

He found Harry in his box, waiting to be wheeled out for exhibition in the adjoining chapel. The casket was open and the old man looked quite snug. Drawn up to a little below his shoulders and folded back to show its fancy lining was an ivory satin coverlet. Under his head was a tiny lace cushion. He was wearing a Tuxedo, or at least had on a black bow tie with his stiff shirt and wing collar. His face had been newly shaved, his eyebrows shaped and plucked and his lips and cheeks rouged. He looked like the interlocutor[2] in a minstrel show.

Tod bowed his head as though in silent prayer when he heard someone come in. He recognized Mrs. Johnson's voice and turned carefully to face her. He caught her eye and nodded, but she ignored him. She was busy with a man in a badly fitting frock coat.

"It's the principle of the thing," she scolded. "Your estimate said bronze. Those handles ain't bronze and you know it."

"But I asked Miss Greener," whined the man. "She okayed them."

"I don't care. I'm surprised at you, trying to save a few dollars by fobbing off a set of cheap gun-metal handles on the poor child."

Tod didn't wait for the undertaker to answer. He had seen Faye pass the door on the arm of one of the Lee sisters. When he caught up with her, he didn't know what to say. She misunderstood his agitation and was touched. She sobbed a little for him.

1. I.e., become a prostitute.
2. Role analogous to master of ceremonies. He appeared in whiteface; the other performers, in blackface.

She had never looked more beautiful. She was wearing a new, very tight black dress and her platinum hair was tucked up in a shining bun under a black straw sailor. Every so often, she carried a tiny lace handkerchief to her eyes and made it flutter there for a moment. But all he could think of was that she had earned the money for the outfit on her back.

She grew uneasy under his stare and started to edge away. He caught her arm.

"May I speak with you for a minute, alone?"

Miss Lee took the hint and left.

"What is it?" Faye asked.

"Not here," he whispered, making mystery out of his uncertainty.

He led her along the hall until he found an empty showroom. On the walls were framed photographs of important funerals and on little stands and tables were samples of coffin materials and models of tombstones and mausoleums.

Not knowing what to say, he accented his awkwardness, playing the inoffensive fool.

She smiled and became almost friendly.

"Give out, you big dope."

"A kiss . . ."

"Sure, baby," she laughed, "only don't muss me." They pecked at each other.

She tried to get away, but he held her. She became annoyed and demanded an explanation. He searched his head for one. It wasn't his head he should have searched, however.

She was leaning toward him, drooping slightly, but not from fatigue. He had seen young birches droop like that at midday when they are over-heavy with sun.

"You're drunk," she said, pushing him away.

"Please," he begged.

"Le'go, you bastard."

Raging at him, she was still beautiful. That was became her beauty was structural like a tree's, not a quality of her mind or heart. Perhaps even whoring couldn't damage it for that reason, only age or accident or disease.

In a minute she would scream for help. He had to say something. She wouldn't understand the aesthetic argument and with what values could he back up the moral one? The economic didn't make sense either. Whoring certainly paid. Half of the customer's thirty dollars. Say ten men a week.

She kicked at his shins, but he held on to her. Suddenly he began to talk. He had found an argument. Disease would destroy her beauty. He shouted at her like a Y.M.C.A.[3] lecturer on sex hygiene.

She stopped struggling and held her head down, sobbing fitfully. When he was through, he let go of her arms and she bolted from the room. He groped his way to a carved, marble coffin.

He was still sitting there when a young man in a black jacket and gray striped trousers came in.

"Are you here for the Greener funeral?"

Tod stood up and nodded vaguely.

3. Young Men's Christian Association.

"The services are beginning," the man said, then opened a little casket covered with grosgrain[4] satin and took out a dust cloth. Tod watched him go around the showroom wiping off the samples.

"Services have probably started," the man repeated with a wave at the door.

Tod understood this time and left. The only exit he could find led through the chapel. The moment he entered it, Mrs. Johnson caught him and directed him to a seat. He wanted badly to get away, but it was impossible to do so without making a scene.

Faye was sitting in the front row of benches, facing the pulpit. She had the Lee sisters on one side and Mary Dove and Abe Kusich on the other. Behind them sat the tenants of the San Berdoo, occupying about six rows. Tod was alone in the seventh. After him were several empty rows and then a scattering of men and women who looked very much out of place.

He turned in order not to see Faye's jerking shoulders and examined the people in the last rows. He knew their kind. While not torch-bearers themselves, they would run behind the fire and do a great deal of the shouting. They had come to see Harry buried, hoping for a dramatic incident of some sort, hoping at least for one of the mourners to be led weeping hysterically from the chapel. It seemed to Tod that they stared back at him with an expression of vicious, acrid boredom that trembled on the edge of violence. When they began to mutter among themselves, he half-turned and watched them out of the corner of his eyes.

An old woman with a face pulled out of shape by badly-fitting store teeth came in and whispered to a man sucking on the handle of a home-made walking stick. He passed her message along and they all stood up and went out hurriedly. Tod guessed that some star had been seen going into a restaurant by one of their scouts. If so, they would wait outside the place for hours until the star came out again or the police drove them away.

The Gingo family arrived soon after they had left. The Gingos were Eskimos who had been brought to Hollywood to make retakes for a picture about polar exploration. Although it had been released long ago, they refused to return to Alaska. They liked Hollywood.

Harry had been a good friend of theirs and had eaten with them quite regularly, sharing the smoked salmon, white fish, marinated and maatjes herrings[5] they bought at Jewish delicatessen stores. He also shared the great quantities of cheap brandy they mixed with hot water and salt butter and drank out of tin cups.

Mama and Papa Gingo, trailed by their son, moved down the center aisle of the chapel, bowing and waving to everyone, until they reached the front row. Here they gathered around Faye and shook hands with her, each one in turn. Mrs. Johnson tried to make them go to one of the back rows, but they ignored her orders and sat down in front.

The overhead lights of the chapel were suddenly dimmed. Simultaneously other lights went on behind imitation stained-glass windows which hung on the fake oak-paneled walls. There was a moment of hushed silence, broken only by Faye's sobs, then an electric organ started to play a recording of one of Bach's chorales, "Come Redeemer, Our Saviour."[6]

4. Fabric of a strong, heavy, corded weave, often used for ribbons.
5. Pickled young herring (Yiddish).
6. A hymn by the German theologian Martin Luther (1483–1546) that was set to music several times by Johann Sebastian Bach (1685–1750).

Tod recognized the music. His mother often played a piano adaptation of it on Sundays at home. It very politely asked Christ to come, in clear and honest tones with just the proper amount of supplication. The God it invited was not the King of Kings, but a shy and gentle Christ, a maiden surrounded by maidens, and the invitation was to a lawn fete, not to the home of some weary, suffering sinner. It didn't plead; it urged with infinite grace and delicacy, almost as though it were afraid of frightening the prospective guest.

So far as Tod could tell, no one was listening to the music. Faye was sobbing and the others seemed busy inside themselves. Bach politely serenading Christ was not for them.

The music would soon change its tone and grow exciting. He wondered if that would make any difference. Already the bass was beginning to throb. He noticed that it made the Eskimos uneasy. As the bass gained in power and began to dominate the treble, he heard Papa Gingo grunt with pleasure. Mama caught Mrs. Johnson eyeing him, and put her fat hand heavily on the back of his head to keep him quiet.

"Now come, O our Saviour," the music begged. Gone was its diffidence and no longer was it polite. Its struggle with the bass had changed it. Even a hint of a threat crept in and a little impatience. Of doubt, however, he could not detect the slightest trace.

If there was a hint of a threat, he thought, just a hint, and a tiny bit of impatience, could Bach be blamed? After all, when he wrote this music, the world had already been waiting for its lover more than seventeen hundred years. But the music changed again and both threat and impatience disappeared. The treble soared free and triumphant and the bass no longer struggled to keep it down. It had become a rich accompaniment. "Come or don't come," the music seemed to say, "I love you and my love is enough." It was a simple statement of fact, neither cry nor serenade, made without arrogance or humility.

Perhaps Christ heard. If He did, He gave no sign. The attendants heard, for it was their cue to trundle on Harry in his box. Mrs. Johnson followed close behind and saw to it that the casket was properly placed. She raised her hand and Bach was silenced in the middle of a phrase.

"Will those of you who wish to view the deceased before the sermon please step forward?" she called out.

Only the Gingos stood up immediately. They made for the coffin in a group. Mrs. Johnson held them back and motioned for Faye to look first. Supported by Mary Dove and the Lee girls, she took a quick peek, increased the tempo of her sobs for a moment, then hurried back to the bench.

The Gingos had their chance next. They leaned over the coffin and told each other something in a series of thick, explosive gutturals. When they tried to take another look, Mrs. Johnson herded them firmly to their seats.

The dwarf sidled up to the box, made a play with his handkerchief and retreated. When no one followed him, Mrs. Johnson lost patience, seeming to take what she understood as a lack of interest for a personal insult.

"Those who wish to view the remains of the late Mr. Greener must do so at once," she barked.

There was a little stir, but no one stood up.

"You, Mrs. Gail," she finally said, looking directly at the person named. "How about you? Don't you want a last look? Soon all that remains of your neighbor will be buried forever."

There was no getting out of it. Mrs. Gail moved down the aisle, trailed by several others.

Tod used them to cover his escape.

18

Faye moved out of the San Berdoo the day after the funeral. Tod didn't know where she had gone and was getting up the courage to call Mrs. Jenning when he saw her from the window of his office. She was dressed in the costume of a Napoleonic vivandiere.[7] By the time he got the window open, she had almost turned the corner of the building. He shouted for her to wait. She waved, but when he got downstairs she was gone.

From her dress, he was sure that she was working in the picture called "Waterloo." He asked a studio policeman where the company was shooting and was told on the back lot. He started toward it at once. A platoon of cuirassiers, big men mounted on gigantic horses, went by. He knew that they must be headed for the same set and followed them. They broke into a gallop and he was soon outdistanced.

The sun was very hot. His eyes and throat were choked with the dust thrown up by the horses' hooves and his head throbbed. The only bit of shade he could find was under an ocean liner made of painted canvas with real life boats hanging from its davits.[8] He stood in its narrow shadow for a while, then went on toward a great forty-foot papier mache[9] sphinx that loomed up in the distance. He had to cross a desert to reach it, a desert that was continually being made larger by a fleet of trucks dumping white sand. He had gone only a few feet when a man with a megaphone ordered him off.

He skirted the desert, making a wide turn to the right, and came to a Western street with a plank sidewalk. On the porch of the "Last Chance Saloon" was a rocking chair. He sat down on it and lit a cigarette.

From there he could see a jungle compound with a water buffalo tethered to the side of a conical grass hut. Every few seconds the animal groaned musically. Suddenly an Arab charged by on a white stallion. He shouted at the man, but got no answer. A little while later he saw a truck with a load of snow and several malamute dogs.[1] He shouted again. The driver shouted something back, but didn't stop.

Throwing away his cigarette, he went through the swinging doors of the saloon. There was no back to the building and he found himself in a Paris street. He followed it to its end, coming out in a Romanesque[2] courtyard. He heard voices a short distance away and went toward them. On a lawn of fiber, a group of men and women in riding costume were picnicking. They were eating cardboard food in front of a cellophane waterfall. He started toward them to ask his way, but was stopped by a man who scowled and held up a sign—"Quiet, Please, We're Shooting." When Tod took another step forward, the man shook his fist threateningly.

Next he came to a small pond with large celluloid swans floating on it. Across one end was a bridge with a sign that read, "To Kamp Komfit." He

7. Female camp-follower selling food and drink to Napoleon's armies.
8. Cranes that project over the side of a ship.
9. Chewed paper (French, literal trans.); a moldable mixture of paper and glue.
1. Alaskan sled dogs.
2. Architectural style of early medieval Europe.

crossed the bridge and followed a little path that ended at a Greek temple dedicated to Eros.[3] The god himself lay face downward in a pile of old newspaper and bottles.

From the steps of the temple, he could see in the distance a road lined with Lombardy poplars. It was the one on which he had lost the cuirassiers. He pushed his way through a tangle of briars, old flats and iron junk, skirting the skeleton of a Zeppelin,[4] a bamboo stockade, an adobe fort, the wooden horse of Troy,[5] a flight of baroque palace stairs that started in a bed of weeds and ended against the branches of an oak, part of the Fourteenth Street elevated station,[6] a Dutch windmill, the bones of a dinosaur, the upper half of the Merrimac,[7] a corner of a Mayan temple, until he finally reached the road.

He was out of breath. He sat down under one of the poplars on a rock made of brown plaster and took off his jacket. There was a cool breeze blowing and he soon felt more comfortable.

He had lately begun to think not only of Goya and Daumier but also of certain Italian artists of the seventeenth and eighteenth centuries, of Salvator Rosa, Francesco Guardi and Monsu Desiderio,[8] the painters of Decay and Mystery. Looking down hill now, he could see compositions that might have actually been arranged from the Calabrian work of Rosa. There were partially demolished buildings and broken monuments half hidden by great, tortured trees, whose exposed roots writhed dramatically in the arid ground, and by shrubs that carried, not flowers or berries, but armories of spikes, hooks and swords.

For Guardi and Desiderio there were bridges which bridged nothing, sculpture in trees, palaces that seemed of marble until a whole stone portico began to flap in the light breeze. And there were figures as well. A hundred yards from where Tod was sitting a man in a derby hat leaned drowsily against the gilded poop of a Venetian barque and peeled an apple. Still farther on, a charwoman on a stepladder was scrubbing with soap and water the face of a Buddha thirty feet high.

He left the road and climbed across the spine of the hill to look down on the other side. From there he could see a ten-acre field of cockleburs spotted with clumps of sunflowers and wild gum. In the center of the field was a gigantic pile of sets, flats and props. While he watched, a ten-ton truck added another load to it. This was the final dumping ground. He thought of Janvier's "Sargasso Sea."[9] Just as that imaginary body of water was a history of civilization in the form of a marine junkyard, the studio lot was one in the form of a dream dump. A Sargasso of the imagination! And the dump grew continually, for there wasn't a dream afloat somewhere which wouldn't

3. The Greek god of love.
4. A passenger-carrying airship. Their popularity declined after 1937, when the *Hindenburg* crashed and burned in New Jersey, killing thirty-six.
5. In Homer's *Iliad*, the city of Troy falls when its Greek besiegers enter the city concealed in a large wooden horse.
6. In New York City.
7. A wood-hulled U.S. Navy ship that was converted into an ironclad warship, one of the first of its kind, by the Confederate navy during the American Civil War (1861–65).
8. Paintings formerly attributed to Monsu Desiderio are now thought to be by several different French Renaissance painters, including François de Nomé (early 17th century) and Didier Barra (1590–1656), both noted for their fantastic paintings of ruins. Nomé's works influenced the surrealist painters of the 1920s and 1930s. Rosa (1615–1673) and Guardi (1712–1793), Italian painters known for their dark and stormy images.
9. *In the Sargasso Sea* (1898), an adventure tale by the American novelist and historian Thomas A. Janvier (1849–1913), in which the protagonist drifts into a floating junkyard of ghost ships at the center of the Sargasso Sea, a section of the Atlantic encircled by the Gulf Stream and other currents and where marine refuse naturally accumulates.

sooner or later turn up on it, having first been made photographic by plaster, canvas, lath and paint. Many boats sink and never reach the Sargasso, but no dream ever entirely disappears. Somewhere it troubles some unfortunate person and some day, when that person has been sufficiently troubled, it will be reproduced on the lot.

When he saw a red glare in the sky and heard the rumble of cannon, he knew it must be Waterloo. From around a bend in the road trotted several cavalry regiments. They wore casques[1] and chest armor of black cardboard and carried long horse pistols in their saddle holsters. They were Victor Hugo's soldiers. He had worked on some of the drawings for their uniforms himself, following carefully the descriptions in "Les Miserables."[2]

He went in the direction they took. Before long he was passed by the men of Lefebvre-Desnouettes, followed by a regiment of gendarmes d'elite, several companies of chasseurs of the guard and a flying detachment of Rimbaud's lancers.[3]

They must be moving up for the disastrous attack on La Haite Santee.[4] He hadn't read the scenario and wondered if it had rained yesterday. Would Grouchy[5] or Blucher arrive? Grotenstein, the producer, might have changed it.

The sound of cannon was becoming louder all the time and the red fan in the sky more intense. He could smell the sweet, pungent odor of blank powder. It might be over before he could get there. He started to run. When he topped a rise after a sharp bend in the road, he found a great plain below him covered with early nineteenth-century troops, wearing all the gay and elaborate uniforms that used to please him so much when he was a child and spent long hours looking at the soldiers in an old dictionary. At the far end of the field, he could see an enormous hump around which the English and their allies were gathered. It was Mont St. Jean and they were getting ready to defend it gallantly. It wasn't quite finished, however, and swarmed with grips, property men, set dressers, carpenters and painters.

Tod stood near a eucalyptus tree to watch, concealing himself behind a sign that read, "'Waterloo'—A Charles H. Grotenstein Production." Near by a youth in a carefully torn horse guard's uniform was being rehearsed in his lines by one of the assistant directors.

"Vive l'Empereur!"[6] the young man shouted, then clutched his breast and fell forward dead. The assistant director was a hard man to please and made him do it over and over again.

In the center of the plain, the battle was going ahead briskly. Things looked tough for the British and their allies. The Prince of Orange commanding the center, Hill the right and Picton the left wing, were being pressed hard by

1. Helmets.
2. The epic novel (1862) of the Napoleonic era and its aftermath by the popular French writer Victor Hugo (1802–1885). A 1935 Hollywood film adaptation was nominated for an Academy Award for Best Picture.
3. Mobile mounted troops. Charles Lefebvre-Desnouettes (1773–1822), a French general during the Napoleonic Wars. "Gendarmes d'elite": members of Napoleon's elite Imperial Guard (French). "Chasseurs": hunters (French, literal trans.); light infantry or cavalry.
4. La Haye Sainte (The holy crown; French), a walled farm, was captured by the French during the course of the battle, giving them the strategic advantage until the Prussian army, lead by Field Marshal Gebhard Leberecht von Blücher (1742–1819), arrived along rain-bogged paths in time to secure victory for the allied armies opposing Napoleon, whose artillery was still more hampered by the wet ground. According to Victor Hugo's famous account of the battle in *Les Miserables*, "If it had not rained in the night between the 17th and the 18th of June, 1815, the fate of Europe would have been different. A few drops of water, more or less, decided the downfall of Napoleon."
5. Marshal Emmanuel de Grouchy (1766–1847) commanded one wing of Napoleon's forces at Waterloo.
6. Long live the Emperor! (French).

the veteran French. The desperate and intrepid Prince was in an especially bad spot. Tod heard him cry hoarsely above the din of battle, shouting to the Hollande-Belgians, "Nassau! Brunswick! Never retreat!" Nevertheless, the retreat began. Hill, too, fell back. The French killed General Picton with a ball through the head and he returned to his dressing room. Alten[7] was put to the sword and also retired. The colors of the Lunenberg battalion, borne by a prince of the family of Deux-Ponts, were captured by a famous child star in the uniform of a Parisian drummer boy. The Scotch Greys were destroyed and went to change into another uniform. Ponsonby's heavy dragoons were also cut to ribbons. Mr. Grotenstein would have a large bill to pay at the Western Costume Company.

Neither Napoleon nor Wellington was to be seen. In Wellington's absence, one of the assistant directors, a Mr. Crane, was in command of the allies. He reinforced his center with one of Chasse's brigades and one of Wincke's.[8] He supported these with infantry from Brunswick, Welsh foot, Devon yeomanry and Hanoverian[9] light horse with oblong leather caps and flowing plumes of horsehair.

For the French, a man in a checked cap ordered Milhaud's cuirassiers to carry Mont St. Jean.[1] With their sabers in their teeth and their pistols in their hands, they charged. It was a fearful sight.

The man in the checked cap was making a fatal error. Mont St. Jean was unfinished. The paint was not yet dry and all the struts were not in place. Because of the thickness of the cannon smoke, he had failed to see that the hill was still being worked on by property men, grips and carpenters.

It was the classic mistake, Tod realized, the same one Napoleon had made. Then it had been wrong for a different reason. The Emperor had ordered the cuirassiers to charge Mont St. Jean not knowing that a deep ditch was hidden at its foot to trap his heavy cavalry. The result had been disaster for the French; the beginning of the end.

This time the same mistake had a different outcome. Waterloo, instead of being the end of the Grand Army, resulted in a draw. Neither side won, and it would have to be fought over again the next day. Big losses, however, were sustained by the insurance company in workmen's compensation. The man in the checked cap was sent to the dog house by Mr. Grotenstein just as Napoleon was sent to St. Helena.[2]

When the front rank of Milhaud's heavy division started up the slope of Mont St. Jean, the hill collapsed. The noise was terrific. Nails screamed with agony as they pulled out of joists. The sound of ripping canvas was like that of little children whimpering. Lath and scantling snapped as though

7. Commanders in the allied forces opposing Napoleon. The Prince of Orange, later William II, king of the Netherlands (1792–1849), was wounded at Waterloo. Rowland Hill (1772–1842) led a crucial charge against the Imperial Guard. Thomas Picton (1758–1815) died in battle, although his troops successfully repulsed the French. Charles Alten (1764–1840), commanding a division in the Allied front lines, was seriously wounded. Nassau and Brunswick were allied troops from states that are now part of Germany. West's account of the battle in these paragraphs draws heavily on Hugo's *Les Miserables*, chapter 6.

8. Hugo's *Les Miserables* names Chassé and Wincke as allied commanders. David Hendrik Chassé (1765–1849) commanded a division from the Netherlands. Wincke may be Hugo's error for August von Klencke, who commanded the Light Field Battalion Luneburg in the army of the German state of Hanover, allied with England.

9. Brunswick, Wales, and Devonshire (in England) and Hanover all contributed to the allied forces.

1. Wellington's high position at Waterloo, attacked at the climax of the battle by armored cavalry under the command of Édouard Jean-Baptiste Milhaud (1766–1833).

2. A small, remote island in the south Atlantic to which Napoleon was exiled.

they were brittle bones. The whole hill folded like an enormous umbrella and covered Napoleon's army with painted cloth.

It turned into a rout. The victors of Bersina, Leipsic, Austerlitz,[3] fled like schoolboys who had broken a pane of glass. "Sauve qui peut!"[4] they cried, or, rather, "Scram!"

The armies of England and her allies were too deep in scenery to flee. They had to wait for the carpenters and ambulances to come up. The men of the gallant Seventy-Fifth Highlanders[5] were lifted out of the wreck with block and tackle. They were carted off by the stretcher-bearers, still clinging bravely to their claymores.[6]

19

Tod got a lift back to his office in a studio car. He had to ride on the running board because the seats were occupied by two Walloon grenadiers and four Swabian foot.[7] One of the infantrymen had a broken leg, the other extras were only scratched and bruised. They were quite happy about their wounds. They were certain to receive several extra days' pay, and the man with the broken leg thought he might get as much as five hundred dollars.

When Tod arrived at his office, he found Faye waiting to see him. She hadn't been in the battle. At the last moment, the director had decided not to use any vivandieres.

To his surprise, she greeted him with warm friendliness. Nevertheless, he tried to apologize for his behavior in the funeral parlor. He had hardly started before she interrupted him. She wasn't angry, but grateful for his lecture on venereal disease. It had brought her to her senses.

She had still another surprise for him. She was living in Homer Simpson's house. The arrangement was a business one. Homer had agreed to board and dress her until she became a star. They were keeping a record of every cent he spent and as soon as she clicked in pictures, she would pay him back with six per cent interest. To make it absolutely legal, they were going to have a lawyer draw up a contract.

She pressed Tod for an opinion and he said it was a splendid idea. She thanked him and invited him to dinner for the next night.

After she had gone, he wondered what living with her would do to Homer. He thought it might straighten him out. He fooled himself into believing this with an image, as though a man were a piece of iron to be heated and then straightened with hammer blows. He should have known better, for if anyone ever lacked malleability Homer did.

He continued to make this mistake when he had dinner with them. Faye seemed very happy, talking about charge accounts and stupid sales clerks. Homer had a flower in his buttonhole, wore carpet slippers and beamed at her continually.

After they had eaten, while Homer was in the kitchen washing dishes, Tod got her to tell him what they did with themselves all day. She said that they lived quietly and that she was glad because she was tired of excitement. All she wanted was a career. Homer did the housework and she was

3. Battles in the Napoleonic wars.
4. Every man for himself! (French).
5. A Scottish regiment.
6. Traditional broadswords.
7. Soldiers from French-speaking Belgium and southwestern Germany, respectively.

getting a real rest. Daddy's long sickness had tired her out completely. Homer liked to do housework and anyway he wouldn't let her go into the kitchen because of her hands.

"Protecting his investment," Tod said.

"Yes," she replied seriously, "they have to be beautiful."

They had breakfast around ten, she went on. Homer brought it to her in bed. He took a housekeeping magazine and fixed the tray like the pictures in it. While she bathed and dressed, he cleaned the house. Then they went downtown to the stores and she bought all sorts of things, mostly clothes. They didn't eat lunch on account of her figure, but usually had dinner out and went to the movies.

"Then, ice cream sodas," Homer finished for her, as he came out of the kitchen.

Faye laughed and excused herself. They were going to a picture and she wanted to change her dress. When she had left, Homer suggested that they get some air in the patio. He made Tod take the deck chair while he sat on an upturned orange crate.

If he had been careful and had acted decently, Tod couldn't help thinking, she might be living with him. He was at least better looking than Homer. But then there was her other prerequisite. Homer had an income and lived in a house, while he earned thirty dollars a week and lived in a furnished room.

The happy grin on Homer's face made him feel ashamed of himself. He was being unfair. Homer was a humble, grateful man who would never laugh at her, who was incapable of laughing at anything. Because of this great quality, she could live with him on what she considered a much higher plane.

"What's the matter?" Homer asked softly, laying one of his heavy hands on Tod's knee.

"Nothing. Why?"

Tod moved so that the hand slipped off.

"You were making faces."

"I was thinking of something."

"Oh," Homer said sympathetically.

Tod couldn't resist asking an ugly question.

"When are you two getting married?"

Homer looked hurt.

"Didn't Faye tell about us?"

"Yes, sort of."

"It's a business arrangement."

"Yes?"

To make Tod believe it, he poured out a long, disjointed argument, the one he must have used on himself. He even went further than the business part and claimed that they were doing it for poor Harry's sake. Faye had nothing left in the world except her career and she must succeed for her daddy's sake. The reason she wasn't a star was because she didn't have the right clothes. He had money and believed in her talent, so it was only natural for them to enter into a business arrangement. Did Tod know a good lawyer?

It was a rhetorical question, but would become a real one, painfully insistent, if Tod smiled. He frowned. That was wrong, too.

"We must see a lawyer this week and have papers drawn up."

His eagerness was pathetic. Tod wanted to help him, but didn't know what to say. He was still fumbling for an answer when they heard a woman shouting from the hill behind the garage.

"Adore! Adore!"

She had a high soprano voice, very clear and pure.

"What a funny name," Tod said, glad to change the subject.

"Maybe it's a foreigner," Homer said.

The woman came into the yard from around the corner of the garage. She was eager and plump and very American.

"Have you seen my little boy?" she asked, making a gesture of helplessness. "Adore's such a wanderer."

Homer surprised Tod by standing up and smiling at the woman. Faye had certainly helped his timidity.

"Is your son lost?" Homer said.

"Oh, no—just hiding to tease me."

She held out her hand.

"We're neighbors. I'm Maybelle Loomis."

"Glad to know you, ma'am. I'm Homer Simpson and this is Mr. Hackett."

Tod also shook hands with her.

"Have you been living here long?" she asked.

"No. I've just come from the East," Homer said.

"Oh, have you? I've been here ever since Mr. Loomis passed on six years ago. I'm an old settler."

"You like it then?" Tod asked.

"Like California?" she laughed at the idea that anyone might not like it. "Why, it's a paradise on earth!"

"Yes," Homer agreed gravely.

"And anyway," she went on, "I have to live here on account of Adore."

"Is he sick?"

"Oh, no. On account of his career. His agent calls him the biggest little attraction in Hollywood."

She spoke so vehemently that Homer flinched.

"He's in the movies?" Tod asked.

"I'll say," she snapped.

Homer tried to placate her.

"That's very nice."

"If it weren't for favoritism," she said bitterly, "he'd be a star. It ain't talent. It's pull. What's Shirley Temple[8] got that he ain't got?"

"Why, I don't know," Homer mumbled.

She ignored this and let out a fearful bellow.

"Adore! Adore!"

Tod had seen her kind around the studio. She was one of that army of women who drag their children from casting office to casting office and sit for hours, weeks, months, waiting for a chance to show what Junior can do. Some of them are very poor, but ho matter how poor, they always manage to scrape together enough money, often by making great sacrifices, to send their children to one of the innumerable talent schools.

8. Temple (1928–2014) was the country's most famous child movie star during the 1930s.

"Adore!" she yelled once more, then laughed and became a friendly housewife again, a chubby little person with dimples in her fat cheeks and fat elbows.

"Have you any children, Mr. Simpson?" she asked.

"No," he replied, blushing.

"You're lucky—they're a nuisance."

She laughed to show that she didn't really mean it and called her child again.

"Adore . . . Oh, Adore . . ."

Her next question surprised them both.

"Who do you follow?"

"What?" said Tod.

"I mean—in the Search for Health, along the Road of Life?"

They both gaped at her.

"I'm a raw-foodist, myself," she said. "Dr. Pierce is our leader. You must have seen his ads—'Know-All Pierce-All.'"

"Oh, yes," Tod said, "you're vegetarians."

She laughed at his ignorance.

"Far from it. We're much stricter. Vegetarians eat cooked vegetables. We eat only raw ones. Death comes from eating dead things."

Neither Tod nor Homer found anything to say.

"Adore," she began again. "Adore . . ."

This time there was an answer from around the corner of the garage.

"Here I am, mama."

A minute later, a little boy appeared dragging behind him a small sailboat on wheels. He was about eight years old, with a pale, peaked face and a large, troubled forehead. He had great staring eyes. His eyebrows had been plucked and shaped carefully. Except for his Buster Brown collar,[9] he was dressed like a man, in long trousers, vest and jacket.

He tried to kiss his mother, but she fended him off and pulled at his clothes, straightening and arranging them with savage little tugs.

"Adore," she said sternly, "I want you to meet Mr. Simpson, our neighbor."

Turning like a soldier at the command of a drill sergeant, he walked up to Homer and grasped his hand.

"A pleasure, sir," he said, bowing stiffly with his heels together.

"That's the way they do it in Europe," Mrs. Loomis beamed. "Isn't he cute?"

"What a pretty sailboat!" Homer said, trying to be friendly.

Both mother and son ignored his comment. She pointed to Tod, and the child repeated his bow and heel-click.

"Well, we've got to go," she said.

Tod watched the child, who was standing a little to one side of his mother and making faces at Homer. He rolled his eyes back in his head so that only the whites showed and twisted his lips in a snarl.

Mrs. Loomis noticed Tod's glance and turned sharply. When she saw what Adore was doing, she yanked him by the arm, jerking him clear off the ground.

9. A large round collar worn with a floppy bow tie, named after a cartoon character created in 1902; out of fashion by the 1930s.

"Adore!" she yelled.

To Tod she said apologetically, "He thinks he's the Frankenstein monster."[1]

She picked the boy up, hugging and kissing him ardently. Then she set him down again and fixed his rumpled clothing.

"Won't Adore sing something for us?" Tod asked.

"No," the little boy said sharply.

"Adore," his mother scolded, "sing at once."

"That's all right, if he doesn't feel like it," Homer said.

But Mrs. Loomis was determined to have him sing. She could never permit him to refuse an audience.

"Sing, Adore," she repeated with quiet menace. "Sing 'Mama Doan Wan' No Peas.' "[2]

His shoulders twitched as though they already felt the strap. He tilted his straw sailor over one eye, buttoned up his jacket and did a little strut, then began:

"Mama doan wan' no peas,
An' rice, an' cocoanut oil,
Just a bottle of brandy handy all the day.
Mama doan wan' no peas,
Mama doan wan' no cocoanut oil."

His singing voice was deep and rough and he used the broken groan of the blues singer quite expertly. He moved his body only a little, against rather than in time with the music. The gestures he made with his hands were extremely suggestive.

"Mama doan wan' no gin,
Because gin do make her sin,
Mama doan wan' no glass of gin,
Because it boun' to make her sin,
An' keep her hot and bothered all the day."

He seemed to know what the words meant, or at least his body and his voice seemed to know. When he came to the final chorus, his buttocks writhed and his voice carried a top-heavy load of sexual pain.

Tod and Homer applauded. Adore grabbed the string of his sailboat and circled the yard. He was imitating a tugboat. He tooted several times, then ran off.

"He's just a baby," Mrs. Loomis said proudly, "but he's got loads of talent."

Tod and Homer agreed.

She saw that he was gone again and left hurriedly. They could hear her calling in the brush back of the garage.

"Adore! Adore . . ."

"That's a funny woman," Tod said.

Homer sighed.

"I guess it's hard to get a start in pictures. But Faye is awfully pretty."

1. The monster created by Viktor Frankenstein in *Frankenstein* (1818), by Mary Shelley (1797–1851). A number of popular film adaptations starring Boris Karloff as the monster were made during the 1930s.

2. Song written in 1931 by Charles Lofthouse and L. Wolfe Gilbert and popularized in a 1938 recording by Jimmy Rushing with Count Basie and his orchestra.

Tod agreed. She appeared a moment later in a new flower print dress and picture hat and it was his turn to sigh. She was much more than pretty. She posed, quivering and balanced, on the doorstep and looked down at the two men in the patio. She was smiling, a subtle half-smile uncontaminated by thought. She looked just born, everything moist and fresh, volatile and perfumed. Tod suddenly became very conscious of his dull, insensitive feet bound in dead skin and of his hands, sticky and thick, holding a heavy, rough felt hat.

He tried to get out of going to the pictures with them, but couldn't. Sitting next to her in the dark proved the ordeal he expected it to be. Her self-sufficiency made him squirm and the desire to break its smooth surface with a blow, or at least a sudden obscene gesture, became irresistible.

He began to wonder if he himself didn't suffer from the ingrained, morbid apathy he liked to draw in others. Maybe he could only be galvanized into sensibility and that was why he was chasing Faye.

He left hurriedly, without saying good-bye. He had decided to stop running after her. It was an easy decision to make, but a hard one to carry out. In order to manage it, he fell back on one of the oldest tricks in the very full bag of the intellectual. After all, he told himself, he had drawn her enough times. He shut the portfolio that held the drawings he had made of her, tied it with a string, and put it away in his trunk.

It was a childish trick, hardly worthy of a primitive witch doctor, yet it worked. He was able to avoid her for several months. During this time, he took his pad and pencils on a continuous hunt for other models. He spent his nights at the different Hollywood churches, drawing the worshipers. He visited the "Church of Christ, Physical" where holiness was attained through the constant use of chest-weights and spring grips; the "Church Invisible" where fortunes were told and the dead made to find lost objects; the "Tabernacle of the Third Coming" where a woman in male clothing preached the "Crusade Against Salt"; and the "Temple Moderne" under whose glass and chromium roof "Brain-Breathing, the Secret of the Aztecs" was taught.

As he watched these people writhe on the hard seats of their churches, he thought of how well Alessandro Magnasco[3] would dramatize the contrast between their drained-out, feeble bodies and their wild, disordered minds. He would not satirize them as Hogarth[4] or Daumier might, nor would he pity them. He would paint their fury with respect, appreciating its awful, anarchic power and aware that they had it in them to destroy civilization.

One Friday night in the "Tabernacle of the Third Coming," a man near Tod stood up to speak. Although his name most likely was Thompson or Johnson and his home town Sioux City, he had the same counter-sunk eyes, like the heads of burnished spikes, that a monk by Magnasco might have. He was probably just in from one of the colonies in the desert near Soboba Hot Springs[5] where he had been conning over his soul on a diet of raw fruit and nuts. He was very angry. The message he had brought to the city was one that an illiterate anchorite[6] might have given decadent Rome. It was a crazy jumble of dietary rules, economics and Biblical threats. He claimed to have seen the Tiger of Wrath stalking the walls of the citadel and the Jackal of

3. Italian painter (1667–1749) noted for representing beggars, criminals, religious enthusiasts, and outcasts.
4. William Hogarth (1697–1764), satirical English painter and printmaker.
5. Resort in southern California's San Jacinto Valley.
6. A hermit.

Lust skulking in the shrubbery,[7] and he connected these omens with "thirty dollars every Thursday and meat eating."

Tod didn't laugh at the man's rhetoric. He knew it was unimportant. What mattered were his messianic rage and the emotional response of his hearers. They sprang to their feet, shaking their fists and shouting. On the altar someone began to beat a bass drum and soon the entire congregation was singing "Onward Christian Soldiers."[8]

20

As time went on, the relationship between Faye and Homer began to change. She became bored with the life they were leading together and as her boredom deepened, she began to persecute him. At first she did it unconsciously, later maliciously.

Homer realized that the end was in sight even before she did. All he could do to prevent its coming was to increase his servility and his generosity. He waited on her hand and foot. He bought her a coat of summer ermine and a light blue Buick runabout.[9]

His servility was like that of a cringing, clumsy dog, who is always anticipating a blow, welcoming it even, and in a way that makes overwhelming the desire to strike him. His generosity was still more irritating. It was so helpless and unselfish that it made her feel mean and cruel, no matter how hard she tried to be kind. And it was so bulky that she was unable to ignore it. She had to resent it. He was destroying himself, and although he didn't mean it that way, forcing her to accept the blame.

They had almost reached a final crisis when Tod saw them again. Late one night, just as he was preparing for bed, Homer knocked on his door and said that Faye was downstairs in the car and that they wanted him to go to a night club with them.

The outfit Homer wore was very funny. He had on loose blue linen slacks and a chocolate flannel jacket over a yellow polo shirt. Only a Negro could have worn it without looking ridiculous, and no one was ever less a Negro than Homer.

Tod drove with them to the "Cinderella Bar," a little stucco building in the shape of a lady's slipper, on Western Avenue. Its floor show consisted of female impersonators.

Faye was in a nasty mood. When the waiter took their order, she insisted on a champagne cocktail for Homer. He wanted coffee. The waiter brought both, but she made him take the coffee back.

Homer explained painstakingly, as he must have done many times, that he could not drink alcohol because it made him sick. Faye listened with mock patience. When he finished, she laughed and lifted the cocktail to his mouth.

"Drink it, damn you," she said.

She tilted the glass, but he didn't open his mouth and the liquor ran down his chin. He wiped himself, using the napkin without unfolding it.

7. The prophet Jeremiah predicts that both Babylon and Jerusalem will become a haunt of jackals for their sins (Jeremiah 9.11, 51.37). According to one of the "Proverbs of Hell" in *The Marriage of Heaven and Hell* (1793) by English poet William Blake, "The tigers of wrath are wiser than the horses of instruction."

8. Popular Christian hymn, English in origin, composed in 1871.

9. A small open car. In the 1930s Buick was a luxury car. "Ermine": a particularly expensive fur.

Faye called the waiter again.

"He doesn't like champagne cocktails," she said. "Bring him brandy."

Homer shook his head.

"Please, Faye," he whimpered.

She held the brandy to his lips, moving the glass when he turned away.

"Come on, sport—bottoms up."

"Let him alone," Tod finally said.

She ignored him as though she hadn't even heard his protest. She was both furious and ashamed of herself. Her shame strengthened her fury and gave it a target.

"Come on, sport," she said savagely, "or mama'll spank."

She turned to Tod.

"I don't like people who won't drink. It isn't sociable. They feel superior and I don't like people who feel superior."

"I don't feel superior," Homer said.

"Oh, yes, you do. I'm drunk and you're sober and so you feel superior. Goddamned, stinking superior."

He opened his mouth to reply and she poured the brandy into it, then clapped her hand over his lips so that he couldn't spit it back. Some of it came out of his nose.

Still without unfolding the napkin, he wiped himself. Faye ordered another brandy. When it came, she held it to his lips again, but this time he took it and drank it himself, fighting the stuff down.

"That's the boy," Faye laughed. "Well done, sloppy-boppy."

Tod asked her to dance in order to give Homer a moment alone. When they reached the floor, she made an attempt to defend herself.

"That guy's superiority is driving me crazy."

"He loves you," Tod said.

"Yeah, I know, but he's such a slob."

She started to cry on his shoulder and he held her very tight. He took a long chance.

"Sleep with me."

"No, baby," she said sympathetically.

"Please, please . . . just once."

"I can't, honey. I don't love you."

"You worked for Mrs. Jenning. Make believe you're still working for her."

She didn't get angry.

"That was a mistake. And anyway, that was different. I only went on call enough times to pay for the funeral and besides those men were complete strangers. You know what I mean?"

"Yes. But please, darling. I'll never bother you again. I'll go east right after. Be kind."

"I can't."

"Why . . . ?"

"I just can't. I'm sorry, darling. I'm not a tease, but I can't like that."

"I love you."

"No, sweetheart, I can't."

They danced until the number finished without saying anything else. He was grateful to her for having behaved so well, for not having made him feel too ridiculous.

When they returned to the table, Homer was sitting exactly as they had left him. He held the folded napkin in one hand and the empty brandy glass in the other. His helplessness was extremely irritating.

"You're right about the brandy, Faye," Homer said. "It's swell! Whoopee!"

He made a little circular gesture with the hand that held the glass.

"I'd like a Scotch," Tod said.

"Me, too," Faye said.

Homer made another gallant attempt to get into the spirit of the evening.

"Garsoon,"[1] he called to the waiter, "more drinks."

He grinned at them anxiously. Faye burst out laughing and Homer did his best to laugh with her. When she stopped suddenly, he found himself laughing alone and turned his laugh into a cough, then hid the cough in his napkin.

She turned to Tod.

"What the devil can you do with a slob like that?"

The orchestra started and Tod was able to ignore her question. All three of them turned to watch a young man in a tight evening gown of red silk sing a lullaby.

> *"Little man, you're crying,*
> *I know why you're blue,*
> *Someone took your kiddycar away;*
> *Better go to sleep now,*
> *Little man, you've had a busy day . . ."*[2]

He had a soft, throbbing voice and his gestures were matronly, tender and aborted, a series of unconscious caresses. What he was doing was in no sense parody; it was too simple and too restrained. It wasn't even theatrical. This dark young man with his thin, hairless arms and soft, rounded shoulders, who rocked an imaginary cradle as he crooned, was really a woman.

When he had finished, there was a great deal of applause. The young man shook himself and became an actor again. He tripped on his train, as though he weren't used to it, lifted his skirts to show he was wearing Paris garters,[3] then strode off swinging his shoulders. His imitation of a man was awkward and obscene.

Homer and Tod applauded him.

"I hate fairies," Faye said.

"All women do."

Tod meant it as a joke, but Faye was angry.

"They're dirty," she said.

He started to say something else, but Faye had turned to Homer again. She seemed unable to resist nagging him. This time she pinched his arm until he gave a little squeak.

"Do you know what a fairy is?" she demanded.

"Yes," he said hesitatingly.

"All right, then," she barked. "Give out! What's a fairy?"

1. Homer's pronunciation of *garçon*, "waiter" (French).
2. From "Little Man, You've Had a Busy Day" (1934), by Al Hoffman (1902–1960), Maurice Sigler (1901–1960), and Mabel Wayne (1890–1978), recorded in the 1930s by Paul Robeson (1898–1976) among other notable singers.
3. A brand marketed to men for holding up dress socks.

Homer twisted uneasily, as though he already felt the ruler on his behind, and looked imploring at Tod, who tried to help him by forming the word "homo" with his lips.

"Momo," Homer said.

Faye burst out laughing. But his hurt look made it impossible not to relent, so she patted his shoulder.

"What a hick," she said.

He grinned gratefully and signaled the waiter to bring another round of drinks.

The orchestra began to play and a man came over to ask Faye to dance. Without saying a word to Homer, she followed him to the floor.

"Who's that?" Homer asked, chasing them with his eyes.

Tod made believe he knew and said that he had often seen him around the San Berdoo. His explanation satisfied Homer, but at the same time set him to thinking of something else. Tod could almost see him shaping a question in his head.

"Do you know Earle Shoop?" Homer finally asked.

"Yes."

Homer then poured out a long, confused story about a dirty black hen. He kept referring to the hen again and again, as though it were the one thing he couldn't stand about Earle and the Mexican. For a man who was incapable of hatred, he managed to draw a pretty horrible picture of the bird.

"You never saw such a disgusting thing, the way it squats and turns its head. The roosters have torn all the feathers off its neck and made its comb all bloody and it has scabby feet covered with warts and it cackles so nasty when they drop it into the pen."

"Who drops it into what pen?"

"The Mexican."

"Miguel?"

"Yes. He's almost as bad as his hen."

"You've been to their camp?"

"Camp?"

"In the mountains?"

"No. They're living in the garage. Faye asked me if I minded if a friend of hers lived in the garage for a while because he was broke. But I didn't know about the chickens or the Mexican. . . . Lots of people are out of work nowadays."

"Why don't you throw them out?"

"They're broke and they have no place to go. It isn't very comfortable living in a garage."

"But if they don't behave?"

"It's just that hen. I don't mind the roosters, they're pretty, but that dirty hen. She shakes her dirty feathers each time and clucks so nasty."

"You don't have to look at it."

"They do it every afternoon at the same time when I'm usually sitting in the chair in the sun having got back from shopping with Faye and just before dinner. The Mexican knows I don't like to see it so he tries to make me look just for spite. I go into the house, but he taps on the windows and calls me to come out and watch. I don't call that fun. Some people have funny ideas of what's fun."

"What's Faye say?"

"She doesn't mind the hen. She says it's only natural."

Then, in case Tod should mistake this for criticism, he told him what a fine, wholesome child she was. Tod agreed, but brought him back to the subject.

"If I were you," he said, "I'd report the chickens to the police. You have to have a permit to keep chickens in the city. I'd do something and damned quick."

Homer avoided a direct answer.

"I wouldn't touch that thing for all the money in the world. She's all over scabs and almost naked. She looks like a buzzard. She eats meat. I saw her one time eating some meat that the Mexican got out of the garbage can. He feeds the roosters grain but the hen eats garbage and he keeps her in a dirty box."

"If I were you, I'd throw those bastards out and their birds with them."

"No, they're nice enough young fellows, just down on their luck, like a lot of people these days, you know. It's just that hen . . ."

He shook his head wearily, as though he could smell and taste her.

Faye was coming back. Homer saw that Tod was going to speak to her about Earle and the Mexican and signaled desperately for him not to do it. She, however, caught him at it and was curious.

"What have you guys been chinning about?"

"You, darling," Tod said. "Homer has a t.l.[4] for you."

"Tell me, Homer."

"No, first you tell me one."

"Well, the man I just danced with asked me if you were a movie big shot."

Tod saw that Homer was unable to think of a return compliment so he spoke for him.

"I said you were the most beautiful girl in the place."

"Yes," Homer agreed. "That's what Tod said."

"I don't believe it. Tod hates me. And anyway, I caught you telling him to keep quiet. You were shushing him."

She laughed.

"I bet I know what you were talking about." She mimicked Homer's excited disgust. "'That dirty black hen, she's all over scabs and almost naked.'"

Homer laughed apologetically, but Tod was angry.

"What's the idea of keeping those guys in the garage?" he demanded.

"What the hell is it your business?" she replied, but not with real anger. She was amused.

"Homer enjoys their company. Don't you, sloppy-boppy?"

"I told Tod they were nice fellows just down on their luck like a lot of people these days. There's an awful lot of unemployment going around."

"That's right," she said. "If they go, I go."

Tod had guessed as much. He realized there was no use in saying anything. Homer was again signaling for him to keep quiet.

For some reason or other, Faye suddenly became ashamed of herself. She apologized to Tod by offering to dance with him again, flirting as she suggested it. Tod refused.

4. From "trade last"; a compliment passed along in hopes of receiving another compliment in exchange.

She broke the silence that followed by a eulogy of Miguel's game chickens, which was really meant to be an excuse for herself. She described what marvelous fighters the birds were, how much Miguel loved them and what good care he took of them.

Homer agreed enthusiastically. Tod remained silent. She asked him if he had ever seen a cock fight and invited him to the garage for the next night. A man from San Diego was coming North with his birds to pit them against Miguel's.

When she turned to Homer again, he leaned away as though she were going to hit him. She flushed with shame at this and looked at Tod to see if he had noticed. The rest of the evening, she tried to be nice to Homer. She even touched him a little, straightening his collar and patting his hair smooth. He beamed happily.

21

When Tod told Claude Estee about the cock fight, he wanted to go with him. They drove to Homer's place together.

It was one of those blue and lavender nights when the luminous color seems to have been blown over the scene with an air brush. Even the darkest shadows held some purple.

A car stood in the driveway of the garage with its headlights on. They could see several men in the corner of the building and could hear their voices. Someone laughed, using only two notes, ha-ha and ha-ha, over and over again.

Tod stepped ahead to make himself known, in case they were taking precautions against the police. When he entered the light, Abe Kusich and Miguel greeted him, but Earle didn't.

"The fights are off," Abe said. "That stinkola from Diego didn't get here."

Claude came up and Tod introduced him to the three men. The dwarf was arrogant, Miguel gracious and Earle his usual wooden, surly self.

Most of the garage floor had been converted into a pit, an oval space about nine feet long and seven or eight wide. It was floored with an old carpet and walled by a low, ragged fence made of odd pieces of lath and wire. Faye's coupe stood in the driveway, placed so that its headlights flooded the arena.

Claude and Tod followed Abe out of the glare and sat down with him on an old trunk in the back of the garage. Earle and Miguel came in and squatted on their heels facing them. They were both wearing blue denims, polka-dot shirts, big hats and high-heeled boots. They looked very handsome and picturesque.

They sat smoking silently, all of them calm except the dwarf, who was fidgety. Although he had plenty of room, he suddenly gave Tod a shove.

"Get over, lard-ass," he snarled.

Tod moved, crowding against Claude, without saying anything. Earle laughed at Tod rather than the dwarf, but the dwarf turned on him anyway.

"Why, you punkola! Who you laughing at?"

"You," Earle said.

"That so, hah? Well, listen to me, you pee-hole bandit, for two cents I'd knock you out of them prop boots."

Earle reached into his shirt pocket and threw a coin on the ground. "There's a nickel," he said.

The dwarf started to get off the trunk, but Tod caught him by the collar. He didn't try to get loose, but leaned forward against his coat, like a terrier in a harness, and wagged his great head from side to side.

"Go on," he sputtered, "you fugitive from the Western Costume Company, you . . . you louse in a fright-wig, you."

Earle would have been much less angry if he could have thought of a snappy comeback. He mumbled something about a half-pint bastard, then spat. He hit the instep of the dwarf's shoe with a big gob of spittle.

"Nice shot," Miguel said.

This was apparently enough for Earle to consider himself the winner, for he smiled and became quiet. The dwarf slapped Tod's hand away from his collar with a curse and settled down on the trunk again.

"He ought to wear gaffs,"[5] Miguel said.

"I don't need them for a punk like that."

They all laughed and everything was fine again.

Abe leaned across Tod to speak to Claude.

"It would have been a swell main," he said. "There was more than a dozen guys here before you come and some of them with real dough. I was going to make book."

He took out his wallet and gave him one of his business cards.

"It was in the bag," Miguel said. "I got five birds that would of won easy and two sure losers. We would of made a killing."

"I've never seen a chicken fight," Claude said. "In fact, I've never even seen a game chicken."

Miguel offered to show him one of his birds and left to get it. Tod went down to the car for the bottle of whiskey they had left in a side pocket. When he got back, Miguel was holding Jujutla in the light. They all examined the bird.

Miguel held the cock firmly with both hands, somewhat in the manner that a basketball is held for an underhand toss. The bird had short, oval wings and a heart-shaped tail that stood at right angles to its body. It had a triangular head, like a snake's, terminating in a slightly curved beak, thick at the base and fine at the point. All its feathers were so tight and hard that they looked as though they had been varnished. They had been thinned out for fighting and the lines of its body, which was like a truncated wedge, stood out plainly. From between Miguel's fingers dangled its long, bright orange legs and its slightly darker feet with their horn nails.

"Juju was bred by John R. Bowes of Lindale, Texas," Miguel said proudly. "He's a six times winner. I give fifty dollars and a shotgun for him."

"He's a nice bird," the dwarf said grudgingly, "but looks ain't everything."

Claude took out his wallet.

"I'd like to see him fight," he said. "Suppose you sell me one of your other birds and I put it against him."

Miguel thought a while and looked at Earle, who told him to go ahead.

"I've got a bird I'll sell you for fifteen bucks," he said.

The dwarf interfered.

5. Metal spurs attached to fighting gamecocks.

"Let me pick the bird."

"Oh, I don't care," Claude said, "I just want to see a fight. Here's your fifteen."

Earle took the money and Miguel told him to get Hermano, the big red.

"That red'll go over eight pounds," he said, "while Juju won't go more than six."

Earle came back carrying a large rooster that had a silver shawl. He looked like an ordinary barnyard fowl.

When the dwarf saw him, he became indignant.

"What do you call that, a goose?"

"That's one of Street's Butcher Boys," Miguel said.

"I wouldn't bait a hook with him," the dwarf said.

"You don't have to bet," Earle mumbled.

The dwarf eyed the bird and the bird eyed him. He turned to Claude.

"Let me handle him for you, mister," he said.

Miguel spoke quickly.

"Earle'll do it. He knows the cock."

The dwarf exploded at this.

"It's a frame-up!" he yelled.

He tried to take the red, but Earle held the bird high in the air out of the little man's reach.

Miguel opened the trunk and took out a small wooden box, the kind chessmen are kept in. It was full of curved gaffs, small squares of chamois with holes in their centers and bits of waxed string like that used by a shoemaker.

They crowded around to watch him arm Juju. First he wiped the short stubs on the cock's legs to make sure they were clean and then placed a leather square over one of them so that the stub came through the hole. He then fitted a gaff over it and fastened it with a bit of the soft string, wrapping very carefully. He did the same to the other leg.

When he had finished, Earle started on the big red.

"That's a bird with lots of cojones,"[6] Miguel said. "He's won plenty fights. He don't look fast maybe, but he's fast all right and he packs an awful wallop."

"Strictly for the cook stove, if you ask me," the dwarf said.

Earle took out a pair of shears and started to lighten the red's plumage. The dwarf watched him cut away most of the bird's tail, but when he began to work on the breast, he caught his hand.

"Leave him be!" he barked. "You'll kill him fast that way. He needs that stuff for protection."

He turned to Claude again.

"Please, mister, let me handle him."

"Make him buy a share in the bird," Miguel said.

Claude laughed and motioned for Earle to give Abe the bird. Earle didn't want to and looked meaningly at Miguel.

The dwarf began to dance with rage.

"You're trying to cold-deck[7] us!" he screamed.

"Aw, give it to him," Miguel said.

6. Balls, testicles (Spanish).

7. To stack the deck; i.e., to cheat.

The little man tucked the bird under his left arm so that his hands were free and began to look over the gaffs in the box. They were all the same length, three inches, but some had more pronounced curves than the others. He selected a pair and explained his strategy to Claude.

"He's going to do most of his fighting on his back. This pair'll hit right that way. If he could get over the other bird, I wouldn't use them."

He got down on his knees and honed the gaffs on the cement floor until they were like needles.

"Have we a chance?" Tod asked.

"You can't ever tell," he said, shaking his extra large head. "He feels almost like a dead bird."

After adjusting the gaffs with great care, he looked the bird over, stretching its wings and blowing its feathers in order to see its skin.

"The comb ain't bright enough for fighting condition," he said, pinching it, "but he looks strong. He may have been a good one once."

He held the bird in the light and looked at its head. When Miguel saw him examining its beak, he told him anxiously to quit stalling. But the dwarf paid no attention and went on muttering to himself. He motioned for Tod and Claude to look.

"What'd I tell you!" he said, puffing with indignation. "We've been cold-decked."

He pointed to a hair line running across the top of the bird's beak.

"That's not a crack," Miguel protested, "it's just a mark."

He reached for the bird as though to rub its beak and the bird pecked savagely at him. This pleased the dwarf.

"We'll fight," he said, "but we won't bet."

Earle was to referee. He took a piece of chalk and drew three lines in the center of the pit, a long one in the middle and two shorter ones parallel to it and about three feet away.

"Pit your cocks," he called.

"No, bill them first," the dwarf protested.

He and Miguel stood at arm's length and thrust their birds together to anger them. Juju caught the big red by the comb and held on viciously until Miguel jerked him away. The red, who had been rather apathetic, came to life and the dwarf had trouble holding him. The two men thrust their birds together again, and again Juju caught the red's comb. The big cock became frantic with rage and struggled to get at the smaller bird.

"We're ready," the dwarf said.

He and Miguel climbed into the pit and set their birds down on the short lines so that they faced each other. They held them by the tails and waited for Earle to give the signal to let go.

"Pit them," he ordered.

The dwarf had been watching Earle's lips and he had his bird off first, but Juju rose straight in the air and sank one spur in the red's breast. It went through the feathers into the flesh. The red turned with the gaff still stuck in him and pecked twice at his opponent's head.

They separated the birds and held them to the lines again.

"Pit 'em!" Earle shouted.

Again Juju got above the other bird, but this time he missed with his spurs. The red tried to get above him, but couldn't. He was too clumsy and heavy to fight in the air. Juju climbed again, cutting and hitting so rapidly that his legs were a golden blur. The red met him by going back on his tail and hooking upward like a cat. Juju landed again and again. He broke one of the red's wings, then practically severed a leg.

"Handle them," Earle called.

When the dwarf gathered the red up, its neck had begun to droop and it was a mass of blood and matted feathers. The little man moaned over the bird, then set to work. He spit into its gaping beak and took the comb between his lips and sucked the blood back into it. The red began to regain its fury, but not its strength. Its beak closed and its neck straightened. The dwarf smoothed and shaped its plumage. He could do nothing to help the broken wing or the dangling leg.

"Pit 'em," Earle said.

The dwarf insisted that the birds be put down beak to beak on the center line, so that the red would not have to move to get at his opponent. Miguel agreed.

The red was very gallant. When Abe let go of its tail, it made a great effort to get off the ground and meet Juju in the air, but it could only thrust with one leg and fell over on its side. Juju sailed above it, half turned and came down on its back, driving in both spurs. The red twisted free, throwing Juju, and made a terrific effort to hook with its good leg, but fell sideways again.

Before Juju could get into the air, the red managed to drive a hard blow with its beak to Juju's head. This slowed the smaller bird down and he fought on the ground. In the pecking match, the red's greater weight and strength evened up for his lack of a leg and a wing. He managed to give as good as he got. But suddenly his cracked beak broke off, leaving only the lower half. A large bubble of blood rose where the beak had been. The red didn't retreat an inch, but made a great effort to get into the air once more. Using its one leg skillfully, it managed to rise six or seven inches from the ground, not enough, however, to get its spurs into play. Juju went up with him and got well above, then drove both gaffs into the red's breast. Again one of the steel needles stuck.

"Handle them," Earle shouted.

Miguel freed his bird and gave the other back to the dwarf. Abe, moaning softly, smoothed its feathers and licked its eyes clean, then took its whole head in his mouth. The red was finished, however. It couldn't even hold its neck straight. The dwarf blew away the feathers from under its tail and pressed the lips of its vent[8] together hard. When that didn't seem to help, he inserted his little finger and scratched the bird's testicles. It fluttered and made a gallant effort to straighten its neck.

"Pit birds."

Once more the red tried to rise with Juju, pushing hard with its remaining leg, but it only spun crazily. Juju rose, but missed. The red thrust weakly with its broken bill. Juju went into the air again and this time drove a gaff through one of the red's eyes into its brain. The red fell over stone dead.

The dwarf groaned with anguish, but no one else said anything. Juju pecked at the dead bird's remaining eye.

"Take off that stinking cannibal!" the dwarf screamed.

8. Cloacal opening.

Miguel laughed, then caught Juju and removed its gaffs. Earle did the same for the red. He handled the dead cock gently and with respect.

Tod passed the whiskey.

22

They were well on their way to getting drunk when Homer came out to the garage. He gave a little start when he saw the dead chicken sprawled on the carpet. He shook hands with Claude after Tod had introduced him, and with Abe Kusich, then made a little set speech about everybody coming in for a drink. They trooped after him.

Faye greeted them at the door. She was wearing a pair of green silk lounging pajamas and green mules[9] with large pompons and very high heels. The top three buttons of her jacket were open and a good deal of her chest was exposed but nothing of her breasts; not because they were small, but because they were placed wide apart and their thrust was upward and outward.

She gave Tod her hand and patted the dwarf on the top of the head. They were old friends. In acknowledging Homer's awkward introduction of Claude, she was very much the lady. It was her favorite role and she assumed it whenever she met a new man, especially if he were someone whose affluence was obvious.

"Charmed to have you," she trilled.

The dwarf laughed at her.

In a voice stiff with hauteur, she then ordered Homer into the kitchen for soda, ice and glasses.

"A swell layout," announced the dwarf, putting on the hat he had taken off in the doorway.

He climbed into one of the big Spanish chairs, using his knees and hands to do it, and sat on the edge with his feet dangling. He looked like a ventriloquist's dummy.

Earle and Miguel had remained behind to wash up. When they came in, Faye welcomed them with stilted condescension.

"How do you do, boys? The refreshments will be along in a jiffy. But perhaps you prefer a liqueur, Miguel?"

"No, mum," he said, a little startled. "I'll have what the others have."

He followed Earle across the room to the couch. Both of them took long, wooden steps, as though they weren't used to being in a house. They sat down gingerly with their backs straight, their big hats on their knees and their hands under their hats. They had combed their hair before leaving the garage and their small round heads glistened prettily.

Homer took the drinks around on a small tray.

They all made a show of manners, all but the dwarf, that is, who remained as arrogant as ever. He even commented on the quality of the whiskey. As soon as everyone had been served, Homer sat down.

Faye alone remained standing. She was completely self-possessed despite their stares. She stood with one hip thrown out and her hand on it. From

9. Backless shoes.

where Claude was sitting he could follow the charming line of her spine as it swooped into her buttocks, which were like a heart upside down.

He gave a low whistle of admiration and everyone agreed by moving uneasily or laughing.

"My dear," she said to Homer, "perhaps some of the men would like cigars?"

He was surprised and mumbled something about there being no cigars in the house but that he would go to the store for them if . . . Having to say all this made him unhappy and he took the whiskey around again. He poured very generous shots.

"That's a becoming shade of green," Tod said.

Faye peacocked for them all.

"I thought maybe it was a little gaudy . . . vulgar, you know."

"No," Claude said enthusiastically, "it's stunning."

She repaid him for his compliment by smiling in a peculiar, secret way and running her tongue over her lips. It was one of her most characteristic gestures and very effective. It seemed to promise all sorts of undefined intimacies, yet it was really as simple and automatic as the word thanks. She used it to reward anyone for anything, no matter how unimportant.

Claude made the same mistake Tod had often made and jumped to his feet.

"Won't you sit here?" he said, waving gallantly at his chair.

She accepted by repeating the secret smile and the tongue caress. Claude bowed, but then, realizing that everyone was watching him, added a little mock flourish to make himself less ridiculous. Tod joined them, then Earle and Miguel came over. Claude did the courting while the others stood by and stared at her.

"Do you work in pictures, Mr. Estee?" she asked.

"Yes. You're in pictures, of course?"

Everyone was aware of the begging note in his voice, but no one smiled. They didn't blame him. It was almost impossible to keep that note out when talking to her. Men used it just to say good morning.

"Not exactly, but I hope to be," she said. "I've worked as an extra, but I haven't had a real chance yet. I expect to get one soon. All I ask is a chance. Acting is in my blood. We Greeners, you know, were all theatre people from away back."

"Yes. I . . ."

She didn't let Claude finish, but he didn't care.

"Not musicals, but real dramas. Of course, maybe light comedies at first. All I ask is a chance. I've been buying a lot of clothes lately to make myself one. I don't believe in luck. Luck is just hard work, they say, and I'm willing to work as hard as anybody."

"You have a delightful voice and you handle it well," he said.

He couldn't help it. Having once seen her secret smile and the things that accompanied it, he wanted to make her repeat it again and again.

"I'd like to do a show on Broadway," she continued. "That's the way to get a start nowadays. They won't talk to you unless you've had stage experience."

She went on and on, telling him how careers are made in the movies and how she intended to make hers. It was all nonsense. She mixed bits of badly understood advice from the trade papers with other bits out of the fan magazines and compared these with the legends that surround the activities of screen stars and executives. Without any noticeable transition, possibilities became probabilities and wound up as inevitabilities. At first she occasionally stopped and waited for Claude to chorus a hearty agreement, but when she had a good start, all her questions were rhetorical and the stream of words rippled on without a break.

None of them really heard her. They were all too busy watching her smile, laugh, shiver, whisper, grow indignant, cross and uncross her legs, stick out her tongue, widen and narrow her eyes, toss her head so that her platinum hair splashed against the red plush of the chair back. The strange thing about her gestures and expressions was that they didn't really illustrate what she was saying. They were almost pure. It was as though her body recognized how foolish her words were and tried to excite her hearers into being uncritical. It worked that night; no one even thought of laughing at her. The only move they made was to narrow their circle about her.

Tod stood on the outer edge, watching her through the opening between Earle and the Mexican. When he felt a light tap on his shoulder, he knew it was Homer, but didn't turn. When the tap was repeated, he shrugged the hand away. A few minutes later, he heard a shoe squeak behind him and turned to see Homer tiptoeing off. He reached a chair safely and sank into it with a sigh. He put his heavy hands on the knees, one on each, and stared for a while at their backs. He felt Tod's eyes on him and looked up and smiled.

His smile annoyed Tod. It was one of those irritating smiles that seem to say: "My friend, what can you know of suffering?" There was something very patronizing and superior about it, and intolerably snobbish.

He felt hot and a little sick. He turned his back on Homer and went out the front door. His indignant exit wasn't very successful. He wobbled quite badly and when he reached the sidewalk, he had to sit down on the curb with his back against a date palm.

From where he was sitting, he couldn't see the city in the valley below the canyon, but he could see the reflection of its lights, which hung in the sky above it like a batik[1] parasol. The unlighted part of the sky at the edge of the parasol was a deep black with hardly a trace of blue.

Homer followed him out of the house and stood standing behind him, afraid to approach. He might have sneaked away without Tod's knowing it, if he had not suddenly looked down and seen his shadow.

"Hello," he said.

He motioned for Homer to join him on the curb.

"You'll catch cold," Homer said.

Tod understood his protest. He made it because he wanted to be certain that his company was really welcome. Nevertheless, Tod refused to repeat the invitation. He didn't even turn to look at him again. He was sure he was wearing his long-suffering smile and didn't want to see it.

He wondered why all his sympathy had turned to malice. Because of Faye? It was impossible for him to admit it. Because he was unable to do anything to help him? This reason was a more comfortable one, but he dismissed it with even less consideration. He had never set himself up as a healer.

Homer was looking the other way, at the house, watching the parlor window. He cocked his head to one side when someone laughed. The four short sounds, ha-ha and again ha-ha, distinct musical notes, were made by the dwarf.

1. Cloth patterned through a wax-relief dying process, brought to a high art in Indonesia.

"You could learn from him," Tod said.

"What?" Homer asked, turning to look at him.

"Let it go."

His impatience both hurt and puzzled Homer. He saw that and motioned for him to sit down, this time emphatically.

Homer obeyed. He did a poor job of squatting and hurt himself. He sat nursing his knee.

"What is it?" Tod finally said, making an attempt to be kind.

"Nothing, Tod, nothing."

He was grateful and increased his smile. Tod couldn't help seeing all its annoying attributes, resignation, kindliness, and humility.

They sat quietly, Homer with his heavy shoulders hunched and the sweet grin on his face, Tod frowning, his back pressed hard against the palm tree. In the house the radio was playing and its blare filled the street.

They sat for a long time without speaking. Several times Homer started to tell Tod something but he didn't seem able to get the words out. Tod refused to help him with a question.

His big hands left his lap, where they had been playing "here's the church and here the steeple," and hid in his armpits. They remained there for a moment, then slid under his thighs. A moment later they were back in his lap. The right hand cracked the joints of the left, one by one, then the left did the same service for the right. They seemed easier for a moment, but not for long. They started "here's the church" again, going through the entire performance and ending with the joint manipulation as before. He started a third time, but catching Tod's eyes, he stopped and trapped his hands between his knees.

It was the most complicated tic Tod had ever seen. What made it particularly horrible was its precision. It wasn't pantomime, as he had first thought, but manual ballet.

When Tod saw the hands start to crawl out again, he exploded.

"For Christ's sake!"

The hands struggled to get free, but Homer clamped his knees shut and held them.

"I'm sorry," he said.

"Oh, all right."

"But I can't help it, Tod. I have to do it three times."

"Okay with me."

He turned his back on him.

Faye started to sing and her voice poured into the street.

"Dreamed about a reefer five feet long
Not too mild and not too strong,
You'll be high, but not for long,
If you're a viper—a vi-paah."[2]

Instead of her usual swing delivery, she was using a lugubrious one, wailing the tune as though it were a dirge. At the end of every stanza, she shifted to an added minor.

2. "If You're a Viper," a popular jazz song about marijuana written and first recorded in 1936 by Stuff Smith (1909–1967). "Viper": a marijuana smoker. "Reefer": a joint, or marijuana cigarette.

"I'm the queen of everything,
Gotta be high before I can swing,
Light a tea and let it be,
If you're a viper—a vi-paah."

"She sings very pretty," Homer said.

"She's drunk."

"I don't know what to do, Tod," Homer complained. "She's drinking an awful lot lately. It's that Earle. We used to have a lot of fun before he came, but now we don't have any fun any more since he started to hang around."

"Why don't you get rid of him?"

"I was thinking about what you said about the license to keep chickens."

Tod understood what he wanted.

"I'll report them to the Board of Health tomorrow."

Homer thanked him, then insisted on explaining in detail why he couldn't do it himself.

"But that'll only get rid of the Mexican," Tod said. "You'll have to throw Earle out yourself."

"Maybe he'll go with his friend?"

Tod knew that Homer was begging him to agree so that he could go on hoping, but he refused.

"Not a chance. You'll have to throw him out."

Homer accepted this with his brave, sweet smile.

"Maybe . . ."

"Tell Faye to do it," Tod said.

"Oh, I can't."

"Why the hell not? It's your house."

"Don't be mad at me, Toddie."

"All right, Homie, I'm not mad at you."

Faye's voice came through the open window.

"And when your throat gets dry,
You know you're high,
If you're a viper."

The others harmonized on the last word, repeating it.

"Vi-paah . . ."

"Toddie," Homer began, "if . . ."

"Stop calling me Toddie, for Christ's sake!"

Homer didn't understand. He took Tod's hand.

"I didn't mean nothing. Back home we call . . ."

Tod couldn't stand his trembling signals of affection. He tore free with a jerk.

"Oh, but, Toddie, I . . ."

"She's a whore!"

He heard Homer grunt, then heard his knees creak as he struggled to his feet.

Faye's voice came pouring through the window, a reedy wail that broke in the middle with a husky catch.

"High, high, high, high, when you're high,
Everything is dandy,

Truck on down to the candy store,
Bust your conk on peppermint candy![3]
Then you know your body's sent,
Don't care if you don't pay rent,
Sky is high and so am I,
If you're a viper—a vi-paah."

23

When Tod went back into the house, he found Earle, Abe Kusich and Claude standing together in a tight group, watching Faye dance with Miguel. She and the Mexican were doing a slow tango to music from the phonograph. He held her very tight, one of his legs thrust between hers, and they swayed together in long spirals that broke rhythmically at the top of each curve into a dip. All the buttons on her lounging pajamas were open and the arm he had around her waist was inside her clothes.

Tod stood watching the dancers from the doorway for a moment, then went to a little table on which the whiskey bottle was. He poured himself a quarter of a tumblerful, tossed it off, then poured another drink. Carrying the glass, he went over to Claude and the others. They paid no attention to him; their heads moved only to follow the dancers, like the gallery at a tennis match.

"Did you see Homer?" Tod asked, touching Claude's arm.

Claude didn't turn, but the dwarf did. He spoke as though hypnotized.

"What a quiff! What a quiff!"[4]

Tod left them and went to look for Homer. He wasn't in the kitchen, so he tried the bedrooms. One of them was locked. He knocked lightly, waited, then repeated the knock. There was no answer, but he thought he heard someone move. He looked through the keyhole. The room was pitch dark.

"Homer," he called softly.

He heard the bed creak, then Homer replied.

"Who is it?"

"It's me—Toddie."

He used the diminutive with perfect seriousness.

"Go away, please," Homer said.

"Let me in for a minute. I want to explain something."

"No," Homer said, "go away, please."

Tod went back to the living room. The phonograph record had been changed to a fox-trot and Earle was now dancing with Faye. He had both his arms around her in a bear hug and they were stumbling all over the room, bumping into the walls and furniture. Faye, her head thrown back, was laughing wildly. Earle had both eyes shut tight.

Miguel and Claude were also laughing, but not the dwarf. He stood with his fists clenched and his chin stuck out. When he couldn't stand any more of it, he ran after the dancers to cut in. He caught Earle by the seat of his trousers.

"Le'me dance," he barked.

Earle turned his head, looking down at the dwarf from over his shoulder.

3. Cocaine (slang). "Conk": head.

4. Derogatory slang for female genitals.

"Git! G'wan, git!"

Faye and Earle had come to a halt with their arms around each other. When the dwarf lowered his head like a goat and tried to push between them, she reached down and tweaked his nose.

"Le'me dance," he bellowed.

They tried to start again, but Abe wouldn't let them. He had his hands between them and was trying frantically to pull them apart. When that wouldn't work, he kicked Earle sharply in the shins. Earle kicked back and his boot landed in the little man's stomach, knocking him flat on his back. Everyone laughed.

The dwarf struggled to his feet and stood with his head lowered like a tiny ram. Just as Faye and Earle started to dance again, he charged between Earle's legs and dug upward with both hands. Earle screamed with pain, and tried to get at him. He screamed again, then groaned and started to sink to the floor, tearing Faye's silk pajamas on his way down.

Miguel grabbed Abe by the throat. The dwarf let go his hold and Earle sank to the floor. Lifting the little man free, Miguel shifted his grip to his ankles and dashed him against the wall, like a man killing a rabbit against a tree. He swung the dwarf back to slam him again, but Tod caught his arm. Then Claude grabbed the dwarf and together they pulled him away from the Mexican.

He was unconscious. They carried him into the kitchen and held him under the cold water. He came to quickly, and began to curse. When they saw he was all right, they went back to the living room.

Miguel was helping Earle over to the couch. All the tan had drained from his face and it was covered with sweat. Miguel loosened his trousers while Claude took off his necktie and opened his collar.

Faye and Tod watched from the side.

"Look," she said, "my new pajamas are ruined."

One of the sleeves had been pulled almost off and her shoulder stuck through it. The trousers were also torn. While he stared at her, she undid the top of the trousers and stepped out of them. She was wearing tight black lace drawers. Tod took a step toward her and hesitated. She threw the pajama bottoms over her arm, turned slowly and walked toward the door.

"Faye," Tod gasped.

She stopped and smiled at him.

"I'm going to bed," she said. "Get that little guy out of here."

Claude came over and took Tod by the arm.

"Let's blow," he said.

Tod nodded.

"We'd better take the homunculus with us or he's liable to murder the whole household."

Tod nodded again and followed him into the kitchen. They found the dwarf holding a big piece of ice to the side of his head.

"There's some lump where that greaser[5] slammed me."

He made them finger and admire it.

"Let's go home," Claude said.

"No," said the dwarf, "let's go see some girls. I'm just getting started."

5. Derogatory slang for a Mexican American.

"To hell with that," snapped Tod. "Come on."

He pushed the dwarf toward the door.

"Take your hands off, punk!" roared the little man.

Claude stepped between them.

"Easy there, citizen," he said.

"All right, but no shoving."

He strutted out and they followed.

Earle still lay stretched on the couch. He had his eyes closed and was holding himself below the stomach with both hands. Miguel wasn't there.

Abe chuckled, wagging his big head gleefully.

"I fixed that buckeroo."

Out on the sidewalk he tried again to get them to go with him.

"Come on, you guys—we'll have some fun."

"I'm going home," Claude said.

They went with the dwarf to his car and watched him climb in behind the wheel. He had special extensions on the clutch and brake so that he could reach them with his tiny feet.

"Come to town?"

"No, thanks," Claude said politely.

"Then to hell with you!"

That was his farewell. He let out the brake and the car rolled away.

24

Tod woke up the next morning with a splitting headache. He called the studio to say he wouldn't be in and remained in bed until noon, then went downtown for breakfast. After several cups of hot tea, he felt a little better and decided to visit Homer. He still wanted to apologize.

Climbing the hill to Pinyon Canyon made his head throb and he was relieved when no one answered his repeated knocks. As he started away, he saw one of the curtains move and went back to knock once more. There was still no answer.

He went around to the garage. Faye's car was gone and so were the game chickens. He went to the back of the house and knocked on the kitchen door. Somehow the silence seemed too complete. He tried the handle and found that the door wasn't locked. He shouted hello a few times, as a warning, then went through the kitchen into the living room.

The red velvet curtains were all drawn tight, but he could see Homer sitting on the couch and staring at the backs of his hands which were cupped over his knees. He wore an old-fashioned cotton nightgown and his feet were bare.

"Just get up?"

Homer neither moved nor replied.

Tod tried again.

"Some party!"

He knew it was stupid to be hearty, but he didn't know what else to be.

"Boy, have I got a hang-over," he went on, even going so far as to attempt a chuckle.

Homer paid absolutely no attention to him.

The room was just as they had left it the night before. Tables and chairs were overturned and the smashed picture lay where it had fallen. To give himself a reason for staying, he began to tidy up. He righted the chairs, straightened the carpet and picked up the cigarette butts that littered the floor. He also threw aside the curtains and opened a window.

"There, that's better, isn't it?" he asked cheerfully.

Homer looked up for a second, then down at his hands again. Tod saw that he was coming out of his stupor.

"Want some coffee?" he asked.

He lifted his hands from his knees and hid them in his armpits, clamping them tight, but didn't answer.

"Some hot coffee—what do you say?"

He took his hands from under his arms and sat on them. After waiting a little while he shook his head no, slowly, heavily, like a dog with a foxtail in its ear.

"I'll make some."

Tod went to the kitchen and put the pot on the stove. While it was boiling, he took a peek into Faye's room. It had been stripped. All the dresser drawers were pulled out and there were empty boxes all over the floor. A broken flask of perfume lay in the middle of the carpet and the place reeked of gardenia.

When the coffee was ready, he poured two cups and carried them into the living room on a tray. He found Homer just as he had left him, sitting on his hands. He moved a small table close to him and put the tray on it.

"I brought a cup for myself, too," he said. "Come on—drink it while it's hot."

Tod lifted a cup and held it out, but when he saw that he was going to speak, he put it down and waited.

"I'm going back to Wayneville," Homer said.

"A swell idea—great!"

He pushed the coffee at him again. Homer ignored it. He gulped several times, trying to swallow something that was stuck in his throat, then began to sob. He cried without covering his face or bending his head. The sound was like an ax chopping pine, a heavy, hollow, chunking noise. It was repeated rhythmically but without accent. There was no progress in it. Each chunk was exactly like the one that proceeded. It would never reach a climax.

Tod realized that there was no use trying to stop him. Only a very stupid man would have the courage to try to do it. He went to the farthest corner of the room and waited.

Just as he was about to light a second cigarette, Homer called him.

"Tod!"

"I'm here, Homer."

He hurried over to the couch again.

Homer was still crying, but he suddenly stopped even more abruptly than he had started.

"Yes, Homer?" Tod asked encouragingly.

"She's left."

"Yes, I know. Drink some coffee."

"She's left."

Tod knew that he put a great deal of faith in sayings, so he tried one.

"Good riddance to bad rubbish."

"She left before I got up," he said.

"What the hell do you care? You're going back to Wayneville."

"You shouldn't curse," Homer said with the same lunatic calm.

"I'm sorry," Tod mumbled.

The word "sorry" was like dynamite set off under a dam. Language leaped out of Homer in a muddy, twisting torrent. At first, Tod thought it would do him a lot of good to pour out in this way. But he was wrong. The lake behind the dam replenished itself too fast. The more he talked the greater the pressure grew because the flood was circular and ran back behind the dam again.

After going on continuously for about twenty minutes, he stopped in the middle of a sentence. He leaned back, closed his eyes and seemed to fall asleep. Tod put a cushion under his head. After watching him for a while, he went back to the kitchen.

He sat down and tried to make sense out of what Homer had told him. A great deal of it was gibberish. Some of it, however, wasn't. He hit on a key that helped when he realized that a lot of it wasn't jumbled so much as timeless. The words went behind each other instead of after. What he had taken for long strings were really one thick word and not a sentence. In the same way several sentences were simultaneous and not a paragraph. Using this key, he was able to arrange a part of what he had heard so that it made the usual kind of sense.

After Tod had hurt him by saying that nasty thing about Faye, Homer ran around to the back of the house and let himself in through the kitchen, then went to peek into the parlor. He wasn't angry with Tod, just surprised and upset because Tod was a nice boy. From the hall that led into the parlor he could see everybody having a good time and he was glad because it was kind of dull for Faye living with an old man like him. It made her restless. No one noticed him peeking there and he was glad because he didn't feel much like joining the fun, although he liked to watch people enjoy themselves. Faye was dancing with Mr. Estee and they made a nice pair. She seemed happy. Her face shone like always when she was happy. Next she danced with Earle. He didn't like that because of the way he held her. He couldn't see what she saw in that fellow. He just wasn't nice, that's all. He had mean eyes. In the hotel business they used to watch out for fellows like that and never gave them credit because they would jump their bills.[6] Maybe he couldn't get a job because nobody would trust him, although it was true as Faye said that a lot of people were out of work nowadays. Standing there peeking at the party, enjoying the laughing and singing, he saw Earle catch Faye and bend her back and kiss her and everybody laughed although you could see Faye didn't like it because she slapped his face. Earle didn't care, he just kissed her again, a long nasty one. She got away from him and ran toward the door where he was standing. He tried to hide, but she caught him. Although he didn't say anything, she said he was nasty spying on her and wouldn't listen when he tried to explain. She went into her room and he followed to tell about the peeking, but she carried on awful and cursed him some more as she put red on her lips. Then she knocked over the perfume. That made her twice as mad. He tried to explain but she wouldn't listen and just went on calling him all sorts of dirty things. So he went to his room and got undressed and tried to go to sleep. Then Tod woke him up and wanted to come in and talk. He

6. I.e., leave without paying.

wasn't angry, but didn't feel like talking just then, all he wanted to do was go to sleep. Tod went away and no sooner had he climbed back into bed when there was some awful screaming and banging. He was afraid to go out and see and he thought of calling the police, but he was scared to go in the hall where the phone was so he started to get dressed to climb out of the window and go for help because it sounded like murder but before he finished putting his shoes on, he heard Tod talking to Faye and he figured that it must be all right or she wouldn't be laughing so he got undressed and went back to bed again. He couldn't fall asleep wondering what had happened, so when the house was quiet, he took a chance and knocked on Faye's door to find out. Faye let him in. She was curled up in bed like a little girl. She called him daddy and kissed him and said that she wasn't angry at him at all. She said there had been a fight but nobody got hurt much and for him to go back to bed and that they would talk more in the morning. He went back like she said and fell asleep, but he woke up again as it was just breaking daylight. At first he wondered why he was up because when he once fell asleep, usually he didn't get up before the alarm clock rang. He knew that something had happened, but he didn't know what until he heard a noise in Faye's room. It was a moan and he thought he was dreaming, but he heard it again. Sure enough, Faye was moaning all right. He thought she must be sick. She moaned again like in pain. He got out of bed and went to her door and knocked and asked if she was sick. She didn't answer and the moaning stopped so he went back to bed. A little later, she moaned again so he got out of bed, thinking she might want the hot water bottle or some aspirin and a drink of water or something and knocked on her door again, only meaning to help her. She heard him and said something. He didn't understand what but he thought she meant for him to go in. Lots of times when she had a headache he brought her an aspirin and a glass of water in the middle of the night. The door wasn't locked. You'd have thought she would have locked the door because the Mexican was in bed with her, both of them naked and she had her arms around him. Faye saw him and pulled the sheets over her head without saying anything. He didn't know what to do, so he backed out of the room and closed the door. He was standing in the hall, trying to figure out what to do, feeling so ashamed, when Earle appeared with his boots in his hand. He must have been sleeping in the parlor. He wanted to know what the trouble was. "Faye's sick," he said, "and I'm getting her a glass of water." But then Faye moaned again and Earle heard it. He pushed open the door. Faye screamed. He could hear Earle and Miguel cursing each other and fighting. He was afraid to call the police on account of Faye and didn't know what to do. Faye kept on screaming. When he opened the door again, Miguel fell out with Earle on top of him and both of them tearing at each other. He ran inside the room and locked the door. She had the sheets over her head, screaming. He could hear Earle and Miguel fighting in the hall and then he couldn't hear them any more. She kept the sheets over her head. He tried to talk to her but she wouldn't answer. He sat down on a chair to guard her in case Earle and Miguel came back, but they didn't and after a while she pulled the sheets away from her face and told him to get out. She pulled the sheets over her face again when he answered, so then he waited a little longer and again she told him to get out without letting him see her face. He couldn't hear either Miguel or Earle. He opened the door and looked out. They were gone. He locked the doors and windows and went to his room and lay down on his bed. Before he knew it he fell asleep and when he woke up she was gone. All he could find was Earle's boots in the hall. He threw them out the back and this morning they were gone.

25

Tod went into the living room to see how Homer was getting on. He was still on the couch, but had changed his position. He had curled his big body into a ball. His knees were drawn up almost to his chin, his elbows were tucked in close and his hands were against his chest. But he wasn't relaxed. Some inner force of nerve and muscle was straining to make the ball tighter and still tighter. He was like a steel spring which has been freed of its function in a machine and allowed to use all its strength centripetally. While part of a machine the pull of the spring had been used against other and stronger forces, but now, free at last, it was striving to attain the shape of its original coil.

Original coil . . . In a book of abnormal psychology borrowed from the college library, he had once seen a picture of a woman sleeping in a net hammock whose posture was much like Homer's. "Uterine Flight," or something like that, had been the caption under the photograph. The woman had been sleeping in the hammock without changing her position, that of the foetus in the womb, for a great many years. The doctors of the insane asylum had been able to awaken her for only short periods of time and those months apart.

He sat down to smoke a cigarette and wondered what he ought to do. Call a doctor? But after all Homer had been awake most of the night and was exhausted. The doctor would shake him a few times and he would yawn and ask what the matter was. He could try to wake him up himself. But hadn't he been enough of a pest already? He was so much better off asleep, even if it was a case of "Uterine Flight."

What a perfect escape the return to the womb was. Better by far than Religion or Art or the South Sea Islands. It was so snug and warm there, and the feeding was automatic. Everything perfect in that hotel. No wonder the memory of those accommodations lingered in the blood and nerves of everyone. It was dark, yes, but what a warm, rich darkness. The grave wasn't in it. No wonder one fought so desperately against being evicted when the nine months' lease was up.

Tod crushed his cigarette. He was hungry and wanted his dinner, also a double Scotch and soda. After he had eaten, he would come back and see how Homer was. If he was still asleep, he would try to wake him. If he couldn't, he might call a doctor.

He took another look at him, then tiptoed out of the cottage, shutting the door carefully.

26

Tod didn't go directly to dinner. He went first to Hodge's saddlery store thinking he might be able to find out something about Earle and through him about Faye. Calvin was standing there with a wrinkled Indian who had long hair held by a bead strap around his forehead. Hanging over the Indian's chest was a sandwich board that read—

TUTTLE'S TRADING POST
for
GENUINE RELICS OF THE OLD WEST
Beads, Silver, Jewelry, Moccasins,
Dolls, Toys, Rare Books, Postcards.
TAKE BACK A SOUVENIR
from
TUTTLE'S TRADING POST

Calvin was always friendly.

" 'Lo, thar," he called out, when Tod came up.

"Meet the chief," he added, grinning. "Chief Kiss-My-Towkus."

The Indian laughed heartily at the joke.

"You gotta live," he said.

"Earle been around today?" Tod asked.

"Yop. Went by an hour ago."

"We were at a party last night and I . . ."

Calvin broke in by hitting his thigh a wallop with the flat of his palm.

"That must've been some shindig to hear Earle tell it. Eh, Skookum?"

"Vas you dere, Sharley?" the Indian agreed, showing the black inside of his mouth, purple tongue and broken orange teeth.

"I heard there was a fight after I left."

Calvin smacked his thigh again.

"Sure musta been. Earle get himself two black eyes, lulus."

"That's what comes of palling up with a dirty greaser," said the Indian excitedly.

He and Calvin got into a long argument about Mexicans. The Indian said that they were all bad. Calvin claimed he had known quite a few good ones in his time. When the Indian cited the case of the Hermanos brothers who had killed a lonely prospector for half a dollar, Calvin countered with a long tale about a man called Tomas Lopez who shared his last pint of water with a stranger when they both were lost in the desert.

Tod tried to get the conversation back to what interested him.

"Mexicans are very good with women," he said.

"Better with horses," said the Indian. "I remember one time along the Brazos,[7] I . . ."

Tod tried again.

"They fought over Earle's girl, didn't they?"

"Not to hear him tell it," Calvin said. "He claims it was dough—claims the Mex robbed him while he was sleeping."

"The dirty, thievin' rat," said the Indian, spitting.

"He claims he's all washed up with that bitch," Calvin went on. "Yes, siree, that's his story, to hear him tell it."

Tod had enough.

"So long," he said.

"Glad to meet you," said the Indian.

"Don't take any wooden nickels,"[8] Calvin shouted after him.

7. River running through Texas.
8. I.e., look out for yourself. During the Great Depression, some banks issued wooden nickels as emergency currency, but most were produced as promotional tokens; many featured variations on the Indian image featured on the "buffalo nickel" issued by the U.S. Mint from 1913 to 1938.

Tod wondered if she had gone with Miguel. He thought it more likely that she would go back to work for Mrs. Jenning. But either way she would come out all right. Nothing could hurt her. She was like a cork. No matter how rough the sea got, she would go dancing over the same waves that sank iron ships and tore away piers of reinforced concrete. He pictured her riding a tremendous sea. Wave after wave reared its ton on ton of solid water and crashed down only to have her spin gaily away.

When he arrived at Musso Frank's restaurant, he ordered a steak and a double Scotch. The drink came first and he sipped it with his inner eye still on the spinning cork.

It was a very pretty cork, gilt with a glittering fragment of mirror set in its top. The sea in which it danced was beautiful, green in the trough of the waves and silver at their tips. But for all their moon-driven power, they could do no more than net the bright cork for a moment in a spume of intricate lace. Finally it was set down on a strange shore where a savage with pork-sausage fingers and a pimpled butt picked it up and hugged it to his sagging belly. Tod recognized the fortunate man; he was one of Mrs. Jenning's customers.

The waiter brought his order and paused with bent back for him to comment. In vain. Tod was far too busy to inspect the steak.

"Satisfactory, sir?" asked the waiter.

Tod waved him away with a gesture more often used on flies. The waiter disappeared. Tod tried the same gesture on what he felt, but the driving itch refused to go. If only he had the courage to wait for her some night and hit her with a bottle and rape her.

He knew what it would be like, lurking in the dark in a vacant lot, waiting for her. Whatever that bird was that sang at night in California would be bursting its heart in theatrical runs and quavers and the chill night air would smell of spice pink. She would drive up, turn the motor off, look up at the stars, so that her breasts reared, then toss her head and sigh. She would throw the ignition keys into her purse and snap it shut, then get out of the car. The long step she took would make her tight dress pull up so that an inch of glowing flesh would show above her black stocking. As he approached carefully, she would be pulling her dress down, smoothing it nicely over her hips.

"Faye, Faye, just a minute," he would call.

"Why, Tod, hello."

She would hold her hand out to him at the end of her long arm that swooped so gracefully to join her curving shoulder.

"You scared me!"

She would look like a deer on the edge of the road when a truck comes unexpectedly around a bend.

He could feel the cold bottle he held behind his back and the forward step he would take to bring . . .

"Is there anything wrong with it, sir?"

The fly-like waiter had come back. Tod waved at him, but this time the man continued to hover.

"Perhaps you would like me to take it back, sir?"

"No, no."

"Thank you, sir."

But he didn't leave. He waited to make sure that the customer was really going to eat. Tod picked up his knife and cut a piece. Not until he had also put some boiled potato in his mouth did the man leave.

Tod tried to start the rape going again, but he couldn't feel the bottle as he raised it to strike. He had to give it up.

The waiter came back. Tod looked at the steak. It was a very good one, but he wasn't hungry any more.

"A check, please."

"No dessert, sir?"

"No, thank you, just a check."

"Check it is, sir," the man said brightly as he fumbled for his pad and pencil.

27

When Tod reached the street, he saw a dozen great violet shafts of light moving across the evening sky in wide crazy sweeps. Whenever one of the fiery columns reached the lowest point of its arc, it lit for a moment rose-colored domes and delicate minarets of Kahn's Persian Palace Theatre.[9] The purpose of this display was to signal the world premiere of a new picture.

Turning his back on the searchlights, he started in the opposite direction, toward Homer's place. Before he had gone very far, he saw a clock that read a quarter past six and changed his mind about going back just yet. He might as well let the poor fellow sleep for another hour and kill some time by looking at the crowds.

When still a block from the theatre, he saw an enormous electric sign that hung over the middle of the street. In letters ten feet high he read that—

"MR. KAHN A PLEASURE DOME DECREED"

Although it was still several hours before the celebrities would arrive, thousands of people had already gathered. They stood facing the theatre with their backs toward the gutter in a thick line hundreds of feet long. A big squad of policemen was trying to keep a lane open between the front rank of the crowd and the façade of the theatre.

Tod entered the lane while the policeman guarding it was busy with a woman whose parcel had torn open, dropping oranges all over the place. Another policeman shouted for him to get the hell across the street, but he took a chance and kept going. They had enough to do without chasing him. He noticed how worried they looked and how careful they tried to be. If they had to arrest someone, they joked good-naturedly with the culprit, making light of it until they got him around the corner, then they whaled him with their clubs. Only so long as the man was actually part of the crowd did they have to be gentle.

Tod had walked only a short distance along the narrow lane when he began to get frightened. People shouted, commenting on his hat, his carriage, and his clothing. There was a continuous roar of catcalls, laughter and yells,

9. Modeled on Grauman's Chinese Theatre in Hollywood, site of many movie premieres, which opened in 1927. The theater's electric sign echoes the opening line of "Kubla Khan" (1816)—"In Xanadu did Kubla Khan a stately pleasure dome decree"—by the English poet Samuel Taylor Coleridge (1772–1834).

pierced occasionally by a scream. The scream was usually followed by a sudden movement in the dense mass and part of it would surge forward wherever the police line was weakest. As soon as that part was rammed back, the bulge would pop out somewhere else.

The police force would have to be doubled when the stars started to arrive. At the sight of their heroes and heroines, the crowd would turn demoniac. Some little gesture, either too pleasing or too offensive, would start it moving and then nothing but machine guns would stop it. Individually the purpose of its members might simply be to get a souvenir, but collectively it would grab and rend.

A young man with a portable microphone was describing the scene. His rapid, hysterical voice was like that of a revivalist preacher whipping his congregation toward the ecstasy of fits.

"What a crowd, folks! What a crowd! There must be ten thousand excited, screaming fans outside Kahn's Persian tonight. The police can't hold them. Here, listen to them roar."

He held the microphone out and those near it obligingly roared for him.

"Did you hear it? It's a bedlam, folks. A veritable bedlam! What excitement! Of all the premieres I've attended, this is the most . . . the most . . . stupendous, folks. Can the police hold them? Can they? It doesn't look so, folks . . ."

Another squad of police came charging up. The sergeant pleaded with the announcer to stand further back so the people couldn't hear him. His men threw themselves at the crowd. It allowed itself to be hustled and shoved out of habit and because it lacked an objective. It tolerated the police, just as a bull elephant does when he allows a small boy to drive him with a light stick.

Tod could see very few people who looked tough, nor could he see any working men. The crowd was made up of the lower middle classes, every other person one of his torch-bearers.

Just as he came near the end of the lane, it closed in front of him with a heave, and he had to fight his way through. Someone knocked his hat off and when he stooped to pick it up, someone kicked him. He whirled around angrily and found himself surrounded by people who were laughing at him. He knew enough to laugh with them. The crowd became sympathetic. A stout woman slapped him on the back, while a man handed him his hat, first brushing it carefully with his sleeve. Still another man shouted for a way to be cleared.

By a great deal of pushing and squirming, always trying to look as though he were enjoying himself, Tod finally managed to break into the open. After rearranging his clothes, he went over to a parking lot and sat down on the low retaining wall that ran along the front of it.

New groups, whole families, kept arriving. He could see a change come over them as soon as they had become part of the crowd. Until they reached the line, they looked diffident, almost furtive, but the moment they had become part of it, they turned arrogant and pugnacious. It was a mistake to think them harmless curiosity seekers. They were savage and bitter, especially the middle-aged and the old, and had been made so by boredom and disappointment.

All their lives they had slaved at some kind of dull, heavy labor, behind desks and counters, in the fields and at tedious machines of all sorts, saving their pennies and dreaming of the leisure that would be theirs when they had enough. Finally that day came. They could draw a weekly income of ten or fifteen dollars.[1] Where else should they go but California, the land of sunshine and oranges?

Once there, they discover that sunshine isn't enough. They get tired of oranges, even of avocado pears and passion fruit. Nothing happens. They don't know what to do with their time. They haven't the mental equipment for leisure, the money nor the physical equipment for pleasure. Did they slave so long just to go to an occasional Iowa picnic? What else is there? They watch the waves come in at Venice.[2] There wasn't any ocean where most of them came from, but after you've seen one wave, you've seen them all. The same is true of the airplanes at Glendale.[3] If only a plane would crash once in a while so that they could watch the passengers being consumed in a "holocaust of flame," as the newspapers put it. But the planes never crash.

Their boredom becomes more and more terrible. They realize that they've been tricked and burn with resentment. Every day of their lives they read the newspapers and went to the movies. Both fed them on lynchings, murder, sex crimes, explosions, wrecks, love nests, fires, miracles, revolutions, wars. This daily diet made sophisticates of them. The sun is a joke. Oranges can't titillate their jaded palates. Nothing can ever be violent enough to make taut their slack minds and bodies. They have been cheated and betrayed. They have slaved and saved for nothing.

Tod stood up. During the ten minutes he had been sitting on the wall, the crowd had grown thirty feet and he was afraid that his escape might be cut off if he loitered much longer. He crossed to the other side of the street and started back.

He was trying to figure what to do if he were unable to wake Homer when, suddenly, he saw his head bobbing above the crowd. He hurried toward him. From his appearance, it was evident that there was something definitely wrong.

Homer walked more than ever like a badly made automaton and his features were set in a rigid, mechanical grin. He had his trousers on over his nightgown and part of it hung out of his open fly. In both of his hands were suitcases. With each step, he lurched to one side then the other, using the suitcases for balance weights.

Tod stopped directly in front of him, blocking his way.

"Where're you going?"

"Wayneville," he replied, using an extraordinary amount of jaw movement to get out this single word.

"That's fine. But you can't walk to the station from here. It's in Los Angeles."

Homer tried to get around him, but he caught his arm.

"We'll get a taxi. I'll go with you."

The cabs were all being routed around the block because of the preview. He explained this to Homer and tried to get him to walk to the corner.

"Come on, we're sure to get one on the next street."

1. Equivalent to an annual income of $15,000–25,000 in present-day U.S. dollars.
2. Beachfront neighborhood of Los Angeles, founded in 1905 as a resort town.
3. Opened in 1922, the Grand Central Airport at Glendale was the first commercial airport in Los Angeles.

Once Tod got him into a cab, he intended to tell the driver to go to the nearest hospital. But Homer wouldn't budge, no matter how hard he yanked and pleaded. People stopped to watch them, others turned their heads curiously. He decided to leave him and get a cab.

"I'll come right back," he said.

He couldn't tell from either Homer's eyes or expression whether he heard, for they both were empty of everything, even annoyance. At the corner he looked around and saw that Homer had started to cross the street, moving blindly. Brakes screeched and twice he was almost run over, but he didn't swerve or hurry. He moved in a straight diagonal. When he reached the other curb, he tried to get on the sidewalk at a point where the crowd was very thick and was shoved violently back. He made another attempt and this time a policeman grabbed him by the back of the neck and hustled him to the end of the line. When the policeman let go of him, he kept on walking as though nothing had happened.

Tod tried to get over to him, but was unable to cross until the traffic lights changed. When he reached the other side, he found Homer sitting on a bench, fifty or sixty feet from the outskirts of the crowd.

He put his arm around Homer's shoulder and suggested that they walk a few blocks further. When Homer didn't answer, he reached over to pick up one of the valises. Homer held on to it.

"I'll carry it for you," he said, tugging gently.

"Thief!"

Before Homer could repeat the shout, he jumped away. It would be extremely embarrassing if Homer shouted thief in front of a cop. He thought of phoning for an ambulance. But then, after all, how could he be sure that Homer was crazy? He was sitting quietly on the bench, minding his own business.

Tod decided to wait, then try again to get him into a cab. The crowd was growing in size all the time, but it would be at least half an hour before it over-ran the bench. Before that happened, he would think of some plan. He moved a short distance away and stood with his back to a store window so that he could watch Homer without attracting attention.

About ten feet from where Homer was sitting grew a large eucalyptus tree and behind the trunk of the tree was a little boy. Tod saw him peer around it with great caution, then suddenly jerk his head back. A minute later he repeated the maneuver. At first Tod thought he was playing hide and seek, then noticed that he had a string in his hand which was attached to an old purse that lay in front of Homer's bench. Every once in a while the child would jerk the string, making the purse hop like a sluggish toad. Its torn lining hung from its iron mouth like a furry tongue and a few uncertain flies hovered over it.

Tod knew the game the child was playing. He used to play it himself when he was small. If Homer reached to pick up the purse, thinking there was money in it, he would yank it away and scream with laughter.

When Tod went over to the tree, he was surprised to discover that it was Adore Loomis, the kid who lived across the street from Homer. Tod tried to chase him, but he dodged around the tree, thumbing his nose. He gave up and went back to his original position. The moment he left, Adore got busy with his purse again. Homer wasn't paying any attention to the child, so Tod decided to let him alone.

Mrs. Loomis must be somewhere in the crowd, he thought. Tonight when she found Adore, she would give him a hiding. He had torn the pocket of his jacket and his Buster Brown collar was smeared with grease.

Adore had a nasty temper. The completeness with which Homer ignored both him and his pocketbook made him frantic. He gave up dancing it at the end of the string and approached the bench on tiptoes, making ferocious faces, yet ready to run at Homer's first move. He stopped when about four feet away and stuck his tongue out. Homer ignored him. He took another step forward and ran through a series of insulting gestures.

If Tod had known that the boy held a stone in his hand, he would have interfered. But he felt sure that Homer wouldn't hurt the child and was waiting to see if he wouldn't move because of his pestering. When Adore raised his arm, it was too late. The stone hit Homer in the face. The boy turned to flee, but tripped and fell. Before he could scramble away, Homer landed on his back with both feet, then jumped again.

Tod yelled for him to stop and tried to yank him away. He shoved Tod and went on using his heels. Tod hit him as hard as he could, first in the belly, then in the face. He ignored the blows and continued to stamp on the boy. Tod hit him again and again, then threw both arms around him and tried to pull him off. He couldn't budge him. He was like a stone column.

The next thing Tod knew, he was torn loose from Homer and sent to his knees by a blow in the back of the head that spun him sideways. The crowd in front of the theatre had charged. He was surrounded by churning legs and feet. He pulled himself erect by grabbing a man's coat, then let himself be carried along backwards in a long, curving swoop. He saw Homer rise above the mass for a moment, shoved against the sky, his jaw hanging as though he wanted to scream but couldn't. A hand reached up and caught him by his open mouth and pulled him forward and down.

There was another dizzy rush. Tod closed his eyes and fought to keep upright. He was jostled about in a hacking cross surf of shoulders and backs, carried rapidly in one direction and then in the opposite. He kept pushing and hitting out at the people around him, trying to face in the direction he was going. Being carried backwards terrified him.

Using the eucalyptus tree as a landmark, he tried to work toward it by slipping sideways against the tide, pushing hard when carried away from it and riding the current when it moved toward his objective. He was within only a few feet of the tree when a sudden, driving rush carried him far past it. He struggled desperately for a moment, then gave up and let himself be swept along. He was the spearhead of a flying wedge when it collided with a mass going in the opposite direction. The impact turned him around. As the two forces ground against each other, he was turned again and again, like a grain between millstones. This didn't stop until he became part of the opposing force. The pressure continued to increase until he thought he must collapse. He was slowly being pushed into the air. Although relief for his cracking ribs could be gotten by continuing to rise, he fought to keep his feet on the ground. Not being able to touch was an even more dreadful sensation than being carried backwards.

There was another rush, shorter this time, and he found himself in a dead spot where the pressure was less and equal. He became conscious of a terrible pain in his left leg, just above the ankle, and tried to work it into a more comfortable position. He couldn't turn his body, but managed to get his head around. A very skinny boy, wearing a Western Union cap, had his back wedged against his shoulder. The pain continued to grow and his whole leg as high as the groin throbbed. He finally got his left arm free and took the back of the boy's neck in his fingers. He twisted as hard as he could. The boy began to jump up and down in his clothes. He managed to straighten his elbow, by pushing at the back of the boy's head, and so turn half way around and free his leg. The pain didn't grow less.

There was another wild surge forward that ended in another dead spot. He now faced a young girl who was sobbing steadily. Her silk print dress had been torn down the front and her tiny brassiere hung from one strap. He tried by pressing back to give her room, but she moved with him every time he moved. Now and then, she would jerk violently and he wondered if she was going to have a fit. One of her thighs was between his legs. He struggled to get free of her, but she clung to him, moving with him and pressing against him.

She turned her head and said, "Stop, stop," to someone behind her.

He saw what the trouble was. An old man, wearing a Panama hat and horn-rimmed glasses, was hugging her. He had one of his hands inside her dress and was biting her neck.

Tod freed his right arm with a heave, reached over the girl and brought his fist down on the man's head. He couldn't hit very hard but managed to knock the man's hat off, also his glasses. The man tried to bury his face in the girl's shoulder, but Tod grabbed one of his ears and yanked. They started to move again. Tod held on to the ear as long as he could, hoping that it would come away in his hand. The girl managed to twist under his arm. A piece of her dress tore, but she was free of her attacker.

Another spasm passed through the mob and he was carried toward the curb. He fought toward a lamp-post, but he was swept by before he could grasp it. He saw another man catch the girl with the torn dress. She screamed for help. He tried to get to her, but was carried in the opposite direction. This rush also ended in a dead spot. Here his neighbors were all shorter than he was. He turned his head upward toward the sky and tried to pull some fresh air into his aching lungs, but it was all heavily tainted with sweat.

In this part of the mob no one was hysterical. In fact, most of the people seemed to be enjoying themselves. Near him was a stout woman with a man pressing hard against her from in front. His chin was on her shoulder, and his arms were around her. She paid no attention to him and went on talking to the woman at her side.

"The first thing I knew," Tod heard her say, "there was a rush and I was in the middle."

"Yeah. Somebody hollered, 'Here comes Gary Cooper,'[4] and then wham!"

"That ain't it," said a little man wearing a cloth cap and pullover sweater. "This is a riot you're in."

"Yeah," said a third woman, whose snaky gray hair was hanging over her face and shoulders. "A pervert attacked a child."

"He ought to be lynched."

4. Hollywood star (1901–1961), known for playing incorruptible American heroes; his movies of the 1930s included *A Farewell to Arms* (1932) and *Mr. Deeds Goes to Town* (1936).

Everybody agreed vehemently.

"I come from St. Louis," announced the stout woman, "and we had one of them pervert fellers in our neighborhood once. He ripped up a girl with a pair of scissors."

"He must have been crazy," said the man in the cap. "What kind of fun is that?"

Everybody laughed. The stout woman spoke to the man who was hugging her.

"Hey, you," she said. "I ain't no pillow."

The man smiled beatifically but didn't move. She laughed, making no effort to get out of his embrace.

"A fresh guy," she said.

The other woman laughed.

"Yeah," she said, "this is a regular free-for-all."

The man in the cap and sweater thought there was another laugh in his comment about the pervert.

"Ripping up a girl with scissors. That's the wrong tool."

He was right. They laughed even louder than the first time.

"You'd a done it different, eh, kid?" said a young man with a kidney-shaped head and waxed mustaches.

The two women laughed. This encouraged the man in the cap and he reached over and pinched the stout woman's friend. She squealed.

"Lay off that," she said good-naturedly.

"I was shoved," he said.

An ambulance siren screamed in the street. Its wailing moan started the crowd moving again and Tod was carried along in a slow, steady push. He closed his eyes and tried to protect his throbbing leg. This time, when the movement ended, he found himself with his back to the theatre wall. He kept his eyes closed and stood on his good leg. After what seemed like hours, the pack began to loosen and move again with a churning motion. It gathered momentum and rushed. He rode it until he was slammed against the base of an iron rail which fenced the driveway of the theatre from the street. He had the wind knocked out of him by the impact, but managed to cling to the rail. He held on desperately, fighting to keep from being sucked back. A woman caught him around the waist and tried to hang on. She was sobbing rhythmically. Tod felt his fingers slipping from the rail and kicked backwards as hard as he could. The woman let go.

Despite the agony in his leg, he was able to think clearly about his picture, "The Burning of Los Angeles." After his quarrel with Faye, he had worked on it continually to escape tormenting himself, and the way to it in his mind had become almost automatic.

As he stood on his good leg, clinging desperately to the iron rail, he could see all the rough charcoal strokes with which he had blocked it out on the big canvas. Across the top, parallel with the frame, he had drawn the burning city, a great bonfire of architectural styles, ranging from Egyptian to Cape Cod colonial.[5] Through the center, winding from left to right, was a long hill street and down it, spilling into the middle foreground, came the

5. Simple, small, gable-roofed houses modeled after 17th-century New England homes and popular during the Depression.

mob carrying baseball bats and torches. For the faces of its members, he was using the innumerable sketches he had made of the people who come to California to die; the cultists of all sorts, economic as well as religious, the wave, airplane, funeral and preview watchers—all those poor devils who can only be stirred by the promise of miracles and then only to violence. A super "Dr. Know-All Pierce-All" had made the necessary promise and they were marching behind his banner in a great united front of screwballs and screwboxes to purify the land. No longer bored, they sang and danced joyously in the red light of the flames.

In the lower foreground, men and women fled wildly before the vanguard of the crusading mob. Among them were Faye, Harry, Homer, Claude and himself. Faye ran proudly, throwing her knees high. Harry stumbled along behind her, holding on to his beloved derby hat with both hands. Homer seemed to be falling out of the canvas, his face half-asleep, his big hands clawing the air in anguished pantomime. Claude turned his head as he ran to thumb his nose at his pursuers. Tod himself picked up a small stone to throw before continuing his flight.

He had almost forgotten both his leg and his predicament, and to make his escape still more complete he stood on a chair and worked at the flames in an upper corner of the canvas, modeling the tongues of fire so that they licked even more avidly at a corinthian column that held up the palmleaf roof of a nutburger stand.

He had finished one flame and was starting on another when he was brought back by someone shouting in his ear. He opened his eyes and saw a policeman trying to reach him from behind the rail to which he was clinging. He let go with his left hand and raised his arm. The policeman caught him by the wrist, but couldn't lift him. Tod was afraid to let go until another man came to aid the policeman and caught him by the back of his jacket. He let go of the rail and they hauled him up and over it.

When they saw that he couldn't stand, they let him down easily to the ground. He was in the theatre driveway. On the curb next to him sat a woman crying into her skirt. Along the wall were groups of other disheveled people. At the end of the driveway was an ambulance. A policeman asked him if he wanted to go to the hospital. He shook his head no. He then offered him a lift home. Tod had the presence of mind to give Claude's address.

He was carried through the exit to the back street and lifted into a police car. The siren began to scream and at first he thought he was making the noise himself. He felt his lips with his hands. They were clamped tight. He knew then it was the siren. For some reason this made him laugh and he began to imitate the siren as loud as he could.

1939

RICHARD WRIGHT
1908–1960

With the 1940 publication of *Native Son* by the Book-of-the-Month Club, Richard Wright became the most famous African American author of his time. *Native Son* is an uncompromising study of an African American underclass youth who is goaded to brutal violence by the oppression, hatred, and incomprehension of the white world. The sensational story disregarded conventional wisdom about how black authors should approach a white reading audience. Bigger Thomas, the main character, embodied everything that such an audience might fear and detest, but by situating the point of view within this character's consciousness Wright forced readers to see the world through Bigger's eyes and thus to understand him. The novel was structured like a hard-boiled detective story, contained layers of literary allusion and symbol, and combined Marxist social analysis with existential philosophy—in brief, it was at once a powerful social statement and a complex work of literary art.

Wright was born near Natchez, Mississippi. When he was five, his father abandoned the family—Wright, his younger brother, and his mother—and for the next ten years Wright was raised by a series of relatives in Mississippi. By 1925, when he went to Memphis on his own, he had moved twenty times. Extreme poverty, a constantly interrupted education that never went beyond junior high school, and the religious fundamentalism of his grandmother, along with the constant experiences of humiliation and hatred in a racially segregated South: all these contributed to Wright's growing sense that the hidden anger of black people was justified and that only by acknowledging and expressing it could they grapple with it. The title of *Native Son* made the point that the United States is as much the country of black as of white; the story showed that blacks had been deprived of their inheritance.

Two years after moving to Memphis, Wright went north to Chicago. There he took a series of odd jobs and then joined the WPA Writers' Project (a government project of the Depression years to help support authors) as a writer of guidebooks and as a director of the Federal Negro Theater. He began to study Marxist theory, contributing poetry to leftist literary magazines and joining the Communist Party in 1932. By 1935 he had become the center of a group of African American Chicago writers and had started to write fiction. He was influenced by the naturalistic fiction of James T. Farrell, whose study of sociology at the University of Chicago had helped give structure to his popular Studs Lonigan trilogy about working people of Irish descent.

Wright moved to New York in 1937 to write for the New York Writers' Project and as a reporter on the communist *Daily Worker.* In 1938 he published *Uncle Tom's Children,* a collection of four short stories. (An earlier novel, *Lawd Today,* was not published until after his death.) Set in the rural South, the stories center on racial conflict and physical violence. Wright's theme of the devastating effect of relentless, institutionalized hatred and humiliation on the black male's psyche was paramount in all of them.

After *Native Son,* Wright turned to autobiographical writings that eventuated in *Black Boy,* published in 1945. Many consider this to be his best book, and such writers as Ralph Ellison and James Baldwin took it as a model for their own work in the 1950s and 1960s. A communist activist in the early 1940s, Wright became increasingly disillusioned and broke completely with the party in 1944. Visiting France in 1946, he was warmly received by leading writers and philosophers. In 1947 he settled permanently in that country, where he was perceived from the first as one of the important experimental modernist prose writers and was ranked on a level with Hemingway, Fitzgerald, and Faulkner. An existential novel, *The Outsider* (1953), was followed by five more books: two novels and three collections of lectures, travel writings, and sociopolitical commentary. The collection *Eight Men,* from which the story printed here is taken, was the last literary project he worked on, and it appeared the year after his death.

Wright's immersion in Marxist doctrine gave him tools for representing society as divided into antagonistic classes and run for the benefit of the few. But in each of his works he portrays individuals who, no matter how they are deformed and brutalized by oppression and exploitation, retain a transcendent spark of selfhood. Ultimately, it is in this spark that Wright put his faith. His writing from first to last affirmed the dignity and humanity of society's outcasts without romanticizing them, and indicted those who had cast them out. As Ralph Ellison expressed it, Wright's example "converted the American Negro impulse toward self-annihilation and 'going underground' into a will to confront the world" and to "throw his findings unashamedly into the guilty conscience of America."

The text was first published in *Harper's Bazaar* (1939) under the title "Almos' a Man." Under its present title it appeared in *Eight Men* (1961), a posthumous collection of Wright's short fiction.

The Man Who Was Almost a Man

Dave struck out across the fields, looking homeward through paling light. Whut's the use talkin wid em niggers in the field? Anyhow, his mother was putting supper on the table. Them niggers can't understan nothing. One of these days he was going to get a gun and practice shooting, then they couldn't talk to him as though he were a little boy. He slowed, looking at the ground. Shucks, Ah ain scareda them even ef they are biggern me! Aw, Ah know whut Ahma do. Ahm going by ol Joe's sto n git that Sears Roebuck catlog n look at them guns. Mebbe Ma will lemme buy one when she gits mah pay from ol man Hawkins. Ahma beg her t gimme some money. Ahm ol ernough to hava gun. Ahm seventeen. Almost a man. He strode, feeling his long loose-jointed limbs. Shucks, a man oughta hava little gun aftah he done worked hard all day.

He came in sight of Joe's store. A yellow lantern glowed on the front porch. He mounted steps and went through the screen door, hearing it bang behind him. There was a strong smell of coal oil and mackerel fish. He felt very confident until he saw fat Joe walk in through the rear door, then his courage began to ooze.

"Howdy, Dave! Whutcha want?"

"How yuh, Mistah Joe? Aw, Ah don wanna buy nothing. Ah jus wanted t see ef yuhd lemme look at tha catlog erwhile."

"Sure! You wanna see it here?"

"Nawsuh. Ah wans t take it home wid me. Ah'll bring it back termorrow when Ah come in from the fiels."

"You plannin on buying something?"

"Yessuh."

"Your ma lettin you have your own money now?"

"Shucks. Mistah Joe, Ahm gittin t be a man like anybody else!"

Joe laughed and wiped his greasy white face with a red bandanna.

"Whut you plannin on buyin?"

Dave looked at the floor, scratched his head, scratched his thigh, and smiled. Then he looked up shyly.

"Ah'll tell yuh, Mistah Joe, ef yuh promise yuh won't tell."

"I promise."

"Waal, Ahma buy a gun."

"A gun? What you want with a gun?"

"Ah wanna keep it."

"You ain't nothing but a boy. You don't need a gun."

"Aw, lemme have the catlog, Mistah Joe. Ah'll bring it back."

Joe walked through the rear door. Dave was elated. He looked around at barrels of sugar and flour. He heard Joe coming back. He craned his neck to see if he were bringing the book. Yeah, he's got it. Gawddog, he's got it!

"Here, but be sure you bring it back. It's the only one I got."

"Sho, Mistah Joe."

"Say, if you wanna buy a gun, why don't you buy one from me? I gotta gun to sell."

"Will it shoot?"

"Sure it'll shoot."

"Whut kind is it?"

"Oh, it's kinda old . . . a left-hand Wheeler. A pistol. A big one."

"Is it got bullets in it?"

"It's loaded."

"Kin Ah see it?"

"Where's your money?"

"What yuh wan fer it?"

"I'll let you have it for two dollars."

"Just two dollahs? Shucks, Ah could buy tha when Ah git mah pay."

"I'll have it here when you want it."

"Awright, suh. Ah be in fer it."

He went through the door, hearing it slam again behind him. Ahma git some money from Ma n buy me a gun! Only two dollahs! He tucked the thick catalogue under his arm and hurried.

"Where yuh been, boy?" His mother held a steaming dish of black-eyed peas.

"Aw, Ma, Ah just stopped down the road t talk wid the boys."

"Yuh know bettah t keep suppah waitin."

He sat down, resting the catalogue on the edge of the table.

"Yuh git up from there and git to the well n wash yosef! Ah ain feedin no hogs in mah house!"

She grabbed his shoulder and pushed him. He stumbled out of the room, then came back to get the catalogue.

"Whut this?"

"Aw, Ma, it's jusa catlog."

"Who yuh git it from?"

"From Joe, down at the sto."

"Waal, thas good. We kin use it in the outhouse."

"Naw, Ma." He grabbed for it. "Gimme ma catlog, Ma."

She held onto it and glared at him.

"Quit hollerin at me! Whut's wrong wid yuh? Yuh crazy?"

"But Ma, please. It ain mine! It's Joe's! He tol me t bring it back t im termorrow."

She gave up the book. He stumbled down the back steps, hugging the thick book under his arm. When he had splashed water on his face and hands, he groped back to the kitchen and fumbled in a corner for the towel. He bumped into a chair; it clattered to the floor. The catalogue sprawled at his feet. When he had dried his eyes he snatched up the book and held it again under his arm. His mother stood watching him.

"Now, ef yuh gonna act a fool over that ol book, Ah'll take it n burn it up."

"Naw, Ma, please."

"Waal, set down n be still!"

He sat down and drew the oil lamp close. He thumbed page after page, unaware of the food his mother set on the table. His father came in. Then his small brother.

"Whutcha got there, Dave?" his father asked.

"Jusa catlog," he answered, not looking up.

"Yeah, here they is!" His eyes glowed at blue-and-black revolvers. He glanced up, feeling sudden guilt. His father was watching him. He eased the book under the table and rested it on his knees. After the blessing was asked, he ate. He scooped up peas and swallowed fat meat without chewing. Buttermilk helped to wash it down. He did not want to mention money before his father. He would do much better by cornering his mother when she was alone. He looked at his father uneasily out of the edge of his eye.

"Boy, how come yuh don quit foolin wid tha book n eat yo suppah?"

"Yessuh."

"How you n ol man Hawkins gitten erlong?"

"Suh?"

"Can't yuh hear? Why don yuh lissen? Ah ast yu how wuz yuh n ol man Hawkins gittin erlong?"

"Oh, swell, Pa. Ah plows mo lan than anybody over there."

"Waal, yuh oughta keep yo mind on whut yuh doin."

"Yessuh."

He poured his plate full of molasses and sopped it up slowly with a chunk of cornbread. When his father and brother had left the kitchen, he still sat and looked again at the guns in the catalogue, longing to muster courage enough to present his case to his mother. Lawd, ef Ah only had tha pretty one! He could almost feel the slickness of the weapon with his fingers. If he had a gun like that he would polish it and keep it shining so it would never rust. N Ah'd keep it loaded, by Gawd!

"Ma?" His voice was hesitant.

"Hunh?"

"Ol man Hawkins give yuh mah money yit?"

"Yeah, but ain no usa yuh thinking bout throwin nona it erway. Ahm keepin tha money sos yuh kin have cloes t go to school this winter."

He rose and went to her side with the open catalogue in his palms. She was washing dishes, her head bent low over a pan. Shyly he raised the book. When he spoke, his voice was husky, faint.

"Ma, Gawd knows Ah wans one of these."

"One of whut?" she asked, not raising her eyes.

"One of these," he said again, not daring even to point. She glanced up at the page, then at him with wide eyes.

"Nigger, is yuh gone plumb crazy?"

"Aw, Ma."

"Git outta here! Don yuh talk t me bout no gun! Yuh a fool!"

"Ma, Ah kin buy one fer two dollahs."

"Not ef Ah knows it, yuh ain!"

"But yuh promised me one."

"Ah don care whut Ah promised! Yuh ain nothing but a boy yit!"

"Ma, ef yuh lemme buy one Ah'll *never* ast yuh fer nothing no mo."

"Ah tol yuh t git outta here! Yuh ain gonna toucha penny of tha money fer no gun! Thas how come Ah has Mistah Hawkins t pay yo wages t me, cause Ah knows yuh ain got no sense."

"But, Ma, we needa gun. Pa ain got no gun. We needa gun in the house. Yuh kin never tell whut might happen."

"Now don yuh try to maka fool outta me, boy! Ef we did hava gun, yuh wouldn't have it!"

He laid the catalogue down and slipped his arm around her waist.

"Aw, Ma, Ah done worked hard alla summer n ain ast yuh fer nothin, is Ah, now?"

"Thas whut yuh spose t do!"

"But Ma, Ah wans a gun. Yuh kin lemme have two dollahs outta mah money. Please, Ma. I kin give it to Pa . . . Please, Ma! Ah loves yuh, Ma."

When she spoke her voice came soft and low.

"What yuh wan wida gun, Dave? Yuh don need no gun. Yuh'll git in trouble. N ef yo pa jus thought Ah let yuh have money t buy a gun he'd hava fit."

"Ah'll hide it, Ma. It ain but two dollahs."

"Lawd, chil, whut's wrong wid yuh?"

"Ain nothing wrong, Ma. Ahm almos a man now. Ah wans a gun."

"Who gonna sell yuh a gun?"

"Ol Joe at the sto."

"N it don cos but two dollahs?"

"Thas all, Ma. Just two dollahs. Please, Ma."

She was stacking the plates away; her hands moved slowly, reflectively. Dave kept an anxious silence. Finally, she turned to him.

"Ah'll let yuh git tha gun ef yuh promise me one thing."

"Whut's tha, Ma?"

"Yuh bring it straight back t me, yuh hear? It be fer Pa."

"Yessum! Lemme go now, Ma."

She stooped, turned slightly to one side, raised the hem of her dress, rolled down the top of her stocking, and came up with a slender wad of bills.

"Here," she said. "Lawd knows yuh don need no gun. But yer pa does. Yuh bring it right back t me, yuh hear? Ahma put it up. Now ef yuh don, Ahma have yuh pa pick yuh so hard yuh won fergit it."

"Yessum."

He took the money, ran down the steps, and across the yard.

"Dave! Yuuuuuh Daaaaave!"

He heard, but he was not going to stop now. "Naw, Lawd!"

The first movement he made the following morning was to reach under his pillow for the gun. In the gray light of dawn he held it loosely, feeling a sense of power. Could kill a man with a gun like this. Kill anybody, black or white. And if he were holding his gun in his hand, nobody could run over him; they would have to respect him. It was a big gun, with a long barrel and a heavy handle. He raised and lowered it in his hand, marveling at its weight.

He had not come straight home with it as his mother had asked; instead he had stayed out in the fields, holding the weapon in his hand, aiming it now and then at some imaginary foe. But he had not fired it; he had been afraid that his father might hear. Also he was not sure he knew how to fire it.

To avoid surrendering the pistol he had not come into the house until he knew that they were all asleep. When his mother had tiptoed to his bedside late that night and demanded the gun, he had first played possum; then he had told her that the gun was hidden outdoors, that he would bring it to her in the morning. Now he lay turning it slowly in his hands. He broke it, took out the cartridges, felt them, and then put them back.

He slid out of bed, got a long strip of old flannel from a trunk, wrapped the gun in it, and tied it to his naked thigh while it was still loaded. He did not go in to breakfast. Even though it was not yet daylight, he started for Jim Hawkins' plantation. Just as the sun was rising he reached the barns where the mules and plows were kept.

"Hey! That you, Dave?"

He turned. Jim Hawkins stood eying him suspiciously.

"What're yuh doing here so early?"

"Ah didn't know Ah wuz gittin up so early, Mistah Hawkins. Ah wuz fixin t hitch up ol Jenny n take her t the fiels."

"Good. Since you're so early, how about plowing that stretch down by the woods?"

"Suits me, Mistah Hawkins."

"O.K. Go to it!"

He hitched Jenny to a plow and started across the fields. Hot dog! This was just what he wanted. If he could get down by the woods, he could shoot his gun and nobody would hear. He walked behind the plow, hearing the traces creaking, feeling the gun tied tight to his thigh.

When he reached the woods, he plowed two whole rows before he decided to take out the gun. Finally, he stopped, looked in all directions, then untied the gun and held it in his hand. He turned to the mule and smiled.

"Know whut this is, Jenny? Naw, yuh wouldn know! Yuhs jusa ol mule! Anyhow, this is a gun, n it kin shoot, by Gawd!"

He held the gun at arm's length. Whut t hell, Ahma shoot this thing! He looked at Jenny again.

"Lissen here, Jenny! When Ah pull this ol trigger, Ah don wan yuh t run n acka fool now!"

Jenny stood with head down, her short ears pricked straight. Dave walked off about twenty feet, held the gun far out from him at arm's length, and turned his head. Hell, he told himself, Ah ain afraid. The gun felt loose in his fingers; he waved it wildly for a moment. Then he shut his eyes and tightened his forefinger. Bloom! A report half deafened him and he thought his right hand was torn from his arm. He heard Jenny whinnying and galloping over the field, and he found himself on his knees, squeezing his fingers hard between his legs. His hand was numb; he jammed it into his mouth, trying to warm it, trying to stop the pain. The gun lay at his feet. He did not quite know what had happened. He stood up and stared at the gun as though it were a living thing. He gritted his teeth and kicked the gun. Yuh almos broke mah arm! He turned to look for Jenny; she was far over the fields, tossing her head and kicking wildly.

"Hol on there, ol mule!"

When he caught up with her she stood trembling, walling her big white eyes at him. The plow was far away; the traces had broken. Then Dave stopped short, looking, not believing. Jenny was bleeding. Her left side was red and wet with blood. He went closer. Lawd, have mercy! Wondah did Ah shoot this mule? He grabbed for Jenny's mane. She flinched, snorted, whirled, tossing her head.

"Hol on now! Hol on."

Then he saw the hole in Jenny's side, right between the ribs. It was round, wet, red. A crimson stream streaked down the front leg, flowing fast. Good Gawd! Ah wuzn't shootin at tha mule. He felt panic. He knew he had to stop that blood, or Jenny would bleed to death. He had never seen so much blood in all his life. He chased the mule for a half a mile, trying to catch her. Finally she stopped, breathing hard, stumpy tail half arched. He caught her mane and led her back to where the plow and gun lay. Then he stooped and grabbed handfuls of damp black earth and tried to plug the bullet hole. Jenny shuddered, whinnied, and broke from him.

"Hol on! Hol on now!"

He tried to plug it again, but blood came anyhow. His fingers were hot and sticky. He rubbed dirt into his palms, trying to dry them. Then again he attempted to plug the bullet hole, but Jenny shied away, kicking her heels high. He stood helpless. He had to do something. He ran at Jenny; she dodged him. He watched a red stream of blood flow down Jenny's leg and form a bright pool at her feet.

"Jenny . . . Jenny," he called weakly.

His lips trembled. She's bleeding t death! He looked in the direction of home, wanting to go back, wanting to get help. But he saw the pistol lying in the damp black clay. He had a queer feeling that if he only did something, this would not be; Jenny would not be there bleeding to death.

When he went to her this time, she did not move. She stood with sleepy, dreamy eyes; and when he touched her she gave a low-pitched whinny and knelt to the ground, her front knees slopping in blood.

"Jenny . . . Jenny . . ." he whispered.

For a long time she held her neck erect; then her head sank, slowly. Her ribs swelled with a mighty heave and she went over.

Dave's stomach felt empty, very empty. He picked up the gun and held it gingerly between his thumb and forefinger. He buried it at the foot of a tree. He took a stick and tried to cover the pool of blood with dirt—but what was the use? There was Jenny lying with her mouth open and her eyes walled and glassy. He could not tell Jim Hawkins he had shot his mule. But he had to tell something. Yeah, Ah'll tell em Jenny started gittin wil n fell on the joint of the plow. . . . But that would hardly happen to a mule. He walked across the field slowly, head down.

It was sunset. Two of Jim Hawkins' men were over near the edge of the woods digging a hole in which to bury Jenny. Dave was surrounded by a knot of people, all of whom were looking down at the dead mule.

"I don't see how in the world it happened," said Jim Hawkins for the tenth time.

The crowd parted and Dave's mother, father, and small brother pushed into the center.

"Where Dave?" his mother called.

"There he is," said Jim Hawkins.

His mother grabbed him.

"Whut happened, Dave? Whut yuh done?"

"Nothin."

"C mon, boy, talk," his father said.

Dave took a deep breath and told the story he knew nobody believed.

"Waal," he drawled. "Ah brung ol Jenny down here sos Ah could do mah plowin. Ah plowed bout two rows, just like yuh see." He stopped and pointed at the long rows of upturned earth. "Then somethin musta been wrong wid ol Jenny. She wouldn ack right a-tall. She started snortin n kickin her heels. Ah tried t hol her, but she pulled erway, rearin n goin in. Then when the point of the plow was stickin up in the air, she swung erroun n twisted herself back on it . . . She stuck herself n started t bleed. N fo Ah could do anything, she wuz dead."

"Did you ever hear of anything like that in all your life?" asked Jim Hawkins.

There were white and black standing in the crowd. They murmured. Dave's mother came close to him and looked hard into his face. "Tell the truth, Dave," she said.

"Looks like a bullet hole to me," said one man.

"Dave, whut yuh do wid the gun?" his mother asked.

The crowd surged in, looking at him. He jammed his hands into his pockets, shook his head slowly from left to right, and backed away. His eyes were wide and painful.

"Did he hava gun?" asked Jim Hawkins.

"By Gawd, Ah tol yuh tha wu a gun wound," said a man, slapping his thigh.

His father caught his shoulders and shook him till his teeth rattled.

"Tell whut happened, yuh rascal! Tell whut . . ."

Dave looked at Jenny's stiff legs and began to cry.

"Whut yuh do wid tha gun?" his mother asked.

"Whut wuz he doin wida gun?" his father asked.

"Come on and tell the truth," said Hawkins. "Ain't nobody going to hurt you . . ."

His mother crowded close to him.

"Did yuh shoot tha mule, Dave?"

Dave cried, seeing blurred white and black faces.

"Ahh ddinn gggo tt sshooot hher . . . Ah ssswear ffo Gawd Ahh ddin. . . . Ah wuz a-tryin t sssee ef the old gggun would sshoot."

"Where yuh git the gun from?" his father asked.

"Ah got it from Joe, at the sto."

"Where yuh git the money?"

"Ma give it t me."

"He kept worryin me, Bob. Ah had t. Ah tol im t bring the gun right back to me . . . It was fer yuh, the gun."

"But how yuh happen to shoot that mule?" asked Jim Hawkins.

"Ah wuzn shootin at the mule, Mistah Hawkins. The gun jumped when Ah pulled the trigger . . . N fo Ah knowed anythin Jenny was there a-bleedin."

Somebody in the crowd laughed. Jim Hawkins walked close to Dave and looked into his face.

"Well, looks like you have bought you a mule, Dave."

"Ah swear fo Gawd, Ah didn go t kill the mule, Mistah Hawkins!"

"But you killed her!"

All the crowd was laughing now. They stood on tiptoe and poked heads over one another's shoulders.

"Well, boy, looks like yuh done bought a dead mule! Hahaha!"

"Ain tha ershame."

"Hohohohoho."

Dave stood, head down, twisting his feet in the dirt.

"Well, you needn't worry about it, Bob," said Jim Hawkins to Dave's father. "Just let the boy keep on working and pay me two dollars a month."

"Whut yuh wan fer yo mule, Mistah Hawkins?"

Jim Hawkins screwed up his eyes.

"Fifty dollars."

"Whut yuh do wid tha gun?" Dave's father demanded.

Dave said nothing.

"Yuh wan me t take a tree n beat yuh till yuh talk!"

"Nawsuh!"

"Whut yuh do wid it?"

"Ah throwed it erway."

"Where?"

"Ah . . . Ah throwed it in the creek."

"Waal, c mon home. N firs thing in the mawnin git to tha creek n fin tha gun."

"Yessuh."

"Whut yuh pay fer it?"

"Two dollahs."

"Take tha gun n git yo money back n carry it t Mistah Hawkins, yuh hear? N don fergit Ahma lam you black bottom good fer this! Now march yosef on home, suh!"

Dave turned and walked slowly. He heard people laughing. Dave glared, his eyes welling with tears. Hot anger bubbled in him. Then he swallowed and stumbled on.

That night Dave did not sleep. He was glad that he had gotten out of killing the mule so easily, but he was hurt. Something hot seemed to turn over inside him each time he remembered how they had laughed. He tossed on his bed, feeling his hard pillow. N Pa says he's gonna beat me . . . He remembered other beatings, and his back quivered. Naw, naw, Ah sho don wan im t beat me tha way no mo. Dam em all! Nobody ever gave him anything. All he did was work. They treat me like a mule, n then they beat me. He gritted his teeth. N Ma had t tell on me.

Well, if he had to, he would take old man Hawkins that two dollars. But that meant selling the gun. And he wanted to keep that gun. Fifty dollars for a dead mule.

He turned over, thinking how he had fired the gun. He had an itch to fire it again. Ef other men kin shoota gun, by Gawd, Ah kin! He was still, listening. Mebbe they all sleepin now. The house was still. He heard the soft breathing of his brother. Yes, now! He would go down and get that gun and see if he could fire it! He eased out of bed and slipped into overalls.

The moon was bright. He ran almost all the way to the edge of the woods. He stumbled over the ground, looking for the spot where he had buried the gun. Yeah, here it is. Like a hungry dog scratching for a bone, he pawed it up. He puffed his black cheeks and blew dirt from the trigger and barrel. He broke it and found four cartridges unshot. He looked around; the fields were filled with silence and moonlight. He clutched the gun stiff and hard in his fingers. But, as soon as he wanted to pull the trigger, he shut his eyes and turned his head. Naw, An can't shoot wid mah eyes closed n mah head turned. With effort he held his eyes open; then he squeezed. *Bloooom!* He was stiff, not breathing. The gun was still in his hands. Dammit, he'd done it! He fired again. *Blooooom!* He smiled. *Blooooom! Blooooom! Click, click.* There! It was empty. If anybody could shoot a gun, he could. He put the gun into his hip pocket and started across the fields.

When he reached the top of a ridge he stood straight and proud in the moonlight, looking at Jim Hawkins' big white house, feeling the gun sagging in his pocket. Lawd, ef Ah had just one mo bullet Ah'd taka shot at tha house. Ah'd like t scare ol man Hawkins jusa little . . . Jusa enough t let im know Dave Saunders is a man.

To his left the road curved, running to the tracks of the Illinois Central. He jerked his head, listening. From far off came a faint *hooof-hoooof; hoooof-hoooof; hoooof-hoooof*. . . . He stood rigid. Two dollahs a mont. Les see now . . . Tha means it'll take bout two years. Shucks! Ah'll be dam!

He started down the road, toward the tracks. Yeah, here she comes! He stood beside the track and held himself stiffly. Here she comes, erroun the ben . . . C mon, yuh slow poke! C mon! He had his hand on his gun; something quivered in his stomach. Then the train thundered past, the gray and brown box cars rumbling and clinking. He gripped the gun tightly; then he jerked his hand out of his pocket. Ah betcha Bill wouldn't do it! Ah betcha. . . . The cars slid past, steel grinding upon steel. Ahm ridin yuh ternight, so hep me Gawd! He was hot all over. He hesitated just a moment; then he grabbed, pulled atop of a car, and lay flat. He felt his pocket; the gun was still there. Ahead the long rails were glinting in the moonlight, stretching away, away to somewhere, somewhere where he could be a man . . .

1939, 1961

Selected Bibliographies

Reference Works and Histories

Chapters on the period may be consulted in the *Columbia Literary History of the United States* (1988), general editor Emory Elliott; the *Columbia History of the American Novel* (1991), general editor Emory Elliot; the *Columbia History of American Poetry* (1993), edited by Jay Parini; *The History of Southern Literature* (1985), edited by Louis D. Rubin et al.; A. LaVonne Brown Ruoff's *American Indian Literature* (1990); and *The Cambridge History of American Poetry* (2015), edited by Alfred Bendixen and Stephen Burt. Relevant volumes in the eight-volume *Cambridge History of American Literature* are volume 5, *Poetry and Criticism*, 1900–1950 (2003), edited by Sacvan Bercovitch, and volume 6, *Prose Writing*, 1910–1950 (2002), edited by Sacvan Bercovitch and Cyrus R. Patell. Reference works dedicated to the period and some of its important movements include *A Companion to Modernist Literature and Culture*, edited by David Bradshaw and Kevin J. H. Dettmar (2006); *The Cambridge Companion to American Modernism* (2005), edited by Walter Kalaidjian; *The Cambridge Companion to the Harlem Renaissance*, edited by George Hutchinson (2007); *A Companion to Twentieth-Century Poetry*, edited by Neil Roberts (2001); *A Companion to Twentieth-Century American Fiction*, edited by David Seed (2010); *The Cambridge Companion to Modernist Poetry*, edited by Alex Davis and Lee M. Jenkins (2007); *A Companion to Twentieth-Century American Drama* (2005), edited by David Krasner; *A Companion to the Modern American Novel 1900–1950* (2009), edited by John T. Matthews; *The Oxford Critical and Culture History of Modernist Magazines*, Volume 2, *North America, 1894–1960* (2012), edited by Peter Brooker and Andrew Thacker; *The Cambridge Companion to the Literature of the American South* (2013), edited by Sharon Monteith; *A Companion to Modernist Poetry* (2014), edited by David E. Chinitz and Gail McDonald; *A Companion to the Harlem Renaissance* (2015), edited by Cherene Sherrard-Johnson; and *The Cambridge Companion to Modern American Poetry* (2015), edited by Kalaidjian.

For early histories of the period authored by critics who were active in the rise of modernism, see Malcolm Cowley's *Exile's Return* (1951), *After the Genteel Tradition: American Writers, 1910–1930* (1964), and *A Second Flowering: Works and Days of the Lost Generation* (1973); and Edmund Wilson's *The Shores of Light: A Literary Chronicle of the Twenties and Thirties* (1952). Other important early surveys include Alfred Kazin's *On Native Grounds: An Interpretation of Modern American Prose Literature* (1942);

Frederick J. Hoffman's *The Twenties: American Writing in the Postwar Decade* (1955); Harold Clurman's *The Fervent Years: The Story of the Group Theatre and the Thirties* (1957); Walter Rideout's *The Radical Novel in the United States, 1900–1954* (1956); Joseph Wood Krutch's *The American Drama Since 1918* (1957); Daniel Aaron's *Writers on the Left* (1961); Louis D. Rubin's *Writers of the Modern South* (1963); Howard Taubman's *The Making of the American Theater* (1965); Warren French's *The Social Novel at the End of an Era* (1966); Brooks Atkinson's *Broadway: Nineteen Hundred to Nineteen Seventy* (1970); Nathan I. Huggins's *Harlem Renaissance* (1971); Hugh Kenner's *The Pound Era* (1971); and Kenner's *A Homemade World: The American Modernist Writers* (1975).

General books on literary and cultural history appearing since 1980 include David Levering Lewis's *When Harlem Was in Vogue* (1981); Daniel J. Singal's *The War Within: From Victorian to Modernist Thought in the South 1919–1945* (1982); Shari Benstock's *Women of the Left Bank: Paris 1900–1940* (1986); *Modernism and the Harlem Renaissance* (1987), edited by Houston Baker Jr.; Cecilia Tichi's *Shifting Gears: Technology, Literature, Culture in Modernist America* (1987); Joan Shelley Rubin's *The Making of Middlebrow Culture* (1992); Michael North's *The Dialect of Modernism: Race, Language and Twentieth-Century Literature* (1994); George Chauncey's *Gay New York: Gender, Urban Culture, and the Making of the Gay Male World, 1980–1940* (1994); George Hutchinson's *The Harlem Renaissance in Black and White* (1995); Cheryl Wall's *Women of the Harlem Renaissance* (1995); Walter Benn Michaels's *Our America* (1995); Ann Douglas's *Terrible Honesty: Mongrel Manhattan in the 1920s* (1995); Ross Posnock's *Color and Culture: Black Writers and the Making of the Modern Intellectual* (1998); William J. Maxwell's *New Negro, Old Left: African-American Writing and Communism between the Wars* (1999); Christine Stansell's *American Moderns: Bohemian New York and the Creation of a New Century* (1999); David G. Nicholls's *Conjuring the Folk: Forms of Modernity in African America* (2000); Michael Szalay's *New Deal Modernism: American Literature and the Invention of the Welfare State* (2000); Edward Pavlic's *Crossroads Modernism: Descent and Emergence in African-American Literary Culture* (2002); Catherine Turner's *Marketing Modernism between the Two World Wars* (2003); Tim Armstrong's *Modernism: A Cultural History* (2005); Daphne Lamothe's *Inventing the New Negro: Narrative, Culture, and Ethnography* (2008); Sarah Wilson's *Melting-Pot Modernism* (2010); Erick King Watts's *Hearing the Hurt: Rhetoric, Aesthetics, and Politics of the New Negro Movement* (2012); Jeffrey Hart's *The Living Moment: Modernism in a Broken World* (2012); Pearl James's *The New Death: American Modernism and World War I* (2013); Hazel Hutchison's *The War That Used Up Words: American Writers and the First World War* (2015); and Ichiro Takayoshi's *American Writers and the Approach of World War II, 1930–1941* (2015).

Literary Theory and Criticism

For an introduction to the ideas of literary criticism during the period, see Rene Wellek's *A History of Modern Criticism: American Criticism, 1900–*

1950, volume 7 (1987); and Vincent B. Leitch's *American Literary Criticism from the 30s to the 80s* (1988). Gordon Hutner's *American Literature, American Culture* (1998) reprints a number of critical statements from the period. Gerald's Graff's *Professing Literature: An Institutional History* (1987); Lawrence H. Schwartz's *Creating Faulkner's Reputation: The Politics of Modern Literary Criticism* (1988); and Mark Jancovich's *The Cultural Politics of the New Criticism* (1994) analyze aspects of American literary criticism in the period and its aftermath.

Theoretical treatments of modernism (often in international perspectives) include Andreas Huyssen's *After the Great Divide: Modernism, Mass Culture, Postmodernism* (1986); Ashadur Eyssteinsson's *The Concept of Modernism* (1991); Joseph N. Riddel's *The Turning Word: American Literary Modernism and Continental Theory* (1996); Leonard Diepeveen's *The Difficulties of Modernism* (2003); Michael Trask's *Cruising Modernism: Class and Sexuality in American Literature and Social Thought* (2003); Susan McCabe's *Cinematic Modernism: Modernist Poetry and Film* (2005); Robert Scholes's *Paradoxy of Modernism* (2006); and John Carlos Rowe's *Afterlives of Modernism: Liberalism, Transnationalism, and Political Critique* (2011).

Criticism of poetry published since 1980 includes M. L. Rosenthal and Sally M. Gall's *The Modern Poetic Sequence: The Genius of Modern Poetry* (1984); William Drake's *The First Wave: Women Poets in America, 1914–1945* (1987); Albert Gelpi's *A Coherent Splendor: The American Poetic Renaissance, 1910–1950* (1987); Lisa M. Steinman's *Made in America: Science, Technology, and American Modernist Poets* (1987); *Shadowed Dreams: Women's Poetry of the Harlem Renaissance* (1989), edited by Maureen Honey; Cary Nelson's *Repression and Recovery: Modern American Poetry and the Politics of Cultural Memory, 1910–1945* (1989); Elisa New's *Fictions of Form in American Poetry* (1993); Frank Lentricchia's *Modernist Quartet* (1994); Elizabeth Gregory's *Quotation and Modern America Poetry: Imaginary Gardens with Real Toads* (1996); Rachel Blau DuPlessis's *Genders, Races, and Religious Cultures in Modern American Poetries, 1908–1934* (2001); Merrill Cole's *The Other Orpheus: A Poetics of Modern Homosexuality* (2003); Jennifer Ashton's *From Modernism to Postmodernism: American Poetry and Theory in the Twentieth Century* (2005); Rachel Potter's *Modernism and Democracy: Literary Culture, 1900–1930* (2006); Charles Altieri's *The Art of Twentieth-Century American Poetry: Modernism and After* (2006); and Joel Nickels's *The Poetry of the Possible: Spontaneity, Modernism, and the Multitude* (2012).

Critical studies of fiction published since 1980 include Hazel V. Carby's *Reconstructing Womanhood: The Emergence of the Afro-American Woman Novelist* (1987); Linda Wagner-Martin's *The Modern American Novel, 1914–1945* (1990); J. Gerald Kennedy's *Imagining Paris* (1993); Barbara Foley's *Radical Representations: Politics and Form in U.S. Proletarian Fiction, 1929–41* (1993); David Minter's *A Cultural History of the American Novel* (1994); Laura Hapke's *Daughters of the Great Depression: Women, Work, and Fiction in the American 1930s* (1995); Gordon Hutner's *What America Read: Taste, Class, and the Novel, 1920–1960* (2009); Lawrence Buell's *The Dream of the Great American Novel* (2014); and David M. Ball's *False Starts: The Rhetoric of Failure and the Making of American Modernism* (2014).

Critical studies of drama published since 1980 include C. W. E. Bigsby's *A Critical Introduction to Twentieth-Century American Drama*, volume 1,

1900–1940 (1985); Ethan Mordden's *The American Theatre* (1981); Brenda Murphy's *American Realism and American Drama, 1880–1940* (1987); David Krasner's *A Beautiful Pageant: African American Theatre, Drama, and Performance in the Harlem Renaissance, 1910–1927* (2002); Julia A. Walker's *Expressionism and Modernism in the American Theatre: Bodies, Voices, Words* (2005); Soyica Diggs Colbert's *The African-American Theatrical Body: Reception, Performance, and the Stage* (2011); and Andrea Most's *Theatrical Liberalism: Jews and Popular Entertainment in America* (2013).

AMERICAN LITERATURE 1914–1945

Sherwood Anderson
In addition to works mentioned in the author's headnote, Anderson published *The Modern Writer* (1925); *Sherwood Anderson's Notebook* (1925); *Alice and the Lost Novel* (1929); *Nearer the Grass Roots* (1929); *The American Country Fair* (1930); and *Home Town* (1940). The Library of America published his *Collected Stories* (2012), edited by Charles Baxter. The Norton Critical Edition of *Winesburg, Ohio* (1996), edited by Charles E. Modlin and Ray Lewis White, includes background materials and critical essays, as does the edition edited by John H. Ferres (1996). White edited a variorum edition of *Winesburg, Ohio* (1997) as well as *Sherwood Anderson's Memoirs: A Critical Edition* (1969). *The Letters of Sherwood Anderson* (1953) were edited by Howard Mumford Jones and Walter Rideout. See also *Sherwood Anderson: Selected Letters* (1984), edited by Charles E. Modlin, and *Letters to Bab: Sherwood Anderson to Marietta D. Finley, 1916–1933* (1985), edited by William A. Sutton. A two-volume biography by Walter Rideout is *Sherwood Anderson: A Writer in America* (2006–7). For critical commentary see *Sherwood Anderson: A Collection of Critical Essays* (1974), edited by Walter Rideout; *New Essays on Winesburg, Ohio* (1990), edited by John W. Crowley; Allen Papinchak's *Sherwood Anderson: A Study of the Short Fiction* (1992); Judy Jo Small's *A Reader's Guide to the Short Stories of Sherwood Anderson* (1994); Ray Lewis White's *Winesburg, Ohio: An Exploration* (1990); and Clarence Lindsay's *Such a Rare Thing: The Art of Sherwood Anderson's Winesburg, Ohio* (2009).

Sterling Brown
Brown's *Collected Poems*, selected by Michael S. Harper (1989, 1996), includes *Southern Road, No Hiding Place* as well as additional individual poems. *A Son's Return: Selected Essays of Sterling A. Brown* (1996) is edited by Mark A. Sanders, and Sanders with John Edgar Tidwell edited *Sterling A. Brown's A Negro Looks at the South* (2007). A special issue of the journal *Callaloo*, 5 (1982), contains a bibliography by Robert G. O'Meally along with reminiscences and critical assessments by several scholars. Full-length studies are Joanne V. Gabbin's *Sterling A. Brown: Building the Black Aesthetic Tradition* (1985), and Mark A. Sanders's *Afro-Modernist Aesthetics and the Poetry of Sterling A. Brown* (1999). There are discussions of Brown in Stephen Henderson's *Understanding the New Black Poetry* (1973); Jean Wagner's *Black Poetry* (1973); Henry Louis Gates, Jr.'s *Figures in Black: Words, Signs, and the "Racial" Self* (1987); Victor Kramer's *The Harlem Renaissance Reconsidered* (1987); and Cary Nelson's *Repression and Recovery* (1989). *After Winter: The Art and Life of Sterling A. Brown* (2009), edited by Tidwell and Steven C. Tracy, includes a wide selection of critical essays.

Willa Cather
Cather's volume of verse, *April Twilights* (1903; rev. 1923; reissued with an introduction by Bernice Slote, 1990), and her collection of essays, *Not under Forty* (1936), supplement the standard edition of her fiction, *The Novels and Stories of Willa Cather* (1937–41), and the scholarly editions (1992–2015) under the general editorship of Guy Reynolds. Her stories, novels, poems, and essays were published in three volumes by the Library of America with notes by Sharon O'Brien (1987, 1990, 1992). *The Selected Letters of Willa Cather* (2013) was edited by Andrew Jewell and Janis Stout. Other sources include *Willa Cather on Writing* (1949); *Writings from Willa Cather's Campus Years* (1950), edited by James Shively; and *The Kingdom of Art: Willa Cather's First Principles and Critical Statements* (1967), edited by Bernice Slote. William M. Curtin collected articles and reviews in the two-volume *The World and the Parish* (1970). Personal memoirs include Edith Lewis's *Willa Cather Living* (1953, 2000), and Elizabeth Sergeant's *Willa Cather: A Memoir* (1953, 1992). Janis P. Stout's *A Calendar of the Let-*

ters of Willa Cather (2002), and the biography *Willa Cather: The Writer and Her World* (2000) are worthwhile. Phyllis C. Robinson's *Willa: The Life of Willa Cather* (1982) is a full-length biography, as is James Woodress's *Willa Cather: A Literary Life* (1987). Sharon O'Brien's *Willa Cather: The Emerging Voice* (1987) concentrates on Cather's early years.

Critical studies of Cather are David Stouck's *Willa Cather's Imagination* (1975); Marilyn Arnold's *Willa Cather's Short Fiction* (1984) and *Willa Cather: A Reference Guide* (1986); Susan J. Rosowski's *The Voyage Perilous: Willa Cather's Romanticism* (1986); Sally P. Harvey's *Redefining the American Dream: The Novels of Willa Cather* (1995); Joseph R. Urgo's *Willa Cather and the Myth of American Migration* (1995); Guy Reynolds's *Willa Cather in Context* (1996); O'Brien's *New Essays on My Ántonia* (1999); Ann Romines's *Willa Cather's Southern Connection* (2000); Joan Acocella's *Willa Cather and the Politics of Criticism* (2000); and David Porter's *On the Divide: The Many Lives of Willa Cather* (2008) on her relationship to the literary marketplace. Janis P. Stout edited *Willa Cather and Material Culture: Real-World Writing and Writing the Real World* (2005). Also useful is *Violence, the Arts, and Willa Cather* (2007), edited by Joseph R. Urgo and Merrill Maguire Skaggs.

Hart Crane

Langdon Hammer edited *Hart Crane: Complete Poems and Selected Letters* (2006) for the Library of America. Crane's *Collected Poems*, edited by his friend Waldo Frank, appeared in 1933. Lawrence Kramer edited *The Bridge: An Annotated Edition* (2011). *Correspondence between Hart Crane and Waldo Frank* (1998) was edited by Steve H. Cook. Other sources of primary and bibliographical material are *My Land, My Friends: The Selected Letters of Hart Crane* (1997), edited by Langdon Hammer and Brom Weber; *Hart Crane: An Annotated Critical Bibliography* (1970), edited by Joseph Schwartz; and *Hart Crane: A Descriptive Bibliography* (1972), edited by Joseph Schwartz and Robert C. Schweik. Gary Lane compiled *A Concordance to the Poems of Hart Crane* (1972). Biographies of Crane are John Unterecker's *Voyager: A Life of Hart Crane* (1969); Paul Mariani's *The Broken Tower: A Life of Hart Crane* (2000); and Clive Fisher's *Hart Crane: A Life* (2002).

Useful earlier studies are R. W. B. Lewis's *The Poetry of Hart Crane* (1967); Monroe K. Spears's *Hart Crane* (1965); and Hunce Voelcker's *The Hart Crane Voyages* (1967). See also Richard P. Sugg's *Hart Crane's "The Bridge"* (1976); Helge Norman Nilsen's *Hart Crane's Divided Vision: An Analysis of "The Bridge"* (1980); Edward Brunner's *Hart Crane and the Making of "The Bridge"* (1984); Paul Giles's *Hart Crane: The Contexts of The Bridge* (1986); Thomas E. Yingling's *Hart Crane and the Homosexual Text* (1990); Brian M. Reed's *Hart Crane: After His Lights* (2006); Daniel Gabriel's *Hart Crane and the Modernist Epic: Canon and Genre Formation in Crane, Pound, Eliot and Williams* (2007); and John T. Irwin, *Hart Crane's Poetry: "Appollinaire Lived in Paris, I Live in Cleveland, Ohio"* (2011).

Countee Cullen

The Library of America issued Cullen's *Collected Poems* (2013), edited by Major Jackson. Cullen's groundbreaking anthology of 1927, *Caroling Dusk*, was reissued in 1993. His poetry volume, *Color*, originally published in 1925, was also reissued in 1993. *My Soul's High Song*, a collection of his writings edited by Gerald Early, appeared in 1991. *And Bid Him Sing: A Biography of Countée Cullen*, by Charles Molesworth, appeared in 2012. Earlier work of interest includes Helen J. Dinger's *A Study of Countee Cullen* (1953); Margaret Perry's *A Bio-Bibliography of Countee P. Cullen* (1969); Blanche E. Ferguson's *Countee Cullen and the Negro Renaissance* (1966); and Alan R. Shucard's *Countee Cullen* (1984).

E. E. Cummings

Complete Poems 1904–62, edited by George J. Firmage, was published in 1991. Firmage also edited *Three Plays and a Ballet* (1967). Cummings's prose fiction includes *The Enormous Room* (1922) and *EIMI* (1933). *E. E. Cummings: A Miscellany Revised* (1965), edited by Firmage, contains previously uncollected short prose pieces. *Six Nonlectures* (1953) consists of the talks that Cummings delivered at Harvard in the same year. A gathering of works is *Another E. E. Cummings* (1999), edited by Richard Kostceanetz. *Selected Letters of E. E. Cummings* (1969) was edited by F. W. Dupee and George Stade. Firmage edited *E. E. Cummings: A Bibliography* (1960). Barry Ahearn edited *The Correspondence of Ezra Pound and E. E. Cummings* (1996).

Several of Cummings's earlier works have been reedited by Firmage in the Cummings Typescript Editions. These include *Tulips & Chimneys* (1976); *No Thanks* (1978); *The Enormous Room*, with illustrations by Cummings (1978); *ViVa* (1979); *XAIPE* (1979); and *Etcetera*, the unpublished poems (1983).

Biographies are Richard S. Kennedy's *Dreams in the Mirror* (1979, 1994) and Susan Cheever's *E. E. Cummings: A Life* (2014). Early studies include Norman Friedman's *E. E. Cummings: The Growth of a Writer* (1964); Robert E. Wegner's *The Poetry and Prose of E. E. Cummings* (1965); and Rushworth Kidder's *E. E. Cummings, An Introduction to the*

Poetry (1979). See also Cary Lane's *I Am: A Study of E. E. Cummings' Poems* (1976), and Richard S. Kennedy's *E. E. Cummings Revisited* (1994). Norman Friedman edited *E. E. Cummings: A Collection of Critical Essays* (1972) and authored *(Re)Valuing Cummings: Further Essays on the Poet* (1996). David G. Farley's *Modernist Travel Writing: Intellectuals Abroad* (2010) compares Cummings and Ezra Pound.

Hilda Doolittle (H.D.)

H.D.'s poetry through 1944 has been collected and edited by Louis L. Martz in *Collected Poems 1912–1944* (1983). *Collected Poems of H.D.* was published in 1925. Subsequent volumes of poetry include *Red Rose for Bronze* (1931); the trilogy of war poems *The Walls Do Not Fall* (1944), *Tribute to the Angels* (1945), and *The Flowering of the Rod* (1946); the dramatic monologue *Helen in Egypt* (1961); the major collection of her late poems, *Hermetic Definition* (1972); and the long poem *Vale Ave* (1992). H.D.'s other book-length verse dramas are *Hippolytus Temporizes* (1927) and the translation of *Euripides' Ion* (1937). *Palimpsest* (1926), *Hadylus* (1928), *Bid Me to Live* (1961), *HERmione* (1981), and *Asphodel* (1992), edited by Robert Spoo, compose her major prose fiction. *By Avon River* (1949) celebrates Shakespeare in prose and verse. *Tribute to Freud* (1956) is her account of her psychoanalysis by Freud. Also important are two autobiographical works: *End to Torment* (1979) and *The Gift* (1982, complete edition 1998). Michael Boughn compiled *H.D.: A Bibliography, 1905–1990* (1993). *Richard Aldington and H.D.: The Early Years in Letters* (1992), edited by Caroline Zilboorg, collects correspondence. Zilboorg also edited a scholarly edition of *Bid Me to Live* (2012).

Barbara Guest's *Herself Defined: The Poet H.D. and Her World* (1984) is a biography; Rachel Blau DuPlessis's *H.D.: The Career of That Struggle* (1986); Susan S. Friedman's *Psyche Reborn: The Emergence of H.D.* (1981); and Janice S. Robinson's *H.D.: The Life and Work of an American Poet* (1982) combine biography and literary analysis. Among critical books are Gary Burnett's *H. D.: Between Image and Epic, The Mysteries of Her Poetics* (1990); Friedman's *Penelope's Web: Gender, Modernity, and H.D.'s Fiction* (1990); Eileen Gregory's *H.D. and Hellenism* (1997); Diana Collecott's *H.D and Sapphic Modernism* (1999); Georgia Taylor's *H.D. and the Public Sphere of Modernist Women Writers 1913–1946* (2001); Adalaide Morris's *How to Live/What to Do: H.D.'s Cultural Poetics* (2003); and Annette Debo's *The American H.D.* (2012). Nephie J. Christodoulides and Polina Mackay edited *The Cambridge Companion to H. D.* (2011).

John Dos Passos

The Library of America reissued *U.S.A.* in a single volume (1997), followed by *Travel Books and Other Writings, 1916–1941* (2003) and *Novels, 1920–1925* (2003). John Rohrkemper's *John Dos Passos, A Reference Guide* appeared in 1980. Two biographies are Virginia Spencer Carr's *Dos Passos: A Life* (1984) and Townsend Ludlington's *John Dos Passos: A Twentieth Century Odyssey* (1980). *Dos Passos: A Collection of Critical Essays* was edited by Andrew Hook in 1974 and *Dos Passos: The Critical Heritage*, edited by Barry Maine, appeared in 1988 and was reissued in 1997. Useful books include Linda W. Wagner's *Dos Passos: The Artist as American* (1979); Robert C. Rosen's *John Dos Passos: Politics and the Writer* (1981); Donald Pizer's *Dos Passos' U.S.A.: A Critical Study* (1990); Janet Casey's *Dos Passos and the Ideology of the Feminine* (1998); and Seth Moglen's *Mourning Modernity: Literary Modernism and the Injuries of American Capitalism* (2007).

T. S. Eliot

Eliot's poetic works have been collected in *Collected Poems, 1909–1962* (1963) and *The Complete Poems and Plays of T. S. Eliot* (1969). *Inventions of the March Hare: Poems 1909–1917* (1997), edited by Christopher Ricks, contains early, previously unpublished poetry. The indispensable manuscript to *The Waste Land* is in *The Waste Land: A Facsimile and Transcript of the Original Drafts Including the Annotations of Ezra Pound* (1971), edited by Valerie Eliot. Michael North edited a Norton Critical Edition of *The Waste Land* (2001), and Lawrence Rainey edited *The Annotated Waste Land with Eliot's Contemporary Prose* (2005). Important critical writings include *The Use of Poetry and the Use of Criticism* (1933), *Poetry and Drama* (1951), *The Three Voices of Poetry* (1953), *On Poetry and Poets* (1957), and *To Criticize the Critic and Other Writings* (1965). Three volumes of social commentary are *After Strange Gods* (1934), *The Idea of a Christian Society* (1939), and *Notes toward the Definition of Culture* (1948). Valerie Eliot's edition of *The Letters of T. S. Eliot* (1988–2015) has reached five volumes, up to 1933. J. L. Dawson edited *Concordance to the Complete Poems and Plays of T. S. Eliot* (1995). Good biographies are Peter Ackroyd's *T. S. Eliot: A Life* (1984); Lyndall Gordon's *T. S. Eliot: An Imperfect Life* (1998, 2000), an updating of her earlier biographies; James E. Miller Jr.'s *T. S. Eliot: The Making of an American Poet, 1888–1922* (2005); and Robert Crawford's *Young Eliot: A Biography* (2015).

Influential earlier studies of Eliot include F. O. Matthiessen's *The Achievement of T. S. Eliot* (rev. 1947); Helen Gardner's *The Art of T. S. Eliot* (1950); Hugh Kenner's *The*

Invisible Poet (1959), Northrop Frye's *T. S. Eliot* (1963); and Stephen Spender's *T. S. Eliot* (1976).

Among numerous critical studies are Helen Gardner's *The Composition of Four Quartets* (1978); Derek Traversi's *T. S. Eliot: The Longer Poems* (1976); Louis Menand's *Discovering Modernism: T. S. Eliot and His Context* (1987); Jewel Spears Brooker and Joseph Bentley's *Reading "The Waste Land": Modernism and the Limits of Interpretation* (1990); Brooker's *Mastery and Escape: T. S. Eliot and the Dialectic of Modernism* (1994); A. David Moody's *Thomas Stearns Eliot, Poet* (1994); Anthony Julius's *T. S. Eliot, Anti-Semitism, and Literary Form* (1996); Ronald Schuchard's *Eliot's Dark Angel: Intersections of Life and Art* (2001); David Chintz's *T. S. Eliot and the Cultural Divide* (2003); and Craig Raine's *T. S. Eliot* (2006). Moody also edited the useful *Cambridge Companion to T. S. Eliot* (1994). For collections of critical essays about Eliot, see *T. S. Eliot: A Collection of Criticism* (1974), edited by Linda W. Wagner (1974); *T. S. Eliot: The Modernist in History* (1991), edited by Ronald Bush; and *Gender, Desire, and Sexuality in T. S. Eliot* (2004), edited by Cassandra Laity and Nancy K. Gish. Gareth Reeves's *T. S. Eliot's "The Waste Land"* (1994) is a comprehensive introduction to the poem.

Donald C. Gallup compiled the standard bibliography, *T. S. Eliot: A Bibliography* (rev. 1969).

William Faulkner

The Library of America issued Faulkner's novels in four volumes: 1930–1935 (1985), 1936–1940 (1990), 1942–1954 (1994), and 1957–1962 (1999). In addition to the volumes mentioned in the author's headnote are *Early Prose and Poetry* (1962), edited by Carvel Collins; *Dr. Martino and Other Stories* (1934); *Pylon* (1935); *The Unvanquished* (1938); *Intruder in the Dust* (1948); *Knight's Gambit* (1949); *Collected Stories of William Faulkner* (1950); *Requiem for a Nun* (1951); *Notes on a Horsethief* (1951); *Big Woods* (1955); and *Essays, Speeches, and Public Letters* (rev. 2004), edited by James B. Meriwether. Transcripts of discussions and interviews with Faulkner include *Faulkner at Nagano* (1956), edited by Robert A. Jelliffe; *Faulkner in the University* (1959), edited by Frederick L. Gwynn and Joseph L. Blotner; *Faulkner at West Point* (1964), edited by Joseph L. Fant and Robert Ashley (1964); and *The Lion in the Garden* (1968), edited by Meriwether and Michael Millgate. Letters are collected in *The Faulkner-Cowley File* (1961), edited by Malcolm Cowley (1961), and *Selected Letters of William Faulkner* (1977), edited by Joseph L. Blotner. Noel Polk has produced editions of several Faulkner novels based on a study of the manuscripts. Michael Gorra and Polk have published a Norton Critical Edition of *The Sound and the Fury* (2014), and Gorra has also published one of *As I Lay Dying* (2010).

Blotner's *Faulkner: A Biography*, 2 volumes (1974) is condensed and updated in *Faulkner* (1984). Two shorter biographies based on Blotner's work are David Minter's *William Faulkner: His Life and Work* (1980) and Judith Wittenberg's *Faulkner: The Transfiguration of Biography* (1979).

Comprehensive guides are Thomas E. Connolly's *Faulkner's World: A Directory of His People and Synopsis of Actions in His Published Works* (1988); and *A William Faulkner Encyclopedia* (1999), edited by Robert W. Hamblin and Charles E. Peek. Teresa Towner's *Cambridge Introduction to William Faulkner* (2008) and John T. Matthews's edited *New Cambridge Companion to William Faulkner* (2015) are useful. Influential early studies include Cleanth Brooks's *William Faulkner: The Yoknapatawpha Country* (1963) and Hyatt H. Waggoner's *William Faulkner: From Jefferson to the World* (1959). Later studies include John T. Irwin's *Doubling and Incest, Repetition and Revenge: A Speculative Reading of Faulkner* (1975); Thadious M. Davis's Faulkner's *"Negro": Art and the Southern Context* (1983); Eric J. Sundquist's *Faulkner: The House Divided* (1983); Robert Dale Parker's *Faulkner and the Novelistic Imagination* (1985); Warwick Wadlington's *Reading Faulknerian Tragedy* (1987) and *As I Lay Dying: Stories out of Stories* (1992); Minrose C. Gwin's *The Feminine and Faulkner: Reading (beyond) Sexual Difference* (1990); André Bleikasten's *The Ink of Melancholy: Faulkner's Novels from "The Sound and the Fury" to "Light in August"* (1990); Richard Moreland's *Faulkner and Modernism: Rereading and Rewriting* (1990); Joel Williamson's *William Faulkner and Southern History* (1993); Diane Roberts's *Faulkner and Southern Womanhood* (1994); David Minter's *Faulkner's Questioning Narratives: Fiction of His Major Phase, 1929–42* (2001); Philip Weinstein's *Becoming Faulkner: The Art and Life of William Faulkner* (2010); and Candace Waid's *The Signifying Eye: Seeing Faulkner's Art* (2013).

Edited collections of critical essays include Louis J. Budd and Edwin Cady's *On Faulkner* (1989); Linda Wagner-Martin's *Faulkner: Six Decades of Criticism* (2002); Annette Trefzer's *Global Faulkner: Faulkner and Yoknapatawpha, 2006* (2009); and Peter Lurie and Ann J. Abadie's *Faulkner and Film* (2014).

F. Scott Fitzgerald

Fitzgerald's novels are *This Side of Paradise* (1920), *The Beautiful and Damned* (1922), *The Great Gatsby* (1925), *Tender Is the Night* (1934; rev. 1939; rpt. 1953), and the unfinished *The Last Tycoon* (1941). His collections of stories are *Flappers and Philosophers*

(1921), *Tales of the Jazz Age* (1922), *All the Sad Young Men* (1926), and *Taps at Reveille* (1935). Two recent editions of his fiction are the Library of America's *Novels and Stories 1920–1922* (2000) and Matthew J. Bruccoli and Judith Baughman's *Before Gatsby: The First Twenty-Six Stories* (2001). The Cambridge Edition of Fitzgerald's works (1991–2014) includes his novels, story collections, and *My Lost City: Personal Essays, 1920–1940* (2005). A satirical play, *The Vegetable, or From Presidents to Postman*, was published in 1923. Among collections of Fitzgerald's writings are *F. Scott Fitzgerald in His Own Time: A Miscellany* (1971), edited by Jackson R. Bryer and Bruccoli, and *Afternoon of an Author* (1957), edited by Arthur Mizener. *The Crack-Up* (1945), edited by Edmund Wilson, collects essays, notebook entries, and letters from the 1930s; youthful work is collected in *F. Scott Fitzgerald: The Princeton Years; Selected Writings, 1914–1920* (1966), edited by Chip Defaa.

The fullest collection of letters is *Correspondence of F. Scott Fitzgerald* (1980), edited by Bruccoli and Margaret M. Duggan. Other volumes of letters are *Dear Scott/Dear Max: The Fitzgerald-Perkins Correspondence* (1971), edited by John Kuehl and Jackson R. Bryer; *As Ever, Scott Fitz* (1972), edited by Bruccoli and Jennifer McCabe Atkinson (letters between Fitzgerald and his literary agent, Harold Ober); and *Dear Scott, Dearest Zelda: The Love Letters of F. Scott and Zelda Fitzgerald* (2002), edited by Jackson R. Bryer and Cathy W. Barks. Biographies include Bruccoli's *Some Sort of Epic Grandeur: The Life of F. Scott Fitzgerald* (1981), Scott Donaldson's *Fool for Love: F. Scott Fitzgerald, A Biographical Portrait* (1983), James Mellow's *Invented Lives* (1984), Jeffrey Myers's *Scott Fitzgerald* (2000), and Andrew Turnbull's *Scott Fitzgerald* (2001).

Among guides are Robert Gale's *An F. Scott Fitzgerald Encyclopedia* (1998); Linda Pelzer's *Student Companion to F. Scott Fitzgerald* (2001); and Kirk Curnutt's *Cambridge Introduction to F. Scott Fitzgerald* (2007). Critical studies include Milton R. Stern's *The Golden Moment: The Novels of F. Scott Fitzgerald* (1970); Brian Way's *F. Scott Fitzgerald and the Art of Social Fiction* (1980); John Kuehl's *F. Scott Fitzgerald, a Study of the Short Fiction* (1991); and Scott Donaldson's *Fitzgerald and Hemingway: Works and Days* (2009). Among collections of critical essays are *The Short Stories of F. Scott Fitzgerald: New Approaches in Criticism* (1983), edited by Jackson R. Bryer; *New Essays on "The Great Gatsby"* (1985), edited by Bruccoli; *The Cambridge Companion to F. Scott Fitzgerald* (2001), edited by Ruth Prigozy; *F. Scott Fitzgerald in the Twenty-First Century* (2003), edited by Jackson R. Bryer, Prigozy, and Milton B. Stern; and *F. Scott Fitzgerald in Context* (2013), edited by Bryant Mangum.

Robert Frost

The Poetry of Robert Frost (1969) incorporated *Complete Poems* (1949) and Frost's last volume, *In the Clearing* (1962). The Library of America issued Frost's *Collected Poems, Prose, and Plays* (1995). Mark Richardson edited *The Collected Prose of Robert Frost* (2007), and Robert Faggen edited *The Notebooks of Robert Frost* (2007). Richardson and Donald Sheehy edited *The Letters of Robert Frost*, volume 1 (2014). Important collections of letters appear in *Selected Letters of Robert Frost* (1964), edited by Lawrence Thompson; *The Letters of Robert Frost to Louis Untermeyer* (1963); and Margaret Anderson's, *Robert Frost and John Bartlett: The Record of a Friendship* (1963). Conversations and interviews with Frost include Edward C. Lathem's *Interviews with Robert Frost* (1966); Reginald L. Cook's *The Dimensions of Robert Frost* (1964); Daniel Smythe's *Robert Frost Speaks* (1954); and Louis Mertin's *Robert Frost: Life and Talks—Walking* (1965).

Lawrance Thompson completed two volumes of the authorized biography: *Robert Frost: The Early Years, 1874–1915* (1966) and *Robert Frost: The Years of Triumph, 1915–1938* (1970). The third volume, *Robert Frost, the Later Years (1976)*, was completed by Richard Winnick, and Lathem produced a shorter version of the biography in *Robert Frost: A Biography* (1981). Other biographies are Jeffrey Meyers's *Robert Frost* (1996) and Jay Parini's *Robert Frost: A Life* (1999). William H. Pritchard in *Frost: A Literary Life Reconsidered* (1984) is interested in the poet's art, not his personal life. James L. Potter's *Robert Frost Handbook* (1980) is a useful guide; Lathem produced a concordance to Frost's poetry (1994).

A brief critical introduction is Mordecai Marcus's *The Poems of Robert Frost* (1991). Other critical studies are Richard Poirier's *Robert Frost, The Work of Knowing* (1977, reissued with new material in 1990); John C. Kemp's *Robert Frost and New England: The Poet as Regionalist* (1979); George Monteiro's *Robert Frost and the New England Renaissance* (1988); Mario D'Avanzo's *A Cloud of Other Poets: Robert Frost and the Romantics* (1990); Judith Oster's *Toward Robert Frost* (1991); George Bagby's *Frost and the Book of Nature* (1993); Mark Richardson's *Robert Frost: The Poet and His Poetics* (1997); and Tim Kendall's *The Art of Robert Frost* (2012). Collections of critical essays include *On Frost* (1991), edited by Edwin H. Cady and Louis J. Budd, and Robert Faggen's *Cambridge Companion to Robert Frost* (2001).

Susan Glaspell
Susan Glaspell: The Complete Plays, edited by Linda Ben-Zvi and J. Ellen Gainor, appeared in 2010. *Major Novels of Susan Glaspell*, edited by Martha C. Carpenter, was published in 1995. Patricia l. Bryan and Martha C. Carnpentier edited *Her America: "A Jury of Her Peers" and Other Stories* (2010). Two biographies are Arthur E. Waterman's *Susan Glaspell* (1966) and Barbara O. Rajkowska's *Susan Glaspell: A Critical Biography* (2000). Critical studies include Marcia Noe's *Susan Glaspell: Voice from the Heartland* (1983); Veronica A. Makowsky's *Susan Glaspell's Century of American Women: A Critical Interpretation of Her Work* (1993); Gainor's *Susan Glaspell in Context: American Theater, Culture, and Politics, 1915–48* (2001); and Brenda Murphy's *The Provincetown Players and the Culture of Modernity* (2005). A collection of critical essays is *Susan Glaspell: Essays on Her Theater and Fiction* (1995), edited by Ben-Zvi.

Ernest Hemingway
There is no collected edition of Hemingway's writings. In addition to works mentioned in the author's headnote, his fiction includes *Today Is Friday* (1926) and *God Rest You Merry Gentlemen* (1933). His tribute to Spain, *The Spanish Earth*, and his play *The Fifth Column* appeared in 1938, the latter in a collection *The Fifth Column and the First Forty-Nine Stories*. His journalism has been collected in *The Wild Years* (1962), edited by Gene Z. Hanrahan, and *By-Line: Ernest Hemingway, Selected Articles and Dispatches of Four Decades* (1967), edited by William White. His *Complete Poems* (1992) has been edited by Nicholas Gerogiannis. *The Letters of Ernest Hemingway*, vols. 1 and 2 (2011, 2013), have appeared under the general editorship of Sandra Spanier. Audre Hanneman's *Ernest Hemingway: A Comprehensive Bibliography* (1967) is thorough. Scribners published *The Complete Short Stories of Ernest Hemingway* (1987).

The authorized biography is Carlos Baker's *Ernest Hemingway: A Life Story* (1969). Jeffrey Meyers's *Hemingway: A Biography* (1985) and Kenneth S. Lynn's *Hemingway* (1987) are important. Michael Reynolds's detailed volumes include *The Young Hemingway* (1986), *Hemingway: The Paris Years* (1989), *Hemingway: The 1930s* (1997), and *Hemingway: The Final Years* (1999). Bernice Kert's *The Hemingway Women* (1983) tells about Hemingway's mother, wives, and lovers; John Raeburn's *Fame Became of Him: Hemingway as Public Writer* (1984) compares the life with the public image.

Paul Smith's *A Reader's Guide to the Short Stories of Ernest Hemingway* (1989) is useful; Peter B. Messent's *Ernest Hemingway* (1992) is a good overview. For collections of critical essays on Hemingway, see *Ernest Hemingway: Eight Decades of Criticism* (2009), edited by Linda Wagner-Martin; *The Cambridge Companion to Hemingway* (1996), edited by Scott Donaldson; and *A Historical Guide to Ernest Hemingway* (2001), edited by Wagner-Martin. Specialized studies include Wirt Williams's *The Tragic Art of Ernest Hemingway* (1982); Mark Spilka's *Hemingway's Quarrel with Androgyny* (1990); Robert W. Trogdon's *The Lousy Racket: Hemingway, Scribners, and the Business of Literature* (2007); Amy L. Strong's *Race and Identity in Hemingway's Fiction* (2008); Robert Paul Lamb's *Art Matters: Hemingway, Craft, and the Creation of the Modern Short Story* (2010); and Mark Cirino's *Ernest Hemingway: Thought in Action* (2012).

Langston Hughes
A sixteen-volume standard edition of Hughes's complete works appeared in 2001–3. Arnold Rampersad and David Roessel edited *The Collected Poems of Langston Hughes* (1994), including *The Weary Blues* (1926), *Fine Clothes to the Jew* (1927), *The Dream Keeper and Other Poems* (1932), *Scottsboro Limited: Four Poems and a Play in Verse* (1932), *Montage of a Dream Deferred* (1951), and *The Panther and the Lash: Poems of our Times* (1967). His short stories were edited by Akiba Sullivan Harper (1996). Faith Berry edited *Good Morning Revolution: Uncollected Social Protest Writings by Langston Hughes* (1973). *Mule Bone* (1991), which he coauthored with Zora Neale Hurston, has been edited with contextual materials by George Houston Pope and Henry Louis Gates, Jr. Hughes's autobiographical volumes include *The Big Sea* (1940) and *I Wonder as I Wander* (1956); both were reissued in 1993. Charles H. Nichols edited *Arna Bontemps–Langston Hughes: Letters 1925–1967* (1980), and Rampersad edited his *Selected Letters* (2015).

Early biographies of Hughes include Charlemae Rollins's *Black Troubador: Langston Hughes* (1970), and James S. Haskins's *Always Movin' On: The Life of Langston Hughes* (1976). Faith Berry's *Langston Hughes: Before and Beyond Harlem* (1983, 1995) contains much about Hughes's life to 1940. Arnold Rampersad's two-volume *Life of Langston Hughes*—volume 1, *1902–1941: I, Too, Sing America* (1986), and volume 2, *1941–1967: I Dream a World* (1988)—is definitive.

Thomas A. Mikolyzk compiled *Langston Hughes: A Bio-Bibliography* (1990). Contemporary reviews were collected by Letitia Dace (1997). Full-length critical studies are Onwuchekwa Jemie's *Langston Hughes: An Introduction to the Poetry* (1976); Richard K. Barksdale's *Langston Hughes: The Poet and His*

Critics (1977); Steven C. Tracy's *Langston Hughes and the Blues* (1988); R. Baxter Miller's *The Art and Imagination of Langston Hughes* (1989); W. Jason Miller's *Langston Hughes and American Lynching Culture* (2011); Vera M. Kutzinski's *The Worlds of Langston Hughes: Modernism and Translation in the Americas* (2012); and David E. Chinitz's *Which Sin to Bear? Authenticity and Compromise in Langston Hughes* (2013). Essay collections include *Langston Hughes: Critical Perspectives Past and Present* (1993), edited by Henry Louis Gates, Jr., and K. A. Appiah; *Langston Hughes: The Man, His Art, and His Continuing Influence* (1995), edited by C. James Trotman; and *A Historical Guide to Langston Hughes* (2003), edited by Steven C. Tracy. Peter Mandelik and Stanley Schatt's *A Concordance to the Poetry of Langston Hughes* (1975) is useful.

Zora Neale Hurston

Robert Hemenway's *Zora Neale Hurston, A Literary Biography* (1977) initiated the Hurston revival; her work is mostly available in paperback editions. The Library of America published Hurston's writing in two volumes: *Novels and Stories* (1995) and *Folklore, Memoirs, and Other Writings* (1995); Jean Lee Cole and Charles Mitchell edited *Collected Plays* (2008). Her letters were edited by Carla Kaplan (2002). Biographies include Valerie Boyd's *Wrapped in Rainbows: The Life of Zora Neale Hurston* (2003) and Virginia Lynn Moylan's *Zora Neale Hurston's Final Decade* (2011). Book-length studies include Karla C. F. Holloway's *The Character of the Word: The Texts of Zora Neale Hurston* (1987); John Lowe's *Jump at the Sun: Zora Neale Hurston's Cosmic Comedy* (1994); Deborah G. Plant's *Every Tub Must Sit on Its Own Bottom: The Philosophy and Politics of Zora Neale Hurston* (1995); Margaret Genevieve West's *Zora Neale Hurston and American Literary Culture* (2005); and Lovalerie King's *Cambridge Introduction to Zora Neale Hurston* (2008). Hurston is linked to other writers in Cheryl A. Wall's *Women of the Harlem Renaissance* (1995); Carla Kaplan's *The Erotics of Talk: Women's Writing and Feminist Paradigms* (1996); and Trudier Harris's *The Power of the Porch: The Storyteller's Craft in Zora Neale Hurston, Gloria Naylor, and Randall Kenan* (1996). Collections of essays are *New Essays on "Their Eyes Were Watching God"* (1990), edited by Michael Awkward; *Zora Neale Hurston: Critical Perspectives Past and Present* (1993), edited by Henry Louis Gates, Jr., and K. A. Appiah; and *Critical Essays on Zora Neale Hurston* (1998), edited by Gloria L. Cronin.

Nella Larsen

Larsen's complete fiction, including *Quicksand, Passing*, and three stories, appeared in 1992, edited by Charles R. Larson; this volume was reissued in 2001. The two novels were also made available in 1986, in an edition introduced by Deborah E. McDowell. The Norton Critical Edition of *Passing* (2007), edited by Carla Kaplan, includes critical and historical backgrounds. Biographies are Thadious M. Davis's *Nella Larsen, Novelist of the Harlem Renaissance: A Woman's Life Unveiled* (1994), and George Hutchinson's *In Search of Nella Larsen: A Biography of the Color Line* (2006). Larsen is also considered in Cheryl A. Wall's *Women of the Harlem Renaissance* (1995). Three critical studies, each connecting Larsen with other African American writers, are Charles R. Larson's *Invisible Darkness: Jean Toomer and Nella Larsen* (1993); Jacquelyn Y. McLendon's *The Politics of Color in the Fiction of Jessie Fauset and Nella Larsen* (1995); and Erika M. Miller's *The Other Reconstruction: Where Violence and Womanhood Meet in the Writings of Wells-Barnett, Grimké, and Larsen* (2000). Pamela L. Caughie discusses *Passing* in "'The Best People': The Making of the Black Bourgeoisie in Writings of the Negro Renaissance," *Modernism/Modernity* 20.3 (2013), 519–537.

Amy Lowell

Lowell's complete poems were published in 1955. Honor Moore edited her *Selected Poems* (2004) for the Library of America. Ferris Greenslet, who was her editor at Houghton Mifflin, has written an excellent family chronicle from the first settler to Amy Lowell, *The Lowells and Their Seven Worlds* (1945). Additional biographical material may be found in S. Foster Damon's *Amy Lowell: A Chronicle, with Extracts from Her Correspondence* (1935), and *Florence Ayscough and Amy Lowell: Correspondence of a Friendship* (1945), edited by Harley Farnsworth MacNair. Critical estimates of Lowell include Jean Gould's *Amy: The World of Amy Lowell and the Imagist Movement* (1975); Glenn Richard Ruihley's *The Thorn of a Rose: Amy Lowell Reconsidered* (1975); Richard Benvenuto's *Amy Lowell* (1985); and Melissa Bradshaw's *Amy Lowell, Diva Poet* (2011). Adrienne Munich and Bradshaw edited *Amy Lowell, American Modern* (2004).

Edgar Lee Masters

An edition of *Spoon River Anthology* annotated by John E. Hallwas appeared in 1992, uncollected Spoon River poems were edited by Herbert K. Russell in 1991, and Masters's autobiography, *Across Spoon River*, was published with an introduction by Ronald Primeau in 1991. His son, Hardin Wallace Masters, published *Edgar Lee Masters: A Biographical*

Sketchbook about a Famous American Author (1978); the definitive biography is by Russell (2001). A brief general estimate and survey is John T. Flanagan's *Edgar Lee Masters: The Spoon River Poet and His Critics* (1974). Ronald Primeau's *Beyond Spoon River: The Legacy of Edgar Lee Masters* (1981) considers Masters's lesser-known work.

Claude McKay

Volumes of McKay's poetry include *Songs of Jamaica* (1912), *Constab Ballads* (1912), *Spring in New Hampshire and Other Poems* (1920)—published in England—and *Harlem Shadows* (1922). William J. Maxwell edited the *Complete Poems* (2004), including many poems previously uncollected. Books of prose published in his lifetime include the novels *Home to Harlem* (1928), *Banjo* (1929), and *Banana Bottom* (1933); a short story collection, *Gingertown* (1932, 1991); an autobiography, *A Long Way from Home* (1937), and an essay collection, *Harlem: Negro Metropolis* (1940). Collections brought out after McKay's death include *Selected Poems* (1953), *The Dialect Poetry of Claude McKay* (1972), *The Passion of Claude McKay: Selected Poetry and Prose* (1973); two books of short stories, *Trial by Lynching* (1977) and *My Green Hills of Jamaica* (1979); and an essay collection, *The Negro in America* (1979).

Three good biographies are James R. Giles's *Claude McKay* (1976); Wayne F. Cooper's *Claude McKay: Rebel Sojourner in the Harlem Renaissance* (1987, 1996); and Tyrone Tillery's *Claude McKay: A Black Poet's Struggle for Identity* (1992). A collection of interpretive essays is *Claude McKay: Centennial Studies* (1992), edited by A. L. McLeod. General works with material on McKay include Harold Cruse's still valuable *The Crisis of the Negro Intellectual* (1967); Kenneth Ramchand's *The West Indian Novel and Its Background* (1970; rev. ed. 2004); Nathan I. Huggins's *Harlem Renaissance* (1971); Addison Gayle's *The Way of the New World: The Black Novel in America* (1975); David Levering Lewis's *When Harlem Was in Vogue* (1981); Bernard W. Bell's *The Afro-American Novel and Its Tradition* (1987); and George Hutchinson's *The Harlem Renaissance in Black and White* (1995). Contrasting treatments of McKay's poetry are in Winston James's *A Fierce Hatred of Injustice: Claude McKay's Jamaican Poetry of Rebellion* (2001) and Josh Gosciak's *The Shadowed Country: Claude McKay and the Romance of the Victorians* (2006).

Edna St. Vincent Millay

Millay's *Collected Sonnets* (1941) and *Collected Lyrics* (1943) were followed by *Collected Poems: Edna St. Vincent Millay* (1956), edited by Norma Millay (1956). The Library of America issued *Selected Poems* (2003). Her prose sketches, *Distressing Dialogue*, published under the pseudonym Nancy Boyd, appeared in 1924. Her three verse plays (*Aria da Capa*, 1920; *The Lamp and the Bell*, 1921; and *Two Slatterns and a King*, 1921) were collected in *Three Plays* (1926). Allan Ross Macdougall edited *Letters of Edna St. Vincent Millay* in 1952. The biographies are Daniel Epstein's *What Lips My Lips Have Kissed* (2001) and Nancy Milford's *Savage Beauty: The Life of Edna St. Vincent Millay* (2001). A chapter on Millay appears in Brett C. Millier's *Flawed Light: American Women Poets and Alcohol* (2009). Essay collections are *Critical Essays on Edna St. Vincent Millay* (1993), edited by William B. Thesing, and *Millay at One Hundred* (1995), edited by Diane P. Freedman. Elissa Zellinger's "Edna St. Vincent Millay and the Poetess Tradition," *Legacy* 29.2 (2012), 240–62, looks at Millay's formal choices in the context of earlier women's poetry.

Marianne Moore

Each collection of Moore's verse excluded some earlier poems while subjecting others to extensive revisions and changes in format. Her separate volumes include *Poems* (1921), *Observations* (1924), *The Pangolin and Other Verse* (1936), *What Are Years?* (1941), *Nevertheless* (1944), *Like a Bulwark* (1956), *O to Be a Dragon* (1959), and *Tell Me, Tell Me* (1966). Collections include *Selected Poems* (1935), *Collected Poems* (1951), and *The Complete Poems of Marianne Moore* (1967, repr. 1981, 1987), which included selections from her translation of *The Fables of La Fontaine* (1954). Grace Shulman's *The Poems of Marianne Moore* (2003) is now the fullest edition. Patricia C. Willis has brought together Moore's published prose in *The Complete Prose of Marianne Moore* (1986). Moore's correspondence with Robert Lowell is published in David Kalstone's *Becoming a Poet* (1991); her relation to Wallace Stevens is considered by Robin G. Schulze in *The Web of Friendship* (1995). Biographies are Charles Molesworth's *Marianne Moore: A Literary Life* (1990) and Linda Leavell's *Holding On Upside Down: The Life and Work of Marianne Moore* (2013). Bonnie Costello edited *The Selected Letters of Marianne Moore* (1997). Book-length studies include Bernard F. Engel's *Marianne Moore* (1963, rev. 1989); Costello's *Marianne Moore: Imaginary Possessions* (1982); John M. Slatin's *The Savage's Romance: The Poetry of Marianne Moore* (1986); Grace Schulman's *Marianne Moore: The Poetry of Engagement* (1987); Margaret Holley's *The Poetry of Marianne Moore: A Study in Voice and Value* (1987); Cristanne Miller's *Questions of Authority* (1995); Leavell's

Marianne Moore and the Visual Arts (1995); Elisabeth W. Joyce's *Cultural Critique and Abstraction: Marianne Moore and the Avant-Garde* (1998); and Victoria Bazin's *Marianne Moore and the Cultures of Modernity* (2010). Bethany Hickock's *Degrees of Freedom: American Women Poets and the Women's College, 1905–1955* (2008) connects Moore with Elizabeth Bishop and Sylvia Plath. Essay collections include *Marianne Moore, Woman and Poet* (1990), edited by Patricia Willis, and *Critics and Poets on Marianne Moore: "A Right Good Salvo of Barks"* (2005), edited by Leavell, Miller, and Schulze. Craig S. Abbott compiled *Marianne Moore: A Descriptive Bibliography* in 1977. Gary Lane's *A Concordance to the Poems of Marianne Moore* appeared in 1972.

Eugene O'Neill

The Library of America collected O'Neill's plays in three volumes, *Complete Plays, 1913–1920*; *Complete Plays, 1920–1931*; and *Complete Plays, 1932–1943* (1988). The standard biography of O'Neill is still that of Arthur and Barbara Gelb, *O'Neill* (1962, rev. 2000). Other biographical treatments are L. Schaeffer's *O'Neill, Son and Artist* (1973, 1990); Stephen A. Bloch's Eugene *O'Neill: Beyond Mourning and Tragedy* (1999); and Robert M. Dowling's *Eugene O'Neill: A Life in Four Acts* (2014). *The Theatre We Worked For: The Letters of Eugene O'Neill to Kenneth Macgowan* (1982), edited by Jackson R. Bryer, documents O'Neill's attitudes to the theater of his day. Brenda Murphy's *O'Neill: Long Day's Journey into Night* (2001) provides a production history. Bryer and Travis Bogard edited *Selected Letters of Eugene O'Neill* (1994). *Conversations with Eugene O'Neill* (1990) is edited by Mark W. Estrin. Literary analysis of O'Neill's plays can be found in Bogard's *Contour in Time: The Plays of Eugene O'Neill* (1972, rev. 1987); Michael Manheim's *Eugene O'Neill's New Language of Kinship* (1982); Judith E. Barlow's *Final Acts: The Creation of Three Late O'Neill Plays* (1985); Kurt Eisen's *The Inner Strength of Opposites* (1994; on O'Neill's techniques); Joel Pfister's *Staging Depth: Eugene O'Neill and the Politics of Psychological Discourse* (1995); Donald Gallup's *Eugene O'Neill and His Eleven-Play Cycle* (1998); Doris Alexander's *Eugene O'Neill's Last Plays: Separating Art from Autobiography* (2005); and John Patrick Diggins's *Eugene O'Neill's America: Desire Under Democracy* (2007).

Essay collections include *Eugene O'Neill's Century* (1991), edited by Richard F. Moorton Jr.; *The Critical Response to Eugene O'Neill* (1993), edited by John H. Houchin; and *The Cambridge Companion to Eugene O'Neill* (1998), edited by Michael Manheim.

Katherine Anne Porter

Primary sources include *Ship of Fools* (1962); *The Collected Stories of Katherine Anne Porter* (1965); *The Collected Essays and Occasional Writings of Katherine Anne Porter* (1970); *The Never-Ending Wrong* (1977), about the Sacco and Vanzetti case; *Letters* (1990), edited by Isabel Bayley; *"This Strange, Old World" and Other Book Reviews by Katherine Anne Porter* (1991), edited by Darlene Harbour Unrue; *Uncollected Early Prose of Katherine Anne Porter* (1993), edited by Ruth M. Alvarez and Thomas F. Walsh; and *Katherine Anne Porter's Poetry* (1996), edited by Unrue. The Library of America's *Collected Stories and Other Writings* (2008), edited by Unrue, includes Porter's literary reviews and her journalism from Mexico. Unrue edited *Selected Letters of Katherine Anne Porter: Chronicles of a Modern Woman* (2012).

Biographies are Joan Givner's *Katherine Anne Porter, A Life* (1982, rev. 1991), and Unrue's *Katherine Anne Porter: The Life of an Artist* (2005). Givner also edited *Katherine Anne Porter: Conversations* (1987). *A Bibliography of the Works of Katherine Anne Porter*, edited by Louise Waldrip and Shirley Ann Bauer, appeared in 1969.

Critical studies include Jane Krause DeMouy's *Katherine Anne Porter's Women: The Eye of Her Fiction* (1983); Unrue's *Truth and Vision in Katherine Anne Porter's Fiction* (1985); Willene and George Hendrick's *Katherine Anne Porter* (rev. 1988); Thomas F. Walsh's *Katherine Anne Porter and Mexico: The Illusion of Eden* (1992); Robert H. Brinkmeyer's *Katherine Anne Porter's Artistic Development* (1993); Janis P. Stout's *Katherine Anne Porter, A Sense of the Times* (1995); Mary Titus's *The Ambivalent Art of Katherine Anne Porter* (2005); and Stout's *South by Southwest: Katherine Anne Porter and the Burden of Texas History* (2013). Unrue edited *Critical Essays on Katherine Anne Porter* (1997).

Ezra Pound

Pound's early poetry, from *A Lume Spento* (1908) through *Ripostes* (1912), is in the authoritative *Collected Early Poems of Ezra Pound* (1976), edited by Michael King. The same volumes, along with later volumes *Hugh Selwyn Mauberley* and *Homage to Sextus Propertius*, are collected in *Personae: The Collected Shorter Poems* (rev. ed. 1949; 2nd rev. ed. 1990). The New Directions edition of *The Cantos* (1993) is definitive. The Library of America's *Poems and Translations* (2003), edited by Richard Sieburth, excludes *The Cantos*. The most important of Pound's critical writings are *The Spirit of Romance* (rev. 1952); *Gaudier-Brzeska: A Memoir* (1916); *Instigations* (1920); *Make It New* (1934); *The ABC of Read-*

ing (1934); *Guide to Kulchur* (1938); and *Patria Mia* (1950). His criticism has been collected in *Literary Essays of Ezra Pound* (1954), edited by T. S. Eliot; *Selected Prose, 1909–1965* (1973), edited by William Cookson; and Ezra Pound's *Poetry and Prose Contributions to Periodicals* (1991), prefaced and arranged by Lea Baechler, A. Walton Litz, and James Longenback in eleven volumes. *Ezra Pound Speaking: Radio Speeches of World War II* (1978), edited by Leonard W. Doob, collects his wartime radio addresses. D. D. Paige edited *The Letters of Ezra Pound, 1907–1941* (1950). Other correspondence is collected in *Ezra Pound and Dorothy Shakespear: Their Letters, 1909–1914* (1984), edited by Omar Pound and A. Walton Litz; *Pound/Lewis: The Letters of Ezra Pound and Wyndham Lewis* (1985), edited by Timothy Materer; *Ezra Pound and James Loughlin* (1994), edited by David M. Gordon; and *Pound/Cummings: The Correspondence of Ezra Pound and E. E. Cummings*, edited by Barry Ahearn. Reviews of Pound are collected in Eric Homberger's *Ezra Pound: The Critical Heritage* (1973, 1997).

James J. Wilhelm's three-volume biography includes *The American Roots of Ezra Pound* (1985), *Ezra Pound in London and Paris, 1908–1925* (1990), and *Ezra Pound: The Tragic Years, 1925–1972* (1994). David Moody also has a three-volume biography, *Ezra Pound: Poet* (2007, 2014, 2015). Also useful are Noel Stock's *The Life of Ezra Pound* (1970, 1982); C. David Haymann's *Ezra Pound, The Last Rower: A Political Profile* (1976); and Wendy Stallard Flory's *The American Ezra Pound* (1989). *The Roots of Treason: Ezra Pound and the Secrets of St. Elizabeth* (1984), by E. Fuller Torrey, focuses on Pound's trial and incarceration.

Hugh Kenner's *The Pound Era* (1972) has been influential. Good introductions are Christine Brooke-Rose's *A ZBC of Ezra Pound* (1971) and James Knapp's *Ezra Pound* (1972). For *The Cantos* see the *Annotated Index to the Cantos of Ezra Pound* (1957) (through "Canto LXXXIV"), edited by John H. Edwards and William W. Vasse; Noel Stock's *Reading the Cantos* (1967); Ronald Bush's *The Genesis of Pound's Cantos* (1976); Wilhelm's *The Later Cantos of Ezra Pound* (1977); Lawrence S. Rainey's *Ezra Pound and the Monument of Culture* (1991); Carrol F. Terrill's *A Companion to the Cantos of Ezra Pound* (1993); George Kearn's *Guide to Ezra Pound's Selected Cantos* (1980); Anthony Woodward's *Ezra Pound and "The Pisan Cantos"* (1980); and William Cookson's updated *Guide to the Cantos of Ezra Pound* (2001). Tim Redman's *Ezra Pound and Italian Fascism* (1991) addresses the poet's politics, as does Leon Surette's *Pound in Purgatory: From Economic Realism to Anti-Semitism* (1999). Cultural approaches to Pound include Michael Coyle's *Ezra Pound, Popular Genres, and the Discourse of Culture* (1995); Daniel Tiffany's *Radio Corpse* (1995); and Rebecca Beasley's *Ezra Pound and the Visual Culture of Modernism* (2007). Marjorie Perloff's *The Dance of the Intellect* (1996) studies poetry in the Pound tradition; Jacob Korg's *Winter Love: Ezra Pound and H. D.* (2003) is a comparative study. Andrew Gibson edited *Pound in Multiple Perspective: A Collection of Critical Essays* (1993), and Ira B. Nadel edited *The Cambridge Companion to Ezra Pound* (1999).

Edwin Arlington Robinson

Collected Poems of Edwin Arlington Robinson (1921) was enlarged periodically through 1937. In addition to shorter verse, Robinson wrote long narrative poems, including the *Arthurian Trilogy of Merlin* (1917), *Lancelot* (1920), and *Tristrum* (1927). Other books include *Roman Bartholomew* (1923), *The Man Who Died Twice* (1924), *Cavender's House* (1929), *The Glory of the Nightingales* (1930), *Matthias at the Door* (1931), *Talifer* (1933), *Amaranth* (1934), and *King Jasper* (1935). Ridgely Torrence compiled *Selected Letters* (1940). Denham Sutcliffe edited *Untriangulated Stars: Letters of Edwin Arlington Robinson to Harry de Forest Smith, 1890–1905* (1947). Richard Cary edited *Edwin Arlington Robinson's Letters to Edith Brower* (1968).

Scott Donaldson's *Edwin Arlington Robinson: A Poet's Life* (2007) is comprehensive. Richard Cary documented *The Early Reception of Edwin Arlington Robinson* (1974). Introductions to Robinson's work include Wallace L. Anderson's *Edwin Arlington Robinson: A Critical Introduction* (1967), Hoyt C. Franchere's *Edwin Arlington Robinson* (1968), and Louis O. Coxe's *Edwin Arlington Robinson: The Life of Poetry* (1969). Ellsworth Barnard edited *Edwin Arlington Robinson: Centenary Essays* (1969). Other collections are *Appreciation of Edwin Arlington Robinson: Twenty-eight Interpretive Essays* (1969), edited by Richard Cary; and *Edwin Arlington Robinson: A Collection of Critical Essays* (1970), edited by Francis Murphy. Richard Hoffpair's *The Contemplative Poetry of Edwin Arlington Robinson, Robert Frost, and Yvor Winters* (2002) links Robinson to other poets.

Carl Sandburg

The *Complete Poems of Carl Sandburg* (1950) was revised and expanded in 1970. *Breathing Tokens* (1978), edited by Margaret Sandburg, prints unpublished poems. *Billy Sunday and Other Poems* (1993), edited by George and Willene Hendrick, contains some of his unpublished, uncollected, and unexpurgated poems. Paul Berman edited his *Selected Poems* (2006) for the Library of America. In addition to eight full-length volumes of poetry, Sandburg wrote a Pulitzer Prize–winning study of Abraham Lincoln: *Abraham Lincoln: The Prairie Years*, 2 vols. (1926), and *Abraham Lincoln: The War Years*, 4 vols. (1939); two collections of journalism and social commentary; *Rootabaga Stories* for children; a novel; and a book of American folk songs. *Fables, Foibles and Foobles* (1988), edited by George Hendrick, is a selection of unpublished humorous pieces. *More Rootabagas* (1993), edited by Hendrick, contains stories for children. *Selected Poems* (1996) was edited by George and Willene Hendrick. *The Letters of Carl Sandburg* (1968, 1988) was edited by Herbert Mitgang. *The Poet and the Dream Girl: The Love Letters of Lilian Steichen and Carl Sandburg* (1987, 1999) was edited by Margaret Sandburg.

Always the Young Strangers (1953) and *Ever the Winds of Chance* (1983), edited by Margaret Sandburg and George Hendrick, are segments of Sandburg's autobiography. A full-scale biography is Penelope Niven's *Carl Sandburg: A Biography* (1991). Critical studies include Richard Crowder's *Carl Sandburg* (1964) and Philip R. Yannella's *The Other Carl Sandburg* (1996). John Marsh's *Hog Butchers, Beggars, and Busboys: Poverty, Labor, and the Making of Modern American Poetry* (2011) includes a chapter on Sandburg.

Gertrude Stein

The Library of America published Stein's writings in two volumes: 1903–32 and 1932–46 (1998). The Yale Edition of the *Unpublished Writings of Gertrude Stein* (1951–58), edited by Carl Van Vechten, contains eight volumes of poetry, prose fiction, portraits, essays, and miscellany. The Norton Critical Edition of *Three Lives and Q.E.D.* (2005), edited by Marianne DeKoven, supplies critical and biographical contexts. Among publications in Stein's lifetime are *Tender Buttons* (1914) and prose fiction, including *Three Lives* (1909), *The Making of Americans* (1925), *Lucy Church Amiably* (1930), *Ida: A Novel* (1941), and *Brewsie and Willie* (1946). *Geography and Plays* (1922), *Operas and Plays* (1932), and *Last Operas and Plays* (1949, 1995), edited by Carl Van Vechten, contain dramatic pieces. Biographical material and portraits of Stein's contemporaries may be found in *The Autobiography of Alice B. Toklas* (1933), *Portraits and Prayers* (1934), *Everybody's Autobiography* (1937), and *Wars I Have Seen* (1945). Other works, including meditations, essays, sketches, and sociolinguistic treatises, are *Useful Knowledge* (1928), *How to Write* (1931), *Lectures in America* (1935), *Narration: Four Lectures by Gertrude Stein* (1935), *What Are Masterpieces?* (1940), and *Four in America* (1947). Donald C. Gallup edited *Fernhurst, Q.E.D. and Other Early Writings by Gertrude Stein* (1971) and also a collection of letters to Stein, *The Flowers of Friendship* (1953). Her correspondence with Mabel Dodge Luhan is edited by Patricia R. Everett (1996), with Thornton Wilder by Edward Burns and Ulla E. Dydo (1996), and with Virgil Thomson by Susan Holbrook and Thomas Dilworth (2010). *Baty Precious Always Shines* (2000), edited by Kay Tarner, has selected love letters written between Stein and her partner, Alice B. Toklas. *Gertrude Stein: An Annotated Bibliography* (1979) was compiled by Maureen R. Liston.

W. G. Rogers's *When This You See Remember Me: Gertrude Stein in Person* (1948) and *Alice B. Toklas's What Is Remembered* (1963) are reminiscences of Stein by friends. Biographies include Howard Greenfield's *Gertrude Stein: A Biography* (1973); James R. Mellow's *Charmed Circle: Gertrude Stein and Company* (1974); Janet Hobhouse's *Everybody Who Was Anybody* (1989); Linda Wagner-Martin's *Favored Strangers: Gertrude Stein and Her Family* (1995); Brenda Wineapple's *Sister Brother: Gertrude and Leo Stein* (1996); and Janet Malcolm's *Two Lives: Gertrude and Alice* (2007).

Critical studies include Robert B. Haas's *A Primer for the Gradual Understanding of Gertrude Stein* (1971); Richard Bridgman's *Gertrude Stein in Pieces* (1970); Wendy Steiner's *Exact Resemblance to Exact Resemblance: The Literary Portraiture of Gertrude Stein* (1978); Marianne DeKoven's *A Different Language: Gertrude Stein's Experimental Writing* (1983); Randa Kay Dubnick's *The Structure of Obscurity: Gertrude Stein, Language, and Cubism* (1984); Lisa Ruddick's *Reading Gertrude Stein: Body, Text, Gnosis* (1990); Jane P. Bowers's *Gertrude Stein* (1993); Linda Watts's *Gertrude Stein: A Study of the Short Fiction* (1999); Barbara Will's *Gertrude Stein, Modernism, and the Problem of "Genius"* (2000); Steven Meyer's *Irresistible Dictation: Gertrude Stein and the Correlations of Writing and Science* (2001); Dana Cairns Watson's *Gertrude Stein and the Essence of What Happens* (2005); and Karen Leick's *Gertrude Stein and the Making of an American Celebrity* (2009). Bruce Kellner edited the useful *Gertrude Stein Companion* (1988). A collection of critical essays, edited by Richard Kostelanetz, is *Gertrude Stein Advanced* (1990).

John Steinbeck

The Library of America issued four volumes of Steinbeck's work, *Novels and Stories 1932–1937* (1994), *The Grapes of Wrath and Other Writings* (1996), *Novels 1942–1952* (2002), and *Travels with Charley and Later Novels*

1947–1962 (2007). Two biographies are Jack J. Benson's *The True Adventures of John Steinbeck, Writer* (1984) and Jay Parini's *John Steinbeck* (1995). Elaine Steinbeck and Robert Wallsten edited *Steinbeck: A Life in Letters* (1975). Critical studies of Steinbeck include R. S. Hughes's *Beyond the Red Pony: A Reader's Guide to Steinbeck's Complete Short Stories* (1987); John H. Timmerman's *The Dramatic Landscape of Steinbeck's Short Stories* (1990); and Warren French's *John Steinbeck's Fiction Revisited* (1994). R. David edited *John Steinbeck: A Collection of Critical Essays* (1972); other collections are *Rediscovering Steinbeck* (1989), edited by Cliff Lewis and Carroll Britch; *Critical Essays on Steinbeck's* Grapes of Wrath (1989), edited by John Ditsky; *Short Novels of John Steinbeck* (1990), edited by Jackson J. Benson; *John Steinbeck: The Contemporary Reviews* (1996), edited by Joseph R. McElrath Jr., Jesse S. Crisler, and Susan Shillinglaw; *Steinbeck and the Environment: Interdisciplinary Approaches* (1997), edited by Susan F. Beegel; and *Beyond Boundaries: Rereading John Steinbeck* (2002), edited by Shillinglaw and Kevin Hearle.

Wallace Stevens

The Collected Poems of Wallace Stevens was published in 1954. Milton J. Bates's *Opus Posthumous* (1957, rev. 1989) includes previously uncollected poems, plays, and essays. *The Necessary Angel: Essays on Reality and the Imagination* (1951) is Stevens's prose statement on poetry. The Library of America issued his *Collected Poetry and Prose* (1997). Other resources are *Letters of Wallace Stevens* (1966, 1996), edited by Holly Stevens; *The Contemplated Spouse: The Letters of Wallace Stevens to Elsie* (2006), edited by J. Donald Blount; *Concordance to the Poetry of Wallace Stevens* (1963), edited by Thomas Walsh; and *Wallace Stevens: A Descriptive Bibliography* (1973), compiled by J. M. Edelstein.

Joan Richardson's *Wallace Stevens: The Early Years, 1879–1923* (1986) chronicles the poet's youth and her *Wallace Stevens: The Later Years, 1923–1955* (1988) completes the story. Another biography is Tony Sharpe's *Wallace Stevens: A Literary Life* (2000). A. Walton Litz's *Introspective Voyager: The Poetic Development of Wallace Stevens* (1972) traces Stevens's thought and style through his early and middle years. Harold Bloom's *Wallace Stevens: The Poems of Our Climate* (1977) considers intellectual influences on Stevens; Joseph N. Riddle's *The Clairvoyant Eye: The Poetry and Poetics of Wallace Stevens* (1969, 1991) reads many individual poems. Other good full-length studies include Eleanor Cook's *Poetry, Word-Play, and Word-War in Wallace Stevens* (1988) and *A Reader's Guide to Wallace Stevens* (2007); James Longenbach's *Wallace Stevens: The Plain Sense of Things* (1991); Alan Filreis's *Modernism from Left to Right* (1994); Janet McCann's *Wallace Stevens Revisited* (1995); and Edward Ragg's *Wallace Stevens and the Aesthetics of Abstraction* (2010). Jacqueline Vaught Brogan's *The Violence within/The Violence without: Wallace Stevens and the Emergence of a Revolutionary Poetics* (2003) and Malcolm Woodland's *Wallace Stevens and the Apocalyptic Mode* (2005) consider the relation of Stevens's poetry to war. Albert Gelpi collects essays on the poet in *Wallace Stevens: The Poetics of Modernism* (1990); other collections are *Critical Essays on Wallace Stevens* (1988), edited by Steven Gould Axelrod and Helen Deese; *Wallace Stevens and the Feminine* (1993), edited by Melita Schaum; and *Wallace Stevens Across the Atlantic* (2008), edited by Bart Eeckhout and Ragg.

Jean Toomer

Toomer's published works include *Cane* (1923, repr. 1975, pub. also in a Norton Critical Edition, 2011), *Essentials* (1931), *Portage Potential* (1932), and an address, "The Flavor of Man" (1949). His *Collected Poems*, edited by Robert B. Jones and Margery Toomer Latimer, was published in 1988. *A Jean Toomer Reader* (1993), containing previously unpublished writings, was edited by Frederik L. Rusch; Robert B. Jones edited *Selected Essays and Literary Criticism* (1996). Mark Whalan edited *The Letters of Jean Toomer, 1919–1924* (2005). Brian Joseph Benson and Mabel Mayle Dillard's *Jean Toomer* (1980); Nellie Y. McKay's *Jean Toomer, Artist: A Study of His Literary Life and Work, 1894–1936* (1984); and Cynthia Earl Kerman and Richard Eldridge's *The Lives of Jean Toomer: A Hunger for Wholeness* (1989) are biographies. Studies include Charles Scruggs and Lee Van De Marr's *Jean Toomer and the Terrors of American History* (1998); Karen Ford Jackson's *Split-Gut Song: Jean Toomer and the Poetics of Modernity* (2005); and Barbara Foley's *Jean Toomer: Race, Repression and Revolution* (2014). Whalan's *Race, Manhood, and Modernism in America: The Short Story Cycles of Sherwood Anderson and Jean Toomer* (2007) is a comparative study. Essay collections are *Jean Toomer: A Critical Evaluation* (1988), edited by Therman B. O'Daniel, and *Jean Toomer and the Harlem Renaissance*, edited by Geneviève Faber and Michel Faith (2000).

Nathanael West

West's published novels are *The Dream Life of Balso Snell* (1931), *Miss Lonelyhearts* (1933), *A Cool Million: The Dismantling of Lemuel Pitkin*

(1934), and *The Day of the Locust* (1939). *Miss Lonelyhearts* and *The Day of the Locust* are reprinted in a combined volume from New Directions (1962, 1969). The Library of America's *Novels and Other Writings* (1997), edited by Sacvan Bercovitch, includes selected letters as well as screenplays and a play. Biographies are Jay Martin's *Nathanael West: The Art of His Life* (1970) and Joe Woodward's *Alive Inside the Wreck: A Biography of Nathanael West* (2011). Critical studies include James F. Light's *Nathanael West: An Interpretive Study* (1961); Victor Comerchero's *Nathanael West: The Ironic Prophet* (1964); Randall Reid's *The Fiction of Nathanael West: No Redeemer, No Promised Land* (1967); Alistair Wisker's *The Writing of Nathanael West* (1990); and Jonathan Veitch's *American Superrealism: Nathanael West and the Politics of Representation in the 1930s* (1997). Chapters on West are in Rita Barnard's *The Great Depression and the Culture of Abundance: Kenneth Fearing, Nathanael West, and Mass Culture in the 1930s* (1995); Karen Jacobs's *The Eye's Mind: Literary Modernism and Visual Culture* (2001); and Chip Rhodes's *Politics, Desire, and the Hollywood Novel* (2008). Ben Siegel's *Critical Essays on Nathanael West* (1994) provides a useful sampling of contemporary reviews and early critical responses. William White compiled *Nathanael West: A Comprehensive Bibliography* (1975).

William Carlos Williams

Williams's poems were first collected in three volumes: *Collected Earlier Poems of William Carlos Williams* (1951), *Collected Later Poems of William Carlos Williams* (1950), and *Pictures from Brueghel* (1962). More recent are *The Collected Poems of William Carlos Williams, volume 1*, 1909–1939 (1996), edited by A. Walton Litz and Christopher MacGowan, and volume 2, 1939–1962, edited by MacGowan (1988). *Paterson*'s five books, published individually between 1946 and 1958, were issued in one volume in 1963 and reedited by MacGowan (1992). The Library of America issued *Selected Poems* (2004), edited by Robert Pinsky. *Kora in Hell*, Williams's volume of prose poetry, is in the collection *Imaginations* (1970), edited by Webster Schott, along with essays, fiction, and creative prose. Williams's short stories are collected in *Make Light of It* (1950) and again, with several additions, in *The Farmers' Daughters* (1961). His novels are *A Voyage to Pagany* (1928), *White Mule* (1937), *In the Money* (1940), and *The Build Up* (1946). His dramatic pieces were published together in *Many Loves and Other Plays* (1961). Important essays are contained in *In the American Grain* (1925, 1940), *Selected Essays of William Carlos Williams* (1954), and *Imaginations* (1970), edited by Webster Schott. Williams's prose also includes *The Autobiography of William Carlos Williams* (1951); a book of recollections dictated to Edith Heal, *I Wanted to Write a Poem* (1958); and *Yes, Mrs. Williams* (1959), a portrait of the poet's mother. J. C. Thirlwall edited *The Selected Letters of William Carlos Williams* (1957). Selections from the Pound–Williams correspondence, edited by Hugh Witemeyer, appeared in 1996. Letters between Williams and Denise Levertov, edited by MacGowan, appeared in 1998. Barry Ahearn edited *The Correspondence of William Carlos Williams and Louis Zukofsky* (2003). *The Humane Particulars: The Collected Letters of William Carlos Williams and Kenneth Burke* (2003) was edited by James H. East. Emily Mitchell Wallace compiled *A Bibliography of William Carlos Williams* (1968). Reed Whittemore's *William Carlos Williams: Poet from Jersey* (1975) is a critical biography, as are Paul Mariani's more detailed *William Carlos Williams: A New World Naked* (1981), and Herbert Leibowitz's *"Something Urgent I Have to Say to You": The Life and Works of William Carlos Williams* (2011).

James E. Breslin's *William Carlos Williams: An American Artist* (1970) is a still-useful overview. Other general introductions are Thomas R. Whitaker's *William Carlos Williams* (1989) and Kelli A. Larson's *Guide to the Poetry of William Carlos Williams* (1995). Among specialized studies are Mike Weaver's *William Carlos Williams: The American Background* (1971); Joseph N. Riddel's *The Inverted Bell: Modernism and the Counter-Poetics of William Carlos Williams* (1974); Henry M. Sayre's *The Visual Text of William Carlos Williams* (1983); Ann W. Fisher-Wirth's *William Carlos Williams and Autobiography: The Woods of His Own Nature* (1989); Ron Callan's *William Carlos Williams and Transcendentalism* (1992); T. Hugh Crawford's *Modernism, Medicine, and William Carlos Williams* (1993); Brian A. Bremen's *William Carlos Williams and the Diagnostics of Culture* (1993); Peter Halter's *The Revolution in the Visual Arts and the Poetry of William Carlos Williams* (1994); Donald W. Markos's *Ideas in Things* (1994); Barry Ahearn's *William Carlos Williams and Alterity* (1994); Julio Marzan's *The Spanish American Roots of William Carlos Williams* (1994); Stanley Koehler's *Countries of the Mind: The Poetry of William Carlos Williams* (1998); and John Beck's *Writing the Radical Center: William Carlos Williams, John Dewey, and American Cultural Politics* (2001).

Linda Wagner's *The Prose of William Carlos Williams* (1970) and Robert Coles's *William Carlos Williams: The Knack of Survival in America* (1975) discuss Williams's prose. For *Paterson*, see Joel Conarroe's *William Carlos Williams' Paterson: Language and Landscape* (1970); Benjamin Sankey's *A Companion to*

William Carlos Williams's Paterson (1971); and Ann Marie Mikkelson's *Pastoral, Pragmatism, and Twentieth-Century American Poetry* (2011). Paul Mariani's *William Carlos Williams: The Poet and His Critics* (1975) considers Williams's critical reception, as does *William Carlos Williams, The Critical Heritage* (1980, 1997), edited by Charles Doyle.

Thomas Wolfe

Arlyn and Matthew Bruccoli edited Wolfe's massive *O Lost: A Story of the Buried Life* (2000). David Madden compiled *Thomas Wolfe's Civil War* (2004) from Wolfe's writings. Among primary documents are *The Notebooks of Thomas Wolfe* (1970), edited by Richard S. Kennedy and P. Reeves; *The Autobiography of an American Novelist, by Thomas Wolfe* (1983), edited by Leslie Field; *The Letters of Thomas Wolfe* (1956), edited by Elizabeth Nowell; *The Letters of Thomas Wolfe to His Mother* (1968), edited by C. Holman and S. Ross; *My Other Loneliness: Letters of Thomas Wolfe and Aline Bernstein* (1983), edited by Suzanne Stutman; *Beyond Love and Loyalty: The Letters of Thomas Wolfe and Elizabeth Nowell* (1983), edited by Richard S. Kennedy; and *To Loot My Life Clean: The Thomas Wolfe–Maxwell Perkins Correspondence* (2000), edited by Matthew Bruccoli. The fullest biography is David Herbert Donald's *Look Homeward: A Life of Thomas Wolfe* (1987). John Lane Idol Jr.'s *A Thomas Wolfe Companion* (1987) is informative and useful. John Earl Bassett compiled *Thomas Wolfe: An Annotated Critical Bibliography* (1996).

There were many critical studies of Wolfe in the 1950s and 1960s. Later books include Carol I. Johnston's *Of Time and the Artist* (1996) and Robert Taylor Ensign's *Lean down Your Ear upon the Earth, and Listen: Thomas Wolfe's Greener Modernism* (2003).

Collections of critical essays are *Thomas Wolfe: The Critical Reception* (1974), edited by P. Reeves; *The Loneliness at the Core: Studies in Thomas Wolfe* (1975), edited by C. Hugh Holman; and *Critical Essays on Thomas Wolfe* (1985), edited by John S. Phillipson.

Richard Wright

Wright's fiction includes *Uncle Tom's Children* (1938), *Native Son* (1940), *The Outsider* (1953), and *Eight Men* (1961). *Black Boy* (1945) is his autobiography; *White Man, Listen!* (1957) is an important work of nonfiction. The Library of America has published his writings in two volumes, including an unexpurgated version of *Native Son* (1991). Earle V. Bryant edited *Byline, Richard Wright: Articles from the Daily Worker and the New Masses* (2015). For a complete bibliography of his writings, see *Richard Wright: A Primary Bibliography* (1982), compiled by Charles T. Davis and Michel Fabre. A good sample of reviews can be found in *Richard Wright: The Critical Reception* (1978), edited by John M. Reilly; a massive bibliography of Wright criticism around the world has been assembled by Keneth Kinnamon (1988). Kinnamon and Michel Fabre edited *Conversations with Richard Wright* (1993). The best critical biography is Fabre's *The Unfinished Quest of Richard Wright* (1993); see also Margaret Walker's *Richard Wright, Daemonic Genius* (1993) and Hazel Rowley's *Richard Wright: The Life and Times* (2001). Critical studies include Russell C. Brignano's *Richard Wright: An Introduction to the Man and His Works* (1970), Kinnamon's *The Emergence of Richard Wright* (1972), Fabre's *Richard Wright: Books and Writers* (1990) and his essays in *The World of Richard Wright* (2007), and Robert Butler's *Native Son: The Emergence of a New Black Hero* (1991). Abdul R. Jan Mohamed's *The Death-Bound-Subject: Richard Wright's Archaeology of Death* (2005) is an ambitious theoretical study. Collections of criticism are Yoshinobu Hakutani's *Critical Essays on Richard Wright* (1982); *Richard Wright: Critical Perspectives Past and Present* (1993), edited by Henry Louis Gates, Jr., and K. A. Appiah; *The Critical Response to Richard Wright* (1995), edited by Robert J. Butler; *Richard Wright: A Collection of Critical Essays* (1995), edited by Arnold Rampersad; Kinnamon's *Critical Essays on Richard Wright's Native Son* (1997); and *Richard Wright: New Readings in the 21st Century* (2011), edited by Alice Mikal Craven, William E. Dow, and Gary Taylor.

PERMISSIONS ACKNOWLEDGMENTS

IMAGE CREDITS

P. 2: Edward Hopper (American 1882–1967), *Nighthawks*, 1942; Friends of American Art Collection 1942.51, The Art Institute of Chicago. Photography © The Art Institute of Chicago; p. 4: Bettmann/Getty Images; p. 5: Library of Congress/Getty Images; p. 8: Smithsonian American Art Museum, Washington, DC/Art Resource, NY; p. 11: Smithsonian American Art Museum, Washington, DC/Art Resource, NY; p. 12: Smithsonian American Art Museum, Washington, DC/Art Resource, NY; p. 16: Merrill C. Berman Collection; p. 20: Provincetown Players, 1916; p. 33: University of Nebraska Lincoln, Archives and Special Collections; p. 185: The Sandor Family Collection. Richard & Ellen Sandor; p. 202: HIP/Art Resource, NY; p. 210: Library of Congress; p. 212: Art & Artifacts Division, Schomburg Center for Research in Black Culture, The New York Public Library, Astor, Lenox and Tilden Foundations; p. 354: Bettmann/Getty Images; p. 516: Library of Congress; p. 538: Library of Congress; p. 608: Harry Ransom Humanities Research Art Collection, UT Austin; p. 667: Courtesy Everett Collection; p. 668: Norton; p. 860: Bettmann/Getty Images.

COLOR INSERT CREDITS

C1: Marcel Duchamp (1887–1968), © ARS, NY, *Nude Descending a Staircase (No. 2)*, 1912. Oil on canvas, 57 7/8 x 35 1/8 inches (147 x 89.2cm). The Louise and Walter Arensberg Collection, 1950. The Philadelphia Museum of Art. Art © 2016 Artists Rights Society (ARS), New York/ADAGP, Paris/Succession Marcel Duchamp. Photo credit: The Philadelphia Museum of Art/Art Resource, NY. C2: Marsden Hartley, *Portrait of a German Officer*, The Metropolitan Museum of Art, The Alfred Stieglitz Collection, 1949 (49.70.42). Image copyright © The Metropolitan Museum of Art/Art Resource, NY. C3: Thomas Hart Benton, American (1889–1975), *Hollywood*, 1937–38. Tempera with oil on canvas, mounted on panel, 56 x 84 inches (142.2 x 213.4 cm). The Nelson-Atkins Museum of Art, Kansas City, Missouri. Bequest of the artist, F75-21/12. Photo by Jamison Miller. Art © T. H. Benton and R. P. Benton Testamentary Trusts/UMB Bank Trustee/Licensed by VAGA, New York, NY; C4: Hampton University Museum, Hampton, VA; C5: Charles Sheeler (1883–1965), *River Rouge Plant*, 1932; oil on Canvas, 20 x 24 1/8 in. Whitney Museum of Art, NY; Purchase 32.43; C6: Georgia O'Keeffe, *From the Faraway, Nearby*, The Metropolitan Museum of Art, Alfred Stieglitz Collection, 1959 (59.204.2). Photograph © 1984 The Metropolitan Museum of Art; C7: Granger, NYC—All rights reserved; C8: Edward Hopper (American 1882–1967), *Nighthawks*, 1942; Friends of American Art Collection 1942.51, The Art Institute of Chicago. Photography © The Art Institute of Chicago.

TEXT CREDITS

Sterling Brown: "Mister Samuel and Sam," "He Was a Man," "Master and Man," "Break of Day," "Bitter Fruit of the Tree," from THE COLLECTED POEMS OF STERLING A BROWN, selected by Michael S. Harper. Copyright © 1980 by Sterling A. Brown. Reprinted by permission of Elizabeth A. Dennis.

Willa Cather: "The Novel Démeublé" from NOT UNDER FORTY by Willa Cather, copyright © 1936 by Willa S. Cather, renewed 1964 by Edith Lewis and the City Bank Farmers Trust Co. "The Sculptor's Funeral" from COLLECTED STORIES by Willa Cather, copyright 1948 by Alfred A. Knopf, a division of Penguin Random House LLC, copyright renewed 1976 by Charles E. Cather. Used by permission of Alfred A. Knopf, an imprint of the Knopf Doubleday Publishing Group, a division of Penguin Random House LLC. All rights reserved. Any third party use of this material, outside of this publication, is prohibited. Interested parties must apply directly to Penguin Random House LLC for permission. MY ÁNTONIA by Willa Cather. Copyright 1918, 1926 by Willa Sibert Cather, © renewed 1946 by Willa Sibert Cather; copyright © renewed 1954 by Edith Lewis. Reprinted by permission of Houghton Mifflin Harcourt Publishing Co. All rights reserved.

Hart Crane: "At Melville's Tomb," "The Tunnel," "To Brooklyn Bridge," "Chaplinesque" and "Powhatan's Daughter," from THE COMPLETE POEMS OF HART CRANE by Hart Crane, ed. by Marc Simon. Copyright 1933, © 1958, 1966 by Liveright Publishing Corporation. Copyright © 1986 by Marc Simon. Used by permission of Liveright Publishing Corporation.

Countee Cullen: "From the Dark Tower," "Uncle Jim," "Yet Do I Marvel," "Incident," and "Heritage," from ON THESE I STAND by Countee Cullen. Copyright © 1947 Harper & Brothers, New York; renewed 1975 Ida M. Cullen. Copyrights held by the Amistad Research Center, Tulane University, administered by Thompson and Thompson, Brooklyn, NY.

E. E. Cummings: "anyone lived in a pretty how town," copyright 1940, © 1968, 1991 by the Trustees for the E. E. Cummings Trust. "Buffalo Bill's," copyright 1923, 1951, © 1991 by the Trustees for the E. E. Cummings Trust. Copyright ©1976 by George James Firmage. "the Cambridge ladies who live in furnished souls," copyright 1923, 1951, © 1991 by the Trustees for the E. E. Cummings Trust. Copyright © 1976 by George James Firmage. "I sing of Olaf glad and big," copyright 1931 © 1959, 1991 by the Trustees for the E. E. Cummings Trust. Copyright © 1976 by George James Firmage. "in Just-," copyright 1923, 1951 © 1991 by the Trustees for the E. E. Cummings Trust. Copyright © 1976 by George James Firmage. "my father moved through dooms of love," copyright 1940, © 1968, 1991 by the Trustees for the E.E. Cummings Trust, "next to of course god America I," copyright 1926, 1954 © 1991 by the Trustees for the E. E. Cummings Trust. Copyright © 1985 by George James Firmage. "O sweet spontaneous," copyright 1923, 1951 © 1991 by the Trustees for the E. E. Cummings Trust. Copyright © 1976 by George James Firmage. "pity this busy monster, manunkind," copyright 1944 © 1972, 1991 by the Trustees for the E. E. Cummings Trust. "somewhere I have never travelled, gladly beyond," copyright 1931, © 1959, 1991 by the Trustees for the E. E. Cummings Trust. Copyright © 1979 by George James Firmage. "Thy fingers make early flowers of," copyright 1923, 1951 © 1991 by the Trustees for the E. E. Cummings Trust. Copyright © 1976 by George James Firmage, from COMPLETE POEMS:

1904–1962 by E. E. Cummings, edited by George J. Firmage. From THE ENORMOUS ROOM, A TYPESCRIPT EDITION WITH DRAWINGS BY THE AUTHOR, ed. by George James Firmage. Copyright © 1978 by the Trustees for the E. E. Cummings Trust. Copyright © 1976 by George James Firmage. Used by permission of Liveright Publishing Corporation.

H.D. (Hilda Doolittle): "Oread" from COLLECTED POEMS 1912–1944 by H.D. (Hilda Doolittle). Copyright © 1914 by Hilda Doolittle. "Fragment 113," "Helen," "Leda," "Mid-day," and "The Walls Do Not Fall (Part 1)" from COLLECTED POEMS 1912–1944. Copyright © 1982 by The Estate of Hilda Doolittle. Reprinted by permission of New Directions Publishing Corp. and Carcanet Press Ltd.

John Dos Passos: From THE BIG MONEY from *U.S.A.* by John Dos Passos. Copyright by Elizabeth H. Dos Passos. Reprinted by permission of Lucy Dos Passos Coggin.

T. S. Eliot: "The Love Song of J. Alfred Prufrock," "Sweeney Among the Nightingales," "Gerontion," and "The Waste Land," reprinted by permission of Faber and Faber Ltd. from COLLECTED POEMS 1909–1962 by T. S. Eliot. "The Hollow Men" and "Journey of the Magi" from COLLECTED POEMS 1909–1962 by T. S. Eliot, copyright 1936 by Houghton Mifflin Harcourt and © renewed 1964 by Thomas Stearns Eliot. "Burnt Norton" from FOUR QUARTETS, copyright 1936 by Houghton Mifflin Harcourt and © renewed 1964 by T. S. Eliot. All rights reserved. Reprinted by permission of Houghton Mifflin Harcourt and Faber and Faber Ltd. From "Tradition and the Individual Talent" from SELECTED ESSAYS by T. S. Eliot. Reprinted by permission of Faber & Faber Ltd.

William Faulkner: *As I Lay Dying*, "Barn Burning," and "A Rose for Emily" from COLLECTED STORIES OF WILLIAM FAULKNER by William Faulkner. Copyright © 1950 by Random House, Inc., and renewed 1977 by Jill Faulkner Summers. Reprinted by permission of W. W. Norton and Company.

Jessie Redmon Fauset: From THERE IS CONFUSION by Jesse Redmon Fauset. Copyright 1924 by Boni & Liveright, Inc., renewed 1951 by Jesse Redmon Fauset. Used by permission of Liveright Publishing Corp.

F. Scott Fitzgerald: "Babylon Revisited" reprinted by permission of Scribner, a Division of Simon & Schuster, Inc., from THE SHORT STORIES OF F. SCOTT FITZGERALD, ed. by Matthew J. Bruccoli. Copyright 1931 by The Curtis Publishing Company. Copyright renewed © 1959 by Frances Scott Fitzgerald Lanahan. All rights reserved.

Robert Frost: "The Pasture," "Mowing," "Mending Wall," "The Death of the Hired Man," "Home Burial," "After Apple-Picking," "The Wood-Pile," "The Road Not Taken," "The Oven Bird," "Birches, "Out, Out-" "Fire and Ice," "Nothing Gold Can Stay," "Stopping by Woods on a Snowy Evening," "Desert Places," "Design," Neither Out Far, Nor in Deep," "Provide, Provide," "The Gift Outright," and "Directive" from THE POETRY OF ROBERT FROST, ed. by Edward Connery Lathem. Copyright © 1916, 1923, 1930, 1934, 1939, 1969 by Henry Holt and Company, copyright 1936, 1942, 1944, 1951,1958, 1962 by Robert Frost. Copyright 1964, 1967, 1970, 1975 by Lesley Frost Ballantine. Reprinted by permission of the publisher Henry Holt and Company, LLC. "The Figure a Poem Makes" from THE SELECTED PROSE OF ROBERT FROST, ed. by Hyde Cox and Edward Connery Lathem. Copyright © 1939, 1967 by Henry Holt and Company. Reprinted by permission of Henry Holt and Company, LLC. All rights reserved.

Ernest Hemingway: "Hills Like White Elephants" from THE SHORT STORIES OF ERNEST HEMINGWAY. Copyright 1927 by Charles Scribner's Sons; copyright renewed © 1955 by Ernest Hemingway. All rights reserved. Published in Great Britain in THE FIRST FORTY-NINE STORIES. From THE SUN ALSO RISES, copyright © 1926 by Charles Scribner's Sons; copyright renewed 1954 by Ernest Hemingway. All rights reserved. Published in Great Britain as FIESTA: THE SUN ALSO RISES. Reprinted by permission of the publishers, Scribner, a division of Simon & Schuster, Inc., and Jonathan Cape c/o The Random House Group Limited. Excerpt from letter from Ernest Hemingway to his family (Aug. 18, 1918). From ERNEST HEMINGWAY, SELECTED LETTERS, 1917–1961, ed. by Carlos Baker. Copyright © 1981 by Carlos Baker and The Ernest Hemingway Foundation, Inc. All rights reserved. Reprinted with permission of Atria/Scribner/Gallery, a division of Simon & Schuster, Inc.

Langston Hughes: "The Negro Speaks of Rivers," "Mother to Son," "The Weary Blues," "I, Too," "Song for a Dark Girl," "Theme for English B," "Vagabonds," "Genius Child," "Madam and Her Madam," "Madam's Calling Cards," "Silhouette," "Note on Commercial Theatre," "Visitors to the Black Belt," "Mulatto," "Freedom (1)," "Words Like Freedom," from THE COLLECTED POEMS OF LANGSTON HUGHES, edited by Arnold Rampersad with David Roessel, Associate Editor. Copyright © 1994 by The Estate of Langston Hughes. Used by permission of Alfred A. Knopf, an imprint of the Knopf Doubleday Publishing Group, a division of Penguin Random House LLC. All rights reserved. Any third party use of this material, outside of this publication, is prohibited. Interested parties must apply directly to Penguin Random House LLC for permission. Electronic rights by permission of Harold Ober Associates, Inc. "The Negro Artist and the Racial Mountain" abridged from *The Nation,* June 23, 1926. Copyright 1926 by Langston Hughes. Used by permission of Harold Ober Associates, Inc.

Zora Neale Hurston: From "The Eatonville Anthology" and "How It Feels to Be Colored Me" reprinted by permission of The Joy Harris Literary Agency, Inc. "Sweat" as taken from THE COMPLETE STORIES by Zora Neale Hurston. Introduction copyright © 1995 by Henry Louis Gates, Jr., and Sieglinde Lemke. Compilation copyright © 1995 by Vivian Bowden, Lois J. Hurston Gaston, Clifford Hurston, Lucy Ann Hurston, Winifred Hurston Clark, Zora Mack Goins, Edgar Hurston, Sr., and Barbara Hurston Lewis. Afterword and Bibliography copyright © 1995 by Henry Louis Gates, Jr. Reprinted by permission of HarperCollins Publishers.

Nella Larsen: PASSING from QUICKSAND AND PASSING is reprinted by permission of Profile Books Limited.

Amy Lowell: "St. Louis" and "New Heavens for Old" from THE COMPLETE POETICAL WORKS OF AMY LOWELL. Copyright © 1955 by Houghton Mifflin Harcourt Publishing Company, © renewed 1983 by Houghton Mifflin Harcourt Publishing Company, Brinton P. Roberts, and G. D'Andelot Belin, Esq. Reprinted by permission of Houghton Mifflin Harcourt Publishing Co. All rights reserved.

Mina Loy: "Feminist Manifesto" from THE LOST LUNAR BAEDEKER by Mina Loy. Works of Mina Loy copyright © 1996 by the Estate of Mina Loy. Introduction and edition copyright © 1996 by Roger L. Conover. Reprinted by permission of Farrar, Straus and Giroux, LLC, and Carcanet Press Ltd.

Claude McKay: "Africa," copyright 1921; "The Harlem Dancer," copyright 1917; "The Lynching," copyright 1920; "Harlem Shadows," copyright 1918; "America," copyright 1921; and "If We Must Die," copyright 1921. Reprinted by permission of the Literary Estate of Claude McKay.

F. T. Marinetti: From "Manifesto of Futurism" from "The Founding Manifesto of Futurism" from MARINETTI: SELECTED WRITINGS by F. T. Marinetti, ed. by R. W. Flint, tr. by R. W. Flint and Arthur A. Coppotelli. Translation copyright © 1972 by Farrar, Straus & Giroux, Inc. Reprinted by permission of Farrar, Straus and Giroux, LLC.

Edgar Lee Masters: From SPOON RIVER ANTHOLOGY (1915). Copyright © by Edgar Lee Masters. Reprinted by permission of the Estate of Edgar Lee Masters and the Estate of Hilary Masters.

Edna St. Vincent Millay: "I, being born a woman," "Apostrophe to Man," "I too beneath Your Moon, Almighty Sex," from COLLECTED POEMS. Copyright © 1923, 1932, 1939, 1940, 1951, © 1962, 1967, 1968, 1982 by Edna St. Vincent Millay and Norma Millay Ellis. "I Forgot for a Moment" from MAKE BRIGHT THE ARROWS. Copyright 1940, © 1968 by Edna St. Vincent Millay and Norma Millay Ellis. Reprinted by permission of The Permissions Company, Inc., on behalf of Holly Pepe, Literary Executor, The Edna St. Vincent Millay Society, www.millay.org.

Marianne Moore: "To a Snail," "Poetry," and "Marriage" with author's notes, copyright © 1935, 1963 by Marianne Moore. All rights reserved. "The Paper Nautilus," copyright 1941 by Marianne Moore and renewed © 1969 by Marianne Moore. All rights reserved. "The Mind Is an Enchanting Thing" and "In Distrust of Merits," copyright 1944 by Marianne Moore and renewed © 1972 by Marianne Moore. All rights reserved. Reprinted from THE COLLECTED POEMS OF MARIANNE MOORE by permission of Scribner, a Division of Simon & Schuster, Inc., Faber & Faber Ltd., and by David M. Moore, Administrator, Literary Estate of Marianne Moore. All rights reserved.

Eugene O'Neill: LONG DAY'S JOURNEY INTO NIGHT, copyright © 1955 by Carlotta Monterey O'Neill. Copyright © renewed 1983 by Oona O'Neill Chaplin and Yale University. Reprinted by permission.

Katherine Anne Porter: "Flowering Judas" from FLOWERING JUDAS AND OTHER STORIES, copyright 1930 by Katherine Anne Porter and renewed 1958 by Katherine Anne Porter. All rights reserved. Reprinted by permission of the publishers, Houghton Mifflin Harcourt Publishing Company and Jonathan Cape c/o The Random House Group Limited. Published in Great Britain in COLLECTED STORIES. Electronic rights by permission of The Permissions Company, Inc., for the Katherine Anne Porter Literary Trust. *Pale Horse, Pale Rider* from PALE HORSE, PALE RIDER: THREE SHORT NOVELS, copyright 1937 by Katherine Anne Porter and renewed 1965 by Katharine Anne Porter. Reprinted by permission of Houghton Mifflin Harcourt Publishing Company. All rights reserved. Electronic rights by permission of The Permissions Company, Inc., for the Katherine Anne Porter Literary Trust.

Ezra Pound: "A Virginal," "Hugh Selwyn Mauberley [Part 1]," "In a Station of the Metro," "Portrait d'Une Femme," "To Whistler, American," "Villanelle: The Psychological Hour," and "A Pact" from PERSONAE, copyright © 1926 by Ezra Pound. "The River-Merchant's Wife: A Letter" original by Rihaku, from PERSONAE, copyright © 1926 by Ezra Pound. Reprinted by permission of New Directions Publishing Corp. and Faber & Faber Ltd. Published in Great Britain in COLLECTED SHORTER POEMS. Canto I and Canto XVII from THE CANTOS OF EZRA POUND, copyright 1934 by Ezra Pound. Canto XLV from THE CANTOS OF EXRA POUND, copyright © 1937 by Ezra Pound. Reprinted by permission of New Directions Publishing Corp. and Faber and Faber Ltd. From "A Retrospect" from THE LITERARY ESSAYS OF EZRA POUND, copyright © 1935 by Ezra Pound. Reprinted by permission of New Directions Publishing Corp. and Faber and Faber Ltd.

Carl Sandburg: "Chicago" and "Fog from CHICAGO POEMS by Carl Sandburg. Copyright 1916 by Houghton Mifflin Harcourt Publishing Company and renewed 1944 by Carl Sandburg. "Cool Tombs" and "Grass" from CORNHUSKERS by Carl Sandburg. Copyright 1918 by Houghton Mifflin Harcourt Publishing Company and renewed 1946 by Carl Sandburg. Reprinted by permission of Houghton Mifflin Harcourt Publishing Company. All rights reserved.

Gertrude Stein: From THE MAKING OF AMERICANS: THE HERSLAND FAMILY by Gertrude Stein, copyright 1934 Houghton Mifflin Harcourt Publishing Company and renewed 1962 by Alice B. Toklas, reprinted by permission of Houghton Mifflin Harcourt Publishing Company. From THE AUTOBIOGRAPHY OF ALICE B. TOKLAS by Gertrude Stein, copyright 1933 by Gertrude Stein and renewed 1961 by Alice B. Toklas. Used by permission of Random House, an imprint and division of Penguin Random House LLC. All rights reserved. Any third party use of this material, outside of this publication, is prohibited. Interested parties must apply directly to Penguin Random House LLC for permission. "Objects" from TENDER BUTTONS by Gertrude Stein is reprinted with permission of the Estate of Gertrude Stein through its Literary Executor, Mr. Stanford Gann, Jr., of Levin & Gann, P.A.

John Steinbeck: "The Chrysanthemums" from THE LONG VALLEY by John Steinbeck, copyright 1937, renewed © 1965 by John Steinbeck. Used by permission of Viking Books, an imprint of Penguin Publishing Group, a division of Penguin Random House LLC and Penguin Books Ltd. Copyright 1938 by John Steinbeck. Copyright renewed 1966 by John Steinbeck.

Wallace Stevens: "The Snow Man," "A High-Toned Old Christian Woman," "The Emperor of Ice-Cream," "Disillusionment of Ten O'Clock," "Sunday Morning," "Anecdote of the Jar," "Thirteen Ways of Looking at a Blackbird," "The Idea of Order at Key West," "Of Modern Poetry," and "The Plain Sense of Things" from THE COLLECTED POEMS OF WALLACE STEVENS by Wallace Stevens. Copyright 1954 by Wallace Stevens. Used by permission of Alfred A. Knopf, an imprint of the Knopf Doubleday Publishing Group, a division of Penguin Random House LLC. All rights reserved. Any third party use of this material, outside of this publication, is prohibited. Interested parties must apply directly to Penguin Random House LLC for permission and Faber and Faber Ltd.

Jean Toomer: "Georgia Dusk," "Fern," "Portrait in Georgia," "Blood-Burning Moon," and "Seventh Street" from CANE by Jean Toomer. Copyright 1923 by Boni & Liveright. Copyright renewed 1951 by Jean Toomer. Used by permission of Liveright Publishing Corporation.

Nathanael West: *The Day of the Locust* from MISS LONELYHEARTS & THE DAY OF THE LOCUST, copyright © 1939 by the Estate of Nathanael West. Reprinted by permission of New Directions Publishing Corp.

William Carlos Williams: "Portrait of a Lady," "The Young Housewife," "Queen-Anne's-Lace," "The Widow's Lament in Springtime," "Spring and All, Section 1" "To Elsie," "The Red Wheelbarrow," "This Is Just to Say," "The Dead Baby" and excerpt from the essay "Spring and All" from THE COLLECTED POEMS OF WILLIAM CARLOS WILLIAMS 1909–1939, volume I. Copyright © 1938 by New Directions Publishing Corporation. "A Sort of a Song," "Burning the Christmas Greens," "The Dance (In Brueghel's)," and "Landscape with the Fall of Icarus," from THE COLLECTED POEMS OF WILLIAM CARLOS WILLIAMS 1939–1962, volume II. Copyright © 1944, 1962 by William Carlos Williams. Reprinted by permission of New Directions Publishing Corp. and Carcanet Press Ltd.

Thomas Wolfe: "The Lost Boy" by Thomas Wolfe. Copyright © 1937 by McCall Corporation. Copyright renewed 1965 by Paul Gitlin, Administrator C.T.A., Estate of Thomas Wolfe. Reprinted with the permission of McIntosh & Otis, Inc.

Richard Wright: "The Man Who Was Almost a Man" from EIGHT MEN by Richard Wright. Copyright 1940, © 1961 by Richard Wright, renewed © 1989 by Ellen Wright. Introduction © 1996 by Paul Gilroy. Reprinted by permission of HarperCollins Publishers, John Hawkins & Associates, Inc., and the Estate of Richard Wright.

Index